A DICKENS COMPANION

A DICKENS COMPANION

NORMAN PAGE

Schocken Books • New York

First American edition published by Schocken Books 1984
10 9 8 7 6 5 4 3 2 1   84 85 86 87
Copyright © Norman Page 1984
Published by agreement with The Macmillan Press Ltd, London

Library of Congress Cataloging in Publication Data

Page, Norman.
    A Dickens companion.

    Bibliography: p.
    Includes index.
    1. Dickens, Charles, 1812-1870—Handbooks, manuals,
etc. I. Title.
PR4588.P33 1984   823'.8   83-16306

Manufactured in Hong Kong

ISBN 0-8052-3883-2

To Valerie and Campbell Purton,
and the Infant Phenomena Dinah and Tom

Contents

List of Plates

Preface

An elderly charwoman employed about the place . . . was told of
the approaching visit, and who it was that was coming. . . .
'Lawk ma'am!' she said. 'Is the young gentleman upstairs the son
of the man that put together *Dombey?*' Reassured upon this point,
she explained her question by declaring that she never thought
there was a man that *could* have put together *Dombey*. Being
pressed further as to what her notion was of this mystery of *Dombey*
(for it was known she could not read), it turned out that she
lodged at a snuff-shop kept by a person named Douglas, where
there were several other lodgers; and that on the first Monday of
every month there was a Tea, and the landlord read the month's
number of *Dombey*, those only of the lodgers who subscribed to the
tea partaking of that luxury, but all having the benefit of the
reading; and the impression produced on the old charwoman
revealed itself in the remark with which she closed her account of
it. 'Lawk ma'am! I thought that three or four men must have put
together *Dombey!*' Dickens thought there was something of a
compliment in this, and was not ungrateful – John Forster, *The
Life of Charles Dickens* (1872–4).

It seems that on a just view of the matter the books we call classics
possess intrinsic qualities that endure, but possess also an
openness to accommodation which keeps them alive under
endlessly varying dispositions – Frank Kermode, *The Classic*
(1975).

It is sometimes said that the study of English literature in our time is
kept alive only by the academic establishment, and that great
authors have come to owe their immortality to the life-support
systems provided by set books and examinations. This mournful
truth admits, however, of not a few happy exceptions. There is, for

example, a company of nineteenth-century novelists who are unquestionably read and re-read by large numbers of people not out of duty but out of delight. This company (which also includes, for example, Jane Austen and Thomas Hardy) surely has Charles Dickens at its head – a position that that vigorous and domineering personality would doubtless have insisted on. For a century and a half people have been reading – or, like the charwoman, listening to – Dickens' novels for pleasure; and even though the custom of reading aloud has sadly declined, the death of the reading habit has been frequently announced, and nearly all of Dickens' work has been made available through other media in countless adaptations, there is no sign that ordinary readers are going to stop turning to his books. At the same time the 'official' revaluation of Dickens by the literary and academic establishment during the past generation has been an extraordinary phenomenon: no other novelist or nineteenth-century author is now so frequently written about by scholars and critics.

There have been numerous guides and companions to Dickens; one of them appeared within a couple of years of his death and is thus more than a century old; and it is probably not unfair to say that, to a greater or lesser extent, most of them have been amateur productions in both the favourable and the pejorative senses of that term – labours of love, products of an admirable energy and enthusiasm, but frequently incomplete and not infrequently inaccurate. Many of them reflect bygone fashions and exhibit a kind of literary tunnel-vision in their preoccupation with, for example, characters, prototypes, or topography.

The present volume has been designed as a reference book that will be found useful by students of Dickens and general readers alike – by scholars needing to check a point quickly, by undergraduates or sixth-formers working on an essay, and by those who simply (and sensibly) want to satisfy their curiosity on some topic relating to this endlessly fascinating man and writer. So far as I know there is no single volume that provides ready answers to such questions as: When did Dickens start writing *Dombey and Son*? When did he finish *Our Mutual Friend*? What alternative titles did he consider for *Edwin Drood*? In what month did the final instalment of *David Copperfield* appear? Who were the prototypes of Mr Merdle and Miss Mowcher? What did Ruskin say about *Hard Times*, and Aldous Huxley about *The Old Curiosity Shop*? Who was Mark Lemon? When did Dickens visit Pompeii, and when did his father die? What are the Dickensian associations of Hampstead and Brighton and Kettering? How many public readings did Dickens give in America? What film versions of *A Tale of Two Cities* have there been? This book enables the answers to any of these – and, I suppose, several thousand others – to be found within a few moments.

The chronology of Dickens' life with which the book opens is followed by an alphabetical 'who's who' of those who were associated with Dickens personally or professionally. Then, as the core of the *Companion*, separate sections are devoted to Dickens' books in the order of their appearance. For each of the novels there is information on composition, publication in serial and volume form, and reception, with an indication of the best available texts and summary discussion of some of the main directions taken by interpretation and criticism, and with indications of material that can be consulted by those wishing to make a more serious study of the work in question. There is also a list of characters, with brief notes on each character's role in the novel and on prototypes and other points of interest; an index of characters at the end of the volume enables a character to be traced even when the reader does not know in which book it appears. In addition to the novels, information will be found on Dickens' travel books, his Christmas books and stories, his letters, speeches, readings, plays, poems, journalism, and other minor writings. Next there are sections on Dickens' illustrators and on the topography of his works; and finally a select bibliography, a filmography, and a list of some of the early dramatizations. The appendices reprint three documents of particular interest that the reader may find it useful to have conveniently to hand, and describe Dickens' notebook and memoranda.

My debts to a large number of those who have written on Dickens will be obvious, but I should like to make special mention of three on whom I have drawn especially heavily: Philip Collins, whose extensive bibliographical work and whose work on Dickens' reputation in *Dickens: The Critical Heritage* (1971), referred to throughout as *Critical Heritage*, form only a part of his total contribution to Dickens studies; Edgar Johnson, whose biography of Dickens (referred to throughout as Johnson) has been indispensable; and Robert L. Patten, whose recent *Charles Dickens and his Publishers* is a mine of precise and accurate information in a complex field in which there has in the past been much inaccuracy and vagueness. I am also grateful to Barnaby Page for compiling the filmography; to Valerie Purton for pointing out some omissions in my original list of the Dickens circle; and to Philip Collins for reading my typescript and suggesting numerous improvements and additions. I am glad to have been able at the last moment to take advantage of Professor Collins' most recent contribution to Dickens studies, *Dickens: Interviews and Recollections* (1981).

Abbreviations

CD	Charles Dickens
AN	*American Notes*
ATTC	*A Tale of Two Cities*
AYR	*All the Year Round*
BH	*Bleak House*
BR	*Barnaby Rudge*
DC	*David Copperfield*
D&S	*Dombey and Son*
ED	*The Mystery of Edwin Drood*
GE	*Great Expectations*
HT	*Hard Times*
HW	*Household Words*
LD	*Little Dorrit*
MC	*Martin Chuzzlewit*
MHC	*Master Humphrey's Clock*
NN	*Nicholas Nickleby*
OCS	*The Old Curiosity Shop*
OMF	*Our Mutual Friend*
OT	*Oliver Twist*
PP	*The Pickwick Papers*
SB	*Sketches by Boz*
UT	*The Uncommercial Traveller*

A Dickens Chronology

(For further information concerning various individuals referred to in this chronology, see the next chapter, 'The Dickens Circle'.)

1812   (7 February) Charles John Huffam Dickens born at 1 Mile End Terrace (now 393 Commercial Road and a Dickens museum), Landport, Portsmouth, Hampshire, second child and eldest son of John Dickens, a clerk in the Navy Pay Office at Portsea, and Elizabeth Dickens (née Barrow). ('Huffham' in the baptismal register is a clerical error: CD was named after his godfather, Christopher Huffam, and always spelt the name thus.)
    (4 March) CD baptized at St Mary's, Kingston, Portsea.
    (June) The Dickens family move, possibly to 16 Hawke Street, a smaller and cheaper house (destroyed in the Second World War).
    (Christmas 1813) they move again, to Wish Street (later renamed Kings Road), Southsea (house now demolished).

1814   At the end of the year John Dickens is transferred to Somerset House, London, and establishes his family in lodgings at 10 Norfolk Street, off Fitzroy Square, St Pancras.

1817   (midsummer) John Dickens is moved to Chatham, Kent, and the family settle at 2 (now 11) Ordnance Terrace. Their servant Mary Weller looks after young Charles, who often plays with their neighbours' children, George and Lucy Stroughill; later he is sent with his sister Fanny to a dame school held over a shop in Rome Lane.

1821   (25 March) The Dickens family move to a smaller and cheaper house, 'The Brook', 18 St Mary Place (now demolished). Charles and Fanny begin to attend a school in Clover Lane kept by William Giles.

1822　　　Towards the end of the year John Dickens is transferred back to London. William Giles gives CD a copy of Goldsmith's *Bee* as a parting present. The Dickens family settle at 16 Bayham Street (now demolished), in Camden Town. CD's schooling is not resumed: 'What would I have given . . . to have been sent back to any other school, to have been taught something anywhere!' (CD, quoted by Forster).

1823　　　(Michaelmas) The family's financial situation growing desperate, CD's mother rents a house at 4 Gower Street North (now demolished) in a vain attempt to establish a school: 'Nobody ever came to the school, nor do I recollect that anybody ever proposed to come, or that the least preparation was made to receive anybody' (CD, quoted by Forster). (Compare Mrs Micawber's similarly unsuccessful attempts: *DC*, Ch. 11.)

1824　　　(9 February) At the suggestion of James Lamert, CD starts work at Warren's Blacking Warehouse, 30 Hungerford Stairs, Strand (on the site now occupied by Embankment Gardens), for six shillings a week: 'My father and mother were quite satisfied. They could hardly have been more so, if I had been twenty years of age, distinguished at a grammar-school, and going to Cambridge'. (For this and other quotations see Appendix A. See also under Dilke in 'The Dickens Circle', below). His job was

> to cover the pots of paste-blacking: first with a piece of oil-paper, and then with a piece of blue paper; to tie them round with a string; and then to clip the paper close and neat all round, until it looked as smart as a pot of ointment from an apothecary's shop. When a certain number of grosses of pots had attained this pitch of perfection, I was to paste on each a printed label; and then go on again with more pots.

By his fellow-workers, who included Bob Fagin and Poll Green, he was nicknamed 'the young gentleman'. Years later he wrote that

> No words can express the secret agony of my soul, as I sunk into this companionship; compared these every day associates with those of my happier childhood; and felt my early hopes of growing up to be a learned and distinguished man, crushed in my breast . . . . My whole nature was so penetrated with the grief

and humiliation of such considerations, that even now, famous and caressed and happy, I often forget in my dreams that I have a dear wife and children; even that I am a man; and wander desolately back to that time of my life.

(20 February) John Dickens is arrested for debt; after three nights in a sponging-house he is sent to the Marshalsea prison.

(25 March) Mrs Dickens and the younger children move into the Marshalsea, leaving CD in lodgings with Mrs Elizabeth Roylance in Little College Street, Camden Town. CD spends his Sundays at the prison; later he moves into an attic in Lant Street, near the Marshalsea, and is able to have his breakfasts and suppers with his family.

(28 May) John Dickens is released from prison, a timely legacy of £450 from his mother, who died on 28 April, enabling him to discharge his debt. The family lodge briefly with Mrs Roylance, and in June take a small house in a poor area, 29 Johnson Street, Somers Town. John Dickens resumes work at the Navy Pay Office and CD continues at the blacking warehouse (now moved to Chandos Street, Covent Garden). John Dickens quarrels with James Lamert, and CD leaves the blacking warehouse after spending four or five months there:

I never afterwards forgot, I never shall forget, I never can forget, that my mother was warm for my being sent back . . . . It was a very long time before I liked to go up Chandos Street. My old way home by the Borough made me cry, after my eldest child could speak.

(Late June) CD begins to attend Wellington House Academy, Hampstead Road, run by William Jones.

1824–7   At Wellington House Academy, where his friends include Daniel Tobin, John Bowden, Henry Danson, Richard Bray and Owen Thomas. He wins a Latin prize.

1827   (March) The Dickens family are evicted from 29 Johnson Street for non-payment of rent, and move into lodgings at 17 The Polygon (now demolished), Somers Town. CD leaves school, and after a few weeks spent working for Charles Molloy, a solicitor with offices at 6 Symonds Inn, Chancery Lane, he begins work (May) as office-boy for Ellis and Blackmore, attorneys, of 5 Holborn Court, Gray's Inn, and subsequently of Raymond Buildings, Holborn. He buys Gurney's *Brachygraphy* and begins to learn shorthand.

1828   (November) He leaves Ellis and Blackmore's to become a free-lance shorthand-reporter at Doctors' Commons, near St Paul's Cathedral.

1829–31   He falls in love with Maria Beadnell; visits the theatre frequently and takes lessons in acting; is a great admirer of Charles Mathews, a celebrated comic actor; arranges an audition with Mathews and Charles Kemble, but is prevented by illness from attending. On his eighteenth birthday CD applies for a reader's ticket at the British Museum. At this time his parents are in lodgings above a greengrocer's shop at 10 Norfolk Street, Fitzroy Square (now 22 Cleveland Street).

1832   CD is employed as shorthand-reporter for the *Mirror of Parliament*, a transcript of parliamentary proceedings started in 1828 by his uncle John Henry Barrow. From 5 March he also works as reporter for a new evening newspaper, the *True Sun*, edited by Samuel Laman Blanchard. He quickly acquires a reputation as a top-rank reporter, outstanding in the gallery of the House of Commons 'not merely for accuracy in reporting, but for marvellous quickness in transcript' (James Grant, quoted by Forster).
    (July) Resigns from *True Sun*. After a period in lodgings in the Strand, he lives with his parents again, now at 13 (later 25) Fitzroy Street.

1833   The Dickens family move to 18 Bentinck Street, near Portland Place, and CD's twenty-first birthday is celebrated there. His four-year-old relationship with Maria Beadnell comes to an end. He begins to write short fictional sketches of London life.
    (December) His first published fiction, 'A Dinner at Poplar Walk', appears in the *Monthly Magazine* 'in all the glory of print', and is quickly followed by other unsigned contributions in 1834.

1834   (August) CD uses the pseudonym 'Boz' for the first time. He becomes a parliamentary reporter for the *Morning Chronicle*, whose offices were at 322 Strand. During parliamentary recesses he travels all over the country to cover political meetings and elections (for example, to Edinburgh in September 1834; to Ipswich and Sudbury in January 1835; to Exeter in May 1835; to Bristol in November 1835; to Kettering in December 1835). 'Boz' continues to publish sketches in the *Morning Chronicle* and elsewhere.

(November) John Dickens arrested for debt; CD comes to the rescue. CD and his brother Frederick move into chambers at 13 Furnival's Inn.

1835   (January) CD agrees to contribute sketches to the *Evening Chronicle*, edited by George Hogarth, at whose home he meets and falls in love with Hogarth's daughter Catherine. They become engaged in April. CD later moves into lodgings at 18 Selwood Place, Brompton, in order to be near the Hogarth home.

(27 September) CD begins to contribute a series of sketches to *Bell's Life in London* (continued to 17 January 1836) under the pseudonym 'Tibbs'. John Macrone agrees to publish a volume of CD's sketches, with illustrations by George Cruikshank, and to pay him £150 for the copyright.

1836   (7 February) *Sketches by Boz* published on CD's twenty-fourth birthday.

(10 February) William Hall, of the publishing firm of Chapman & Hall, invites him to write the text to accompany a series of plates by the artist Robert Seymour illustrating the adventures of the Nimrod Club; CD's suggestion that the plates should illustrate the text, and that publication should be in twenty parts issued monthly at a shilling each, is accepted. As CD remarked later, 'I thought of Mr Pickwick', and work on *Pickwick Papers* is promptly begun.

(29 March) CD obtains a special licence from the Vicar General's office.

(31 March) The first number of *PP* appears.

(2 April) CD and Catherine Hogarth are married quietly at St Luke's Church, Chelsea; they go for a week's honeymoon to the village of Chalk, near Chatham, then begin married life at Furnival's Inn, Kate's younger sister Mary living with them.

(19 April) Seymour commits suicide. After Robert Buss has been tried as his successor and found wanting, H. K. Browne is selected to illustrate *PP* and soon afterwards adopts the pseudonym of 'Phiz'.

(May) CD accepts Macrone's offer of £200 for a three-volume novel to be called *Gabriel Vardon, the Locksmith of London*. CD goes to Ipswich to report a speech by Daniel O'Connell.

(June) CD publishes a political pamphlet *Sunday under Three Heads* under the pseudonym of Timothy Sparks, attacking attempts to prohibit all work and recreation on the Sabbath. He reports the celebrated Melbourne-Norton trial.

(July) Following the introduction of Sam Weller in the June number, sales of *PP* rise dramatically.

(August) CD contracts to write two novels for Richard Bentley.

(September) CD's farce, *The Strange Gentleman*, is produced at the St James' Theatre and is published in December by Chapman & Hall.

(November) CD accepts Bentley's invitation to edit a new monthly magazine, *Bentley's Miscellany*, and resigns from the *Morning Chronicle*.

(December) Second series of *Sketches by Boz* is published. *The Village Coquettes*, a musical play with words by CD, is produced at the St James' Theatre and published by Bentley. CD and Macrone quarrel over the contracted novel *Gabriel Vardon*; on 5 January 1837 a compromise is reached, releasing CD from his contract. On Christmas Day, Harrison Ainsworth introduces CD to John Forster.

1837   (6 January) CD's first child, Charles (later known as Charley), is born.

(January) *Bentley's Miscellany* begins publication.

(February) Serialization of *Oliver Twist* begins in *Bentley's Miscellany*.

(March) CD's one-act farce, *Is She his Wife?*, is produced at the St James' Theatre. CD assumes a three-year lease of 48 Doughty Street (now a Dickens museum).

(7 May) Death of Mary Hogarth. No number of *PP* appears at the end of the month, and no instalment of *OT* appears in June, *Bentley's Miscellany* carrying an explanatory announcement.

(July) CD, Kate and Browne spend a week's holiday in France and Belgium.

(Part of August and September) CD, Kate and Charley are on holiday at Broadstairs, Kent.

(18 November) Banquet to celebrate the completion of the serialized *Pickwick*.

(November) CD and Kate spend a few days at Brighton.

(9 December) Charley is christened.

1838   (30 January) CD and Browne set off for Yorkshire to gather material for a novel dealing with the notorious boarding schools. On his return, CD promptly begins *Nicholas Nickleby*, and by 9 February has written the first chapter.

(6 March) CD's second child, Mary, is born.

(1 April) First number of *NN* appears.

(June) CD becomes a member of the Athenaeum Club.

(June–July) CD and his family holiday in a rented cottage at Twickenham.

(October) CD and Browne tour the Midlands and North Wales. Forster joins them in Manchester, where they visit cotton mills.

(9 November) *Oliver Twist* published in three volumes.

1839   (January) CD attends a public dinner given in his honour at Manchester.

(February) CD relinquishes the editorship of *Bentley's Miscellany*. He agrees to deliver *Barnaby Rudge* to Bentley by 1 January 1840.

(April) Serialization of *OT* is concluded.

(July) Chapman & Hall agree to publish a weekly periodical, *Master Humphrey's Clock*, for which CD will write a new novel as well as shorter papers.

(20 July) CD attends a banquet in honour of Macready.

(August–September) The Dickens family holiday at Broadstairs, where CD works at the closing portion of *NN* (completed on 20 September).

(29 October) CD's third child, Kate, is born.

(October) CD resumes work on *BR* (begun and abandoned in January), but it makes very slow progress.

(November) CD takes a twelve-year lease of 1 Devonshire Terrace, Regent's Park.

(December) CD's solicitors inform Bentley that he will not deliver the manuscript of *BR* on 1 January. The Dickens family move to Devonshire Terrace.

1840   (February) Dickens and Forster visit Walter Savage Landor in Bath.

(4 April) The first number of CD's weekly magazine *Master Humphrey's Clock* is published.

(25 April) The first episode of *The Old Curiosity Shop* appears in the fourth number of the *Clock*.

(June) The Dickens family are at Broadstairs; CD continues work on *OCS*.

(July) CD witnesses the execution of the murderer Courvoisier.
(September) The Dickens family are at Broadstairs again.

1841   (23 January) CD's fourth child, Walter, is born.
(6 February) Serialization of *OCS* is concluded.
(13 February) Serialization of *BR* begins.
(June and July) CD and Kate visit Scotland; CD is lionized in
Edinburgh, where a public dinner is given for him on 25 June and
the freedom of the city bestowed upon him; they tour the Highlands.
(August and September) The Dickens family are at Broadstairs;
CD works on the concluding portion of *BR*.
(September) CD tells Forster that he has made up his mind to go
to America.
(October) CD undergoes an operation for a fistula.
(November) Serialization of *BR* is concluded. CD convalesces at
Richmond and Windsor.
(December) *BR* published in one volume.

1842   (4 January) CD and Kate sail from Liverpool on the
packet *Britannia* bound for Boston.
(22 January) They land in Boston after a very bad crossing. CD is
lionized, and writes to friends in England: 'There never was a king
or emperor upon the earth so cheered and followed by crowds, and
entertained in public at splendid balls and dinners'; 'There never
was, and never will be such a triumph.' (For his subsequent
disenchantment with the USA, especially over the copyright question, see pp. 132–3.) Their subsequent itinerary includes Harvard,
Worcester, Springfield, Hartford, New Haven, New York (where
they spend three weeks), Philadelphia, Washington, Baltimore,
Pittsburgh, Cincinnati, Louisville, St Louis, Columbus, Cleveland,
Buffalo, Niagara, Toronto, Kingston, Quebec, Montreal. In
Montreal CD directs and acts in an amateur theatrical production.
(7 June) CD and Kate sail from New York on the˙ *George
Washington*; they reach Liverpool on 29 June. CD quickly begins
work on *American Notes*, and continues during a holiday at
Broadstairs in August.
(October) *AN* is published. Henry Wadsworth Longfellow visits
CD in London. CD, Forster, Maclise and Stanfield tour Cornwall.
(November) CD begins work on *Martin Chuzzlewit*.

1843   (January) Serialization of *MC* begins.

(August–September) The Dickens family are on holiday at Broadstairs; work continues on *MC*.

(5 October) CD presides at the first annual soirée of the Manchester Athenaeum; on returning to London he begins work on *A Christmas Carol* (completed by the end of November) in such 'odd moments of leisure' as he can spare from completing *MC*.

(17 December) *A Christmas Carol* is published.

1844 (15 January) CD's fifth child, Francis, is born.

(February) Disappointed by his earnings from *A Christmas Carol* and by the poor serial sales of *MC*, CD decides to sever his connexion with Chapman & Hall, and also resolves to reduce his living expenses.

(26 and 28 February) CD speaks in Liverpool and Birmingham.

(1 June) CD signs an agreement with his new publishers, Bradbury & Evans.

(July) Serialization of *MC* is concluded; the novel is published in volume form.

(2 July) The Dickens family set off for Italy, CD having purchased a travelling coach and hired Louis Roche as courier. The party – including Kate, five children, Georgina Hogarth, servants, courier and dog – travel via Boulogne, Paris, Lyons, by boat down the Rhone, Avignon, Marseilles, Nice, Genoa. They stay at the Villa di Bella Vista, Albaro, two miles from Genoa, until the end of September; then move to the Palazzo Peschiere, Genoa.

(October) After difficulties in making a start, CD begins work on *The Chimes*, designed as a successor to *A Christmas Carol*, to be ready for the Christmas trade of 1844.

(3 November) CD finishes *The Chimes*.

(6 November) CD and Roche set off for England, via Parma, Bologna, Ferrara, Venice, Verona, Mantua, Milan, Lake Maggiore, the Simplon Pass, Vévey, Fribourg, Basle, Strasbourg, Paris. They arrive in London on 30 November for an eight-day visit.

(3 December) CD reads *The Chimes* to a group of friends in Forster's chambers in Lincoln's Inn Fields. On the return journey to Italy, he spends three days in Paris with Macready, and meets Victor Hugo, Alexandre Dumas, Théophile Gautier, Eugène Delacroix, and others; he then proceeds by coach to Marseilles and by boat to Genoa.

1845 (19 January) CD and Kate set out for an extended tour that includes Spezzia, Carrara, Pisa, Leghorn, Rome, Naples (where they are joined by Georgina Hogarth), Sorrento, Paestum, Pompeii, Herculaneum, Vesuvius (where, in appalling conditions, they ascend to the brink of the crater), Monte Cassino, Florence, Fiesole.

(June) The Dickens family leave Genoa and return to England.

(20 September) CD stages and plays Bobadil in an amateur production of Ben Jonson's *Every Man in his Humour*.

(October) CD begins work on his third Christmas book, *The Cricket on the Hearth* (finished by 1 December).

(28 October) CD's sixth child, Alfred, is born.

(20 December) *The Cricket on the Hearth* is published.

1846   (21 January) The *Daily News* begins publication under CD's editorship.

(9 February) CD resigns his editorship of the *Daily News* (he is succeeded by Forster), but continues to contribute occasional pieces. Later he enquires about the possibility of obtaining paid employment as a London magistrate.

(April) He agrees to write a novel in twenty monthly parts for publication by Bradbury and Evans.

(May) *Pictures from Italy* is published.

(31 May) The Dickens family set out for Switzerland via Ostend; they travel by Rhine steamboat to Strasbourg, then on by railway to Basle and by coach to Lausanne, where they rent a house.

(27 June) CD begins *Dombey and Son* ('a plunge straight over head and ears into the story').

(September) CD visits Geneva.

(17 October) He finishes *The Battle of Life*, his fourth Christmas book, written concurrently with *Dombey and Son*.

(October) The first number of *Dombey and Son* appears.

(16 November) The Dickens family leave Geneva for Paris.

(19 December) *The Battle of Life* is published; a dramatic version of the story, staged with CD's co-operation, opens at the Lyceum Theatre two days later.

1847   (March) Charley Dickens, who is in England, catches scarlet fever, and the family return to London.

(18 April) CD's seventh child, Sydney, is born.

(June–July) The Dickens family are on holiday at Broadstairs.

(26 and 28 July) CD stages an amateur production of *Every Man in his Humour* in Manchester and Liverpool.

(1 December) CD presides at a soirée of the Leeds Mechanics' Institute.

After Christmas, he and Kate travel to Scotland; on the train from Edinburgh to Glasgow Kate has a miscarriage.

1848   (April) Serialization of *D&S* is concluded.

(May) CD produces *Every Man in his Humour*, *The Merry Wives of Windsor*, and other plays at the Theatre Royal, Haymarket; Queen Victoria and the Prince Consort attend the theatre on 17 May.

(June) There are further performances at Manchester, Liverpool and Birmingham; and (July) in Edinburgh and Glasgow.

(August) The Dickens family are on holiday at Broadstairs.

(2 September) Death of CD's sister Fanny.

(30 November) CD finishes his fifth and last Christmas book, *The Haunted Man*, which is published on 19 December; before the end of the year a dramatic version by Mark Lemon is staged at the Adelphi Theatre.

1849   (7 January) CD sets out for a short holiday in Norfolk with Leech and Lemon; they visit Norwich, Yarmouth and Lowestoft.

(16 January) CD's eighth child, Henry, is born.

(January–April) CD publishes several articles in the *Examiner* concerning the notorious Tooting baby-farm.

(February) CD begins work on *David Copperfield*. He and Kate take a holiday in Brighton, where they are joined by Leech and his wife.

(May) Serialization of *DC* begins.

(12 May) Thackeray dines at Devonshire Terrace; among the other guests are the Carlyles, Mrs Gaskell, H. K. Browne and Douglas Jerrold.

(July) The Dickens family are on holiday at Broadstairs; later in the month they go to Bonchurch on the Isle of Wight.

(November) CD witnesses the hanging of Mr and Mrs Manning, and writes two letters to *The Times* protesting against public executions; a lively controversy ensues. CD visits the Watsons at Rockingham Castle in Northamptonshire.

(December) He receives a letter of protest from Mrs Seymour Hill (see 'The Dickens Circle').

1850   (6 February) CD addresses the Metropolitan Sanitary Association (and again on 10 May 1851).

(30 March) The first number of CD's weekly magazine *Household Words* appears.

(June) CD takes ten days' holiday in Paris with Maclise.

(August-October) The Dickens family are at Broadstairs; Kate remains in London until September.

(16 August) CD's ninth child, Dora, is born.

(21 October) CD finishes *David Copperfield*.

(November) Serialization of *DC* is concluded.

(18–20 November) CD takes part in amateur theatricals at Knebworth, Bulwer-Lytton's Hertfordshire country house. During this year, CD works energetically for the establishment of the Guild of Literature and Art (incorporated in 1854).

1851   (7 January) CD goes to Rockingham Castle for amateur theatricals.

(February) Dora Dickens is seriously ill. Joseph Paxton shows CD the Crystal Palace. CD takes a five-day holiday in Paris. He attends Macready's last stage appearance, and organizes and speaks at the farewell dinner held on 1 March. Kate Dickens is unwell and goes to Malvern for treatment; CD visits her there.

(18 March) Rehearsals begin for CD's production of Bulwer-Lytton's comedy *Not So Bad As We Seem*.

(31 March) Death of John Dickens, father of CD.

(14 April) Death of Dora Dickens, aged almost eight months. CD receives the news after making a speech at a dinner held for the General Theatrical Fund; CD and Mark Lemon sit up all night beside the child's body. Kate returns from Malvern.

(May) The Dickens family go on holiday to Broadstairs (until 20 October).

(16 May) Queen Victoria attends a performance of *Not So Bad As We Seem* at Devonshire House.

(18 June) Public performances of *Not So Bad As We Seem* begin at the Hanover Square Rooms and continue until 4 August.

(November) CD moves into Tavistock House, Tavistock Square; later in the month he begins *Bleak House*. Provincial performances of *Not So Bad As We Seem* begin, and continue in 1852, including Manchester and Liverpool (February), Shrewsbury and Birmingham (May), Nottingham, Derby and Sheffield (August), Manchester and Liverpool again (September), CD accompanying his troupe throughout.

1852   (1 March) Serialization of *BH* begins.

(13 March) CD's tenth child, Edward, is born.

(July–September) The Dickens family are on holiday in Dover.

(August) Death of CD's friends Richard Watson and Count D'Orsay.

(October) CD is on holiday in Boulogne.

1853   (March) CD spends two weeks in Brighton.

(May) He receives a visit from Professor Cornelius Felton.

(June) CD is confined to his bed for six days with kidney trouble (a chronic complaint since childhood).
After a few days in Folkestone, the Dickens family go on holiday to Boulogne.

(August) CD finishes *BH*.

(10 October) CD sets out for an extended tour of France, Switzerland and Italy with Wilkie Collins and Augustus Egg. They visit Paris, Strasbourg, Lausanne, Geneva, Genoa, Naples, Rome, Florence, Venice.

(11 December) CD returns to England.

(27 December) He reads *A Christmas Carol* at the Birmingham Town Hall in aid of the Birmingham and Midland Institute – the first of his public readings. (Others followed on 29 and 30 December.)

1854   (January) CD visits Preston, Lancashire, to observe the millworkers' strike

(1 April) Serialization of *Hard Times* begins in *Household Words*.

(June) The Dickens family set off to spend the summer in Boulogne.

(17 July) CD finishes *HT*.

(12 August) Serialization of *HT* is concluded.

(17 September) CD's daughter Mary falls ill with cholera, but makes a rapid recovery.

(19 December) CD reads *A Christmas Carol* at Reading; also at Sherborne (20th) and Bradford (28th).

1855   (10 February) CD receives a letter from Mrs Maria Winter (née Beadnell).

(11 February) He sets off on a trip to Paris with Wilkie Collins.

(25 February) He meets Maria Winter.

(7 March) The Winters dine with the Dickenses.

(May) CD begins work on *Little Dorrit*.

(15–19 June) CD's production of Wilkie Collins' play *The Lighthouse* is staged in the schoolroom theatre at Tavistock House; it is repeated on 10 July at Campden House, Kensington, for the benefit of the Bournemouth Sanatorium for Consumptives.

(27 June) CD presides at a meeting of the Administrative Reform Association.

(July) The Dickens family are on holiday in Folkestone; in October they go to Boulogne, then to Paris; CD makes brief visits to England in early November and mid-December. On 18 December he is at Rockingham; on 19th, he gives a reading at Sheffield; on 24th he returns to Paris.

(1 December) Serialization of *LD* begins.

(31 December) CD finishes the fourth number of *LD*.

1856   (February) CD visits London briefly, and again in March.

(14 March) He buys Gad's Hill Palace, near Rochester.

(April) CD returns to England.

(June) The Dickens family go on holiday to Boulogne (until August).

(October) CD begins to plan the production of Wilkie Collins' melodrama *The Frozen Deep*; rehearsals begin on 16 October and continue for the rest of the year.

1857   (6 January) The first performance of *The Frozen Deep* takes place in the schoolroom theatre at Tavistock House (other performances follow on 8, 12 and 14 January).

(17 May) A housewarming is held at Gad's Hill, where the family are installed by 1 June.

(June) Serialization of *LD* is concluded. Hans Andersen stays at Gad's Hill. CD declines Queen Victoria's invitation to him to perform *The Frozen Deep* at Buckingham Palace, and proposes that she attend a private performance at the Gallery of Illustration in Regent Street.

(1 July) Victoria, Albert, and the King of the Belgians attend the special performance of *The Frozen Deep*.

(8 July) First public performance of *The Frozen Deep*, in aid of the Douglas Jerrold Fund (further performances on 18 and 25 July).

(July) CD gives two readings of *A Christmas Carol* in London and one in Manchester in aid of the Jerrold Fund.

(20 July) Walter Dickens sails for India.

(21–2 August) Two performances of *The Frozen Deep* take place in the Free Trade Hall, Manchester, for the Jerrold Fund; three professional actresses, Mrs Ternan and her daughters Maria and Ellen, are engaged to join the cast.

(September) CD and Wilkie Collins go on holiday to Cumberland.

1858   (9 February) CD speaks at a dinner on behalf of the Hospital for Sick Children.

(15 April) CD gives a reading for the Children's Hospital.

(29 April) CD's first reading for profit takes place at the St Martin's Hall, followed by sixteen other London readings (continuing to 22 July).

(14 May) Catherine Dickens, having separated from CD, accepts a settlement; Charley goes with her, while the other children and Georgina Hogarth remain with CD. CD is infuriated by gossip that Ellen Ternan – or Georgina Hogarth – is his mistress.

(12 June) CD publishes in *Household Words* a statement concerning his 'domestic trouble' and denying 'all the lately whispered rumours', and sends it to the newspapers to be copied. He quarrels with Mark Lemon for declining to publish it in *Punch*. A more explicit letter appears in the New York *Tribune* and is copied by English newspapers.

(2 August–13 November) CD gives eighty-three readings in the provinces and in Scotland and Ireland.

(December) CD gives eight readings in London during the Christmas period.

1859   (30 April) First issue of CD's weekly magazine *All the Year Round* appears, containing the opening instalment of *A Tale of Two Cities*, CD having withdrawn from *Household Words* following a quarrel with his publishers, Bradbury & Evans, proprietors of *Punch*.

(28 May) The last number of *Household Words* appears, CD having acquired ownership of the magazine on 16 May.

(Summer) CD is at Gad's Hill, working on *ATTC*.

(September) CD visits Broadstairs.

(10–27 October) Second provincial reading tour (fourteen readings).

(December) CD gives three readings in London over the Christmas period.

1860   (17 July) Kate Dickens, daughter of CD, marries Charles Allston Collins.

(27 July) Death of Alfred Dickens, brother of CD.

(September) CD sells Tavistock House.

(October) CD begins work on *Great Expectations*.

(1 November) CD and Wilkie Collins visit North Devon.

(26 November) Serialization of *ATTC* is concluded.

(1 December) Serialization of *GE* begins in *All the Year Round*.

1861   (March–April) CD gives six readings in London.

(June) CD visits Lytton at Knebworth.

(3 August) Serialization of *GE* is concluded.

(28 October) CD begins a provincial reading tour (forty-six readings).

(November) Marriage of Charley Dickens; CD does not attend the wedding.

1862   (30 January) Conclusion of provincial reading tour.

(March–June) CD gives eleven readings in London.

(June) CD is offered £10,000 for an eight-month reading tour of Australia; after some hesitation, he declines.

(16 October) CD goes to Paris, and is joined there by Georgina Hogarth and Mary Dickens.

1863   (January) After spending Christmas at Gad's Hill, CD returns to Paris; he gives three charity readings at the British Embassy.

(March–June) CD gives thirteen readings in London.

(13 September) Death of Elizabeth Dickens, mother of CD.

(24 December) Death of Thackeray.

(31 December) Walter Dickens dies in India.

1864   (May) Serialization of *Our Mutual Friend* begins.

(June) CD goes for short holiday to France and Belgium.

1865   (29 May) Alfred Dickens sails for Melbourne. CD then goes to Paris for a short holiday; on the return journey on 9 June, he and Ellen Ternan are involved in a serious railway accident at Staplehurst, Kent.

(November) Serialization of *OMF* is concluded.

1866   (April–June) CD gives thirty readings in London and the provinces.

1867   (January–May) CD gives fifty-two readings in England and Ireland.

(2 November) CD is given a farewell dinner at the Freemasons' Hall.

(9 November) CD sails on the *Cuba* from Liverpool, arriving in Boston on 19th.

(2 December) CD begins a series of seventy-five readings; his itinerary includes New York, Philadelphia, Washington (where he is invited to the White House), New Haven, Hartford, Worcester, Providence.

1868   (20 April) CD's final reading of his American tour. His profit on the tour is about £20,000.

(22 April) CD sails from New York on the *Russia*.

(July) Longfellow visits Gad's Hill.

(26 September) Edward Dickens sails for Australia.

(October) Henry Dickens begins his studies at Cambridge. Death of Frederick Dickens, brother of CD.

(6 October) CD begins a farewell tour with seventy-two readings in England, Scotland and Ireland.

(14 November) CD reads 'Sikes and Nancy' for the first time to an invited audience of friends.

1869   (5 January) First public reading of 'Sikes and Nancy' takes place.

(20 April) The series of readings begun in October is abandoned after CD's collapse.

(23 April) CD, now seriously ill, consults an eminent physician.

(May) CD makes a will, including a bequest to Ellen Ternan.

(August) CD begins work on *The Mystery of Edwin Drood*.

1870   (11 January) CD begins his final series of twelve London readings.

(15 March) He gives the last of his readings.

(March) CD is received by Queen Victoria at Buckingham Palace.

(April) *ED* begins publication in monthly numbers. Death of Maclise.

(May) Death of Mark Lemon.

(8 June) After working all day on *ED*, CD suffers a stroke at dinner.

(9 June) CD dies at 6.10 p.m. without regaining consciousness.

(14 June) His body is conveyed by special train from Gad's Hill to Charing Cross for a private funeral, and buried in Westminster Abbey. For three days, thousands of members of the public pass by the open grave to pay their respects.

The Dickens Circle

AINSWORTH, WILLIAM HARRISON (1805–82), novelist and editor, met CD in 1834 and introduced him to his first publisher, Macrone, and to John Forster. In 1838, CD, Ainsworth and Forster formed a 'Trio Club'. Ainsworth succeeded CD as editor of *Bentley's Miscellany* in 1839. His historical novels *Rookwood* (1834) and *Jack Sheppard* (1839) were very popular; the latter appeared in *Bentley's Miscellany*, was illustrated by Cruikshank, and was often compared with *Oliver Twist*, to CD's annoyance (he wrote in 1840 that he was 'by some jolter-headed enemies most unjustly and untruly charged with having written a book after Mr Ainsworth's fashion'). See also Henry Fielding Dickens.

ANDERSEN, HANS CHRISTIAN (1805–75), Danish author best remembered for his fairy tales, of which the first English translation appeared in 1846. CD met him at Lady Blessington's in 1847, and invited him to Broadstairs; when Andersen visited England again in 1857 his prolonged stay at Gad's Hill was something of a trial to the Dickens family. Andersen admired CD greatly and dedicated three books to him. See E. Bredsdorff, 'Hans Andersen and Charles Dickens: A Friendship and its Dissolution', *Anglistica* (1956).

AUSTIN, HENRY, was an early friend of CD. In 1837 he married CD's younger sister Letitia, and the couple often joined the Dickens family at home or on holiday. Austin was an architect who directed alterations carried out at Tavistock House and Gad's Hill. As Secretary of the Sanitary Commission he provided CD with material for a series of articles in *HW* on this topic. CD wrote numerous letters to him.

BARROW, CHARLES (1759–1826), CD's maternal grandfather, was Chief Conductor of Moneys in the Navy Pay Office. His wife was born Mary Culliford.

BARROW, ELIZABETH (1789–1863), maiden name of Mrs John Dickens, CD's mother (see Elizabeth Dickens).

BEADNELL, MARIA (later Mrs Henry Winter) was CD's first love. He met her in 1829 when he was seventeen, became infatuated with her, and often visited the family home in Lombard Street next to the bank where her father, George Beadnell, was manager. Her parents, unimpressed by the young man's prospects, dispatched her to Paris to finish her education (probably late in 1831); when she returned, her behaviour towards him was distinctly cooler, but the relationship dragged on until 1833, when he resigned himself to failure and gave her up (on 13 May 1833 he wrote: 'I never have loved and I never can love any human creature breathing but yourself'). She later married Henry Winter, a merchant, and in February 1855 CD received a letter from her; he commented that 'three or four and twenty years vanished like a dream and I opened it with the touch of my young friend David Copperfield when he was in love'. (A few years earlier he had portrayed Maria as Dora in *DC*, and he now told Maria that the novel contained 'a faithful reflection of the passion I had for you'.) Their meeting dealt a devastating blow to his romantic memories, for the enchanting girl was now middle-aged, stout and affected, with a fondness for brandy in her tea. Thereafter he resolutely avoided her somewhat importunate overtures, and put her into *LD* as Flora Finching (the echo Dora/Flora is hardly accidental). For a version of their reunion, see *LD*, Ch. 13.

BEARD, FRANCIS CARR (FRANK), brother of Thomas Beard, became CD's doctor.

BEARD, THOMAS, was a fellow-reporter in the House of Commons in CD's early years when he was working for the *Mirror of Parliament* and Beard for the *Morning Herald*. Beard obtained a post on the *Morning Chronicle* for him in 1834, was best man at his wedding, and became a lifelong friend.

BENTLEY, RICHARD (1794–1871), publisher. In 1836, when *Pickwick* was first establishing itself as a popular success, he invited CD to write two novels; and on 22 August a contract was signed specifying a payment of £500 for each novel. He started the magazine *Bentley's Miscellany* in 1837, with CD as editor, and *Oliver Twist* was serialized there (1837–9). CD also revised a life of the clown Grimaldi for Bentley. They quarrelled over financial arrangements, and in 1839 CD resigned the editorship.

BLANCHARD, SAMUEL LAMAN (1804–45). As editor of the *True Sun*, he employed CD as a reporter from the first day of publication (5 March 1832). They later became friends, and Blanchard was one of the group who assembled in Forster's rooms in Lincoln's Inn on 3 December 1844 to hear CD read *The Chimes*. When Blanchard committed suicide in 1845, CD wrote: 'No philosophy will bear these dreadful things, or make a moment's head against them, but the practical one of doing all the good we can, in thought and deed'. His son Sidney Laman Blanchard (1827?–83) became a reporter on the *Daily News* under CD's editorship, and later contributed to *HW* and *AYR*.

BLESSINGTON, COUNTESS OF (1789–1849), stepmother and mistress of Count D'Orsay, had been a friend of Byron and was a witty hostess famous for the literary salon she held at Gore House, which was frequented by Wellington, Disraeli, Sydney Smith and others. CD was introduced there in 1836; in 1842 he wrote that 'Lady Blessington wears brilliantly, and has the gloss upon her, yet.' She contributed to the *Daily News* under CD's editorship.

BOYLE, THE HONOURABLE MARY (1810–90), niece of Mrs Richard Watson. CD met her at Rockingham Castle in 1849; they became very close friends, and she was at Gad's Hill on the day he died (having dashed there as soon as she heard of his collapse). His letters to her indicate how deeply he involved himself in his theatrical roles. CD described her as 'the very best actress I ever saw off the stage, and immeasurably better than a great many I have seen on it'.

BROWNE, HABLOT KNIGHT (1815–82), artist and illustrator who worked under the name of 'Phiz'. After the suicide of Robert Seymour, he took over the task of illustrating *Pickwick*, and a long and close collaboration followed. In the summer of 1837, he accompanied CD and Kate on a holiday trip to Belgium; and at the end of the same year, shortly before CD began work on *Nicholas Nickleby*, they went together to Yorkshire 'to look up the Cheap Schools in that county' (Forster). Browne illustrated ten of CD's fifteen novels; with *Great Expectations* he was dropped in favour of Marcus Stone. CD's letters to Browne contain many detailed instructions and valuable insights into his conception of character and scene; and our visual apprehension of many of CD's characters from Mr Pickwick and Sam Weller onwards owes much to Browne's work. See the section on 'Dickens' Illustrators' below; also John Harvey, *Victorian Novelists and their*

Illustrators (1970) and Michael Steig, *Dickens and Phiz* (1978).

BROWNING, ROBERT (1812–89), poet. He and CD knew and corresponded with each other. In 1842 CD read Browning's play *A Blot on the 'Scutcheon* in manuscript (Browning having lent it to Forster, who passed it on to CD) and wrote enthusiastically that it had thrown him into 'a perfect passion of sorrow . . . . It is full of genius . . .'.

BULWER, EDWARD, *see* LYTTON, EDWARD BULWER-

BURDETT COUTTS, MISS ANGELA (1814–1906), later Baroness Burdett Coutts, wealthy heiress and philanthropist. She was the daughter of Sir Francis Burdett, politician and reformer, and granddaughter of Thomas Coutts, banker. She met CD in 1838 or 1839 and they became lifelong friends. CD 'became the guiding conscience of her philanthropic career, and she the power through which Dickens was to bring about many a practical achievement in which the world did not even suspect his hidden hand' (Johnson). In 1843 he investigated the Field Lane Ragged School for her and wrote her a long, vivid and moving letter describing the appalling conditions: the premises were 'like an ugly dream', but 'the moral courage of the teachers is beyond all praise . . . . Their office is worthy of the apostles.' CD was not optimistic about the response to a public appeal ('There is a kind of delicacy which is not at all shocked by the existence of such things, but is excessively shocked to know of them'); but he urged Miss Coutts to come to the rescue ('I deem it an experiment most worthy of your charitable hand'), and threw himself energetically into the practical details of amelioration, including 'a good supply of running water, soap, and towels'. In 1846 he drew up a plan for another charitable enterprise: a home for the rehabilitation of prostitutes to be established by Miss Coutts. When the home, Urania Cottage in Shepherd's Bush, was opened, he chose the premises, appointed the matron, and organized its running. In 1852 he supervised in detail another of her projects, slumclearance and the building of model flats in Bethnal Green. Dickens made Miss Coutts his confidante as his marital troubles moved towards a crisis, and she tried in vain to effect a reconciliation between him and his wife. *The Heart of Charles Dickens*, ed. Edgar Johnson (New York, 1952), is a selection of CD's letters to Miss Coutts (published in England [1953] as *Letters from Dickens to Angela Burdett Coutts, 1841–65*).

CARLYLE, THOMAS (1795–1881), author and sage. CD's friendship with Carlyle was an important influence on his writings, and *A Tale of Two Cities* in particular shows his debt to Carlyle as a historian. CD greatly admired his *French Revolution*, and the scenes of mob violence in *Barnaby Rudge* owe something to that work. He asked Carlyle for advice on source-materials when he was working on *ATTC*, and was staggered when Carlyle dispatched two cartloads of books from the London Library. *Hard Times* is dedicated to him. See Michael Goldberg, *Carlyle and Dickens* (1972) and William Oddie, *Dickens and Carlyle: The Question of Influence* (1972). When CD died, Carlyle wrote:

No death since 1866 [when his wife, Jane Welsh Carlyle, died] has fallen on me with such a stroke; no Literary Man's hitherto ever did. The good, the gentle, ever friendly noble Dickens, – every inch of him an Honest Man!

On another occasion, in conversation, he was less enthusiastic:

Dickens, he said, was a good little fellow, and one of the most cheery, innocent natures he had ever encountered. But he lived among a set of admirers who did him no good . . . . His theory of life was entirely wrong. He thought men ought to be buttered up, and the world made soft and accommodating for them, and all sorts of fellow have turkey for their Christmas dinner . . . . Dickens had not written anything which would be found of much use in solving the problems of life . . . . Thackeray had more reality in him and would cut up into a dozen Dickenses . . . .

CATTERMOLE, GEORGE (1800–68), artist, executed many illustrations, mainly of architectural subjects, for *OCS* and *BR*. It was in a letter to Cattermole, giving details for the illustration of Little Nell lying dead, that CD wrote: 'I am breaking my heart over this story.' Cattermole also acted with CD's company of players in a production of *Every Man in his Humour*.

CHISHOLM, MRS CAROLINE (1808–77), philanthropist, lived in India (1832–8) and Australia (1838–46). On her return to England she established the Family Colonization Loan Society to assist those emigrating to Australia, and published pamphlets on emigration. She met CD in February 1850, and contributed to the first number of *HW* ('A Bundle of Emigrants' Letters', jointly with

CD). The references to Australian emigration near the end of *DC* no doubt owe something to CD's contacts with Mrs Chisholm and her work, and she is probably the prototype of Mrs Jellyby in *BH* (after visiting Mrs Chisholm's home, CD wrote to Miss Burdett Coutts: 'I dream of Mrs Chisholm, and her housekeeping. The dirty faces of her children are my constant companions').

CHORLEY, HENRY FOTHERGILL (1808–72) was for nearly forty years on the staff of the *Athenaeum* and wrote reviews of many of CD's novels for that journal, as well as his obituary. From 1854 he was a close friend of CD and a frequent visitor to Gad's Hill, where he took part in amateur theatricals (Mary Dickens wrote that 'My father was very fond of him').

COLLINS, CHARLES ALLSTON (1828–73), artist, author, and younger brother of Wilkie Collins. He married CD's daughter Kate in 1860. CD originally wished him to illustrate *Edwin Drood*; in the event, he executed only the cover-design, ill-health preventing him from continuing the work. Collins also contributed to *HW* and *AYR*.

COLLINS, WILLIAM WILKIE (1824–89), novelist and close friend of Dickens in his later years (Forster described him as 'one of [CD's] dearest and most valued friends'). They met in 1851 and from 1852 Collins contributed frequently to *Household Words*, joining its staff in 1856. In 1853, CD, Collins and Augustus Egg went together on a tour of France, Switzerland and Italy. CD produced Collins' melodrama *The Frozen Deep*, and they collaborated on *The Lazy Tour of Two Idle Apprentices* and *No Thoroughfare*. Collins' novel *Hide and Seek* (1854) is dedicated to CD 'as a token of admiration and affection'; *The Woman in White* (1860) and *The Moonstone* (1868) were serialized in *AYR*. Collins' unconventionality made him a congenial companion, and the elements of mystery and detection in CD's later novels may well owe something to his influence (see T. S. Eliot's essay, 'Wilkie Collins and Dickens', in his *Selected Essays* [1932].) CD wrote numerous letters to Collins, who is the subject of a biography by Kenneth Robinson (1951).

CORNWALL, BARRY, *see* PROCTER, BRYAN WALLER.

COWDEN-CLARKE, MARY (Mrs Charles Cowden-Clarke) (1809–98), authoress, played in CD's amateur theatricals, her roles including that of Mistress Quickly in *The Merry Wives of Windsor*. In her *Recollections of Writers* (1878) she wrote that, when she read the news of CD's death, 'the sun seemed suddenly blotted out'.

CRUIKSHANK, GEORGE (1792–1878), artist and illustrator. He illustrated *Sketches by Boz* and *Oliver Twist* (see the section on 'Dickens' Illustrators' below). His earlier work included illustrations for Pierce Egan's *Life in London* (1821).

DANA, RICHARD HENRY, JR. (1815–82), American author best known for *Two Years before the Mast* (1840). CD met him during his first American tour in 1842 and found him 'a very nice fellow indeed'. Dana for his part described CD in far from flattering terms: 'a dissipated looking mouth with a vulgar draw to it, a muddy olive complexion, stubby fingers, and a hand by no means patrician. A hearty off hand manner, far from well bred, and a rapid dashing way of talking'; he found him, however, 'full of life', and added, 'I never saw a face fuller of light'. Dana's father said of CD, 'He has the finest of eyes; and his whole countenance speaks life and *action* the face seems to flicker with the *heart's* and *mind's* activity. You cannot tell how dead the faces near him seemed.' Dana and CD met again when CD returned to America in 1867.

DAVIS, MRS ELIZA, wife of J. P. Davis, a Jewish banker who purchased Tavistock House from CD in 1860. In 1863 she wrote to him 'telling him that Jews regarded his portrayal of Fagin in *Oliver Twist* as "a great wrong" to their people' (Johnson); as a result CD introduced the character of Riah – a good Jew exploited by a Christian moneylender – into *Our Mutual Friend*.

DE LA RUE, MRS EMILE, the English wife of a Swiss banker, was living in Genoa when CD and his wife visited Italy in 1844–5, and the two couples struck up a friendship. Mrs De La Rue suffered from serious psychological disturbance, including hallucinations, and CD treated her on many occasions by 'mesmerism' (he had previously exerted his hypnotic powers on both Kate and his sister-in-law Georgina). Kate was annoyed and jealous as a result of her husband's ministrations, which were often required during the night. CD visited the De La Rues again when he was in Genoa, this time without Kate, in 1853. He corresponded frequently with M. De La Rue. In his fiction, his interest in mesmerism is most clearly manifested in *Edwin Drood*. See F. Kaplan, *Dickens and Mesmerism* (1975).

DICKENS, ALFRED, brother of CD and third child of his parents. Born in 1813, he died in childhood.

DICKENS, ALFRED D'ORSAY TENNYSON, CD's sixth child and fourth son, born in 1845 and named after his godfathers, Alfred Tennyson and Count D'Orsay. (Edward FitzGerald saw in the names evidence of CD's 'Snobbishness and Cockneyism'.) Alfred emigrated to Australia in 1865 and died in America in 1912. He published 'My Father and his Friends', *Nash's Magazine*, IV (1911). See Mary Lazarus, *A Tale of Two Brothers* (1973) for an account of Alfred's Australian career.

DICKENS, ALFRED LAMERT, brother of CD and seventh child of his parents, born in 1822. He became an engineer and was engaged in railway construction. When he died in 1860 he left a widow and five children in need of CD's financial support.

DICKENS, AUGUSTUS, youngest brother of CD and eighth child of his parents. CD's nickname for Augustus was Moses, 'in honour of the *Vicar of Wakefield*'; the child's nasal pronunciation of this as 'Boses' was shortened in the family to 'Boz', and CD adopted this as his pseudonym very early in his career as an author. Augustus, born in 1827, died in Chicago in 1866.

DICKENS, CATHERINE (KATE) (1815–79), born Catherine Hogarth, was the wife of CD and the mother of his ten children. She was the eldest child of George Hogarth, and CD met her in 1835 at her parents' home in York Place, Chelsea. They were married at St Luke's Church, Chelsea, on 2 April 1836. They were legally separated in 1858. Their children – Charles, Mary, Kate, Walter, Francis, Alfred, Sydney, Henry, Dora and Edward – are given under separate entries. See Hebe Elsna, *Unwanted Wife: A Defence of Mrs. Charles Dickens* (1963); also Appendix B.

DICKENS, CHARLES CULLIFORD BOZ (Charley), CD's eldest child, was born in 1837 and educated at Eton. He followed a career in business but went bankrupt in 1868, whereupon CD placed him in the office of *AYR*. He subsequently became sub-editor and was left a share in the magazine in CD's will. He married Bessie Evans, whose father was a partner in the publishing firm of Bradbury & Evans, in 1862; CD had quarrelled with the firm, disapproved of the match, and did not attend the wedding. Charley published 'Glimpses of Charles Dickens', *North American Review*, CLX (1895) and 'Reminiscences of my Father', *Windsor Magazine*, Christmas Supplement (1934). He died in 1896.

DICKENS, DORA ANNIE, CD's ninth child and third daughter, was born on 16 August 1850 while *David Copperfield* was in process of serialization and she was named after Dora in that novel. She died in infancy on 14 April 1851.

DICKENS, EDWARD BULWER LYTTON (nicknamed Plorn), CD's seventh son and youngest child, born on 13 March 1852, was named after his godfather Edward Bulwer-Lytton. He became a favourite of his father, but did badly at school (CD lamented 'his want of application and continuity of purpose') and was dispatched to Australia ('I hope he may take better to the Bush than to Books'). He died there in 1902. See Mary Lazarus, *A Tale of Two Brothers* (1973).

DICKENS, ELIZABETH, née Barrow (1789–1863), mother of CD, married John Dickens in 1809 and bore him eight children, of whom CD was the second. She taught him to read and tried unsuccessfully to start a school. CD felt bitterly about her wish that he should be sent back to the blacking warehouse after his father had terminated his employment there. He portrayed her as Mrs Nickleby in *Nicholas Nickleby*. She became senile in old age.

DICKENS, FRANCES ELIZABETH (Fanny), sister of CD and the eldest child of her parents, was born on 28 October 1810. As a child she sang comic songs with CD. She won a scholarship to the Royal Academy of Music, did well there, and was launched on a musical career. She married Henry Burnett, and died of tuberculosis in 1848. Her crippled son Harry is said to have given CD the idea of Paul Dombey.

DICKENS, FRANCIS JEFFREY (Frank), fifth child and third son of CD, was born in 1844 and named after his godfather Francis Jeffrey. He was employed for a time in the office of *AYR*, but proved of little use there and in 1863 went to India to join the Bengal Mounted Police. He died in America in 1886.

DICKENS, FREDERICK (1820–68), brother of CD and sixth child of his parents, visited CD in Genoa in September 1844. Chronically impecunious, he was continually sponging on his brother, who told him in 1856 that 'the possibility of your having any further expenses from me is absolutely and finally past'. When Fred died in 1868, CD wrote to Forster: 'It was a wasted life, but God forbid that one should be hard upon it, or upon anything in this world that is not deliberately and coldly wrong.' He married Anna Weller (see under Christiana Weller).

DICKENS, HARRIET, sister of CD and fifth child of her parents, was born in 1819 and died in childhood.

DICKENS, HENRY FIELDING (Harry), CD's eighth child and sixth son, was born in 1849. His godfather was Harrison Ainsworth. In 1863 he started a family newspaper, *The Gad's Hill Gazette*. He did well at school and at Trinity College, Cambridge, where he was awarded a mathematical scholarship. He subsequently had a successful career at the Bar, became a QC, was knighted, and died in 1933. He published *Memories of my Father* (1928); 'A Chat about my Father', *Harper's Magazine*, cxxix (1914); and *Recollections* (1934).

DICKENS, JOHN (1785/6–1851), father of CD, was the son of the butler and housekeeper at Crewe Hall, Lord Crewe's country house, and was appointed to the Navy Pay Office at Somerset House in 1805. He married Elizabeth Barrow in London in 1809, and she bore him eight children. When Charles, the second, was born, John Dickens was a clerk in the Navy Pay Office at Portsea with an annual salary of £110. In 1815 he was moved back to London, in 1817 to Chatham, and in 1822 to London again. Improvident and chronically impecunious, he was arrested for a debt of forty pounds in 1824 and imprisoned in the Marshalsea for three months; there he became chairman of the prisoners' committee and author of a petition for a royal bounty to drink the King's health on his birthday. On his release, he became a reporter; but he was arrested for debt again in 1834. This time he was rescued by CD, to whom he was thereafter a tiresome financial burden (on one occasion he remarked of his father, 'How long he is, growing up'). CD settled him in Exeter in 1838, but he later moved back to London. CD was with him when he died in 1851. Micawber (*DC*) and William Dorrit (*LD*) reflect different aspects of John Dickens' character.

DICKENS, KATE MACREADY (Katey), third child and second daughter of CD, was born in 1839. Her godfather was CD's friend Macready. She married Charles Allston Collins. After her parents' separation, although continuing to live with her father, she frequently visited her mother. In her old age she told her version of the story of the breakdown of CD's marriage and his affair with Ellen Ternan to Gladys Storey; see G. Storey, *Dickens and Daughter* (1939). She died in 1929. As well as publishing various reminiscences of her father, she is the author of unpublished recollections (ms. in the Pierpont Morgan Library, New York).

DICKENS, LETITIA, sister of CD and fourth child of her parents, was born in 1816. She married Henry Austin in 1837 and died in 1874.

DICKENS, MARY (Mamie), second child and eldest daughter of CD, was born in 1838. Her godfather was John Forster. She never married, but remained a lifelong companion to her father and after the separation never visited her mother until after his death. She died in 1896 and is the author of *My Father as I Recall Him* (1897) and other reminiscences. See also HOGARTH, GEORGINA.

DICKENS, SYDNEY SMITH HALDIMAND, fifth son and seventh child of CD, was born in 1847 and named after Sydney Smith (1771–1845), author and wit, whom CD had met at London literary salons, and William Haldimand, a former MP resident in Lausanne whom CD met during his visit to Switzerland in 1846. CD nicknamed Sydney 'the Ocean Spectre' because he habitually had a faraway look in his eyes as if he were contemplating some spectre out at sea. Appropriately enough, he joined the Royal Navy as a cadet, and rose to be a lieutenant; but his extravagance and dissipation caused his father much anxiety. He died at sea of bronchitis in 1872.

DICKENS, WALTER LANDOR, fourth child and second son of CD, was born in 1841 and named after his godfather Walter Savage Landor. With the help of Miss Burdett Coutts he obtained a cadetship in the East India Company's 26th Native Infantry, and sailed to India in July 1857. CD said on that occasion that 'he felt the parting was like having great teeth drawn with a wrench'. Walter distinguished himself during the Indian Mutiny, but died in Calcutta in 1863.

DILKE, CHARLES WENTWORTH (1789–1864), journalist and critic. He was a friend of CD's father and is said to have visited the blacking-warehouse on one occasion and to have met the young CD there. In the second chapter of his biography Forster relates the episode and its distant aftermath as follows:

I asked [Dickens] if he remembered ever having seen in his boyhood our friend the elder Mr Dilke, his father's acquaintance and contemporary, who had been a clerk in the same office in Somerset House at which Mr John Dickens belonged. Yes, he said, he recollected seeing him at a house in Gerrard Street, where his uncle Barrow lodged during an illness, and Mr Dilke had visited him. Never at any other time. Upon which I told him that someone else had been intended in the mention made to me, for that the reference implied not merely his being met accidentally, but his having had some juvenile employment in a warehouse near the Strand; at which place

Mr Dilke, being with the elder Dickens one day, had noticed him, and received, in return for the gift of a half-crown, a very low bow. He was silent for several minutes; I felt that I had unintentionally touched a painful place in his memory; and to Mr Dilke I never spoke of the subject again. It was not, however, then, but some weeks later, that Dickens made further allusion to my thus having struck unconsciously upon a time of which he never could lose the remembrance while he remembered anything, and the recollection of which, at intervals, haunted him and made him miserable, even to that hour.

Very shortly afterwards, I learnt in all their detail the incidents that had been so painful to him, and what then was said to me or written respecting them revealed the story of his boyhood.

Dilke had known Keats and Shelley, and was editor of the *Athenaeum* (1830–46) and for a time business manager of the *Daily News*. His son and namesake became an MP and a baronet, and was one of those responsible for proposing the Great Exhibition of 1851.

DOLBY, GEORGE (died 1900) was from 1866 CD's manager for his reading tours. He later published *Charles Dickens as I Knew him: The Story of the Reading Tours, 1866–1870* (1885).

D'ORSAY, ALFRED COUNT (1801–52), French aristocrat and artist, a 'glittering cosmopolitan dandy' and 'dilettante man-about-town' (Johnson) who settled in England and lived at Gore House with Lady Blessington. CD met him in 1836 and is said to have been influenced by his flamboyant taste in dress. He became godfather to CD's sixth child, Alfred.

EGG, AUGUSTUS (1816–63), artist, became a friend of CD and a fellow-actor in amateur theatricals. He travelled to Italy with CD and Wilkie Collins in 1853. He proposed to Georgina Hogarth, CD's sister-in-law, but was refused.

FAGIN, BOB, one of the boys employed at Warren's blacking warehouse (see also Paul Green). He lived with his brother-in-law, a Thames waterman, befriended CD when he worked alongside him, and presumably provided the name for Fagin in *Oliver Twist*.

FECHTER, CHARLES (1824–79), actor and dramatist of German origin, was one of the group of younger men who were friends of

CD in his later years. CD greatly admired his acting: when he saw Fechter in *La Dame aux Camélias* in Paris, he remarked that 'A man who can do this can do anything.' After making a name in the French theatre, Fechter settled in England in 1860. He acted in a dramatized version of *No Thoroughfare*, a Christmas story by CD and Wilkie Collins, when it was produced at the Adelphi Theatre in London in 1868. In 1865 he sent CD a present of a Swiss chalet packed in fifty-eight boxes; it was erected in the garden at Gad's Hill, and it was there that CD wrote the last lines of the uncompleted *Edwin Drood*. CD contributed an essay 'On Mr Fechter's Acting' to the *Atlantic Monthly* in August 1869.

FELTON, CORNELIUS (1807–62), Professor of Greek at Harvard University, was a lively and somewhat Pickwickian character whom CD met on his first American tour in 1842. CD described him as 'a most delightful fellow – unaffected, hearty, genial, jolly; quite an Englishman of the best sort'; later he said that 'he was one of the jolliest and simplest of men, and not at all starry, or stripey'. Felton said of CD: 'I had been convinced since the first number of Pickwick, that one of the greatest minds of the age was coming out and . . . that Dickens was the most original and inventive genius since Shakespeare!' When *American Notes* was published, Felton said: 'Opinions are various, but we agree pretty well here, in thinking it a capital book; lively, spirited, true and good humored' (a view that was not shared by all his country-men). His enthusiastic review of Dickens' book in the *North American Review* for January 1843 (reprinted in *Critical Heritage*, pp. 130–5) delighted CD and was a notable exception to the generally cool welcome given to that work in America. Felton visited CD in England in 1853.

FIELDS, JAMES T. (1817–81), Boston editor and publisher. As a young man he attended a dinner for CD in Boston during the 1842 American tour. Fields and his wife Annie (1834–1915), a prominent literary hostess, became warm admirers of CD. They visited him at Gad's Hill in 1859 and saw a good deal of him during his second American tour, which Fields organized. In 1869 they again visited him in England, and CD accompanied them on sight-seeing tours of London, Rochester and Canterbury. With Fields he visited the unsavoury neighbour-hood of the Ratcliffe Highway in London's East End, where they encountered in an opium den the old woman portrayed in *ED* as 'the Princess Puffer'. In October 1869 CD read to Fields the newly written opening chapters of that novel. Fields' reminiscences of CD are included in his *Yesterdays with Authors* (Boston, 1872). Annie Fields' diaries contain many references to CD: see *Memories of a Hostess*, ed. M. A. DeWolfe Howe (1923).

FILDES, SIR LUKE (1844–1927), artist and illustrator, executed the illustrations for *The Mystery of Edwin Drood*. When he queried the curious length of Jasper's black neckerchief, CD is said to have told him, 'I must have the double necktie! It is necessary, for Jasper strangles Edwin Drood with it' (reported by Fildes in a letter to *The Times* in 1905). On the day of CD's death, Fildes painted the well-known picture 'The Empty Chair'.

FITZGERALD, PERCY (1834–1925), Irish author and journalist, was one of a group who became known as 'Mr Dickens's young men' (see also Payn, Sala, Yates). CD met him in Dublin in 1858. Fitzgerald was a frequent contributor to *HW* and *AYR*. He visited CD at Gad's Hill and made him a present of an Irish bloodhound; subsequently he published *The History of Pickwick* (1891), *Memories of Charles Dickens* (1913), and other books on Dickens and on John Forster.

FONBLANQUE, ALBANY (1793–1872), journalist and friend of CD, was for a time editor of *The Examiner* and a leader writer on the *Daily News* under CD's editorship.

FORSTER, JOHN (1812–76), CD's most intimate friend and first biographer, attended Newcastle Grammar School and came to London in 1828, where he studied at University College and entered the Inner Temple. He moved in literary circles, was a friend of Leigh Hunt and Charles Lamb, and became a successful journalist. In 1832 he joined the staff of the *Examiner* and later contributed a favourable review of *Sketches by Boz* to that journal. From 1847 to 1855, he edited the *Examiner* and published there some significant reviews of CD's novels. He met CD on Christmas Day 1836, the introduction being performed by Harrison Ainsworth. As their friendship grew, they spent much time together and corresponded frequently, and Forster read and corrected CD's proofs. The Library Edition of CD's works (1858) is dedicated to him. He advised CD on business and personal matters, representing him in negotiations with his publishers (Robert L. Patten aptly describes him as CD's 'unofficial literary agent from the days of *Pickwick* onward') and also over the legal separation from his wife. He was one of the executors of CD's will. He briefly succeeded CD as editor of the *Daily News* in 1846 and became part-proprietor of *HW*. Forster was a man of quick temper, and he and CD sometimes quarrelled; he was also jealous of CD's friendships with younger men such as Wilkie Collins, whose role in CD's later life is somewhat played down in Forster's biography. Forster is caricatured as Podsnap in *Our Mutual Friend*. His *Life of Charles Dickens* appeared in 1872–4 and is still a major source. He bequeathed his collection of CD's manuscripts to what is now the Victoria and Albert Museum.

FRITH, WILLIAM (1819–1909), artist, met CD in 1842 and became a member of his circle of friends. He painted a portrait of CD in 1859.

GASKELL, MRS ELIZABETH CLEGHORN (1810–65), novelist, made important contributions to *HW* and *AYR*. CD much admired her first novel, *Mary Barton* (1848), and met her in 1849. On 31 January 1850 he wrote inviting her to contribute 'a short tale, or any number of tales' to *HW*. ('I do honestly know', he wrote in the same letter, 'that there is no living English writer whose aid I would desire to enlist in preference to the authoress of Mary Barton (a book that most profoundly affected and impressed me).') The result was 'Lizzie Leigh', serialized in the first three numbers of the newly established magazine. *Cranford* appeared in eight parts published at irregular intervals (1851–3), and her 'industrial novel' *North and South* was serialized in 1854–5, immediately following CD's own exercise in the same sub-genre, *HT*. This last work involved her in a certain amount of disagreement with CD: she objected to his editorial interference, refusing to allow what she had written to be subjected to revision ' "even by Mr Dickens" ' (who quoted her phrase in a letter of 24 March 1855); for his part he was not surprised that her story caused the sales of the magazine to fall and confessed to finding it, 'so divided, wearisome in the last degree' (14 October 1854). Her husband William Gaskell (1805–84), a Unitarian minister, was acquainted with CD, who visited the Gaskells when he was in Manchester.

GILES, REV. WILLIAM, was the minister of the Zion Baptist Chapel in Chatham, Kent, during CD's boyhood residence in that town. Giles was an acquaintance of the Dickens family, and his son William ran a school to which CD and his sister Fanny were sent. William Giles, a young Oxford graduate, is said to have recognized in CD the signs of exceptional promise, and to have given him special attention.

GREEN, PAUL (Poll), was a boy employed in Warren's blacking warehouse during CD's time there (see also Bob Fagin). He was the son of a fireman employed at Drury Lane Theatre.

HILL, MRS SEYMOUR, was the prototype of Miss Mowcher in *David Copperfield*. Edgar Johnson recounts this curious episode as follows:

> [In December 1849] he received a curious and touching communication. This was from a chiropodist and manicurist named Mrs. Seymour Hill, a tiny dwarf, whom he had seen trotting around on short legs in the neighborhood of Devonshire Terrace, and whose grotesque oddity of physique he had used for Miss Mowcher in his story, never imagining it would meet her eyes. But she had seen it, and been bitterly hurt. 'I have suffered long and much,' she wrote, 'from my personal deformities but never before at the hands of a Man so highly gifted as Charles Dickens . . .' What made injury worse was that the character was clearly intended to be odious. 'Now you have made my nights sleepless and my daily work tearfull.'
>
> Dickens was moved to remorse. He was unfeignedly sorry, he replied, to have given her a moment's distress. It was true that he had partly had her in mind, but a great portion of the character was based on someone quite different, and even in appearance Miss Mowcher resembled almost as much still another person, unknown to him, whom he had passed in the streets. 'Pray consider all these things and do not make yourself unhappy.' He was so pained by her distress that to prevent her passing 'another of those sleepless nights' he would alter the entire design of the character from his original intention 'and oblige the Reader to hold it in a pleasant remembrance'. This offer Mrs. Hill accepted, and in the later numbers of the novel Dickens faithfully kept his promise.

HOGARTH, CATHERINE, maiden name of Mrs Charles Dickens: see Catherine Dickens.

HOGARTH, GEORGE (1783–1870), CD's father-in-law and father of Catherine Dickens and Georgina and Mary Hogarth, had been a lawyer in Edinburgh and a friend of Sir Walter Scott. He moved to London in 1834, met CD, and in 1835 became editor of a newly established newspaper, the *Evening Chronicle*, to which he invited

CD to contribute. Hogarth contributed a favourable review of *SB* to the *Morning Chronicle*. CD became a friend of the Hogarth family, and met his future wife at her father's house in Chelsea (18 York Place). Hogarth became music critic of the *Daily News* under CD's editorship in 1846, and held the position for twenty years.

HOGARTH, GEORGINA (1827–1917), fifth child and third daughter of George Hogarth, sister of Catherine Dickens, and hence CD's sister-in-law. She joined the Dickens household after the first visit to America in 1842, accompanied them on the Italian tour of 1844–5, and became a permanent member of the family. As time went on, she assumed control of domestic affairs; she sided with CD over his separation from her sister, and remained with him after Kate's departure. She was with CD when he suffered his fatal stroke, and he made her (with Forster) co-executrix of his will, in which he wrote:

I solemnly enjoin my dear children always to remember how much they owe to the said Georgina Hogarth, and never to be wanting in a grateful and affectionate attachment to her, for they know well that she has been, through all the stages of their growth and progress, their ever useful self-denying and devoted friend.

She co-edited (with Mamie Dickens) the first important collection of CD's letters (1880–2).

HOGARTH, MARY (1819–37), third child and second daughter of George Hogarth, sister of Catherine Dickens, and hence CD's sister-in-law. She came to stay with him and Kate shortly after their marriage, and lived with them at Furnival's Inn and then at 48 Doughty Street. On 7 May 1837, at the age of seventeen, she died very suddenly in CD's arms, apparently of heart disease. He was devoted to her and was overwhelmed with grief; the serialization of *Oliver Twist* in *Bentley's Miscellany* was interrupted, his announcement there referring to 'the sudden death of a very dear young relative to whom he was most affectionately attached, and whose society had been for a long time the chief solace of his labours'. He composed the inscription on her tombstone: 'Mary Scott Hogarth/ died 7th May 1837/ Young, beautiful, and good/ God in his mercy/ Numbered her with his angels/ At the early age of/ Seventeen.' The death of Little Nell in *The Old Curiosity Shop* expresses something of his feelings: of that episode he wrote that 'Dear Mary died yesterday, when I think of this sad story.' He dreamed of Mary repeatedly, wore her ring until his death, and for years wished to be buried in the same grave. To a friend he wrote: 'Thank God she died in my arms, and the very last words she whispered were of me . . . . I solemnly believe that so perfect a creature never breathed . . . . She had not a fault.'

HOLLAND, LADY AUGUSTA-MARY (1770–1845), was the hostess of a celebrated political and literary salon at Holland House. CD was introduced to her in 1838.

HOLLINGSHEAD, JOHN (1827–1904), journalist and theatre manager, contributed frequently to *HW* from 1857 and subsequently joined its staff; later he contributed to *AYR*. His *My Lifetime* (1895) includes reminiscences of CD.

HOOD, THOMAS (1799–1845), poet and wit, met CD about 1840. He reviewed *The Old Curiosity Shop* and *Barnaby Rudge* in the *Athenaeum* (see *Critical Heritage*, pp. 94–8, 103–5). CD refers to the former review in the 1848 preface to *OCS* ('an essay of which [Little Nell] was the principal theme, so earnestly, so eloquently, and tenderly appreciative of her, and of all her shadowy kith and kin, that it would have been insensibility in me, if I could have read it without an unusual glow of pleasure and encouragement').

HORNE, RICHARD HENGIST (1803–84), poet and journalist, was a reporter on the *Daily News* under CD's editorship and a sub-editor of *HW* in 1850–1. He emigrated to Australia in 1852. There is a chapter on CD in his *A New Spirit of the Age* (1844).

HUFFAM, CHRISTOPHER, CD's godfather, a prosperous naval rigger, lived at Limehouse, and CD as a boy sometimes visited him there.

HUNT, WILLIAM HOLMAN (1827–1910), artist and member of the Pre-Raphaelite Brotherhood, was best man at the wedding in 1860 of CD's daughter Kate to Charles Allston Collins and was a friend and former fellow-student of the bridegroom. CD admired his work.

HUNT, LEIGH (1784–1859), a versatile and prolific author, had been a friend of Byron, Lamb and others, and had introduced Keats and Shelley to each other. Forster introduced him to CD in 1838, and Hunt commented: 'What a face is his to meet in a drawing-room! It has the life and soul in it of fifty human beings.' *Sketches by Boz* owes something to the influence of Hunt's work as an essayist. In 1847 he received a civil list pension. In *Bleak House* Hunt is caricatured as Harold Skimpole. CD wrote in a letter: 'I suppose he is the most exact portrait that was ever painted in words! . . . It is an absolute reproduction of a real man'; and a contemporary remarked that he 'recognized Skimpole instantly . . . and so did every person whom I talked with about it who had ever had Leigh Hunt's acquaintance'. After Hunt's death, CD regretted his caricature and claimed that it had been intended to capture only certain of Hunt's qualities and not to stand as a complete portrait (see 'Leigh Hunt: a Remonstrance', *AYR*, 24 December 1859). See also Edmund Blunden, *Leigh Hunt and his Circle* (1930).

IRVING, WASHINGTON (1783–1859), American author, met CD in New York in 1842 after having previously corresponded with him. It has been suggested that the character of Tony Weller in *Pickwick Papers* owes something to that of the coachman in Irving's *Sketch-Book*, published in 1820.

JEFFREY, FRANCIS (Lord Jeffrey) (1773–1850), Scottish judge, founder and editor of the *Edinburgh Review*, and a notoriously severe critic of Wordsworth and others. He was one of the most notable of CD's early admirers: he praised *Oliver Twist*, and his grief over the deaths of Little Nell and Paul Dombey is famous. The two men became friends, and CD visited him in Scotland in 1841. CD named his third son after Jeffrey, and dedicated *The Cricket on the Hearth* to him. There is a chapter on Jeffrey in J. W. T. Ley's *The Dickens Circle* (1918).

JERDAN, WILLIAM. As editor of the *Literary Gazette* he published (in June 1836) one of the earliest criticisms of *PP*, which had at that time reached only the fourth number and was still little known, and wrote to CD urging him to develop the character of Sam Weller 'to the utmost'. CD later invited him to the dinner held to celebrate the completion of *PP*. He contributed to *Bentley's Miscellany* and acted as Bentley's representative in CD's dispute with the publisher in 1840.

JERROLD, DOUGLAS (1803–57), humorist and dramatist, was a popular contributor to *Punch* in its early years. He met CD in 1838, was a member of the sub-editorial staff of the *Daily News* under his editorship, and was a fellow-actor in various amateur theatricals. They quarrelled in 1849 over the issue of capital punishment, but were soon reconciled. His son, William Blanchard Jerrold (1826–84), was a journalist and author who contributed frequently to *HW*.

JONES, WILLIAM, was the principal and owner of Wellington House Academy in Hampstead Road, where CD was a pupil in 1824–7. He was a Welshman and a savage disciplinarian who has been proposed as a prototype for Mr Creakle in *David Copperfield*. His staff included Mr Taylor, who was lame and played the flute (cf. Mr Mell in *David Copperfield*); Mr Manville (or Mandeville); Mr Shiers, who coached CD in Latin; a dancing-master; and a French master. For CD's later account of the school, see 'Our School', *HW*, 11 October 1851.

KENT, CHARLES (1823–1902), journalist and author, contributed to *HW* and *AYR* and organized the farewell banquet given to CD on 2 November 1867 before his departure for America. He edited the *Sun* from 1845 to 1871, and published an interesting study, *Charles Dickens as a Reader* (1872). For his enthusiastic reviews of *Dombey and Son* in the *Sun*, see *Critical Heritage*, p. 227; it was this that led to a meeting, and a lifelong friendship, between Kent and CD.

KNIGHT, CHARLES (1791–1873), journalist and publisher, and friend of CD. He contributed to *HW*, and was a fellow-member of the Shakespeare Society, whose membership also included Forster, Thackeray, Macready, Talfourd, Procter, Blanchard, Jerrold, Maclise, Cattermole, Charles and Edwin Landseer, and others. His *Passages of a Working Life* (1864) includes references to CD.

KNOWLES, JAMES SHERIDAN (1784–1862), dramatist. In March 1832 CD arranged to audition for a part in his play *The Hunchback*, but was prevented by a cold from attending and never again attempted a theatrical career. CD was later energetic in securing financial aid for Knowles in his old age.

KOLLE, HENRY, was a friend of CD during his period as a lawyer's clerk. He married Anne, sister of Maria Beadnell, and was involved in CD's courtship of Maria.

LAMERT, JAMES, was a stepson of CD's aunt and lodged with the Dickens family at Chatham during CD's boyhood. During this period Lamert often took the boy to the Theatre Royal. After the move to Camden town, he continued to live with the Dickens family, made CD a toy theatre, and offered him ('in an evil hour for me', as CD later said) a job in the blacking warehouse that he managed for his brother-in-law George Lamert.

LANDOR, WALTER SAVAGE (1775–1864), poet and prose-writer, became godfather to CD's fourth child, Walter. It was during a visit to Landor in Bath in 1840 that CD conceived the idea of little Nell, the heroine of *The Old Curiosity Shop*. Landor is the prototype of Boythorn in *Bleak House*: Henry Crabb Robinson said that in CD's portrait Landor's 'fierce tones, tenderness of heart, and exaggeration in all his judgements' are 'described with great truth and force'. Boythorn is referred to in CD's review of Forster's biography of Landor (*AYR*, 24 July 1869).

LANDSEER, SIR EDWIN (1802–73), animal-painter, designer of the Trafalgar Square lions, and one of the numerous artist-friends of CD. He and his brother Charles were members of the dining-club called 'The Portwiners', to which CD belonged; other members included Forster, Thackeray, Bulwer, Macready, Lemon and Maclise. During CD's Italian tour Landseer looked after his pet raven Grip and was responsible for the much-quoted joke that CD was 'raven mad'.

LAYARD, SIR AUSTEN HENRY (1817–94), traveller, archaeologist and author: he excavated Nineveh and other Middle Eastern sites in the 1840s, and published accounts of his findings; later he became a radical politician (he was a Liberal MP from 1852) and eventually a privy councillor and diplomat. He accompanied CD on an ascent of Vesuvius during the later's Italian tour. CD supported his campaign against administrative incompetence. After a visit to the Crimea during the war there, Layard returned to England determined to press for reform. CD published a series of articles in *HW* in 1855 attacking the government, and was a subscribing member of Layard's Administrative Reform Association. (He addressed the Association on 27 June 1855: see *Speeches*, pp. 197–208). The satire on bureaucracy in *Little Dorrit* needs to be read with this background in mind.

LEECH, JOHN (1817–1864), artist, illustrator and caricaturist and a frequent contributor to *Punch*, executed four illustrations for *A Christmas Carol*, and was one of the illustrators for *The Chimes* and *The Haunted Man*. Leech went to Norfolk with CD in January 1849; he and his wife accompanied CD and Kate on holiday at Brighton in the following month; and CD took a short holiday in Paris with him in 1851. When Leech died, CD wrote: 'This death of poor Leech . . . has put me out woefully.'

LEMON, MARK (1809–70), dramatist and journalist, was one of the founders and at first joint editor and later editor of *Punch*. He was a member of CD's sub-editorial staff on the *Daily News* and contributed to *HW*. He became a close friend of CD, went to

Norfolk with him in January 1849, acted with him in amateur theatricals, and was known to the Dickens children as 'Uncle Mark' and 'Uncle Porpoise'. In 1848 he adapted CD's Christmas story *The Haunted Man* for the stage; he also dramatized *The Chimes* (jointly with Gilbert à Beckett). When CD's baby daughter Dora died in 1851, Lemon sat up with him all night beside the body. (See CD's letter of 26 April 1855). In 1858 CD quarrelled with him when Lemon refused to print in *Punch* CD's statement (see Appendix A) concerning his separation from his wife. He and Lemon were reconciled in 1867 at Clarkson Stanfield's deathbed.

LEWES, GEORGE HENRY (1817–78), versatile author, reviewer and scientist, and consort of George Eliot, was a friend of CD and a member of his troupe of amateur actors when benefit performances of Jonson's *Every Man in his Humour* were staged in London, Manchester and Liverpool in 1847 in aid of Leigh Hunt. Forster says that CD had 'an old and great regard for' Lewes. In 1852–3 CD and Lewes engaged in a controversy over the episode of Krook's spontaneous combustion in *Bleak House*: Lewes attacked it as unscientific, CD defended it, and the argument continued for some time both in the public press and in private letters. (See Dickens' preface to the novel; also Gordon S. Haight, 'Dickens and Lewes on Spontaneous Combustion', *Nineteenth-Century Fiction*, x, 1955.) In February 1872 Lewes reviewed the first volume of Forster's *Life* in the *Fortnightly Review* and took the occasion to stigmatize CD's intellectual limitations ('an almost unique example of a mind of singular force in which, so to speak, sensations never passed into ideas . . . an *animal* intelligence, i.e., restricted to perceptions'). Forster responded at length to the 'studied depreciation', which he described as 'odious', in his second volume.

LINTON, MRS LYNN (1822–98), was introduced to CD by Landor and became a frequent and highly regarded contributor to *HW* and *AYR*. CD purchased Gad's Hill from her in 1856, she having inherited the house from her father. In *My Literary Life* (1899) she wrote of CD that he had 'a strain of hardness in his nature' despite his writing 'so tenderly, so sentimentally, so gushingly'.

LOCKHART, JOHN GIBSON (1794–1854), biographer of Scott and Burns, was the editor (1825–53) of the influential *Quarterly Review*, in which there appeared several important early criticisms of CD's work, including (October 1837) the celebrated remark that 'he has risen like a rocket, and he will come down like the stick'. Lockhart is said to have described *PP* as 'all very well – but damned low!'. In Edinburgh he had been a friend of George Hogarth, CD's father-in-law. According to Forster, in 1839 CD 'had pleasing communications with Lockhart, dining with him at Cruikshank's a little later; and this was the prelude to a *Quarterly Review* article on *Oliver Twist* by Mr Ford, written at the instance of Lockhart . . . in which amends were made for previous less favourable notices in that Review'. (Substantial extracts from Ford's review are given in *Critical Heritage*.)

LONGFELLOW, HENRY WADSWORTH (1807–82), American poet. CD visited him during his first and second American tours (1842, 1867–8), and Longfellow visited CD in England on two occasions.

LYTTON, EDWARD BULWER-, first Baron Lytton (1803–73), novelist, dramatist and politician, became a friend of CD. In 1850 CD acted in three private performances of Ben Jonson's *Every Man in his Humour* at the Lytton family seat, Knebworth Park, in Hertfordshire. CD and Lytton jointly set up a charitable scheme for needy authors, the Guild of Literature and Art, CD believed it would 'entirely change the status of the literary man in England', but after a promising start its success was not lasting. *Bleak House* is dedicated to CD's 'companions' in the Guild. It was Lytton who persuaded CD to change the ending of *Great Expectations* (see under the section on that novel). In 1861 CD published Lytton's novel *A Strange Story* as a serial in *AYR*.

McCARTHY, JUSTIN (1830–1912), Irish politician and author. His *Reminiscences* (1899) include references to his meetings with CD after he arrived in London in 1852 (e.g., 'Dickens rather frightened me . . . . His manner was full of energy; there was something physically overpowering about it, as it then seemed to me; the very vehemence of his cheery good-humour rather bore one down'). He also has a chapter on CD in *Portraits of the Sixties* (1903).

MACLISE, DANIEL (1806–70), Scots-Irish painter and Royal Academician, was introduced to CD by Harrison Ainsworth in 1838. He painted the fine 'Nickleby' portrait of CD in 1839 (it was commissioned by the publishers Chapman & Hall as frontispiece to the three-volume edition of *Nicholas Nickleby*). He also painted Georgina Hogarth and did a small group portrait of the Dickens children for Kate to take with her to America in

1842. In 1844 he executed the well-known sketch of a group listening to CD reading *The Chimes*. He accompanied CD to watch the hanging of the murderer Courvoisier in 1840, made a holiday trip to Cornwall with CD and others in 1842, and visited Paris with CD in 1850. When Maclise died in 1870, CD described him at a Royal Academy dinner as 'the gentlest and most modest of men'.

MACREADY, WILLIAM CHARLES (1793–1873), Shakespearean actor, manager of Covent Garden Theatre (1837–9) and Drury Lane Theatre (1841–3), was introduced to CD by Forster in 1837; they remained friends for life. CD visited Macready in Paris in December 1844. When he retired from the stage in 1851, CD arranged the farewell dinner and attended his last performance (in *Macbeth*). Macready's grief at the death of Little Nell is well known, and he wept at CD's reading of *The Chimes* ('If you had seen Macready last night', CD wrote to Kate, 'undisguisedly sobbing, and crying on the sofa as I read, you would have felt, as I did, what a thing it is to have power'). He wept again at CD's reading from *David Copperfield*, and described the 'Sikes and Nancy' reading from *Oliver Twist* as 'two Macbeths'. His daughter Catherine Macready (1834–69) contributed poems to *HW*.

MACRONE, JOHN, CD's first publisher. He published *Sketches by Boz*, and *Gabriel Vardon* (which later became *Barnaby Rudge*) was originally intended for him.

MARRYAT, CAPTAIN FREDERICK (1792–1848), novelist and friend of CD. Like CD he was a frequent guest at Lady Blessington's salon at Gore House. His *Diary in America* (1839) anticipated *AN* (which Marryat admired) in its unflattering portrayal of American life and manners. Marryat also shared CD's views on the question of international copyright. In 1842 he presided at a dinner held at Greenwich to welcome CD home from America.

MARTINEAU, HARRIET (1802–76), novelist, popularizer of political economy and advocate of social reform, was a frequent contributor to *HW* from 1850 to 1855. She criticized the accuracy of CD's presentation of industrial life in *Hard Times* and elsewhere, and in 1855 described a series of articles in *HW* on factory accidents as containing 'unscrupulous statements, insolence, arrogance, and cant'. Elsewhere she said of CD that 'we may wish that he had a sounder social philosophy' (see Humphry House, *The Dickens World* [London: Oxford University Press, 1941], pp. 74–5). CD remarked of her that 'there never was such a wrong-headed woman born – such a vain one – or such a Humbug'. She has sometimes been regarded as the model for Mrs Jellyby in *BH*.

MATHEWS, CHARLES (the elder) (1776–1835), comic actor much admired by CD at the period in his life when he hoped to go on the stage himself. *The Dictionary of National Biography* says of Mathews that 'as a mimic he had no equal', and CD told Forster that in his early years he went 'always to see Mathews whenever he played'. From 1818 to 1833 Mathews presented a series of one-man shows in which he performed a large number of parts in rapid succession; and CD's subsequent techniques of character-individuation may well owe something to Mathews' acting techniques.

MILLAIS, SIR JOHN (1829–96), was an artist and one of the originators of the Pre-Raphaelite movement in 1848. In 1850 CD attacked his Royal Academy painting, 'The Carpenter's Shop', which depicts the boy Jesus with one of his hands cut by an accident in the workshop, as exhibiting 'the lowest depths of what is mean, odious, repulsive, and revolting'. He and Millais later became friends, however, and the artist made a pencil sketch of CD's head on the day after his death.

MITTON, THOMAS, was an early friend of CD who borrowed money from him on various occasions. He acted as CD's representative in some of his dealings with publishers.

MORLEY, HENRY (1822–94), was on the staff of *HW* and *AYR* and was a very frequent contributor to both journals. He subsequently edited the *Examiner* and became Professor of English Literature at University College, London.

PAYN, JAMES (1830–98), contributed frequently to *HW* from 1855 and met CD in 1856. He subsequently published novels and edited the *Cornhill Magazine*. His *Some Literary Recollections* (1884) contains references to CD.

PHIZ, *see* BROWNE, HABLOT KNIGHT

PRESCOTT, WILLIAM H. (1796–1859), American historian. CD met him in America in 1842, and Prescott became one of the circle of his American friends. He visited CD in England in 1849.

PROCTER, BRYAN WALLER (1787–1874). Under the pseudonym of 'Barry Cornwall' he was in his day a popular poet. He had been a friend of Lamb and Hazlitt, was a member of Lady Blessington's salon at Gore House, and became a lifelong friend of CD. He attended the dinner to welcome him home from America in 1842.

In a letter of 2 March 1845 CD refers to him as 'our dear good Procter'. He contributed to *HW* and *AYR*. His daughter Adelaide Anne Procter (1825–64) was a very popular poetess who contributed frequently to *HW* and *AYR* as 'Mary Berwick'; CD was not at first aware that the pseudonym belonged to one he had known since her childhood, and he accepted her poems on their merits. He wrote a touching introduction for a posthumous edition of her *Legends and Lyrics* (1866).

PUTNAM, GEORGE W. (1812–96), was a New Englander whom CD engaged as his secretary during the first American tour in 1842. He published reminiscences of CD in *Atlantic Monthly*, XXVI (1870) and is the subject of an article by N. C. Peyrouton, *Dickensian*, LIX (1963).

ROCHE, LOUIS, was a native of Avignon who acted as courier for the Dickens family on the Italian trip in 1844–5 and for the journey to Switzerland in 1846. CD described him as 'a most faithful, affectionate, and devoted man'.

ROGERS, SAMUEL (1763–1855), poet, whose *Pleasures of Memory* (1792) and *Italy* (1822–8) enjoyed a wide popularity. He was a wealthy banker, moved in high society, and gave famous breakfasts. CD met him often and dedicated *Master Humphrey's Clock* to him, but described him unflatteringly in 1852: 'Vivacious enough and vicious enough – tells the same words, to the same people, twenty times in a day, and has his little dinner parties of four, where he goes mad with rage if anybody talks to anyone but himself.' Rogers' *Recollections* appeared in 1859.

ROYLANCE, MRS ELIZABETH, was 'a reduced old lady' and an acquaintance of the Dickens family with whom CD lodged in Little College Street, Camden Town, in 1824, when the rest of his family were living in the Marshalsea prison and he was employed at Warren's blacking warehouse. She had formerly taken children in to board at Brighton and, according to CD, 'unconsciously began to sit for Mrs. Pipchin in *Dombey* when she took me in'.

RUSSELL, LORD JOHN (later Earl Russell) (1792–1878), radical politician, Prime Minister 1846–52. As a young reporter CD covered many of his speeches, including those in support of the Reform Bill of 1832. Later they became acquainted. In 1846 CD sent him information concerning the Ragged Schools. He had a high regard for Russell – an exception to his usual opinion of politicians – and dedicated *ATTC* to him.

SALA, GEORGE AUGUSTUS (1828–96), journalist and author, was a frequent contributor to *HW* from 1851, and subsequently to *AYR*. He published a book on CD in 1870, and there are further reminiscences in *Things I have Known* (1894). He and CD quarrelled in 1856 but were reconciled in 1858.

SEYMOUR, ROBERT (1800–36), artist and illustrator, enjoyed a considerable popularity for his burlesque sporting pictures. In 1835 he suggested to the publishing firm of Chapman & Hall a 'series of plates depicting the mishaps of a "Nimrod Club" of Cockney sportsmen' (Johnson). After several other authors had declined, CD – then unknown – was invited to write the accompanying humorous text; but in his hands the scheme was reversed, the text assumed primacy, and it became clear to Seymour that 'he would be playing second fiddle to the hack originally called in merely to concoct a story around his plates' (Johnson). In this almost fortuitous way was *Pickwick Papers* born and CD's fame established. Seymour took his own life between the publication of the first and second numbers of the novel, leaving CD without an illustrator; his successor was H. K. Browne ('Phiz'). Angus Wilson has suggested that, although Seymour's suicide was the result of a congenital depression, it 'was perhaps also brought on somewhat by Dickens's masterfulness'. CD's phrase in his preface to *PP*, 'My views being deferred to . . . ', is quietly eloquent. In the same preface he found it necessary to state that Seymour 'never originated or suggested an incident, a phrase, or a word, to be found in this book'.

SHAW, WILLIAM, was the one-eyed headmaster of Bowes Academy, Yorkshire, which CD and 'Phiz' visited in 1838 in quest of material for the novel that became *Nicholas Nickleby*. Even though CD used an alias and appeared under the pretext of seeking a school for a friend's son, Shaw was suspicious. He is depicted in *NN* as Squeers. For some graphic details of Shaw's regime, see Johnson, p. 217.

SMITH, ARTHUR, became the business manager for CD's public readings in 1858. When Smith died in 1861 CD said that it was 'as if my right arm were gone'. According to Johnson, 111 readings had been given under his management. Albert Smith, brother of Arthur, was responsible for a dramatization of *The Cricket on the Hearth* produced at the Lyceum Theatre at Christmas 1845.

SMITH, SYDNEY (1771–1845), author and wit, was a frequent visitor at Holland House and met CD early in his career. At first inclined, like some other prominent literary figures, to disparage the phenomenal popular success of 'Boz', Smith was converted by reading *Nicholas Nickleby*: as Forster says, 'Sydney Smith confessed himself vanquished by a humour against which his own had long striven to hold out. "*Nickleby* is *very good*," he wrote to Sir George Phillips after the sixth number. "I stood out against Mr Dickens as long as I could, but he has conquered me".' Smith later praised the pathetic figure of Chuffey, the old clerk in *Martin Chuzzlewit*, and wrote to Dickens that 'Chuffey is admirable . . . . I never read a finer piece of writing: it is deeply pathetic and affecting' (he had just perused the fourth number). After Smith's death CD referred to him as 'poor dear Sydney'.

SMITH, DR THOMAS SOUTHWOOD, sent CD in 1840 a copy of the report of the Children's Employment Commission (of which he was Chief Commissioner); its account of child labour in the mines filled CD with horror and indignation. In 1843 Smith sent him a government blue book on sanitary conditions among the poor; CD's response was similar, and he promised in a letter to Smith that in his writings he would come down like 'a sledgehammer' on these social evils. *The Chimes* was one of the results of this vow.

STANFIELD, CLARKSON (1793–1867), artist and Royal Academician, was a friend of CD. They met in 1838, and Stanfield was one of the group who toured Cornwall with CD in 1843. He was one of the illustrators of *The Battle of Life* and *The Haunted Man*, and painted scenery for several of the amateur productions in which CD was involved. It was over Stanfield's deathbed in 1867 that CD and Mark Lemon were reconciled. After Stanfield's death, CD wrote to his son: 'No one of your father's friends can ever have loved him more dearly than I always did, or can have better known the worth of his noble character.' He also wrote an obituary of Stanfield for *AYR* (1 June 1867).

STONE, MARCUS (1840–1921), artist and illustrator, was the son of Frank Stone (1800–59), artist and friend of CD, who was a prominent member of CD's troupe of amateur actors and did three illustrations for *The Haunted Man*. Marcus Stone succeeded H. K. Browne as CD's illustrator, and executed the illustrations for *Our Mutual Friend* and for several volumes in the Library Edition of 1862. It was Stone who showed CD the curious shop in St Giles's on which is based Mr Venus's establishment in *OMF*.

STROUGHILL, GEORGE AND LUCY, two children who were Chatham neighbours and friends of the young CD. They lived at

1 Ordnance Terrace (the Dickens family were at number 2), and George and CD would act plays together.

TALFOURD, SIR THOMAS NOON (1795–1854), serjeant-at-law and later a judge, knighted in 1849, was one of CD's early friends. Talfourd had been a journalist and man of letters in his early years and the friend of Wordsworth, Coleridge and Lamb; later he became an active MP. It was he who introduced CD to Count D'Orsay and to Gore House and Holland House; and in 1838 he proposed him for membership of the Athenaeum Club. *Pickwick Papers* is dedicated to him in recognition of his efforts to improve the protection given to authors by the copyright laws. In 1844 he was CD's counsel in a lawsuit against publishers who pirated his work. When Talfourd died in 1854, CD wrote: 'So amiable a man, so gentle, so sweet-tempered, of such a noble simplicity, so perfectly unspoiled by his labours and their rewards, is very rare indeed upon this earth.' He is said to have been the original of Tommy Traddles in *David Copperfield*. CD's obituary of Talfourd appeared in *HW* on 25 March 1854.

TENNYSON, ALFRED (Lord Tennyson) (1809–92), poet, was godfather to CD's son Alfred. In 1842 CD wrote: 'I have been reading Tennyson all the morning on the seashore' (no doubt the important 1842 collection of poems); and from Italy in 1844 he wrote that 'Tennyson I have also been reading, again and again. What a great creature he is.'

TERNAN, ELLEN LAWLESS, was an actress and the daughter of a well-known actress. She, her mother and her sister were all given parts by CD in a production of *The Frozen Deep* in Manchester in 1857, Ellen playing a minor role; and CD seems to have fallen quickly in love with her. When a bracelet ordered for her fell accidentally into the hands of his wife Kate, the latter was violently resentful. Soon rumours spread that Ellen was CD's mistress: he denied them, but there seems to be little doubt that sooner or later she filled that role. When he was involved in the Staplehurst railway accident on 9 June 1865, she was certainly with him, and had probably been with him in Paris, whence he was returning. He seems to have taken a villa in Peckham for her and to have visited her there in the years 1867–70. She came to Gad's Hill immediately after his death. In his will he left her a legacy of a thousand pounds, 'almost as if he desired to defy convention from his grave' (Johnson). Her influence on CD's later heroines has often been suggested: certainly their names – Estella (*GE*), Bella

(*OMF*), Helena Landless (*ED*) – bear a striking resemblance to hers. In 1876 Ellen Ternan married a clergyman who was headmaster and proprietor of a private school. She died in 1914. Her affair with CD was first made known by Thomas Wright in 1934 (see his *Life of Charles Dickens* [1935] and *Autobiography* [1936]). In *Dickens and Daughter*, Gladys Storey states that Ellen's child by CD died in infancy. See also Ada Nisbet, *Charles Dickens and Ellen Ternan* (1952).

THACKERAY, WILLIAM MAKEPEACE (1811–63), novelist, was a friend of CD and also his closest rival. In 1848, during the serialization of *Vanity Fair*, Thackeray wrote to his mother: 'I am become a sort of great man in my way – all but at the top of the tree: indeed there if the truth were known and having a great fight up there with Dickens.' They had met while *Pickwick Papers* was in progress: after Robert Seymour's death, Thackeray had offered himself as illustrator for that novel, but was turned down. Edgar Johnson says that 'Thackeray was acutely conscious of rivalry with Dickens. . . . He was bowled over by the pure brilliance of some of Dickens's achievements, but on the whole critical of his literary art, which he regarded as a mere caricature of reality.' On his part, CD deplored Thackeray's lack of seriousness. (In his obituary of Thackeray published in *The Cornhill Magazine* in February 1864, CD wrote: 'I thought that he too much feigned a want of earnestness, and that he made a pretence of undervaluing his art, which was not good for the art that he held in trust.') They quarrelled in 1858 (see YATES, EDMUND below), but were reconciled in 1863 (some months before Thackeray's sudden death) on the occasion of a chance meeting at the Athenaeum Club and apparently on Thackeray's initiative.

THOMPSON, JOHN, was CD's servant for some twenty years. After he was dismissed for theft, CD set him up in business.

THOMPSON, T. J., *see* WELLER, CHRISTIANA

TOBIN, DANIEL, was CD's closest friend at Wellington House Academy. They remained in touch after leaving school.

TOWNSHEND, REV. CHAUNCY HARE (1798–1868). CD met him in 1840 and discovered a common interest in mesmerism (Townshend had published *Facts in Mesmerism*). A letter of 2 June 1841 (to Lady Blessington) refers to 'Townshend's magnetic boy' and declares 'I am a believer in earnest.' CD dedicated *GE* to Townshend and presented him with the manuscript. Townshend died in 1868, naming CD as his literary executor and requiring him to publish 'without alteration as much of my notes and reflections as may make known my opinions on religious matters'. In Edgar Johnson's words,

> When the notes were sent from Townshend's home in Lausanne they proved so bulky, repetitious, and chaotic that publishing them 'without alteration' was impossible. Dickens murmured that the volume would fall stillborn from the press, and he privately gave it the title *Religious Hiccoughs*, but he faithfully arranged, collated, and selected, and saw the volume published in the following year.

The book appeared as *Religious Opinions* in 1869, with an introduction by CD. On Townshend's death, CD wrote to Georgina Hogarth (12 March 1868): 'It is not a light thing, to lose such a friend, and I truly loved him.'

VICTORIA, QUEEN (1819–1901), reigned from 1837. She and the Prince Consort attended CD's production of *Every Man in his Humour* at the Theatre Royal, Haymarket, in 1848, and she subsequently attended other productions by CD and his company of amateur actors. In March 1870 he had an interview with the Queen: 'they talked of his American trip, the servant problem, and the high cost of food' (Johnson), and she presented him with an autographed copy of her *Journal of Our Life in the Highlands* and asked for a set of his works. In her diary for 1838, she confessed to finding *Oliver Twist* 'excessively interesting'.

WATSON, HON. MR AND MRS RICHARD, lived at Rockingham Castle, Northamptonshire. Watson (1800–52) was a son of the 2nd Lord Sondes. CD met them when he was in Lausanne in 1846. In 1849 he visited Rockingham; there he met Mary Boyle (see above) and organized amateur theatricals, playing Sir Peter Teazle to Mary's Lady Teazle in scenes from Sheridan's *The School for Scandal*. Another visit and more theatricals took place in 1851. When Watson died CD wrote: 'I loved him as my heart, and cannot think of him without tears.' The Dedlock mansion in *Bleak House* is said to be based on Rockingham Castle.

WELLER, CHRISTIANA, was a young lady whom CD met when he was presiding at a soirée of the Liverpool Mechanics' Institute in 1844 and found himself introducing her performance on the piano. He was strongly attracted to her, and confessed his infatuation to his friend T. J. Thompson; but when Thompson announced that *he* had fallen in love with Christiana, and asked CD's advice, he was urged to propose to her. After twice breaking off the engagement, with CD intervening to mend matters, she married Thompson in 1845. CD visited them in Lausanne in 1846 and found the reunion with Christiana disillusioning: 'She seems (between ourselves) to have a devil of a whimpering, pouting temper.' The Thompsons settled in Italy and CD visited them there in 1846. Christiana's younger sister Anna married Frederick Dickens, brother of CD, in spite of opposition from her father.

WELLER, MARY, was a servant of the Dickens family during their residence in Chatham in CD's boyhood. She told blood-curdling stories to the young Dickens, including the tale of Captain Murderer (see 'Nurse's Stories' in *The Uncommercial Traveller*). Later she recalled his boyhood recitations: he would, for instance, declaim Isaac Watts' 'The Voice of the Sluggard', as she said, 'with *such* action and *such* attitudes!'. CD presumably remembered her when naming Sam Weller in *Pickwick Papers*; Sam's wife is called Mary.

WILKIE, SIR DAVID (1785–1841), painter. CD met him on social occasions in London. When Wilkie died suddenly in 1841, CD proposed a toast to his memory at a dinner held in Edinburgh (25 June).

WILLS, WILLIAM HENRY (1810–80), journalist, contributed to *Bentley's Miscellany* in 1837 and joined the staff of *Punch* when it was founded in 1841. He was CD's secretary when he was editing the *Daily News*, and later became a sub-editor and one-eighth proprietor of, and contributor to, *HW*, and a sub-editor and quarter-owner of *AYR*. The modest title of 'sub-editor' hardly does justice to the importance of Wills's role: he was in effect CD's right-hand man in the conduct of his periodicals for nineteen years, and became a close personal friend. He was CD's confidant in the arrangements made for Ellen Ternan during CD's absence in America in 1867.

WINTER, MRS HENRY, *see* BEADNELL, MARIA

YATES, EDMUND (1831–94), journalist, was a son of the actor Frederick Yates, who had known CD. Edmund Yates contributed to *HW*. He met CD in 1854, became an intimate friend, and seems to have been in his confidence regarding the relationship with Ellen Ternan. He was at the centre of the

'Garrick Club affair' in 1858 which led CD (who defended Yates) to quarrel with Thackeray. See Yates's *Recollections and Experiences* (1884). Yates was joint author of a parody of *Hard Times*: see *Critical Heritage*, pp. 309–13. Yates's mother was also acquainted with CD; she was a former actress who 'had played Dolly Varden and Sikes's Nancy in the old days at the Adelphi' (Johnson), and it was she who, having wept copiously at Dickens' performance in the melodrama *The Lighthouse*, exclaimed: 'O Mr Dickens what a pity it is you can do anything else!'

DICKENS' WRITINGS

Sketches by Boz

Text   Oxford Illustrated Dickens (1957).

Composition   In the Preface to the Cheap Edition (1847) of *Pickwick Papers*, Dickens writes of

> the Magazine in which my first effusion – dropped stealthily one evening at twilight, with fear and trembling, into a dark letter-box, in a dark office, up a dark court in Fleet Street – appeared in all the glory of print; on which occasion by-the-bye, – how well I recollect it! – I walked down to Westminster Hall, and turned into it for half-an-hour, because my eyes were so dimmed with joy and pride, that they could not bear the street, and were not fit to be seen there.

The 'Magazine' was the *Monthly Magazine* and the 'effusion' was 'A Dinner at Poplar Walk' (subsequently retitled 'Mr. Minns and his Cousin'), which 'appeared in all the glory of print' on 1 December 1833. During 1834–6 Dickens contributed numerous other sketches to the *Monthly Magazine* and other periodicals; at first they were unsigned, but he soon adopted the pseudonym of 'Boz' (for its origin, see p. 26).

Periodical publication   Most of the sketches appeared initially in periodicals as follows:

1833	Dec. 1	'A Dinner at Poplar Walk', *Monthly Magazine*.
1834	Jan.	'Mrs. Joseph Porter, "Over the Way"', *Monthly Magazine*.
	Feb.	'Horatio Sparkins', *Monthly Magazine*.
1834	April	'The Bloomsbury Christening', *Monthly Magazine*.
	May	'The Boarding-House', *Monthly Magazine*.

1834 June 7   'Sentiment', *Bell's Weekly Magazine.*

Aug.   'The Boarding-House – No. II', *Monthly Magazine.*

Sept. 26   'Omnibuses' (Street Sketches No. 1), *Morning Chronicle.*

Oct.   'The Steam Excursion', *Monthly Magazine.*

Oct. 10   'Shops and their Tenants' (Street Sketches No. 2), *Morning Chronicle.*

Oct. 23   'The Old Bailey' (Street Sketches No. 3), *Morning Chronicle.*

Nov. 5   'Shabby-Genteel People' (Street Sketches No. 4), *Morning Chronicle.*

Dec. 15   'Brokers' and Marine Store Shops' (Street Sketches No. 5), *Morning Chronicle.*

1835 Jan.   'Passage in the Life of Mr. Watkins Tottle, Chapter the First', *Monthly Magazine.*

Jan. 31   'Hackney Coach Stands' (Sketches of London No. 1), *Evening Chronicle.*

Feb.   'Passage in the Life of Mr. Watkins Tottle, Chapter the Second', *Monthly Magazine.*

Feb. 7   'Gin Shops' (Sketches of London No. 2), *Evening Chronicle.*

Feb. 19   'Early Coaches' (Sketches of London No. 3), *Evening Chronicle.*

Feb. 28   'The Parish' (Sketches of London No. 4), *Evening Chronicle.*

March 7   'The House' (Sketches of London No. 5), *Evening Chronicle.*

March 17   'London Recreations' (Sketches of London No. 6), *Evening Chronicle.*

April 7   'Public Dinners' (Sketches of London No. 7), *Evening Chronicle.*

April 11   'Bellamy's' (Sketches of London No. 8), *Evening Chronicle.*

April 16   'Greenwich Fair' (Sketches of London No. 9), *Evening Chronicle.*

April 23   'Thoughts about People' (Sketches of London No. 10), *Evening Chronicle.*

May 9   'Astley's' (Sketches of London No. 11), *Evening Chronicle.*

1835   May 19   'Our Parish' (Sketches of London No. 12), *Evening Chronicle*.

       June 6   'The River' (Sketches of London No. 13), *Evening Chronicle*.

       June 18   'Our Parish' (Sketches of London No. 14), *Evening Chronicle*.

       June 30   'The Pawnbroker's Shop' (Sketches of London No. 15), *Evening Chronicle*.

       July 14   'Our Parish' (Sketches of London No. 16), *Evening Chronicle*.

       July 21   'The Streets – Morning' (Sketches of London No. 17), *Evening Chronicle*.

       July 28   'Our Parish' (Sketches of London No. 18), *Evening Chronicle*.

       Aug. 11   'Private Theatres' (Sketches of London No. 19), *Evening Chronicle*.

       Aug. 20   'Our Parish' (Sketches of London No. 20), *Evening Chronicle*.

       Sept. 27   'Seven Dials' (Scenes and Characters No. 1), *Bell's Life in London*.

       Oct. 4   'Miss Evans and "The Eagle"' (Scenes and Characters No. 2), *Bell's Life in London*.

       Oct. 11   'The Dancing Academy' (Scenes and Characters No. 3), *Bell's Life in London*.

       Oct. 18   'Making a Night of It' (Scenes and Characters No. 4), *Bell's Life in London*.

       Oct. 25   'Love and Oysters' (Scenes and Characters No. 5), *Bell's Life in London*.

       Nov. 1   'Some Account of an Omnibus Cad' (Scenes and Characters No. 6), *Bell's Life in London*.

       Nov. 22   'The Vocal Dressmaker' (Scenes and Characters No. 7), *Bell's Life in London*.

       Nov. 29   'The Prisoners' Van' (Scenes and Characters No. 8), *Bell's Life in London*.

       Dec. 13   'The Parlour' (Scenes and Characters No. 9), *Bell's Life in London*.

       Dec. 27   'Christmas Festivities' (Scenes and Characters No. 10), *Bell's Life in London*.

1836   Jan. 3   'The New Year' (Scenes and Characters No. 11), *Bell's Life in London*.

1836 Jan. 17   'The Streets at Night' (Scenes and Characters
                   No. 12), *Bell's Life in London*.

      March 31   'The Tuggs's at Ramsgate', *Library of Fiction*
                   No. 1.

      May 31   'A Little Talk about Spring and the Sweeps',
                   Library of Fiction No. 3.

      Aug. 6   'The Hospital Patient', *Carlton Chronicle*.

      Sept. 24   'Meditations in Monmouth Street' (Sketches by
                   Boz, New Series No. 1), *Morning Chronicle*.

      Oct. 4   'Scotland Yard' (Sketches by Boz, New Series
                   No. 2), *Morning Chronicle*.

      Oct. 11   'Doctors' Commons' (Sketches by Boz, New
                   Series No. 3), *Morning Chronicle*.

      Oct. 26   'Vauxhall-Gardens by Day' (Sketches by Boz,
                   New Series No. 4), *Morning Chronicle*.

Dickens' first 'effusion' was not the only sketch to be later retitled:
'The Old Bailey' became 'Criminal Courts'; 'Love and Oysters'
became (less suggestively, since oysters were believed to be an
aphrodisiac) 'Misplaced Attachment of Mr. John Dounce'; 'Some
Account of an Omnibus Cad' was expanded and retitled 'The Last
Cab-driver and the First Omnibus Cad'; 'Christmas Festivities'
became 'A Christmas Dinner'; and 'A Little Talk about Spring and
the Sweeps' became 'The First of May'. 'The House' and
'Bellamy's' were conflated to form 'A Parliamentary Sketch'.
(Details taken from Appendix F to Volume I of the Pilgrim Edition
of Dickens' letters.)

Volume publication   John Macrone, who had been co-publisher of
the *Monthly Magazine* in 1834 and had set up in business for himself
in September of that year, suggested to Dickens that his sketches
should be collected in a volume with illustrations by the well-known
artist George Cruikshank, and offered him £100 for the copyright.
In *Charles Dickens and his Publishers* Professor Robert Patten has
drawn attention to the significance of the partnership of author and
illustrator:

   The idea developed of combining Dickens's closely observed
   sketches of London life with the illustrations of Cruikshank, the
   great popular favourite famous for his London street scenes.
   Macrone could capitalize on Dickens's growing reputation and

Cruikshank's already established one. The proposed titles all emphasized the combination: 'Bubbles from the Bwain of Boz and the Graver of Cruikshank,' 'Sketches by Boz and Cuts by Cruikshank,' 'Etchings by Boz and Wood Cuts by Cruikshank' . . . . the collaborators were soon on friendly terms, with Cruikshank selecting subjects for illustrations from copies of Dickens's published pieces

Before the end of October 1835 Dickens had begun, at Macrone's suggestion, to collect his sketches for volume publication. After various delays *Sketches by Boz* appeared in two volumes on 8 February 1836; it sold well, and a second edition was called for before the end of July and a third in February 1837. Before the end of the month of publication, indeed, Dickens was able to refer to 'the great success of my book'. Early in the summer he began to put together a second series; this was published in one volume on 17 December 1836, and includes all the items published in periodicals during 1833–5 but omitted from the first series. Subsequently Chapman & Hall purchased the copyright of both series from Macrone and issued a combined edition; this appeared in monthly parts from November 1837 to June 1839 and as a single volume in May 1839. For this edition the sketches were arranged in four groups, an arrangement followed in modern editions.

In his preface to the Cheap Edition issued in 1850, Dickens wrote that 'The whole of these sketches were written and published, one by one, when I was a very young man' and that they were 'collected and republished while I was still a very young man; and sent into the world with all their imperfections (a good many) on their heads'. In *Dickens at Work* Kathleen Tillotson has demonstrated convincingly that Dickens is guilty of 'manipulation of facts'. In the first place, 'six out of the total of over fifty had made no previous periodical appearance, and . . . some at least were written especially for the collection'. More importantly, Dickens' revisons of the collected sketches were extensive:

This description [in the 1850 preface] would not lead one to suppose that when Dickens first collected his sketches he made extensive cuts, rewrote whole paragraphs, and made innumerable minute changes both of substance and style; nor that he continued to revise in successive editions including the very one for which this Preface was written.

Professor Tillotson also shows that the 1850 edition involved expurgations: for example, 'cursedly' and 'the deuce' were omitted; the 'legs' of a young lady became the 'ankles'; and a coarsely comic 'two grain calomel pill' became a simple 'pill' – evidence of a growing squeamishness as Victoria's reign got into its stride. Professor Tillotson concludes that 'the suppression of the original versions in modern editions brings some loss of understanding, both of Dickens's methods and of the very nature of the original sketches'.

Reception   Forster recalled in the *Life* that the *Sketches* were 'much more talked about than the first two or three numbers of *Pickwick*', and the reviewers were generally encouraging. The *Metropolitan Magazine* (March 1836) praised the collection's 'startling fidelity'; the *Spectator* (20 February 1836) found in it 'the romance . . . of real life'; the *Sun* (15 February 1836) referred to 'great powers of observation, and fidelity of description, combined with . . . humour'; and *Chambers's Edinburgh Journal* (9 April 1836) predicted that Dickens stood a good chance of becoming 'a successful and popular author'.

Forster makes it clear that Dickens himself was prone to undervalue the *Sketches*:

> Richly did it merit all the praise it had, and more, I will add, than he · was ever disposed to give to it himself. He decidedly underrated it. He gave, in subsequent writings, so much more perfect form and fullness to everything it contained, that he did not care to credit himself with the marvel of having yet so early anticipated so much. But the first sprightly runnings of his genius are undoubtedly here. Mr. Bumble is in the parish sketches, and Mr. Dawkins the dodger in the Old Bailey scenes.

This seems psychologically shrewd and convincing.

Forster is also perceptive in noting that Dickens' province in the *Sketches* is the 'quite unhackneyed ground' of 'a sort of life between the middle class and the low'. We may surmise that the richness of this field discovered and exploited by the young Dickens derived partly from its freedom from the constraints of middle-class notions of decorum in speech and behaviour and from the standardizing effects of middle-class education, as well as from the comic potential of unsuccessful attempts to ape bourgeois manners.

Although the *Sketches* have been overshadowed by their great successors, their originality was genuine and substantial. Forster's tribute to 'the marvel of having yet so early anticipated so much' has been echoed by some recent critics: J. Hillis Miller, for instance, pushes Forster's view further (and perhaps too far) in claiming that the *Sketches* 'contain all of Dickens's later work in embryo'. (Miller's observation that 'the full implications of the *Sketches* are only visible in the light of their relations to the later work of Dickens' seems more acceptable.) Kathleen Tillotson has argued that the modern reader unfamilar with the popular prose of the 1830s is apt to underrate the sheer originality of *Sketches by Boz*. That originality consisted partly in the quality that contemporary reviewers recurringly designated as 'fidelity' – a shunning of literary stereotypes in favour of a scrupulous and vivid realism. Here, again, Forster shows himself a highly perceptive critic.

> The observation shown throughout is nothing short of wonderful. Things are painted literally as they are; and, whatever the picture, whether of every-day vulgar, shabby genteel, or downright low, with neither the condescending air which is affectation, nor the too familiar one which is slang.

In his original preface (February 1836) Dickens stated that his object had been 'to present little pictures of life and manners as they really are'; and, obvious enough as this sounds a century and a half later, there had been nothing quite like it before. Robert Browning (not the Victorian poet but a modern critic) points out that 'Dickens's realism, unlike the superficial realism of Pierce Egan's *Life in London* [published in 1820–1 and also illustrated by Cruikshank], does not confer glamour on the sordid and squalid'. Browning also notes that Dickens 'takes in the whole metropolis with its rapidly extending suburbs, such as Stamford Hill, Camberwell, Norbury, and Richmond', and adds that 'it is the distinction of the *Sketches*, as it is that of Joyce's *Dubliners*, that the reader senses the life of a whole city'.

Not all critics have taken issue with Dickens' disparagement of his first book. Chesterton found the *Sketches* 'not manifestations of the man of genius' and turned his judgment into an all too characteristic paradox: 'We might almost say that this book is one of the few books by Dickens which would not, standing alone, have made his fame. And yet standing alone it did make his fame.' K. J. Fielding has said that 'their interest is chiefly in the way in which they foreshadow the works to come'. Sylvère Monod has deplored 'the poverty of the style' in comparison with the great novels that followed: he finds in the *Sketches* 'spurious refinements', 'vulgarity of tone', incorrect grammar, and such features as circumlocutions, foreign words, superficial literary and classical allusions, legal terms, and other 'borrowed plumes'. Monod concludes that it is a young man's book with 'the makings of a style, but no real style as yet', and suggests that the really remarkable thing is the way these defects disappeared within the few months between the *Sketches* and *Pickwick*.

And yet the *Sketches* surely display an extraordinary linguistic variety and inventiveness: here is a writer capable of responding to and exploiting the power of words to an extent very unusual, if not unheard of, in other prose writers of the 1830s. Consider, for instance, the brilliance of the sustained comic imagery in 'The Four Sisters': these virgins, 'formal, stiff, and cold' as their furniture, have decided 'to winter through life together' and live 'in Polar harmony among themselves', 'occasionally iceing the neighbours'. The cliché ('frigid') has taken on fresh life: the animate and the inanimate are no longer distinct categories, the resuscitated dead metaphor (a cold woman) is pursued to the end of a long paragraph, where a 'thaw' sets in with the marriage of one of the sisters. The passage seems to look forward to the even more brilliant set piece of the christening scene in *Dombey and Son* a decade later.

Again, Dickens can already exploit the vigour of common speech uninhibited by considerations of propriety: we recall that he was born in the Regency and that Victoria is not yet on the throne (but see above for the effect of his subsequent revisions). The broker's man who speaks of being 'as lonesome as a kitten in a wash-house copper with the lid on' and 'as seedy as a cheap cowcumber' anticipates Sam Weller and Mrs Gamp, just as the 'poor clerk' in 'Thoughts about People' anticipates Newman Noggs; 'gallantry in its dotage' in the same sketch anticipates Mr Turveydrop; 'A Visit to Newgate' anticipates *Little Dorrit* (already Dickens shows a preoccupation with prisons and a horrified fascination with capital punishment and the condemned cell); and the Christmas dinner at which 'one little seat may be empty' anticipates *A Christmas Carol*. (J. Hillis Miller has noted the far-reaching significance of the reference in 'Our Next-door Neighbour' to 'the physiognomy of street-door knockers' and the detective-like skill Dickens shows at reading an individual life-history in a heap of old clothes in

'Meditations in Monmouth Street'.) Characters exhibit their delight in holding forth in a style often incongruously and hilariously formal, as ardent performers on the instrument of language, happiest in the role of soloist: the very earliest of the sketches, indeed, 'A Dinner at Poplar Walk', lays down the pattern that Mrs Gamp and other major creations are to follow.

In addition to an important chapter in Butt and Tillotson's *Dickens and Work*, the following discussions of *Sketches by Boz* are worth consulting: Robert Browning's essay in *Dickens and the Twentieth Century*, ed. Gross and Pearson; J. Hillis Miller, 'The Fiction of Realism: *Sketches by Boz, Oliver Twist*, and Cruikshank's illustrations', in *Charles Dickens and George Cruikshank* (California, 1971) (the same essay appears in *Dickens Centennial Essays*, ed. Ada Nisbet and Blake Nevius [California, 1971]); C. B. Cox, 'Comic Viewpoints in *Sketches by Boz*', *English*, XII, 1959. Walter Dexter has discussed the reception of the book in *Dickensian*, XXXI (1935) and XXXII (1936).

The Pickwick Papers

Text Penguin English Library, ed. Robert L. Patten (1972).

Composition Towards the end of 1835 Robert Seymour, a well-known artist and illustrator, proposed to the publishing firm of Chapman & Hall a series of illustrations, to be issued monthly, based on an imaginary 'Nimrod Club' of Cockney sportsmen. There was nothing very original about Seymour's notion, which drew on the popularity of Pierce Egan's *Life in London* (issued monthly in 1820–1) and of such collections of sporting sketches as Surtees' *Jorrocks' Jaunts and Jollities* (1831–4). Seymour needed a hack-writer to provide the letterpress to accompany his illustrations; and on 10 February 1836 William Hall approached Charles Dickens with an invitation to undertake this task, which had already been declined by several others. Dickens' response, which showed an astonishing confidence for a struggling author of just twenty-four, was recalled by him in the 1847 Preface to *Pickwick*:

> I objected, on consideration, that although born and partly bred in the country I was no great sportsman, except in regard of all kinds of locomotion; that the idea was not novel, and had been already much used; that it would be infinitely better for the plates to arise naturally out of the text; and that I should like to take my own way, with a freer range of English scenes and people, and was afraid I should ultimately do so in any case, whatever course I might prescribe to myself at starting.

In other words, he would accept the commission provided that the subject were changed and his own role became dominant rather than subordinate! The publishers agreed to the expansion of the literary element but stuck to the original plan that the work should deal with 'manners and life in the Country'. Seymour's cover-design has a border of sporting activities and accessories surrounding the title: *The Posthumous Papers of the Pickwick Club Containing a Faithful Record of the Perambulations, Perils, Travels, Adventures and Sporting Transactions of the Corresponding Members. Edited by 'Boz'.*

Given his other commitments, Dickens had taken on a great deal: he wrote fast and furiously, and by mid-March was 'tired and worn out', but by the end of the month had completed the first two numbers, amounting to 24,000 words. Seymour continued with his share in the joint task, but Dickens made it quite clear who was in charge (he asked the artist to do another drawing to illustrate 'The Stroller's Tale', on the grounds that his first attempt lacked 'sympathy and solicitude'). Seymour, plagued by debts and with a history of mental trouble, committed suicide on 20 April. For Dickens this can only be described as a stroke of luck; it had, as Professor Patten says, the effect of 'transforming *Pickwick* from another example of illustrated comic sporting sketches to a novel whose pace and design were controlled by the author, not the illustrator'. After some delay H. K. Browne ('Phiz'), who was even younger than Dickens, was engaged to replace Seymour as illustrator.

Composition did not proceed without difficulties. As Patten says, Dickens 'vastly overextended himself' at this stage in his career: in November 1836, for example, he was busy with *Pickwick*, which still had another year to run, but was also occupied with the second series of *Sketches by Boz*, two plays, the editing of *Bentley's Miscellany* (due to begin in January 1837), for which he was committed to writing a substantial article every month, and other projects; and from February 1837, when *Oliver Twist* began to appear, he was writing two novels simultaneously. No wonder he fell behind with the *Pickwick* instalments: the wonder is that he wrote so much and so well in the circumstances. The only interruption was in May 1837, when Mary Hogarth's sudden death prevented him from writing the number due to appear at the end of that month.

Serialization   As Patten says, 'The prodigious success of *Pickwick* in parts signals a revolution in publishing.' Dickens did not invent serial publication, which has eighteenth-century and early nineteenth-century precedents; but he made it popular and thus was a major force in shaping the English novel during the middle years of the nineteenth century. Serial publication both 'opened up a new reading and buying public' and 'yielded profits hitherto thought impossible for any publisher or author' (Patten). Not that the format became universal: the three-volume novel retained its position until late in the century, though its cost was such that purchases were made by the circulating libraries rather than by individual buyers. The serialized novel was in effect a method of buying fiction by easy payments, the cost being spread over nineteen months (of the twenty 'parts' into which the novel was divided, the last was normally a double number). Its implications for both writers and readers were far-reaching. For an excellent discussion of the subject, see Part I of Kathleen Tillotson's *Novels of the Eighteen-Forties* (1954).

The Pickwick Papers appeared in nineteen monthly parts (the last being a double number) from April 1836 to November 1837 (no part appeared in June 1837: for the reason, see above). Eight illustrations by Seymour; two by R. W. Buss; the remainder by 'Phiz'. Division of the numbers was as follows: I (Chs 1–3); II (Chs 3 (conclusion), 4–5); III (Chs 6–8); IV (Chs 9–11); V (Chs 12–14); VI (Chs 15–17); VII (Chs 18–20); VIII (Chs 21–3); IX (Chs 24–6); X (Chs 27–9); XI (Chs 30–2); XII (Chs 33–4); XIII (Chs 35–7); XIV (Chs 38–40); XV (Chs 41–3); XVI (Chs 44–6); XVII (Chs 47–9); XVIII (Chs 50–2); XIX–XX (Chs 53–7).

Publication   The novel appeared in volume form in November 1837 and included a preface and a dedication to Thomas Talfourd. Dickens wrote new prefaces for the 'Cheap Edition' (1847) and the 'Charles Dickens Edition' (1867).

Reception   Sales of the early numbers were modest, and the printing order for the second number was a mere five hundred. But with the introduction of Sam Weller in the fourth number (July 1836) the astonishing rage for *Pickwick* began to get under way, and 'by the turn of the year it was clear that *Pickwick* was a gold mine' (Patten): by February 1837 sales reached 14,000 copies for the month, rising to 20,000 in May, 26,000 in September, and nearly 40,000 by the end of serialization. The publishers made the substantial profit of £14,000 on the monthly numbers alone. Dickens' fame quickly became international, the novel 'appearing in English-speaking countries and colonies from America to Van Diemen's land' (Patten):

There were Pickwick hats, canes, cigars, fabrics, coats, song books, china figurines, Weller corduroys and jest books, and Boz cabs. There were imitations, plagiarisms, parodies, sequels, extra illustrations, Pickwick quadrilles, stage piracies, and adaptations.

As Patten points out, the enthusiasm did not quickly fade: 'within a hundred years, the public bought up at least ninety-six separate English editions, and 127 American ones'. Edgar Johnson does not exaggerate in saying that 'It is doubtful if any other single work of letters before or since has ever aroused such wild and widespread enthusiasm in the entire history of literature.'

The reading version devised by Dickens and variously known as 'Bardell and Pickwick' and 'The Trial from Pickwick' became one of Dickens' most popular public readings. It was first given in Birmingham on 19 October 1858, and 'immediately became a great favourite' (Collins). Dickens based another reading, 'Mr Bob Sawyer's Party', on Ch. 32 of the novel.

One of the side-effects of serialization was that a novel published in this way received much more than the usual share of attention from critics, since there were reviews of the monthly instalments as well as of the complete book. As early as August 1836 Dickens was already 'Boz the magnificent' (*Fraser's Magazine*). Even earlier, the *Metropolitan Magazine* had provided free – and welcome – publicity for the novel by describing it as 'laugh-provoking', and eleven months later the same periodical was still responding regularly to Dickens' offerings and finding them even 'more uproarious in their fun, and more rich in their drollery'. The *Athenaeum* reviewer, having perused rather less than half the novel month by month, found 'great cleverness' in it (December 1836) but drew attention to its debts to literary predecessors ('The *Pickwick Papers*, in fact, are made up of two pounds of Smollett, three ounces of Sterne, a handful of Hook, a dash of a grammatical Pierce Egan – incidents at pleasure, served with an original *sauce piquante*'); comparisons with Egan, Hogarth, Cervantes, and even Shakespeare were made by other reviewers. But there were some disapproving murmurs: 'extravagance' was diagnosed as a fault by many, and Abraham Hayward wrote in the *Quarterly Review* (October 1837) that Dickens 'has risen like a rocket, and he will come down like the stick' – a prediction that could hardly have been farther from the truth.

Ian Watt has suggested that, if Samuel Richardson was the father of the English novel, there was something unplanned and accidental about his firstborn, *Pamela*; and much the same may be said about *The Pickwick Papers*, which launched Dickens' career as a novelist so early, so brilliantly, and so decisively. As Professor Patten points out, 'Though *Sketches* [*by Boz*] inaugurated Dickens's career, *Pickwick* made it [and] ushered in the age of the novel. . . . The success of the flimsy shilling parts, issued in green wrappers . . . , was unprecedented in the history of literature.' During the next thirty years and more, the graph of Dickens' popularity was to show slight variations; but he remained 'at the top of the tree' (in Thackeray's phrase) to the end of his days.

Seymour's notion of 'sporting sketches' had only a limited effect on the novel, but it did determine the appearance of Pickwick and his circle of friends. More important as an influence were the eighteenth-century novels Dickens had read in childhood; for *Pickwick*, like *Nickleby*, has strong picaresque elements. Dickens' 1837 preface opens by declaring that 'The author's object in this work, was to place before the reader a constant succession of characters and incidents'; and, having referred to the method of publication in monthly numbers, adds that in such circumstances 'no artfully interwoven or ingeniously complicated plot can with reason be expected'. He was obviously conscious of the loose structure of the novel, and anxious to disarm criticism; yet for many readers the 'succession of characters and incidents' is part of the book's attraction.

Having said that Dickens owes a debt to the picaresque tradition, however, one must quickly add that it was a picaresque modified: Mr Pickwick is no Tom Jones, and the episode at the Ipswich inn takes a very different turn from Tom's sexual escapade at Upton-on-Severn. The preface already quoted expresses the hope that 'throughout this book, no incident or expression occurs which could call a blush into the most delicate cheek' – an interesting anticipation of the attitude that Dickens was to satirize thirty years later in Mr Podsnap. His hero is no lusty young man ambitious to make his way in the world, but elderly, retired, and possessed of a comfortable income and a remarkable innocence. The frankness of Fielding and the coarseness of Smollett have been refined and sentimentalized for a readership largely composed of women and what Podsnap would call the young person; and the influence of Sterne, whose *Sentimental Journey* is alluded to in *Pickwick* Chapter 51, has been added to that of the picaresque novelists.

These eighteenth-century influences are appropriate in a novel so generously nostalgic; for Mr Pickwick (if one may for a moment speak biographically of a fictional character) was born and grew up in that century, and the novel as a whole – though written and published in the Railway Age – looks back to a vanishing England of coaches and coaching-inns when it is not (as in the Dingley Dell episodes) celebrating a timeless English idyll. The cast of characters is a very large one, the essence of picaresque being the hero's encounters with a wide variety of human types; many appear only briefly, but those who persist (Pickwick's friends, the Wardles, Jingle and Job Trotter, above all Sam and Tony Weller) help to give the book a rough coherence.

Movement is essential to the picaresque, and Pickwick does not stay in one place at a time for long. His first tour takes him into Kent (Rochester, Gravesend, and so on; Dingley Dell has been variously located in that county); his second into Suffolk, 'Eatanswill' being Sudbury (see, however, p. 307 below), and Pickwick travelling thither on the Norwich coach and then proceeding to Bury St Edmunds; his third to Ipswich; his fourth to Bath and Bristol; and his fifth again west to Bristol, Clifton, Gloucester, Tewesbury, Worcester, and on a wide clockwise circuit back to London via Birmingham, Coventry, Daventry and Towcester; throughout one has a vivid sense of fictional characters moving over a real landscape (for which Dickens drew on his recent travels as a reporter) and even pausing at actual inns and other buildings. The London scenes, too, are located with precision, and are bounded by Bishopgate on the northwest, the Borough High Street on the southwest – for Dickens is writing of a time when the West End was literally that. (The Penguin edition has useful maps of the Pickwickians' tours and of Pickwickian London – the latter identifying, rather strikingly, some sixty locations actually referred to in the novel.)

As noted above, the *Pickwick* craze – which, as Edgar Johnson tells us, led people to name their dogs and cats Sam, Jingle, Mrs Bardell and Job Trotter – began with the introduction of Sam Weller in the fourth number; and Sam is certainly the most oft-quoted character in the book. The wisecracking comic to Mr Pickwick's straight man, he has an endless fund of witticism and anecdote, rendered even more colourful by the stylized Cockney dialect that Dickens painstakingly reproduces; he also has Dickens' own energy, confidence and resourcefulness, as well as a knowledge of the ways of the world that reverses his quasi-filial relationship to his master and establishes what was to become a favourite

Dickensian pattern – the older man dependent upon a younger person or even a child (Nell's grandfather, Mr Dorrit, and 'Mr Dolls' are all variations on this theme). It is interesting that, in order to illustrate 'the thing that cannot be imitated' in Dickens, his 'fertility of invention', George Orwell should have taken two examples from this novel: Mr Jack Hopkins' story of the child who swallowed his sister's necklace, and Sam's story (Ch. 44) of the obstinate patient. Both, like so much else in this novel, are tall stories, fictions within the fiction, which lead us to laugh both at the anecdotes and at the gullibility of those who credit them.

The novel's early and continuing popularity gave rise to a vast mass of Pickwickiana, little of which can be called critical but all of which represents a tribute to the inexhaustible fun and infectious good humour of the book. C. S. Calverley's *Pickwick* examination paper, which not many of us would pass, demonstrates what one would not necessarily have taken for granted: the immense popularity of Dickens in undergraduate circles in the 1850s (Calverley's *Autobiography* later named Dickens as 'of course the first favourite' among contemporary authors, and Philip Collins notes that '*Pickwick* was, clearly, already a cult-book'). Later came a host of such books as *A Pickwickian Pilgrimage* (1881), *Pickwickian Manners and Customs* (1897), *An Index to Pickwick* (1897), *Mr Pickwick's Kent* (1899), and even *The Eatanswill Gazette*, which flourished briefly in 1907–8; the titles of these publications are sufficient to demonstrate the nature of the enthusiasm that prompted them. More recently, the mills of academic criticism have taken even *Pickwick* as grist; and, broadly speaking, there have been two main tendencies in coming to terms with it – one, to see it as anticipating the qualities of the later work; the other, to recognize it as *sui generis*.

For the former school, the role-playing of Jingle and others begins a lifetime's fascination with theatricality in all its aspects and with living as a kind of performance (Jingle is, of course, both an actor by profession and a swindler who imposes on others). Crucial, too, to such an interpretation is the part played in the novel by the Fleet Prison, in which Jingle, Pickwick, Mrs Bardell and others are all reunited, and in which pretence and comedy give way to a confrontation with stark reality. As Edmund Wilson's seminal essay showed over forty years ago, the prison is one of the most dominant and potent symbols in Dickens' work; and the tone of the book certainly changes when, in the aftermath of the exuberantly funny trial scene, Mr Pickwick is confined. John Killham has drawn attention to Dickens' own use of the term 'emblem', in a sense roughly approximating to that of 'symbol', in describing the withered plant watered, without much result, by the wife of a Fleet prisoner: 'too true an emblem, perhaps, of the office she had come there to discharge'. Killham also points out that 'When Mr Pickwick was greeted on his first arrival in the prison by the sight of a Dutch clock and a bird-cage, Sam Weller was quick to point out the meaning of these objects. "Veels within Veels, a prison in a prison".'

Some modern critics have made much of the interpolated tales, those gloomy short stories, so intensely preoccupied with poverty, drunkenness and madness, inserted within the main narrative. Dickens was drawing, again, on a precedent to be found in *Tom Jones* and elsewhere; the leisurely progress of his novel did not exclude such delaying tactics, and the contrast between the comedy and farce of the main story and the Gothic grimness of the tales seems a sufficient reason for their existence. However, many recent commentators have found this too tame an explanation and have suggested a more organic relationship between novel and tales; as Philip Collins says, 'the burden of these articles generally is that the interpolated tales are more relevant and/or better than has been recognized'.

In contrast to the attempts to make *Pickwick* sound like a late rather than an early Dickens novel, Sylvère Monod has argued in detail, and (I think) persuasively, that 'the book does not possess one firmly designed, self-evident, plot, but is composed of four plots – three of which are secondary – interwoven, and broken by many interludes'. Professor Monod defines these various plots as follows:

The main plot, main at least in the sense that it has greater importance than any other for the narrative as a whole and covers the largest number of chapters, is the misunderstanding between Mrs. Bardell and Mr. Pickwick, with all its consequences. An excellent 'digest' of *Pickwick* could be produced by printing a version that would begin with that story in Chapter XII, with Sam's engagement, and take it as far as its winding-up in Chapter XLVIII; thus could be presented a 'Bardell *v.* Pickwick Trial,' which would of course have to omit many delightful passages, but nothing essential; the result would be a poorer book, but a better novel, than *Pickwick* is.

The novel obviously contains several elements scarcely connected with the main plot: (a) a group of episodes whose center is old Wardle (repeated invitations and visits, sporting scenes, Winkle's and Snodgrass' love affairs); (b) the pursuit of Jingle, his tricks, his punishment, pardon, and final conversion; (c) the Weller Saga, with the family relationships of the Wellers and their contacts with the Temperance Society and the 'Reverend' Mr. Stiggins. The third subplot, in accordance with the tradition of the French classical theater and the eighteenth century English drama, reproduces at an inferior level, among the servants, their masters' adventures.

In addition to these four plots, *Pickwick* contains a number of episodes artificially and loosely connected with one or other of them which interrupt the progress of the general story. The chief episodes – without counting the nine 'inserted tales' – are the quarrel with the cabman and Mr. Winkle's abortive duel with Slammer; the antiquarian discovery; the Eatanswill election (it is Tupman's friendship with Wardle that takes the Pickwickians to Dingley Dell; it is Wardle's friendship with Perker, then Perker's with Pott, that takes them to Eatanswill; it is Pott's with Mrs. Leo Hunter that takes them to the fancy-dress party – through this primitive principle of association, it was easy enough to go on, apparently forever); the second hunting-party; the meeting with Peter Magnus and his fiancée; the whole of the Christmas number; the evening at Bob Sawyer's; the parties at Bath (masters and servants); the interview between Pott and Slurk.

Monod concludes that, with four plots, nine inserted tales, and ten 'interludes', one may well question Dickens' claim that the novel constitutes 'a tolerably harmonious whole' – unless one grants that 'harmony' refers to no more than a prevailing consistency of tone and atmosphere (though the prison scenes and the interpolated tales make this open to question). Of deliberate structuring, of the kind that Dickens was to execute with such masterly effects in his later work, there is little trace; and claims that the novel makes significant use of symbolism, in the sense in which this can be said of (for instance) that other prison-novel, *Little Dorrit*, are usually found to lean heavily on details that form only a tiny part of this rich and multifarious book. But this is not to deny, of course, that in many ways *Pickwick* anticipates elements in Dickens' later work – among much else, in the satirical treatment of the legal world and of religious hypocrites, in some of the comic types (artful landladies, predatory widows, windbag politicians, and so on), and in the stylistic variety and originality and the ready impulse to parody. The novel's opening, like the chapter-titles and much of the conversation of the Pickwickians, has a conscious formality that is clearly tongue-in-cheek on Dickens' part, and acts as a foil to the pace and vivacity of Sam Weller and Alfred Jingle. Again, Dickens has cleverly emulated, and improved on, the vigour of Smollett without offending the susceptibilities of a generation whose manners were very different from those of the mid-eighteenth century; so that Miss Mitford could write to a friend in June 1837 that the book contained 'fun – London life – but without anything unpleasant: a lady might read it all *aloud* . . . '. The remark is an appropriate epigraph to the history of the novel in the new reign that began in that year.

F. R. and Q. D. Leavis describe the novel as 'callow', but most readers will probably rejoice to concur with Rachel Trickett's verdict that it is 'one of the funniest books ever written'. Such a disarming quality has not, however, prevented it from being very widely discussed by modern critics – more widely, according to Philip Collins, than any other pre-*Copperfield* novel by Dickens. Sylvère Monod's discussion in his *Dickens the Novelist* has been referred to above, and Steven Marcus's book also has a good chapter. Among a large number of essays may be mentioned those by W. H. Auden (in his *The Dyer's Hand*, 1962), D. M. Bevington (*Nineteenth-Century Fiction*, xvi, 1962), John Killham (in *Dickens and the Twentieth Century*, ed. John Gross and Gabriel Pearson), and Barbara Hardy (*London Review*, ii, 1967). Among those who have discussed the structure of the novel, including the function of the interpolated tales, are William Axton (*Studies in English Literature 1500–1900*, v, 1965), Robert Patten (*Dickens Studies*, i, 1965) and M. Colwell (*Dickens Studies*, iii, 1967). On the composition and serialization of the novel, see John Butt and Kathleen Tillotson's *Dickens at Work*.

CHARACTERS

ALLEN, ARABELLA. Pretty young lady, sister of Ben Allen. In Ch. 47 Winkle presents her to Pickwick as his wife. Her brother BENJAMIN (Ben) is a medical student and a friend of Bob Sawyer.

He is described in Ch. 30 as 'a coarse, stout, thick-set young man, with black hair cut rather short, and a white face cut rather long'. MISS ALLEN, Arabella's aunt, also appears.

AYRESLEIGH, MR. One of the debtors detained at Mr Namby's sponging-house.

BAGMAN, THE ONE-EYED. Teller of two of the interpolated tales (Chs 14, 49).

BAMBER, JACK. Referred to in 'The Old Man's Tale about the Queer Client' (Ch. 21).

BANTAM, ANGELO CYRUS. Master of Ceremonies at Bath when Pickwick visits that town (see Ch. 35).

BARDELL, MRS (Martha). A widow, and Mr Pickwick's landlady, 'a comely woman of bustling manners and agreeable appearance' (Ch. 12). She lives in Goswell Street. She misunderstands his intentions and brings a breach of promise action against him (Ch. 18). Later she is herself sent to the Fleet Prison by the lawyers she has employed (see the end of Ch. 47, which also provides the curtain at the close of the sixteenth number), and meets Pickwick there. Her young son TOMMY also appears.

BETSY. Servant-girl to Mrs Raddle, the landlady of Bob Sawyer.

BLADUD, PRINCE. Appears in one of the interpolated tales (Ch. 36).

BLOTTON, MR. Member of the Pickwick Club; he is briefly argumentative in the opening chapter.

BOLDWIG, CAPTAIN. Choleric landowner, 'a little fierce man in a stiff black neckerchief and blue surtout' (Ch. 19), on whose property Mr Pickwick is found asleep in a wheelbarrow. He has Pickwick conveyed to the pound.

BUZFUZ, SERJEANT. Barrister representing Mrs Bardell at the trial (Ch. 34). He is said to have been based on a Serjeant Bompas.

CLUPPINS, MRS (Elizabeth). Friend of Mrs Bardell, 'a little brisk, busy-looking woman' (Ch. 26). She also appears at the trial and gives evidence.

CRADDOCK, MRS. Pickwick's landlady at Bath.

CRIPPS, TOM. Servant to Bob Sawyer when he visits Bristol.

DODSON, MR. Lawyer of the firm of Dodson and Fogg, who act for Mrs Bardell: 'a plump, portly, stern-looking man, with a loud voice' (Ch. 20), physically contrasting with his partner. The two of them are described by Mr Pickwick in Ch. 53 as ' "mean, rascally, pettifogging robbers" '.

DOWLER, MR. Retired army officer, 'a stern-eyed man of about five-and-forty, who had a bald and glossy forehead . . . and large black whiskers' (Ch. 35). He visits Bath with the Pickwickians, and is accompanied by his pretty wife.

DUBBLEY, MR. Leader of an Ipswich division of special constables.

EDMUNDS, JOHN. Appears in 'The Convict's Return' (Ch. 6).

FAT BOY, THE *see* JOE.

FIZKIN, HORATIO. The Buff party candidate at the Eatanswill election (Ch. 13).

FLASHER, WILKINS. A stockbroker (Ch. 35).

FOGG, MR. Lawyer of the firm of Dodson and Fogg, who act for Mrs Bardell: 'an elderly, pimply-faced, vegetable-diet sort of man'. See also DODSON.

GOODWIN. Servant to Mrs Pott of Eatanswill (Ch. 18).

GRUB, GABRIEL. The sexton in the interpolated tale of the goblins who stole a sexton (Ch. 29).

GRUMMER, DANIEL. A special constable in Ipswich, an elderly man 'chiefly remarkable for a bottle-nose, a hoarse voice, a snuff-coloured surtout, and a wandering eye' (Ch. 24), and with some affinity with Shakespeare's Dogberry and Verges.

GRUNDY, MR. Appears at the Magpie and Stump (Ch. 20) and declines 'to oblige the company with a song'.

GUNTER, MR. One of Bob Sawyer's guests at his bachelor party (Ch. 32).

GWYNN, MISS. 'The writing and ciphering governess' at the seminary for young ladies into which Mr Pickwick inadvertently intrudes (Ch. 16).

HARRIS, MR. A greengrocer at Bath.

HEYLING, GEORGE. The 'queer client' in the interpolated tale told in Ch. 21.

HOPKINS, JACK. Medical student and a friend of Bob Sawyer; he appears in Ch. 32.

HUMM, ANTHONY. President of the Brick Lane Branch of the United Grand Junction Ebenezer Temperance Association (Ch. 33).

HUNTER, LEO. Citizen of Eatanswill; his name refers to his wife's passion for seeking out literary lions. MRS LEO HUNTER is herself a poetess ('Ode to an Expiring Frog') and appears in Ch. 15.

HUTLEY, JEM ('Dismal Jemmy'). A down-at-heel actor, the brother of Job Trotter. He tells 'The Stroller's Tale' in Ch. 3 and at the end of the book emigrates to the New World.

JACKSON, MR. Lawyer's clerk to the firm of Dodson and Fogg (Ch. 20).

JINGLE, MR (Alfred). Strolling actor, introduced in Ch. 2. He reappears at the cricket-match in Ch. 7; deceives Miss Rachael Wardle into thinking that Mr Tupman is after her money, and elopes with her himself (Chs 8–9), but is bought off by her brother (Ch. 10). He turns up again at Mrs Leo Hunter's soirée at Eatanswill, this time dressed as a naval officer and posing as Captain Charles Fitz-Marshall (Ch. 15), but is recognized by Pickwick. Later he. joins Pickwick in the Fleet Prison; and eventually, with Pickwick's help, emigrates to Demerera. Jingle's tall stories resemble those of Sam Weller, but his staccato, fragmentary style of speech is entirely his own and may well have been modelled on that of Goldfinch, a character in Thomas Holcroft's play *The Road to Ruin* (1792), though debts to Surtees and Hook have also been proposed. Dickens himself made a brief excursion into the Jingle style in a letter of 27 April 1841 ('Post just going – compression of sentiments required – ', and so on).

JINKS, MR. Clerk to Mr Nupkins, the Mayor of Ipswich (Ch. 24).

JOE ('The Fat Boy'). Servant to Mr Wardle, notable for his gargantuan appetite and his habit of falling asleep at every opportunity. In these respects he is said to be an accurate representation of the symptoms of a rare disease known as the Kleine-Levin syndrome. He is introduced in Ch. 4; observes Tupman making love to Miss Rachael Wardle in Ch. 8; and reappears in Ch. 28.

LOBBS, MR. Wealthy and disagreeable saddler in the story 'The Parish Clerk' (Ch. 17), in which his daughter Maria also appears.

LOWTEN, MR. Clerk to Mr Perker of Gray's Inn.

MAGNUS, PETER. The jealous suitor of Miss Witherfield, introduced as 'a red-haired man with an inquisitive nose and blue spectacles' (Ch. 22).

MALLARD, MR. Clerk to Serjeant Snubbin (Ch. 31).

MARTIN, MR. There are two characters of this name: (1) groom to Arabella Allen's aunt; (2) prisoner in the Fleet Prison. There is also a JACK MARTIN who appears in the story of the bagman's uncle (Ch. 49).

MARY. At first a housemaid in the employ of Mr Nupkins, Mayor of Ipswich, she later becomes maid to Arabella Allen. She is kissed by Sam Weller in Ch. 25, and marries him at the end of the book, becoming Mr Pickwick's housekeeper and bearing Sam two sons. *On the significance of her married name, see under* WELLER.

MILLER, MR. One of the guests at Dingley Dell.

MIVINS, MR ('The Zephyr'). A prisoner in the Fleet (Ch. 41).

MUZZLE. 'Undersized footman' to Mr Nupkins, Mayor of Ipswich; he appears in Ch. 24.

NAMBY, MR. Sheriff's deputy involved in the arrest of Mr Pickwick (Ch. 40). He is 'a man of about forty, with black hair, and carefully combed whiskers', and is 'dressed in a particularly gorgeous manner, with plenty of articles of jewellery about him'.

NODDY, MR. One of Bob Sawyer's guests in Ch. 32.

NUPKINS, MR (George). Mayor of Ipswich; he appears in Ch. 24. His disagreeable wife appears in Ch. 25, as does his daughter HENRIETTA.

PAYNE, DR. Friend of Dr Slammer.

PELL, SOLOMON. Attorney at the Insolvent Debtors' Court, 'a fat flabby pale man, in a surtout which looked green one minute and brown the next' (Ch. 43).

PERKER, MR. Mr Pickwick's solicitor; he has chambers in Gray's Inn and is introduced in Ch. 10.

PHUNKEY, MR. Barrister who acts as junior counsel for the defence in the trial of Bardell v. Pickwick. He is introduced in Ch. 31.

PICKWICK, MR (Samuel). Retired man of business and founder of the Club named after him. He is introduced in the opening chapter of the novel ('the bald head, and circular spectacles') and portrayed in Seymour's illustration 'Mr Pickwick addresses the Club'. The publisher Edward Chapman suggested to Seymour 'a figure modelled on a friend, a fat, genial beau from Richmond addicted to drab tights and black gaiters. Seymour knew this type equally well, having drawn him on several occasions, and thus the immortal Pickwick was born' (Patten). Later Dickens said, 'I thought of Mr Pickwick, and wrote the first number'; he is said to have derived the name Pickwick from Moses Pickwick, a Bath coach proprietor. Among other adventures and misadventures, Pickwick lodges with Mrs Bardell, who misunderstands his intentions (Ch. 12); is the defendant in a breach of promise action brought by her (Ch. 18), announces his determination to pay no damages (Ch. 31), and appears at the trial (Ch. 34); is arrested (Ch. 41) and sent to prison; and leaves prison, 'far more sad and melancholy, for the moment, than when he had first entered it' (Ch. 47). He also falls asleep in a wheelbarrow (Ch. 19) and is put in the pound; has an adventure at Ipswich with a lady in yellow curlpapers (Ch. 22); spends Christmas at Dingley Dell (Ch. 28); and slides on the ice (Ch. 31). Throughout most of the book he is accompanied by his manservant Sam Weller. The Penguin edition includes useful sketch-maps of the Pickwickians' tours and of London sites associated with Mr Pickwick.

PIPKIN, NATHANIEL. Hero of the story 'The Parish Clerk' (Ch. 17).

POTT, MR. Editor of the *Eatanswill Gazette*, 'a tall, thin man, with a sandy-coloured head inclined to baldness, and a face in which solemn importance was blended with a look of unfathomable profundity' (Ch. 13). His wife also makes an appearance.

PRICE, MR. One of the prisoners at Mr Namby's sponging-house (Ch. 40).

PRUFFLE. Servant to an 'elderly scientific gentleman' (Ch. 39).

RADDLE, MRS. Termagant landlady of Bob Sawyer, introduced in Ch. 32. She lives in Lant Street, and is a sister of Mrs Cluppins. Her husband also appears.

ROGERS, MRS. Lodger at Mrs Bardell's house (Ch. 46).

ROKER, TOM. Turnkey in the Fleet prison (Ch. 41).

SANDERS, MRS (Susannah). Friend of Mrs Bardell, introduced in Ch. 26, where she is described as 'a big, fat, heavy-faced personage'.

SAWYER, BOB. Medical student (his name suggesting 'sawbones'), described in Ch. 30. Ch. 32 gives an account of his bachelor party and provided the material for one of Dickens' public readings.

SIMMERY, FRANK. A betting gentleman introduced in Ch. 55.

SKIMPKIN, MR. Counsel for Mrs Bardell in her breach of promise action (Ch. 34).

SLAMMER, DR. 'Surgeon to the 97th' at Chatham barracks. He is introduced in Ch. 2 as 'a little fat man, with a ring of upright black hair round his head, and an extensive bald plain on the top of it'. He sends a challenge to Jingle, which is delivered in error to Winkle.

SLUMKEY, THE HON. SAMUEL. One of the candidates in the Eatanswill election.

SLURK, MR. Editor of the *Eatanswill Independent*.

SMANGLE, MR. Prisoner in the Fleet (Ch. 41).

SMART, TOM. Appears in the interpolated tale told in Ch. 14.

SMAUKER, JOHN. Footman to Angelo Cyrus Bantam of Bath. He sends an invitation to Sam Weller (Ch. 37).

SMORLTORK, COUNT. Introduced to Mr Pickwick by Mrs Leo Hunter in Ch. 15 as ' "the famous foreigner – gathering materials for his great work on England" ', he represents a satirical portrait of the confident but superficial and ill-informed observer.

Contemporary readers might well have been reminded of Prince Pückler-Muskau and Professor Friedrich von Raumer, both of whom had recently published accounts of their visits to England (see Kathleen Tillotson's article in *The Times Literary Supplement*, 22 November 1957).

SMOUCH, MR. Assistant to Mr Namby.

SNODGRASS, AUGUSTUS. Introduced in the opening chapter; a former ward of Mr Pickwick and an aspiring poet.

SNUBBIN, SERJEANT. Barrister who appears for Mr Pickwick in the trial of Bardell v. Pickwick (Ch. 34): 'a lantern-faced, sallow-complexioned man, of about five-and-forty, or – as the novels say – he might be fifty' (Ch. 31). He lives in Lincoln's Inn Old Square.

SNUPHANUPH, LADY. Card-player at Bath (Ch. 35).

STARELEIGH, MR JUSTICE. Judge at the trial of Bardell v. Pickwick (Ch. 34): 'a most particularly short man, and so fat, that he seemed all face and waistcoat'. He is said to have been based on Mr Justice Gazelee.

STIGGINS, REV. MR. 'A prim-faced, red-nosed man, with a long, thin countenance, and a semi-rattlesnake sort of eye' (Ch. 27), 'deputy shepherd' of an evangelical congregation, a friend of Sam Weller's step-mother, and one of the earliest of Dickens' satirical portraits of nonconformist clergymen. As a climax to the eighteenth number (Ch. 53), he is kicked by Tony Weller.

TAPPLETON, LIEUTENANT. He acts as Dr Slammer's second when the latter challenges Jingle.

TOMKINS, MISS. Prim principal of the Westgate House Establishment for Young Ladies, the scene of one of Mr Pickwick's nocturnal misadventures (see Ch. 16).

TROTTER, JOB. Manservant to Jingle (see Chs. 16, 23) and brother of Jem ('Dismal Jemmy') Hutley.

TRUNDLE, MR. Husband of Isabella Wardle, and son-in-law of Mr Wardle.

TUCKLE, MR. Bath footman (see Ch. 37).

TUPMAN, TRACY. Friend of Mr Pickwick and member of the Club, introduced in the opening chapter. A portly middle-aged bachelor of amorous disposition, he makes love to Miss Rachael Wardle (Ch. 8) and is observed and betrayed by the fat boy.

WARDLE, MR. Owner of the Manor Farm at Dingley Dell, introduced in Ch. 4. The second number of the novel ends (Ch. 5) with his welcoming Mr Pickwick and his friends to his home. He has an unmarried daughter EMILY and another daughter, ISABELLA, who marries Mr Trundle: also a spinster sister, RACHAEL, who is loved by Mr Tupman (Ch. 8) and elopes with Jingle (Ch. 9); and a deaf mother, introduced in Ch. 6.

WELLER, SAMUEL (Sam). Mr Pickwick's manservant, and arguably the hero of the novel, he is introduced in Ch. 10 'busily employed in brushing the dirt off a pair of boots' in the yard of the White Hart inn in the Borough. For his contribution to the success of the novel, see above (p. 70). He accompanies Pickwick on his travels, his knowingness contrasting with Pickwick's innocence and his vigorous demotic speech and informal manners with the other's conventionality. His witticisms, tall stories and outlandish comparisons quickly became the rage; couched in a painstakingly rendered Cockney dialect, they are eminently quotable. Also memorable is his father TONY Weller, a coachman, whose second wife SUSAN, is landlady of the Marquis of Granby at Dorking. Sam meets his stepmother (referred to, according to the usage of the time, as his 'mother-in-law') in Ch. 27; hears of her death and visits his father in Dorking (Ch. 52). Sam eventually marries MARY, Mr Nupkins' pretty housemaid, whose name thus becomes identical with that of the Dickens' servant in CD's childhood (see p. 50).

WHIFFERS, MR. Footman at Bath (see Ch. 37).

WICKS, MR. Clerk to Dodson and Fogg (Ch. 20).

WINKLE, NATHANIEL. One of Mr Pickwick's friends and a member of the Club, he is introduced in the opening chapter. His role as an amateur sportsman is a vestige of the original conception of the work as a series of sporting sketches. He appears, nervously, at the trial of Bardell v. Pickwick (Ch. 34), and is bullied by the judge.

WITHERFIELD, MISS. The middle-aged lady in yellow curlpapers encountered in Ipswich by Mr Pickwick (Ch. 22).

WUGSBY, MRS COLONEL. Card-player at Bath (Ch. 35).

Oliver Twist

Texts Penguin English Library, ed. Peter Fairclough, introduction by Angus Wilson (1966); Clarendon Dickens, ed. Kathleen Tillotson (1966).

Composition In November 1836 Dickens accepted the publisher Richard Bentley's invitation to edit a new monthly magazine to be entitled *Bentley's Miscellany*, and by an agreement dated 4 November he contracted 'to furnish an orginal article of his own writing, every monthly Number, to consist of a sheet of about 16 pages'. The *Miscellany* began publication in January 1837, and the following month Dickens contributed not 'an original article' but the first instalment of a new novel. He was still engaged in writing *Pickwick Papers*, and his plan seems to have been to devote the first fortnight of each month to *Oliver Twist* and the second to *Pickwick*. Between November 1837 and February 1838 Dickens enjoyed a brief respite from his double task, with *Pickwick* concluded and *Nickleby* not yet begun; apart from this, he carried the staggering burden of writing two novels simultaneously throughout the composition of *Oliver Twist*. There was an interruption in May 1837 when Mary Hogarth died and Dickens felt unable to go on with his work; the June issue of the *Miscellany* accordingly carried an announcement that the instalment due would not appear. But by the beginning of June he was evidently back at his desk again. On 14 July he confessed himself to be 'terribly behindhand'; a year later (15 July 1838), working towards a deadline (not in the event met) of September for volume publication, he had only just begun the last of the three volumes and admitted that he was 'sadly harassed to get it finished in time' and had 'several very important scenes . . . yet to write'. Towards the end he was 'incessantly occupied, night and day', and the book was not finished until

October. (For a detailed account of the stages of composition, see Kathleen Tillotson's introduction to the Clarendon edition.)

Serialization   Unlike Dickens' later novels, the instalments of which appeared at regular intervals and were of more or less uniform length, *Oliver Twist* was published somewhat irregularly and in portions of varying length, in twenty-four instalments from February 1837 until April 1839. Illustrations by George Cruikshank. Division as follows: monthly from February to May 1837, with two chapters in each issue of *Bentley's Miscellany*; no June instalment (for the reason, see above); Chs 9–11 in July, 12–13 in August, 14–15 in September; no October instalment; Chs 16–17 in November, 18–19 in December; 20–2 in January 1838; 23–5 in February (originally numbered 1–3 of Book II); 26–7 in March; 28–30 in April; 31–2 in May; 33–4 in June; 35–7 in July; 38 and part of 39 in August (originally numbered 1–2 of Book III); no September instalment; the rest of 39 and 40–1 in October; 42–3 in November; 44–6 in December; 47–9 in January 1839; 50 in February; 51 in March; 52–3 in April. (In the original version the chapter-divisions were somewhat different from April 1838 onwards and the total number of chapters was 51. The numbers above follow the arrangement in modern editions, which was adopted in 1846.)

Publication   Published in three volumes by Richard Bentley on 9 November 1838 (that is, several months before magazine serialization was concluded). The title was *Oliver Twist; or, the Parish Boy's Progress* (perhaps with a punning allusion to *The Pilgrim's Progress*). The original title-page indicated the author as 'Boz', but at Dickens' request a new title-page was substituted a week after first publication naming the author as 'Charles Dickens. Author of "The Pickwick Papers"'. Dickens revised the text significantly in subsequent editions (1846, 1850, 1858, 1867: see below). No preface (a preface was added in 1841; a different preface was included in the Cheap Edition of 1850). The novel was serialized again in 1846 (10 monthly parts) and in 1849–50 (19 weekly parts; also in 5 monthly parts). It was thus, as Kathleen Tillotson says, 'published in an unusual number of different forms – magazine, three volumes, monthly parts, one volume, and collected editions; it passed through the hands of three different publishers; and it was revised four times, once with exceptional thoroughness'. It occupied

Dickens, on and off, for over thirty years, since he based on it his celebrated public reading 'Sikes and Nancy' as late as 1868.

Reception Philip Collins notes that 'Reviewers of *Oliver Twist* mostly hailed its greater "earnestness" and "purpose", and recognized its advance on *Pickwick* in constructional skill.' The *Spectator* praised its realism in the presentation of low life: 'the thieves, their comates, and the Londoners of Boz, are flesh and blood – living creatures'; 'very remarkable skill in making use of peculiarities of expression, even to the current phrase of the day'. It had some reservations, however, about the novel's topicality: 'These things tell with many readers, but they must detract from the permanence of the writer who freely uses them.' Not all readers welcomed the graphic realism: Henry Fox wrote in a letter, 'I know there are such unfortunate beings as pickpockets and street walkers. I am very sorry for it and very much shocked at their mode of life, but I own that I do not much wish to hear what they say to one another' (a faint anticipation, perhaps, of Mr Podsnap). The young Queen Victoria found the book 'excessively interesting'; she persuaded Lord Melbourne to read it, but he was unimpressed ('"I don't *like* those things; I wish to avoid them; I don't like them in *reality*, and therefore I don't wish them represented"').

Kathleen Tillotson has argued that *Oliver Twist*, Dickens' second novel to be published, may have been his first to be conceived, its origins going back as far as 1833. Be that as it may, the contrast with *Pickwick* was a marked one for his first readers and is still striking as we contemplate the two books today. As Angus Wilson says,

> the sombre tone of *Oliver Twist*, coming after *Pickwick Papers*, was a surprise, though no disappointment, to contemporary readers . . . . With *Oliver Twist* Dickens the master of grand guignol, and Dickens the journalist, come to the front of the stage, while Dickens the comedian of *Pickwick Papers* retires into comparative shadow.

It is as if Dickens were eager to demonstrate his own versatility and to avoid being typecast as the author of a particular kind of fiction: in the context of the 1830s it is hard to think of a more abrupt change than the one he makes – from the cheerful, middle-class world of Mr Pickwick to the squalid, violent criminal milieu ('the very dregs of life', as Dickens later said in his preface) of Fagin and

Sikes. The contrast is not a complete one, however; for *Pickwick*, in its macabre and melodramatic interpolated tales, had hinted at the darker side of life, and *Oliver Twist*, in one group of its characters, proclaims the survival of Pickwickian benevolence and a genteel and ordered way of life.

As Angus Wilson has shown in his excellent introduction to the Penguin edition, Dickens drew on various literary and dramatic models in his second novel. The Gothic novel may well have contributed 'a certain supernatural element implied in the diabolic character of Fagin, and in the mysterious absence of his footprints after he has peered in upon Oliver in his country retreat, and in the whole phantom character of Monks'. The eighteenth-century picaresque novel may have suggested 'the disputed-inheritance-cum-illegitimate-son plot' (cf. *Tom Jones* and *Humphry Clinker*). Popular melodrama of the kind that Dickens enjoyed in the London theatres made its contribution, notably to the stylized and implausible dialogue at certain points. Most obvious of all to Dickens' first readers would have been the influence of the so-called 'Newgate novel', which flourished in the 1830s; to this category belong such once-popular works as Bulwer-Lytton's *Paul Clifford* (1830) and *Eugene Aram* (1832), and Harrison Ainsworth's *Rookwood* (1834). Such novels glamourized the criminal classes (the heroes of the first and third are highwaymen). At the end of the decade, Thackeray satirized this school of fiction in his *Catherine* (serialized in 1839–40), narrated by 'Ikey Solomon, junior' (Ikey Solomon had been the prototype of Fagin); and in *Fraser's Magazine* (August 1840), describing the crowd at a public execution, he contrasted the real-life Nancys with those depicted by Dickens:

> I was curious to look at them, having, in late fashionable novels, read many accounts of such personages. Bah! what figments these novelists tell us! Boz, who knows life well, knows that his Miss Nancy is the most unreal fantastical personage possible; . . . He dare not tell the truth concerning such young ladies.

Dickens for his part was annoyed at having *Oliver Twist* classified as a Newgate novel ('I am by some jolter-headed enemies most unjustly and untruly charged with having written a book after Mr Ainsworth's fashion': letter of February 1840).

Certainly, although the presentation of criminal life is still vivid, there is more to *Oliver Twist* than that. Most obviously, there is the satire on the Poor Law Amendment Act of 1834 and its effects. Peter Fairclough notes that the opening chapters of the novel appeared when a campaign by *The Times* attacking the Act was at its height. As Fairclough says,

> The chief object of the new Act was to stop the benevolent Allowance System – a development of the granting of wholesale outdoor relief by many humane J.P.s, whereby labourers' wages were supplemented to subsistence level by contributions to the Poor Rate – by abolishing out-relief to the able-bodied.

It also made the workhouses themselves as uncongenial as possible, in order to discourage 'able-bodied paupers' from resorting to them: the diet was sparse, discipline strict, exercise very limited and the work done hard and monotonous. Oliver is born into the pre-1834 system, and sent to one of the baby farms which were a feature of the early nineteenth-century provision for pauper orphans. But by the time he is nine years old (Ch. 2) the new Act is in effect and his fate is settled by one of the elected Boards of Guardians that had been newly established. Humphry House has commented that Bumble's still being beadle after the introduction of the new Act was perfectly possible: 'all the details did not change at a stroke, and the early reports of the Commissioners are full of complaints of unsuitable officers taken over from the old system'.

House also points out that although Dickens' account of the workhouse diet – 'three meals of thin gruel a day, with an onion twice a week, and half a roll on Sundays' – was an exaggeration, the diet was in fact meagre and monotonous, and gruel played a prominent part in the menus ($1\frac{1}{2}$ pints a day for seven days a week, according to a Dietary approved in 1836).

Dickens was to continue his attack on the inhumanity of the workhouse system: almost thirty years later, in his last completed novel, *Our Mutual Friend*, it is still a target. But it is not the only topical aspect of this early novel; indeed, according to House, 'A novel could hardly have been more topical than *Oliver Twist*.' Saffron Hill, where much of the action takes place, was notorious in the period as a haunt of thieves, prostitutes and fences, and in making it the base of Fagin's activities 'Dickens was . . . using a contemporary topical allusion with which a great number of his readers would have been quite familiar beforehand' (House). The brief reference to Oliver's narrow escape at being apprenticed to a chimney-sweep alludes to the plight of the climbing boys, another contemporary scandal. And Mr Fang the magistrate is based on a real-life prototype whom Dickens had actually observed in action (see entry for 'Fang' below).

Dickens obviously saw these topical and realistic elements as part of the strength of the novel, and he defends them in the 1841 preface. But, as so often in Dickens, they exist alongside elements that belong to quite a different order of fiction; for Oliver's situation owes something to fairytale and folktale, with Oliver as a male Cinderella or princess disguised as a goosegirl; and his innate gentility (manifested, for example, in his speech – a product of his birth rather than his environment) is flagrantly non-realistic.

Similarly, there is a problem arising from the conflict between the impulse on Dickens' part to satirize with righteous indignation and the impulse to turn anything and everything to comedy. Bumble is not, *a priori*, a figure of fun but the corrupt representative of an evil system. In the novel, however, he is a comedian, and some of the scenes in which he appears (for example, his courtship of Mrs Corney) have little or nothing to do with the attack on the poor law. This is an aspect of Dickens' art not confined to this novel (compare, for instance, the treatment of Mrs Gamp in *Martin Chuzzlewit*, where the exposure of her incompetence as a nurse is almost lost sight of in the rich eccentricity of her monologues); but it has left some of Dickens' critics very uncomfortable. John Carey, for instance, has remarked in his stimulating book on Dickens that starving children are no laughing matter; but this is perhaps to view too narrowly the function of laughter, which for Dickens could be not only a means of escaping from the serious issues with which life presents us but a means of coming to terms with them and even bringing home their seriousness with a special kind of emphasis. Certainly in reading *Oliver Twist*, especially its early chapters, the response is of a complex kind, with compassion, indignation and amusement strangely blended.

As noted above, Dickens revised the text of this novel at intervals, and his revisions included some significant changes. Peter Fairclough has commented that in the early editions 'the Maylies and Mr Brownlow were treated more sentimentally than in the later editions, and Dickens also gradually eliminated a good deal of crude and clumsy early writing'. He also played down the anti-Semitism of the original version by avoiding the expression 'the Jew' in reference to Fagin (for his attempt to make reparation for the harm done by the portrait of Fagin, see p. 25). Moreover, he softened the 'strong language' given to Sikes and other characters: Fairclough, again, notes the 'gradual elimination of many oaths throughout all texts as the novel left the pages of a man's magazine for an audience including females and "Young Persons"'. These last revisions also, of course, reflect the changing threshold of tolerance as the Victorian age got into its stride. The pressure on the novelist to observe the proprieties produced from him the claim in the 1841 preface that he had attempted 'to banish from the lips of the lowest character I introduced, any expression that could by possibility offend' – an attitude that he himself was later to satirize in his portrayal of Mrs General and Mr Podsnap. The reading version, 'Sikes and Nancy', that Dickens prepared in 1868 (see p. 267) goes even further in bowdlerizing Sikes' language – 'Hell's fire', for instance, being omitted, and 'Damme' becoming 'Hello' – as the printed text was adapted for oral delivery.

Angus Wilson has suggested plausibly that the characters of this novel can be divided into three groups: the genteel (Mr Brownlow, the Maylies), the criminal (Fagin, Sikes, Nancy, the boy-pickpockets), and the inhabitants of the town where Oliver spends his childhood (Bumble, Mrs Corney, Mr Gamfield, the Sowerberrys). The last group belongs to the social satire of the novel, the other two to its almost allegorical moral drama of the struggle between good and evil – and, as Graham Greene has argued in his essay on this novel, evil is rendered with much more conviction than good. Beside Fagin, the benevolent Mr Brownlow is insubstantial; even Nancy, though her activities as prostitute are scarcely touched on (Dickens never uses the word in the novel) and her sexuality is played down, is a *human* portrait in a way that the virtuous Rose Maylie is not. Between these groups, as Wilson says, move 'the passive figure of Oliver himself and the mechanical figure of his sinister half-brother Monks'. Oliver is the weakest of Dickens' heroes; but Wilson, while conceding that it is 'a great artistic failure' on Dickens' part to have 'this vacuum at the centre of the novel', suggests that Oliver's 'total passivity' may serve a purpose: 'Oliver on the surface-level totally fails to win our feelings for orphan paupers, yet Oliver at a deeper level, as childhood threatened by obscure evil, is a satisfactory device'. Certainly such moments as the end of Chapter 34 (coinciding with the end of one of the original instalments) have a nightmare quality that belongs less to realistic fiction than to myth.

Apart from the important introductions by Kathleen Tillotson and Angus Wilson referred to above, there are good discussions of this novel by John Bayley (in Gross and Pearson's *Dickens and the Twentieth Century*), Graham Greene (*The Lost Childhood*), and Michael Slater (in a special *Oliver Twist* number of *The Dickensian*, 1974). The books by John Carey, Humphry House and Steven Marcus all contain relevant material, as does Philip Collins' *Dickens and Crime*. Collins' edition of the reading versions includes a full account of Dickens' extraordinary last fling in devising public readings and his almost obsessive passion for thrilling an audience with 'Sikes and Nancy' in the closing months of his life.

CHARACTERS

BARNEY. Jewish character, 'younger than Fagin, but nearly as vile and repulsive in appearance' (Ch. 15).

BATES, CHARLEY. One of Fagin's gang of young thieves. He ends as an honest man (Ch. 53).

BEDWIN, MRS. Housekeeper to Mr Brownlow; she takes care of Oliver during his stay in Mr Brownlow's house.

BLATHERS. Bow Street officer (Ch. 31).

BRITTLES. Servant at Mrs Maylie's house (Ch. 28).

BROWNLOW, MR. Kindly old gentleman who, after Oliver has been wrongly charged with picking his pocket, befriends him and takes him to his own home (Chs 11–12). He is led to believe that Oliver is an impostor (Ch. 17), but later learns the truth and is reunited with the boy (Ch. 41). He turns out to have been a friend of Edward Leeford, father of Oliver and Monks (Ch. 51).

BUMBLE, MR. Beadle (parish officer) in the town where Oliver is born. He names the child; proposes to Mrs Corney (Ch. 27); finds his marriage to be a great disappointment (Ch. 37), since he has 'fallen from all the height and pomp of beadleship, to the lowest depth of the most snubbed henpeckery'; is present when Monks obtains and disposes of the locket taken from Oliver's dying mother (Ch. 38); is exposed and deprived of his parochial office (Ch. 51); and ends, fittingly, as a pauper in the workhouse in which he had reigned as beadle (Ch. 53).

CHITLING, TOM. One of Fagin's young men, about eighteen years old.

CLAYPOLE, NOAH. Charity-boy employed by Mr Sowerberry. He

bullies Oliver and is treated affectionately by Charlotte
Sowerberry. Later he goes to London and is employed by Fagin
to spy on Nancy.

CORNEY, MRS. Workhouse matron, the object of Bumble's romantic
attentions (Ch. 23); he proposes to her (Ch. 27); she turns out to
be a shrew (Ch. 37). She is present at the death of Old Sally
(Ch. 24), who attended Oliver's birth, and secures from her
evidence of Oliver's parentage which is obtained and destroyed
by Monks (Ch. 38).

CRACKIT, TOBY. Housebreaker, in league with Fagin and Sikes
(Ch. 19).

DAWKINS, JOHN (Jack) (The Artful Dodger). Young pickpocket, a
member of Fagin's gang. He befriends Oliver (Ch. 8); is later
arrested and appears in court (Ch. 43).

DICK. Friend and playmate of Oliver at the workhouse.

DODGER, THE ARTFUL, see DAWKINS, JOHN

DUFF. Bow Street Officer (Ch. 31).

FAGIN. Introduced in Ch. 8: 'a very old shrivelled Jew, whose
villainous-looking and repulsive face was obscured by a quantity
of matted red hair'. The red hair and the toasting fork with which
he is cooking sausages (Dickens' text being reinforced at this point
by Cruikshank's illustration, 'Oliver introduced to the
Respectable Old Gentleman') suggest a diabolical quality (for
the red hair combined with villainy, compare Uriah Heep in
David Copperfield). On the origin of Fagin's name, see p. 30. On
the accusation of anti-Semitism brought against Dickens, see
p. 25. Fagin is the ringleader of a gang of juvenile pickpockets.
He welcomes Oliver to their number and later plots with Monks
to deprive Oliver of his birthright. He is eventually arrested,
tried, and condemned to death; is visited by Oliver and Mr
Brownlow in the condemned cell (Ch. 52); and finally executed.
The trial scene (Ch. 52) shows a brilliant use of psychological
detail, and Fagin's last hours are memorably illustrated by
Cruikshank's 'Fagin in the Condemned Cell'. 'Fagin was, as
everyone saw, based on the famous Jewish fence, Ikey Solomon,
and his methods of employing and training boy pick-pockets were
the standard practice, and remained so for several decades'
(Philip Collins, *Dickens and Crime*, p. 262). (This identification
has, however, been queried by J. J. Tobias in his *Prince of Fences:
The Life and Crimes of Ikey Solomons* [1974].) Saffron Hill, where
Fagin lives, was notorious for its criminal population.

FANG, MR. Bullying and inhuman magistrate before whom Oliver appears (Ch. 11), based on the Hatton Garden magistrate Allan Stewart Laing, dismissed from the bench in January 1838. Fang was drawn from life: on 3 June 1837 Dickens wrote to a Mr Haines, who was in charge of Press reporters for the City Courts:

> In my next number of Oliver Twist, I must have a magistrate; and, casting about for a magistrate whose harshness and insolence would render him a fit subject to be 'shewn up' I have, as a necessary consequence, stumbled upon Mr Laing of Hatton Garden celebrity. I know the man's character perfectly well; but as it would be necessary to describe his personal appearance also, I ought to have seen him . . . .

He asked Haines to arrange for him to spend a short time in Laing's court.

FLEMING, AGNES. Oliver's mother; she dies at the beginning of the story in giving birth to him and is only identified by that name in Ch. 51.

CAMFIELD, MR. Brutal chimney-sweep. Oliver has a narrow escape from being apprenticed to him (Ch. 3).

GILES. Butler and steward at Mrs Maylie's house (Ch. 28).

GRANNETT, MR. Overseer at the workhouse. For his inhuman treatment of a vagrant, see Ch. 23.

GRIMWIG, MR. Argumentative and cynical friend of Mr Brownlow (Ch. 14).

LEEFORD, EDWIN. Father of Oliver and Monks, identified only in Ch. 51.

LIMBKINS, MR. Chairman of the workhouse board of management before which Oliver appears (Ch. 3).

LOSBERNE. Doctor who attends Oliver (Ch. 30). He is a family friend of the Maylies.

MANN, MRS. Keeper of a baby-farm to which parish orphans, including Oliver, were sent (Ch. 2).

MAYLIE, MRS. Well-to-do lady, 'well advanced in years', who befriends Oliver (Ch. 29). Her adopted daughter ROSE (later ROSE FLEMING), seventeen years old, becomes Oliver's champion; meets Nancy (Ch. 46); and is revealed as Oliver's aunt (Ch. 51). Rose marries HARRY MAYLIE, son of Mrs Maylie, who becomes a clergyman.

MONKS. Villain in league with Fagin (Ch. 26), later revealed as Oliver's half-brother and as involved in a plot to deprive Oliver of his rights. With Fagin he appears mysteriously to Oliver at the Maylies' house (Ch. 34). He obtains proof of Oliver's parentage from Mrs Corney and destroys it (Ch. 38); is confronted by Mr Brownlow (Ch. 49); discloses the story of Oliver's rightful inheritance (Ch. 51); emigrates to America and dies in prison there (Ch. 53).

NANCY. Young woman, mistress of Sikes, and a prostitute (though her profession, like her language, is very delicately touched on by Dickens). By pretending to be Oliver's sister she forces him to return to Fagin (Ch. 15); later she feels tenderly towards Oliver and confesses to Rose Maylie what she has done, warning her of Monks and telling her that he is Oliver's half-brother (Ch. 40). She is spied on by Noah Claypole (acting on Fagin's instructions) and suspected of betraying the gang (Ch. 46). At Fagin's prompting she is murdered by Sikes (Ch. 47).

SALLY, OLD. Workhouse inmate present at the death of Oliver's mother (Ch. 1). On her own deathbed she tries to confess to Mrs Corney the theft of a locket from Oliver's dead mother (Ch. 24).

SIKES, BILL. Housebreaker in league with Fagin; a brutal man of violent temper. He murders Nancy (Ch. 47), is pursued and cornered, and dies (Ch. 51). His guilty flight is described with great pace and vividness. He is 'about five-and-thirty' (see description in Ch. 13).

SOWERBERRY, MR. 'The parochial undertaker' to whom Oliver is apprenticed (Ch. 3). His wife and his daughter CHARLOTTE also appear. His name is, of course, a grim pun.

TWIST, OLIVER. Born in a workhouse, his unmarried mother (later named as Agnes Fleming) dying at his birth, he is sent to a baby-farm; lives in the workhouse, picks oakum, and asks for more; is apprenticed to Mr Sowerberry, an undertaker; goes to London and meets Fagin and his gang; is befriended by Mr Brownlow but later forced to return to Fagin's; accompanies Sikes on a housebreaking expedition; is befriended by the Maylies; is reunited with Mr Brownlow; visits Fagin in the condemned cell; is revealed as the son of Edwin Leeford, who is also the father of Monks (who has been plotting to deprive his half-brother of his rightful inheritance); and is adopted by Mr Brownlow.

Nicholas Nickleby

Text   Penguin English Library, ed. Michael Slater (1978).

Composition   Just as the composition of *Oliver Twist* overlapped with that of *Pickwick*, Dickens began a new novel while *Oliver Twist* was still in progress (its composition was in the event to occupy him for about another nine months, that is, until he was well into *Nickleby*). Nor was this by any means the whole tale of his staggering commitments at this stage of his career. Towards the end of January 1838 he wrote that 'my month's work has been dreadful – Grimaldi, the anonymous book for Chapman and Hall, Oliver, and the Miscellany. They are all done, thank God, and I start on my pilgrimage to the cheap schools of Yorkshire (a mighty secret of course) next Monday Morning'. 'Grimaldi' was his edition of a life of the famous clown; 'the anonymous book' was *Sketches of Young Gentlemen*; 'Oliver' was of course the current number of the novel; and at the same time he was planning to collaborate with Harrison Ainsworth on a book to be entitled *The Lions of London* – a project that was, not surprisingly, abandoned. On 30 January he set out with his illustrator Browne on the 'pilgrimage' to Yorkshire, to see at first-hand the notorious boarding schools and, as it turned out, to make the acquaintance of Mr Squeers' prototype. He was obviously eager to begin the new book and, back in London, began it on 6 February; within three days the first chapter was finished.

As time went on the gruelling programme he had prescribed for himself caused a certain tardiness in producing the copy of *Nickleby* on time: 'The pressures of his other work made it impossible for Dickens to adhere strictly to his contractual agreements to have his *Nickleby* copy ready for the fifteenth of the month: . . . he was nearly always late, and was never able to get a month or two ahead' (Patten). The pace was terrific, and Professor Patten has described vividly and in detail the pressure under which Dickens worked at this time. The final instalment of the novel was finished on 20 September 1839 and published ten days later – a striking reminder of the speed with which, in those days, printing, proof-reading and distribution were executed. (The number was officially published in October, but in accordance with normal practice was actually available on the last day of the previous month.)

Serialization   In nineteen instalments, published monthly from April 1838 to October 1839. Illustrations by 'Phiz'. Division as follows: I (Chs 1–4); II (Chs 5–7); III (Chs 8–10); IV (Chs 11–14); V (Chs 15–16); VI (Chs 18–20); VII (Chs 21–3); VIII (Chs 24–6); IX (Chs 27–9); X (Chs 30–3); XI (Chs 34–6); XII (Chs 37–9); XIII (Chs 40–2); XIV (Chs 43–5); XV (Chs 46–8); XVI (Chs 49–51); XVII (Chs 52–4); XVIII (Chs 55–8); XIX–XX (Chs 59–65).

Publication   Published in one volume by Chapman & Hall in October 1839, with the title *The Life and Adventures of Nicholas Nickleby*. Dickens added a preface and a dedication to W. C. Macready. The edition had as a frontispiece Maclise's portrait of Dickens (usually known as the 'Nickleby portrait'). For the 1848 edition (Cheap Edition) Dickens wrote a new preface and extensively revised the text; Michael Slater notes that the revisions have the effect of 'toning down the exuberance of the original: "a scowl of deadly hatred" becomes merely "a scowl"; "rising with the sneer of a devil" becomes simply "rising", and so forth'.

Reception   The novel sold well as a serial: the initial circulation of 50,000 was 'nearly maintained' (Patten) throughout the run and 'the profits upon the numbers alone equalled those from *Pickwick*: £14,000'. As Patten says, 'The contemporary reception was far more enthusiastic than the current one': ten years after its first appearance, the *Athenaeum* could still describe *Nickleby* as 'perhaps the best of Mr Dickens's works' – not a verdict that many modern critics would endorse. Dickens celebrated the success of the novel with a banquet (held on 5 October 1839). The 'Nickleby' portrait, sold separately, was greatly in demand and made Dickens' features familiar to an eager public. The *Spectator* reported in 1863 that sales of *Nicholas Nickleby* in volume form had exceeded 100,000.

The covers of the monthly parts bore the title *The Life and Adventures of Nicholas Nickleby, containing a Faithful Account of the Fortunes,*

Misfortunes, Uprisings, Downfallings and Complete Career of the Nickleby Family – the kind of elaborate, whimsical and consciously old-fashioned title that Dickens was to use again for *Martin Chuzzlewit*. This title was followed by the formula: 'Edited by "Boz"'. For publication in volume form a shorter title was adopted (noted above), and Dickens was named as the author. The 'life and adventures' promise in both titles is reminiscent of the eighteenth-century authors whom Dickens, like David Copperfield, read as a child; and the novel is picaresque in structure and spirit. Like Smollett's *Roderick Random*, Nicholas is an impoverished young man of good family driven by circumstances to make his own way in the world. He is mobile, likeable, and thoroughly conventional. The speed with which Dickens embarked on writing this novel, and the rapidity of composition, suggest that there was a large element of improvisation; the contrast with his intensively meditated and painfully composed later work is very striking.

As in *Oliver Twist*, Dickens blends social criticism with conventional romance and melodrama. The exposure of the sinister boarding schools occupies only a minor place in the novel, and the hero quits Dotheboys Hall before the story is one-quarter complete. But Squeers – who, like Bumble, is both a monster and a figure of fun – is one of the most celebrated of all the characters in the whole very extensive Dickensian gallery, partly at least because (like Quilp) his villainy expresses itself with such remarkable energy and what one can only call sense of style. Like all of Dickens' great comedians and villains, he is supremely a *performer*; and, as with Bumble, the question arises whether the effectiveness of the satire is not diminished by the laughter that frequently seems to overcome the reader's indignation and compassion. In Chapter 8, Dickens makes a comment that indicates his own awareness of this complex and even contradictory response; after describing the school and its wretched inmates, he adds:

> And yet this scene, painful as it was, had its grotesque features, which, in a less interested observer than Nicholas, might have provoked a smile.

– and then goes on to describe the spectacle of Mrs Squeers stationed beside 'an immense basin of brimstone and treacle'. Such a comment seems to place both narrator and reader in a category of persons 'less interested . . . than Nicholas', and thereby to undercut the hero's social indignation and human compassion. Again, the description of the porridge served to the boys – 'which looked like diluted pincushions without the covers' – is comic, though the point about the inadequate and unpleasant diet is serious enough.

On quite another level of fictional convention is the part of the novel dealing with that other villain, Nicholas's uncle Ralph, whose speech is as stagily conventional as Squeers' is inventively individual. The dialogue assigned to Ralph Nickleby is absurdly theatrical; on the other hand, as Michael Slater has said, 'theatricality and role-playing are the living heart of *Nicholas Nickleby*', and Dickens' love affair with the drama, which took many forms and continued to the end of his life, finds happier manifestations in this book. The Crummles troupe, through whom Dickens expresses in detail, with affection and delight, the absurdities of contemporary conventions of drama and acting, are the most obvious examples of this theatricality; but as Slater says, 'Nearly everybody else in this crowded book is playing a role.' Steven Marcus has drawn attention to the apt symbolism of Miss La Creevy's miniatures, which depict people as they would wish to be rather than as they are. Dickens was to explore this human tendency further in *Martin Chuzzlewit*, where one of the most memorable characters, Mrs Harris, does not even 'exist' in the same way as the other characters, being a figment imagined by a figment of Dickens' imagination. Not all the characters who act a part are conscious of doing so, however: Mrs Nickleby, for example, whose very funny stream-of-consciousness dialogue anticipates Flora Finching and Mrs Lirriper, is quite spontaneous in her endearing absurdity.

Michael Slater can hardly be contradicted when he says that 'the main plot of the novel is largely a lifeless bore', lacking the 'mythic or fabular' power that goes far to redeeming the plot of *Oliver Twist*. Nor can much be said for some of the leading characters, including Nicholas and his uncle, who remain thin stereotypes lacking the individualization that, at his best, Dickens is capable of bestowing upon even the most minor characters. Some of the characters admired by an earlier generation are little to the taste of modern readers – for example, the Cheeryble brothers, whose benevolence is as embarrassing as their name and for whom Orwell's description ('two gruesome old Peter Pans') is not really too harsh. The novel stands or falls – and for many readers emphatically stands – by virtue of its comedy and the rich gallery of characters that includes the Squeers family, Mantalini, Mrs Nickleby and the Crummles troupe. More pervasively, the novel has that extraordinary exuber-ance and fertility of inventiveness that Dickens displays perhaps more strikingly than any other writer – the superabundant creative energy that endows any character or scene, however peripheral, with its own uniqueness:

> Mr Crummles lived in Saint Thomas's Street, at the house of one Bulph, a pilot, who sported a boat-green door, with window-frames of the same colour, and had the little finger of a drowned man on his parlour mantel-shelf, with other maritime and natural curiosities. He displayed also a brass knocker, a brass plate, and a brass bell-handle, all very bright and shining, and had a mast, with a vane on the top of it, in his back-yard [Ch. 23].

That 'little finger of a drowned man' leaves in the memory the unmistakable Dickensian fingerprint; irrelevant yet intensely mem-orable, it is evidence of a continuing fascination with detached or detachable portions of the human body. Or consider the ghastly yet infectious relish of Squeers: ' "I never thrashed a boy in a hackney-coach before. . . . There's inconveniency in it, but the novelty gives it a sort of relish, too!" '; and again in the same chapter, ' "What's come of my milk of human kindness? It turns into curds and whey when I look at him" ' (Ch. 38) – the fact that this dialogue occurs in the episode of the wretched Smike's recapture rendering the effect all the more complex and surprising. *Nicholas Nickleby* is not one of Dickens' greatest novels; but no-one but Dickens could have written certain pages of it. Alongside writing that is merely routine and no doubt resulted from haste and almost intolerable pressure (see, for example, the opening of Ch. 58: 'They procured a humble lodging . . . ', and so on) are passages not inferior to the most brilliant of Dickens' later comic writing.

Though a great favourite with earlier generations of Dickensians, this novel has not offered much grist to the mills of modern criticism; and the recent revival of interest in Dickens' early work – a reaction against the reaction, a generation ago, in favour of the late, 'dark' novels – has not in itself succeeded in rehabilitating it, though the book has recently been given fresh currency as a result of the Royal Shakespeare Company's marathon theatrical version. It is, com-ments Philip Collins, 'not the sort of novel we now find it easy to write about' – which may reflect on the limitations of modern criticism and its failure to deal adequately with comedy as well as on the limitations of this particular novel. Michael Slater's account of its composition and serialization is authoritative (1973), and his introduction to the Penguin edition is stimulating. W. W. Robson (*Publications of the Manchester Literary and Philosophical Society*, 1967–8), Bernard Bergonzi (in Gross and Pearson's collection), and Jerome Meckier (*Dickens Studies Annual*, 1971) have also written on this novel, and Steven Marcus's book contains a chapter on it. Earlier generations of students were much preoccupied with the human and scenic prototypes, and the back numbers of *The Dickensian* contain a large amount of material on this and other topics. Dickens' own reading, 'Nicholas Nickleby at the Yorkshire School', was popular.

CHARACTERS

ADAMS, CAPTAIN. Lord Frederick Verisopht's second in the duel fought in Ch. 50.

ALPHONSE. Page to Mrs Wititterly (Ch. 21).

BELVAWNEY, MISS. A member of Vincent Crummles' troupe; she appears in Ch. 23.

BOLDER. Boy at Dotheboys Hall, beaten by Squeers in Ch. 8.

BONNEY, MR. He attends the meeting of the United Metropolitan Improved Hot Muffin and Crumpet Baking and Punctual Delivery Company (Ch. 2).

BORUM, MR AND MRS. Nicholas and Miss Snevellicci call on them in Ch. 24 to solicit their patronage at the 'bespeak'.

BRAVASSA, MISS. Member of the Crummles troupe.

BRAY, MR WALTER. Described in Ch. 46 as 'scarce fifty, perhaps, but so emaciated as to appear much older': reduced to penury and invalidism by a life of dissipation, he is prepared to marry off his daughter MADELINE to the old miser Arthur Gride in order to recoup his fortunes, but dies suddenly in Ch. 54 before the plot can be carried out. Madeline is loved by, and eventually marries, Nicholas.

BROOKER. Dishonest character, formerly clerk to Ralph Nickleby.

BROWDIE, JOHN. Bluff, loud-voiced and good-hearted Yorkshire-man, introduced in Ch. 9. He befriends Nicholas and rescues Smike (Ch. 39). He marries Matilda Price. His speech represents a broad north-country dialect.

CHEERYBLE, CHARLES AND EDWIN. Twin brothers, business partners, and genial philanthropists introduced in Ch. 35. They befriend Nicholas. Their nephew Frank eventually marries Kate Nickleby.

CHOWSER, COLONEL. One of the guests at Ralph Nickleby's house in Ch. 19.

COBBEY. Boy at Dotheboys Hall (see Ch. 8.).

CROWL, MR. Fellow-lodger with Newman Noggs.

CRUMMLES, MR VINCENT. Manager of a company of strolling players, introduced in Ch. 22. Nicholas joins his troupe. Crummles reappears in Ch. 48. Crummles' speech is strongly coloured by his profession ('"There's genteel comedy in your walk and manner, juvenile tragedy in your eye, and touch-and-go farce in your laugh"', as he tells Nicholas in Ch. 22). His wife and daughter NINETTA ('the Infant Phenomenon') also appear.

CURDLE, MR AND MRS. Nicholas and Miss Snevellicci call on them in Ch. 24 to solicit their patronage at the 'bespeak', and Dickens takes the opportunity to satirize amateur pseudo-scholarship (Mr Curdle has 'written a pamphlet of sixty-four pages, post octavo, on the character of the Nurse's deceased husband in Romeo and Juliet').

DICK. Pet blackbird belonging to Tim Linkinwater and kept in the Cheerybles' counting-house. He is not overlooked in the general round-up of characters in the novel's final chapter.

FOLAIR, THOMAS. Member of the Crummles troupe, introduced in Ch. 23.

GRAYMARSH. Boy at Dotheboys Hall (Ch. 8).

GREEN, MR. Friend of the Kenwigs family (Ch. 14).

GREGSBURY, MR. Member of Parliament who offers Nicholas a post as his secretary, which is declined (Ch. 16).

GRIDE, ARTHUR. Old miser and moneylender, introduced in Ch. 47: 'a little old man, of about seventy or seventy-five years of age, of a very lean figure, much bent, and slightly twisted . . . the whole expression of the face was concentrated in a wrinkled leer, compounded of cunning, lecherousness, slyness, and avarice'. He plots with Ralph Nickleby to obtain the hand of Madeline Bray – one of Dickens' versions of the 'beauty and the beast' theme – but is outwitted. His housekeeper Peg Sliderskew robs him of vital papers (Ch. 56).

GRUDDEN, MRS. Member of the Crummles troupe.

HAWK, SIR MULBERRY. Gambler and man about town, the

villainous associate of Lord Frederick Verisopht. He is introduced in Ch. 19, where Ralph Nickleby introduces him to Kate
Nickleby; and meets her again, imposing on her gullible mother
(Chs 26–7). He kills Verisopht in a duel (Ch. 50) and flees
abroad.

KENWIGS, MR AND MRS. With their daughter MORLEENA and other
children they are fellow-lodgers of Newman Noggs. The family is
introduced in Ch. 14, where Mr Kenwigs is described as 'a turner
in ivory' and his wife as 'quite a lady in her manners, and of a very
genteel family, having an uncle [Mr Lillyvick] who collected a
water-rate'.

KNAG, MISS. The forewoman in Madame Mantalini's establishment, she is introduced in Ch. 17. Her brother MORTIMER, 'an
ornamental stationer and small circulating library keeper', also
makes an appearance (Ch. 18).

LA CREEVY, MISS. Affected but good-natured painter of miniatures,
'a mincing young lady of fifty' (Ch. 3), who befriends the
Nicklebys. At the end of the novel she marries Tim Linkinwater.

LANE, MISS. Governess to the Borum family (Ch. 24).

LEDROOK, MISS. Member of the Crummles troupe.

LENVILLE, MRS. Member of the Crummles troupe.

LILLYVICK, MR. A collector of water-rates and uncle of Mrs
Kenwigs. He marries Miss Petowker.

LINKINWATER, TIM. Chief clerk to the Cheeryble brothers: 'a fat,
elderly, large-faced clerk, with silver spectacles and a powdered
head' (Ch. 35). At the end of the novel he marries Miss La
Creevy.

MANTALINI, MADAME. Milliner and dressmaker who employs Kate
Nickleby (her name being a facetiously Italianate version of
'mantle'). She later goes bankrupt and Kate loses her job (Ch.
21). Her husband ALFRED is lazy, dissipated, and extravagantly
affected in dress, speech and manner: when he is introduced in
Ch. 10, he speaks 'in a mincing tone' and is 'dressed in a gorgeous
morning gown, with a waistcoat and Turkish trousers of the same
pattern, a pink silk neckerchief, and bright green slippers.
. . . He had whiskers and a moustache, both dyed black and
gracefully curled.' He has 'married on his whiskers', the lady
being 'much older' than he; his name is actually Muntle. He is
frequently unfaithful, pretends to poison himself (Ch. 44), and
makes his final appearance turning a mangle (Ch. 64).

NICKLEBY, NICHOLAS. Hero of the novel, introduced in Ch. 3. His father, Nicholas Nickleby senior, the younger brother of Ralph Nickleby, has speculated with his small inheritance, been ruined, and has died, leaving a widow and daughter dependent upon Nicholas's exertions (Ch. 1). He meets Squeers (Ch. 4) and sets off for Yorkshire (Ch. 5); befriends Smike (Ch. 8); interferes when the latter is beaten by Squeers, and leaves the school (Ch. 13); returns to London and is employed as a tutor to teach French to the Kenwigs children (Ch. 16); quarrels with his uncle (Ch. 20); sets off with Smike and meets Vincent Crummles, whose troupe he joins under the alias of Johnson (Ch. 22); leaves the company after enjoying a considerable success as an actor (Ch. 30); returns to London (Ch. 32); is befriended by the Cheeryble brothers (Ch. 35); falls in love with Madeline Bray and rescues her from marriage with Arthur Gride (Ch. 54), finally marrying her himself (Ch. 65). His foolish and garrulous mother is a delightful comic creation and, in the surrealistic absurdity of her monologues, a precursor of Flora Finching and Mrs Lirriper. She is eccentrically courted by 'The Gentleman Next Door' (Chs 37, 41, 49), who throws cucumbers and vegetable marrows over the garden wall and eventually comes down her chimney. Nicholas's sister KATE is an innocent young girl harried by the plots of her uncle Ralph and the unwelcome attentions of Sir Mulberry Hawk and Lord Frederick Verisopht (see Chs 26–8); she eventually marries Frank Cheeryble. RALPH Nickleby is the stagey villain of the piece; he lives in Golden Square and is described in Ch. 2. He plots against Nicholas and his sister but is finally outwitted and hangs himself (Ch. 62). He is depicted in the stylized terms of the melodramatic stage, foaming at the mouth and uttering such speeches as ' "My curse, my bitter, deadly curse upon you, boy!" ' (Ch. 54).

NOGGS, NEWMAN. Clerk to Ralph Nickleby, introduced in Ch. 2: 'a tall man of middle-age, with two goggle eyes whereof one was a fixture, a rubicund nose, a cadaverous face, and a suit of clothes . . . much the worse for wear'. He befriends Nicholas, spies on his employer, learns of his plots, and finally confronts him (Ch. 59).

PETOWKER, MISS HENRIETTA. Friend of the Kenwigs family. She joins the Crummles troupe and marries Mr Lillyvick (Ch. 25).

PITCHER. Boy at Dotheboys Hall (Ch. 7).

PLUCK, MR. Guest at Ralph Nickleby's house (Ch. 19) and toady of Sir Mulberry Hawk.

PRICE, MATILDA. Friend of Fanny Squeers. She marries John Browdie.

PUGSTYLES, MR. He leads the deputation to Mr Gregsbury in Ch. 16.

PUPKER, SIR MATTHEW. Chairman of the meeting of the United Metropolitan Improved Hot Muffin and Crumpet Baking and Punctual Delivery Company held in Ch. 2.

PYKE, MR. Guest at Ralph Nickleby's house (Ch. 19) and toady of Sir Mulberry Hawk.

SLIDERSKEW, PEG. Housekeeper to Arthur Gride, whom she robs and abandons (Ch. 56). She is eventually transported.

SMIKE. Pathetic boy of 'eighteen or nineteen years old', introduced in Ch. 7 as a member of Squeers' household, ill-treated, half-starved, and mentally subnormal. Nicholas befriends him and, when Smike is recaptured after running away, interferes to prevent Squeers from thrashing him (Ch. 13). He accompanies Nicholas (a vestige of the picaresque tradition) when the latter leaves Yorkshire; joins the Crummles troupe, where he is known as Digby; is seized again by Squeers (Ch. 38) but rescued by John Browdie (Ch. 39); falls ill (Ch. 55) and dies (Ch. 58); and is revealed as the son of Ralph Nickleby (Ch. 60).

SNAWLEY, MR. Unctuous rascal who appears in Ch. 4 and reappears in Ch. 45, where he is alleged by Ralph Nickleby to be the father of Smike.

SNEVELLICCI, MISS. Member of the Crummles troupe. She is introduced in Ch. 23 as one 'who could do anything, from a medley dance to Lady Macbeth'.

SNEWKES, MR. A friend of the Kenwigs family (Ch. 14).

SNOB, MR. A guest at Ralph Nickleby's house (Ch. 19).

SQUEERS, MR WACKFORD. Brutal and incompetent master of a Yorkshire boarding school (for the topicality of this theme, see p. 95 above). He is introduced in Ch. 4 (his appearance is 'not prepossessing. He had but one eye, and the popular prejudice runs in favour of two . . . his expression bordered closely on the villainous') in the coffee-room of the Saracen's Head in London, Dickens' verbal description being reinforced by Phiz's illustration. He employs Nicholas, ill-treats Smike, and is beaten by Nicholas (Chs 4–13); reappears in Ch. 34; conspires with Ralph Nickleby; and ends by being imprisoned and transported. His wife, 'of a large raw-boned figure', is introduced in Ch. 7, as is his daughter FANNY, 'in her three-and-twentieth year' (Ch. 9).

Fanny's famous letter is quoted in Ch. 15. On a likely prototype of
Squeers, see p. 45.

TIMBERRY, MR SNITTLE. Member of the Crummles troupe.

TRIMMERS, MR. Charitable friend of the Cheeryble brothers (see
Ch. 35).

VERISOPHT, LORD FREDERICK. Foolish and dissipated aristocrat and
boon companion of Sir Mulberry Hawk, introduced in Ch. 19.
He has an affected drawling manner of speech. With Hawk's
encouragement, he plots against Kate Nickleby's virtue. Hawk
later kills him in a duel (Ch. 50).

WESTWOOD. SIR MULBERRY HAWK's second in the duel fought in
Ch. 50.

WITITTERLY, MR AND MRS. (Henry and Julia). Pretentious middle-
class couple living in Cadogan Place, Sloane Street, and
introduced in Ch. 21. She has 'an air of sweet insipidity' and is
described by her husband as ' "a hothouse plant, an exotic" ';
Kate Nickleby is for a time employed by her.

Master Humphrey's Clock

Two of Dickens' novels, *The Old Curiosity Shop* and *Barnaby Rudge*, first appeared within the clumsy framework of Dickens' weekly periodical, *Master Humphrey's Clock*, which began on 4 April 1840 and ceased publication with the conclusion of *Barnaby Rudge*. In his childhood Dickens had read and loved the *Spectator*, the *Tatler*, and Goldsmith's *Bee*, and his plan was to produce a Victorian version of the eighteenth-century periodical miscellany. Edgar Johnson has described the intended result as an 'Arabian Nights-Gulliver-Mr Spectator Salmagundi', and the opening chapters of the *Clock* seem to indicate a certain feverish anxiety to cram in as many diverse elements as possible. As Angus Wilson has not unfairly said,

> It was, it must be confessed, a lazy scheme of an over-pressed young man in which he hoped to use the popularity of Mr Pickwick and Sam Weller all over again; in which a quaint old narrator, Master Humphrey, should link a series of stories; in which a contemporary taste for whimsical legend (exemplified in [R. H. Barham's] *The Ingoldsby Legends* of 1837) should be exploited by making the mythical giants of London, Gog and Magog, tell many of the tales; in which travel sketches like those made so popular by the American writer, Washington Irving, would give reason for Dickens the editor to travel to Ireland and America.

The scheme offered several advantages for Dickens. He would share in the profits; and by presiding over the *Clock*'s fortunes he would maintain his relationship with his public, whilst at the same time, since contributions by other hands were to be included, some of the creative pressure would be taken off him.

Dickens was gratified by the initial success of his periodical: nearly 70,000 of the first number were sold (the modest price of threepence no doubt contributing to its success), and he wrote jubilantly that 'the Clock goes gloriously indeed'. But sales fell off dramatically, and Edgar Johnson has suggested that many readers may have discovered their error in supposing that the periodical would contain a continued story. It was clear that what the public wanted from Mr Dickens was not a miscellany but a new novel, and he came promptly to the rescue with a decision to extend beyond its originally intended compass the 'little child-story' that had occurred to him during a visit to Bath at the end of February 1840 and which he had felt, even before publication of the *Clock* began, was 'SURE to be effective'. The first episode of the story of Little Nell appeared in the fourth number, the second episode in the seventh number; thereafter it displaced all else and ran continuously, reaching its conclusion in the forty-fifth number (6 February 1841). The work that became *The Old Curiosity Shop* was thus initially conceived as a short story but, under the pressure of circumstances, and as the periodical changed its nature, developed into a full-length novel serialized weekly. One side-effect was the abrupt change of narrative point of view after the third number from first- to third-person, leaving an inconsistency that Dickens never troubled to remove by revising the opening chapters. *Barnaby Rudge* immediately followed *The Old Curiosity Shop*, running from 13 February to 27 November 1841 and bringing the *Clock* enterprise to an end, the final number appearing on 4 December 1841.

The *Clock* included illustrations by 'Phiz' and George Cattermole. As Robert Patten has said, it 'appeared in a bewildering variety of formats': apart from the 88 weekly numbers, which sold at threepence each, it was issued in monthly parts and in three volumes published at half-yearly intervals. Testimony of an unusual kind to its popularity is found in a doggerel poem of the period, 'Humphrey's Clock', which appeared in an underground directory of prostitutes and used the 'clock' as the occasion for a sexual *double entendre* (the poem is quoted by Ronald Pearsall in *Collapse of Stout Party: Victorian Wit and Humour* [1975], p. 200).

The Old Curiosity Shop

Text   Penguin English Library, ed. Angus Easson, introduction by Malcolm Andrews (1972).

Composition   Begun early in 1840, completed at the beginning of 1841 (the final number appearing on 6 February). For details, see below. For the composition of the closing chapters, Dickens made his first known number-plans – memoranda to assist him in working out the plot. Manuscript and portion of corrected proofs in Forster Collection.

Serialization   40 instalments in *Master Humphrey's Clock* (see above): the first on 25 April 1840, the second on 16 May, and thereafter weekly until 6 February 1841. Division as follows: I (Ch. 1); II (Ch. 2); III (Chs 3–4); IV (Ch. 5); V (Chs 6–7); VI (Ch. 8); VII (Chs 9–10); VIII (Chs 11–12); IX (Chs 13–14); X (Chs 15–16); XI (Chs 17–18); XII (Chs 19–20); XIII (Chs 21–2); XIV (Chs 23–4); XV (Chs 25–6); XVI (Chs 27–8); XVII (Chs 29–30); XVIII (Chs 31–2); XIX (Chs 33–4); XX (Chs 35–6); XXI (Ch. 37); XXII (Chs 38–9); XXIII (Chs 40–1); XXIV (Chs 42–3); XXV (Chs 44–5); XXVI (Chs 46–7); XXVII (Chs 48–9); XXVIII (Chs 50–1); XXIX (Chs 52–3); XXX (Chs 54–5); XXXI (Chs 56–7); XXXII (Chs 58–9); XXXIII (Chs 60–1); XXXIV (Chs 62–3); XXXV (Chs 64–5); XXXVI (Ch. 66); XXXVII (Chs 67–8); XXXVIII (Chs 69–70); XXXIX (Chs 71–2); XL (Ch. 73). Illustrations by 'Phiz' and George Cattermole. Portions of the manuscript were omitted from the serial version for reasons of space; since the first volume-edition follows the text of the serial issue in most respects, these passages have usually not been restored. A selection of the cancelled passages is included in the notes to the Penguin edition. See also Angus Easson's essay in *Dickens Studies Annual* (1970). The serialization of *The Old Curiosity Shop* restored the failing fortunes of *Master*

Humphrey's Clock, which had started with a sale of 70,000 but quickly dropped to 50,000. By the end of its serialization the circulation of the periodical had reached the staggering figure of 100,000 – a record unequalled by any other of Dickens' major novels.

Publication   Published in one volume by Chapman & Hall in 1841. A preface and a dedication to Samuel Rogers were added. Another preface was later written for the 'First Cheap Edition' in 1848.

Reception   For details of the public response to Little Nell, see below. The circulation figures for the final part of the story (see above) speak for themselves. Nell was hailed as a character of Shakespearean profundity, and 'comparisons with Cordelia and Imogen were frequent' (Philip Collins). As Professor Collins also notes, the enthusiasm was not restricted to unsophisticated readers or popular and middle-brow periodicals: even the *Westminster Review* could regard Nell as 'the happiest and most perfect of Dickens's sketches'. Other important elements in the novel – for example, the comedy associated with Dick Swiveller and the grotesque figure of Quilp – received less attention.

The novel was hugely successful on both sides of the Atlantic. Forster said that it served 'more than any other of [Dickens'] works to make the bond between himself and his readers one of personal attachment'. Dickens' emotional involvement in his heroine's fate was considerable: Forster commented that he 'never knew him wind up any tale with such sorrowful reluctance as this. He caught at any excuse to hold his hand from it . . . '; and Dickens wrote in a letter to Forster (?8 January 1841), 'I am the wretchedest of the wretched. It [Nell's death] casts the most horrible shadow upon me, and it is as much as I can do to keep moving at all. . . . Nobody will miss her like I shall. . . . Dear Mary died yesterday, when I think of this sad story.' (Mary Hogarth, Dickens' sister-in-law, had died on 7 May 1837 at the age of seventeen.)

Dickens' emotions were shared by at least some of his readers. His actor-friend Macready noted in his diary (21 January 1841): 'Asked Dickens to spare the life of Nell in his story'; when the instalment containing Nell's death arrived, he wrote, 'I dread to read it, but I must get it over.' The once-ferocious critic Lord Jeffrey was found in tears: 'You'll be sorry to hear', he remarked, 'that little Nelly, Boz's little Nelly, is dead.' (It is a sign of how quickly fashions in taste and sensibility can change, however, that a generation later, in 1873, a critic in the *Atlantic Monthly* could recall Jeffrey's reaction 'with amazement' and enquire 'Does any peer of the realm now shed tears for [Nell's] fate?') Another reader reacted more violently: flinging down the book in a passion of indignation, he exclaimed 'The Villain! The Rascal!! The bloodthirsty Scoundrel!!! . . . He killed my little Nell – He killed my sweet little child' (letter to Forster from Mrs Jane Greene of Dublin, referring to her uncle). Daniel O'Connell, the Irish politician, is said to have groaned, 'He should not have killed her.' As these examples show, Nell's story and fate caught the public imagination, or at least touched the public sensibility. In New York, crowds waiting for the ship bringing the latest instalment to dock are said to have shouted impatiently, 'Is Little Nell dead?' Edward FitzGerald called the book a 'Nelly-ad', and a popular song of the 1840s contained the lines: 'She has departed,/ The gentle hearted,/ Her soul no longer by grief invaded;/ And music lingers,/ From angel fingers,/ Around the death bed of Little Nell.'

Dickens was gratified not only by the commercial success of the novel but by its emotional impact. It brought him considerable fan-mail from the bereaved; as he wrote to an American correspondent,

Some simple and honest hearts in the remote wilds of America, have written me letters on the loss of their children; so numbering my little book, or rather heroine, with their household gods, and so pouring out their trials and sources of comfort in them, before me as a friend, that I have been inexpressibly moved . . . .

He made a similar point in a speech in Boston on 1 February 1842 (*Speeches*, p. 20). In a letter written on (?) 17 January 1841, he had told Forster:

When I first began (on your valued suggestion) to keep my thoughts upon this ending of the tale, I resolved to try and do something which might be read by people about whom Death had been, with a softened feeling, and with consolation.

He cannot have doubted, after the reception of the novel, that his aim had been fulfilled.

But before the end of the century the anti-Nell reaction had set in. Ruskin said that Dickens killed Nell as a butcher slaughters a lamb –

for the market; Oscar Wilde declared that 'one must have a heart of
stone to read the death of Little Nell without laughing'; and for
Aldous Huxley the 'pathetic parts' of the novel were even poorer
than Florence Barclay's sentimental best-seller *The Rosary*. Today
the novel is, of all Dickens' books, one of the most difficult to
approach with an open mind, but it richly and perhaps surprisingly
rewards the effort.

In the first place, to regard the novel as monopolized or
dominated by Little Nell is to ignore the evidence; and the
experience of actually reading it – as opposed to recalling it, or to
heeding the witty but hyperbolic verdicts of Ruskin or Wilde –
produces a very different impression. There are long stretches of the
narrative from which Nell is absent and in which she is barely
mentioned, and these portions – less a Nellyad than a Quilpiad or a
Dickiad – contain some of Dickens' best writing in the comic and
grotesque modes. Nell may not be far at times from the maudlin,
self-indulgent world of the Victorian sentimental ballad or religiose
engraving (though this, too, is open to argument); but some scenes
in the novel are, as A. E. Dyson has said, closer to the world of Lewis
Carroll and Franz Kafka (consider, for example, the extraordinary
dialogue in which the enquiry as to what happens to superannuated
giants elicits the information that they are kept in caravans to wait
on dwarfs). In the first dozen chapters, Dick Swiveller is introduced
(Ch. 2), Quilp is shown at home (Chs 4–5), Dick is further
developed (Chs 7–8), and Sampson Brass appears (Ch. 11): here's
richness, indeed; and it looks as though Dickens were concerned to
create as boldly contrasting a setting as possible for the pathos and
sentiment attaching to Nell. Some of his contemporaries did not
altogether miss the point: the *Ecclesiastic and Theologian* referred in
1855 to the novel's 'mingling of a conception of great poetical
beauty with the events and persons of common life', and Thackeray
confessed as early as 1843 that he had 'never read the *Nelly* part of
the *Old Curiosity Shop* more than once; whereas I have Dick Swiveller
and the Marchioness by Heart' (both quoted in *Critical Heritage*,
p. 91).

It will not quite do to suggest, as F. R. Leavis has suggested of
George Eliot's *Daniel Deronda*, that what we encounter here is a case
of two different books on different levels of achievement coexisting
between the covers of a single novel: *The Old Curiosity Shop* has a
unity derived partly from the interlacings of the plot, which links
Nell and her grandfather with the comic and low-life characters,

and partly from an element of the grotesque in the presentation of Nell herself (the original idea was of childish innocence and freshness amid the mouldering decay of the shop's antiques and lumber, and the contrast recurs at the close of the novel when Nell comes to rest in the crumbling Gothic of the village church). But for many present-day readers, one suspects, the parts of the novel in which Nell is least prominent will turn out to be most satisfying.

Dick Swiveller seems to embody a change of intention on Dickens' part: the initial emphasis on his dissoluteness and moral weakness soon gives way to a more affectionate portrayal, and Angus Wilson has made the point that Dick is what Dickens might easily have been if he had remained a clerk (the similarity of names is perhaps suggestive). Swiveller is certainly one of Dickens' symbolic namings, though it is probably going too far to connect it, as one commentator has done, with the archaic 'swive' (copulate). Like that of Dickens, Dick's mind has a 'figurative and poetic character' and is given to many a 'flight of fancy' (Ch. 7); and Chesterton's apt phrases – he observes that Dick has 'a lonely literary pleasure in exaggerative language' and an 'unerring instinct for the perfect folly of a phase' – apply no less to Dickens himself. In his letters (and the same was presumably true of his conversation) we frequently find Dickens assuming for facetious purposes the role of one of his own characters; and towards the end of the composition of this novel he wrote to Maclise (January 1841) that he was 'at the moment inflamed with wine and "the Mazy"', thus borrowing a word used by Dick in Chapter 56. The latter's discovery and befriending of the Marchioness, and her nursing of him through his illness, are genuinely touching; and their marriage is no mere gesture dictated by the convention of a tidy ending but entirely appropriate. For Dick inhabits the real world, as the Marchioness also does but Nell (whom in some ways she parallels) does not; and Dick's social world is substantial and documented in detail, in contrast to the timelessly idealized world – the world of allegory or fairy tale – through which, with only a few exceptions, Nell and her grandfather move.

Dick's spontaneous wit and verbal inventiveness remind us of his creator; but Quilp too has 'an extraordinary flow of language' (Ch. 33), and psychological criticism has seen his demonic energy as related to the artistic impulse. The 'original' of Quilp was a hideous dwarf at Bath who let out donkeys on hire, beat his donkeys professionally and his wife as a hobby, and was introduced to

Dickens by Rose Paynter. Thomas Hood was troubled by the
'association of moral with physical deformity' in Quilp; but for
Dickens, and for the kind of non-realistic art that can exist in his
novels alongside efforts at the most scrupulous realism, the connection is crucial. While Nell's childlike figure moves towards death,
this 'elderly . . . dwarf' (Ch. 3) displays a riotous and outrageous
vitality. For all the exactness of his local habitation on Tower Hill,
he is a figure out of fairy tale or nightmare: the Beast to Nell's
Beauty, the wolf to her Red Riding-hood, the allegorical Evil to
her Goodness. In this novel, written very near the beginning of the
Victorian period, Dickens can still permit himself very strong
suggestions of Quilp's powerful sexuality; and Gabriel Pearson, who
perhaps goes too far in claiming that 'Quilp's very vitality savages
Nell's pallid heroics', is right in seeing Mrs Quilp as 'starkly
. . . implicated in sexuality' and the smoking scene as 'the closest we
get to downright copulation in early-Victorian fiction'. Quilp's
nearest relation in the Dickensian gallery is not that other dwarf,
Miss Mowcher, but the diabolical arch-plotter Rigaud in *Little
Dorrit*, though Rigaud's melodramatics are forced and tedious in
comparison with the self-delighting humour of Quilp. A villain who
can enjoin silence with the words ' "not so much as a creaking
board, or a stumble against a cobweb" ' (Ch. 49) is a villain whose
reappearances delight us.

Sampson and Sally Brass are studies in selfishness and avarice at a
time when Dickens could still see these qualities as comic. The
traditional sex-roles are reversed: the ironically named Sampson
(Dickens at first called him Septimus) is weak, his sister no frail
vessel but mannish and domineering. A cancelled passage reveals
her as the mother of the Marchioness, and gives a more serious
undertone to her ill-usage of the girl. The Brasses' plot against Kit is
thwarted, good in this instance triumphing over evil, for Kit and his
family offer a sentimental portrait of the deserving poor, the 'happy
families' idyll of working-class life that had a permanent attraction
for Dickens. Kit's name provides Dickens with the opportunity for
what may well be his most daring sexual pun:

> 'Kit, eh!' said Brass. 'Strange name – name of a dancing-
> master's fiddle, eh, Mr. Richard? Ha, ha! . . . '

Sampson's laughter seems excessive unless we remember that, in
nineteenth-century low slang, 'kit' could mean the male and 'fiddle'

the female genitals – a double joke for which Dick was no doubt a fit audience.

If Dick seems to emerge from the closely observed metropolitan world of *Sketches by Boz* and Quilp from fairy tale or popular entertainment of the Punch and Judy variety, Nell owes something to Shakespeare, as contemporary reviewers were quick to note. Echoes of *King Lear* are particularly in evidence, with Nell's grandfather as Lear to her Cordelia (see, for example, in Ch. 12, the dialogue between the child and the old man – ' "Let us wander barefoot through the world" ', etc.); and in some passages the writing moves perilously close to blank verse. In their conversation at the beginning of Ch. 24, for instance, we find the following (here slightly rearranged):

' . . . How can you bear to think that we are safe,
When they are searching for me everywhere . . . '

' . . . Judge for yourself, dear grandfather; look round,
And see how quiet and still it is . . .
Could I feel easy – did I feel at ease –
When any danger threatened you?'
                                                    'True, true . . . . '

' . . . But here, while the sun shines above our heads,
And everything is bright and happy, we
Are sitting sadly down, and losing time.
See what a pleasant path; and there's the bird . . . . '

Characteristically, though, the wholly serious Shakespearean echoes are counterpointed by Dick Swiveller's bibulous allusions to *Hamlet* and *Macbeth*.

Chesterton raised a question about the title of this novel:

There seems no reason in particular, at the first and most literal glance, why the story should be called after the Old Curiosity Shop. Only two of the characters have anything to do with such a shop, and they leave it for ever in the first few pages. It is as if Thackeray had called the whole novel of 'Vanity Fair' 'Miss Pinkerton's Academy'

and then answered it himself by suggesting that 'this title is something in the nature of a key to the whole Dickens romance',

since 'his tales always started from some splendid hint in the streets'.
The nature of the shop seems more precisely significant, however:
an antique shop, or junk shop, represents the past in the present, a
little piece of extraterritoriality in which time remembered takes
visible shape; and the shop (doubly old, for it is an old shop selling
old things) is initially the setting for a heroine who herself exists out
of time, detached from the contemporary world inhabited by the
likes of Dick, the Marchioness and the Brasses. Nell's journey across
England is also a journey back in time. As Angus Easson points out,
'Dickens deliberately creates a dream landscape by the omission
of names', and the Grand Union Canal is merely 'some water'; but it
is clear that Nell and her grandfather travel slowly through the
England of the industrial revolution (Birmingham and the Black
Country) to a pre-industrial landscape and a rural life strongly
reminiscent of Goldsmith's *The Deserted Village*.

The original illustrations, from that of the sleeping Nell surrounded by ancient lumber in the opening chapter to the comp-
lementary one of the dead Nell near the end of the book (this last
effectively placed opposite the page on which stands the verbal
description of her corpse), admirably catch the world, or rather the
two worlds, of the story: and John Harvey has shown how the two
artists principally involved, Browne and Cattermole, divided
between them the two main areas of the novel: that dominated by
Quilp, 'boisterous, comic, and fantastical', became Browne's
province, while that dominated by Nell, 'subdued, solemn, and
pathetic', became Cattermole's. (For further details of the illustrations, see the section on 'Dickens' Illustrators'.)

Dickens' manuscript and proofs provide abundant evidence of his
striving, even thus early in his career, for the maximum stylistic, and
especially comic, effect; and many of his happiest touches are found
to have been afterthoughts. When Dick Swiveller remarks in his first
appearance (Ch. 2), ' " . . . the wing of relationship should *never be
clipped but* be always expanded and serene. Why should a grandson
and grandfather peg away at each other with mutual violence when
all might be *bliss and* concord?" ', the words italicized were added
above the line in the manuscript; and when Dick laments the
faithlessness of Sophy Cheggs in Ch. 50– ' "Yet loved I as man never
loved that *hadn't wooden legs*, and my heart, my heart is breaking for
the love of Sophy Cheggs" ' – we find that Dickens first wrote
'walked on human legs'. At the proof stage, he added the passage
containing the reference to Buffon in Ch. 51 (from 'Kit' to ' "that's

enough"'"); the delectable comment on the Marchioness's drink made out of orange-peel in Ch. 56 (the comparatively feeble '"it hasn't much flavour"' being replaced by '"it seems as if it would bear a little more seasoning, certainly"'); the splendid final sentence of Ch. 66 (Dick's '"And she shall walk in silk attire, and siller have to spare, or may I never rise from this bed again!"'); and (as blurb-writers say) many, many others.

Modern criticism has done less than justice to *The Old Curiosity Shop*. Essays that repay study include those by Gabriel Pearson in *Dickens and the Twentieth Century*, ed. Gross & Pearson; Lawrence Senelick in *Dickens Studies*, III (1967); Robert L. Patten in *Dickens the Craftsman*, ed. R. B. Partlow, Jr.; and A. E. Dyson in *Critical Quarterly*, VIII (1966). The general studies of Dickens by John Lucas and Steven Marcus also contain good chapters on this novel.

CHARACTERS

BACHELOR, THE. Brother of Mr Garland; he lives with an elderly clergyman, a college friend, in the village where Nell settles after her second meeting with the schoolmaster.

BRASS, SAMPSON. 'An attorney of no very good repute from Bevis Marks in the city of London' (Ch. 11). He is Quilp's legal adviser, cunning but pusillanimous, and (like Fagin and Uriah Heep) a red-haired villain. His mannish sister and colleague SALLY ('a kind of amazon at common law': Ch. 33) turns out to be the Marchioness's mother.

CHEGGS, MR (Allick). Market-gardener and Dick Swiveller's rival for the hand of Sophia Wackles (see Ch. 8). His sister Miss CHEGGS also appears.

CHUCKSTER, MR. Foppish clerk employed by Mr Witherden.

CODLIN, THOMAS. Codlin and Short are the owners of a travelling Punch and Judy show; Nell meets them at an early stage of her travels. Short's real name is Harris; his nickname, Short Trotters ('by reason of the small size of his legs': Ch. 17), is usually abbreviated to Short. Codlin is of a sour disposition, Short cheerful and friendly – a Dickensian pairing repeated in the Spenlow and Jorkins of *David Copperfield*.

EDWARDS, MISS. Poor apprentice at Miss Monflathers' boarding-school; she shows sympathy towards Nell and is reproved for it (Ch. 30).

GARLAND, MR AND MRS. Benevolent couple who employ Kit
Nubbles at their Finchley home, Abel Cottage (named after their
only son, ABEL). Their pony WHISKER (a 'self-willed pony': Ch.
22) provides comic interludes. Their servant girl BARBARA loves
Kit.

GROOVES, JAMES (Jem, Jemmy). Keeps the Valiant Soldier, a public
house where Nell and her grandfather take shelter from a storm
and the latter gambles at cards (Ch. 29).

JARLEY, MRS. Stately, corpulent and kind-hearted proprietress of a
travelling waxwork show. She befriends and employs Nell at one
stage of her wanderings. Dickens' manuscript shows that on
second thoughts he played down some of the non-standard
elements initially inserted in the dialogue assigned to Mrs Jarley.

JINIWIN, MRS. Mother of Mrs Quilp; she lives with her daughter and
son-in-law and is terrorized by the latter.

LIST, ISAAC. Gamester with whom Nell's grandfather plays cards
(Ch. 29).

MARCHIONESS, THE. Diminutive servant-girl employed by Sampson
and Sally Brass. Bullied and half-starved by the latter, she is
befriended by Dick Swiveller, whom she nurses during an illness
and eventually marries. Dickens originally revealed in Ch. 66
that Sally Brass was her mother and implied that Quilp was her
father, but subsequently deleted the passage. It is printed in the
Penguin edition, pp. 715–16. See also G. G. Grubb, *Modern
Language Notes*, LXVIII (1953), and Angus Easson, *Modern Language
Review*, LXV (1970).

MARTON, MR. (usually referred to as 'the Schoolmaster'). He
befriends Nell and her grandfather during their wanderings and
by chance encounters them again and provides them with a home
(Ch. 52). The death of his favourite pupil foreshadows that of
Nell.

MONFLATHERS, MISS. Snobbish and disagreeable principal of a girls'
boarding-school (Chs. 28, 30).

NELL, LITTLE. Heroine of the novel. She first appears in the opening
chapter and dies in Ch. 71. Nell is 'nearly fourteen' (Ch. 7) when
the story opens, and is the grand-daughter of old Trent.

NUBBLES, CHRISTOPHER (Kit). Boy employed and then dismissed by
Nell's grandfather and subsequently employed by Mr Garland.
He loves Nell devotedly and is the victim of a plot devised by the
Brasses at Quilp's instigation. He is the son of a poor industrious
widow who frequents a Little Bethel (see Ch. 22).

QUILP, DANIEL. Elderly dwarf of hideous appearance (described in Ch. 3) and sadistic tastes. Dick Swiveller tells him, ' "You have the queerest and most extraordinary way with you" ' (Ch. 21), and Sampson Brass pays obsequious tribute to his ' "amazing flow of spirits" ' (Ch. 33). His wife, MRS BETSY QUILP, is 'a pretty little, mild-spoken, blue-eyed woman' (Ch. 4) who is terrified of him. Quilp is the villain of the novel, a plotter who delights in making mischief, and the self-described 'evil genius' (Ch. 67) of Nell and her grandfather.

SCHOOLMASTER, THE, see MR MARTON.

SCOTT, TOM. Boy employed by Quilp.

SHORT, see CODLIN, THOMAS.

SINGLE GENTLEMAN, THE. A mysterious figure who takes lodgings with the Brasses and is revealed as searching for Nell and her grandfather. In Chapter 69 his identity is disclosed (he is a younger brother of Nell's grandfather). In a postscript to the novel he is identified as Master Humphrey, the supposed narrator of the story.

SLUM, MR. Poet who composes verses to publicize Mrs Jarley's waxwork display (Ch. 28).

SWIVELLER, DICK. Cheerful, disreputable and endearing anti-hero of the novel, first introduced as a friend of Fred Trent. He is employed by Sampson Brass and later marries the Marchioness.

TRENT, FRED. Brother of Nell and friend of Dick Swiveller; a wastrel.

WACKLES, SOPHIA. 'A fresh, good-humoured, buxom girl of twenty' (Ch. 8), she is loved, briefly, by Dick Swiveller (see Ch. 7). With her mother and two sisters she conducts a 'Ladies Seminary' at Chelsea.

WITHERDEN, MR. Attorney to Mr Garland, whose son Abel is articled to him.

Barnaby Rudge

Text Penguin English Library, ed. G. W. Spence (1973).

Composition An indication of the complex origins of this novel is provided by Kathleen Tillotson's observation that it 'was the fifth of Dickens' novels to be published, but had nothing interfered with his original plan it would have been the first'. That original plan goes back to May 1836, when Dickens contracted to write for John Macrone, the publisher of *Sketches by Boz*, 'a work of Fiction (in Three Volumes of the usual size) . . . to be entitled *Gabriel Vardon, the Locksmith of London*'. A few months later, he seems to have considered himself released from this contract, for on 22 August he agreed to write a three-volume novel for Richard Bentley; in an earlier letter he had referred to this work as *Barnaby Rudge*. Meanwhile, *Pickwick* had achieved its resounding success; it was quickly followed by *Nickleby* and *Oliver Twist*, and for the next couple of years Dickens did nothing about his promise. In September 1838 it was agreed that *Barnaby Rudge: A Tale of the Great Riots* should succeed *Oliver Twist* as a monthly serial in *Bentley's Miscellany*, of which Dickens was now editor; and in January 1839 he began work on the new novel. It was, however, quickly abandoned: Dickens obviously found the longstanding commitment irksome (a letter of 21 January speaks of 'slavery and drudgery'), and he was irritated at having agreed long ago to supply Bentley with a novel on terms (£500 for the outright copyright) that his new fame made appear very disadvantageous. It was not until October 1839 that he took up the novel once more. On 30 October he announced that he was 'going forthwith tooth and nail at Barnaby'. In spite of the upheaval of moving house, he continued to work at it in the closing weeks of 1839; but it was clearly not going to be ready for delivery on 1 January 1840 for publication in three volumes, as he had promised Bentley. Not surprisingly, therefore, he

was considerably startled to find Bentley advertising it on 14
December as 'preparing for publication'. A quarrel followed, with
threats of legal action from both sides. At last, in July 1840, he
severed all connexion with Bentley, and transferred the copyright of
the novel to Chapman & Hall. Before the end of the year it was
decided that it should follow *The Old Curiosity Shop* as a weekly serial
in the miscellany *Master Humphrey's Clock* (see in the chapter on 'Master
Humphrey's Clock'). Its forthcoming appearance was announced
on 9 January 1841, and Dickens took up again the two or three
chapters he had written more than a year earlier and set to work
with a will. On 29 January he wrote to Forster:

> I didn't stir out yesterday, but sat and *thought* all day; not writing
> a line . . . . I imaged forth a good deal of *Barnaby* by keeping my
> mind steadily upon him; and am happy to say I have gone to
> work this morning in good twig, strong hope, and cheerful spirits

– an account which gives some insight into his creative method at
this early stage of his career. Not for the last time, he came to chafe
at the constrictions of the short weekly instalments: on 5 August he
exclaimed to Forster, 'Oh! If I only had him, from this time to the
end, in monthly numbers.'

The novel occupied Dickens' thoughts, then, on and off for some
five years, and was at different times conceived as a three-decker, a
monthly serial, and a weekly serial. One result of all this was that it
was able to take shape in Dickens' mind in a more leisurely fashion
than any other of his early novels. As G. W. Spence has said, 'To the
fact that he had been living with the subject for so long before he
began publication may be attributed the signs in *Barnaby Rudge* of
careful planning and structural control which distinguish it from his
other novels of this period.' Professor Tillotson suggests that
Dickens' persistence in going ahead with the novel in spite of
difficulties and delays 'is evidence of his tenacity of purpose and the
grip of the original idea on his imagination; not, as has been
suggested, of the grudging performance of a task'. Manuscript and
portion of corrected proofs (Chs 17–18 only) in Forster Collection.

Serialization   Weekly in *Master Humphrey's Clock* from 13 February
to 27 November 1841. Ch. 1 of the novel occupied the first
instalment; Ch. 12 the seventh instalment. With these exceptions,
each number of the *Clock* contained two chapters. The *Clock*, which

concluded with the termination of *Barnaby Rudge*, was also issued concurrently in monthly parts, each containing four or five weekly numbers. Illustrations by George Cattermole and 'Phiz'.

Publication. By Chapman and Hall, December 1841, in one volume.

Reception Philip Collins notes that the work 'attracted little serious discussion, and not much enthusiasm'; even Forster, in his *Examiner* review, admitted that 'The interest with which the story commences, has ceased to be the interest before it closes.' It has always been, critically speaking, one of the least regarded of Dickens' novels. But the heroine Dolly Varden and the raven Grip were widely admired, and the scenes involving the Maypole Inn were also popular. Edgar Allan Poe, writing in the *Saturday Post*, praised Dickens' power of creating atmosphere; his poem 'The Raven' probably owes something to Barnaby's Grip.

Barnaby Rudge is one of Dickens' two historical novels, the other being *A Tale of Two Cities* nearly twenty years later. It deals, however, with the fairly recent past: its opening sentence contains the date 1775, and the main action (the Gordon Riots) belongs to 1780, only a couple of generations before the date of composition (its subtitle is 'A Tale of the Riots of 'Eighty'). Dickens was entering into conscious rivalry with the most famous and successful of his predecessors, Sir Walter Scott, and K. J. Fielding is not the only critic to have found 'faint traces of Scott all through the book' (for example, the Gordon Riots and the attack on Newgate Prison parallel the Porteous riots and the storming of the Tolbooth in *The Heart of Midlothian*). As Professor Fielding points out, the novel really falls into two halves: the first half is 'a plain historical novel about comic innkeepers, mysterious strangers, an unsolved murder, and a missing steward', and the second – to which the first is no more than a preparation – an account of the famous 'No Popery' riots of 1780 instigated by Lord George Gordon and his followers.

As well as being a historical novel, however, it is also a highly topical book. Kathleen Tillotson has argued convincingly that it is 'related to the events and mood of the exact years of its writing and publication', and that 'the five years' delay between design and publication had increased the novel's topicality'. She adds that 'the events of 1836–41 made the novel almost journalistically apt':

behind it are the Poor Law riots, the Chartist risings at various towns, mass meetings, 'and most pointed of all, the Newport rising of 1839 with its attempt to release Chartist prisoners'. Furthermore, the foundation in 1839 of the Protestant Association, with its mass meetings, petitions, and local branches, gave fresh point to Dickens' exposure of sectarian bigotry.

Dickens undertook a certain amount of research for his novel. His main source was contemporary newspapers, together with a pamphlet by Thomas Holcroft; he also knew and admired Carlyle's recent *French Revolution* (1837), with its accounts of mob violence. Professor Tillotson suggests that he read published reminiscences of the period and talked to eyewitnesses. (See Chs 39 and 65 of the novel for Dickens' own references to his sources.) In the preface Dickens claims that 'reference has been had to the best authorities of that time, such as they are'.

Jack Lindsay finds in the novel 'a discrepancy between the tremendous force of the poetic motives that surround the characters, and the characters themselves', and cites Simon Tappertit as a case in point: he is 'the figure who ostensibly represents the wrongs and grievances of the workers; but he is a figure of fun and we do not feel any real relation between his fulminations and the shattering upheaval – except in the sense of a parody'. It is certainly true that the comic figures of Tappertit and Miggs are much more successful and memorable than the melodramatic villain Gashford or the demented Barnaby; on the other hand, the central crowd scenes have a genuine power and reflect a preoccupation with mob violence that was again to find expresssion in *A Tale of Two Cities*.

As noted above, most critics regard the novel as among Dickens' lesser achievements, and even when they grant that it was a grand and ambitious subject they regard it as an incomplete success. A notable exception is Steven Marcus. Conceding that it is 'customarily dismissed as a failure', that its prose is 'relatively undistinguished', and that it 'seems laboriously slow in getting up steam' and 'except for the descriptions of the riots . . . tends to be of a curiously uniform flatness', he nevertheless argues that it is 'a vastly better novel than its reputation in any way suggests'. Professor Marcus sees Dickens' theme as 'authority in political and social relations, as well as in personal and private ones', and finds 'intelligence and skill' in his connecting of these two kinds of relations. Marcus's long essay on this novel in *Dickens: From Pickwick to Dombey* is probably the most sustained attempt to demonstrate its importance in Dickens's development – less in his technical development as a novelist than in his growing insight into the ills of society.

Dickens' preoccupation throughout his work with the theme of parents and children finds full expression in *Barnaby Rudge*: Sir John Chester's treatment of his two sons (as with Gloucester in *King Lear*, one is legitimate, the other illegitimate); Mr Willet's insistence on treating Joe as a child; the Vardens' spoiling of Dolly; Mrs Rudge's relationship with Barnaby – these represent variations on the idea of 'natural bonds' and 'natural affections', and 'nature' is indeed a key concept in this novel, viewed sometimes literally and seriously and sometimes sceptically and ironically. Like Wordsworth's idiot boy, Barnaby is a child of nature; Hugh is a natural child in another sense; natural goodness is to be found in Gabriel Varden and Joe Willet (in contrast to the hypocrisy of Sir John Chester, Gashford and Miggs). A Wordsworthian view of nature is expressed directly in Ch. 25:

> Ye men of gloom and austerity, . . . Listen to the million voices in the summer air, and find one dismal as your own. Remember, if ye can, the sense of hope and pleasure which every glad return of day awakens in the breast of all your kind who have not changed their nature; and learn some wisdom from the witless, when their hearts are lifted up they know not why, by all the mirth and happiness it brings.

and ironically in Ch. 75, when Sir John 'glanced approvingly at an elegant little sketch, entitled "Nature," on the wall'.

In *Barnaby Rudge*, then, Dickens has given us both a historical novel dealing with the Gordon Riots and a novel dealing with natural affections and duties. Kathleen Tillotson has argued that the two are closely connected: 'Through Hugh and Barnaby the fictitious and historical parts of the novel are firmly related.' H. F. Folland has said that the controlling theme of the novel is 'the deceptive and complex relationships between the doer and his deed, deeds and their consequences, and the doer's responsibility for them'. One obvious aspect of this is the parent's responsibility for the child; another is the political agitator's responsibility for the violence that ensues. Sylvère Monod suggests that 'Hugh has been violent, brutal, evil, because he is the product of a violent, brutal, evil society' – a line of argument that sees society rather than (or as well as) the individual as bearing responsibility for deeds, and looks forward to the vision of society in such later novels as *Little Dorrit* and *Our Mutual Friend*.

Gissing found this novel 'not characteristic of Dickens', but there are some highly characteristic elements. The Vardens' servant Miggs begins as a Smollettian stereotype – the vinegary, spiteful, man-hungry spinster – but turns into a memorable comic figure and is given the most inventive dialogue in the whole novel: when she remarks in Ch. 41 that ' "I wouldn't stay . . . and make dissensions, not for a annual gold mine, and found in tea and sugar" ', or when in Ch. 71 she describes herself ironically as a 'potter's wessel' and the likes of Dolly as 'young flaunting pagins' who 'comb and titiwate theirselves into whitenining and suppulchres', we are reminded not only of Smollett's Win Jenkins in *Humphry Clinker* but of Mrs Gamp. Dolly herself anticipates the spoiled and wilful heroines of Dickens' later period (Estella, Bella); by the end of the novel, however, she has learned wisdom – which for Dickens means the meek acceptance of a properly subordinate wifely role (she declares in Ch. 78, ' "I will never know a wish or care beyond our home and you, and I will always study how to please you with my best affection and my most devoted love" '). As a ' "patient, gentle, never-tiring wife" ' she dons the mantle that was later to be worn by Agnes Wickfield and Esther Summerson. Sir John Chester, like Squeers and Pecksniff, is a round-the-clock villain; and like Carker, his smile is the smile on the face of the tiger: in Ch. 25 he is found 'smilingly asleep – for even sleep, working but little change in his dissembling face, became with him a piece of cold, conventional hypocrisy'; and as he dies (Ch. 81) there is 'scorn and hatred in his look: but seeming to remember, even then, that this expression would distort his features after death, he tried to smile'. His brother in villainy is Gashford, who also 'smiled as if for practice' (Ch. 35).

Professor Marcus sees *Barnaby Rudge* as 'the last work of Dickens' apprenticeship to his art'. At the same time, as some of the above examples have suggested, there are striking anticipations of later elements. Very prominent throughout the book is an evident interest in the nature of perception: 'Perhaps a man never sees so much at a glance as when he is in a situation of extremity', Dickens writes in Ch. 58, and the scene in which old Willet watches the destruction of the Maypole Inn is of great psychological interest. The Maypole itself has provoked a Freudian interpretation, and Professor Marcus has praised the 'shameless brilliance' of the symbolism of the master-key forged by Simon Tappertit.

This novel has attracted less critical attention than most of the others, and is rarely if ever studied in academic circles; but it provides plenty of food for thought and should not be overlooked by the serious student of Dickens. The most stimulating discussion is that by Steven Marcus (in *Dickens: From Pickwick to Dombey*). Jack Lindsay's essay in *Dickens and the Twentieth Century,* ed. Gross & Pearson, H. F. Folland's 'The Doer and the Deed' (*Publications of the Modern Language Association,* LXXIV, 1959), Sylvère Monod's 'Rebel with a Cause: Hugh of the Maypole' (*Dickens Studies,* I, 1965) and A. E. Dyson's 'The Genesis of Violence' (*Critical Quarterly,* IX, 1967; reprinted in *The Inimitable Dickens*) are all worth consulting. Some of these interpretations stress the social and political aspects of the novel and the evidence it furnishes for an understanding of Dickens' attitude to history. Butt and Tillotson's *Dickens at Work* contains a chapter on the composition of the novel. The Penguin edition has an introduction by G. W. Spence, and Georg Lukács' *The Historical Novel* (1950) offers a Marxist view. Angus Wilson refers to this novel as 'the turning point in Dickens's growth from an extraordinary to a great novelist' in his essay 'Dickens on Children and Childhood', in *Dickens 1970,* ed. Michael Slater (1970); the same essay suggests that the novel's hero is 'heir to Wordsworth's idiot boy tradition'.

CHARACTERS

AKERMAN. Head jailer at Newgate Prison.

CHESTER, EDWARD. In love with Emma Haredale, niece of Geoffrey Haredale, who is his father's enemy. He rescues her from Gashford during the riots, and they eventually marry. His father SIR JOHN CHESTER, is a smooth villain who secretly foments the Anti-Catholic riots. He is killed by Haredale in a duel. Hugh is his natural son.

COBB, TOM. Chandler and keeper of the post office at Chigwell.

DAISY, Solomon. Parish clerk at Chigwell.

DENNIS, NED. Brutal hangman and leader of the Gordon Riots, he is himself eventually executed.

GASHFORD. Secretary to Lord George Gordon. He captures Emma Haredale during the riots. A melodramatic and unconvincing villain.

GILBERT, MARK. Member of a secret society formed by London apprentices.

GORDON, LORD GEORGE. A Member of Parliament who instigates the Anti-Catholic riots named after him.

GRIP. Raven belonging to Barnaby. Dickens himself later had a pet raven named Grip.

GRUEBY, JOHN. Servant to Lord George Gordon.

HAREDALE, MR. GEOFFREY. A Roman Catholic gentleman who lives at The Warren, a house that Steven Marcus has described as representing 'that secret, mouldering past in which all order and authority have been overthrown'. He has inherited the family property from his elder brother Reuben, a country gentleman mysteriously murdered before the novel opens (see Ch. 1); he is suspected of murder, though his innocence is later proved. The house is burned down in the riots. He is guardian of his niece Emma, an orphan, who is loved by Edward Chester.

HUGH. Surly ostler at the Maypole Inn at Chigwell, later revealed as Sir John Chester's natural son. He becomes a leader in the Gordon Riots and is executed.

MIGGS. The Vardens' domestic servant, 'a tall young lady . . . of a sharp and acid visage' (Ch. 7) and a fine comic creation.

PARKES, PHIL. A ranger in Epping Forest.

RUDGE, BARNABY. Described in Ch. 3, he is the half-witted son of Mrs Rudge, whose husband has formerly been steward to Mr Reuben Haredale and turns out to have been his murderer.

STAGG. Blind proprietor of a drinking-cellar. Discussing the influence of Sir Walter Scott on *Barnaby Rudge*, K. J. Fielding has written: 'it has even been suggested that, merely as a joke, Dickens introduced a somewhat thirsty character named Stagg into the story in order to echo the famous line in *The Lady of the Lake*, "The stag at eve had drunk his fill." This is too good *not* to be true.'

TAPPERTIT, SIMON (Sim). Apprentice to Gabriel Varden the locksmith. Physically insignificant and labouring under an intense feeling of resentment, he becomes captain of the 'Prentice Knights, a secret society formed by London apprentices to combat the tyranny of their masters. He aspires to be the lover of Dolly Varden. He is mutilated in the riots and the legs of which he is inordinately and comically vain become 'shattered limbs' (see the curious ending of Ch. 71). One of the characters in whom Dickens contrives, partly through suggestive symbolism, to convey an impression of powerful sexual feelings without ever making them quite explicit. For Jack Lindsay's comment on Simon Tappertit, see above (p. 124).

VARDEN, GABRIEL. Locksmith with a shop at Clerkenwell (Ch. 4). His wife, MARTHA VARDEN, is 'a lady of what is commonly called an uncertain temper' (Ch. 7). His daughter DOLLY, attractive but spoiled and coquettish, is vainly loved by Simon Tappertit, is captured by the rioters, rescued by Joe Willet, and later marries him. She proved a popular character; W. P. Frith's painting 'Dolly Varden' (1842) is now in the Victoria & Albert Museum.

WILLET, JOHN. Landlord of the Maypole Inn at Chigwell in Essex, 'a burly, large-headed man with a fat face' (Ch. 1). Steven Marcus has said that the inn represents 'a vision of the idyllic past, which has come to be dominated by tyrannic and imbecile authority' and thus is closely related to the social and political themes of the novel. His son Joe is in love with Dolly Varden. As a result of his father's tyranny (he insists on treating him as a child), Joe runs away from home, joins the army, loses an arm, but later saves Dolly from the rioters. She eventually marries him.

American Notes

Text   Penguin English Library, ed. J. S. Whitley and A. Goldman (1972)

Composition   Written during the summer of 1842 and based partly on letters written to Forster during the visit to America (see below).

Publication   Published in two volumes in October 1842.

Reception   As Philip Collins points out, 'Dickens's first attempt at a serious and sustained non-fictional work . . . got a far worse press than any of his previous books.' All the 'heavy quarterlies' in England attacked it with 'unique unanimity', while in America 'injured pride led to some fierce reviewing and dark threats'. Edgar Johnson quotes some of the enraged vituperation directed at Dickens by American reviewers: the 'famous penny-a-liner' had 'the most coarse, vulgar, impudent, and superficial' mind 'that ever had the courage to write about . . . this original and remarkable country'; he was a 'flash reporter' with the feelings of 'a low-bred scullion', and was of all visitors 'the most flimsy – the most childish – the most trashy–the most contemptible'. Some individuals, including Dickens' American friends Longfellow and Felton, recognized the book's merits. (For Felton's enthusiastic notice in the *North American Review*, see *Critical Heritage*, pp. 130–5.) Like many another book panned by critics, however, it sold well in America: Johnson notes that

> cheap editions . . . flooded the country at six cents a copy. The
> *New York Herald* printed the work in nineteen hours after the
> arrival of copy from England and sold fifty thousand in two days.

In Philadelphia three thousand copies went in half an hour. Such sales brought Dickens fame (or notoriety) but not fortune, since existing copyright laws permitted American publishers to issue his work without payment of royalties.

In England the price of the two-volume *Notes* (one guinea) discouraged large sales; but, comments Robert Patten,

> The sales figures do not entirely support a conclusion that the *Notes* were a failure; travel books in two volumes for a guinea a copy appealed to a much more limited audience than fiction for 3*d.* a week. But there is much truth to the argument that the hostile – or, even worse, condescending – critical reception of the book affected the public's feeling about Dickens. And some truth, perhaps, to Forster's attribution of the disappointing sales of *Chuzzlewit* to a capricious lull in popular taste.

K. J. Fielding has discussed the English reception of *American Notes* in *Modern Language Review*, LIX, 1964.

Dickens announced his decision to go to America in a letter to Forster dated 19 September 1841, and his initial mood was one of high enthusiasm: he told an American correspondent that he would soon arrive 'upon the soil I have trodden in my day-dreams many times and whose sons (and daughters) I yearn to know and be among'. The anti-American prejudices of some of his friends (Lady Holland asked, 'Why cannot you go down to Bristol and see some of the third and fourth class people there and they'll do just as well?') did not deter him. He and Kate sailed from Liverpool on 4 January 1842 and after a very bad crossing lasting fourteen days reached Halifax. Edgar Johnson has vividy described the lionization that greeted Dickens in the United States: in Boston, 'ladies pressed into the studio to stare at him until Dickens bolted for the door, only to be mobbed there and forced to retreat'; when he fell into their clutches they seized his hand and 'furtively snipped bits of fur from his coat to treasure as souvenirs'.

Dickens travelled widely in the eastern parts of the USA and Canada, made many acquaintances (including some who remained friends for life), and visited many public institutions such as schools and prisons. His enthusiasm soon gave way to disillusion, however; and he found himself irritated and even disgusted by many aspects of American life and manners, including the universal spitoon. As Robert Patten has said,

The American trip put a considerable strain on his budget; and his speaking out on behalf of International Copyright strained his relations with press and public. The precarious financial state of the nation, its fierce and licentious journals, its hypocrisy about slavery, the crudeness of the culture, the unrestrained curiosity about Boz all contributed to Dickens's discomfort.

He was not sorry to return home, sailing from New York on 7 June.

From America he had written long journal-letters to Forster, and these formed the basis of the book that was quickly assembled after his return to England. (His trip had been financed by his publishers to enable him to write a travel book.) There was naturally some retouching as well as some selection of the material, and Forster later said that whereas certain passages quoted in the *Life* but not utilized in the *Notes* possessed the 'freshness of first impressions', other passages incorporated in the published book by Dickens had not been improved by 'rhetorical additions in the printed work' (he instances the description of Niagara). Now that the relevant letters are readily available in the third volume of the Pilgrim edition, it is interesting to read them in conjunction both with the *Notes* and with an artistically more significant portion of the invisible luggage Dickens brought home – the American chapters of *Martin Chuzzlewit*.

The Pilgrim editors suggest that the original title of the work – *American Notes for General Circulation* – is 'a pun on the American monetary situation, with perhaps a secondary reference to the kind of circulation the book could expect, thanks to the lack of an international copyright'.

There have been few critical discussions of *American Notes*, but the introduction to the Penguin edition contains some suggestive observations relating it to Dickens' subsequent work: for example, that 'the trip appears . . . to have given Dickens further insight into the nature of evil. Depths of hypocrisy, malice, duplicity appear to have been unveiled to him'. These depths were soon to be sounded in *Martin Chuzzlewit*, and not only in the American chapters of the novel. See also the substantial introduction to Michael Slater's *Dickens on America and the Americans* (1979) and a useful article by Harry Stone in *PMLA* (1957).

Martin Chuzzlewit

Texts Penguin English Library, ed. P. N. Furbank (1968); Clarendon Dickens, ed. Margaret Cardwell (1982).

Composition Dickens began work on *Martin Chuzzlewit* in November 1842, *American Notes* having appeared in the previous month. He had recently returned from a holiday in Cornwall, and his first notion was to set the opening scene in a lighthouse or on some lonely spot on the Cornish coast; instead, he wrote an introductory chapter in the manner of Fielding with a heavily ironical account of the genealogy of the Chuzzlewits. Dickens' routine, as with his previous serials, was to devote the first two weeks of the month to writing the current instalment, leaving the other two weeks free for correcting the proofs and other tasks. In March 1843 he wrote that he was 'in great health and spirits, and powdering away at Chuzzlewit, with all manner of facetiousness rising up before me as I go on'. But his high spirits did not last, for sales were disappointing (see below). The hero's sudden departure for America, announced at the end of the fifth number, was a response to this situation. Manuscript and corrected proofs (incomplete) in Forster Collection.

Serialization In nineteen monthly parts, from January 1843 to July 1844. Illustrations by Phiz. Division as follows: I (Chs 1–3); II (Chs 4–5); III (Chs 6–8); IV (Chs 9–10); V (Chs 11–12); VI (Chs 13–15); VII (Chs 16–17); VIII (Chs 18–20); IX (Chs 21–3); X (Chs 24–6); XI (Chs 27–9); XII (Chs 30–2); XIII (Chs 33–5); XIV (Chs 36–8); XV (Chs 39–41); XVI (Chs 42–4); XVII (Chs 45–7); XVIII (Chs 48–50); XIX (Chs 51–4). Sales were disappointing, and Dickens wrote to his publishers on 2 March 1843 that he would 'be glad to hear of any improvement in Chuzzlewit'. The monthly circulation of about 20,000 parts compared badly with 40,000–50,000 for *Pickwick* and 100,000 for *The Old Curiosity Shop*, and various explanations of the indifferent sales have been advanced. The success of a novel was influenced by the fortunes of its immediate predecessors, and *Barnaby Rudge* had not been popular, and *American Notes* had provoked many attacks; so that a general waning of Dickens' popularity caused the new novel to suffer accordingly. Moreover, as Robert Patten has said, the opening number was 'slow, uneven, and unfocused'. Professor Patten has also shown that there was in the early 1840s a widespread depression in publishing on both sides of the Atlantic: 'economic depression, social turbulence, political instability, and a flood of cheap publications' hurt most publishers during this period, and Dickens' novel 'could scarcely have come out at a worse time'. Even the device of sending Martin to America failed to increase sales by more than about 2000. Philip Collins has suggested that the moral world of *Chuzzlewit* – 'a world of knaves and fools, destitute of any one quality that could command respect', as the *Westminster Review* put it – was little to the taste of readers. See also Forster's chapter on '*Chuzzlewit* Disappointments', and Ada Nisbet's 'The Mystery of *Martin Chuzzlewit*', in *Essays Critical and Historical, Dedicated to Lily B. Campbell* (Berkeley, 1950).

Publication   Published by Chapman & Hall in one volume in 1844. Dickens wrote a preface for this edition and further prefaces for the 'Cheap Edition' (1849) and the 'Charles Dickens Edition' (1867).

Reception   Although *The Critic* noted in January 1844 that it was 'just now the rage to decry Dickens, by pronouncing his *Chuzzlewit* a failure', the reviewers did not share the widespread lack of appreciation and their verdict was generally favourable. (Professor Collins endorses Forster's summarizing comment that 'It was felt generally to be an advance upon his previous stories.') Tom Pinch was particularly admired.

The title printed on the cover of the first monthly number of *Martin Chuzzlewit* was, as Professor Monod says, 'the longest, most cumbersome, and most jovial [Dickens] had coined so far': *The Life and Adventures of Martin Chuzzlewit, His Relatives, Friends and Enemies, Comprising All his Wills and his Ways: With an Historical Record of what he did, and what he didn't: showing, moreover, Who inherited the Family Plate, Who came in for the Silver Spoons, and Who for the Wooden Ladles, The whole forming a complete Key to the House of Chuzzlewit, edited by 'Boz,' with illustrations by 'Phiz'.* Mercifully this was dropped in favour of *The Life and Adventures of Martin Chuzzlewit*, but the longer title is of interest as indicating that old Martin rather than his grandson and namesake was originally conceived as the central figure.

Philip Collins has said of this novel that 'its place in Dickens's development is crucial', and a paragraph in the 1844 preface suggests that Dickens himself was aware of this;

> I have endeavoured in the progress of this Tale, to resist the temptation of the current Monthly Number, and to keep a steadier eye upon the general purpose and design. With this object in view, I have put a strong constraint upon myself from time to time, in many places; and I hope the story is the better for it, now.

What seems to be implied here is a renunciation of the loose episodic structure of *Pickwick* and *Nickleby* in favour of a more disciplined organization derived from an overall 'purpose and design'. Dickens' device for achieving this was to construct his novel around a dominant central idea, that of selfishness: the 'life and adventures' formula, with its hint of the easy-going picaresque, thus yields place to a story whose main purpose is the expounding of a *moral* theme. Rigorous artistic control over his material and self-restraint did not come to Dickens overnight, however; and *Chuzzlewit* retains many traces of the earlier manner. Professor Monod has drawn attention to its 'extravagant coincidences' and the 'blatant unlikelihood' of some of its incidents; and the dispatching of the hero to America is a famous instance of the adaptability of Dickens' narrative. Monod has further suggested that the ending of the novel is 'probably the most fantastic of all the prize-giving scenes staged by Dickens in his fiction'.

For all its claims to expose and anatomize the vice of selfishness, moreover, *Martin Chuzzlewit* is above all a *comic* novel and Dickens' greatest work in this mode. Such a simple statement, though likely to command general assent, needs immediate qualification, however; for this supreme comic novel also accommodates bitter satire, social comment, murder and melodrama, and the pathos of unrequited love, while one of the novel's two great comic creations is a hypocrite whose egotism is all-consuming and the other is a predatory representative of a barbarous system crying out for reform. Evidently, the comedy of *Martin Chuzzlewit* is not as simple a

matter as the laboured facetiousness of the longer title and the
opening chapter might lead one to suppose.

Steven Marcus, in a stimulating discussion of this novel, has said
that its greatness 'begins in its prose': it is a novel in which 'the
influence of Shakespeare . . . is everywhere to be found', and also of
all Dickens' novels 'the most Joycean, for language itself is one of its
subjects'. Selfishness involves hypocrisy and dissimulation, which
in turn involve the distortion of language: thus Pecksniff and
Mrs Gamp, for instance, 'speak in the language of piety, and
embody the ethos of Bible-reading Protestantism'. Pecksniff, who
'warm[s] his hands before the fire, as benevolently as if they were
somebody else's, not his' (Ch. 3), is a master of illusion in speech and
act; indeed the word 'illusion' is used in connexion with his horse,
who is said to resemble him in many respects, at the beginning of the
fifth chapter. Ch. 8 opens with a splendid passage in which
Pecksniff, starting a coach journey on a winter day, argues that 'it is
always satisfactory to feel, in keen weather, that many other people
are not as warm as you are':

> 'And if we were no better off than anybody else, what would
> become of our sense of gratitude; which,' said Mr Pecksniff with
> tears in his eyes, as he shook his fist at a beggar who wanted to get
> up behind, 'is one of the holiest feelings of our common nature.'

Pecksniff's language creates a situation in which the tears and the
fist-shaking alike seem appropriate; and the Wordsworthian vocabulary encourages us to read this as a parody of Wordsworth's
encounter with the leech-gatherer or the old Cumberland beggar.
Pecksniff pays lip-service to the Christian ideal of benevolence, and
at times Dickens' parody sails dangerously close to the wind – as
when he makes Pecksniff say to old Martin, ' "Bless you for hating
me" ' (Ch. 3). But Pecksniff can cite Scripture for his purpose (see
the opening of Ch. 24), and indeed in his speech touches nothing
that he does not pervert and corrupt, whether it is classical allusion
(' "those fabulous animals (pagan, I regret to say) who used to sing
in the water" ': Ch. 4), Biblical reference (' "We shall go forth tonight by the heavy coach – like the dove of old, my dear Martin –
and it will be a week before we again deposit our olive-branches in
the passage" ': Ch. 6), figurative language (' "And if it comes to pass
that either of us be run over, in any of those busy crossings which
divide the streets of life, the other will convey him to the hospital in

Hope, and sit beside his bed in Bounty!"' Ch. 5), or metrical speech
(' "Some few there are who walk between; who help the needy as
they go; and take no part with either side" ': Ch. 2). The narrator
tells us early in the novel that Pecksniff's enemies 'asserted . . . that
a strong trustfulness in sounds and forms was the master-key to
Mr Pecksniff's character', and this is one of the key-sentences of a
novel that continually sets the power of 'sounds and forms' against
the strength of human realities. In the brilliant scene (Ch. 9) where
Pecksniff gets drunk, 'sounds and forms' still dominate his speech as
he quotes confusedly from his prospectus; but Dickens daringly
shows a genuine salaciousness momentarily breaking the surface as
Pecksniff expressed a wish ' "to see Mrs. Todgers's notion of a
wooden leg" '.

The other great comic creation in this novel is, of course,
Mrs Gamp, and for all the differences she has much in common with
Pecksniff. Notwithstanding the responsibilities of her calling (she
presides over the hazardous business of childbirth and the solemn
business of dying) she is wholly selfish and self-indulgent, and her
closest friend is a convenient invention to enable her to transmit self-
praise. Like Pecksniff, but more extravagantly, she plays havoc with
language, perverting common speech (*rager* for *razor*, *parapidge* for
parapet, etc.) no less than Biblical texts (' "Rich folk may ride on
camels, but it ain't so easy for 'em to see out of a needle's eye" ': Ch.
25). In Mrs Gamp's speech Dickens makes what is perhaps his most
effective use of a highly characteristic feature of style – what George
Orwell, missing the point, stigmatized as 'unnecessary detail' but
what is in its effects most tellingly and memorably comic and
therefore of the essence.

While Pecksniff and Mrs Gamp are illusionists, Tom Pinch is the
victim of an illusion; and there are grounds for regarding Tom as a
more interesting character than young Martin, though critics who
have seen him as the hero of the novel have surely gone too far.
Tom's unrequited but uncomplaining devotion to Mary Graham is
as selfless as Martin's feelings towards her are selfish; and Tom
changes more profoundly in the course of the novel than its
eponymous hero. His change involves the loss of an illusion, and his
discovery of the truth about Pecksniff turns into a larger discovery
about the nature of the world:

He began to think, 'there are more Pecksniffs than one, perhaps,'
. . . An uneasy thought entered Tom's head; a shadowy

misgiving that the altered relations between himself and Pecksniff
were somehow to involve an altered knowledge on his part of
other people, and were to give him an insight into much of which
he had had no previous suspicion. (Chs. 36–7)

Not only does Tom undergo more impressively than Martin the
inner growth and development that we are entitled to expect of a
hero, but we are made aware of his inner life in a way that has no
counterpart in the presentation of Martin. When the latter, in
thanking Tom for his devotion to duty (Ch. 48), mentions Mary's
name, Tom's unexpressed feelings are vividly conveyed. For all the
familiar external oddity of Tom Pinch, there are signs that Dickens
was trying to do something new with this character; further
evidence may be found in Tom's conversation with Ruth Pinch in
Ch. 50, when he tells her that she thinks of him ' "as if I were a
character in a book" '.

Dickens' manuscript contains much evidence of his striving by
means of additions and revisions for comic effect through sharpness
of detail. For example, in Mrs Gamp's recollections of her deceased
husband the reference to 'Guy's Hospital' is added above the line,
and 'long home' was originally 'last home'. As usual, Dickens took
great pains with proper names, and tried out Chubblewig,
Sweezleden, Chuzzletoe, Chuzzleboy, Chuzzlewig, Sweezleback
and Sweezleway, before settling on Chuzzlewit. His note for the
third number includes the interesting phrase 'Old Martin's plot to
degrade and punish Pecksniff in the end' – an indication that this
feature of the plot was long premeditated rather than improvised at
a later stage.

In spite of the disappointing initial sales, this novel became from
the eighteen-fifties onwards one of Dickens' most popular works. In
1847 he wrote a further fragment dealing with Mrs Gamp; it was not
published during his lifetime but was included in Forster's *Life*. On
17 June 1858 he gave the first performance of what was to become a
successful reading, *Mrs Gamp*.

Modern critics have paid less attention to *Chuzzlewit* than to some
of Dickens' later novels, and some of the recent interpretations have
been far-fetched. Dorothy Van Ghent's 'The Dickens World: A
View from Todgers's' (*Sewanee Review*, LVIII, 1950) has been
influential. Barbara Hardy, whose lively essay in *Dickens and the
Twentieth Century*, ed. Gross & Pearson, starts by endorsing the
nineteenth-century view that it is 'a badly organized novel',

observes: 'I can truthfully say that the *Martin Chuzzlewit* of Jack Lindsay . . . Dorothy Van Ghent . . ., and J. Hillis Miller . . . is a novel – or rather, three different novels – which I should like to read'. The novel's serialization is examined by John Butt in *Pope, Dickens and Others* (1969). P. N. Furbank's introduction to the Penguin edition ought not to be overlooked. The discussions by Steven Marcus and Sylvère Monod are referred to above.

CHARACTERS

BAILEY, BENJAMIN (known as 'Young Bailey' and 'Bailey Junior'). An undersized youth who works as boots at Mrs Todgers' boarding-house. He is later employed by Tigg Montague; is shaved, in a brilliant scene of absurdist comedy, by Poll Sweedlepipe (Ch. 29); and is wrongly supposed to be dead (Ch. 49).

BEVAN, MR. Massachusetts doctor visiting New York. Martin meets him in Ch. 17.

BRICK, JEFFERSON. The youthful war correspondent of the New York Rowdy Journal. Martin meets him on arriving in America (Ch. 16); Brick is accompanied on this occasion by his equally juvenile wife.

BULLAMY. Porter at the Anglo-Bengalee Assurance Company.

CHOKE, GENERAL CYRUS. American militia officer, and a member of the Eden Land Corporation. Martin meets him on a train (Ch. 21) and is persuaded to invest in the Eden speculation.

CHOLLOP, MAJOR HANNIBAL. American ruffian, 'a man of roving disposition' who 'in any less advanced community, might have been mistaken for a violent vagabond' (Ch. 33).

CHUFFEY, OLD. Ancient, near-senile clerk to Anthony Chuzzlewit; as Jonas says, he has been 'addling his old brains with figures and book-keeping all his life' (Ch. 11). He denounces Jonas in Ch. 51.

CHUZZLEWIT, ANTHONY. Brother of old Martin Chuzzlewit and father of Jonas. He is a grasping man of business who has a fatal stroke in Ch. 18. His son JONAS marries Mercy Pecksniff after his father's death. He later murders Montague Tigg and on being arrested poisons himself (Ch. 51).

CHUZZLEWIT, MARTIN JUNIOR, his great nephew, is the eponymous hero of the novel. He becomes a pupil of Pecksniff but after a quarrel announces at the end of the fifth number (Ch. 12) that he will ' "go to America!" ' He returns to England in Ch. 35 after much hardship and many disappointments, and eventually marries Mary Graham.

CHUZZLEWIT, MARTIN SENIOR is the brother of Anthony, the grandfather of Martin junior and a cousin of Pecksniff. He is a wealthy old gentleman obsessed by a conviction of man's selfishness (' "Oh self, self, self! At every turn nothing but self!" ': Ch. 3, at the end of the first number); his suspicions are reinforced by the designs of those members of his family who hope to be his heirs (see SLYME, CHEVY; SPOTTLETOE MR).

CICERO. A negro, a former slave who has bought his freedom. Martin and Mark Tapley meet him in New York (Ch. 17) and he is the occasion for Dickens' brief satire on slavery.

CODGER, MISS, *see* TOPPIT, MISS.

CRIMPLE, DAVID. Pawnbroker who becomes Secretary to the Anglo-Bengalee Assurance Company and absconds when the company crashes (Ch. 49).

DIVER, COLONEL. Editor of the New York Rowdy Journal. Martin meets him on arriving in America (Ch. 16).

FIPS, MR. A lawyer (Ch. 39).

FLADDOCK, GENERAL. American militia officer, a passenger on the boat that takes Martin from Liverpool to New York. Martin meets him again in New York (Ch. 17).

GAMP, MRS SARAH. Professional nurse, midwife and layer-out of the dead, and Dickens' greatest comic creation. She is introduced, with a wealth of circumstantial detail, in Ch. 19, when Mr Pecksniff summons her after the death of Anthony Chuzzlewit. She is a widow and lodges in Kingsgate Street, High Holborn, 'at a bird-fancier's, next door but one to the celebrated mutton-pie shop . . . '. Dickens is said to have based her on a real-life nurse described to him by Miss Burdett Coutts.

GRAHAM, MARY. Young lady, companion to old Martin Chuzzlewit. She is loved by his grandson, young Martin, and also by Tom Pinch.

HARRIS, MRS. Alleged friend of Mrs Gamp, often alluded to and quoted by her but actually non-existent.

HOMINY, MRS. American lady, 'a philosopher and an authoress' and a member of 'one of our most aristocratic families'. Martin meets her in Chs 22 and 34. She is the occasion for some of Dickens' satire directed at the oddities of American English.

JINKINS, MR. One of the boarders at Mrs Todgers' establishment.

JOBLING, DR JOHN. Medical officer to the Anglo-Bengalee Assurance Company (Ch. 27).

KEDGICK, CAPTAIN. Landlord of the National Hotel, where Martin stays (Ch. 22) en route from New York to Eden.

KETTLE, LAFAYETTE. Boastful and jingoistic American whom Martin meets on a train (Ch. 21).

LEWSOME, MR. Assistant to a doctor; he tells of Jonas Chuzzlewit's part in the death of Anthony Chuzzlewit (Ch. 48).

LUPIN, MRS. A widow and landlady of the Blue Dragon inn in the Wiltshire village where Pecksniff lives: 'broad, buxom, comfortable, and good-looking' (Ch. 3), she later marries Mark Tapley.

MODDLE, AUGUSTUS. Boarder (the 'youngest gentleman') at Mrs Todgers' establishment. He is engaged to Charity Pecksniff but deserts her at the last moment (Ch. 54).

MONTAGUE, TIGG, see TIGG, MONTAGUE.

MOULD, MR. Undertaker called in when Anthony Chuzzlewit dies. He is well known professionally to Mrs Gamp and is the occasion for Dickens' satire on the ostentatious pomp and commercialism of Victorian funeral customs (see Ch. 19).

NADGETT, MR. Inquiry agent employed by Tigg Montague (Ch. 38).

NORRIS FAMILY. Martin meets them in New York (Ch. 17) and discovers that they have a passionate interest in the British aristocracy.

PAWKINS, MRS. Owner of a New York boarding-house where Martin stays (Ch. 16).

PECKSNIFF, SETH. Architect living in 'a little Wiltshire village' near Salisbury; he receives Martin as a pupil. Pecksniff is Dickens' portrait of an unctuous hypocrite, and one of his greatest comic creations. He was partly based on S. C. Hall, philanthropist and author. Pecksniff is exposed, denounced and struck down by old Martin in Ch. 52. His elder daughter CHARITY (Cherry) hopes to marry Augustus Moddle but he flees to Australia at the last moment. Her sister MERCY (Merry) marries Jonas Chuzzlewit and is made unhappy by him.

PINCH, TOM. Assistant to Pecksniff, 'an ungainly, awkward-looking man, extremely short-sighted and prematurely bald' (Ch. 2). Unworldly and credulous, and a kind of saintly fool, he is at first deceived by Pecksniff's pretensions; but is later sent away by Pecksniff (Ch. 31) and comes to realize the truth. He plays the organ and entertains an unrequited love for Mary Graham. His sister RUTH is a quiet and modest girl who is 'governess in a . . . lofty family' in Camberwell. She eventually marries John Westlock.

PIP, MR. 'Theatrical man' and an acquaintance of Montague Tigg.

POGRAM, HON. ELIJAH. Member of the US Congress. Martin meets him in Ch. 33.

PRIG, BETSEY. Nurse and friend of Mrs Gamp. She appears in Ch. 25, and they quarrel in Ch. 49.

SCADDER, ZEPHANIAH. Agent of the Eden Land Corporation, through whom Martin invests in that fraudulent enterprise (Ch. 21).

SLYME, CHEVY. Self-seeking relative of old Martin (see Ch. 4). He later becomes an ally of the confidence trickster Tigg Montague.

SPOTTLETOE, MR. One of a group of self-seeking relatives of old Martin (see Ch. 4).

SWEEDLEPIPE, PAUL (Poll). Barber, bird-fancier and landlord of Mrs Gamp. He is introduced in Ch. 26 and shaves Young Bailey in Ch. 29.

TAPLEY, MARK. Young man employed as an ostler at the Blue Dragon. He becomes a manservant to Martin Chuzzlewit and accompanies him to America, the relationship following the picaresque tradition and paralleling such eighteenth-century instances known to Dickens as Tom Jones and Partridge and Roderick Random and Strap. Mark is obstinately cheerful under every adversity. He eventually marries his former employer, Mrs Lupin.

TIGG, MONTAGUE (alias Tigg Montague). Friend of Chevy Slyme and himself a confidence trickster. He becomes Chairman of the fraudulent Anglo-Bengalee Assurance Company, and is later murdered by Jonas Chuzzlewit.

TODGERS, MRS. Keeper of a 'Commercial Boarding-House', 'a very dingy edifice' situated 'near the Monument' in London. The Pecksniffs stay there (Chs 8–9), and Young Bailey is employed there as a boots.

TOPPIT, MISS. She and MISS CODGER are 'two literary ladies' whom Martin meets in Ch. 34 and who represent Dickens' satire on Emersonian Transcendentalism ('"Howls the sublime . . ."').

WESTLOCK, JOHN. Former pupil of Mr Pecksniff and friend of Tom Pinch. He later marries Ruth Pinch.

WOLF, MR. Journalist and acquaintance of Montague Tigg (Ch. 28).

Pictures from Italy

Dickens' second travel book aroused less interest than his first, and it is not a work that many who have once read it will be impatient to re-read. It was the outcome of his sojourn and his extensive travels in Italy in 1844–5 – experiences that were to be drawn upon more memorably in the next decade in the Italian scenes of *Little Dorrit*. Before leaving Genoa in June 1945 Dickens was already entertaining the notion of another travel book. *American Notes* had been partly based on the journal-letters written to Forster, and during his time in Italy Dickens had been sending to England material of the same kind; but he was puzzled as to how best they could be shaped into a book – as he told Forster on 7 June 1845, 'I cannot for the life of me devise any plan of using them to my own satisfaction, and yet think entirely with you that in some form I ought to use them.'

Once written, he used part of his material in a series of articles in the *Daily News* from 21 January to 11 March 1846, under the title 'Travelling Letters – Written on the Road'. The volume was published by Bradbury and Evans in May. The choice of an illustrator had given Dickens some trouble: his original arrangement with Clarkson Stanfield fell through (perhaps, it has been suggested, because the Catholic Stanfield was offended by Dickens' anti-Catholicism: see David Paroissien's article in *Dickensian*, LXVII, 1971), and an unknown artist named Samuel Palmer – later to become one of the greatest of nineteenth-century English painters – was engaged.

The book sold respectably but was largely ignored by reviewers: as Philip Collins notes, 'none of the heavies reviewed it except the *Dublin Review*, which predictably was offended by Dickens's attitude to Roman Catholicism'. *The Times* was highly unfavourable: 'There is nothing new in the book from beginning to end . . . . Had John Jones been its author it would never have been heard of.' Such a verdict is not entirely fair, however, for there are some unmistakably

Dickensian touches in the book. Dickens' 'clutching eye' (as Macready called it) spotted the loungers in an apothecary's shop in Genoa: 'so still and quiet, that either you don't see them in the darkened shop, or mistake them – as I did one ghostly man in bottle-green, one day, with a hat like a stopper – for Horse Medicine' – where the punning reference to 'bottle-green' and the surrealistic vision of a man transformed into a bottle are entirely characteristic. Again, in Verona Dickens records an encounter with a lady who 'at least resembled the Capulets in the one particular of being very great indeed in the "Family" way' – a joke that would surely not have been admitted into his fiction. Particularly striking is the description of the mummy of San Carlo Borromeo dressed in pontifical robes and laden with jewels that Dickens saw in Milan:

> The shrunken heap of poor earth in the midst of this great glitter, is more pitiful than if it lay upon a dunghill. There is not a ray of imprisoned light in all the flash and fire of jewels, but seems to mock the dusty holes where eyes were, once. Every thread of silk in the rich vestments seems only a provision from the worms that spin, for the behoof of worms that propagate in sepulchres.

There is a good modern edition of *Pictures from Italy* by David Paroissien (1973).

Dombey and Son

Texts   Penguin English Library, ed. Raymond Williams (1970); Clarendon Dickens, ed. Alan Horsman (1974).

Composition   On 30 January 1846 Dickens wrote to Forster of his plan for 'going abroad to write a new book in shilling numbers'. His last novel, *Martin Chuzzlewit*, had been completed in July 1844, so that a new one was certainly due; and Alan Horsman has shown that the plan of writing a novel during a period spent abroad had originated as early as 1843. On 2 March 1846 Dickens wrote that 'Vague thoughts of a new book are rife within me just now; and I go wandering about at night into the strangest places, according to my usual propensity at such a time, seeking rest, and finding none.' A month later he refers again to the notion of going abroad. On 18 April his publishers announced 'A NEW ENGLISH STORY, by Mr Dickens', and on 18 May the first number was promised for October. The title was announced at the end of August – this in spite of Dickens' earlier insistence on secrecy ('The very name getting out, would be ruinous'); though, as Butt and Tillotson point out, 'The title kept a bigger secret than it disclosed.' Meanwhile, Dickens had left England with his family on 31 May and had settled at the Villa Rosemont in Lausanne. On 27 June he had written the opening of the new book, 'a plunge straight over head and ears into the story'. The manuscript shows that the opening number was 'written with remarkable fluency' (Horsman); later portions, however, show heavy revision. Manuscript and corrected proofs in the Forster Collection.

Serialization   Nineteen monthly parts, in the by now familiar green paper covers, published from October 1846 until April 1848. Illustrations by Phiz. Division as follows: I (Chs 1–4); II (Chs 5–7); III (Chs 8–10); IV (Chs 11–13); V (Chs 14–16); VI (Chs 17–19);

VII (Chs 20–2); VIII (Chs 23–5); IX (Chs (26–8); X (Chs 29–31);
XI (Chs 32–4); XII (Chs 35–8); XIII (Chs 39–41); XIV (Chs 42–
5); XV (Chs 46–8); XVI (Chs 49–51); XVII (Chs 52–4); XVIII
(Chs 55–7); XIX–XX (Chs 58–62). The first number was a great
success: Robert Patten has shown that the first printing of 25,000
was sold out within hours, successive reprintings were called for, and
the printers put in 'at least ninety hours of overtime' on this part
alone. Dickens wrote gleefully to Forster on 11 October that 'The
Dombey sale is BRILLIANT!' The sales of the next few numbers
held up well, and for the third and fourth the press-run was 32,000.
After the death of little Paul in the fifth number, it was raised to
33,000. After a slight decline later, it touched 33,000 again after
Edith's dramtic flight, and rose even higher before the end. The
success of the early numbers of *Dombey* marked a turning-point in
Dickens' financial position and brought him an economic security
he had never known before. His total profits on the serial were in
excess of £9000. Patten makes a telling comparison with
Thackeray's sales and profits on *Vanity Fair*, which was running
almost simultaneously in a similar format: a sale of fewer than 5000
copies per number, and a payment of a mere £60 per number. For
Thackeray's own comment on their rivalry, see in Chapter 'The
Dickens Circle'.

Publication   Published in one volume by Bradbury & Evans on 12
April 1848. Dickens added a short preface and a dedication to the
Marchioness of Normanby. He wrote another preface for the Cheap
Edition of 1858.

Reception   A common view was that there was some falling off of
interest after the fifth number, in which Paul dies. The reaction is
anticipated by Lord Jeffrey's comments in a letter to Dickens (31
January 1847), where, after some extravagant praise ('Oh, my dear
Dickens! what a No. 5 you have now given us! I have so cried and
sobbed over it last night, and again this morning . . . '), he asks:
'But after reaching this climax in the fifth number, what are you to
do with the fifteen that are to follow?' To the impact of the opening
numbers there is ample testimony, and Jeffrey was not the only
distinguished reader to be deeply moved: Macaulay wept 'as if my
heart would break' over the plight of Florence in the opening
number; Thackeray exclaimed, on reading the fifth, that 'There's
no writing against such power as this!'; and another commentator

declared that Paul's death 'flung a whole nation into mourning' (a hyperbole echoed by the well-known critic David Masson in 1859: 'It is scarcely an exaggeration to say that the death of Little Dombey caused a national mourning'). Some reviewers complained of Dickens' 'fine writing' and found the symbolism of river and sea overdone. One or two found Paul unconvincingly precocious. On the other hand, the satire directed at Dr Blimber's educational methods was often praised.

According to Forster, Dickens told him at a very early stage in the genesis of *Dombey and Son* that 'it was to do with Pride what its predecessor had done with Selfishness'. It is thus a logical successor to *Martin Chuzzlewit*; on the other hand a common (though not unanimous) verdict is that it represents a marked advance on the earlier novel in design and construction. Kathleen Tillotson describes it as 'the earliest example [in Dickens' work] of responsible and successful planning; it has unity not only of action, but of design and feeling'; and F. R. Leavis goes even further in designating it 'the first major novel': it 'marks a decisive moment in Dickens's career; he offered it as a providently conceived whole, presenting a major theme, and it was his first essay in the elaborately plotted Victorian novel'. It is true that there is in *Dombey* no evidence of the open-ended planning that permitted Dickens to dispatch Martin to America; but Alan Horsman has sensibly reminded us that the contrast between the two novels ought not be exaggerated. Dickens had, after all, had 'old Martin's plot to degrade and punish Pecksniff' in mind as early as the third number; contrariwise, he announced his resolve to conduct the story of *Dombey* 'through all the branches and offshots and meanderings that come up', and foresaw 'an opportunity for good scenes between Captain Cuttle and Miss Tox' – a hint of self-indulgence, and of indulgence of his readers, since such scenes would hardly be essential to his central theme.

Kathleen Tillotson is right, however, in pointing out that 'the comedy is in lower relief and is subordinated to the design of the whole'; she adds that 'Not only the comedy, but all the characters and all the action are subordinated to Mr Dombey.' Dickens himself wrote in the 1858 preface that 'an obstinate nature exists in a perpetual struggle with itself', and that 'Mr Dombey undergoes no violent change . . . . A sense of his injustice is within him, all along.' Such psychological complexity is new in Dickens' work: 'In

Mr Dombey Dickens achieves the remarkable feat of making us aware of the hidden depths of a character, while keeping them largely hidden' (Kathleen Tillotson); 'the theme is the opposition of pride and love, with Mr Dombey as the meeting-point. The novel is thus to be a new departure for Dickens – a novel founded upon a relation, and upon a character's inner conflict' (Butt and Tillotson).

Another noteworthy feature of the novel is its contemporaneity. To quote Kathleen Tillotson again, it is the first of Dickens' novels in which 'a pervasive uneasiness about contemporary society takes the place of an intermittent concern with specific social wrongs'; in other words, Dickens is now preoccupied not with the Poor Law, or with boarding-schools, but with the changing nature of English life in its physical, social and moral aspects – a preoccupation that was to develop and deepen in the great 'dark' novels of his later period. The most powerful symbol of change in the novel is the railway – transforming the landscape, uprooting people from their homes, modifying the rhythms of life, and ultimately slaying the villain.

Kathleen Tillotson finds the prevailing mood of this novel one of 'deep disquiet about contemporary values': it 'suggests the gloom of wealth . . . and its capacity to petrify or poison human relations, in the family and in society'. Mr Dombey is a man whose springs of feeling are frozen at the source – the metaphor being Dickens' own and brilliantly developed in, for example, the episode of little Paul's christening. (Dickens' use of the recurring symbol, which no doubt owes much to his awareness of the 'iterative imagery' of Shakespeare's tragedies, was one of the ways in which he solved the problem of imposing unity on a very long, diverse and complex work, and is one of his major contributions to the art of fiction.) It is of course no accident that Mr Dombey is a business man, for the Dickensian diagnosis sees the growing materialism of an expanding industrial and commercial society as the enemy of human brotherhood and, in a Wordsworthian sense, the natural instincts. Nor is it irrelevant that his manager Carker, the villain of the piece, should be a representative (as Kathleen Tillotson says) of the managerial revolution, a 'new man' as firmly enclosed in his egotism, ambition and sensuality as Dombey is in his pride. Against the world of business (the firm that is indicated by one of the meanings of the novel's ambiguous title) stands the world of the Wooden Midshipman, another business indeed, but archaic, unaggressive, and hopelessly ineffective in the competitive world of the 1840s. The

power of wealth to destroy human sensibilities and human relationships has no place in the world of *Pickwick*, where the hero's solution
to most human ills is to distribute half-crowns and the mercenary
motives of Jingle are a good-natured joke. There are hints of this
theme in *The Old Curiosity Shop* and *Martin Chuzzlewit*, but in *Dombey*
it is a central concern of the novel; and it remains of the first
importance in Dickens' work through the later masterpieces (*Little
Dorrit, Great Expectations*) up to and including *Our Mutual Friend*
nearly twenty years later.

The title, concealing the importance of Florence, is a trick: that
Dickens was anxious not to show his hand too quickly is indicated by
his second thoughts in the edition of 1859 (the Library edition),
where he removed the final words of the fifth number, in which
Miss Tox exclaims after Paul's death, ' "To think . . . that Dombey
and Son should be a Daughter after all!" '. Exceptionally, Dickens
seems not to have tried out alternative titles for this novel but to
have hit on the final one right away; and it is indeed highly
felicitous, with its artful concealment of Paul's death and its ironical
allusion to the true subject of the book, which is (as Kathleen
Tillotson says) Dombey and Daughter. Florence's passivity does not
make her a very dramatic heroine; like Fanny Price in *Mansfield
Park* her role is mainly one of silent suffering. But she represents the
strength of love, as other quiet heroines (Amy Dorrit, Lizzie
Hexam) were later to do. Edith Dombey, in any case, offers drama
enough and to spare: 'Not a tragic heroine, but a tragedy queen' is
Kathleen Tillotson's verdict, and it points appropriately to Edith's
relationship to Victorian melodrama. Edith belongs to another line
of Dickensian women characters: the cold, haughty, self-destructive
figures incapable of love (Lady Dedlock, Louisa Bounderby,
Miss Wade, Estella – not, of course, all cast in precisely the same
mould, but showing significant similarities).

It is tempting to see Paul Dombey as Dickens' endeavour to
repeat, in a masculine variation, his earlier success with Little Nell.
But it has to be added that Paul – in, for example, his conversations
with Mrs Pipchin and his schooldays at Dr Blimber's – is a good deal
closer to being an acceptable realistic portrait of a young child; and
although there is undeniably some sentimentality in his presentation there is also humour, charm and observation. Dickens'
reading 'The Story of Little Dombey' was understandably popular.

The portrayal of Carker has genuine power and in one respect at
least represents a considerable achievement on Dickens part:

without offending Mrs Grundy, he has managed to suggest Carker's concealed sexuality and even to indicate, without actually saying it in so many words, that his luxurious suburban home contains pornographic paintings and books. Carker's ruthless, predatory nature is conveyed through recurring images drawn from the feline species: he waits like a cat at a mouse-hole, his smile is the smile on the face of the tiger, and when he is killed the dogs sniff at his blood. The flexibility of Dickens' art is shown by comparing Carker with Bagstock: the Major is one of Dickens' most brilliant grotesques, a figure of caricature rather than social realism, but he shares Carker's sensuality (even his name looks like a double sexual pun) as well as his egotistical aggressiveness, and again he is partly described through animal imagery (his digestive processes are compared to those of a snake). Among the other lesser characters, a special word must be said for Mrs Skewton, Edith's mother and another grotesque: as a merciless, almost Swiftian satire on the artificiality of the 'polite' world, she is the medium of an attack on debased romantic notions that is to be repeated in Mrs Merdle (*Little Dorrit*).

Dombey and Son has provoked some excellent criticism. Kathleen Tillotson's essay in her *Novels of the Eighteen-Forties* (1954) and the essay in Butt and Tillotson's *Dickens at Work* are referred to above, as is F. R. Leavis's essay in *Dickens the Novelist*. Other important discussions include those by John Lucas (in *Tradition and Tolerance in Nineteenth-Century Fiction*, ed. David Howard *et al.*, 1966), Denis Donoghue (*Nineteenth-Century Fiction*, 1970), Julian Moynahan (in *Dickens and the Twentieth Century*, ed. Gross and Pearson), and Raymond Williams (introduction to the Penguin edition). Paul Herring has discussed Dickens' number-plans for this novel (*Modern Philology*, 1970). A recent study is the dauntingly titled *Interpreting Interpreting: Interpreting Dickens's Dombey* (1979), by S. R. Horton.

CHARACTERS

BAGSTOCK, MAJOR JOSEPH (Joe). 'A wooden-featured, blue-faced, Major, with his eyes starting out of his head' (Ch. 7); he is a choleric bachelor who tyrannizes his NATIVE SERVANT ('The Native, who had no particular name, but answered to any vituperative epithet': Ch. 20). He becomes a friend of Mr Dombey.

BAPS, MR. Dancing-master at Dr Blimber's school.

BERRY, MISS, *see* PIPCHIN, MRS.

BITHERSTONE, MASTER. Pupil at Mrs Pipchin's school at Brighton.

BLIMBER, DR. Headmaster of a school at Brighton to which Paul Dombey is sent, 'a great hothouse, in which there was a forcing apparatus incessantly at work' (Ch. 11) – Dickens' satire on a narrowly academic system of education and the classical curriculum in particular. MISS CORNELIA BLIMBER, his daughter, is a teacher at the school, 'dry and sandy with working in the graves of deceased languages' (Ch. 11). MRS BLIMBER also appears.

BLOCKITT, MRS. Nurse present at the birth of Paul Dombey (Ch. 1).

BRIGGS. Pupil at Dr Blimber's school.

BROGLEY. 'Sworn broker and appraiser' (Ch. 9); he keeps a second-hand furniture shop and takes possession of Sol Gills' property when the latter cannot meet a debt.

BROWN, GOOD MRS. Hideous old woman who abducts Florence and steals her clothes (Ch. 6). She later encounters Edith Granger and Carker, and offers to tell their fortunes (Ch. 27). Her daughter is Alice Marwood (see below).

BUNSBY, JACK. Old sailor, friend and adviser of Captain Cuttle (see Ch. 23). Bluff and taciturn, he later unwillingly marries the redoubtable Mrs MacStinger.

CARKER, MR JAMES. Manager of Mr Dombey's offices in the City of London. He is described in Ch. 13 ('thirty-eight or forty years old'); an ambitious, sensual, ruthless man and a patient plotter. His house is described in Ch. 33. He is employed by Mr Dombey to rebuke Edith for her failings as a wife (Ch. 45). When she flees from her home he follows her to France; at a Dijon inn she rejects him; he is pursued by Mr Dombey and is killed by an express train (Ch. 55). His elder brother JOHN (known in the firm as 'the junior' on account of his inferior position) is a clerk in Mr Dombey's employ. He is a white-haired and broken man constantly humiliated by his brother and taunted with his disgrace (he has been detected as an embezzler many years earlier: see Ch. 13). Their sister HARRIET lives with John; their home is described in Ch. 33.

CHICK, MRS LOUISA. Sister of Mr Dombey. She appears in the opening chapter of the novel, and her husband, Mr John Chick, is introduced in Ch. 2.

CUTTLE, CAPTAIN EDWARD (Ned). Friend of Sol Gills, introduced in Chapter 4. He has 'a hook instead of a hand attached to his right wrist'. The soul of goodness, he is a kind of fairy godfather to Walter Gay and Florence Dombey.

DIOGENES (DI). Dog, a pet of the Dombey family; Paul becomes fond of him (Ch. 14) and after Paul's death he comforts Florence (Ch. 18). On the last page of the novel he is referred to again ('an old dog is generally in their company') – a statement added in Forster's handwriting to Dickens' manuscript.

DOMBEY, MR PAUL. 'About eight-and-forty years of age' when the story opens, he is a wealthy merchant who sets all his hopes on his son, little PAUL, who dies young. He is uniformly cold towards his daughter FLORENCE. His second marriage, to Edith Granger, is a failure. His business collapses (Ch. 58); a broken man, he is reunited with Florence. His first wife, FANNY, dies in the opening chapter of the novel in giving birth to little Paul, who goes to school at Brighton (first at Mrs Pipchin's, then at Dr Blimber's), suffers from a lingering illness, and dies (Ch. 16). Florence (Floy) is six years old when the story opens, and becomes a great favourite of her brother but is shunned by her father. She flees from his home (Ch. 47) and takes refuge with Captain Cuttle. She promises to marry Walter Gay (Ch. 50); after their marriage they go on a voyage to China and her child is born on the way home. She returns to her father (Ch. 59) to take care of him in his old age. On EDITH DOMBEY, *see* GRANGER, EDITH.

FEEDER, MR ('Mr Feeder, B.A.'). Dr Blimber's assistant. He later marries Cornelia Blimber.

FEENIX, COUSIN. Elderly clubman, a relative of Edith Dombey resident at Baden-Baden. He attends her wedding (Ch. 31). See also Edith Granger.

FLOWERS. Maid to Mrs Skewton. Like that of Withers, the name has a symbolic appropriateness.

GAME CHICKEN, THE. Professional boxer who gives lessons to Toots.

GAY, WALTER. Nephew of Sol Gills; he is fourteen years old when first introduced (Ch. 4). He is employed in Mr. Dombey's office, falls in love with Florence, is sent to Barbados by Mr Dombey on the ship *Son and Heir* (Ch. 12), and is presumed drowned when the ship is reported lost (Ch. 26). He reappears (Ch. 49) and later marries Florence. Dickens' original notion was to show Walter going to the bad ('gradually and naturally trailing away . . . into negligence, idleness, dissipation, dishonesty, and ruin', as he told Forster); it appears to have been Forster who discouraged this plan.

GILLS, SOLOMON (Sol). Ships' instrument maker, friend of Captain Cuttle, and uncle of Walter Gay. He goes away in mysterious circumstances (Ch. 25); after a long absence in search of his nephew Walter, he returns home and they are reunited (Ch. 56).

GLUBB. Old Brighton fisherman who pushes Paul's carriage on the beach during his illness and entertains him with stories of the sea.

GRANGER, EDITH (later EDITH DOMBEY). Young widow introduced in Ch. 21, 'very handsome, very haughty'. She becomes the second Mrs Dombey and befriends Florence (Ch. 28). Her relationship with her husband, never very cordial, rapidly deteriorates; and when he refuses her request for a separation she runs away. After fleeing to Dijon with Carker she scornfully rejects him (Ch. 54: see Phiz's 'Mr Carker in his hour of triumph'). She later returns and is briefly reunited with Florence (Ch. 61) before going off to permanent exile in Italy with Cousin Feenix. Her mother is Mrs Skewton.

HOWLER, REV. MELCHISEDECH. Preacher 'of the Ranting persuasion'. Mrs MacStinger attends his meetings.

MACSTINGER, MRS. Captain Cuttle's landlady, a virago who later marries Mr Bunsby very much against his wishes.

MARWOOD, ALICE. Daughter of Good Mrs Brown; she is introduced in Ch. 34. An abandoned woman and an ex-criminal, she receives charity from Harriet Carker (Ch. 33) but rejects it on learning who Harriet is. It later turns out that Alice has been seduced and set on the road to ruin by Mr Carker. She dies in Ch. 58. Her fate is clearly intended to be seen in relation to that of Edith Granger; the title of Ch. 34, 'Another Mother and Daughter', stresses the parallel. Alice, Edith, and their two mothers all meet in Ch. 40 (see Phiz's illustration 'A Chance Meeting').

MIFF, MRS. 'Wheezy little pew-opener' at the church where Mr Dombey and Edith are married (Ch. 31). She is also present at the wedding of Florence and Walter (Ch. 57).

MORFIN, MR. Employed at Mr Dombey's office; he helps to expose Carker's villainy and to rescue the honour of John Carker: see Ch. 53. He marries Harriet Carker.

NIPPER, SUSAN ('Spitfire'). Servant in Mr Dombey's household; she is in charge of Florence during her childhood and later becomes her maid. Her manner is 'so desperately sharp and biting that she seemed to make one's eyes water' (Ch. 3). She is fiercely loyal and loving towards Florence and is dismissed for defending her to her father (Ch. 44), but later is reunited with Florence. She marries Mr Toots.

PANKEY, MISS. Pupil at Mrs Pipchin's school.

PEPS, DR PARKER. Fashionable doctor ('one of the Court

Physicians') in attendance at the birth of little Paul (Ch. 1).

PERCH. Messenger at Mr Dombey's offices in the City.

PILKINS, DR. 'Family practitioner' in attendance at the birth of little Paul (Ch. 1).

PIPCHIN, MRS. Ugly and elderly lady, an 'ogress and child-queller' (Ch. 8), who keeps a dame's school at Brighton to which little Paul Dombey is sent. On her prototype, see p. 44. See also Phiz's fine illustration, 'Paul and Mrs Pipchin'. Her niece Berinthia (Miss Berry) assists on the domestic side. Mrs. Pipchin is later employed by Mr Dombey as a housekeeper.

SKETTLES, SIR BARNET. An MP. His son becomes a fellow-pupil of little Paul at Dr Bimber's school.

SKEWTON, MRS. ('Cleopatra'). Mother of the young widow Edith Granger (later Edith Dombey). Grotesquely affected in her pretence of eternal youth (her nickname is derived from the Shakespearean phrase, 'Age cannot wither her'). She is stricken with paralysis (Ch. 37) and soon dies (Ch. 41).

SOWNDS, MR. Beadle present at Mr Dombey's wedding (Ch. 31).

TOODLES, MR. Stoker of a steam engine; he lives at Staggs's Gardens with his wife POLLY, who becomes wet-nurse to little Paul (during her employment Mr Dombey insists that she be known as Richards: see Ch. 2). Mr Toodles meets Mr Dombey at the railway station (Ch. 20). Their eldest son ROBIN (also known as Rob and Biler) is nominated by Mr Dombey to a place at the Charitable Grinders' School; he gets into bad company there and deteriorates sadly; Mr Carker arranges for him to work at Sol Gills's shop as a spy on Florence's visits there.

TOOTS. Head boy at Dr Blimber's school, simple-minded but amiable and loyal. On leaving school he moves in sporting circles and aspires to the hand of Florence. He is much preoccupied by sartorial matters (his tailor, as he is fond of telling people, is Burgess and Co.). He later marries Susan Nipper.

TOX, MISS LUCRETIA. Friend of Mrs Chick. She is described in Ch. 1 and lives at Princess's Place (described in Ch. 7). She has unsuccessful matrimonial designs on Mr Dombey and Major Bagstock; her name seems to be a humorous allusion to Shakespeare's Lucrece.

TOZER. Pupil at Mr Blimber's school.

WITHERS. Page to Mrs Skewton, employed to push her wheelchair. His name is appropriate to his employer's faded charms.

David Copperfield

Text Penguin English Library, ed. Trevor Blount (1966); Clarendon Dickens, ed. Nina Burgis (1981).

Composition Begun February 1849, finished October 1850. From 23 to 28 February Dickens was trying out titles and names (see below) — for him an indispensable preliminary to the business of writing. Progress at first was slow: with the first number due on 1 May, he confessed on 19 April that 'My hand is out in the matter of Copperfield. Today and yesterday I have done nothing. Though I know what I want to do, I am lumbering on like a stage-wagon .... I am quite aground ... and the long Copperfieldian perspective looks snowy and thick, this fine morning.' Soon, however, his writing gathered momentum: halfway through the third number, he told Forster (6 June) that he felt 'quite confident in the story'; and by 17 November he was able to tell him, 'I am wonderfully in harness, and nothing galls or frets.' Some of the later portions were written very rapidly — Chs 23–4, for instance, within four days. Manuscript and corrected proofs in Forster Collection.

Serialization 19 monthly numbers, from May 1849 to November 1850. Illustrations by Phiz. The opening number sold about 25,000; thereafter sales dropped slightly. Division as follows: I (Chs 1–3); II (Chs 4–6); III (Chs 7–9); IV (Chs 10–12); V (Chs 13–15); VI (Chs 16–18); VII (Chs 19–21); VIII (Chs 22–4); IX (Chs 25–7); X (Chs 28–31); XI (Chs 32–4); XII (Chs 35–7); XIII (Chs 38–40); XIV (Chs 41–3); XV (Chs 44–6); XVI (Chs 47–50); XVII (Chs 51–3); XVIII (Chs 54–7); XIX–XX (Chs 58–64).

Publication Published in one volume by Bradbury & Evans in 1850. Preface and dedication to the Hon. Mr and Mrs Richard

Watson added. New preface written for the Cheap Edition (1858) and revised for the Charles Dickens Edition (1867).

Reception   DC was warmly admired by many readers from the first number onwards; its humour and sentiment made a strong appeal, and it quickly came to be regarded as Dickens' masterpiece. His rival Thackeray was generous in his praise, and even Matthew Arnold, who normally had little time for novels, later expressed a high regard for it: 'What treasures of gaiety, invention, life, are in that book! what alertness and resource! what a soul of good nature and kindness governing the whole!' (1881). The storm scene was especially admired – by, among others, Tolstoy.

Dickens said in the 1867 preface that this was his 'favourite child'; it is also his most autobiographical novel. In 1847, in response to an enquiry from Forster about his early life, Dickens had written an autobiographical fragment (printed for the first time in the second chapter of Forster's biography) that is of the greatest interest and that showed Dickens, as he neared forty, turning to memories that would be heavily drawn on in the novel. In January 1849 Dickens toured Norfolk, visiting Great Yarmouth and talking to fishermen there. He told Forster that 'Yarmouth . . . is the strangest place in the wide world . . . . I shall certainly try my hand at it', and within a few weeks he was creating the Peggotty family.

This is Dickens' only full-length novel narrated throughout in the first person, a point of view he had tried but quickly abandoned in *Master Humphrey's Clock*. (As a weekly serial, *Great Expectations* is much shorter.) It was Forster who proposed 'that he should write it in the first person, by way of change', but it is possible that the popularity of Charlotte Brontë's *Jane Eyre* (published in October 1847 and quickly reprinted) may also have contributed to Dickens' decision.

Names and titles were always important for Dickens, and he seems to have taken peculiar pains over this novel. Towards the end of February 1849 he wrote to Forster of 'My mind running, like a high sea, on names – not satisfied yet, though' (the sea-image is striking in view of both the recent visit to Yarmouth and the novel he eventually wrote). It seems that he could not proceed with the writing until a suitable title was found, and the manuscript contains many draft title-pages. Some earlier notions were: *Mag's Diversions, The Copperfield Disclosures, The Copperfield Records, The Copperfield*

David Copperfield 159

Survey of the World as It Rolled, and *Copperfield Complete.* The final title has an eighteenth-century fullness: *The Personal History, Experience, and Observations of David Copperfield the Younger, of Blunderstone Rookery, which he never meant to be published on any account.* The hero's name also underwent numerous transmogrifications before reaching its familar form: a sheet of paper in Dickens' hand includes such possibilities as Wellbury, Flowerbury, Magbury, Copperboy, Topflower and Copperstone. Having decided on David Copperfield, 'Dickens was much startled when Forster pointed out to him that the initials were his own reversed, and exclaimed that it was "just in keeping with the fates and chances that were always befalling him. 'Why else,' he said, 'should I so obstinately have kept to that name when once it turned up?' " ' (Johnson).

The novel begins with the hero's birth and thereafter moves forward steadily in time; but it is also concerned with the past, with memory and the uncovering of buried experiences. This double movement, at once forwards and backwards, gives the narrative much of its richness of texture and is signalled at the outset: David is 'a posthumous child'; the first page mentions his birth, but also refers to 'ghosts and spirits'; the first chapter is titled 'I am born', but ends with a vivid picture of a grave. David's father, dead before the narrative opens, is frequently mentioned; and in the oppressively feminine Copperfield household there is a sense of something missing (reinforced by the references to a rookery without rooks, a kennel without a dog). With the advent of the Murdstones (one of Dickens' many symbolic names), the gap is filled, and the first number ends with David's discovery that 'the empty dog-kennel was filled up with a great dog' which 'sprang out to get at me'. In *Dombey and Son* a little earlier Dickens had conveyed with great power a sense of sexuality, rampant or covert, in the figures of Bagstock and Carker; now he does it with Murdstone, in whose nature there is also a strong flavour of sadism ('I am certain he had a delight in that formal parade of executing justice' as he takes David to his room to be beaten in Ch. 4). David's mother in her foolish affection and 'her pettish wilful manner' anticipates both Dora a little later in the novel and some of Dickens' later heroines: the second epithet in the last phrase quoted, indeed, is a verbal anticipation of Bella Wilfer in *Our Mutual Friend.* Clara Peggotty's domesticity, efficiency and undemanding loyalty are, as it were, the Georgina Hogarth to Clara Copperfield's Kate Dickens, and the curious and striking detail of the two women in David's early life

having the same Christian name has been commented on: it is as if
Dickens were polarizing his feelings about women – separating the
feminine idea into housekeeper and sex-object – as, later in the
novel, he does with Agnes and Dora.

Since the narrator of the novel is the adult David, there is from
the outset a double perspective of childhood relived but also seen
and judged from the viewpoint of maturity. The second chapter
opens with some observations on memory, and in some passages
later in the novel Dickens' narrative briefly abandons the normal
past tense for either the present tense (for example, 'Here we stand,
all three, before me now': Ch. 11) – a device perhaps influenced by
its striking use in *Jane Eyre* – or employs the verbless, and therefore
timeless, sentence. In the following passage we see a transition from
past tense through verbless sentence to a present that relives the
past:

> If the funeral had been yesterday, I could not recollect it
> better. The very air of the best parlour, when I went in at the
> door, the bright condition of the fire, the shining of the wine in the
> decanters, the patterns of the glasses and plates, the faint sweet
> smell of cake, the odour of Miss Murdstone's dress, and our black
> clothes. Mr Chillip is in the room, and comes to speak to me.
> (Ch. 9)

When the past is recalled, the 'future' of the narrative is of course
already irrevocable, and this gives momentum to the narrative and
helps to counteract the digressiveness and formlessness to which the
autobiographical mode is prone. As Dickens writes in Chapter 31
(and the passage is characteristic of many instances of what he liked
to call 'foreshadowing' in this novel):

> It is no worse, because I write of it. It would be no better, if I
> stopped my most unwilling hand. It is done. Nothing can undo it;
> nothing can make it otherwise than as it was.

In the presentation of Steerforth, Dickens very strikingly mingles
the child's hero-worship with the man's moral censure in the light of
subsequent events (see the paragraph in Ch. 21 beginning 'He
maintained all his delightful qualities'). Complementarily, the final
glimpse of the dead Steerforth is of his 'lying with his head upon his
arm, as I had often seen him lie at school' (Ch. 55).

Dickens does not always allow David to interpret the events of childhood and youth in the light of *a posteriori* knowledge, however; and sometimes the reader is left to perceive David's misinterpretation of a situation through his innocence – a guilelessness that can be both comic and touching, like so much in this bitter-sweet novel. Some examples are the boy's failure to realize that Mr Murdstone is courting his mother, David's misunderstanding of Steerforth's motives in patronizing the Peggotty family, and his failure to understand Miss Mowcher's sibyl-like warnings of Little Em'ly's fate.

Critics and common readers have generally agreed that this novel contains some of Dickens' most vivid portrayals of character, and the list below of about sixty characters includes some of the most familiar in the whole Dickens canon. However, the novel has attracted the attention of recent critics less than some others; and although many readers of earlier generations would have concurred with Dickens in regarding it as their favourite, its merits have seemed less indubitably outstanding to most recent commentators. Perhaps its limited topicality, and its lack of the comprehensive vision of society offered by (say) *Little Dorrit*, offer relatively little grist to the mills of contemporary criticism. Stylistically, though, it is of particular interest, and nobody has written better on this aspect of the novel than Sylvère Monod in his *Dickens the Novelist*.

Monod is especially illuminating on the emotional vocabulary of *David Copperfield*. He notes that the epithet *little* ('the most characteristic word in the whole Dickensian vocabulary') occurs no fewer than 186 times in fourteen chapters (9–23); other recurring words are *own* (85 times in the same chapters), *old* (97 times in Chs 11–21, usually in the emotional sense of 'familiar' rather than the more objective sense), and *great* (85 times in Chs 11–21 and, like *little*, emotional rather than physical in its favourite connotations). Among other stylistic features peculiarly frequent in this novel are an addiction to the superlative and a curious fondness for such phrases as 'a kind of' and 'a sort of' (77 examples noted in Chs 9–21). I think Professor Monod errs, however, in seeing this latter feature, which he describes as 'a curious hesitancy which nothing in [Dickens'] character seems to suggest', as puzzling: one must surely take into account the extent to which the individual voice of David as narrator is created and maintained, and the extent to which it differs from Dickens' more customary and more rhetorical narrative voice. The same critic rightly notes that this novel possesses 'a simplicity [of style] which is decidedly a novelty in Dickensian fiction', and it can be argued that Dickens was here embarking on a deliberate experiment in style – an experiment that is carried further (perhaps too far) in his next novel, in the portion of *Bleak House* narrated by Esther Summerson.

The manuscript and corrected proofs provide, indeed, evidence that he quite consciously curbed the exuberance of language that came naturally to him. At the proof stage, for example, there are many deleted passages that, left in the final text, would have given the novel a less restrained, more emotionally explicit tone. In Chapter 9 there is a passage describing David woken from sleep by the sound of the spade digging his mother's grave: he weeps and sobs, and Peggotty wrings her hands and gives vent to her grief. In Chapter 23, references to Aunty Betsey weeping and David furiously angry are struck out. Even in the comic passages there is some playing down of extravagant, characteristically 'Dickensian' effects: thus, when the Micawbers' furniture is sold (Ch. 11), the description of their living 'like a party of domesticated Arabs' disappears; and elsewhere Mr Dick's eccentric behaviour is toned down in Dickens' revisions. Butt and Tillotson in *Dickens at Work* draw attention to some of these second thoughts and note that there is 'some adjustment in the pathos' – though the revisions, as I have suggested, are not confined to the pathetic passages. The manuscript shows that some of Dickens' more felicitous effects, and some of the most notable instances of stylistic simplicity, were arrived at only after much effort: the famous account of Barkis's death, for example – 'And it being low water, he went out with the tide' – achieved its apparent ease only after heavy revision.

Apart from the essay by Butt and Tillotson referred to above, which reproduces and discusses Dickens' number-plans for this novel, significant criticism and scholarship include Q. D. Leavis's 'Dickens and Tolstoy: The Case for a Serious View of *David Copperfield*' (in *Dickens the Novelist*): like Professor Monod, Mrs Leavis argues at length the now unfashionable case for taking the whole novel, not just the childhood chapters, seriously, and for ranking it high in Dickens' total achievement. Among other critics, G. B. Needham has written on 'The Undisciplined Heart of David Copperfield' (*Nineteenth Century Fiction*, IX, 1955) and J. R. Kincaid on the novel's structure (*Dickens Studies*, II, 1966). An earlier essay is Virginia Woolf's, first published in 1925 and collected in *The Moment* (1947). K. J. Fielding has some interesting comments on

'*David Copperfield* and Dialect' (*The Times Literary Supplement*, 30 April 1949), and there is a monograph on the novel by Philip Collins (1977), as well as good discussions in Angus Wilson's book on Dickens and in J. H. Buckley's *Season of Youth* (1974).

CHARACTERS

BARKIS. Carrier who conveys David and Peggotty to Yarmouth (Ch. 3), 'of a phlegmatic temperament, and not at all conversational' (Ch. 5). He sends a message to Peggotty that 'Barkis is willin' ', later marries her (Ch. 10), and dies ('went out with the tide': Ch. 30). Strindberg said that his entire character was confined to a single word ('willin' '); whether or not this is exaggerated, he is certainly a good example of what E. M. Forster designated the 'flat' Dickensian character.

CHILLIP, MR. Doctor present at the birth of David.

COPPERFIELD, CLARA. Mother of David. A 'nursery-governess in a family where Mr Copperfield came to visit' (Ch. 1), she is 'not yet twenty' at the time of her marriage (Dickens originally wrote 'only twenty' but made the change at the proof stage). Widowed early, she later marries Mr Murdstone and dies in childbirth.

COPPERFIELD, DAVID. Hero and narrator of the novel.

CREAKLE, MR. Proprietor of Salem House, the school near Blackheath to which David is sent. Self-described as 'a Tartar', he exercises a tyrannical and sadistic style of discipline (see Ch. 7: 'I should think there never can have been a man who enjoyed his profession more than Mr Creakle did. He had a delight in cutting at the boys, which was like the satisfaction of a craving appetite. I am confident that he couldn't resist a chubby boy, especially; that there was a fascination in such a subject, which made him restless in his mind, until he had scored and marked him for the day'). He reappears in Ch. 61. An interesting cancelled passage in Dickens' corrected proofs makes him a Calvinist. For a likely prototype, see under 'William Jones' in 'The Dickens Circle'.

CRUPP, MRS. Landlady to David Copperfield during his bachelor days in London (Ch. 23).

DARTLE, ROSA. Companion to Mrs Steerforth; she is described in Ch. 20 ('dark, and not agreeable to look at . . . and had a scar upon her lip'). Embittered and sarcastic, she is a striking study in repression and anticipates Miss Wade in *Little Dorrit*.

DICK, MR. Mentally deranged but kindly gentleman who resides with Betsey Trowood at Dover, she having rescued him from a private madhouse (Ch. 14). He is fond of kite-flying and is composing 'a Memorial about his own history' into which Charles I cannot be prevented from intruding. (1849, the date of composition of this portion, was the bicentenary of that monarch's execution; Dickens' original notion was to make Mr Dick's *idée fixe* the proverbial bull in a china shop.) As noted above, Dickens toned down at the proof stage his original, more extravagant description of Mr Dick's eccentric behaviour. The proofs also contain an amusing example of the printer's misreading of Dickens' sometimes difficult handwriting, the last word in 'Mr Dick was very partial to gingerbread' appearing as 'going abroad'.

DOLLOBY, MR. Dealer in old clothes in the Kent Road. David sells some garments to him on his painful journey to Dover (Ch. 15).

ENDELL, MARTHA, *see* MARTHA

FIBBITSON, MRS. Old lady who lives with Mrs Mell, the mother of a master at Salem House.

GRAINGER. Friend of Steerforth, introduced to David in Ch. 24.

GRAYPER, MR. Neighbour of Mrs Copperfield; he attends her funeral (Ch. 9).

GULPIDGE, MR. Guest at Mr and Mrs Waterbrook's home when David is present (Ch. 25).

GUMMIDGE, MRS. Widow of Mr Peggotty's 'partner in a boat', she lives with Mr Peggotty at Yarmouth. At first much given to complaining self-pity ('"I am a lone lorn creetur"' is her characteristic phrase), she later shows resolution and eventually accompanies Mr Peggotty to Australia.

HEEP, URIAH. Red-haired (he is compared to a 'red fox') and cadaverous-faced youth first described in Ch. 15. He is a clerk to Mr Wickfield, over whose affairs he eventually gains control, whose business partner he becomes, and whose daughter Agnes he plans to marry. Denounced by Mr Micawber in Ch. 49 and exposed in Ch. 53, he is eventually jailed (Ch. 61). Like Fagin, he is one of those Dickensian villains who conveys a hint of diabolism: see the curious passage that ends Ch. 25, where he is explicitly referred to as a devil. Uriah's unusual name suggests the Old Testament story of King David, Bathsheba, and Uriah the Hittite; but the parallel, if one was intended, seems to be unclear. Uriah's mother, Mrs Heep, is the widow of a sexton and is described by her son as 'a very umble person' (Ch. 16).

HOPKINS, CAPTAIN. Fellow-prisoner of Mr Micawber in the King's Bench Prison. Dickens' autobiographical fragment indicates that Captain Porter, a fellow-prisoner of John Dickens in the Marshalsea Prison, was the prototype of Captain Hopkins.

JANET. Servant to Betsey Trotwood at her house in Dover.

JIP. Dora Spenlow's pet spaniel.

JORAM. Employed by Mr Omer at his Yarmouth shop and in love with Minnie Omer (Ch. 9). Later he marries her and becomes her father's partner.

JORKINS, MR. Partner of Mr Spenlow in the law firm to which David is articled. David meets him in Ch. 35. He is a nonentity whose supposed objections are used as an excuse by Mr Spenlow.

LARKINS, MISS. Young lady briefly loved by David when he is 17 (Ch. 18). She marries 'Mr Chestle, a hop-grower'.

LITTIMER. Manservant to Steerforth, described in Ch. 21. He ends in prison (Ch. 61).

MALDON, JACK. Cousin of Annie Strong, he is a ne'er-do-well who tries to conduct a flirtation with her under the eyes of her unsuspecting husband. He goes to India but soon returns.

MARKHAM. Friend of Steerforth, introduced to David in Ch. 24.

MARKLEHAM, MRS. (nicknamed 'the Old Soldier'). Mother of Annie Strong; she is described in Ch. 16.

MARTHA (Endell). A fallen woman. She first appears (Ch. 22) as a 'black shadow' following Emily (and foreshadowing her fate). See Ch. 47 for her part in the finding of Emily. She emigrates with the Peggotty family and marries in Australia (see Ch. 63). For Dickens' interest in the social problem of prostitution, see under Burdett Coutts on p. 22.

MEALY POTATOES, see WALKER, MICK.

MELL, MR (CHARLEY). Master at Salem House, the school near Blackheath to which David is sent. He meets David on his arrival in London and they call on his mother, a poor old woman (Ch. 5). Mell is insulted by Steerforth (Ch. 7). He is 'wretchedly underpaid' (Ch. 6) and plays the flute for consolation: for a prototype, see in chapter 'The Dickens Circle' (under Jones).

MICAWBER, MR. The Micawber family take David as a lodger at their house in Windsor Terrace when he goes to work in London (Ch. 11); at the time Mr Micawber is employed taking orders on commission for Murdstone and Grinby, wine merchants. Chronically insolvent, he is arrested for debt and sent to the

King's Bench Prison. His moods swing between despair and an exuberant and groundless optimism. Later he exposes Heep (Ch. 53), emigrates to Australia and becomes a magistrate there (Ch. 63). Dickens' father, John Dickens, has often been proposed as the model of Micawber. Mrs Micawber is 'a thin and faded lady, not at all young' (Ch. 11); the reference to her unsuccessful attempt to start a school perhaps recalls the similar effort made by Dickens' mother (see p. 2). In *Aspects of the Novel* E. M. Forster cites Mrs Micawber as an example of Dickensian 'flat' characterization.

MILLS, JULIA. Friend and companion of Dora Spenlow when the latter is courted by David.

MOWCHER, MISS. Dwarfish lady, manicurist by profession; she is acquainted with Steerforth, and David meets her in Ch. 22. Shrewd and perceptive, she comments obliquely on Steerforth's plan to seduce Little Em'ly. On the curious origin of Dickens' change of intention with regard to Miss Mowcher, see p. 34.

MURDSTONE, MR. (Edward). Handsome and black-haired, he becomes the second husband of Mrs Copperfield and hence David's step-father. His spinster sister JANE is 'a gloomy-looking lady' (Ch. 4). She joins the Copperfield household on her brother's marriage and quickly takes over the housekeeping. For an arresting passage on her repressed sexuality, see Ch. 4 (she was 'constantly haunted by a suspicion that the servants had a man secreted somewhere on the premises').

OMER, MR. Yarmouth draper who fits out David with mourning clothes after his mother's death. David revisits him later (Ch. 21) and finds that Em'ly is employed at the shop. His daughter MINNIE marries Joram.

ORFLING, THE (i.e., the Orphan). Servant in the Micawber household (Ch. 11). She is an orphan from St Luke's Workhouse.

PEGGOTTY, CLARA. Servant and companion to Mrs Copperfield, deeply devoted to David. She marries Barkis. Her brother DAN, a 'bacheldore' (bachelor) and head of the Yarmouth household, receives David as a guest and later visits him at school. He sets out in search of Little Em'ly after her seduction by Steerforth (Ch. 31): ' "I'm going to seek my niece through the wureld." ' He finds her (Ch. 50); resolves to emigrate to Australia (Ch. 51); and returns to tell of his success (Ch. 63). In the article cited earlier, K. J. Fielding has shown that in representing Mr Peggotty's broad dialect Dickens drew not only on his very brief visit to Yarmouth but on Moor's *Suffolk Words and Phrases* (1823), where he found such words as *bein, dodman, mawther* and *mavish*. Mr Peggotty's niece EMILY is a childhood friend of David on his visits to Yarmouth. In Ch. 3 she tells him, significantly, that she wants to be a lady. She is fascinated by Steerforth when he visits her home with David (Ch. 21), and is seduced by and elopes with him (Ch. 31), travelling through Europe as his mistress (Ch. 46) while her uncle searches for her. She is found (Ch. 50) and accompanies her uncle to Australia. The character of Martha represents a warning of Emily's potential fate. Mr Peggotty's nephew HAM is also a member of the Yarmouth household, and is vainly in love with Little Em'ly.

QUINION, MR. Friend of Mr Murdstone and manager of the London firm of Murdstone and Grinby, wine merchants, where David is employed after his mother's death (see Ch. 11).

SHARP, MR. Underpaid usher at Salem House.

SHEPHERD, MISS. A 'boarder at the Misses Nettingalls' establishment', at Canterbury, briefly loved by David (Ch. 18) during his school days.

SPENLOW, MR (Francis). Lawyer to whom David is articled (Ch. 23). He is indignant when he learns that David wishes to marry his daughter Dora, but dies suddenly (and, for David and the plot, very conveniently) in Ch. 38. See also Jorkins. His daughter DORA becomes David's first wife; for a delightful description of their courtship, see Ch. 33. She is a hopelessly incompetent housewife (Ch. 44) and dies in Ch. 53. Her maiden aunts LAVINIA and CLARISSA grant permission to David to become Dora's suitor after her father's death (Ch. 41).

SPIKER, MR (Henry). Guest at Mr and Mrs Waterbrook's house when David is present (Ch. 25).

STEERFORTH, JAMES. Senior pupil at Salem House; he patronizes David (whom he nicknames Daisy) and insults Mr Mell. David meets him again by chance in London (Ch. 19), visits his home, and introduces him to the Peggotty family at Yarmouth. He seduces and elopes with Emily; takes her on a Byronic tour of Europe; and is drowned, Shelley-like, at sea. His body is cast up on Yarmouth beach, where it is found by David (Ch. 55). His mother, who has indulged him from childhood, is the employer of Rosa Dartle.

STRONG, DR. Elderly headmaster of the school in Canterbury attended by David; he is described in Ch. 16, where his age is given as 62. He is compiling a Dictionary – a task that shows no signs of ever reaching a conclusion. An unworldly, unsuspicious, old-fashioned scholar, he marries a young wife, ANNIE (née Markleham), who is at first mistaken by David for his daughter. She is the object of the attentions of her cousin Jack Maldon, an irresponsible young man, but in Ch. 45 declares her love for her husband – her words forming an unconsciously ironic commentary on David's own marriage to Dora (see the fine ending to Ch. 45).

TRADDLES, TOMMY. Fellow-pupil of David at Salem House. David later meets him in London. Traddles becomes engaged to Sophy, one of the ten daughters of a Devonshire curate (Ch. 27), and after long delays is happily married to her (Ch. 59). A cheerful, patient, uncomplaining figure, he acts as a foil to both David and Steerforth. On a possible prototype, see under 'Talfourd' in 'The Dickens Circle'.

TROTWOOD, BETSEY. Paternal great-aunt of David. She is in the house when he is born (Ch. 1) and is seen no more until he seeks help from her in Dover (Ch. 14, where she is described). She confronts the Murdstones when they call on her (Ch. 14), adopts David and gives him the name Trotwood. It later emerges that she has been unhappily married.

TUNGAY. Wooden-legged assistant to Mr Creakle, the proprietor of Salem House school.

WALKER, MICK. One of the boys employed at Murdstone and Grinby's when David works there (Ch. 11). Another is known as MEALY POTATOES.

WATERBROOK, MR. London agent of Mr Wickfield. Agnes stays at his house in Ely Place, Holborn, and David visits her there (Ch. 25).

WICKFIELD, MR. A widower and Betsey Trotwood's lawyer. A weak and half-senile man, he is victimized by Uriah Heep. His daughter AGNES keeps house for him: with her basket of keys and her domestic efficiency (contrasting with Dora's incompetence) she anticipates Esther Summerson in *Bleak House*. David marries her (Ch. 62) after Dora's death.

Bleak House

Texts Penguin English Library, ed. Norman Page, introduction
by J. Hillis Miller (1971); Crowell Critical Library, ed. Duane
DeVries (1971); Norton Critical Edition, ed. George Ford and
Sylvère Monod (1977).

Composition Dickens wrote on 21 February 1851 that 'the first
shadows of a new story' were 'hovering in a ghostly way' about him,
but the novel was not begun until November of that year. It was
completed in August 1853 – 'by the third week of August', according to Forster. Edgar Johnson states that 'Dickens wrote more
easily, or at least with fewer groans of misery and despair, than for
years past.' Manuscript and corrected proofs in Forster Collection.

Serialization Nineteen monthly parts, the last a double number,
from March 1852 to September 1853, as follows: I (Chs 1–4); II
(Chs 5–7); III (Chs 8–10); IV (Chs 11–13); V (Chs 14–16); VI (Chs
17–19); VII (Chs 20–2); VIII (Chs 23–5); IX (Chs 26–9); X (Chs
30–2); XI (Chs 33–5); XII (Chs 36–8); XIII (Chs 39–42); XIV
(Chs 43–6); XV (Chs 47–9); XVI (Chs 50–3); XVII (Chs 54–6);
XVIII (Chs 57–9); XIX–XX (Chs 60–7). Illustrations by 'Phiz'.
The serial was a great success. By the end of the day of publication,
the first number had sold out and reprinting had begun. On 4
March Dickens wrote that it was 'blazing away merrily'. By the end
of June, 38,500 copies of the first number had been printed. Nor was
there any falling-off in its success: on 8 May he wrote that 'It is a
most enormous success, all the prestige of Copperfield (which was
very great) falling upon it, and raising its circulation above all my
other books'; in November he said that 'its circulation is half as large
again as Copperfield!'; and on the day that he completed the novel,
he wrote that 'it has retained its immense circulation from the first,
beating dear old Copperfield by a round ten thousand or more. I

have never had so many readers.' (He repeats this final phrase at the
end of his Preface to the first edition.) Robert Patten has calculated
that by the end of 1853 a total of 686,853 parts had been sold, 'the
equivalent of 34,342 complete novels'; Professor Patten adds that,
although there was a slight falling off in sales towards the end, 'to
have sustained such readership over such a long period of time is a
signal achievement'.

Publication   Published in one volume by Bradbury & Evans in
1853. Preface added. Dedication to 'my companions in the Guild of
Literature and Art' (see p. 41).

Reception   Noting that *Bleak House* is a crucial item in the history of
Dickens' reputation, Professor Collins points out that this contention means different things as applied to, respectively, the contemporary and the twentieth-century verdicts: whereas 'for many
critics in the 1850s, '60s, and '70s, it began the drear decline of "the
author of *Pickwick*, *Chuzzlewit* and *Copperfield*"', for many modern
critics it is seen as having 'opened the greatest phase of his
achievement'. The immediate reception was not unfavourable,
though particular elements, predictably enough, gave offence to
particular sections of the public (for example, Mrs Jellyby and the
satire on philanthropy and missionary efforts; the attack on
Chancery; Mr Chadband). Krook's spontaneous combustion ig-
nited a controversy to which Dickens provided a rejoinder in his
preface to the 1853 edition. Jo's pathetic death was widely praised,
and Mr Bucket proved popular. In private letters, Charlotte Brontë
found Esther Summerson's narrative 'too often weak and twaddling', and John Stuart Mill complained that Dickens had had 'the
vulgar impudence . . . to ridicule rights of women'. Ruskin later
ridiculed the high mortality rate in the novel.

Writing on 'Dickens and *Punch*' (*Dickens Studies*, III, 1967), Philip
Collins has said that

> more of [Dickens'] jokes and social references than is often
> realized were right up-to-date, concerned with events, issues and
> personalities prominent in the previous month or so. To read the
> *Punch* issues published concurrently with an instalment of a
> Dickens novel is one good way of noticing this.

Bleak House is a particularly good example of the topicality of Dickens' fiction; on the other hand, topical references coexist with details suggesting an earlier period, so that the dating of the action is not a simple matter. Humphry House suggests (in *The Dickens World*) that 'Dickens seems to have gone out of his way to leave the imaginary time of the story vague': Esther says at one point 'I omit the date', no year is ever mentioned, and 'there is scarcely even the name of a month'. House comments acutely that 'This is more surprising because the sense of the passage of time is so peculiarly vivid, and makes more impression on the memory, perhaps, than the chronology of any of the novels.' The legal terms and vacations alternate regularly in the Court of Chancery, the seasons revolve at Chesney Wold; but 'the tempo of events in the two main strands of the plot is curiously dissimilar'. House goes on to suggest that a kind of double time operates in *Bleak House* (as it does in *Othello*): 'we think of Richard Carstone's failure, entanglement, and decay as slow and long-drawn-out, but of the events which hurried Lady Dedlock to discovery and death as a swiftly moving series of crises'.

House concludes that what Dickens was doing in this novel was to draw on distant memories for certain parts of his story ('the whole atmosphere of the legal parts of the book and a number of the small details . . . are drawn out of the inexhaustible store of memories from Dickens's early days'), but to overlay this evocation of the past with 'a reformist's anger with the immediate present', for 'Both the Court of Chancery and the slums were topical subjects in 1852, for other reasons than because Dickens made them so. People were then in fact dying of litigation and of cholera.' Generalizing about Dickens' work as a whole, House suggests that 'whatever may be the imaginary date of the plot, the material most likely to be contemporary with the time of writing, and most topical to it, is the "Reformism" and the more deliberate social satire'.

John Butt has summarized some of the issues that the first readers of *Bleak House* would have recognized as topical – issues that they might well have ecountered already, for example, in the news columns and the leaders of *The Times*. 'What had directed Dickens's attention to the Court of Chancery in 1851 was the interest which everyone was taking in chancery that year': *The Times* carried a leading article on the subject on the first day of that year, and this was only one of a number of prominent references (on the last day of January it reported at length a meeting of the Chancery Reform Association). Butt goes so far as to say that 'Dickens's indictment of

Chancery was more than merely topical. It followed in almost every respect the charges already levelled in the columns of *The Times*.' Another contemporary issue was 'the public anxiety caused by the establishment of the Roman Catholic hierarchy in England', and Dickens clearly has this in mind in his satiric portrayal of Mrs Pardiggle and of the ladies in Ch. 8 who are collecting subscriptions for 'the Sisterhood of Mediaeval Marys'. Butt identifies 'female emancipation and female management' as another object of Dickens' contemporary satire: for a likely prototype of Mrs Jellyby, see in chapter 'The Dickens Circle (under Caroline Chisholm, whose Family Loan Colonization Society was established in May 1850), while behind Borrioboola Gha is the ill-fated Niger expedition of 1841, a published account of which Dickens had reviewed in the *Examiner* in 1848.

Inspector Bucket is yet another topical figure: the detective branch of the Metropolitan Police force had been formed in the forties, and Dickens had written about it extensively in *Household Words*, where 'Inspector Wield' is based on a detective named Field who also became the model for Bucket. *Household Words*, indeed, frequently offers a non-fictional gloss on Dickens' fictional writing of the same period: Mrs Bagnet can be linked with a note (6 September 1851) on the hardships endured by soldiers' wives. The notorious Tooting baby-farm, referred to in Ch. 10, also belonged to recent history, and Dickens had contributed several articles on this scandal to the *Examiner* early in 1849. The foreign murderess Hortense would certainly have reminded readers of a recent husband-and-wife trial and execution (the latter attended by Dickens) that had attracted enormous public interest: on the Manning case of 1849, see Albert Borowitz, *The Woman Who Murdered Black Satin* (1981). As for the outcast Jo, Dickens' own *Household Narrative* (the monthly supplement to *Household Words*) had reported at the beginning of 1850 the evidence given by George Ruby in a case of assault heard at the Guildhall: fact and fiction resemble each other strongly, and Jo almost certainly owes a good deal to the wretched Ruby. In the same year the *Household Narrative* also carried a report of the Sloane Scandal, which involved the sadistic ill-treatment of a parish girl, Jane Wilbred; and Professor Collins has argued plausibly that this case may lie behind the heartless exploitation of Charley Neckett by Judy Smallweed.

Alongside these allusions, for the most part unmistakably contemporary, are others which seem to belong to a considerably earlier period. The curious reference to the 'Spanish refugees' in Ch. 43, for instance, evokes the world of Dickens' childhood and youth, for these were 'the exiles of the Torrijos party, well known around St. Pancras between 1823 and 1830' (House). The account in Ch. 55 of the coming of the railway to Lincolnshire also suggests a period considerably earlier than the date of composition, and the portrait of Chancery is in some respects outdated. Since Esther concludes her narrative, as she says, 'full seven years' after the action, and if she may be supposed to be writing at about the same time as Dickens, Richard's death would be dated about 1846 and the action would have begun in the early forties a dating impossible to reconcile with the allusions cited in this paragraph. But these are, after all, only details; the costumes in the illustrations belong to the 1850s; and Butt sensibly concludes that the minor inconsistencies are not enough to counteract

the strong flavour of contemporaneity in the action and in the characters. *Bleak House* began as a tract for the times, and the more fully this is recognized, the more fully we shall appreciate the 'esemplastic power' which imposed upon a mass of seemingly heterogeneous material a significant and acceptable form.

Not that all of Dickens' contemporaries found the form of the novel 'significant and acceptable': a critic in the *Spectator* wrote (24 September 1853) that *Bleak House* was,

even more than any of its predecessors, chargeable with not simply faults, but absolute want of construction . . . . Mr. Dickens discards plot, while he persists in adopting a form for his thoughts to which plot is essential, and where the absence of a coherent story is fatal to continuous interest.

This seems to miss the point entirely – a point implicit throughout the novel, and explicit in a key-paragraph in Ch. 16:

What connexion can there be, between the place in Lincolnshire, the house in town, the Mercury in powder, and the whereabout of Jo the outlaw with the broom, who had that distant ray of light upon him when he swept the churchyard-step? What connexion can there have been between many people in the innumerable histories of the world, who, from opposite sides of great gulfs, have, nevertheless, been very curiously brought together!

This is a novel about connexions at the same time as it depicts and dramatizes the separation of individuals living in the same society (a striking case in point is the episode in which, encountering Jo and seeking his aid, the disguised Lady Dedlock is quite literally unable to understand the language he speaks – a language as debased and barbarous as Jo's own appalling state). Hence the comprehensiveness of Dickens' vision, which brings together a large cast of characters from all levels of society – landed aristocracy, professional middle classes, petty bourgeoisie, working classes, submerged tenth – and insists on their interdependence, the fever (both undeniable contemporary fact and powerful symbol) linking the comfortable world of John Jarndyce with the slum of Tom-all-Alone's. The superb scene of Jo's death in Ch. 47 – unashamedly rhetorical, but triumphantly successful in its rhetoric – places the final stress on our common involvement and common responsibility: the pronoun in 'And dying thus around us every day' startlingly involves narrator and reader along with all those in the novel who accept or shrug off that responsibility.

The second, generalizing sentence in the passage from Ch. 16 quoted above shows Dickens defending himself against the charge of relying too heavily on coincidence; and elsewhere Forster refers to Dickens' views on this subject:

> On the coincidences, resemblances, and surprises of life, Dickens liked especially to dwell, and few things moved his fancy so pleasantly. The world, he would say, was so much smaller than we thought it; we were all so connected by fate without knowing it; people supposed to be far apart were so constantly elbowing each other; and to-morrow bore so close a resemblance to nothing half so much as to yesterday.

Here, again, the stress is on 'connexion'. In its range and variety, Dickens' fictional world resembles the real world and accommodates a great diversity of attitudes and effects – satire, comedy, pathos, melodrama, mystery – with further differentiations within these categories, so that we find (for example) satirical comedy in the presentation of the parasitical Dedlock relatives, black comedy in the ghoulish figure of Vholes, farce (again of Beckettian black) in the Smallweeds, caricature in Boythorn, sentimental comedy in Guppy. London itself is an image of this diversity in unity, and the coincidences on which the plot so much depends often take the form of chance encounters in the city streets. Barbara Hardy has suggested that *Bleak House* initiates Dickens' later period, to which belongs a series of 'novels of the sociological imagination' in which he 'set out a full map and large-scale criticism, in the expressive form of art, of Dickens's England'. Coming as it does almost exactly at the mid-point of his career, *Bleak House* is plainly (to quote Professor Collins yet again) 'crucial' in the development of his art.

How deliberate that art was can be seen from the number-plans, which recorded different stages in his conception and execution of the exacting task of writing a novel in nineteen monthly parts. These plans are reproduced in the three editions cited above and repay careful study.

The narrative method of *Bleak House* is unique in Dickens' work and can be seen as combining the fruits of the experience gained in writing his previous two novels: the third-person narrative of *Dombey and Son* and the autobiographical narrative of *David Copperfield*. In *Bleak House* Dickens boldly experiments with what W. J. Harvey has called a 'double narrative': Esther Summerson and the third-person narrator tell almost exactly equal portions of the story, alternating frequently but irregularly. One of the technical problems involved was to distinguish with sufficient clarity between the two narrators, and Dickens does this partly by a tense-difference (Esther speaks of the past, the third-person narrator of a dramatic present) but also more pervasively by a sharp contrast in the two narrative styles. Esther's tone is quiet, conversational, confidential, intimate; her language is for the most part unaffected and even commonplace – on the first page of her narrative, for example (which Dickens's manuscript reveals to have caused him considerable pains), typical adjectives are *little, great, beautiful, dear*. The third-person narrator's voice, established immediately in the famous description of London fog with which the novel opens, is rhetorical and emphatic, his style experimental: the tone is declamatory, and typical adjectives in the opening passage are *implacable, elephantine, undistinguishable, haggard*. W. J. Harvey has suggested that the deliberate flatness of Esther's style represents Dickens' conscious attempt to put a brake on his own exuberance. It has to be said, though, that he was not always successful, and at times (for example, the description of Mrs Guppy's 'holding her pocket-handkerchief to her chest, like a fomentation, with both hands', and of Turveydrop – 'I almost believe I saw creases come into the whites of his eyes' when he bowed) the voice seems to be unmistakably and unrepentantly that of the Inimitable Boz.

Esther represents one of the problems of the novel: she is clearly important, but has often received a bad press (though she has found many defenders in recent years). One critic, F. W. Boege, found in her 'positive bad qualities, such as the simpering affectation of innocence'. As with many of Dickens' heroines, the problem seems to arise because of the gulf between his ideal of womanhood and our own; and it is serious enough when the character is of major importance, as with Amy Dorrit or Agnes Wickfield, but even more so when she is also the narrator of half the novel. Esther's role, it needs to be remembered, is largely that of observer: Dickens needed to create a character whose unassuming personality would enable her to mingle freely with a large variety of characters without determining the tone of the episode by the force of her own qualities – for after all, though she is in a sense the heroine of the story (perhaps owing something in that capacity to the immense and recent popularity of *Jane Eyre*), she is not a protagonist on the scale of David Copperfield or Pip and does not dominate this novel as they dominate theirs. A reviewer in the *Athenaeum* praised the accuracy of Esther's powers of observation and found in her 'the immediate power of the daguerrotype in noting at once the minutest singularities of so many exceptional people', and this seems to hit the nail neatly on the head: like Isherwood, she seems to offer herself (with, as we have seen above, only occasional lapses) as a camera.

As usual Dickens took considerable trouble over finding a title that satisfied him, and ten slips of paper now bound in with the manuscript in the Forster Collection record some alternatives. They include *Tom-All-Alone's/The Ruined House*; *Tom-All-Alone's/Building/ Factory/Mill/The Ruined House/That got into Chancery/and never got out*; *Tom-All-Alone's/The Solitary House/Where the Wind howled*; *Bleak House/and The East Wind/How they both got into Chancery/and never got out*; and other variations on these ideas.

Bleak House has been very widely discussed by recent critics. There are important chapters in two books: Butt and Tillotson's *Dickens at Work* and the Leavises' *Dickens the Novelist*, this novel being considered by, respectively, John Butt and Q. D. Leavis. The general studies of Dickens by Humphry House, J. Hillis Miller, Sylvère Monod and Angus Wilson contain useful material on *Bleak*

1 Drawing of Dickens by Samuel Lawrence, 1837

2   Painting of Dickens by Daniel Maclise

3   Dickens at 50

4   Dickens: the final reading

5   A page from the manuscript of *Martin Chuzzlewit*

6 Dickens' number-plan for no. 5 of *Dombey and Son*

7 'First appearance of Mr Samuel Weller' by Phiz, from *The Pickwick Papers*

" A black and dreadful place !" exclaimed the child.

" Look in," said the old man, pointing downward with his finger.

The child complied, and gazed down into the pit.

" It looks like a grave, itself," said the old man.

" It does," replied the child.

" I have often had the fancy," said the sexton, "that it might have been dug at first to make the old place more gloomy, and the old monks more religious.   It's to be closed up, and built over."

The child still stood, looking thoughtfully into the vault.

" We shall see," said the sexton, " on what gay heads other earth will have closed, when the light is shut out from here.   God knows !   They'll close it up, next spring."

" The birds sing again in spring," thought the child, as she leant at her casement window, and gazed at the declining sun.   " Spring ! a beautiful and happy time !"

9 'The Dombey Family' by Phiz, from *Dombey and Son*

10   'Fagin in the Condemned Cell' by George Cruikshank, from *Oliver Twist*

11 'Florence and Edith on the Staircase' by Phiz, from *Dombey and Son*

12   Cover design by Charles Collins for *The Mystery of Edwin Drood*

House. Trevor Blount has written a series of articles on particular aspects (*Modern Language Review*, LX, 1965; *Essays in Criticism*, XV, 1965; and others); W. J. Harvey has some good things to say in his *Character and the Novel* (1965) and in the essay he contributed to Gross and Pearson's symposium; and Michael Steig deals with this novel in 'Dickens' Excremental Vision' (*Victorian Studies*, XIII, 1970). M. E. Grenander has examined Dickens' use of point of view (*Nineteenth-Century Fiction*, X, 1956), G. J. Worth has discussed 'The Genesis of Jo the Crossing-Sweeper' (*Journal of English and Germanic Philology*, LX, 1961), and K. J. Fielding has taken up the question of Leigh Hunt as a model for Harold Skimpole (*Notes and Queries*, April 1955). Among the many who have written on Esther are William Axton (*Modern Language Quarterly*, XXVI, 1965) and A. E. Dyson (in his 1969 casebook, which also brings together a selection of critical material). There are good monographs devoted to *Bleak House* by Philip Collins (1971) and Grahame Smith (1974). Ford and Monod's Norton edition and DeVries's Crowell edition both include critical extracts.

CHARACTERS

BADGER, BAYHAM. Doctor with 'a good practice at Chelsea' (Ch. 13) who takes Richard Carstone as a pupil. He basks comically in the reflected glory of his wife's two deceased husbands, 'Captain Swosser of the Royal Navy' and 'Professor Dingo . . . of European reputation', to whom he constantly refers in conversation.

BARBARY, MISS. Sister of Lady Dedlock; she brings up Esther Summerson in her home at Windsor, having told her sister that her child has died at birth and leading Esther to believe that she is her godchild. She represents a gloomy and unforgiving variety of religious temperament that Dickens later depicted more fully in Mrs Clennam (in *Little Dorrit*). *See also under* BOYTHORN, LAWRENCE.

BAGNET, MATTHEW, nicknamed 'Lignum Vitae'. Ex-artilleryman and bassoon-player, he keeps a small shop selling musical instruments and is a friend of George Rouncewell. His wife is a paragon of loyal, unpretentious resourcefulness; it is she who reunites George with his mother. Their children are known by the names of the military bases at which they were born: QUEBEC, MALTA, WOOLWICH.

BLINDER, MRS. Old woman who shows kindness to Neckett's children after they are orphaned (see Ch. 15).

BOYTHORN, LAWRENCE. Country gentleman, bachelor friend of Mr Jarndyce, and a compound of apparent ferocity and real gentleness. He conducts a running battle with his neighbour Sir Leicester Dedlock on minor legal disputes; it is through visiting him that Esther Summerson is brought in contact with Lady Dedlock. We learn in Ch. 43 that in youth he was to have married Miss Barbary, until (using him barbarously) she broke off the engagement without explanation. He is based on the writer Walter Savage Landor who, like Boythorn, was known for his loud laughter and fondness for exaggeration; Henry Crabb Robinson said that Dickens' portrait had 'great truth and force'. Forster published in 1869 a life of Landor which Dickens reviewed in *The Examiner*.

BUCKET, MR. Detective officer largely instrumental in unravelling the mystery surrounding Lady Dedlock and in solving the Tulkinghorn murder case. As his name suggests, he is 'deep' and secretive in manner. He has been called the first detective in English fiction and is modelled on Inspector Charles Field, concerning whom Dickens had written three articles in *Household Words* (Aug.–Sept. 1850). His wife assists him in his investigations.

CARSTONE, RICHARD. Orphan; *see also* CLARE, ADA. He lives under the care of Mr Jarndyce but, corrupted by the law-suit, conceives a groundless distrust of him; taught at Winchester only to compose Latin verses, he is unable to settle to any profession. A victim of the Chancery suit (cf. Gridley), he dies shortly after its termination.

CHADBAND, MR. Minister 'of no particular denomination' (Ch. 19) and one of Dickens' eloquent religious hypocrites, he is without compassion or concern for actual human need (manifested by Jo the crossing-sweeper). His speech parodies a catechistical style of evangelical preaching. His wife is the former Mrs Rachael.

CLARE, ADA. Orphan and a distant cousin of Richard Carstone, whom she later marries; like him she is involved in the Chancery suit of Jarndyce versus Jarndyce. She lives with her cousin John Jarndyce and becomes a close friend of Esther Summerson.

DEDLOCK, SIR LEICESTER. Elderly baronet, ultra-conservative in politics, with houses in Lincolnshire (Chesney Wold) and London: 'his family is as old as the hills, and infinitely more respectable. . . . He is an honourable, obstinate, truthful, high-spirited, intensely prejudiced, perfectly unreasonable man' (Ch. 2). His wife, LADY HONORIA DEDLOCK (her Christian name is, of course, ironic), is the mother of Esther Summerson; she is considerably younger than her husband and 'at the top of the fashionable tree' (Ch. 2). VOLUMNIA Dedlock, a faded spinster, is the most prominent of a chorus of parasitical cousins who visit Chesney Wold; others include the HONOURABLE BOB STABLES and the unnamed 'debilitated cousin'; all caricature types of aristocratic idleness and affectation.

DONNY, MISS. Twins of this name keep a small boarding school, Greenleaf, at Reading, where Esther Summerson is educated for 'six happy, quiet years' (Ch. 3) to be a governess.

FLITE, MISS. Half-crazy old lady who has spent years in attending the Court of Chancery and expects 'a judgment. Shortly. On the Day of Judgment' (Ch. 3). She is lodger at Krook's shop and tells her story to Esther in Ch. 35.

GRIDLEY, MR, 'the man from Shropshire'. His life has been laid waste and his temperament embittered by a protracted Chancery suit described in Ch. 15. His death in Ch. 25 foreshadows that of Richard Carstone.

GUPPY, WILLIAM. Employed by Kenge and Carboy, London solicitors; he meets Esther Summerson when she arrives in London (Ch. 3) and later aspires unsuccessfully to marry her. His eccentric mother is a Dickensian grotesque of a type later developed more fully and brilliantly as Mr F's Aunt (in *Little Dorrit*).

GUSTER (AUGUSTA). Servant to the Snagsbys and given to fits, she is a product of the notorious Tooting baby-farm, concerning which there was a much-publicized scandal in 1849.

HORTENSE. French maid employed, and later dismissed, by Lady Dedlock; murderess of Tulkinghorn. Dickens modelled her on Mrs Maria Manning, former lady's maid of Swiss extraction, whose execution for murder he had witnessed in 1849.

HAWDON, CAPTAIN (also known as 'Nemo,' Latin for 'nobody'). Formerly an army officer, he has been the lover of Lady Dedlock before her marriage and is the father of her child (Esther Summerson). He is reduced to poverty, lives in squalor at Krook's, and copies legal documents for Mr Snagsby; Lady Dedlock's reaction to a chance glimpse of his handwriting gives Tulkinghorn the first clue to her secret (Ch. 2).

JARNDYCE, JOHN. Middle-aged bachelor-hero of the novel; he is an unwilling party to the Chancery suit of Jarndyce versus Jarndyce, and becomes the guardian of Esther Summerson. His paternal benevolence recalls Mr Brownlow (*Oliver Twist*), but by now Dickens is acutely conscious of the limitations of benevolence in dealing with the world's evil. Jarndyce's frequent references to the 'East Wind' (one of the ideas for the novel's title was 'Bleak House and the East Wind') are both an example of the Dickensian identifying catch-phrase and a reminder of Jarndyce's reluctant awareness that we inhabit a fallen world.

JELLYBY, MRS. 'Telescopic' philanthropist (see Ch. 4); the vehicle of Dickens' satire on those who could not or would not grasp that charity begins at home, she fixes her eye firmly on missionary work in Africa whilst her own children are shamefully neglected and the needy on her doorstep are destitute and uncared for. Her daughter Caroline, known as CADDY, becomes a friend of Esther Summerson, marries Prince Turveydrop, and (puzzlingly) bears a child who is deaf and dumb. PEEPY JELLYBY is also an object of his mother's inattention. Mr Jellyby is reduced to both despair and bankruptcy by his wife's indifference to domestic duties; in this respect she is the antithesis of Esther Summerson.

JENNY. Wife of a brutal brickmaker and living in conditions of poverty and squalor, she is visited by Mrs Pardiggle and Esther Summerson; when Jenny's baby dies in their presence, Esther covers its face with her handkerchief, and this object plays a role later in the novel. Jenny aids Lady Dedlock in her final flight.

JO. A crossing-sweeper; a boy without home or friends, filthy, half-starved and ignorant, he presents a moral and practical problem to which different people (Snagsby, Skimpole, Chadband, and so on) respond in very different ways. He carries infection, literally and symbolically, from the slum of Tom-all-Alone's to the middle-class world of Bleak House. He dies in Ch. 47.

JOBLING, TONY. Friend of Guppy, he occupies (under the assumed name of Weevle) the room in Krook's house in which Captain Hawdon has died.

KENGE, ('Conversation'.) London lawyer of the firm of Kenge and Carboy, he acts for Mr. Jarndyce, though his imperturbable complacency with the legal *status quo* contrasts with his client's impatience and indignation. Like many other characters in this novel and in Dickens' work generally, Kenge 'appeared to enjoy beyond everything the sound of his own voice' (Ch. 3).

KROOK, MR. Nicknamed the Lord Chancellor, he keeps a junk shop popularly known as Chancery and also lets rooms to Miss Flite and Captain Hawdon. Filthy, illiterate and suspicious of everyone, his only companion is his vicious cat Lady Jane. Krook dies of spontaneous combustion: see Dickens' Preface (1853) for a defence of this episode, which is at once richly symbolic and rendered with a vivid and gruesome sense of actuality.

NECKETT, nicknamed COAVINSES. 'Follower' or broker's man who calls in connexion with Skimpole's debts (Ch. 6). After his death Mr Jarndyce befriends his orphaned children, and his daughter CHARLEY (Charlotte) becomes Esther's maid.

PARDIGGLE, MRS. Puseyite do-gooder, an example of 'rapacious benevolence' (Ch. 8), she represents, like Mrs Jellyby, officious, insensitive and ill-judged charity; while she devotes her energies to various 'causes' her children are 'ferocious with discontent'.

QUALE, MR. Philanthropist with a 'power of indiscriminate admiration' (Ch. 15).

RACHAEL, MRS. Servant to Esther Summerson's aunt; she later marries Mr Chadband and thus reappears in the novel.

ROSA, see ROUNCEWELL, WATT.

ROUNCEWELL, MRS. 'The old housekeeper at Chesney Wold' (Ch. 7), unswerving in her loyalty to the Dedlock family. Her elder son GEORGE (referred to also as Mr George and 'the trooper') is a scapegrace ex-army man who has lost touch with his mother for many years but is reunited with her; he runs a shooting-gallery in the neighbourhood of Leicester Square and is accused of the murder of Tulkinghorn. Her younger son is a prosperous 'ironmaster' or manufacturer in the north of England, a representative of the new industrial and democratic age as Sir Leicester Dedlock is of the old aristocratic landed order; his son WATT (whose name recalls the rebel Wat Tyler, Sir Leicester's *bête noire*) falls in love with Rosa, Lady Dedlock's maid and protégée, and she becomes the occasion of a confrontation between the ironmaster and the aristocrat.

SKIMPOLE, HAROLD. Heartless sponger who exploits Jarndyce's generosity and idealism; he affects indifference to material possessions and money (as Inspector Bucket says, ' "he takes it, though" '). He is also a portrait of the romantic artist in a debased form, dabbling in many artistic fields but taking nothing seriously (cf. Gowan in *Little Dorrit*). Dickens kills him off in Ch. 61. Skimpole (originally *Leonard* Skimpole in Dickens' manuscript and even at some points in the first edition) is based on Leigh Hunt, poet and essayist; Dickens boasted in a letter that 'it is an absolute reproduction of a real man', and the resemblance was recognized by contemporaries.

SMALLWEED, GRANDFATHER (Joshua). Grotesque, partly paralysed and insatiably avaricious moneylender. His wife is in a state of advanced senility. His granddaughter JUDY and his grandson BARTHOLOMEW (Bart, Young Smallweed) are twins; the latter is a friend of Guppy.

SNAGSBY, MR. Law-stationer with premises in Cook's Court, Cursitor Street. He undertakes copying for Tulkinghorn, employs Captain Hawdon, and befriends Jo, his unostentatious charity contrasting with the empty professions of Chadband and the indifference of such do-gooders as Mrs Jellyby and Mrs Pardiggle to what is before their eyes. His unwitting involvement in the web of secrets and mysteries arouses the suspicions of his termagant wife.

SQUOD, PHIL. Physically grotesque assistant at George Rouncewell's shooting-gallery; a former waif who has survived by an act of individual, unorganized compassion – hence, a luckier Jo.

SUMMERSON, ESTHER. Narrator of almost exactly one-half of the novel, its unorthodox heroine, and an embodiment of the domestic virtues as Dickens conceived them. She is brought up as an orphan by her aunt Miss Barbary, whom she believes to be her godmother (the influence of *Jane Eyre* may be detected); she is actually the illegitimate daughter of Lady Dedlock and Captain Hawdon. Mr Jarndyce becomes her guardian and has her educated; instead of becoming a governess, however, she acts as his housekeeper. The question of whom she will marry contributes to the plot-interest, and her illness (smallpox), which leaves her face seriously disfigured but her moral beauty unimpaired, provides one of the novel's dramatic and sentimental crises. She is known by a variety of nicknames (cf. David Copperfield), including Dame Durden, Old Woman, Little Old Woman and Cobweb: see Ch. 8 and W. Axton's article in *Dickensian*, LXII, 1966.

SWILLS, LITTLE. Comic vocalist at the Sol's Arms (Ch. 11).

TULKINGHORN, MR. Elderly bachelor and attorney; he handles Sir Leicester Dedlock's legal affairs and, on his own account, tracks down Lady Dedlock's secret. The mystery of his murder provides some of the plot-interest in the later portions of the novel.

TURVEYDROP, MR. Elderly gentleman who is 'a model of Deportment' (see Dickens' brilliant description, somewhat implausibly relayed by Esther Summerson, in Ch. 14); his hero is the Prince Regent, and like Sir Leicester Dedlock he represents a survival from a vanished age. He is one of many instances of parental irresponsibility in this novel. His son PRINCE is an overworked dancing-master who marries Caddy Jellyby.

VHOLES, MR. Solicitor to Richard Carstone; physically as well as morally repulsive, he is variously referred to in terms suggestive of a predatory animal (the illustration 'Attorney and Client' accompanying Ch. 39 is relevant) and of a cannibal. His blood-sucking (he has 'something of the Vampire in him': Ch. 60) is conducted under the guise of a bleakly complacent respectability. He exemplifies 'the one great principle of the English law . . . to make business for itself' (Ch. 39).

WEEVLE, MR, see JOBLING, TONY.

WOODCOURT, ALLAN. Noble-hearted and handsome young physician devoted to tending the poor, he is present at the death of Jo and comes to love, and be loved by, Esther Summerson. His professional dedication (cf. Bucket) contrasts with the idleness of the Dedlocks. His mother is fiercely proud of her descent from an old Welsh family.

Hard Times

Texts Norton Critical Edition, ed. George Ford and Sylvère Monod (1966); Penguin English Library, ed. David Craig (1969).

Composition On 23 January 1854 Dickens wrote to Miss Burdett Coutts: 'there is such a fixed idea on the part of my printers and co-partners in *Household Words*, that a story of me, continued from week to week, would make some unheard of effect that I am going to write one'. A month later he was asking Mark Lemon (20 February) to 'note down and send me any slang terms among the tumblers and circus-people that you can call to mind' for use in 'my new story'; and on 18 April he wrote to Wills that he was 'in a dreary state, planning and planning the story of *Hard Times* (out of materials for I don't know how long a story) . . . '. Dickens' decision to embark on a weekly serial was prompted by concern over the falling sales of *Household Words* (an episode of history that repeated itself a few years later when *Great Expectations* came to the rescue of the ailing *All the Year Round*). A *Household Words* article by Dickens, 'Frauds on the Fairies' (1 October 1853), shows that the theme of the under-nourished imagination had recently been in his mind:

> In an utilitarian age, of all other times, it is a matter of grave importance that Fairy tales should be respected . . . every one who has considered the subject knows full well that a nation without fancy, without some romance, never did, never can, never will hold a great place under the sun.

At about the same time that the composition of *Hard Times* began, at the end of January 1854, Dickens visited Preston in Lancashire, which has often been identified with Coketown, to see for himself something of the strike of cotton-mill operatives in progress there; one of the results was a *Household Words* article, 'On Strike' (11

February). In this way, from different directions, the preoccupations that were to find expression in the novel and to be conveyed through, respectively, Mr Gradgrind and Stephen Blackpool came together. Manuscript and corrected proofs in Forster Collection.

Serialization   Twenty weekly numbers published in *Household Words* from 1 April to 12 August 1854. No illustrations. The serial achieved the desired effect in boosting the flagging sales of the magazine: Professor Patten notes that the circulation 'rose dramatically' on its appearance, and for the six months ending September 1854 net receipts rose 237 per cent. Division as follows: I (Chs 1–3); II (Chs 4–5); III (Ch. 6); IV (Chs 7–8); V (Chs 9–10); VI (Chs 11–12); VII (Chs 13–14); VIII (Chs 15–16); IX (Ch. 17); X (Chs 18–19); XI (Chs 20–1); XII (Ch. 22); XIII (Ch. 23); XIV (Ch. 24); XV (Chs 25–6); XVI (Chs 27–8); XVII (Chs 29–30); XVIII (Chs 31–2); XIX (Chs 33–4); XX (Chs 35–7).

Publication   Published in one volume by Bradbury & Evans in 1854 as *Hard Times, for These Times*. The dedication to Carlyle was added, as was the division into three books ('Sowing', 'Reaping', 'Garnering') and the chapter-titles. No preface or illustrations. It was assumed that the large sales of the magazine had exhausted most of the public interest, and only 5000 copies were printed; however, another 3000 were quickly called for.

Reception   Early reviews were unenthusiastic and fairly perfunctory (Professor Collins notes their 'unaccustomed brevity'). Forster's praise in the *Examiner* was exceptional: the *Athenaeum* found it 'scarcely wrought out with Mr Dickens's usual felicity', and Richard Simpson in the *Rambler* judged the novel 'stale, flat and unprofitable; a mere dull melodrama, in which character is caricature, sentiment tinsel, and moral (if any) unsound'. Macaulay's verdict in his diary was harsh: 'One excessively touching, heartbreaking passage, and the rest sullen socialism.' Within a few years, however, there were signs of more genuine appreciation: the French critic Taine discussed it in his *History of English Literature* (1856; English translation, 1871), and in 1860 Ruskin published a remarkable encomium in the *Cornhill Magazine*, repeated in his volume *Unto This Last* (1862):

> let us not lose the use of Dickens's wit and insight, because he chooses to speak in a circle of stage fire. He is entirely right in his

main drift and purpose in every book he has written; and all of them, but especially *Hard Times*, should be studied with close and earnest care by persons interested in social questions.

He found the novel 'in several respects, the greatest he has written' – a verdict that remained highly unfashionable until it was revived in 1948 by F. R. Leavis.

Butt and Tillotson subtitle their chapter on *Hard Times* in *Dickens at Work* 'The Problems of a Weekly Serial', and Dickens ran into difficulties at an early stage of composition. In February 1854 he wrote to Forster: 'The difficulty of the space is CRUSHING. Nobody can have an idea of it who has not had an experience of patient fiction-writing with some elbow-room always, and open places in perspective.' *Hard Times* is the shortest of his completed novels, and the lack of elbow-room is manifested in a certain enforced economy of effect that can make for strength (as in the opening account of the schoolroom) but also for thinness of texture. The cast of characters is restricted to about twenty; uncharacteristic, too, is the provincial setting and the necessary renunciation of the London scenes that add so much variety and richness to most of Dickens' novels.

As usual, Dickens took great pains with the title of his novel, noting twenty-five possibilities (later whittled down to fourteen), including *According to Cocker, Prove it, Stubborn Things, Mr Gradgrind's Facts, The Grindstone, Two and Two are Four, Something Tangible, Our Hard-headed Friend, Rust and Dust, Simple Arithmetic, A Matter of Calculation, A Mere Question of Figures, The Gradgrind Philosophy, Hard Heads and Soft Hearts, Heads and Tales* and *Black and White*. The antitheses of some of these, including the last two listed, hint at the bold contrasts of the book (schoolroom v. circus, Bitzer v. Sissie Jupe, and so on). Butt and Tillotson have noted that the novel was firmly in line with the policy of *Household Words* as defined by Dickens in inaugurating his magazine on 30 March 1850:

No mere utilitarian spirit, no iron binding of the mind to firm realities, will give a harsh tone to our *Household Words* . . . we would tenderly cherish that light of Fancy which is inherent in the human breast; which, according to its nurture, burns with an inspiring flame, or sinks into a sullen glare, but which (or woe betide that day!) can never be extinguished.

In his 1839 essay 'Chartism', Thomas Carlyle – to whom *Hard Times* was to be dedicated – had spoken of the 'Condition-of-England question', and in the ensuing years a number of novels appeared to which this label has been attached. Disraeli's *Sybil* (1845) gave wide currency to the phrase 'the two nations' and the notion of a Christian society in which a great gulf stretched between rich and poor. Other novels described more specifically the life of the urban masses, bringing scenes of squalor, misery, brutish labour and grinding poverty into the homes and hearts of a mainly middle-class novel-reading public: still remembered in this category are Charles Kingsley's *Yeast* and Mrs Gaskell's *Mary Barton* – both published in 1848, the year of revolutions, and the latter somewhat defiantly subtitled 'a tale of Manchester life'. *Hard Times* is Dickens' diagnosis of the 'condition of England' and his contribution to the sub-genre of the 'industrial novel'. He had earlier written memorably of the landscape and life of industrial England in *The Old Curiosity Shop*, sending Nell and her grandfather on a journey that takes them through Birmingham and the Black Country to a pre-industrial rural haven; but in *Hard Times* he writes more extensively and exclusively of 'Coketown', a northern industrial town whose very architecture seems a denial of the human spirit.

After all, however, this is only to a limited extent an industrial novel: the two chief representatives of the ruling classes are, respectively, a retired merchant and a parvenu banker, and we see little of the factory-system at close range. Its main representative is, of course, Stephen Blackpool; but even here the issue is complicated – Stephen is a victim of his fellow-workers who send him to Coventry, of the drunken wife who adds to his miseries, and of the laws that make divorce a luxury for the wealthy, as well as of the hardships of industrialism – and we see Stephen only *outside* the factory where most of his life is spent. The industrial theme is in fact subordinate to the dominant educational theme: the 'wisdom of the head' represented by the utilitarian philosophy of the Gradgrind school, and the 'wisdom of the heart' that ultimately demonstrates its superiority.

Dickens' recurring interest in education finds prominent expression in this novel which opens in a schoolroom where the contrasting figures of Bitzer and Sissie foreshadow their respective roles throughout the story. His concern with parent-child relationships also recurs as the childhood of Tom and Louisa Gradgrind is shown as a prelude to their later unhappiness. In a book that contains some notably realistic elements, the grotesque figure of Bounderby and the mysterious old woman who all-too-predictably turns out to be his mother seem to strike a jarring note; yet they ought to be seen – and the phenomenon is a widespread one in Dickens' fiction – as components in an art that even in a single work can range widely between realistic and non-realistic extremes. Gradgrind's house (Stone Lodge), the circus, the abandoned mine-shaft into which Stephen falls – these are some obvious instances of poetic symbolism. On the other hand, the novel also contains scenes and characters that would not be out of place in a work of conscientious realism. In this category are the powerful scenes (one near the end of Book the First, the other at the end of Book the Second) between Gradgrind and his daughter, as is also the figure of James Harthouse, who seems to have escaped from a society novel and who, as a study in the effete and amoral upper-class idler, recalls Steerforth in *David Copperfield* and looks forward to Henry Gowan in *Little Dorrit* and Eugene Wrayburn in *Our Mutual Friend*. Dickens' manuscript shows that he took considerable pains over one of the more obvious concessions to realism in this novel, the broad north-country dialect of Stephen Blackpool.

As noted above, *Hard Times* was not much relished by contemporary critics, probably because it lacks the characteristically Dickensian comprehensiveness, variety and humour. But F. R. Leavis's claim that it went unappreciated until his 1948 revaluation does not really (as it were) stand up to scrutiny. Ruskin's encomium has already been quoted. In 1906 G. K. Chesterton wrote that '*Hard Times* is not one of the greatest books of Dickens; but it is perhaps in a sense one of his greatest monuments', and noted the intensity of feeling in the novel and the 'almost unexpected note of severity':

> The characters are indeed exaggerated but they are bitterly and deliberately exaggerated; they are not exaggerated with the old unconscious high spirits of Nicholas Nickleby or Martin Chuzzlewit. Dickens exaggerates Bounderby because he really hates him. He exaggerated Pecksniff because he really loved him.

A few years later G. B. Shaw wrote enthusiastically and at length concerning *Hard Times*.

Leavis's influential essay appeared as an appendix to *The Great Tradition* (1948) and praises the novel's imaginative power, poetic symbolism, concentration of effect and 'clear insight into the

English social structure'. Startlingly (since the essay appeared in a period when Dickens was still unfashionable in academic circles), he makes comparisons with Shakespeare and D. H. Lawrence. His position was challenged by a number of critics, including E. D. Hirsch (*Criticism*, VI, 1964). Among other important discussions are David Lodge's analysis of the rhetoric of *Hard Times* in his *Language of Fiction* (1966); the relevant chapter in Butt and Tillotson's *Dickens at Work*; and Geoffrey Carnall's 'Dickens, Mrs. Gaskell and the Preston Strike' (*Victorian Studies*, VIII, 1964). Gross and Pearson's *Dickens and the Twentieth Century* includes John Holloway's '*Hard Times*: A History and a Criticism'. There are also some relevant pages in Philip Collins' *Dickens and Education*. The Norton Critical Edition by Ford and Monod includes many of the items mentioned above as well as much useful information concerning textual revisions. David Craig's introduction to the Penguin edition offers a Marxist approach.

CHARACTERS

BITZER. Pupil at Mr Gradgrind's school, 'light-eyed and light-haired . . . he looked as though, if he were cut, he would bleed white' (I,2: cf. Sissy Jupe). Employed as porter and 'general spy and informer' (II,1) at Bounderby's bank. He attempts to prevent Tom Gradgrind's escape, motives of self-interest overriding all considerations of humanity or gratitude.

BLACKPOOL, Stephen. Factory-worker at Coketown, 'forty years of age' (I,10): 'a good power-loom weaver, and a man of perfect integrity'. In love with Rachael, a fellow-worker and a good woman, he is inescapably chained to a drunken wife, 'foul to look at . . . but so much fouler than that in her moral infamy'. Mr Bounderby advises him that he has no hope of a divorce (I,11). He is sent to Coventry by his fellow-workers (II,4), suspected of the bank robbery (III,4) and dies after falling down Old Hell Shaft, a disused mine-shaft (III,6) – in his death, as in his life, a victim of the heartless industrial system. His name suggests both martyrdom and his Lancashire origins.

BOUNDERBY, JOSIAH. 'A rich man: banker, merchant, manufacturer, and what not' (I,4); a prominent citizen of Coketown and a self-advertising self-made man. He marries Louisa Gradgrind. His pretence of humility is exposed by the appearance of his mother (*see* PEGLER MRS).

CHILDERS, E. W. B. Performer at 'Sleary's Horse-riding'; his son
KIDDERMINSTER is a partner in his act (see I,6).

GRADGRIND, Thomas. 'A man of fact and calculations' (I,2), he lives
in the aptly-named Stone Lodge with his wife and his children
THOMAS (Tom), LOUISA, MALTHUS and JANE. Thomas junior
attends his father's school and is later employed in Bounderby's
bank, which he robs (II,8). Upon detection he is smuggled out of
the country with Mr Sleary's help and in the face of Bitzer's
attempt to prevent his escape. Louisa also attends her father's
school and later, at his urging, makes an unsuitable marriage to
Bounderby (see I,15). In the dramatic scene ending the second
Book of the novel, she tells her father what his teaching has
brought her to and confesses her affair with Harthouse (adding,
however – to placate Mrs Grundy – that ' "I have not disgraced
you" '). The unhappy fates of Tom and Louisa constitute a
damning criticism of Gradgrind's Utilitarian philosophy.
(Gradgrind's name may well reflect that of James and John
Stuart Mill, prominently associated with the doctrine of
Utilitarianism, as well as hinting at the mills or factories of
Coketown.) Mrs Gradgrind is a woman 'of surpassing feebleness'
(I,4) whose quite unsentimental deathbed (II,9) is one of
Dickens' most memorable.

HARTHOUSE, JAMES. Effete gentleman; he enters politics in a mood of
cynical boredom, having been advised of 'a good opening among
the hard Fact fellows' (II,2). In Coketown he meets and (to
relieve his boredom) makes love to Louisa Gradgrind; when she
terminates the affair he departs (III,2). One of Dickens' portraits
of a recurring *bête-noire*: the idle and immoral scion of a 'good'
family who has received an upper-class education (cf. Steerforth
in *DC* and Henry Gowan in *LD*). G. B. Shaw describes him as a
study of 'the Victorian "swell"'.

JUPE, CECILIA (Sissy). Pupil at Mr Gradgrind's school; her father
'belongs to the horse-riding' (I,2) at Mr Sleary's travelling circus.
She is 'so dark-eyed and dark-haired that she seemed to receive a
deeper and more lustrous colour from the sun when it shone upon
her' (cf. her antithesis, Bitzer). When she is abandoned by her
father, she is received into Mr Gradgrind's family (I,7).

M'CHOAKUMCHILD, MR. Teacher at Mr Gradgrind's school, and
member of the first generation of trained teachers who passed
from state-aided training colleges into the schools in 1853. For an
ironical comment on such a training see the final paragraphs of

I,2. His name, as well as being obviously and improbably appropriate to his teaching methods, may be intended to recall that of J. R. McCulloch, author of *A Descriptive and Statistical Account of the British Empire* (1837) and one of the first Fellows of the Statistical Society of London (founded 1834). In a comparison of *HT* and *D&S*, Philip Collins (*Dickens and Education*, p. 144) describes M'Choakumchild as 'a poor man's Blimber – equally well-meaning, but equally engaged in "Murdering the Innocents," denying them the right to any childhood, zealously suppressing their imagination and individuality'.

MERRYLEGS. Performing dog at 'Sleary's Horse-riding'. His death is described (III,8).

PEGLER, MRS. Mysterious old woman who appears in Coketown (I,12) and later turns out to be Mr Bounderby's long-lost and unjustly maligned mother (III,5).

RACHAEL. A good woman 'five and thirty years of age' (I,10): *see* BLACKPOOL, STEPHEN.

SLACKBRIDGE. Mob-orator and agitator (II,4): Dickens' unsympathetic and (according to some verdicts) ill-informed portrait of a trade-unionist. On his origins, see Geoffrey Cornall's essay cited earlier.

SLEARY, MR. Proprietor of 'Sleary's Horse-riding', a genial, brandy-sodden philosopher (see end of III,8) with a comically lisping speech. He helps to smuggle Tom Gradgrind out of the country. His daughter JOSEPHINE is a performer at the circus.

SPARSIT, MRS. Housekeeper to Mr Bounderby; she is a 'highly connected' elderly lady (I,7) in a much-vaunted state of decayed gentility, and a satirical portrait of groundless esteem for family connexions. She spies on Louisa's affair with Harthouse and is finally dismissed (IV,9).

Little Dorrit

Texts Penguin English Library, ed. John Holloway (1967); Macmillan College Classics, ed. R. D. McMaster (1969): Clarendon Dickens, ed. H. P. Sucksmith (1979).

Composition According to Forster, Dickens started to make notes for a new novel in January 1855, 'six months before the first page of *Little Dorrit* was written'. He seems to have experienced great difficulty over the early stages of composition, and the preliminary planning occupied him for months: gone were the days when he dashed rapidly into the writing of a novel and even kept two novels going simultaneously. Dickens himself referred to the book for the first time in a letter of 10 March 1855, where he described himself as 'In the ghostly unrest of going to begin a new book': at about the same time he said he was 'writing and planning and making notes over an immense number of little bits of paper', and 'in the first stage of a new book, which consists in going round and round the idea, as you see a bird in his cage go about and about his sugar before he touches it'. As Harvey Peter Sucksmith has said, this stage of the creative process was characterized by 'intense unease, much difficulty in making progress, and considerable uncertainty and hesitation'. One sign of his uncertainty is in the memoranda he jotted down for the opening number: 'People to meet and part as travellers do, and the future connexion between them in the story, not to be now shewn to the reader but to be worked out as in life.' This idea was not in the event very thoroughly pursued, though Dickens seems to have returned to it at the opening of the second book. Among other ideas first noted and then rejected in Dickens' planning of the early numbers are: 'Family and two daughters?'; 'Working jeweller and *his* daughters?'; 'Miss Wade in the prison?'; 'Her father?'. We also know that Dickens entered the following in his notebook: 'The people who lay all their sins negligences and ignorances, on Providence.' Forster's version of this is as follows:

> The book took its origin from the notion he had of a leading man for a story who should bring about all the mischief in it, lay it all on Providence, and say at every fresh calamity, 'well, it's a mercy, however, nobody was to blame, you know!'.

Dickens' first title for the novel, *Nobody's Fault*, reflects this theme; but the 'leading man' never materializes.

By 8 May Dickens had hit on a 'capital' title, presumably *Nobody's Fault*, but was still in 'a state of restlessness impossible to be described'; and he repeated the phrase almost word for word on 21 May ('in a state of restlessness not to be described or imagined'), though he had by now begun to write the opening chapter. Progress was slow, and it was not until mid-August that he was able to tell Forster that he had begun the second number, and not until the end of September that he had 'almost finished No. 3'. The publishers announced the novel in mid-October, serialization began on the last day of November, and as usual it proceeded *pari passu* with composition. On 11 May 1857 he told Wilkie Collins that he had finished the novel two days earlier – none too soon, since it appeared in volume form only three weeks later. From first to last it had taken well over two years.

Serialization   In nineteen monthly parts, from December 1855 to June 1857. 'Though challenged by other cheap forms of serialization, shilling monthly parts continued through the fifties to hold their own' (Patten). Illustrations by Phiz. Division as follows: I (Book One, 'Poverty', Chs 1–4: hereafter abbreviated as I, 1–4, etc.); II (I, 5–8); III (I, 9–11); IV (I, 12–14); V (I, 15–18); VI (I, 19–22); VII (I, 23–5); VIII (I, 26–9); IX (I, 30–2); X (I, 33–6); XI (Book Two, 'Riches', Chs 1–4); XII (II, 5–7); XIII (II, 8–11); XIV (II, 12–14); XV (II, 15–18); XVI (II, 19–22); XVII (II, 23–6); XVIII (II, 27–9); XIX–XX (II, 30–4). The opening number sold very well: the 32,000 copies printed went quickly and the sale eventually reached 38,000. On 2 December, Dickens told Forster, 'Little Dorrit has beaten even Bleak House out of the field. It is a most tremendous start, and I am overjoyed at it.' In his preface, written a year and a half later, he was to echo this proud boast: 'In the Preface to *Bleak House* I remarked that I had never had so many readers. In the Preface to its next successor, *Little Dorrit*, I have still to repeat the same words', for the sales held up well throughout the run of the serial. (*Little Dorrit* was, of course, the 'next successor' to *Bleak House* in the sense that it was the next novel published in twenty monthly numbers; *Hard Times*, which comes between them, was a weekly serial.) Sales were no doubt helped by an extensive publicity campaign which involved the distribution of 4000 posters and 310,000 handbills.

Publication   Published in one volume by Bradbury & Evans on 30 May 1857. Dickens added a preface and a dedication to Clarkson Stanfield. Again, sales were good and Sucksmith states that 'With regard to sales, *Little Dorrit* was Dickens's greatest success since his earliest triumphs.'

Reception   The critical reception of this novel contrasts strikingly both with its popularity among contemporary readers (evinced by sales figures) and the high esteem in which it is now held, 'For many critics indeed *Little Dorrit* became a by-word for the bad Dickens' (Philip Collins). Even before serialization was concluded, *Fraser's Magazine* had roundly pronounced it 'decidedly the worst' of all Dickens' novels to date, and a reviewer in *Blackwood's Magazine* (April 1857) significantly deplored Dickens' 'tendency to abandon his strong point as humourist and comic writer. . . . For as a humourist we prefer Dickens to all living men.' The same reviewer's regret at the vanishing of 'the old natural, easy, unconscious Pickwickian style' – 'Alas, alas! shades of Gamp, Hominy, Swiveller, and all the Pickwickian host!' – was often to be repeated by reviewers of Dickens' later novels. The widespread nostalgia for Dickens' early manner may well have been, as Collins shrewdly suggests, a nostalgia for the reviewers' own departed youth (the undergraduate who roared at *Pickwick* was turning forty when *Dorrit* appeared); but in the case of this novel there were also more specific reasons for disgruntlement. Dickens' political views offended many; and (to quote Collins again) many were 'put off by the general "darkness" of the novel, and its sad middle-aged unglamorous hero'.

Little Dorrit   is, says Sucksmith, 'not only the most topical of Dickens' novels but also the one in which he draws most widely and overtly upon the events of his life and times'. Even though the action is ostensibly set in a period considerably anterior to the date of composition, it is in most respects very much a novel of the fifties, and there are even references to events that took place while composition was in progress. Some of the most important of the topical allusions are:

(1) 'Almost all the satire on the Circumlocution Office, from Number III onwards, was inspired by contemporary events' (Sucksmith). The Northcote-Trevelyan Report of 1853 had sharply criticized modes of recruitment into the civil service and recommended (among other things) competitive examinations for entrants and promotion by merit.

(2) The existing administrative machinery and personnel were put to the test when Britain entered the Crimean War in March 1854:

> soon an appalling record of muddle, nepotism, misery, and brave but needless death emerged. With the aid of the telegraph, William Russell, special correspondent for *The Times*, gave an unprecedented immediacy to the tale of confusion and horror in camps, battlefields, and hospitals . . . . When in January 1855 John Arthur Roebuck . . . demanded a parliamentary inquiry into the mismanagement of the war, Aberdeen's government fell' (R. D. McMaster).

Dickens' friend, the Liberal MP Henry Layard, was one of the leaders of the Administrative Reform Association; Dickens joined the Association and addressed it in June 1855, soon after beginning work on *Little Dorrit*. During 1855 he also published a series of articles in *Household Words* attacking governmental muddle and incompetence.

(3) The reference in Dickens' preface to 'a certain Irish bank' is to the failure of the Tipperary Bank; one of its directors, John Sadleir, an MP, who had overdrawn £200,000 from the bank, committed suicide on Hampstead Heath on 16 February 1856. Sadleir is the prototype of Merdle, with further hints borrowed from the career of George Hudson, the 'railway king', who rose from obscurity, moved in high society, enjoyed the friendship of the Prince Consort, and went into exile in about 1850 after a stock crash involving some eighty million pounds.

(4) 'The portrait of Lord Decimus Tite Barnacle . . . as an arrogant aristocrat, a glib, evasive, and obstructionist politician, was stimulated by Dickens's view of Lord Palmerston who became Prime Minister on Aberdeen's fall in January 1855' (Sucksmith).

Although, then, the action of the novel begins 'thirty years ago' (the novel's opening words), its world is less that of the twenties than of the fifties. Probably the most important element in the novel suggestive of an earlier period is the Marshalsea Prison, which had been closed in 1849. But chronological consistency or historical verisimilitude was never an overriding concern for Dickens. In one instance, what looked like a topical allusion was denied by Dickens and was apparently an example of life coming close to copying art. The collapse of Mrs Clennam's house was said to have been based on 'the recent fall of houses in Tottenham Court Road'; but Dickens rejected this suggestion, pointing out that the fictional event had been 'carefully prepared for from the very first presentation of the old house in the story' – additional evidence, if any is needed, of the close-knit planning of the novel from start to finish.

Dickens drew widely on his continental travels for the account in Book Two of the Dorrit family's journeyings. And he drew on a recent experience that had touched a long-standing but still sensitive memory in basing Flora Finching on Maria Winter (née Beadnell), whom he had loved a quarter of a century earlier and met again in 1855 (see 'The Dickens Circle'). He went further back for memories of the Marshalsea and of his father, to whom Mr Dorrit owes much.

As noted above, Dicken's original title was *Nobody's Fault*, on which Butt and Tillotson comment that, despite the change,

'Nobody's Fault' survives and not only in the Barnacles. Its meanings are multiple. Beginning as irony, a comment on the tendency to shift responsibility, it becomes a gloomy truth pervading all parts of the novel, as a ground-tone of despair about society. As in *Bleak House*, the calamities of the novel spring not so much from a single evil will but from the corruption of the whole condition of things; Mr Merdle and Mrs. Clennam are them- selves victims. The Marshalsea is more than a prison; it is a microcosm of the world. Gaining wealth, Mr Dorrit escapes only from one prison into another: the prison of society – with Mr Merdle's butler and Mrs. General as half-comic jailers. We are shown the prison of poverty in Bleeding Heart Yard, the prison of administration in the Circumlocution Office, the prison of heredity and temperament in Mrs. Clennam and Miss Wade. We are all each other's prisoners; there is no way out, for it is 'nobody's fault'.

This makes it sound like a sad, depressed and depressing, even embittered novel – as indeed it is, though it is perhaps going too far to say that *all* parts of the novel are pervaded by gloom and despair. If Dickens exacts a full look at the worst, he also expresses a faith in human goodness and in the power of love: in Amy Dorrit's love (not only for her father and her family but, touchingly, for the mentally defective Maggy), the Plornishes' unenvious contentment and neighbourliness, Daniel Doyce's solid worth, Flora's endearing and effusive generosity, and in the love that brings together Arthur Clennam and Little Dorrit at the end of the novel (Dickens is not yet ready for the uncompromisingly painful ending that he first wrote for *Great Expectations*). John Wain has called *Little Dorrit* 'Dickens's most tragic novel', but it is a tragedy that, unorthodoxly, ends with a marriage that we are clearly meant to believe will bring deep and abiding happiness. Dickens' conclusion resembles, in fact, that of Matthew Arnold in 'Dover Beach', written only a few years earlier than *Little Dorrit*: just as Arnold, contemplating 'human misery' and seeing life as a struggle on 'a darkling plain', comes to the conclusion 'Ah, love, let us be true/To one another!', Dickens sees private love (charity rather than eros) as constituting the only hope for mankind in a world of public evil and corruption.

The plot of this novel is complex, not so much in the sense that it is full of event – John Wain has gone so far as to suggest that it is really 'plotless' and static, a labyrinth rather than a road – but in the sense that the machinations of Mrs Clennam, Flintwinch and others are highly involved. (The editor of the Penguin edition usefully provides an appendix summarising the dénouement of the story.) As in many of Dickens' novels, there is plot in two senses of the word: a fictional structure partly composed by plotting on the part of some of the characters. But its main outlines are clear enough, and the contrast between the two 'books' is a bold one: for Mr Dorrit, with his release from prison and his new-found wealth everything changes and yet nothing is different. The prison symbolism is indeed dominant throughout, in the way that Shakespeare's tragedies are permeated by recurring symbols that give unity to a complex work of art. *Little Dorrit* opens in a literal prison; moves in the second chapter to one that is only half-literal (the travellers in quarantine are temporary 'prisoners' of the regulations); and moves again in the third chapter to the metaphorical prison of an English Victorian Sunday and the self-induced prison of Mrs Clennam's paralysis. Dickens has solved triumphantly the problem of giving an extraordinary degree of cohesion to a very long narrative that can at the same time accommodate very diverse elements.

For once again the remarkable flexibility of Dickens' art must be stressed. There are passages of sentiment (the early presentation of Amy Dorrit), of satire (Mrs General's concern for the proprieties), of high comedy (Flora Finching deserves to stand alongside Mrs Gamp as one of Dickens' supreme comic creations), of highly conventional and absurd melodrama (Rigaud-Blandois), of acute psychological observation (the self-deceiving behaviour of Mr Dorrit), and of genuinely moving and exciting drama (Mr Dorrit's collapse, and Mr Merdle's suicide) – to touch on only some of the components of this rich and varied novel. And if there is an almost Gissing-like realism in such passages as the homecoming of Arthur Clennam, what are we to make of the surrealistic scenes involving Mrs Merdle, her bosom, and her parrot? Such a spectrum of fictional modes reminds us of the danger and the folly of attempting to sum up any novel by Dickens, and especially any of the late, 'dark' novels, by a single or simple formula.

Dickens' manuscript and proofs show that his effects did not always come easily or quickly. When Flora is introduced in Ch. 13, for instance, the manuscript shows some significant shifts of intention and a sharpening of the verbal art in many places. Flora, finally described as 'very broad', was originally 'very fat'; the verb 'said' is replaced by more expressive words ('giggled', 'tittered'); and in the following passage the words here italicized were added above the line:

> for five days I had a cold *in the head* from crying which I passed entirely in the back drawing room – there is the back drawing room *still* on the first floor *and still at the back of the house* to confirm my words . . .'.

The effect of spontaneity and fluency was achieved only by patient revision. Again, when Mrs Merdle is introduced in Chapter 20, Dickens first wrote 'The lady was not young but she was got up to appear young' (a commonplace and unincisive formulation), then revised it to 'The lady was not young *and fresh from the hand of Nature* but was young and fresh from the hand of her maid', the italicized words being added above the line. Clearly the later Dickensian felicities were not always, perhaps not generally, spontaneous but had to be worked at and worked for; and there is a world of difference between the flowing, relatively unrevised early manuscripts (for example, the surviving fragments of *Oliver Twist*) and the crabbed, heavily corrected later work, which must have caused the printers many a headache. One might even risk a generalization and suggest that the most brilliant stylistic effects were most heavily worked over – Flora's dialogue, for example, often showing thickets of revisions. Nor had Dickens finished revising when the manuscript left his hands. At the proof stage he paid careful attention, for instance, to the punctuation of Flora's speeches, at one point cutting out seven commas and a dash in less than four lines to indicate her breathless flow of words; and in Mrs Merdle's interview with Fanny Dorrit (Ch. 20) the former's patronizing and glacial manner is stressed in the corrected proofs, 'frostily' being added at one point, and 'my dear' being changed to 'Miss Dorrit', and 'friendly' to 'obliging'. Much detailed work remains to be done on Dickens' language and style, and can more readily be done now that textual editions of many of the novels have become available.

The introductions to the three editions mentioned above can all be recommended; Sucksmith's in particular gives a very full and useful account of the origins and composition of the novel. There is a short chapter in Butt and Tillotson's *Dickens at Work*; John Butt has also discussed the serialization of the novel in his *Pope, Dickens and Others* (1969); and Paul Herring has analysed Dickens' number-plans (*Modern Philology*, LXIV, 1966). John Wain's essay, referred to above, is in Gross and Pearson's *Dickens and the Twentieth Century*, and there is a longer and more rewarding essay by F. R. Leavis in *Dickens the Novelist*. Leavis's, indeed, has claims to be considered one of the two most important essays on this novel, the other being Lionel Trilling's (first published in 1953, in *Kenyon Review*, XV, and as the introduction to the New Oxford Illustrated edition; reprinted in *The Opposing Self*, 1955). R. D. McMaster has written on the structure of the novel (*Queen's Quarterly*, LXVII, 1961), and William Myers has discussed 'The Radicalism of *Little Dorrit*' (in *Literature and Politics in the Nineteenth Century*, ed. John Lucas, (1971). There is a monograph on this novel by J. C. Reid (1967).

CHARACTERS

BANGHAM, MRS. 'Charwoman and messenger' in the Marshalsea Prison (see I,6).

BARNACLE, TITE. First referred to (I,9) as 'a man of great power. . . . a commissioner, or a board, or a trustee, "or something" . . . under Government – high in the Cirumlocution Office'. We learn later (I,10) that 'The Barnacle family had for some time helped to administer the Circumlocution Office . . . . The Barnacles were a very high family, and a very large family.' They represent the nepotism and inefficiency in the civil service: on the contemporary satire, and on Lord Palmerston as a possible prototype of Lord Decimus Tite Barnacle, see above. Barnacle Junior (FERDINAND) is described in I,10 and later visits Arthur Clennam in prison (II,28).

BLANDOIS, see RIGAUD.

BOB. Turnkey at the Marshalsea (see I,6).

CASBY, CHRISTOPHER ('the Patriarch'). Owner of property in Bleeding Heart Yard and formerly town-agent to Lord Decimus Tite Barnacle. He is described in the chapter named after him, 'Patriarchal' (I,13) and lives off the Gray's Inn Road with his widowed daughter and only child FLORA (see FINCHING, FLORA). Actually a grasping and extortionate landlord, he pretends benevolence but is exposed and physically humiliated by Pancks (II,32).

CAVALLETTO, JOHN BAPTIST. Italian described in the opening chapter of the novel, where he is found in the Marseilles prison together with Rigaud. He reappears in I,11 and meets Rigaud again by chance, running away from him in fear. On arriving in London he is run over and injured in a street accident, and found by Arthur Clennam, who befriends him (I,13). He settles in Bleeding Heart Yard and later tells Clennam that Rigaud is a murderer.

CHIVERY, JOHN. 'The sentimental son of a turnkey' at the Marshalsea; he is in love with Amy Dorrit (see I,18). He visits Mr Dorrit (II,18) and later tells Arthur Clennam that Amy loves him (II,27). His mother appears also (I,22).

CLENNAM, ARTHUR. The subdued, melancholy, entirely unromantic hero of the novel, described in I,2 as 'a grave dark man of forty' who 'has been more than twenty years in China'. He returns home in I,3, to the scenes of a bleak and repressive childhood;

takes an interest in Amy Dorrit and her family; falls in love with Minnie Meagles, but discovers that she is engaged to Gowan (I,28); meets his old love, Flora Finching; goes into partnership with Daniel Doyce; is ruined when Merdle's bank collapses, and enters the Marshalsea prison (II,26); is nursed there during an illness by Amy Dorrit; and marries her in the final chapter. His mother MRS CLENNAM (later revealed not to be in fact his real mother) is a widow and a stern woman, narrow and harsh in her religious doctrines, who has lost the use of her limbs and never leaves her room. Later she rises from her couch and flees the house (II,30–1), and goes to the Marshalsea in an attempt to make restitution for a wrong committed many years before and to ask Amy Dorrit for her forgiveness.

DORRIT, AMY ('Little Dorrit', 'the child of the Marshalsea'). Introduced (I,5) as a girl who visits Mrs Clennam's house to do needlework: 'her diminutive figure, small features, and slight spare dress, gave her the appearance of being much younger than she was. A woman, probably of not less than two-and-twenty, she might have been passed in the street for little more than half that age.' She was born in the Marshalsea prison (I,6), and is devoted to her father, of whose good fortune she learns in I,35. She accompanies him to France and Italy, writing to Arthur Clennam from Venice (II,4) and from Rome (II,11). She visits Arthur in prison (II,30); later nurses him through an illness; and finally marries him, having learned from Mrs Clennam that she is entitled to a legacy under a will suppressed by the latter. Amy's father WILLIAM DORRIT, 'the Father of the Marshalsea', is introduced and described in I,6, which narrates his arrival at the prison more than twenty years earlier. He learns of his fortune from Arthur Clennam (I,35), leaves prison (I,36), is found at the opening of the second book travelling through the Alps, en route for Italy, in great style as an affluent gentleman accompanied by his family. In Rome he has a breakdown and believes he is back in prison (II,19); and soon dies. EDWARD (Tip) Dorrit, the feckless brother of Amy, has a series of jobs: 'But whatever Tip went into, he came out of tired, announcing that he had cut it' (I,7). Her sister FANNY, two years older than Amy, becomes a dancer, and is as proud and impulsive as Amy is quiet and modest. Resentful of slights, she marries Edmund Sparkler largely to spite his mother, Mrs Merdle (see II,14–15). FREDERICK DORRIT, brother of

William and hence Amy's uncle ('a ruined uncle': I,6), is a broken old man who plays the 'clarionet' in a small theatre orchestra.

DOYCE, DANIEL. 'A smith and engineer' whose efforts to bring an invention to official notice have been frustrated by the Circumlocution Office for many years: see I,10. His factory is in Bleeding Heart Yard. His history is related in I,16. In conjunction with Arthur Clennam, he establishes an engineering firm: for a pointed contrast between the firm's genuinely useful work and middle-class dilettantism and parasitism, see the opening of II,8. Doyce, who represents a type new in the Victorian period, is contrasted with the archaic and obsolete survivals of an earlier period (cf. Rouncewell in *Bleak House*). He is ruined in the collapse of Merdle's bank but prospers abroad, where he wins a recognition denied him by his own country (II,34).

FINCHING, FLORA (née Casby). Daughter of Christopher Casby, a garrulous but good-hearted widow and formerly the beloved of Arthur Clennam (for the superb scene of their reunion and the abrupt collapse of Clennam's romantic image of the past, see I,13). On Maria Beadnell, the prototype of Flora, see 'The Dickens Circle'. Dickens wrote in 1856: 'There are some things in Flora in number seven that seem to me extraordinary droll, with something serious at the bottom of them after all'; 'It came into my head one day that we have all had our Floras, and that it was a half-serious, half-ridiculous truth which had never been told.' Flora's aunt by marriage, referred to only as MR F's AUNT, is a formidable old lady, eccentric if not senile, and a brilliant comic creation (see I,13).

FLINTWINCH, AFFERY. An old servant to Mrs Clennam. Her husband JEREMIAH is one of the plotters of the novel; he receives a mysterious visitor, apparently his double (actually his twin brother EPHRAIM), in I,4; conspires with Rigaud; and disappears when the Clennam house collapses, eventually turning up in Holland (II,31).

GENERAL, MRS. Described in II,2, she is employed as companion and preceptress to Mr Dorrit's daughters and represents the Victorian proprieties incarnate:

> Mrs. General had no opinions. Her way of forming a mind was to prevent it from forming opinions . . . . Even her propriety

could not dispute that there was impropriety in the world; but
Mrs General's way of getting rid of it was to put it out of sight,
and make believe that there was no such thing.

GOWAN, HENRY. Cynical artist and upper-class idler, introduced in
I,17, where Daniel Doyce observes that he has '"sauntered into
the Arts at a leisurely Pall-Mall pace"'. His family is 'a distant
ramification of the Barnacles', and his late father has been
'originally attached to a legation abroad' but 'had been pen-
sioned off as a Commissioner of nothing particular somewhere or
other, and had died at his post with his drawn salary in his hand,
nobly defending it to the last extremity'. Gowan courts Minnie
Meagles, whose father ' "has twice taken his daughter abroad in
the hope of separating her from Mr Gowan"'. He marries her
and appears in II,1, en route for Italy with his new wife. Gowan
owns a Newfoundland dog LION, which is poisoned by Rigaud
(II,6). Gowan's mother (described in I,25) lives in a grace-and-
favour apartment at Hampton Court and is an insufferable snob
who patronizes Mr Meagles, affecting to believe that her son is
being trapped into marriage; whereas Mr Meagles is far from
desiring it, and the advantage is all on Gowan's side (see II,8 for a
highly effective scene).

LAGNIER, *see* RIGAUD.

LION, *see* GOWAN, HENRY.

MAGGY. A grotesque, mentally retarded young woman (the
medical authenticity of her portrayal has been confirmed by
Russell Brain). She is befriended by Amy Dorrit, whom she calls
'Little Mother' (for a vivid description of Maggy, see I,9). She
and Amy encounter a prostitute in the London streets (I,14).

MEAGLES, MR. Introduced in I,2, in Marseilles, where he and his
family have been delayed by quarantine in the course of a
continental tour. He meets Arthur Clennam on that occasion and
again in London; later Arthur visits him at his Twickenham
home (I,16). He and his wife are prosperous, good-hearted but
simple people; see also under Henry Gowan. Their daughter
MINNIE (Pet) is described in I,2; she is a beautiful but spoilt girl
whose twin sister had died in early childhood. She is loved by
Arthur Clennam but is courted by Gowan and marries the latter:
for Mr Meagles' pathetic resignation to her loss, see the end of
II,33. *See also* TATTYCORAM.

MERDLE, MR. Financier, described in I,21: 'Mr Merdle was

immensely rich; a man of prodigious enterprise; a Midas without
the ears, who turned all he touched to gold.' An unattractive
man, he moves in society (with a house 'in Harley Street,
Cavendish Square') but with obvious discomfort, and is despised
by his own butler. He is 'in Parliament, of course' and 'in the
City, necessarily'. He gives a dinner party (II,21) at which are
present such semi-allegorical guests as Bar, Bishop, Horse
Guards, Treasury, Bellows and Bench. He commits suicide
(II,25), his bank collapses, and he is exposed as 'simply the
greatest Forger and the greatest Thief that ever cheated the
gallows'. On the contemporary prototypes of Merdle, see above.
The collapse of his bank ruins, among many others, Arthur
Clennam, Daniel Doyce, Pancks, and Amy, Fanny and Edward
Dorrit. His wife, described in I,20, is a proud, unfeeling woman:
affecting a desire for the simple life, she conforms to the dictates of
society ('"We know it is hollow and conventional and worldly
and every shocking, but unless we are Savages in the Tropical
seas (I should have been charmed to be one myself–most
delightful life and perfect climate, I am told), we must consult
it"'; later she describes herself, unconvincingly, as '"pastoral to a
degree, by nature"'). She reproaches Mr Merdle for not living
up to his position in society (I,33). Her son by a previous
marriage, EDMUND SPARKLER, is 'chuckleheaded'–'"almost an
idiot"', according to Fanny Dorrit–and is 'monomaniacal in
offering marriage to all manner of undesirable young ladies'
(I,21). He proposes to Fanny, who at first refuses but later marries
him (II,15). He is appointed to the Circumlocution Office (II,12).

MR. F's AUNT, see under FINCHING, FLORA.

PANCKS. Rent-collector for Casby, described in I,13 and compared there to 'a little labouring steam-engine'. He lives in
Pentonville. His employer compels him to press the impoverished
dwellers in Bleeding Heart Yard for payment with the utmost
ruthlessness; he thus acts as a catspaw for the apparently
benevolent Casby (cf. a similar relationship between Riah and
Fledgeby in *Our Mutual Friend*). He is responsible for discovering
that Mr Dorrit is heir to a fortune (I,32). He later cuts off Casby's
hair (II,32), thus revealing the truth about his physical appearance and moral nature.

PLORNISH. Mr and Mrs Plornish live in Bleeding Heart Yard and
are introduced in I,12. They befriend Cavalletto and represent
the instinctive generosity and goodheartedness of the poor

(compare the quotation from one of Dickens' speeches on pp. 268–9 below). Mr Plornish is a plasterer; his wife is referred to as SALLY in I,12 but as MARY in II,27.

RIGAUD. Foreign villain of the novel, described in its opening chapter, where he is found in the Marseilles prison and proclaims himself 'a cosmopolitan gentleman' and 'a citizen of the world'. A stagey willain (even Dickens refers to 'his theatrical air') with a strong hint of diabolism (like the prince of darkness, he is a gentleman – a word Rigaud uses habitually and which invites comparison with other specimens in the novel such as Gowan). He reappears in I,11, now under the name of Lagnier; and again in I, 30, where he visits Flintwinch in London, having assumed the name of Blandois. He turns up once more in the Alps (II,1) and accompanies Gowan to Venice (II,6); revisits Flintwinch (II,10), and attempts to blackmail Mrs Clennam, having obtained possession of the suppressed codicil. He is killed in the collapse of the Clennam house (II,31).

RUGG, MR. Agent and debt-collector. Pancks is a lodger in his Pentonville home (I,25). MRS AND MISS RUGG (the latter has 'a little property' derived from the damages in a breach of promise suit) also appear.

SPARKLER, EDMUND, *see* MERDLE, MR.

TATTYCORAM. Nickname of an orphan from the Foundling Hospital (there named HARRIET BEADLE) who has been adopted by the Meagles family after the loss of their own daughter (Minnie's twin). The nickname has been devised, somewhat insensitively, by Mr Meagles (after Captain Thomas Coram, founder of the Foundling Hospital, and Tatty, a form of Harriet). She acts as companion and attendant to Minnie, and her inferior status fills her with resentment. She is described in I,2; confides in Miss Wade; runs away from the Meagles family (I,27) and takes refuge with Miss Wade; but eventually returns to the Meagles (II,33).

TICKIT, MRS. Elderly lady who looks after the Meagles' home in their absences.

WADE, MISS. A 'reserved' and 'handsome young Englishwoman' with 'a proud observant face'; she is introduced in I,2 as one of the English travellers in Marseilles. She harbours Tattycoram after the latter has run away. Her life story is recounted in II,21 ('The History of a Self-Tormentor').

WOBBLER, MR. Official in the Circumlocution Office (see I,10).

A Tale of Two Cities

Text   Penguin English Library, ed. George Woodcock (1970).

Composition   Although he had conceived the idea for *A Tale of Two Cities* much earlier, Dickens did not begin writing the novel until a few weeks before serial publication was due to start. On 21 February 1859 he confessed that 'I cannot please myself with the opening of my story, and cannot in the least settle at it or take to it.' Once started, he found the compressed form of short weekly instalments very taxing, as he had earlier done with *Hard Times*. To Forster he wrote on 25 August 1859 that 'Nothing but the interest of the subject, and the pleasure of striving with the difficulty of the forms of treatment, nothing in the mere way of money, I mean, could also repay the time and trouble of the incessant condensation.' It was finished before he set off on a provincial reading tour on 19 October. Manuscript in Forster Collection.

Serialization   31 weekly instalments in *All the Year Round*, which the novel was designed to launch, from 30 April to 26 November 1859. The first instalment appeared in the opening number of the new periodical. Divison as follows: I (Book I, Chs 1–3); II (Ch. 4); III (Ch. 5); IV (Ch. 6); V (Book II, Chs 1–2); VI (Ch. 3); VII (Chs 4–5); VIII (Ch. 6); IX (Chs 7–8); X (Ch. 9); XI (Chs 10–11); XII (Chs 12–13); XIII (Ch. 14); XIV (Ch. 15); XV (Ch. 16); XVI (Chs 17–18); XVII (Chs 19–20); XVIII (Ch. 21); XIX (Chs 22–3); XX (Ch. 24); XXI (Book III, Ch. 1); XXII (Chs 2–3); XXIII (Chs 4–5); XXIV (Chs 6–7); XXV (Ch. 8); XXVI (Ch. 9); XXVII (Ch. 10); XXVIII (Chs 11–12); XXIX (Ch. 13); XXX (Ch. 14); XXXI (Ch. 15). Also serialized monthly, as described by Dickens:

> I have struck out a rather original and bold idea. That is, at the end of each month to publish the monthly part in the green cover,

with the two illustrations at the old shilling. This will give All the Year Round always the interest and precedence of a fresh weekly portion during the month; and will give me my old standing with my old public, and the advantage (very necessary in this story) of having numbers of people who read it in no portions smaller than a monthly part.

In other words, Dickens combined periodical publication with serialization in monthly parts. The latter included illustrations by 'Phiz'.

Publication   Published in one volume by Chapman & Hall in 1859.

Reception   The novel aroused little enthusiasm among contemporary reviewers and some were positively hostile – notably James Fitzjames Stephen in the *Saturday Review* (17 December 1859). Later, however, its brevity, its strong plot, and its popularity on the stage made it one of the most widely-read of Dickens' novels.

Before settling on the final title, Dickens considered in turn various alternatives, including *One of these Days, The Thread of Gold, Buried Alive* and *The Doctor of Beauvais*.

A Tale of Two Cities comes nearly twenty years after Dickens' other historical novel, *Barnaby Rudge*. Like that work, it shows the influence of Carlyle, whom Dickens deeply admired and whose *French Revolution* he had read with enthusiasm. (On Carlyle's assistance with source-materials, see in chapter 'The Dickens Circle'.) In the preface to *The Woman in White*, Wilkie Collins described Dickens' novel as his 'most perfect work of constructive art'; although strongly plotted, however, it is far from being fully representative of Dickens' mature art, and this probably helps to account for both its cool reception by contemporary reviewers and its relative neglect by modern critics. Forster's *Life* concedes that 'there was probably never a book by a great humourist, and an artist so prolific in the conception of character, with so little humour and so few rememberable figures'.

The idea for the story was derived from Wilkie Collins' play *The Frozen Deep*, which Dickens produced in 1857. Collin's absurd plot, a compound of melodrama and sentiment, concerns a woman loved by two men, one of whom gives his life to save the other. The theme of rivalry, renunciation and sacrifice is carried over into the triangular situation of Lucy Manette, Charles Darnay and Sydney Carton. (In the production Dickens himself had played the role corresponding to the last of these.) For a full account of Dickens' involvement in Collins' play, see, R. L. Brannan, *Under the Management of Mr Charles Dickens: his Production of 'The Frozen Deep'* (1966).

Another aspect of the background to this novel is Dickens' heavy involvement in his public readings immediately before and after its composition. The rhetorical and declamatory style of his narrative, from the opening paragraph onwards, may well owe something to his experience of the power of the spoken word as he faced the large and responsive audiences who came to hear him read. In 1861 he prepared a reading, 'The Bastille Prisoner', based on the first of the three books of the novel; it was never performed.

Coming as it does between two novels that stand among Dickens' finest achievements (*Little Dorrit* and *Great Expectations*), *A Tale of Two Cities* has, for all the power of its set pieces, a thinness of texture. Dickens' characteristic and highly idiosyncratic humour and satire are almost wholly absent; in their place are only melodrama and sentiment. As Forster conceded, characterization is thin. Lucie is a doll-like heroine; like Ruth Pinch and Esther Summerson she enshrines the domestic virtues as Dickens conceived of them ('true to her duties . . . as all the quietly loyal and good will always be': III, 5) – but the conception is, as often, damagingly narrow and schematic. Charles Darnay, although sharing his creator's initials and Christian name, is a pasteboard hero. Dr Manette, potentially of greater interest, is unreal, and his sufferings, so important to the plot, are rendered only conventionally, though there is some psychological interest in his lapses into the obsessive behaviour of his imprisonment. Sydney Carton is a more interesting figure than any of these: as Darnay's *alter ego* he exemplifies Dickens' interest in the double in a much less crude form than (say) Flintwinch's mysterious twin brother in *Little Dorrit*, and illustrates his fondness for creating a pair of characters who, while sharing certain characteristics, are moral antitheses (for a more extreme instance, compare David Copperfield and Uriah Heep, united by their love of Agnes Wickfield). As a public school boy (never a type much favoured by Dickens) who has gone to the bad – in ways not fully specified, though alcohol is largely involved – he anticipates Eugene Wrayburn, who also finds redemption, though his death-bed is not as conclusive as Carton's.

The other characters are little more than stock types: the fussy, old-fashioned, and thoroughly admirable loyalty of Jarvis Lorry; the bullying sham of Stryver; the contemptible Barsad; and the mannish, absurd, but devoted Miss Pross. The French characters suffer from the artificiality of the dialogue put in their mouths: Dickens' notion of creating an impression of French-speaking characters is to write speeches that are neither English nor French.

The plotting of this novel has been praised, but it leans heavily on far-fetched coincidences and the 'foreshadowing' (as Dickens liked to call it) is sometimes heavy-handed: the reader can, for instance, easily become weary of those stone faces outside the chateau of the bad Marquis. Sylvère Monod has drawn attention to the absurdity of the crucial letter written in the Bastille by Dr Manette: literally penned in his own blood, it is nevertheless inordinately long-winded.

Though long a favourite as a school text (no doubt on account of its lack of subtlety and its relative brevity), *A Tale of Two Cities* has received short and unenthusiastic shrift from most recent critics, and Philip Collins describes it as 'the least admired and least discussed of the later novels'. There is a good discussion in Monod's *Dickens the Novelist*, including some examination of the use in this novel of the stylistic device of *anaphora* (repetition). The debt to Carlyle is considered in the books by Goldberg and Oddie. Monod has also contributed essays on this novel to *Nineteenth Century Fiction* (1970) and *Dickensian* (1970), and there is an essay by John Gross in Gross and Pearson's *Dickens and the Twentieth Century* which considers it as 'a tale of two heroes' and includes an interesting analysis of the way in which 'Carton's and Darnay's fates are entwined from their first meeting'. *Twentieth Century Interpretations of 'A Tale of Two Cities'*, ed. C. E. Beckwith (New Jersey, 1972), contains a selection of criticism, including an interesting extract from Sergei Eisenstein's *Film Form*.

CHARACTERS

BARSAD, JOHN, *see* PROSS, SOLOMON (*under* PROSS, MISS).

CARTON, SYDNEY. Educated at Shrewsbury School, he has been a law student in Paris and is presented as a London barrister, brilliant but dissipated, working as 'jackal' for the ruthless careerist Stryver, who takes all the credit for Carton's legal insights. He bears a strong physical resemblance to Charles Darnay and – for the sake of Lucie, whom he loves – dies for him on the scaffold, thus redeeming his wasted life.

CLY, ROGER. Old Bailey spy (the name suggests both spy and sly), supposedly dead and buried, but 'resurrected' by Jerry Cruncher (see II,14).

CRUNCHER, JERRY. Messenger at Tellson's Bank in London and spare-time 'resurrection man', stealing corpses from graveyards for sale as anatomical specimens. His knowledge that Roger Cly is not actually dead is important as the plot works to its climax. His son YOUNG JERRY is ambitious to follow in his father's footsteps. His wife, addicted to 'flopping' or praying for him, is a small-scale satirical sketch directed at popular evangelical religious fervour.

DARNAY, CHARLES. French aristocrat (see ST EVRÉMONDE) who renounces his title, settles in England and marries Lucie Manette; he returns to France on a mission of mercy, is arrested and sentenced to death, and is rescued from the guillotine by Sydney Carton.

DEFARGE, ERNEST. Keeper of a wine-shop in the Paris suburb of Saint Antoine, and local organizer of a group of revolutionaries. His wife THÉRÈSE is the implacable enemy of the Evrémonde family and has vowed to exterminate the entire race (including Charles Darnay, his wife and his child). Her knitting constitutes a secret record of aristocratic despotism. She becomes one of the women who sit around the guillotine and is accidentally killed by Miss Pross while trying to prevent Lucie's escape.

GABELLE. Postmaster of the village forming part of the Evrémonde estate.

GASPARD. Murderer of the Marquis St Evrémonde.

JACQUES ONE, TWO, THREE. Revolutionaries associated with Defarge, the name recalling the term 'Jacquerie' (rising of French peasants in 1358).

JACQUES FOUR. Name assumed by Defarge.

JACQUES FIVE. Road-mender, later an associate of Defarge and a wood-sawyer in Paris.

LORRY, JARVIS. Elderly confidential clerk at Tellson's Bank in London; a bachelor, a friend of the Manette family, and a paragon of honour, loyalty and devotion to duty.

MANETTE, DR ALEXANDER. Paris physician imprisoned in the Bastille for eighteen years, later liberated and taken to London. His golden-haired daughter LUCIE is the heroine of the novel;

she marries Charles Darnay and is loved by Sydney Carton.

PROSS, MISS. Formidable red-haired Englishwoman, devoted servant and companion to Lucie Manette. She kills Madame Defarge
in a struggle. Her brother SOLOMON, alias John Barsad, is a spy
and informer who is blackmailed into aiding Sydney Carton in
his rescue of Darnay from imprisonment and execution.

ST EVRÉMONDE, MARQUIS DE. Twin brothers and oppressive French
aristocrats who hold the title in turn. The elder is the father of
Charles Darnay. The younger is murdered by Gaspard.

STRYVER, MR. Bullying London barrister whose success is built on
the work of his 'jackal' Sydney Carton. Said to be based on Edwin
James, 'a pushing and unscrupulous barrister who was later
debarred for malpractice' (Johnson): Dickens visited James'
chambers with Edmund Yates.

VENGEANCE, THE. Female revolutionary in the Paris suburb of
St Antoine, associated with Madame Defarge.

Great Expectations

Texts   Macmillan College Classics, ed. R. D. McMaster (1965); Penguin English Library, ed. Angus Calder (1969).

Composition   Like *Hard Times*, *Great Expectations* was written at the prompting of urgent external circumstances. As Robert Patten says, 'though there are some indications that Dickens had been thinking about the theme of *Great Expectations* for a while, both the timing and the form of the story were once again determined by economic considerations'. Dickens had launched his weekly periodical *All the Year Round* in April 1859 with *A Tale of Two Cities* as the lead-story, and the *Tale* was followed by Wilkie Collins' immensely popular *The Woman in White*. As the latter drew towards a close in August 1860 a new serial was introduced – Charles Lever's *A Day's Ride*. This turned out to be, as Patten says, 'deadly dull', and 'Dickens feared, then saw confirmed, a drop in sales'. Just as *Hard Times* had been written and published in response to the falling sales of *Household Words*, Dickens now conceived the notion of coming to the rescue of *All the Year Round* by writing a new novel himself. His letters to Forster in October 1860 communicate and justify his decision:

> It was perfectly clear that the one thing to be done was, for me to strike in. I have therefore decided to begin a story, the length of the Tale of Two Cities, on the First of December . . . by dashing in now, I come in when most wanted.

He also told Forster that 'the book will be written in the first person throughout' and that the hero would be, in the first three numbers, 'a boy-child, like David [Copperfield]' and later 'an apprentice'. The novel was completed by early June 1861. On the problems created by weekly serialization, see below. Manuscript in Wisbech Museum; portion of corrected proof in Forster Collection.

Serialization   Weekly instalments in *All the Year Round*, from 1 December 1860 to 3 August 1861. Division as follows: I (Chs 1–2); II (Chs 3–4); III (Ch. 5); IV (Chs 6–7); V (Ch. 8); VI (Chs 9–10); VII (Ch. 11); VIII (Chs 12–13); IX (Chs 14–15); X (Chs 16–17); XI (Ch. 18); XII (Ch. 19); XIII (Chs 20–1); XIV (Ch. 22); XV (Chs 23–4); XVI (Chs 25–6); XVII (Chs 27–8); XVIII (Ch. 29); XIX (Chs 30–1); XX (Chs 32–3); XXI (Chs 34–5); XXII (Chs 36–7); XXIII (Ch. 38); XXIV (Ch. 39); XXV (Ch. 40); XXVI (Chs 41–2); XXVII (Chs 43–4); XXVIII (Chs 45–6); XXIX (Chs 47–8); XXX (Chs 49–50); XXXI (Chs 51–2); XXXII (Ch. 53); XXXIII (Ch. 54); XXXIV (Chs 55–6); XXXV (Ch. 57); XXXVI (Chs 58–9). The division of Pip's story into three 'stages' was made in the serial version.

Publication   Published in three volumes by Chapman & Hall in July 1861. No illustrations. No preface. Dedication to Chauncy Hare Townshend. 'Three volumes post 8vo for 31s. 6d. is surely not a format predictable from anything which had gone before in Dickens' life. No other work of his had been issued in that form at that price' (Patten). The first printing was a small one (1000 copies) and sold quickly.

Reception   The serial version achieved its objective of restoring the failing fortunes of *All the Year Round*. The novel was immediately successful ('an immense success', 'universally liked', declared Dickens soon after it began). A more far-reaching effect was its role in reversing the decline in Dickens' popularity that had taken place during the half-dozen years since *Hard Times*. Reviewers hailed it as a welcome return to the earlier manner: 'after passing under the cloud of *Little Dorrit* and *Bleak House*', said the *Saturday Review*, ' . . . he has written a story that is new, original, powerful, and very entertaining'; the same reviewer deemed it 'quite worthy to stand beside *Martin Chuzzlewit* and *David Copperfield*'. E. S. Dallas wrote somewhat ambiguously in *The Times*:

> Mr Dickens has good-naturedly granted to his hosts of readers the desire of their hearts . . . . The public insist upon seeing in Mr Dickens chiefly the humourist; and, however great he may be in

other directions, they count all as nothing beside his rare faculty of humour. To those who may not be satisfied with a work of this author's unless humour superabounds most, we can heartily commend *Great Expectations*.

An American critic, Edwin Whipple, wrote in the *Atlantic Monthly* that the novel was 'a masterpiece'. Mrs Oliphant, hower, was not amused and wrote in *Blackwood's Magazine* that it was 'feeble, fatigued, and colourless'.

Modern criticism of *Great Expectations* has generally seen it as one of Dickens' 'dark' novels (a term used by Lionel Stevenson) and have stressed its sombre, disillusioned quality; so that it comes as something of a surprise to find not only that Dickens' contemporaries hailed it as a refreshing return to his earlier manner of robust comedy but also that Dickens himself spoke of it, at any rate initially, as primarily comic and grotesque in conception. 'I have made the opening, I hope', he told Forster, 'in its general effect exceedingly droll', and he went on to speak of the 'pivot' of the story – the relationship of Pip and the convict, 'on which the story will turn' – as a 'grotesque tragi-comic conception'. To Mary Boyle he wrote: 'Pray read Great Expectations. I think it is very droll.' These are not quite the terms in which most recent discussions of this novel have been conducted. And yet, while the presentation of the hero and of society at large is sufficiently sober and even melancholy, there is a good deal of comedy in the novel – certainly much more than in its predecessors as weekly serials, *Hard Times* and *A Tale of Two Cities*. Such characters as Mr Wopsle, Mr Trabbs and Bill Barley might have strayed from *Martin Chuzzlewit* or even *Nicholas Nickleby*, and such episodes as Wemmick's wedding seem self-indulgently light-hearted, whilst the home life of the Pocket family is distinctly a throwback. But these are minor characters and minor episodes; and while they render intelligible the response of Dickens' earliest readers, the novel as a whole is profoundly serious.

Perhaps the clue to its tone is given by Dickens' own term 'tragi-comedy'. It is (at least with the substituted ending) a comedy in the sense that enables *Measure for Measure* or *A Winter's Tale* to be classified among Shakespeare's comedies; and although, for example, Dickens told Forster at the outset that he had 'put a child and a good-natured foolish man, in relations that seem to be very funny', this is a very incomplete account of Joe Gargery's role in the story – a role that can show him both as a figure of fun (the hen-pecked husband of music-hall jokes, the comic illiterate, the rustic absurdly tricked out in his uncomfortable Sunday best) and as possessing genuine dignity and the power to touch our feelings deeply (as in his visit to Pip's London chambers and his nursing of Pip back to health). What Dickens achieved in *Great Expectations* was a subtle blending of genres and effects that had earlier been kept separate: in *The Old Curiosity Shop*, for instance, farce and sentiment usually occupy different blocks of the novel, but in *Great Expectations* they are shown to be different aspects of the same character or experience.

Like *David Copperfield*, the novel is told in the first person, and a remark of Dickens' already quoted makes it clear that his earlier novel was in his mind when composition began. The auto-biographical narrative enables Pip both to recreate the past with a vivid sense of immediacy and to comment on it, often ironically, from the standpoint of a man who is older, wiser and sadder. Thus, when he describes himself (Ch. 19) leaving his village to go to London, he recalls: 'I promised myself that I would do something for them one of these days, and formed a plan in outline for bestowing a dinner of roast-beef and plum-pudding, a pint of ale, and a gallon of condescension upon everybody in the village'; 'pint of ale' neutrally records his memory of the younger man's state of mind, but 'gallon of condescension' – the wordplay not precluding bitterness – conveys a judgement made on his earlier self by the mature Pip. Dickens often, indeed, uses the contrast between 'then' and 'now' (or 'then' and 'later') as a kind of rhetorical device: 'I thought it a strange thing then, and I thought it a stranger thing long afterwards' (Ch. 8); 'I was inwardly crying for her then, and I know what I know of the pain she cost me afterwards' (Ch. 11); 'I did not know then, though I think I know now' (Ch. 12). At such points the narrator gives a double or even triple perspective on his experience that, like the blending of comedy and seriousness, produces a subtly ambiguous and bitter-sweet flavour.

Even an experience at a particular point in time can be revealed as existing in the memory only as a result of the layers accumulated through subsequent experiences: thus when Pip has described his first impressions of Miss Havisham (Ch. 8), he adds: 'It was not in the first few moments that I saw all these things, though I saw more of them in the first moments than might be supposed'; the claim made for the child's acute powers of observation is qualified by the adult's honesty as to the sources of his memories. Naturally the plot precludes total honesty at every stage of the narrative; at least, if the narrator is not actually dishonest he chooses to remain silent at certain crucial points. For example, the ambiguous dialogue between Pip and Miss Havisham near the end of Ch. 19 misleads the reader as Pip himself was misled, though on re-reading it becomes clear that the reader's deductions have been as hasty and ill-founded as Pip's own: the *suggestio falsi* is mainly contained in the dialogue and in the fanciful comparison of Miss Havisham to a fairy godmother, rather than in narrative comment.

As with his earlier weekly serials, Dickens found the short instalments of *Great Expectations* very irksome: 'As to the planning out from week to week', he told Forster, 'nobody can imagine what the difficulty is without trying.' As the details given above (under *Serialization*) indicate, some instalments contained a single chapter and none contained more than two chapters. Not only was the finished novel appreciably shorter than, say, *Copperfield* or *Dorrit*, but the effect of each portion had to be made in a much smaller compass than the thirty-two pages of the monthly numbers. Dickens' creative struggles were not in vain, however, and the narrative of *Great Expectations* has a pace and an economy that make for artistic success: beside it *Copperfield* seems, in places at least, leisurely, diffuse, even rambling. (Compare the lengthy account of David's visit to Switzerland with the brief allusion to Pip's years abroad.)

Bernard Shaw, writing in 1937, found this 'the most perfect of Dickens' works' – with one exception. He deplored the happy ending that was substituted, at the instigation of Bulwer-Lytton, for the ending Dickens originally wrote; and his disapproval is echoed by a large though not unanimous chorus. Lytton, who read the original ending in proof, felt that Dickens' readers would not care for it and convinced Dickens that he was right. Considerations of sales can hardly have been the overriding motive, since *All the Year Round* was firmly on its feet again long before the serialization of the novel was concluded (Professor Patten estimates that the circulation of the periodical may have approached 100,000). It seems likely that what was in question was the relationship between Dickens and his public and their confidence in him as a great popular entertainer who, while showing the darker side of life, would make everything come right in the end. The original ending, first printed by Forster, ran as follows (after Biddy's question, referring to Estella, ' "you are sure you don't fret for her?" '):

'I am sure and certain, Biddy.

It was two years more, before I saw herself. I had heard of her as leading a most unhappy life, and as being separated from her husband, who had used her with great cruelty, and who had become quite renowned as a compound of pride, brutality, and meanness. I had heard of the death of her husband (from an accident consequent on ill-treating a horse), and of her being married again to a Shropshire doctor, who, against his interest, had once very manfully interposed on an occasion when he was in professional attendance on Mr. Drummle, and had witnessed some outrageous treatment of her. I had heard that the Shropshire doctor was not rich, and that they lived on her own personal fortune. I was in England again – in London, and walking along Piccadilly with little Pip – when a servant came running after me to ask would I step back to a lady in a carriage who wished to speak to me. It was a little pony carriage which the lady was driving, and the lady and I looked sadly enough on one another. 'I am greatly changed, I know, but I thought you would like to shake hands with Estella too, Pip. Lift up that pretty child and let me kiss it!' (She supposed the child, I think, to be my child.) I was very glad afterwards to have had the interview; for in her face, and in her voice, and in her touch, she gave me the assurance that suffering had been stronger than Miss Havisham's teaching, and had given her a heart to understand what my heart used to be.

Forster commented that 'the first ending . . . seems more consistent with the drift, as well as the natural working out of the tale', and many others have seen the substitution as a kind of selling short of the book's moral seriousness. As David Lodge has recently said:

Estella was, after all, the sexual symbol of all the false values on which Pip based his early life, and to reward him for his renunciation of these values with marriage to her is a kind of contradiction. It also compromises the novel's sober recognition that not all the damage we do to ourselves and to others is reparable. In the original version, Pip, having realized belatedly that Estella is incapable of love, turns too late to the loving Biddy, and, twice disappointed, accepts his single, childless state as in a sense his just deserts (hence the irony, in the cancelled conclusion, of Estella's assumption that little Pip is his own child)

('Ambiguously Ever After', in *Essays by Divers Hands*, n.s. XLI [1980], p. 43).

The novel has been widely discussed – indeed Professor Collins declares that 'As a candidate for the most discussed of Dickens' novels, *Great Expectations* rivals or surpasses *Bleak House*.' Critics from Chesterton (1906) onwards have praised its psychological truth and moral power: see, among others, Christopher Ricks' essay in Gross and Pearson's *Dickens and the Twentieth Century* and Julian Moynahan's 'The Hero's Guilt – the Case of *Great Expectations*' (*Essays in Criticism*, x, 1960). Others have drawn attention to the excellence of the novel's construction and the handling of narrative point of view: see Robert B. Partlow Jr's 'The Moving I: A Study of Point of View in *Great Expectations*' (*College English*, XXIII, 1961–2) and T. E. Connolly's 'Technique in *Great Expectations*' (*Philological Quarterly*, XXXIV, 1955). Other important general discussions include Ada Nisbet's 'The Autobiographical Matrix of *Great Expectations*' (*Victorian Newsletter*, xv, 1959) and the appropriate chapters in Dorothy Van Ghent's *The English Novel: From and Function* (1953), the Leavises' *Dickens the Novelist* (1970), where Q. D. Leavis writes on this novel, and Barbara Hardy's *The Moral Art of Dickens* (1970). On more specialized topics, Mary Edminson has written on the dating of the action (*Nineteenth-Century Fiction*, XIII, 1958); Harry Stone on the orgins of Miss Havisham (*Victorian Newsletter*, XXIV, 1968); and Martin Meisel on both Miss Havisham (*Publications of the Modern Language Association*, LXXXI, 1966) and the novel's endings (*Essays in Criticism*, xv, 1965). Dickens prepared a reading version of *Great Expectations*, probably before the end of the summer of 1861. It was privately printed but never performed. Philip Collins notes that it 'runs from Pip's first meeting with Magwitch in the churchyard to Magwitch's death in prison'; Estella and Biddy are never mentioned, nor are Orlick, Drummle, and other minor characters.

CHARACTERS

AVENGER, THE. Young manservant employed, and endured, by Pip when he is in London.

BARLEY, CLARA. Fiancée and later wife of Herbert Pocket. She lives with her old father, BILL BARLEY, an eccentric retired ship's purser, in a house overlooking the Thames.

BIDDY. Grand-daughter of Mr Wopsle's great-aunt; an orphan and a friend to Pip. She later marries Joe Gargery (Ch. 58).

CLARRIKER & CO. Firm that employs Herbert Pocket and later Pip; the latter eventually becomes a partner (Ch. 58).

COILER, MRS. 'Toady neighbour' (Ch. 23) of the Pocket family.

COMPEYSON. Criminal, an earlier associate of Magwitch (see Ch. 42), later a fellow-convict and deadly enemy, and the villain of the novel. Like so many of Dickens' bad lots, he has been educated at a public school before turning gentleman-forger. He is revealed (Ch. 42), in one of the novel's numerous coincidences, as the lover who abandoned Miss Havisham. He is eventually drowned in attempting to prevent Magwitch from fleeing the country (Ch. 54).

DRUMMLE, BENTLEY. Disagreeable and unattractive young man, a pupil of Matthew Pocket and 'the next heir but one to a baronetcy' (Ch, 23). He marries and ill-treats Estella; his death (from an accident resulting from his ill-treatment of a horse) is referred to in both the original and the substituted endings.

ESTELLA, *see* HAVISHAM, MISS.

FLOPSON. Nurse to the Pocket children.

GARGERY, JOE. Village blacksmith, brother-in-law to Pip and the intimate friend and ally of his childhood. He visits Pip in London (Ch. 27) and nurses him through an illness (Ch. 57). His wife, MRS JOE, is the shrewish sister of Pip, 'tall and bony' (Ch. 2), more than twenty years older than he, and frequently 'on the rampage'. Later she is attacked by an unknown assailant (subsequently identified as Orlick) and left paralysed (Ch. 15). She dies in Ch. 34, and Pip returns to his old home to attend her funeral. Joe later marries Biddy and their child is named Pip.

HAVISHAM, MISS. Rich and eccentric lady whose house (Satis House) Pip visits: 'the strangest lady I have ever seen, or shall ever see' (Ch. 8). Abandoned by her lover (see Compeyson) on her wedding day, she has stopped the clocks and remained in her bridal dress. She encourages Estella to wreak revenge on her behalf on the male sex; misleads Pip into believing she is his benefactress; is rescued by Pip when, after a dramatic confrontation, she accidentally sets fire to herself (Ch. 49); and dies (Ch. 57). On a possible prototype for Miss Havisham, see under Berners Street in the section on 'Topography'; see also the articles by Meisel and Stone cited above. ESTELLA HAVISHAM is the adopted daughter of Miss Havisham and is a proud young lady who treats Pip with undisguised scorn on his first visit to the house. Encouraged by Miss Havisham, Pip falls in love with Estella, who is sent to France and later lives with a family at Richmond. She marries Bentley Drummle and is eventually revealed as the daughter of Magwitch and Molly. She sees Pip again after a long interval (Ch. 59): on the two versions of Estella's final fate, see above. ARTHUR HAVISHAM, referred to in Ch. 42, is a brother of Miss Havisham and has been a criminal associate of Compeyson.

HUBBLE, MR. Wheelwright in the village where Pip grows up.

JAGGERS, MR. London lawyer described in Ch. 11. He acts, coincidentally, both for Miss Havisham and for Magwitch. It is he who tells Pip about his great expectations (Ch. 18) and, at any rate by default, is guilty of nourishing Pip's illusions as to their origins.

LAZARUS, ABRAHAM. Lisping Jewish client seen by Pip in Jaggers' office (Ch. 20).

MAGWITCH. Appears in the opening chapter as an escaped convict; is befriended by Pip, recaptured, and transported; becomes a prosperous sheep-farmer in Australia and, through the agency of Jaggers, Pip's unknown benefactor; reappears at Pip's rooms in London (Ch. 39) in one of the finest scenes in the novel, where Pip learns the bitter truth concerning the source of his money (Ch. 39). He assumes the name of Provis. He is subsequently revealed as the father of Estella (Ch. 50). An escape attempt is foiled by Compeyson, and Magwitch is seriously injured (Ch. 54); he dies in the prison hospital (Ch. 56) after learning that his daughter is alive and 'a lady', and that Pip loves her. The development of Magwitch from the Gothic monster of the opening scenes to the dignified and moving figure of the later portions of the book is a remarkable achievement.

MIKE. Disreputable character employed by Mr Jaggers (Ch. 20).

MILLERS. Nurse to the Pocket children.

MOLLY. Mr Jaggers' housekeeper, an acquitted murderess (see Ch. 48), later revealed as the mother of Estella.

ORLICK, DOLGE. Morose journeyman blacksmith employed by Joe Gargery. He quarrels with Mrs Joe and makes a murderous attack on her (Ch. 15). He subsequently attempts to murder Pip

(Ch. 53). Psychological critics have seen him as the 'double' or *alter ego* of Pip – whom, incontrovertibly, he stands next to in the alphabet.

PIP, *see* PIRRIP, PHILIP

PIRRIP, PHILIP, usually known as Pip. Hero and narrator of the story, he is an orphan, 'brought up by hand' by his sister, Mrs Joe Gargery; later apprenticed to his brother-in-law the blacksmith. He visits Miss Havisham's house and meets Estella; tells Biddy he wants to be a gentleman (Ch. 17); hears of his great expectations (Ch. 18); and goes to London. He is nicknamed Handel ('The Harmonious Blacksmith') by Herbert Pocket, with whom he forms a close friendship. He lives beyond his means. He loves Estella, and is heart-broken by her marriage. When Magwitch returns from Australia, Pip learns, in a scene (Ch. 39) that is the turning-point of the action, the truth about the source of his money. Orlick makes an attempt on his life (Ch. 53). Pip tries to smuggle Magwitch out of the country (Ch. 54); after Magwitch's death Pip falls ill and is nursed by Joe (Ch. 57) – an illness that, as often in Dickens, acts as a spiritual rebirth (cf. Eugene Wrayburn in *Our Mutual Friend*). Later he goes abroad as a clerk for the firm of Clarriker and Co. (Ch. 58), returns after eleven years and sees Estella again in London (Ch. 59: on the two endings, see above). In *The Dickens World*, Humphry House comments that 'It is a remarkable achievement to have kept the reader's sympathy throughout a snob's progress.'

POCKET, HERBERT. First appears as a boy whom Pip meets on one of his visits to Satis House (Ch. 11), when they fight. Some years later they meet again, and Pip stays with Herbert at his rooms in Barnard's Inn when he first arrives in London. He nicknames Pip 'Handel', becomes a close friend, and marries Clara Barley. His father MATHEW POCKET, educated at Harrow and Cambridge, is a crammer and private tutor to whom Pip goes when he moves to London. He lives at Hammersmith with his wife BELINDA and six children 'in various stages of tumbling up' (Ch. 22). CAMILLA AND SARAH POCKET are predatory relatives of Miss Havisham.

PROVIS, *see* MAGWITCH.

PUMBLECHOOK, MR. Uncle of Joe Gargery, a pompous well-to-do corn chandler who first bullies Pip and then claims to have been his friend and benefactor. He is comically manhandled by burglars (Ch. 57) – a scene on which George Orwell has some interesting comments.

SKIFFINS, MISS. Lady 'of a wooden appearance' who marries Wemmick (Ch. 55).

STARTOP. Pupil of Matthew Pocket.

TRABB, MR. Tailor who makes Pip a suit of clothes when he goes to London (Ch. 19) and is comically obsequious at the news of his great expectations. Trabb's boy, his cheeky assistant, also appears.

WEMMICK, JOHN. Clerk to Mr Jaggers. A highly efficient and drily business-like man who reveals a totally different side of his nature, affectionate and boyish, at his Walworth home, where he lives with his amiably senile father (the 'Aged Parent'). He marries Miss Skiffins (Ch. 55).

WOPSLE, MR. Parish clerk in the village in which Pip grows up. His great-aunt keeps a dame-school to which Pip is sent (Ch. 7). He become an actor, changes his name to Waldengarver, and is seen in a disastrous performance of *Hamlet* when Pip attends the theatre in London (Ch. 31). He reappears in Ch. 47.

Our Mutual Friend

Text Penguin English Library, ed. Stephen Gill (1971).

Composition Nearly three years passed between the completion of the serialization of *Great Expectations* and the first number of *Our Mutual Friend*. Dickens' rate of production of his novels had slowed down markedly since the earlier part of his career – partly, perhaps, because he was getting older and suffering periods of ill-health as well as family anxieties, but also because he was expending much of his energy on his weekly magazine *All the Year Round*, his public readings, and his regular Christmas stories, and not least importantly because composition had become for him a slower, more painful and deliberate process. According to Forster, he had devised the title of the novel as early as 1861, and he wrote to Forster in the same year indicating what were to turn out to be some of its main elements:

> I think a man, young and perhaps eccentric, feigning to be dead, and being dead to all intents and purposes external to himself, and for a few years retaining the singular view of life and character so imparted, would be a good leading incident for a story . . . . A poor impostor of a man marrying a woman for her money; she marrying *him* for *his* money; after marriage both finding out their mistake, and entering into a league and covenant against folk in general; with whom I propose to connect some Perfectly New People . . . I must use somehow the un-educated father in fustian and the educated boy in spectacles whom Leech and I saw at Chatham.

Dickens had planned to begin writing the novel during 1862, but he found it hard to make a start: 'Alas!', he lamented in April of that year, 'I have hit upon nothing for a story. Again and again I have tried.' More than a year later he was still trying; in August 1863 he declared himself 'full of notions . . . for the new twenty numbers' and in October 'exceedingly anxious to begin my book'. Another comment at the same time indicates the significance that the opening scene of the novel was to possess: 'I see my opening perfectly, with the one main line on which the story is to turn.' He had resolved not to allow publication to begin before he had five numbers in hand – evidence that he was aware that the writing would go slowly, as indeed it did through the winter of 1863–4. By 25 January two numbers were finished ('a combination of drollery with romance which requires a great deal of pains and a perfect throwing away of points that might be amplified'). He confessed to feeling 'at first quite dazed in getting back to the large canvas and the big brushes' – that is, to the spaciousness of monthly numbers after the constricted weekly portions of his previous two novels. After serialization began, progress was still slow: he told Forster on 29 July 1864 that 'although I have not been wanting in industry, I have been wanting in invention, and have fallen back with the book . . . I . . . have a very mountain to climb before I shall see the open country of my work'. Professor Patten has suggested that the novel's 'relative commercial failure . . . may have contributed its share to Dickens's evident depression during the summer of 1864'. At last, on 31 July 1865, he was able to say that he was 'but now finishing Our Mutual Friend'. Manuscript in the Pierpont Morgan Library, New York.

Serialization   Nineteen monthly parts, published from May 1864 to November 1865. Illustrations by Marcus Stone. Division as follows: I (I, 1–4); II (I, 5–7); III (I, 8–10); IV (I, 11–13); V (I, 14–17); VI (II, 1–3); VII (II, 4–6); VIII (II, 7–10); IX (II, 11–13); X (II, 14–16); XI (III, 1–4); XII (III, 5–7); XIII (III, 8–10); XIV (III, 11–14); XV (III, 15–17); XVI (IV, 1–4); XVII (IV, 5–7); XVIII (IV, 8–11); XIX–XX (IV, 12–16). The opening circulation was 40,000, an increase on that of his last monthly serial, *Little Dorrit*. 30,000 had been sold within three days of publication, no doubt helped by an extensive advertising campaign which had cost Chapman & Hall a thousand pounds and included the distribution of a million handbills, 145,000 catalogues, and 'plastering virtually the whole of England with posters' (Patten), while a hundred omnibuses carried advertisements. As Professor Patten says, 'All parties expected a large sale for the new serial.' But sales dropped, 'the print order declined steadily', and by the final double number 'only 19,000 copies . . . were stitched into the green leaves'.

Publication   Published in two volumes by Chapman & Hall. The first volume appeared in February 1865 (coinciding with the publication of the tenth number), the second the following November. Dickens added a 'Postscript in lieu of Preface' and a dedication to Sir James Tennent.

Reception   Although Collins describes the novel's original reception as 'fairly cordial', it was distinctly mixed and some reviewers were notably harsh. The influential *Saturday Review* judged it 'a very tedious performance' and 'rather hard reading'; the young Henry James found it 'the poorest of Mr Dickens's works'; and later on even Forster (in the *Life*) was to express the view that 'it wants freshness and natural development' and 'will never rank with his higher efforts'. In contrast, Henry Chorley in the *Athenaeum* considered it 'one of Mr Dickens's richest and most carefully-wrought books', and E. S. Dallas in *The Times* declared, perceptively but unorthodoxly, that it was 'infinitely better than *Pickwick* in all the higher qualities of a novel'. As Collins says, 'it never became a general favourite'.

As noted above, *Our Mutual Friend* was slow to win recognition as a major achievement; as Professor Collins states elsewhere, even today 'there is less agreement about the status of *Our Mutual Friend* than about that of any of Dickens' other mature novels'. Even when it is praised by earlier critics, the praise seems curiously off-centre: Swinburne, for example, waxed ecstatic about a minor character, Betty Higden ('the most nearly intolerable tragedy in all the tragic work of Dickens', 'the unsurpassed and unsurpassable grandeur and beauty of the martyred old heroine's character'), and Chesterton regarded the novel as a 'sort of Indian summer of [Dickensian] farce'. Jack Lindsay's claim in 1950 that it is 'in many ways [Dickens'] supreme work' and 'one of the greatest works of prose ever written. A work which finally vindicates Dickens's right to stand, as no other English writer can stand, at the side of Shakespeare' would not have found much support even at that date, though it was to be endorsed a dozen years later by Arnold Kettle. Angus Wilson is right in describing it as 'a novel before its time'; it is, it has been significantly said, Dickens' *Waste Land*, and it has had to wait for full appreciation until critics and readers had absorbed modernist writing. For *Our Mutual Friend* is a masterpiece of fictional symbolism and, as such, almost without parallel in English writing of the 1860s.

Just as *Little Dorrit* opens with a prison and is haunted by that image, recurring in many forms, to its last page, *Our Mutual Friend* opens with the river, which flows throughout the novel and is an element in many of its most important scenes, serving as an agent of death but also of rebirth. Gaffer Hexam, Bradley Headstone and Rogue Riderhood all die in the river; but for Eugene Wrayburn his near-drowning is the means of his being born again and beginning a new life. We may observe a preoccupation in Dickens' later novels with the theme of rebirth: Mr Dorrit and Dr Manette are released into the world after long periods of imprisonment, and John Harmon starts afresh after he is believed to be dead.

The other dominant symbol of the novel is of the dustheaps: as Stephen Gill says, 'Harmon's Dust Mounds lower over *Our Mutual Friend* just as they did over suburban London', for they are both rich poetic symbol and contemporary fact. Henry Mayhew's *London Labour and the London Poor* (1861–2), which provides a number of parallels to elements in this novel, speaks of the 'dust-yards' where ashes and cinders from the hearths of London are 'piled up to a great height in a conical heap, and having much the appearance of a volcanic mountain'. (Mayhew also refers to 'the dredgers . . . the men who find almost all the bodies of persons drowned, – the grisly occupation described in the novel's opening chapter.) As early as 1850 Dickens had published in *Household Words* an article by R. H. Horne on the sifters, who made a living by searching through the heaps of refuse for anything saleable.

The significant shift here is that 'dust' appears to have been a euphemism for any kind of rubbish; and Humphry House went so far as to argue that not only were valuable articles discovered that had been accidentally thrown away ('gold and silver articles were sometimes found in them, and in the one heap in 1847 a banker's cheque for a considerable amount turned up'), but that the dust-contractors also collected 'the contents of the privies and the piles of mixed dung and ashes which were made in the poorer streets'. More recently, the accuracy of this latter claim has been questioned. Even without this vivid reinforcement, however, the symbol remains a powerful one: the idea of wealth and splendour being based on rubbish (and Stephen Gill notes that 'The value of the dust-heaps was, literally, legendary. Horne and Mayhew relate tales of mounds fetching from £10,000 to £40,000') obviously took hold of Dickens' imagination. Wealth is seen as corrupting in *Our Mutual Friend*, whether the angle of vision is comic (as in Wegg's cupidity), satirical (as with the Veneerings), or serious (as in Bella Wilfer's mercenary impulses). Dickens had always been interested in problems of sanitation: he had, written in the 1849 preface to *Martin Chuzzlewit* that he hoped he had, in all his writings, 'taken every possible opportunity of showing the want of sanitary improvement in the neglected dwellings of the poor', and in *Household Words* he had referred to sanitation as 'the most momentous of all earthly questions'. In *The City of Dickens*, Alexander Welsh quotes a passage written by Henry Austin, Dickens' brother-in-law, in a report to the General Board of Health in 1857:

> In towns of rich and of poor population the quality of the sewage may also materially differ . . . . The value of the refuse of Belgravia would, no doubt, exceed that of Bethnal Green.

It is in this kind of context of contemporary experience and consciousness that we must approach the 'dust' of this novel: there is, as Arnold Kettle points out, nothing abstract or schematic about Dickens' symbols, which are at the same time precise and potently suggestive, giving a new and disturbing resonance to the cliché 'stinking rich'.

Dickens sees Victorian England as a society in danger of moral collapse: the choice of reading matter for Wegg's sessions with Mr Boffin is not random but points towards the central theme, for Gibbon's *Decline and Fall of the Roman Empire* suggests a contemporary parallel. Yet Dickens' vision is not wholly one of despair: as Kenneth Muir says, while the novel has as its theme 'the danger of wealth', 'some of its most moving scenes occur when the human affections triumph over the corruption of the world'. Bella can be unattractively calculating, but her fondness for her father is genuine enough and her change of heart is permanent (Dickens has come a long way since the static early heroines, personifications of limited notions of what was deemed desirable in a young woman). Mr Boffin's miserliness turns out to be assumed. Fledgeby is offset by Riah, Dickens' portrait of a good Jew (itself offsetting that of Fagin). Betty Higden represents simple goodness (though Sloppy, like Maggy in *Little Dorrit*, is another version of a favourite character-type, the Wordsworthian idiot or child of nature; and Johnny is, as Ruskin would have said, led to the slaughter, though now less from unashamed sentimentality than in order to give needed publicity to the Hospital for Sick Children).

Alongside much that is stylized and much that is familiar, the character of Bradley Headstone stands out as a masterpiece of psychological realism. The 'respectable' self-made man, prickly in the face of slights real or imagined, is a portrait of a member of society observed (as Philip Collins has shown) with accuracy – the trained schoolmaster. The scenes in which he is taunted by Wrayburn and vainly declares his love to Lizzie have great dramatic power without ever lapsing into melodrama. That characters such as Headstone and Wrayburn (the latter seeming to anticipate one of Wilde's drawing-room comedies of the nineties in some of his dialogue) should coexist with others such as Twemlow, Podsnap and Venus is evidence that, in his last completed novel, Dickens had not lost the power of sustaining a richly varied and yet unified art.

One of the most remarkable features of the book is its language, often extraordinarily experimental by the standards of its period. One of its most brilliant set-pieces, the Veneerings' dinner-party in Ch. 2, has been analyzed by J. Hillis Miller in *The Form of Victorian Fiction* (1968); Miller finds it 'seemingly inexhaustible in the complexity of its implications'. Sylvère Monod had also written well on the style of this novel – a style as nervous, intense and highly-charged as much of Dickens' early writing is fluent and relaxed. Monod notes the habit of repetition in Dickens' later style: the word 'new', for example, occurs eighteen times in the first two paragraphs of Ch. 2, and when Bradley Headstone is introduced in the opening chapter of Book Two the word 'decent' is repeated so often as to acquire heavy irony. More generally, Monod draws attention to a significant shift in some of Dickens' favourite epithets of approval for human qualities: 'genteel' and 'manly' in the early work give place to 'cheerful' and 'self-possessed'.

As so often, Dickens took pains over the naming of his characters and arrived at the final and familiar forms only by a process of trial and error. Lizzie Hexam was originally to have been called Jenny, Silas Wegg Solomon, and Mr Boffin Teddy, while Amos Deadstone and other variations were considered for Bradley Headstone. And once again Dickens' number-plans (unfortunately not reproduced in the Penguin edition, but printed and discussed in the article by

Ernest Boll referred to below) are of great interest.

The novel's reputation has been discussed by Philip Hobsbaum (*Essays in Criticism*, XIII, 1963). H. S. Nelson has demonstrated the relationship of *Our Mutual Friend* to Mayhew's writings (*Nineteenth-Century Fiction*, xx, 1966). Three very good essays on this novel referred to above are: by Kenneth Muir (*Essays & Studies*, XIX, 1966); by Ernest Boll (*Modern Philology*, XLII, 1944); and by Sylvère Monod (*Etudes Anglaises*, x, 1957; in French). Arnold Kettle has contributed an essay on it to Gross and Pearson's collection, and Harry Stone has discussed the character of Riah in his 'Dickens and the Jews' (*Victorian Studies*, II, 1959). Other useful essays are by R. D. McMaster (*Dalhousie Review*, XL, 1960) and F. X. Shea (*Papers on Language and Literature*, IV, 1968).

CHARACTERS

ANALYTICAL, THE. A 'melancholy retainer' or butler at the Veneerings' house; he serves the wine 'like a gloomy Analytical Chemist' (I,2).

BLIGHT. Office boy to Mortimer Lightwood (I,8).

BOFFIN, MR NICODEMUS (Noddy; also known as 'the Golden Dustman'). He has inherited a dust-heap from his former employer, old Harmon, and lives nearby in a house known as Boffin's Bower. He employs Silas Wegg to read to him (I,5); offers a reward for the apprehension of John Harmon's supposed murderer (I,8); hires John Rokesmith as secretary (I, 8); he and his wife welcome Bella Wilfer into their home, but soon Mr Boffin's benevolence and geniality turn to surliness and he displays a great interest in misers (III,5–6); he discharges his secretary after accusing him of mercenary intentions towards Bella (III, 15); and later discloses that his miserliness was a pretence assumed for the benefit of Bella (IV,13). Henry Dodd, who owned a dust-yard in Islington and was reputed to have given his daughter a dust-heap as a wedding present, has been suggested as a prototype of Boffin; Dickens certainly knew Dodd.

MRS. HENRIETTA ('Henerietty') Boffin, a kindly lady who befriends Bella, is introduced (I,5) as 'a highflyer at Fashion': 'a stout lady of rubicund and cheerful aspect, dressed . . . in a low evening-dress of sable satin, and a large black velvet hat and feathers' even in her own home.

BOOTS, BREWER. Guests at Veneering's dinner-party in I,2.

DOLLS, MR. Nickname of Jenny Wren's father: see Wren.

FLEDGEBY, 'Fascination'. Vain, malicious and undersized, he is introduced as 'an awkward, sandy-haired, small-eyed youth, exceeding slim (his enemies would have said lanky)' in II,4, and later referred to as 'the meanest cur existing, with a single pair of legs' (II,5). He lives in Albany and employs Riah as an agent for his extortionate money-lending. He is soundly thrashed by Lammle and has his wounds peppered by Jenny Wren (IV,9).

FOREIGN GENTLEMAN. He is condescendingly interviewed by Podsnap at his daughter's birthday party (I,11).

GLIDDERY, BOB. Pot-boy at the Six Jolly Fellowship Porters, a riverside public house.

HANFORD, JULIUS, *see* JOHN HARMON, *under* HARMON, OLD.

HARMON, OLD. ' "A tremendous old rascal who made his money by Dust" ' (I,2), he dies before the story opens; Mortimer Lightwood (I,2) refers to the stipulation in his will that his son will inherit his property only on condition that he marries a certain young woman (later identified as Bella Wilfer). Mortimer announces at the end of the same chapter that the son has been drowned; however, JOHN HARMON appears in I,3 under the name of Julius Handford (retaining his own initials), and later takes rooms at the Wilfers' house and is employed by Mr Boffin as secretary under the name of John Rokesmith. He is described as 'A dark gentleman. Thirty at the utmost' (I,4). Mr Boffin refers to him as Our Mutual Friend (I,9). He resolves not to disclose his true identity (II,13); is discharged by Mr Boffin (III,15); marries Bella, still under an assumed name (IV,4); and discloses his true identity only after he has been suspected of his own murder (IV,12–13).

HEADSTONE, BRADLEY. A schoolmaster introduced in II,1: to all appearances 'a thoroughly decent young man of six-and-twenty' – only the epithet 'decent' by repetition becomes tinged with irony, and we learn in the same paragraph that he has 'a manner that would be better described as one of lying in wait', with 'a kind of settled trouble in the face'. He befriends Charley Hexam, takes an interest in Lizzie, and calls on Eugene Wrayburn (II,6), where his acute consciousness of social inferiority is powerfully conveyed. He declares his love for Lizzie (II,15) and develops a passionate jealousy of his rival Eugene; goes to Plashwater Weir Mill Lock dressed in clothes similar to those of Riderhood (IV,1); makes a murderous attack on Eugene and attempts to throw the blame on Riderhood, who later blackmails him; they drown together (IV,15).

HEXAM, JESSE (Gaffer). Thames waterman; he and his daughter LIZZIE appear on the first page of the novel, she as 'a dark girl of nineteen or twenty'. Gaffer is later found dead (I, 14). Lizzie is loved by Bradley Headstone but dislikes and fears him; Eugene Wrayburn takes an interest in her, though his motives seem unclear even to himself. She later rescues Eugene after he has been attacked and left for dead, and marries him. CHARLEY HEXAM is an ambitious youth, introduced in I, 3 and suggested to Dickens by the 'uneducated father in fustian and the educated boy in spectacles' he had seen at Chatham and mentioned in a letter to Forster.

HIGDEN, MRS BETTY. Old woman who 'minds' children and, with the aid of Sloppy, takes in mangling (I,16): she has 'an indomitable purpose and a strong constitution' which have enabled her to 'fight out many years' (I,16), but has a terror of dying in the work-house. She resolves to run away (II,14); falls ill; declares that she has ' "fought against the Parish and fled from it, all my life, and I want to die free of it!" '; and dies in the presence of Lizzie Hexam ('and lifted her as high as Heaven': closing words of III,8). For Swinburne's dithyramb on Betty Higden as heroine, see above. H. S. Nelson notes that an old woman mentioned by Mayhew speaks in very similar terms to Betty; and Stephen Gill points out that 'Dickens's offensive against the tyrants who administered the Poor Law began in *Oliver Twist* and concluded in the ringing tones of the Postscript to *Our Mutual Friend*' (Dickens writes there: 'I believe there has been in England, since the days of the STUARTS, no law so often infamously administered, no law so often openly violated, no law habitually so ill-supervised'). Humphry House suggested that 'what may seem to some the tedious pig-headedness with which she refuses all Boffin's offers of help can be regarded as a gallant dying gesture of independence; her very stupidity is the reverse of many virtues the English Poor Law was destroying'.

INSPECTOR, MR. Policeman who joins in the hunt for Gaffer Hexam (I,13–14) – further evidence of Dickens' keen interest in and admiration for the police force (cf. Bucket in *Bleak House*).

JOHNNY. Orphan 'minded' by Betty Higden and adopted by the Boffins. He dies in hospital at the end of II,9 – the last of Dickens's child-deathbeds, and the opportunity for Dickens to advertise the work of the Great Ormond Street Hospital for Sick Children, founded in 1852, for which he had appealed for funds in a speech of 9 February 1858 (see *Speeches*, pp. 246–53).

LAMMLE, ALFRED. An unscrupulous adventurer, he marries Sophronia Akersham, an adventuress, in I, 10; after the wedding they discover that each has erroneously supposed the other to possess property, and resolve to make the best of a loveless and penniless marriage by teaming up to exploit the rest of the world. Mrs Lammle obtains an influence over Georgiana Podsnap (II,4), intending to make a match between her and Fledgeby; but she is overcome by scruples of conscience and begs Twemlow to save the girl (II,16). Lammle later thrashes Fledgeby (IV,9). The Lammles represent the predatory, fortune-hunting aspect of fashionable society; for Dickens' early notion of these characters, see p. 225.

LIGHTWOOD, MORTIMER. An intimate and confidant of Eugene Wrayburn, he first appears at Veneering's dinner-party (I,2). He has practised law for five years without success.

MARY ANNE. 'Favourite pupil' and household assistant of Miss Peecher (see II,1).

MILVERY, REV. FRANK. Conscientious clergyman in a slum district: 'quite a young man, expensively educated and wretchedly paid, with quite a young wife and half a dozen quite young children' (I,9) – an unexpectedly sympathetic portrait of a truly Christian pastor. He and his wife MARGARETTA are asked by the Boffins to find an orphan for them to adopt.

PEECHER, MISS. 'Small, shining, neat, methodical, and buxom' teacher (II,1); she has unsuccessful matrimonial designs on Bradley Headstone.

PODSNAP, MR. 'A too, too smiling large man' introduced in I,2, where he is a guest at the Veneerings' dinner-party. In his jingoism and his concern for the Young Person, he represents middle-class complacency and hypocrisy: see especially I,11 ('Podsnappery'). His wife is mercilessly described in I,2: 'fine woman for Professor Owen [anatomist and an expert on dinosaurs], quantity of bone, neck and nostrils like a rocking-horse, hard features, majestic head-dress in which Podsnap has hung golden offerings' – she recalling Mrs Merdle in *Little Dorrit*, as he in some respects recalls Mrs General in the same novel. Their daughter GEORGIANA is a timid girl whose eighteenth birthday is celebrated (I,11); she becomes the object of Mrs Lammle's attentions and of Fledgeby's self-seeking matrimonial plans.

POTTERSON, MISS ABBEY. Landlady of the Six Jolly Fellowship Porters, a riverside pub (see I,6).

RIAH. Elderly Jew of gentle manners and speech, introduced in II,5. He is employed by Fledgeby in his money-lending transactions (compare a somewhat similar relationship between Pancks and Casby in *Little Dorrit*). On Riah as a response to the appeal made by Mrs. Eliza Davis to Dickens, see under 'Davis' in 'The Dickens Circle'. See also the article by Harry Stone referred to above.

RIDERHOOD, ROGUE. Disreputable waterside character; he lives at Limehouse Hole. He visits Mortimer Lightwood and accuses Gaffer Hexam of the Harmon murder (I,12). He is run down by a steamer and almost drowned (III,2–3); blackmails Bradley Headstone and, in spite of his conviction that he cannot die by water, drowns with him (IV,15). His daughter PLEASANT, introduced in II,12, is 'an unlicensed pawnbroker'.

ROKESMITH, JOHN, *see under* HARMON, OLD.

SAMPSON, GEORGE. Disappointed lover of Bella Wilfer.

SLOPPY. An ungainly, simple-minded, but good-hearted orphan (a 'love-child'), brought up in the workhouse: 'Full-Private Number One in the Awkward Squad of the rank and file of life', 'a very long boy, with a very little head, and an open mouth of disproportionate capacity' (I,16). Betty Higden, for whom he turns the mangle, says that ' "speaking quite correctly, he has no right name. I always understood he took his name from being found on a Sloppy night" ' (cf. Oliver Twist; also Tattycoram in *Little Dorrit*). He is adopted by the Boffins after Johnny's death. The penultimate chapter of the novel hints that he will marry Jenny Wren.

TIPPINS, LADY. Decayed, impecunious and snobbish lady, a member of the social chorus ('The Voice of Society') at the Veneerings', and 'relict of the late Sir Thomas Tippins, knighted in mistake for somebody else by His Majesty King George the Third'. She is introduced in I,2 ('charming old Lady Tippins . . . with an immense obtuse drab oblong face, like a face in a tablespoon, and a dyed Long Walk up the top of her head, as a convenient public approach to the bunch of false hair behind'). A brilliantly savage portrait in some respects reminiscent of that of Mrs Skewton in *Dombey and Son*.

TWEMLOW, MR. 'First cousin to Lord Snigsworth', he is a harmless, innocent-minded gentleman, a bachelor who moves (with some bewilderment) in fashionable society and lives in Duke Street, St James's; introduced in I,2 ('grey, dry, polite, susceptible to east wind, First-Gentleman-in-Europe collar and cravat, cheeks drawn in as if he had made a great effort to retire into himself some years ago, and had got so far and had never got any farther').

VENEERING, MR. He and his wife ANASTATIA are the 'Perfectly New people' referred to in Dickens' indication of his first notions for this novel: in I,2 they appear as 'bran-new people in a bran-new house in a bran-new quarter of London'. He is 'forty, wavy-haired, dark, tending to corpulence, sly, mysterious, filmy'; she 'fair, aquiline-nosed and fingered, not so much light hair as she might have, gorgeous in raiment and jewels, enthusiastic, propitiatory . . .'. They represent the *nouveaux riches* of the period, vulgar and ambitious social upstarts; they are, of course, expressively named.

VENUS, MR. Taxidermist and articulator of skeletons; he has a shop at Clerkenwell and 'a sallow face with weak eyes, surmounted by a tangle of reddish-dusty hair' (I,7). His stock-in-trade includes Mr Wegg's amputated leg and he becomes a fellow-conspirator of Wegg in the plot against Mr Boffin. He has been disappointed in love. His shop is based on one in Saint Giles's pointed out to Dickens by his illustrator Marcus Stone (see letter of 25 February 1864). See also the paper by F. X. Shea referred to above.

WEGG, SILAS. 'A man with a wooden leg' (his name being a portmanteau form of the phrase), introduced in I,5 as a street-hawker of ballads (an occupation referred to by Mayhew). He is employed as a reader by Mr Boffin, becomes envious of the latter's wealth, and, with Venus as a fellow-conspirator, determines to exploit and blackmail him – a comic instance of the mercenary and predatory impulses treated more seriously elsewhere in the novel. He is finally exposed and deposited in a 'scavenger's cart' (IV,14), thus suffering the physical humiliation that is the frequent fate of Dickensian comic villains (cf. Casby in *Little Dorrit* and Fledgeby in this novel).

WILFER, REGINALD. 'A poor clerk' (I,4) of a 'chubby, smooth innocent appearance' – one of Dickens' boy-men, the father of a family but himself an overgrown child, united to a formidable

wife (cf. Mr Jellyby in *Bleak House*). He lives in Holloway and is
employed by Chicksey, Veneering and Stubbles. His wife is 'a tall
woman and an angular. Her lord being cherubic, she was
necessarily Majestic, according to the principle which matri-
monially unites contrasts.' Their large family includes three
daughters, BELLA, LAVINIA and CECILIA, the first of these being
one of the novel's two heroines. Mr Wilfer and Bella dine at
Greenwich (II,8). She is the girl to whom old Harmon has
betrothed his son: II,9 ends with her wishing 'now that the
deceased old John Harmon had never made a will about her, now
that the deceased young John Harmon had lived to marry her'.
She is taken up by the Boffins, goes to live with them, and
confesses that ' "I have money always in my thoughts and my
desires; and the whole life I place before myself is money, money,
money, and what money can make of life!" ' (end of III,4 and
also of the eleventh number). It is for her benefit that Boffin stages
his pretence of being corrupted by avarice. After Rokesmith has
been discharged she leaves the Boffins and tells her father that she
and Rokesmith (whom she does not know to be the John Harmon
with whose destiny her own is linked) are in love (III,16). She
and John marry (IV,4); she tells him she is expecting a baby
(IV,5); they return to the Boffins, and Bella is reconciled with
them; she also learns her husband's true identity and that Mr
Boffin's miserliness was a pretence and a test (IV,12–13). As an
'alternative' heroine, Bella stands in contrast with Lizzie Hexam
socially and temperamentally. She is also one of a group of later
heroines (which includes Estella and Helena Landless) whose
vivacity contrasts markdly with the self-effacing heroines more
common in Dickens. It has been suggested that this new
character-type owes something to Dickens' involvement with
Ellen Ternan, and indeed that their names are variations on hers.
Wilfer obviously and appropriately suggests *wilful*.

WRAYBURN, EUGENE. Introduced as 'a friend of Mortimer' at
Veneering's dinner-party in I,2; they have been at the same
public school and, like Mortimer Lightwood, Eugene is an
unsuccessful lawyer (he has been a barrister for seven years and
has ' "had no business at all" ': I,3). He takes a rather equivocal
interest in Lizzie Hexam (Dickens never actually says in so many
words that he plans to seduce her, but the possibility is clearly
present). He has her educated; receives a visit from Bradley
Headstone and Charley Hexam, and is reproached by Mortimer

Lightwood with having designs on Lizzie's innocence (II,6); finds out where she is from 'Mr Dolls', visits her, and is attacked and rescued (IV,6); thinks he will die, marries her, and recovers (IV,10). Wrayburn is a familiar Dickensian type – the upper-class idler, socially useless and morally irresponsible (cf. Steerforth, Gowan) – but with a difference, in that he is changed by a good woman's love.

WREN, JENNY. A shrewd, sharp-tongued, crippled figure – a child in appearance, a woman in fact and manner – who works as a dolls' dressmaker; she is introduced in II,1 as 'a child – a dwarf – a girl – a something'. She has a drunken father, nicknamed MR DOLLS and their relationship reverses the natural order, she treating him as a naughty child. She becomes a friend of Lizzie Hexam and refuses to tell Eugene Wrayburn where the latter is hiding (III,10). She visits Riah in his roof-top garden (II,5) – a curious scene in which she pretends that she is dead and the roof-top heaven. Mr Dolls betrays Lizzie's hiding-place to Eugene for money to buy rum (III,17); and dies (IV,9). The penultimate chapter of the novel hints that Jenny will marry Sloppy.

The Mystery of Edwin Drood

Texts   Clarendon Dickens, ed. Margaret Cardwell (1972); Penguin English Library, ed. Arthur J. Cox, introduction by Angus Wilson (1974).

Composition   By the early summer of 1869 three-and-a-half years had elapsed since Dickens had published a novel; he had been busy during that period editing *All the Year Round* and delivering his public readings, but the gap between *Our Mutual Friend* and its successor turned out to be unprecedented in Dickens' career. According to Dolby, the manager of his reading tours, he began 'to cast about for a subject for a new book' in May 1869 or thereabouts; and in July he wrote to Forster:

> What should you think of the idea of a story beginning in this way? – Two people, boy and girl, or very young, going apart from one another, pledged to be married after many years – at the end of the book. The interest to arise out of the tracing of their separate ways, and the impossibility of telling what will be done with that impending fate.

By the end of August, however, a different notion had taken hold of him:

> I laid aside the fancy I told you of, and have a very curious and new idea for my new story. Not a communicable idea (or the interest of the book would be gone), but a very strong one, though difficult to work.

Forster claims (and there is no way of checking his claim) that 'immediately afterward' he learned from Dickens that the story

239

was to be that of the murder of a nephew by his uncle; the originality of which was to consist in the review of the murderer's career by himself at the close, when its temptations were to be dwelt upon as if, not he the culprit, but some other man, were the tempted. The last chapters were to be written in the condemned cell . . .

In the same passage Forster also mentions the importance in Dickens' plot of the gold ring ('which had resisted the corrosive effects of the lime into which he had thrown the body') in bringing Jasper to account, and says that Rosa was to have married Tartar, Crisparkle to have married Helena Landless, and Neville Landless to have died in helping Tartar to 'unmask and seize the murderer'. Forster's reliability in this instance has been questioned, but his main point – that Dickens' conception was of a 'sensation novel' in which the main focus of interest should be the psychological state of the murderer – sounds plausible enough: Dickens had, after all, shown a profound interest in the criminal mind from Bill Sikes to Bradley Headstone.

On a sheet of paper dated 'Friday Twentieth August, 1869' Dickens set down a list of seventeen titles for his new story: the list includes *The Loss of James Wakefield, James's Disappearance, Flight and Pursuit, Sworn to avenge it, One Object in Life, A Kinsman's Devotion, The Loss of Edwyn Drood, The Mystery in the Drood Family, The Flight of Edwyn Drood, Edwin Drood in hiding, The Disappearance of Edwin Drood, The Mystery of Edwin Drood,* and *Dead? Or alive?.* It will be noted that, while a few of these place the emphasis on Jasper's wish to solve and revenge his nephew's murder, most hint ambiguously at Edwin's fate. Before the end of September Dickens had settled on a title and chosen Charles Collins as his illustrator; and during October he was busy writing the first number. We know that during the period preceding composition he had paid at least one visit to Shadwell, where he had found the 'original' of the Princess Puffer in the person of 'Opium Sal'. (James T. Fields, the American publisher who accompanied Dickens, later recorded that 'The identical words which Dickens puts into the mouth of this wretched creature in "Edwin Drood" we heard her croon as we leaned over the tattered bed on which she was lying.')

Dickens wrote the final words of his uncompleted novel a few hours before his fatal stroke on 8 June 1870. At the time of his death three numbers had been published and nearly another three had been written. He never saw the proofs of the last two chapters he wrote. Manuscript and partial proofs in the Forster Collection.

Serialization Monthly numbers from April to September 1870. Division as follows: I (Chs 1–5); II (Chs 6–9); III (Chs 10–12); IV (Chs 13–16); V (Chs 17–20); VI (Chs 21–3). The novel was originally planned to occupy twelve numbers: thus it was roughly half-complete when Dickens died. On the decision to abandon the pattern of twenty numbers that Dickens had followed from *Pickwick* to *Our Mutual Friend*, Robert Patten has written:

> The commercial reception of *Our Mutual Friend* bore out the general impression that the shilling part had had its day. So Dickens proposed two alternatives to Chapman: weekly instalments in *All the Year Round*, or twelve monthly numbers. The smaller compass is probably not primarily related to Dickens's ill health. He did find the large canvas of his last serial disconcerting at first; he was now comfortable in more confined and compact instalments; he was anxious about his condition; but he was also being realistic about the market.

The serial sold well, with an opening circulation of 50,000. But Dickens had found himself hard pressed even before publication began (he wrote to G. H. Lewes on 26 February 1870: 'Between my readings, my book, my weekly journal . . . I am really hard put to it occasionally'); and a week after the first number appeared he confessed himself to be 'making headway but slowly', though he was naturally delighted by the sales ('We have been doing wonders with No. 1 of Edwin Drood'; he told Fields; '*It has very, very far outstripped every one of its predecessors*'). When he came to an agreement with his publishers,

> There was one clause that had never been in a Dickens contract before. It was included by Dickens's own desire: that if he should die or for any other reason be unable to finish the story in twelve numbers, Forster was to serve as an arbitrator to decide what amount should in fairness be repaid to Chapman [Johnson].

Publication By Chapman & Hall in one volume in September 1870 (on the same day at the sixth and last monthly number). The illustrations executed for the serial by Luke Fildes were included.

Reception   The Mystery of Edwin Drood was welcomed as a return to
Dickens' early manner; significantly, Durdles was a particularly
popular character. The *Athenaeum* breathed an audible sigh of relief
at finding 'a favourite author in a shape and fashion in which he has
not been seen for many a weary day', and gratification at Dickens'
creative longevity was more in evidence than appreciation of his
attempt at a new sub-genre (as the *Graphic* said, reviewing the
opening number, 'What other story-teller, English or foreign, ever
maintained so great and increasing a popularity for six and thirty
years!').

Dickens' last novel, like his first, has attracted an enormous
amount of attention for reasons largely unconnected with literary
criticism. Just as many books have been written on Mr Pickwick's
journeyings, many have been devoted to 'completing' Dickens'
unfinished book or otherwise 'solving' the mystery of *The Mystery of
Edwin Drood*. (The most recent venture is Charles Forsyte's *The
Decoding of Edwin Drood* [1980].) As Arthur Cox has said, 'The
literature on [this novel] is extremely extensive, though much of it is
of doubtful value'; in terms of literary criticism, the book is an
exception to the rule that Dickens' work has in recent years received
attention on a scale undreamed of by earlier generations – as Philip
Collins says, 'The old breed of Droodians has almost died out,
leaving no alternative critical regime.' It is, however, not only the
adventitious fact of its remaining half-finished that justifies us in
regarding it as one of Dickens' lesser novels; there seems little reason
to suppose that, even had it been completed, it would have stood
among his major achievements. To my mind it is comparable with,
say, *Hard Times*: in other words it is readable, often brilliant,
representative of some aspects of Dickens' genius and art, but
lacking the scope and vision of the major novels. Part of the reason
for this is no doubt that it was, quite consciously, an exercise in a
specialized genre or sub-genre – the so-called 'sensation novel'.

Contemporary reviewers made comparisons with Trollope, on
the rather flimsy basis of the cathedral city setting; but there is no
real point of contact between these two authors, and the real affinity
of *The Mystery of Edwin Drood* is with the novels that Wilkie Collins
and others were publishing in the last decade of Dickens' life.
Collins, a dozen years younger than Dickens, was taken up by him
in the fifties and joined the staff of *Household Words* (revealingly,
Dickens told Wills that Collins was 'very suggestive and exceedingly
quick to take my notions'). Collins' *The Dead Secret* appeared in

Dickens' journal in 1857, and his *The Woman in White* followed *A Tale of Two Cities* in the newly launched *All the Year Round* – a significant choice on Dickens' part, implying confidence in the other novelist's powers of sustaining the appeal that his own novel had held for readers. *The Woman in White* was a brilliant success and was described as 'probably the most popular novel of the year' (*National Review*). It set a fashion for novels of mystery and intrigue with strong, well-constructed plots and vivid characterization; later successes in this genre included Mary Elizabeth Braddon's *Lady Audley's Secret* (1862) and Collins' own *The Moonstone* (1866). Arguably *Great Expectations* owes something to this tradition; but it is also true that Dickens had anticipated some elements in sensation fiction in such earlier novels as *Bleak House*. (See T. S. Eliot's 1927 essay, 'Wilkie Collins and Dickens', reprinted in his *Selected Essays*.)

The date of the action is not precisely stated, but various clues suggest the early 1840s. In Ch. 17 there is a reference to 'the yet unfinished and undeveloped railway station' at Cloisterham, and in a cancelled passage in Ch. 9 (given in a note to the Penguin edition) Mr Grewgious speaks to Jasper of 'the new railroad yonder'.

The notes to Arthur Cox's Penguin edition, and the textual notes in Margaret Cardwell's Clarendon edition, record other variations between Dickens' manuscript and the printed text. At the outset, Dickens, who after all had not written a serial novel for several years, made an unprecedented blunder: usually very skilful at judging how much of his manuscript was required to fill a monthly number, and scrupulous at giving readers value for money (exactly thirty-two pages, with no short measure), he found when he received the proofs of the first two numbers from the printers that he had underwritten each by no less than six pages. As he wrote to Georgina Hogarth, 'Consequently I had to transpose a chapter from number two to number one, and remodel number two altogether!'. Nor was this the only, or the first, problem besetting the new serial. Charles Collins, brother of Wilkie and son-in-law of Dickens, had been engaged as illustrator but, after making a start, was unable to continue on account of ill-health. Luke Fildes was engaged in his place, and it was Fildes, who, many years later, recalled in a letter to *The Times* (27 October 1905) that Dickens insisted on the importance of showing, in his illustration to Chapter 14, the unusually long scarf worn by Jasper, 'for Jasper strangles Edwin Drood with it'.

From the first, readers of the unfinished novel were much

exercised as to how Dickens had intended to bring it to a conclusion. Attempts at finishing it off according to one theory or another started very early; in a crowded field a few samples will illustrate the popularity of this kind of game of wits:

H. Morford and others, *John Jasper's Secret* (Philadelphia, 1871).
R. A. Proctor, *Watched by the Dead* (1887).
W. E. Crisp, *The Mystery of Edwin Drood Completed* (1914).
'A Loyal Dickensian', *Dickens' Mystery of Edwin Drood* (1927).

J. C. Walters' *The Complete Mystery of Edwin Drood* (1912) contains an extensive bibliography, and Felix Aylmer's *The Drood Case* (1964) shows that the problem had not altogether lost its charm for a much later generation.

As S. C. Roberts notes, 'The two main questions on which so much labour and ingenuity have been expended are (1) Was Drood murdered? and (2) Who was Datchery?' As we have seen above, some of Dickens' projected titles, like the final title chosen, preserved a careful ambiguity as to Edwin's fate; but this was probably no more than a canny wish to avoid letting the cat out of the bag prematurely. Dickens was reported by his eldest son to have replied 'Of course; what else do you suppose?' when asked whether Edwin was murdered (recalled by Charles Dickens junior in his introduction to an edition of the novel); and the number-plans are explicit that a murder has been committed. But R. A. Proctor's book mentioned above develops the theory that Jasper's murder attempt failed and that Edwin, rescued from the quicklime by Durdles, disguised himself as Datchery; Andrew Lang and M. R. James found some merit in this theory, and such projected titles as *Edwin Drood in Hiding*, along with the suggestive title of Ch. 14 ('When shall these three meet again?'), gives it modest support. Most verdicts, however, have been against it. Roberts says that 'The one point on which there is general agreement is that Jasper was the murderer, or at least that he attempted the murder.' (See, however, Aylmer's book noted above, which appeared after Roberts' introduction to the Oxford Illustrated Dickens and offers a dissenting view of Jasper.)

The references in the text to Datchery strongly suggest that he is one of the other characters in disguise, and there is no shortage of candidates – Drood, Neville and Helena Landless, Bazzard, Tartar, and Grewgious have all found supporters. Some of the details in the text can be invoked in support of one or other candidate, though one must remember that Dickens was perfectly capable of introducing red herrings. Thus we learn that Helena has had experience of disguising herself as a boy in the manner of a Shakespearean heroine; that Tartar is a man of leisure able to go where he wishes; and that Bazzard has theatrical ambitions. Would-be solvers of the mystery have not neglected the wrapper-illustration, though this seems to provide not so much clues as further mysteries.

An additional minor problem is posed by the so-called 'Sapsea fragment', found among Dickens' papers after his death and published by Forster. This introduces a new character, Poker, and according to Forster represents an attempt on Dickens' part to open up 'some fresh veins of character incidental to the interest, though not directly part of it'. Margaret Cardwell, in rejecting this suggestion, has persuasively argued that 'Poker's introduction is a parallel too close to that of Datchery to be a likely additional interest; the more reasonable assumption would be that this was a first draft later rejected'. (Since the fragment is not given in all editions, it is reproduced below.)

As already indicated, specifically critical discussions of this novel are relatively scarce. Particularly worthy of mention are essays by Edmund Wilson (in *The Wound and the Bow*, 1941), V. S. Pritchett (in *The Living Novel*, 1946), George H. Ford (*Nineteenth-Century Fiction*, VI, 1952), A. O. J. Cockshut (in Gross and Pearson's collection, 1962), and Philip Collins (*Dickensian*, LX, 1964). There is more good material in Collins' *Dickens and Crime*, and Angus Wilson's introduction to the Penguin edition should not be missed.

THE SAPSEA FRAGMENT

Wishing to take the air, I proceeded by a circuitous route to the Club, it being our weekly night of meeting. I found that we mustered our full strength. We were enrolled under the denomination of The Eight Club. We were eight in number; we met at eight o'clock during eight months of the year; our annual subscription was eight shillings each; we played eight games of four handed cribbage at eightpence the game; our frugal supper was composed of eight rolls, eight mutton chops, eight pork sausages, eight baked potatoes, eight marrow bones with eight toasts, and eight bottles of ale. There may or may not be a certain harmony of colour in the ruling idea of this (to adopt a phrase of our lively neighbours) reunion. It was a little idea of mine.

A somewhat popular member of the Eight Club was a member by the name of Kimber. By profession dancing-master. A common-place hopeful sort of man, wholly destitute of dignity or knowledge of the world.

As I entered the Club-room, Kimber was making the remark: "And he still half believes him to be very high in the Church."

In the act of hanging up my hat on the Eighth peg by the door, I caught Kimber's visual ray. He lowered it, and passed a remark on the next change of the moon. I did not take particular notice of this at the moment, because the world was often pleased to be a little shy of Ecclesiastical topics in my presence. For I felt that I was picked out (though perhaps only through a coincidence) to a certain extent to represent what I call our glorious constitution in church and state. The phrase may be objected to by captious minds; but I own to it as mine. I threw it off in argument some little time back. I said, Our Glorious Constitution in Church and State.

Another member of the Eight Club was Peartree, also member of the Royal College of Surgeons. Mr Peartree is not accountable to me for his opinions, and I say no more of them here than that he attends the poor gratis, whenever they want him, and is not the parish doctor. Mr Peartree may justify it to the grasp of *his* mind thus to do his republican utmost to bring an appointed officer into contempt. Suffice it that Mr Peartree can never justify it to the grasp of *mine*.

Between Peartree and Kimber there was a sickly sort of feeble-minded alliance. It came under my particular notice when I sold off Kimber by auction. (Goods taken in execution.) He was a widower in a white under waistcoat and slight shoes with bows, and had two daughters not ill-looking. Indeed, the reverse. Both daughters taught dancing in Scholastic Establishments for Young Ladies – had done so at Mrs Sapsea's; nay, Twinkletons – and both, in giving lessons, presented the unwomanly spectacle of having little fiddles tucked under their chins. In spite of which the younger one might, if I am correctly informed – I will raise the veil so far as to say I KNOW she might – have soared for life from this degrading taint, but for having the worst class of mind alloted to what I call, the common herd, and being so incredibly devoid of veneration as to become painfully ludicrous.

When I sold off Kimber without reserve, Peartree (as poor as
he can hold together) had several prime household lots knocked
down to him. *I* am not to be blinded, and of course it was as plain
to me what he was going to do with them, as it was that he was a
brown hulking sort of revolutionary subject who had been in
India with the soldiers and ought (for the sake of society) to have
his neck broken. I saw the lots shortly afterwards in Kimber's
lodgings – through the windows – and I easily made out that there
had been a sneaking pretence of lending them 'till better times. A
man with a smaller knowledge of the world than myself might
have been led to suspect that Kimber had held back money from
his creditors and fraudulently bought the goods. But besides that
I knew for certain he had no money, I knew that this would
involve a species of forethought not to be made compatible with
the frivolity of a caperer, innocculating other people with
capering, for his bread.

As it was the first time I had seen either of those two since the
Sale, I kept myself in what I call Abeyance. When selling him up,
I had delivered a few remarks – shall I say a little homily? –
concerning Kimber, which the world did regard as more than
usually worth notice. I had come up into my pulpit, it was said,
uncommonly like; and a murmur of recognition had repeated his
(I will not name whose) title, before I spoke. I had then gone on to
say that all present would find, in the first page of the Catalogue
that was lying before them, in the last paragraph before the first
lot, the following words: 'Sold in pursuance of a Writ of execution
issued by a Creditor.' I had then proceeded to remind my Friends
that however frivolous, not to say contemptible, the pursuits by
which a man got his goods together, still his goods were as dear to
him, and as cheap to society (if sold without reserve) as though his
pursuits had been of [a] character that would bear serious
contemplation. I had then divided my text (if I may be allowed so
to call it) into three heads; firstly, Sold; secondly, In pursuance of
a writ of execution; thirdly, Issued by a creditor; with a few moral
reflections on each and winding up the "Now to the first Lot" in a
manner that was complimented when I afterwards mingled with
my hearers.

So not being certain on what terms I and Kimber stood, I was
grave, I was chilling. Kimber however, moving to me, I moved to
Kimber. (I was the creditor who had issued the writ. Not that it
matters.)

"I was alluding, Mr Sapsea," said Kimber, "when you came in, to a stranger who entered into conversation with me in the street as I came to the club. He had been speaking to you just before, it seemed, by the churchyard; and though you had told him who you were, I could hardly persuade him that you were not high in the Church."

"Idiot!" said Peartree.

"Ass!" said Kimber.

"Idiot and Ass!" said the other five members.

"Idiot and Ass, gentlemen," I remonstrated, looking around me, "are strong expressions to apply to a young man of good appearance and address." My generosity was roused. I own it.

"You'll admit that he must be a Fool," said Peartree.

"You can't deny that he must be a Blockhead," said Kimber.

Their tone of disgust amounted to being offensive. Why should the young man be so calumniated? What had he done? He had only made an innocent and natural mistake. I controlled my generous indignation, and said so.

"Natural," repeated Kimber. "*He's* a Natural!"

The remaining six members of the Eight Club laughed unanimously. It stung me. It was a scornful laugh. My anger was roused in behalf of an absent friendless stranger. I rose (for I had been sitting down.)

"Gentlemen," I said with dignity, "I will not remain one of this club allowing opprobrium to be cast on an unoffending person in his absence. I will not so violate what I call the sacred rites of hospitality. Gentlemen, until you know how to behave yourselves better, I leave you. Gentlemen, until then I withdraw from this place of meeting whatever personal qualifications I may have brought into it. Gentlemen, until then you cease to be the Eight Club, and must make the best you can of becoming the Seven."

I put on my hat and retired. As I went down stairs I distinctly heard them give a suppressed cheer. Such is the power of demeanour and knowledge of mankind – I had forced it out of them.

II

Whom should I meet in the street, within a few yards of the door of the inn where the Club was held, but the selfsame young man whose cause I had felt it my duty so warmly – and I will add so disinterestedly – to take up!

"Is it Mr Sapsea," he said doubtfully, "or is it –"

"It is Mr Sapsea," I replied.

"Pardon me, Mr Sapsea; you appear warm, Sir."

"I have been warm," I said, "and on your account." Having stated the circumstances at some length (my generosity almost overpowering him), I asked him his name.

"Mr Sapsea," he answered, looking down, "your penetration is so acute, your glance into the souls of your fellow men is so penetrating, that if I was hardy enough to deny that my name is Poker, what would it avail me?"

I don't know that I had quite exactly made out to a fraction that his name was Poker, but I dare say I had been pretty near doing it.

"Well, Well," said I, trying to put him at his ease by nodding my head, in a soothing way. "Your name is Poker, and there is no harm in being named Poker."

"Oh Mr Sapsea!" cried the young man in a very well-behaved manner. "Bless you for those words!" He then, as if ashamed of having given way to his feelings, looked down again.

"Come Poker," said I, "let me hear more about you. Tell me. Where are you going to, Poker, and where do you come from?"

"Ah Mr Sapsea!" exclaimed the young man. "Disguise from you is impossible. You know already that I come from somewhere, and am going somewhere else. If I was to deny it, what would it avail me?"

"Then don't deny it," was my remark.

"Or," pursued Poker, in a kind of despondent rapture, "or if I was to deny that I came to this town to see and hear you Sir, what would it avail me? Or if I was to deny

CHARACTERS

BAZZARD. Mr Grewgious's clerk, described in Ch. 11.

BILLICKIN, MRS. Landlady resident in Southampton Street, Bloomsbury Square; she lets rooms to Rosa Bud (Ch. 21).

BUD, ROSA (Rosebud). Orphan and pupil at Miss Twinkleton's boarding-school; engaged from childhood to Edwin Drood, who nicknames her 'Pussy'. They break off their engagement (Ch. 13).

She is the object of the unwelcome attentions of John Jasper, and it has been suggested that the illustration 'Jasper's Sacrifices' may show his exerting some kind of 'mesmeric' or hypnotic power over her, just as she is disturbed by the 'resounding chord' he plays on the organ and, even more so, by the curious feature of his piano accompaniment to her singing (he 'ever and again hinted the one note, as though it were a low whisper from himself').

CRISPARKLE, REV. SEPTIMUS. One of the minor canons at Cloisterham Cathedral, a muscular Christian and a bachelor, tutor to Neville Landless. He lives with his mother, whom he affectionately nicknames 'the China Shepherdess', at Minor Canon Corner.

DATCHERY, DICK. A mysterious man with a mane of white hair, he appears in Ch. 18 in Cloisterham. His appearance suggests a disguise (his hair is 'unusually thick and ample', and he has black eyebrows); for theories as to his identity, see above.

DEPUTY ('Winks'). Urchin ('a hideous small boy in rags') employed by Durdles to throw stones at him if he is out late (Ch. 5). He is also 'man-servant' at the Travellers' Twopenny, a doss-house.

DROOD, EDWIN. Orphan nephew of John Jasper, he is engaged to Rosa Bud, quarrels with Neville Landless, and disappears (announced in Ch. 14).

DURDLES. Stonemason and drunkard, familiar with the cathedral crypt (see Ch. 4) and evidently to be used without his knowledge by Jasper in disposing of Edwin's body.

GREWGIOUS, MR HIRAM. 'Receiver and Agent . . . to two rich estates' (Ch. 11), and guardian to Rosa Bud, he has chambers in Staple's Inn, London. He is described in Ch. 9.

HONEYTHUNDER, MR LUKE. Philanthropist and guardian of Helena and Neville Landless.

JASPER, JOHN. 'A dark man of some six-and-twenty' (Ch. 2), music-teacher, chorister, and in charge of the cathedral music. He is the uncle of Edwin Drood, who calls him Jack, and, according to most interpretations, his murderer. He is infatuated with Rosa Bud, who is engaged to Edwin. The opening scene of the novel shows him in an opium-den (perhaps thanks to the influence of Wilkie Collins' *The Moonstone*). Philip Collins suggests convincingly (in *Dickens and Crime*, pp. 306–7) that 'Certainly it is Jasper, as the murderer, who is to suffer destruction . . . by some miscalculation, or over-reaching himself – such as, [Dickens] firmly believed, all murderers made at some point in their most cunning plans – Jasper would betray his own guilt through trying to convict Neville.' George Gissing was unimpressed by Jasper, finding him 'a very vulgar assassin, and we care not at all what becomes of him'.

LANDLESS, HELENA. Orphan, ward of Mr Honeythunder, hand-some and darkskinned, 'of almost the gipsy type' (Ch. 6): she has been brought up in Ceylon by her stepfather. Her twin brother NEVILLE is similar in appearance and comes to Cloisterham to 'read' with Mr Crisparkle. He and Edwin Drood quarrel (Ch. 8), egged on by Jasper. He is arrested on suspicion of Edwin's murder (Ch. 15); and there are strong indications that his sister, who is devoted to him, was intended to play a role in proving his innocence.

'PUFFER, 'Er Royal Highness the Princess.' Nickname given by Durdles to an old woman who keeps an opium den in London's dockland (Ch. 1); she appears in Cloisterham (Ch. 14), and Jasper visits her again in London in Ch. 22. On her prototype, see p. 240 above.

SAPSEA, MR THOMAS. Self-important auctioneer and 'the purest Jackass in Cloisterham' (Ch. 4). He becomes mayor (Ch. 12).

TARTAR, MR. Stranger who appears in Ch. 17 and introduces himself to Neville Landless as a neighbour. He is 'a handsome gentleman' of twenty-eight or thirty and 'extemely sunburnt'; he has been a lieutenant in the Navy but has resigned on receiving a legacy. He turns out to have been Mr Crisparkle's fag at school (Ch. 20).

TISHER, MRS. Widow employed at Miss Twinkleton's boarding-school.

TOPE, MR. Chief verger of Cloisterham cathedral. His wife also appears in the novel.

TWINKLETON, MISS. Proprietress of Nuns' House, a seminary for young ladies at Cloisterham, at which Rosa Bud is a pupil.

Christmas Books

Between 1843 and 1848 Dickens published five Christmas Books. They enjoyed a wide (though not a uniform) popularity and in the mid-forties became a national institution – as, indeed, the first and best of them, *A Christmas Carol*, has remained. They are described individually below, but a few observations on them as a group are in order. In a lively essay on Dickens and Christmas (*Etudes Anglaises*, 1970), Philip Collins has pointed out that, when Dickens died, many of the obituaries referred to 'the centrality of Christmas in his work and outlook'. Certainly the association of Dickens with Christmas, and vice versa, is still potent: as Professor Collins says, 'The *Carol* must be one of the tiny handful of literary works that (say) three-quarters of the population could attribute to their author, and name a character from.' Not that Dickens' contemporaries spoke with a unanimous voice on this question. Mrs Oliphant, never one of Dickens' keenest fans, could scarce forebear to sneer (she said that he was 'the first to find out the immense spiritual power of the Christmas turkey'); Edwin Whipple said that he 'christianizes eating and drinking, and contrives to make the stomach in some odd way an organ of the soul'; Carlyle, though moved by the *Carol* when it appeared, later objected to what he saw as its soft centre ('He thinks men ought to be buttered up, and the world made soft and accommodating for them, and all sorts of fellow have turkey for their Christmas dinner'). Dickens himself would no doubt have set more store by the costermonger's girl in Drury Lane who was reported to have exclaimed, on hearing of Dickens' death: 'Then will Father Christmas die too?' As some of the details cited below illustrate, there was at times a notable disparity between the critical reception of these works and their popularity with the public, as evinced by sales.

John Butt suggested in 1951 (in a lecture printed in his *Pope, Dickens, and Others*, 1969) that the Christmas Books mark 'an important stage in Dickens's development as a novelist', since they provide evidence of his premeditation, his attention to construction, and his use of such structural devices as repetition and contrast – qualities less in evidence in his earlier work but increasingly important from *Dombey* onwards. Kathleen Tillotson has suggested (in a lecture included in the *Dickensian* supplement, *Dickens Memorial Lectures*, 1970) that they also look forward to the novels that succeed them in 'their treatment of time': the ghost-machinery enables Dickens to 'play tricks with time, breaking through the barriers of ordinary experience'. It may be no coincidence that, not long after completing the last of the Christmas Books, Dickens began work on *David Copperfield*, the novel in which he most fully explores time and memory (and which, appropriately enough, appeared in volume form in the same year as Tennyson's *In Memoriam* and Wordsworth's *Prelude*).

Michael Slater, who has written more fully and authoritatively on the Christmas Books than anyone else, has made some interesting comments on their homogeneity considered as a group. He points out that the first two, *A Christmas Carol* and *The Chimes*, have much in common:

> Both these little books, products of the Hungry Forties, overflow with benevolence towards the poor and appeal urgently to the reader's charitable feelings. Both are distinctly seasonal, the *Carol* having a Christmas setting and *The Chimes* a New Year's Eve one. In both stories the supernatural plays a crucial part, the main character being converted by its means from an undesirable state of mind to a joyful and generous one.

Slater add that 'All these features reappear in the last of the Christmas Books, *The Haunted Man*'; the two intervening ones, however, show significant differences, though there are two other elements that run through the whole series – the emphasis laid upon 'family love and the delights of home', and 'the theme of memory and its beneficial effects on the moral life'.

The Christmas Books are the most obvious examples of an interest in Christmas that recurs throughout Dickens' work. On 27 December 1835 he published a sketch titled 'Christmas Festivities', and followed it a week later with 'The New Year'; both were later incorporated in *Sketches by Boz*. One of the most famous episodes in *Pickwick* is the account of Christmas at Dingley Dell, published in

December 1836. At the other end of his career, there is the
Christmas episode in *Great Expectations* and the Christmas Eve
chapter of *Edwin Drood* – this last a doom-laden scene that is as far
removed as possible from the high spirits and benevolence of
Mr Pickwick and the Cratchits.

Apart from separate publication (described below), the
Christmas Books were collected by Dickens and published in 1852
and subsequently. For the 1852 edition Dickens wrote a preface that
is partly apologetic and partly self-justifying:

> The narrow space within which it was necessary to confine
> these Christmas Stories when they were originally published,
> rendered their construction a matter of some difficulty, and
> almost necessitated what is peculiar in their machinery. I never
> attempted great elaboration of detail in the working out of
> character within such limits, believing that it could not succeed.
> My purpose was, in a whimsical kind of masque which the good
> humour of the season justified, to awaken some loving and
> forbearing thoughts, never out of season in a Christian land.

A CHRISTMAS CAROL

Published on 17 December 1843 by Chapman & Hall, with four
coloured illustrations by John Leech. Dickens began writing it at
the beginning of October and finished it by the end of November.
He was a little more than halfway through *Martin Chuzzlewit* at the
time, and must have worked under considerable pressure; but his
emotional involvement in the *Carol* was considerable: as he wrote to
Cornelius Felton,

> Charles Dickens wept and laughed and wept again, and excited
> himself in a most extraordinary manner in the composition; and
> thinking whereof he walked about the black streets of London,
> fifteen and twenty miles many a night when all the sober folks had
> gone to bed . . . .

It sold well: 6000 copies (at the high price of five shillings) had gone
by Christmas Eve, and orders were still 'coming in fast from town
and country'. Nor did sales end with the end of the holiday season:
as Patten points out, 'More copies were printed and sold between

January and April [1844] than during the Christmas season of
1843.' Dickens was able to boast that the book was 'a most
prodigious success – the greatest, I think, I have ever achieved'. His
profits, however, were bitterly disappointing; and a dispute over
them with Chapman & Hall led to his break with the firm.

The *Carol* quickly established for itself a special place in English
literature, such that it was 'not to be talked about or written of
according to ordinary rules', as one contemporary critic observed
(*Blackwood's Magazine*, January 1844). Lord Jeffrey found Tiny Tim
'in life and death almost as sweet and touching as Nelly [in *The Old
Curiosity Shop*]'; and Thackeray, while registering mild objections
('I am not sure that the allegory is a very complete one, and
protest . . . against the use of blank verse in prose'), proclaimed:
'Who can listen to objections regarding such a book as this? It seems
to me a national benefit, and to every man or woman who reads it a
personal kindness.' It was quickly plagiarized – something which,
whether or not the sincerest form of flattery, caused Dickens much
annoyance and involved him in litigation.

Dickens read the *Carol* at the British Consulate in Genoa in the
summer of 1845, and it was his first public reading when he began to
perform for charity in 1853; thereafter it remained the most popular
item in his repertoire and loomed large in his farewell reading at the
end of his life. There were numerous dramatizations, and it seems to
have been the most popular of all Dickens' works on the screen (see
'Filmography'). A facsimile of the manuscript, which is now in the
Pierpont Morgan Library, New York, was published in 1967; and a
facsimile of Dickens' prompt-copy for the reading version in 1971.

A Christmas Carol contains elements shared by some of Dickens'
other books – for example, he was exploring in *Martin Chuzzlewit*
(part of which was written concurrently with the *Carol*) the themes
of avarice, selfishness and benevolence; benevolence indeed had
been a favourite theme from *Pickwick* onwards; and the Cratchits
have near relations in other humble and impoverished but happy
families, such as the Nubbles in *The Old Curiosity Shop* and (a few
years after the *Carol*) the Toodles in *Dombey and Son*; while Tiny Tim,
as Jeffrey's comment cited above reminds us, is one of Dickens'
doomed (though, in the outcome, reprieved) children. For this, as
for the other Christmas Books, the best edition is that by Michael
Slater (Penguin English Library, two volumes, 1971), which has a
general introduction, separate introductions for each story, and
notes.

THE CHIMES

The Chimes: A Goblin Story of Some Bells that Rang an Old Year out and a New Year in was published on 16 December 1844 (1845 on the title-page), with illustrations by Daniel Maclise, John Leech, Richard Doyle and Clarkson Stanfield. According to Forster, when Dickens signed a contract with his new publishers (Bradbury & Evans) on 1 June 1844 there was 'an understanding . . . that a successor to the *Carol* would be ready for the Christmas of 1844'. Dickens wrote the story in Genoa in the autumn and had finished it by 3 November. Again, the composition of this Christmas story worked him up to a high pitch of excitement: 'I am in a regular, ferocious excitement with *The Chimes*', he declared; ' . . . I am fierce to finish in a spirit bearing some affinity to those of truth and mercy, and to shame the cruel and the canting'. When he finished it, he confessed that he 'had what women call "a real good cry"'. At the beginning of December he dashed to London and gave two private readings to friends which were, as Philip Collins says, 'the germ of his later career as a public reader'. Maclise, one of his illustrators, was present in Forster's rooms on 3 December and later described the 'shrieks of laughter' and 'floods of tears': he added, 'I do not think there was ever such a triumphant hour for Charles'. Dickens later read the story in public, for the first time in 1858.

Michael Slater points out that this story, with its 'intensely topical satire', was 'far more of an overt political manifesto than the *Carol*':

> Dickens was out to strike the heaviest blow in his power on behalf of the poor and oppressed of early Victorian England by fiercely attacking a number of prominent theories and attitudes held by the upper and middle classes which tended to see the swarming ranks of the underprivileged as at best a superfluous nuisance and at worst 'born bad', naturally vicious and depraved.

Examples of the story's topicality are the references to treating attempted suicide as a crime (Sir Peter Laurie's campaign to achieve this, launched in 1841, had caused much controversy); to infanticide (the recent case of Mary Furley, sentenced in April 1844, had caused a public outcry); and to the plight of agricultural labourers in Dorset (the manuscript refers to Hertfordshire, and Dickens made the change – Dorset at that time being a by-word for agrarian poverty and wretchedness – at the proof stage). (These and

other allusions are fully annotated in Dr Slater's excellent edition.)
Dickens makes ironic references to 'a bold peasantry' and (a
particular *bête-noire* of his) 'the good old times', and in a cancelled
passage provides a particularly striking example of his attitude to
the past:

> a small party were enjoying rustic sports, while another rather
> larger party were being hanged on trees in the background and a
> third were having brazen collars soldered round their necks as the
> born vassals of an undeniably picturesque Baron; singing at
> the same time 'oh the good old times, the grand old times, the
> glorious old Feudal times, the Genuine Genteel Millennium!'

Slater's argument that *The Chimes* is a less satisfactory work of art
than the *Carol* is compelling: not only is it overcrowded with
characters and overburdened with plot, but the ending is unsatisfactory and represents something of an evasion of the serious
issues raised. The vision of poverty, prostitution, sweated labour,
suicide and infanticide produces on the reader an effect of 'gloomy
reflection which is not really dispelled by the sudden burst of merry-
making at the end of the story'.

The book sold well and Dickens described it as 'a most sweeping
success'. But the critical reception was very mixed, though for
political rather than literary reasons. The *Globe* said on 31
December 1844 that it was being 'attacked and defended with a
degree of ardour which scarcely any other subject is capable of
inspiring'; and as Slater points out 'the critics' reactions were
governed by their political affiliations'. Richard Holt Hutton, who
was later to become one of the Victorian age's most perceptive
critics, wrote in a private letter that it was 'the finest thing Dickens
had ever written'.

The manuscript and corrected proofs are in the Forster
Collection.

THE CRICKET ON THE HEARTH

The Cricket on the Hearth: A Fairy Tale of Home was published by
Bradbury & Evans as Dickens' Christmas Book for 1845 (1846 on
the title-page). It was illustrated by a team consisting of the four
artists who had illustrated *The Chimes*, with the addition of Edwin

Landseer, and was dedicated to Lord Jeffrey. During 1844 Dickens had projected a weekly periodical to be titled *The Cricket*; it would have as its epigraph 'A cheerful creature that chirrups on the Hearth' and would embody, as Dickens said,

> *Carol* philosophy, cheerful views, sharp anatomization of humbug, jolly good temper; papers always in season, pat to the time of the year; and a vein of glowing, hearty, generous, mirthful, beaming reference in everything to Home, and Fireside.

The project came to nothing, but the title was revived for a Christmas Book, in which the cricket would be (as Dickens told Forster) 'a little household god – silent in the wrong and sorrow of the tale, and loud again when all went well and happy'.

He was thinking hard about the book by the end of September 1845, but composition did not begin until mid-October; it went slowly and with difficulty (at the beginning of November Dickens was 'hard at it, grinding my teeth'); and it was finished by 1 December.

The *Cricket* was very popular and sold better than either of its predecessors: 'the habit of his Christmas books – "as regularly expected as a pantomime" – had caught on' (Patten). Professor Patten has shown, however, that Forster's claim that initial sales 'doubled that of both its predecessors' is exaggerated. Still, the seventeen different dramatizations staged within a month of publication attest to a remarkable popularity – and this in spite of a widely unfavourable critical reception. Philip Collins notes that among reviewers there was 'general disappointment' at the third of the Christmas books. *The Times* was particularly savage, finding it 'a twaddling manifestation of silliness almost from the first page to the last'.

'As a Reading, it featured both in Dickens's first charity performances in 1853 and in his first paid series in 1858; but, while the *Carol* enjoyed sustained popularity, The *Cricket* proved much less successful, and it soon disappeared from the repertoire' (Collins).

There is a certain fairy-tale or pantomime quality about this story, especially about those parts concerning the old toymaker Caleb, his blind daughter Bertha, and his long-lost sailor son who turns up and marries young May instead of the ogre for whom she had been destined. As in *The Chimes*, the story ends with marriage,

feasting and dancing, with even the ogre repenting and joining in
the festivities. As Michael Slater says, Dickens offers us a world of
animated toys. One might add that, again, there is some shirking of
serious issues that Dickens raises but does not develop – notably in
relation to the Peerybingles' marriage and mutual trust. The most
resonant passage in the whole story refers to John Peerybingle's
having seen his young wife with another man and having instantly
(and wrongly) suspected her of infidelity. As his wife says,
' " . . . oh, dear John, how could you, could you, think so!" ' – but
the moral and psychological depths of a potentially powerful
situation remain undisturbed.

THE BATTLE OF LIFE

As noted above, this fourth Christmas book seems to have nothing in
common with the others. Michael Slater describes it as 'a savagely
foreshortened Dickens novel'. It was published, with the subtitle *A
Love Story*, by Bradbury & Evans for the Christmas trade of 1846,
having been written concurrently with an early portion of *Dombey
and Son*. The latter had been begun at the end of June and Dickens,
not surprisingly, found it 'too difficult to begin two books simultaneously' (Patten). Late in September he described himself to
Forster as 'capriciously despondent' and feared that he was 'wasting
the marrow of the larger book'; there seemed to be some doubt
whether the Christmas book would be persevered with or abandoned, though a few days later he said that he would not abandon
it 'until after a most desperate fight'. The book even gave him bad
dreams.

The *Battle of Life* sold well, 23,000 copies on the day of publication
alone; and the scale of Dickens' success and popularity can be
measured, as Professor Patten points out, by Thackeray's very
different success with *his* Christmas book, *Mrs. Perkins's Ball*, issued
at the same time, which sold 1500 copies. As with *The Cricket on the
Hearth*, the contrast between popular acclaim and critical denigration was very striking. Wilkie Collins said that it was a book which
'everybody abused, and which, nevertheless, everybody read',
though the abuse and the enthusiasm surely came from different
quarters. Again, *The Times* was markedly hostile, finding it 'of all
the bad Christmas books . . . *the worst* . . . *the very worst*'. Even Lord
Jeffrey, in a letter to Dickens, ventured to suggest that 'The general

voice . . . persists in refusing it a place among your best pieces'.

Michael Slater, whose verdict on the book is that it is 'an interesting failure', points out that it possesses none of the urgent and deeply-felt topicality of Dickens' best work in this genre:

> The England of the Hungry Forties disappears altogether and Dickens gives us instead a middle-class eighteenth-century setting and a story which dispenses entirely with the supernatural element and does not relate in any way to Christmas, despite the snow-scene at the end of the second part.

The book was illustrated by the same team as *The Chimes* (Maclise, Leech, Doyle and Stanfield).

THE HAUNTED MAN

There was no Christmas book in 1847 and *The Haunted Man and the Ghost's Bargain: A Fancy for Christmas Time*, which appeared in 1848, was Dickens' last exercise in this genre. It was illustrated by John Leech, Clarkson Stanfield, John Tenniel and Frank Stone. Dickens read it on 11 December 1848 to a group of friends and later prepared a prompt-copy with a view to using it in his programmes of public readings; but it was in the event never performed.

The story is based on a 'ghostly and wild idea' first noted by Dickens in July 1847 and briefly returned to in September 1847. He began to ponder the story seriously in September 1848, began writing it during October, and dispatched the manuscript of the third and final part on 1 December. By the end of the year, about 18,000 copies had been sold. This was more than 6000 down from *The Battle of Life*: 'Clearly the year's break between Christmas books had interrupted the habit of buying Dickens's offerings and allowed others to garner a share of the market . . . there was no disguising the fact that . . . the *Haunted Man*, though profitable, was not especially successful, either in 1848 or subsequently' (Patten).

In this final Christmas book Dickens returned to the Christmas setting and 'something like the same blend of features that produced the *Carol* and *The Chimes*' (Slater). Once again, the conditions of the poorer classes are evoked, the happiness of hearth and home is idyllically represented, and the protagonist is converted by the agency of the supernatural. There is also an interesting exploration of the theme of memory (significant in view of the fact that *David Copperfield* was to be begun early in the New Year). The story insists that memories of good and ill are inextricably bound together, and that we cannot abandon the memory of misfortunes without also losing something precious. As the hero Redlaw says, drawing a moral analogy from a scientific fact, at the end of the second chapter:

'In the material world, as I have long taught, nothing can be spared; no step or atom in the wondrous structure could be lost, without a blank being made in the great universe. I know, now, that it is the same with good and evil, happiness and sorrow, in the memories of men . . . .'

Redlaw is an intellectual who has to become as a little child in order to learn an essential truth: as Forster puts it, 'What the highest exercise of the intellect had missed is found in the simplest form of the affections.' The story also makes striking use of the *Doppelgänger* motif (see the passage in Ch. 1, reinforced by Leech's illustration, where the ghostly visitant is a duplicate of Redlaw himself) – a motif to be repeated in *David Copperfield* and elsewhere.

Dickens wrote no more Christmas books after 1848: as Slater points out, in 1849 he was busy with *Copperfield* and by 1850 he had launched *Household Words*, rendering the extra annual burden out of the question.

Christmas Stories

Dickens is not often thought of as a writer of short stories, but he published one or more Christmas stories annually from 1850 to 1867. The first of them, 'A Christmas Tree', appeared in *Household Words* on 21 December 1850; then, from 1851 to 1858, he published each year an Extra Christmas Number of that journal which included contributions by Dickens and others; and from 1859 to 1867 there appeared a series of Extra Christmas Numbers of *All the Year Round*. On several occasions Dickens co-operated with Wilkie Collins in the composition of a story – for example, in the final Christmas story, 'No Thoroughfare', in 1867. A number of the stories were dramatized, and Dickens made reading versions of seven of them (see below).

Not all these stories hold great interest for the modern reader. Sylvère Monod has noted that 'The Signalman', a chapter in one of the later stories, 'Mugby Junction' (1866), gives 'a disturbing picture of the power and mystery of railroads'. Probably the most remarkable of the group is 'Mrs. Lirriper's Lodgings' (1863), in which Dickens created a surrealistically garrulous character worthy to stand beside Mrs Gamp and Flora Finching. His contemporaries were quick to recognize her as an outstanding achievement – 'entitled to rank with Mrs. Nickleby and Mrs. Gamp', as the *Saturday Review* said: and Dickens revived her the following year ('Mrs. Lirriper's Legacy'). The verbal inventiveness associated with Mrs Lirriper anticipates the stream of consciousness novelists of the twentieth century: Mrs Lirriper's style is always eloquent but frequently in defiance of logic ('the Adelphi Hotel which would not have been much above a quarter of a mile if the weather had been less severe' recalls Mrs Gamp's '"A pleasant evenin' . . . though warm, which . . . we must expect when cowcumbers is three for twopence"').

Dickens turned frequently to the Christmas stories in his quest for material suitable for adaptation as readings. 'The Poor Traveller' (1854) was first given in 1858; 'Boots at the Holly-Tree Inn' (1855) also in 1858; 'Mrs. Lirriper's Lodgings', devised in late 1865 or early 1866, was never performed; 'Dr Marigold', based on the story 'Dr Marigold's Prescriptions' (1865), was read in 1866; 'Barbox Brothers', based on a story published in 1866, was read in the following year but repeated only a few times; 'The Boy at Mugby', adapted from the same story, was also read in 1867 but, as Philip Collins says, 'never caught on'; 'Mr Chops, The Dwarf', based on a story published in 1858, was prepared in 1861 but not performed until 1868; and 'The Signalman' was never performed (though Emlyn Williams, using his own version rather than Dickens', has done so with success).

Readings and Speeches

The definitive edition of the readings, *Charles Dickens: The Public Readings*, ed. Philip Collins (Oxford: Clarendon Press, 1975), has a long and valuable introduction and contains 21 items as follows (those marked * were never performed):

A Christmas Carol
The Cricket on the Hearth
The Chimes
*The Haunted Man
The Story of Little Dombey
The Poor Traveller
Boots at the Holly-Tree Inn
Mrs. Gamp
Bardell and Pickwick
David Copperfield
Nicholas Nickleby at the Yorkshire School
*The Bastille Prisoner
Mr Chops, The Dwarf
*Great Expectations
Mr Bob Sawyer's Party
Doctor Marigold
*Mrs. Lirriper's Lodgings
Barbox Brothers
The Boy at Mugby
*The Signalman
Sikes and Nancy

Between 1853 and his death in 1870, Dickens gave (on Professor Collins' reckoning) a total of 472 readings, the majority of them after 1858, when he began doing so for money. This total includes numerous London seasons and provincial tours, as well as the tour of

America in 1867–8. The most frequently performed items were 'The Trial from Pickwick' and 'A Christmas Carol' – the latter being, in Collins' phrase, 'the quintessential Dickensian reading', the first public reading he ever gave, prominent in his repertoire throughout his career, and included as the main item in his final reading.

The preparation of his reading-copies involved abridgement and some rewording of the novel-text, with the insertion (as an aid to his memory) of stage-directions. In his later years the readings took a heavy toll of Dickens' energies and eventually of his health and strength, and reduced the time he was able to give to writing. On the other hand they brought him not only substantial financial rewards (about £45,000 in all, or nearly half of the fortune he left) but also a large measure of emotional gratification, since they enabled him to exchange the novelist's solitary task for the performer's immediate awareness of his audience's response. (Significantly, he asked the *Carol* audience in Bradford in 1854 that 'if you feel disposed as we go along to give expression to any emotion, whether grave or gay, you will do so with perfect freedom from restraint, and without the least apprehension of disturbing me': see *Speeches*, p. 169). The readings proved to Dickens all over again, and repeatedly, that his public loved him and were moved to laughter and tears by his work; it is, in psychological terms, noteworthy that the beginning of his career as a professional reader dates from the same period as the breakdown of his marriage.

Collins' edition provides full information on each reading, and there is space here for reference to only a handful of the individual items. Dickens had read *The Chimes* to selected groups of friends on two occasions in December 1844, and this marks the first step in what was later to become an ambitious and time-absorbing second career; as Collins observes, 'it was not surprising that he thought of including this piece in his first charity readings in 1853', and Forster described the 1844 private readings as 'the germ of those readings to larger audiences by which, as much as by his books, the world knew him in his later life'. *The Story of Little Dombey*, first given on 10 June 1858, was the first reading extracted from one of the novels; Dickens wrote to Forster from Edinburgh in the autumn of that year that the *Dombey* reading – primarily pathetic, but not without humour also – was 'our greatest triumph everywhere'. It has been analysed by Alan Horsman in Appendix D of the Clarendon edition of *Dombey and Son*. 'Bardell and Pickwick' (known also as 'The Trial from

Pickwick') was second only to 'A Christmas Carol' in popularity; Collins notes that Dickens 'particularly relied upon the combination of these two favourite items for such outstanding occasions as his American débuts and his final farewell performances'. This reading is based almost entirely on Ch. 34 of *The Pickwick Papers*, and contemporary evidence suggests that Dickens' impersonation of Mr Justice Stareleigh was an especially memorable instance of his remarkable histrionic gifts. In her *Pen Photographs of Charles Dickens's Readings, Taken from Life* (1871), Kate Field writes:

> Dickens steps out of his own skin which, for the time being, is occupied by Mr Justice Stareleigh. His little round eyes, wide open and blinking; his elevated eyebrows that are in a constant state of interrogation; his mouth, drawn down by the weight of the law; the expression of the *ensemble*, which clearly denotes that everybody *is* a rascal whether found guilty or not; and the stern, iron-clad voice, apparently measuring out justice in as small quantities as possible, and never going faster than a dead march, – make up an impersonation that is extraordinary, even for Dickens.

Effective in quite a different way was 'David Copperfield', Dickens' own favourite among all his readings. Long afterwards Lord Redesdale wrote: 'Never shall I forget the effect produced by his reading of the death of Steerforth; it was tragedy itself, and when he closed the book and his voice ceased, the audience for a moment seemed paralysed, and one could almost hear a sigh of relief.' 'Sikes and Nancy' was the last of the readings to be devised: Dickens' first attempt was made in 1863, when he found the material 'so horrible . . . that I am afraid to try it', and it was not until the early autumn of 1868 that he prepared the reading version – 'very horrible, but very dramatic', as he told Dolby. He gave a trial performance to an invited audience at the St James's Hall on 14 November, and was gratified to note that, when he had finished reading, his guests were 'unmistakably pale, and had horror-stricken faces'. Ignoring the advice of Forster, Dolby, and his eldest son Charley, who were anxious that he should not impose on himself the strain of this reading, Dickens went ahead and gave the first public performance on 5 January 1869. Thereafter he included it in his programmes almost obsessively, sometimes as often as four times in a single week (see Philip Collins, *'Sikes and Nancy*: Dickens' Last

Reading', *Times Literary Supplement*, 11 June 1971). Collins provides
(pp. xxvii–xxviii) an interesting list of the number of performances
of each of the readings, headed by 'The Trial from Pickwick' (164)
and 'A Christmas Carol' (127).

In addition to Collins' major edition and the short book by Kate
Field referred to above, the following contain useful material on
Dickens' readings: George Dolby, *Charles Dickens as I Knew him*
(1885; reprinted in 1970); John D. Gordan, *Reading for Profit: The
Other Career of Charles Dickens* (1958); Charles Kent, *Charles Dickens as
a Reader* (1872). Dickens' letters and Forster's *Life* may also be
consulted.

The Speeches of Charles Dickens, ed. K. J. Fielding (Oxford: Clarendon
Press, 1960), contains the texts of 115 speeches delivered between
1837 and 1870. In an introductory essay, Professor Fielding states
that 'As an orator there is no doubt [Dickens] was outstanding.'
Edmund Yates said that he 'was by far the best after-dinner speaker
I have ever heard', and this testimony is echoed by many others.
Dickens' speeches were carefully prepared, but he spoke without
notes except for citing facts and figures or giving a quotation; after
delivering a speech he was capable of repeating it in private
verbatim, as (for example) he did in New York in 1868. A
contemporary account of the 1841 Edinburgh banquet given in his
honour, which Professor Fielding describes as 'Dickens' first
triumph in public speaking', records that his speech-making
'seemed entirely spontaneous' and that he employed 'entirely a
conversational tone'.

Many passages in the speeches touch on his aims in writing and
suggest parallels with his published work. Early in his career he said
that he wrote 'to increase the stock of harmless cheerfulness' and 'to
show that virtue may be found on the by-ways of the world, that it
was not incompatible with poverty and even with rags' (*Speeches*,
pp. 9–10; the sentiments were repeated in slightly different terms in
Boston in 1842: see pp. 19–20). Later he said that 'Every effort of my
pen has been intended to elevate the masses of society to give them
the station they deserve among mankind' (p. 34). He spoke often of
the poor: 'It surely cannot be allowed that those who labour day by
day, surrounded by machinery, shall be permitted to degenerate
into machines themselves' (p. 61: speech given at Birmingham in
1844); 'No one who had any experience of the poor could fail to be
deeply affected by their patience, by their sympathy with one

another, and by the beautiful alacrity with which they helped one
another in toil, in the day of suffering, and at the hour of death'
(pp. 107–8). As an example of the speeches reinforcing the message
of the fiction, two speeches may be referred to that echo the teaching
of *Hard Times*: on the question of a child's need to play, Dickens
declared 'with what a determined self-assertion nature declares that
play they must' (pp. 271–2); and a little later – appropriately
enough, in Manchester – he repeated the head and heart, fact and
fancy antitheses of the novel: 'Let the child have its fables: let the
man or woman into which it changes, always remember these fables
tenderly . . . . The hardest head may co-exist with the softest heart'
(pp. 284–5).

M. H. Miller's 'Charles Dickens at the English Charity Dinner',
Quarterly Journal of Speech, XLVII, 1961, may also be consulted.

Letters

The first collection of Dickens' letters, edited by Georgina Hogarth and Mamie Dickens (respectively, his sister-in-law and daughter), appeared in three volumes in 1880–2. For subsequent editions, see p. 313. The Pilgrim edition, now in progress (and likely long to be so), is making available a large number of Dickens' letters never previously printed; for those who live to see its completion it will provide an edition fully worthy of its subject. Dickens was an extraordinarily prolific and fluent letter-writer; and even though large numbers of letters were systematically destroyed by Forster, Georgina Hogarth and others (Dickens himself destroyed on 3 September 1860 'the accumulated letters and papers of twenty years', though these were presumably in the main letters to rather than by him), a very large number survive. As Humphry House has said, 'Dickens was so famous so young; long before he was thirty, people were treasuring his letters.' The Pilgrim edition is fully annotated, the annotations in themselves constituting a valuable work of reference.

Plays and Poems

These are of only minor interest. For details of editions, see p. 313.
Complete Plays and Selected Poems of Charles Dickens (London: Vision
Press, 1970) includes the texts of six plays: *The Strange Gentleman, The
Village Coquettes, Is She his Wife?, The Lamplighter, Mr Nightingale's
Diary* (written jointly with Mark Lemon), and *No Thoroughfare*
(jointly with Wilkie Collins). This is in no sense a scholarly edition.

Other Minor Writings

Dickens wrote extensively for his various periodicals; and while much of his work was collected (in, for example, *The Uncommercial Traveller*) much more was uncollected. The question is complicated by the fact that many contributions had a joint authorship and by Dickens' editorial practice of rewriting the articles submitted by some of his contributors. Anne Lohrli's useful book on *Household Words* (Toronto: University of Toronto Press, 1973) makes clear Dickens' contributions to that periodical. On Dickens as editor, see various articles by Gerald G. Grubb (for example, *Studies in Philology*, XL, 1943; ibid., XLII, 1945); also Philip Collins in *Dickensian*, LII, 1956, and LXI, 1965, and in *Review of English Literature*, II, 1961. For various collections of Dickens' journalism, see pp. 313–14.

Among other items too numerous to list completely, the following may be singled out for mention:

Sunday under Three Heads (1836). Illustrated by Phiz.

Sketches of Young Gentlemen (1838). Illustrated by Phiz.

Memoirs of Joseph Grimaldi (1838). Dickens abridged the text and added a preface. Illustrated by Cruikshank.

Sketches of Young Couples (1840). Illustrated by Phiz.

An Appeal to Fallen Women (1847). Pamphlet written in connexion with Miss Burdett Coutts' charitable efforts.

Letters to *The Times* on public executions, 14 and 19 January 1849; reprinted as a pamphlet (1849).

The Life of Our Lord (1849, 1934). Written for his own children and not intended for publication.

A Child's History of England (three volumes, 1852–4). Originally serialized in *Household Words*, 1851–3.

Translations

Dickens has long been one of the most widely translated of English authors. Anyone interested in this topic should consult the *General Catalogue* of the British Library. According to an article published in the *British Museum Quarterly* (1940), describing a collection presented to the Library, it appears that his work has been translated not only into most western languages (including, for example, Icelandic, Ukrainian and Catalan) but also into numerous oriental languages. Those inclined and competent to do so can (to select only a handful of instances) read *David Copperfield* in Armenian, *A Tale of Two Cities* in Arabic, *Little Dorrit* in Chinese, 'Mugby Junction' in Finnish and 'The Chimes' in Lithuanian. There are also Braille and shorthand versions. The most popular candidate for translation has been *David Copperfield* – the world's as well as Dickens' favourite child, it would seem – with *Oliver Twist* and *A Christmas Carol* competing for second place.

Dickens' Illustrators

In the past few years there has been a considerable amount of attention paid to the original illustrations of Dickens' novels and stories – as Philip Collins says, 'More work of high quality on Dickens and his illustrators has been produced in the past decade [to 1978] than in the century preceding' – and a radical readjustment has taken place in our understanding of their function and their relationship to the text. F. G. Kitton's pioneering study *Dickens and his Illustrators* (1899) has now been superseded by Jane R. Cohen's *Charles Dickens and his Original Illustrators* (1980), a comprehensive study of all eighteen artists who at various times worked for, and with, Dickens. Other significant work includes John Harvey's *Victorian Novelists and their Illustrators* (1970), Q. D. Leavis's essay 'The Dickens Illustrations: Their Function' (in F. R. and Q. D. Leavis, *Dickens the Novelist*), and Michael Steig's major study of Dickens' most important collaborator, *Dickens and Phiz* (1978). Important shorter discussions are: J. Hillis Miller's 'The Fiction of Realism: *Sketches by Boz, Oliver Twist*, and Cruikshank's Illustrations', in *Dickens Centennial Essays*, ed. Ada Nisbet and Blake Nevius (1971); *George Cruikshank: A Revaluation*, a symposium edited by Robert L. Patten (*Princeton University Library Chronicle*, xxxv, 1973–4); and various essays by Patten (*English Literary History*, 1967 and 1969; *Dickensian*, 1970) and Joan Stevens (*Studies in Bibliography*, 1967). There is a useful annotated bibliography, *Victorian Novel Illustration: A Selected Checklist 1900–1976* (1979) by John Olmsted and Jeffrey Welch.

In the listing below I have drawn on Thomas Hatton's 'A Bibliographical List of the Original Illustrations to the Works of Charles Dickens . . . ' in *The Nonesuch Dickens: Retrospectus and Prospectus* (1937), which also includes an essay by Arthur Waugh on 'Charles Dickens and his Illustrators'.

279

The following is a list of Dickens' major publications, with brief details of the illustrations included in the original editions.

Sketches by Boz   28 small etchings by George Cruikshank in the original edition of the two series published by Macrone; this number was increased to 40 in the combined edition published by Chapman & Hall in 1837–9.

The Pickwick Papers   Robert Seymour executed the pictorial wrapper and produced seven plates for the first two numbers; after his death, Robert Buss provided two for the third number (omitted from subsequent editions at Dickens' request); and the remainder were provided by H. K. Browne. The total number of illustrations (including wrapper) was 46; all are reproduced in the Penguin edition.

Oliver Twist   24 etchings by George Cruikshank.

Nicholas Nickleby   39 etchings by Browne.

Master Humphrey's Clock   19 wood-engravings – 6 by Cattermole (who also did the pictorial wrapper and frontispiece), the rest by Browne.

The Old Curiosity Shop   73 wood-engravings, mainly by Cattermole and Browne; also initial vignettes, frontispiece and tailpiece.

Barnaby Rudge   75 wood-engravings by Browne and Cattermole; also initial vignettes and frontispiece.

Martin Chuzzlewit   38 etchings by Browne, also wrapper and frontispiece.

Pictures from Italy   4 woodcuts by Samuel Palmer.

American Notes   No illustrations.

A Christmas Carol   4 woodcuts and 4 etchings by Leech.

The Chimes   12 illustrations (11 woodcuts and one steel engraving) and an engraved frontispiece, by Maclise, Leech, Doyle and Stanfield.

The Cricket on the Hearth   Frontispiece and 12 wood-engravings by Masclise, Leech, Doyle, Stanfield and Landseer.

The Battle of Life   Frontispiece and 11 woodcuts by Maclise, Doyle, Leech and Stanfield.

The Haunted Man   Frontispiece and 15 woodcuts by Tenniel, Stanfield, Frank Stone, and Leech.

Dombey and Son   Wrapper (woodcut) and 38 etchings by Browne.

David Copperfield   Wrapper (woodcut) and 38 etchings by Browne.

Bleak House   Wrapper (woodcut) and 38 etchings by Browne.

Hard Times   No illustrations.

Little Dorrit   Wrapper (woodcut) and 38 etchings by Browne.

A Tale of Two Cities   Wrapper and 14 etchings by Browne.

Great Expectations   No illustrations. (Marcus Stone later executed 8 wood-engravings for the Illustrated Library Edition.)

Our Mutual Friend   Wrapper and 40 wood-engravings by Marcus Stone.

Edwin Drood   Wrapper by Charles Alston Collins; 12 illustrations by Luke Fildes.

Of the illustrators named above, most can be quite summarily dealt with; but George Cruikshank and, above all, Hablôt Knight Browne call for more extended discussion.

R. W. Buss's relationship with Dickens was confined to the third number of *Pickwick*, for which he produced two illustrations, 'The Cricket Match' and 'The Arbour Scene'. He was a well-known artist who had exhibited at the Royal Academy; but, although he had experience of wood-engraving, 'he knew nothing about etching . . . he could not make himself even passably competent in so brief a time' (Johnson). To his chagrin, Buss was brusquely dismissed.

For a brief biographical note on George Cattermole, see in chapter 'The Dickens Circle'. He was, as John Harvey notes, 'chiefly an architectural and historical artist' – he had contributed drawings to *Cathedral Antiquities of Great Britain*, and his first Academy picture was a view of Peterborough Cathedral – and so he was well equipped to render the solemn, pathetic and antiquarian elements in *The Old Curiosity Shop*, while Browne depicted the comic and fantastic elements. Cattermole came fully into his own in the illustrations for the latter part of the novel, including Nell's deathbed. For *Barnaby Rudge* he was responsible for depicting 'the picturesque setting and the queer buildings; the locksmith's house, "The Boot", The Warren, Westminster Hall, and of course The Maypole' (Harvey). Dickens was delighted with his drawing of the Maypole Inn ('Words cannot say how good it is').

For a note on Charles Alston Collins, see in chapter 'The Dickens Circle'. The special interest of his cover-design for *The Mystery of Edwin Drood* is that it has been regarded as offering clues to Dickens' unfulfilled intentions, and it has for that reason been subjected to close scrutiny.

Richard Doyle's contribution was limited to a few illustrations for *The Chimes*, *The Cricket on the Hearth* and *The Battle of Life*. Of the first of these, Johnson writes that Dickens was 'delighted' with the illustrations, but 'One woodcut of Doyle's, to be sure, and another of Leech's, he found so unlike his idea that he invited the two artists to breakfast, he wrote Kate, "and with that winning manner which you know of, got them with the highest good humour to do both afresh"'.

For a note on Luke (later Sir Luke) Fildes, Dickens' last illustrator, see in chapter 'The Dickens Circle'. John Harvey writes that Fildes, like Marcus Stone, represents 'a new style in illustration which differed radically from that of Browne and Cruikshank' – a more realistic, less emblematic, allusive and caricatural style.

Edwin (later Sir Edwin) Landseer was one of the five artists who contributed illustrations to *The Cricket on the Hearth*: for his friendship with Dickens, see in chapter 'The Dickens Circle'.

On Daniel Maclise, another member of the *Christmas Books* teams, see in chapter 'The Dickens Circle'.

Samuel Palmer, one of the greatest of nineteenth-century English artists, was still virtually unknown when he executed the illustrations for the original edition of *Pictures from Italy*.

On Robert Seymour's role in the genesis of *The Pickwick Papers*, see the section on that novel. Long after his death, his widow claimed that he had had a larger share in originating the novel than Dickens had admitted, and she published a pamphlet on the subject. Dickens repudiated the claim in a letter to the *Athenaeum* and in his preface to the Charles Dickens Edition of the novel (1867). See also Appendix C to the Penguin edition of *Pickwick*.

On Clarkson Stanfield, who produced illustrations for the four Christmas books from *The Chimes* to *The Haunted Man*, see in chapter 'The Dickens Circle'.

Frank Stone was one of the illustrators of *The Haunted Man*. His son Marcus Stone (see in chapter 'The Dickens Circle') illustrated *Our Mutual Friend*. John Harvey suggests that Dickens 'never took the younger Stone seriously as a collaborator' and 'took little interest in his work': 'he let the artist take whatever subject he liked, and even neglected to inspect the sketches before the illustrations were engraved'.

John (later Sir John) Tenniel was one of the illustrators of *The Haunted Man*. He was a young man at the time; he later became famous as a *Punch* cartoonist and is remembered as the original illustrator of Lewis Carroll's Alice books.

A further name can be added to this list: that of Samuel Williams, a wood-engraver who was responsible for the only Dickens illustration both drawn and cut by the same man – the picture of Nell asleep in *The Old Curiosity Shop*.

George Cruikshank was twenty years older than Dickens and already a well-known artist when Macrone engaged him to illustrate *Sketches by Boz*; indeed, it was no doubt his reputation that the publisher relied on to sell the book. Contemporary reviewers praised his work highly and often compared him to Hogarth. John Harvey has made the very interesting point that Cruikshank's graphic art has much in common with what was to become the characteristically Dickensian style – for example, the mode of vision that merges the animate with the animate and the human with the animal; to cite a single instance, young Jerry Cruncher's nightmarish sensation that he is being pursued by a coffin 'hopping on behind him, bolt upright upon its narrow end' (*A Tale of Two Cities*, Ch. 14) is thoroughly in the spirit of Cruikshank.

Cruikshank also illustrated *Oliver Twist*, but Q. D. Leavis has suggested that he was at his best in the *Sketches*; she singles out for particular praise 'Public Dinners', 'Seven Dials', and 'Monmouth Street'. ('Public Dinners' has a special kind of interest since it incorporates a self-portrait – the bearded figure on the right is the artist – as well as a portrait of Dickens, in the centre of the picture and bearing a strong resemblance to the slightly later Maclise portrait.) In *Oliver Twist*, according to Mrs Leavis, Cruikshank missed some opportunities:

> [he] did not adequately illustrate the recapture of Oliver, or illustrate at all the intensely dramatic court scene where Fagin feels the moral condemnation of the court in the accusing eyes focused on him; and when he takes such an opportunity as the important scene of Oliver's trance (in which Oliver *feels*, without seeing, the terrifying presence of Fagin and Monk at the window) there is nothing supernatural, no thrilling sense of the mystery of Oliver's vision, and no horror, all of which the text demands. The pictures of Bill Sikes after the murder of Nancy are crude and none of these drawings containing the Artful Dodger and his set convey the combination of a degraded humour with brutality that Dickens has created there.

Mrs Leavis's explanation of the relative failure of these illustrations is that Cruikshank worked largely independently, taking little in the way of direction from the novelist, so that there is no intimate and integral relationship between text and picture. It must be said, though, that two of the *Oliver Twist* illustrations, 'Oliver asking for More' and 'Fagin in the Condemned Cell', are among the most memorable of all the Dickens illustrations. For an excellent discussion of the latter, see John Harvey's book (p. 210).

Of all the Dickens illustrators, however, far and away the most important is Hablôt Knight Browne (see in chapter 'The Dickens Circle'), who adopted the name 'Phiz' to harmonize with Dickens' 'Boz' and worked closely with him for over twenty years, illustrating ten novels from *The Pickwick Papers* to *A Tale of Two Cities*. Three years younger than Dickens and almost unknown when he was first engaged, Browne was biddable and co-operative in a way that Cruikshank was not; and his relationship with Dickens is the most important one between artist and novelist in the period. Apart from Michael Steig's authoritative study mentioned above, there are recent books on 'Phiz' by Albert Johannsen (1965) and John Buchanan-Brown (1978).

Browne worked in a tradition of graphic art that goes back through Gillray to Hogarth, and it is significant that Dickens' verbal art was often compared to the latter: 'The Soul of Hogarth has migrated into the Body of Mr Dickens' declared Sydney Smith in 1837, and such comments were commonplace. The general view among modern commentators is that Browne's best work for Dickens belongs to the years 1836–50 (that is, up to and including *David Copperfield*). By the sixties his style of illustration – Hogarthian, iconographic, caricatural – had gone out of favour, to be replaced by a more severe, less extravagent realism.

As Professor Steig makes clear, in the ten novels (out of fifteen) that Browne illustrated for Dickens a 'complex relationship' developed between text and picture that is rare in Victorian fiction. No other major novelist enjoyed a relationship as close, sustained and fruitful as Dickens enjoyed with Browne. The precise nature of their creative relationship has been debated. According to Mrs Leavis, 'For "Phiz" there was no question of independence.' Browne burned his correspondence in 1859 and only a few of Dickens' instructions to him survive; but it has been argued that, while Dickens certainly exercised some control over the subject, content and style of the illustrations, Browne enjoyed 'a high degree of independence', was 'a collaborator rather than a mere employee or drudge', and was in fact 'the very first interpreter of each of the novels he illustrated' (Steig). More generally, Professor Steig suggests that by 'revealing implications of which the novelist himself may not be fully conscious', 'the illustrators are Dickens' first critics' (though it should be added that it would be unwise to underestimate Dickens' self-awareness).

The first collaboration between novelist and artist was on a small scale: Browne executed three wood-engravings for Dickens' 'Sunday under Three Heads' (1836). After Seymour had died and the short-lived services of Buss had been dispensed with, Browne took over as illustrator of *Pickwick* and Dickens, to his immense satisfaction, was enabled to reverse the original relationship between author and illustrator: the text was now paramount, with two illustrations accompanying each monthly number (four in the final double number). The normal practice developed between them whereby Dickens would give Browne the subjects of the two illustrations and usually include a portion of his manuscript or a copy of the proof; Browne then submitted drawings for Dickens' approval; any proposed alterations were incorporated; and Browne etched the design on steel. Within this framework, however, there was scope for the artist to make his own contribution – for example, in the use of emblematic detail. A good example of an illustration that is close to Dickens' text and yet possesses its own specifically visual quality and conveys its own message is 'Mrs Bardell encounters Mr Pickwick in the prison.' Of this, Steig comments:

[It] adds nothing not specified in the text, but nonetheless it can be 'read', and is a good example of Phiz's early mastery of the iconography of space and form. In this plate, the horizontal band formed by the main characters is juxtaposed both to the vertical of the gateway and to the dynamic thrust of the jailer, who appears to have just pushed the ladies and child down the steps. One reads from top to bottom left, and then to the right, just as one 'sees' in the text the arrival at prison, the revelation to Mrs. Bardell that she is a prisoner, and then the encounter with Mr Pickwick. The triangular arrangement, however, makes it possible to read the illustration in two directions, as though causally: from Mrs. Bardell up to the jailer and down to Pickwick, implying that her lawsuit has brought him to prison; or in reverse, beginning with Pickwick, implying that his stubborn adherence to principle has caused him unwittingly to make a victim out of his former landlady. Yet Pickwick and Mrs. Bardell also are part

of the same compositional horizontal band, linked as victims of a
vicious system.

Such an illustration, if Steig's interpretative method is accepted, is
doing much more than emphasize a point in the text: it is providing
its own moral comment on the situation. These often crowded and
meticulously detailed plates need to be studied in a manner that, as
the eye travels over them, constitutes a 'reading'; as Steig says, 'the
paramount problem . . . is how to "read" the text and illustrations
in conjunction with one another'.

The Old Curiosity Shop is a particularly striking example of
Browne's work. As indicated above, he shared the task of illustrating
this novel with Cattermole, the two artists becoming respectively
responsible for the two predominant modes of the novel – the one
comic, grotesque, exuberant, the other sentimental, pictureque and
idealized. Steig argues very interestingly that the effect of Browne's
contribution (for example, his portrayal of Quilp) was to 'emphasize the unruliness of the energies unleashed by Dickens's imagination' and to shift the balance of the work: instead of the novel
being dominated by the 'idealizing and religious sentiments' that
were Dickens' starting-point, and that represented his conscious
intention, those sentiments are in danger of being submerged by the
demoniacal figure of Quilp and the vigorous, relatively coarse
humour of Dick Swiveller and Sampson and Sally Brass. Browne's
illustrations 'emphasize embedded sexual nuances and . . . bring
to the novel the vital energy of comic rascality'.

For many students of Browne's work, *Martin Chuzzlewit* and
Dombey and Son in the forties represent the climax of his partnership
with Dickens. John Harvey states that 'The illustrations improved
during the publication of *Chuzzlewit*, and the overall growth in
Browne's talent since the days of *Pickwick* is striking.' Harvey also
suggests that 'The new sharpness and life in the *Chuzzlewit* drawings
is due partly to Browne's discovery of Daumier'; and he shows the
remarkable resemblance between Browne's portrayal of Mrs Gamp
and the French artist's 'La Garde-Malade' of 1842. The influence of
Hogarth is still present, too; and Steig points out that the title-page
of *Chuzzlewit*, depicting Pecksniff greeting a new pupil who has just
arrived by coach, appears to echo the first plate in Hogarth's 'A
Harlot's Progress', where a young girl freshly arrived from the
country is met by a bawd – the parallel implying, of course, a
comment on Pecksniff's pretensions. Steig makes the general point

that, in his plates for this novel, Browne's 'ability to interpret the text by means of parallelism, antithesis, and emblematic details emerges brilliantly'.

One of the *Chuzzlewit* illustrations, 'Warm Reception of Mr Pecksniff by his Venerable Friend', provides an insight into the working methods of novelist and artist. Dickens' instructions were as follows:

> The room in the Temple, Mrs. Lupin, with Mary in her charge, stands a little way behind old Martin's chair. Young Martin is on the other side. Tom Pinch and his sister are there too. Mr Pecksniff has burst in to rescue his venerable friend from this horde of plunderers and deceivers. The old man in a transport of burning indignation, arises from his chair, and uplifting his stick knocks the good Pecksniff down; before John Westlock and Mark who gently interpose (though they are very much delighted) can possibly prevent him. Mr Pecksniff on the ground. The old man full of fire, energy & resolution.

As Steig observes, these instructions are very general: although Dickens indicates the position of some of the characters, there is no sign that he has attempted to visualize the scene in detail, or at least no evidence that he is anxious to foist his own conception of the scene on Browne. His indications are novelistic ('the good Pecksniff') rather than strongly visual. At the bottom of these instructions, Browne wrote: 'Mrs. Lupin & Mary – behind Mary's chair. Yg. Martin on other side. Tom & his sister. Old man – Pecksniff. John Westlock & Mark' – the raw materials given by Dickens, to which Browne adds such details as two books clearly titled *Tartuffe* and *Paradise Lost* (both, of course, relevant to the situation). Steig concludes, persuasively, that 'Despite the prevailing assumption that Browne always acted strictly under Dickens' directions, it is plain . . . that he had a good deal of freedom – and responsibility – to interpret the subjects, and thus, the novel.' There are other examples of Browne's exercise of this freedom: for instance, in the title-page illustration already referred to, he not only invokes Hogarth by association but adds the symbolically significant detail of the broken finger-post.

The illustrations for *Dombey and Son* are richly, sometimes excitingly, emblematic, and Dickens from the start attached great importance to them: as he told Forster, 'The points for illustration,

and the enormous care required, make me excessively anxious.'
Steig's book includes excellent analyses of some of the *Dombey* plates
(too long to quote here), and Harvey also has good comments on
'Coming Home from Church' and other plates. On 'The Dombey
Family', Harvey comments:

> Here there is no facetiousness or exaggeration, although we might
> infer that the artist was an expert caricaturist from the very sharp
> sensitivity of the line that touches in Dombey's face. It is done
> with a few strokes, but the Dombey of the text is caught to the life:
> proud and handsome, but with his meanness showing in the
> contracted mouth, in the nose pinched in a fastidious sniff, and in
> the tired eyes which wander uneasily and resentfully towards his
> daughter, while he keeps his head turned away.

As Harvey points out, the scene depicted does not actually occur in
the novel precisely as shown: what Browne has done is to catch the
essence of Dombey rather than merely presenting a particular
moment in the narrative.

The autobiographical *David Copperfield*, in which the narrator
allows his memory to dwell on moments from the past, involves a
somewhat different style of illustration – less intensely dramatic,
more affectionately nostalgic. To see the difference one has only to
compare 'Our Pew at Church' or 'We arrive unexpectedly at
Mr Peggotty's fireside' with 'Florence and Edith on the staircase' or
'Mr Carker in his hour of triumph'. The contrast is one between a
loving and humorous delight in the domestic and the familar, and
the high melodrama of stylized gesture, faces registering strong
emotion, and emblematic detail. Harvey suggests that

> The chief feature of the *Copperfield* illustrations is the greatly
> extended use of the 'tableau'. In this novel Dickens will
> momentarily arrest his characters in a significant grouping which
> he describes as a 'picture' and which is evidently conceived with
> an illustration in mind.

The 'vein of Christian sentiment' in this novel is expressed visually
through the favourite device of pictures within the picture – in this
case, of biblical scenes such as the paintings of the prodigal son and
of the infant Moses in 'Changes at Home' (another contrast with the

classical and mythological statuary and paintings in the *Dombey* illustrations).

Steig's verdict is that 'In *Dombey and Son* and *David Copperfield* Browne reaches his highest concentration of allusive, emblematic interpretation, as well as continuing to emphasize meanings implicit in these novels' structures through visual parallels among the illustrations.' Mrs Leavis finds the *Bleak House* illustrations 'disappointing': in her view Dickens no longer needed an illustrator, his verbal art being sufficiently visual in quality, and the illustrations were no more than the persistence of an established convention. Although Steig finds them 'far more uneven in quality than those for the three preceding novels', he suggests that the 'new and striking use of the dark plate' gives them a special interest and serves to reinforce the darkness of Dickens' social vision. There is also evidence in the cover-design of *Bleak House*, with its identifiable characters, hints of plot, and foreshadowings of the 'symbolic and thematic parallels of the text', that Dickens explained his intentions to Browne in some detail. By general consent there is a further decline in the *Little Dorrit* illustrations, and those for *A Tale of Two Cities* are weak. Before the end of the fifties not only had the long productive partnership of Browne and Dickens come to an end: Dickens' novels were never again to be so richly complemented by their illustrations, and the new style of novel-illustration was to relegate the plates to a minor role. It was Browne's achievement to produce illustrations that are an indispensable part of the total work – an edition that lacks them is in a real sense incomplete – and his renderings of the great Dickensian characters fix them for ever in the minds of readers. As Steig says, 'Phiz's Micawber is *the* Micawber of our visual imaginations'; and the same is true of a host of characters from Pickwick and Sam Weller onwards.

No collaboration between novelist and artist in the nineteenth century is more important than that between Dickens and Browne – indeed, it is hard to think of one that comes near to rivalling it; and for no novelist are the illustrations now by general consent regarded as being of more importance, complementing and not merely adorning the text. Other novelists were abundantly illustrated; but it is significant that, while virtually all modern editions of, say, Trollope or Hardy dispense with the illustrations that accompanied their first appearance, and few readers complain about or are even conscious of their absence, there is a distinct sense of something vital being missing in an unillustrated Dickens. (Significantly, a dimension seems to be permanently absent from the unillustrated *Hard Times*.) Even before the close of Dickens' career, however, fashions in book-illustration had changed sufficiently for the illustrations to fall off in quality and to become less integral to the text. As John Harvey says,

> *Bleak House* (1852–3) had in fact been the last novel in which Browne could feel that his style of illustration was the style of the time, for 1855 is generally acknowledged as the year in which a new mode of illustration, represented pre-eminently by Millais, began its rapid and victorious invasion of the whole field of book-illustration . . . . By 1860 the new style was clearly dominant . . . .

The older tradition of illustration quickly went out of fashion; and before the end of the century it was possible for Joseph Pennell to dismiss the work of Browne, Cruikshank, and others as 'simply rubbish'. In recent years, however, this judgment has been reversed, and the later style of illustration has been seen as insipid in comparison with the tradition inherited and developed by Browne.

Q. D. Leavis's important essay begins by raising some fundamental questions concerning the importance of the illustrations for the Victorians and for us:

> Was it necessary or desirable to have Dickens's novels illustrated? Why did Dickens's original publishers, all of them, think it essential to pay artists to illustrate novels, to illustrate even short pieces of light reading like *Sketches by Boz*? And even if illustrations were desirable or necessary then, do we, sophisticated intellectually, and capable readers of far more difficult novels than Dickens's, need them now?

For Dickens' original audience, the illustrations served several purposes. In our time, bombarded as we are by an incessant and exhausting barrage of visual stimuli of many kinds, it is hard for us to appreciate the extent to which the early Victorians were visually starved; and the illustrations must have been seized upon with an eagerness, and perused with a closeness of attention, that we are unlikely to emulate without conscious effort. Furthermore, in the conditions of serial publication, the illustrations would provide an aid to memory: Browne's Pickwick and Cruikshank's Fagin are as unforgettable as the mannerisms of speech and behaviour and the outlandish names that Dickens attached to his characters partly for the same reason. Beyond this, a particular plate could serve to stress a particular moment in the action or a particular thematic feature, and even to interpret and supplement Dickens' text. When we see, in a corner of Mr Vholes' office in *Bleak House*, a cat watching a mousehole, we receive a shock that may be greater than is provided by any particular moment in the reading of the novel up to that point. The answer to Mrs Leavis's final question is that we are not so sophisticated as to dispense with the illustrations and regard them as a concession to a childlike age that needed pictures to make its stories palatable; some recent interpreters (notably Michael Steig) have argued that we are actually likely to see more in the illustrations than the first readers ever saw. Dickens' own interest in them, sometimes intense, at any rate up to the midpoint of his career, confirms the modern view that they must be regarded as an integral part of the total experience offered by the novel – which is, indeed, not a book with illustrations but a work in which verbal and graphic art richly complement each other.

Topography

There is a long tradition of enthusiastic interest in the topography of
Dickens' writings, extending from T. E. Pemberton's *Dickens's
London* (1876) to a flurry of guidebooks published in the centenary
year of 1970 and including Michael and Mollie Hardwick's useful if
sometimes inaccurate *Dickens's England*, Geoffrey Fletcher's *The
London Dickens Knew*, and an excellent alphabetical guide to
Dickens' London produced by London Transport. It is not difficult
to accuse such undertakings of sentimentality, irrelevance, or
downright muddleheadedness; and it is true that to speak of visiting
Little Nell's church or photographing Joe Gargery's cottage may
betoken a confusion concerning the relationship of literature to
actuality and a grossly over-simplified view of the creative process.
At the same time, however, even at their most unfashionably hearty
or peripheral – how characteristic of their periods are the very titles
of William R. Hughes' *A Week's Tramp in Dickens-Land* (1891), and
B. W. Matz's *Dickensian Inns and Taverns* (1922)! – they pay tribute in
their own way to Dickens' compelling powers of description and to
the intensity of the reader's response to his rendering of a physical
world that is sometimes real, sometimes imagined, and often
somewhere between the two.

Certainly his powers of observation and the vigour of his response
to place are beyond question. Nor can there be any argument about
the importance of physical settings in his fiction. This chapter first
briefly outlines the main places associated with the course of
Dickens' own experience: his homes, the places he visited, and those
associated with his work and his leisure; then it offers two mini-
guides to the most important places with Dickensian associations,
biographical or fictional – or both; for even a cursory enquiry into
this topic reveals the extent to which the world of the novels overlaps
with the real world.

I

Since, like many other novelists, Dickens made extensive and detailed use of first-hand experience in creating the settings of his fiction, the student of Dickensian topography finds himself moving repeatedly between the world of the novels and other writings and the world their creator inhabited. Sometimes, like George Eliot searching England for a landscape suitable for the action of *The Mill on the Floss*, he 'researched' his fictional backgrounds: hence the 1838 journey to Yorkshire and the 1854 visit to Preston. Much more often, like Joyce writing of Dublin in European exile, he drew on the resources of memory, or on recent experience. Practically always his fiction uses settings that are more or less precisely specified, and the reader often has a strong sense of the novelist exploiting contrasted settings as characters and action move from one locality to another – from East End to West End, from town to country, from England to abroad. London streets and public buildings are usually (though not invariably) referred to by their familiar names; outside London names are sometimes unspecified or fictitious, though identifications can often be plausibly made.

Dickens' early life was geographically unsettled, the moves incident to his father's career in the Navy Pay Office combining with the changes of domicile resulting from the fluctuations of the family fortunes. Although he was born in what is nowadays Portsmouth, he is often regarded as a Londoner – not altogether inappropriately, since much of his childhood and much of his adult life was spent there. Before he was three years old the first move to London took place, into the first of what was to become a long series of lodgings and rented houses, their varying size and neighbourhood serving as a barometer of the intermittently precarious state of the Dickens family's finances. When the child was five, a move to Chatham followed, and during a stay of more than five years in this town he had his first schooling. Even at that time, Chatham and Rochester, on either side of the Medway, were almost joined; and as he moved between the two towns the boy must have felt the contrast between the busy dockyards of Chatham and the quiet cathedral city of Rochester. It was to this area that, forty years later, he was to make his last move; in a fictional version of Rochester that he was to set his last novel; within a few miles of Rochester that he was to die; and in Rochester that he wished to be buried – a wish that went unfulfilled.

Before he was eleven, the family was back in London, in Camden Town, later to be the residence of Bob Cratchit. A little more than a year later there followed the period when the young boy worked in the blacking warehouse while his father was in a debtor's prison – not a long period as measured by the calendar, but profound and permanent in its effect on Dickens' sensibility and imagination, and far-reaching in its influence on his creative work. At this period the lonely child spent hours wandering the streets and, largely uncons- ciously, laid the foundations of that 'extensive and peculiar' knowledge of the metropolis that he attributes to Sam Weller in his first novel and that he himself so often displays. On his Sunday visits to the Marshalsea prison he absorbed impressions that were to be used in the prison scenes in *Pickwick* and *Copperfield*, and, most importantly, in *Little Dorrit*. During the lean years at this stage of his life, Dickens came to know intimately the world of pawnshops and cheap eating-houses, of shabby and scantily furnished lodgings situated in seedy neighbourhoods, with their population of rootless tenants and suspicious landlords, and their moonlight flittings and frequent evictions. A timely legacy, combined with his father's vanity, restored his family life and enabled him to resume his education; but as the family fortunes again declined yet another move was made down the social scale into lodgings at The Polygon, Somers Town.

Dickens left school and began work as an attorney's office-boy; then, having painfully acquired shorthand, he became a reporter at Doctors' Commons, thus plunging into the world of legal London with its mixed population of prosperous lawyers (Tulkinghorn, Jaggers) and ill-paid clerks working long hours and existing on the verge of penury (Dick Swiveller, Guppy, and – outside the legal world but within the same stratum of society – Bob Cratchit), not to mention assorted hangers-on of the powerful legal establishment (in *Bleak House* alone, Captain Hawdon is a 'law-writer', Snagsby a legal stationer, Krook a dealer in old documents discarded as waste- paper, Bucket a detective). More cheerfully, he haunted the theatres and confirmed a taste for the stage that was to manifest itself in the amateur theatricals and professional readings of later years. *Sketches by Boz*, containing his first published writings, stands as a record of the metropolitan scenes, occupations and amusements on which Dickens became an expert.

As a political reporter he travelled widely to cover elections and major speeches; and the picaresque form of *Pickwick* and *Nickleby* may owe as much to first-hand experience as to literary models. The world of *Pickwick* is partly Dickens' own London, ranging from Mrs Bardell's furnished lodgings to the law courts and the Fleet prison, and partly the world of his provincial journeyings by coach (he had, for instance, stayed in 1835 at the Great White Horse inn at Ipswich, where one of Mr Pickwick's nocturnal misadventures takes place), which took him as far afield as Exeter and Edinburgh.

Success in his career as a journalist made possible a more settled mode of existence; and near the end of 1834 he exchanged the succession of temporary lodgings for the dignity of chambers in Furnival's Inn. It was there that, a few months later, he began married life. The success of *Pickwick* shortly afterwards, and the contracts and offers that it prompted, encouraged him to take a lease of the gracious house at 48 Doughty Street (now an admirable Dickens Museum) early in 1837. Later in the same year came his first visit to the Continent and his first holiday at what was to become a favourite haunt – the Kentish seaside resort of Broadstairs. In 1838 there were two significant excursions: a visit to Yorkshire in quest of material concerning the notorious boarding-schools for use in *Nickleby*, and a tour of the Midlands and North Wales that provided vivid glimpses of industrial England that were later to be used in *The Old Curiosity Shop*.

The move to Devonshire Terrace in November 1839 suggests increasing confidence in his earning powers and marks another stage of his ascent up the social ladder. The visit to Scotland in 1841 served as a curtain-raiser for the 1842 American tour, which was itself an extraordinary testimony to the fame Dickens had achieved by the age of thirty, as well as the source of material for *Chuzzlewit* and *American Notes*. (For details of his American itinerary, see p. 8.) In the summer of 1844 followed a journey to Italy, where the Dickens family resided for almost a year. During this period Dickens travelled widely in Italy and accumulated impressions that are recorded in *Pictures from Italy*. His letters of this period, like his letters from America, are highly readable. In 1846 the Dickens family again travelled to the Continent, this time spending several months in Switzerland.

From 1847 Dickens' base was London, with occasional provincial and continental forays in the company of his male friends (for example, a Norfolk holiday with Leech and Lemon in 1849; a short trip to Paris with Maclise in 1850); visits to country-houses such as

Rockingham Castle and Knebworth; tours with his company of amateur actors (such as those taken extensively in 1848 and 1851–2); and family holidays at Broadstairs, Brighton, Dover, Folkestone, Boulogne, and on the Isle of Wight. His most extensive journey during these years was the two-month continental tour with Wilkie Collins and Augustus Egg in 1854.

At the end of that year Dickens gave a public reading in Birmingham, the first of what was to develop into a long series extending to the year of his death and involving him in thousands of miles of travel in Britain and the United States. The purchase of Gad's Hill in 1856 inaugurates a new period in which Dickens spent less time in London – showing in middle age, indeed, a marked waning of his youthful relish for metropolitan life ('London is a vile place', he wrote on 10 February 1851) – and more in the seclusion of his home in Kent. Tavistock House, his London home since 1851, was given up in 1860. From the late fifties, the public readings involved him in extensive travels throughout the British Isles: for example, a series of 83 readings in the provinces and in Scotland and Ireland in 1858; 46 provincial readings in 1861–2; 52 readings in England and Ireland in 1867. There were readings in Paris in 1863. A reading-tour of Australia mooted in 1862 failed to materialize; but towards the end of 1867 he set off for a tour of America that involved 75 readings and continued until April 1868. Later in that year he was again touring England, Scotland and Ireland on an extensive farewell tour. During this last decade of his life, his journeys for pleasure were relatively few, though he did go to Devon in 1860 with Collins (with whom, in 1857, he had visited the Lake District), to Paris in 1862, to Paris and Belgium in 1864, and to Paris again (probably with Ellen Ternan) in 1865. The later novels make considerable use of the Kentish scenes in the neighbourhood of Dickens' last home: *Great Expectations* moves between the Kent marshes and the metropolis, and *Edwin Drood* is largely set in a cathedral town closely modelled on Rochester. His last completed novel (*Our Mutual Friend*), however, is, very strikingly and power-fully, a novel of London's streets and London's river. Dickens' last journey took his body from Gad's Hill, where he died, to burial in Westminster Abbey.

The remainder of this chapter lists a selection of the places most prominent in Dickens' life and writings. Anything more than a selective listing would be far beyond the scope of the present volume: for works devoted to Dickensian topography, see the

Bibliography. The locations identified here are divided into two groups: (1) Dickens' London; (2) Outside London.

II DICKENS' LONDON

ASTLEY'S. Theatre in Westminster Bridge Road celebrated for its 'equestrian drama', a combination of circus, music-hall and melodrama. There is a description of Astley's in *SB*, and visits are paid to it by Kit Nubbles and Barbara and their families (*OCS*, Ch. 39) and by Trooper George (*BH*, Ch. 21).

ATHENAEUM. Famous club in Waterloo Place. Dickens was elected a member in 1838, and it was in the lobby of the Athenaeum that he and Thackeray were reconciled on the occasion of a chance meeting.

BARNARD'S INN. Pip and Herbert Pocket move into chambers here: for Pip's first impressions, see *GE* Ch. 21.

BAYHAM STREET. The Dickens family lived at Number 16 (now demolished) in 1823. There is a tradition that Dickens had this house in mind in describing the Cratchit home in *A Christmas Carol*.

BERNERS STREET. This street (off Oxford Street) is mentioned in the essay 'Where we stopped growing' (*Miscellaneous Papers*) in connexion with an eccentric character who may have been the prototype of Miss Havisham (*GE*):

> The White Woman is her name. She is dressed entirely in white, with a ghastly white plaiting round her head and face, inside her white bonnet . . . . She is a conceited old creature, cold and formal in manner, and evidently went simpering mad on personal grounds alone – no doubt because a wealthy Quaker wouldn't marry her. This is her bridal dress . . . .

See also an article by M. Meisel in *PMLA* (1966).

BEVIS MARKS. Sampson Brass (*OCS*) is described as 'an attorney . . . from Bevis Marks in the City of London'. Dickens wrote to Forster in 1840: 'I intended calling on you this morning on my way back from Bevis Marks whither I went to look at a house for Sampson Brass.'

BLACKHEATH. Among numerous references, this is the site of Salem House, the school to which David Copperfield is sent, and of the cottage where John and Bella Rokesmith settle. A glimpse of the dangers of crossing blackheath in an earlier period is given in the second chapter of *ATTC*.

BOROUGH, THE. That is, Southwark, the scene of numerous episodes. We first meet Sam Weller 'busily employed in brushing the dirt off a pair of boots' in the yard of the White Hart (*PP*, Ch. 10), demolished in 1889. The Marshalsea Prison in the Borough High Street dated from the fourteenth century and by Dickens' time was used for debtors: his father was imprisoned there, as was William Dorrit, and Little Dorrit was born there (see *LD*, Bk I, Chs 6, 8, and so on, and Preface). During his father's imprisonment, Dickens lived for a time in Lant Street, which is also the scene of Bob Sawyer's lodging (see *PP*, Ch. 30). Mr Micawber was put into the King's Bench Prison (demolished 1880), also in the Borough High Street.

BRIDEWELL. Workhouse and 'house of correction' near Blackfriars, demolished in 1864. Noah Claypole insults Oliver by saying that if his mother were alive she might be 'hard labouring in Bridewell' (*OT*, Ch. 6).

BRITISH MUSEUM. Dickens applied for a readers' ticket on his eighteenth birthday; the Reading Room is mentioned in 'Shabby-genteel People' (*SB*).

BUCKINGHAM PALACE. Dickens was received there by Queen Victoria in March 1870 (see under 'Victoria' in 'The Dickens Circle'), and a few days later attended a levee.

CAMDEN TOWN. For a description of the 'euphonious locality' of Staggs's Gardens, see *D&S*, Ch. 6. *See also* BAYHAM STREET.

CHANCERY LANE. This figures prominently in *BH*, where, according to T. W. Hill, 'the London scenes are nearly all within a half-mile radius from Chancery Lane'. Cook's Court, where Mr Snagsby's law-stationery business is situated, is based on Took's Court, off Cursitor Street, and the house occupied by the Neckett family is in Cursitor Street.

CHEAPSIDE. There are numerous references to this famous thoroughfare: for example, Mr Pickwick and Sam meet Tony Weller there (*PP*, Ch. 20), Mr Mould the undertaker lives 'within the ward of Cheap' (*MC*, Ch. 25), and Pip meets Mr Jaggers there (*GE*, Ch. 48). As a boy CD arrived in London at the Cross Keys Inn (128 Wood Street), and Pip arrives there in *GE* (Ch. 20).

CURSITOR STREET, *see* CHANCERY LANE.

DEVONSHIRE TERRACE. Dickens lived at Number 1 from 1839 to 1851 (the house was demolished in 1962).

DOCTORS' COMMONS. Ecclesiastical and Admiralty courts near St Paul's Cathedral, abolished in 1858. In *SB* ('Doctors' Commons') it is described as 'the place where they grant marriage-licences to love-sick couples, and divorce to unfaithful ones; register the wills of people who have property to leave, and punish hasty gentlemen who call ladies by unpleasant names'. Dickens became a freelance shorthand-reporter there in 1828. It appears in *PP* (Chs 10, 55) and in *DC* (Chs 23, 33), where David becomes an articled clerk in Mr Spenlow's law-firm.

DOUGHTY STREET. Dickens lived at Number 48 in 1837–9: his first child was born there, and Mary Hogarth died there. The house is now occupied by the Dickens Fellowship and is open to the public as a Dickens Museum.

FLEET PRISON, THE. Latterly a debtors' prison, it was demolished in 1848; its site is now occupied by the Memorial Hall, Farringdon Street. Mr Pickwick is imprisoned there (*PP*, Chs 40, 43).

FURNIVAL'S INN (now demolished). Dickens had chambers here (in 1834–5), as do John Westlock in *MC* (Ch. 36, etc.) and Rosa Bud in *ED*.

GERRARD STREET (Soho). As a boy Dickens used to visit his maternal uncle, Thomas Barrow, who lived there. It is also the residence of Jaggers in *GE*.

GREAT ORMOND STREET. The Hospital for Sick Children was opened in 1852. On 3 April of that year CD drew attention to it in an article in *HW* ('Drooping Buds'), and on 9 February 1858 he took the chair at a charity dinner and made an appeal for contributions. Little Johnny dies there in *OMF* (Bk II, Ch. 9).

HAMMERSMITH. The Pocket family live there in a riverside house: see *GE*, Ch. 22.

HAMPSTEAD. Dickens lived for a short time at Wylde's Farm (formerly Collins's Farm), North End, Hampstead, after the death of Mary Hogarth in 1837. Later he frequently walked on the Heath and visited the inn known as Jack Straw's Castle, described by Forster as 'memorable for many happy meetings'. ('Oh for Jack Straw's!' wrote Dickens from America in 1842.) Dick Swiveller settles in a cottage at Hampstead after his marriage (*OCS*, Ch. 73), Bill Sikes traverses the Heath after the murder of Nancy (*OT*, Ch. 48), and Mr Pickwick is the author of a paper 'Speculations on the Source of the Hampstead Ponds' (*PP*, Ch. 1).

HIGHGATE. Dickens' parents and his baby daughter Dora are buried in Highgate Cemetery. Dickens lived in Highgate for a time in 1832. David Copperfield and Aunt Betsey live there.

HUNGERFORD STAIRS. The site of the blacking warehouse where Dickens was employed ('the last house on the left-hand side of the way at old Hungerford Stairs', according to the autobiographical fragment).

LIMEHOUSE. Christopher Huffam, Dickens's godfather, lived there at 5 Church Row; and as a boy Dickens would visit him. The neighbourhood figures in *OMF* as the home of the Hexams and of Rogue Riderhood, who lives 'deep and dark in Limehouse Hole'.

LINCOLN'S INN. The High Court of Chancery, described in the opening chapter of *BH*, sat in Lincoln's Inn Hall after term-time in Dickens' day. Guppy works for 'Kenge and Carboy's . . . of Lincoln's Inn'; their offices are in Old Square, as are those of Serjeant Snubbin (*BH*, Ch. 3; *PP*, Ch. 31). Miss Flite describes the garden of Lincoln's Inn as 'quite a bower in the summer-time' (*BH*, Ch. 5). Forster lived at 58 Lincoln's Inn Fields, and it was there that on 3 December 1844 Dickens read *The Chimes* to a group of friends. Mr Tulkinghorn's house (*BH*) is based on Forster's.

MARSHALSEA, *see* BOROUGH, THE

MONUMENT, THE. Todgers' boarding-house (*MC*, Ch. 9) is near the Monument.

NEWGATE. Prison dating from the twelfth century, burnt down by the Gordon rioters in 1780 (see *BR*, Chs 64–6), rebuilt and finally demolished in 1902; the Central Criminal Court now stands on its site. Lord George Gordon and Fagin are imprisoned and die there (*BR*, Ch. 81; *OT*, Ch. 52), Kit Nubbles is confined there (*OCS*, Ch. 63), and Pip visits the prison with Wemmick (*GE*, Ch. 20).

NORWOOD. Carker's luxurious residence is 'in the green and wooded country near Norwood' (*D&S*, Ch. 33).

PENTONVILLE. Mr Brownlow (*OT*, Ch. 12) and Mr Pancks (*LD*, Bk 1, Ch. 25) live there.

PICCADILLY. Dickens gave the last of his public readings on 15 March 1870 at the St James's Hall (now demolished, the Piccadilly Hotel occupying the site). At Devonshire House (demolished 1924) he appeared in Lytton's comedy *Not So Bad As*

We Seem before Queen Victoria on 16 May 1851. Chapman & Hall, Dickens's publishers, had offices at 193 Piccadilly. In the novels, Fascination Fledgeby had chambers in Albany and the Lammles were married at St James's Church (*OMF*, Bk 3, Ch. 1; Bk I, Ch. 10); Mr Pickwick and Sam Weller caught the coach for Bath (*PP*, Ch. 35) at the White Horse Cellar near the corner of Dover Street, and Esther Summerson was met there by Guppy (*BH*, Ch. 3) when she arrived in London.

RICHMOND. Estella goes to live there 'at a great expense, with a lady who has the power – or says she has – of taking me about and introducing me', and Pip visits her there in 'a house by the Green' (*GE*, Ch. 33). At the Star and Garter Hotel at the top of Richmond Hill Dickens celebrated the completion of *DC* with a party whose guests included Tennyson and Thackeray.

SAFFRON HILL, off Clerkenwell Road, Fagin's neighbourhood; at a public house, The Three Cripples, Sikes is depicted (*OT*, Ch. 15).

ST PAUL'S CATHEDRAL. The subject of numerous references in the novels: for instance, Eugene Wrayburn and Mortimer Lightwood walk in the churchyard there with Bradley Headstone (*OMF*, Bk 3, Ch. 10).

SEVEN DIALS. Notorious slum district, described in *SB* ('Seven Dials') as a 'maze of streets, courts, lanes and alleys'. Mantalini turns a mangle and finds life ' "one dem'd horrid grind" ' in the cellar of a house in a 'labyrinth of streets . . . between Seven Dials and Soho'. In his childhood, according to Forster, if Dickens 'could only induce whomsoever took him out to take him through Seven-dials, he was supremely happy. "Good Heaven!" he would exclaim. "What wild visions of prodigies of wickedness, want, and beggary, arose in my mind out of that place!" '

SHADWELL. Dickens visited an opium den in Shadwell in 1869 and later wrote: 'The opium smoking I have described in *ED*, I saw (exactly as I have described it, penny ink bottle and all) down in Shadwell.' The American publisher, James T. Fields, who accompanied him, wrote that 'In a miserable court, at night, we found a haggard old woman blowing at a kind of pipe made of an old ink bottle.' In *ED*, John Jasper travels eastward through the city 'until he reaches his destination: a miserable court, specially miserable among many such'.

SOHO. Dr Manette's house is here (*ATTC*, Bk 2, Ch. 6).

STRAND. The offices of the *Morning Chronicle*, where Dickens was employed as a reporter, were at 332 Strand.

SYMONDS INN. Dickens was employed by Charles Molloy, a solicitor with offices at 6 Symonds Inn, Chancery Lane, for a few weeks in 1827. Mr Vholes also has offices there (*BH*, Ch. 39).

TAVISTOCK HOUSE. Dickens's home from 1851 to 1860. The offices of the British Medical Association now occupy the site.

THAMES. Especially prominent in *OMF*, which opens with a river scene, and in the escape episode of *GE* (Ch. 54).

TOWER HILL. The site of Quilp's residence (*OCS*, Ch. 4).

WALWORTH. Wemmick and his Aged Parent live here in 'a little wooden cottage in the midst of plots of garden' (*GE*, Ch. 25), Wemmick's 'Walworth sentiments' contrasting sharply with those associated with his professional life.

WELLINGTON STREET. The office of *HW* (now demolished) was opposite the Lyceum Theatre, that of *AYR* at Number 11 (now 26), at the corner of Tavistock Street.

III   OUTSIDE LONDON

BARNARD CASTLE (Durham). Dickens and H. K. Browne stayed at the King's Head there at the beginning of February 1837, during their visit to Yorkshire (*see also* GRETA BRIDGE; BOWES).

BATH. Dickens visited Bath in February 1840, accompanied by Forster, and called on W. S. Landor, who had lodgings in St James's Square. Dickens is said to have conceived the idea of Little Nell on this occasion.

BIRMINGHAM. Dickens often visited the city and gave speeches and public readings there. In *Dickens on England and the English*, Malcolm Andrews writes that it was Dickens' first visit to the Birmingham–Wolverhampton area in 1838 that gave him 'the basis for his remarkable description of England's Black Country through which Little Nell and her grandfather travel' (see *OCS* Chs 44–5). In a letter to his wife (1 November 1838) Dickens wrote of travelling 'through miles of cinder-paths and blazing furnances and roaring steam-engines, and such a mass of dirt, gloom and misery as I never before witnessed'. At a prize-giving at the Birmingham and Midland Institute on 6 January 1870, Dickens made his well-known remark that he had 'very little faith in the people who govern us' but 'great confidence in the People whom they govern'.

BLUNDESTON, village near Lowestoft in Suffolk, said to be the 'original' of Blunderstone in *DC* (or at least to have suggested the name of the fictional village: Dickens seems not to have visited Blundeston but noticed the name on a signpost in January 1849).

BOWES (Yorkshire). William Shaw (see in chapter 'The Dickens Circle') kept Bowes Academy; Dickens and 'Phiz' called on him early in February 1837 in quest of material concerning the Yorkshire boarding-schools for use in *NN*.

BRIGHTON. Dickens was there in 1837 and subsequently. Paul Dombey is sent to school there; when Mr Dombey visits his son he stays at the Bedford Hotel, as Dickens did in 1848.

BROADSTAIRS (Kent). Seaside resort of which Dickens became very fond and where he spent many family holidays (in his case usually combined with work on the current novel). The Dickens family stayed in various lodging-houses; later they leased Fort House (subsequently renamed Bleak House, though the house has no connection with the novel beyond the fact that it was partly written there). The picture of Dover in *DC* may be based on Dickens's knowledge of Broadstairs. The town is described in 'Our English Watering-Place' (*HW* 2 August 1851; *Reprinted Pieces*).

BURY ST EDMUNDS. The Angel, which figures in *PP*, is still standing.

CANTERBURY. David Copperfield passes through this city on his way to Dover, and later in the same novel it is depicted as the home of Mr Wickfield and Agnes.

CHALK. Village near Gravesend in Kent. Dickens honeymooned there, and a cottage in the village has been said to have been the original of Joe Gargery's cottage in *GE*.

CHATHAM. Dickens lived there as a child (1817–22). The marsh country depicted in *GE* is based on the Chatham–Gravesend area. Two papers in *UT*, 'Dullborough Town' and 'Chatham Dockyard', relate to the town.

CHIGWELL (Essex). This village is depicted in *BR*; the Maypole Inn in that novel is based on the King's Head, still standing.

CORNWALL. Dickens toured Cornwall in 1842 in the company of Forster, Maclise and Stanfield. After his return he wrote to Cornelius Felton (31 December 1842): 'I never laughed in my life as I did on this journey . . . . I was choaking and gasping and bursting the buckle off the back of my stock all the way . . . . I do believe there never was such a trip.'

DOVER. Prominent in *DC* and *ATTC*.

FOLKESTONE. The Dickens family spent the summer of 1855 at this seaside resort, and part of *LD* was written there.

GRANTHAM. Dickens and H. K. Browne stayed at the George in January 1838 en route for Yorkshire. The town is mentioned in Ch. 5 of *NN*.

GREAT YARMOUTH. Dickens, with Leech and Lemon, visited this seaside resort during a tour of Norfolk in January 1849. Local tradition holds that talking to fishermen on the beach gave him material used in the portrayal of the Peggotty family in *DC*. In a letter to Forster, Dickens described Yarmouth as 'the strangest place in the wide world: one hundred and forty-six miles of hill-less country between it and London . . . . I shall certainly try my hand at it.'

GRETA BRIDGE (Yorkshire). Dickens and H. K. Browne stayed at the George and New Inn on the night of 31 January 1838 at the beginning of their brief Yorkshire visit.

IPSWICH. As a young reporter Dickens covered an election there in May 1835 and 'reported O'Connell's speech . . . amid intense excitement and fears of mob violence' (Johnson). The Great White Horse in the scene of one of Mr Pickwick's misadventures.

KENILWORTH. Dickens and H. K. Browne visited Kenilworth in October 1838, en route for the industrial Midlands and North Wales. Dickens admired the castle and later sent Dombey, Carker, Mrs Skewton and Edith for 'a stroll among the haunted ruins of Kenilworth' in *D&S*, Ch. 27, Mrs Skewton's enthusiasm being the occasion for some satire on nineteenth-century medievalism (' "Oh!" cried Mrs. Skewton, with a faded little scream of rapture, "the Castle is charming! – associations of the Middle ages – and all that . . ." ').

KETTERING (Northamptonshire). Dickens went there in December 1835 to report a by-election for the *Morning Chronicle*. In a vivid letter (16 December) to Catherine Hogarth he described the violence and brutality of electioneering, 'just stopping short of murder and a riot . . . . Anything more sickening and disgusting, or anything that roused my indignation so much, I never beheld.' *See also Sudbury*.

KNEBWORTH (Hertfordshire). Knebworth Park was the family seat of Dickens' friend Edward Bulwer-Lytton (see 'The Dickens Circle').

LAKE DISTRICT. Dickens went there with Wilkie Collins in 1857 on 'a little tour in search of an article and in avoidance of railroads' (letter to Forster). The result was a joint production by the two authors, *The Lazy Tour of Two Idle Apprentices*.

LEAMINGTON. Dickens was there in 1838 (*see also* KENILWORTH). Mr Dombey goes there after the death of Paul, and there meets Edith (*D&S*, Chs 20–1).

NORWICH. Dickens went to Norwich with Leech and Lemon in January 1849 at the start of a short Norfolk holiday. They visited the cathedral and saw 'the place of execution, which we found fit for a gigantic scoundrel's exit' (letter to Forster, 12 January 1849).

PORTSMOUTH. Dickens' birthplace (see 'A Dickens Chronology'). He left there in 1814 when his family moved to London, and revisited the town in 1838 while writing *NN* (the hero's adventures with Mr Vincent Crummles' company of strolling players take place in Portsmouth).

PRESTON (Lancashire). Often regarded as the prototype of Coketown in *HT* (though Manchester is another claimant). Dickens went there in January 1854 to observe a strike in progress, and described the town in a letter to Forster as 'a nasty place'. Much later he wrote to Charles Fechter: 'When I did Hard Times I called the scene Coketown. Everybody knew what was meant, but every cotton-spinning town said it was the other cotton-spinning town' (4 September 1866).

ROCHESTER. Cathedral town just across the river Medway from Chatham, where Dickens lived as a child. It is the Cloisterham of *ED* and its cathedral figures prominently in that novel. The Gatehouse at Rochester has been identified with John Jasper's house; Restoration House has been identified with the Satis House of *GE*; and the village of Dingley Dell in *PP* is nearby. Significantly, on completing *DC* in October 1850 Dickens wrote in a letter to Miss Coutts that he had 'an idea of wandering somewhere for a day or two – to Rochester, I think, where I was a small boy'. In 1856 he purchased Gad's Hill Place, a few miles from Rochester; it remained his home for the rest of his life, and he died there. He had seen the house in his childhood and told Miss Coutts (9 February 1856) that he 'used to look at it as a wonderful Mansion (which God knows it is not) when I was a very odd little child with the first faint shadows of all my books in my head – I suppose'.

ROCKINGHAM (Northamptonshire). Dickens visited his friends, the Hon. Mr and Mrs Richard Watson, at Rockingham Castle. The castle is said to be the prototype of the Dedlock mansion in *BH* (removed to the neighbouring county of Lincolnshire), and the Dedlock Arms to be based on the Sondes Arms in Rockingham village.

SALISBURY. The 'little Wiltshire village' where Mr Pecksniff lives is 'within an easy journey of the fair old town of Salisbury' (*MC*, Ch. 2).

SCOTLAND. Dickens and Kate toured Scotland in the summer of 1841. In Edinburgh Dickens was given the freedom of the city and fêted at a public dinner. His letters to Forster give a vivid impression of his reaction to the Highlands (see especially 5, 9 and 11 July); Glencoe in particular he found 'an awful place', 'tremendous', 'perfectly horrific', and he felt that the scenes he passed through would 'live in my dreams for years'.

SUDBURY (Suffolk). Dickens visited this small market town as a young reporter and depicted it as Eatanswill in *PP* (Ch. 13), though its election scenes derive largely from his memories of an 1835 by-election in Kettering.

TONG (Shropshire). The quiet village where Little Nell ends her wanderings and dies has been identified with Tong.

WARWICK. Dickens and Browne visited Warwick and Stratford during their tour of the Midlands in 1838 (*see also* BIRMINGHAM; KENILWORTH; LEAMINGTON).

Outside England, a substantial portion of *Chuzzlewit* is set in America; the first part of *Little Dorrit* opens in Marseilles and the second part in Switzerland, the Dorrits continuing their travels into Italy; Paris and the French countryside are depicted in *A Tale of Two Cities*; a group of characters in *Copperfield* emigrate to Australia (Mr Peggotty returning to give an account of their experiences in Ch. 63); Pip and Herbert Pocket leave England to work in 'the East'; Edith Dombey's confrontation with Carker (*Dombey*, Ch. 54) takes place at Dijon, and she later goes into Italian exile. Dickens also wrote two travel-books, *American Notes* and *Pictures from Italy*. Some of Dickens' essays and sketches – for example, 'Our French Watering-Place' (*Reprinted Pieces*) – also describe or refer to his periods of residence and travel on the Continent.

Select Bibliography

This bibliography is divided into the following sections:

1. Bibliographies.
2. Reference books.
3. Manuscripts.
4. Dickens' novels and stories.
5. Other writings by Dickens.
6. Biographies and reminiscences.
7. Critical studies: general.
8. Critical studies: special aspects.
9. Topography.
10. Journals.

The place of publication is London unless otherwise indicated. Books, essays and articles devoted to single works are noted under the appropriate headings earlier in this volume.

1 BIBLIOGRAPHIES

British Museum, *Dickens: An Excerpt from the General Catalogue* (1960).
Churchill, R. C., *A Bibliography of Dickensian Criticism, 1836–1975* (1975).
Collins, Philip, Dickens entry in *The New Cambridge Bibliography of English Literature*, III (1800–1900) ed. George Watson (Cambridge, 1969); published separately (1970) by the Dickens Fellowship.
Collins, Philip, Dickens entry in *Victorian Fiction: A Second Guide to Research*, ed. George Ford (New York, 1978) (see also Nisbet below).
Eckel, J. C., *The First Editions of the Writings of Charles Dickens* (1932).

Fenstenmaker, John J., *Charles Dickens, 1940–1975: An Analytical Subject Index to Periodical Criticism of the Novels and Christmas Books* (Boston, Mass., 1979).

Ford, George H. and Lauriat Lane, Jr, *The Dickens Critics* (Ithaca, 1961). (This useful anthology contains a checklist of Dickens criticism covering the period 1840–1960.)

Gold, Joseph, *The Stature of Dickens: A Centenary Bibliography* (Toronto, 1971).

Hatton, T. and A. H. Cleaver, *A Bibliography of the Periodical Works of Dickens* (1933).

Kitton, F. G., *Dickensiana* (1886); *The Novels of Dickens* (1897); *The Minor Writings of Dickens* (1900).

Miller, W. *The Dickens Student and Collector* (Cambridge, Mass., 1946).

Nisbet, Ada, Dickens entry in *Victorian Fiction: A Guide to Research*, ed. Lionel Stevenson (Cambridge, Mass., 1964). (For an updating of this important bibliography of Dickens criticism, see Collins above.)

Slater, Michael, Dickens entry in *The English Novel: Select Bibliographical Guides*, ed. A. E. Dyson (1974).

Garland Press has in preparation a comprehensive annotated bibliography, *The Works of Charles Dickens*, planned to appear in 18 volumes. The first volume (on *David Copperfield*, by Richard J. Dunn) was published in 1981.

2 REFERENCE BOOKS

Fyfe, T. A., *Who's Who in Dickens* (1912).

Greaves, J., *Who's Who in Dickens* (1972).

Hardwick, Michael and Mollie, *The Dickens Companion* (1965); *The Charles Dickens Encyclopedia* (1973).

Hayward, A. L., *The Dickens Encyclopaedia* (1924).

Philip, A. J., *A Dickens Dictionary* (1909).

Pierce, G. A., *The Dickens Dictionary* (Boston, Mass., 1872).

Stonehouse, J. H., *Catalogue of the Library of Dickens from Gadshill* (1935).

Williams, M., *The Dickens Concordance* (1907).

3 MANUSCRIPTS

By far the most important repository of Dickens manuscripts is the Forster Collection in the Victoria & Albert Museum, South Kensington. It contains the complete manuscripts of the following novels.

American Notes
Barnaby Rudge
* *Bleak House*
* *The Chimes*
* *David Copperfield*
* *Dombey and Son*
The Mystery of Edwin Drood
* *Hard Times*
* *Little Dorrit*
Martin Chuzzlewit
The Old Curiosity Shop
A Tale of Two Cities

For the items marked * the complete proofs with corrections by Dickens (often of considerable interest) are also available in the Forster Collection. In addition, the Collection possesses portions of the proofs of *Barnaby Rudge, Edwin Drood, Great Expectations, Martin Chuzzlewit*, and *The Old Curiosity Shop*; proofs of the dedication and preface of *The Pickwick Papers* and the preface to *Nicholas Nickleby*; portions of the manuscript and proof of *Master Humphrey's Clock*; and part of the manuscript of *Oliver Twist* (Chs 12–43). Minor items include manuscripts of *Sketches of Young Couples, Travelling Letters* (an early version of *Pictures from Italy*; portion only), *A Child's History of England*; a volume of dedications, prefaces and memoranda; and four volumes of articles, reviews, and miscellaneous material.

Other Dickens manuscripts are widely scattered. That of *Great Expectations* is in Wisbech Museum, Cambridgeshire; that of *A Christmas Carol* and *Our Mutual Friend* in the Pierpont Morgan Library, New York; that of *The Cricket on the Hearth* at Austin, Texas; and that of *The Life of Our Lord* in the Free Library, Philadelphia. The British Library possesses a few pages of the *Pickwick* manuscript (other fragments of which exist in various collections and in the hands of private owners), as well as a fragment of the manuscript of *Nicholas Nickleby*, the 1850 Preface to *Oliver Twist*, a portion of the corrected proofs of *The Old Curiosity Shop*, and other items. Other important collections include those held by the Dickens House, London; Yale University Library; the Rosenbach Museum, Philadelphia; the Berg Collection, New York Public Library; the VanderPoel Collection at Austin, Texas; the Huntington Library, San Marino, California; and the Reed Collection, Dunedin Public Library, New Zealand. Dickens' letters are widely scattered, and many are still unpublished.

Microfilm versions of the major manuscripts at South Kensington and Wisbech are available, as well as of other material at the Dickens House. A facsimile version of the manuscript of *A Christmas Carol* has been published (see p. 256).

4 DICKENS' NOVELS AND STORIES

The following are the most important collected editions of Dickens' works published or inaugurated during his lifetime (it should be noted that not all editions include the minor and non-fictional writings):

The 'first cheap edition', published in 17 volumes in 1847–67. (This was reissued in 1865–7 as 'The People's Edition' in 25 volumes.)

The Library Edition, published in 22 volumes in 1858–9 and reissued in 30 volumes in 1861–74 (the reissue including the later works).

The Charles Dickens Edition, published in 21 volumes in 1867–75.

There have been many subsequent editions, of which the most important are:

The Nonesuch Dickens, published in 23 volumes in 1937–8.

The New Oxford Illustrated Dickens, published in 21 volumes in 1947–58 (with introductions of very varying quality).

The Clarendon Dickens, begun in 1966, still in progress, and likely to be so for many years. So far, the following have appeared: *Oliver Twist, Dombey and Son, The Mystery of Edwin Drood, Little Dorrit, David Copperfield*. This will take its place as the standard scholarly edition; textually it is unlikely to be excelled, but unfortunately it lacks annotation.

The Penguin English Library has published (from 1966) all the major novels and the *Christmas Books*; regrettably the minor writings have been excluded from this series, apart from a volume of *Selected Short Fiction*. There is no consistent editorial policy, but all volumes contain introductions and notes.

For editions of individual novels, see under the appropriate section earlier in this volume.

5 OTHER WRITINGS BY DICKENS

The Pilgrim edition of Dickens' letters, under the general editorship of Madeleine House and Graham Storey, is the first complete edition and, when concluded, will form a fitting monument both to modern Dickens scholarship and to a writer who put a full share of his characteristic vitality into his letters. The first volume appeared in 1965, and to date four others have been published, the most recent (1981) covering the years 1847–9. On the early stages of this edition, see some attractive essays by Humphry House in his *All in Due Time* (1955). For those who survive to see this great edition completed, it is likely to prove one of the finest examples of its kind. Previously, the fullest available collection was the Nonesuch edition, ed. Walter Dexter (three volumes, 1938). There have been numerous collections of Dickens' letters to various individuals – for example, to Wilkie Collins (1892), W. H. Wills (1912), Mark Lemon (1917), Angela Burdett Coutts (1931), Catherine Dickens (1934), and Maria Beadnell (1936).

F. G. Kitton has edited *The Poems and Verses of Charles Dickens* (1903), and there is an edition of the *Complete Plays and Selected Poems* (1970). *The Speeches of Charles Dickens* have been edited by K. J. Fielding (Oxford, 1960), and *Charles Dickens: The Public Readings* by Philip Collins (Oxford, 1975), both these editions being models of their kind.

For twenty years Dickens expended enormous energies on his periodicals: *Household Words* (weekly from 30 March 1850 to 28 May 1859), and *All the Year Round* (weekly from 30 April 1859 to his death). *The Household Narrative*, a monthly supplement to *Household Words*, ran from April 1850 to December 1855. Dickens' own contributions to his periodicals have been collected in various volumes, including *Reprinted Pieces* (1858), *The Uncommercial*

Traveller (1861; second series, 1868), and *Miscellaneous Papers* (1908); and in *Charles Dickens' Uncollected Writings from 'Household Words'*, ed. Harry Stone (Bloomington, 1968). Anne Lohrli has compiled a useful listing of the contents of *Household Words* (Toronto, 1973).

For a select list of Dickens' other minor writings, see p. 275. For a comprehensive list, see Philip Collins' contribution to *The New Cambridge Bibliography of English Literature*.

6 BIOGRAPHIES AND REMINISCENCES

Aylmer, Felix, *Dickens Incognito* (1959).
Carlton, William J., *Charles Dickens, Shorthand Writer* (1926).
Collins, Philip (ed.), *Dickens: Interviews and Recollections* (1981).
DeVries, Duane, *Dickens's Apprentice Years* (Hassocks, 1976).
Dickens, Henry F., *Memories of My Father* (1928).
Dickens, Mamie, *Charles Dickens, by his Eldest Daughter* (1885); *My Father As I Recall Him* (1897).
Dolby, G., *Charles Dickens As I knew Him* (1885).
Forster, John, *The Life of Dickens* (1872–4).
Hibbert, Christopher, *The Making of Dickens* (1967).
Johnson, Edgar, *Dickens: His Tragedy and Triumph* (New York, 1952).
Kent, Charles, *Charles Dickens as a Reader* (1872)'.
Kingsmill, Hugh, *The Sentimental Journey: A Life of Dickens* (1934).
Kitton, F. G., *Charles Dickens* (1902).
Langton, Robert, *The Childhood and Youth of Charles Dickens* (1883).
Lindsay, Jack, *Dickens: A Biographical and Critical Study* (1950).
MacKenzie, Norman and Jeanne, *Dickens: A Life* (New York, 1979).
Maurois, André, *Dickens* (1934).
Pearson, Hesketh, *Dickens: His Character, Comedy and Career* (1949).
Pope-Hennessy, Una, *Charles Dickens* (1945).
Priestley, J. B., *Dickens: A Pictorial Biography* (1961).
Shore, W. T., *Charles Dickens and his Friends* (1909).
Storey, Gladys, *Dickens and Daughter* (1939).
Straus, Ralph, *Charles Dickens: A Biography from New Sources* (1928).
Ward, A. W., *Dickens* (1882).
Wilkins, W. G., *Charles Dickens in America* (New York, 1911).
Wilson, Angus, *The World of Charles Dickens* (1970).
Wright, Thomas, *The Life of Dickens* (1935).

7 CRITICAL STUDIES: GENERAL

Axton, W. F., *Circle of Fire* (Lexington, Kentucky, 1966).

Blount, Trevor, *Dickens: The Early Novels* (1968).

Butt, John and Kathleen Tillotson, *Dickens at Work* (1957).

Carey, John, *The Violent Effigy: A Study of Dickens's Imagination* (1973).

Chesterton, G. K., *Charles Dickens* (1906); *Appreciations and Criticisms of the Works of Dickens* (1911). (The latter reprints Chesterton's introductions to editions of Dickens' novels.)

Cockshut, A. O. J., *The Imagination of Dickens* (1961).

Collins, Philip(ed.), *Dickens: The Critical Heritage* (1971).

Dyson, A. E., *The Inimitable Dickens: A Reading of the Novels* (1970).

Engel, Monroe, *The Maturity of Dickens* (Cambridge, Mass., 1959).

Fielding, K. J., *Charles Dickens: A Critical Introduction* (1958).

Ford, George H. and Lauriat Lane, Jr (eds), *The Dickens Critics* (Ithaca, 1961).

Garis, Robert, *The Dickens Theatre* (1967).

Gissing, George, *Dickens: A Critical Study* (1898); *The Immortal Dickens* (1925). (The latter reprints Gissing's introductions to Dickens' novels.)

Gross, John and Gabriel Pearson (eds), *Dickens and the Twentieth Century* (1962).

Hardy, Barbara, *Dickens: The Later Novels* (1968); *The Moral Art of Dickens* (1970).

Hobsbaum, Philip, *A Reader's Guide to Charles Dickens* (1977).

House, Humphry, *The Dickens World* (Oxford, 1941).

Jackson, T. A., *Dickens: The Progress of a Radical* (1937).

Kincaid, J. R., *Dickens and the Rhetoric of Laughter* (Oxford, 1971).

Leavis, F. R. and Q. D., *Dickens the Novelist* (1970).

Lucas, John, *The Melancholy Man: A Study of Dickens's Novels* (1970).

Manning, Sylvia, *Dickens as Satirist* (New Haven, Conn., 1971).

Marcus, Steven, *Dickens from Pickwick to Dombey* (New York, 1964).

Miller, J. Hillis, *Dickens: The World of his Novels* (Cambridge, Mass., 1958).

Monod, Sylvère, *Dickens the Novelist* (Norman, Oklahoma, 1968). (Originally published as *Dickens romancier* in 1953.)

Orwell, George, 'Charles Dickens', in *Inside the Whale* (1940); reprinted in *Critical Essays* (1946).

Quiller-Couch, A., *Dickens and Other Victorians* (Cambridge, 1925).

Stewart, Garrett, *Dickens and the Trials of Imagination* (Cambridge, Mass., 1974).

Sucksmith, Harvey Peter, *The Narrative Art of Charles Dickens* (Oxford, 1970).

Swinburne, A. C., *Charles Dickens* (1913).

Trilling, Lionel, 'The Dickens of Our Day', in *A Gathering of Fugitives* (Boston, Mass., 1956).

Walder, Dennis, *Dickens and Religion* (1981).

Welsh, Alexander, *The City of Dickens* (Oxford, 1971).

Williams, Raymond, *The English Novel from Dickens to Lawrence* (1970).

Wilson, Edmund, 'Dickens: The Two Scrooges', in *The Wound and the Bow* (Boston, 1941).

Wing, George, *Dickens* (1969).

8   CRITICAL STUDIES: SPECIAL ASPECTS

Andrews, Malcolm, *Dickens on England and the English* (1979).

Bodelsen, C. A., ' "The Physiognomy of the Name" ', *Review of English Literature*, II (July 1961).

Boll, E., 'Charles Dickens and Washinton Irving', *Modern Language Quarterly*, V (1944).

Brannan, R. L., *Under the Management of Mr Charles Dickens: His Production of 'The Frozen Deep'* (Ithaca, 1966).

Brook, G. L., *The Language of Dickens* (1970).

Brain, Russell, 'Dickens, Neuro-psychiatrist', 'Dickensian Diagnoses', in *Some Reflections on Genius* (1960).

Collins, Philip, *Dickens and Crime* (1962); *Dickens and Education* (1963); 'Dickens in Conversation', *Dickensian*, LIX (1953); 'The Significance of Dickens's Periodicals', *Review of English Literature*, II (July 1961).

Cruikshank, R. J., *Dickens and Early Victorian England* (1949).

Eliot, T. S., 'Wilkie Collins and Dickens', in *Selected Essays* (1932).

Fleissner, Robert F., *Dickens and Shakespeare* (New York, 1965).

Ford, George H., *Dickens and his Readers* (Princeton, 1955).

Frye, Northrop, 'Dickens and the Comedy of Humours', in *Experience in the Novel*, ed. R. H. Pearce (New York, 1968).

Fyfe, T. A., *Dickens and the Law* (Edinburgh, 1910).

Gerson, Stanley, *Sound and Symbol in the Dialogue of the Works of Charles Dickens* (Stockholm, 1967).

Goldberg, Michael, *Carlyle and Dickens* (Athens, Georgia, 1972).

Grubb, G. G., 'Dickens's Editorial Methods', *Studies in Philology*, XL (1943).

Harbage, Alfred B., *A Kind of Power: The Shakespeare–Dickens Analogy* (Philadelphia, 1975).

Holdsworth, W. S., *Dickens as a Legal Historian* (New Haven, 1928).

Kaplan, Fred, *Dickens and Mesmerism* (Princeton, 1975).

Lary, N. M., *Dostoevsky and Dickens* (1973).

Manning, J., *Dickens on Education* (Toronto, 1959).

Matthews, William, *Cockney Past and Present* (1938).

Page, Norman, *Speech in the English Novel* (1973) (Includes a chapter on 'Dickens and Speech'.)

Patten, Robert L., *Charles Dickens and his Publishers* (Oxford, 1978).

Pope, Norris, *Dickens and Charity* (1978).

Pugh, E. W., *The Dickens Originals* (1912).

Quirk, Randolph, 'Charles Dickens, Linguist', in *The Linguist and the English Language* (1974).

Rosenberg, M., 'The Dramatist in Dickens', *Journal of English and Germanic Philology*, LIX (1960).

Sanders, Andrew, *The Victorian Historical Novel 1840–1880* (1979).

Simpson, Evelyn, 'Jonson and Dickens', *Essays and Studies*, XXIX (1944).

Slater, Michael, *Dickens on America and the Americans* (1979).

Smith, Grahame, *Dickens, Money, and Society* (Berkeley, 1968).

Spilka, Mark, *Dickens and Kafka* (Bloomington, 1963).

Stone, Harry, *Dickens and the Invisible World: Fairy Tales, Fantasy, and Novel-making* (1980); 'Dickens and the Jews', *Victorian Studies*, II (1959); 'Dickens and Interior Monologue', *Philological Quarterly*, XXXVIII (1959).

Sutherland, J. A., *Victorian Novelists and Publishers* (1976).

Wierstra, F. D., *Smollett and Dickens* (Amsterdam, 1928).

9 TOPOGRAPHY

Addison, William, *In the Steps of Charles Dickens* (1955).

Allbut, Robert, *London and Country Rambles with Charles Dickens* (n.d.).

Anon., *Charles Dickens and Southwark* (1974).

Cooper, T. P., *With Dickens in Yorkshire* (1923).

Dexter, Walter, *The Kent of Dickens* (1924); *The London of Dickens* (1924); *The England of Dickens* (1925).
Fletcher, Geoffrey, *Pocket Guide to Dickens's London* (1969).
Frost, Thomas, *In Kent with Charles Dickens* (1880).
Hardwick, Michael and Mollie, *Dickens's England* (1970).
Hughes, William R., *A Week's Tramp in Dickens-Land* (1891).
Kent, William, *London for Dickens Lovers* (1935).
Matz, B. W., *Dickensian Inns and Taverns* (1922).
Moreland, Arthur, *Dickens Landmarks in London* (1931).

10 JOURNALS

The Dickensian is the organ of the Dickens Fellowship and has appeared regularly since 1905. Its volumes are a mine of detailed information and, especially in recent years, have included many articles of scholarly significance. A comprehensive index (1905–74) is available. The *Dickens Studies Newsletter* was launched in the centenary year of 1970 and is published four times a year by the Dickens Society. *Dickens Studies* (Boston), inaugurated in 1965, was short-lived. Its successor, the *Dickens Studies Annual*, was established in 1969 and appears irregularly; nine volumes have so far been published, and it has recently enlarged its scope and adopted the subtitle 'Essays on Victorian Fiction'. The *Dickens Studies Newsletter* and the journal *Victorian Studies* both publish regular bibliographies of Dickens criticism.

Filmography

The advent of the cinema as a medium of popular entertainment gave a considerable boost to the international popularity of Dickens; and from the early days of the silent cinema to the present time (and latterly through the medium of television) his works have provided a favourite source of dramatic adaptations. Of the seventy-six productions included in this selective listing, *A Christmas Carol* leads the fields with fifteen versions, with *Oliver Twist* (14) a close runner-up.

In the following list, the title of the film is the same as that of the novel unless otherwise noted. For each item some or all of the following information is given (as available): country of origin, year of production, director, screenwriter, leading actors/actresses.

In compiling this list, the following sources have been useful: Rachael Low, *The History of the British Film*; Ian F. Finlay, 'Dickens in the Cinema' (*Dickensian*, 1958); Ana Laura Zambrano, 'Feature Motion Pictures Adapted from Dickens: A Checklist' (*Dickens Studies Newsletter*, 1974–5).

BARNABY RUDGE
(1) USA, 1913; (2) GB, 1915 (director and screenwriter: Thomas Bentley; with Tom Powers, Violet Hopson); (3) GB, 1921 (directed by Thomas Bentley).

BLEAK HOUSE
GB, 1920 (directed by Maurice Elvey; with Constance Collier).

THE CHIMES
GB, 1914, two versions (one directed by Thomas Bentley, one by Herbert Blanche).

319

A CHRISTMAS CAROL

(1) as *Scrooge; or, Marley's Ghost*, GB, 1901(directed by W. R. Booth); (2) US, 1908; (3) US, 1910; (4) as *Scrooge*, GB, 1913 (director: Leedham Bantock; screenplay: Seymour Hicks; with Seymour Hicks, William Lugg); (5) GB, 1913; (6) GB, 1914 (director and screenwriter: Harold Shaw; with Charles Rock, George Bellamy); (7) as *The Right to be Happy*, US, 1916 (directed by Rupert Julian); (8) as *Scrooge*, GB, 1922 (directed by George Wynn; with H. V. Esmond); (9) as *Scrooge*, GB, 1923 (directed by Edwin Greenwood; with Russell Thorndike, Jack Denton); (10) as *Scrooge*, GB, 1928 (director: Hugh Croise; screenplay: Bransby Williams; with Bransby Williams); (11) as *A Dickensian Fantasy*, GB, 1923 (directed by Aveling Ginever; with Lawrence Manray); (12) as *Scrooge*, GB, 1935 (director: Henry Edwards; screenplay: Seymour Hicks and others; with Seymour Hicks); (13) US, 1938 (director: Edwin L. Marin; screenplay: Hugo Butler; with Reginald Owen, Jean Lockhart); (14) as *Scrooge*, GB, 1951 (director: Brian Desmond Hurst; screenplay: Noel Langley; with Alastair Sim, Mervyn Johns); (14) GB, 1960 (directed by Robert Hartford-Davis); (15) as *Scrooge*, GB, 1970 (director: Ronald Neame; screenplay: Leslie Bricusse; with Albert Finney, Alec Guinness).

THE CRICKET ON THE HEARTH

(1) US, 1909 (directed by D. W. Griffith); (2) US, 1914 (directed by Alan Hale); (3) US, 1914 (directed by Lorimer Johnston); (4) US, 1922 (directed by Lorimer Johnston); (5) US, 1949 (directed by Sobey Marin).

DAVID COPPERFIELD

(1) US, 1911; (2) GB, 1912; (3) GB, 1913 (directed by Cecil Hepworth and Thomas Bentley; with Master Eric Desmond, Alma Taylor); (4) Denmark, 1922 (directed by A. W. Sandberg; with Martin Hertzberg); (5) US, 1935 (director: George Cukor; screenplay: Hugh Wright and others; with Freddie Bartholomew, W. C. Fields); (6) US/GB, 1969 (filmed for television) (director: Delbert Mann; screenplay: Jack Pulman; with Alistair MacKenzie, Ralph Richardson).

DOMBEY AND SON

(1) GB, 1917 (director: Maurice Elvey; screenplay: Eliot Stannard; with Norman McKinnel, Heyford Hobbs); (2) as *Rich Man's Folly*,

US, 1931 (director: John Cromwell; screenplay; Grover Jones and others; with George Bancroft, Robert Ames).

GREAT EXPECTATIONS
(1) US, 1917 (directed by Paul West; with Jack Pickford); (2) Denmark, 1922 (directed by A. W. Sandberg; with Gerhard Jessen, Martin Hertzberg); (3) US, 1934 (directed by Stuart Walker); (4) GB, 1946 (director: David Lean; screenplay: Ronald Neame and others; with John Mills, Martita Hunt, Bernard Miles); (5) GB, 1975 (filmed for television) (director: Joseph Hardy; screenplay: Sherman Yeller; with Michael York, Margaret Leighton).

HARD TIMES
GB, 1915 (with Bransby Williams).

LITTLE DORRIT
(1) US, 1913; (2) GB, 1920 (director and screenwriter: Sidney Morgan; with Joan Morgan); (3) Denmark, 1924 (directed by A. W. Sandberg; with Karina Bell); (4) Germany, 1934 (directed by Carl Lamac; with Anni Ondra).

MARTIN CHUZZLEWIT
(1) US, 1912; (2) US, 1914.

THE MYSTERY OF EDWIN DROOD
(1) GB, 1909 (directed by Arthur Gilbert; with Copper Willis, Nancy Bevington); (2) GB, 1915 (directed by Herbert Blanche; with Tom Ferriss, Vinnie Burns); (3) US, 1935 (director: Stuart Walker; screenplay: John L. Balderston and others; with Claude Rains, Heather Angel).

NICHOLAS NICKLEBY
(1) US, 1902; (2) US, 1912; (3) GB, 1947 (director: Alberto Cavalcanti; screenplay: John Dighton; with Derek Bond, Cyril Fletcher).

OLIVER TWIST
(1) US, 1909; Denmark, 1910 (directed by August Blom; with Agnes Norlund); (3) France, 1910; (4) Italy, 1911; (5) US, 1912; (6) GB, 1912 (directed by Thomas Bentley); (7) US, 1916 (directed by James Young; with Marie Doro); (8) Hungary, 1920 (directed by

Peter Lubinsky); (9) US, 1921 (directed by Millard Webb); (10) US, 1922 (director: Frank Lloyd; screenplay: Harry Weil; with Jackie Coogan, Lon Chaney); (11) as *Fagin*, GB, 1922 (directed by H. B. Parkinson; with Ivan Berlyn); (12) US, 1933 (directed by William J. Caven; with Dickie Moore, Irving Pichel); (13) GB, 1948 (director: David Lean; screenplay: David Lean and others; with John Howard David, Alec Guinness); (14) as *Oliver!*, GB, 1968 (musical version) (director: Carol Reed; screenplay: Vernon Harris and others; with Mark Lester, Ron Moody).

OUR MUTUAL FRIEND
Denmark, 1919 (directed by A. W. Sandberg with Peter Malberg, Aage Fonss).

THE OLD CURIOSITY SHOP
(1) France, 1912; (2) GB, 1912 (directed by Frank Powell); (3) GB, 1913 (director and screenwriter: Thomas Bentley; with Mai Deacon, E. Felton); (4) GB, 1914 (directed by Cecil Hepworth); (5) GB, 1921 (director: Thomas Bentley; screenplay: J. A. Atkinson; with Mabel Poulton, Pino Conti); (6) GB, 1934 (director: Thomas Bentley; screenplay: Margaret Kennedy and others; with Elaine Benson, Hay Petrie); (7) as *Mr Quilp*, GB, 1974 (director: Michael Tuchner; screenplay: Louis and Irene Kamp; with Anthony Newley, Sarah-Jane Varley).

THE PICKWICK PAPERS
(1) US, 1912; (2) US, 1913; (3) GB, 1952 (director and screenwriter: Noel Langley; with James Hayter, James Donald).

A TALE OF TWO CITIES
(1) US, 1917 (directed by Frank Lloyd; with William Farnum); (2) GB, 1922 (directed by W. C. Rowden; with J. Fisher White, Ann Trevor); (3) as *The Only Way*, US, 1926 (directed by Herbert Wilcox; with Martin Harvey); (4) US, 1935 (director: Jack Conway; screenplay: W. P. Lipscomb and others; with Ronald Colman, Elizabeth Allan); (5) GB, 1958 (directed by Ralph Thomas; with Dirk Bogarde, Dorothy Tutin).

Not all the above are faithful to the original: the second item under *Dombey and Son*, for instance, is a free adaptation in modern dress; and there are other items which owe even less to Dickens. A 1904 one-reeler, *Mr Pecksniff Fetches the Doctor*, is described thus by Ana Laura Zambrano:

> The film borrows only its title from *Martin Chuzzlewit*. A man is shown quietly sleeping when a nurse wakes him. He dresses, fetches the doctor and waits in an adjoining room. The nurse enters with three babies and the father faints.

Such curiosities constitute nevertheless a minor tribute to Dickens' fame, as in our time do such nomenclatorial oddities as the singer who called himself Tiny Tim and the rock group Uriah Heep.

Early Dramatizations

Many of Dickens' novels and stories were promptly, and some of them repeatedly, adapted for the stage: Professor Patten notes, for instance, that within a month of the publication of *The Cricket on the Hearth* no fewer than seventeen different versions were produced, one of them opening at the Lyceum Theatre on the day of publication. As the following highly selective listing indicates, different adaptations sometimes selected for emphasis different aspects of the work in question, and stage versions were apt to follow very hard on the heels of the published work. The place of production is London unless otherwise stated.

BARNABY RUDGE
Barnaby Rudge: A Domestic Drama, by C. Selby and C. Melville, produced 28 June 1841.
Barnaby Rudge, or the Murder at the Warren: A Drama, by T. H. Higgie, published in 1854.
(See also Malcolm Morley, 'Plays in *Master Humphrey's Clock*', *Dickensian*, 1947.)

THE BATTLE OF LIFE
The Battle of Life, produced 21 December 1846. The printed version indicates that it was 'dramatised from early proofs of the work, by the express permission of the author'.
The Battle of Life: A Drama, produced January 1847.
(See also Malcolm Morley, '*The Battle of Life* in the Theatre', *Dickensian*, 1952.)

BLEAK HOUSE
Lady Dedlock's Secret, by J. P. Simpson, produced 1874.
Bleak House, or Poor Jo: A Drama, by G. Lander, produced 1876.

THE CHIMES

The Chimes: A Goblin Drama in Four Quarters, by Mark Lemon and Gilbert à Beckett, authorized by Dickens and produced 19 December 1844.

The Chimes; in Three Peals, by E. Stirling, produced 26 December 1844.

(See also Malcolm Morley, 'Ring up *The Chimes*', *Dickensian*, 1951.)

A CHRISTMAS CAROL

A Christmas Carol; or the Miser's Warning, by C. Z. Barnett, produced 5 February 1844.

A Christmas Carol; or Past, Present and Future, by E. Stirling, produced 4 February 1844.

(See also Malcolm Morley, 'Curtain Up on "A Christmas Carol" ', *Dickensian*, 1951.)

THE CRICKET ON THE HEARTH

The Cricket on the Hearth: A Drama, in three acts, produced 20 December 1845. The printed version indicates that the adaptation was made 'by the express permission of the author'.

The Cricket on the Hearth, A Fairy Tale of Home, by E. Stirling, produced 31 December 1845.

The Cricket on the Hearth: A Fairy Tale of Home in Three Chirps, by W. T. Townsend, produced 5 January 1846.

(See also Malcolm Morley, 'The Cricket on the Stage', *Dickensian*, 1952.)

DAVID COPPERFIELD

David Copperfield: A Drama, by J. Brougham, produced (New York) 6 January 1851.

Little Emily: A Drama, by A. Halliday, produced 9 October 1869.

(See also Malcolm Morley, 'Stage Appearances of Copperfield', *Dickensian*, 1953.)

DOMBEY AND SON

Dombey and Son, by J. Brougham, produced (New York) 1848.

Captain Cuttle, by J. Brougham, produced (New York) 1850.

(See also Malcolm Morley, 'Enter Dombey and Son', *Dickensian*, 1952.)

GREAT EXPECTATIONS

Great Expectations: A Drama, by W. S. Gilbert, produced 29 May
1871.
(See also Malcolm Morley, 'Stages of *Great Expectations*',
Dickensian, 1955.)

HARD TIMES

Hard Times: A Domestic Drama, by F. F. Cooper, produced 14
August 1854.
Under the Earth; or the Sons of Toil, by W. H. C. Nation, produced 22
April 1867.
(See also Malcolm Morley, '*Hard Times* on the Stage', *Dickensian*,
1954.)

LITTLE DORRIT

Little Dorrit, by F. F. Cooper, produced 10 November 1856.
(See also Malcolm Morley, 'Little Dorrit, On and Off',
Dickensian, 1954.)

MARTIN CHUZZLEWIT

Martin Chuzzlewit: A Drama, by E. Stirling, produced 9 July 1844.
Mrs. Sarah Gamp's Tea and Turn Out: A Bozzian Sketch, by B. Webster,
produced 26 October 1846.
Martin Chuzzlewit, or his Wills and his Ways: A Drama, by T. Higgie
and T. H. Lacy, produced 29 July 1844.
Tom Pinch: A Domestic Comedy, by J. J. Dilley and L. Clifton,
produced 10 March 1881.
(See also Malcolm Morley, 'Martin Chuzzlewit in the Theatre,'
Dickensian, 1951.)

MASTER HUMPHREY'S CLOCK

Master Humphrey's Clock: A Domestic Drama, by F. F. Cooper,
produced 26 May 1840.

THE MYSTERY OF EDWIN DROOD

Lost: A Drama, by W. Stephens, produced 4 November 1871.
(See also Malcolm Morley, 'Stage Solutions to the Mystery',
Dickensian, 1957.)

NICHOLAS NICKLEBY

Nicholas Nickleby: A Farce, by E. Stirling, produced 19 November
1838.

The Fortunes of Smike; or A Sequel to Nicholas Nickleby, by E. Stirling, produced 2 March 1840.
(See also Malcolm Morley, 'Nicholas Nickleby on the Boards', *Dickensian*, 1947.)

OLIVER TWIST

Oliver Twist, or the Parish Boy's Progress: A Domestic Drama, by C. Z. Barnett, produced 21 May 1838.
(See also Malcolm Morley, 'Early Dramas of Oliver Twist,' *Dickensian*, 1947.)

OUR MUTUAL FRIEND

Our Mutual Friend, by G. F. Rowe, produced in New York on 4 June 1866.
The Golden Dustman, by H. B. Barnie, produced 16 June 1866.
(See also Malcolm Morley, 'Enter Our Mutual Friend', *Dickensian*, 1955.

THE PICKWICK PAPERS

The Peregrinations of Pickwick, by W. L. Rede, produced 3 April 1837.
The Pickwick Club: A Burletta in Three Acts, by E. Stirling, produced 27 March 1837.
Sam Weller, or The Pickwickians, by W. T. Moncrieff (i.e., W. T. Thomas), produced 10 July 1837.
(See also Malcolm Morley, 'Pickwick Makes his Stage Début', *Dickensian*, 1946.)

A TALE OF TWO CITIES

A Tale of Two Cities: A Drama, by T. Taylor, produced 16 February 1860 (dramatized with Dickens' assistance).
The Tale of Two Cities; or the Incarcerated Victim of the Bastille, by F. F. Cooper, produced 7 July 1860.
(See also Malcolm Morley, 'The Stage Story of *A Tale of Two Cities*', *Dickensian*, 1955.)

Appendix A   The Autobiographical Fragment

(Dickens told no-one, not even his wife, about the period of his childhood spent in the blacking-factory (for the relevant dates and some details, see pp. 2–3). But some time before beginning *David Copperfield* he embarked on the composition of an autobiography; and in the spring of 1847, as Forster relates in his *Life of Charles Dickens*, a casual conversation that accidentally 'touched a painful place in his memory' led him to confide to Forster 'the story of his boyhood', apparently by giving him a copy of the autobiographical fragment. When he came to write *David Copperfield*, he found (as Forster says) that 'those warehouse experiences fell then so aptly into the subject he had chosen, that he could not resist the temptation of immediately using them'. The autobiography was abandoned, though Dickens refers to it again in a letter to Mrs Maria Winter, née Beadnell, dated 22 February 1855. The most substantial extracts published by Forster in his *Life* are reproduced here.)

This speculation was a rivalry of 'Warren's Blacking, 30, Strand,'—at that time very famous. One Jonathan Warren (the famous one was Robert), living at 30, Hungerford Stairs, or Market, Strand (for I forget which it was called then), claimed to have been the original inventor or proprietor of the blacking recipe, and to have been deposed and ill-used by his renowned relation. At last he put himself in the way of selling his recipe, and his name, and his 30, Hungerford Stairs, Strand (30, Strand, very large, and the intermediate direction very small), for an annuity; and he set forth by his agents that a little capital would make a great business of it. The man of some property was found in George Lamert, the cousin and brother-in-law of James. He bought this right and title, and went into the blacking business and the blacking premises.

In an evil hour for me, as I often bitterly thought. Its chief manager, James Lamert, the relative who had lived with us in Bayham Street, seeing how I was employed from day to day, and knowing what our domestic circumstances then were, proposed that I should go into the blacking warehouse, to be as useful as I could, at a salary, I think, of six shillings a week. I am not clear whether it was six or seven. I am inclined to believe, from my uncertainty on this head, that it was six at first, and seven afterwards. At any rate, the offer was accepted very willingly by my father and mother, and on a Monday morning I went down to the blacking warehouse to begin my business life.

It is wonderful to me how I could have been so easily cast away at such an age. It is wonderful to me that, even after my descent into the poor little drudge I had been since we came to London, no one had compassion enough on me—a child of singular abilities: quick, eager, delicate, and soon hurt, bodily or mentally—to suggest that something might have been spared, as certainly it might have been, to place me at any common school. Our friends, I take it, were tired out. No one made any sign. My father and mother were quite satisfied. They could hardly have been more so, if I had been twenty years of age, distinguished at a grammar-school, and going to Cambridge.

The blacking warehouse was the last house on the left-hand side of the way, at old Hungerford Stairs. It was a crazy, tumble-down old house, abutting of course on the river, and literally overrun with rats. Its wainscotted rooms and its rotten floors and staircase, and the old grey rats swarming down in the cellars, and the sound of their squeaking and scuffling coming up the stairs at all times, and the dirt and decay of the place, rise up visibly before me, as if I were there again. The counting-house was on the first floor, looking over the coal-barges and the river. There was a recess in it, in which I was to sit and work. My work was to cover the pots of paste-blacking: first with a piece of oil-paper, and then with a piece of blue paper; to tie them round with a string; and then to clip the paper close and neat all round, until it looked as smart as a pot of ointment from an apothecary's shop. When a certain number of grosses of pots had attained this pitch of perfection, I was to paste on each a printed label; and then go on again with more pots. Two or three other boys were kept at similar duty downstairs on similar wages. One of them came up, in a ragged apron and a paper cap, on the first Monday morning, to show me the trick of using the string and tying the knot. His name was Bob Fagin; and I took the liberty of using his name, long afterwards, in *Oliver Twist*.

Our relative had kindly arranged to teach me something in the dinner-hour; from twelve to one, I think it was; every day. But an arrangement so incompatible with counting-house business soon died away, from no fault of his or mine; and for the same reason, my small work-table, and my grosses of pots, my papers, string, scissors, paste-pot and labels, by little and little, vanished out of the recess in the counting-house, and kept company with the other small work-tables, grosses of pots, papers, string, scissors and paste-pots downstairs. It was not long before Bob Fagin and I, and another boy whose name was Paul Green, but who was currently believed to have been christened Poll (a belief which I transferred, long afterwards, again, to Mr. Sweedlepipe, in *Martin Chuzzlewit*), worked generally, side by side. Bob Fagin was an orphan, and lived with his brother-in-law, a waterman. Poll Green's father had the additional distinction of being a fireman, and was employed at Drury Lane theatre; where another relation of Poll's, I think his little sister, did imps in the pantomimes.

No words can express the secret agony of my soul as I sunk into this companionship; compared these everyday associates with those of my happier childhood; and felt my early hopes of growing up to be a learned and distinguished man crushed in my breast. The deep remembrance of the sense I had of being utterly neglected and hopeless; of the shame I felt in my position; of the misery it was to my young heart to believe that, day by day, what I had learned, and thought, and delighted in, and raised my fancy and my emulation up by, was passing away from me, never to be brought back any more; cannot be written. My whole nature was so penetrated with the grief and humiliation of such considerations, that even now, famous and caressed and happy, I often forget in my dreams that I have a dear wife and children; even that I am a man; and wander desolately back to that time of my life.

My mother and my brothers and sisters (excepting Fanny in the royal academy of music) were still encamped, with a young servant-girl from Chatham Workhouse, in the two parlours in the emptied house in Gower Street North. It was a long way to go and return within the dinner-hour, and, usually, I either carried my dinner with me, or went and bought it at some neighbouring shop. In the latter case, it was commonly a saveloy and a penny loaf; sometimes, a fourpenny plate of beef from a cook's shop; sometimes, a plate of bread and cheese, and a glass of beer, from a miserable old public-house over the way; the Swan, if I remember right, or the Swan and something else that I have forgotten. Once, I remember tucking my own bread (which I had brought from home in the morning) under my arm, wrapped up in a piece of paper like a book, and going into the best dining-room in Johnson's alamode beef-house in Clare Court, Drury Lane, and magnificently ordering a small plate of alamode beef to eat with it. What the waiter thought of such a strange little apparition, coming in all alone, I don't know; but I can seen him now, staring at me as I ate my dinner, and bringing up the other waiter to look. I gave him a halfpenny, and I wish, now, that he hadn't taken it.

(Forster intervenes at this point: 'I lose here for a little while the fragment of direct narrative, but I perfectly recollect that he used to describe Saturday night as his great treat. It was a grand thing to walk home with six shillings in his pocket, and to look in at the shop windows, and think what it would buy. Hunt's roasted corn, as a British and patriotic substitute for coffee, was in great vogue just then; and the little fellow used to buy it, and roast it on the Sunday. There was a cheap periodical of selected pieces called the *Portfolio* which he had also a great fancy for taking home with him. The new proposed "deed," meanwhile, had failed to propitiate his father's creditors; all hope of arrangement passed away; and the end was that his mother and her encampment in Gower Street North broke up and went to live in the Marshalsea. I am able at this point to resume his own account.')

The key of the house was sent back to the landlord, who was very glad to get it; and I (small Cain that I was, except that I had never done harm to anyone) was handed over as a lodger to a reduced old lady, long known to our family, in Little College Street, Camden Town, who took children in to board, and had once done so at Brighton; and who, with a few alterations and embellishments, unconsciously began to sit for Mrs. Pipchin in *Dombey*, when she took in me.

She had a little brother and sister under her care then; somebody's natural children, who were very irregularly paid for;

and a widow's little son. The two boys and I slept in the same room. My own exclusive breakfast, of a penny cottage loaf and a pennyworth of milk, I provided for myself. I kept another small loaf, and a quarter of a pound of cheese, on a particular shelf of a particular cupboard: to make my supper on when I came back at night. They made a hole in the six or seven shillings, I know well; and I was out at the blacking warehouse all day, and had to support myself upon that money all the week. I suppose my lodging was paid for, by my father. I certainly did not pay it myself; and I certainly had no other assistance whatever (the making of my clothes, I think, excepted), from Monday morning until Saturday night. No advice, no counsel, no encouragement, no consolation, no support, from anyone that I can call to mind, so help me God.

Sundays Fanny and I passed in the prison. I was at the academy in Tenterden Street, Hanover Square, at nine o'clock in the morning, to fetch her; and we walked back there together at night.

I was so young and childish, and so little qualified—how could I be otherwise?—to undertake the whole charge of my own existence that, in going to Hungerford Stairs of a morning, I could not resist the stale pastry put out at half-price on trays at the confectioners' doors in Tottenham Court Road; and I often spent in that the money I should have kept for my dinner. Then I went without my dinner, or bought a roll, or a slice of pudding. There were two pudding shops between which I was divided, according to my finances. One was in a court close to St. Martin's Church (at the back of the church), which is now removed altogether. The pudding at that shop was made with currants, and was rather a special pudding, but was dear: two penn'orth not being larger than a penn'orth of more ordinary pudding. A good shop for the latter was in the Strand, somewhere near where the Lowther Arcade is now. It was a stout, hale pudding, heavy and flabby; with great raisins in it, stuck in whole, at great distances apart. It came up hot, at about noon everyday; and many and many a day did I dine off it.

We had half an hour, I think, for tea. When I had money enough, I used to go to a coffee-shop, and have half a pint of coffee, and a slice of bread and butter. When I had no money, I took a turn in Covent Garden Market, and stared at the pineapples. The coffee-shops to which I most resorted were, one in Maiden Lane; one in a court (non-existent now) close to Hungerford Market; and one in St. Martin's Lane, of which I only recollect that it stood near the church, and that in the door there was an oval glass plate, with COFFEE-ROOM painted on it, addressed towards the street. If I ever find myself in a very different kind of coffee-room now, but where there is such an inscription on glass, and read it backward on the wrong side MOOR-EEFFOC (as I often used to do then, in a dismal reverie), a shock goes through my blood.

I know I do not exaggerate, unconsciously and unintentionally, the scantiness of my resources and the difficulties of my life. I know that if a shilling or so were given me by anyone, I spent it in a dinner or a tea. I know that I worked, from morning to night, with common men and boys, a shabby child. I know that I tried, but ineffectually, not to anticipate my money, and to make it last the week through by putting it away in a drawer I had in the counting-house, wrapped into six little parcels, each parcel containing the same amount, and labelled with a different day. I know that I have lounged about the streets, insufficiently and unsatisfactorily fed. I know that, but for the mercy of God, I might easily have been, for any care that was taken of me, a little robber or a little vagabond.

But I held some station at the blacking warehouse too. Besides that my relative at the counting-house did what a man so occupied, and dealing with a thing so anomalous, could, to treat me as one upon a different footing from the rest, I never said, to man or boy, how it was that I came to be there, or gave the least indication of being sorry that I was there. That I suffered in secret, and that I suffered exquisitely, no one ever knew but I. How much I suffered, it is, as I have said already, utterly beyond my power to tell. No man's imagination can overstep the reality. But I kept my own counsel, and I did my work. I knew from the first that, if I could not do my work as well as any of the rest, I could not hold myself above a slight and contempt. I soon became at least as expeditious and as skilful with my hands as either of the other boys. Though perfectly familiar with them, my conduct and manners were different enough from theirs to place a space between us. They, and the men, always spoke of me as 'the young gentleman.' A certain man (a soldier once) named Thomas, who was the foreman, and another named Harry, who was the carman and wore a red jacket, used to call me 'Charles' sometimes, in speaking to me; but I think it was mostly when we were very confidential, and when I had made some efforts to entertain them over our work with the results of some of the old readings, which were fast perishing out of my mind. Poll Green uprose once, and rebelled against the 'young-gentleman' usage; but Bob Fagin settled him speedily.

My rescue from this kind of existence I considered quite hopeless, and abandoned as such, altogether; though I am solemnly convinced that I never, for one hour, was reconciled to it, or was otherwise than miserably unhappy. I felt keenly, however, the being so cut off from my parents, my brothers, and sisters; and, when my day's work was done, going home to such a miserable blank; and *that*, I thought, might be corrected. One Sunday night I remonstrated with my father on this head, so pathetically and with so many tears, that his kind nature gave way. He began to think that it was not quite right. I do believe he had never thought so before, or thought about it. It was the first remonstrance I had ever made about my lot, and perhaps it opened up a little more than I intended. A back-attic was found for me at the house of an insolvent court agent, who lived in Lant Street in the Borough, where Bob Sawyer lodged many years afterwards. A bed and bedding were sent over for me, and made up on the floor. The little window had a pleasant prospect of a timber-yard; and when I took possession of my new abode, I thought it was a Paradise . . . .
[Forster notes at this point a hiatus in the narrative which he tries to make good with fragmentary evidence from Dickens' letters and from his own recollections.]

Bob Fagin was very good to me on the occasion of a bad attack of my old disorder. I suffered such excruciating pain that time, that they made a temporary bed of straw in my old recess in the counting-house, and I rolled about on the floor, and Bob filled empty blacking-bottles with hot water, and applied relays of them to my side, half the day. I got better, and quite easy towards evening; but Bob (who was much bigger and older than I) did not like the idea of my going home alone, and took me under his protection. I was too proud to let him know about the prison; and after making several efforts to get rid of him, to all of which Bob Fagin in his goodness was deaf, shook hands with him on the steps of a house near Southwark Bridge on the Surrey side, making believe that I lived there. As a finishing piece of reality in case of his looking back, I knocked at the door, I recollect, and asked, when the woman opened it, if that was Mr. Robert Fagin's house . . . .

My usual way home was over Blackfriars Bridge, and down that turning in the Blackfriars Road which has Rowland Hill's chapel on one side, and the likeness of a golden dog licking a golden pot over a shop door on the other. There are a good many little low-browed old shops in that street, of a wretched kind; and some are unchanged now. I looked into one a few weeks ago, where I used to buy boot-laces on Saturday nights, and saw the corner where I once sat down on a stool to have a pair of ready-made half-boots fitted on. I have been seduced more than once, in that street on a Saturday night, by a show-van at a corner; and have gone in, with a very motley assemblage, to see the Fat Pig, the Wild Indian, and the Little Lady. There were two or three hat-manufactories there, then (I think they are there still); and among the things which, encountered anywhere, or under any circumstances, will instantly recall that time, is the smell of hat-making . . . .

It was necessary, as a matter of form, that the clothes I wore should be seen by the official appraiser. I had a half-holiday to enable me to call upon him, at his own time, at a house somewhere beyond the Obelisk. I recollect his coming out to look at me with his mouth full, and a strong smell of beer upon him, and saying good-naturedly that 'that would do,' and 'it was all right.' Certainly the hardest creditor would not have been disposed (even if he had been legally entitled) to avail himself of my poor white hat, little jacket, or corduroy trowsers. But I had a fat old silver watch in my pocket, which had been given me by my grandmother before the blacking days, and I had entertained my doubts as I went along whether that valuable possession might not bring me over the twenty pounds. So I was greatly relieved, and made him a bow of acknowledgment as I went out . . . .

I was such a little fellow, with my poor white hat, little jacket, and corduroy trowsers, that frequently, when I went into the bar of a strange public-house for a glass of ale or porter to wash down the saveloy and the loaf I had eaten in the street, they didn't like to give it me. I remember, one evening (I had been somewhere for my father, and was going back to the Borough over Westminster Bridge), that I went into a public-house in Parliament Street, which is still there though altered, at the corner of the short street

leading into Cannon Row, and said to the landlord behind the
bar, 'What is your very best—the VERY *best*—ale, a glass?' For,
the occasion was a festive one, for some reason: I forget why. It
may have been my birthday, or somebody else's. 'Twopence,'
says he. 'Then,' says I, 'just draw me a glass of that, if you please,
with a good head to it.' The landlord looked at me, in return, over
the bar, from head to foot, with a strange smile on his face; and
instead of drawing the beer, looked round the screen and said
something to his wife, who came out from behind it, with her
work in her hand, and joined him in surveying me. Here we
stand, all three, before me now, in my study in Devonshire
Terrace. The landlord, in his shirt-sleeves, leaning against the
bar window-frame; his wife, looking over the little half-door; and
I, in some confusion, looking up at them from outside the
partition. They asked me a good many questions, as what my
name was, how old I was, where I lived, how I was employed, etc.
To all of which, that I might commit nobody, I invented
appropriate answers. They served me with the ale, though I
suspect it was not the strongest on the premises; and the landlord's
wife, opening the little half-door and bending down, gave me a
kiss that was half-admiring and half-compassionate, but all
womanly and good, I am sure . . . .

I mention the circumstance because it illustrates, to me, my
early interest in observing people. When I went to the
Marshalsea of a night, I was always delighted to hear from my
mother what she knew about the histories of the different debtors
in the prison; and when I heard of this approaching ceremony, I
was so anxious to see them all come in, one after another (though
I knew the greater part of them already, to speak to, and they
me), that I got leave of absence on purpose, and established
myself in a corner, near the petition. It was stretched out, I
recollect, on a great ironing-board, under the window, which in
another part of the room made a bedstead at night. The internal
regulations of the place, for cleanliness and order, and for the
government of a common room in the ale-house, where hot
water and some means of cooking, and a good fire, were provided
for all who paid a very small subscription, were excellently
administered by a governing committee of debtors, of which my
father was chairman for the time being. As many of the principal
officers of this body as could be got into the small room without
filling it up supported him, in front of the petition; and my old

friend Captain Porter (who had washed himself, to do honour to so solemn an occasion) stationed himself close to it, to read it to all who were unacquainted with its contents. The door was then thrown open, and they began to come in, in a long file; several waiting on the landing outside, while one entered, affixed his signature, and went out. To everybody in succession Captain Porter said, 'Would you like to hear it read?' If he weakly showed the least disposition to hear it, Captain Porter, in a loud, sonorous voice, gave him every word of it. I remember a certain luscious roll he gave to such words as 'Majesty—gracious Majesty—your gracious Majesty's unfortunate subjects—your Majesty's well-known munificence'—as if the words were something real in his mouth, and delicious to taste: my poor father meanwhile listening with a little of an author's vanity, and contemplating (not severely) the spikes on the opposite wall. Whatever was comical in this scene, and whatever was pathetic, I sincerely believe I perceived in my corner, whether I demonstrated or not, quite as well as I should perceive it now. I made out my own little character and story for every man who put his name to the sheet of paper. I might be able to do that now, more truly: not more earnestly, or with a closer interest. Their different peculiarities of dress, of face, of gait, of manner, were written indelibly upon my memory. I would rather have seen it than the best play ever played; and I thought about it afterwards, over the pots of paste-blacking, often and often. When I looked, with my mind's eye, into the Fleet Prison during Mr. Pickwick's incarceration, I wonder whether half a dozen men were wanting from the Marshalsea crowd that came filing in again, to the sound of Captain Porter's voice! . . .

I am not sure that it was before this time, or after it, that the blacking warehouse was removed to Chandos Street, Covent Garden. It is no matter. Next to the shop at the corner of Bedford Street, in Chandos Street, are two rather old-fashioned houses and shops adjoining one another. They were one then, or thrown into one, for the blacking business; and had been a butter shop. Opposite to them was, and is, a public-house, where I got my ale, under these new circumstances. The stones in the street may be smoothed by my small feet going across to it at dinner-time, and back again. The establishment was larger now, and we had one or two new boys. Bob Fagin and I had attained to great dexterity in tying up the pots. I forget how many we could do in five minutes.

We worked, for the light's sake, near the second window as you come from Bedford Street; and we were so brisk at it, that the people used to stop and look in. Sometimes there would be quite a little crowd there. I saw my father coming in at the door one day when we were very busy, and I wondered how he could bear it.

Now, I generally had my dinner in the warehouse. Sometimes I brought it from home, so I was better off. I see myself coming across Russell Square from Somers Town, one morning, with some cold hotch-potch in a small basin tied up in a handkerchief. I had the same wanderings about the streets as I used to have, and was just as solitary and self-dependent as before; but I had not the same difficulty in merely living. I never, however, heard a word of being taken away, or of being otherwise than quite provided for.

At last, one day, my father and the relative so often mentioned quarrelled; quarrelled by letter, for I took the letter from my father to him which caused the explosion, but quarrelled very fiercely. It was about me. It may have had some backward reference, in part, for anything I know, to my employment at the window. All I am certain of is that, soon after I had given him the letter, my cousin (he was a sort of cousin, by marriage) told me he was very much insulted about me; and that it was impossible to keep me, after that. I cried very much, partly because it was so sudden, and partly because in his anger he was violent about my father, though gentle to me. Thomas, the old soldier, comforted me, and said that he was sure it was for the best. With a relief so strange that it was like oppression, I went home.

My mother set herself to accommodate the quarrel, and did so next day. She brought home a request for me to return next morning, and a high character of me, which I am very sure I deserved. My father said I should go back no more, and should go to school. I do not write resentfully or angrily: for I know how all these things have worked together to make me what I am: but I never afterwards forgot, I never shall forget, I never can forget, that my mother was warm for my being sent back.

From that hour until this at which I write, no word of that part of my childhood which I have now gladly brought to a close, has passed my lips to any human being. I have no idea how long it lasted; whether for a year, or much more, or less. From that hour, until this, my father and my mother have been stricken dumb upon it. I have never heard the least allusion to it, however far off and remote, from either of them. I have never, until I now impart it to this paper, in any burst of confidence with anyone, my own wife not excepted, raised the curtain I then dropped, thank God.

Until old Hungerford Market was pulled down, until old Hungerford Stairs were destroyed, and the very nature of the ground changed, I never had the courage to go back to the place where my servitude began. I never saw it. I could not endure to go near it. For many years, when I came near to Robert Warrens' in the Strand, I crossed over to the opposite side of the way, to avoid a certain smell of the cement they put upon the blacking-corks, which reminded me of what I was once. It was a very long time before I liked to go up Chandos Street. My old way home by the Borough made me cry, after my eldest child could speak.

In my walks at night I have walked there often, since then, and by degrees I have come to write this. It does not seem a tithe of what I might have written, or of what I meant to write.

Appendix B   Dickens' Separation from his Wife

Dickens and Kate separated early in May 1858. On 12 June Dickens published on the front page of *Household Words* a statement headed 'Personal', signed with his name and reproduced in full below. On 29 May he had written to Arthur Smith – the manager for his reading tours – a letter to which he had attached a covering note stating that 'You have not only my full permission to show this, but I beg you to show it to anyone who wishes to do me right.' This letter appeared in the *New York Tribune* on 16 August, and was copied by some English newspapers – to the chagrin of Dickens, who referred to it as a 'violated letter' and wrote to his solicitor on 5 September that he wished Kate to know that he was 'no consenting party to this publication'.

1   THE *HOUSEHOLD WORDS* STATEMENT

Personal

Three-and-twenty years have passed since I entered on my present relations with the Public. They began when I was so young, that I find them to have existed for nearly a quarter of a century.

Through all that time I have tried to be as faithful to the Public, as they have been to me. It was my duty never to trifle with them, or deceive them, or presume upon their favour, or do any thing with it but work hard to justify it. I have always endeavoured to discharge that duty.

My conspicuous position has often made me the subject of fabulous stories and unaccountable statements. Occasionally, such things have chafed me, or even wounded me; but, I have always accepted them as the shadows inseparable from the light of my notoriety and success. I have never obtruded any such personal uneasiness of mine, upon the generous aggregate of my audience.

For the first time in my life, and I believe for the last, I now deviate from the principle I have so long observed, by presenting myself in my own Journal in my own private character, and entreating all my brethren (as they deem that they have reason to think well of me, and to know that I am a man who has ever been unaffectedly true to our common calling), to lend their aid to the dissemination of my present words.

Some domestic trouble of mine, of longstanding, on which I will make no further remark than that it claims to be respected, as being of a sacredly private nature, has lately been brought to an arrangement, which involves no anger or ill-will of any kind, and the whole origin, progress, and surrounding circumstances of which have been, throughout, within the knowledge of my children. It is amicably composed, and its details have now but to be forgotten by those concerned in it.

By some means, arising out of wickedness, or out of folly, or out of inconceivable wild chance, or out of all three, this trouble has been made the occasion of misrepresentations, most grossly false, most monstrous, and most cruel—involving, not only me, but innocent persons dear to my heart, and innocent persons of whom I have no knowledge, if, indeed, they have any existence—and so widely spread, that I doubt if one reader in a thousand will peruse these lines, by whom some touch of the breath of these slanders will not have passed, like an unwholesome air.

Those who know me and my nature, need no assurance under my hand that such calumnies are as irreconcileable with me, as they are, in their frantic incoherence, with one another. But, there is a great multitude who know me through my writings, and who do not know me otherwise; and I cannot bear that one of them should be left in doubt, or hazard of doubt, through my poorly shrinking from taking the unusual means to which I now resort, of circulating the Truth.

I most solemnly declare, then—and this I do, both in my own name and in my wife's name—that all the lately whispered rumours touching the trouble at which I have glanced, are abominably false. And that whosoever repeats one of them after this denial, will lie as wilfully and as foully as it is possible for any false witness to lie, before Heaven and earth.

2 THE 'VIOLATED LETTER'

Mrs. Dickens and I lived unhappily together for many years. Hardly anyone who has known us intimately can fail to have known that we are in all respects of character and temperament wonderfully unsuited to each other. I suppose that no two people, not vicious in themselves, ever were joined together who had a greater difficulty in understanding one another, or who had less in common . . . .

Nothing has, on many occasions, stood between us and a separation but Mrs Dickens's sister, Georgina Hogarth. From the age of fifteen she has devoted herself to our house and our children. She has been their playmate, nurse, instructress, friend, protectress, adviser and companion . . . . Mrs Dickens has often expressed to her her sense of her affectionate care and devotion in the house never more strongly than within the last twelve months.

For some years past, Mrs Dickens has been in the habit of representing to me that it would be better for her to go away and live apart; that her always increasing estrangement made a mental disorder under which she sometimes labours—more, that she felt herself unfit for the life she had to lead as my wife, and that she would be better far away. I have uniformly replied that we must bear our misfortune, and fight the fight out to the end; that the children were the first consideration, and that I feared they must bind us together 'in appearance'.

At length, within these three weeks, it was suggested to me by Forster that, even for their sakes, it would surely be better to reconstruct and rearrange their unhappy home. I empowered him to treat with Mrs Dickens, as the friend of both of us for one-and-twenty years. Mrs Dickens wished to add, on her part, Mark Lemon, and did so. On Saturday last, Lemon wrote to Forster that Mrs Dickens 'gratefully and thankfully accepted' the terms I proposed to her. Of the pecuniary part of them, I will only say that I believe they are as generous as if Mrs Dickens were a lady of distinction and I a man of fortune. The remaining parts of them are easily described—my eldest boy to live with Mrs Dickens and take care of her; my eldest girl to keep my house; both my girls, and all my children but the eldest son, to live with me, in the continued companionship of their aunt Georgina . . . .

Two wicked persons, who should have spoken very differently of me in consideration of earned respect and gratitude, have (as I am told, and indeed to my personal knowledge) coupled with this separation the name of a young lady for whom I have great attachment and regard. I will not repeat her name—I honour it too much. Upon my soul and honour, there is not on this earth a more virtuous and spotless creature than that young lady. I know her to be innocent and pure, and as good as my own dear daughters. Further, I am quite sure that Mrs Dickens having received this assurance from me, must now believe it, in the respect I know her to have for me, and in the perfect confidence I know her in her better moments to repose in my truthfulness.

On this head, again, there is not a shadow of doubt or concealment between my children and me. All is open and plain among us, as though we were brothers and sisters. They are perfectly certain that I would not deceive them, and the confidence among us is without a fear.

Appendix C   Dickens' Will

(Reproduced from Forster's biography. According to Forster, Dickens left about £93,000.)

I, CHARLES DICKENS, of Gadshill Place, Higham in the county of Kent, hereby revoke all my former Wills and Codicils and declare this to be my last Will and Testament. I give the sum of £1000 free of legacy duty to Miss Ellen Lawless Ternan, late of Houghton Place, Ampthill Square, in the county of Middlesex. I GIVE the sum of £19 19 0 to my faithful servant Mrs. Anne Cornelius. I GIVE the sum of £19 19 0 to the daughter and only child of the said Mrs. Anne Cornelius. I GIVE the sum of £19 19 0 to each and every domestic servant, male and female, who shall be in my employment at the time of my decease, and shall have been in my employment for a not less period of time than one year. I GIVE the sum of £1000 free of legacy duty to my daughter Mary Dickens. I also give to my said daughter an annuity of £300 a year, during her life, if she shall so long continue unmarried; such annuity to be considered as accruing from day to day, but to be payable half-yearly, the first of such half-yearly payments to be made at the expiration of six months next after my decease. If my said daughter Mary shall marry, such annuity shall cease; and in that case, but in that case only, my said daughter shall share with my other children in the provision hereinafter made for them. I GIVE to my dear sister-in-law Georgina Hogarth the sum of £8000 free of legacy duty. I also give to the said Georgina Hogarth all my personal jewellery not hereinafter mentioned, and all the little familiar objects from my writing-table and my room, and she will know what to do with those things. I ALSO GIVE to the said Georgina Hogarth all my private papers whatsoever and wheresoever, and I leave her my grateful blessing as the best and truest friend man ever had. I GIVE to my eldest son Charles my library of printed books, and my engravings and prints; and I also give to my son Charles the silver salver presented to me at Birmingham, and the silver cup presented to me at Edinburgh, and my shirt studs, shirt pins, and sleeve buttons. AND I BEQUEATH unto my said son Charles and my son Henry Fielding Dickens, the sum of £8000 upon trust to invest the same, and from time to time to vary the investments thereof, and to pay the annual income thereof to my wife during her life, and after her decease the said sum of £8000 and the investments thereof shall be in trust for my children (but subject as to my daughter Mary to the proviso hereinbefore contained) who being a son or sons shall have attained or shall attain the age of twenty-one years, or being a daughter or daughters shall have attained or shall attain that age or be previously married, in equal shares if more than one. I GIVE my watch (the gold repeater presented to me at Coventry), and I give the chains and seals and all appendages I have worn with it, to my dear and trusty friend John Forster, of Palace Gate House, Kensington, in the county of Middlesex aforesaid; and I also give to the said John Forster such manuscripts of my published works as may be in my possession at the time of my decease. AND I DEVISE AND BEQUEATH all my real and personal estate (except such as is vested in me as a trustee or mortgagee) unto the said Georgina Hogarth and the said John Forster, their heirs, executors, administrators, and assigns respectively, upon trust that they the said Georgina Hogarth and John Forster, or the survivor of them or the executors or administrators of such survivor, do and shall, at their, his, or her uncontrolled and irresponsible direction, either proceed to an immediate sale or conversion into money of the said real and personal estate (including my copyrights), or defer and postpone any sale or conversion into money, till such time or times as they, he, or she shall think fit, and in the meantime may manage and let the said real and personal estate (including my copyrights), in such manner in all respects as I myself could do, if I were living and acting therein; it being my intention that the trustees or trustee for the time being of this my Will shall have the fullest power over the said real and personal estate which I can give to them, him, or her. AND I DECLARE that, until the said real and personal estate shall be sold and converted into money, the rents and annual income thereof respectively shall be paid and applied to the person or persons in the manner and for the purposes to whom

and for which the annual income of the monies to arise from the
sale or conversion thereof into money would be payable or
applicable under this my Will in case the same were sold or
converted into money. AND I DECLARE that my real estate shall
for the purposes of this my Will be considered as converted into
personalty upon my decease. AND I DECLARE that the said trustees
or trustee for the time being, do and shall, with and out of the
monies which shall come to their, his, or her hands, under or by
virtue of this my Will and the trusts thereof pay my just debts,
funeral and testamentary expenses, and legacies. AND I DECLARE
that the said trust funds or so much thereof as shall remain after
answering the purposes aforesaid, and the annual income thereof,
shall be in trust for all my children (but subject as to my daughter
Mary to the proviso hereinbefore contained), who being a son or
sons shall have attained or shall attain the age of twenty-one
years, and being a daughter or daughters shall have attained or
shall attain that age or be previously married, in equal shares if
more than one. PROVIDED ALWAYS, that, as regards my copyrights
and the produce and profits thereof, my said daughter Mary,
notwithstanding the proviso hereinbefore contained with reference to her, shall share with my other children therein
whether she be married or not. AND I DEVISE the estates vested
in me at my decease as a trustee or mortgagee unto the use
of the said Georgina Hogarth and John Forster, their heirs
and assigns, upon the trusts and subject to the equities
affecting the same respectively. AND I APPOINT the said GEORGINA
HOGARTH and JOHN FORSTER executrix and executor of this my
Will, and GUARDIANS of the persons of my children during their
respective minorities. AND LASTLY, as I have now set down the
form of words which my legal advisers assure me are necessary to
the plain objects of this my Will, I solemnly enjoin my dear
children always to remember how much they owe to the said
Georgina Hogarth, and never to be wanting in a grateful and
affectionate attachment to her, for they know well that she has
been, through all the stages of their growth and progress, their
ever useful self-denying and devoted friend. AND I DESIRE here
simply to record the fact that my wife, since our separation by
consent, has been in the receipt from me of an annual income of
£600, while all the great charges of a numerous and expensive
family have devolved wholly upon myself. I emphatically direct
that I be buried in an inexpensive, unostentatious, and strictly

private manner; that no public announcement be made of the time or place of my burial; that at the utmost not more than three plain mourning coaches be employed; and that those who attend my funeral wear no scarf, cloak, black bow, long hat-band, or other such revolting absurdity. I DIRECT that my name be inscribed in plain English letters on my tomb, without the addition of 'Mr.' or 'Esquire.' I conjure my friends on no account to make me the subject of any monument, memorial, or testimonial whatever. I rest my claims to the remembrance of my country upon my published works, and to the remembrance of my friends upon their experience of me in addition thereto. I commit my soul to the mercy of God through our Lord and Saviour Jesus Christ, and I exhort my dear children humbly to try to guide themselves by the teaching of the New Testament in its broad spirit, and to put no faith in any man's narrow construction of its letter here or there. IN WITNESS whereof I the said Charles Dickens, the testator, have to this my last Will and Testament set my hand this 12th day of May in the year of our Lord 1869.

CHARLES DICKENS . . . .

I, CHARLES DICKENS of Gadshill Place near Rochester in the county of Kent Esquire declare this to be a Codicil to my last Will and Testament which Will bears date the 12th day of May 1869. I GIVE to my son Charles Dickens the younger all my share and interest in the weekly journal called *All the Year Round*, which is now conducted under Articles of Partnership made between me and William Henry Wills and the said Charles Dickens the younger, and all my share and interest in the stereotypes stock and other effects belonging to the said partnership, he defraying my share of all debts and liabilities of the said partnership which may be outstanding at the time of my decease, and in all other respects I confirm my said Will. IN WITNESS whereof I have hereunto set my hand the 2nd day of June in the year of our Lord 1870.

CHARLES DICKENS . . . .

Appendix D   The Berg Notebook

During his later years Dickens kept a notebook, now in the Berg Collection at the New York Public Library, in which he recorded ideas for use in his fiction. According to Forster, who has a chapter discussing it ('Hints for Books Written and Unwritten': Book Ninth, Chapter VII), Dickens made the first entry 'in January 1855, six months before the first page of *Little Dorrit* was written'. H. P. Sucksmith has said that the ideas noted therein include 'character traits, the "germs" of plots and incidents, scraps of dialogue and occasional settings for a story'. Sucksmith adds that 'Almost invariably each idea recorded in the notebook already creates a strong effect', and that 'most of the ideas create either an ironic or a sympathetic effect (or both effects together)'. Notions for titles and names are also included. A good instance of Dickens' interest in the oddities of actual speech is cited by Forster:

> A confidential servant at Tavistock House, having conferred on some proposed changes in his bedroom with the party that was to do the work, delivered this ultimatum to her master. 'The gas-fitter says, sir, that he can't alter the fitting of your gas in your bedroom without taking up almost the ole of your bedroom floor, and pulling your room to pieces. He says, of course you can have it done if you wish, and he'll do it for you and make a good job of it, but he would have to destroy your room first, and go entirely under the jistes.'

Forster quotes several passages later developed in *Little Dorrit*; for example:

> Bed-ridden (or room-ridden) twenty – five-and-twenty – years; any length of time. As to most things, kept at a standstill all the

while. Thinking of altered streets as the old streets – changed
things as the unchanged things – the youth or girl I quarrelled
with all those years ago, as the same youth or girl now. Brought
out of doors by an unexpected exercise of my latent strength of
character, and then how strange!

which is the germ of Mrs Clennam's situation in that novel, and of
an episode towards the end of the book.

Similarly, the roles of Carton and Stryver in *A Tale of Two Cities*
are adumbrated by a succinct note:

The drunken? – dissipated? – What? – LION – and his JACKAL
and Primer, stealing down to him at unwonted hours.

and the eccentric relationship of Boffin and Wegg in *Our Mutual
Friend* is anticipated by

Gibbon's Decline and Fall. The two characters. One reporting it
to the other as he reads. Both getting confused as to whether it is
not all going on now.

The stresses of family relationships appear in

The man who is governed by his wife, and is heartily despised in
consequence by all other wives; who still want to govern *their*
husbands.

and

The agreeable (and wicked) young-mature man, and his devoted
sister.

One wishes that Dickens had contrived to make use of some of the
ideas noted, such as

The man who marries his cook at last, after being so desperately
knowing about the sex.

Like Henry James in his notebooks, Dickens made lists of names
for possible future use, his sources including the Privy Council
Education Lists. These lists illustrate the truism, which Dickens

never tired of repeating, that actuality is stranger than fiction – for the real-life Joly Stick, Henry Ghost, Catherine Two, Miriam Denial and Ambrosina Events are odder than all but the oddest of his fictional namings. Among the lists it is interesting to find some that were actually used; for instance, Pleasant and Bradley, both of which appear in *Our Mutual Friend*.

It should be added that Forster's transcription of the notebook is not entirely trustworthy; an edition of it is in course of preparation.

Appendix E   The Number-plans

Brilliant and endlessly resourceful improvisation was the hallmark of Dickens' earlier work; but for his later novels he paid increasing attention to construction, and evidence for this is to be found not only in the novels themselves but in the memoranda or 'number-plans' that survive for many of them. Their precise nature has been debated, but their general purpose seems reasonably clear. These memoranda are usually of two kinds: a kind of repertoire or stock-pot of ideas (incidents in embryo, characters, names, fragments of speech) to be drawn on in a given number or instalment of a novel, and more detailed jottings organized under individual chapter-headings. Not surprisingly, the notes tend to become fuller and more detailed towards the end of the book; given the kind of conclusions that Dickens favoured, with rewards and punishments being appropriately distributed and the subsequent fates of even minor characters often being disclosed, some aid to memory was clearly necessary to ensure that no-one was overlooked.

Thus, in his notes for the penultimate number (XVIII) of *Bleak House*, Dickens writes:

All Esther's Narrative? No.
Pursuit interest sustained throughout.
Ending with the churchyard gate, and Lady Dedlock lying dead upon the step.
Mr Bucket and Esther.
Snagsby's and Guster? Yes.
Mr Boythorn? No.
Allan Woodcourt? Yes.
Explain the change of clothes or leave it? Explain it at the last.

These notes seem to show Dickens in the act of thinking on paper, and the manner of proceeding by asking himself questions is very characteristic. In these brief phrases he settles some of the crucial technical questions relating to this portion of the novel: what narrative point of view is to be used; what is to give unity to the 'part'; what is to form its climax (in the event the number closes with the words: 'And it was my mother, cold and dead'); which characters are to be introduced (a recurring problem, for with the large cast only a selection of characters could be referred to in any given number); what was to be disclosed concerning the mysterious circumstances of Lady Dedlock's flight. In the notes for each of the three chapters constituting this number, Dickens (again very characteristically) sets down fragments of dialogue – 'No idea of money – But he takes it though' (Bucket's sardonic comment on Skimpole); 'I have got it by the Lord!' (Bucket's excitement at solving the mystery); 'who will tell him' (referring to Sir Leicester Dedlock); 'Bring her round somehow in the Lord's name!' – which catch the dramatic flavour of an episode.

For the final (double) number of the same novel, the memoranda are naturally fuller. The general notes are as follows, and we can assume that Dickens ticked off each item as he disposed of it in the course of composition:

Richard's death.√
Vholes and Conversation Kenge at the end of the suit.√
Grandfather Smallweed and the will?√
George and his brother. Betrothal day√
Esther and Allan Woodcourt√
Her father. – The letter of instructions George gave Mr
    Tulkinghorn√
Sir Leicester, in connexion with
                    Boythorn√
                    Mrs Rouncewell√
                    Volumnia√
                    Debilitated cousin√
                    George?√
The old girl and the Bagnet family√
Mr Snagsby. No√
Mr Guppy's handsome proposal – His mother. Tony Jobling√
Jellybys and Turveydrop's – Deportment.
Chesney Wold Picture. Sir Leicester and George – Boythorn

obliged to pretend to be still in opposition – Lady Dedlock in
the Mausoleum – without being found very much to disturb
the deceased Dedlocks.
Charley.
Miss Flite and her birds –
Mr Skimpole.

All this, in accordance with Dickens' usual habit, went on the left-
hand side of a sheet of paper, the right-hand side carrying further
notes for the eight chapters.

The opening chapter of *Our Mutual Friend* provides an example of
a scene growing from the sketchiest outline. What I have referred to
as the general memoranda contain the simple phrases

Open between the bridges
It in tow

this time on the verso of a sheet; on the other side, the chapter
begins to take a more definite shape, and the names of characters
and even a crucial piece of dialogue are settled:

The man in his boat, watching the tide. The Gaffer. Gaffer.
Gaffer Hexham. *Hexam.*
His daughter rowing. Jenny. Lizzie.
Taking the body in tow
His rejected partner, who has 'Robbed a live man!' Riderhood
this fellow's name.

Naturally enough, the number-plans for *The Mystery of Edwin
Drood* have been perused with special eagerness by Droodians
hoping for a clue to the outcome. Dickens' notes for Ch. 14 show him
shaping the narrative and reminding himself of important details
that need to be included:

When shall these three meet again?

How each passes the day
Watch and shirt pin   Neville   Watch to the
all Edwin's jewellery   Edwin   Jeweller
                            Jasper
'And so *he* goes up the postern stair'

Storms of wind

The number-plans for *Bleak House* are printed in full in the Penguin edition; those for *Our Mutual Friend* in E. Boll's article cited on p. 231; those of *Dombey and Son, David Copperfield* and *Edwin Drood* as an appendix to the Clarendon edition of those novels. Nothing short of a photographic reproduction, however, can reveal some of the suggestive details of the originals – for example, that the evident use of a different pen and/or different ink indicates that the replies Dickens made to the questions he asked himself were added not immediately but after an interval. The best general discussion of the number-plans is in John Butt and Kathleen Tillotson's *Dickens at Work*.

Index of Dickens' Characters

The following list enables a character to be traced to the novel in which it appears; an entry for each character will be found in the section of this book devoted to the individual novels. For a key to the abbreviations used, see p. xv.

There are well over five hundred names here, representing something like twice that number of characters; and although the list makes no claim to be exhaustive (for there are many characters, especially in the early novels, that appear only very briefly and are often unnamed), it suggests both Dickens' fecundity as a creator of characters and his inventiveness in naming them. Some of the early names have a certain obviousness that recalls Ben Jonson and the eighteenth-century comedy of manners: Verisopht for an effete aristocrat, Grimwig for a cantankerous gentleman, Crackit for a housebreaker and Sowerberry for an undertaker. Others, as C. A. Bodelsen says, 'sound farcical in themselves and would render anybody ridiculous, like a false nose': Snodgrass, Snubbin, Todgers, Wackles, Wugsby, and even Pickwick. Some, like Tupman for an aspiring lady's man, are impudent jokes. Dickens gradually grew out of this style of name and moved on to such hauntingly suggestive namings as Dombey, Merdle, and Vholes. But he never abandoned it entirely; and his last work of fiction includes Rosa Bud and Honeythunder, which one would be inclined to dismiss as improbable were it not that some of the actual names Dickens recorded (see p. 351) far exceed them in outlandishness. It should be added that, as well as human characters, the list includes a horse, a raven, and several dogs.

General Index

Handbook of Psychotherapy for Anorexia Nervosa and Bulimia

The
One Best
Way

THE
ONE BEST
WAY

FREDERICK WINSLOW TAYLOR
AND THE ENIGMA OF EFFICIENCY

ROBERT KANIGEL

LITTLE, BROWN AND COMPANY

A *Little, Brown* Book

First published in the United States
in 1997 by Viking Penguin
First published in Great Britain in 1997
by Little, Brown and Company

Copyright © 1997 by Robert Kanigel

The moral right of the author has been asserted.

*Grateful acknowledgment is made to the following for
permission to use archival materials from their collections:*
Elise W. Carr; Frederick Winslow Taylor Collection,
Stevens Institute of Technology, Hoboken, New Jersey; Kheel
Center for Labor-Management, Documentation & Archives,
M. P. Catherwood Library, School of Industrial and
Labor Relations, Cornell University

Page 676 constitutes an extension of this copyright page.

A CIP catalogue record for this book
is available from the British Library.

ISBN: 0 316 88294 1

Printed and bound in Great Britain
by Clays Ltd, St Ives plc

Little, Brown and Company (UK)
Brettenham House
Lancaster Place
London WC2E 7EN

For Saul Wolshine, Charles Kanigel,
and all the others who worked at
Egyptian Polishing and Plating Works
Brooklyn, New York
1926–1989

CONTENTS

PROLOGUE

Outside, washington lay dark and cold, the thermometer hovering all day near freezing. Inside, within a House of Representatives committee room almost beneath the Capitol dome, Frederick Winslow Taylor faced his enemies. At a long table beneath a high vaulted ceiling the congressmen and labor leaders sat, interrogating him, poking and pecking at him, making him bleed. Earlier, for six hours, virtually nonstop, he'd held forth on the origins of what all America now knew as the Taylor system, serving up autobiography, history lesson, and sermon all at once. That was Thursday and Friday. On Saturday morning, the inquisition had begun. Now, on Tuesday, January 30, 1912, it continued, recessing for dinner, picking up at eight, grinding on till almost midnight.

Taylor was the first efficiency expert, the original time-and-motion man. To organized labor, he was a soulless slave driver, out to destroy the workingman's health and rob him of his manhood. To the bosses, he was an eccentric and a radical, raising the wages of common laborers by a third, paying college boys to click stopwatches. To him and his friends, he was a misunderstood visionary, possessor of the one best way that, under the banner of science, would confer prosperity on worker and boss alike, abolishing the ancient class hatreds.

Taylor was a product of the Philadelphia Quaker aristocracy. Now he faced Congressman William Bauchop Wilson, from the coal mines of central Pennsylvania. And it was Wilson, the committee chairman, a former union organizer battle-scarred by jailings, beatings, and blacklistings, who asked the questions. As a young shop foreman bent on squeezing more from his men, hadn't Taylor set times for each job "in which the work could be done rather than the length of time in which it should be done?"

No, insisted Taylor, it was "a perfectly proper pace."

But, Wilson pressed, didn't the fact "that your people were in better

1

financial circumstances than the average workman remove from your mind the same fear of ultimate exhaustion" faced by the workers?

How, he was saying, could Taylor understand? Taylor had worked beside the men, but was not of them. His father was a wealthy landowner with holdings up and down the lower Delaware. His mother came from a prominent New England whaling family. As a boy, he'd traveled through Europe, viewing Raphaels in Munich, riding veloci-pedes along the lakefront in Lucerne, hiking through the Alps. He'd attended an elite New England prep school. His way through life was smoothed by family connections, sweetened by wealth. What did he, Taylor, know of the worker's plight?

Trim, fit, fifty-five years old, with a thin blond mustache and impe-rious gaze, Taylor was used to deference and respect. He'd burst onto the national scene the previous fall and had been the darling of the press ever since. He lectured around the country. He was Mr. Scientific Management, a name to rival Edison or Ford. But even before, for at least a decade, he'd been accustomed to blandishments of praise from a smaller circle of engineers and industrialists. Followers hung on his word. He'd deliver messianic, hours-long monologues without fear of interruption. In workplaces run in obedience to his design, authority flowed implacably down from the top and brooked no back talk or resistance.

Yet now, commanded to appear before elected officials, he had to explain himself, give an accounting of his views. Since September, the House Committee to Investigate the Taylor and Other Systems of Shop Management had met in four cities, heard from iron molders and machinists, steamfitters, army officers, union officials, other efficiency experts—sixty witnesses in all; testimony taken so far would fill almost 1,400 pages of printed text. The original December 10 report deadline had been pushed back four months. Taylor had done all he could to orchestrate the proceedings—coaching witnesses, closeting congress-man, pelting them with letters, articles, and books. But now events lay beyond his control. Others asked the questions; he answered them. Wilson and the others could take any fool direction they wished. They could play to their constituents, or to the press, or to the unions. They could flit from subject to subject. They could surrender to wild illogic. They could go as their whims, not his, dictated.

At one point, Taylor outlined for the committee what he viewed as a science of shoveling. Materials of varying density—coal, gravel, powdery dirt—demanded shovels of varying size and shape; for each, you wanted one that gave you the 21$^1/_2$-pound shovelfuls that, he had discovered, left you with the largest pile of material at day's end.

"You have told us the effect on the pile," observed John Q. Tilson, one of the panel's three congressmen. But "what about the effect on the man?"

Taylor's strength lay in his zeal and tenaciousness; he locked his jaws around an idea the way a lion did the throat of its prey. But at pirouetting with the sudden turns of another's attack he was not so adept, and he sometimes fell into what he'd later term "traps" laid by Chairman Wilson.

Wilson, who would soon become the first secretary of labor in the Woodrow Wilson administration, had come from Scotland as a boy of eight, gone down into the pits at nine, joined the union at eleven, later organized most of the mines in his district, and ultimately helped shape the nascent United Mine Workers Union. And he believed with all his heart in a say-so for everyone, in workmen having a voice, in negotiation, compromise, democracy. For him, the vaunted Taylor system was just bosses being bosses, driving the men too hard and too fast, making them unwilling victims of an unyielding clock. Elected to the House six years before, he'd helped shepherd through its Resolution 90. "Whereas," it began, "the 'Taylor system' appears to be of such a character and nature as to be detrimental to the best interests of American workingmen, being in its essential parts a "high-speed" process, where none but the strong survive. . . ."

Wilson had grown up black with coal dust. But he was no ordinary rough-hewn miner. Not much for drinking and carousing, something of a loner, he was earnest, fair-minded, idealistic to the point of utopian, and had a philosophical streak to him. "A very smooth old fellow," Taylor called him (though Wilson was six years younger). The two of them clashed at one point over Taylor's wish to define what he meant by a "first-class man." The phrase, a staple of Taylor's rhetoric, was forever getting him in trouble; he wanted to set the record straight.

Don't want to hear it, said Wilson. Whatever Taylor meant by first-class man, what happened to the man who wasn't? That's what he wanted to know.

"I cannot answer that question until I define what I mean by 'first class,'" replied Taylor. "You and I may have a totally different idea as to the meaning of these words."

But, insisted the chairman, "the very fact that you specify 'first class' would indicate that in your mind you would have some other class than 'first class.' "

Mr. Taylor: If you will allow me to define it I think I can make it clear.
The Chairman: You said a "first-class" workman can be taken care of under normal conditions. That is what you have already said. Now, the other class . . .

"Mr. Chairman," put in Congressman William C. Redfield of Brooklyn, "the witness has now four times . . . said that until he is allowed to define what he means by 'first class' no answer can be given, because he means one thing . . . and he thinks that you mean another."

For another half hour it went on like this. Consider, said Taylor, a stable filled with horses. A big dray horse might be suited to haul a coal wagon, a more delicate saddle horse to recreational riding. Would you mount the dray for a ride in the country, or hitch a saddle horse to a heavy wagon? Of course not. The same went for men. Big strong horses for heavily laden wagons. Big strong men for the grunt work of the world. Same thing. Each suited to its destiny. Each, in its own way, "first class."

But "how does scientific management propose to take care of men who are not 'first-class' men in any particular line of work," asked the chairman.

"I give it up," said Taylor, disgusted.

"Scientific management has no place for such men?"

"Scientific management has no place for a bird that can sing and won't sing . . ."

"We are not . . . dealing with horses nor singing birds," said Wilson—and today, most of a century later, we can hear the frustration steaming up from the transcript—"but we are dealing with men who are a part of society and for whose benefit society is organized . . ."

For eight hours, punctuated occasionally by questions posed by other committee members, Wilson went at him. Taylor, who until now had largely enjoyed praise from the nation's opinion makers, now stood in the witness's docket, parrying attacks, snarling at his inquisitors, his opinions contested, his replies interrupted, his life and work picked apart.

During breaks in the questioning, he could step to the single window at the room's far end, and look out over the broad stone terrace of the Capitol to the Mall below. Or else wander out into the marble hallway, and up the steps to the Rotunda, with its paintings and frescoes and friezes, lush with color and history, encircling the great space beneath the dome. By comparison, the committee room was a cell. Eight steps wide, with an alcove at one end and a marble fireplace along one wall, it was more like a large living room than a great public chamber. You could hear a door close, papers rustling. So when the shouting started, it filled the room, echoing from its century-old stone walls.

In his direct testimony, giving a version of the talk he'd given countless times to visitors to his home outside Philadelphia, Taylor had sometimes spoken too quickly and too indistinctly to be heard; the stenographer missed snatches of it. But now, during the cross-examination, no one had trouble hearing him. All that Tuesday afternoon and evening, as lamps were lit over Washington and new logs heaped on the committee room fireplace, the questioning continued, tempers grew short, voices rose.

Ten months earlier, in the same committee room, unions hostile to Taylor had fired their opening salvos. His system, they said, overworked and enslaved the men; denied them a voice; reduced skilled mechanics to common laborers; left no room for the average man, but only the superhumanly strong. Old Samuel Gompers himself, longtime head of the American Federation of Labor, produced a recent *Washington Post* story meant to damn Taylor. At the very steel mill that launched the Taylor system, a plug fell out of a huge ladle filled with molten steel. The men steadying it took fright, threw down their long tongs, and fled. The ladle tilted over, raining death on the men below. Six died. A dozen others were left badly burned. It might be "interesting," Gompers concluded meaningfully, to trace the tragedy's ties to "this sort of system"—meaning Taylor's.

"Organized labor's campaign against all things Taylor," a journalist sympathetic to him later wrote, "was no soft, pretty, plaintive cry, but the cry of those who were out for blood and weren't overly particular how they got it." For most of a year they'd attacked from afar, through broadsides, editorials, and pronouncements. But now their enmity found its target in the flesh. Wilson, though never heard to utter a generous word about Taylor or his system, was among the more temperate of his adversaries. At least two of the labor leaders on hand, however, let loose their rage. What actually was said, and by whom, what curses and taunts, what sneers and insinuations, does not come down to us today; Wilson, who'd earned a reputation as a peacemaker, struck it all from the record. But certainly Taylor, bludgeoned and baited, lost control. "With flushed face," wrote Frank Copley in his 1923 biography, "Taylor flew up at them, hurled denunciations." Wilson shouted for order. Shaken, Taylor left the stand and soon, his testimony over, was on a train out of Washington.

A year and a half before, he had become famous overnight, as an industrial messiah. Now he came away shaking with hurt and rage. Taylor's letters immediately after his Washington testimony seem distant and blurred, as if caught up in someone else's nightmare. A few days later, recuperating at a hotel in Atlantic City, New Jersey, he decided to leave with his wife, who was herself under a doctor's care, on a cruise to the Mediterranean. Little more than three years later, he was dead.

~

Frederick Winslow Taylor, in the words inscribed on his tombstone, was the father of scientific management. To us, that means almost nothing, and says almost nothing about his impact, because the term itself is virtually extinct: "scientific management," as well as its near synonym, "Taylorism," have been absorbed into the living tissue of American life.

Back in 1912, Taylor would ask those inquiring about his system to visit him at his estate outside Philadelphia, then join him for a factory tour. When brought before Congress and asked about factories incorporating his principles, he could cite specific industries, companies, employees. No one today, though, speaks of Taylorized factories, or factories working under scientific management. Because, as the authors of one labor movement history could observe even by 1936, the tenets of scientific management "have been so widely accepted and applied by so many thousands of engineers and managers that they have become commonplaces of American industrial practice." In 1959, two writers used the word "assimilation" to describe Taylorism's impact on Britain; it had become part of British life the way an ethnic minority, say, enriches a culture while disappearing within it.

Taylor's thinking, then, so permeates the soil of modern life we no longer realize it's there. It has become, as Edward Eyre Hunt, an aide to future President Herbert Hoover, could grandly declaim in 1924, "part of our moral inheritance." Taylor's name is not as familiar today as in 1912, when controversy swirled around him and his ideas leaped from every newspaper. And many of the specific industrial practices he prescribed, in their thoroughness and technical detail tedious even to describe, are no longer in use. But scholars and writers who plumb the roots of twentieth-century life inevitably come back to Frederick Winslow Taylor and his pervasive—to many, insidious—influence.

By one definition, Taylorism is "the application of scientific methods to the problem of obtaining maximum efficiency in industrial work or the like." *Or the like.* And in that slight, almost parenthetical extension lies a hint of Taylorism's hold. Because while Taylor got his start in the factories of the industrial Northeast in the 1870s, it's not just industry that bears his imprint today but all of modern life.

Taylor bequeathed a clockwork world of tasks timed to the hundredth of a minute, of standardized factories, machines, women, and men. He helped instill in us the fierce, unholy obsession with time, order, productivity, and efficiency that marks our age. Foreign visitors to America often remark on the rushed, breathless quality of our lives. Taylor—whose life, from 1856 to 1915, almost exactly coincided with the Industrial Revolution at its height—helped make us that way. "Speedy Taylor" they called him in the shop. "I never found Mr. Taylor in any period of relaxation," a colleague once said. "Even when we were sitting still there was always something to study, consider or plan." Always, he was consumed with finding the one best way to grind a tool or shovel coal; and he applied the same principles to highly skilled work, office work, and even to the tennis and golf he played in off-hours.

Taylor left a distinctive mark on American life and the world. He was not himself a classic workaholic; if he worked hard, it was not demonically so. But he quickened the tempo of our lives, left us more nervous, speedy, irritable. Today, news magazines and books with titles like *Timelock* and *The Tao of Time* say that Americans suffer from "time poverty." Whatever their points of difference, all concur that if we obsessively value time, jealously guard what we have of it, and contrive to use it "efficiently," we must look to Taylor for the reasons why.

"Why is it so easy," asked Michael Munley in a 1991 doctoral dissertation, "to hear and see reminders of Frederick Taylor in the brusque efficiency with which affluent American professionals organize their lives . . . [with] personal planning calendars, car telephones, voice mail, [and] beepers to track them anywhere, even on vacation?" No time to stop and smell the roses? Taylor deserves a dollop of the blame.

For populist critic Jeremy Rifkin, in *Time Wars*, Taylor "made efficiency the *modus operandi* of American industry and the cardinal virtue of American culture. His work principles have been transported to every sector of the globe and have been responsible for converting much of the world's population to the modern time frame." Taylor, Rifkin declared, "has probably had a greater effect on the private and public lives of the men and women of the twentieth century than any other single individual."

This is not the overstatement it seems.

Apart from mechanization itself, writes historian Anson Rabinbach, "no other development in the history of industrial work had an impact equivalent to Frederick Winslow Taylor's ideas of industrial organization."

Automation? For author and management guru Peter Drucker, that's just "a logical extension of Taylor's Scientific Management."

Japanese industrial prowess flourished on Taylor's ideas, which reached Japan about when they did Europe. A book dealer specializing in management literature reports that, after World War II, the Japanese saw Taylor's ideas as vital to their nascent economic miracle. "They were buying his books like crazy," he says. In 1961, when Taylor's son Robert visited Japan, he was beseeched by Toshiba executives for a pencil, a picture, *anything* that had been associated with his father. "They wanted to feel or touch," he wrote, "something that Fred Taylor had touched or handled."

Today, Taylorism is intellectually out of fashion, and few admit sympathy with its precepts; one management consultant told me he spent most of his professional life trying to undo Taylor's damage. When John Sculley, Apple Computer chairman, spoke at President-elect Clinton's economic conference in Little Rock before the inauguration in 1994, it was Taylor, along with Henry Ford, whom he invoked to represent the heavy hand from which the American economy must free itself.

But in the meantime, Taylorism lives. A manager at the automobile factory jointly operated by General Motors and Toyota in Fremont, California, pinned its success squarely on " 'the intelligent interpretation and application of Taylor's time-and-motion studies . . .' The reference to Taylor may be jarring," observed a student of the venture, Paul Adler, writing in *Harvard Business Review*, "but it fits." A trade unionist, Mike Parker, interprets new participatory management schemes as "an intensification, not an abandonment, of the essence of classical Taylorism." In *White-Collar Blues*, Charles Heckscher sees middle managers "treated increasingly as cogs in the machine." What's this, he says, but "a kind of Taylorization of management."

Taylor saw knowledge, not muscle power, as the prime productive resource, and today the "knowledge industry" is looked to as the source of most new jobs—while well-paid blue-collar jobs, the kind blending head and hand, disappear. Robert Reich, labor secretary in the Clinton administration, lays this divorce of brain from brawn in the modern workplace squarely at Taylor's door, adding: "One cannot overstate the importance of this split to the way America organized itself" since. When in the 1940s, a labor union commissioned a study of Taylorist time-study practices, its author, William Gomberg, pictured a *Brave New World*-like future in which "the simplification of jobs at one end of the job-rating scale and the increasing demands for skills at the other end would . . . create a society in which only geniuses and morons would survive."

Today, mention Taylor or Taylorism in the right crowd—and the right crowd can be as various as managers, industrial engineers, Old Leftists, historians, skilled machinists, sociologists of work, economists, and industrial relations specialists—and all nod in recognition. At one conference of historians of science and technology in 1991, a scholar commenting on, of all things, astronomy's turn-of-the-century preoccupation with getting more data at lower cost paused and then observed ruefully, "You have to love the notion of Frederick Winslow Taylor organizing observatories . . ." Everyone knew what she meant.

When it comes to the areas of modern life he touched, Taylor is the gold standard against which all else must be compared, the natural benchmark. *La période prétaylorienne*, a French encyclopedia begins its article on work organization; then, inevitably, it's on to *le taylorisme*. One French scholar, analyzing what was seen as an anti-Taylorist drift in industrial management, concluded that in the end "anti-Taylorism is neo-Taylorism." In 1991, an American scholar came to a kindred insight; breaking down management theories after World War II into two presumably antagonistic camps, Stephen Waring concluded that in the end they were merely "opposite sides of the same Taylorist coin."

In 1977, a pair of management scholars, Daniel A. Wren and Robert D. Hay, asked historians of business and economics to rank seventy-one contributors to management thought and practice. Taylor won handily, ahead of John D. Rockefeller, Andrew Carnegie, Alfred P. Sloan, Thomas Edison, and Henry Ford. When the same task was put to members of the management history division of the Academy of Management, Taylor again topped the list, scoring thirty-one first-place votes; the next person down had three.

~

Taylor's credo of rational efficiency has burned its way into the modern mind. As scholar Samuel Haber rightly observed of Taylor, "Many who vigorously disparaged his accomplishment came to share his aspiration. . . . His system had some of the inevitableness and objectivity of science and technology. A Taylor plant became one of those places where an important segment of the American intelligentsia saw the future—and saw that it worked." Taylorism was the express train that, early in the twentieth century, bore us full tilt to the future, one from which, like it or not, we could never get off. Such was its seductive hold that it could seem as if all of modern life was bewitched by a Taylorist demon. Taylor came along and something in his insistent message lodged in the mind, stuck.

It stuck in mine, certainly, when I first heard of him. I was fifteen, reading John Dos Passos's masterful *U.S.A.* trilogy. In it, the novelist used a variety of innovative literary devices to capture the country's twentieth-century pulse, among which was a kind of capsule biography, strung out across the page in irregular lines of text more like poetry than prose. Ford, among seminal figures of the day, got the Dos Passos treatment. So did the Wright Brothers, J. P. Morgan, Rudolph Valentino, and William Jennings Bryan. And so did Taylor. There, in *The Big Money*, the trilogy's concluding volume, I read: *He couldn't stand to see an idle lathe or an idle man. Production went to his head and thrilled his sleepless nerves like liquor or women on a Saturday night.*

And this, where Dos Passos quoted from Taylor's testimony before Congress, recalling his battles with his men: *I was a young man in years, but I give you my word I was a great deal older that I am now, what with the worry, meanness, and contemptibleness of the whole damn thing. It's a horrid life for any man to live, not being able to look any workman in the face without seeing hostility.*

"The American Plan" was the title Dos Passos gave his luminous eight-page portrait of Taylor. But Taylor's vision was "American" only in that it bubbled up from American soil and bore its flavor, not that its influence was limited to this country.

Peter Drucker has called Taylor's perhaps "the most powerful as well as the most lasting contribution America has made to Western thought since the Federalist Papers." When Taylor's immensely influential book, *The Principles of Scientific Management*, first appeared in 1911, it was lapped up for translation into Chinese, Dutch, French, Lettish (the language of the Latvians), German, Italian, Japanese, Russian, Swedish, and even Esperanto. Later it was published in Spanish. In World War I, French premier Georges Clemenceau directed that Taylor's principles be placed in the service of the war effort. An English army officer raptly read one of Taylor's books, which he'd had his mother send him, beside a battle-scarred château on the Western front. "In Russia his name is almost as well known as in America," a college president observed in 1933, and "in every country men who have never heard his name are moving to the rhythm of his thought."

During the first half of the twentieth century, Taylor became the paradigmatic American figure, bearer of a potent strain in modern life, decried by some, lauded by others, but always inescapably American. "The Taylor System is to Europe not only 'an American lesson,' " declared a Finnish professor after Taylor's death, "it is *the* American lesson." A League of Nations document called scientific management "a characteristic feature of American civilization." For Germans enamored of Taylor and Henry Ford during the years before Hitler, Thomas Hughes wrote in *American Genesis*, the prevailing attitude was, "Taylorism + Fordismus = Amerikanismus."

Scholars debate Taylor's influence on Henry Ford's assembly line, though influence there plainly was. But of the two, it may well be Taylor who had the more profound, lasting, and wide-ranging impact. As Yale scholar David Montgomery has pointed out, the assembly line found use only in certain industrial settings; whereas Taylor's contribution was an approach, a state of mind, applicable to every aspect of life. Taylor himself said as much. "The same principles" of scientific management, he wrote, "can be applied with equal force to all social activities: to the management of our homes; the management of our farms; the management of the business of our tradesmen, large and small; of our churches, our philanthropic institutions, our universities, and our governmental departments."

In researching this book I was struck repeatedly by how many strands of modern life wend back to Taylor—in every one of the areas Taylor cited, but in many others besides, including offices, hospitals, libraries, and schools. Look back to 1910 and the first explosion of interest in scientific management and you see field after field absorbing its message. The influence of *The Principles of Scientific Management* "went far beyond the industrial world itself," writes Hubert Zapf; "indeed, Taylor seems to have expressed in his book with almost visionary clarity the general spirit of his age."

It was an age when factories were going up, not coming down; when production, the clamor of things being made, bore the excitement we invest today in Silicon Valley. Hopes for a new era of boundless prosperity surged through American life. Social problems were enormous; but, it was felt, if only enough cool reason could be brought to bear on them, they too would submit. Faith in benign science knew no bounds.

Today, when a home improvement contractor sells a new kitchen, its arrangement, the placement of its appliances, and the like owe something to Taylor and his vision. In 1911, a New Jersey housewife, Mary Pattison, who had formed a women's group to seek ways to reduce housework drudgery and already thought in terms of "elements and factors," came across an article about scientific management. She tracked down Taylor and soon was applying his principles, even his time-study methods. *Add salt and baking powder—10 seconds. Stir and mix dry ingredients—62 seconds . . .* That, of course, was how you made biscuits. Later, Pattison wrote a book to which Taylor contributed the foreword. Influenced by Pattison, Christine Frederick applied motion study to kitchen design and layout, and wrote books with titles like *Household Engineering: Scientific Management in the Home.*

Likewise in education. By the turn of the century, school boards and administrators had already absorbed the business ethos of the day, creating what Raymond Callahan, in *Education and the Cult of Efficiency*, called "a situation of readiness—readiness for the great preacher of the gospel of efficiency, Frederick W. Taylor, and his disciples." Journals and lecture platforms were soon littered with the likes of "The Principles of Scientific Management Applied to Teaching Music in the Public Schools"; sight-reading, wrote one of them, was "an inviting problem for the efficiency expert." To Callahan, application of industrial methods to the schools had tragic consequences. But for better or for worse, Taylor's influence "extended to all of American education from the elementary schools to the universities."

While many of Taylor's principles meant little outside a factory, his broader outlook crossed to other fields largely intact—certainly his emphasis on efficiency and productivity. But perhaps even more, the model of applying scientific thinking to problems that, on their face, were not "scientific" at all, had never been "scientific," and did not seem to lend themselves to scientific methods. In this respect, Taylor's impact was like that of Darwin, Marx, and Freud. Each brought a deeply analytical, "scientific" cast of mind to an unruly, seemingly intractable problem—Darwin to the chaos of life on the planet; Marx to the vagaries of social and economic systems; Freud to the swirling depths of the mind; Taylor to the physical, economic, and psychological complexities of human work. That none of them was, in every way, truly "scientific" made their impact no less profound.

Some, of course, felt misgivings about applying science to these nonscientific realms. A school superintendent entranced by scientific management admitted "momentary doubt" that it could be applied to the education of children. As for "systematizing the household," Martha Bensley Bruere wrote in a 1911 article, it hardly seemed like something you could "reduce to an equation." Still, inspired by Taylor's model, that's just what she set out to do.

And that's how it was in field after field. "Efficiency, Taylorism, and Libraries in Progressive America": this was the title of a 1981 paper by Marion Casey in the *Journal of Library History*. "Scientific Management in American Protestant Churches," by Peter B. Petersen: another typical title. In the science of work, in industrial psychology, management, and machine-shop practice—in all these areas, one expects Taylor to have left a deep imprint. But in so many other areas far removed from business and industry, a look back reveals that something happened early in

the twentieth century to give that field its present form, and that this
something was rooted in Taylor's ideas.

Today it is only modest overstatement to say that we are all Taylorized, that from assembly-line tasks timed to a fraction of a second, to
lawyers recording their time by fractions of an hour, to standardized
McDonald's hamburgers, to information operators constrained to
grant only so many seconds per call, modern life itself has become
Taylorized.

～

Taylor's ideas had a way of breaking loose from their moorings,
drifting with the intellectual currents, and anchoring in unlikely places
far downstream. Scholars have found, for instance, surprising links
between Taylor and a number of literary figures.

For example, critic Hubert Zapf pictured D. H. Lawrence's *Women
in Love*, written during World War I, soon after scientific management
came to wide public notice, as unequivocally influenced by Taylor. In
it, one of the two central male characters, Gerald Crich, installs an efficiency system in his coal mines so in accord with Taylor's vision, and
justified in such similar terms, as to "leave little doubt that D. H.
Lawrence used the historical model of Taylorism" to depict modern
industrialism. Wrote Lawrence of young Crich's mine:

> The working of the pits was thoroughly changed, all the control
> was taken out of the hands of the miners, the [traditional hiring]
> system was abolished. Everything was run on the most accurate
> and delicate scientific method, educated and expert men were in
> control everywhere, the miners were reduced to mere mechanical
> instruments.

According to Zapf, Taylor's vision served Lawrence as a symbol of the
withered, spiritually impoverished materialism he held in contempt.

In Russia, a few years later, Yevgeny Zamyatin described a totalitarian dystopia in his novel *We*, which would be hailed as "the literary
ancestor" of both Aldous Huxley's *Brave New World*, published eight
years later, and of George Orwell's *1984*. In it, Taylor's memory is
revered. Taylor's Tables—the railroad timetables of Zamyatin's day

taken to their ultimate Taylorized lengths—regiment every aspect of life. And whereas Huxley would reckon time Before Ford and After Ford, Zamyatin measured dates A.T.—After Taylor. A professor in Petrograd around the time Taylor's book was translated into Russian, Zamyatin wrote sardonically of a geometric, mathematicized world, where the hours of the day are regulated by the Tables, where men and women walk in lockstep files four across for exercise, where each mouthful of food gets fifty bites. Most haunting of all, as one critic has observed, the people accept the regimentation. "I see myself as a part of an enormous, vigorous, united body," records the hero, D-503, a mathematician and engineer tempted by the unknown, disordered world beyond the Green Wall.

> And what precise beauty! Not a single superfluous gesture, or bow,
> or turn. Yes, this Taylor was undoubtedly the greatest genius of the
> ancients . . . I cannot understand the ancients. How could they
> write whole libraries about some Kant and take only slight notice
> of Taylor, of this prophet who saw ten centuries ahead?

In Austria, about the time of Hitler's rise to power in neighboring Germany, Rudolf Brunngraber wrote a peculiar novel, *Karl und das 20. Jarhhundert*, which American journalist Dorothy Thompson noticed in a Viennese bookshop, bruited about as the European book of the year on her return to the States, and arranged to have published in the United States. In *Karl and the Twentieth Century*, Brunngraber plays out the thin thread of the life of an Everyman, Karl Lakner, against the social crises, army movements, and political machinations of early twentieth-century Europe and America. And periodically, Taylor appears as a haunting figure, a symbol of the cruel, impersonal forces that oppress Karl. Indeed, the opening chapter, "The Maximum of Order," begins with Taylor: "When, at Philadelphia in 1880, Frederick W. Taylor became the first consistent advocate of scientific management, Karl Lakner had not yet been born in Vienna. . . ."

> Fate held him in reserve, with some eighteen hundred million
> others, to live through the most turbulent epoch yet known to
> history.

Mr. Taylor did what he could to straighten the rails along
which that epoch was to run. Our vaunted civilization was his
hobby . . .

For workers touched by Taylor's theories, wrote Brunngraber,

what yesterday had been simply "work" was being transformed
into "industrial management." The boss and his foremen watched
your fingers as though you were a criminal. Tools were continually
being improved; working processes were incessantly being
changed. . . . None of the hands could deny (damn it all!) that the
new methods were better, and yet there was something sinister
about the whole affair.

Each of these novels suggests a grim Faustian bargain. Lawrence's
miners, for example, "were satisfied to belong to the great and wonderful machine, even whilst it destroyed them." Brunngraber's character, soon to throw himself to his death, hears a professor intone that
"Mankind has become the unhappy victim of . . . material superfluity,
to attain which he has sacrificed his inward goods." It is a pact with
the devil these Taylorized souls strike. In each case, much is gained—
regularity, order, material prosperity, efficiency. The mines produce
more, D-503 enjoys economic well-being, and in Karl's world, at least,
"the new methods were better. . . ." But always, beneath the surface, lies
a spiritual emptiness, a something-right-gone-wrong, a cool, quiet
dread.

In *Technopoly*, cultural historian Neil Postman, groping for a date
to mark the onset of the "totalitarian technocracy" he intends his ne-
ologism to represent, considers first the Scopes Trial of 1925, when
Evolution stared down the Bible; but no, he catches himself, not quite
the sense of "technology *as* faith" he seeks. Rather, he selects for the
epochal moment the fall of 1910, when Taylor's ideas first came before
the nation. Those ideas, Postman writes, constitute "the scaffolding of
present-day American Technopoly." And he adds: "In the work of
Frederick Taylor we have, I believe, the first clear statement of the idea
that society is best served when human beings are placed at the disposal
of their techniques and technology, that human beings are, in a sense,
worth less than their machinery."

On the Left, of course, one can scarcely utter Taylor's name without a sneer or shudder, amenities of the capitalist workplace being seen as no more than a cloak for Taylorism's mailed fist. Political scientist Richard Pfeffer, who donned workman's overalls to work in a piston-ring plant, could observe that "Beneath current managerial cosmetics ... the body of Taylorism lives in all its ugliness." In *Labor and Monopoly Capital*, another left-wing critic, Harry Braverman, writes that in the productive world Taylorism dominates, "the practitioners of 'human relations' and 'industrial psychology' are [merely] the maintenance crew for the human machinery."

Thinking out loud about the respective influences of Taylor and Henry Ford, German historian Ulrich Wengenroth, of Munich's Deutsches Museum, slips into a kind of rhythmic dialectic: "Ford exerted control through the machine, Taylor directly on the person. With Ford, the power was behind the veil of a machine. With Taylor the power was blunt. Taylor wanted to improve people. Ford didn't care." And this sense of almost unseemly intimacy in Taylorism's dominion over the individual haunts the imagination of our age. For it conjures up the specter of one human being *exacting his will* on another. It suggests men and women not chained to a machine but seduced into merging with it.

Yet if Taylor were merely a destroyer of souls, some dark satanic stain on modern life, he might captivate us less. But Taylor viewed himself as the workingman's dearest friend, as the Great Harmonizer intent on doing good for worker, capitalist, and public alike. Even today, for every critic who views him as devil, another sees him as saint. And the split doesn't hew to easy left-right lines. Only the slightest shift in perspective, it turns out, changes Taylor's hat from black to white.

In American history classes, Taylor is usually studied along with the Progressive movement; the same workplace practices seen today as crudely authoritarian were by the lights of his own day, at least to some, a model of enlightened reform. His champions included Louis Brandeis, "the People's Lawyer" and future Supreme Court justice, and Ida Tarbell, legendary muckraking journalist and scourge of the great trusts. Several Taylor disciples would take leading roles in the New Deal administration of Franklin D. Roosevelt; indeed, as Robert Reich has noted, FDR's system of national planning, "in which the principles of scientific management would largely supplant the price system," was in part modeled on Taylor's ideas. Lenin, exhorting his compatriots to greater production, wrote, "We must introduce in Russia the study and teaching of the new Taylor System and its systematic trial and adaptation."

Such sympathy for Taylorism need not be seen as some bizarre historical anomaly, a holdover from a past whose inhabitants wore blinders. The world into which Taylor was born enjoyed nothing like the material prosperity of ours, where ballpoint pens are made so inexpensively that they're handed out free; where a color television goes for a day's wages; where all but a small aggrieved underclass, oppressed by cruel historical circumstances, enjoy a material bounty unknown in any previous epoch. Taylor's world was one where making pumps, sewing machines, books, steam engines, springs, stoves, and shirts was *hard;* where cutting things, shaping them, fitting them, assembling them, and carrying them across rivers, mountains, and plains roused the imagination and intelligence of the nation's most energetic citizens. Taylor promised the chance to do all these things faster and cheaper.

Some today see manufacturing as potentially the agriculture of the twenty-first century, an activity destined to engage the interests of as few people, and occupy as culturally peripheral a role, as farming does now. As we push buttons, crunch numbers, send faxes, merge address lists, type contracts, and write books, it can be easy to forget that in the 1870s and 1880s, when Taylor was coming up, making things was not so taken for granted. When he died, his old friend Wilfred Lewis said of him that "no one has done more to raise the standard of living throughout the civilized world as he." Amid the postwar prosperity of the 1950s, British management scholar Lyndall Urwick observed that to Taylor "the United States owe a large, if incalculable proportion of their immense productivity and high standard of living." Both men were, indisputably, right.

And so, decry his influence, damn his practices, and condemn his insensitivity as we may, we cannot forget that some part of our material prosperity can be laid at his door, and that with only a slight shift in focus, Taylor's influence can be seen as primarily a benign one.

It is this murky territory, then, between the dark country to which Taylor's critics consign him and the sunny utopia of his own vision, that compels our attention. Taylor, the author in his own mind of a revolution that would augur a thousand years of industrial peace, was reviled during his lifetime by both labor and management; he still is. A man of immense spirit, intelligence, and tenacity, he managed to alienate, or at least irritate, almost everyone, including many among his own circle of admirers. He was irascible, hard-cussing, forever landing in trouble. Even his sanitized 1923 biography, subject to the ever solicitous blue pencil of his wife and disciples, often refers to his tactlessness and bullish insensitivity. He advanced ideas that, even by the standards of his time, much less those of today's, could seem autocratic and cruel, yet he felt profoundly misunderstood. His declared purpose was to take all control from the hands of the workman (whom he regularly compared to oxen or horses), and place it in those of management, yet he insisted that he aimed only to substitute "hearty brotherly cooperation for contention and strife."

Taylor was not a profoundly original thinker, if by that we mean someone who creates something new where nothing had been before. Though some of his disciples liked to picture him that way, he was no genius in the way Einstein or Picasso were. Rather, he took fragments of thought and practice drifting through the nineteenth century and directed them down one tight channel, focused them, packaged them, sold them as a single idea—and projected it into the twentieth century.

He believed that idea and sold it, without letup, for the best part of four decades. First to the few skilled machinists who worked under him. Then to the rest of the company for which he worked. Then to other engineers, businessmen, and industrial leaders. Finally to everyone else. He sold it with tenacity, purpose, and force, with theatrical flair, in a million words, from a thousand speaker's platforms until, in 1910 and 1911, it burst upon the world.

In Taylor's vision, man and machine worked together like clockwork. In that vision lies the great paradox of modern life. Each day we reap the material benefits of the cult of workplace efficiency that he championed; yet we chafe—we scream, we howl, we protest—at the psychic chains in which it grips us. When young people during the 1960s sniped at the System, it was in part the Taylor system itself, institutionalized in corporate America, that they opposed. It was Taylor, after all, who first said in 1911, explicitly and without apology:

> In the past the man has been first. In the future the System must be first.

And it is.

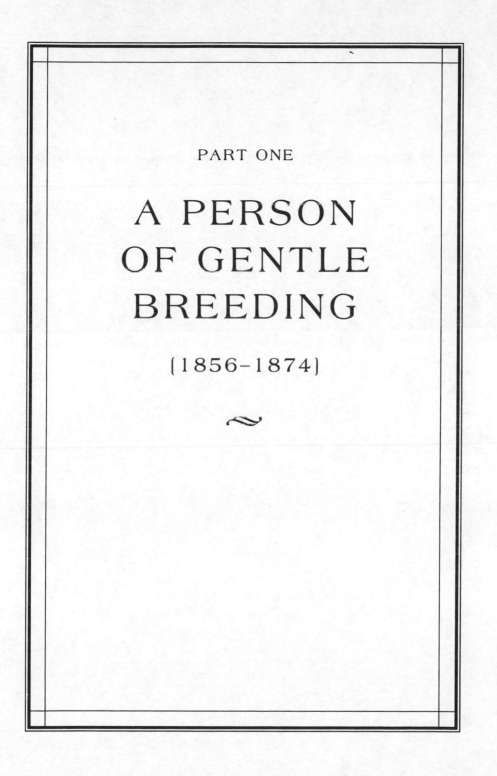

PART ONE

A PERSON
OF GENTLE
BREEDING

(1856–1874)

THE BRIDGE AT FINSTERMUNZ

~

T HEY WERE STUCK AT A SMALL HOTEL squeezed up against the side of a mountain high in the Tyrol, in a corner of Europe where the modern states of Austria, Switzerland, and Italy converge. It was the summer of 1869, and a thin-featured thirteen-year-old boy with straight blond hair, Fred Taylor, was traveling with his family through Europe.

That winter, they had stayed in Berlin. Then, in June, they had headed south for Dresden, Prague, Nuremberg, Munich, and Salzburg. Finally, they'd reached the Alps. In Innsbruck, where individual peaks gave way to a solid wall of mountains, they hired a carriage for an eight-day trip, over the switchbacking mile-and-a-half-high Stelvio pass into Italy, then back into Switzerland and over two other passes to the spa town of Bad Ragaz. For the first two days their route paralleled the Inn, the river that gave Innsbruck its name, along a road flanked by sudden upthrusts of rock to which greenery clung where it could. Higher up the slopes, green yielded entirely to rock, then, higher still, to snow.

If the scenery was unspeakably beautiful, the ride itself was dusty and unpleasant. Hour after hour, the team of horses hauled their heavily laden carriage up the dirt road. But at last, concluding a long, gradual ascent of a stretch of new road hacked from the solid rock face of the mountain, they reached Finstermunz. From their hotel, looking out across the road and beyond a tiny, dollhouse-like stone chapel that memorialized the men who had died building it, they could see Switzerland. South of the Finstermunz pass, not many miles distant, lay Italy.

The Taylors had planned to spend only a night here. But as they slept, a thunderstorm swept over the pass. Even on a cloudless summer day, the Inn, tinged an almost Caribbean blue-green, swept across the valley floor with a roiling ferocity. And the stream at the southern end of the pass that tumbled down a sheer, rocky cliff to feed the Inn was a barely contained waterfall. Now, swollen by the rain, it had swept away the wooden bridge that spanned it, depositing on the road heaps of rock and debris. The road was out. The bridge leading out of the pass was down. The Taylors were trapped in Finstermunz.

On Sunday, July 25, 1869, two dozen local men worked at clearing away what Fred, in his youthful, German-inspired spelling, called "rub-bisch." A twenty-minute hike up from the hotel, the bridge stood beside a stone fortress, all hulking granite and firing slits, built into the cliffs twenty years before. While the men worked—with no great industry, it seemed to Fred—he, brother Winslow, and cousin George climbed amid the tumble of rocks, hiked with their alpenstocks, even joined soldiers from the fort in their gymnastics exercises.

For the boys, it was all great fun. But Fred's father wanted to get going and, by that evening, was losing his patience. He, Fred, and the old coachman they'd hired to drive them through the Alps went up to the bridge site again to check on progress. By then, wrote Fred, "there were but a few common workmen" left, trying to fashion a temporary structure strong enough to bear the weight of their heavy carriage. It ought to be ready, they were told, by noon the following day.

It had better be, Mr. Taylor advised the coachman; if they couldn't leave the next morning, he'd have no recourse but to dismiss him. They would leave him and the carriage behind, and get their baggage carried across whatever ramshackle structure was by then in place, to the vil-lage on the other side. Then they'd continue to the Stelvio in one of the big mail coaches that regularly plied the pass.

Well, wrote Fred, "this stirred the old man up." The coachman returned the next morning to the bridge site, remonstrated with the road crew chief to hurry, conveyed Mr. Taylor's offer of twelve guldens for getting their carriage across, and even shouldered several loads of boards himself to speed progress. By early that afternoon, the bridge was finished, their carriage was borne across, and they were on their way to the Stelvio.

Mr. Taylor had gotten his way.

On almost every page of the journal Fred kept in Europe, money talks, just as it did at Finstermunz. One time, just back in Lucerne from a few days' sightseeing across the lake, they arrived at a boardinghouse during a heavy rain, only to be told by the proprietor they could not stay; there was a three-night minimum. "Father induced her, however," noted young Fred matter-of-factly, "to take us in at a higher price than usual."

A week later, they were riding in a large, open traveling carriage up toward the Furka pass, out of Hospentahl, the little town on the floor of a green, secluded Alpine valley where they'd spent the night. An hour into the climb, with the town a speck below them, there were only the mountains, the fields of wildflowers, the winding road, and the clip-clop of the horses. Their seat backs pressed gently against them with each rhythmic surge of the horses against their harnesses. And then abruptly, eighteen-year-old Edith Wright, with whom they were traveling, realized she had left her watch back at the hotel.

Turn right around and return to Hospentahl? No need. Rather, the Taylors offered a guide they met along the road fifteen francs to bring it back. The guide sped down the pass and within an hour had caught up with them again; the watch was safe, aboard the next mail coach. The day was saved. The boys leisurely explored a glacier's clear green ice. That evening at the hotel, Edith had her watch.

In Europe, as all through his youth, Fred saw money—the promise of its gain or the threat of its loss—bending others to the service of him and his family. The Taylors weren't rich like the Rockefellers, but they were rich enough to experience life in all its sumptuous variety. They didn't wallow in luxury, but they were not ascetic, either. They spent freely to taste life's pleasures for themselves and their children. Money granted them freedom and release, bought convenience, compelled cooperation.

Earlier that year, in Berlin, we "had our windows thoroughly washed up today," wrote Fred. "It makes our rooms much lighter." The Taylors attended the theater. They bought works of art, lace, firearms. They employed servants. They stayed at fine hotels. Later, back in the States, when Fred was off at school and wanted a boat, he got a boat. When his father had a pair of fine boots made for him but worried they might not fit, he wrote to say that Fred could always send them back and they'd have another pair made.

For Fred Taylor as he was growing up, "privilege" wasn't luxury but that richness of experience made possible by means. The Taylors used their wealth to travel where they wished, for however long they wished, to nourish the highest and best parts of themselves, to buy reprieve from the grind endured by legions of the poor. And it all flowed so naturally from their circumstances in life that young Fred would have had to be far more alive to the nuances of social inequality than he was to realize how much it shaped him.

Later, in recounting his life before congressional committees, to college students and businessmen, or in court, Taylor did not deny his privileged circumstances. "My father had some means," he'd allow. But if he noted this fact, he did so in passing, as one among many, immediately swallowed up in his customary account of his days as apprentice, laborer, machinist, and engineer. By the time he became famous, his stint in the shop could seem all of a piece with his status as a gentleman, like two equal weights, occupying opposite ends of a balance scale and emblematic of the evenhanded regard for workman and boss with which he credited himself.

So delicate was this balance that, shift it but slightly and it could seem, as in abridged encyclopedia accounts, as if he'd worked his way up from nothing, Abe Lincoln–style. "He was apprenticed as pattern-maker and machinist in a small Philadelphia firm" one encyclopedia entry had it, without reference to his family's wealth or social position. When Taylor died, a French champion of his views, Charles de Freminville, noted that many had attributed to him "a workingman's mentality" but that this was "an error very promptly dissipated" by the facts.

And a great error it was. When he was older, Taylor did serve an apprenticeship and did work as a laborer and machinist. But by then his values were formed. Looking back upon a period early in their marriage when he and his wife "were obliged to mingle with people from all parts of the country," Taylor would write, "we found the finest kind of men and women living in all ranks of society, and in the smallest and most out-of-the-way places. We both valued this experience, because of the enlarged sympathies it gave us," he concluded, "for our own kind."

∽

Frederick Winslow Taylor was born on March 20, 1856, the second son of Franklin and Emily Taylor, in Germantown, a suburb of Philadelphia. His brother, Edward Winslow Taylor, known as Win, was two years older. A sister, Mary Newbold Taylor, was born in 1858.

As a boy, he attended a Germantown private school.

Around the spring of 1868, when he was twelve, the family traveled to Europe, where they stayed for three years.

Soon after their return to Philadelphia, Fred was sent to Exeter Academy, in New Hampshire. The plan was for him to enroll at Harvard and become a lawyer.

In June 1874, after two years at Exeter, he took the Harvard admissions examination and passed with honors.

But he didn't go to Harvard, and he didn't become a lawyer. He went to work.

These are the raw facts of his early years. Taylor's life, even more than most, draws us irresistibly to this period. For the events that shaped his thinking all took place by the time he was twenty-five, and the great turn in his life, away from Harvard and the law, came when he was eighteen. Until then, his life had proceeded on a comfortably predictable course. Afterward, claiming almost religious insight granted by experiences normally alien to those of his own station, he would set out to preach a new industrial gospel to the nation and the world.

2

BROOKDALE FARM

∼

BUZZING BEES SWARM UNDER THE EAVES of the old New Jersey manor house. Brookdale Farm the place is called. It sits on a low rise at the end of a milelong drive from the main road, a sprawling bay-windowed house of brick. And burned into the bricks beneath the gable are letters several feet high and visible from a considerable distance: T at the gable's apex, A.A. just below, and then 1766.

Anthony and Ann Taylor built it in 1766. Anthony—grandson of Samuel Taylor, who came over from England and settled here in Burlington County, New Jersey, in 1677—was great-grandfather of Frederick Taylor. The land he owned remains within the larger family today, an oddly angled homestead covering a square mile or so, lush with wildflowers, brambles, and greenery, still much as it was in 1766. Or, for that matter, as it was when the British laid it waste during the

Revolution, when Anthony embraced the colonial cause a little too ardently, supplying food to rebel troops. Hessian mercenaries in the pay of the British, family tradition has it, came to arrest Anthony but, finding him absent, left and said they'd return—only to be waylaid by General Washington's army at Trenton.

Fred's grandfather, another Anthony, was born at Brookdale, apprenticed to a Philadelphia merchant, went into business for himself, and formed a partnership with his future brother-in-law, with whom he traded with the East Indies. In 1810, at thirty-eight, he retired with a sizable fortune, settling at Sunbury, another big estate, not far from Brookdale in Bucks County, Pennsylvania, looking over Neshaminy Creek. Comfortably ensconced on Sunbury's four hundred acres, he helped found a bank, Farmer's National, and started buying land in earnest. When he died (before Fred was born) he was the county's biggest landholder.

He was fifty when, in 1822, his wife gave birth to Franklin, Fred's father, youngest of their eleven children. Frank's brother Anthony died at twenty-eight. Brother Robert apparently earned a medical degree but may never have practiced. Brother Caleb became active in Whig and Republican politics, was a delegate to state and national conventions, failed three times to win election to Congress and finally succeeded after the Civil War; later, he became president of the family bank and amassed three thousand acres of land. Then there were brothers William, Edward, Michael, who died in 1833, and Thomas. And sisters Sarah, Mary, who died in her youth, and Emma . . .

And Franklin, the baby. As a child, his mother, forty-three when he was born, was often sick. His eldest sister Sarah—"my almost mother," he described her, a full generation older than himself, to whom "I owe all that I have of good"—cared for him. After attending Doylestown Academy, he went to Princeton, where he was the youngest in a class of eighty students; he graduated in 1840, took up the study of law, and was admitted to the bar in 1844. At least during Fred's childhood, all through the Civil War, Franklin kept an office on Walnut Street, near Independence Square in Philadelphia, but practiced little, if at all.

It was a story common among Old Philadelphia families, particularly those of Quaker stock, as the Taylors were: you'd go to school, earn a degree, establish yourself in a profession like law or medicine, then never so much as draw up a brief or treat a patient. Or else, as variation on a theme, cease practice after only a few years. The true Old Philadelphian, writes Nathaniel Burt in *The Perennial Philadelphians*, "is born retired. His education and training are not designed to make him Get Ahead. He's already Ahead." Burt writes of a William Camac, from a distinguished Philadelphia family. Wooing a girl from a strict Quaker background, Camac had almost won her over—except, she worried, he had no profession. So the lovesick young man enrolled in medical school, got his M.D., and "presented the diploma to his beloved on bended knee. She took him. The formalities over with, he never thereafter did one stroke of medical work."

Likewise for Franklin Taylor. A lawyer by training, he was a gentleman by birth; he didn't have to spend his life poring over legal briefs. Instead, he studied the languages and history that were his love, and served on the board of a school for retarded children.

And, of course, oversaw his properties; that, it seems, the Taylors always did well. Later, it would astound Fred's son, Robert, to see the records of Franklin's estate, consisting mainly of mortgages on farm property in Pennsylvania and New Jersey. "It started off on the first page, mortgage on such and such for so many acres and so forth," listing its value and the interest rate, Robert recalled. "It was $8000, $6500, $5400, $4300 all spelled out, page after page after page. My eyes got bigger and bigger." And then at the end: the total. In an era before income taxes, when a live-in maid earned five dollars a week, its value came to just short of a million dollars—worth, in our terms, ten to twenty million.

Four days after his father's death, at the age of eighty-seven, Fred Taylor wrote his friends with the news: "I can hardly think of any man of his age who will be more missed." Frank Copley, author of the family-sanctioned 1923 biography of Taylor, pictured Fred's father as unwilling to speak about himself; the kind of man so sensitive, so delicate, that in the journal he kept during his courtship, he retreated to French to mask his feelings; who might turn a beggar away from the door, then pause, stand there, wondering whether he had done right. "A very sweet, quiet man, not the least a go-getter," Robert Taylor described him later. Frank Taylor was content—it is mild language as befits a mild man—to be a fine person, a responsible father, a good and loyal friend. Tall and trim, his bald, oval head made thinner in photographs by sideburns culminating in a modest fringe of beard, he was

known for making his carriage available to friends at the slightest sign
of need. When the family went to Europe in the late 1860s, he was there
with his children all the while, strolling through the Tiergarten with
them, or reading Dickens to them at night. He seemed always to have
time. Fred Taylor spoke of his father's "soft, mild manner and a gentleness which was almost that of a woman"—qualities, he took care to
add, which hid "a man of very unusual bravery and strength."

His son was not just being dutiful. When in 1852, James B.
Richards, a pioneer Boston educator of the retarded, came to Philadelphia to start a school, Franklin Taylor helped organize it. Founded the
following year, the Pennsylvania Training School for Feeble-Minded
Children soon migrated from two small buildings in Germantown to a
campus about ten miles west of Philadelphia in Media. By the late
1870s, it cared for three hundred children, some of whom were successfully readied for public school and thus spared, in the language of
one account, "the misery and ejection of hopeless idiocy." That the
retarded could be educated was still a new idea; Frank Taylor's school
was for its time a progressive one. It absorbed his energies from its
founding, when he was thirty-one, to his death fifty-seven years later.
He served as secretary of its board of managers, spoke at official functions, welcomed visitors, helped preserve its history and, one suspects
from the number of his friends listed among its "life subscribers and
donors," solicited financial support.

Frank Taylor was no Milquetoast. Letters written to his son when he
was away at school are peppered with vigorous opinion and firm
advice:

> I am glad that you are in good health and trust that you will be
> careful of your diet without being anxious or fussy, eat moderately
> and of those viands which you know do not disagree with you.
> Keep up your regular exercise and be careful not to strain yourself
> with the heavy clubs. Oft repeated exercise with lighter weights is
> much more advantageous than when heavy weights are used. I
> regret that you did not do yourself more credit in your
> examination in mathematics. But . . . try again without being
> discouraged. . . . I think with care you will do better next time. But
> whatever you do, maintain your self respect. Don't use any trick
> work. In short be true to yourself and good.

Our more skeptical age is apt to greet a performance like this with a smirk, as just more fussy Victorian moralism. But Franklin did not quite hew to type. His letters were leavened by a caring he did not disguise. He addressed them to "my dear son," and signed them with love. In between, he urged Fred to keep warm in the New England cold and asked interested questions: "Where do you all study? Does [brother Win] study in your room or in his? Does he sleep upstairs alone? Has he a fire in his room?" He showed concern for Fred's health, delight at the receipt of his letters. He was no cold fish.

Then, too, right beside the moralizing lay a deep and thoroughgoing tolerance. Even a sermonlike tract he once wrote, "On Self-Control," seemed somehow bighearted. Unattractive personal qualities, he observed, are part of human nature; they can't be rooted out, and shouldn't be: "I do not think that the evil passions which we have should be eradicated," he wrote, "but that they should be under proper control; then they would not be a curse to us, but a blessing."

Franklin's letters staked out the moral high ground but didn't dwell on lapses from it. At one point, Fred cheated on an exam. His father upbraided him but lauded his confession: "I don't believe that you will ever again copy or act unfairly."

Early into his first year, Fred, sixteen at the time, took a book into church, in conflict with school rules. When his father sided with the school, Fred wrote back insisting that bringing a book into church defied no written proscriptions: *Where's it say you can't?* But Fred's nervy obstinacy was, to his father, no reason to condemn but an opportunity to instill values. "I am sorry you do not take a broader, juster view of your rights and duties," he wrote Fred:

> He who limits and guides his activities by the written law alone
> will be very small and will become more and more selfish and
> narrow. There is no written law that men should not smoke in
> drawing rooms, or come in with muddy boots or soiled clothes, or
> should not read when in company, or very many other cases. Yet
> one's educated sense of propriety and what is due to others will not
> allow persons of gentle breeding to do any of those things. . . .
> [Whoever] does so does what is unbecoming a gentleman.

3

"THEE ONLY DO I WANT"

~

IT IS A SLENDER PIECE OF WHALEBONE four or five feet long. A gentle
ridge running along its length supplies a common waterline for all the
whaling scenes carved upon it. Scrimshaw, this folk art is called; sailors
on long voyages used sail needle or knife to carve whalebone or whale
teeth with scenes and designs, then etch them in black, the effect reminiscent of the fine-line work seen on currency.

This one, belonging to Marie Clark Hodges, great-great-grand-
daughter of Isaac Winslow, Fred Taylor's grandfather on his mother's
side, may have been done by a sailor as his ship neared Le Havre,
France, in August 1834, the place and time it records. With a light,
graceful hand, the anonymous artist depicts the little six-man whale
boats approaching the great mammals; a dead whale is being hauled up
beside the ship by a wide strap suspended from two of its three masts.
"Officer Plunging His Harpoon in a Whale," one scene reads in French.
"The Whale in Its Death Agony," reads another. From the main mast
billows a small triangular pennant. And on the pennant, perfectly clear,
the single letter: W, for Winslow.

If the Taylors were content to look after their properties and collect
their 6 percent, Winslows were doers from way back. Even a spare, tele-
graphic sketch of Isaac Winslow leaves you breathless: commanded
whaling vessels at sea, lived for years in France, invented, launched
businesses, financed troublemaking abolitionists, *was* a troublemaking
abolitionist.

Born to Quaker parents in Portland, Maine, in 1787, one of eleven
children, Isaac Winslow was five generations distant from Kenelm
Winslow, who came to America in 1629, nine years after the *Mayflower*
brought two of his brothers to Plymouth Rock; a Winslow House is
included on tours of Plymouth today. Isaac's brother, Jeremiah,
apprenticed to a New Bedford, Massachusetts, family with interests,
like everybody else in town, in whaling.

Bustling New Bedford, home port to hundreds of ships, was the whaling capital of the world. The Quakers who owned the ships and set wages for their crews, writes historian Samuel Eliot Morison, were "as tight-fisted, cruel, and ruthless a set of exploiters as you can find in American history." Jeremiah himself was soon one of them (an owner, that is; we don't know how well he fit Morison's harsh portrait), out-fitting ships and hiring crews for two-year voyages that yielded whale oil for lighting and whale bone for corset stays. Soon after the War of 1812, the French government invited Americans to establish a whaling industry in their country. Jeremiah responded. Letters of refer-ence in hand, he sailed a fully equipped ship to France, established his credentials in Paris, and by 1817 was settled in Le Havre. Brother Isaac followed.

"For sale at their stores, No. 1 Exchange Row, just below the Hay Market, Winter and Summer strained Spermaceti Oil, by the cask and retail." The ad, in a Portland, Maine, newspaper, carried under the sign of the whale the names of Nathan and Isaac Winslow. It was late 1816, and Isaac, who the year before had married Sarah Hussey, daughter of a prominent Quaker preacher, was twenty-nine. Two years later, he was a sea captain, in command of the *Bourbon* for a two-year voyage to the South Atlantic. It yielded twenty-five whales, seventeen hundred bar-rels of oil, and three tons of whalebone. Later, he owned a share in two other whalers. When Jeremiah returned briefly to the United States in 1829, he left Isaac, at Le Havre, in charge. "Delaroche has recently sold for the lighting of Paris nearly all his oil, with the exception of about three hundred thousand [kilograms], at 46 francs," Isaac wrote his brother in a typical business-stuffed letter. "He keeps three hundred thousand to sell at a higher price."

Jeremiah became something of a whaling legend and even the sub-ject of "La Chanson du Père Winslow," a wry toast to the ardor with which he discouraged spirits on board his ships; French sailors sang it as late as the 1870s. He was awarded French citizenship, and his descendants today in France are numerous. Later, in 1829, Isaac also sought naturalization, but perhaps due to a nationalistic backlash to Winslow successes, the authorities denied his request.

Early that summer, Isaac's wife, Sarah, returned to America. With her was their French-accented daughter, Emily Annette, born in Le Havre in 1822, her little French trunk heaped with pretty clothing. "I hope my dear little Emily will do all she can to help and please her Mama," Isaac wrote from Le Havre. A few months later, to Sarah: "All that is dearest to me is far from me. With a busy world around me I am lonely and solitary."

Probably around 1833, Isaac returned to the United States for good. Over the next few years, he sold off his whaling interests and by 1835 was comfortably enough settled to buy a hundred thousand dollars' worth of Maine woodlands. During his whaling career, he had invented various items of shipboard gear. Now, living in Danvers, near Salem, Massachusetts, he concocted a "tonic mixture" for the relief of fever (or maybe scurvy), launched a factory to make it, and shipped barrels of it to his brother in Le Havre before liquidating the business in 1837. Having learned of a French method for preserving food in sealed cans, he developed and ultimately patented a variation of it and, with brother Nathan, worked at ways to refine it.

One thing on his mind the previous winter, he wrote a friend in the spring of 1835, was his land deals; the other was the antislavery movement. In the years before the Civil War, slavery stirred fierce passions. And not just in a simplistic North-South way; many up north feared a radical abolitionist movement that threatened to flood their cities with freed black workers. The nation seethed. Unruly mobs broke up abolitionist rallies. A Philadelphia hall where three thousand men and women met for an antislavery convention in 1838—in the City of Brotherly Love, seventy-five miles north of the Mason-Dixon Line— was attacked by a rock-throwing mob and left a smoking ruin.

The abolitionist movement itself was split over how far to push, and how fast, for slavery's end. Crusading journalist William Lloyd Garrison represented the radical fringe. "I do not wish to think, or speak, or write, with moderation," he wrote in the maiden issue of the paper he founded in 1831 and published for more than thirty years, *The Liberator*. "I am in earnest—I will not equivocate—I will not excuse—I will not retreat a single inch—AND I WILL BE HEARD." Isaac Winslow and his brother Nathan were among Garrison's most ardent supporters.

Isaac—who refused to vote and so grant legitimacy to government morally stained by the sin of slavery—bankrolled Garrison's *Thoughts on African Colonization* in 1832; Garrison would recall him fondly as "my very early and attached friend." He and Nathan attended the 1833 founding session of Garrison's American Anti-slavery Society in Philadelphia, and signed Garrison's "Declaration of Sentiments." In 1837, he led a five-member committee charged with shoring up the finances of *The Liberator*; its financial failure, they wrote, "would dishearten many a friend, and would be received with sneers, and hailed with savage triumph, by the enemies of freedom." In 1840, when the call went out to "friends of the Slave of every nation" for a World Anti-Slavery Convention, set for June 12 in London, fifty-three-year-old Isaac Winslow was among those who set out for England. With him were his niece, Abby Southwick, and—named a delegate by the Massachusetts Anti-Slavery Society—his only daughter Emily, now seventeen, who would marry Franklin Taylor and bear a child, Frederick.

On May 9, 1840, their second day out into the Atlantic, they were all aboard the *Roscoe* when a fierce storm broke; "a real neat little gale," Emily wrote in her diary. The ship took on water. Passengers got soaked. It was like that for much of the three-week crossing. The violent foaming seas mesmerized them all. Philadelphia abolitionist Lucretia Mott recorded in her journal that Isaac Winslow came "well supplied with oranges, lemons, soda and other comforts & luxuries, freely distributed in his abundant kindness." Others among the three dozen cabin passengers were Mary Grew, twenty-seven, and Sarah Pugh, forty, both already prominent abolitionists. They were an intelligent and spirited group "whose philosophical and theological diversities," wrote Grew, "are sufficient to produce animated and interesting discussions, which pleasantly employ our time and our thoughts. We roam at will over the wide fields of theology, each earnestly contending for his or her own faith."

On May 27, the *Roscoe* anchored in the River Mersey, outside Liverpool. Ten days later, after touring England and Wales, the Winslows reached London. Isaac, Emily, and cousin Abby stayed with the Motts and Garrison, who had arrived on another ship from America. At the convention, attended by five hundred, a battle broke out over whether to seat women. By a wide margin, they were consigned to a gallery as mere "visitors"; Garrison, in sympathy, sat with them for the rest of the convention. On the last day, a formal protest was read out; among the signers was Isaac Winslow. At one point, Lucretia Mott, dubbed the Lioness of the Convention, met Elizabeth Cady Stanton, on her honeymoon at the time, and the two resolved to work for women's rights as

well as those of slaves. That, Stanton wrote later, was the beginning of
the women's rights movement in England and America.

Emily, all of eighteen, did not confine her European trip to anti-
slavery business. One companion from the *Roscoe*, Elizabeth Neall
from Philadelphia, recalled their time together in Rotterdam and that
"very interesting evening with our young friends; subsequently, our
united attack upon Mr. Smith—alias Lord Somebody—on the R[otter-
dam] steamboat. . . . You have not forgotten any of our old adventures,
I know." But whereas Neall and Abby Southwick returned home in
October with Isaac Winslow, who wrangled with slaveholding passengers the whole way, Emily stayed in Europe. "You don't know how
much astonishment you caused all your friends," Neall wrote her, "by
allowing your father to come to America without you."

A six-month trip stretched into three years. Emily stayed with her
uncle Jeremiah, his French wife, and her three cousins in Le Havre, but
also traveled; she saw the valley of the Rhine, the Alps, the Champs-
Elysées. Her infrequent letters home—she was probably having too
much fun to bother writing—were judged "common property," a New
England cousin wrote her, and "run after and borrowed like a village
newspaper." In July 1843, three years into Emily's adventure, cousin
Sarah Southwick felt moved to urge her home, but then, how could
she, she went on, "when you are constantly telling us of so much enjoyment"? Friends wondered whether she'd ever come back. So did
her father. "I think thou are preparing much future misery for thyself
by choosing France for thy place of residence," he wrote from
Philadelphia.

Isaac had settled in Philadelphia soon after returning from the
London congress, for a time living with his sister Maria, who had married a Philadelphia man. When Emily finally did return to America,
probably early in 1844, she moved to Philadelphia, too. But like her
widowed father, she spent as much time in New England, in and out of
the homes of aunts, uncles, and cousins in Portland and Boston.
Among these were her Southwick cousins, including Abby, her traveling companion to London. And her uncle Nathan's three daughters,
with whom she was bound by blood more closely yet; Nathan's wife
and her mother were sisters—making Harriet, Louisa, and Lucy Ellen
her double first cousins.

Uncle Nathan, someone said of him once, was a "desperate unrelenting Quaker abolitionist." He would shortly be "disowned"—

excommunicated from the Society of Friends—for taking a second wife not herself a Quaker. His two eldest daughters already had been disowned, Harriet for "departing from plainness" and Louisa for marrying outside the fold. Louisa's husband was Samuel Sewall, a prominent Boston attorney powerfully drawn to transcendentalism, the liveliest intellectual and literary movement of its day.

"I suppose you do not hear much about the Transcendental philosophy," Louisa had written Emily in Le Havre. "Here it is the chief subject of conversation. It is impossible to tell you what it is, for I have never found two persons who gave the same definition of it." Billowing up from around Concord, Massachusetts, outside Boston, its leading spokesman was Ralph Waldo Emerson, a former Unitarian minister who'd adopted a philosophical position that trusted in insight transcending logic and experience. After leaving the church, he'd moved to Concord, gathered around him such like-minded thinkers as Henry David Thoreau, formed a group called the Transcendental Club, and started a journal. Transcendentalism held heretical views of God. It bore a tinge of anarchism and socialism. It produced a short-lived experiment in communal living called Brook Farm.

Emily had, by age eighteen, witnessed stirring and historic events. And back in America, at the Sewall home in Boston, she would indeed meet Emerson, Thoreau, and other leading lights of the movement. But did she herself figure in it? Write essays? Philosophize and debate? No evidence comes down that she did. Her family brimmed over with every species of moral fervor. But by now, in her mid-twenties, Emily Winslow fretted less about the great social movements of her day than about the ordinary business of everyday social life.

During these years, she did not want for suitors. Her father had settled on her a dowry of ten thousand dollars, and she was spirited, intelligent, and attractive besides; in their letters, her cousins spoke of her beauty, her winning smile on entering a room, and her "conquests." To one young Philadelphia man visiting her in Europe, Edward Wright, she made "quite a pleasant impression." Then, there was a mysterious "young patrician"; cousin Anna girlishly warned her to "beware of his many enticing attractions lest you . . . find yourself incurable." Back in America, she became engaged to Charles Wright, a cousin of Edward's; but in late 1846, she broke it off, one cousin writing of the "awkward, ugly job [Emily had] to perform—of telling Charlie Wright she did not wish to marry him." Emily dismissed one suitor on account of his looks. "If you are ever married," cousin Harriet, another of Uncle Nathan's daughters, chided her, "you will find that goodness and sense and affection have infinitely more charms for you than beautiful eyes and fine hair."

It was during this period that Emily met Franklin Taylor. Just how and when is unclear, but at one point—early 1846 is the best guess—they apparently lived in the same Philadelphia boardinghouse where, for about six months, they saw each other almost daily. For Emily, Franklin at first seemed only the proverbial "friend"; he, on the other hand, was bewitched. But fearing Charles Wright was still in the picture, and shy and quiet anyway, he said nothing. In time, they went their separate ways, Franklin briefly to Europe.

A little later, Emily embarked on a teaching career. In the fall of 1848, she enrolled in the West Newton State Normal School in Massachusetts, one of the early teachers colleges. With cousin Abby she cherished hopes of starting her own school. The following year, Elizabeth Cady Stanton's sister, Kate Wilkeson, wrote Emily from Buffalo, suggesting that she and Abby start one there. "You might as well make the experiment here as in any other place." Soon, glowing references in hand, Emily was in Buffalo with Abby and issuing a flyer for their Young Ladies' School—embracing "all the branches of a thorough English education, together with the French, German and Italian languages, drawing, needlework and music"—set to open in a private home, on October 1, 1849. "Miss Winslow, who is a native of France will give particular attention to the pronunciation of the French language"; the flyer gave her name as Emilie.

The school was apparently a failure; by the following spring Emily was set to return to Philadelphia. And just then, in April 1850, Franklin Taylor made his move. Visiting Buffalo, he contrived to see her but again did not express his feelings for her. But a week later, back in Philadelphia, the floodgates opened. "My sole object in visiting Buffalo was to see you," he wrote her:

> I love you and have long loved you. I am fully aware that I have
> nothing to offer you, no inducements, nothing to give you in
> exchange. I have neither wealth, eminence in my profession, nor
> high social position. I have nothing but my love

—that and a rare, heartfelt eloquence:

I have thought long. My judgment joins my heart. 'Tis not a feeling
of yesterday, to be effaced by the first pretty face which crosses
my path. I have been in and of the world. I have mingled in scenes
of gaiety. I have met many beautiful and intelligent [people]. But
still I turn to thee. Thee only do I want. As thou sayest, so be my
future lot.

Emily, it seems, did not know what to think and took enough
trouble with her reply to prepare a rough draft, scribbling it in the margins of the flyer for her school. She expressed surprise, noted their relatively slight acquaintance, and worried that "on those movements
which seem to me the great hope and prophecy of the future our views
are altogether opposed."

But she did not close the door. She knew not what the future held
but hoped in the meantime he would esteem her his "sincere and
grateful friend."

For Franklin, Emily's letter aroused "mingled feelings of pleasure
and pain." He wrote back with a brief autobiography. A correspondence ensued in which Franklin methodically—but with wisdom and
eloquence, too—responded to her objections, empathizing with "the
immensity of the step you would take." She was, he knew, alone in her
weighty decision; it was "a step second only to that great step, when we
shall stand before our God."

Late that summer he visited her at her Aunt Ruth's, in Portland.
The next day, he wrote to her from Boston. "This last week has been
to me a dream. . . . To feel that I do possess thy love is happiness
indeed. . . . My lips have touched thy forehead, once. That touch did
send a thrill of joy through every nerve, and gave a foretaste of a future
bliss." A week later, at Sunbury, the Taylor family home alongside
Neshaminy Creek, he was telling everyone of their engagement.

On June 26, 1851, the abolitionist journal *Pennsylvania Freedman*,
edited by Mary Grew, Emily's friend from the *Roscoe*, reported the
news of their wedding:

Married—on the 19th inst., by Friends ceremony, before the
Mayor, Charles Gilpin, Franklin Taylor, esq., to Emily, only
daughter of Isaac Winslow, all of this city.

4

FOOT SOLDIER

~

T HE WEDDING TOOK PLACE at the house of Benjamin Jones, father-in-law of Frank's brother Robert. On hand were Isaac Winslow and a whole slew of Newbolds—Frank's mother's family, a locally prominent one stitched into the Taylors through marriage across many generations. That afternoon the couple boarded the train for New York; later they went up to Boston, where they saw cousin Abby and her family. After a side trip to Cape Cod, it was on to the White Mountains and Portland, where they visited more family, not returning to Philadelphia until early August.

They were married as Quakers, and Frank Taylor always remained one. But the wedding took place on a Thursday, out of meeting (the Quaker worship assembly); and Emily, in the eyes of her coreligionists, had married virtually outside the faith. In 1827, a fierce schism had shaken the Quaker community. A group led by Elias Hicks, a Long Island Quaker mystic who advocated heeding one's own inner light even at the expense of traditional Christian teachings, broke off from the mainstream. In time, about two thirds of Philadelphia Quakers, including the Taylors, became Liberal, or Hicksite. The rest, hewing to more traditional belief, remained Orthodox; the Winslows were among them.

The Orthodox, in particular, barred marriage with Hicksites or even attending their weddings. Soon after her return with Franklin from New England, two of Emily's Orthodox brethren called, met with her and Franklin for about an hour, and calmly discussed their "disorderly" marriage. Emily, unmoved by their pleas, expressed no wish to remain a member and was soon read out of her own Quaker community.

Did their son Fred, child of Quakers by birth, grow up in a Quaker home? The answer is as blurred as it is in the families of so many ethnic or religious minorities today: yes and no. Quakers traditionally frowned on theater and art; the Taylors enjoyed both. There is no evidence that they were thoroughgoing pacifists. They forswore the Quaker practice of using the scriptural names of the months—"first month" for January and so on—though Frank's sister Sarah, for one, did. And it was the Unitarian church Sunday school, not Quaker meeting, in which Fred grew up (though on at least one occasion, in London, he did attend meeting with his father).

Still, a Quaker tinge remained. "As soon as you entered their house the language was all thee and thou," recalled Taylor's own son Robert of his grandparents, who had changed little, he suspected, from when his father was a boy. The gentleness imputed to Franklin was pure Quaker in spirit. So was his tolerance. So were their abolitionist convictions. In short, what Nathaniel Burt has written of an Old Philadelphia whose Quaker families had mostly left the fold could apply at least broadly to Fred's family as well: what remained was "a Quaker facade—subdued, careful, moderate, puritanical but never ascetic, honest but shrewd, modest but firm."

$$\sim$$

Science has not yet found a genetic basis for such traits as tenacity, moral fervor, and contentiousness nor otherwise been able to trace how a parent imprints her personality on her child's. But knowing all we do of Frederick Winslow Taylor, and of Isaac Winslow and of Emily, it is tempting to conclude that whatever she passed down— along with the blue-and-gold satin banner, still in the family's possession, that she and her friends hoisted at the London antislavery convention—influenced him more than anything from her husband's side. The gentleness Taylor lauded in his father, after all, was hardly a quality upon which, on the strength of his own life, he placed high value. And his mother's more remarkable history, flavored with great events and important personages from the nation's early days, makes it easier to see her hand in the development of his personality. That, certainly, has been the prevailing view, even within the family. "Fred Taylor," his son Robert once told an interviewer, "got all his drive from his mother. She had it." When John Dos Passos wrote of Taylor, he made it seem as if his mother, that "fervent abolitionist," had forged his character almost single-handedly.

Did she? Or was she, like her husband, a more conventional

influence on him, a woman quite as willing to accept things as they were as to overturn them?

She was not, first of all, "a prominent anti-slavery agitator," as one account of the Taylor family has it. Her trip to London for the congress, in 1840, came long before her marriage to Frank Taylor and sixteen years before Fred's birth. At an impressionable eighteen, in company with her father and his abolitionist friends, Emily's passions may have been more volatile, lain closer to the surface. Her father, certainly, was a major abolitionist figure, with firmly held convictions and "an unusual force of character." Did she feel all her father's passion? Or was she aboard the *Roscoe* largely as Isaac Winslow's daughter?

She was not, as we've seen, all serious business during the three years of her European sojourn. In a letter to her near the end of her stay, Elizabeth Neall, who'd returned with cousin Abby and Isaac Winslow back in 1840, pictured her "surrounded . . . by so much that is attractive in society's gaiety, splendors and taste. You have been perhaps 'whirling thro' the gay cotillion,'" and "going to midnight balls and entertaining plays." Did Neall drop a gentle barb in referring to abolitionist meetings in New York, "which once you were pleased to attend"?

The abolitionist fervor in America passed Emily by. Her cousin Sarah Southwick, Abby's sister, wrote her early in 1842 "of the exciting scenes we have been through within the last two or three days. . . . [Without being there herself Emily could not] comprehend the glorious, thrilling, soul-stirring meetings we have held."

Emily's aunt Ruth Morrell wrote of a friend to whom Emily had seemed "so conscientious. She hopes the gaiety of France will not change Emily from what she once was." Her father likewise worried. "The tho't occurred," Isaac wrote her from Philadelphia on July 25, 1841, when she'd been in Europe about a year, "Does my daughter . . . no longer take an interest in our various benevolent moral and religious movements?"

Like the "red diaper babies" of the American Left a century later, Emily had grown up amid the zealous, slightly disreputable radical politics of her family and their circle of friends; it would have been odd had they not influenced her at all. "You have lived intimately with persons holding your present views," Frank wrote her in a letter just before they became engaged. "Perhaps time and circumstances might change them somewhat."

However firm Emily's personal convictions may once have been, her marriage to Frank doubtless softened them. "I cannot agree with you in many of your ideas," he wrote her early in their correspondence. "I confess it freely. I cannot receive them. I cannot see them practicable." And then, in language capturing all the wisdom of the great middle way, he added: "My moderation tells me, yield not a certainty for an uncertainty, hesitate ere you plunge society into chaos, that out of darkness may arise one knows not what."

Something of this moderate vision colored their life together. Divergent views on "abstract questions" need not undermine their marriage, Frank wrote Emily in another letter. More important were one's "love of the domestic circle, the chain of social intercourse, the communion of friendship, the similarity of temper, disposition and tastes." Whereas, "the abstract question of slavery or the amelioration of the condition of the human race—I cannot see why they . . . [need] disturb the harmony of the private circle."

Unlike others aboard the *Roscoe* during that storm-swept voyage— Lucretia Mott, Sarah Pugh, Mary Grew, and Isaac Winslow himself— Emily disappeared from the pages of history. For more than twenty years after she moved back to Philadelphia with her father, she remained a member of the Philadelphia Female Anti-Slavery Society. Mott, Sarah Pugh, and a few others sparked the group, forever organizing, writing, moving resolutions, reporting back to the rank and file. Emily was among the two hundred or so women who signed its constitution early in 1845. But she was never an officer and, the society's minutes suggest, never known to offer a motion or otherwise take a leadership role. At one point, she joined four other women to help collect subscription money. Another time, she helped Sarah Pugh distribute copies of the society's annual report to local sewing circles. And over the years she often, along with thirty or forty others, served on the arrangements committee for the society's annual antislavery fair, its chief fund-raiser.

After the Taylors returned from Europe in 1871, Emily pushed to build their new house on the other side of town, east of Main Street— so, it was said, to be nearer Sarah Pugh. Emily's small, delicately formed friend was "one of those silent little Quakeresses who devoted themselves wholly to great causes," someone once said, "an eager abolitionist, an advocate of woman suffrage, free trade, peace, and the single standard of morals for men and women." Pugh, in short, was the real thing. She ate no sugar and wore only linen underwear. "Cotton was grown by slaves, and sugar also," she would explain.

But Emily wasn't like that. Hers was the record of, at best, a foot soldier in the feminist and abolitionist struggles of her day. A biography of Sarah Pugh, littered with names, scarcely mentions hers. The same goes for those of Lucretia Mott and Mary Grew. Emily joined Sarah at the Germantown Library, which was something of a feminist creation, run and managed exclusively by women. But she was not one of its founders; it had begun, as a little room over a dry goods store, when the Taylors were still in Europe. Emily would remain active in the library for the next quarter century, occupying various offices, giving German lessons on its behalf, helping to round up speakers, selling tickets to theatrical benefits. "Mrs. Sharp, Mrs. Taylor and Mrs. Wells were appointed a standing committee on entertainments," the library's minutes noted in 1873.

Years later, at a pressured moment in testimony before a federal commission, Taylor would abruptly recall how when the Emancipation Proclamation was issued in 1863, his parents and some of their abolitionist friends seemed unhappy about it. "I remember," Taylor said, using the story to impugn, in a roundabout way, what he saw as similarly impure motives among his union leader foes, "a great many of these antislavery happenings and their disappointment because it abolished their society. . . . I was only a young boy at the time; but these women had won their cause, and they felt darned sorry about it." Fred, at seven, could scarcely appreciate the real issues involved; Sarah Pugh, for example, wrote to an English friend that abolitionists "accept the Emancipation Proclamation variously, depending on the temperament as well as the principles of the individual." Still, it may be a mistake to wholly dismiss Taylor's contemptuous recollection. Childhood antennae, often exquisitely sensitive to signs of phoniness or bluster, may have discerned in his mother, or among her coterie of friends, something less than purity of purpose, some little gap between word and action, some sign of high moral resolve lost in the easy affability of a social club.

Emily Taylor was not frivolous, not insincere. But she was no firebrand, no disturber of the peace, either. However ardent her temperament may have been at eighteen, years passed, marriage intervened, and by the time Fred Taylor was a boy, with Emily in her forties, the fires had cooled further. Surely, Fred's European journal during the years after the Civil War, when he was a teenager and his mother was approaching fifty, reveals no outward sign of fiery social conscience and every sign of a woman happy to traipse through museums and shops. "Mother and Sis went out lace hunting today and have found two places which they like very much," Fred notes in Brussels on September 5, 1870. Three days later: "Took a long walk with Father this morning, but I have not seen much of Mother or Sis, as they are always out lace hunting."

Likewise, Emily's letters to Fred a little later in his teens are occupied not with the burning issues of the day but with details of the new house they are having built, speakers she has lined up for the library, recent purchases, and conventional if heartfelt advice. She observes, in asking after brother Win, that "so much depends upon making a good impression on the teachers at first." In another letter, she reports on the arrival of a dress made for her in Europe. "The silk is handsome and it was tastefully made by Mrs. Knapp, the dressmaker whom I employed in Paris." That a lecturer at the Ladies Club was "a strong woman's rights and suffrage man" is about as close as she gets to revealing social convictions. And, not surprisingly for a woman who lived out of trunks for five years, hoped-for pleasures of hearth and home loom large: "It is just after dinner," she writes Fred on November 2, 1873, "and I am sitting looking over at our [new] house with a good deal of satisfaction. Not that it is so very handsome, but the idea of having a house once more seems very pleasant."

While Fred is at school, apparently troubled by what may have seemed her son's inclination toward atheism, she expresses her belief that "he is much more fortunate and happy who believes in an all wise and benevolent ruler of the universe." She goes on to offer something like a personal creed:

> I think an unselfish, useful life gives us more comfort than
> anything else, whatever our beliefs about the future may be. . . .
> Every period of life brings with it certain . . . duties which at best
> become our pleasures. So that what is usually called pleasure, if not
> connected with some usefulness or if not conducive to the
> happiness of others, soon becomes dull and unsatisfactory. I hope
> both my dear boys will lead useful and unselfish lives and I know

that they will not only make others happier but be much happier themselves. And be able to look with more calmness and trust to the future.

And she adds, "I know that my happiness in this world depends on the good and noble character of my dear children."

In the end, Emily Taylor was more like her husband than unalike. Like Frank, she tried to instill in her children firm and, in the context of the day, progressive values. But she did not leave them uneasy with the social order or moping with guilt over their comfortable circumstances in life. She was not, during the years Fred was growing up, driven to change the world, nor did she, to all outward appearances, chafe at the bonds of home and family. Rather, she was comfortable with her station, enjoyed life, kept social conscience in a fine and equanimitous balance with personal pleasure and comfort, and generally conformed to the expectations, values, and interests of her neighbors and friends in Germantown.

5

GERMANTOWN DAYS

~

I N THOSE DAYS A LITTLE STREAM, which furnished power to a mill, flowed through Germantown from the northeast. Later, the Wingohocking would be channeled into a sewer—you'd be able to hear the flow of water during a heavy rain—and an alley would be built above it. But in 1853, the area was still largely woods and fields, and the stream passed behind the house on Willow Avenue to which the Taylors moved that year. The land was owned by their friends Isaac and Elizabeth Pugh, who lived in an ivy-clad house across the street with his sister, Sarah Pugh. The Taylor house, occupying a long, narrow lot, just a few paces wide but reaching two hundred feet back to the stream, was a plain, two-story structure. Later, Fred Taylor's widow decreed that a picture of it be dropped from the family-commissioned biography because, in Frank Copley's words, of "its lack of esthetic charm." In 1854, Winslow was born there, followed by Fred in 1856.

But it was Germantown where Fred Taylor lived over the years, more than any particular home there; the Willow Avenue house was the first of at least five. While absorbed by Philadelphia in the city's 1854 expansion, Germantown lay eight miles northwest of the city center. Its slip into the city's shadow was recent, its roots in the nation's past were its own; a major Revolutionary War battle was fought there in 1777. But beginning in the 1840s, with the coming of America's first commuter railroad up from Philadelphia along the town's east side, well-off old families and newly wealthy businessmen began to flock there. Through the center of town snaked the old Indian trail that was Main Street, later Germantown Avenue; and in 1859, horsecars began plying its length. Supplanting slower, less comfortable omnibuses, which were handicapped by rutted and cobblestoned streets, the horsecars soon carried twenty-five hundred passengers a day on the fifty-minute run into the city. Germantown became the city's premier suburb. Over one five-year span, property values doubled. Everywhere on the hills north and east of Main Street, great stone houses shot up, all turrets, gables, and porches; gray stone was everywhere, in the houses themselves, in the stables behind the houses, in the long snaking walls that bordered the great estates.

In 1857, the Taylors moved to Cedron, a house on a dozen-acre property owned by Franklin Taylor's sister Sarah and her husband. The prior owner, Redwood Wright, had toyed with calling the place Redwood, only to be confounded by its dearth of redwoods; but there were plenty of cedars, so Cedron it became, or so the story goes. Cedron was a hilly, wooded preserve off Indian Queen Lane that would later be reckoned the largest estate in Germantown, home to a vast mansion where Fred's sister and brother-in-law would live. It was more modestly scaled when Frank and Emily and their two boys moved there, but it was already sacred ground: Washington's army had camped there before and after the battle of Brandywine. Fred's sister was born there a few days before Christmas, 1857, and there Fred spent his next eleven years amid a tight coterie of some of the neighborhood's wealthiest and most respected families.

In 1864, when Fred was eight, some of them—seeking, so the record of their first meeting has it, "a religious ministration more liberal than the existing churches in Germantown afforded"—formed the Unitarian Society of Germantown. Growing out of New England Congregationalism's liberal wing, and influenced by the Transcendentalists,

Unitarians rejected any hint of creed, emphasized tolerance, and embraced science, rationalism, and this world rather than the next. Among the forty-nine to sign the founding statement in 1865 was Emily W. Taylor. (Franklin, at least in name always a Quaker, did not.) Also among the signers, and laying the cornerstone two years later for their new church, were James A. Wright and E. W. Clark. Neither man can stake claim to a big place in the history books, and their overly familiar English names tend to recede from memory. But they were important in their time, and their families were bound up with Fred Taylor all his life.

James A. Wright was the son of a Maryland Quaker who had moved to Philadelphia in 1817 and the following year established a crockery import business. In 1836, James joined his father's firm and soon became, by one account, its "ruling spirit." He and his brother built it into a large business, with a five-story headquarters in downtown Philadelphia, branches around the world, and interests in pottery, breadstuffs, coal, and petroleum; the first export of petroleum, two years after the first well was drilled in Titusville, Pennsylvania, went through the Wright firm. In 1864, he formed the Atlantic Petroleum Storage Company to store, refine, and ship oil. He was part owner of the Red Star Line, one of whose ships in 1867 crossed the Atlantic in what was then record time, just over eight days.

Like many Taylor family friends, Wright was a longtime abolitionist. He witnessed the burning of Pennsylvania Hall in 1838 and, while on honeymoon with his first wife that year, was set upon by a mob for his beliefs. At twenty-six, he was treasurer of a Philadelphia abolitionist group. During the Civil War, he aided newly emancipated slaves.

With his second wife, he fathered eight children, many of whom became part of Fred's life. Ernest N. Wright wrote how "we children grew up with" the Taylor children, how Fred would bring him over to Cedron for dinner after Sunday School. The Wright estate, Oakley, almost backed up to Cedron; indeed, it was from Redwood Wright that the Taylors had bought it. The two families, which had distant kinship ties and nearly grew closer still with Emily's engagement to Charles Wright, would travel together through Europe; it was George Wright, along with brother Win, with whom Fred climbed among the rocks at the bridge site in Finstermunz. Fred would room with James Wright, Jr., at school. He would work with Ernest Wright at his first job.

If the Wrights were rich, the Clarks were probably the richest family in Germantown. Formed in 1837, their banking house had become by the 1850s, after helping finance the Mexican-American War, one of the most important in the country, with branches in St. Louis, New Orleans, and New York. Edward White Clark, son of the founder, who with his brother would sponsor archaeology expeditions to the Mideast and was first president of the Unitarian Church, lived in a great estate at the edge of Germantown, not far from Cedron. His son Clarence would marry Fred's sister Mary, become a close friend to Fred, and manage his finances.

The Wrights and the Clarks, it is not far wrong to say, were the only kinds of people young Fred Taylor knew. They and the Taylors were wealthy, white Protestants of English stock long established in America. They lived in big houses a few minutes' walk from one another. They were important figures in their community. And they (along with the wider Taylor-Winslow-Newbold clan and a few other local families who probably deviated from the mold less than any of them could have known) made for a rich network of personal connections that would nurture and sustain Fred Taylor all his life.

～

Fred grew up during the Civil War; he was five when rebel troops fired on Fort Sumter, nine when Lee surrendered at Appomattox. At least two of his cousins, sons of his uncle Robert, served in the war, one of them earning a Medal of Honor. In Germantown, the war was never far out of sight. A glimpse into a factory's dark interior might reveal the glint of newly made bayonets or bolts of cloth for army uniforms, both of which were made in Germantown. Soldiers, in half-mile-long columns, paraded through town. Funeral services were held at Haines Street Methodist Church for soldiers killed at Fair Oaks or Antietam. In July 1862, a recruiting station was opened in the office of a coal company on Main Street. In September, the home guards could be seen drilling in the evenings above Shoemaker's Lane. By March 1863, military hospitals in Germantown and nearby communities held almost two thousand wounded soldiers.

A boyhood friend about a year and a half Fred's senior, Birge Harrison, remembered "the occasional mysterious appearance and disappearance of a black face at 'Cedron' " during the war, persuading him that it served as a stop on the Underground Railroad for conducting fugitive slaves to safety in Canada. Harrison remembered them staying there for days at a time and that when visiting he was "expected to kiss them good morning and good night quite as if they were distant relatives who had unexpectedly appeared on the scene."

On March 11, 1862, former slaves Prince Rivers and Brian White appeared before the Philadelphia Female Anti-Slavery Society, Emily's group. Rivers was a sergeant in a South Carolina regiment of black volunteers. White told how he had repeatedly tried to escape, been twice captured, twice imprisoned, finally condemned to death. But "with almost superhuman effort," the meeting minutes recorded, he escaped once more, "traveling six days and nights, without food and with his manacles," before reaching Union forces. The inspiring account helped energize abolitionists demoralized by early Union defeats. "Events since our last meeting," the minutes noted, "have not realized the hopes with which we [last] separated of the speedy triumph of freedom."

In late June 1863, Confederate forces under Robert E. Lee approached Gettysburg, little more than a hundred miles west of Philadelphia. Despite the threat, a strange apathy hung over the city, which was defended by only four hundred trained soldiers and ten pieces of artillery. The city had strong Southern leanings and politically was deeply divided. People were sick of the war. Recruiters banged at their drums, yet crowds of young men filled the streets, unmoved and unresponsive. Some older men did enlist in the home guards and could be seen drilling each morning and evening. And recent graduates of area schools joined hastily formed regiments. Aping their elders, boys in Fred's group formed themselves into ragtag youth squads. But, Birge Harrison would recall, a wry smile lodged in his written reminiscence, "I cannot remember that Fred," seven at the time, "displayed any enthusiasm in regard to this movement."

For most of the war Fred was in school, at Germantown Academy, twenty minutes on foot from Cedron. Just a few years before, in peacetime, on an April Saturday in 1860, bustling crowds, streaming flags, and bands of musicians had thronged Germantown's cobbled Main Street to mark the hundredth anniversary of the school's founding. But with the war on, the local economy was depressed. Enrollment dropped. The school, used as a hospital during the Battle of Germantown in 1777 and still bearing the remains of six British soldiers interred on its grounds, occupied a broad two-story stone building erected on a knoll a few steps up from the street. But it felt almost empty now, with fewer than three dozen students enrolled, just nine of them in the primary department with Fred.

Soon after Gettysburg, the school's principal resigned. The new one, Cyrus V. Mays, stressed what we might today call the holistic approach. Education, he wrote, "should be organic and complete, not mechanical; it should penetrate and regulate the entire being. The growth should be from within . . . should be free and natural instead of being cramped." After the bonfires and bell-ringing that greeted the news of Lee's surrender in 1865, Academy enrollments rose, to about fifty-five by the time Fred left. Classes were extended an hour earlier into the morning. Mays urged the installation of parallel bars and other gymnastics equipment, saying regular exercise would give "elasticity to the spirits and freshness to the mind." But how much these and others of May's lofty precepts reached down into the daily classroom experience of young Fred Taylor we do not know.

We do know that on July 5, 1867, when Fred was eleven, his eighty-year-old grandfather, Isaac Winslow, in Maine for the funeral of a relative, was admitted—perhaps following a sudden stroke, for until then he had seemed in good health—to a gray granite structure a mile outside Augusta known as the Maine Insane Hospital; that on July 25, he died, the news coming as a shock to his old friend William Lloyd Garrison; and that perhaps with the help of an inheritance from him, less than a year later Emily, Franklin, twelve-year-old Fred, and his brother and sister left for Europe.

6

RITE OF PASSAGE

～

"I WOKE UP THIS MORNING with the thought that I was thirteen years old," Fred wrote in his journal on Saturday, March 20, 1869. He came down to breakfast surprised to find cakes and candies heaped high on his plate. For a birthday present, his parents had given him five thalers, the large silver coins from which the dollar takes its name.

Fred and his family were in Berlin, near the end of their first winter in Europe. The previous summer they had visited England, Belgium, the Alps. Over the winter, Fred had been in school, studying religion, arithmetic, German, French, geography, and history. Yet that probably counted for the least of his learning. "Mother has commenced with our grammar lessons again," he noted on March 30. In the evenings, his father read to them, usually in German. He practiced the piano two hours a day and sometimes spent most of the day on needlework. ("I can now sew quite fast and it looks very regular.") He and the family visited museums and galleries and went to the zoo. They toured castles in the royal estates of Charlottenburg and Potsdam.

They strolled down the Unter den Linden, the stately tree-shaded axis of leisured Berlin life; once, they saw the crown prince with his wife, in a carriage drawn by four horses. At the Monbijou palace, on the other side of the River Spree, they saw Frederick the Great's favorite horse, stuffed and dressed to look as it had in life, ready to ride. Fred found a wheeled chair that had belonged to the Prussian king's father, plunked himself down in it, and pushed himself around the room. Then, on his piano, he played "Yankee Doodle." Next day it was off to the Tiergarten, the great wooded park that began just beyond the Brandenburg Gate.

On June 3, the family boarded a train for Lubbenau, a picturesque little town fifty miles across the sandy plain south of Berlin. Then it was off to Dresden, Prague, Nuremberg, Munich, Salzburg, and the Tyrol; to Innsbruck, Zurich, Lucerne, Interlaken, Zermatt, and Geneva. Early that fall, they reached Paris.

But this itinerary of their second summer in Europe warps the shape of their experience. For its headlong recital of the places they visited suggests speed or urgency, and little of either marked their years in Europe. The Taylors didn't reach Paris, their winter quarters, until four months after leaving Berlin. Just getting to Interlaken, about as far from Berlin as Cleveland is from Milwaukee, took them seven weeks.

For wealthy Americans, Europe was the ultimate educational experience, a way to instill in their children what mere books could not, a rite of passage. The world had not yet shrunk; a trip abroad was still the preserve of the well-born and the well-off. The Civil War's end had made European travel the thing to do, and the Taylors were doing it, along with Henry James, the young Edith Wharton, the family of

Theodore Roosevelt, and Jefferson Davis, the former Confederate president.

For the Taylors, though, Europe meant more even than the sort of grand tour upon which the Roosevelts, for example, had embarked. They were not traveling in Europe but living there. Their pace was leisurely. They stopped often. And wherever they stopped, they sampled. After Berlin, their first destination was little Lubbenau, a village in the Spreewald, a marshy wooded region where the River Spree broke off into a little Venice of canals used by the locals, in long spidery boats, to transport their crops. Arriving by train, they parked their trunks at a hotel near the station and went sightseeing by boat along quiet flowing waterways overhung by birch and alder trees.

In Nuremberg, Fred witnessed his first wedding. They visited the fourteenth-century Frauenkirche that towered over the central market place, bought cherries from local vendors, went to the theater. They strolled beside the city's seventy-five watchtowers, through its narrow, crooked medieval streets, past gabled houses, under arched gates, and along the moat between the old castle walls.

In Munich, they settled into their suite at a hotel on the Karlsplatz and soon were visiting the Alte Pinakothek, a masterfully proportioned museum five hundred feet long that somehow looked little larger than a big house. Inside, one great gallery passed into the next, like railcars, nine of them, so you could sight down from one end to the other. In between were the Raphaels, the Van Dycks, the glorious Rubenses. The Taylors returned again and again.

Later in their three weeks in Munich, they climbed the steps that wound up toward the top of *Bavaria*, the great bronze figure of a woman that looked out over the city a mile and a half to the east; a dozen people, wrote Fred in his journal, could fit inside its head. Behind it stood the marble-columned Hall of Fame, built by Ludwig I a quarter century before to house busts of Bavaria's famous men. In front, at the base of the ridge upon which it was built, lay the open plain where Oktoberfests had been held since 1819.

The Taylors visited galleries, bought paintings, took day trips into the surrounding countryside, toured the Südlischer Friedhof, a wedge-shaped cemetery crisscrossed by quiet lanes for strolling and filled with the remains of Munich's notables. The next day they took the train to Salzburg.

On July 9, Fred climbed up from town to the Hohensalzburg
fortress, begun by a papal loyalist archbishop in the eleventh century as
a bulwark against the king, replete with turrets and towers, heavy wood
doors with rude iron hinges, thick iron grates, and sudden twists in
narrow stone walkways that took you through tunnels and up stone
steps. Looking out over one of its great stone parapets, Fred could see
the town far below, with the river that divided Salzburg curving
through it. But from an adjoining parapet, the town disappeared, and
in its place was a shimmering tableau of mountain peaks receding into
the distance until they faded into sky.

The flatlands were gone now, not to return until the Taylors left
Geneva for Paris; for eleven weeks it was the Alps. They traveled mostly
by carriage, which for people like the Taylors were great, imposing
affairs that bore eight or ten people in lushly appointed, spring-
mounted compartments high above the rutted road. Some of them
plying the Swiss passes weighed three tons and were pulled by four or
five horses. To anyone at roadside as they passed, they left an indelible
image, of a driver perched high, his whip snapping, horses' hooves
pounding, a swirl of dust in their wake.

The refinement of museum and *Schloss* now yielded to the physical
exuberance of the mountains; Fred's journal is filled with accounts of
rowing, velocipede rides, hiking, and climbing. The family explored the
mountainous resort areas around Salzburg, then continued on to Innsbruck, Finstermunz (where the bridge repairs delayed them), then over
the Stelvio and a chain of other high mountain passes, finally reaching
Zurich on August 1. A few days later, they were in Lucerne, climbing
Mount Pilatus, the town's signature peak. At the top, at a little hotel
perched between two rocky promontories seven thousand feet above
sea level, Fred "had a very good cup of chocolate, and I believe the
honey was pure."

In Kleine Scheidegg, high above Interlaken, the family stayed at
the Bellevue Hotel, which from any angle looked insignificant against
the primeval snow-laden peaks, shrouded in mist, rising round it.
Kleine Scheidegg stood at an altitude of sixty-seven hundred feet, about
that of the Pilatus summit. But here that barely got you to the foothills
and a saddle-shaped pass between two valleys. Above it, along the
ridgeline up the slope, you reached the Eiger Glacier and then the
unforgettable jagged mass of the Jungfrau, which rose to nearly fourteen thousand feet.

With a young Englishman they'd met, Fred climbed the Lauber-horn, its summit a thousand feet or so above their hotel, up a steep slope of dense, green ground cover broken by rocky folds that harbored islands of snow. The matted, mossy stuff under their feet felt like sponge. Alpine wildflowers—delicate red petals, flecks of yellow, vel-vety blue funnels holding pearls of moisture—dotted the slope. As they climbed, the vista changed constantly as thick, gray mists swirled in and out, obscuring or revealing this peak or that, the sun occasionally cut-ting through a break in the clouds to illuminate a snowy summit, mir-roring back a painful white glare.

For Fred, by now something of a connoisseur of Alpine scenery, the view from the top of the Lauberhorn disappointed him. "Just as we reached the summit," he wrote, "the mist thickened in and obscured the prospect," though they could see a flurry of avalanches off the steeply sloped sides of the Jungfrau. For a time, they just stood there, taking it in. Then, perhaps curious about the effects of the thinner air, Fred reached for his watch and took a deep breath.

∾

For the minute and a half he held his breath, he was exquisitely aware of time passing, watch ticking. But more often, for Fred in Europe, time passed heedlessly, innocent of hurry or constraint. He and his family didn't taste Europe, they savored it. They had time for boat trips, excursions, long hikes. By the time they left Berlin, Fred knew all the shops that sold bird's eggs. He and Win were groomsmen at a wedding. Fred began thinking in German: the frescoes at the New Museum in Berlin were located on the *Treppenhaus,* or stairway. He noticed *Kasernes,* or barracks. The rolls in Salzburg were *Semmels.*

This rich, leisurely experience, even down to the smallest details of where they went and what they did, differed little from that of other well-off travelers. Indeed, a prescient investor in that summer of 1869 who got his hands on the Taylor itinerary could have bought up prop-erties along the way and made a fortune. For almost without exception, wherever the Taylors went then are tourist meccas to millions now. His parents took him to places that were idyllic, memorable, historic—but always conventionally so.

The Taylors didn't slum, never sampled the offbeat or sordid, had no taste for worlds alien to their own. In 1856, an Englishman wrote a sightseeing guide to Germany and the Tyrol that would uncannily foretell the Taylor itinerary thirteen years later, even down to the pass at Finstermunz. When the Taylors reached Zurich, they stayed at the Baur au Lac, built up against the lakefront at the foot of the Bahnhofstrasse, a grand, gloriously proportioned place with rooms so large and ceilings so high they seemed engorged with the clear mountain air; the *Tagblatt der Stadt Zürich* noted their arrival, along with that of Baron Morpurgo from Trieste, Gräfin Bentheim, and other personages from Chicago, Marseilles, Paris, and London. In 1871, *Sights and Sensations of Europe* observed that for American tourists in Paris "the Grand Hotel is their rallying point and rendezvous." When the Taylors reached Paris, they headed straight there.

To all this, no sign of rebellion on Fred's part comes down to us, no wish for things to be other than they were. His interests and activities in Europe were always thoroughly conventional, invariably those of his family, their circle, and their time.

On March 24, 1869, in Berlin, Fred recorded in his journal that he

> ran over to the bird's egg places and got twenty-seven eggs for a groschen a piece. There was a boy in the store and he sold us several eggs which cost respectively in the other store two thalers, twenty groschen and such like prices. One very valuable egg that we got was the snow bunting's. It is a very pretty and rare egg.

Fred's early journal entries refer often to the eggs he'd collected and the prices he paid for them; at one point he had 180 different kinds. For a while in Germany he fed all his spare money into buying them or books about them. In Munich, he and Win ventured into the woods looking for them, and when he returned from Europe he had a substantial collection. (The egg's insides are extracted through a tiny hole made in one end, leaving a bare shell that can retain its distinctive color and pattern, unchanged, for a century or more.)

To us, collecting bird's eggs might suggest rare and refined sensibilities, perhaps a taste for the idiosyncratic. Indeed, the eggs are delicate and lovely, ranging in color from mottled ochers, to solid avocado greens, to pointillistic baby blues, in size from that of a thimble to a cannonball. But this was no hobby for an effete minority; it was extremely popular, almost a "rite of passage for young boys, both here and in England," as one account has it. Naturalists recruited boys to hunt specimens, established price lists, advertised in popular magazines. Young Teddy Roosevelt did it. So did Fred Taylor.

In so much else that interested or occupied him in Europe, Fred mirrored prevailing taste. "We . . . went to our turning lesson this afternoon," he wrote on May 22. "I practice an hour and a half now." All through that summer of 1869 his journal refers to turners and turning. This was a kind of gymnastics, pioneered earlier in the century by Friedrich Ludwig Jahn, a fervent nationalist who believed that in physical exercise lay the basis for German national strength. Jahn died in 1852, but his legacy lived in the parallel bars, balance beams, and other staples of the modern gym that he invented, and in the *Turnverein*, or gymnastics societies that, by Taylor's time, had spread around the world. Turning was in the air and Taylor, as usual, took great heaving gulps of it. Wherever he went in Germany, Austria, and Switzerland, he found groups of gymnasts and joined in.

Bird's eggs. Turning. Velocipedes?

In Lucerne, the day after they came down from Pilatus, Fred and Win tried riding bicycles, or, rather, a forerunner called the velocipede, in which the pedal turns the front wheel without chain or gears as intermediary. It weighed fifty pounds or more, had a thick, wrought-iron frame, wooden wheels supported by wooden spokes half an inch thick, and a brake, applied by a twist of the handlebar, that drew a leather strap against the rear wheel. At the end of their forty-five-minute lesson, they "could ride a little alone," Fred recounted. An hour of practice the next day and he could get a hundred yards without falling. The day after that they were back for more, practicing on a level stretch of road between the Schweizerhof Hotel and the lakefront. By the time they reached Interlaken, they were renting velocipedes by the week and riding up to Lauterbrunnen, an eight-hundred-foot climb out of town.

This was 1869, a quarter century before the great bicycle boom, a time before bicycles were bicycles at all. But these primitive velocipedes, which had been around for fifty years, were just then immensely popular. Two years earlier, the 1867 world's fair in Paris had established the reputation of the Michaux velocipede, and, about the time Fred was puffing up the hill to Lauterbrunnen, the Michaux factory in Paris had three hundred workers churning them out. A century later, a museum exhibit devoted to early bicycles would display no fewer than six models from 1865 to 1870, the most densely represented by far in its collection. This was the first bicycle boom, the velocipede was in, and the Taylors were among many who took it up.

All his life, it could be fairly said of Fred Taylor, he did not anticipate trends but seized upon them. He had no taste for what was not yet in the air. He was always, if unconsciously, in fashion.

7

THE CRYSTAL PALACE, AGAIN

~

W E KNOW IN SOME DETAIL how Fred and his family lived in Europe, because beginning about a year after their arrival there, on March 15, 1869, a few days before his thirteenth birthday, Fred began to keep his journal. It scarcely qualifies as a literary document. It is riddled with misspellings (corrected in excerpts here). It shows no special grace or flair and offers no explicit revelations of Fred's inner life. But he wrote in it every day, scrupulously, and kept it up all that spring in Berlin. He told of the family's travels that summer, up to their arrival in Paris in October. He took it up again on leaving Paris the following July and maintained it all through the Franco-Prussian War summer of 1870. It is long, sometimes detailed, and spans a key period of his youth, one just a few years before the great turn in his life of 1874. Drawing too-firm conclusions from a teenager's diary, of course, poses risks; who would care to be represented by his or her adolescent scribblings? Still, it offers precious clues, giving us our closest, most sustained view of Fred Taylor during those years.

Fred's journal is no work of youthful genius. True, it begins only after the family's first year in Europe, after his earliest and keenest impressions may have dulled. And its author certainly shows himself to be bright enough, in every ordinary sense. But if there were any exceptional brilliance to him, you might expect to see a glint of it at thirteen or fourteen, and you don't. Anne Frank, hiding from the Nazis in Amsterdam, was just the same age, after all, when she kept her diary. Fred's language reveals no literary gifts. It is not, on the whole, the record of a particularly close observer, nor does it show a young man with precocious insight into human nature or into himself.

What it does reveal is a teenager, to every outward appearance comfortable with his lot. Read it too fast and you could miss the fourteen-year-old's offhand comment, in Oslo, that "this evening the American consul called on us"; or that rock formations he'd seen at Schandau, near Dresden, impressed him more than any in Switzerland; or that London's Crystal Palace was, on second view, not "quite as pretty as it was before when we were there." He had seen it all but seems blissfully unaware that he has. He doesn't act superior, just no differently from any other son of privilege.

Not that this matters much, except for Taylor's later contention that he knew what the workingman really wanted and was indeed his close and sympathetic friend. In fact, no special sympathy for working-class life bubbles up from Fred's journal. He shows no urge to rub shoulders with the lower orders but, if anything, a tendency to keep his distance. While settling accounts upon leaving their boardinghouse in Berlin, the proprietress harangues Fred's father, claiming, in Fred's account, "that we had always been so impolite to her and treated her as if she were a boarding house keeper." To which he adds, "(What is she but a boarding house keeper?)" Traveling by carriage in Norway the following year, he records that "Just as we were going away, the peasants were all having their breakfast. They were all eating out of the same dish with wooden spoons. They were extremely dirty." On the train to Cologne, unaccountably in a third-class compartment with Win, he describes their compartment as "full of peasants, and very disagreeable." All this in a single key, with no overtones or embellishments: *We are us, and they are them.*

The only doubt or discontent evident in Fred's journal lies in his occasional impatience with inactivity. "I think that the long staying in the house after the measles is much worse than the disease itself," he writes on March 15, 1869. At a Munich museum, he sees fine tapestry worked "by rich ladies who had nothing else to do." In London, the following year, he writes, "We lead a very lazy life here." A little later, the day's entry consists of, "Did about the same thing as yesterday, which amounts to nothing." A certain distaste seeps up from these entries.

Fred's life in Europe, it seems, was not always busy and productive enough to suit him.

He craved effort, especially mental effort. On the train from Nuremberg to Munich, on June 17, 1869, he studies geometry. "I enjoy studying it very much," he writes. On July 6, the headaches from which he has suffered for three days let up enough that geometry lures him back. "Lately it has become harder," he writes, now halfway through the textbook, "but I like it all the better to have something more to think about." Impatient when doing nothing, he scrupulously logs all he does do—read, study math, make lists, devise magic tricks, practice the piano. In Norway, in 1870, "We were obliged to stay here today so I have been writing and reading pretty much all the time."

~

Fred's journal is littered with the prices of things. Outside the Frauen-kirche in Nuremberg, "we bought a pound or two of cherries very cheap." In Antwerp, he records, they could buy black silk for 85 francs per yard, "10 francs cheaper than two young American ladies had to pay yesterday for the same silk."

This silk is "remarkably thick and soft." But often, the taste of the cherries or the quality of the silk interests him less than their price. "We went swimming for the first time this winter," Fred writes in Berlin. "Father got 15 tickets yesterday at two groschens a ticket. Singly they cost two and a half groschens." Two weeks later, they go rowing. "It cost 2 $^1/_2$ groschen for an hour and three quarters, the cheapest that I have yet seen it." He says nothing of the swimming or rowing but only—after more than a year in Europe, when the novelty of foreign coins and currencies ought presumably to have faded—of the price.

Works of art can seem to him like commodities. In Munich, they see

> a very pretty picture called "The Wounded Huntsman." The price
> of it was eight hundred guldens, but [the dealer] reduced the price
> to six hundred. At this store, we bought four [pictures] of dogs and
> deer. They only cost 20 guldens each, but look as if they cost
> almost fifty. After coming home we found that the dog pictures
> were not nearly so well painted as some of the others, so took one
> of them back and got it changed for another deer picture.

Two days later, Mrs. Taylor goes back and bids once more for *The Wounded Huntsman*. Five hundred guldens, she offers. Five hundred fifty including the frame, responds the dealer. No deal. So Emily goes to another gallery, sees several paintings she likes, and "offered them their prices less 10 percent." In the end, Fred records, they buy "1400 guldens worth of pictures." *The Wounded Huntsman* is not among them.

On a single page of his journal, recorded in Berlin in April 1869, Fred declares he's bought "the handsomest specimen of a raven's egg that I ever saw," rates a group of gymnasts as the best he's ever seen, some French "pudels" as "the most intelligent dogs that I ever saw," and the acting at the Schauspielhaus in Berlin, "the best of any place that I ever saw."

Such pronouncements fill his journal; he rates, judges, evaluates, forever stalking the grandest and the best. On one page, he grades all the Swiss hotels at which he's stayed by price or quality. The Bellevue in Kleine Scheidegg is "excellent," the Hotel de la Poste in Meiringen merely "tolerable." The following summer in London, while shopping for a cricket bat, his journal fills with prices and estimates of quality. Peters & Son, a store carrying ship models and archery equipment along with cricket bats, particularly draws his attention. On the back of their card, he writes:

best bats whale bone set in cane handle cost 15/

one very nice one

The best bat I have seen yet on the Strand not very far from Charing Cross costs <u>18/6</u>

The one best bat . . .

8

A STAGE, A BATTLEFIELD

~

I N MAY, BEFORE LEAVING BERLIN, Fred and his family visited Potsdam, southwest of the city, the former home of Frederick the Great. That morning, his mother had roused him from a sound sleep, they had boarded the train, and now they were touring a few of the two hundred rooms of the New Palace, where the current crown prince lived. They had just passed through a hall that bore a huge porcelain vase, a gift from the czar, when they entered the shell room.

Perhaps fifty feet wide and twice that long, it comprised a great marble-floored hall and two wings set off by massive columns, with painted ceiling, crystal chandeliers, and arched windows that looked out over the royal grounds. And virtually every square inch of it—the columns, the walls, the arches over the doorways—was encrusted with seashells and polished minerals. There were raw stones and crystal growths, seas of mica, quartz explosions, gleaming stone in every color, silicon in every variety, all artfully contrived into flowers, dragons, geometric shapes. It was fabulous, gorgeous in its excess, the ultimate realization of some untrammeled private fantasy.

What Fred wrote about it in his journal, filled in with historical background probably gleaned from a guide, was altogether prosaic. And yet the room lingered with him: two pages after having passed on to descriptions of Frederick the Great's apartment, library, and private theater, he interrupted his account to declare, "The shell room must look very beautiful of an evening." In his mind's eye, he could see it lit as he never had in life, with the shimmering play of lights dancing across the crystals, the great tableau alive with light.

Must we know all the rest of Frederick Winslow Taylor's life to see this sudden vision as the product of a deeply theatrical imagination? And would it be entirely misleading to say that young Fred—not so different from the sons and daughters of traveling vaudevillians—had "grown up in the theater"?

Quakers, of course, traditionally abjured theater and other spectacle; but whatever lingered of Quaker sensibilities among the Taylors plainly didn't extend that far. In Europe, the whole family attended the theater regularly, Fred often recording his impressions in his journal. In Berlin, they squeezed into the narrow seats of the Schauspielhaus, home to the Royal Theater, refitted with more but smaller seats to accommodate the city's theater-hungry crowds. They went to Kroll's Theater, on the Königsplatz; "Father bought six tickets for Kroll's theater this morning," wrote Fred on April 17, summarizing the plot and critiquing, as ever, the performances. "There is one very fine comic actor at Kroll's," he noted. "All of the principal actors sing as well as play." In Munich, "We went to the theater and enjoyed both plays very much," though one featured "Tyrolean peasants [who spoke a] patois scarcely any of which we could understand."

All his life, Fred Taylor would exhibit a theater lover's weakness for show and spectacle, a taste for the dramatic that would turn up in his dealings with workers, in his speeches before businessmen, in his appearances in court and before Congress. Repeatedly, he would become involved in tense, angry confrontations that were the stuff of high drama; he may not have actually enjoyed them, but he probably never felt quite so alive as when he became embroiled in them and could play the part he had written for himself. He loved theater. He sang. As a young man he even performed at Philadelphia's Academy of Music. His friends enjoyed his flights into foreign accents and mimicry. Despite a formal, etiquette-bound modesty, he was never shy about placing himself and his ideas at stage center, sometimes delivering an hours-long monologue and demanding silence from his audience for its duration.

Early hints of this fondness for the dramatic percolate through his journal. Almost invariably, the events, places, and sights upon which he lavishes the most description bear a certain theatrical quality, as in the case of the shell room; he has little to say about the quiet, the small, or the subtle. As an adult, several of Fred Taylor's friends and business associates were big-egoed, blustering figures, veritable P. T. Barnums of industry, happily full of themselves; and even as a boy in Europe, Fred apparently wasn't put off by, and may even have been drawn to, showy people. One California woman the family met in Stuttgart was "a very good talker and entertained us very well." His new piano teacher, Mr. Ruthling, was an actor on the side; Fred liked him very much.

Fred's first response to Sans Souci in Potsdam, graced by some of the loveliest rooms Europe's finest craftsmen could create, was that "it is quite a small palace compared to what I thought it would be"; it was intimate, almost delicate, only a single story high—not heroically enough scaled, apparently, to suit Fred. It took the view from below, after they'd toured the historic rooms and descended the steps of the terraced gardens, to capture his fancy. Surrounded by sculptures of classical figures on pedestals, he stood beside a magnificent marble statue of Frederick the Great on horseback, looking through the mist thrown up by a fountain that spewed a hundred-foot-high gusher from the center of a great circular pond. Before him stood the six formal terraces of vegetation, cascades of green loveliness, the orange trees and flowers, and only then the palace itself, like a diamond tiara atop a regal brow. That was more like it. "One of the most beautiful views of the sort that I ever saw," he wrote.

When Fred hiked through Alpine meadows, he didn't note the wildflowers trembling in the breeze (though once, in Nuremberg, he did ooh and ahh at an infant's tiny finger); it took snow-topped magnificence to move him. When he visited the museums, he didn't comment on sedate portraits and delicate, finely worked miniatures; always he went for the dramatic or the melodramatic. At Munich's Alte Pinakothek, the only painting he mentioned in his journal was one of Jesus by Carlo Dolci, very likely *Christ Child with a Garland of Flowers*, painted in 1680, one of several by the artist at the museum. Dolci was a seventeenth-century Florentine artist of middling talent but rabid faith whom, one critic pointed out, "even his contemporaries found . . . something of a religious fanatic." Critics today invariably see the religious fervor in his paintings, even for its time, as exaggerated and overdone, marred by what one describes as "their oversweet and languid piety." To appeal to young Fred, it seems, things had to be larger than life, bigger than big, sweeter than sweet.

What had captivated him earlier at Berlin's New Museum were the huge murals that lined its three-story grand stairway, or Treppenhaus ("Treppenhouse" in Fred's typically fractured spelling): "They are the most beautiful pictures that I have ever seen." Fred was given to such pronouncements, of course, but here he lavished several pages on the immense compositions. "The first one is the fall of the tower of Babel, away from which go the descendants of Ham," and so on through the next five, culminating in, "Last and best is in the time of the Reformation. In the middle stands Luther holding a bible high above his head. . . ." For Fred, for whom a sentence or two would usually do for a whole day at the museum, here was testimony to the hold on him of the flamboyant in scale and spirit: the Treppenhaus murals, as one book about Berlin had it, depicted nothing less than "the chief events in the civilization of the human race."

Despite everything said and written of Taylor's presumably meticulous, well-ordered sensibilities, it was this taste for stark extremes, for the biggest, boldest, and best, for epic struggle and operatic emotion, that marked him more deeply. Indeed, what he owed most to his mother and her abolitionist friends, perhaps, was a sense of life as a titanic struggle—between freedom and slavery, good and evil—steeped in human drama and played out on the great stage of the nation's life.

~

Fred kept a stamp album while in Europe, an *album timbres-poste* published in France a few years before with a red cloth cover and a foldout map. It devoted pages to *Allemagne* (Germany) but also to Bavaria, the duchy of Brunswick, and the free city of Hamburg, each with its own flag and coat of arms. A united Germany, under Prince Otto von Bismarck, was only just then emerging from shifting confederations of duchies and small states. "Not by speeches and majority decisions will the greatest problems of the time be decided," Bismarck thundered in 1862, "but by blood and iron."

Germany warred with Denmark in 1864. It warred with Austria in 1866. In between, German workers laid the cornerstone for a victory monument, of *Siegesäule*, near the Brandenburg Gate, a huge column surmounted with a great gilded figure of Victory. At the column's base, sculptors and mosaicists would portray scenes unrivaled in their martial exuberance, from the 1864 and 1866 wars and then, later, from the destructive frenzy against France that would erupt in 1870, replete with soundings of trumpets, imperial eagles, soldiers in pointed helmets, and swords raised high overhead.

Fred Taylor would later profess dislike for Germans, and his journal offers hints of it. A girl visiting his sister is "unusually good looking for a German." Later, at a Paris boarding school, Fred takes a liking to its director; but Herr Kornemann's easy laugh soon gives way to an ugly belligerence, and he "proves himself a thorough German." This was no fleeting adolescent antipathy: ever since his youth in Europe, Taylor would write forty years later, "I have disliked [the Germans] exceedingly."

A bias borne of slights suffered at the hands of German boys? "We can't play with them," Fred told his mother once when urged to play with some German children. "They always cheat."

But perhaps there was more to it. Did he see in German bellicosity the reflection of a coarse, combative streak within himself?

One day while in Berlin, Fred and his father visited the battle monument atop the Kreuzberg hill at the southern edge of town, a great Gothic obelisk with sculptures of mythological figures in flowing robes. Beneath each was an iron cross and the record of some bloody Prussian victory over Napoleon from half a century before—"Leipzig, 18 October 1813 . . . Paris, 30 March 1814."

A little later, they walked to the Hasenheide, a large parklike preserve at the southern edge of the city, flat but for a few stunted undulations of terrain, the site of formal reviews of the guards each spring and fall. While walking down a path, a Prussian soldier stopped them. Shooting exercises were under way nearby; their presence was *verboten*.

This was the Germany young Fred Taylor knew, everywhere bristling with cannon, cavalry, and soldiers in bright uniforms, puffed up with martial pride. And to none of this does Fred's journal record the slightest aversion or any remnant of Quaker pacifism.

In Berlin, he admired the soldiers' uniforms. "The prettiest, I think, is that of the lancers—dark blue with a red bust." In Munich, he, Win, and Mary watched soldiers at a parade ground, in iron-wire masks and breastplates, fencing with muskets while others practiced shooting. Mary thought a young recruit seemed to be crying; Fred didn't notice. A few days later, they inspected instruments of torture at a museum, then went up to the third floor to see what Fred found to be "the most beautiful arms that I have yet seen . . . made of steel or iron very richly inlaid with gold." At another museum, the statues he liked best were of "Grecian and Roman heroes fighting over the dead bodies of their friends." In Oslo, the following summer, Fred bought a dagger and sheath. In Brussels, he spent days shopping for a gun.

Whatever else he was, a taste for battle was part of Fred Taylor, too. A pugnaciousness—a warlike bravado, a looking-for-trouble insouciance—warred with his father's mildness and with any Quaker precepts of social harmony he learned at home. Along with Win, he was forever making mischief.

Back in Germantown, Fred had led raids on the cherry trees of a pair of old ladies who lived nearby, not for the cherries, writes Copley, "but for the unholy joy of getting the ladies to come out and scold." When a school-age girl who had spent the weekend visiting the Taylors at Cedron showed up for class on Monday morning too agitated to do her work, the teacher was quick to blame "those Taylor boys"; the brothers already had a reputation.

In Europe, Fred was no readier to keep out of trouble. Once, again at Berlin's Hasenheide, Fred and a friend encountered some boys—*strassen Jungen*, or street kids, Fred called them—who "were impudent to us and we got in a quarrel with them." A crowd formed. Tension mounted. Fred's journal reveals no hint of any principled turning of the other cheek. But finally, outnumbered and probably scared, he and his friend hailed a carriage and escaped.

Another time, Fred and Win were walking down the street when they saw a soldier coming their way. In Bismarck's Germany, soldiers took civilian deference as a given; surely these boys would step aside. But the brothers didn't. Instead, discreetly locking arms and bracing themselves, they kept walking and plowed into the soldier, sending him sprawling. The soldier rose, dusted himself off, pulled out his card, and presented it to the two boys. *A duel?* Fred put on a show of examining it, then shrugged his shoulders, tore it up, scattered the pieces to the wind, and sauntered off with his brother, leaving the enraged soldier standing there, nonplussed.

This, at least, is how the story comes down to us through the family, and perhaps it profits from embellishments heaped up over the years. Still, it suggests the combativeness Fred shared with his brother. Fred Taylor "knew" to avoid conflict, yet some part of him gloried in it. All his life, even as he extolled the virtues of harmony, he was brawling and bullheaded, forever getting into fights.

～

On October 4, 1869, soon after arriving in Paris, Fred and Win entered Kornemann's, located at 12, rue de Boulogne, a narrow street near the Place de Clichy and the St. Lazare train station. "Korny," as the boys called him, seemed pleasant at first, but, as Fred recollected, "I was not there over a week when I commenced to see his real character." At mealtimes, Kornemann would rail at his wife in front of the boys, reducing her to tears.

Fred and Win had a little room with two narrow beds. They would be awakened before daybreak and by eight had already had prayers and a math or science lesson. After a breakfast of coffee and bread, it was more math, then French dictation and translation. Then a big lunch of meat and vegetables and a half-hour break, and on to music lessons. Then, gymnastics in the yard, two hours of German with Kornemann, piano practice, dinner at 6:30, then more classes until bedtime at nine.

Fred's journal suggests a long dark winter under the lash of a thoroughly unlikable man, mostly away from his parents, whom he saw only on Sundays "except when we were punished." When he left Kornemann's the following summer, his music teacher was "the only one whom I was really sorry to leave. He was so kind to me." Except for a handful of the most obligatory sights—the Louvre, Luxembourg Gardens, the Sorbonne, and a few others—he had seen little of Paris.

On July 4, 1870, the Taylors spent the day packing. At eight that night, their train slipped away from the platform at the Gare du Nord and, as Fred wrote, "I did not have any regrets at all."

Just two weeks into their summer travels, after docking in Copenhagen on July 16, they learned that war had been declared between France and Prussia. The news was a little premature; the history books, at least, record Bismarck still scheming and the formal declaration still three days away. But war it was. "We boys go for France and the others for Prussia," Fred wrote.

Scant war news reached them in Norway, where they traveled by coach, mostly with their Germantown friends the Wrights. "Our baggage is strapped up behind and the boy who goes with us to take back the horses sits there on it." Scandinavian flat bread, Fred found, "sure is flat enough. The people eat five or six thicknesses of it together. It is about as good stale as fresh and hard as a brick."

On July 30, seventeen-year-old George Wright, his nineteen-year-old sister Edith, and two of the others split off from the rest of the party and headed off for Bergen by a different route. The Taylors spent August 2 sailing up Stor Fjord. The scenery was breathtaking, Fred marveling at a mountain dropping so sharply into the water that a few feet away from its sheer face the depth could reach three hundred feet. His mother made friends with a young artist, with whom she spoke English, French, and German with equal ease.

Toward evening, the weather turned and, as they approached the dock, the sky was gray and misty. Rain threatened. They had not yet disembarked when someone from shore came on board with the news: George was hurt. "We hurried on shore and up at the hotel met one of the Miss Pierces who told us that he was dead."

It had happened the day before, after a morning and afternoon of hiking, rowing, and horseback riding. Crossing a rickety log bridge slung about ten feet above a swift-flowing river, he'd slipped, fallen into the water, and been washed downstream. He was found hours later, his clothes ripped and torn, his body battered. "We all of us feel very sad," wrote Fred. A few days later, George was buried in a Bergen churchyard.

On August 15, back from Norway now and staying in London, Fred noted that "everyone is full of the war news here and the Strand is fairly covered with paper boys screaming and yelling all around. It seems that the French have received two very bad defeats and are now retreating." That evening, Edith Wright left to join her father in Ireland. But before boarding the train, she gave Fred her brother's soap bag and his sleeve buttons, made from coins.

In Brussels three weeks later, his mother and sister shopped for lace, while Fred and Win made the rounds of gun stores. "Father has given his consent to our taking two guns home," Fred recorded on September 5. At a store the next day, they found a gun shop to their liking. "Win is thinking of getting *un fusil à deux coups,*" a double-barreled rifle, the technical details of which Fred recorded in French. The price was 205 francs. Fred himself liked *un fusil ordinaire* for 115 francs.

In Cologne, on September 10—a week after the disastrous French defeat at Sedan, where eighty thousand troops surrendered, and a week before the Germans began their siege of Paris—Fred found the city "full of soldiers of all sorts who are lounging around the streets. On the way down to the hotel we saw two trains full of soldiers going to the war. . . . Another train was almost entirely filled with horses."

It was a time when war was not yet total war; armies battled on battlefields and life for civilians could pass almost unchanged. Fred went to the cathedral to hear High Mass and then, in what his journal makes sound almost like a tourist expedition, crossed the Rhine to see eight thousand French soldiers said to be held there as prisoners—only to find they had already been taken away. On a steamer trip down the Rhine, they saw not only castles but also captured French troops along the shore. In Mainz, Fred wrote, French officers, presumably prisoners of war, "seemed to be perfectly free, and went around the town, as it seemed, perfectly unnoticed."

It was probably around this time that Fred and Win toured a battle-field—presumably after the bodies had been carted off but still littered with guns, helmets, and swords—trying to scavenge what they could. A Prussian soldier spotted them and demanded the return of their booty. Hiding it under his cap, Win managed to get away with a pressed-metal uniform insignia, about the size of a cigarette pack, that bore a 96 and the figure of an eagle.

Later that month, they reached Stuttgart, where Emily found them a boarding school for the winter with a Frau Erpf. "While we were in Stuttgart," wrote Fred,

> Mrs. Erpf's sister was married and gave a grand wedding party. Win, Foster and I were all groomsmen. About two o'clock we drove down to the Stiftskirche and were introduced to our bridesmaids in the sacristy. (Mine was the prettiest of them all.) After being introduced we marched arm in arm into the church and deposited our bridesmaids opposite us on the other side of the altar and then sat down. After we had been sitting so about five minutes the bride and her man came marching in, which seemed to be the sign for everyone to commence a blubbering, which they kept up regularly through the whole ceremony . . .
>
> [At the reception], I was away from all the Americans, down near the bride with my bridesmaid on my right and another German lady on my left. At my plate was a card marked Mr. Tholer, instead of Taylor. I put as many questions as I could think of to my bride [sic], to all of which she answered yes! no! and such answers. But after a while she got more talkative and at the end of the evening she talked very well.

Though they would be at least another year in Europe, this was Fred's last entry in his journal.

9

"WE WELCOME YOUR RETURN"

∿

Y EARS LATER, asked for a brief account of his life, Taylor would devote a single sentence to the three and a half years with his family in Europe, concluding with a dismissive phrase, "all of which I disapprove of for a young boy." By then, he was an important man with a deep stake in the gritty virtues of physical work and hard, practical experience. He had, as it were, an image to protect, an image those soft, easy years in Europe did nothing to advance.

Europe for Fred was probably something like what public school education has traditionally been for the upper-class English boy: a crucial, abstractly rewarding experience that would help fit him to rule but which, in its dailiness, may not have been particularly pleasant.

What in Europe—an enchanted kingdom to millions who could never hope to go there—was not to like? For one thing, summer adventures aside, Europe meant long, gray winters in school. On May 14, 1869, Fred recorded in his journal that "Today is the last day of our school in Berlin, and I can't say that I am very sorry of it." About the school year in Paris he felt similarly. Then, too, repeated visits to cultural monuments doubtless palled in time, natural curiosity withered by sheer surfeit. Or maybe he was just too young. In any case, however much his parents thought they were conferring upon him the blessings of culture and civilization, to young Fred it never quite took.

And yet he took from the experience more than he thought. When they returned from Europe, Fred boasted a command of German and French that he deemed "almost equal to my knowledge of English." On a visit to France in 1909, he found that within ten days he spoke French "nearly as fluently as ever." And when one of his books appeared in German, he could pass knowingly on its translation. He would return often to Europe, where his ideas had lasting influence.

What resources of initiative and self-confidence did Fred Taylor gain through those three years in Europe that others less fortunate did not?

Certainly, he came back a richer, fuller person. He had seen the reflected glory of kings and princes, experienced the artistic genius of the Renaissance. He had stayed at the best hotels, eaten in the finest restaurants. For the kreuzers, francs, guldens, thalers, and pounds he and his family commanded, common people in half a dozen lands had done their bidding. Whether or not he preferred Carlo Dolci to Raphael, or cared ever to see either of them again, he had at least seen them. And that forever set him apart, as a ruler and not one of the ruled.

∿

"My very dear friends," it began.

> In spirit, we welcome your return to your home and your friends and we shall welcome you most heartily to the old home.
> Will not you come to us for a while? We shall be so glad to have you. Without any trouble we can give you these comfortable rooms, and plenty of peaches and sweet potatoes and I must not forget tomatoes. I will not promise much for the rest of the table, but come and we will make out, to give you all plenty to eat.

The letter was from Elizabeth Pugh, across the street from whose house on Willow Avenue the Taylors had lived early in their marriage. It was dated August 10, 1871. After more than three years, the Taylors were back in Germantown.

They came back to a new president; the 1868 vote had gone to Ulysses S. Grant. Philadelphia's population had swelled to seven hundred thousand. Allegations of fraud had tainted recent municipal elections. News of a double murder trial filled the papers. Early in 1870, the city's blacks joyously celebrated the adoption of the Fifteenth Amendment, which gave them the vote; later that year, the Pennsylvania Anti-Slavery Society held a final meeting and disbanded. On May 15, the city's large ethnic German population, celebrating the victory of German arms over France, held a huge procession, nine miles long. In 1871, with the volunteer fire department having disbanded the previous winter, a paid, municipal fire department was established in its stead. North in Germantown, meanwhile, the YMCA opened its new rooms on Main Street, and fights were breaking out nearly every Sunday at Biffert's Skating Park Hotel, over toward the Wissahickon.

Fred returned to what he would call "the healthy out-of-door life of Germantown, than which I believe there is nothing finer in the world, in which sport is the leading idea, with education a long way back." He fell in again with old friends, including Birge Harrison. "With our brothers and our boyhood friends," Harrison remembered later, "we led a healthy normal life in the woods and fields about Germantown, playing cricket and rounders, football and mumble-the-peg, and scouring the countryside for thirty miles about in search of minerals and 'specimens' of various kinds." Some of Fred's friends had set up a Germantown Scientific Society, which occupied a room in the Langstroth Building (where the Unitarian Society had met before getting its own building) stocked with collections of minerals, birds, and scientific books. Fred, now fifteen, became active in it. With a copy of Greenleaf's *New Higher Algebra* in hand, he took to studying math, apparently on his own.

The Taylors were back in Germantown, but not at Cedron, which belonged to Frank's sister, Sarah, and where sister Emma lived as well. Over the next couple of years, they would go there often for dinner with Aunt Sarah and her husband. "We drove over to Cedron this morning, found your aunts pretty well, Peyton [a horse] improving slowly and the new man, William, was busy hauling manure on the potato patch for rye," Fred's father wrote him a little later. Clearly, their ties to the place remained, and no discord or rivalry over it seeps into family correspondence. Still, for unclear reasons, the house in which they had lived for more than a decade was not theirs to live in now.

For much of the three years after their return, and certainly by about November 1872, Fred and his family lived with friends, Ed and Phoebe Houghton, in a big house up the hill from Main Street. Here on Germantown's east side, across town from Cedron, they planned to build a new house; Emily, for one, wanted to be near Sarah Pugh, the high-minded abolitionist who lived with her brother Isaac and his wife at the base of the hill, near the train depot. For three years in Europe, they'd lived out of their bags. They still had no place of their own but by the fall of 1872 were working up the plans for one. By early the following year, they had purchased property on Ross Street, a sizable plot that backed up to a nursing home.

Fred heard about his parents' ambitious plans in detail, but mostly by mail. For by this time, he was away at school in New England.

10

THE GREAT TRIUMVIRATE

~

H E WASN'T BORN THERE, didn't die there, and for most of his life didn't live there, but New England occupies almost as central a place in Fred Taylor's story as Philadelphia. Isaac Winslow's whaling history, and Emily's brush with the great Transcendentalist thinkers, were quintessential New England stories; both maintained lifelong links to the region. And Fred Taylor would be said to have, in the words of his first biographer, "one whale of a New England conscience." At least in broad brushstrokes he did possess those Puritan sensibilities of self-restraint and inner mission which we associate with New England, and which Max Weber had in mind when he wrote *The Protestant Ethic and the Spirit of Capitalism* in 1904.

All his life Taylor kept coming back to New England. He vacationed in the great north woods of Maine (or the Adirondack wilderness in nearby New York), to canoe, camp, hike, and hunt. Later in his career, for three years, he worked in Maine. He played golf on the courses of Augusta and Rockland, Maine. He spent Julys at the home of his wife's family in Plymouth, Massachusetts, literally down the road from where the Pilgrims landed. He spent Augusts with his sister and brother-in-law in the mountains around Manchester, Vermont. Later, after he was famous, the first great challenge to his life's work surfaced in an industrial town a few miles outside Boston.

And beginning in 1872, when he was sixteen, Fred attended Phillips Exeter Academy, in Exeter, New Hampshire. Exeter was a prime feeder school to Harvard, year after year placing twenty to thirty boys in its freshman class, many more than Boston Latin—or, for that matter, any other school; of one group of 631 Exeter boys going on to earn college degrees, 413 did so from Harvard. Founded in 1781, Exeter was well-endowed and well-connected, with a glorious pedigree. Daniel Webster had gone there, as had Robert Todd Lincoln, Abe Lincoln's son. But prep schools still drew their students regionally, and Exeter was an uncommon choice for a Philadelphian. Of 162 students at Exeter in 1872, most hailed from New Hampshire, Massachusetts, and elsewhere in New England; only eight were from Pennsylvania.

At Exeter, Fred found himself surrounded by the same relaxed wealth he had always known. Even the school's catalog complained, on behalf of the trustees and instructors, about "the excessive amount of money furnished [students] by parents and guardians." No one at Exeter, it is hard to think otherwise, ever wanted for anything. Take the sheer excellence of illustrations appearing in the *Peun* (or PEA'n, the acronym for Phillips Exeter Academy). Or the quality of student furnishings revealed in old photographs. Or the frequent references in local publications to one new endowment or another. "Phillips Exeter Academy is to receive a legacy of $50,000 by the will of Jeremiah Kingman of Barrington," the *Exeter News-letter* reported on December 27, 1872; tuition at the time was twenty dollars per term.

Fred enrolled in the fall of 1872 in the middle class (between junior and senior), and moved into a big house on Eliot Street presided over by Mrs. L. B. Cilley, mother of the school's Greek teacher. Mrs. Cilley, his father wrote Fred after leaving him in her charge and returning to Philadelphia, struck him as "a kind motherly person one with whom we felt great confidence in leaving you." Having borne ten children, the two youngest of whom probably still lived at home, she was then in her mid-fifties. While the school had just bought a hotel to use as its second dormitory, most students lived with families in town, the walls of their rooms cluttered with a Victorian excess of photos, prints, rugs, fringed tablecloths, mementoes of every sort, and (a few years later, at least) lacrosse sticks and tennis rackets.

With Fred at Mrs. Cilley's was, along with three other students, James A. Wright, Jr., one of the Wright boys from Philadelphia, George's fifteen-year-old younger brother. At least a week before the start of class on September 14, they were already up at Exeter, getting off to a good start as housemates, presumably, by keeping scrupulous track of how many nightshirts, stockings, and collars, at six cents each, they sent out for laundering. Fred was either less fastidious than Jamie, or less extravagant, normally getting about half as many garments cleaned.

First settled in 1638, Exeter resembled any other New England town in winter, with great denuded trees set against low gray skies, and white clapboard houses on silent, snowbanked streets; snow fell half a dozen times a month from November to April, with a couple of yards of the stuff accumulating by May's thaw.

But this busy little manufacturing town of thirty-five hundred was just fifty miles from Boston, an hour and a half away on the Boston and Maine Railroad; trains came six times daily. With the academy supplying hungry audiences, the town enjoyed a cultural life that belied its size. On December 13, 1872, at the Exeter town hall, Frederick Douglass offered "Reminiscences of Slavery and Anti-Slavery." The following October, the knife-edged editorial caricaturist Thomas Nast appeared and "by a few happy strokes" of colored chalk on a large easel, the local paper reported, skewered the corrupt and rapacious Boss Tweed.

Fred wasn't at Exeter two months before the town was visited by excitement of quite another kind.

A FIEND OF FIENDS!

———

Revolting Tragedy in Northwood!

———

AN OLD MAN OUTRAGES AND
MURDERS HIS NIECE!

———

The Body Mutilated and Concealed in the Woods!

———

THE MURDERER CONFESSES HIS CRIME!

———

THE BODY RECOVERED!

———

THE CORONER'S INQUEST!

———

OTHER VICTIMS OF THE DEMON!

———

It seldom falls to the lot of the journalist to record so brutal and revolting a crime as has recently been perpetrated in the town of Northwood, in this county . . . one of the most shocking and fiendish ever recorded in the criminal annals of the country. . . .

After this typographic treat, readers learned how a certain Evans had committed unspeakable crimes. Two months later, there was more. A local bank official, N. Appleton Shute, left desperate by stock and gambling losses, took the evening train into Boston and failed to return the following morning. He had embezzled, or "defalcated," $170,000. "You seem to have had two very exciting circumstances in the usually quiet little town of Exeter, the defalcation and the trial for murder," Emily wrote Fred that winter. "Did you see Evans? What a wretch he must be."

Fred's first months at Exeter were hard going. Math was fine, but plunked down into Greek grammar and Cicero's *Orations Against Catiline* in Latin, he felt panicky. "Does Latin become any easier to you?" Emily wondered in a letter a few weeks into the term. And though his grades each week never varied much from 9 and 10, it was only by dint of hard work. At some point, he yielded to the pressure. Early in November, Fred wrote his parents that he had cheated on an exam.

His parents took the news with equanimity. Of course, he got a lecture—from his father he could always expect one—urging him never to do it again. "I would ten thousand times rather have you stand honorably and honestly low in your marks," his father wrote, "than to have you wanting in honesty, honor, and self-respect. The first is of small importance, but the latter is vital, no matter what you may acquire or what you may accomplish." But his confession eased their pain. "Your mother desires me to say that though she would have been proud and pleased to hear you [illegible] first in your class, she is still more delighted that you have confessed to doing wrongly and acted up to your conscientious sense of duty. Better be right than be king."

A week later followed the incident, mentioned earlier, in which Fred took a book into church and then insisted he had defied no written rules in doing so. (The school prided itself, it was said, on how it had "no rules, only absolute freedom, tempered by expulsion.") His father had replied that "persons of gentle breeding" did not defy the rules, written or not, nor did they try to get around them:

> My dear boy, I have written a good deal on this subject for I have
> felt very much about it and I trust when you come to think over
> the matter you will take a juster, truer view. Do not do violence to
> your better, truer self, and never seek to justify sophistically
> anything which your enlightened conscience tells you there may be
> a doubt about, for where your conscience doubts walk carefully

and slowly. And remember 'tis better to follow thy doubts than to violate your inner light.

But Fred was not finished with trouble. The following spring, Mrs. Cilley, with whom they boarded, learned that Fred and Win, who had joined him at Exeter, were dipping into books less high-minded than Cicero. "Your mother and I both feel very great objection to reading those dime novels," wrote his father. "Many of them are vicious [immoral], all are trashy, and I hope that neither of you will read them, and if there were no other reason you should feel a regret and hesitation to do anything to offend or hurt Mrs. Cilley's feelings in the matter." Emily had her say, too. "My dear boys," she squeezed into the top of the letter, "I sincerely join in all your father says about the discipline of the school and those weak injurious novels."

But a second postscript softened their reproach: "I am so glad, dear Fred, that you tell us about the . . . novels, Mrs. Cilley, etc. I hope my dear boy will continue to be free and candid." An incident that might just as easily have prompted only parental rebuke became a way to laud Fred's honesty and preserve his self-esteem.

Though two years older than Fred, Winslow had entered Exeter as a junior, a year behind him. He joined his brother and Jamie Wright at Mrs. Cilley's and was followed that spring by a native New Hampshirean whom Fred had met earlier, James Tufts. Fred and the new boy became friends. "For more than a year," recalled Tufts, a fixture at Exeter for more than fifty years as professor of English, "we played, rowed, studied, ate, and slept together."

The two of them were avid rowers. "I have a remembrance of very pleasant times on the Old Salt," Taylor wrote. He meant the Squamscott River, which passed through town and bore the salt tide up from Portsmouth; you always had to reckon with the tide, Exeter boys learned, because when it ebbed you faced mudflats instead of river and had to carry your boat back. Fred wanted a boat and his father relayed word that a family friend would loan him his. It needed repairs, painting, and oars, so it would be a while before Fred had it—and not until the school had a boathouse for it. A boat club formed that year, gaining use of a church cellar for the boats, and Fred got the twenty-six-foot craft the following spring.

On a fine fall afternoon in October, the local paper reported, the shores of the Squamscott were "thronged with spectators and its waters thickly dotted with sail and row boats filled with those who had come out to witness the Third Annual Regatta of the students of Phillips Academy." The third race was for four-oared boats, and Taylor and Tufts rowed for the winning crew.

Since the end of the Civil War, baseball had grown popular at Exeter, but the school did not play outside teams until 1875, and the sport was still in its adolescence—no gloves, masks, or catcher's mitts, and the pitcher threw underhand. A species of curveball was just coming in; a classic jock named Shillito, who barely scraped by academically, was the first Exonian to throw one. Fred, club captain at one point, was also a pitcher and gave his deliveries a peculiar twist that caused batters to pop the ball into harmless outs. Batters called his pitch illegal, but the umpires sustained him.

When Exeter boys gathered for reunions later or reminisced about the school, they dwelled not on sports but on the harsh academic climate. In Taylor's memory, half the students were dropped each year, and the others scrambled to head the class. "Hard work" is what John Olmstead, who graduated the year Taylor entered, always remembered about Exeter. "It was a place where one learned to appreciate Sunday, mail time, and his nightgown." Much initiative was demanded of students. If you didn't understand something, you had to get it on your own; the teachers weren't there to spoon-feed you. The place fairly reveled in the cold justice with which it applied its standards. "Young man," the principal once advised Olmstead, "I think it probably impossible for you to remain in the senior class and it is doubtful whether you can stay in the Academy at all."

Classes met in the Third Academy Building, a new, brick-and-sandstone structure, centerpiece of the campus, built to emulate in more permanent materials a wooden predecessor destroyed by fire. Upstairs, under the clock tower, a great hall—with a rose window at its center and the massive wood beams of an open timbered roof above—served as chapel and auditorium. On the first floor were six large classrooms, each with forty or fifty desks.

Curricular revolution was in the air just then; Harvard, to which Exeter's eyes always turned, had widened its focus from the classics. Soon, Exeter would respond, offering courses in English, geography, French, physics, and American history—but not soon enough to influence Fred's years there, which came under the old regime. The curriculum remained largely as it always had been—algebra and geometry, Virgil, Cicero, Homer, Plato, Euclid, Thucydides. A good teacher could use the classics as the wedge into a wider world: translating Greek, for example, honed skills in English composition. But always, and only, it was mathematics, Latin, Greek.

Olmstead remembered the Greek master, Cilley, scratching his thighs and scowling as a student stuttered through an irregular Greek verb and the mathematics teacher, George A. Wentworth, irascibly taunting a geometry-fearful student, "Do you expect ever to get into Harvard, Collins?"

"Well, I hope so, sir," said Collins.

"How many in this class think Collins will ever get in?" he asked the class, who sided with their classmate.

"Well, they seem to be with you, Collins," Wentworth muttered with what somebody remembered as an inscrutable smile, "but I don't agree with them, and I never will."

Cilley and Wentworth were two thirds of what school historians would dub the Great Triumvirate. But during Fred's time, they were much more; the old principal, the third of the three, had retired the year before and the new principal was no match for the two entrenched figures. Cilley and Wentworth, both Exeter graduates, had entered Harvard, as sophomores, in the fall of 1855 and roomed together there. Wentworth returned to Exeter to teach in 1858, Cilley a year later. Now, during Fred's tenure, they were in their mid-thirties and had been at Exeter more than fourteen years. Their personalities were forceful, their classroom demeanors unforgettable.

Neither had an overly refined temperament. Cilley, his beady eyes fairly popping out of his head, was "gruff with those who did not put forth their best effort, and by roaring sometimes intimidated those of little courage," wrote one school historian. "If there was one thing that he hated fervently it was affectation and cant. Outspoken to the verge of rudeness in all matters, public and private, even in class he would not brook a stilted or overfine translation."

And Cilley was, if anything, the meeker of the two.

Wentworth was a big man with a broad forehead, thick, dark, wavy hair, his ears lost in the touseled locks that curled around them; a long, bristly beard, full sensual lips, and sleepy, drooping eyes that looked as if they held bottomless reservoirs of menace. In a snapshot taken of him in the 1880s as he strolled past the Exeter town hall in a top hat, he seemed to fix his eyes on the camera, daring its lens to linger. No Hollywood director would have the imagination to cast him as anything but a thug.

This son of a poor New Hampshire farmer was called "Bull" Wentworth. He looked like a bull and bellowed like one. He cared not a whit how he dressed or how he looked and had no use for rules other than his own. "Due attention should be paid to deportment," he was advised at a school where he briefly taught before returning to Exeter. "A little regularity in passing to and from the seat, and decorum in the several classes at recitation, serve to give that finished appearance which is very desirable, but which was greatly wanting in this school during the past term." At Exeter, he was known to show up in class half an hour late and to admit students who had been expelled. In the words of one account, he was the "confidant of every troublemaker in the school." He brooked no interference with his authority and was seen by at least one alumnus as "uncouth, savage."

Yet parents sent their boys to Exeter expressly for his sake. Students loved and never forgot him; Fred Taylor would tell a congressional committee about him forty years later. He was, first of all, an inspired teacher; while he raged and blew and blustered, substance stood behind it. Like Cilley, he had been Phi Beta Kappa at Harvard. He wrote thirty-four mathematics texts, several of them translated into foreign languages, mostly based on his Exeter teaching. He made a fortune from them, which he later bequeathed to the school that was his life.

Then, too, he had a softer side. When a student contracted scarlet fever and had to be moved from the dormitory, Wentworth "marched into my room, wrapped me up as tenderly as a mother and carried me down to a warm, heated carriage that he had prepared, took me to a private house, carried me up again and himself put me to bed." A school historian saw him as a complex brew of "savagery and tenderness; of withering sarcasm and the refined gentleness of a woman; of biting personal remarks and of unasked aid and comfort to the poor and helpless."

After the mildness of his father, the sheer virility of the two men surely must have stirred sixteen-year-old Fred. All his life, he'd respond to the heroically scaled; and the two legendary teachers, alive in the

memories of so many Exeter boys, were surely that. For Fred, the loving
severity with which they stamped the school, where "no excuse was
taken for any delinquency whatever, and in which every boy had to toe
the mark in all respects," would linger. Exeter was "perhaps the very
best experience of my early life." In Cilley and Wentworth, he had
living models for an uncompromising personal style that nodded to the
gentlemanly virtues yet roared with a brazen, outlaw individualism.

~

Letters from home came weekly, crammed with family news and local
gossip. Fred heard that his parents had stayed with the Sewalls in
Boston, that the old Germantown railroad depot had been supplanted
by a new one, that the Justices had turned down a thirty-thousand-
dollar offer for their house, that the horse disease decimating Germantown had run its course, that his father had been busy chauffeuring
sister Mary to parties, that Uncle Michael continued to decline and,
finally, in May, that he had died. "His last moments were exceedingly
quiet and peaceful," wrote Emily. At the funeral, "it was raining when
we got to the burying ground and we had to walk through the wet
grass, there being no path. He was buried next to your Uncle William,
and in a row with the rest of the family."

Early in Fred's second year, on September 18, 1873, his Aunt Sarah
wrote him and Win from Cedron. "Edward rang just as Sister and Self
were at tea and confirmed the failure of J. Cooke & Co., also that of
E. W. Clark and Co.—an intense excitement on 3rd Street."

She was describing the first tremors of the panic of 1873, which
started in the very bowels of the Taylor circle, spread from Philadelphia, and induced a nationwide business depression that would last for
five years. Financier Jay Cooke had gotten his start in the offices of
E. W. Clark (the Clarks being friends of the Taylors), went on to help
finance the Civil War, and was a banking figure of rocklike solidity. But
now, his huge railroad investment had burst its bubble. When Jay
Cooke closed its doors, David McCullough has written in *Mornings on
Horseback*, his biography of Theodore Roosevelt, "it was as if the Bank
of England had failed."

Succeeding weeks brought more grim news. "There has been such a
terrible panic," his father wrote Fred early the following month, "that it
will require some time to pass before men regain any confidence in
each other."

In early November, Emily wrote Fred, "I am afraid there will be a good deal of suffering among the poor this winter. Mr. Collum has not paid his workmen for seven weeks and Pete, Bridget's husband, is all out of money, so that they have no coal and no provisions. I suppose this will be the case with a good many."

The panic little influenced the family's day-to-day lives, certainly not Fred's at Exeter, but it did force them to sell at an inconvenient time. To pay for the new house they were having built, wrote Emily, "I am obliged to sell my stock . . . at a very low price, so that we shall not escape loss."

∾

Mostly, however, and even from the very beginning, letters from home bore advice, much of it prompted by troubling news from Fred about his study habits, aggravated by reports from the Wrights through Jamie, or from Win: The boy was driving himself.

Five hours a night on homework and other class preparation, maybe two on math, two on Latin translation—that was average. Thirty years later, Taylor chose not to send one of his own boys to Exeter. "He thought it was too severe for me," recalled Robert Taylor, who, after Cornell, went on to a successful career as engineer and investor and was about as bright as anyone would want to be. In any case, Fred worked, worried, plugged away. After a slow start, he ended the first term with a 91 in Latin, a 92 in Greek, and an 89 in mathematics, grades that placed him near the top of the class.

His grades would only improve as he went along, but that, paradoxically, worried his parents all the more. He was a bright boy but no genius; what was he doing to himself?

From home, Frank and Emily held out a rudder of moderation. Curb your excesses, they as much as said; seek the middle ground. Yes, study hard, his father advised, but every hour or so "take a few minutes exercise with your clubs"—weights of some kind—"just long enough to relieve the strain on your mind." Emily was pleased that Fred had not been among those dropped to a lesser requirement, 15 lines, in Latin. "But I should much rather that you should have 15 lines than to make yourself sick by study." It's doubtful Fred heard them though, or eased up on their account. His parents' injunctions continued. Nothing they heard from New Hampshire gave them reason to relent in the slightest.

Advice, especially from his father, ranged over matters large and small. With Fred off at school that first term, Frank ordered made for him a pair of boots with cork liners to better keep out the New England cold. He sent them up to Exeter with Cosmoline for waterproofing, socks Emily had knitted for him, and several pages of advice on how best to maintain them. Later that fall, with Fred returning home for Christmas, he issued elaborate plans and weather contingencies, advised him what he needed to do at the depot, and the like:

> Should it be stormy you would better take the rail all the way,
> coming by way of Worcester and Springfield and leaving the
> Worcester station opposite the United States Hotel. You will find
> an express man at the station on your arrival in Boston who will
> take your baggage where you desire and give you a check from one
> depot to the other. You would better check your trunk only to
> N.Y. . . .

It was sound fatherly advice. One day, Fred Taylor would issue similarly elaborate instructions, and for him, we must guess, they did not represent the cruel emasculation of the workman that his harshest critics would assert but, rather, the parental concern on which he had been raised. The Victorian era comes down to us today mired in images of distance and reserve. But it is impossible to read letters from Fred's parents during his Exeter days and not find them full of kindness, concern, caring, and love.

～

Leaving aside those small unrecorded slights, hurts, and injustices which every child suffers at the hands of his parents and which forever mark his inner psychic terrain, Fred Taylor had an enviable childhood and adolescence.

Deep in the interstices of daily life, no doubt, frustrations gnawed at him and resentments festered. Tales of Fred's sleeping problems and of a harness he contrived to combat them, of the contempt his European journal reveals for the lazy and useless life, and of his compulsive striving at Exeter all suggest he was scarcely immune from neurosis or the usual teenage turmoil. But for the most part he was a normal teenager who looked with confidence to the world soon to open to him. His was a privileged childhood, in the best sense of the word.

Though his upbringing was stripped of all want, he had been taught the value of the dollar. His parents had firm standards; yet they moderated their expectations with tolerance and compassion. He grew up surrounded by well-born, prosperous people who took a lively interest in the big world around them and who mattered in it. He had plenty of family and friends—good family, good friends. His parents evidently did not suffer from drunkenness, gluttony, or excesses of marital discord. They did not withhold affection. All his life the sun of his parents' regard would warm Fred in its glow, leaving him with not the slightest want of self-confidence.

In this respect, at least, Fred and his brother reached adulthood similarly shaped, though Win's "self-confidence," if that is what it was, verged on something like narcissism. Edward Winslow Taylor did not do as well as Fred at Exeter, but he did well enough; he was no slouch intellectually. After school, he worked briefly in an import-export firm probably tied to friends of the family (perhaps the Wrights), went to medical school (where he began smoking cigars in anatomy class to ward off the smell), and got an M.D. degree from Philadelphia's Jefferson Medical College in 1881. But he practiced only briefly.

Early in his career, the story goes, a patient appeared with some minor ailment. Win was eating breakfast and couldn't be bothered. "Let him wait until I'm finished," he ordered. The disgruntled patient stalked off to find another doctor, whereupon Dr. Taylor took down his shingle and never practiced again. The story is no doubt apocryphal, but family members tell it with such relish that it probably strikes close to his personality. Handsome and even distinguished looking, he married well—to a Sharpless, an old Philadelphia family—and spent his life eating and drinking well, outliving his brother by more than twenty years. "He didn't accomplish a damn thing," his nephew Robert would put it.

A damn thing, that is, but hunt and fish. "He hunted from Florida to Maine, shooting anything that flew," recalls his grandson, Frank Wallace, who grew up at Cedron, where Win lived for many years. (Once or twice he shot himself, as telltale black dots in his neck and arms, shotgun pellets migrating to the skin's surface, would testify.) In later years, Win went up to Canada and Maine and sent salmon, trout, quail, duck, and pheasant back to Philadelphia. The summer before Win enrolled at Exeter, back in August 1872, he got a letter from his friend John Peet from Elizabethtown, New Jersey, fairly reeking of guns and game: "Shot four quail ..." The following month, Aunt Sarah wrote Fred that Win had arrived with Edward Wright at Cedron with guns, ammunition, kills. Such stuff was about all that ever mattered to Win, and to listen to family members tell of his later years, he apparently remained perfectly comfortable doing what he did, untroubled by his own lapses from kindness and tact, for the rest of his life.

"I loved him, but he was a horror," recalls Marie Hodges, granddaughter of Fred and Win's sister Mary, who pictures him as insufferably coarse, bereft of gentility and, all in all, "a disagreeable ogre." "I would not have him in our home if he were not your brother," she remembers her grandfather saying to Mary. Win could take his mother's candor and twist it into cruelty. Grandson Frank Wallace, known in the family as "Cappy," brought to Christmas dinner a girl who, whatever her other charms, was cross-eyed. "Can't Cappy do any better than that?" Win sneered in front of her, sending the young lady to her room in tears.

"He thought the world was designed for him and him alone," remembers Wallace, who idolized him; "Grandfather-said-so" they called him in school. And yet, he could see in his grandfather a shameless self-importance, a profound sense of entitlement. Winslow would call his sleeping chauffeur near midnight, demand to have the car brought around, and think nothing of it. "He thought," says Wallace simply, "it was his due."

Fred's largely unknown brother did nothing the world acclaims or remembers, yet enjoyed a healthy (or maybe not so healthy) self-regard. That, apparently, is what growing up in this family—at least for a boy—meant. "The ego in his cosmos seemed to be exceptionally vigorous," a sympathetic writer said of Fred Taylor, "and there were frequent flashes of a nature not only pugnacious but domineering and imperious." The Taylor children were bright, rich, loved. And having all that made them strong.

Indeed, if there was any lack in Fred Taylor's childhood, it was one that all children should suffer: in the words of that tired parental lament, he never realized how good he had it. He did not trouble himself over his fortunate circumstances. And he lacked the insight or motivation to get inside the skin of those not as favored as he; indeed, he regularly chose as friends the bright and the blessed, not those scarred by ill luck or inarticulate with hurt. Left relatively unscathed by life, he probably would have been at a loss to understand why all the aggrieved, unlucky, and impoverished people of the world didn't just push themselves up off the floor.

But just once in his youth, as far as we can tell, he did feel disappointment's chill wind.

1 1

THE WISEST COURSE

~

O N SEPTEMBER 19, 1873, Fred's father wrote him, hoping he was "well and free from headaches."

The following week, he wrote to say he was sorry to hear Fred still had them, offering dietary advice: "Fried and fatty things are not generally wholesome and few persons with delicate stomachs can eat them with impunity." And then he added, "You would be better to leave the school, and go on with your studies in mathematics, etc. elsewhere, if you decide to become an engineer, than ruin your health."

Leave the school . . . become an engineer.

This extraordinary prospect—what about Harvard? the law?—was no new element in Fred's correspondence with his parents. Five months earlier, on April 24, near the end of Fred's first year, his father had written, "If you intend to become an engineer you cannot master too thoroughly the elementary branches of mathematics," which reads as if the idea could have been Fred's. September's letter, however, sounded a new note, one exhibiting a logic we today might find alien: staying at Exeter, said his father, risked Fred's health, whereas leaving Exeter to become an engineer meant saving it.

In a letter Emily wrote to Fred a few days later we can make out the thinking more clearly: "And now dear Fred, what about yourself? Have you less headache? If the lessons do not become easier and you continue to have headaches will it not be better for you to leave and go to an engineering school at Troy, Hoboken—where Archie Richards has just entered—or the school of technology at Boston?" The school in Troy, New York, was Rensselaer Polytechnic Institute, the nation's first engineering school, founded in 1824. Hoboken meant Stevens Institute of Technology, in New Jersey. The Boston school was Massachusetts Institute of Technology. "I think the wisest course," she went on, "would be for you to drop down lower in your class. We shall think it no disgrace for you. On the contrary, it will show much more good sense to retain your health for life than to study to be one of the first in your class."

In Fred's second year at Exeter, the heavy, leather-jacketed book with marbled endpapers that bore the record of his grades showed him doing exceedingly well. But he was killing himself to do it, Emily felt; his terrible headaches proved as much. Options? Continue in the velvet-lined pressure cooker that was Exeter, but go easier on himself, accepting an inevitably lower class position; this was the second possibility she mentioned. Or else, drop out altogether and choose a less demanding discipline, engineering.

Today, a Harvard B.A. and an engineering degree from Rensselaer or one of the other schools Emily mentioned represent very different educational experiences. But in 1873 they stood even further apart. Today, engineering courses are often highly abstruse, with undergraduates sometimes vying with one another over how theoretical their courses are, with the textbooks a glut of Greek letters representing mathematical quantities, and with academic pressure as high as or higher than at the best liberal arts schools. But not in 1873. While engineering curricula included science and mathematics, they were still rooted in the shop floor. Students learned drafting, how to run machine tools and regulate boilers. In such a setting, the severe academic pressure undermining Fred's health would, his parents felt, be absent.

In succeeding weeks, the headaches eased but not his parents' counsel. At the first sign of their return, he was advised, he should let up on his study. In Fred Taylor's time, more than ours, good health was seen as fragile, rare, and precious. You couldn't count on getting sick and taking a pill to get better. Seemingly healthy people died at 15, or 30, or 40, of tuberculosis, pneumonia, typhus, and scarlet fever. They died in epidemics of yellow fever, cholera, and smallpox. Even wealth didn't unfailingly protect parents from the agony of a child's illness or death. More than today, people got sick and never got well. And his parents' letters were shot through with such worry.

Certainly by November 6, 1873, but probably before, their fears had found a definite object, Fred's eyes. Wrote Emily, "I feel a little anxious about what you say about not getting to bed until 11 o'clock. I think you must need more sleep and I am afraid it will injure your eyes. I hope you will not care in the least about your marks. They are of so little consequence in comparison to your health and your eyesight."

Modern thinking inverts the cause-and-effect relationship that Emily's letter implied. Long hours of study, even by kerosene lamp late into the night, don't by themselves injure eyes. Rather, poor eyesight uncorrected by glasses and harshly taxed by use may produce symptoms of strain, including headaches. And Fred's vision *was* left uncorrected.

As a boy, he did not wear glasses and had no vision problems that come down to us. He had always been an avid reader; when he had a book in his hand, you had to scream at him, sister Mary would say, to gain his attention. In Europe—on the trains, in the jouncing carriages—he was always reading, in French as well as in English. On the train to Hamburg, he finished *Le Collier de la Reine*, an 1850 novel by Alexandre Dumas *père*. Between spells of seasickness traveling from Oslo to England, he spent all day reading *The Knight of Gwynne* by Charles Lever, a popular Anglo-Irish novelist.

But Fred's headaches long predated his Exeter period. Leaving the Pinakothek in Munich, on July 4, 1869, for example, he was struck by one, "in consequence of which I did not go down to dinner"; it persisted all day. Four days later, he reported, "I still have this bad headache." He attributed it to the effects of something he'd eaten, coupled with a cold, but it could have stemmed from vision problems.

Fred would later be diagnosed as seriously astigmatic, a condition in which asymmetry of the lens or cornea causes blurred vision; the attempt to compensate for it can cause serious headaches. Why didn't he wear glasses at Exeter, as he did later? Why wasn't his astigmatism detected and treated with the proper glasses, leaving the headaches, as seems likely, to disappear?

The family hardly shunned eye doctors; in 1869, in Salzburg, Emily went to see one. And probably by January 1874, Fred's parents did take him to see what his future wife would term "a noted eye specialist." (He apparently commanded princely fees. In what sounds like a family joke based on their experience with one, Emily suggested in a letter to the

boys that "one [of you] might be[come] an oculist"—an ophthalmolo-
gist—"and earn $10 for a 15 minutes consultation.")

But astigmatism, routinely treated today, was then still unfamiliar.
While described as far back as 1793, it was thought to be rare until the
Dutch physician Frans Cornelis Donders demonstrated its relatively
ubiquity and pointed up the use of special cylindrical lenses for its correction. But that came only in 1862 and apparently failed to win instant
acceptance; even by 1886, Donders's breakthrough was still seen as
recent.

That headaches could be caused by vision problems like uncorrected astigmatism was a new enough notion that an article making
much of the idea, "Headaches from Eye Strain," could appear in a
medical journal as late as 1876. The effort needed by the farsighted,
"especially with astigmatic trouble," wrote Philadelphia physician S.
Weir Mitchell, "is extreme, owing to the instinctive craving for distinct
vision—and hence the source of fatigue. The use of the eyes is so incessant that it is impossible for the victim, by any means save glasses, to
put the eyes at rest."

But either these new ideas about the links between headaches, eye-
strain, and astigmatism hadn't reached the Taylors and their doctors,
or they were not applied to Fred; he got no corrective lenses. The prescription instead was simpler still. Fred must go easy on his eyes. He
mustn't use them so much.

But what was "so much"? By what yardstick was Fred abusing his
eyes? As it turns out, the whole edifice of the family's thinking rested on
a hidden foundation stone and, in a letter Emily wrote the boys just
before Christmas, it was laid bare: "I am afraid, Fred, you have been
studying too hard or you would not be likely to get high marks in
Greek and mathematics." Indeed he had been, consistently pulling
down 9 and 10 each week and destined for a 94 average in one and a 95
in the other, highest in the class. Grades so high, she was saying, must
reflect excessive study. What else could account for them? Certainly
Fred was no genius.

This was not the first time his parents had intimated that they
thought Fred only ordinarily able. Encouraging his involvement with
the debate society, for example, Frank had observed that speaking skills
"can be acquired by dull boys by care, attention, and perseverance."
Did this and similar comments represent a lack of faith in his abilities
or a level-headed assessment of them?

Or, more likely, were they trying to discourage him from so over-valuing his abilities that he set his goals too high, and so protect him from his own blind, bulldog vision? Were they nudging a temperament given to extremes back to the middle?

At least for public consumption, Fred came to share his parents' estimation of him and, implicitly, their view of the whole problem. Competition to head the class at Exeter, he would later write, was so severe that those "not very brilliant had to work away late into the night in order to get there." This hard work, he believed in what we now know to be medically fallacious reasoning, "broke my eyes down."

Early the following year, with the boys back in school after Christmas vacation, Franklin—who was suffering from a "great weakness of my eyes" that barred reading or writing without pain—set out in full the logic that informed the coming decision: He hoped Fred's eyes were better, he began, but they needed rest in any case. "I fear very greatly," he went on,

> that any hard study or severe application to the classics will produce the same condition, as the looking [up of] . . . words in the dictionary and the Greek text are trying to the eyesight. . . . My own feeling is that it would be more prudent for Fred to give up Latin and Greek and apply himself to mathematics and the exact sciences, in the study of which he would not be obliged to overstrain his eyes. I want Fred to consider maturely the matter and if he thinks better he can come home at once or he can remain until the end of this term and then decide. You are now old enough to think soberly of the matter.

So the choice, it seems, was Fred's and he made it. In Exeter records his name is listed for the term beginning January 7, 1874, but no grades have been entered. "Appears to have left school at end of first term," a notation reads. Sometime, probably in March, he went home to Germantown.

PART TWO

IRON, FIRE, SAND, AND SMOKE

[1874–1879]

1

MATERIAL WORLD

∾

A SECOND PHILLIPS EXETER ACADEMY EXISTED beside the one Fred Taylor and his classmates knew, one remote from Wentworth's mathematics and Cilley's Greek, from ideals passed down by the school's founder, from the delight Fred felt as his slim boat skimmed across the water, from anything immaterial at all. Though visible and tangible, this other Exeter normally went unnoticed.

What, after all, was there to say about the wooden desk at which Fred sat in Bull Wentworth's class? Or the boilers that delivered steam to heat the rooms? Or the kerosene lamps in whose glow Fred and his classmates studied? Once such things existed, it seemed they'd always existed. How could these, set beside Plato and Euclid, stir the mind and heart?

And yet they, too, ranked as human achievements. For they represented neither nature's benevolence alone nor mere wish, but human thought, effort, and will. Creating them, and the other things men and women made, came hard.

In 1874, huge factories powered by great engines and human sweat were still a relatively new idea. It was forty years before Ford's assembly line. Workplaces were ill-lit, ramshackle sheds, or wood-floored lofts in brick buildings with high arched windows and banks of skylights. It was a world of wood, iron, rope, leather, cloth. Horse-drawn carriages counted as an important industry; blacksmiths were a fixture of everyday industrial life. Tall-masted, wood-hulled ships shared the seas with steamers. The incandescent lamp was five years away.

If you reckoned costs on the basis of what the average person, on average wages, could acquire, in a sense everything was expensive: the things of middle-class life—the beautiful things, the useful things, the conveniences and comforts—all were in short supply, cost too much, or couldn't be had at any price. A wagon wheel was no trifle; neither was a stove. The great mass of people, at least by the standards of our time, had little. You could, as Karl Marx and others did, point to inequities in the distribution of wealth and indict capitalism. But with equal justice, you could point simply to how much trouble it was, how much labor and material it took, to make a plow, or dig a ton of coal, or generate even as much power as a horse.

It was the age of steam; the hissing, puffing, leisurely churning steam engine, fueled by coal, lovingly tended, was everywhere, powering lathes and looms. Yet most manufacturing still relied heavily on human labor. Steam was bulky. You still had to get its power, through belts and pulleys, to wherever it was needed; and often, you couldn't, at least not without much trouble and expense. The compact gasoline engine didn't exist. Nor did the cheap, ubiquitous little motors used today even for so trifling a task as adjusting a car's rearview mirror. But human muscle, amplified mechanically by levers, blocks and tackles, and winches, was amply available, to dig trenches and lay rails, to pound the rivets that held boilers together, to load railcars with bars of pig iron. To sweep, to carry, to push.

The world didn't fret much about making things in an "environmentally responsible" way; it was happy to be able to make them at all. The country's most fertile minds—engineers, inventors, entrepreneurs, visionaries—*thought* about how to make them bigger, or faster, or cheaper. It took almost twenty years after 1836 for the U.S. Patent Office to record its first twelve thousand patents, but by the early 1870s it was issuing that many each year.

A new machine or household product existed first as idea, then perhaps as rude sketch. Only later did it become a brass, iron, or wood contrivance that could grind coffee, pump water, harvest wheat, or spin cotton. This was creative work in the most literal sense of the word, and engineers and mechanics of the day appreciated as much. In 1878, the magazine *American Machinist* was born. Its editor was James Waring See, at twenty-eight already an experienced machinist and entrepreneur but also a gifted writer; the letters to the editor he wrote to himself, under the name Chordal, fairly brimmed with succulent morsels of machine shop lore and mechanical wisdom. "You and I," Chordal wrote, "have hundreds of friends engaged in changing dull and heavy material into moving mechanism, a process akin to the creation of life."

And it was.

Some months after leaving Exeter, probably late in 1874, Fred Taylor stepped into this world of industrial creation, as apprentice in a small Philadelphia pump works.

Enterprise Hydraulic Works occupied two attached brick buildings together fronting fifty-six feet along Race Street and reaching back from it a similar distance to a tiny alley. Occupying about three thousand square feet, the size of a large suburban house, it had been used as a machine shop off and on for at least fifteen years. Behind it to the south was another, slightly wider alley, with the implausibly grand name of McCormicks Avenue. And then, on the other side, the far more substantial works of the Creswell iron foundry, established on the site a few years before and employing nearly a hundred people.

The pump works lay near Philadelphia's teeming industrial heart, bristling with energy, humming, vital. Workshop of the World, its boosters would dub it with scant exaggeration. Unlike commercial New York, Philadelphia was primarily industrial; it made things, more than words or ideas. More than two hundred thousand of its seven hundred thousand residents worked directly in manufacturing. It was a skilled worker's paradise; young men with brains, ambition, and a little money would leave their jobs, find a building somewhere, or a corner of a mill, and launch a business.

The city had prospered during the Civil War, its metalworking plants transformed into a Union arsenal. Still, no one industry dominated. Philadelphia made ships, shoes, tools, textiles, carpet, locomotives, hats, stoves; of three hundred forms of industrial activity the U.S. Census charted, the city had a stake in almost 90 percent of them. Its industrial districts, one historian has written, "supported an array of mills and plants whose diversity has scarcely been matched anywhere in the history of manufacturing."

Philadelphia had but few large firms with many hundreds or thousands of employees. Biggest by far was the Baldwin Locomotive Works, the Boeing Aircraft of its day, whose hulking thirty-ton black engines, all boilers and cranks, forgings and heavy castings, were shipped across the world, to Mexico, Australia, Africa, and Brazil. Its plant, occupying three square blocks, employed up to three thousand workers and sometimes turned out a dozen locomotives a week.

Compared to Baldwin, Enterprise Hydraulic Works, also known as Ferrell & Jones, after its two owners, was a zero. But set against most of the city's eleven thousand manufacturers—one- or two-person hole-in-the wall operations launched on a few hundred dollars in savings, like doll makers, cigar box makers, broom manufacturers, and nail makers—it was a substantial business. In today's money, the machinery it made in a year might be worth a million dollars. A few years later, with Fred gone and the company under partially new management, it represented an investment of thirty-five thousand dollars, employed thirty-five people and reported sales of almost fifty thousand dollars a year—at a time when skilled mechanics earned two dollars a day. When Fred started there, however, with the economy reeling from the panic of 1873, the business was probably smaller.

Just beyond Vine Street, to the north, began the highly industrialized Fifteenth Ward, home to Baldwin and other large works, their great smokestacks and foundry cupolas billowing smoke and soot across the city. But here on Race Street, just within the city's old northern border, shops and small factories lay stitched in among homes. Narrow, two-story, brick row houses flanked the pump works on either side. Across the street stood others, including that of William H. Jones, one of the owners, at 2215 Race. The Tenth Ward, which included the works and ran in a band four blocks wide from Broad Street to the Schuylkill, was home to about twenty-three thousand people.

A minute or two's stroll from Ferrell & Jones brought you to a phalanx of small manufacturers, none of which employed more than about a hundred workers. Along St. David Street was Edgewood Worsted Mills, Girard Bolt Works, Philadelphia Firebrick Works and, backing onto the piers along the Schuylkill to the west, the Parafine Oil Works. A little south, almost hard up against the river, was Townsend, Wilson, and Hubbard, which made wrought carriage bolts. Back on Race Street, at 2130, was Philadelphia Galvanizing. Due south, at 22nd and Arch, was American Meter.

It was a little enclave here almost by the banks of the Schuylkill, at the far western edge of the two-mile, between-the-rivers breadth of William Penn's original Philadelphia. As late as 1853, before they were integrated into the main city system and Race Street was still Sassafras Street, the north-south streets here were still numbered up from the river, as Schuylkill Third. The river was *there,* a block and a half down the street, alive with coal barges, canal boats, and other craft, masts and rigging looming over it. Its banks were studded with docks and storage yards, many of them Philadelphia and Reading Railroad properties, for lumber, coal, sand, and stone. A few blocks south, the graceful iron arches of the Chestnut Street Bridge soared across the river to the west.

Ferrell & Jones made steam pumps and other hydraulic machinery. It had been to pump out mines that the earliest steam engines were developed in England. By Taylor's time, however, "steam-pump" meant more than just a steam-powered pump. Back in 1840, as Chordal had occasion to advise his readers, steam moved pistons in a straight line, and pistons moved water in a straight line. "But what a world of complicated, intermediate machinery ... between these simple terminal elements!" So in that year American engineer Henry Worthington scrapped the intervening mechanism and made the steam piston drive the pump piston directly, through "a single transmitting piece of metal." First in twenty-three-year-old Worthington's imagination and then in iron and brass, a steam-operated pump became the steam-pump, the hyphen virtually embodying its working principle.

Ferrell & Jones was one among a half dozen or so steam-pump manufacturers in Philadelphia. It never made a great name for itself, and no one today remembers its pumps; a few years later, in new hands, the firm was making elevator machinery. At the centennial exhibition of 1876, it would enjoy the nineteenth-century equivalent of today's fifteen minutes of fame by showing a few of its pumps there. But we remember it today only because it was there, a stone's throw from the Schuykill, that eighteen-year-old Frederick Taylor first stepped out onto the industrial landscape of his day.

Fred had seen Bismarck's Berlin and Louis Napoleon's Paris. He could tell a Michelangelo from a Raphael, knew geometry, Latin grammar, and mealtime manners. Back in Germantown, among his family and their friends, he was almost an adult. But here on Race Street, he was a child.

Almost the first day on the job, the head of the shop confronted him. "Do you know the rule?" he asked.

"What rule?" Fred replied.

"Do you know the rule?" the man repeated, seemingly exasperated, virtually assaulting the new boy.

"I don't know what you mean," Fred fumbled.

"Do you mean to come here and ask to be an apprentice and do not know this foot rule?"

Oh, he knew a foot rule, of course.

So the man laid a foot rule on the table in front of him—but a foot rule with a difference. It had no numbers engraved upon it, only bare lines. The man laid the point of his knife on one of the lines. "Tell me quick what that means."

Fred couldn't. With a moment's trouble, he could have counted the lines and determined that it was, say, five and three sixteenths inches. But he couldn't do it instantly; he didn't know the rule. So far as any self-respecting mechanic was concerned, he knew nothing.

In the coming weeks and months, he'd see men in the shop go up to a lathe, mount in it rough pieces of wood, and turn them down to any diameter they wished, by eye, finished as accurately "as if they had used gauges"; thirty years later Taylor would recall the scene, still full of wonder. Revelations like that, large and small, came all through his early months as an apprentice.

2

"AN EMPLOYMENT OF SOME OTHER KIND"

∾

I N 1906, when Frederick Taylor was named president of the American Society of Mechanical Engineers, a biographical account marking his elevation briefly alluded to the events of 1874 and the beginning of his apprenticeship:

> Disappointed at not being able to carry out the plan which he had
> formulated of laying a broad foundation for a subsequent
> professional training, he returned home, determined to apply
> himself to securing practical experience in the trades which
> pertained to his proposed profession of engineering, and at the

same time to develop his physical strength until his eyesight should become sufficiently restored to resume his studies.

The story reads like one made to fit subsequent events and suggests that rounding-off of rough and uncertain edges that an important person sometimes enjoys in official histories. In fact, we know little about the months between when Taylor left Mrs. Cilley's house in Exeter and began his apprenticeship at the pump works. But the ASME statement does, at least, include the major compositional elements of any sketch we might make of that time: Fred was disappointed. His eyesight was a factor. He did set out to secure work experience. And he was sufficiently drawn to mathematics, science, and orderly habits of thought to make the choice of engineering, as his "proposed profession," a sensible one.

~

Salzburg, Austria. July 18, 1869.

After an early breakfast, Fred, thirteen, records that they "got into a crazy old carriage with a pair of crazy old horses hitched to it and rode up a dirty little valley with very pretty mountains on each side of it to a dirty little hotel where the horses were fed." From there, they continue on to the Königssee, a long finger of deep, clear water nestled among mountain peaks rising around it to eight thousand feet and more. The mountains, some of them snowcapped, are so steep, writes Fred, they "come down almost perpendicular to the lake." One rower fires a pistol. "The echo of it was as loud as a clap of thunder."

They spend the morning there and at around one o'clock are driven to the mouth of a salt mine, near Berchtesgaden, in continuous operation since at least 1559, the stone-arched portal to it tucked into the side of a mountain. "At five o'clock," writes Fred, "[we] went into a room and were dressed up to go into the mine":

> Our dress consisted of a pair of pants (of very coarse cloth) which we put on over our pants, a coat of the same material, and lastly a very broad brimmed black cloth hat. The ladies were dressed up in white pants and with a black coat on, and I forgot to say that both women and men wore a black leather apron which came down behind instead of in front. The women wore little hats

which look like smoking caps. And thus attired, each of us having a
lantern in our hands, we went into the salt mine.

There was a sudden chill as they entered, a sense of leaving the
world behind:

> We first walked eleven hundred feet in a straight line into the
> mountain. The passage way I should think was about 10 feet high
> and six wide. There is a rail road which runs down it. When we
> were there a car came down it but we stepped into a little sort of a
> room made on each side of the railway. We had scarcely got in
> there before the train came whizzing past at a great rate. . . . We
> walked along [another] passageway until we came to a large
> apartment from which we walked down a pair of steps to the salt
> lake, which was lighted up when we were there. It looked very
> beautiful, as the lights were reflected so vividly from the water that
> it looked as if there were two sets of them. We were rowed across it
> in a boat. All the sides all around the lake were salt.

On the lake, within the broad, flat, disklike hollow of the mountain,
it was like being in a low-ceilinged club basement, the flat salt roof lying
just overhead:

> The way they get the salt is they fill it entirely up with water from
> above and, after it has stayed in a sufficient time to take up all of
> the salt which it is possible to hold, then it is let out by means of
> pipes and evaporated. We next went to a large place where they
> were running the salt. (The guide said that there were 36 such lakes
> as I have just mentioned in the mine). Here the leather aprons
> came into play. In order to go down into the mine we had to sit
> astride two logs and, holding on to a rope, slide down. It was real
> good fun to feel yourself sliding down, but you can stop yourself at
> pleasure by holding on tight to the rope.

Slide down the logs too quickly and you could actually feel the
warmth, from the friction, radiate up from your seat:

> From the bottom of the mine there is a shaft put down to the
> distance of about 500 feet and, there being a distance of 700 feet to

the surface above us, the mine is a thousand two hundred feet
deep. From there we went up a pair of stairs into another
passageway out of which we turned into one in a branch of which
is the mineralogical cabinet. In it are the different specimens of salt
which are found in the mine, some of the red and white crystals. At
the head of it is a very large white crystal with the king's initials cut
in it. From there we went by car (the cars are made by cushioning a
long board which is put up on four wheels like a bench. On this are
elevated two chairs which are meant for the ladies. The gentlemen
sit astride. One of the guides sits in front and puts on the brake
when it is necessary).

The tiny, narrow-gauge train, perhaps two feet across, made an
awful clatter as it hurtled along the tracks:

[There was] no daylight [across] a distance of 5000 feet, which we
did in five minutes. After taking off our aprons with which we
went into the mine we bought several boxes of salt in which there
were quite a number of varieties and then drove back to Salzburg
at about 9 o'clock in the evening.

This is the longest sustained description Fred Taylor offered during
the two years he kept his European journal—more space, by far, than
he devoted to any incident, work of art, museum, palace, person, place,
or thing he had seen. In it, he shows perfect ease with number, dimension, and technical detail. His description of the underground chamber
is vivid, his account of the saltmaking process surprisingly thorough.

In 1970, an Indian psychiatrist, Sudhir Kakar, would paint a
psychoanalytic portrait, *Frederick Taylor: A Study in Personality and
Innovation*, in which he interprets Taylor's turn toward engineering
and industry as a rejection of his father. Of several reviewers who took
issue, Edwin Layton wrote in *Technology and Culture* that Kakar "overlooks the possibility that scientific management might have been
shaped in some fundamental way by science."

As boy and man, Fred Taylor was genuinely moved by matters
scientific and technical. They were not the only things that moved
him and perhaps not even the chief ones. And later, he and his supporters would exaggerate the extent to which his system, scientific
management, was truly "scientific." Still, it is indisputable that

numbers, facts, rules, and *things* occupied a large part of his mental universe.

When Taylor was a teenager, probably during the year between the family's return from Europe and his departure for Exeter, he joined his friends in a Germantown Scientific Society, which maintained collections of minerals, birds, and the like; "under Fred's leadership," recalled Birge Harrison, "we were all more or less 'scientific.' " Even a tad too scientific to suit young Birge, who was a year and a half older and would go on to become a landscape painter of some repute. "Fred was always a bit of a crank in the opinion of our boyhood band, and we were inclined to rebel sometimes from the strict rules and exact formulas to which he insisted that all of our games must be subjected." Fred marked off the field they used for rounders, an early form of baseball, with a precision that left Harrison wondering why "the whole of a fine sunny morning should be wasted in measuring it off by feet and by inches."

Fred's other quirks also impressed Harrison. They and their friends would take long cross-country hikes in and around Germantown. And Fred, in Harrison's memory, was "constantly experimenting with his legs, in an endeavor to discover the step which would cover the greatest distance with the least expenditure of energy; or the easiest method of vaulting a fence, [or] the right length and proportions of a walking staff."

Fred's European journals are studded with references to mathematical problems. In Lucerne, he gets Mrs. Prentice's help with square roots and notes that another American, a Mr. Osgood, had also been fond of geometry as a boy. "He had found over 100 original ways of proving different things," writes Fred, and twenty-eight proofs of the Pythagorean theorem. Later, Osgood gave him a problem that captivated Fred for days; when he solved it, he drew the figure in his journal and set out the steps of the proof.

At Finstermunz, where the family was stuck when the storm swept away the bridge, he admired the new roadway, which "is a great piece of engineering. It is a good deal of the way cut out of the precipice. There are several places made to protect the road from avalanches." He referred to thick-walled, arched stone structures reminiscent of castle battlements, built below sheer cliffs, within which the road passed.

And in Norway, where they traveled by carriages that changed horses every seven miles, "or one Norwegian mile," as Fred took care to note, he kept track of their departure and arrival times at each:

Left Piggestad 9:43		Reached Listad 11:05	
"	Listad 11:45	"	Oien 12:30
"	Oien 3:15	"	Storkelstad 4:30

and so on, station after station, down the page, like data in a laboratory experiment. That was late July. Early in August he recorded even more extensive data, covering four days and seventeen stations. "The ones marked with a star," he noted, are "where we stopped to get something to eat."

Until he was eleven, Fred saw in his grandfather, Isaac Winslow, a life at least as steeped in practical things as in the pretty words and cultured sensibilities of his parents. Winslow, who as a whaler had devised a variety of shipboard gear, was something of an inventor, with several patents to his credit. One, awarded in 1849, was for a metal cap, slipped onto the neck of a bottle below its thick glass lip, intended to stop a cork from blowing out due to built-up pressure from within. Another, awarded only two years before his death, described a knife used to strip corn from its cob: to its curved blade was attached a gauge, set for the height of the kernels, that permitted a workman to smoothly shave off the kernels at their root without gouging the cob.

Early on, Fred displayed evidence of an inventive bent himself. He put a long-toothed rake into service as a brake for the bobsleds on which he and his friends sped down snowy Germantown hills. He disclosed another to his friend Birge when he was about twelve, a peculiar sleep harness. Vexed by nightmares, he had noticed that he always awoke from them on his back, not in some other position. So he devised a harness of straps and pointed wooden rods, perhaps like little pencils, designed to prick him into wakefulness should he start to roll onto his back. Masochism in fullest flower? Perhaps not. The less flavorful explanation is that, quite simply, he had hit upon a technical solution to what he saw as a technical problem. And solution it was, Harrison records: "The thing worked and Fred ceased to be the victim of his unquiet dreams," at least for a time.

~

Given his bent for science and invention, it is possible to see in Taylor's headaches and eye problems at Exeter a handy way out of a life planned for him but for which he had no relish; his shift to industry entirely willing; the whole story just so much grist for legend—of a Great Man, visited by adversity, who accepts the cruel cards that fate deals him yet triumphs anyway:

> In early life he had planned a career
>   Of work and study, to him most dear;
> But diligently studying by day and by night
>   Seriously impair his tender eyesight.
> Thus obliged to renounce the work he loved best
>   He wasted no time in idle rest,
> But sought an employment of some other kind,
>   Even tho' not suited quite to his mind.

This piece of doggerel, prepared by Fred's mother-in-law for his fiftieth birthday, does seem suspiciously pat. And Sudhir Kakar is not alone in viewing the canonical account of Taylor's turn to industry with skepticism. "Clearly," writes Samuel Haber in *Efficiency and Uplift: Scientific Management in the Progressive Era*, "this troublous period of impaired vision hinged as much upon problems of the mind as of the body."

But it's not clear. His parents' fears for Fred's eyes at Exeter were real. And their solicitousness did not flag once he had changed course; when he returned to school some years later, his mother actually read to him some of his texts. In 1883, Taylor himself wrote Exeter friend Tufts—to whom, we might expect, he needn't dissemble—how "I was almost entirely debarred from all correspondence for five years after leaving school"—or until about 1879—"on account of my eyes." Years later, replying to a French interviewer, his wife gave four years as the time his doctors specified. Five years? Four? Plainly, the doctors had spoken. Reports of Fred's disappointment come from sources many and varied enough, with not a discordant note among them, that seeing the Taylor family's account of the events of 1874 as some elaborate charade stretches credulity.

On the other hand, that his eye problems were real, his options limited, and the choice of engineering, in retrospect, a happy and natural one, hardly mean that the change in course came with stoic acceptance of the inevitable. More likely, it was fraught with terrible ambivalence. Certainly, his whole future was not preordained the moment he packed his bags to leave Exeter; for at eight in the morning on Thursday, June 25, 1874, three months *after* his return home from Exeter, Fred Taylor sat down with others in Harvard Hall in Cambridge, Massachusetts, for the college's admissions examination, and faced one more blitz of the classics:

> Translate into Greek:-When these ten thousand Greeks had come in their march to the great river Euphrates, they found a barbarian soldier . . .
>
> . . .
>
> Translate into English:-Restat ut doccam omnia, quae sint in hoc mundo, quibus utantur homines . . .

Taylor would later dismiss the Greek and Latin so meaningful to his father as "dead languages." But at the time, part of him no doubt resisted letting go of what had become so safe and familiar, not to mention all they represented of Harvard and the law. Eighteen-year-old Fred Taylor, it can be safely said, was a confused young man during that spring of 1874. At some point, he must have decided he had not worked so hard at Exeter to just throw it all over, and so went ahead, as planned, with the Harvard examination.

The exam, which included mathematics as well, would stretch across three days. But with it, Fred was through with the classics at last. That fall, his friend Tufts enrolled at Harvard. Later, the Harvard admissions book for the class of 1878, listing the two hundred or so students admitted that summer and fall, recorded no fewer than twenty-six from Exeter, more than from any other school.

Fred Taylor, who had passed the examination with honors, was not among them.

~

But if not Harvard, why not MIT or another engineering school? That possibility, after all, was the one his parents had broached in their letters to him at Exeter, not that of dropping school altogether and starting as an apprentice.

In fact, apprenticeship, not school, was still the far more customary path into industry for a young man, even for those blessed by circumstances and certain that, thirty years later, they would be running the company and not a lathe. "We know of a number of cases," declared a Wilmington, Delaware, newspaper, known as the *Every Evening*, in 1871,

> where the sons of our most highly respected citizens are either apprentices or journeymen in our machine shops. . . . Such do not, of course, expect to remain journeymen always, but until opportunity does offer for them to engage in similar enterprises for themselves, they daily don their blue overalls and blouses and work amidst the dust and grease, veritable "greasy mechanics," without any thought that their employment in any way compromises their honor and dignity, and without any loss of social position.

In years to come, engineers would much debate the merits of shop education versus formal university studies rooted in mathematics and science. But in Taylor's time, just seven schools offered degree programs in mechanical engineering; from all of them together, graduates numbered only about thirty in 1874. Rensselaer went back to 1824, but its mechanical engineering course only to 1862, and by 1870 it had been eliminated. A new program at Stevens had started only in 1871. Thus, for the Taylors, engineering school may never have been entertained seriously at all. An apprenticeship, on the other hand, was so natural and obvious a course as to merit scarcely a word.

A colleague from later years, Carl Barth, would intimate that Taylor's apprenticeship went "much against his family's wishes." And no doubt, like any parents seeing their child deflected from a desirable course, they had misgivings. Leaving Harvard and the law behind represented a break from the quiet, leisured life of Franklin Taylor, a life that could have been their son's as well. Still, as the Wilmington paper suggested, an apprenticeship represented no radical turn. In Philadelphia especially, Taylor would comment, it had long "been customary for many young men with parents who are well-to-do to start at the bottom in our machine shops, industrial establishments and mercantile houses, and work absolutely on the same level as the regular employees of the shop."

In 1874, the nation endured its worst depression in two decades.

Across Philadelphia, thousands were out of work; at Baldwin Locomotive alone, fourteen hundred men had lost their jobs in the past year. Yet just then, amid industrial calamity, Taylor landed his apprenticeship. Whatever their reservations, his parents probably helped arrange it, perhaps through Joseph L. Ferrell, a Germantown neighbor, and the money behind Ferrell & Jones. Or through James Wright, whose own son, Ernest, five years Fred's junior, would shortly join him at the same small firm. It would not have been the first time Franklin Taylor had intervened on behalf of his sons. Two years before, with Fred at Exeter and Winslow still at home, he had tried to get the older boy a job in the coast survey through their friends the Harrisons. "If W goes," he wrote Fred in relaying the news, "I want him to work as the others do, take his full share." A charmingly egalitarian sentiment, surely; any rich man's son proud to have worked "as the others do" might justly be pardoned for overlooking how the way had been greased for him.

In any case, late in 1874 or perhaps early in 1875, after months of rattling around his parents' big new house on Ross Street, hefting stones for the hotbeds his mother was installing and performing other odd jobs, Fred began his apprenticeship as a patternmaker.

3

POURING DAY

~

O N POURING DAY, the fire at the base of the tall brick-lined furnace burning slowly, men at a platform halfway up heave through its gaping iron door alternating loads of iron and coal. Maybe a ton or two of fresh, pig iron ingots mixed with scrap, perhaps flawed castings from previous melts; and a lesser weight of coal—or else coke, the porous, cleaner-burning black material, about the consistency of pumice, that coal becomes once purged of impurities by slow baking. Then, someone turns on the "blast," and a blower injects the furnace with a powerful draft of forced air. Blow into the embers of a campfire and you'd get similar results: the red-orange fire at the base of the cupola roars to life, burns hotter, yellower, spews sparks. For half an hour, the great fan blows, and iron melts, gathering at the base of the furnace. Finally, they shut down the blast, pull the plug, and down a shallow open trough, into a huge ladle, pours liquid iron in a blinding yellow-white stream, not sluggish like honey, but loose and sloshy like water.

The ladle, an iron pot lined with fireclay, sits nestled in a large metal ring supported from above by a crane, yet free to tilt. With the ladle filled, a man wielding a long rod with a plug of clay at its end inserts it in the cupola's taphole to halt the iron's flow. Another man skims off the gooey, crusty slag that's formed on the surface of the molten iron. A third, operating the crane, which commands the entire foundry floor, hoists the ladle. Two thick rods, handles of a sort, project from opposite ends of the iron ring that surrounds and supports the ladle; men now grip these rods, steadying the ladle, then push, pull, and prod it into position over the mold, a hard-packed bed of sand within a wooden frame.

Finally, ladle poised over the mold's open mouth, they tip it over until iron pours in a narrow stream; it's like a waiter decanting wine, aiming for the glass and not the patron's lap—except the bottle weighs a couple of tons and the wine is served at twenty-seven hundred degrees Fahrenheit. For five or ten seconds, the men scarcely move, a few feet from the stream of searing liquid iron, until the mold fills. Then they tip up the ladle and proceed to the next mold. They work fast; the molten iron must not cool enough to become sluggish.

Behind them as they work, from the molds already filled, smoke and steam puff up from vent holes pricked in the sand; sometimes stray gases take fire, the flames resembling the faint blue pilot light of a gas stove. Men looking down upon the foundry floor from high beside the furnace's charging door see a dark sandy expanse, crowded with dozens of wooden boxes filled with sand, some of them by now steaming, their mouths dull red circles of molten metal. It is like looking down from an airplane at a landscape of softly glowing volcanoes.

Within each mold had lain intricate hollows; now they are filled with red-hot iron, slowly cooling. The sand serves as natural insulator, and some of the more massive pieces take long to cool. When, perhaps the following day, the molds are shaken out, the foundry floor is left a mess of crumbled sand, from which men extract finished castings of cold gray iron.

～

The foundry was the hot, dirty, dangerous place where molds were prepared, iron poured, and most of the metal products of the nineteenth century first took shape. The pump works on Race Street, too small to have one of its own, had parts for the machinery it made cast elsewhere—the Creswell foundry across the alley, perhaps, or any of dozens of others in Philadelphia. Out went the wooden pattern, back came the iron part.

Today, consumer and industrial products draw from a wider menu of materials—plastics, graphite composites, aluminum, titanium, stainless steel. We are used to wondrous new glues, metals with bizarre properties, materials squeezed, shaped, and processed into unrecognizable forms. But Taylor's world was still largely one of iron and wood. And casting—along with forging, where hot metal is pounded the way blacksmiths did but with huge, powered hammers—was the most common way to make parts of brass, bronze and, especially, iron. Today, a stove door or the bed of a machine tool might be stamped from steel plate; back then they would have been cast. A kitchen appliance part today injection-molded from plastic then would have been cast from iron. Engine parts were made from cast iron. Handles and cranks, architectural facades, and pump housings were cast-iron.

Fresh from the foundry, its contours bearing the sand's grainy imprint, a casting was still far from a finished product. In the machine shop, it would have holes drilled, bored, and reamed, surfaces planed, milled, ground, and polished. Only then, typically, would it become part of a steam engine, gearbox, or pump.

But even the simplest casting, one not bound for the machine shop, came from the sand with protruding appendages to be broken off (and thrown back into the furnace for remelting). These were artifacts of the foundry process itself—heavy conical "sprues" through which the iron was poured, "gates" and "risers" that controlled the passage of the hot iron through the mold, paper-thin "flash" at the seam between the mold's two halves. Shaken free from its sand, a casting looked like nothing so much as a grotesque mutation of the final part.

The molder, a foundry worker, made the mold that made the casting. His medium was sand, which might be a secret, much-prized blend of several types or just good local sand from a nearby riverbank. In any case, he shook it through a sieve to fix its grain size and added just enough water. Too little, and the sand taking up the pattern would crumble as he worked with it; too much, and the hot iron would release too much steam. His object: to create within the mold's wooden frame a perfect little island of sculptured sand, its hollows as fine and smooth as the swirls along the beach after a wave has retreated into the sea.

But the wooden forms that fashioned those hollows were the work not of the molder but of a patternmaker, Fred's new trade. Often, the two breeds of craftsman worked for different companies; Ferrell & Jones, as we have seen, made the patterns but farmed out the molding. When they worked for the same company, the patternmakers might have a shop upstairs from the molders or in another building. In any case, they typically occupied an oasis of relative calm, at some remove from the rough-and-tumble of the foundry floor.

While rooted in the metalworking trades and intimate with foundry practice, the patternmaker functioned more like a carpenter. His materials were white pine, mahogany, cherry. Since his patterns were often one of a kind, he relied little on machinery. Many pattern shops had only a simple wood lathe, perhaps foot treadle–operated like an old-fashioned sewing machine, whose operator simply elbowed his cutting tool into the spinning work. Marking out, sawing, planing, and assembly were the work of traditional hand tools. Glue figured in, too, the final pattern typically being built up from smaller pieces.

But unlike a carpenter, a patternmaker worked at one or two removes from the final object, just as a photographer works with a negative of the final picture. And while carpenters normally sought crisp, sharp edges and perfect right angles, the patternmaker's mental landscape was all soft contours, bizarre involutions, labyrinthine voids.

In principle, patternmaking could hardly be simpler: the pattern should presumably look like the part you wish to make from it. After all, what did the molder do but place the pattern in the middle of a wooden box, shovel sand around it, pound it in tight with a wooden mallet, take out the pattern, and pour in molten metal to fill the voids the pattern had left? He'd let it cool and break open the mold—and, presto, a casting. So, it might seem, pattern equals casting.

But one nagging question proved the neat equation false: how do you get the pattern out of the mold so you can get the iron in? And in that single, maddening constraint lay all the patternmaker's worry and grief, all the knowledge he brought to his craft—and all the skill that eighteen-year-old Fred Taylor, apprentice patternmaker, sought to acquire.

Even the simplest object didn't get a pattern of precisely identical shape. When hot metal cooled, it shrank, in iron's case an eighth of an inch or so for every foot; so you had to make the pattern overlarge or else find your four-foot pump housing off by a crucial half inch.

Then, too, a casting was typically the starting point for subsequent metal-cutting operations. So you had to understand the final use of the part to know where the pattern needed machining allowances built into it.

Even something as absurdly simple as a perfect cylinder or cube could not, in its foundry pattern, be a perfect cylinder or cube. Try pulling a pickle jar straight up out of wet sand at the beach. The sides of the jar, smooth as they are, grab at the sand, pull it out in granules and clumps, destroying the bottle's impression in the sand.

Now imagine the jar no longer cylindrical but conical, like an ice-cream cone, the wider end at the surface. Pulling that out would be a snap; the first tug would forever free it from the sand's grip. And just such a departure from straight up and down was what every pattern needed—"draft," it was called. It meant three or four degrees of taper on most surfaces, cylindrical surfaces slightly conical. And the pattern-maker had to build it into every pattern he made.

The molder's moment of truth came when he tried to pull the pattern from the mold, holding his breath, hoping it pulled away cleanly, the sand left behind perfectly imprinted with its shape. The enemy? Sand clinging to the pattern. So a good patternmaker sanded his wooden form, which was feathery light, like stage scenery, compared to the iron part it made. He painted it with several coats of varnish to slick it up. He used beeswax or putty to build rounded "fillets" where otherwise there would be sharp corners partial to sand. He built into his pattern a "rapping plate" that the molder could use to jiggle the pattern free of the sand's grip. And when otherwise finished, he would take a file and smooth out any nicks or edges that might stick to the sand. His hand was more reliable than his eyes; he'd run his fingers over every square inch of the wood, feeling for undercuts, irregularities, little globs of glue—any spot that might catch and hold a grain of sand and thereby tug at the pattern as it rose from the mold.

But forget nicks, sharp corners, and draft; a more fundamental question influenced the design of every pattern: how could you bury something in the earth, then neatly unbury it? That is, how could you build a pattern so that in removing it from the sand you didn't destroy the very cavity you'd just made?

This was no new problem, and the general solution went back to the dim reaches of early industrial technology: You make the mold in two halves, and you make the pattern in two pieces, with the seam, or "parting line," between them at the object's broadest extent. This way, you can lift each part of the pattern from its own half of the mold, then assemble the two halves into one finished mold.

To cast a globe, for example, you make a pattern consisting of two solid hemispheres. You bury one hemisphere in one bed of sand round end down, flat side flush with the top of the mold. You do the same with the other. Then you pop both hemispherical patterns from their respective beds of packed sand, leaving a hemispherical hollow in each, and invert one half of the mold so that it sits, duly aligned, atop the other. The result? A perfect spherical hollow. Drive a tunnel down from the surface through which to admit the molten metal, and you've got the rudiments of a finished mold.

Of course, the piece to be cast—a gear, a housing, a valve—was never that simple. Often, it was not just its exterior you wanted cast but its interior as well. If you need a hollow roller, like the cardboard sleeve of a paper towel roll but in metal, you could cast the roller solid, without the hole, and drill it out later. But could you cast it that way in the first place and save the subsequent work?

Here, again, the general solution was an old one, in the form of a "core." The core was a sand form, shaped by the internal contours of a wooden box, held together with binders like molasses or flour, baked in a special oven that gave it the color and consistency of crusty brown sugar, and placed in the mold once the pattern itself had been removed; the pattern gave the casting its outer shape, a core its internal shape. On pouring day—with the mold closed up, the wooden pattern removed, but the sand core in place—passage of the molten iron was blocked, thus forming a hollow. Later, with the casting cooled and shaken free from the sand, the core, too, was reduced to loose sand and could be removed.

Here, the patternmaker's job was to make the wooden box whose internal shape gave the core its outer shape—which, in turn, gave the casting its internal shape. A foundry might keep cylindrical cores and a few other common shapes in stock sizes. But often the patternmaker had to individually craft cores of fabulous complexity, corresponding to the intricate cavities of steam engine or pump components. The final mold, just before closing up for the pour, with the cores resting in the sand, made for an often lovely sculpture with rounded contours of smooth sand and dark grottoes of empty space.

As one patternmaker's manual from the turn of the century observed, a machinist had the rough casting itself to guide his work, something to see and touch; but the patternmaker "must *imagine* the casting before him, and must build something in wood which will pro duce that casting in metal." Some of what he made corresponded to the final shape, some to the negative of the final shape. And he had always to travel, in his mind's eye, between those abstract realms, to imagine dark recesses that twisted, bent, and curled in space and through which white-hot metal would ultimately flow.

Patternmaking demanded intelligence, skill, and creativity; give two men the same job, and you might get back two different patterns. Around the turn of the century, a young German theology student intent on sampling industrial workers' lives, Paul Gohre, took a job with a large manufacturer and saw patternmakers up close. "The patterns were often of the strangest shapes," he marveled. Patternmakers were "not skilled workmen only, but men of intelligence." They might wear coarse clothes and speak coarsely, but they got respect from the boss and contributed freely to the pattern's design. "Thus a certain independence of action was assured to the individual workman, and what he produced was not a fragment, but a thing complete and excellent in itself."

So, too, did patternmakers leave their mark on Chordal, that close observer of 1870s shop culture, who verged on faulting them for being too good. "A good pattern-maker can, if he sees fit, make a pattern which will stand daily use and storage for fifteen years," he noted. "His work will be solid, wood to wood all over, five coats of varnish, and an exterior impervious to moisture." But such fine work was not always needed. "If he wants to," Chordal went on, the man for such a job "could make the pattern in one-sixth the time, and the exterior shape would be the same, the castings from them identical" to one designed for long service. But good men, typically, did *not* want to. They knew how to make it only one way: good.

Chordal described an exemplar of the craft, Bob. With him,

you don't have to measure to see if there's shrinkage here, and rappage there. You don't have to find out if this core will cut through where you don't want it to, or if that core is in such form that it can't be set. You need have no anxiety about sizes, or about bosses coming in the right place, or about sharp work where you want fillets. You need not bother about the matter at all . . .

It's Bob's business to make patterns which will make castings like the drawings, and he understands his business, and attends to it. He don't stand around with sharp tools and wait for instructions how to make this, how to part that, how to dowel this, where to glue that, and where to put these rapping plates on, and where to put cores, and where to draw in green sand, and all such. That's his business. Bob's a pattern-maker and a good one.

In many small shops without draftsmen and "lordly engineers with square roots, and cube roots, and logarithms, and torsion equations," observed Chordal, a patternmaker like Bob was "the man called on to furnish the high art for the establishment," a genius in overalls.

If any trade was apt to subvert a rich boy's stereotypes about men who worked with their hands, that of the patternmaker was it. At Ferrell & Jones in 1874, Fred Taylor worked with three or four of them, close up, every day. And at the head of the group, under whom he served at least the first six months of his apprenticeship, was a man named John R. Griffith.

4

BIOGRAPHY OF AN UNKNOWN MAN

≈

HISTORY IS NOT CONSIDERATE of the lives of people like John Griffith. He is not an important man in the eyes of the world. No biographies have been written about him, and none ever will be. Most knowledge of him died when he did.

We know that Griffith was about twenty-six when Taylor came into the shop; that he was born in Pennsylvania, of Pennsylvania-born parents; that during the years Fred served as apprentice, he never stayed long in any one place; that at the beginning of Fred's term, he lived down near the oldest part of Philadelphia, by the Delaware River, at 215 Spruce Street; that during the following year he moved across town to a house, directly across from the pump works, at 2215 Race Street, where William H. Jones, one of the firm's principals, and also a patternmaker, lived; and that the following year, perhaps now working for another company, he moved to 921 Buttonwood Street, near the heart of Philadelphia's industrial district. He probably earned something like eight hundred dollars a year—not a princely sum but toward the high end for Philadelphia workmen—and may well have seen his wages drop in the wake of the depression, as they did throughout the country beginning in 1873 and all through the rest of the decade.

Beyond this, we know only that Griffith touched Fred Taylor deeply. "The very best training I had was in the early years of [my] apprenticeship in the pattern shop," he wrote, "when I was under a workman of extraordinary ability, coupled with fine character. I there learned appreciation, respect and admiration for the everyday working mechanic." And nothing we know of Taylor's later life causes us to doubt his sincerity in the slightest or to think his time with Griffith made on him anything less than the most profound and lasting impression.

The Griffiths of the world may be hidden from history, yet they leave their mark, seeming to embody in their calloused hands and plain talk cons of secret knowledge. Even today, many a young engineer fresh from college finds his Griffith, a machinist, mechanic, or technician placed in his service, yet years his senior and far more knowledgeable, unschooled yet keenly intelligent, a virtuoso in the arts of making and doing.

Scholars sometimes find them, too. In Sheffield, England, historian Geoffrey Tweedale befriended master cutler Stan Shaw, last of the old-time Sheffield knife makers, fifty years at his trade. In a brief biography he introduced readers to Shaw's world of hand-cut and tempered blades, burnished springs, and stag handles. Shaw had come up, in local vernacular, as a "little mester," renting bench space in a factory, gradually learning every skill that went into knife making, and ultimately making huge exhibition knifes, collector's knifes, even one for Queen Elizabeth. Shaw knew just when to pull his blade from the flame, just how to tap the rivet so that the mother-of-pearl handle didn't shatter. Tweedale's admiration bubbles up from every page.

In America, Douglas Harper met another of the breed. His name was Willie, and he repaired old Saabs in particular and old wrecks of every other kind in the rural wastes of northern New York State. Harper, a sociologist, took to him, photographed him at work, placed him in scholarly perspective, and wrote a book about him, *Working Knowledge.* But at the root of his interest, plainly, was simple awe at what the tall hawk-faced man with the crew cut could fashion out of a pile of scrap metal with a welder's torch and little else. He could repair a furnace on the coldest night of the year, fix a sawmill or a silo blower, redesign and build the door to an old stove. But something more than ingenuity impressed Harper, a nobility of spirit that found expression in welded steel, and that rows of accounting figures, or fine words on paper, or lofty ideas, could never match.

So it was, or something like it, for Fred Taylor and John Griffith. A little after Taylor went to work at the pump works, Ernest Wright, yet another of the Wright children, then about fourteen, also started working there (perhaps after school, as he must have still been a student at Germantown Academy). Wright worked beside Taylor for several years before going on to Stevens Tech and a career as an engineer, and he must have seen Fred every day. Through a friend, whose family owned one of Philadelphia's two biggest machine tool manufacturers, Wright was already steeped in shop ways. But, in his recollection, Taylor was not. Before his apprenticeship, he wrote, Taylor "had never shown any particular interest in things mechanical." And several of Taylor's colleagues would confirm that, for all his scientific bent, he showed real antipathy to working with his hands. But, Wright went on, "the influence and teaching of John Griffith, head pattern maker at Ferrell & Jones, made a permanent impression on Fred and laid the foundation for his life work."

~

Just before starting his apprenticeship, Taylor wrote later—he was, as usual, making a point, and so may have let the story take flight from literal truth—his father's unmarried older brother Caleb, then sixty, a bank president just back from a term in Congress, summoned his nephew to the family's Bucks County estate at Sunbury. "If you want success," Uncle Caleb intoned, "do what I say," and launched into homiletic discourse. If you are due at work at seven, get there at ten to seven. If the workday ends at six, don't leave until ten after six. Hold your temper. Don't talk back to the boss. And don't quit a job without thinking it over for a couple of days.

Uncle Caleb's wisdom apparently sat well with young Fred, who fell right into the workplace routine. He breakfasted each morning at half past five and took the train (or, less likely, the horsecar) to work. By half past six, he was sweeping the floor of the shop. Soon, the steam engine powered up and the other workmen at their places, he was busy taking orders, doing as he was told. For ten hours or more, he worked amid patterns, and pieces of patterns, in pine or mahogany, almost comically light and soft compared to the iron pieces they made; lengths of wood and pots of glue, jack planes and grinding wheels, routers, rabbet planes, chisels and gouges, squares and calipers.

All day long, the soft gloom of the shop enveloped him; in that era before the electric light, only areas near the windows facing Race Street or, perhaps, the alley out back or beneath a skylight, enjoyed bright light. During the winter, especially, nightwork left the men hunched over candles, lanterns, or gaslight— making for, in Chordal's phrasing, "a black immensity with little spots of light," feeble and glaring all at once.

During those early months, everything was new for Fred Taylor: working with his hands, doing menial jobs, coming home exhausted. So, especially, was working beside men who, unlike him and his friends, had to earn a living, as three quarters of seventeen-year-old Philadelphia boys did. Euclid and Cicero were a distant memory now. The gentleman's son from Germantown had stepped into the rough-hewn world of working-class Philadelphia.

Unlike those of many other cities, Philadelphia's working ranks fell heavily on the skilled side of the ledger and were largely native-born; Irish and German immigrants, for example, were less a fixture than in many other cities. The cobblestoned, gaslit city boasted housing conditions better by far than New York; one account from the period claimed that Philadelphia's "working classes are better housed, better fed, and better clothed than those of any city in the world." While the twenty-five to forty-dollar monthly rent of a six- or eight-room row house lay beyond the means of most, a bare three-room house might rent for just twelve dollars, a week's wage for a skilled worker. The building boom after the Civil War had thrown up tens of thousands of narrow, two- and three-story row houses, which sold for around twelve hundred dollars and made home ownership, at least for some skilled workers in some industries, relatively common.

That, at least, was the happy long view from later, a view collapsing one decade of the late 1800s into another. But in 1874—not ten years earlier or later—city and nation endured a painful pause in the march of progress. Taylor would recall the "bad industrial conditions which prevailed" during his apprenticeship. The effects of the panic of 1873, about which his parents had written to him at Exeter, lingered. Factories had closed, and thousands were out of work, without unemployment insurance to soften the blow. Hunger was widespread. The trade union movement, resurgent during the heady 1860s, had collapsed. As one historian recounts, "the year 1873 had brought a depression like none before, a vale of tears that grew wider and deeper until by 1876 it seemed like the valley of death itself."

Male laborers in Philadelphia earned about $1.50 per day, skilled workers $2.00 to $3.00, occasionally higher. Women, like one who lived on the little alley called Ashton Place, up Twenty-third Street from the pump works, and advertised in the *Public Ledger* for work as a chambermaid or seamstress, typically earned far less; paper bag makers, seed packers, or button makers, mostly women, might earn as little as fifty or seventy-five cents a day.

The horsecars that plied the dusty streets in that drought-ridden fall of 1874 might bustle with activity, but they were largely filled with better-off shoppers and leisured parkgoers, not ordinary workers. For the poorly paid, the twelve-cent round-trip fare could eat up 10 percent or more of their wages. Most people walked to work. Those losing their jobs but able to find new ones in another part of town didn't commute; they moved.

On the job, workers lay in fear of the caprices of the foreman; life was insecure, hours long, the workplace dangerous. At the Paschall Iron Works at Fifth and Tasker streets, around the time Fred started his apprenticeship, a pulley broke, the steam engine's governor failed, the engine "ran away," and the flywheel broke apart, killing a worker. Over at the Hynemann carpet factory on North Second, a carpet weaver with a little too much to drink staggered down the stairs, fell two flights, fractured his skull, was left to lie unconscious and untended all day, and died that night.

At a low point in his life in 1903, the novelist Theodore Dreiser also took a menial job, recording his impressions in *An Amateur Laborer*, a fragmentary account published long after his death. "These houses on the hill," he wrote of the simple homes of workers in Kingsbridge, New York, that he passed at the end of each long day, "—how they loomed up with that atmosphere of tenderness and comfort which appeals to the home-loving instinct in man. Toil and the comfort of the night— how these loomed large in the hour of weariness." Equally so, it must have been, for a tired Fred Taylor as he trudged up the hill to his parents' new house in Germantown at the end of each day.

The house on Ross Street, just six miles from the pump works, was a world away. There, the smell of fresh paint may have lingered yet. Many of the furnishings were almost virginally new. Two years before, Frank and Emily had had a young architect—Charles McKim, soon to become a principal in the famous New York firm of McKim, Mead & White—design it, or at least review their own plans for it. All the time Fred was away at Exeter, construction progressed, his parents writing him when the slaters arrived or the carpenters left, about the choice of stone, about cornices and dormer windows.

"Our home is so nearly done," Emily had written the boys on February 15, 1874, "that it is quite time to look for servants. I hope the colored woman who lived with Mrs. Houghton will get me some. She has promised to try." When the boys were home, she told them, they'd get their choice of rooms on the third floor. Within the next month, Fred was home and, presumably, exercising his choice. He would live at the big house on Ross Street for the next ten years, all through his apprenticeship and all through his early years in industry.

The mansard-roofed house wasn't flashy—that wasn't the Taylor style—but it was comfortable and spacious. A walkway from the street, set off from the sidewalk by a stone wall, led to a side entrance. On a ward map from the period, the Taylor house hardly stood out from similar places in the neighborhood, with their L-shaped extensions and big bay windows. It was only later maps, which showed the neighborhood filling in with closely packed row houses, any four or five of which could fit onto the Taylor property, that hinted at the scale of the house and its grounds. In the back, toward a nursing home with its great Victorian steeple within sight to the west, stood stables; in photographs taken in the 1890s, you could see the family retainer, Thomas Hughes, putting horses through their paces, jumping a stockade fence. There would be room for a tennis court, too. When cousin Ben came to see the house during construction, he commented that the closets, as Emily wrote, "looked more like rooms than closets."

It was doubtless during his apprenticeship that, as Fred told the story later, he'd come home at the end of a hard day on Race Street, tired and drained, only to be greeted with a light supper of rhubarb. Afterwards, as a servant scurried about taking care of the dishes, he would listen to his father read in French the first volume of Hippolyte Taine's *Les Origines de la France contemporaine*.

Around the table, certainly, he heard about family friends, perhaps about how the Wrights were making out with the steamship service, known as the Red Star Line, they had recently established to Liverpool and Antwerp. Or about the new marble fireproof building, downtown on Chestnut Street, that was home to Fidelity Insurance, Trust and Safe Deposit Company, over which their friends the Clarks presided. No doubt, he heard his mother tell of her work at the Germantown library and of Sarah Pugh and her other friends there. In that fall of 1874, the library board fretted over low evening attendance, resolved to advertise the library's Saturday evening hours in the paper and erect a sign, facing the street, to list them. With two other women, Emily was named to its new advertising committee.

That was home. And every morning, often before dawn, Fred would walk down the steep hill, flanked by low stone walls, board the train, and soon find himself down on Race Street again. The mind-bludgeoning contrast of people, scenes, and experiences could scarcely be lost on anyone. "I look back upon the first six months of my apprenticeship as a patternmaker as, on the whole, the most valuable part of my education," he wrote. "Not that I gained much knowledge during that time," he went on, "nor did I ever become a very good patternmaker; but the awakening as to the reality and seriousness of life was complete, and, I believe, of great value."

Griffith and the others might be ill-suited to appear at a Germantown party. They might be coarse and unread, slouch along the street in greasy overalls, scarcely looking up at you as you passed (to borrow images Taylor would use later); they might chew tobacco, spit and cuss, delight in conning the boss. But he liked them, and maybe he loved them, and certainly he respected them. "I remember very distinctly," he would write later, "the perfectly astonishing awakening at the end of six months of my apprenticeship, when I discovered that the three other men who were with me in the pattern shop were all much smarter than I was." And out of this came the realization, startling to sheltered Fred, that he was "made of the same kind of clay, physically as well as mentally, as these other men."

Make no mistake, this was a discovery, and a thrilling one for an eighteen-year-old. Many years later, an English novelist, David Lodge, would thrust his protagonist into the gritty world of the foundry, where she, too, would find her life shaken and enriched. In *Nice Work*, a scholar inured to academic values and comforts finds foundry life

> so bizarre, so totally unlike her usual environment, that there was a
> kind of exhilaration to be found in it, in its very discomfort and
> danger, such as explorers must feel, she supposed, in a remote and
> barbarous country. . . . She derived a subtle satisfaction from her
> association with the factory, and a certain sense of superiority over
> her friends. . . . She led a double life these days, and felt herself to
> be a more interesting and complex person because of it.

So it must have been for Fred. It was like striking gold or falling rapturously in love: he possessed secret knowledge that his Germantown friends could scarcely imagine. And he treasured this new knowledge— so unexpected, so exhilarating—all his life.

He was, strangely, happy. Later, he'd tell his wife about those days, and she would report how, early in his apprenticeship, he "threw himself entirely into the life of the shop, leaving each morning . . . in overalls, lunch pail under his arm. From then on, he showed such enthusiasm for his new work that his old friends . . . wondered if perhaps they ought to be following his example."

～

Then, as now, "apprenticeship" was a charged word, steeped in myth, musty with images of the Middle Ages, of boys in coarse clothes absorbing wisdom from a grizzled old master in a tiny shop. But the 1870s

were not the 1370s, and amid rapid industrialization, apprenticeship
was nothing like it once was. Back in the 1840s, seventy-year-old
J. F. Holloway recalled during a lapse into nostalgia at an American
Society of Mechanical Engineers meeting in 1895:

> the apprentices were in small shops. The machine shops of this
> country were individual shops: they were owned by the man who
> operated them, or by a small partnership, and the apprentice had
> the privilege, the inestimable privilege, of living in the family, of
> getting up in the early morning and making the fire, milking the
> cow and taking care of the horse, before he went to work in the
> shop. There was a certain community of feeling, in those days,
> between the boys in the shop and the master.

But now, the old skein of mutual responsibility was unraveling.
Abuses went both ways. Apprentices had traditionally been "bound"
for so many years, so that the master might ultimately recoup losses
suffered while the boy was still awkward, ignorant, and useless. But by
the time of Taylor's apprenticeship, fathers only rarely signed their sons
over like that. So boys often quit, leaving for regular jobs, long before
their time was up. On the other hand, apprentices were often exploited
as cheap labor. "The new factory system confused many Americans,
who accepted uncritically the belief that whatever was called an
apprenticeship must in fact be one," writes W. J. Rorabaugh in *The
Craft Apprentice*. It was "not always easy to tell the difference between a
true apprenticeship and a false one."

Surely, Fred Taylor's differed markedly from the norm, even from
the more ambiguous one of his time. That even in its fourth and
final year he earned only three dollars a week—pin money, less than
the lowest-paid servant—was not unusual, nor that he earned nothing at all during his first year; besides, he didn't need the money. What
was unusual, he allowed later, was that "I was given, perhaps, special
opportunities to progress from one kind of work to another." He had
told the shop's owners, or his father had, that he "wanted an opportunity to learn fast rather than [earn high] wages, and for that reason, I think, I had specially good opportunities to progress." Taylor's
apprenticeship bore something in common with an executive training
program.

Even late in the nineteenth century, an apprentice normally spent his entire four, five, or seven years learning a single trade—patternmaking, say, at the start, patternmaking at the end, then into a regular job as journeyman patternmaker. But not Fred Taylor. Sometime into his term at the pump works, perhaps early in 1876, he began a second apprenticeship as a machinist. That was one departure from the norm.

Another, perhaps more unusual, was that beginning around May 1876, Fred took six months off, to take a job at the centennial exposition across the river in Fairmont Park.

5

CENTENNIAL

～

By THE HUNDREDS, fair visitors gathered around the great man-made waterfall—the Cataract, as they called it. It was thirty-six feet wide and as high as a three-story building. Over it, water cascaded into a half-million-gallon pool, then was driven back to the top by steam-powered pumps. Or else fed through huge pipes to other pumps that spewed it back in lazy streams and jetting parabolic arcs. The refreshing spray was much savored by visitors to the fair during that hot summer of 1876. Around the pool, benches were lined up, and well-dressed men and women, tired and hot from tramping through the exhibits, stopped there to rest, under the glass roofs and lacy cast ironwork, talking loud over the rumble of the water, or quietly enjoying the cool mist.

The great centennial exposition of 1876, marking a hundred years of American independence, filled 236 acres in west Philadelphia's Fairmont Park. Under a light drizzle, flanked by bunting and the flags of every nation, the emperor and empress of Brazil at his side, President Ulysses S. Grant officially opened it on May 10. But after the hoopla, the exposition slumped, admissions at first numbering only fifteen or twenty thousand per day; Sunday closings—despite the efforts of abolitionist Lucretia Mott, among others—kept most working people away. But by the fall, following a long spell of horrendously hot weather—

one stretch of hundred-degree highs in late July persisted for ten days—the crowds returned. Fifty, sixty, a hundred thousand people came streaming through the turnstiles every day.

They came to see the Bohemian glass, French silks, and Spanish shawls, to see fine cabinetry, jewelry, silver, and fine art; someone counted two and a half miles of art exhibits. Maybe they also came to reaffirm a sense of nationhood barely a decade after the agony of civil war. Visitors ranged over two hundred buildings, including a prefabricated Japanese pavilion with rich ornamental carving and elaborate tile work, and Horticultural Hall, filled with flowers and plants. The Main Hall—largest building in the world, a third of a mile long—covered twenty-one acres.

Even the most pedestrian product could became the focal point of elaborate display. The Nicholson File Company, of Providence, Rhode Island, established in 1864, hung hundreds of its files—as large as meat cleavers and as small as toothpicks—against a cloth-faced display, six feet by ten, each individually attached with screws and neatly twisted wires. But not merely hung: Together they formed a pattern, fanning out from a framed engraving of the Nicholson factory at its center, tiny ones arranged mostly up and down, huge ones horizontally, the overall effect worshipful, if to our eye comically so. Bristle brushes, tacks, and candles got similar treatment.

The world of 1876 ran to the rhythm of great rumbling machinery, and in Machinery Hall lay the heart of the exposition, a fourteen-acre tribute to the mechanical arts. In England, James Clerk Maxwell had only recently worked out the elegant equations representing the mysterious kinship between electricity and magnetism. Edison was at the fair with his quadruplex telegraph, which transmitted several messages at once. And Alexander Graham Bell was showing off his new telephone; "My God, it talks!" said the Brazilian emperor. But all this only whispered of an electronic future still far off. Mechanical power still held sway, power transmitted through gears and belts, power that clacked and whirred, hammered and hissed. Earlier in the century, the English genius Charles Babbage had developed plans for a computer, an "analytical engine" that could perform any mathematical operation; it was intended to work with punch cards, pulleys, and gears.

Under the vast seventy-foot-high roof of Machinery Hall lay a clattering mechanical paradise of blowers, shingle makers, lathes, milling machines, sewing machines, knitting machines, steam engines, looms, cotton presses, printing presses, paper-cutting machines—their beds and housings of heavy cast iron, lavishly painted, ornamented with scrollwork and fanciful designs. A bright green flywheel with decorated spokes. A metal-cutting machine with an eagle cast into its iron base, painted in gold, accented in red, white, and blue. And powering all eight hundred or so working machines—through pulleys and eight miles of shafting, through chains and wide leather belts, some of them two and a half feet wide—was the great Corliss engine, symbol of the exposition, ultimate expression of the Age of Steam.

In a steam engine, no fuel burned within its cylinders, as it does in our automobile engines. Rather, somewhere—maybe across the room or down in the basement—a boiler's coal-stoked fire turned circulating water into high-pressure steam. You'd inject it first to one side of the piston, driving it one way; then, at the end of its stroke, through a timed valve, to the other, driving it back the opposite way. A weighty, rotating mass, the flywheel, smoothed out the jerk. It was almost silent, just the soft hissing of steam and the muted rumble of the reciprocating piston, the whole mass of iron and steel turning, steadily, relentlessly. And slowly, not two or three thousand revolutions per minute like your car engine, but maybe two hundred

The giant Corliss engine turned thirty-six times a minute; you had to wait almost two seconds for its fifty-six-ton flywheel to come around again. A whole shop the size of Ferrell & Jones might run off a ten- or twenty-horsepower engine; the gargantuan six-story Corliss, its pistons almost four feet in diameter and working through a stroke of ten feet, turned out fourteen hundred. It was a wonder of the world. It gripped the imagination of fairgoers more than all the art and architecture. A march was written to celebrate it. Frédéric Bartholdi, sculptor of the Statue of Liberty, rhapsodized that "it had the beauty and almost the grace of the human form." When the American president and Brazilian emperor officially opened the exposition, the silver-plated cranks they turned controlled its valves.

Down a wide aisle from the engine, at the south end of Machinery Hall, was the Hydraulic Annex. Here was that fairgoer's delight, the Cataract, the areas abutting it crowded with hydraulic rams and water-wheels, propeller pumps, steam pumps and deck pumps, from Chicago, Baltimore, Brooklyn, Philadelphia. A Connecticut firm displayed five hundred pumps. In section 8, beside the pool to its southwest, making its modest contribution to the watery din, was Ferrell & Jones, with a steam pump and two others.

All through Machinery Hall, salesmen and exhibit reps guided would-be buyers through the intricacies of a steam engine's new valve or a hydraulic ram's automatic regulator; upward of eleven thousand people with exhibitor passes entered the fairgrounds daily, and one of them was twenty-year-old Fred Taylor. He wasn't hawking Ferrell & Jones pumps. A new opportunity had come his way, typically enough through the family, in this case a cousin, Edward I. H. Howell. Back at the Unitarian church that Fred's mother had helped found, Howell had long been active and would remain so until his death more than half a century later; he had been chairman of the church's entertainment committee, would become superintendent of its Sunday school. But as the centennial neared, he approached Fred with quite a secular proposition.

The centennial was to be a truly international showcase, a chance to show off American wares to visitors from around the world, to learn from foreign exhibitors, buy from them, sell to them. A delegation from Philadelphia had visited Europe to drum up interest and, to the amazement of all, every European country had signed on to come. In the final reckoning, of 30,864 fair exhibitors, more than two thirds were foreign, including more than six hundred machinery exhibitors. "The Centennial," it would be said, "was the first occasion on which a large number of foreigners came to visit the United States at the same time and for the same purpose." And American machinery makers were determined to get their business—in some slight measure, it seems, through Fred Taylor.

By now, Fred had some knowledge of machines; but, less than two years into his apprenticeship, it was knowledge matched by half the men his age in Philadelphia. Of course, he was bright, hardworking, and well-spoken, and he had an extra credential: he was fluent in French and German. He could speak to buyers from France, Germany, Belgium, Switzerland, and Austria with ease and confidence. Would he, asked Howell, take time off from his apprenticeship to represent a group of New England machine tool manufacturers?

He would.

New England and Philadelphia were the two big centers of machine tool manufacturing in the United States. Prentice & Company from

Worcester, Massachusetts, had lathes and drills on exhibit. Putnam Machine, from Fitchburg, Massachusetts, had hand tools, shafting, and planers. Benjamin Laurence, from Lowell, Massachusetts, the great tex- tile center, had milling machines. At the exhibits of one of these, or one of many other New England machine tool makers, Fred Taylor stood duty. For six months, while thousands of other Philadelphia appren- tices toiled in ill-lit shops, Fred enjoyed the glitter of the fair.

One day, a forty-six-year-old man visited his stand and started asking questions. It was Lucian Sharpe, who headed Brown & Sharpe, a large machine tool manufacturer that, at its exhibit virtually in the shadow of the Corliss engine, was showing off its new universal grinder. Sharpe was a devotee of world's fairs. At the Paris exposition of 1867 his company had helped open the whole European market to American machine tools; now he attended them religiously. Fred had no reason to recognize him by sight, and Sharpe didn't at first reveal his identity. But he asked good questions, Fred thought, and clearly knew what he was about. Could he interest the gentleman in something?

Sharpe was scarcely about to buy anything from the boy, but he was enough taken with him to bestow a little fatherly advice. Sitting there, Fred by his side, he asked him to define his idea of success.

Fred fumbled, saying he had no particular idea.

"Why, you must have something that you are working for."

Yes, he did. "I am working to get to be a machinist and earn $2.50 a day," a top wage, probably about what John Griffith made.

No, no, he didn't mean that, Sharpe interjected, and went on to offer a homily about the virtues of working a little more precisely than the next man.

He had settled on that course himself while an apprentice thirty years before; maybe Fred's mention of his own apprenticeship stirred the middle-aged man's memory. At eighteen, Sharpe had gone to work for Joseph R. Brown, and they had developed such an affinity that they formed a new company that would together bear their names. In the beginning, it employed fourteen men, but expanded and went on to employ hundreds, then thousands. And perhaps due to its very birth in an apprenticeship, the company had taken special interest in its young workers, setting up a shop library stocked with two thousand volumes, even encouraging apprentices to meet during working hours for lec- tures and self-improvement.

Old Man Sharpe, as he styled himself, stressed precision workmanship, but that's not what impressionable Fred took from his little speech. Indeed, it was not the content of Sharpe's message that impressed him but, rather, the focus, concentration, and tenacity with which he hewed to it—a single, simple idea, adhered to tenaciously, relentlessly pursued, year in and year out. *That's* what bred success.

~

American machine tools like those which Fred Taylor peddled in Philadelphia stunned the world. "Large sales of machinery have been made, both to foreign and native customers," reported the head of the exposition's bureau of machinery. A British engineer came back "immensely impressed." A French observer advised his compatriots not to worry that Americans might steal European designs; on the contrary, he wrote, "the Americans possess the genius of invention to the highest degree" and had as much to teach Europeans as to learn.

Above all, the Germans were struck by the quality and technical inventiveness of what they'd seen. In *Letters from Philadelphia*, one distinguished professor, Franz Reuleaux, condemned German products as "cheap and bad" compared to what he'd seen in America, and urged German industry to emulate the Americans and take the technological high road. The message took; German quality became legendary. In 1941, a buoyant Adolf Hitler, lecturing his entourage at the height of Germany's battlefield success in World War II, cited the Philadelphia centennial exposition as having given German industry just the kick in the pants it needed, from which nadir it had risen to its present glorious heights.

As the summer heat eased and word of the fair's marvels spread, people swarmed to Philadelphia. On one day alone, in late September, more than a quarter million people showed up. In the end, total attendance reached almost ten million. After a grand display of fireworks the night before, the fair closed on a cold and rainy November 10. The tourists returned to Berlin, Paris, Pittsburgh, and Peoria. Fred Taylor returned to the pump works.

6

THE MASTER TOOLS

∾

Probably before the centennial hiatus, Fred had taken up the machinist's trade, and machine shops would be his home for almost his entire working life.

"Machinist" is not a general term for an operator of machines; nor is the "machine tool" he shepherds just any kind of powered tool; nor is the "machine shop" in which he works simply a shop with machines in it. Though no clue resides in the words themselves, all three now refer, and have since the mid-nineteenth century or a little before, to a particular class of machines: those that cut and shape metal.

But this spare, literal definition fails to suggest the privileged place that machine tools occupy in the industrial world. Fred Colvin, a contemporary of Taylor and editor of *American Machinist*, wrote that machine tools were "distinguished by a remarkable feature that places them almost in the category of living things and permits one to speak literally and not figuratively of their organic evolution. For machine tools are the *only class of machines that can reproduce themselves*." Or, as others have said, they are "the master tools"—the tools that make the tools that make the machines that make the products of home and farm.

If a casting shaken free of sand on the foundry floor represents a rough draft of the final part, the machinist is the editor who shapes it into final form. Machine tools all cut metal. But they go under various names—lathe, shaper, planer, drill press, milling machine, and many more specialized machines—depending on how they cut it; each implies a particular relationship between the work to be cut—locked in place within heavy metal jaws, by clamps, or other contrivances—and the cutting tool.

In a planer, for example, the work moves back and forth against a stationary cutter of hardened tool steel, a thin layer of metal stripped off with each pass, leaving a flat, straight, smooth surface; in a shaper, normally used for smaller cuts, the relationship is reversed, the cutting tool moving back and forth over the stationary work.

In the modest drill press, a rotating drill bit is pulled straight down into work clamped in place, simply cutting a hole to a specified depth.

In the milling machine, work held in a movable vise is guided across the path of a spinning, many-edged cutter suspended from above in a fixed position.

But the prototypical machine tool, first among equals of the master tools, is the lathe. No machine shop, then or now, can be a machine shop without it. The second machine tool you buy might be a drill press, planer, or milling machine, but the first will always be a lathe. And it comes first for one simple reason: civilization rolls on wheels, and lathes make wheels.

More precisely, lathes makes cylindrical surfaces: the machinist places the work within the jaws of a chuck, sets it to spinning, and edges the tool bit, secure in its tool post, slowly into it, shaving away metal. A lathe makes round outsides and round insides. A piston destined to shuttle back and forth within a cylinder will be made on a lathe. So might the bearing surface of a shaft, as well as the sleeves in which it fits, pulleys that transmit power, the great revolving cylinders that go into textile machinery or printing presses, railroad car wheels, pins that fit into holes, screws that fit into nuts. The work might even start out as an irregular casting of some sort, a lump of iron; but once the lathe finishes, there'll be something round to it. So ubiquitous is the lathe, and so easy to shave away metal with it, that even things that need not be round, but can be, are often made on it. Thus a crank handle, or knob, or cannon barrel—not just its inside but its outside surface as well— often bears the telltale marks of the lathe.

The nineteenth-century lathe and its cousins were powered not by electricity but indirectly, by steam or sometimes waterpower, which drove a network of overhead shafts. These, in turn, fed power through long leather belts, four or five inches wide and thick as a finger, to "countershafts" or "jackshafts" above each machine, which in turn fed power, again through belts, down to the shop floor. At each lathe or planer, the belt looped around one of a nest of pulleys of various diameters, the gearboxes of the nineteenth century, thus driving it at the machinist's chosen speed.

The steadily turning overhead shaft was like the electricity today accessible at every socket—on standby, ready. Even turning the switch had its analogy. On "OFF" the belt from each machine was disengaged from the main line of shafting; slipped around a motionless overhead pulley, it sat there, leaving the machine still and impotent. For "ON" your hand went to a pivoted wooden lever, the "shipper," its handle at about the height of your head, which nudged the belt from side to side; with a reach and a pull across a foot or so of arc, you slipped the belt, until now motionless, onto the adjacent "live" pulley, which was just a spinning metal cylinder. After an instant's flapping and settling in, the belt down to the machine turned. That, in the case of a lathe, set the work to spinning, ready for the bite of the small, sharp piece of hardened steel that was the tool bit.

To even the most lightly practiced eye, each machine tool looked different from every other. But to a newcomer, the individual machines might recede into a blur of mechanical shapes, the lingering image that of long, snaking leather belts rising up to the resolutely turning, clanking overhead shafts. A shop full of machines—each with its belt, each with its long, narrow wooden shipper—resembled nothing so much as a forest of spindly trees.

It was a scene repeated around the world in every branch of manufacture. Thomas Edison needed a machine shop to fashion the models for his inventions. The railroads needed them to keep their rolling stock rolling. Guns, textiles, clocks, heavy machinery—all needed the master tools. All needed a machine stop to make parts or repairs.

More than foundry or forge, the machine shop was the quintessential nineteenth-century workplace, turning out not just pistons and valves but also men. Machinists formed the industrial world's broadest class of skilled worker. They worked on lathes a hundred feet long that stretched across the factory floor, making cannon or heavy machinery; on little machines tucked into a corner of the shop, making intricate working parts that could fit on a fingertip; in production shops, making thousands of the same part for rifles or sewing machines; in job shops, making a single item or a very few. The machinists' own elite were the tool-and-die makers, who made the jigs, fixtures, and dies upon which industrial civilization rests.

But all, in a sense, inhabited the same industrial home. The machine shop left hundreds of thousands of men with shared memories: The whirring and flapping of the belts. The first bite of the cutting tool into the gray iron casting; its dull, scraping growl; the sudden streak of freshly cut metal. Iron dust floating down from the tool bit, glittering, caught in a shaft of light penetrating the shop's gloom.

"How that steel curled off as I dug the tool into it," remembered one machinist. "Somehow when a machine acts that way you feel like petting it, as you would a horse. It becomes almost human, part of the man who is running it." Iron and steel were hard and unyielding, yet here in the machine shop, you cut them like butter. Even at its most workaday, shop life held a hint of drama and spectacle.

With factories going up and the mechanical arts in their glory, machine shops drew the bright and the ambitious. Within them, futures were forged. Within them resided the hopes of a still-young nation. "This country is awfully big," wrote Chordal, but

> with all respect for the thousands and thousands of lathes which this very minute are revolving while some chap leans over them with outside calipers; for the thousands of planers, which are at this instant knocking their dogs against their tumblers; for the thousands of drill presses, which this instant would show their spindles gradually descending; for the thousands of vises which this instant have a death grip on some piece of metal; for the shower of chips flying before the thousands of chipping chisels now creeping slowly forward before thousands of ball-peen hammers—with all respect for these many evidences of the existence of machine shops in this land, I venture the opinion that the machine shops haven't got started yet.

You would, went the dream, complete your apprenticeship, take a journeyman's job, save your money, start your own shop, and make your fortune. And some did live out the dream. Taking big advertisers in *American Machinist* as representative of successful machinist-entrepreneurs in general, Chordal set out what he imagined as their origins. At eighteen, he observed, most of them

> were working in shops, drilling set screw holes in pulleys, cutting bolts, chipping new holes in old boilers, contriving ways and means to get old broken studs out of old cylinders, forging square keys out of round iron, butt-welding erroneous connecting rods, gouging out core boxes, gluing up segments, spitting white pine

dust, cutting up old boilers, building up new boilers, putting in new rivets, cutting out old rivets, bedding floor moulds, ramming copes, filing cores, and doing everything one man does for another man's money. They were not preparing themselves to take charge of probated fortunes. They were working.

The vast majority of them, he added, "did not, at the age of eighteen, have fifty dollars they could call their own."

In this last respect, of course, Taylor didn't fit the mold. But in most other ways, their experience was his. It could hardly help but shape him.

7

THE EDUCATION OF AN APPRENTICE

〜

I N PRINCIPLE, EVERY APPRENTICESHIP WAS AN EXCHANGE: the apprentice's labor for the master's knowledge. But in practice, while as an apprentice you surely worked, the master didn't teach, and you didn't learn. Rather, you picked up your trade as best you could.

At first, you swept up, you oiled the overhead shafting. When one of the men asked for a tool, you fetched it. "They work at what they can do and gradually learn," one molder told a state industrial board. The great steel man, John Fritz, recalled of his apprenticeship in a blacksmith and machine shop that his first days were spent pumping the bellows and wielding the sledgehammer. When an apprentice did get something substantive to do, as Entropy, an anonymous Chordal-like correspondent to *American Machinist,* observed of the traditional "shop-trained boy," he was "set to work doing things [he could not] spoil by any chance."

There was wisdom in this. How better to learn the layout of the shop than to find a tool for someone? How better to learn to take orders? How better to ensure that the new boy didn't wreck the shop?

But what about the exchange? Where was the learning?

Certainly, book learning counted for little. In his day, Taylor would testify, "all of my reading was confined to Joshua Rose's book on machine-shop practices." Later, scores of such books would flood the market. But then, as Taylor remembered it, "that was the only one available." Rose, an Englishman, was a consulting engineer in New York whose later *Modern Machine Shop Practice*, a two-volume tome stuffed with gorgeous engravings of machine tools, would go through many editions. But in 1876, midway through Taylor's apprenticeship, it was only Rose's *Complete Practical Machinist*, drawn from articles he had written for *Scientific American*, that Taylor could have seen.

Its baroque subtitle, *Embracing Lathe Work, Vise Work, Drills and Drilling, Taps and Dies, Hardening and Tempering, The Making and Use of Tools, etc. etc.*, suggested comprehensiveness. And to a novice, it might have seemed crammed with knowledge. To cut cast iron with a bright, smooth finish, apply water and keep the cutting speed to about seven feet per minute. To make a drill bit extremely hard, heat it in a charcoal fire to a dull red heat, then quench it in mercury, not water. But apparently its 376 pages struck Fred as meager fare. "I think I read it through in two hours and a half."

If books did not supply apprentices with much, neither did formal training programs, which scarcely existed. Nor could you expect some sage old workman to take you under his wing and bestow upon you his store of knowledge. Rather, all the apprentice learned in the small machine shops of his youth, a veteran machinist recalled, was "what he could discern from personal observation. Machinists, as a rule, were not very liberal with information of the right kind. Once in a while someone would give you some good advice, but that was the exception rather than the rule."

Education? Why, it hardly warranted the name. One report on apprenticeship around the time of Fred's found that apprentices got little attention and that whether or not they became skilled workmen depended mostly on themselves. There lay the "chief vice" of the apprenticeship system, a Philadelphia civic association heard it argued: that it had "scarcely anything of an educational character, and is exceedingly wasteful of the time of the learner."

At first, the apprentice learned plenty: to keep his limbs out of gears and the overhead couplings, to keep the oil lamp out of the jaws of the chuck, to button his top shirt button to keep hot chips off him. The price of such knowledge was scars, severed fingers, and burns. But beyond such grim, expensive lessons?

A veteran machinist might instruct the new boy in the use of a special tool, favor him with odd bits of shop knowledge. "To straighten a reamer which has sprung in hardening," one apprentice recorded in his journal in 1858, "heat it with the hot tongs and suck plunger of straightening machine down very lightly—so Bob Bolton says." In time, the tips and teaching did add up.

But only with glacial slowness. Especially as the century wore on, resentment grew among apprentices who felt they were exploited, working too hard and learning too slowly. Too often, learning was blind, unthinking, profoundly conservative, based on simply doing what you were told, keeping your eyes open, doing things as others in the shop did them.

Taylor would later recall how during his apprenticeship he'd fashion a tool bit, the business end of the piece of steel that actually cut the work. "We would heat the metal" in the blacksmith's forge, "lay it on the edge of the anvil one way and ask a friend to hit it a crack, and then turn it around and repeat the process," giving it a diamond-shaped point. But why that shape? Why not rounded or blunted? "In the primitive shops, such as the one in which I served my apprenticeship," he explained, the diamond point was what you used, period. Like so much of shop practice, "It was a tradition. It had no scientific basis." So they just banged away, "turning it and hitting it with the sledge," just as it had always been done.

"Our trades are learned just as they were in the Middle Ages," Taylor told the Commission on Industrial Relations in 1912. "We always used to say, 'I am picking up a trade,' and you do it; you literally pick up your trade. You look at this fellow and that fellow to see what they are doing." Left largely alone, you did what you thought you had been told to do, blindly, sometimes fearfully.

One machinist with mostly fond memories of his 1870s apprenticeship, W. D. Graves, nonetheless pointed out to *American Machinist* readers in 1910 that "after a few half-days in the manual training department of a good public school" a boy would learn more than "in a month of shop apprenticeship." And, he went on, "that we were taught to swim by being unceremoniously thrown into deep water does not argue that we cannot teach our boys in a gentler manner." Taylor, too, would argue for what he, at least, conceived to be a "gentler manner." In his system, he would say, apprentices really learn. They "are not left to pick up a trade as I was." Taylor system "teachers . . . stand right there and show them. . . . [It's like] having a friend" by your side.

And there, in that wistful claim, we see the long shadow of his apprenticeship, some lingering residue of pain at being left at sea, alone and confused, in an alien world.

At an American Society of Mechanical Engineers meeting in Chicago in 1886, a speaker outlining Cornell University's engineering program suggested that one year in an engineering school shop might serve better than seven years in a working machine shop. Nonsense, Fred Taylor as much as said, "I think it would be more nearly the contrary. I think one year of actual service in a machine shop would in certain respects supplant twenty years of practice in a school shop." For at school, the young man would be surrounded by men much like himself. As a result, he would miss the one thing that was otherwise of

> greatest use to him in his experience with men; that is the
> knowledge of the character of the men with whom he is dealing.
> [At school] he . . . fails to appreciate properly the feeling of
> apprentices toward their teachers, of workmen toward their
> foreman, and of foremen to their employees, which will enable
> him afterwards to manage men successfully.

He can never get such experience at school. "He can only have it by passing through the mill himself; getting there at seven in the morning and leaving at six, and being knocked about to a certain extent as an apprentice."

Being knocked about to a certain extent. If, Taylor wrote later, a college boy placed in a shop for six months "were handled rather brutally and made to understand from the start that he must sweep the floor of the shop in a thoroughly satisfactory manner or perform some other manual or routine duties so as to give entire satisfaction to his employer"—and that he stood to be fired if he didn't—he'd return to school a better man.

In an essay written about 1908 and entitled "Why Manufacturers Dislike College Students," Taylor would observe that college-educated engineers were so spoiled by interesting studies, by the sheer pleasure of learning, by their college freedoms, that shop life almost always disappointed them. Better to stick them in a shop for a year right from the start. "They then begin to learn the greatest lesson of life, that almost nine tenths of the work that every man has to do is monotonous, tiresome and uninteresting. They then start to develop the character which enables them to do unpleasant, disagreeable things." He was probably thinking of himself during his apprenticeship, a callow teenager fresh from Exeter, too spirited and ambitious, too well-educated—too damned fine—to simply do as he was told, fit in, and serve.

On coming to Ferrell & Jones, Ernest Wright recalled, Taylor was alien to mechanical ways. He inclined toward abstractions and ideals, loved the idea of the one best cricket bat, we may suppose, more than any physical embodiment of it. "He had a natural aversion to manual work," a friend from later, Carl Barth, observed, "only brain work being fully to his liking."

Taylor would later portray himself as a practical man, a veteran of the shop floor; and surely he was, compared to the men in the front office who got no closer to the shop than a ledger book. But it hadn't come naturally; it was an acquired taste. He had been raised on words—his father reading to them at dinner, lofty abolitionist sentiments, fine conversation in the hotel lobbies of Europe, Homer's Greek in Cilley's class at Exeter.

But at the pump works, words wouldn't do. He felt the tool's heat as it cut. He lifted awkward, gray iron castings. His hands turned black, his nostrils filled with soot. The shapes he encountered—stubs, shoulders, and sleeves, rods and flats—were not Platonic forms but rusted steel bolts, oily bronze bearings, castings rough from the foundry, metal polished mirror-smooth. A Euclidian radius on the drawing became a few swipes with the file. The Idea was gone, transmuted into steel.

A sense of awakening and of quiet, hard-won triumph runs through Taylor's recollections of his apprenticeship. He had entered it soft and self-indulgent; he emerged tempered, serious, and strong. It had been his trial by fire. All his life it would loom bittersweet in memory.

In time, its pains would be mostly forgotten, its triumph forever recalled. Years later, brought before the House investigating committee, he was asked whether it was not natural for a machinist to resist overwork. Oh, you couldn't overwork yourself on the lathe, Taylor replied. Why, back in 1895, middle-aged and "physically soft," he'd run a big experimental lathe himself for a whole winter, working harder than he ever had before. "And I tell you," he said, staring his inquisitors in the face, "it was the easiest and happiest year I have had since my apprenticeship."

~

1906. Taylor is president of the American Society of Mechanical Engineers. Fame is four years off. But he is a distinguished figure in his profession and has been asked to appear before a congressional committee to testify against the Littauer bill, which would replace the English system of inches and pounds with the metric system of meters and grams.

For the men in the shop, says Taylor, meters and millimeters are alien, whereas good old fractions of an inch are friends. "The half inch is one of the important facts of their lives," he says. "They live with it. It is a language to them. They talk and think more in inches than in words while at work, and they are doing that all their lives long."

Of course, he adds, "these workmen have not appeared before your committee and stated their side." But since they cannot leave their lathes to address the distinguished gentlemen, "that is what I am trying to do for them." He, Fred Taylor, is their voice. Perhaps, he allows, some engineers and scientists favor the metric system, but "Gentleman," he pleads, "remember the workingmen who are really the sufferers," the anonymous men for whom he feels obliged to speak.

"I am a mechanic," he claims, though he has not worked as one for thirty years; a switch to the metric system "hits me hard. Probably none of you gentlemen are mechanics, and therefore the change contemplated by the Littauer bill would not trouble you in the least."

When his questioner points out that a high army officer advocates the metric system, Taylor pulls rank, if in reverse: "I doubt, however, whether he has ever worked as a workman, or come into intimate personal contact with the workmen." Worked as a workman, that is, *as he has.*

Again and again, all through his crusades for scientific management, Taylor would trade on his early years in the shop, stressing to workmen his credentials as one of their own, to employers his insight, born of shop experience unusual among them, into what the worker really wants.

A rhetorical device with which to disarm his critics? Yes, but not just that. His identification with skilled workers, forged at the pump works, was real. All through his correspondence, as well as his published writings and public testimony, we see an abiding respect for skilled workmen and for knowledge gleaned not from books but, rather, amid the heat of the foundry and the clatter of the machine shop.

At one point during his 1906 testimony, he bridles at the idea that it is the lathe that produces work and not its operator. "I do not think that you understand what a lathe is," Taylor shoots back. "A lathe is not like a loom which, after it is set, can only weave the one particular pattern which it is set for. A lathe is run from morning till night by an intelligent man who is obliged to guide it, as it were, just as if it were a high-spirited horse. . . . He has to have a lot of brains to use his machine."

Even the work practice known as soldiering—over a lifetime of writing and public speaking Taylor would give the word currency, forever linking it to his name—did not diminish Taylor's respect for the breed.

You go to work and toil at a hard, steady pace all day, accomplishing as much as you can? You do not. Rather, you deliberately make fewer patterns, or turn fewer shafts, than you otherwise could. When the boss comes along, you sputter and flutter into activity, then ease up once he leaves. Never do you charge ahead at full speed all day long. And you never let on what you could manage to do if pressed.

This was soldiering, and it was the rule in industry, Taylor would maintain, not the exception. He saw it "all through my apprenticeship," he told Congressman Wilson forty years later, "from the time I started as an apprentice until I got through; the thing was practically universal in the shop."

To intense, hardworking young Taylor, the practice could scarcely have seemed like anything but the most shameless sloth. Still, something in how he learned of it—perhaps through men like John Griffith or others whom he esteemed, or by seeing the hostile glares greeting any who brooked it—left soldiering a shop floor institution he did not then care to challenge.

Besides, the practice drew on a logic of its own. As a workman, you need to husband your strength. And you need to conserve the shop's perhaps limited work; who knows when business might slacken and you are cast jobless into the street? Moreover, if only out of manly self-respect, you want some say-so over your day. The boss wants all of you, your substance, your very life force; as a man, you owe it to yourself to yield as little of it as possible. Hence, GO SLOW.

That Taylor could make the workman's case for soldiering, and that he had done it himself, was always one weapon he used in his crusade to end it. He had stood among workmen as one of their own, been through what they'd been through, counted them as his friends. And that, in his own mind, gave him the right to speak for them.

For him, his apprenticeship was the ultimate credential, one he would invoke all his life.

~

And yet, Taylor's intimacy with his co-workers and insight into their world was less than he claimed and less than he thought. The evidence suggests that his knowledge of working-class life all came on the job—working with the men elbow to elbow, yet always across a gulf born of their differing circumstances in life.

How often did Fred Taylor visit the homes of friends from the shop or otherwise see them outside work hours? How often did he meet their families or drink with them at day's end? Probably almost never. Later, even to serve the parables he used to such effect to drive home his points, he never mentioned being welcomed in a workman's home. Never in a lifetime of letters, speeches, reminiscences, books, and articles did he begin, "One time, when I was over at Jim Marley's house . . ."

What we know of Taylor's apprenticeship comes mostly from his own recollections or from those of his own circle—never, even as brief snippets, from workmen themselves. For Fred Taylor, the pump works offered an intoxicating whiff of the workingman's world, not deep insight into it. Years later, he confided that, when younger, he had "worked for two and a half years in a machine shop," probably that of the pump works, "before the workmen found out that I was a gentleman's son."

Such a deception—for that, of course, is what it was—hints at relationships extending only so far. For what could he say when asked where he lived or why he never invited his friends to his house? Or when the conversation veered, as it must sometimes have, to schooling, family, friends? And how could he disguise his well-bred manners and speech?

In every outward, conventional way, Fred Taylor was forthright, honest, and direct—sometimes brutally so; his scientific side, certainly, sought truth or, at least, fact. And yet all his life, his integrity warred with a flair for the theatrical, a fondness for tall tales. For the sake of a story, he was willing to improve upon some facts, omit others. At the pump works, he was already showing himself willing to assume a role, to present things not quite as they were.

Taylor would sometimes be compared to Theodore Roosevelt, a man similarly favored by circumstances and with a personality no less vigorous. But as David McCullough writes of him in *Mornings on Horseback*, Roosevelt never tried to be anything other than what he was. He "was every inch the 'dude' the newspapers portrayed; he made no pretense by word or dress at being anything other than wellborn, never resorted . . . to being 'one of the boys.' "

Not so Taylor, who did try to act like one of the boys; for someone with his gift for mimicry, that came easily. Stories come down to us of the Uncle Remus stories Taylor told, in Negro dialect, that left his audience howling; of how he played a stiff German professor, complete viss a dhick cggzent; Copley suggests he could have succeeded on the stage. Now, at the pump works, he took to cussing with abandon. Hells and damns, and who knows what stronger stuff, erupted from him. "He not only picked up a habit of swearing," reports Copley, "but deliberately cultivated and retained it."

Copley wrote at a time, the 1920s, when propriety counted for more than it does now. One Taylor loyalist standing guard over the official biography, Harlow Person, complained that a Copley draft reproduced Taylor's swearing too faithfully: "Cuss words . . . may sometimes charm, but in cold print they are repellent." So Copley toned it down, devoted three pages to his subject's "Chesterfieldian manners," and quoted Ida Tarbell, the famous muckraking journalist, to the effect that "Mr. Taylor never seemed to be more of a gentleman than when he was swearing."

But the compulsive swearing revealed something of him. To hear Copley explain it, Taylor sought "whatever advantage there might be in as nearly as possible speaking the language of those with whom he dealt." But more likely, Taylor genuinely wanted acceptance from those rough-hewn men, sought to bridge the painful gap between himself and them. He was, at eighteen or nineteen, less like Teddy Roosevelt than Marcel Proust's protagonist in *Remembrance of Things Past*, Swann, "who behaved simply and casually with a duchess, [but] . . . would instantly begin to pose when in the presence of a housemaid."

Of course, it didn't quite take. Those working with him, Copley tells us, "appear invariably to have been first puzzled and then amused by [his swearing]. They easily could feel the incongruity between this habit and his general character."

Taylor's later writings suggest an ear uneasily cocked to the shop floor, resolved to root out anything professorial, flowery, or high-falutin from his vocabulary. "Regarding the word 'gang boss,'" he would write a colleague later, "I have personally a strong predilection for Anglo-Saxon words, and for that reason do not like 'supervisor' . . . Anglo-Saxon words are to my mind much more virile."

Race Street inhabited him forever. He spent the rest of his life thinking about workmen, claiming to speak for them, championing his system on their behalf, acting always as if he held their approval and respect.

Speaking before a group of engineering educators, he would lament that young men straight out of college lacked "the slightest knowledge of the great raw material" with which they were they were to work: the workman. He, presumably, did possess such knowledge.

No one can manage workmen, he went on, "who cannot say ten sentences consecutively to a workman" and be recognized as a former workman himself. He, presumably, would pass the test.

A year spent working closely "with a totally different class of men from those with which they have been brought up" counted for more than a similar time spent traveling abroad. He, presumably, knew; he'd had both experiences.

But did Taylor protest too much?

All his life, he made workmen objects of study—human data points from which to tease knowledge. The "management of the future," he would say, meant the "patient, analytical, almost microscopic study of men," which was best made "side by side and shoulder to shoulder" with them. You had to become "intimate with them, so that they forget that you are not one of their kind, and genuinely tell you what they think." Always, "they" were *they*.

Taylor's lectures at Harvard and elsewhere, purporting to give the lowdown on "Workmen and their Management," sound like advice for the care and feeding of children: "If one hopes to get into close and friendly touch with workmen, it is above all desirable that they should be talked to on their own level by those who are over them."

All this smacks of paternalistic remoteness, not fraternity. The worker intimacy he would always claim as his was more coveted than possessed. If on Race Street he was presumably made new, the transformation was imperfect and incomplete.

8

CONNECTIONS

~

"WHILE MUCH DISAGREEABLE DRUDGERY fell to the lot of the apprentice," W. D. Graves wrote in 1910 of his own experience some forty years before, "he was occasionally put to *making something*—given a job which he could complete and show as his own." For Graves, it was a set of wagon wheels. "I can well remember the pride which swelled in my boyish bosom as I watched the first pair of wagon wheels which I myself had wholly built, roll their somewhat wobbly way out of the yard."

But if an apprentice got little chance to make things whole through most of his term, he did toward the end. An apprenticeship typically concluded with the making of a model intended to showcase one's abilities, demonstrate mastery of one's skills; "masterpiece" goes back to these capstone projects. Sometime, perhaps around 1877, Fred made his, a miniature steam pump in iron and bronze.

Snap a picture of it against a featureless drape with no reference scale beside it, and you might think it just another Ferrell & Jones steam pump. But the whole assemblage—steam engine, flywheel, and pump, with its voluptuous, onion-shaped pressure vessel on top—sat on a cast-iron pedestal only about two feet long and four or five inches wide. Later, Taylor gave it to his son who prized it, disassembling it to see how it worked. Robert Taylor knew little of its origins, he wrote later, but: "It was tested and worked satisfactorily, that I know."

From the foundry patterns for the pedestal down to the fine machining, Taylor had presumably done it all. It was not of museum quality, but it was as good as it needed to be. Outer surfaces were nicely polished, some internal components rough, fine tool marks still plainly visible. The dozen or so nuts used to assemble the thing varied one from the other, even to the naked eye: You couldn't interchange them; their threads didn't match. They had all been made by the hand of Fred Taylor.

∾

Sometime after the centennial, probably in late 1877 or early 1878, he met Wilfred Lewis. The son of an iron manufacturer's representative, Lewis had graduated from MIT in 1875, begun a kind of postcollegiate apprenticeship as a mechanic at a Philadelphia machine tool maker, and had recently moved up to draftsman. Both men were of similar back-ground—Philadelphia-born, of Quaker stock, well-off, and within a year and a half in age—and could commiserate about their fledgling experiences in the shop world. Soon, Lewis was drifting down to "the little pump works" on Race Street to visit. "There was a bond of sym-pathy in our vocations," he recalled, "and we soon became great friends." In time, he later wrote Taylor's wife, "I loved him as a brother."

Not much later, the two of them and about half a dozen others, most in their early and mid-twenties—the men largely constituting the charter membership of the Engineers Club of Philadelphia—traveled to Boston, visited briefly at the house where Lewis had lived while at MIT, then continued on to the White Mountains of New Hampshire. Mem-bers of the party included Fred's sister Mary, now about twenty; Edith Wright, eldest sister of the Wright boys; and Coleman Sellers, Jr.

Sellers, twenty-five, was kin to William Sellers, head of the big machine tool manufacturing company that bore his name and that functioned as a Hewlett-Packard, say, does in the computer industry today: as a prime training ground for technical talent. Coleman Sellers, Jr. worked there, as did his father, Coleman Sellers, Sr., who was chief engineer. So did Fred Lewis. William Sellers, fifty-four, owned another company, located down the Delaware near Wilmington, Edgemoor Iron, which supplied iron to the Brooklyn Bridge, then under construc-tion. Five years before, he had bought a controlling interest in a third company, Philadelphia's Midvale Steel.

Midvale's other big investor was Edward W. Clark, of the Philadelphia banking house, and a friend of the Taylors; Clark's son Clarence, Fred's future brother-in-law, would join Midvale in 1878, after his graduation from the University of Pennsylvania. Also soon to own a piece of Midvale was James A. Wright, father of Edith, one among the party that traveled to Boston, of Ernest, Fred's young friend at the pump works, and of Jamie, Fred's classmate at Exeter.

People stuck in dead-end jobs while others, of seemingly no greater merit, advance rapidly, sometimes bitterly indict "connections," even while leaving their precise nature to conjecture. We must resort to just such a formula in the case of Fred Taylor, who, probably in late 1878, also got a job at Midvale and would spend his next twelve years there, rising quickly. Certainly, he had abundant connections to the upper reaches of the company hierarchy. But precisely how they helped— through what means they were invoked, who said what to whom, under what circumstances and when—fail to come down to us.

We do know that by early 1878 Taylor was finishing up his apprenticeship. In better times, he might have marched into a good journeyman's job as patternmaker or machinist. But times were still bad. The depression of 1873 lingered; wages were down a quarter from five years before. "During the last few years," Chordal wrote at about the time Taylor sought work, "an owner has been thankful if he could keep his front door open and the line shaft turning around, and the men have been thankful for a job at any pay." Still, at Midvale, Taylor got a job, if only as a laborer, on the floor of the machine shop.

He worked only briefly as such. The shop clerk's hand was found in the till, causing him to be fired. Taylor was never convinced that the clerk had done anything wrong, but he got his job in any case.

With little taste for pushing paper, though, Taylor trained another man for the job and asked the foreman for work as a machinist. This time, "because I had made good as a clerk when they needed one," he wrote, but also perhaps thanks to better business conditions and his connections, he got as he wished.

He was an ordinary machinist for about two months. Sometime probably in 1879, he was promoted to a job that left him still at the lathe but also overseeing the work of others. At the age of twenty-three, Fred Taylor became a gang boss.

PART THREE

THE CREATION

(1879–1886)

1

AN INTERESTING AND CAPRICIOUS MATERIAL

~

LITTLE REMAINS BUT WEEDS IN THIS LOW, flat basin at the foot of the shallow rise leading up to Germantown. Tall, brown grasses rise from sodden soil, whipped by the winter wind. Midvale Steel is gone now; back in the 1970s, the local papers bore bitter reminiscences of steelworkers who'd lost their jobs and knew they'd never get them back. Then, the buildings came down. Now it is just a vast, desolate flatness, studded here and there with torn-up concrete, mounds of weed-topped rubble, old tires, rotting railroad ties. Here and there, a buried sliver of wood juts up, like a bayonet from a battlefield.

The steam hammers, the clattering machine shop, the rolling mills and open hearth furnaces are gone. Only feeble hints of the hot, noisy past remain, like a black, oil-soaked checkerboard of wooden flooring, disks of timber cut across the grain and laid out like bricks, under the open sky. If you stoop and elbow aside the high grasses, you find flecks of brick from the old mills sown like seeds through the soggy clay soil. Sometimes a chunk big enough to fit in the palm of your hand, but mostly small red shards, mixed into the mud, everywhere, numberless, without end.

On the southeastern corner of the property, one final slim reminder: a sweeping curve of railroad track. You see it even in the oldest photographs, in all the oldest maps, where the Philadelphia & Reading rolled by. And here it is today, overrun by weeds, but still that same ribbon of steel, gently arcing around the spot where Midvale Steel began.

Just beyond the tracks to the north, when Fred Taylor started work here in 1878, ran a wooden fence that enclosed the entire works. And within that fence—may we step through its long vanished gate now?—seven closely packed acres of modestly scaled structures, lined up north-south and east-west, their roofs surmounted by superstructures of windows and louvers to admit light and air. Water tanks, storage sheds, and coal piles were scattered across the site. Loops and spurs of railroad track laced it all together.

To the south, nearest the P & R tracks, stood the smoky blacksmith shop. Behind it, a foundry's two squat smokestacks rose twenty or thirty feet above neighboring roofs. Then came the molding shop with its brick core ovens and their heavy iron doors; another foundry; rolling mills; hammer shop; and finally, circling around to near the blacksmith shop again, the "tire mill," with its attached machine shop. Some of the buildings were little more than sheds, with frame walls and gravel or corrugated iron roofs; others, formidable slate-roofed structures with brick walls a foot and a half thick, pierced by banks of rhythmically arched windows reminiscent of a Roman aqueduct.

In the machine shop of the tire mill, Fred Taylor got his start. It was a low, prematurely ramshackle, frame structure with three shallow gables breaking up its eighty-foot length, filled with lathes and boring mills; someone would remember it as "a small, dark, smoky little building [that] . . . was never lighted and never cleaned." Here Taylor began a twenty-six-year search for the laws that governed the cutting of metal. Here he tore up work, timed its parts, and reconstituted them into the new work of the twentieth century.

∾

One summer morning in 1866, about twelve years before Taylor arrived, two men trudged across the marshy field down the hill from Germantown, in an area still known as Nicetown, from a Neisse family of local repute. One of them was Philip Syng Justice, a trim, bespectacled forty-seven-year-old who had started out in the wholesale hardware business in Philadelphia. During the Civil War, he'd gone into manufacturing, making bayonets and guns. In 1863, he also established the Philip S. Justice Car and Locomotive Springs Manufactory, employing about forty men, which imported from Europe what were known as "tyres."

"Tyre" is the British spelling for our word "tire," and long before automobiles with rubber tires came along, it was in ordinary usage. The metal band on the outside of a wagon wheel was a tire. So was the metal ring on the outside of a locomotive wheel; the idea, of course, was to replace *it*, rather than the whole wheel. These metal tires, some of them weighing a ton or more, would be machined to precise inner dimensions, then shrink-fitted over the wheel. To install a four-foot-diameter tire, you'd heat it enough to expand a sixty-fourth or so of an inch, slip it over the wheel, and hammer it into position. When it cooled, shrinking, it locked around the wheel in an unshakable grip.

It was such tires that late in 1867, Philip Syng Justice proposed to manufacture. Tires were big business and many American companies made them. But they made them of iron, and Justice proposed to make them from the new miracle material, steel. Locomotives weighing thirty or forty tons caused havoc where wheel met rail, iron rails sometimes needing replacement every two years. Iron tires, too, quickly wore out, getting thinner and thinner, until nothing remained. But those made of steel lasted five times as long, and the number sold in the United States climbed precipitously, from 466 in 1863 to 48,000 by 1871. At first, virtually all were imported, from Krupp, the huge German steelmaker, or from manufacturers in Sheffield, England. Justice was among the importers, supplying Philadelphia's vast Baldwin Locomotive works, which routinely ordered five hundred at a clip.

Now, rather than continue bringing in tires from abroad, which took two or three months and incurred steep import tariffs, Justice hoped to make them himself. He wrote Baldwin with his plan: "It is proposed to start an Establishment in this city or neighborhood, immediately, for the manufacture of Cast Steel Tyres and heavy forgings of Cast Steel with the ultimate intention of making Cast Steel Rails as well." He and William Butcher, a Sheffield, England, engineer and member of a prominent family of steelmakers, would join him in the enterprise.

Midvale veterans would recall frantically pumping out buildings frequently flooded in the low basin at the foot of Germantown. But though forewarned, Justice and Butcher were not about to let a little marsh interfere with their plans; seven acres passed into Justice's hands on November 16, 1866. For whatever the cost in money and trouble on account of the inhospitable ground, a look at local maps revealed the compelling argument for building there: coal.

To melt iron and steel, to get it hot enough to work under great steam hammers and squeeze between rollers, to power the steam engines that drove the lathes and other machine tools that would cut it to size—all required enormous quantities of coal. Earlier in the century, huge deposits of anthracite coal had been discovered in the hills of northeastern Pennsylvania; black diamond, they called it. Almost rocklike, anthracite was harder and stronger than bituminous coal; you could heap it higher into a furnace without the ore crushing it. And it burned hotter; it was like a natural form of coke, which ordinary coal became only after its impurities burn off. All told, it was vastly superior. Men had grown rich just finding ways to get it to market. Steep, inclined tracks helped get it over the mountain ridges. Networks of canals bore little boats, each piled with a few tons of it, downstream to the Schuykill and thence to Philadelphia, where it was unloaded and transferred to railcars. The tracks of the Philadelphia & Reading Railroad, which tied the anthracite fields to the great network of wharves at Port Richmond on the Delaware, passed west-to-east right next to the property Justice bought for his steelworks; day and night, trains of coal cars rattled by. This was anthracite's own "Main Line," and the new steelworks would go up beside it.

Soon advertisements for the new company, forerunner of Midvale Steel, appeared:

The Wm. Butcher
STEEL WORKS
of
Philadelphia

———

William Butcher,
President and Superintendent, Philadelphia
Philip S. Justice, Selling Agent,
14 North Fifth Street, Philadelphia,
and 42 Cliff Street, New York

———

Manufacturers of
Solid Toughened
CAST STEEL LOCOMOTIVE TYRES
Cast-Steel Reversible Frogs and Switches,
   "   "   Crank Pins, Piston Rods, Shafts, etc.
   "   "   Connecting Rods, Frog Points & Bars,
   "   "   Cast-Steel Spring Steel for Railway Use,

CASTINGS & FORGINGS
in Steel to Pattern

But things weren't as rosy as the ad suggested, and the company's early years were fraught with trouble; steel, in the 1860s and 1870s, was nothing but trouble.

∾

Steel itself wasn't "new." It couldn't have been long into the Iron Age, beginning around 1200 B.C., that humans observed that raw iron, melted in charcoal fires and absorbing carbon, sometimes came out harder, stronger, and more ductile than usual. What was new, at the time Midvale was founded in the 1860s, was steel in quantity, as a commonplace of industrial production. Before then, you could make steel, but never much of it at a time.

Steel is iron that contains just the right amount of carbon. Iron's physical properties depend, with exquisite sensitivity, on its carbon content. Extracted from iron ore in the furnace, pig iron—the sight of molten iron fed from a broad common channel into smaller cavities surrounding it must have reminded someone of piglets feeding at a sow—is stiff and strong but brittle. It contains so much carbon, three or four percent, that a handful of chips retrieved from the bed of a machine tool will leave your hands soiled and gray, as if by the shavings from a pencil sharpener.

Pig iron reheated and beaten while hot, burning off virtually all its carbon and leaving it with a pronounced grain, is known as wrought iron. If pig iron was the staple of the foundry, the stuff of castings, wrought iron was that of the forge, easily hammered, stretched, and welded.

So different are the properties of the two materials—wrought iron devoid of carbon and pig iron rich with it—that their common designation as iron is almost a lexical accident. Indeed, the material intermediate between them in carbon is never known as iron at all but enjoys its own name: steel.

Steel itself exhibits a wide range of physical properties, again based on its carbon content (and, also, on any other materials, like nickel, manganese, or tungsten, with which it may be alloyed). "Mild" steel, with one or two tenths of a percent carbon, is similar to wrought iron in its properties, being easy to work and cut. Steel with five or six tenths of a percent or more can be dramatically modified by sudden or gradual heating and chilling that together constitute "heat treatment";

from such steel you can fashion swords, hammers, or tool bits of uncanny toughness and resilience.

So sensitive is steel to its heat treatment and precise formulation—half a cup of carbon in a hundred pounds of steel will make a difference—so maddeningly difficult to keep consistent, that its making has always been veiled in legend. Methods of making steel a few pounds at a time, by antique processes known as cementation or blistering, were closely guarded; steelmaking was a cottage industry, the work of veritable alchemists who might supply prized samples of fine steel for a knife or tool. Before the mid-nineteenth century, metal bound for anything as large as a bridge, or cannon, or cauldron—anything demanding large amounts of material—was almost certainly iron, not steel.

In 1854, a Sheffield, England, engineer named Henry Bessemer contrived a way to use the carbon in molten pig iron to fuel its own elimination: with a powerful blast of air, you literally burn it off, the process's volcanic shower of sparks testimony to its success. Of course, you had to stop just short of eliminating the last vestige of carbon, which was tricky. Another Englishman, Robert Mushet, took to burning off all the carbon, thus establishing a zero point, then reintroducing carbon in small and measured amounts to make steel. Within a few years came a competing process, open hearth, in which pig iron and scrap steel were heated in a dishlike furnace capable of especially high temperatures. The process lent itself to precise control of the steel's final composition, to recipes that could be readily doctored, manipulated, and refined—and to large-quantity production.

It wasn't just that Bessemer, open hearth, and other innovations made steel cheap, though they did: the Bessemer process, for example, cut the price of steel from a hundred sixty dollars per ton to sixty, and by 1889 steel rails went for twenty-nine dollars a ton. But more, in the years after the Civil War, you now measured output not in pounds, but tons. Steel, once limited to tool bits weighing a few ounces or swords weighing a few pounds, could go by the ton into bridges, buildings, or armor plate—or locomotive tires.

At Butcher's, the future Midvale, they took the red-hot bloom of steel from the furnace, flattened it under a steam hammer, and punched a small hole in its middle. Then, they slung it, still hot, on the horn, or beak, of a contoured anvil, on which it turned while a hammer repeatedly struck blows on its periphery, the hole in the middle enlarging with each blow; the result was a "beaked bloom." It was then allowed to cool, its surface defects were chipped away, it was reheated, rolled to the desired shape, and finally finished to precise dimensions in the machine shop.

But in the 1870s, steelmaking was still fussy and temperamental, with any company that attempted it almost by definition cutting-edge, like a software or biotechnology company today. Butcher's tire-rolling mill, which rolled a finished tire from the bloom in ten minutes, had been made by a British firm and shipped to Philadelphia; the technology simply didn't exist in America. The four-hundred-horsepower steam engine that drove it was said to have "no equal in this country." A huge lifting crane that hefted cylinders of red-hot steel and moved them around the mill invited whispered superlatives. As for the recipes for the steel, Butcher kept them all to himself, in the tradition of the alchemists. All was new, untried, provisional, and risky.

At first, they rolled tires from crucible steel, a method predating Bessemer and the other recent innovations. But in 1869, the company turned to the new open-hearth process and bought a furnace under the key Siemens-Martin patents. Here, presumably, was the gateway to the future. The furnace's capacity "was only $3^1/_2$ tons," an old hand reminisced in 1915, by which time steelmaking was a science and steel a commodity, "but this cupful of metal gave the bosses more agony than any combination of 50-ton furnaces can possibly cause our present-day experts." Troubles mounted. The company had agreed to make two thousand tons of rails for the Philadelphia & Reading Railroad, but the steel bore too much phosphorus and the rails broke.

The new company, begun with so much hope, foundered. In the early days, "good and willing men were not lacking, the bone and sinew had been there, practical skill in melting, heating and working steel had been there," a key figure from the company's history, Russell Davenport, would recall. Needed was a "more accurate chemical knowledge of the difference between good and bad steel and a common sense" in applying it. And cash.

In 1868, the Butcher works had bought a big steam hammer from William Sellers, the machine tool maker, and Sellers took payment in stock. Now, in the wake of costly production problems, the company borrowed more money from him and from the great banking house,

Edward W. Clark & Company. Clark was one of the forty-nine founding members of the Germantown Unitarian Church, along with Philip Syng Justice and Emily Winslow Taylor. Soon, Butcher was gone and so was his name: Sellers renamed the company Midvale Steel Works (because it was about midway between the Schuykill and Delaware rivers), which now rested more firmly than ever in his hands and those of Clark and a few other investors.

At one point, Sellers went to England, trying to scare up a buyer for the firm. But he got no takers, doubtless because the company's prospects were grim, its reputation blackened. For a time, only seventy-five men worked there. "One small, open-hearth furnace was in operation," Davenport recounted later. "No. 1 hammer ran a few days a week; some tool steel was melted in the crucibles and hammered at old No. 3 hammer." Meanwhile, he recalled, "something like 3000 tons of steel of various kinds and in various conditions of manufacture were piled about the yard regarding which little or nothing was known."

Enter Charles Augustus Brinley, who joined the firm in 1872. A young chemist not long out of Yale, Brinley would never win any popularity contests among the men; he carried his head a little too high, seemed aloof and imperturbable. Taylor, who worked for him later, remembered him for his expressionless eyes, the silk handkerchief poking up from the breast pocket of his coat, and the scent of perfume that trailed after him. But Brinley was a real metallurgy expert, and now, at Midvale, at the age of twenty-five, he set out to break this temperamental bronco that was steel. It was, as he would himself argue later, the great transition point. Steelmaking was still a rule-of-thumb enterprise. But now, he would write, "men who had come from classrooms and laboratories directly to the practical conduct of a manufacture for which they were solely responsible were forced to adopt the scientific method, and stand or fall by it."

And adopt it he did. First, he set about salvaging those thousands of tons of steel in the yard. He and Mickey Kelly, a fellow from the previous regime whose head unaccountably clung to details of their production history, trudged through the yard, stopping at this pile or that, Kelly reciting all he knew. The two of them wrote it all down on numbered placards they left with each pile. Then Brinley pulled samples, took them to a rudimentary lab, and analyzed them. "By careful selection and mixing with high grade pig iron purchased for the purpose,"

Davenport would recall, "all this old stuff was successfully worked into rail blooms."

With Butcher's alchemic formulations reduced to chemistry and mathematics, his failed experiments into steel rails, Midvale was on its way to becoming a "scientific" steelmaker. Brinley began working with the unsuccessful open-hearth operation, keeping copious records of what had been tried, what worked, what didn't. He was half in the mill, half in the laboratory, his notes growing ever richer and more detailed. "From this time forward," a company history relates, "not a month passed without improvement in orderliness and system throughout the works."

Two years later, in 1874, after being named superintendent, Brinley hired his old Yale roommate, Russell Davenport, just back from travels in Switzerland and Germany, as his assistant. Davenport, also a chemist, moved with him into a plain, four-room, two-story house, the first floor of which Brinley had fashioned into a laboratory; they ate their meals, prepared for them by a neighborhood woman, beside a mechanical testing machine.

The two men, so near in age and background, would live together for the next four years, until about the time Taylor came and Brinley married. All day they'd work, and "not a night passed," Brinley remembered, "without a visit to the furnaces, followed by a round of the Works." Together, they explored what Brinley would call that "most interesting and capricious material," steel, whose working and composition they sought to precisely control. Midvale, in the words of one company history, became "a large laboratory."

The ultimate overseer of their "lab" was William Sellers himself, the third of the great Midvale triumvirate. Sellers, from an old Pennsylvania family, was no common lug of an engineer but a towering figure in American industry. After apprenticing in his uncle's machine shop in Wilmington, Delaware, he worked for a few years in New England, as foreman in another relative's shop; there he met, among others, George Corliss, the future centennial exhibition engine builder. He soon launched his own machine tool company in Philadelphia; within a decade, it was the city's leading firm. In 1856, his second cousin Coleman Sellers, a brilliant inventor, joined him from Cincinnati. Design after design bubbled up from the Sellers shops; William Sellers would be awarded some ninety patents. By the 1870s, he presided over a complex of foundries, forges, machine shops, and erecting shops spread across six acres of prime industrial real estate. In its two pedestrian-linked complexes, close to seven hundred people worked. In 1869, Sellers set up Edgemoor Iron on the Delaware River, just outside Wilmington. Four years later, he gained control of Midvale.

During the late Civil War years, Sellers had served as president of Philadelphia's Franklin Institute, perhaps America's most distinguished scientific body. He helped plan the centennial, and his machines took up a great stretch of Machinery Hall: big lathes, little lathes, shapers, slotters, steam hammers, riveters, punches, and shears —thirty-three in all. More than half the hall's overhead shafting was his, as was all of its structural ironwork, which like that of most other centennial buildings had been supplied by Edgemoor Iron Company. The centennial jury awarding his company a medal observed that in its size, variety, and originality, its exhibit was "probably without a parallel in the past history of international exhibitions." It was impossible, the jurors declared, by now falling all over themselves, "to realize the full measure of such refined mechanical, scientific, and artistic merit."

Sellers, it would be said, was the Whitworth of American engineering, a reference to Joseph Whitworth, Britain's most celebrated engineer. If, in his letters to *American Machinist*, Chordal took affectionate potshots at country machine shops that indulged in hopelessly sloppy, rule-of-thumb practices, William Sellers & Company represented their polar opposite, the company's machine tools pictured "as exponents of perfection, as test channels for design." Whitworth himself would label Sellers "the greatest mechanical engineer in the world."

Years before, the two men had competed. Whitworth, in England, had championed a standardized screw thread, a system of thread shapes, angles, and proportions meant to ensure that a half-inch nut, say, from one shop would match a half-inch bolt from another. By the Civil War, however, America had no such standard; many systems vied, each shop adopting its own. Finally, in 1864, stepping in to fill what one scholar would call a "vacuum" in American industrial leadership, Sellers used the platform of the Franklin Institute to advocate a standard thread with subtle but key differences from that of Whitworth's. The federal government adopted it for all government work in 1868, the powerful Pennsylvania Railroad the following year, and soon it was universal. The Sellers standard is largely that in use today.

Compared to Whitworth's, the Sellers thread lent itself to the rough-and-ready practices of the average machine shop; you could cut it on any lathe without special tools. A naval review panel later derided the Whitworth thread for demanding "such skill on the part of the workmen" as to discourage uniformity, while the Sellers thread boasted the "very important advantage of ease of production." This utilitarian emphasis lay at the heart of William Sellers's mechanical philosophy.

Sellers machine tools were innovative, clever, and supremely functional, even to what one scholar, Merritt Roe Smith, has termed "their severe, even chaste, lines." Especially since the 1850s, the prevailing machine-tool aesthetic had emphasized scrollwork, adornments, and floral patterns, fire-engine red and hunter green paint jobs, metal beads and moldings highlighted in gilt; one Massachusetts-built planer sat on four feet shaped like those of a turtle. To a modern eye, wearied by minimalism, all this might seem pleasingly fanciful. But just as Whitworth was leading the movement in England toward more narrowly functional design, so was Sellers in America. Out of his big shops north of the old city came machine tools from which such frivolity had been ruthlessly expunged, heralding the modern way. "What is right, looks right," Sellers would say of a machine; and for him what looked right was spare, unadorned, and painted a "machine gray" that in time became universal.

For Sellers, a thread profile ought to be no more difficult to cut than it had to be, the bed of a machine tool no more ornate. For him and the companies his personality dominated, including Midvale, the idea was to apply to every problem and every decision the austere and unforgiving forces of reason, without undue regard to all that came before, without obeisance to sentiment or fuzzy guesswork.

In March 1875, the navy, which customarily got its steel cannon from foreign suppliers, awarded Midvale an order for little three-inch howitzers, used for throwing lines to ships in distress; it wasn't much as cannon go, but it was the first time the navy felt enough confidence in an American steelmaker to buy cannon from it. It was the first of many such contracts. The following year, Brinley began routine tensile tests for steel. At the centennial exhibition in 1876, Midvale exhibited tires, axles, and cutting tools never before made by the open-hearth process. Brinley, Davenport, and Sellers were making Midvale into a company as congenial to a scientific approach to industrial problems as could be found anywhere in America.

In 1878, Fred Taylor came to Midvale. He had been there only about a year, perhaps less, when Brinley promoted him to gang boss. Taylor testified later: "As soon as I became gang boss, the men who were working under me . . . came to me at once and said, 'Now, Fred, you are not going to be a damn piece-work hog, are you?' "

2

FIGHTING BLOOD

～

M OST MIDVALE WORKERS, as well as many in other companies and industries, were paid not an hourly, daily, or weekly wage, but on piece rate. That meant you got paid so much per piece: the more work done, the more you earned.

Nonsense, a workman from those days might have objected, if perhaps with an imprecation earthier and more vehement. It didn't really work that way. The more work done, the more you earned—up to the point where the boss decided you were making too much and promptly cut the rate. The practice was almost universal. Later, when Taylor had built a system based, in part, on never cutting a piece rate once established, and tried to sell it, businessmen would stare at him. Why, then you'd be paying the men too much! You *had* to cut the rate. It was ridiculous to imagine otherwise. One manufacturer boasted to William Redfield, a future secretary of commerce in the Woodrow Wilson administration, that he had lowered the rate five times on a single job. "I think he should be locked up," said Redfield in telling the story. But he said it in 1911, at a conference on scientific management, by which time the practice was no longer so enshrined.

For the man footing the bill, it made a self-interested sort of sense to lower the rates. For the worker, it made equally good sense to limit output and thereby ward off a rate cut. If everyone in the shop made two dollars a day and then one man started hustling enough to make three, it became obvious to the boss that the rate was set too high: *See how much they're making?* The same went for some resourceful fellow who devised a faster way to do the job. Brain or brawn, it didn't matter.

Too high an output and the rate would be cut, as sure as the sunrise, and all the men would suffer.

And everyone, in every shop, knew it.

A man producing too much on piece rate was seen as sacrificing his friends on the altar of his own greed; he was hogging higher pay, heedless of the rate cut it was sure to provoke. If on day rate, he was sucking up to the boss, likewise to his own gain and at the expense of his fellows.

So every sort of pressure and persuasion went toward ensuring that no one worked much faster than anyone else. Early on, a new employee learned what was OK and what was not, the veterans passing the word down and enforcing it. Taylor himself recalled how, while still one of the men, "we had the work carefully laid out so we were doing [at least by Taylor's reckoning] about a third of a day's work. Every young man who came in there was told, 'Here, don't do more than two or three pieces before noon. We will tell you the game at noon.' " More than factory owners might have cared to admit, the workmen set limits on what they actually did each day.

From before Taylor's time to our own, accounts proliferate of workmen together restricting output, sending false signals about what they could produce, or otherwise slowing down in defiance of the boss. Morris Cooke, a future Taylor disciple, would tell how on entering the Cramp shipyards in Philadelphia as an apprentice machinist in the 1890s, his co-workers assigned him to take an armful of burlap bags and, each afternoon, make a bed for a stocky Irishman named Billy Gallagher on which to nap; he was also to look out for the boss and signal his coming. Mr. Cramp, it seems, liked noise. When he was reported near, Cooke's biographer reported, "sheer bedlam ensued," with Cooke and the other men banging away on any metal at hand. The shipyard owner would smile, nod approvingly, and march off, not to be seen for the rest of the day.

All this came under the broad heading of "soldiering," a word with nautical roots. Soldiers transported by ship, according to the *Morris Dictionary of Word & Phrase Origins*, "acted as privileged passengers," and were exempt from the chores seamen had to perform: to the sailors, goofing off became known as soldiering. As early as 1840, Richard Henry Dana had used the word in his novel *Two Years Before the Mast*: "There is no time to be lost—no 'sogering,' no hanging back then." By the late 1870s, when Chordal was around to notice, the word was as entrenched as the practice. "When the boss comes around," he wrote, workers were apt to "antic about," seeming to

> work their skins off. . . . [But] every smart foreman knows very
> well that during this effervescence the men are not doing anything
> at all. They are making unusual, idle, quick motions for a few
> minutes, just as our energetic chap does all day long. If they kept
> on they would get nothing done. . . . If you see a man reaching out
> lively when a boss comes around, you can make up your mind that
> that chap has been soldiering.

To ward off a rate cut was one reason to soldier. To thumb his nose at the boss, protest wages deemed too low, or husband shop work otherwise apt to run out were others. Sometimes, it was simply to revel in what Taylor himself would picture as that "natural instinct and tendency of men to take it easy."

All this, in any case, was to him "natural soldiering" and almost excusable. More insidious was the "systematic soldiering" he found at Midvale, where the whole shop conspired to restrict production. As an ordinary lathesman, he had gone along with the boys himself, never broken a rate. But now he was gang boss; he represented management and was responsible for both his own work on the lathe and that of those under him. Sorry, he said, things would have to be different now. He had to get more work out of them.

"Take it from us," they said, if we can believe Taylor's version of events. Make waves and "We will have you over that fence inside of three weeks. That means war."

He was determined to increase output and knew there was plenty of room to do so. "But I do not think I had in mind what measures I was going to take; at first I do not think I had any policy clearly in mind. Maybe," he figured, he'd "be able to persuade a lot of my friends"—they were always his "friends"—"to do more work." But he found them unwilling to oblige.

Persuasion wouldn't do, and charm wasn't in his repertoire. So Fred Taylor resorted to what every foreman and boss had always done, in every workshop, factory, atelier, and mill. The men said they would work no harder? Well, by God, they would. And if they wouldn't do it happily, with good grace, he would grind it out of them.

Taylor took a man off to the side, got on the lathe himself, and showed him how to run a piece more quickly. The man went back to his job, worked as leisurely as ever, and turned out the same amount of work as he always had.

So Taylor fired him and hired someone else in his place.

This man, too, he tried to train, cajole, and threaten into submission. And this man, too, in Taylor's recollection, "refused to do any more work than the rest."

More firings followed. Still he got nowhere.

He appealed to their craft pride, their common heritage as mechanics and machinists. "I am a machinist," he reminded them. He did not want to resort to the next step, he said; it would run counter "to what you and I look upon as our interest as machinists." But he would, if they refused to work up to their potential. Having seen dozens of foreman come and go, the men were scarcely about to give ground to this callow twenty-three-year-old, friend of the boss or not. So Taylor escalated the war.

The nation had finally emerged from the long depression. Business had improved and Midvale had secured new contracts; one of them, in 1879, was for steel beams, angles, and channel sections for the Brooklyn Bridge, then going up across the East River in New York. That same year, construction began on a new twelve-ton, open-hearth furnace, designed by William Sellers, to supplant the troublesome $3^1/_2$-ton furnace built ten years before. Soon the machine shop was running on two shifts, day and night. Employment swelled, from 175 in 1877 to about 450 by 1882, and to 600 not long after. At one point, the need for workers was so great that a hundred or so were virtually scraped up off the street, most of them common laborers.

Now, Taylor scoured the plant for those of them who seemed especially intelligent and competent, men who, under luckier circumstances, might have served apprenticeships as skilled workers. Make you a deal, he said. He'd teach them the machinist's trade. His old "friends" in the machine shop wouldn't do the full, fair day's work he expected of them? Maybe these new men would. He'd teach them himself "how to work fast and right."

And yet each responded in the same way. Caught in the maw of the shop's culture, pervasive and inescapable, "every solitary man . . . turned right around and joined the rest of the fellows and refused to work one bit faster."

He reminded them of their promise. "Every one of you has broken his word with me. Now, I have not any mercy on you . . . I am going to cut your rate in two tomorrow and you are going to work for half price from now on." Only if they turned out what Taylor deemed a full day's work would he restore their rates. It was the same nasty hardball every workman knew to expect.

The men protested. Their young boss, they made it known to his superiors, was "a tyrant, and a nigger driver." But it was to no avail; Taylor had friends in high places. A few of the machinists began to fall in line. The shop's five big vertical boring mills—basically a spinning table to which the half-ton steel tire was firmly clamped while a cutting tool gripped from overhead bit into it—worked a little closer to their limits. The men mounted the tires with motions a little crisper now, set cutting speeds a little higher, unclamped the tires with a bit more brio. Production rose.

But among some of the men, bitterness boiled up. Taylor was warned that, come day's end, he'd best be careful. He was given to walking home beside the railroad tracks, which swung past the works, the cricket grounds where Taylor played tennis, and finally the knitting mills beside Wingohocking Creek in Germantown, down the hill from his parents' house. The lonely, two-mile stretch was not unsuited to ambush. Friends and family remonstrated with him to alter his routine. He didn't. Rather, he got the word out in the shop that if they jumped him, he'd gouge and bite and battle back, but would not bear a gun in self-defense; as he told the story, "They could shoot and be damned."

They didn't shoot, but some of the men upped the stakes a little more. Taylor would raise the speed on a machine tool, for example, and one of them would throw a monkey wrench—and not just a metaphoric one—into it. "Almost every day," recalled Taylor, "ingenious accidents were planned," afflicting machines around the shop. And always, the men claimed, it was that "fool foreman who was driving the men and the machines beyond their proper limit."

But Taylor, as he told it later (forever hinting at the depths of his insight into the workingman's mind), had anticipated them. Even before being named gang boss, he'd gone to Brinley, or perhaps Sellers himself, warning them of what was in store. "Now, these men will show you, and show you conclusively, that in the first place I know nothing about my business; and that in the second place, I am a liar, and you are being fooled, and they will bring any amount of evidence to prove these facts beyond a shadow of a doubt." For him to do his job, he went on, they would have to take his word over any number of men in the shop, whatever they said. And since he "happened not to be of working parents," he wrote later in the third person, "the owners of the company believed that he had the interest of the works more at heart than the other workmen [did]," and agreed.

When the men protested what they saw as his brutality or claimed that his incompetence, not their vandalism, had wrecked the machines, Brinley backed him up.

Thus emboldened, Taylor counterattacked. An accident to a machine? Well, from now on, he let it be known, the man in charge of it would either have to contribute to the cost of its repair or quit. "I don't care if the roof falls in and breaks your machine, you will pay all the same." He instituted a system of heavy fines, the proceeds of which ultimately came back to the men at large through what in 1883 became a formal Midvale Beneficial Association. Maybe two dollars for a broken machine part, close to a day's pay. Lesser fines for getting to work late, or leaving early, or failing to report a problem with a machine. It wasn't their fault? Too bad. The fine stood.

For more than two years it went on like this, the air in the shop thick with resentment.

～

Fred Taylor, just a year or two past his apprenticeship, was new to the shop, cruelly ill suited to the arts of compromise, but cocksure, bubbling over with plans and ideas. Imagine their reaction as he blithely informed the men, so recently his "friends," that "he was now working on the side of the management," and that he intended to get a fair day's work from them, not the sad excuse for one they had turned out before.

Taylor would win no prizes for softness and sympathy. Even friends used words like "tactless" and "pugnacious" to describe him. To all outward appearance, he looked benign enough, with a mild, unsullied face, the perfect choirboy. His blond or light brown hair, straight but for the slight wave it sometimes took, was parted straight down the middle; he probably sported a modest mustache by now, as he did a little later and for most of his life. He stood five feet nine and carried about a hundred forty-five pounds on a trim, tight frame, the more so from the tennis he played regularly on weekends. His was no particularly prepossessing figure. He commented once on how many of the legendary steelmen of the era were physically large and daunting; he was not one of them.

But later, people often remarked upon the curious split between Taylor's affable veneer and the tense, tightly coiled steel just beneath, always set to spring. At a memorial service after his death, Rudolf Blankenburg, then mayor of Philadelphia, would describe Taylor as "born and bred to a gentle manner. His sweet smile and courtly bearing were only the surface indications of an innate and broad-spreading sympathy and kindliness." But, Blankenburg grasped, "those whose contacts with him were, like my own, only casual and who went to him as converts, rather than to be converted, could hardly sense his power."

Lillian Gilbreth, half of the Gilbreth efficiency team celebrated in the popular book *Cheaper by the Dozen*, had feelings for Taylor that ranged from enmity to adulation. She, too, saw the split: "His was a face that reflected many moods," she wrote. "The eyes, keen and penetrating, the lips thin and tightly closed when he was presenting an argument or meeting opposition." Yet he was also "the most genial conversationalist in a sympathetic audience."

Amiable and expansive Fred or biting, combative Mr. Taylor—it all depended on whether he was among friends or enemies, at peace or war, whether his will was accepted or challenged. "Taylor was not as tactful as some men," Charles Brinley told Copley, "and did not show a marked ability at that time to keep on good terms with the men in the shop." Whatever peace and harmony meant to him in principle, they were nothing he went to any great trouble to preserve if it meant going back on his convictions, curbing his sarcasm, or otherwise buttoning his lip.

Years later, at an American Society of Mechanical Engineers meeting where a paper given by Taylor had drawn criticism, another engineer, William Kent, commented that he was "glad that Mr. Rogers has attacked Mr. Taylor's paper. There are very few men who have the courage to do so. I hope there will be others who will rise up and attack it, and I know of no man stronger than Mr. Taylor to repel such attacks." The same contentiousness, the same zest for provocation that had pushed him into the path of the German soldier when he was a boy, took only the mildest stimulus to awaken.

When wound up, which was often, his words fairly tumbled out. He was shamelessly cocky and confident. He wouldn't kid-glove you if he could pound you over the head. "I do not care who turns out my work," he said at the ASME meeting where his paper was attacked. "So much work is worth so much money, whether done by an apprentice or by a man just tottering to his grave."

At a lecture he gave in 1906: "In our scheme, we do not ask for the initiative of our men. We do not want any initiative. All we want of them is to obey the orders we give them, do what we say, and do it quick."

You could see it even in his testimony in court, before Congress or government commissions—layers of courtly politeness abruptly giving way, at the first sign of challenge, to sharp rejoinders and impatient attacks. Perhaps not a single transcript of his testimony goes unmarked by sarcasm, impatience, or outburst. Asked during a patent case whether the work he did in reorganizing a company was intended to make it more efficient, he shot back, "Certainly. I didn't intend to make it worse than it was." And when the chairman of a congressional committee weighing metric system legislation tried to open another line of questioning, Taylor demanded to continue: "Won't you allow me to get through first?"

William Fannon, who worked with Taylor at Midvale and who otherwise admired him, observed that, "I often thought he would have made more rapid progress if he had been more tactful and not so willing to combat in such an intense way anybody that saw fit to oppose him." For Fannon, Taylor seemed to live by the maxim, " 'He that is not with me is against me.' "

Taylor lacked the personal skills, the seductive blarney charm, to worm cooperation from the men, to get more out of them and have them love him for it. So at Midvale, he bludgeoned the men, cajoled them, threatened them, and drove them in the only way his temperament permitted. A man less bullheaded might have taken their enmity as reason to approach matters differently—indeed, might have relented and allowed things to return to the status quo. But those early days as gang boss, assistant foreman, and finally foreman at Midvale had stirred in Fred Taylor what he called his "fighting blood." What at first was still "a friendly war" spiraled into a painful struggle that, over more than two years, only grew more bitter.

After a while, an uneasy truce was reached. Taylor still wasn't getting what he deemed a full day's work out of the men; but he was getting twice as much as before. The men weren't happy; the fight wasn't over. It was just a lull in the age-old struggle that pitted bosses against workers, stirred Karl Marx to see an unbridgeable conflict between capital and labor, and fueled the violent labor strife that followed the nationwide railroad strike of 1877.

The men might be cowed for the time being; Taylor's bosses might be happy with the results he had achieved. But Fred himself was miserable. "I was a young man in years," he said later,

> but I give you my word I was a great deal older than I am now with
> the worry, meanness, and contemptibleness of the whole damn
> thing. It is a horrid life for any man to live, not to be able to look
> any workman in the face all day long without seeing hostility there
> and feeling that every man around is his virtual enemy.

The breed of men who, back at the pump works, were his friends now were his enemies, grappling with him in the muck of this ugly fight. He'd get the hell out of the whole damned business or else, as he said later, "find some remedy for this unbearable condition."

3

CUTTING EDGE

~

THE REMEDY, AS HE CAME TO SEE IT, was knowledge.
By late 1880 and his elevation to foreman, Taylor was twenty-four. He had, including his apprenticeship, six years of shop experience and he was a competent machinist. But compared to some of the men, with decades on the shop floor behind them, he didn't know nothin'. And set against their collective knowledge—with their experience at other companies, in other lines of work, with other machine tools, and under other foremen—he knew less than that. "Those fellows know ten times more than you do," he told the Commission on Industrial Relations in 1914, trying to help them grasp his predicament at Midvale.

The struggle with his men was no simple, mindless screaming match of "Yes, you will!" versus "No, I will not!" It was more civil and grown-up than that, no mere contest of wills but of wits. "Hardly a competent workman can be found in a large establishment," Taylor would say with his usual exaggeration, "who does not devote a considerable part of his time to studying"—*studying!*—"just how slowly he can work and still convince his employer that he is going at a good pace." If they could push their machines any harder, of course they would, his men were saying; it's just that they could not. Taylor believed otherwise. He was not so much insisting, "Yes, you will" as "Yes, you can."

He would have liked to be able to say, "You say you can't do this job any faster? Nonsense. You're running it way too slow. With this kind of steel, and that depth of cut, and that feed, you should be able to go at twenty feet per minute, easy. Go ahead and do it at twenty. Use these pulleys here. It'll be fine." But he couldn't say that, because he didn't know—not for sure, anyway. Grizzled old machinists were saying, "Hell, no, that's too fast. It'll burn up the tool. It'll wreck the machine." Was he supposed to call them liars? For all his confidence, he must have sometimes thought, who am I to say they're wrong? They knew, and he didn't.

Of course, often they didn't really know either; much of their wisdom was shop lore, guesswork, built up over the years into serviceable rules of thumb, based on what they'd heard from others, or on what worked well enough day by day, or on chance remembered incidents. But why acknowledge doubt when, just as easily, they could intimate realms of secret knowledge to which they alone were privy? Sticking to what they knew left shop life less rushed and fitful. For them, the old rules of thumb were good enough.

For Taylor, they were not.

~

View a lathe or boring mill for the first time and, unless it were just then cutting metal, you might not at first spy the tool bit itself. Set against the bulk of the machine that held it, the tool was small, almost insignificant, ounces as against tons.

In its simplest form, the tool was just a length of fine steel, roughly square in cross-section and proportioned like a stubby pencil, one end of which was ground into a cutting edge. A small lathe tool might be three eighths of an inch square, two inches long, and fit comfortably in your palm; a big one like that used in the Midvale shop might be an inch and a half square and a foot long. In any case, all of the machine's great mass served only to contain and control the tool's hot, violent encounter with the work. For the machinist, the colossus looming over him, with its cranks, clamps, pins, pulleys, and belts, was just so much stage set for the great drama played out as tool dug into iron or steel and chips started to fly.

Before being ground to shape, the tool was just a piece of steel; before use, the machinist took it to the grinding wheel and, holding it with both hands against the spinning stone, conferred upon it its cutting edge, shaped so as to give the chip room to roll off and form the helical curls of metal that littered every machine tool bed; these were a machine shop's counterpart to the shavings and sawdust of a woodshop.

Like any knife—which, at bottom, it was—the tool cut only while it was sharp, and it stayed sharp only if it was hard. You could form a pair of cutting tools from two pieces of metal indistinguishable to the naked eye—one made of low carbon steel, the other of the finest tool steel—set them both to cutting, and see the first rubbed into impotent dullness by its first swipe at the work; while the second cut for hours, whittling steel as if it were pine. No one, then or now, would dream of making a cutting tool from low-carbon steel. But even fine tool steel, duly heated in the forge to the right color, quenched, and otherwise metallurgically manipulated, then finally ground to its proper profile, would lose its edge if it were run too fast.

But what was too fast? That question beset every machine shop in the world, Midvale's among them.

The Midvale shop was largely in the business of machining the steel tires it had been Justice's vision to make in America. Some had to be lightened, by boring out the inside; others, to correct some imperfection in rolling, or to remove rough seams, or to have their flanges or treads altered; and most of them to be finished to the precise inside diameter needed to fit around a locomotive wheel. The fifteen-hundred-pound ring of steel would be set onto the table of a big vertical boring mill, centered and clamped down, and set to spinning. Then the cutting tool, gripped from overhead by big bolts, would be edged into its path.

How fast the tool cut was set by the machine's "gearbox," which was no gearbox at all but an array of pulleys and belts. All day, the steam engine drove the overhead shafting at a more or less constant rate, which in turn drove a countershaft above each machine, with its four or five adjacent pulleys of varying diameter that together resembled a stepped cone. Ten or twelve feet below, on the machine tool itself, another cone-shaped constellation of pulleys fell in diameter as those above increased. The two sets of pulleys were tied together by a single, long leather belt. Depending on the particular pair of pulleys around which you looped it—large-to-small, small-to-large, and so on—you got different cutting speeds.

In those days, even the highest cutting speeds were almost absurdly low. To senses inured to the modern machine shop, with its urgent, noisy clatter and its spiraling curlicues of blue chips practically boiling up from the tool and hot enough to scald your skin, the scene might seem comical, as if run in slow motion. Cutting speed was normally expressed in feet per minute; that is, tool and work met at a relative speed of, say, fifteen feet per minute. It might take a minute and a half for the table of a big vertical boring mill like those in the Midvale shop to make one complete revolution.

As the work slowly spun, the tool was fed gradually deeper into it. (Were it not, the first complete turn of the work into the fixed tool would bite off a thin sliver of metal, but then, with the very next revolution, all cutting would cease: there would be nothing left to cut, it having already been removed in the first pass.) From ancient times into the nineteenth century, the tool was fed by hand, as it still often is, for example, on wood lathes. But in 1843, Whitworth invented the automatic cross-feed, where the rotation of the work and the advance of the cutting tool were mechanically linked; for example, each revolution of the work might be set to feed the tool one sixty-fourth of an inch.

Speed and feed, together with the depth of the cut, determined how long it took to pare away a given amount of metal—and thus, directly, the job's cost. Because for all that time, the machinist mostly just stood there, monitoring the cut, waiting for it to finish—and drawing his pay. Remove steel faster and the cost dropped. But how much faster could you get away with?

At the right speed and feed, the tool cut merrily away, never getting so hot as to undermine its metallurgical properties; you might be able to cut for an hour or two and never have to regrind the tool. But cut too fast, and you'd slip over the line, heating up the end of the tool so much that it lost its edge and soon was ineffectually grating and scraping, smoke pouring from any grease on the work, once-lovely helices of chip now ragged, steaming, metallic crud.

So you had to stop the machine, unclamp the tool, wander over to the grindstone and, by eye, hold the tool against the whirling stone, grind away the dulled and abraded surface, and restore the cutting edge to its proper contours. Then it was back to the machine, clamping the tool back in place, to pick up where you'd left off. All the while, the machine tool's tons of iron and steel sat there lifeless and impotent, costing money.

One solution was to play it safe: cut at speeds and feeds low enough that you needn't worry about burning up the tool. That way you weren't forever shutting down the machine to regrind it. But then you lost out the other way: your tool was cutting, making a show of chips, but too slowly, well short of its potential. Chordal wrote how the ordinary machinist, finding he had bolted a job to his lathe's faceplate a little insecurely, rarely stopped to rechuck it. Rather, he preferred "to take tender, nibbling cuts on the uncertain thing, because he is *cutting iron all the time*"; he was making progress anyone could see. The same applied to safe, leisurely cutting speeds far below a tool's capabilities. Why fuss? The boss could see you were working.

How far off the tool's potential were you? How much closer could you get? What combination of settings left you with the biggest pile of chips at day's end? These were the essential questions. Yet in the average shop, they received scant attention; rather, they were left to hearsay, hunch, and opinion—to the discretion of the machinist himself; it was part of the dark mystery that surrounded his craft. As Joshua Rose's machinist's manual put it,

> there is no part of the turner's art in which so great a variation of practice exists or is possible, no part of his art so intricate and deceptive, and none requiring so much judgment, perception, and watchfulness, not only because the nature of the work to be performed may render peculiar conditions of speed and feed necessary, but also because a tool may appear to the unpracticed or even to the experienced eye, to be doing excellent duty, when it is really falling far short of the duty it is capable of performing.

But what if you really knew how fast a tool could cut?

In 1880, Taylor didn't know and couldn't have named the dozen relevant variables he'd later identify, much less assign to them relative weights or offer a formula embodying their contributions. Nobody knew any of that in 1880.

On the other hand, everybody knew it was a rich and multifaceted problem. Everybody had an educated guess to offer, a firm opinion, a pet prejudice; at Midvale, Taylor wrote later, some men were sure that fast speeds and light feeds removed metal faster, others said slow speeds coupled to heavy feeds. In any case, that the problem might yield to a coordinated attack was no new idea. In 1867, a machine shop text written by Egbert P. Watson had outlined the problem, even listing variables that needed to be taken into account. "Some enterprising foreman or manufacturer," suggested Watson, might profitably conduct experiments. Meanwhile, Joshua Rose could write, in the preface to his book on machine shop practice, that his aim, while incompletely realized, had been "to develop from the promiscuous practice of the workshop its inherent science."

Science. A spirit of rational inquiry hung heavily in the air in the 1880s, and nowhere more than at Midvale Steel. The whole company, under William Sellers, and those steel-obsessed sons of Yale, Brinley and Davenport, was a testament to the redeeming powers of reason.

Around the fall of 1880, Fred Taylor asked Sellers to approve a series of metal-cutting experiments. Sellers, now fifty-four, was, in the words of Taylor's friend Wilfred Lewis, "of commanding presence and stern appearance." White beard, formidable mustache, and bushy white eyebrows did nothing to make him look grandfatherly.

Taylor later painted himself as the Young Turk innovator in approaching Sellers. But what he proposed fell squarely within the thinking of Sellers's great metalworking fiefdom. "It has been said that good workmen can do work with poor tools," a Sellers treatise on its own machine tools had observed in 1877, reciting from a paper its chief engineer had written for the *Journal of the Franklin Institute* a few years before, "but the problem of the day is not only how to secure more good workmen, but how to enable such workman as are at our command to do good work, and how to enable the many really skillful mechanics to accomplish more and better work than heretofore." This was just what Taylor hoped to do through his metal-cutting experiments. To Sellers, they could scarcely have seemed as radical as Taylor would picture it.

A few years earlier, the Sellers shops had taken some early stabs at the problem. They had adopted compromise cutting angles and begun grinding tools to them with a special machine. Taylor wanted to take this work further, to establish not just ready compromises but optimal practice. But they had tried that, to no avail, Taylor has Sellers saying. Still, he wrote later, referring to himself in the third person, as if that alone deflected the attention his story focused on him, "his conviction . . . was so strong that he obtained the permission of the management to make a series of experiments to investigate the laws of cutting metals with a view to obtaining a knowledge at least equal to that of the combined machinists who were under him." Six months, he figured, ought to do it.

Maybe two years, he came to think once he'd begun.

The experiments went on for twenty-six years.

～

The first object was to resolve once and for all that much-disputed issue of every machine shop, the precise profile to which the tool's cutting edge should be ground.

Consider the square-sectioned tool's tip, its business end. On the grinding wheel, you bevel one right angle so it's a few degrees short of a right angle. Then the same for the two adjacent surfaces, so that whether viewed from top, side, or front, it's always wedge-shaped. Everyone knew these angles were crucial; they had their own names— clearance angle, side slope, back slope. Together, they gave the tool an edge that properly dug into the work, was structurally supported by the rest of the tool, and gave the chips clearance with which to curl up and away. Get those three angles just right, machinists felt, and you could cut faster. But of course each machinist had his own idea as to what "just right" meant.

What were the right angles?

After six months, Taylor had an answer: it didn't much matter. The angles were necessary, but within wide limits, they little influenced maximum cutting speed. Taylor had ground a series of tools with angles systematically varied, set them to cutting metal, and established the fastest speed at which each could be run for some fixed period, typically twenty or forty minutes. But none of the variations exerted a marked effect.

Taylor went to Sellers with the results. Sellers laughed; money down the drain, just as he'd thought. No, Taylor insisted, "We have got to the top of the gold mine." He was onto something and wanted Sellers' approval to continue. In the end, he promised, he'd be getting more work out of the shop.

All right, replied Sellers, spend the money.

Why? Perhaps in appreciation of the young man's grit at facing down the men on the shop floor, despite his slender years and unprepossessing appearance. Or perhaps out of real curiosity about a problem he must have long wondered about. Or else because business was booming, the money was there, and the experiments might just possibly pay off some day. In any case, around the spring of 1881, Taylor's experiments resumed.

They were real experiments, too, with more than a nod to scientific controls. In one early series, as in many others, he used a sixty-six-inch vertical boring mill, which was really just a lathe flipped upright, so that the work revolved like a merry-go-round; the table of this one could accommodate a tire of five and a half feet diameter. Completely overhauling it, he replaced worn parts, restored bearings, installed a new double-drive belt; the idea was to eliminate the machine as a variable, leaving only the tool itself to test.

From a single heat of tool steel, Taylor had a number of one-inch-square cross-section tools forged, "all of the bars from which they were made being treated as nearly alike as possible in hammering, etc. They were," he reported later, "dressed and tempered, always by the same smith, like one sample tool, and ground to gauges and issued from the tool room."

Precautions were taken "to insure against the unconscious and almost unavoidable bias, that there is in the mind of nearly every experimenter, toward making the results of his experiment conform to the law which he thinks exists or should exist." Variables such as depth of cut were recorded in code. Results were left untabulated until the experiment was largely finished, "so that the experimenter had no opportunity of anticipating the law where one existed."

In one series of experiments, Taylor varied the feed, in small increments, from about one thirty-second of an inch per revolution of the work to about three sixteenths. Depth of cut ranged from one sixty-fourth to a full quarter of an inch. The table could be turned at any of ten different speeds. At the end of a set time interval, typically twenty or forty minutes, the tool was examined for wear, discoloration, and other markers of its condition. The test object for these experiments was a single tire, #19642, a ring of steel five feet in diameter and weighing more than half a ton, made in Midvale's new No. 2 open-hearth furnace. In the end, after more than four hundred individual tests, it had been reduced almost entirely to chips.

To what end? For one thing, Taylor could furnish an illuminating, if purely qualitative, description of a tool's decline into uselessness:

> The cutting edge, at first keen, becomes very slightly dull, so that it shines when held in the light, and then gradually rounds off, the metal seeming to be crushed in or made to "flow" . . . rather than to wear. The top or lip of the tool at first becomes polished without much wear, where the shaving slides over it; then gradually becomes worn and deeply guttered, but still polished; then it turns white and becomes rough, through the "cutting" of the shaving, and finally the shaving adheres to it, and mounts up on it. . . .

Taylor concluded that, other variables held constant, the amount of metal removed was a fixed product of speed and feed (though later experiments apparently contradicted this result); that if you reduced cutting speed to let your tool go longer without regrinding, the metal removed failed to increase proportionately with duration of cut; that cutting speed and depth of cut were related by certain fixed ratios.

None of this was earth-shattering. The results represented only small steps toward equipping Taylor with the knowledge he needed to challenge the combined experience of the men. Moreover, for more than two years, the experiments exacted a heavy toll on the rest of the shop: since the cone pulleys permitted only coarse gradations of cutting speed, he had to slow down the steam engine powering the whole shop, sometimes from hour to hour, using a special adjustable engine governor. That was a real nuisance.

Still, he was embarked on a promising course, and Sellers let the experiments continue. John Sellers Bancroft, a leading Wm. Sellers &

Company engineer, suggested that Taylor try a tool with a softly rounded nose, rather than the traditional diamond point; sure enough, Taylor confirmed for it the higher cutting speed Bancroft had found on his own back in 1869. He also found that, by playing upon the tool a vigorous stream of water, he could boost cutting speed 40 percent, presumably because the water kept the tool from overheating.

Moreover, even early results let Taylor draw up tables listing the best feeds and speeds for specific conditions. Guided by them, he reported, he had been able to get 30 percent more work out of the shop's six tire boring mills. And whereas the machines had always needed first-class machinists to run them, now they were "run almost entirely by men who are trained up from a lower class of work—either laborers or machinists' helpers." The men didn't need to have all the knowledge in their hands and heads; Taylor's tables told them what they needed to know.

Traditional craft know-how was being reduced to scientific data and passing from workman to manager, from shop floor to front office. On the big boring mills of the Midvale shop, Taylor was creating a new world of work.

But there was a hitch. Taylor had begun all this to ease the hard feeling in the shop; by recourse to the rulings of an impartial arbiter, ever fair-minded science, there would be no need to wrangle over how to set the machines for greatest productivity. They could rise above mere opinion, with its sharp words and raised voices, to serene and stable fact.

That didn't happen. Taylor concluded one account of an early experiment, drawn from a report he submitted to Midvale management on March 20, 1882, with the observation that there did indeed exist "a large field for improvement in present machine shop practice [and] that many operations now conducted under rule of thumb law, should be brought into the province of scientific law." But, he added, with a bitterness that even today stuns by its abruptness, the greatest obstacle faced by the experimenter was

> the blind and almost unaccountable prejudice on the part of most
> machinists to any improvement or change, although it may be
> more for the interest of the workman than the employer. He will
> find himself opposed by this at every step, and upon entering on

such an undertaking must bid good-bye to all ideas of personal popularity among his fellow workmen.

4

SPECIAL ARRANGEMENTS

~

ON APRIL 20, 1878, Frederick W. Taylor was admitted to the Engineers Club of Philadelphia, whose ranks included distinguished engineers, professors, and luminaries like William and Coleman Sellers. One charter member was Taylor's friend Wilfred Lewis. Another was Mark Richards Muckle, Jr., the son of a German-American newspaper executive decorated by the emperor for his services to Germany in the Franco-Prussian War. Lewis was an MIT graduate, but twenty-one-year-old Muckle, Jr. (who the following year would buy into Ferrell & Jones, making it Ferrell & Muckle), was a "graduate" only of a Sellers apprenticeship. Much the same went for Taylor. The club listed him as a mechanical engineer, but at the time, he had never taken an engineering course and had no work experience beyond his apprenticeship. That neither he nor Muckle qualified by education or experience apparently mattered little. What did matter was that they were from good families.

In well-born family and friends, Taylor had a credential worth more than any college degree. Still, working at Midvale, influenced as it was by Yale-educated chemists Brinley and Davenport, he worried that his advance might be blocked without one. His friend Clarence Clark, son of a principal Midvale shareholder, had joined the company in 1878 after his graduation from the University of Pennsylvania. Guillemeau Aertsen, his father a business associate of the Clarks, had come to Midvale two years earlier and was now a foreman, moving up fast; he'd also graduated from Penn. Taylor's friend Wilfred Lewis had his MIT degree. At the time, only one American engineer in nine had a college degree; but the men whom Taylor knew all did. Then, too, he was driven enough to remedy his ignorance of metal cutting to experiment on his own; he coveted technical knowledge.

At first, he wrote later, he took correspondence courses "given by the scientific professors at Harvard," though the record is murky on this point. He wrote a mathematics teacher associated with a Society for the Promotion of Study at Home that he wished "to get enough knowledge of calculus to study applied mechanics," seeking a course of study "as concise as possible"; how long, he wondered, might it take to complete for "an average student" studying three hours a day, six days a week?

In the end, however, probably early in 1881, Taylor enrolled at Stevens Institute of Technology in Hoboken, New Jersey, high over the Hudson River across from New York City, one of the engineering schools his mother had mentioned in her letters to him at Exeter. Very likely, he landed there through the good offices of William Sellers, whose personal secretary while president of the Franklin Institute during the 1860s had been Henry Morton.

A colorful, many-sided graduate of Penn, where he had done his own translation of the Rosetta stone, Morton had studied law, ultimately turned to chemistry and physics, and began teaching those subjects at a private school. For his lectures, he designed demonstration apparatuses so "novel . . . entertaining and instructive," in the words of one account, that the lecture room had to be enlarged to accommodate the crowds. "We are in a valley among snow-capped mountains," he'd set the scene for a science lecture, "and before us a lake spreads its mirror to the sky. No breath of air ripples its surface, no wavelet breaks upon its beach." Partly on the strength of such performances, which the head of its search committee had witnessed, the new Stevens Institute, founded by the wealthy son of a family of inventors and naval architects, asked Morton to become its first president.

Morton accepted but always maintained links to Sellers in Philadelphia, a hundred miles to the south. His diaries during the years after 1870 record numerous meetings with Sellers there. A tour by Class of '81 students to Philadelphia included visits to the Sellers machine shops and, the next day, his ironworks down the Delaware. It could hardly have taken much arm twisting by Sellers, then, to get Morton, his former aide, a dozen years his junior, to accept Taylor as a Stevens student.

And yet, for so bright and well-prepared a young man as Fred Taylor, why might his admission require special attention at all? Some years earlier, he had passed the Harvard examination with honors. And after Exeter, Stevens admissions requirements in algebra, geometry, composition, and English grammar could surely have held no terror.

But Taylor's arrangement with Stevens was highly unusual. For though enrolled there and ultimately earning a degree, Taylor was, in the words of one scholar, Myron Johnson, a "phantom student." He never attended classes and never left his ten-hours-a-day, six-days-a-week job at Midvale. He scarcely visited Hoboken at all, at a time when other students were complaining to college authorities that the schedule of recitations, study, and shop periods—demanding long spells on Saturdays as well as the rest of the week—left time "altogether inadequate to enable them to perform conscientious work."

Taylor's arrangement was not wholly without precedent. Until 1881, faculty minutes report, Alexander C. Humphreys had been enrolled as a student yet gave only two days a week to school, "being engaged in business the rest of the time." Humphreys had excelled; he later became a Stevens president. "It was doubtless the excellent scholastic work of Humphreys just proceeding Taylor's application," another Stevens president, Franklin Furman, later observed, "that influenced the Stevens professors to admit Taylor on most unusual terms."

Most unusual they were; the freedom Taylor enjoyed went far beyond that of Humphreys. He claimed to have taken entrance examinations for Stevens, but no records remain. Faculty minutes likewise make no mention of any admissions decision concerning him. Humphreys himself later advised Taylor's son that Taylor had sidestepped anything so prosaic as regular attendance "through some special arrangement with President Morton." In 1933, at the time of the fiftieth anniversary of its most famous son's graduation, festivities at Stevens included a one-act play, *The Young Man from Philadelphia*, based on Taylor's account of how he'd importuned a faculty committee to let him enroll on his own terms. But likely as not, the decision was more Morton's, by executive fiat, than it ever was the faculty's.

Later, when a professional society to which he belonged asked Taylor to solicit memberships among his Stevens classmates, he demurred, saying, "I knew the members of this class very slightly." Likewise, his classmates remembered scarcely ever seeing him in Hoboken; Taylor himself said he showed up only for examinations.

Humphreys wrote in 1933 that he had no record of Taylor even paying tuition. And with a single exception—on January 17, 1882, when Taylor is listed as having passed a physics examination (apparently one administered by President Morton back in November)—his academic progress goes unmentioned in faculty minutes.

And yet, the evidence suggests, Taylor merited the Mechanical Engineer degree awarded him in 1883. One student from his class, Harold M. Plaisted, recalled talking to him once during a shop course; but he doubtless erred. For while Stevens boasted a well-stocked and modern machine shop, Taylor hardly needed to demonstrate mastery of machine tools; he probably knew more than most of his instructors. The same applied, in lesser degree, to required instruction in black-smithing, molding, and patternmaking. Taylor was well prepared in mathematics, and his fluency in French and German exempted him from language requirements.

But what of the physics that Stevens also prescribed—the laws of thermodynamics, the pressures and temperatures of steam engines, the electrical resistance of conductors and insulators? And what of chem-istry? How was he to learn all that? Moreover, Stevens required its stu-dents to complete a thesis on a mechanical subject, like steam injectors, floating derricks, or waterwheels.

The thesis was the least of his worries. Taylor submitted two, both lifted from long reports submitted to Midvale, as part of his work, the previous year; he apologized that he'd had "no time to rearrange his notes and put them in better form." One constituted a series of methodical, months-long tests of two kinds of fans used to force air into the open-hearth furnaces, concluding that the annual cost of one greatly exceeded that of the other. The second told of his metal-cutting experiments.

His academic work was more of a problem, but again he enjoyed gentle assists. Taylor's old friend from the pump works, his cousin Ernest Wright, was enrolled at Stevens at the time (although barely; for much of his three years, passing grades eluded him, and he was periodi-cally warned, dropped, and reinstated, only to finally earn his degree the same year as Fred). But Wright, with whom Fred shared member-ship in a fraternity, Theta Xi, would mark those areas of their textbooks on which the professors set most store, thus easing Fred's exam prepa-ration. Meanwhile, Taylor's eyes were still deemed fragile and, the family story goes, his mother read to him from his texts—though, as Taylor remarked later, this hardly suited the study of calculus.

Toward the end of this period, during the academic year 1882–1883, Taylor enrolled as a special student at the University of Pennsylvania's Towne Scientific School. He was listed as pursuing studies in the "chemical section," which at Towne included metallurgy, ores and fuels, assays, and other subjects vital not only to students warmed by the thought of big jobs in the mining regions out west but also, perhaps, to a Midvale employee influenced by chemists like Brinley and Davenport. Indeed, a Stevens alumni roster later listed Taylor as a chemist at Midvale, perhaps reflecting his preoccupation, just then, with metallurgical matters.

Taylor held himself to an impossibly arduous schedule, apparently experimenting with it, the better to cram everything in. By one account, he'd rise at two in the morning, study until four, take a bath, don his work clothes, then lie quietly in bed for a while before breakfast, mustering his strength for the day ahead at Midvale. By another, this one from Wilfred Lewis, he never slept more than four or five hours and would take a half-hour jog through the silent streets of Germantown each morning before work. By a third account, that of his son Robert, he was up at five, at work by seven, and on the job till five, followed by a walk home, dinner, study until eleven, and then, toward midnight, a run through the neighborhood.

His Stevens studies, together with his Midvale job, Taylor wrote a friend in February 1883, have "completely filled my time night and day."

YOUNG AMERICA

~

CERTAIN FACTS ABOUT THE LIFE of Frederick Winslow Taylor, seemingly implausible, must be dispensed with at once.

In its long entry entitled "Sporting Records," the *Encyclopaedia Britannica* names the winners of the U.S. Open Tennis Championship in doubles for 1881. There you will find mention of F. Taylor.

That year and the period leading up to it saw *our* Mr. Taylor embroiled in conflict with his men in the machine shop, pursuing his metal-cutting experiments, studying calculus, and getting by on four or five hours' sleep.

The two Taylors are one and the same. The Tiffany-engraved gold medal he received for his achievement, with its crossed tennis rackets crafted delicately enough to reveal the articulation of their webbing, is in the possession today of Mrs. Marie Clark Hodges, the granddaughter of Taylor's sister Mary.

Around 1873, a retired British major named Clopton Wingfield got the idea of taking three popular court games—tennis, badminton, and racquets—and packaging for sale in a big wooden box the rackets, nets, balls, and other implements needed to play them. The following year, an American, James Dwight, returned home from a college-graduation trip abroad with one of Wingfield's boxes, introduced it to his medical school classmates at Harvard, and, almost overnight, helped launch a tennis craze among the upper crust.

In Philadelphia, tennis began to supplant the ever-popular cricket. The city's first tennis court went up at the great Clark estate on Schoolhouse Lane and Wissahickon. Two of the Clark boys, Clarence and brother Joseph, took up the sport around 1877, and were joined by their friend Fred Taylor, whose parents' property on Ross Street soon got its own court. There Taylor played after work, on holidays—and on Sundays, at first much to the consternation of the neighborhood. Sometimes in the summer, when his parents were away and only the servants were around, he gave spirited dinner parties for his tennis pals.

Taylor, who was right-handed, typically delivered his ground strokes with neither topspin nor undercut. Playing singles, he never got far, preferring instead the strategic intricacies of doubles. He paired up with Clarence Clark, the two of them representing Germantown's Young America Cricket Club and doing far better together than either ever did individually.

Taylor and Clark, who was three years younger, had known each other as children and, it seems, were picking up the thread of their friendship. Clark had finished up at Germantown Academy in 1874, gone on to Penn, and graduated in 1878. That same year he went to work at Midvale Steel, soon being placed in charge of a forge, at the age of nineteen. A short man, about five foot six, with a warm, likable face, Clark never developed high-flown ideas about saving the world, the way Taylor did. But as an adult, he gave away hundreds of thousands of dollars to his alma mater and philanthropies. His grandchildren adored him. He was kind, civil, and well-mannered—the perfect counterpoise to Taylor at his worst.

In the fall of 1880, about when Taylor was named foreman and set to begin his Stevens studies, he and Clark challenged the other big tennis power, the Outerbridge team from Staten Island. They lost, in what one account described as "a desperate contest" aggravated, it seems, by the six-inch disparity in net height between Philadelphia and New York courts. Other controversies, over such matters as the proper size and weight of the ball, led twenty-one-year-old Clark to call a conference, which was attended by upward of a hundred tennis enthusiasts at the Fifth Avenue Hotel in New York the following May. Thus was born the U.S. Lawn Tennis Association, now the U.S. Tennis Association.

That spring and summer, matches were held leading to the first national championships. At Beacon Park, near Boston, Taylor and Clark won. Back in Philadelphia, against a Princeton club, it looked "as though the glory of [the] Young America [Cricket Club] was in danger of having its lustre dimmed," according to one report. But the scare was short-lived, and "Young America came through a winner, as usual," Clark and Taylor winning three of four games. All that summer, they advanced toward the finals, accounts invariably citing their impeccable teamwork.

On August 31, 1881, the finals began at the posh Newport Casino, in Rhode Island; Taylor and Clark were among thirteen teams competing. But whereas many pairings were made only on the day of the competition, Clark and Taylor had played together for years. So while their opponents were forever stepping on one another's toes, the Philadelphians played coolly and consistently, one close to the net, the other in the backcourt, a style later aped by others. In the finals they were pitted against two other top players, James Dwight, who had first introduced the Wingfield Box to America seven years before, and his protégé Richard Sears. By day's end, they were national doubles champions, the two of them bound for *Britannica*, Clark ultimately for the Tennis Hall of Fame.

Taylor continued to compete actively all through his years at Midvale, though never with as much success. He teamed again with Clark the following year, then with Wilfred Lewis until about 1886. Lewis recalled them playing at Taylor's Ross Street home or else at the Young America Cricket Club grounds at Stenton, to which the club moved in 1879, a wide expanse of lawn behind a mansion where George Washington had briefly stayed during the Revolution.

Early on, Taylor used a racket he'd had made shaped like a large, long-handled spoon; viewed from the side, the plane of the netting and the axis of the handle did not coincide but, rather, were set at an angle of perhaps fifteen degrees. With it, you could better scoop up low balls or reach high over the net and slam the ball back into the opposite court with some confidence that it might land within bounds; this, anyway, is what Taylor's 1886 patent asserted. When they played at Newport in the early 1880s, recalled Wilfred Lewis, the racket produced "abundant merriment and derision," which Taylor volleyed right back.

During these years, too, Taylor invented, patented, and assigned to the Spalding sports equipment company several improvements—he actually made money on them—in tennis nets and posts; one, for example, maintained the net's tautness without the guy ropes, windlasses, pulleys, and other paraphernalia then used.

To Taylor, tennis and metal cutting could seem quite alike—as problems to think about, analyze, solve, reduce to a science, or otherwise improve and refine. This was his habit of mind. Over the years, golf, grass, and roses—not to mention tool grinders, steam hammers, and men—would get the Taylor treatment.

~

The Young America Cricket Club, under whose blue-and-white colors Taylor, Clark, and Lewis competed, did indeed have its roots in the English game of cricket. In the 1840s, immigrant millworkers from the textile centers of northern England had brought the sport to Philadelphia, their proletarian vices, drinking and gambling, giving it an unsavory aroma among the local gentry. But new clubs sprouting up in Philadelphia before the Civil War helped legitimize it. The Germantown Cricket Club was established in 1854, and Young America spun off from it the following year, after a spat over age eligibility that had unaccountably escalated into an apple-throwing riot. In the words of one history, Young America clubmen were "a cocky, irreverent, contentious lot, quick to turn on anyone who seemed to invade their rights." By 1879, however, probably a little after Taylor joined, rules barred profanity, betting, or the sale of drink on the grounds, better suiting them to the presence of young ladies.

The clubs, one writer records, became "the community centers of their respective neighborhoods," summers there aglow with tennis and other social activities, not just cricket. "Young men sparkled in the new club uniforms, as they placed a hand on the top rail and vaulted the fence where ladies under parasols mincing through the turnstiles could see them. In mid-afternoon, white tables would sprout under the shade of the elms, and there would be a claret cup and sun-lit china." Club ballrooms hosted elaborate dinners, private balls, and amateur theatricals.

This was the social world Taylor inhabited—not just peripherally or reluctantly but, by all accounts, as ardently as any empty-headed Germantown swell who had nothing better to do than fill his leisure hours with gay socializing. But Taylor worked six days a week at Midvale and studied chemistry and calculus on the side.

In Young America, Taylor threw himself into amateur theatricals. The club was all-male, and sometimes he would play a woman. His sister Mary helped him with the costumes, but he furnished the rich falsetto, routinely deceiving even his friends. Once, he and a friend, also dressed as a woman, made an appointment to have stage photographs taken. They arrived at the set time, only to be told by the photographer that he already had an appointment with two men due any moment.

Taylor protested; he was sure the photographer could fit them in. When the photographer began to lose patience, Taylor dropped his voice a couple of registers. "Now, look here," he barked, "why the hell can't you take our pictures?"

He was good. Once, Wilfred Lewis recalled later, Taylor "was the whole show at the Academy of Music in a very amusing monologue which brought down the house, and, by way of encore, he gave another equally effective." Amid the glorious columned arches and baroque ornamentation of the Academy, Frederick Taylor commanded center stage.

He could pound out Weber's "Invitation to the Dance" on the piano, he could mimic, he could mince, he could ham it up, he could sing:

> In days of old, when knights were bold,
> And barons held their sway,
> A warrior bold, with spurs of gold,
> Sang merrily his lay . . .

a lay being just a poem or song. *Con spirito* the score instructs the singer of "A Warrior Bold," and Taylor apparently supplied plenty of it:

> So what care I, tho' death be nigh,
> I'll live for love or die.

The tempo slowed toward the end, and we can imagine Taylor and his friends lustily belting out the hopelessly syrupy lyrics—holding those last, long notes, milking them:

> I've fought for love,
> I've fought for love,
> For love, for love, I die-ie-ie.

Sometimes Taylor sang with David Bispham, who later went on to the Metropolitan Opera, made a big name for himself, and wrote an autobiography, *A Quaker Singer's Recollections*. Very early in his career, in late 1880, Bispham sang in the premier of an operetta called *Golden-Haired Gertrude*, at the home of its author, Elinor Parish. It was performed again at a local theater, and on this occasion, playing the principal female part beside Bispham, was a friend of Parish, a soprano who had studied voice in Europe, Louise Marie Spooner, who became Fred Taylor's wife.

~

Her mother's side of the family went straight back to the *Mayflower*. Her father's side missed the boat a little, arriving in Plymouth only in 1637, but they'd lived there ever since. Louise's grandfather, Bourne Spooner, had started a rope-making firm, Plymouth Cordage. There, since 1824, men with lengths of Manila hemp tied around their waists stepped backward along a ropewalk, while a waterwheel-powered machine wound fibers into rope later drawn through great tanks of tar to increase its strength. Lou, an only child, would recall "the smell of the tar from the rope walk near my Grandfather Spooner's house," where she'd stay on visits up from Philadelphia. She remembered the wild rose her grandfather wore in his buttonhole when he returned from the works for lunch—that, and the faint whiff of tar as she kissed him.

Her parents and grandparents were friends of the Taylor family and fellow abolitionists. Her grandfather had given up an earlier rope-making business in New Orleans, a family history has it, because he refused to use slave labor. And when her parents were married in 1856, William Lloyd Garrison was there for the ceremony. 'It is safe to say that our acquaintance began when the Taylor and Spooner babies were introduced," she wrote later. When the Taylors were still at Cedron, the Spooners would come up from Philadelphia, where her father was a physician, and she'd play with the Clark boys and the Taylor boys. Once, horsing around, she fell, fainted, and was carried into the house and placed on a sofa. "I made my first impression on young Fred, he told me later, lying there with my rumpled golden curls."

Was there a streak of smugness or self-satisfaction to Lou Spooner? When, years later, she began an autobiography, she titled the first chapter "Recollections of a Happy Childhood," and, indeed, it all came out in flat, unvariegated shades of sunny. "My mother's early life was a very restricted one," she writes, "which I think accounted for my indulgent bringing up." She tells of summer trips to Plymouth "very much to the envy of my Philadelphia friends who did not have New England

ties"; of watching her Uncle Charles, the prosperous family firm's treasurer, opening his mail, she "gloat[ing] over the checks received"; of
visits from friends, with "picnics and sailing parties" on local ponds; of
the "joyous times we had on the many moonlight picnics, singing our
college songs by the music of the katydids"; of traveling in Europe
when she was eighteen, while America sweltered through the summer
of 1876, "lovely evening dresses" being made for her presentation at the
Saxon court.

Frederick Taylor's choice of life's mate fell squarely within his
family's social orbit, departing not one whit from the respectable. "It
almost seems as if my married life with Fred Taylor was ordained," Lou
would write after he was dead and she could look back. Of the closeness
between the families, she would pronounce this opinion: "I have a
feeling there would be fewer divorces if the early family ties were more
carefully considered." We don't know just how those ties, that early
sight of Lou's tangled curls, and their common interest in singing and
amateur theatricals ripened into affection and love. We do know that
by February 1883, and probably much before, they were engaged to be
married.

Fred's early history suggests that, when it came to girls and women,
the usual juices flowed, in their usual abundance, at the usual times.
While a teenager in Europe, as a member of a wedding party in
Stuttgart, he pronounced the bridesmaid with whom he was paired
"the prettiest of them all." In Munich, while visiting the Alte
Pinakothek, brother Win and George Wright both fell for a girl who
was "quite pretty," wrote thirteen-year-old Fred, "but not half pretty
enough for me." Later, at Exeter, Fred got little epistolary rib nudges
from one of the Wright boys, E. N. Wright, Jr., who wrote in November
1872 that he hoped "neither you nor Jim [Wright] are going [at] it too
strong with the young ladies." Then again, three weeks later: "You
speak of Jimmy and certain other persons with whom he is acquainted.
Are you certain you also do not go in for some of the fun, for if reports
are true, you certainly have an interest in that line."

When it came to the physical attributes that Fred plainly valued,
Lou Spooner passed muster. As a young woman, she was pretty, slender, and graceful and she remained so with the passing years. Once,
after they were married and had adopted three children, Fred was
coming back up from the beach with his son Robert, walking behind

Lou, who wore a bathing suit. "My," Taylor said to his son, of his pushing-fifty wife, "hasn't she got a beautiful figure?"

Before they were married in 1884, the minister's wife advised her, "Enjoy the days of your engagement. They are the happiest in life." And in the case of Lou and Fred, she may have been right; following the announcement of their engagement, Lou wrote later, she walked on air. Not so the ensuing years. Frank Copley could write of her to an acquaintance, "I think I have never met an unhappier person." Much later, one of their grandnephews, F. W. Clark, would write, "She gave me the impression that much of her married life was unhappy and full of turmoil." Indeed, the last years of Taylor's life would largely be spent caring for a woman who suffered from what was then called neurasthenia, which left her in bed, almost wholly an invalid, depressed and unable to see friends, for weeks at a time.

And yet, not long after her husband's death, she experienced what Robert Taylor remembered as "almost a complete turnaround. Within two years, she was really getting back on her feet and getting more and more like her grandmother, who loved people and loved company and liked to entertain." She took charge of efforts to preserve her husband's memory. She painted and traveled to Bermuda, Panama, Cuba, Egypt; in Paris, she saw Monet's water lilies. She rented a villa on the Mediterranean with her distant cousin Mathilde, a French descendant of the Winslow clan.

After Fred's death, in short, she seemed to recover youthful enthusiasms perhaps stifled during her marriage. "In her laugh was something so unaffectedly merry and gigglish," Copley wrote a friend about two years after Taylor's death, that "I almost felt as if I were having a lark with a young girl. . . . I know I heard echoes of a long-lost happy girlhood."

And it may be just this blithe lightheartedness, those simple girlish charms still fresh and vibrant in youth, to which Fred, working long days at the steel mill, was irresistibly drawn.

～

Before air conditioning, well-off folks who could escape the sweltering summers of the cities made for the sea, the mountains, and the cooling breezes of the north. And that's what Fred and his friends did every summer, all through his young adult years. Always, it was up north for vacations, to New York or the Maine woods, to camp, fish, hunt, and hike.

With Ernest Wright and brother Win, for instance, he'd head up to Long Lake, in the Adirondacks of upstate New York, hiring the same guide and boat for several years running. The locals, apparently, looked with gleeful anticipation to the coming of city folks with fat wallets; Winslow called the place "Gougeville." Or else it was up to Moosehead Lake in north central Maine, then further up still to the great Allagash waterway and its raging white waters, which Thoreau had come to a quarter century before and written about in *The Maine Woods.*

Thoreau had made the Maine woods, along with Walden, a symbol of freedom from the cares of city life. So it was for Taylor. Even today, civilization thins out as you near Moosehead Lake, which at map scale resembles a moose's antlers. Thirty miles long by ten wide, it is studded with islands, surrounded by smaller ponds, fed by rivers and streams. And everywhere, trees—trees to satisfy the country's need for wood pulp and paper, trees pushing up against every lake shore, trees as far as you can see. Back in Massachusetts or Connecticut, steepled church, town hall, and white clapboard houses, quaint and compactly clustered, made the town itself star. But here, towns lay in the shadow of the landscape. Here, you felt at civilization's edge, that first step into the woods bearing you into the primal wilderness itself.

The town of Greenville, where expeditions to explore the lake and the wild country to the north hired their guides and equipped themselves, was just the old Sanders store at the tip of East Cove, a church, and a few houses. Well-heeled adventurers reached here by rail or, before the Bangor & Piscataquis Railroad pushed its way this far in 1884, by stagecoaches drawn by six- or eight-horse teams. It was unforgiving country, real wilderness, especially if you were headed up further north, to the rapids of the Allagash where Thoreau had canoed. You didn't want anything to go amiss this far from a doctor's care. Taylor would insist that no one in his party carry an ax along the trail—too easy for a chance swing to hurt someone. And years later, when he sent his sons up here, they always spent two weeks in camp first, as an incubation period, to make sure they weren't coming down with measles or chicken pox that, left untreated in the wilderness, could be dangerous.

On one trip to Moosehead Lake with Clarence Clark, another of his regular companions, they were coming around a point when their canoe abruptly tipped over, dumping Fred into the lake for twenty minutes. He must have gasped with the first icy shock of it; water sucks heat from you twenty-five times as fast as still air. Vessels delivering blood to the skin constrict. Blood rushes to the body's deep recesses. Kidney function can be disrupted, the body's temperature regulating system permanently impaired. Indeed, according to his son Robert, Taylor paid a lasting price for his brush with hypothermia. The spill caused his father unspecified "stomach problems" all his life. And while the medical reasoning for it is is not self-evident today, he was apparently ordered not to swim, take a bath, or shower (he took sponge baths instead), and to wear a band of flannel around his middle; a "belly-band," Robert called it. In some later photos of Taylor, you can see what looks like a lumpy layer of swaddling beneath his otherwise trim clothes.

But the scare never stopped Taylor from coming back north. Year after year, at least through his twenties and thirties, before his marriage and after, he and his friends would return to these lovely, rustic places, far from the clamor of the machine shop and the heat of the open hearths. Fred's friend Wilfred Lewis was often asked to go, never did, and regretted it later. They would hoist their guns and fishing tackle, load up their pack baskets with sometimes one hundred pounds of gear, and hike along the trails in their heavy boots, eight or ten miles a day. At night, they lay on beds made from the branches of balsam firs. The next morning, as Lou remembered her trips to Maine with Fred as a young bride, "the large pile of balsam boughs was lighted, sending the sparks high in the air to mingle with the twinkling of the stars."

∿

It was a good life that Fred Taylor led outside Midvale, and never did he show any inclination to forsake it. "He was quite a social favorite," Lewis recalled of him, "and did not wholly renounce the demands of society." He dismissed coming-out parties and the like as "ridiculous nonsense," and since the pump works, he identified with more forthright working-class charms. But unlike those of more ascetic temperament or greater revolutionary zeal, he did not throw over his old life for the sake of the new. The miracle of his nature was that he said yes to both. "His physician told me," recalled Lou Taylor many years later, that "he had led the life of five men."

Not long ago, a scholar confronting the life of Thomas Jefferson reopened an old, painful question: "How could the man who wrote that 'All men are created equal' own slaves?" And yet, he observed, one might invert the question to see Jefferson more sympathetically: "How did a man who was born into a slaveholding society, whose family and admired friends owned slaves, who inherited a fortune that was dependent on slaves and slave labor, decide at an early age that slavery was morally wrong and forcefully declare that it ought to be abolished?"

Something like the same inversion might apply to Frederick Taylor. How could a man so insulated from the hard, circumscribed lives led by most workers advance an industrial order that left their working lives harder and more circumscribed yet? That's one way to frame the question. But another is: How did a man who need never work at all, and who actually disdained manual labor, throw himself onto the shop floor, confront what was arguably the thorniest social problem of his day and devote his life to creating what he conceived as an industrial utopia?

In a sense, Frederick Taylor was every bit the rebel his most devoted champions insisted he was. But he rebelled not against pleasure and privilege but at the shallowness of life in which pleasure and privilege were deemed enough, life that dismissed serious concern for the outside world or earnest effort to improve it.

A poem heard at Harvard, around the time Taylor was there, reads in part:

> We deem it narrow-minded to excel.
> We call the man fanatic who applies
> His life to one grand purpose till he dies.
> Enthusiasm sees one side, one fact;
> We try to see all sides, but do not act.
> . . . We long to sit with newspapers unfurled,
> Indifferent spectators of the world.

That would have been anathema to Taylor and earned his contempt. At Midvale, he was anything but an indifferent spectator. He did act. And did excel. And did, indeed, consecrate his life to "one grand purpose."

6

THE LEANING TOWER OF MIDVALE

~

O<small>VER THE NEXT FEW YEARS</small>, Taylor's responsibilities at Midvale grew, from foreman by the end of 1880, to master mechanic, chief draftsman, and chief engineer. The precise chronology is muddy, in part thanks to Taylor himself who, writing his Exeter friend Tufts in early 1883, already called himself chief engineer; he wasn't and wouldn't be, at least formally, until 1887. Still, his duties steadily broadened. On February 2, 1884, Russell Davenport, who had succeeded Brinley as superintendent two years before, advised "Colonel" James Thompson, the irreplaceable clerk, timekeeper, and paymaster through whose hands most of the routine business of the works passed, "From this date, all boilers, pumps, engines, yard cranes, electric dynamos and circuits, steam, water & drain pipes will be in charge of Mr. Taylor and all orders or other memoranda concerning alteration or repairs to these will be sent to him at Engineers Office (old drawing room)."

Perhaps significantly, Davenport's order extending Taylor's authority also circumscribed it: the steam pipes within Taylor's jurisdiction extended only "up to throttle valve of each engine or tool using steam." Among Midvale Steel's hundreds of employees, perhaps a dozen young men, most of them bright, eager, and ambitious college graduates, exercised substantial authority; Frederick Winslow Taylor, age twenty-eight at the time of Davenport's order, did not run the place. Most of the work he did was entirely unglamorous, devoted to the workaday details of running a shop and solving all the mechanical and human problems that went with hard, hot, dirty work. Most of it would never be celebrated in trade union broadsides, congressional hearings, or management textbooks.

One problem at Midvale was drunkenness. "Each day at noon," Taylor wrote later, "a large wagon, loaded with whiskey and beer, drove into the middle of the works and the men flocked around it like

ants." Everyone among the largely English immigrant workforce
drank, or so it seemed. Determined to stop it, Taylor barred the
booze-laden lunch wagons from the works. In response, the men
started going out for lunch and returning drunk. So they were ordered
not to leave the grounds but to bring lunch with them. Showing up for
work drunk brought a stern rebuke; a third offense meant a stiff fine
and a yearlong no-drinking pledge, or else outright dismissal. Within a
few years, to hear Taylor tell it, Midvale's drinking problem was no
more.

Or take the leaning tower episode. Exhaust from the twelve-ton
open-hearth furnace erected around 1880 had been routed up through
the squat brick smokestack that also served Midvale's original, much
smaller furnace. But the stack failed to create sufficient draft, and it was
decided to extend it forty or fifty feet. Taylor took transit observations
and found that the existing chimney, its foundation having settled,
wasn't plumb. Extended along the same axis, its new section would lie
outside the stack's point of support and doubtless collapse. So Taylor
had the leaning tower of Midvale doubled back on itself at an ever-so-
slight angle; with the original section, it made a broad, shallow V set on
its side. Construction didn't shut down the open hearths for so much
as a day, and for years it worked fine though, a company history conceded, it was "by no means a thing of beauty."

Once, a drain clogged and Taylor's men reported to him they
couldn't clear it. One option was to dig twenty or thirty feet beneath
the foundations and clear it out. But that meant shutting down the mill
for several days. So, as Taylor wrote later of himself, in the third person,
"he took off all of his clothes,

> put on overalls, tied shoes on to his elbows, shoes on to his knees,
> and leather pads on to his hips to keep from getting cut in the
> drain, and then crawled in through the black slime and muck of
> the drain. Time and again he had to turn his nose up into the arch
> of the drain to keep from drowning. After about 100 yards,
> however, he reached the obstruction, pulled it down, and when the
> water had partly subsided, backed out the same way that he had
> come in. He was covered with slime perhaps half an inch thick, all
> over, which had to be scraped off with a scraper, and his skin was
> black for a week or two where the dirt had soaked in.

Taylor tells the story anonymously, with an aw shucks bravado. And yet one senses his delight in occupying center stage. "He was, of course, very much laughed at," Taylor continues, "and finally the anecdote was told as a good joke at a meeting of the Board of Directors." Hero, knave, or fool—it almost didn't matter, as long as he could strut his stuff and hear the gasps, or even the muffled chortling, of the crowd.

In his late twenties, Taylor was the proverbial man in a hurry, filled with ideas, eager to make his mark. Later, his admirers would credit him with infinite patience and tenacity, but these traits were acquired, not innate. "I used to be excessively impatient for immediate results in everything that I went into," he wrote later. Another time, he recalled how at Midvale he felt "that I ought to do in a month what it takes me three months to do." That urgency, that "uneasy, hurried feeling," he allowed, was "most wearing."

Even while still foreman, Taylor's "chief interest and hope in life was that of doing some great thing" at Midvale. "My head was full of wonderful and great projects to simplify the processes, to design new machinery, to revolutionize the methods of the whole establishment." Sometimes, he'd forget or ignore more pedestrian tasks he had been assigned. One day, Davenport had enough, stormed into Taylor's office, and "swore at me like a pirate."

Another time, feeling mistreated, Taylor went over Davenport's head to William Sellers—but got none of the sympathy he expected. "Do you know that all of this [has] impressed me with the fact that you are still a very young man?" Sellers lectured him. "Long before you reach my age you will have found that you have to eat a bushel of dirt, and you will go right ahead and eat your dirt until it really seriously interferes with your digestion."

Let us say it plainly: the boy—for that is what he was in this respect—was full of himself. At the pump works it had come to him with the force of revelation that he was made of mortal stuff, that others were as good as he, that he occasionally had to do as he was told. But all his life he would need to relearn the lesson. Those recurrent self-doubts that often afflict artists or other gifted individuals were rarely visited upon Frederick Taylor.

Once, a workman came to his house in the middle of the night to report that a crucial valve had failed, shutting down part of the works. "I took the earliest train at 6 o'clock down into Philadelphia," Taylor wrote later, "hired a carriage and drove all over the city to every dealer who might possibly have the valve in hand." No luck. And, it seems, no shame at his failure to get it; about noon, he returned to Midvale "feeling very well satisfied" that he'd done what he could. His boss, though, ranted at him and ordered him to New York to get the valve. That he might not merit feeling "very well satisfied" with himself was, for Taylor, almost a new idea.

At Midvale and elsewhere, he would invent machines and other contrivances, a number of which he patented. And each time, flush with the thrill of creation, the thought of his own inventive powers left him aglow. "Well, Freddy," he would say to himself, "that last invention of yours was probably the greatest thing that ever happened." But in fact, few came to much, at least commercially.

Later, he would speak to young engineering students about "success," his lectures littered with nostrums about doing what your boss expects of you and reining in your own ambitions for the sake of the company. "Let your common sense guide and control your ambition," he told them. "Don't try for perpetual motion; don't look for a diamond mine in the coal fields of Indiana; don't make a machine to fly to the moon." But only someone with just such grandiose dreams would need to tell himself that at all. His lectures on success spoke of lessons learned only at great cost, and perhaps incompletely.

~

Late in 1883, manufacturers began to inundate Taylor with trade catalogs. Queen City Malleable Iron Company sent information about yokes and axle clips. C. H. Weston promised a 10 percent discount on his Yarmouthville, Maine, company's eight-inch scaffer, used for cutting leather belts. Taylor had probably solicited most of this. Because around the summer or fall of 1883, soon after his graduation from Stevens, he'd been charged with designing and building a new machine shop north of the foundry, in what had not long before been open fields.

Midvale was on a roll. Between 1881 and 1885, its assets doubled. Total earnings for the period came to about three quarters of a million dollars, and each year 8 percent dividends, sixty thousand dollars, were paid to the owners. Business grew. Tires and axles were its bread-and-butter. But now, Midvale told the government, it was prepared to forge the new rifled cannon that the army and navy wanted. Soon it received the first of many government contracts. Big money poured into Midvale's physical plant. "A fine new office is being erected on the front toward the Blabon Oil Cloth mills," the *Germantown Independent* told its readers on May 19, 1883. "The new building," a three-story brick structure that would accommodate the company's drawing room and laboratory, as well as its business offices, "will be luxuriously furnished and will have toilet, dressing and waiting rooms and every modern improvement."

That was one harvest of the company's improved fortunes; another was the new machine shop. Placed in charge, Taylor had written to vendors, requesting catalogs and price lists, and now they descended upon him. The Gutta Percha and Rubber Manufacturing Company boasted that its Maltese Cross Brand of belting was "made of 32 oz. cotton duck woven especially for belting purposes. . . . A strictly first-class belt, and one that we will fully guarantee." One company offered steel-bottomed oilcans, at thirteen dollars a dozen. Another let you order pipe through a cipher system, to save on telegraph charges. EGYPT DANUBE HICKORY, for example, meant five hundred feet of three-quarters-inch galvanized pipe shipped by rail. Soon the specifications were going back out: "Build external and internal relieving arches . . . Sheathing of roof to be of 1 1/4″ hemlock . . . best material . . . straight and true grain." Painting meant "four coats of the best white lead with such addition of color as selected hereafter." Lightning rods, carpentry, and brickwork—all were spelled out, arrayed on legal-sized paper across seventeen numbered sections.

The new machine shop, two hundred feet long by a hundred wide, was quadruple the size of the old. It was a one-story structure, but only if you think of a Gothic cathedral as one story. This was an industrial cathedral; light streamed in through four tiers of arched windows that paraded across the north and south walls, much as it did through the high stained-glass windows of Chartres. Except, no pews caught the shafts of sunlight, but rather big lathes, laid out across the broad central bay.

The results of Taylor's metal-cutting experiments had become part of Midvale shop practice almost from the beginning. But now, in 1883 and 1884, one of the earliest discoveries, that a cooling stream of water aimed at the tool raised its cutting speed by more than a third, was felt in the very design of the new shop. Beneath each machine a wrought-iron pan was installed to collect the water, which contained carbonate of soda to prevent rust. Funneled by drains to a central well, the water was then pumped to an overhead tank, from which it was fed back to the machines. What were once just numbers from Taylor's early experiments were now finding expression in iron and steel.

The new machine shop became Taylor's laboratory for more experiments, to study the great leather belts that, looped over pulleys, delivered power to the machine tools. The belts, made by close to a hundred manufacturers and easy to take for granted, were an unfailing source of trouble. Sometimes thirty or more feet long and a foot and a half wide, they obviously didn't come from a single stretch of hide; they had to be spliced, glued, laced, riveted into a continuous band. In daily use, they stretched, loosened, slipped, and broke. And when they failed, a machine, or group of machines, or the whole factory, went down with them.

Of course, belts were not normally included in any mental catalog of the triumphs of the age. A Philadelphia manufacturer of them noted years later how the belt enjoyed no respect and "can only retaliate by the infliction of annoyance and indirect loss:

> Sodden with oil, or parched, or mayhap scorched with slip, or
> tortured on the rack as men were once upon a time, it goes upon
> its weary way—goes somehow—and does its work well, [though]
> not *so* well . . . if 'twere better cherished or better understood.

While failing to cherish them, some engineers had at least tried to understand them, establishing rules for their widths, thicknesses, and running speeds, for the horsepower they could transmit or their coefficient of friction. "The width of the belt in inches, multiplied by forty five, gives its strain," Chordal would assert in a typical pronouncement. Every mechanic's notebook was filled with advice like this.

But it began to seem to Taylor that most of it wasn't just inconsistent or downright contradictory but preoccupied with the wrong questions. It wasn't its coefficient of friction, or any of its other physical properties, or even its cost to purchase or maintain, that should dictate a belt's design. Rather, the shop's lost productive time, for which a broken or loosely flapping belt was so often responsible, ought to govern. Most belts, it struck him, were too light, not to transmit the load but to ward off the costly cycle of breakdown and repair that plagued Midvale and every other factory.

In designing the new machine shop, he installed pulleys of larger diameter and greater width; they could bear meatier belts able to transmit double or triple the power and last far longer. And he began experiments in which half the belts conformed to existing practice, while half were made three times heavier. For nine years, Taylor and his assistants would record how much production time was lost to tightening or replacing each belt, the tension maintained, the costs incurred, and so on. In 1893, his work culminated in a mammoth paper written in a language not of physics but of dollars and cents.

In the years leading up to his theory of relativity, Albert Einstein worked in the Swiss patent office. In his most creatively prosperous years as a poet, William Carlos Williams, M.D., treated patients. In a crudely analagous way, during the years that spawned scientific management, Fred Taylor was fretting about lightning rods, roof sheathing, and leather belts.

7

A FAUSTIAN BARGAIN

〜

"ONE BRICKLAYER AND HELPER will average about 480 bricks in 10 H[ours]" Taylor recorded on January 29, 1880, in a "Book Containing Notes of Importance" that he'd begun the day before. Next day, he wrote that a laborer could load a wheelbarrow with loose dirt and wheel it a hundred feet two hundred and forty times in a ten-hour day, though he added the qualifier, "not reliable."

The important notes that Taylor began to keep about the time he became gang boss, which he kept up as foreman and during the next ten years, included odd rules of thumb, names of technical books, first aid treatments for burns, rude sketches of drafting-room furniture, chemical recipes, steel classifications, and much else. From the start, he recorded how long it took the men to perform specific tasks:

It is safe to allow one carpenter and one laborer one day for each [of a particular structure] that is put up. These data are taken from the time occupied in erecting the large trusses which support the hammer shop roof and framework for overhead machinery in grinding room, etc., at Midvale S[teel] W[orks].

This and similar notations come long before the date that Taylor later gave for the origins of "time study." In fact, it was *not* time study, at least not what it came to mean. It was just the sort of straightforward observation made a hundred years before by Adam Smith in *The Wealth of Nations*, that so many workers could make so many pins in a day, or like those made by thousands of other foremen and shop owners in the everyday course of their work. Such knowledge was a foreman's stock in trade, enabling him to estimate future jobs and set piece rates. As Taylor described it later, a foreman looks back to an old job "as nearly like the new one as can be found, and then guesses at the time required to do the new job."

But probably soon after he had begun his metal-cutting experiments, Taylor began to take these raw observations, so squarely within the range of existing practice, one step further and to ask a different question—not, How long did a job take to complete but, How long should it take?

His notebook entries recorded how long various jobs took to complete; these, corrupted by laziness, ineptness, confusion, and inefficiency, were history. The new question was, What were the men capable of? What was possible? What, in effect, was the ideal to which any human performance must be compared? This, viewed the right way, was science, aimed not only at discovering how fast lathes and boring mills could cut metal but at how fast men could work. And this second element now seized Taylor's attention.

"Almost as soon as I started with this idea at the Midvale Steel Works in 1881," Taylor recalled, "I started to collect what information could be had that was written and published on what constituted a day's work." He looked into the German and French literature, as well as that written in English—perhaps the early work of Helmholtz or Marey or, in America, John Nystrom's *A New Treatise on Elements of Mechanics*, published in 1875 and dedicated to William Sellers. At one point, he hired a young college graduate to help.

Most of the scant research had been devoted to finding how much energy—as expressed, say, in the physical unit known as foot-pounds—a man could produce over a course of time. In a typical experiment, a man cranked a winch from which weights were hung. The experimenter recorded how much he could lift how fast. Then, by elementary calculations, these data could be translated into horse-power, which since the days of James Watt, inventor of the steam engine, had been defined as so many foot-pounds per minute or per hour.

Taylor found that existing research results were hopelessly contra-dictory. Sources he might have consulted gave figures for a man's output over ten hours as anywhere from one and a half to four million foot-pounds—far too broad a range on which to base wages. And so, in the account he rendered later, Taylor asked William Sellers if he might conduct experiments of his own. They'll come to nothing, Sellers pre-dicted, while acceding as usual to his earnest young foreman's wish.

Taylor picked two good workers, offered them double pay for the duration, warned them that their windfall was over at the first sign of slacking off, gave them a variety of arduous tasks, calculated the work they performed in foot-pounds and thence into horsepower. He found that on some tasks you could count on only about an eighth of a horsepower out of them, on others fully a half. Again a wide discrep-ancy, a factor of four; again nothing consistent. For the time being, Taylor gave up.

In these experiments, Taylor and his assistant had used a stopwatch to time the work they gave the men. Click and the watch hand impetu-ously starts. Click, and it stops, the moment imprisoned on the face of the watch. Perhaps simply having the stopwatch around led to the next step. His notebook had typically recorded what a man did in ten hours; with the stopwatch you could just as easily measure what he did in ten seconds. But, more to the point, you could determine how long any *part* of a job took to do.

Sometime in 1883, Taylor wrote later, it "occurred to [me] that it was simpler to time each of the elements" of a job and establish an overall time for it "by summing up the total times of its component parts" than to search through records of past jobs and guess how they might apply to a future one. With this strategy, work was no longer an undifferentiated lump. It consisted of discrete pieces, each of which could be timed and studied.

Say you have a casting, to use an illustration Taylor employed later, on which several surfaces, of specified dimensions, must be planed flat and smooth. How many is it fair to expect from a workman in a day? You might look through old records until you found a job that in weight, surface area, material, and so on wasn't too far off, and then you'd estimate up or down; but often, the estimate was little more than a guess. In Taylor's embryonic system, you divide the work into that done by the machine and that done by the workman. For the first, the metal-cutting experiments supply an increasingly accurate guide. For the second, formal time studies do—time studies not of the whole job but of each element making it up.

Start with a five-hundred pound piece of cast iron sitting on the floor. You have to hook it up to a chain or pulley, winch it up, and gently lower it onto the planer table, four feet above the floor. This takes time.

Once on the table, you have to line it up so that the tool takes just the right swipe at the casting, along just the right axis. Machinists worry about getting things level and straight. They establish reference points and reference lines. Two holes previously drilled, for example, might establish a line, or perhaps a surface previously ground smooth and flat. In any case, orienting the piece on the table also takes time.

Then you need to hold it in position; the table has slots into which bolts can be slid, to which "dogs," or clamps, can be screwed on, maybe three or four of them, and tightened down onto the work to cinch it in place. Sometimes, you have to grip it in seemingly odd ways, so as to counter the tendency of even a heavy piece of steel to spring into a curve under the pressure of the clamps. This, too, can be tricky and takes time.

You break down the whole job like this: adjust machine for each cut. Cut metal. Adjust. Cut. Remove bolts and stops. Lift finished piece from table. Return it to floor. Clean away chips—and so on.

The first time you followed a machinist, timing each operation, it might seem a colossal waste of effort. But many of those operations were repeated, in a variety of combinations and permutations, on other jobs. You were always lifting quarter-ton castings into position; you were always tightening clamps. Once you had a time for any one operation, Taylor reasoned, you could use it to help set the rate for any job in which it figured. Two jobs might seem wildly different yet be built up from operations that Taylor termed "elementary"—not in the sense of simple but referring to individual elements of the job. Reduce the work to a series of such elements, time them, add up the times, and, presto, you knew how long the job ought to take.

But it was some time before Taylor took it this far. Early on, he was stumbling in the dark, trying this and that. One problem was simply describing, recording, and indexing each elementary movement—after all, what, exactly, was an elementary movement? Amid the blur of activity of human work, where did one element end and another begin? And how did you classify these elements once you had them? Taylor "threw away his first two years of time study" results, he wrote later, because they were so poorly indexed he couldn't find what he needed when he looked for them.

But in time study, Taylor found, lay a hidden payoff. To do it, you needed to really look at the work; in breaking it into components, you were almost forced to study it. What got in the workman's way? Which machines could be modified? Which operations could be improved or eliminated? To an outsider, the work might at first seem no more than a featureless smear of movement. But after a while, it was as if you were seeing it in slow motion, each element highlighted, dissected, splayed open for view.

Early subjects of time study were the locomotive tires Taylor had used in his earliest metal-cutting experiments. Formerly, the men were paid a set rate "for all of the work that could be done on a tire at a single setting," however much or little metal had to be trimmed. But by the time Taylor was through, the machinist's job was no longer to machine a tire. It was a succession of much smaller tasks:

Set tire on machine ready to turn . . .
Rough face front edge . . .
Finish face front edge . . .
Rough bore front . . .
Finish bore front . . .

and so on, right through to

Rough turn flange . . .
Finish turn edge . . .
Clean fillet of flange . . .
Remove tire from machine and clean face plate . . .

For each of these, the machine settings were specified and a time established. And, perhaps reflecting later, more refined practice, they were
all set down on what Taylor termed an instruction card.

In many ways, the instruction card lay at the new system's heart.
Sometimes, it was nothing more than a penciled memo on a slip of
paper, sometimes several pages permanently mounted, for use again
and again, and often elaborately detailed. In one instance, Taylor asked
his assistant to prepare one for overhauling boilers, probably those furnishing steam to the engine that powered the shop, and hence a job
needing particular dispatch. Because his assistant hadn't a clue, Taylor,
over a period of three months, did the job himself, chipping, cleaning,
and overhauling the boiler, timing his own progress all the while.

The final instruction card, detailing the tools needed and the order
in which each operation was to be performed, filled several pages. "Put
a chain and padlock onto the blow-off valve," the workman was
instructed,

> and onto the valve on top of boiler, leading to main steam
> pipe, and onto the valve which supplies O.H., and after locking
> them bring the keys immediately to the Assistant Engineer. Take
> off the upper and lower man-hole covers, and put wooden plugs
> (numbered in tool room #1371) into openings for blowing off
> respective feed pipes. . . .

The machinist was told to take samples of scale from specified points in
the boiler, place them into envelopes numbered one through eight, and
bring them to the engineer's office. Tools were numbered; a scraper for
removing the mud from the #5 set of boilers was immortalized as
#1165.

"The whole scheme was much laughed at when it first went into
use," Taylor wrote later, but the cost to overhaul the boilers plum-
meted from sixty-two dollars—representing perhaps fifteen hundred
today—to eleven. And these were no mere paper savings. If you were
analyzing work, tearing it down into its components, you didn't put it
back together again without simplifying as you went along. In the
boiler overhaul, for example, Taylor found that a worker lost much
time because of his constrained position. So he had thick pads made for
elbows, knees, and hips; special tools were made and kept ready in a
box in the toolroom.

For Taylor, the instruction card was "to the art of management what the drawing is to engineering." On it, the results of management's work—observing, recording, analyzing, thinking, planning—were neatly set out, in clear black and white, with the time each task ought to take noted to the fraction of a minute. Now, the workman didn't have to think out the job anew; management did it for him. Now, a day was no longer the unit of work, nor was the job as a whole; both were too crude, left the workman too many options. With Taylor's detailed instructions, he had fewer opportunities to hesitate, wander, or err.

By January 1884, Taylor's stopwatch studies had progressed enough to have forms printed up detailing each operation, one copy of which he annotated, more precisely defining each step. Thus the form's clipped "Getting chain on and tightened," he wrote, "includes the running of hoist or crane to where it is wanted and continues until the chain is drawn tight."

Through time study, Taylor was tearing work apart, then putting it back together in new, presumably more efficient form. He was scarcely the first foreman to come along intent on securing efficiencies; that was always part of the job. But at Midvale it was soon no longer the foreman's job. The observations, measurements, and analysis needed to set piece rates became the job of a distinct "rate-fixing" department.

Presumably, once a clerk had finished adding up his columns of figures, the time needed to machine a tire or overhaul a boiler no longer warranted discussion or debate. This, after all, was science; the numbers spoke for themselves. How could there be back talk or grumbling in the face of mathematical exactitude? But there always was. Even at the beginning, Taylor wrote, "there was naturally great opposition to the Rate-Fixing Department, particularly to the man who was taking time observations."

Over the years, Taylor's defenders would point to his sense of fair play. So ingrained was it, the story goes, that when as a young man he went to dances he'd consciously alternate the pretty with the plain among his partners. At Midvale, Taylor must soon have realized that to work under another man's unremitting gaze, timed like a racehorse all the while, might not be pleasant, and that to do a job the way another man set down—with tools he specified, at a pace he established—inflicted injury on men accustomed to deriving pleasure and pride from their work.

That the pace had been scientifically determined didn't matter. Why work more industriously to reach the new standard? Just because the numbers added up? "It is one thing to know how much work can be done in a day," wrote Taylor, "and an entirely different matter to get even the best men to work at their fastest speed or anywhere near it."

And not just because the man had to sweat and strain harder; sometimes, after a time-study man had finished, the job was actually easier, at least physically. Later, Taylor denied that more arduous work was ever demanded of the men in his shops. Scientific management meant improved methods, standardized practices, better-maintained machines. Management did its own job better, and that let the men produce more with perhaps only an extra dollop of diligence, not harder work.

Privately, Taylor was more candid. A few years later, talking to a Midvale visitor, Frank Steele, he said, in Steele's words, that "no man will continue working at the top of his speed under high pressure ('busting himself all day long,' as Mr. Taylor expressed it), without some inducement." And later, in a talk to a group of industrialists, he defined this inducement as what "you had to pay to an ordinarily capable man, a first class man, to get him to work like the devil."

Perhaps, in Taylor's mind, this didn't mean harder work. And yet, to yield to instruction card and stopwatch, to keep relentlessly on task, took something out of you that the old, looser ways didn't. A machinist who worked at Midvale after Taylor left, Harry J. Ruesskamp, told the Special House Committee in 1912 that Taylor's methods at Midvale impaired the worker's "nervous condition":

He is irritable at the least thing among his fellow workmen. . . .
One fellow said that his wife told him that if he didn't soon change
his tactics she would leave him. . . . The continuous strain is
wearing, and he is educated that he dare not waste a movement
which would be detrimental to the company.

The work itself might be no more physically demanding, but somehow, by day's end, it felt as if it were. Going strictly by somebody else's say-so, rigidly following directions, doing it by the clock, made Taylor's brand of work distasteful. You had to do it in the one best way prescribed for you and not in your old, idiosyncratic, if perhaps less efficient way. And many workmen didn't like that.

So what do you do if you wish people to work harder, faster, under conditions repellent to them? You do what Taylor had seen his father do at the storm-wrecked bridge at Finstermunz. You pay them.

～

It was in all probability during the month of June, 1884, that Mr. Chas. V. Shartle called at my home in Philadelphia and stated that Mr. Fred W. Taylor of Germantown wanted to meet Mr. Shartle and myself at the home of a mutual friend, Mr. Jos. B. King, also living in Germantown, on the following Sunday morning, to submit and discuss a new system of cooperative management.

William Fannon, the author of this recollection, and Charles Shartle were well versed in shop ways. Shartle, twenty-two, had served an apprenticeship as a machinist, worked until recently at Philadelphia's venerable Southwark Foundry and Machine Company and would go on to a career as an inventor and entrepreneur. Young Fannon, too, was an experienced machinist. Joseph King was head of the Midvale machine shop under Taylor, who by now was chief engineer in all but title. Would the two men leave their current jobs, Taylor wanted to know, and join him at Midvale?

They did. "Mr. Taylor seemed to inspire confidence in us," Fannon recalled. He was not merely offering them a job but describing a new kind of job, or at least a new way of being paid for it. "Mr. Taylor presented his proposition with great force, so much so that Mr. Shartle and I talked of nothing else on our way home."

Even as a boy, Fannon had worked on piece rate, threading carriage bolts, his pay fixed at so much per thousand bolts. Right before meeting Taylor, at another job, he had had a piece rate cut from under him; the boss simply came around and declared, in Fannon's bitter memory, "that we were making more money than he was." So on that bright Sunday morning when Taylor described a system that would end such abuses, Fannon paid attention. In Taylor's scheme, the rate would be established scientifically, not by whim, leaving the employer no grounds for cutting it. And there was another twist: in the new system there was not one rate but several.

A system of "accumulative rates," Fannon called it, but he was the only one who ever did; Taylor called it the differential rate. You didn't earn a set amount per piece; you earned an amount that depended on your output for the whole day: thirty-five cents per piece, say, for producing less than what Taylor's science decreed, fifty cents for exceeding it.

This was generous or brutal, depending on how you looked at it. Up to the cutoff point, you earned so much per piece. But past it, you earned the higher figure—and not just for that first tire or axle but for the whole day's work. Result: an almost irresistibly seductive inducement to work harder and more efficiently.

Taylor was not the first to install piece rates at Midvale or the first to crow over the increased production he got with them. Plainly, he owed much to Charles Brinley who, long before Taylor's coming, had banned work on verbal orders and instituted a system of written notes that anticipated Taylor's instruction cards. Likewise, he had installed piece rates. For instance, men known as guide rollers making a fixed $2.67 a day in April 1875 were earning 10.15 cents per eight-hundred-pound tire in July 1876. Under piecework, cost per pound dropped from two-and-a-quarter cents to one-and-a-quarter cents. At some point, Brinley had apparently even flirted with a differential rate.

But the threshold in Taylor's scheme was much higher than anyone had ever dreamed of. And why not, Taylor might have shot back. Had he not established it scientifically, through his stopwatch studies? He knew just what the machines could do, just what the men could do. He supplied the right tools; they had only to use them. He supplied precisely detailed instructions; they had only to follow them.

His time studies had convinced Taylor that whereas his men were rough-turning between three and five axles a day—a showing impressive enough that lathe manufacturers sent prospective customers to watch—they could do ten with no great pain. This was "a most fanciful and chimerical air-castle," said William Sellers, in Taylor's telling. "I know you are a fool and I want to prove it to you, and the only way I can prove it to you is to let you go ahead and fail." So Taylor picked out the best machinist in the shop, promised him 40 percent over his regular pay, and demanded that he turn ten axles, each of which required the removal of some eighty pounds of steel.

Impossible, the man replied. Taylor insisted he try. "The man immediately began to 'show off,' " Taylor recalled, "loosening up his tool and machine, so as to make a terrible racket and flying around himself, until the perspiration fairly rolled off him." Six axles a day was it; he could do no more. "In the meantime," according to another account, "the whole shop had heard of this performance, and began to have all sorts of fun at the expense of Mr. Taylor and his new idea."

After two weeks, the time Taylor had given the man to get up to speed, six was still all he could do. So he was fired.

Other men assigned the task suffered similar fates. Once they managed to meet the standard, they felt, Taylor was sure to cut their rate, however fervent his claim to the contrary. But finally, one man with a family who had recently bought a house, and could ill afford to lose his job, was given the task and did it.

It could be done; you just had to do it Taylor's way.

That was the beginning. The differential rate's "effect in increasing and then maintaining the output of each machine to which it was applied was almost immediate, and so remarkable that it soon came into high favor, with both the men and the management," Taylor wrote later. Fannon recalled that by the time he left Midvale in 1887, men previously earning $1.50 per day turning axles earned double that and produced two to three times as much work.

In history's long sweep, the differential rate warrants only a footnote; Taylor himself never placed undue stock in it, viewing it largely as a temporary expedient. Later, many other payment schemes would be advanced, each worth a paper in a technical journal, each with its own merits and failings, and Taylor would be able to discuss them with equanimity. At least once, he would be disappointed when engineers hearing one of his papers responded only to the differential rate and not to the larger principle, of work broken down into its elements and timed individually as a basis for setting piece rates.

But there was one other principle, which Taylor had set out in capital letters in that same paper: "MEN WILL NOT DO AN EXTRAORDINARY DAY'S WORK FOR AN ORDINARY DAY'S PAY." You had to pay them more.

How much more?

Maybe earning fifty cents per piece, a worker could take it easy, turn four or five axles, and come home with a respectable $2.00 or $2.50 for the day. How much more would you have to pay him to keep him on track, day after day, doing the job precisely as it was laid out for him to do, and turn out ten per day? $2.75? $3.00? $5.00? Maybe no amount of money would do.

Taylor had the answer. It was not, he would write with a shrug of sarcasm years later, "a subject to be theorized over, settled by boards of directors sitting in solemn conclave, nor voted upon by trade unions." Rather, it was dictated by "human nature," and he had established it, by trial and error, through experiments into human nature. Indeed, Taylor told the Commission on Industrial Relations, meeting in the Shoreham Hotel in Washington, D.C., less than a year before his death, it had been made the object of what he regarded as a scientific study.

Back at Midvale, he had approached half a dozen men and made them a deal: they were to perform a particular job for which they would receive a 15 percent premium. The hitch? They had to do it in precisely the way Taylor decreed. "Mind you," he emphasized, "you are now subject to limitations you were not subject to before. Someone [will now come and tell you] just how fast you are to do things and how you have to do them." That, he realized, as he told the commissioners, "is disagreeable. No one likes that." The feeds and speeds at which the machines ran were no longer their business but were handed down to them from the planning department. "When we tell you we want you to use such and such feed and such and such speed," Taylor has himself telling the men, "we want you to use it." But in the end—it was simple justice, was it not?—they were free to reject the whole scheme. At the end of six or eight months, they could go back to the old way, at the old wages. Or they could continue in the new way, at the new wages.

It was their decisions that formed the data of Taylor's experiment. Because, in addition to the group of men earning 15 percent more, he set up other groups paid 20, 25, 30, 35 percent more. What would it take to keep them happy? How much to buy them off? That's what the experiment was designed to reveal.

And he found out. Fifteen percent wouldn't do it; at the end of the allotted time, most of the men clamored to return to the old way. But the higher the premium, the more of them stuck with it; at 35 percent, he told the commissioners, "every man stuck and was satisfied with the new thing."

Other kinds of work, Taylor found over the years, demanded higher premiums. For example, "for work requiring especial skill or brains, coupled with close application, but without severe bodily exertion, such as the more difficult and delicate machinist's work," Taylor wrote in "Shop Management," you might have to pay 70 to 80 percent more; sometimes you'd actually have to double their wages. But there was always some point at which the higher pay overcame any resentment at keeping to the stern beat of Taylor's drum and not their own.

There it was, the Faustian bargain in embryonic form: You do it my way, by my standards, at the speed I mandate, and in so doing achieve a level of output I ordain, and I'll pay you handsomely for it, beyond anything you might have imagined. All you have to do is take orders, give up your way of doing the job for mine.

If you went along with the bargain, the promise went, efficiency improved, production and wages shot up. Indeed, many of the men made a lot more money. Yet "the rate-fixing department far more than paid for itself from the very start," Taylor reported later, though "it was several years before the full benefits of the system were felt." Years of refinement lay ahead, generations of industrial engineers to work out the details, to write books and treatises on it. But at Midvale, according to Taylor's account, the men were ultimately won over, leading to "the final result of completely harmonizing the men and the management, in place of the constant war that existed under the old system."

Here was a case of a no longer tenable thesis, the men's old work ways, butting up against its antithesis, Taylor's implacable demand that they abandon them, the conflict spewing forth a volcano of hateful sparks. Solution? A higher synthesis, one ushering in a new reign of peace and harmony, under a benign and ever just science.

In the great drama of Taylor's life, as he wrote the dialogue and stage directions later, he had overcome angry resistance and, through fairness and goodwill, triumphed, not for himself but for the sake of all. At Midvale, by about 1884, most of the essential elements of what would one day be scientific management were in place. Ahead lay a harmonious new industrial future.

Or that, anyway, was the idea.

The Taylors, in a photo taken early in the 1860s. From left, Fred; maternal grandfather, Isaac Winslow; brother, Winslow; father; mother; sister, Mary.

Frederick Taylor, at about fifty. Amiable and expansive Fred or biting and combative Mr. Taylor: It all depended on whether he was among friends or enemies, at peace or war, his will accepted or challenged.

The *W* in the ship's pennant, high atop the forward mast, stood for Winslow. Emily's father and uncle both made fortunes in whaling.

Franklin Taylor. "There is no written law that men should not smoke in drawing rooms, or come in with muddy boots or soiled clothes," he once wrote Fred. But "persons of gentle breeding" simply didn't do such things.

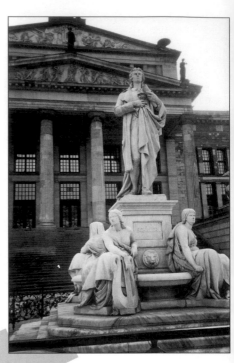

Right. Fred and his family traveled in Europe for three and a half years. Here, in a recent photo, a statue of the poet Schiller in front of the Schauspielhaus in Berlin, where the Taylors attended plays.

Boston March 30

Emily A Winslow

You have been duly appointed by the Massachusetts Anti-Slavery Society ~~at the~~ one of their delegates to represent the society at the Convention of the Friends of Freedom throughout the World, to be held in London on the twelfth day of June next.

Francis Jackson Pres't

Wm. Lloyd Garrison, Cor. Sec.

Above left. Like the "red diaper babies" of the American Left a century later, Emily Winslow Taylor grew up amid the radical politics of her family and their circle of friends. *Above.* When she was named one of a handful of American women to attend a world anti-slavery congress in London, Emily was seventeen years old.

Thanksgiving dinner at the Taylors, some years after Fred Taylor's death. Beginning seventh from the left stands Fred's brother, Win, his widow, Lou, and brother-in-law, Clarence Clark.

Finstermunz, in an old post card. The image at upper right shows where the bridge leading out of the Finstermunz pass was washed out after a storm, temporarily trapping Fred Taylor and his family in 1869.

Germantown Academy, which Fred attended during the Civil War, before going to Europe with his parents.

George Wentworth, Fred's mathematics instructor at Phillips Exeter, was a complex brew of "savagery and tenderness; of withering sarcasm and the refined gentleness of a woman."

Academically, Fred did well in the velvet-lined pressure cooker that was Phillips Exeter Academy, shown here in a recent photo. But it took so much out of him that he never finished.

An ad for Enterprise Hydraulic Works in a local engineering magazine, shortly after Fred left the small firm where he had served his apprenticeship as patternmaker and machinist.

A simple pattern, in two halves, made from wood, at left; and the final product, in cast iron, at right. When the two half-patterns are removed from the sand that's been tightly packed around them, a hollow is left that, filled with molten metal, creates the finished piece.

Pattern shop scene, in a recent photo taken at an industrial museum.

An ad for Wm. Butcher Steel Works, the company that became Midvale Steel, from around 1867.

The Taylor home on Ross Street (today known as Magnolia Street) in Germantown. Taylor lived here all the years of his apprenticeship and until his marriage in 1884 to Lou Spooner. Small row houses now occupy the site.

The boys of Midvale: company managers, around 188. Could that be Taylor, one row down from the top, middle, in front of the man with the high-brimmed hat?

Above. Midvale Steel Company, as shown in an insurance survey map in 1878, about the time Taylor started there. In the building complex numbered 10, center, towards the front, locomotive tires were made; the gabled structure part of it that is nearest the railroad tracks was the machine shop, shown in an interior view below, where they were cut to size. *Right.* H. L. Gantt, who joined Taylor at Midvale Steel and became one of his most devoted disciples.

A corner of the old Midvale machine shop, where Taylor did his first metal-cutting and time-study experiments.

The great steam hammer at work. Taylor designed this forging hammer, which delivered a 75-ton blow, in the mid-1880s. In color, the white cylindrical mass at the bottom would be yellow with heat.

Taylor's wife, Louise; detail from a formal portrait that now hangs in the Taylor Collection, Stevens Institute of Technology, Hoboken, N.J.

Taylor, around the time he worked at Midvale.

Taylor's fiefdom: The new Midvale machine shop, around 1887, which incorporated many of the innovations he had developed since the beginning of his metal-cutting experiments.

8

EDEN RECLAIMED

~

I N 1912, while giving testimony before the Special House Committee, Taylor was telling of the special state of mind that scientific management sought to cultivate among workers and managers. Perhaps it was this reference to inaccessible mental precincts that got Congressman Redfield thinking, because he asked Taylor how you could time a workman "in that part of the work that is purely mental?" What he actually did physically, before your eyes, was one thing. But how could you set a time for "making up his mind how work should be done or in reading and grasping a drawing?"

Instantly, Taylor was taken back forty years, to the big classroom on the first floor of the Third Academy Building at Phillips Exeter where Bull Wentworth held sway. There he had experienced "the first piece of time study that I ever saw made by anyone." Sitting behind his desk, Wentworth would assign Taylor and his fifty or so classmates a series of algebra or geometry problems, maybe five at a time, to work out in class. When finished, each boy was to raise his hand and snap his fingers to be acknowledged. But Wentworth never got through the whole roster. "That's enough," he'd say, about halfway through. "That will do."

His watch hidden behind the desk, he was timing them, Taylor realized, determining how long it took the average boy—twenty-fifth in a class of fifty, say—to complete the problems. He'd compare that boy's time with how long he, Wentworth, took for them, and compute a ratio. In setting homework assignments, he'd use it to calculate backward from how long he needed for the problems. Why, Taylor had wondered, did it always take about two hours to complete his homework? Because Wentworth had set it up that way, through a form of time study.

Indeed, even in time-study sheets that Taylor drew up in late 1883 or early 1884, he left room for the "purely mental" part of the work.

"Learning what is to be done," Taylor listed as the first job element to be timed. "This ends," his annotations to one such sheet explain, "when [the] man knows all that is to be done on the job." From almost the beginning, it seems, work's intellectual component was never hidden from Taylor's gaze, never something added merely as an afterthought.

This was one detail of time study that needed working out in the early days. Another was the unanticipated snags, trips to the bathroom, rests, and other inevitable delays that were the human equivalent of a machine's frictional losses. This was a kind of science, but it needed its fudge factors, too. So Taylor routinely factored one in. A percentage—typically about 25 percent but sometimes more—presumably transformed the mechanical summation of "elementary" times into a total that was fairer and more palatable to the workman.

Between about 1880 and 1884, Taylor worked out a hundred such details of time study, developed his differential rate, and continued his metal-cutting experiments. All the while, he was dealing with everyday shop crises, studying physics and mathematics at home, singing in choral groups, courting Louise Spooner, and jogging through the dark streets of Germantown. Taylor's was not an infinitely fertile mind, but he did have one powerful idea that, elaborated over the years, would ripple through modern life: a workplace ruled by science. Why now, when he was doing so much else, did he work out the insights that would set Taylorism, for good and ill, upon the world?

Maybe it was not despite the "so much else" but because of it. One clue resides in Wilfred Lewis's recollection that around this time Taylor's "play was so nicely fitted in with his work that one helped the other." A cross-fertilization at work? The various parts of his life vitalizing all the others?

During these years, in his early and mid-twenties, Taylor inhabited two worlds, that in which he had grown up and that of the shop floor. He played tennis at the club and worked ten- or eleven-hour days at the shop. He cared for his Germantown friends and the men who worked under him, too. He issued orders and added up columns of numbers but sometimes still felt the weight of a wrench in his hand, smelled burnt oil steaming up from metal cut too fast. He was a protege of William Sellers—but also of John Griffith.

Never again would the juxtapositions of his life seem so sharp and ever-present. If ever creative leaps were going to issue from Fred Taylor, it was now.

That Taylor turned to science for a solution to problems others might deem human, social, or economic need not unduly surprise us. He did have a scientific bent and so might naturally feel at home with metal-cutting experiments, time-measuring instruments, forms for recording data, and the other stigmata of science. To split up work into its components mirrored the intellectual tradition of calculus. To determine through "experiment" how much extra to pay his men took science just one bizarre step further.

Then, too, his thinking had hardly dropped out of the blue. We've seen how Brinley and Davenport had applied science to a steelmaking process traditionally almost alchemical in its mysteries. And almost a decade earlier, in 1872, Coleman Sellers *père*, chief engineer at Wm. Sellers & Company, and father of one of Taylor's friends from the Engineers Club, had argued that designers needed to build into their machine tools simple, standardized actions less vulnerable to the whims of the men who ran them, and in defiance of their prejudices. "Such motions as screwing up the spindle of the popper head, stopping and starting feeds, setting up the slide rests, etc., are motions of habit, and should, if possible, be uniform in all lathes." Withdraw the choice, in other words, from the workman's capricious hands. Such, then, was the spirit that informed the Sellers empire, and Taylor breathed it in.

A hundred years before, Adam Smith had studied the division of labor in his famous pin factory. In 1832, Charles Babbage had recorded the mechanical operations, costs, and quantities of pins made in another English factory. Since the French philosopher Auguste Comte came along in the mid-1800s, the notion that human activity might yield its secrets to science as obediently as did nature had entered the very spirit of the age.

His system, Taylor would one day observe, meant the "gathering in" by management of "all the great mass of traditional knowledge which in the past has been in the heads of the workmen." And just such gathering in was Taylor's intellectual style. He originated comparatively little, but he had sensitive antennae for what was in the air, picking up the slightest currents, amplifying them, and synthesizing them into something new.

Like the Brooklyn Bridge then rising in New York, he took slim steel wires of thought and practice and wove them into a thick, muscled cable: Taylorism.

~

None of this, then—the turn to science for a solution to his problems in the shop, while he was busy with so much else besides—seems terribly difficult to understand. What remains to answer is a deeper question, Why did he so relentlessly seek a solution in the first place? Why did the hostility of those few men in the Midvale machine shop trouble him so much?

After Taylor was named gang boss and foreman, shop tensions might have dissipated in any number of ways. Taylor could have capitulated from the start, meekly gone along with the status quo, countenanced soldiering, and enjoyed the men's goodwill, while finding some way to placate his superiors. He could have learned to charm and wheedle cooperation from them, and similarly avoided a fight. In time-honored foremanly fashion, he could have simply slugged it out with them, bludgeoning them until he got what he wanted. He could have joined battle, lost, and opted for some face-saving rapprochement.

Whatever the case—victory for one side, or the other, or a compromise—that, presumably, would have been the end of it. But Fred Taylor won—got more work out of his men—yet came away shaken. In a sense, he felt the sting of the biblical admonition, What shall it profit a man to gain the whole world but lose his soul? His victory had been a Pyrrhic one, costing too much in the lost friendship of the men.

But not, in his mind, only of the men at Midvale. He had worked there only briefly before his promotion, perhaps too briefly to form strong ties. Rather, it was the four years of his apprenticeship, only just past, that haunted him. Taylor would later give contradictory accounts of just how long he worked at the lathe before being named gang boss. A normal fading of memory? Maybe. But just as likely, his brief time alongside the men at Midvale ran together with his years at the pump works. To us, a century later, his life might seem to divide naturally between Enterprise Hydraulic Works and Midvale Steel. But this split may have meant less to him than another: between an early, idyllic period, comprising both his apprenticeship and his first few months at Midvale, and a second, terribly painful period that began when he was made gang boss.

At the pump works, divisions between management and workers would have seemed slight compared to those at much larger Midvale. Patternmaker John Griffith lived for a while in the same building, across the street from the shop, as William Jones, one of the owners. At least in Fred's memory, the pump works may have seemed like one big happy, if patriarchal, family. There, after an initial adjustment, he was one of the boys. By his own account, he soldiered and cussed with them, working and learning by their side. If only in retrospect, it must have seemed to him idyllic, a kind of personal Eden.

He was cruelly ejected from paradise the day he became a boss at Midvale. Then began the ugly fight he would recount all his life, the palm-sweating responsibility, the ache of facing down angry men whose scowling faces had once borne smiles. Might a nostalgia have overtaken him, a yearning for a sweeter time just past? In the pattern room at the pump works, and perhaps again briefly at Midvale, he had won acceptance, maybe genuine warmth. Then, as gang boss, he had lost it all. And he was determined to get back what he once had, to make his "friends" in the shop his friends once more.

In Taylor's recollections of this period, he insists repeatedly that only as their demanding boss, duty-bound to represent management, did the men bear him ill will; that when he talked with them man to man, he commiserated with them, offered them advice, as one of them; that he truly was their friend, and they his. Plainly, the split between the two roles was painful. He would spend the rest of his life trying to transcend it.

Some of his earliest co-workers at Midvale later took a sort of proprietary pride in Taylor. "They boasted," Copley reported, "that he had told them he cared more for them than for any of his later men, because, they said, 'we were his first pals.'" But now, as gang boss and foreman, his "first pals" were his enemies. *I was a young man in years, but I give you my word I was a great deal older than I am now with the worry, meanness, and contemptibleness of the whole damn thing.*

How many, over the years, had stood in something like Taylor's shoes? How many, named foreman and charged with getting out the work, had turned to harsh language and harsher actions? How many felt uncomfortable in their new positions as they sought to balance their loyalty to their friends among the workmen with that to the company that paid their salaries?

But Taylor alone, it seems, was driven enough to try to reconcile the irreconcilable, to earn the plaudits of his superiors, ruthlessly eliminating the work practices that inhibited production, while also enjoying the friendship of the men. What colossal conceit, what sheer hubris, in the idea that he could have both! Perhaps only someone as favored by circumstances as he, with the deepest reserves of self-assurance, who had been raised to expect from life nothing less than everything, could have thought it possible.

Taylorism grew out of Frederick Winslow Taylor's attempt to reclaim a lost Eden. In his mind, an impersonal arbiter—cool, neutral science—would step in, take the hands of workman and boss, whisper truth to each, and return them gently to the garden to live in peace.

9

A MECHANICAL HEAVEN

≈

O N MAY 3, 1884, at the old, octagonal, brick Unitarian Church at Tenth and Pine streets in Philadelphia, Fred Taylor and Louise Spooner were married by eighty-two-year-old Dr. William Henry Furness, a prominent abolitionist minister, in one of the last weddings he ever performed. "How proud I was to walk up the aisle of the church on the arm of my handsome father," Lou wrote, "and to find Fred waiting for me." The wedding party repaired to the Spooner home, at 1430 Spruce Street, a block south of the Academy of Music, near the heart of proper Philadelphia around Rittenhouse Square. From there, under a spray of rice, it would have been off to the station for their honeymoon, but Lou's trunk and trousseau had been left behind, so it was back to the house and a fevered rush to catch the train. "My first feelings of jealousy came at Niagara Falls," she wrote later, "where Fred's fascination and interest in the power of the falls seemed greater than in me."

Back in Germantown, they moved into a house on Locust Street, not far from Taylor's parents, that Lou set about decorating in blues and yellows. Often, while Fred was at work, she would visit her in-laws for lunch, sewing, and the customary reading aloud. It was a hard time for her. Her hard-driving husband—he made, by one report, seven thousand dollars a year, the equivalent of a hundred fifty thousand or more today—was gone most of the day. And she may have quarreled with Fred's sister Mary who, later that year, married Fred's old friend and tennis partner Clarence Clark. "Those were the days when my nose was a little out of joint, awaking to the realization" that her husband's family might occasionally match "the only child of the Spooner family" in his affections.

While he had no particular moral scruple against drinking, Fred didn't drink, and Lou would later give that as one reason they were "not noted for gay dinners or many social activities." She apparently had but the flimsiest idea of how to run a house. Soon after they were married, a dinner for Fred's boss, Midvale superintendent Russell Davenport, was cause for acute embarrassment. In their newly decorated dining room, alive with rich, warm reds, the grand repast consisted of three meager chops.

Fred didn't rub it in. Indeed, during their married life he mostly pampered her. On their trips to the north woods, Lou wrote, "Walks of over twelve miles, and carries through the wild woods were strenuous for the young bride. Result: a chair with poles must be constructed and guides to carry her to the lake, where a 'lean-to' had been built in preparation for our camping out." At home, Lou told a French interviewer later, her husband would apply

> scientific method to the simplest details of domestic life. He came
> to establish a theory for cooking eggs in their shells, for making
> creams and pies. When I told him that I liked sorrel, he interested
> himself in the various species of this plant, in its properties and
> preparation,

and other such matters. "One could not live with a nature like Fred's," she observed at another time, "without its dominating one's whole life."

As to his work at Midvale, she knew little. It was only on reading his testimony before the Special House Committee, she wrote after he was dead, "that I realized the strain he was under." Mostly, he was just gone, from six, or seven, or eight in the morning until seven at night, the intervening hours spent making Midvale into what one of his men there would call "a regular little mechanical heaven."

∼

Taylor was bringing to the machine shops at Midvale, and increasingly to the rest of the works, a new paradigm of order, standardization, and system. For the very act of close looking, central to time study, revealed not only useless motions by the worker but also deficiencies in the machines, bottlenecks in the flow of material, and other impediments to production. It was as if once you decided to really look, there was no end to what you could find.

Midvale's lathes and boring mills, presumably state-of-the-art, now began to seem susceptible to improvement; each order for a new machine now invariably called for modifications. Sometimes, the company was "obliged," as Taylor wrote later, "to superintend the design of many special tools which would not have been thought of had it not been for elementary rate fixing," with its requisite time study.

One future disciple who later saw some of Taylor's innovations up close, King Hathaway, reported that the practice of marking cuts on a forging set on a special surface plate—to reduce the time needed for machining itself—was, at Midvale, extended "far beyond [that] prevailing even in the best shops of that day." Likewise, inspection methods, a visitor to Midvale wrote later, were made "as automatic as possible. The most careful thought was directed towards devising jigs, templates and gauges, so that the work of inspection should be reduced to a minimum."

Or take tool grinding. Metal-cutting experiments or no, tools still had to be reground, which meant removing the tool from the machine, wandering across the floor to the wheel and, squinting in the shop's gloom, grinding it down until it looked right. The Sellers company had devised a grinding machine to speed the process, but Taylor designed a better one, comprising, according to the patent, thirty "new and useful features." You mounted the tool in the machine along with a special template; when you pressed the template against a guide, the tool was correspondingly pressed against the wheel, its final contour thus automatically established. Later, after Taylor left, someone reported that "the grinding was all done by two young boys." Did the machinist miss his occasional stroll across the floor, the little break from the day's routine? No matter. The new practice was efficient, $3.00-a-day machinist's time replaced with that of a $1.25 boy.

As "master mechanic," one of the titles he held on his way up the Midvale ladder, Taylor had occasion to visit a large Philadelphia foundry, the I. P. Morris Company, where one old lathe dated from the 1820s. It was so worn and ragtag that only one man, who was in his seventies and had run it all his life, could get it to work. The company took perverse pride in the relic and liked to show it off, but Taylor would come away shaking his head. "A few more such old machines, and old men to run them," he wrote, and "the I. P. Morris Co. would soon cease to exist." Neither of them had much place in Fred Taylor's world.

Sometime in 1886, Taylor's assistant, George Sinclair, a twenty-five-year-old Stevens graduate who'd come to Midvale two years before, was asked to develop a system for managing the company's voluminous store of engineering drawings—no trifling task. A company the size of Midvale might have thousands of drawings, in a crazy quilt of different sizes. They'd get lost in the back of drawers, be gone when you needed them or get so dirty you couldn't use them. Now, Sinclair was being asked to improve on a Dewey decimal–like plan being considered by Wm. Sellers & Company. Sinclair submitted his report, complete with samples of eight standard forms that the new system would use. Taylor came back with suggestions. All drawings should be kept not in two but three forms: the original pristine tracings from which blueprints could be made, a set of blueprints in the drawings office, and a third for the shop, the only ones allowed to get dirty.

But we need not fret over the details. What is extraordinary is that the control and care of drawings were being studied at all. Taylor was old enough to remember the legendary John Fritz, an early steel pioneer, most of whose machinery drawings, Taylor would reminisce, "were done with a piece of chalk on the floor of the pattern room, or with a stick on the floor of the blacksmith shop." Fritz often didn't know what he wanted until he'd seen a pattern or a model made. "One of his favorite sayings, whenever a new machine was finished was, 'Now, boys, we have got her done, let's start her up and see why she does not work.' "

It was a long way from sketches in the sand to a study, a report, a system, devoted to keeping track of drawings. But that was the treatment everything at Midvale was getting. Nothing was too slight to escape study and improvement. Not just the grinding of tools, the care of belting, or the oiling of machine tools, but also such intangibles as methods, processes, ways of issuing work orders, or returning materials. Such details, wrote Taylor, normally left to the judgment of foreman and workmen, could now be seen, under the lens of scientific rate fixing, "to be of paramount importance in obtaining the maximum output, and to require the most careful and systematic study and attention."

Taylor was dragging Midvale into a new industrial epoch where John Fritz's way, the messy, casual way of the old shops, would no longer do. Chordal's letters to the *American Machinist* were filled with horror stories of industrial disarray. Castings and patterns lie forlornly about. Material is nowhere at hand when needed. Components that ought to fit don't; a pulley fits one two-inch shaft but not another made by the same machine shop. The Sellers thread is supposed to be standard? Well, writes Chordal, "if I order screws or taps from half the screw shops, I never know what I am going to get." Brown & Sharpe, the machine-tool maker, reviews the existing system of standard gauges, industry's master measuring sticks, and finds they jump from size to size in weird, irregular increments. If American coinage were similarly haphazard, observes Chordal, denominations might be 5 cents, 7, 20, 60, $1.00, $2.00, $2.15, $2.18. All these, and a hundred thousand other obstacles to productivity, testified to a want not of mechanical knowledge but of something else entirely—of system, organization, management.

Taylor had probably read Chordal, either in the *American Machinist* or in compilations of his work appearing in book form after 1880; one Taylor notebook contains a printed list of shop practices, dated March 1880, very likely snipped from a Chordal "letter." The real Chordal, James W. See, was no mere observer. A charter member of the American Society of Mechanical Engineers, he would in 1888 present a long paper on the need for industrial standards. One trio of management historians would go so far as to call him "among the earliest originators of management thought in the late 19th century."

Many of Chordal's wry, superbly articulated views probably influenced Fred Taylor; certainly they were shared by him. More than mere mechanical proficiency and hard work figured in the success of a shop, Chordal wrote. It needed "system" as well, by which he meant "not work, but ... simply a law of action for reducing work. It does not require special executors, but permits few to accomplish much. It loads no man with labor, but lightens the labor of each by rigidly defining it." It was this spirit that Taylor was trying to bring, on a dozen fronts at once, to Midvale.

Time and again Taylor had seen "a workman shut down his machine and hunt up the foreman to inquire, perhaps, what work to put into his machine next, and then chase around the shop to find it or to have a special tool or template looked up or made." Whose fault was that, the worker's? Not at all. It was neither poor workmanship to blame, nor poor machinery, but poor management. Management's duty was to keep tools in good condition, belts maintained, machines oiled, standards established, the right men assigned the right jobs, work flowing smoothly to each. When it failed, the shop failed, however modern its lathes or able its lathesmen.

The point man for any managerial innovation was always the foreman, forever hunkering down on the battle-tortured front line between worker and boss. "There are more bad skillful workers than good ones," wrote Chordal, referring to those lacking in judgment or common sense, "and the thing must be equalized by supervision. The foreman is to supply the judgment, and the workman the skill." But how? Left virtually on his own by higher management, he was hopelessly overworked, perennially distracted. He had to parcel out the work, discipline the men, fire them up, keep track of their hours, resolve conflicts, solve technical problems, see to the maintenance of machinery—and always keep production rolling. No one could possibly do it all.

It was a case of finite time and brainpower too broadly dissipated, Taylor came to think. And sometime before 1883, he began to break the traditional foreman's job into five specialized functions, each assigned a different man: an instruction-card clerk, time clerk, inspector, traditional gang boss, and shop disciplinarian; this last role Taylor himself normally assumed. Later, he'd add three others.

All this went counter to the received wisdom of nineteenth-century business, which emphasized keeping the proportion of "nonproductive" people—clerks, draftsmen, managers, and the like—to a minimum; you wanted everybody out there producing, as few people as possible back in the office. This, Taylor concluded, was all wrong. A factory needed intelligence and stores of knowledge, brains to direct the hands. It needed a sharp, permanent split between thinking and doing.

~

The compulsive traits evident from Taylor's childhood—his pickiness over game rules, his carefully measured strides over the hills and fields of Germantown, his preoccupation with the highest, biggest, and best of everything—now found an appropriate outlet. The one best cricket bat of his youth was becoming the one best Midvale. His attraction to the larger-than-life and the operatically grand, like the frescoes in Berlin that recounted the history of Western civilization, now found expression in the great, manifold system he was building, study upon study, rule upon rule, at Midvale.

Perversely, Taylor's time studies, rate setting, and standardizing, his whole baroque assemblage of methods, rules, and orders, sometimes usurped the daily work of the shop itself. Once, Davenport gave the machine shop a rush order for a government job. But when he showed up next morning, expecting to find it finished, he found instead a single bleary-eyed machinist who'd been working all night under the eye of a time-study man, Davenport's rush job forgotten.

Taylor ruled that any man starting on a machine had to oil it, a fifteen-minute job. Further, he had to replace the round-headed plugs in its hundred or so oil holes with square-headed ones, or vice versa, thus signaling the task done. "Tin tags and plugs," the men sneered, and later one old Midvale hand would dismiss the system as "successful only in increasing the number of cut-out [ruined] bearings and making its users finished liars." Once, recounted Charles Shartle, a gear broke and needed replacement. He kicked a tire off the boring mill, mounted a gear in its stead, bored it out to size, but did not stop to reoil the machine—it had been oiled an hour before. Taylor found out and stormed at him, stressing the inviolability of the system, and slapped a fine on him. By mid-1885, faced with "the antipathy of the men to any innovation," which sounds like Taylor but was actually one of his assistants, Taylor was assigning a single man to lubricate all the shop's two dozen or so machine tools.

Shartle admired Taylor but bristled under what he experienced as his despotism. "I remember he said to me many times," he recalled, " 'I have you for your strength and mechanical ability, and we have other men paid for thinking.' " Shartle, who went on to become a successful inventor and manufacturer, didn't like that. "I would never admit to him that I was not allowed to think," he recalled. "We used to have some pretty hot arguments just over that point."

They had some pretty hot arguments over everything. Once, toward quitting time, a planer taking heavy cuts on a casting pulled free of its brick foundations—which meant it needed to be reset on new ones, an all-night job. Shartle wanted to jack up the machine, set long anchor bolts in the foundation to line up with holes in the planer propped above it, lay the machine back down, tighten down the nuts, and saw off the projecting bolts. Taylor wanted to move the planer clear out of the way and position the anchor bolts by means of a template. As usual, they fought. "I think he was about as mad as ever I saw him," Shartle recalled. But so urgent was getting the planer working that this time Taylor yielded. Shartle, doing it his way, had it running the next morning when Taylor arrived. A smile of approval? Hardly. Taylor pulled Shartle into his office "and [tried] to drive into my dull brain again the reasons for obeying orders."

Taylor was forever indulging in what Copley calls "violent outbreaks during which he would indeed exhaust the resources of the English language—and the German, too," for the benefit of some of the men. Once, Taylor designed a piston for the tire-rolling mill with special grooves for its leather gaskets, and ordered a template made to help in machining it. But, as William Fannon wrote of the incident to Taylor years later, the template "did not meet with your entire approval and you scolded me like a 'Dutch uncle.' "

One mechanic complained to Taylor of being ill-treated, declaring he would endure it no longer. This incurred not Taylor's sympathy but his wrath. "What I took from Mr. Taylor that day I never would have taken from another human being. I was a coward, a damned quitter. I had no guts. I was a little yellow dog. Never before had I heard, much less had directed at me, such a stream of abuse." But he did take it. "I could not help but feel," he said later, "that Mr. Taylor meant it for my own good."

No one questioned Taylor's sincerity or good intentions, but the gap between his personality and his professed goal of workplace harmony seemed vast and inexplicable. At the slightest sign of resistance he'd resort to verbal bludgeoning. "Sometimes," Fannon wrote, "when

Mr. Shartle or I discussed a proposition with him, he would act as if we had no right to oppose him or argue the matter." Taylor's actions "seemed to be of the most contradictory character. He was working hard and quarreling with many people to establish a unique system the aim of which was to make a permanent peace between employer and employee." Harmony, it seems, would come when everybody did it his way, and until then he could abide a struggle of any degree or duration.

Some snickered over Taylor's excesses and eccentricities. A Midvale friend, Theophilus Stork, recalled that at first Taylor's time studies struck everyone in the shop as "a hopeless and useless undertaking." In 1883, Taylor had taken on an assistant, Emlin Hare Miller, to help with his stopwatch studies. And it was probably Miller that Stork had in mind when he referred to

> a young cadet of industry, a student just out of the technical
> school, with a stop watch and a huge diagram before him,
> stationed by Taylor opposite a workman to note minute by
> minute, aye, almost second by second, each and every movement.
> Now he takes up a tool; click goes the stop watch, and down on the
> prepared diagram goes the number of seconds that are required for
> the movement; and so on, day after day, month after month, until
> stacks of these diagrams of the time required for the workman to
> do the simplest act were collected.

A hint of scorn lurks in this recollection. It wasn't just that Taylor did time studies; it was the uncompromising way in which he did them—did everything. Everybody thought he was a crank. Carl Barth, a Norwegian immigrant then working at Sellers as a draftsman, recalled the smirks whenever Taylor came around to check on the design of a machine that he wanted for Midvale, because of his "assertive ways of criticizing."

It was easy to make fun of Fred Taylor and what some called his "monkey mind." Yet he managed to extract the best from everybody; on that, all agreed whether they liked him or not. "I do not believe I ever met a man who could get more out of me than Mr. Taylor did," Shartle wrote. "The time I spent with him was of more benefit to me than [any] other man I ever came in contact with."

Some of his admirers would later term him a true democrat, by which they meant he treated workers equally, with consummate fairness, which he did. But being a "democrat," in this narrow sense, never blunted the emperor in him. His job was to give orders, others' to execute them; his to think, others' to do. His combativeness, his almost preternatural self-assurance, his certitude about what constituted the one best way, lent him all the personality trappings of a tyrant.

Not that he looked the part. In photos from this period, the flinty gaze is not yet apparent. He was still sweet-looking; there was something laughably incongruous between the steel of his temperament and the softness of his appearance that made him a little easier to take.

Besides, he brought an element of theater to Midvale: Silly, overly elaborate rules and procedures that sometimes bordered on farce; frequent shouting matches, tantrums and dramatic monologues, workmen at their lathes "performing" for the prickly director.

Taylor's personality figured large in all he achieved at Midvale. "I cannot help but believe," wrote Shartle, "that we ... worked as hard as we did, just because we wanted to please Mr. Taylor." He never understood that for all his system's science and method, his success owed as much to the vigor of his speech and the strength of his will.

In 1894, after Taylor had left Midvale, but with most of his innovations still in place, a visitor reported that "the company has made money, [has] greatly enlarged [its] business, and [has] a reputation in this country second to none for doing good work." Machining a locomotive tire, he reported, was now done in one fifth the time. Once it had taken ten hours to turn a particular cannon projectile; now it took an hour and a half. Twelve hundred people worked at Midvale, but the figure would have been closer to two thousand were it not for Taylor. At one point, monitoring piece rates kept eight clerks busy; now, with "their files ... full of data on which to base estimates," the company could get by on many fewer. Virtually all of Midvale was on piece rate, regulated by time studies. "They even sweep out the shops by piece rate."

The visitor, George F. Steele, was not wholly unbiased. From 1891 to 1893 he had worked with Taylor at another company and come away a believer. Now, as vice president of the Chicago-based Deering Harvester Company, he was reporting back to his employer about

piece-rate systems he had observed on a trip to factories in Schenectady, Lowell, and Philadelphia.

Midvale was the showcase of his sixteen-page typewritten report.
The piece-work system "which appeals to me most strongly," he wrote,
"is known as the Differential Rate System. This system is employed in
the shops of the Midvale Steel Works, at Philadelphia, Pa., with most
remarkable results." He explained its workings, told something of its
introduction, all without a critical word. "When I visited the Midvale
shops," he wrote,

> I was much interested in noting the evident interest the men took
> throughout the entire works, and from the conversation I heard
> between Mr. Taylor and common workmen in the shops, I am
> thoroughly convinced that the men themselves are heartily in favor
> of the system. The entire force . . . down to the humblest piece rate
> workers are heart and soul believers in the Midvale System.

Whether he knew it or not, Steele was serving as a publicist for Fred
Taylor and his ideas. The whole report bears Taylor's stamp. Taylor
had toured the works with him, introduced him to workmen, pointed
out this or that feature, supplied figures, told his story, impressed upon
Steele his own very personal vision.

By the spring of 1886, Midvale was well on its way to becoming
what Steele would see in 1894. Though Taylor was gone by then, Midvale had not simply disappeared into his past. It was the living embodiment of his most passionate convictions.

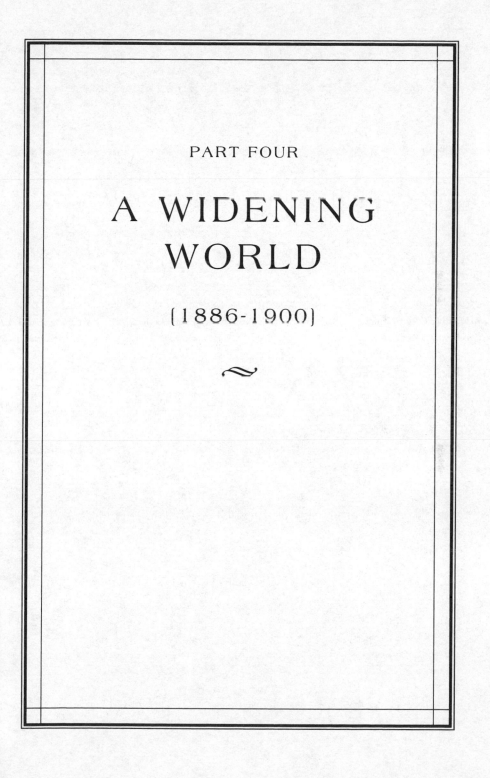

PART FOUR

A WIDENING
WORLD

[1886-1900]

1

THE SIGN OF THE DOLLAR

∼

O N THE AFTERNOON OF WEDNESDAY, MAY 16, 1886, before members of the American Society of Mechanical Engineers gathered in a large hall in downtown Chicago, Henry Towne delivered a paper, "The Engineer as an Economist," that some historians would look back to as the founding document of a new science of management. "The monogram of our national initials, which is the symbol of our monetary unit, the dollar," Towne began, "is almost as frequently conjoined to the figures of an engineer's calculations as are the symbols indicating feet, minutes, pounds or gallons."

Every engineer knew that dollars-and-cents issues figured in his work, right along with boiler pressures and stress factors. But who, asked Towne, ever addressed them? No professional society did, no journal. Old-line manufacturers slogged along on their own, "receiving little benefit from the parallel experience of other similar enterprises." New companies, meanwhile, reinvented the wheel, learning nothing from the past.

This, declared Towne, must stop. Shop management was just as important as engineering itself, and everyone knew it. "The *management of works* has become a matter of such great and far reaching importance as perhaps to justify its classification also as one of the modern arts." And engineers—not just businessmen, clerks, and accountants—were the ones to make it into one.

Henry Robinson Towne, the young professional society's forty-one-year-old acting president, was the Towne of Yale & Towne, the lock maker. Son of a self-made man who would leave a million dollars to the University of Pennsylvania, Towne had served his apprenticeship with an old Philadelphia machine shop, became assistant superintendent, and during the Civil War worked on some of the new ironclad warships. Later, he went to Paris for six months, studied physics at the Sorbonne, then returned to Philadelphia and worked for William Sellers.

Sellers introduced him to Linus Yale, a Connecticut inventor who had once hoped to become a painter but whose fertile imagination erupted instead with the 'Yale Infallible Bank Lock," the "Yale Magic Bank Lock," and finally the modern pin-and-tumbler lock. Towne knew a good thing when he saw it and in October 1868 went into business with Yale to make them.

Two months later, his partner was dead of a heart attack suffered in a New York hotel room, and Towne, at twenty-four, was left alone with their bright plans. The company started with thirty workers; by the 1870s, it had several hundred; by the early 1890s, a few years after Towne's ASME talk, fourteen hundred. If the inventive genius behind its success was Yale's legacy, its management was Towne's. An engineering magazine would later hold it up as an exemplar of "successful shop management." "The yards inside the works are perfectly clean," the article noted, "not a dead leaf or a scrap of paper being allowed to lie on the ground."

Towne's Chicago paper was coupled with two others on kindred themes. One was by Henry Metcalfe, a thirty-nine-year-old army officer stationed at Watervliet Arsenal near Troy, New York, and author the previous year of an early text on workshop management. Metcalfe outlined a system for keeping track of work and material through a shop, using cards and routing slips. "Administration without records is like music without notes—by ear," he said. "Good as far as it goes . . . it bequeaths little to the future."

In the audience that spring afternoon was Fred Taylor, who had joined the ASME the year before. He had read Metcalfe's paper with interest, he said during the discussion, "as we at the Midvale Steel Co. have had the experience, during the past ten years, of organizing a system very similar" to his. But Metcalfe's system erred in leaving a checkbook of sorts—with sheets to fill in, tear out, and return to the central office—in the hands of the worker. "Any record," said Taylor, "which passes through the average workman's hands, and which he holds for any length of time, is apt either to be soiled or torn." So at Midvale, paper passed only between clerks, orders they wrote under a foreman's direction being locked up in bulletin boards behind glass doors, "so that the men can see but not handle them." Besides, Metcalfe's few cards just didn't go far enough. At Midvale, they used upward of two hundred printed forms.

Metcalfe's paper, and Towne's, contained no formulas, no details of machine design; they were about organizing things, watching over them, monitoring their costs. In this, they differed from anything engineers had heard before at professional meetings. Indeed, Towne's paper had been accepted only with misgivings by the society's publications committee. Critics said then, and would continue to say, that such matters were no fit concern of engineers.

Frederick Taylor, needless to say, was not among them; the three papers, especially Towne's, legitimized his natural bent. As a teenager with his family in Europe, he'd been preoccupied with the cost of things, with getting good value. The two papers constituting his Stevens thesis had dealt not only with cutting tools and blowers but also with their costs. His belting experiments, too, focused on costs more than on horsepower or coefficients of friction. Even the paper he was to present that evening, his first before the ASME, fell under the same heading; it was entitled "The Relative Value of Water Gas and Gas from the Siemens Producer, for Melting in the Open-Hearth Furnace." Henry Towne was urging that engineers deliberately bring to their work what Fred Taylor had always brought to everything: a preoccupation with cost, value, dollars and cents.

Over the years, Taylor would say repeatedly that his system had not emerged full-blown as theory, to be applied to practical problems only later, but, rather, that it had bubbled up from the cauldron of shop experience. "Scientific management at every step has been an evolution not a theory," he would say. "In all cases the practice had preceded the theory, not succeeded it."

But before it could become system, theory, or anything of the sort, Taylor's cherished "practice" had to become, as it were, self-conscious. And that, apparently, is what happened in Chicago. Later, Towne would say that nothing he'd done had inspired Taylor in his work. But, he allowed, "there appears to be some reason for the belief that my [Chicago] paper may have awakened him to a realization of the significance of his own work, to the realization of the fact that a new Science was in process of development."

2

NEW FACES

⌇

A T CHICAGO, Taylor's world had widened beyond lathes and locomotive tires. But any thought for a "new Science," Towne's or
any of his own making, would have to wait. For not long after his
return, Midvale—now like a family to him, if sometimes a fractious
one—began to unravel.

A tangled, long-standing suit by a previous coowner from the
Butcher years, who accused Sellers and Clark of having cheated him,
weakened the company enough to make it ripe for takeover. Late in
1886, the Charles Harrahs, father and son, bought a controlling
interest. Harrah the elder was a headstrong, luxuriantly bearded man
who had made and lost fortunes building shipyards, railroads, and
street railways in Brazil and Philadelphia. On March 29, 1887, the company's new Harrah-ruled board named Davenport manager, Aertsen
superintendent, Clarence Clark assistant superintendent, and Taylor
engineer—a seeming endorsement of the status quo. But things were
not as they were. The elder Clarks and the Wrights had sold off their
stakes. Sellers retained his but, quarreling with the new owners, was
debarred from active management.

The Harrahs were quick to assert authority, even on small matters:
"On and after Monday, April 4th," the order went out, "no smoking
will be allowed in any part of the works by any employees of the works,
excepting between the hours of 12 noon and 1 pm on the day turn, and
11:30 p.m. and 12:30 a.m. on the night turn." On July 23, 1888: "Please
note that the President requires all employees who have business with
the Main Office to appear in the Main Office always with coats on."

Taylor remained on good terms with the new owners. He later
included the senior Harrah on his list of "great industrial leaders," right
beside William Sellers. And later correspondence between Taylor
and the younger Harrah, who took over when his father retired in
1888, suggests a shared delight in sarcasm and playful invective. Taylor

probably suffered little interference under the new regime; his compe-
tence was respected, his authority secure. To do his bidding, he later
said, he had "very many assistants and helpers, both in the drafting
room, on the engineering force, and in the practical execution of the
work." Among the brisk, written orders that pushed work through the
factory, Taylor's name appeared with increasing frequency, in, for
example, "blue orders" authorizing new construction:

> Blue Order No. 221, May 17, 1887
> Mr. Thompson:
> Erect 6 ton Yale and Towne trav. crane in M. S. per drawings &
> directions.
> In charge of Mr. Taylor.
> A per D,

which meant that Aertsen, at Davenport's direction, was ordering a
new traveling crane for the machine shop.

In July 1887, Joseph King, at whose house Fannon and Shartle had
first met Taylor three years before, was named the new head of the
machine shop. That same month, Taylor's assistant, George Sinclair,
left Midvale. But before he did, he recommended as his replacement
Henry Gantt, a prematurely bald young Johns Hopkins University
graduate from Maryland. Gantt had taught science, gone on to Stevens
to study engineering, worked as a draftsman, and taught manual
training back at his old prep school. Someone who knew him as a
teacher described him as "a keen, sharp-tongued chap, able and far-
visioned, but not too affable or suave." Five years Taylor's junior, he
started at Midvale in July 1887, stayed until 1893, was won over to
Taylor's ideas and became a disciple, his life and career forever
entwined with that of his mentor.

Taylor put Gantt to work on a vexing problem grown out of the
metal-cutting experiments. In principle, you could now calculate the
right cutting speed and feed for any job. But too often, the calculations
took so long that, had you simply gone with your guess and started cutting, you'd be done already. In 1887, data were typically represented
through graphs, charts, and other visual means. The point where two
curves intersected, for example, might spit out a number you could use
as starting point for the next step of the calculation. That worked, but

could be tedious and slow, especially when, as with speed-and-feed cal-culations, the solution hinged on many variables. Sinclair had spent a year or so working out formulas, graphing them and generating answers by shuttling back and forth between the graphs. But the proce-dure was "so exceedingly slow and laborious," Taylor wrote, as to make it useless. Gantt took up the problem, substituting logarithmic graph paper for the ordinary, evenly divided kind, which helped bring the whole range of solutions before them, not just a small piece of it. Applied to metal cutting it yielded, as Taylor wrote later, "quite rapid approximations."

Also demanding Taylor's attention in the three years following the Harrah takeover were the big cannon that Midvale was making for the navy. The problem was their sheer size. Only colossal hubris let you even think about making a huge steel ingot, white with heat, conform to some human whim of shape and design; and only brute force let you pound a piece of steel, square in cross section and heavier than any hundred men could lift, into a long thin tube with a hole down its middle. Until then, the government bought big cannon and other heavy forgings overseas, from Krupp in Germany or Whitworth in England. When it asked steel manufacturers in America about making them, all said they couldn't do it. "Like all other steel manufactories in the United States," the Cambria Iron Company wrote back, "we have no apparatus capable of forging the large ingots required for modern guns." The navy's new cannon needed a steam hammer bigger than anything America had. Taylor set about designing one for Midvale.

A steam hammer was just what it seemed: a many-tonned hammer lifted not by a man's muscled arm but by the force of steam. In its ear-liest incarnation, which went back to 1842 and James Nasmyth, a Man-chester, England, engineer, steam pressure applied to a piston lifted a heavy hammer. The steam's sudden release sent the hammer, by gravity alone, like a guillotine, crashing down on the work to be forged, each successive strike bringing it closer to final form. Soon, engineers learned to introduce steam to the opposite side of the piston just as the hammer began its fall, sometimes doubling the force contributed by gravity alone.

By the late 1880s there was nothing terribly mysterious about getting a steam hammer to deliver a blow of so many tons. The problems came in absorbing the shock. The hammer's Achilles' heel was its anvil and the foundation on which it lay; these garnered all the designer's attention. This florid account of a big English steam hammer (also used for forging cannon) dates from about the time Taylor designed Midvale's:

> Huge tablets of foot-thick castings alternate with concrete, and enormous baulks of timber, and lower down, beds of concrete, and piles driven deep into the solid earth, for a support for the uppermost plate, upon which the giant delivers his terrible stroke. . . . As the monster works—soberly and obediently though he does it—the solid soil trembles, and everything movable shivers, far and near, as, with a scream of the steam, our "hammer of Thor" comes thundering down, mashing the hot iron into shape as easily as if it were crimson dough, squirting jets of scarlet and yellow yeast.

Steam hammers, in short, tended to batter themselves to death.

Taylor familiarized himself with existing designs, borrowing features from several. But at first glance, his own might have seemed to offer little hope of withstanding its seventy-five-ton impact. The great steam hammer at the Royal Gun Factory at Woolwich, England, boasted a massive two-legged frame that loomed over the anvil like a Goliath with thick, muscled steel thighs straddling its fallen victim. Taylor's, a spidery collection of steel members, looked more like an overwrought erector set and, according to one account, "was greeted with misgivings and even ridicule."

But it seemed puny only compared to other steam hammers; it dwarfed the men who worked with it and scarcely fit the building within which it was housed. Its pretensioned oil-tempered steel bolts were four inches in diameter and twenty feet long—hardly toothpicks. Once up and running, an old hand recalled much later, you could hear the whistle of its exhaust across the neighborhood, "and its tremendous thump shook Tioga [the immediate neighborhood] off the map."

But it didn't shake itself to pieces the way other hammers did. The components of Taylor's hammer were designed to give, like a big spring—flexing, stretching, and recoiling rather than just enduring. And for a dozen years, long after he had left Midvale, Taylor's hammer pounded away, at triple the speed of other hammers, and with less upkeep and repair.

~

In the years following Henry Towne's Chicago paper, the shop floor at Midvale, for so long Taylor's home, was no longer his only one. A new member of the American Society of Mechanical Engineers, just past thirty, he began to be heard at its meetings. On December 2, 1886, in a large Stevens Institute lecture room, he got into a heated debate about his paper from the previous meeting in May. The following November, in Philadelphia, he commented on a colleague's paper about railroad car axles. Taylor was speaking up and in a larger, more visible forum, where he met engineers from around the country.

During this period, as if tying up loose ends from the past decade, he began applying for patents for some of his Midvale inventions. He had secured his first patent, for his spoon-shaped tennis racket, in early 1886. Later that year, just after the Harrah wind blew through Midvale, he filed for a patent on his tool-grinding machine; after he left Midvale, a Philadelphia machine shop, Arthur Falkenau, built and sold it. Over the next three years Taylor filed for, and ultimately received, patents for a boring and turning mill, a new kind of railroad car wheel, an improved chuck, a tool-feeding mechanism, and his big steam hammer. In June 1889, two months after getting the patent, he contracted with A. G. Spalding & Brothers, the sporting-goods supplier, to make and sell his special tennis nets.

Beginning around this time, Taylor had another sideline—his patented tennis net posts, from which he earned a 10 percent royalty. His business associate, who had them made up and shipped out, was John R. Griffith, head patternmaker at the pump works during Taylor's apprenticeship. Griffith worked out of the cellar of his house while moonlighting from a job he held at Midvale.

But many others among Taylor's old friends at Midvale were drifting away now. On May 9, 1887, one of Taylor's young lieutenants, William Fannon, left to go into business with Charles Shartle in Ohio. George Sinclair, as we've seen, left two months later. On September 20, Aertsen left for Homestead Steel. The following year, Davenport, after a moving farewell speech to the men, left for Bethlehem Steel. Meanwhile, the once-brotherly relations between Midvale and Sellers had ruptured; the Sellers drafting room, once a welcome and friendly second home to Taylor, was now off-limits.

However secure his relationship with the Harrahs, Midvale must no longer have felt the same to him. The old familiar faces and family feeling were gone. Indeed, Taylor might have felt that with Sellers, the Clarks, and James Wright no longer around, the ladder he'd been climbing at Midvale now led nowhere. When a wonderful opportunity came Taylor's way late in 1889, could he reasonably affect a lack of interest?

~

The events leading to Taylor's departure went back to 1884. In that year, Grover Cleveland, the staunchly reform-minded governor of New York State, was elected president. His new secretary of the navy was William Collins Whitney, a forty-three-year-old lawyer active in Democratic party politics who, fifteen years before, had married the sister of a Standard Oil multimillionaire. When Taylor met him, he was among the nation's most influential men, a friend of diplomats, an intimate of Roosevelts, Astors, and Adamses. He and his wife set new standards of lavish entertaining in the still provincial national capital. The Gilded Age that Mark Twain had immortalized in his 1873 novel of that name, with its intimations of vast wealth in the hands of new legions of industrialists, of government engorged on business influence and businessmen's money, found in Whitney its veritable incarnation.

This particular Gilded Ager was a thoroughly able one. Having helped eject William Marcy ("Boss") Tweed from New York City politics, he had a reputation as a reformer—and the post-Civil War navy, now in Whitney's hands, certainly needed reform. "In March 1885," he wrote of the date he took office, "the United States Navy had no one vessel of war which could have kept the seas for one week as against any first rate naval power." Its ships were still mostly wood, its few ironclads obsolete; "the Spanish or Chilean fleet could anchor off Coney Island and bomb Madison Square," one newspaper declared. The navy was riddled with what another newspaper called "a long record of crookedness, jobbery [using public office for private gain], inefficiency, and failure."

The new secretary set out to run the navy like a business. He retired obsolete ships, set out on a building program for new, modern vessels (the USS *Maine*, of "Remember the *Maine*" fame, was among them), built munitions plants and gun factories. And he put out for bid new rifled cannon, demanding that they be made by American firms. One successful bidder was Midvale Steel; soon naval inspectors, extended every courtesy, had the run of the Midvale shops.

One of Whitney's problems was the Washington navy yard, located on the banks of the Potomac just outside the capital. A veritable icon of inefficiency, it had been almost wholly neglected since early in the Civil War. Who could come in and do something about it? Who could superintend the gun factory Whitney wanted built there? One day in 1885, he sent for Caspar Goodrich, an up-and-coming thirty-eight-year-old Naval Academy graduate whom the previous navy secretary had named to a board overseeing the Naval War College in Newport, Rhode Island. Now Whitney gave him new orders: find someone to run the Washington yard.

Goodrich conferred with naval inspectors stationed at defense suppliers, including Midvale, learned of Taylor, and met with him, never intimating that a job was in the offing. In the end, he submitted Taylor's name to Whitney. The navy secretary summoned Taylor to Washington, talked with him at length, and offered him the position. But Taylor turned him down.

Four years passed. The Harrahs swept into Midvale, President Cleveland was swept out of Washington, and in 1889, Whitney returned to New York. But in the interim, he and some of his rich friends had been approached about a new papermaking process that looked as if it ought to make all of them more millions still.

～

The first paper mill in America went up in 1690 a few miles from Taylor's birthplace in Germantown, on a little stream that flowed into the Wissahickon. But the paper it produced differed from that most in use today. The fibrous material ground, mashed, beaten, or chemically processed into a slurry, dried on wire screens, and squeezed between rollers to make paper is today wood. In the seventeenth century, it was cotton and linen or, rather, fiber derived from rags, for which there was always a big market. In the early 1800s, women were entreated for their old clothes, and large quantities had to be imported—a hundred and fifty million pounds of rags, for example, as late as 1872.

By 1854, straw was being used; the invention of a process to use it for paper had raised its price from six dollars to twenty dollars a ton almost overnight. But, as one industrial historian wrote two years later, "we have not yet heard the great shout which will go up when rags are no longer king." Straw-based paper, it turned out, wore down metal type prematurely, so the search for ways to use wood pulp, and so harness the world's forests, never abated. Chemical methods were introduced that broke down wood chips in huge disgesters and separated out the nonfibrous elements; these were versions of the sulfite process, a reference to the acid of bisulfite that was the chemical stew's key constituent. The big problem was that the acid ate through the digester's lining.

But a new process promised a solution. Alexander Mitscherlich, a German chemist, had taken out seemingly airtight patents on pulp-making technology that featured, among other innovations, a special liner for the digester. Through an intermediary, he approached a big-time Michigan lawyer who looked after the state's nascent sulfite industry, Don Dickerson, soon to become postmaster general under President Cleveland. He and others bought the North American rights, set up a pilot plant in Michigan, and ultimately approached William Collins Whitney. Soon Whitney and a coterie of his rich friends had bought rights to the Mitscherlich patents, the Manufacturing Investment Company had been formed, and mills employing the new process began going up in Appleton, Wisconsin, and Madison, Maine.

Both mills were under the authority of naval officers on leave. Needed now was a general manager, a real engineer, to run them. Through Captain Goodrich, who had brought Taylor's name to his attention four years before and now oversaw the Maine mill, Whitney summoned Taylor to Washington. They made a deal, signed a contract. On May 28, 1890, Taylor submitted his resignation from Midvale, effective October 1.

But it had not been that bloodless. Taylor, William Fannon recalled, had received and declined "many flattering offers" over the years. This time, too, he'd been reluctant. He talked to relatives and friends, including Wilfred Lewis, even wondering out loud whether perhaps Lewis might want the job instead. Was there, in Taylor's indecisiveness, some flicker of self-doubt? Taylor, it seemed to Lewis, felt "unqualified for so much responsibility."

But how could he not accept? How could any man resist? At a time when skilled workers made six or seven hundred dollars a year, and when his would-be successor as chief engineer at Midvale set his salary requirement at four thousand per year, Whitney and his pals were dangling fifteen thousand dollars in front of him; today that would feel like three or four hundred thousand. And stock options gave Taylor, now thirty-four, the chance to make a fortune when the Mitscherlich process yielded its promised millions.

Taylor was scarcely immune to wealth's unholy allure. But more, the offer recognized, in the most tangible and generous terms, all he had achieved at Midvale. Whitney and his friends were the highest rollers of American capitalism, the closest thing to an American aristocracy. Whitney himself had, bare-handed, resurrected the navy. He had been mentioned as a possible presidential candidate and, more seriously, for governor of New York. According to Henry Adams, he had "gratified every ambition, and swung the country almost at his will; he had thrown away the usual objects of political ambition like the ashes of smoked cigarettes; had turned to other amusements, satiated every taste, gorged every appetite." No offer from a man like that could fail to exert its magic.

"How would you like to go to Maine to live?" Taylor asked his wife one day. It meant giving up their Germantown house, placing their belongings in storage, leaving family and friends behind. "The thermometer goes to 20 below zero," Fred warned her, "and there will be no social life whatsoever." But Lou, recalling idyllic camping trips to Maine "and the fragrance of the balsam in my nostrils," signed on for the rustic adventure.

3

BOOMTOWN ON THE KENNEBEC

~

JUST FIFTEEN YEARS BEFORE, the only way to reach Madison, in central Maine, two thirds of the way north from Portland to Moosehead Lake, was by four-horse stage. Then, in 1875, the Somerset Railroad arrived, snaking into town along the east bank of the Kennebec River. That brought new business, including two woolen mills.

But by 1890, when construction began on what was locally reputed to be the nation's biggest pulp mill, or maybe the world's, Madison's population was still less than two thousand. When Fred and Lou visited that year, "it was an awakening," she wrote later, "to find a drummers' hotel [one frequented by traveling salesmen], with soiled wall paper and a dining room with flies and two-pronged forks!"

Today, interstate highways, national chains, and television have erased contrasts between rural and urban, and few know what it means to live in a real small town, as opposed to those that haunt the national imagination. Back then, to move from Philadelphia or Boston to Madison, Maine, or Appleton, Wisconsin, site of the other Investment Company mill, meant an even more drastic change than would a similar move today. When Taylor asked some of the boys at Midvale to join him in the back country, all but William Fannon refused. And Fannon needed much convincing, having "no grievance at the steel works and . . . about as near being perfectly contented with my position as I ever expect to be." He visited the Michigan mill where the Mitscherlich process was in use, returned to Philadelphia, talked with Taylor, haggled over salary, and finally resigned from Midvale in early January 1891, bound for Appleton as its new assistant manager. "Mrs. Fannon and I came out here away from relations and friends and left every comfort that a large city affords, and against the advice of my relatives," he wrote later.

But he did come, in part thanks to his "confidence in Mr. Taylor's ability and integrity" and in part, perhaps, for the sheer adventure. Indeed, great things were happening in Appleton and Madison.

In Madison, the cornerstone for the mill was laid on August 23, 1890. Old photographs show dynamiting along the riverbank to open up a water channel, and stone strewn about for the foundations of the new buildings; the main one was to stretch nine hundred feet beside the Kennebec and rise to a height of four stories. Freight cars filled with granite, lumber, and brick rumbled into town daily. Everywhere, wooden scaffolding. Everywhere, buildings rising. Bricks that got wet in transit were piled in circular tiers six feet in diameter, at the center of which fires were built to dry them, so they could be pressed into service right away. In the fall of 1890, a starch factory occupying the site where the pulp mill was to go was torn down; nothing, it seems, was too good to give up for the new mill. "The tall pine tree, that ancient landmark, dear to every old resident, was the first to fall" for the sake of progress, a local account had it, "and where it once stood and sighed in the breeze, stands the northerly pier of this great pulp mill." "Madison Booming" the local paper, the six-year-old *Bulletin*, headlined its account of the town's transformation early in 1891. Five hundred men were at work; "Every tenement, every boarding house, is occupied." Lovingly, the paper reported the mill's magnificent statistics: some five million bricks would go into it. . . . Three hundred thousand special acid-proof bricks, needed for the digesters, had arrived from Germany. "Madison," the paper trumpeted, "may safely be reckoned as the busiest village in New England today."

Taylor's contract specified that he start full-time on October 1, 1890, but receive $16.66 for any day he could give the company earlier (this, presumably, on top of his Midvale pay). Indeed, long before fall, Taylor was devoting much of his time to the new venture. He visited Madison and Appleton, met with Goodrich and Robley Evans, the naval officer who presided over the Appleton mill, inspected equipment, conferred with suppliers, toured other mills. He was in New York on June 3, presumably for meetings at the Mills Building, where Whitney had his offices (along with former President Cleveland); then he was on to Saratoga, New York, Detroit, Appleton, and Chicago a week later, with scattered half-days on company business here and there, before proceeding on to New York and Philadelphia.

In August, on his annual north country jaunt—this one to Parmachenee Lake, in the northwest corner of Maine—Taylor stopped in Madison, where he visited with Goodrich. At the end of October, he was back with Lou, presumably scouting for a site on which to build a house; while there, they were both thrown from their carriage and were seriously enough hurt for the local paper to report the accident.

In early December, Taylor returned briefly to Madison, but for most of the following winter he and Lou stayed in Appleton, a Wisconsin town of about five thousand located at the northern tip of Lake Winnebago, near where the Fox River originates on its course to Green Bay and the Great Lakes. Since the 1850s, the area had burgeoned with paper mills, located in towns along the Fox with old Indian names like Neenah, Menasha, and Kaukauna, and new names like Kimberly—for Kimberly & Clark, the biggest of the paper companies. By 1892, the Fox River valley was home to almost two dozen mills, producing more than a quarter of a billion pounds of paper a year.

But Madison, Taylor had decided, would be their home. When Lou suggested they have a house built, he'd replied that it was fine with him, "provided I am not called upon to help in any way"; he had a pulp mill to run. Lou was delighted. She found a local farmer, perhaps on their scouting trip the previous fall, and on his old buckboard scoured the area for a place on which to build. She settled on a wooded bluff high over the Kennebec about a quarter mile from the mill, just a few minutes' walk from Goodrich's house on Pine Street, yet peaceful and apart.

By the following July, the house was finished. Its long axis parallel to the river, you could step out back, away from the road, and watch the sun setting low over the Kennebec. The local papers made much of how the house made "no pretension to finish," and that without plasterwork and lathing, it was merely "a summer cottage suggestive, in its style and finish, of the fields and woods." But it sported touches like deacon seats by each window and bedrooms set around an upstairs gallery, each opening up to the sitting room below, with its big fireplace. Three large fireplaces warmed the house, each five or six feet wide and built from stones hauled up from the river. At a time when a respectable middle-class house in Philadelphia could be had for twelve hundred dollars, their spartan "cabin" cost more than five thousand. On July 14, Lou and her mother, probably coming from Plymouth, arrived in town. Four days later, Taylor himself arrived and, reported the paper, "moved into his new house on the hill near Old Point Crossing."

In Madison, they sometimes called him "Colonel Taylor," which was understandable considering that the locals saw the new mill as a military operation run, in the words of one account, "according to Capt. Goodrich's idea of naval discipline." When a workman made a suggestion about unloading a piece of machinery, Goodrich "fixed him with his stern and steely [gaze] and said, 'Sir, do not speak to me until you are spoken to.'" Goodrich had watched sail yield to steam, wood to steel. As naval attaché, he'd watched the British bombard Alexandria in 1882, in the wake of a nationalist Egyptian revolt, and written a history of the campaign. Described as "a man of unusual charm and sophistication," he would ultimately rise to the rank of rear admiral. But at community relations, it seems, he was little adept, being best remembered for his quick temper and the pumped-up ways of the military men and college boys he brought to town. "The sailor on horseback," they called him. His "exploits," according to one reminiscence, "finally became so ludicrous" that someone set the locals chanting, to the tune of "Yankee Doodle,"

> And there was Captain Goodrich
> Upon a snow-white charger,
> He looked as big as all outdoors
> And sometimes looked much larger.

At least in local memory, the country bumpkins finally got the best of Goodrich. He'd had built a long, one-story "Club House," with a big stone fireplace, down near the Kennebec within view of the mill, a kind of officers' mess cut off from the locals. One day, local men were detailed to unload barrels of wine, destined for Goodrich and his boys, into an adjacent storehouse. When they were done, he made a show of locking up and pocketing the key. But that evening, pulp mill workers crept beneath the building and bored through the floor and into the barrels stored there. Soon, "two-inch streams of wine were flowing" into pails and kegs. "When Captain Goodrich and his fellow executives next entered their storehouse in search of refreshments, they found every barrel empty and the floor as full of holes as a colander."

Just two or three months into its construction, Goodrich quarreled with the architect of the mill, who threw up his hands and walked off the job. Like Taylor, Goodrich was a bristly sort. With the two men working closely until Goodrich returned to sea in November 1891, they and their families grew close. "I venture to call it intimate," Goodrich would say of their friendship at the memorial service following Taylor's death, "although it is quite possible that, through pride, I use too strong a term." Intimate or merely warm, it endured for the rest of Taylor's life, fueled by regular correspondence when Goodrich was away at sea and by family visits when he returned.

~

Late each spring in northern Maine, after the long winter, local residents looked forward to the breakup of the frozen river, harbinger of the new season. As the wait grew longer and the day nearer, expectation filled the air. Lou Taylor remembered seeing an older resident just sitting, by the doorway of her house, quietly waiting. Finally the great day came, Lou recalled, and "the ice would quietly steal away in the night, leaving the long, black curve of the river."

With the breakup, felled logs floated downriver. Lou saw "the driving of many logs by the river men with the resultant jams, and the men poling and jumping from log to log." The lumber collected behind a boom, from which it was lifted by crane into the maw of the mill. First, logs were debarked; to protect workers against someone brushing up against them in the tight, noisy, dangerous workroom, Taylor stationed them in what amounted to cages, occasioning much derision and protest. The debarked logs were sawed into disks an inch and a half thick by a "gang" of monstrous forged-steel saws; at Appleton, there were seventeen of them, each three and half feet in diameter, fixed to a steel shaft ten feet long that spun at nine hundred and fifty revolutions per minute. The machinery could dispatch fifty to sixty cords of wood—a hundred tons—in ten hours. Then the disks went to the digester, the heart of the process, where wood met acid.

The tower in which the acid was made stood as the most visible symbol of the new mill; at 180 feet, it was the tallest man-made structure within miles. When it was finished in 1891, they'd haul cameras to the top to take pictures of the town below—the neighboring woolen mill, the simple frame houses parading up Main Street, the open countryside just beyond. Up through its wooden envelope rose a dozen, hollow, octagonal cylinders, also wood, each connected by cast-iron piping to sulfur burners. From the top of the tower, through chutes to each cylinder, was dumped limestone, which supplied the calcium carbonate that the chemistry required; you could hear the rumble all over town when they did it.

With sulfur percolating through the limestone from below, and water trickling down from above, the acid formed where all the ingredients met, collecting in two tanks at the tower's base. The fumes given off from the tower, it was said, reminded the locals of the hellfire and brimstone they heard preached in church.

The tower sat atop a small hill. So the acid simply flowed by gravity to the digester. It met the wood in massive cylinders, thirteen feet across, made of inch-thick wrought-iron plates riveted together. There it "cooked" at high temperature and pressure for two or three days.

These digesters, in particular their special linings, were the heart of the Mitscherlich technology. In other sulfite mills, the acid often found a way to reach the iron, with which it reacted chemically; the Mitscher-lich lining prevented that. First, inside the iron vessel, was a layer of lead sheeting. Then, special brick imported from Germany was tongue-and-grooved together. Finally, there was another layer of lead. Each digester held twenty-five cords of wood, about fifty tons. After a few days, it became a pasty, semisolid mass that, after further processing and drying, became the raw material for paper and was sold by the car-load at three or four dollars per hundred pounds.

The Appleton mill was quicker off the mark, and by 1892 its hun-dred and fifty men were turning out twelve million pounds of pulp a year. Madison, however, produced nothing at all until November 17, 1891. "We have during the past few days," Taylor wrote the company's lawyer, "been undergoing the agonies of starting the mill. . . . I send you tonight a sample of the very first 20 feet of pulp that went through the dryers. This pulp is dirty, of course, but it is of much better quality than I expected to see for the very first run."

Taylor sent Goodrich a sample, too, which reached him just before he set sail from Hampton Roads aboard the USS *Jamestown*. "My soul rejoiced at the sight of the little sample of pulp," Goodrich wrote back; it seemed "of much better color" than Appleton's. Taylor may have cleaned it up for him: early Madison pulp, it seems, was riddled with knots and black specks, and local boys were paid to stand beside the moving belt and pick them out by hand as the pulp passed by.

By October 26, 1892, Taylor reported to the Investment Company's board that a round of construction begun that April was three-quarters complete. New waterwheels were finished, as were new pumps and exhaust blowers for the acid towers. And the knot catchers, presumably to replace those truant boys, were about half-done. That December, the Madison mill shipped forty-one carloads of pulp.

~

"Owing to our large output," it said on the inside back cover of the leather-bound, vest-pocket notebooks the Investment Company printed up, probably as salesmen's gifts,

> we are able to secure absolute uniformity in the quality of our
> sulphite, and we guarantee that no shipment shall include a bundle
> worse than the sample on which we sell. Our sulphite has been

shown by a recent test to be 29 2/3 per cent stronger than that
made by one of the best quick-cooking plants in this country.

But like advertisements run twenty-five years before by a Butcher Steel
Company still scrambling to make steel that didn't shatter on impact,
the company's claims masked serious problems. Launched with so
much promise, hope, and cash, the pulp mill venture turned into a
debacle.

Many things went wrong, but Taylor largely blamed the Mitscher
lich process itself, the very basis of the business. It was, he declared, "an
enormous fraud." First, the patent rights to it cost too much for what
they delivered in protection from competitors—which is to say
nothing; other companies found ways to circumvent them. And technical information central to the design of the mills proved fatally inaccurate. Perhaps two hundred and fifty to three hundred and fifty
horsepower would suffice to drive the mill's machinery, they'd been
told; instead, Taylor complained, it took eighteen hundred. And the
three hundred horsepower presumably needed to cook and dry the
pulp? They needed more like 1,250. "Owing to the misrepresentations
of the promoters of the process," Taylor would write, "our shafting was
. . . strained beyond its proper limit." Pulleys and belts were forever
splitting and tearing.

The sites in Maine and Wisconsin selected for the new mills were far
from ideal. In 1889, there were no vast regionals grids to supply electric
power; a pulp mill relied on its own water for power, as it relied on it at
every stage of the manufacturing process—fifty thousand or so gallons
for each ton of finished paper. Just a month after the new company was
formed, on October 18, 1889, Whitney and some of his investor friends
visited sites on the Androscoggin, Kennebec, and Penobscot rivers. On
November 24, they came to Madison and chose it, for reasons still
obscure, over more water-blessed locations. At Appleton, too, the
water supply proved wanting; in May 1891, before leaving Appleton for
Madison, Taylor wrote that the mill turned out twenty tons of pulp a
day but could be making thirty "were it not for the shortness in water."

Both Goodrich and Evans, who presided over early construction of
the two mills, would rise to admiralty rank and write autobiographies,
both passing over their pulp mill interludes in a few sentences. "I was
directed to erect a sulphite-fibre mill at Appleton, Wisconsin," Evans

wrote, "which I did." But in fact, competition between the two men to produce the first pulp led to hurried, thoughtless design.

For one thing, the mill buildings, at least in Madison, were simply too small. "It is merely necessary for anyone to walk through the buildings and see how closely the machinery is packed," Taylor would write. The machinery gave more than the usual trouble; shafting and belting wore out prematurely. In Appleton, the saws didn't work right. In Madison, in late 1891, a bin holding three thousand tons of coal collapsed; three men narrowly escaped with their lives. In February of the following year, a large pulley burst, shooting metal fragments through a window into the river and halting production for several days. A few months later, a fire broke out in the digester house, where it raged unchecked for over two hours. "The fumes of the acid and sulphur were almost stifling," a local paper reported. "The heat was so intense that the iron girders of the roof were bent and warped so that a new roof will have to be put on. The damage is considerable, probably $3000." "This is a serious setback to the company," the account went on, "which has not yet got its great plant into full running order."

And it never did. On April 24, 1893, a paper-industry friend, John H. King, wrote Taylor, commiserating with him about another fire, and expressing hope that "you may now find things more encouraging." But by this time, with six months left on his contract, Taylor was soured on the whole business. The great venture had brought him not riches and pride but frustration.

In the spring of 1892, Taylor had begun improvements and new construction that, over the next year, dropped more than a hundred thousand dollars into the Madison mill. Trade journals had pictured the company as overspending right from the start. And with this new round of expenditures, Taylor was installing a whole alternate power plant, along with duplicate line shafting, measures that would strike even ever-sympathetic Copley as "a little too thorough." Inevitably, Whitney and the board called him to account.

On December 19, Taylor answered his inquisitors with a lengthy report, defending himself against charges that the Madison mill had been built too extravagantly; it cost no more than another mill downstream, he insisted. But having perhaps already conveyed its substance to the board, he was not sanguine about the report's reception. "I do not think," he'd written Goodrich six days before, that the comparison between the two mills "has the slightest effect on any of our directors," several of whom were due soon up in Madison. To them, the mill cost more than planned—period—and so therefore was extravagant.

But if Taylor was guilty of extravagance, there was method to it. Once, just after a pulley had broken, someone sitting outside his office heard him upbraid a subordinate who'd been a little too leisurely about restoring production. "Clamp the broken pulley together," the eavesdropper heard Taylor harangue him, "replace it with some sort of spare pulley, make a wooden one, no matter what or how, but keep that shaft revolving."

But while an incident like that made for a good story, it was bad business. Taylor's strategy was to forestall such incidents entirely, however much company money it took. "If a belt breaks once, it is excusable," he'd tell his right-hand man, Sanford Thompson—but not a second time. The first break meant you needed regular inspection and preventive maintenance; you had to get ahead of the problem. One time, a messenger from the mill woke a bleary-eyed Thompson at three o'clock on a cold winter's morning. Taylor wanted to see him immediately. "Mr. Thompson," Taylor told him when he arrived, "I told you to have an idler built for every belt in this mill. Why was this not done? I don't want any excuses—I won't have any excuses—why wasn't it done?"

In his sometimes almost laughable profligacy with the company's money and the labors of his men, you could see one evidence of Taylor's hand. In his efforts to replace skill with system, you could see another.

The men tending the digesters were, by one account, "low grade, unintelligent, illiterate, and even unable to understand the English language," referring presumably to the French speakers among them. As part of their job they were to take a sample of digester fluid and, at regular intervals, submit it to a chemist. Taylor devised a scheme by which a man had only to withdraw a sample at set times and compare it, by eye, to a rack of test tubes filled with digester fluid each taken under standard conditions. Which tube did it best match? The answer told him all he need know and eliminated part of a high-priced chemist's job. In the Midvale machine shop, Taylor's tables and charts supplanted a skilled worker's knowledge and experience. Here at the pulp mill, the rack of test tubes did the same.

The Madison mill's workers, French Canadians and longtime State of Mainers set in their ways, were, according to Copley, "the most difficult class of labor he ever had to deal with." But Taylor was determined to place them on piecework and, eventually, the differential rate. Can't be done, veteran pulp and paper men told him. But he was, as he wrote a fellow pulp and paper executive, "absolutely certain" it could.

He never wholly succeeded at Madison but largely did at Appleton. Within a year and a half, virtually every operation there—"from the time our materials arrive in the yard," Taylor wrote, "until they are shipped in the [railroad] cars"—was on piecework, mostly applied to work gangs rather than individuals. On January 3, 1893, the word went out that, beginning the next day, each man in the six-man crew supplying the sawmill with lumber from the yard would receive 2.55 cents per cord. Some tasks got a differential rate. Men operating the debarking machines would earn seventeen cents per cord if they completed less than eight cords per shift, twenty cents per cord for between eight and twelve, and twenty-one cents per cord for more than twelve.

But these rates were not set "scientifically"; they simply were based on how many cords the men typically did in ten hours; no evidence comes down to us of Midvale-style "elementary time studies." The Appleton rates, wrote the man who set them for Taylor, were "arbitrary . . . established as an additional incentive to rapid work." Moreover, the maximum incentive wasn't the 30–100 percent increase Taylor always promised, but only 23 percent. And Taylor's first paper about his nascent system, which appeared just two years after he left the mill, referred to his time there only in passing.

For Taylor never got the chance to turn his mills into the kind of "mechanical heaven" he had fashioned at Midvale. He had all he could do just to catch the trains forever shuttling him between Appleton, Madison, and New York, keep his boss in the Mills Building off his back, get out the pulp, and put out fires.

∼

Later, Lou Taylor pictured herself as happily surrendering to the rusticity of Maine. She wrote with evident delight of her dealings with "the natives." She made much of their house being simple and spare and of how she secured water for it through the good offices of a local diviner, "a very tall man, with an old worn-out stove pipe hat and frock coat"— and witch hazel stick.

Once, with the company directors due to visit, she was urged to send down to Portland for a caterer. No, she replied, the New Yorkers arriving at her country doorstep by private railcar would already have had their fill of posh treatment. She would give them instead "a native dinner," which turned out to be turkey and mince pie, served by "our old colored servant . . . with white gloves and jacket." But only cider was served, not the champagne their guests might have preferred. "Oh boy—cider," she has them saying. "Just what we wanted."

The Taylors' shingled house above the Kennebec became the social center for those Lou called the mill's "college boys," who would come up to sing around the piano and open fire, and meet Lou's friends and family from the city. As if they were soldiers in wartime needing R and R, Taylor felt "obliged" to invite them—or so he said later, in justifying household expenses of seven thousand dollars a year, when most mill workers made less than seven hundred. Of course, Fred and Lou both loved to sing; socializing around the piano was to them no dreary social chore, and Lou even brought up a musician from Augusta to enhance their "musical evenings." She was pleased to learn that mothers of the men enjoying the Taylor hearth during these years were duly grateful, presumably for keeping their wholesome boys out of trouble.

Rural life in Maine had other compensations, not the least of which, after winters that seemed never to end, was spring itself, when Fred and Lou—and, during that first year the Goodriches—would ride horses through the flower-speckled countryside. But ultimately, Madison had to wear thin for these city folks, even the relentlessly cheerful Mrs. Taylor, whose unmet needs were evident to all. The town "seemed more like a romantic wilderness than a home for Mrs. Taylor," wrote Wilfred Lewis later. Lou herself noted that "impressions of my isolated life brought me an invitation from Secretary Whitney's wife to visit them in New York the following winter," where she heard *Faust* sung at the Metropolitan Opera.

Meanwhile, Fred's worries at the mill gnawed at them. Fannon had warned him not to jump industries midway through his career. And surely he must have asked himself sometimes—on yet another overnight train to Appleton, or after yet another fire in Madison, or during yet another tense meeting with the busybody moneymen in New York—why they had ever left Midvale.

After leaving, he'd had photographs of himself taken, copies made, and delivered to Midvale, asking that they be distributed among his old friends. On December 6, W. H. Colby wrote back with a list of a hundred or so recipients—Harrah, Gantt, "Colonel" Thompson, Joseph King in the machine shop, John Griffith, and others who had figured in his years there, adding, "We hope that we have given them out as you would have done."

Over the next three years, Taylor kept in touch with several of his Midvale friends, their correspondence sometimes taking a personal turn that revealed a wisp of nostalgia for good times now past or even, on Taylor's part, a hint of loneliness. With John Griffith, their little tennis-pole business gave them reason to write, but invariably their letters ranged further afield. "My dear John," wrote Taylor, who normally addressed even friends of long standing by their last names,

> I know it must be a nuisance to you to write, but if you can find a
> little time, I should be very glad to hear how everything is getting
> along—that is, how you are overcoming the various difficulties
> with the new plant, the matter with the hammer and crane, and in
> fact, any of the machinery of the new plant. . . . How are the boring
> lathes in the machine shop doing? And how is that hydraulic steam
> engine of Charley Berkelbach doing? It seems an age since I heard
> from either one of you.

Taylor had left Midvale before ever seeing the big steam hammer work, but his friends kept him apprised of its progress. In November 1890, Colby, his correspondent at Midvale, wrote that Charles Harrah himself had marked the occasion of its maiden blows. "Mr. Taylor would have liked to see the hammer start," Colby quoted him, "and I should like to have him here to see how successfully it works." Then, early the following year, bad news: an accident with the new hammer. The steam had driven up the piston too violently, breaking several parts. "It was [fortunate] it did not kill half a dozen people," wrote W. E. Firth, later named Taylor's successor as chief engineer, "as there was quite a crowd round looking on." No mere pile of machinery, the hammer served as a link to Taylor in Maine. "Thinking that you would be interested to learn that #10 hammer has at last started in earnest," another old friend began a letter to Taylor early the following year.

Meanwhile, Joseph Entwistle, a clerk in the Midvale office and proud master of his new Remington typewriter, complained to Taylor about Harrah. Cavorting in the white-collar dining room, Entwistle wrote him, a few of the men had broken a chair. When everyone, guilty or not, was docked fifty cents, some of them, including Entwistle, wrote Harrah to complain—and *they* were docked fifty cents more,

> for saying we didn't do it. I want to say frankly to you that, had I
> been unmarried, I should have told Mr. H. to take my name off his
> rolls and let me go to some other place where the Boss did not
> place a premium on raising the D—l. I really think I should have
> been on the point of writing to you and asking for a laborer's job
> or something. I have a little manhood left.

Entwistle closed playfully: "Your humble servant cannot get into last summer's clothes, on account of either shrinkage on the part of the clothes, or increase in the size of the aforesaid humble servant."

With Harrah, too, Taylor reestablished ties. Early in 1893, he wrote him, receiving a sample of his old boss's mocking best. "My dear Taylor, " it began

> I owe you an apology and I hereby tender it to you. When I heard
> in the newspapers of your elevation to the position of Assistant
> Secretary of War [presumably a jibe at his appointment by the
> former navy secretary], I and for the matter of that all the boys at
> Midvale made up their minds that for the next four years we would
> hear nothing of our former companion in arms . . . and [that] we
> would be debarred from the privilege of calling upon you in
> Washington, from the fact that we wish to keep unsullied our
> reputation for integrity, which would be endangered by our
> breathing the contaminated air of Washington government circles.
>
> This morning's mail brings me your letter of the 15th inst. and
> calls forth these expressions of regret that I should have misjudged
> you. I see that the official honors which have devolved upon you
> have not altered you yet and that you feel as friendly towards us
> now as before the lightning struck you . . .

In like fashion, Harrah continued for three pages before dispensing with the substance of Taylor's letter, adding, "I have as high a regard for your opinion as an engineer as I have utter contempt for your political beliefs and your views on the economic questions of the United States, though I hope in due time to reform you."

A kindred lightheartedness flavored other correspondence between Madison and Philadelphia during these years, including a playful exchange of claim and counterclaim between Taylor and Axel Petre, Midvale's superintendent, over a certain forty-cents-a-pound packing material. "Why do you stay up in Maine?" Petre wrote finally in August. "Why don't you come down to more civilized parts of the world. Or have your tastes deteriorated so much that you like it better . . . there?"

~

Meanwhile, the mills in Taylor's charge chugged along, slowly making headway. Indeed, he might have surmounted his problems in the end had the economy not gone bust.

Years later, they made it sound in Madison as if Maine itself had defeated Captain Goodrich and the Investment Company. "None of them were familiar with manufacturing and all were city men unused to country people, lumbering, or backwoods conditions," read one account. With the company's money spent and little paper produced, it went on, "Capt. Goodrich and his crew departed, and the Club House and wine shed were closed up." Of course, Goodrich had left long before, by October 1891, to resume his naval career. It was the panic of 1893, heaped atop the company's other woes, that delivered the real coup de grâce.

By 1893, the economy had been weakened by six years of agricultural depression in the western states and a steep decline in foreign trade following the imposition of new tariff barriers. On April 21, federal gold reserves fell below a long-sacrosanct psychological barrier, one hundred million dollars. Confidence was shattered, banks and financial houses failed, prices fell. Workers lost their jobs; Coxey's Army of the unemployed would march the following year on Washington.

It was 1873 all over again, and the nation sank into a depression that lasted more than four years. At the pulp mill, orders dried up, along with any remaining hope for the Investment Company. At the Chicago world's fair, held that summer, pulp from the Madison mill won a prize, and Taylor would later receive from the fair's Board of Lady Managers a diploma of honorable mention attesting to his role "in the production and perfection" of the company's exhibit. But by then, the mill had shut down and Taylor was long gone.

"I think you will be pleased to hear," he wrote a fellow paper company executive, George Hammond, on May 18, 1893,

> that I have succeeded in getting out of the Manufacturing
> Investment Company. . . . I feel that the time has arrived when I
> can honorably leave the Company, as our western mill will be now
> doing finely (for a Mitscherlich mill) and our Madison mill,
> mechanically speaking, is all straightened out and we are
> progressing fairly with the piece work system.

Whitney apparently asked him to stay on, relieving him of an onerous stock-purchase requirement, intimating future wealth, and suggesting that, to avoid the ceaseless travel, he limit his responsibilities to Madison. But Taylor had had enough. By now sour on financiers, he would later express contempt for those who made only money, not things. A month later, he was "happy to say that I am now entirely out of the M. I. Co, and have not felt so well and free from care for a great many years."

For Taylor, the pulp mill had cost him heavily. He had bought fifteen thousand dollars' worth of its common stock, for which he'd sold securities that had cost him nineteen thousand, making for a four-thousand-dollar loss. And he'd been stuck paying interest on the loan that financed his purchase of forty-five thousand dollars in preferred stock. All told, by his bitter reckoning, he had lost twenty-five thousand dollars, or what we might today experience as half a million dollars. "This loss," he wrote around the time he left, "has more than absorbed all of my savings for the past 20 years."

Not that he was destitute. His out-of-pocket loss, he noted, had been "met by a gift from my father," and in 1895, the company would buy back their house for five thousand dollars. But the failure had left him drained. So great was his disappointment, observed William Fannon, "that I think it affected his health." Indeed, while precise symptoms fail to come down to us, Taylor scholar Sudhir Kakar has suggested that they amounted to the first of several nervous breakdowns Taylor later said he had suffered. One correspondent, Benjamin Frick, wrote him after learning of his departure that he and his wife both feared that, had Taylor continued to work as he had, "you would soon completely break down."

Lou's health, too, it seemed to Frick, had been sapped by the long struggle. Taylor had written Goodrich the previous August that "Mrs. Taylor is . . . very much run down. She is unable to sleep and has been so for several months past. . . . Perhaps she has caught the malady from me, as I have been more or less in this condition for a year past."

In the months just after pulling free of the Investment Company but before leaving Madison, palpable relief floods Taylor's letters—along with defenses of his record. They'd said it was "an utter impossibility" to install piecework in a pulp mill, and yet at Appleton, he wrote Hammond, he had done it:

> All the coal, wood, sulphur and limestone, as they arrive in the mill are unloaded from the cars and piled on piece work. They are then transported to the rooms in which they are worked up on piece work and the wood is barked and sawed on piece work. Our digesters are filled, emptied and cooked on piece work and the pulp, when it arrives in the wash room, passes through a long series of machines which take about $2^1/_2$ hours to wash it, and it finally runs on to a paper machine and is bundled into rolls, weighed, sampled and shipped—all on piece work.

Was it coming to seem that the fixed star of his ambition, more important to him than any ups and downs of his career or fortune, was piecework? Ideally, piecework based on time studies and refined by the differential rate, but piece rate in any case?

Taylor had hardly transplanted Midvale to the north woods. But piece rates *had* made a difference. Figures he supplied about the time he left—though an apples-and-oranges lack of parallelism taints the comparison—showed that Appleton costs per ton had dropped from more then seventy-five to thirty-five dollars, output rising from twenty to thirty-six tons a day. Labor costs dropped from more than thirty dollars per ton to eight dollars. The mill employed seventy-five fewer men. And, he added, "our mill at Madison is rapidly getting on to piece work in the same way as our western mill." In Taylor's mind, piecework and other elements of the system he'd brought from Midvale had emerged from the three years with their value intact—and now seemed bigger than any one company.

"We expect to remain in Madison all through this summer," he wrote Hammond, "during which time I hope to have a thorough rest. This is the first time that I have been free for over two weeks at a time for twenty years." He later noted that he had made no "endeavors toward securing other employment as yet and propose to rest here till I feel as well as ever."

But Taylor's angry postscript was sharply at odds with the rest of the letter. Several unfriendly newspaper articles about the company had appeared recently—vengeance exacted, he suspected, for his refusal to be interviewed. "Personally," he assured Hammond, "it does not affect me in the least." But "as a rather curious coincidence," he went on,

> just at the time that the articles were written, slandering the management of our mills, two of the young men employed by us were offered [top jobs], one the position of superintendent and the other position of foreman, in the next two largest sulphite mills in the country to ours. Evidently, our system of management is not regarded so contemptuously by those who ought to know about it as it is by the newspaper men.

Our system of management.

4

ON THE ROAD

᠎

FRED TAYLOR'S LIFE from the fall of 1893 to the spring of 1898 was a period of fitful wanderings, of imperfect success and partial failure, of bright hopes and dead ends.

It was a fractured time, Taylor's attention drawn off in many directions. He worked for many companies, in many industries, in many cities and towns, doing many things. He learned cost accounting, testified in a patent suit, delivered professional papers, sketched tools, wrote reports, toured factories, put together a cartel, paid off industrial spies, and even ran a lathe. He stayed two weeks here, six months there—electric motors in Wisconsin, ball bearings in Massachusetts, a shipyard in Pennsylvania. He was forever on the clattering train, sleeping, working, dictating letters. Sometimes Lou accompanied him, but more often he went alone. He stayed at the Arlington in Boston, at the Virginia Hotel in Chicago, at the Belknap on the Jersey shore. "For the next five years," Lou recalled later," it was travel—travel, pack and unpack, wherever Fred was called . . . always with Fred's large case of books, blueprints, and drawings, and my piano, pictures and chairs to make an atmosphere of home." Lou didn't like it much. Taylor himself would call the period "trying."

He had set out on a new career, as a management consultant, still an oddball way to make a living. There were management consultants before Taylor, but no one called them that. Back in the 1870s, Chordal had limned an admiring portrait of a breed he called Yankee contractors, men from out of town who would contract with a machine shop to take over its production. Introducing their own methods, which emphasized system and organization, they promised lower costs and higher profits, of which they took a cut. "He had on nice boots, and nice clothes, and a white shirt, which would do credit to a lobbyist," Chordal describes one "Doolittle," probably a fictionalized composite. "He wore a plug hat. He looked smart and starchy, and had the manner and approach of a business man." Doolittle kept workmen busy for weeks just making the special tools, fixtures, and jigs that most foreman never found time to make but that spelled lower costs in the long run. And, in best Taylorist fashion—but Taylor was still an apprentice!— the men earned more, yet on lower piece rates.

Taylor was not one of Chordal's Yankee contractors. But as an outside hired expert, unhampered by tradition or personal history, and largely free to kick out old ways and introduce new, he was their lineal descendant. His letterhead read, Frederick Taylor, Consulting Engineer in Management. At first, he charged thirty-five dollars a day. Later he got forty, occasionally fifty. In today's money, he was getting something like a thousand dollars a day.

To keep track of where he went, whom he worked for, and how much he spent, from 1890 to 1897 he kept little vest-pocket notebooks, each roughly the size of a modern audio cassette. "Time working for the Northern Electrical Mfg. Co. of Madison, Wisconsin," he'd squeeze into the top of the little page, then list the days and half days he'd worked, the date of his bill, when he was paid, and how much, along with a separate record of expenses. He recorded details of industrial processes, listed the names of suppliers and their products, made sketches of mill layouts and machinery. He noted the addresses of new business contacts and old friends. He detailed his purchases of fruit, cologne, flowers, candy (he must have had an insatiable sweet tooth), and theater tickets; whenever he had the chance, wherever he was— Philadelphia, New York, Boston—he found time to see a show, usually a play, but sometimes the opera or circus. He wrote down the names of songs and books, occasionally sayings or song lyrics. When his pocket was picked, of twenty-six dollars, he recorded that, too.

All through the period—the heyday after all, of the robber barons— Taylor rubbed up close to the underbelly of American business life, with its sometimes rapacious competition, mistrust, and greed. If he had illusions left after seeing a William Sellers or William Collins Whitney up close, they were gone by the end of this time. Indeed, however idealistic or "progressive" his ideas would later seem to some, they would also bear the stamp of the cruel struggles for business survival, little checked by nobler sentiments, that he had witnessed all around him.

For Taylor, it was a difficult time. As the outsider, he was often pitched into some roiling muddle of a problem, veined with personality conflicts, and with long-entrenched work practices, whether of shop or back office, that needed rooting out. Always he had a new client to please, typically someone with his own large ego, unwilling either to cede him all the authority he requested or reach down in his pockets deep enough to suit his grand visions. So during this period, Taylor never had carte blanche to develop his ideas, as he'd enjoyed at Midvale; rather, it was one element of his system here, another there, depending on who was footing the bill.

That was the downside of these years. The upside was that companies and industries began to blur into each other, while his own ideas stood out bold and fresh against them. At Midvale, he had been part of a specific community, with its own technology and industrial heritage. Now, called in to systematize, organize, or reform this firm or that, he had fleeting encounters with many enterprises, broadening his experience and making his embryonic ideas seem to him truer and more broadly applicable. Could he be blamed if, by 1898, the particular industry scarcely seemed to matter anymore? If it seemed to him that his gift lay not in making electric motors or paper pulp or ball bearings, but in his methods, the larger principles governing them, his system?

∾

Fitchburg, Massachusetts. October 1893.

On August 25, 1893, while still in Madison, Taylor wrote a business associate that he had spent the past six weeks studying bookkeeping and accounting. Shuttling between Madison and New York, he'd several times visited the Investment Company's main office and watched in frank amazement the keeping of its books. "I saw all of these statements made out in pencil by the secretary of the company and the bookkeeper, and the whole work was done in less than two hours. This was really a remarkable piece of work as the transactions for that month footed up more than $200,000—three days or more with any other system. Taylor's correspondent was Chauncey Smith, vice president of the Simonds Rolling Machine Company, of Fitchburg, Massachusetts, a town of about twenty-five thousand located forty miles west of Boston. Taylor would be involved with the company for most of the next decade and even now sat on its board of directors.

After the Civil War, a Fitchburg native, George F. Simonds, had returned home and gone into business with his brother, in their father's old scythe- and pickax-manufacturing shop, making knives and reaper parts. Four years later, they'd moved across town, built a new factory out on Main Street to the east, and soon were making piles of money.

Yet then, in 1888, at the age of forty-five, Simonds pulled out, left the company to his brother, and went his own way. Four years earlier, he'd begun playing with an idea for a new machine that could take any piece of cylindrical stock, roll it between upper and lower dies, and deliver it in any shape you pleased; he'd tried it first using bits of putty or dough in wooden "dies." Starting with ordinary rods, you could churn out projectiles, spindles, pedal pins, machine handles, screws, or boot calks (the cleats projecting from lumbermen's boots); a single machine could make eighteen thousand of these calks daily, versus two thousand by older methods. Brainchild in hand, Simonds set up a company and built a brick factory on Willow Street, across the street from that of the family business.

In 1888, Simonds invited two hundred industrialists and engineers from around the country to see the new works, brought them up from Boston on a special train, let them watch the fourteen rolling machines spewing forth work, treated them to a plush repast by a famous Boston caterer, and sent them away with dropped jaws. "It is the greatest thing in half a century," one of them said. "No one can ever compete with that contrivance, or the corporation that will control it," said another, a Boston engineer. "And as for profit, why, sir, it will coin wealth like a mint."

Simonds' new rolling machines could make anything round in cross section. But its bread and butter was ball bearings, the smooth, hard spheres of steel, precise down to a few ten-thousandths of an inch, on which the wheels of the world would run over the next century. Until Simonds came along, you had to cut them one by one on a lathe or a screw machine, which was just a lathe automatically fed stock from which to turn out identical copies. Simonds's invention made balls cheaper, quicker, better. In 1894, the company issued a sixty-four-page brochure bursting with testimonials. Its balls found use in baby carriages, skates, giant cranes, in anything where friction was the foe—including, Simonds crowed, "the bearing for revolving the dome of the Lick Observatory," the great telescope on California's Mount Hamilton finished a few years before.

But most Simonds balls went into bicycles. With air-filled tires, diamond frames, and chain-driven rear wheels replacing the precarious high wheelers, the bicycle had assumed something like its present form. Everyone was riding. In 1895, Chicago alone supported five hundred cycling clubs, each with distinctive colors and uniforms. Even in little blue-collar Fitchburg, members of the nascent League of American Wheelmen numbered one hundred. "Voluminous petticoats of women gave way to the divided skirt or bloomers topped by colorful jackets with leg o'mutton sleeves," one local history had it. "Men appeared at their offices in knickerbockers, knee-length stockings, gay sweaters and peaked caps." Bicycle production—by 27 manufacturers in 1890, 312 in 1900—shot up into the millions per year with no sign of slackening.

Each cost anywhere from twenty-five to more than one hundred and fifty dollars.

And each needed ball bearings, in which perfect eighth-inch or three-sixteenth-inch balls, entirely hidden from view, rolled within finely ground doughnut-shaped hollows called races. Ball bearings wasted in friction much less of a rider's limited muscle power. And they were safer: before them, bearings were just primitive bushings, cylinders turning within cylinders that were apt to abruptly seize, bringing the wheel up short as if by a powerful brake, and sending the rider over the handlebar. Bicycles needed balls in prodigious quantities. A wheel bearing might use a couple of dozen of them; a bicycle, perhaps a hundred. And a Simonds rolling machine could churn them out like nothing had before.

The flexible new machine could make artillery projectiles, too, and on display for George Simonds's visitors in 1888 were inch-thick slabs of armor penetrated by the steel projectiles that his rolling machines made. It was these projectiles that had brought Taylor and Simonds together. In 1889, a Simonds official wrote Taylor at Midvale, inquiring about forging patents Taylor held and suggesting a possible collaboration. The projectile business never amounted to much, but Taylor was smitten by the Simonds technology and bought stock in the company. By October 1889, he had entered into an agreement to peddle Simonds stock among his friends, his commission as high as thirteen dollars per share. Within six months, he had sold about a hundred thousand dollars' worth; cousin Ernest Wright and Midvale associate H. L. Gantt were among the buyers.

The following August, George Simonds wrote Taylor about the company's management headaches and suggested they meet. Taylor had problems enough at the pulp mill by now, and the meeting apparently never came off. Still, by 1892 and probably earlier, he was on the company's board of directors and could see its growing pains up close: Simonds should be able to dominate the burgeoning ball market yet hadn't. And it had little control over its production costs. "In pursuance of our recent conversation regarding the keeping of costs," Taylor wrote vice president Chauncey Smith in December 1892, "I beg leave to enclose a description of the method of keeping costs which we used at the Midvale Steel Co.," which helped them decide, for example, which products they could profitably manufacture.

Taylor was writing not of machines, or pulp digesters, or piecework, or even of cost reduction; the subject was simply *keeping track* of costs. He was stepping into a territory of charts and long columns of figures—bookkeeping and accounting—that back then was not at all cut-and-dried. Today, when computerized credit card statements spit out the cost of mail-order purchases and hotel stays, all broken down by category, it may be difficult to appreciate how primitive accounting was then. In his little notebooks, Taylor would record how much money he started with, add the amount advanced by the company, subtract what he had spent for personal items like theater tickets or candy, note how much was left at trip's end, and bill the company for the difference. This system was not appreciably less refined than that used by many big companies for monitoring their costs. And in his letter to Chauncey Smith, he was saying that something more finely nuanced was needed if Simonds was to pin down its true costs of production.

Before the industrial revolution made firms larger and widened the area over which they operated, it hadn't mattered all that much, and you could get by with almost anything. A company might have one account listing the money paid into the business, another its expenses, another its revenues. Then, at year's end, it would tote up the figures and glean some rude sense of how well or poorly it had done. This was all you needed or wanted, since most small companies bought most goods and services from outside. If you needed a boiler fixed, you called in a boiler mechanic and paid him, and the transaction duly appeared on the company's books.

But now, with the expanded scale of late nineteenth-century business, critical information was getting lost. Now, very likely, you fixed your boiler in-house. But how did you establish its real cost and apportion it among the company's many products? Just what sorts of numbers did you need to gather, how often, and how would you track them, and how manipulate them, and just what would they mean? In treating transactions within the company, the old accounting was largely mute. Moreover, the information it provided was often useless by the time you got it—last year's figures hopelessly dated. Needed was a system of "managerial accounting," designed to supply cost and other data to company managers fast enough to help them make today's decisions today.

Learn bookkeeping? He'd sooner kill himself, Taylor once blustered to a friend. But at the Investment Company, he was answerable to Whitney, who worried more about dollars than wood pulp. Besides, bookkeeping and accounting weren't all that alien to him: like time study, they brought seeming precision to decisions otherwise ruled by hunch.

In the summer of 1893, Taylor set about to master the latest in accounting practice and bring it to Simonds. During late June or early July he went to New York, where the Investment Company's accounting staff showed him their methods. These constituted "an exceedingly valuable system," Taylor wrote Chauncey Smith, "as we are able to make out monthly statements from our books showing almost everything that anyone might ask about the state of our business," complete with a balance sheet of the sort ordinarily prepared only once a year.

Demonstrating the system in New York was company accountant William Basley, who had worked with financier Jay Gould and consulted for several railroads. It was the far-flung railroads, early prototypes of the modern company, that had pioneered and spread the new methods. For example, Carnegie Steel, which had one of the most modern accounting systems, had picked up its methods from the railroads, to which its early Bessemer mills supplied rails. The accounting techniques that Taylor absorbed from Basley likewise had their origins in railroad practice.

On July 12, a little after Taylor's visit, Basley wrote him with a detailed summary of the system. "All book entries . . . should be made in such a manner that the accounts will of themselves detect errors," he began without preamble, going on to describe each account and the principles on which it was based. The system that Taylor absorbed from Basley, made into his own, and altered to suit his clients, was one he would apply at company after company. It gave you, monthly, a statement of expenses, broken down by jobs labeled by letters and numbers and, later, by a special mnemonic system. It applied overhead not only to wages but to each machine, with time spent on a job the basis for its proportion of the overhead. And, as with most anything Taylor touched, it grew more baroque in its complexity over the years.

Taylor's accounting system was just one piece of what he offered his clients, along with time study, piece rates, standardization, and the rest. By the spring of 1895, but probably much before, he had a stamp made to advertise his business:

FRED W. TAYLOR, M.E.

Ross Street, Germantown, Philadelphia

CONSULTING ENGINEER

Systematizing Shop Management and

Manufacturing Costs a Specialty

If cost accounting was a sideline to him, his contributions to it would be enough to earn the attention of accounting historians a century later and be deemed "a basis for all modern industrial accounting."

∼

By August 1893, when he wrote Chauncey Smith, Taylor had met with Basley, studied what he called "our New York system of bookkeeping," called for linking it to the system of shop records he had developed at Midvale, and was pushing it on Smith and Edward Sawyer, Simonds's treasurer. Anything less than a full, accurate reckoning of product costs, he wrote Smith, was "more misleading almost than no system at all." It would lead to grievous error. "If it comes to a question, next fall, of how much we need to cut prices in order to meet competition," the partial system risked distorting their decisions.

On August 7, Sawyer wrote back, "How long would it take you to reorganize our system at Fitchburg?" Taylor should come and visit him in Boston, spend the night at his house, and plan to discuss the issue.

Later that week, Lou and her mother traveled to a resort on the Isle of Shoals, a group of islands just south of Portsmouth, New Hampshire, that straddled the border with Maine. If Fred joined them, it was briefly. "I found the hotel restful," Lou wrote about one of their trips there, "but—alas—Fred could find little enjoyment in, as he said, 'idle moments rocking on the piazza.'" While Lou enjoyed the ocean breezes, Taylor was on the road, headed for Boston and New York.

When he wrote Hammond again on August 25, Lou back in Madison with him now and the two of them horseback riding again, he mentioned no definite plans. But a month later, the future had firmed up. After October 1, he wrote Hammond, "I expect to be busy in and near Boston."

They moved into the city's Arlington Hotel, which for most of the following fall and winter would be their home. By mid-October, Taylor was shuttling between Boston and Fitchburg, busy installing a new

system of accounts, a task that would occupy him until February of the
following year.

~

New York. December 1893.

"The more I look into the belt record at Midvale the more interesting it becomes," Taylor wrote Joseph B. King, Midvale machine
shop foreman, on March 22, 1893, while still with the Investment
Company. He referred to the voluminous data built up since 1884 in
the Midvale belting experiments, which King had kept up since he'd
left. Now, with belts giving him such grief at the pulp mill, he was
working on a paper on the subject for the American Society of
Mechanical Engineers. In June, he wrote John H. Cooper, a well-
known belting expert, requesting a critique of what he'd written. "I
hesitate to take the emphatic ground which I have taken as to the
proper rules for belting," he wrote, "without having all possible light
thrown on to the subject."

It's hard to imagine Taylor slinking away from emphatic ground on
anything. Indeed, his paper, which he delivered in New York that
December, ran roughshod over conventional wisdom, pronouncing a
new last word on belting. Not surprisingly, it stirred what one sup-
porter called "ill-bred and bitter feelings" against it. The following year,
someone would write Sanford Thompson, Taylor's friend from the
pulp mill, "From what I hear from practical men and members of the
ASME, I should think Taylor would wish he had never presented that
paper on belting." But in fact, Taylor's paper was consulted and quoted
all over. And more than twenty-five years later, in 1919, with Taylor
dead and his every utterance plumbed for wisdom, a British publisher
would reprint it in book form, calling it "the basis for all subsequent
studies, remaining the chief authority on its subject."

"Notes on Belting," the paper was called, but as Henry Towne
observed at the New York meeting, it "could more fittingly be
described as a treatise." Its first ten pages comprised a copious index,
summarizing its conclusions and directing readers to the paragraph
number in which a point was substantiated or developed:

No. 23. The speed at which belting runs has comparatively little
effect on its life until it passes 2,500 to 3,000 ft. per min.

Refer to Paragraph No. (86) to (89) and (71), Life not affected by speed.

and so on through thirty-six numbered conclusions.

Oak tanned belts and rubber, splices, coefficient of friction, load per square inch, stretch, slack side and tight side, cones and counter-shafts—it was all there. But boiled down, Taylor's paper called for belts twice as thick as current practice ordained. "This great difference," another engineer, William Kent, pointed out, reflected a wholesale shift in emphasis. Taylor was actually tackling a new problem: for him it wasn't how wide and thick a belt must be to transmit so much horse-power but, rather, to transmit it "with the minimum cost for belt repairs, the longest life to the belt, and the smallest loss and inconve-nience from stopping the machine while the belt is being tightened or repaired." The belts were the same, but Taylor's way of looking at them was new. To him, they weren't so much transmitters of power as poten-tial impediments to production. When the belts broke, the machines stopped, and the factory grew still. And *this must not be.*

Even by 1895, the forests of belts were beginning to thin. The over-head shafting, countershafts, and leisurely looping lines of belting were, around the country, starting to give way to powerful electric motors, one to each machine tool. The complex diagrams of pulleys and belts that engineers from this period made in their notebooks—*36-inch diameter pulley drives 80-inch diameter pulley through 12-inch wide belt, which is tied by 3¹/₂-inch shaft to . . .* , and so on, across the factory, down through the ceiling, up from the floor below—were yielding to schematic diagrams showing power lines and electrical components. Belting was like a biological species snuffed out by the survival pres-sures of evolution.

Still, in Taylor's treatise on it, one could see that same exhaustive-ness of treatment.

~

Philadelphia. September 1894.

When Taylor started there the morning of September 14, 1894, William Cramp & Sons Ship and Engine Building Company of Phila-delphia esteemed itself "the greatest naval arsenal in the Western Hemisphere." Founded in 1839, when a dozen other shipyards hugged the Philadelphia riverfront, it almost alone among them made the great shift from wood to iron after the Civil War. Cramp's made steamers for the New York to Havana run. It made tugboats and yachts. It made ten-thousand-ton battleships for Japan, Russia, and other nations, as well as the United States; soon, the USS *Maine* would slide down the ways at its docks along the Delaware River. When Taylor went to work there, the shipyard employed fifty-six hundred men—machinists, riveters, plumbers, riggers, and molders, from eighteen-dollar-a week patternmakers to eight-dollar-a week laborers. His job was to reorganize its vast machine shops, both those of Cramp's proper, and those of I. P. Morris, the old-line Philadelphia company that Cramp's had absorbed.

He wasted no time. He started on a Friday and by the following Wednesday had submitted a five-page "preliminary report" to Edwin Cramp, superintending engineer, based on his initial tour of the shops. He wanted to see all belting spliced, instead of laced and hooked, the tools required for the job henceforth to be kept in the toolroom. He had prepared a statement on belting practice, drawn from his ASME paper, that he wished to see applied to the shop from then on; Mr. Cramp should please see Exhibit B. The countershafts, which transmitted power through belts down to the individual machines, needed to be changed—Exhibit C, enclosed, explained how—and new ones ordered. The shop's machine tools would have to be respeeded. But of course, that could not be done all at once, and he was going along with Mr. Johnson, one of three Cramp's employees assigned to help him, that they should begin with one of the forty-eight-inch planers. Mr. Cramp ought to know, too, that he had talked to Wm. Sellers & Company, manufacturers of the planer, who had advised a cutting speed slower than the twenty-four feet per minute that he, Taylor, deemed best. Their opinion, he added, "does not in the least alter my judgment in the matter." Fred Taylor was blowing through the shops.

Back in April, he had done further work for Simonds and afterward put in a brief stint with Chicago's William Deering Company. He spent the spring and summer back in Philadelphia, probably at the home of his parents, except for a month of ocean breezes in Belmar, on the New Jersey coast near Atlantic City. Now, with his new client, Cramp's, he would remain the next six months, into the following spring. At least for a while, he and Lou stayed at the Hamilton Hotel, a couple of blocks south of City Hall. Lou saw old friends. Taylor worked, usually six days a week, issuing a stream of reports and recommendations.

Less than two weeks into the job, he recommended that tools for everyday work be made from self-hardening steel, an expensive alloy normally reserved for cutting only the very hardest forgings. Self-hardening steel went back to an 1868 discovery in England by Robert Mushet, son of a Scottish ironmaster. He found that a dollop of tungsten added to steel, about 7 percent, made for an alloy that, unlike ordinary carbon steel, need not be quenched in water to harden; instead, you left it out in the air to cool and wound up with a steel that cut forgings others could not. Mushet took out no patent on his breakthrough but kept the knowledge to himself and had a Sheffield company make it for him. "The whole manufacturing process . . . was shrouded in secrecy," writes English historian Geoffrey Tweedale:

> The mixtures for the steel were compounded at Mushet's Works deep in the Forest of Dean. . . . Elaborate methods were devised to conceal the destination of the mixture . . . , workmen were sworn to secrecy, and not even all the partners knew the secrets of manufacture.

Taylor had first seen self-hardening steel as an apprentice, back at the pump works. Now, twenty years later and notwithstanding Mushet's elaborate secrecy, many companies made versions of it, like Sanderson and Midvale. But they were all a little different, and no one knew which cut best. To find out once and for all, Taylor urged a careful experiment. He was soon shuttling between Cramp's and Wm. Sellers & Company, which had a readily adjustable electric motor–driven lathe and had agreed to share with Cramp's the cost of the experiments.

And who was on the lathe, tightening down the tool, selecting the speeds and feeds, and taking the cuts? Fred Taylor himself. Years later, he would compare this winter only to his apprenticeship as a pleasant, relaxed time. "I worked more steadily on that lathe than I had ever worked in my whole lifetime as a workman," he testified before a congressional committee. "I give you my word, Mr. Chairman, that during that winter there was never a day that I was overworked, and I was physically soft; I was a comparatively middle-aged man"—he observed his thirty-ninth birthday in March 1895—"and had not done any work by hand for twelve or fourteen years." The comparison was not entirely apt, of course. Taylor was his own boss; if he worked hard or long it was his own doing. He selected every cut, determined the feed and speed. No one stood over him with a stopwatch.

That winter he filled his notebooks with cleanly rendered sketches of tool-edge contours, tables of results and, in his closely packed but legible hand, descriptions of his experimental protocols: "This tool was set in the tool post of Sellers 48" lathe #1106 with a packing piece 1 inch thick underneath it. It was used on diameters of forgings ranging from 8 inches down to $6^1/_2$ inches. It was fed in the direction of the arrow on the sketch."

For these experiments, Taylor often did his own forging and heat treating. (He ordered the tool's identifying labels removed but was familiar enough with some of them to sometimes recognize them just from how they cut.) Each tool had to be heated, hammered into its proper shape, then heated again to a temperature that left it with just the right qualities of hardness and toughness. This key temperature was reckoned not in degrees Fahrenheit but by the color of the glowing tool—a "bright cherry red." Even engineering papers routinely used such terms, but, as Taylor learned to his cost, they were imprecise at best.

The area of the Sellers shops where he worked had a northern exposure, which furnished what for Taylor became a kind of "standard light" by which to gauge the color of the tool he was heating. But at Cramp's, the shop was darker, making "bright cherry red" a bit cooler than at Sellers. Taylor realized as much, tried to compensate, but failed to get the tools hot enough. As a result, the Midvale steel that in his Sellers experiments performed so well did poorly when heat-treated at Cramp's, and he was "laughed at by both the tool dressers and machinists."

In the end he never settled on which brand was better, only that both were better than anything else. But more important, he found that these self-hardening steels had no business being kept locked in a vault, as it were, for use only on special jobs with particularly hard forgings, the existing practice. They were more expensive, but it was false economy, concluded Taylor, to save them for special cases. They cut so much faster, on all sorts of jobs, to warrant their general use around the shop.

This was big news, but in a report to Edwin Cramp the following spring, the big news was buried. Taylor spelled out the measures he'd taken to date or was recommending—new tool-grinding machines in place, toolrooms planned and partly completed, belt maintenance by schedule, a play of soda water on the cutting tool; only in passing did he urge that self-hardening steel be used routinely around the shop. With these innovations in place, he said, the shop's machine tools could be speeded up by 60 percent.

But a personal letter to Cramp, dated the day before, put a different spin on this. "I regard it of the highest importance for your concern that the exact considerations which govern your speeding up in the shop should only be known to yourself and as few of the members of your firm as practicable." All of the measures in the report mattered, but using self-hardening steel mattered much more. If Cramp's employees knew that, he wrote, word would reach his competitors. So, for public consumption, he had prepared the other report, which "purposely does not show the exact weight" of each factor.

The whole contrived business bore what would emerge as a distinctive Taylor stamp. As an engineer, he was alive to the power of the scientific method, doggedly in search of experimental truth; but he was not above shading facts or omitting inconvenient details. He was at home not only with the stopwatch but also with the conjurer's bag of rhetorical tricks. He was a high-minded philosopher-engineer, and a huckster; a scientist, and a showman ever disposed to throw a spotlight onto one part of the stage while leaving another in shadow.

On May 5, two months after submitting his report to Cramp, Taylor handed in his final bill, for the last twelve days of his work. While the circumstances surrounding his departure are hazy, his penchant for spending big money now for the sake of big savings later invariably tested the patience and the pocketbooks of his clients. At Cramp's, as at the Investment Company, the story was the same: if Fred Taylor got his hands on your shop, you could expect to part with a fortune.

Taylor, Copley writes delicately, "did not escape from Cramp's with spirit unwounded." Just a few months later, when a future disciple, Morris Cooke, started at the shipyard, Taylor's influence was nowhere evident. And three years later, when Edwin Cramp's former assistant, Leighton Lee, wrote Taylor that the toolroom had been expanded in the part of the works that were the old I. P. Morris shop, it was all news to Taylor. "It is very satisfactory indeed to hear that my work was not entirely thrown away there," he wrote Lee with chagrin. "Judging from what Mr. Cramp has written, I should have thought my work was worse than useless."

Fitchburg, Massachusetts April 1895.

Two weeks before finishing at Cramp's, on March 23, 1895, Taylor was on the train to Fitchburg, busy with Simonds and the ball bearing business once more. But now it was not accounting that occupied him. Five years after passage of the Sherman Antitrust Act prohibited "any contract, combination, or conspiracy . . . in restraint of trade," but before it was wielded against anyone but labor unions, Fred Taylor was getting paid to help establish just such a combination.

The bicycle was still in its heyday, but the entry of more manufacturers into the ball bearing business had forced down prices and squeezed profits. George F. Simonds had died the previous November, at age fifty-one, after falling off a train, and Simonds company executives suspected their competitors of stealing the patented technology that was his legacy. The industry was chaotic, with mutual suspicion rampant and competition ruinous, the rich nutrient stew that made for combination and cartel: simply agree to limit production and prop up prices, and you could ensure profits for all. The makers of welded-steel tubing did it; so did the steel rail manufacturers. Why couldn't the ball makers?

"The object of this Association," the working draft for an American Ball Association constitution declared,

> is to consolidate the profits which its members may derive from
> the manufacture and sale of steel balls, and secure an equitable
> division of said profits among such members. . . . [They shall
> agree] to the minimum selling price at which any balls shall be
> sold.

Price-fixing, generations of antitrust lawyers would call it, but in the 1890s, everyone was doing it.

Taylor apparently embraced his role with enthusiasm. On April 20, from Philadelphia, he wrote George Weymouth, Simonds's vice president and general manager, that he had looked into how the steel rail manufacturers worked their cartel, and wished to recommend something along the same lines:

> 1st—Find the total consumption of balls throughout the country for this year.

> 2nd—Determine the percentage of the total year's output with which each [firm] . . . will be satisfied . . .

> 3rd—A minimum price to be determined below which . . . no orders are to be accepted.

And so on for ten numbered paragraphs, relentless in their cold logic.

The stumbling block to any such agreement, Taylor allowed, was "the intense suspicion with which each man regards his neighbor," the problem in other cartels whose meetings he had attended. They must keep their eyes on the prize: higher prices and the elimination of competition. And they must "keep the fact quiet, if possible, that there is any such combination whatever."

The following Thursday morning the association was to meet at the Murray Hill Hotel in New York. But the "intense suspicion" about which Taylor had warned enfeebled the combination before it got started. Letters, telegrams, and phone calls among these gentlemen conspirators were riddled with threats and pressure: "Frankly, if I were in your position . . . I should not be over-particular to hold for what I consider my full rights. . . . The matter cannot be delayed." John Grant, of Cleveland Screw Machine, threatened to start a second competing company. And wasn't Excelsior Machine Works infringing on the Simonds patents?

On June 24, 1895, Alfred Bowditch, president of Simonds, wrote Eben W. Clark, of the Chicago company presumably acting as clearinghouse for the combination, "I think you must have misunderstood my conversation to you on Saturday over the telephone." To clear up the confusion, Bowditch suggested he look up Taylor who, until June 28, would be in Detroit at the Russell House Hotel.

In Taylor's record of the time for which he charged Simonds there is a four-day gap, corresponding to his Detroit stay. The ball combination counted for nothing in the end, but in those four unpaid days in Detroit he took his first steps onto the world stage. He was in Detroit for the thirty-first biannual meeting of the American Society of Mechanical Engineers. There, before a hundred and forty engineers, he presented a paper that for the first time publicly outlined the rudiments of what would later be called the Taylor system.

5

"A PARTIAL SOLUTION"

$\sim$

I N THE YEARS BEFORE TAYLOR DELIVERED HIS PAPER, the idea that science could cure the ills afflicting humankind, and that progress could rein unchecked and bountiful, had become an article of faith among many engineers.

In 1881, Robert Thurston, first ASME president, reminded his audience of engineers how earlier mechanical pioneers had prophesied "suites of carriages" whizzing over railroad tracks at forty or fifty miles per hour; some day, inventor Oliver Evans, a contemporary of Thomas Jefferson, had written, "a carriage will start from Washington in the morning, the passengers will breakfast at Baltimore, dine in Philadelphia, and sleep in New York the same day." The miracle had come to pass. Improved weapons and self-propelled torpedoes, Thurston went on, heralded a day "of freedom on the high seas and of cessation of all naval warfare." That newest wonder, electricity, promised still greater boons: "For the occasional mild light of the moon, or the yellow sickly flare of the gas flame, will soon be substituted the less uncertain and always available, and always beautiful and mellow, radiance of the electric flame."

Seven years later, another ASME president could be more sanguine yet. "In ancient times it was known only as the thunderbolts of Jove," said George H. Babcock of electricity. But now, already,

> it rings our call bells, lights our gas, watches sleeplessly in our
> dwellings for burglars, regulates the heat in our rooms to a fraction

of a degree, makes our plated ware and our electrotypes, duplicates
our medals, and starts our exhibitions at the nod of a president or
a king a thousand miles away. . . . [Thanks to 1.7 million miles of
telegraph line,] we read at our breakfast tables in the morning the
news of the whole world of the events of the evening before, some
of it at an earlier hour than it occurs, and business men trade with
customers one thousand or three thousand miles away with almost
the same facility as with their next door neighbors.

"In looking about for fields to conquer," Babcock went on, "the
question springs to mind, Shall we ever fly?" The weight of steam
engines was dropping; so was that of dynamos and electric motors:

When man has learned to generate power with, say, one-tenth the
weight of apparatus that is now required, then by making the
framework of his flying machine of aluminum tubes, there is no
good reason to doubt that he will become master of the air, as he is
now master of the water, and will be able to fly from place to place
with all the certainty and safety of a bird.

In 1887, sixteen years before the Wright Brothers flew at Kitty
Hawk, hopes and dreams were still in bountiful supply. Clouds of
poison gas washing over the artillery-raked trenches of the Western
Front had not yet befouled the pristine ideal of progress. For lucky, able
men like Babcock, progress was still humanity's birthright.

But even for them, an obstacle remained: the relations between men
and men. In the workplaces from which the new wonders came—the
sewing machine factories, cotton mills, steel mills—teeming masses of
workers sweated and strained to make a living. The gap between the
rich and everyone else had never seemed greater. Andrew Carnegie
enjoyed yachts and mansions, a castle back in Scotland. His workers
endured twelve-hour days in the mills, then crawled home exhausted to
two-room houses. Conditions were better than in Europe; you could
still start at the bottom and make a fortune as Carnegie, an impoverished weaver's son, did. Still, the nation's workplaces seethed, and the
threat of strikes gnawed at every big-bellied businessman's composure.

In another ASME address, in November 1882, around the time
Taylor was doing his first, primitive time studies at Midvale, Robert

Thurston broadened his presidential purview from the narrowly technical. "In singular and discreditable contrast" to progress in mechanical engineering, he said,

> stands one feature of our work which has more importance to us
> and to the world . . . than any modern invention or than any
> discovery in science. I refer to the *Relations of the Employers and
> the Working Classes* and to the mutual interests of labor and
> capital. It is from us, if from any body of men, that the world
> should expect a complete and thorough satisfactory practical
> solution of the so-called "labor problem."

Needed, he went on, was

> a *Scheme of Industrial Organization*, that shall exhibit highest
> possible efficiency—one that will prepare the children and youth
> of the country to enter upon lives of maximum usefulness, and to
> do the work that may be given them to do with ease and comfort,
> while, at the same time aiding them to attain health, happiness and
> content[ment], even if not independence and wealth.

The masses need not enjoy all the advantages of the few, just enough to keep their discontent below a full boil.

A few industrial leaders had embraced the novel idea that holding wages just barely above subsistence might not be the only, or the best, way to maintain social peace and their own favored circumstances. They noted the superiority of American wages to those in England, for example, observed the healthier state of American industry, and suggested there might be a connection. At the Chicago ASME meeting where Towne delivered "The Engineer as an Economist," Captain Metcalfe had argued in support of the precept "that cheap labor is not always profitable." Later that year, at the New York meeting, W. E. Partridge made so bold as to argue that high wages weren't a problem but a solution. Every cent that went to workmen weakened the company and cheated the stockholders? Not so, he said. For if you dug a little deeper into the company's pockets than the cruel exigencies of the labor market required, you'd gain a more compliant, harder-working labor force—which meant more profit, not less. Such were the radical notions to which reasonable men were driven by the "labor problem."

By 1895, the problem had grown still more pressing, with the bloody Homestead strike of July 1892 still raw in the nation's memory. During those awful summer days, three hundred Pinkerton guards hired by the Carnegie Steel Company battled with workers who had taken over the company's mill at Homestead, Pennsylvania. The two sides exchanged thousands of rifle shots and shotgun blasts. The workers got hold of a cannon and fired it at a barge bearing the Pinkerton men; a man's head was blown off. Only the arrival of the state militia quelled further violence, but not before dozens of both sides were wounded and ten men lay dead.

Frederick Taylor's paper, "A Piece Rate System," was set squarely against this backdrop. "The ordinary piece-rate system involves a permanent antagonism between employers and men," he began. "The system introduced by the writer, however, is directly the opposite, both in theory and in its results. It makes each workman's interests the same as that of his employer." This was no narrow technical offering, like his paper on belting, but, rather, a prescription for workplace harmony framed, with Taylor's usual keen affinity for his times, in terms any nervous industrialist could understand. "One of the chief advantages . . . of the system," he wrote, the national mood reflected in every word,

is that it promotes a most friendly feeling between the men and their employers, and so renders labor unions and strikes unnecessary.

There has never been a strike under the differential rate system of piece-work, although it has been in operation for the past ten years in the steel business, which has been during this period more subject to strikes and labor problems than almost any other industry.

No more the hell of Homestead; enter, please, the radiant mechanical heaven of Midvale.

Taylor began by dissecting existing pay plans, as well as those intended to remedy their failings; the "labor problem" focused not only on how much you paid your workers but on how you paid them. Might there be some clever system that better roused them to productive effort yet left them happier, too? In 1889, Henry Towne had advanced one candidate, called gain sharing, in which workers earned a share of however much more they produced than they had before; at Yale &

Towne, where it covered about three hundred workers, the plan typically yielded dividends of about 5 percent beyond base pay.

Two years later, at the Providence meeting, Frederick Halsey, a Cornell engineering graduate four months Taylor's junior, weighed in with his premium plan. With it, workers producing no more than they had before earned no less. But those producing beyond past levels earned a premium, typically about one third, of any labor costs thus saved. If in the past you made ten pieces in a ten-hour day, earning three dollars, or thirty cents per hour, then twelve pieces represented a two-hour saving, or sixty cents. Your share, at one third, came to twenty cents, your total pay to $3.20. As Halsey pictured it, the plan was something like a saleman's salary-plus-commission. It would enjoy a wide following, both in America and abroad, in coming years.

The Towne and Halsey schemes, Taylor allowed, were the best around. Yet both were flawed and, despite their seeming differences, for the same reason: they both took historical precedent, the worker's past output, as the starting point. This, to him, represented feeble surrender to the dead past, to layers of workplace tradition, guesswork, and error built up over the years and ossified, like fossil fragments, into daily shop practice.

Taylor proposed—and at Detroit, in 1895, this was a bold new idea—to throw the past aside and start afresh with a true, scientific reckoning of what constituted a fair day's work. Management's duty was to study, analyze, and improve each job; set new, higher levels of production; and help the men achieve them. This was not just another payment scheme, like Towne's or Halsey's; it was a whole new way of running shops and managing workmen. Rooted in science, it erected a new, higher wall between mind and muscle, planning and execution. To one scholar, Horace Drury, it depended on a management that was "supposed to know more about the work than the men themselves—to know more than they know at present, and more than they can discover in the future."

Taylor called the paper "A Piece Rate System, A Step Toward Partial Solution of the Labor Problem." But behind the false modesty—it is hard to view it as anything else—he was aiming his sights on the premier problem of the industrial world. He was trashing "the old system," as he referred to it, and setting out a new one that placed the shop entirely in management's expert hands; you did the work its way, met its production standards, in return for much higher pay. Towne and Halsey offered a carrot for higher production; Taylor's was a bigger, more scrumptious one. Everyone, worker and boss, would get what they wanted.

$\sim$

It was twenty-one years since Fred Taylor, fresh from Exeter and living with his parents on Ross Street, had begun his apprenticeship. At the pump works, a new world had opened up to him. But whether or not he'd have sanctioned the idea, "A Piece Rate System" bore the flavor of his old world, represented a nod to the ethical preoccupations of his parents and their abolitionist friends back in Germantown.

However caustically he would describe it later, Germantown's Quaker-influenced social agenda was hard to entirely throw off. It had already surfaced in the lives of at least two close family friends. His cousin Edith Wright, sister of Exeter roommate Jamie and Stevens classmate Ernest, had visited a slum in the Point Breeze section of Philadelphia owned by her abolitionist father and came away horrified. She prevailed on him to lease her the property and let her turn it into a model community, which she and another woman did.

Florence Kelley—mentioned frequently in his mother's letters to him at Exeter, with whom his sister Mary had played as a child, and whose grandaunt, Emily Taylor's friend Sarah Pugh, would always be an icon of right thinking—had become an ardent socialist. A vision of the ten-year-olds she had once seen working in a steel mill lingered with her always. After Cornell and a stint at the University of Zurich, she had, by the time of Taylor's Detroit paper, translated into English the work of Marx's colleague, Friedrich Engels, worked with Jane Addams at Hull House in Chicago, and successfully lobbied for an Illinois law regulating sweatshops and child labor.

Taylor's paper could be seen to lie comfortably within this tradition. He had painted his Midvale experience onto a broader canvas, transmuted his youthful shop-floor angst into a statement of social idealism:

> Whether cooperation, the differential plan, or some other form
> of piece-work be chosen in connection with elementary rate-fixing,
> as the best method of working, there are certain fundamental facts

and principles which must be recognized and incorporated in any
system of management, before true and lasting success can be
attained; and most of these facts and principles will be found to be
not far removed from what the strictest moralists would call
justice.

Taylor wrote, too, of a "moral effect" and of "acts of personal kindness
and sympathy." Such softer sensibilities stood right beside the belligerent shop boss in him and hint that he still sought a neighborly nod
of approval from Quaker Germantown.

The social and ethical side of his paper was not lost on those who
heard him in Detroit. "The paper we have just listened to and the presentation made by Mr. Taylor," said John Penton, no engineer but
rather the former president of an iron molders' union, "strikes me as
being perhaps the most remarkable thing of its kind I have ever heard
in my life." The mere thought of the piecework abuses that he and his
co-workers had suffered over the years, he said, "causes me to
shudder." But Taylor's system promised to eradicate them and to
peacefully resolve problems like those "solved by the military at Homestead a year or two ago. . . . As a workman, I want to congratulate Mr.
Taylor and to say that his paper . . . is a landmark in the field of political
economy."

Other listeners were not so rhapsodic. Several questioned the undue
complexity of Taylor's scheme. And Halsey, a butt of Taylor's criticism,
questioned whether time study could really bathe shop work in such a
cold, clear light as its originator claimed; if so, he dared its author, furnish "the fullest possible details." Halsey left scant doubt that he
thought the task impossible, his own plan superior. But pro or con, the
men of the ASME recognized that Taylor had taken aim at broader
social concerns. The issue first addressed by Towne in "Gain Sharing"
and now by Taylor, said William Kent, was "one of the most important
questions, not only before this Society, but before the world today—the
harmonizing of labor and capital."

But unrooted in technical terrain, the discussion drifted, from
apprenticeships to, of all things, equal pay for women, the "labor
problem" perhaps suggesting a kindred "women question." And by the
end, Taylor was fed up that his colleagues had missed his central point:
that piece rates ought to be based on time study. "I am much surprised

and disappointed," he concluded, "that the elementary rate-fixing"—still his name for it—"has not received more attention during the discussion."

It was his own fault, of course. He could have framed his subject narrowly and technically, probably spawning narrow, technical responses. But he had chosen to give it a more global sweep. In responding, his listeners had merely drunk from the same cup.

$\sim$

Fred Taylor was not a gifted writer, nor were his papers ever notably graceful. Yet they did carry a peculiar force—in the strength of their conviction, which resonated in every line; in their sometimes hypnotizing repetition; in their seeming acknowledgment of objections that were then swept aside. To read a Taylor paper was to be borne along a highway from which turnoffs were barred until you'd reached the destination; letters from his father while he was at Exeter—long, leisurely sermons—shared something of this quality. Rarely did a Taylor sentence, by itself, charm. Yet a Taylor paper, as a whole, locked you in its embrace like a bear hug.

Taylor tried to avoid puffed-up language, preferring Anglo-Saxon words to those of Latin vintage because they were more "virile." Back at Exeter, his Greek master Cilley was remembered as "singularly fond of plain English, and had little patience with flowery translations"; grandiloquence didn't sit well with him. Nor would it have sat well among Taylor's friends at the pump works, nor at Midvale. From every side, then, he was pushed toward modesty of expression. The language of "A Piece Rate System" was, for its time, mostly unadorned. Taylor referred to himself as "the writer," avoiding the first person, and he projected himself as the soul of practicality, shop wisdom, and common sense.

Just once, or so it seemed to him later, another side of him surfaced. It came in the paper's very last paragraph:

> The level of the great mass of the world's labor has been, and
> must continue to be, regulated by causes so many and so complex
> as to be at best but dimly recognized.
> The utmost effect of any system, whether of management,
> social combination, or legislation, can be but to raise a small ripple

or wave of prosperity above the surrounding level, and the greater
hope of the writer is that, here and there, a few workmen, with
their employers, may be helped, through this system, towards the
crest of the wave.

This was neither plain, nor simple, nor modest. Rather, it ranked as
what he would contemptuously call "fine writing," and later, talking to
his son Kempton, he cited it as such. "I used to think a lot of 'fine
writing' myself once," he told his son, "but this is the only specimen of
[it] . . . which found its way into print." And, he added, "I am quite
ashamed of it." Ashamed, one suspects, because of its do-gooder ora-
tory; because he had failed to expunge every trace of the son of Germantown he still was; because real shop men didn't talk like that.

"A Piece Rate System" didn't make Taylor famous overnight. But
only in retrospect, in comparison to the splash made by his subsequent
papers and books, could one call it ignored. The editor of *Engineering
Magazine*, which reprinted it in 1896, called it "one of the most valuable contributions that have ever been given to technical literature."
Cassiers, an American popular engineering magazine, reprinted it, too.
And in June the following year, the American Economic Association
combined Taylor's paper with those of Towne and Halsey in a separate
publication, *The Adjustment of Wages to Efficiency*, observing that the
three papers were "not easily accessible to economic students" but
should be.

The paper also sparked what must have been Taylor's first puff of
international controversy when, in its August 9, 1895, issue, a London
trade magazine, *Electrical Review*, its correspondent apparently at the
Detroit meeting, took note of it. "Mr. Taylor's system does not strike us
as altogether satisfactory," he observed. Time studies were just too
complicated, and the setting of any piece rate, on any basis, was apt to
lead to workplace quarrels.

Still, Taylor's paper had crossed the Atlantic. A small stone cast into
a still pool, it had made its modest ripple.

6

ON THE ROAD, AGAIN

∾

BUFFALO, NEW YORK. *July 1895.*
"Do not pretend to be too smart," Taylor wrote H. S. Shadbolt on July 3, 1895, "as I think Jones will have a suspicion of a really first class mechanic."

Jones was Edward Jones, whose firm, the Excelsior Machine Company, of Tonawanda, New York, an industrial town north of Buffalo, was a Simonds competitor. Shadbolt, staying at the Stafford Hotel in Buffalo, was a detective, hired to infiltrate Excelsior and learn whether it used Simonds methods to manufacture balls. Taylor, just back from Detroit and off for a week's vacation at a hotel off Buzzards Bay, in Massachusetts, was overseeing his top spy.

A trip to Buffalo that May on ball combination business had convinced Taylor that Excelsior had infringed the Simonds patents. A rumpled "tit" of metal, nearly as large as the final ball itself, was formed at one stage of their manufacturing process—just as in the Simonds process. This and other hints, he wrote Bowditch, furnished "pretty direct evidence that Jones is using dies similar to ours."

That was at the end of May. Since then, he'd put Shadbolt, to whom he'd apparently been introduced by his friend Frank Steele, on the case. By June, Shadbolt was reporting back to him. Now, on July 3, Taylor wrote him that his chances of getting a job with Jones were better as laborer than as a mechanic. But if he failed to find work right away, he should "hire out as a farm laborer somewhere in the neighborhood. Before you leave your present employer be sure and get a recommendation from him for sobriety, hard work, etc."

Over the next three years, Taylor led industrial espionage against at least five companies, using no fewer than six professional detectives, amateur industrial spies, and company turncoats. To himself he reserved the role of string-puller and paymaster. "You will have to send me a little money," read a typical plea from one of his boys. Beginning in June 1895, expense statements, fifty-dollar weekly checks, signed receipts, ungrammatical appeals for money, and stolen information streamed through the mail.

One Taylor detective, W. A. Willard, infiltrated the Pope Manufacturing Company of Hartford, Connecticut, the country's premier bicycle manufacturer. "Well this is the worst job of geting what you want that could be," he wrote Taylor from Hartford on July 3, "but I dont dare to be very bold if I do the fat will be in the fire at once. but I think I shall fix them in the end and that is what I am here for."

Taylor had a recent Stevens graduate, Newcomb Carlton, approach Simonds competitors posing as advance man for a nonexistent group of capitalists on the prowl for worthy bicycle companies to buy. Carlton, who went on to become president of Western Union, later received "two rather savage letters" from a victim of his deception. But, as he wrote Taylor toward the end of the year, "I find that the lying I have lately done has hardened me beyond any ordinary forms of reproach."

Shadbolt meanwhile had posed as mechanic and laborer, got drunk with the boys, and, at Taylor's suggestion, placed false newspaper ads for jobs apt to attract mechanics working at a company he sought to infiltrate. "Your scheme of advertising worked fine, as all your schemes do," he wrote Taylor.

As it turned out, the bicycle maker Pope and Hathorn Manufacturing Company, but not Jones and the Excelsior company, were clearly violating the Simonds patents. Pope settled out of court. But when a Hawthorn machinist, a short, thin man with a dark brown mustache named A. B. Purington, stepped forward with eyewitness confirmation, Simonds brought an infringement suit against the Maine company. That was on July 2, 1896. Over the next two years, there were affidavits to collect, depositions to give, drawings to prepare, models to make, expert testimony to secure. When Purington, last seen working in a little bicycle shop in Bangor, disappeared into the trackless wilds of Maine, Taylor hired an eight-dollar-a-day Pinkerton detective to find him. Not content with vicarious thrills, in 1897 Taylor went so far as to secure a Massachusetts state engineer's license, don overalls, and, seeking evidence, hire himself out to one of his competitors.

Later, Taylor regaled his old buddy Wilfred Lewis with accounts of these escapades. And though by 1915 Lewis had forgotten the details, "the impression made by their recital some fifteen years ago was one of admiration and amusement not excelled by any of the Sherlock Holmes stories I have since read." In Taylor's telling, he recalled, it was all "very thrilling and amusing."

~

Madison, Wisconsin. November 1895.

As Taylor neared his fortieth birthday and, perhaps, with that perennial preoccupation of midlife, looked back over his years and reflected on their worth, his Detroit paper, in the comparative luster of its reception, may have reassured him. More certainly, it brought him business.

"Send Piecework paper to following when they are printed in full," he wrote himself a reminder, listing a dozen or so names. After its appearance in print, the paper routinely went to potential clients and other professional contacts—and to good effect. "Edward J. James, pres't, American Academy of Political & Social Science, Station B Philadelphia, wants me to read Piecework paper before them," Taylor jotted it down. Of course, sometimes he could write off an inquiry as unpromising. "Will you please advise me where I can obtain a copy of your paper entitled "Piece Road System," wrote one company plainly in need of more help than even Taylor could provide. It was addressed to "Mr. F. W. Taylor, c/o Mid Dale Steel Co., Mid Dale, Pa."

Around this time, a Chicago man named John Markoe learned of Taylor and his system and offered his services as broker. An electrical equipment company employing three thousand men was "running around the country looking for a time system," he wrote. If Taylor would make it worth his while, he would bring the two of them together. Taylor wrote back, offering two hundred dollars for any contact netting him a client.

This particular job didn't materialize; but another, also with an electrical equipment manufacturer and also arising from the Detroit paper, did. "Dear Sir," the letter began. "A corporation has recently been formed, of which I am one of the members, for the purpose of manufacturing electrical machinery, such as dynamos, motors, electric cranes, etc."

I am casting about for a system of books for shop record which shall show labor cost and machinery cost, together with what would constitute the day rate on such product. I desire to have all

of the work done by the piece as far as is possible, and I desire to
start with the very best system that can be devised. I recently had
the pleasure of reading a pamphlet containing an article on the
piece rate system written by yourself. . . . I am willing to go to even
extraordinary expense to get this matter started right.

The letter, dated August 6, 1895, was signed A. O. Fox, secretary and
treasurer of the new firm. He was writing from a farm in Wisconsin
where, if his letterhead was to be believed, he bred horses, sheep, and
cattle when not launching new businesses.

Taylor wrote back three days later; his rate was thirty-five dollars
per day plus expenses. On November 2, he stepped off the train from
Chicago and met with the men of the Northern Electrical Manufacturing Company, of Madison, Wisconsin. Mostly working on setting
up the new company's books, Taylor gave the job two weeks that
month, tendered his bill, left for Boston in mid-January, and returned
to Wisconsin for two more stints before finishing up in April.

Total time charged the company: 42½ days.

Total income to Taylor, beyond reimbursed expenses: $1,487.50—
three years' income for the average worker, six months' even for many
a company executive.

A succession of jobs like this, coupled to the sagacious investments
he made in the depression years following the panic of 1893, soon
made his troubles from the pulp mill debacle no more than an
unpleasant memory. "For my own part," he wrote Frank Steele the
following year, "the dull times have been a decided advantage. I have
done better pecuniarily this year than any in my life. . . . During the
dull times," he noted, "money can be invested to so much better
advantage."

∾

Boston. December 1895.

Fred Taylor was not given to slumming; his democratic instincts
never extended to staying at any but the finest hotels. After some weeks
in Wisconsin, Taylor had put up in Boston at the Hotel Vendome, a
vast five-story structure with a semicircular stone arch marking its
entrance. With its mansard roof, the hotel loomed over the street like a
great hulking apparition from Paris. From here, his regular berthing

place in Boston during this period, Taylor wrote Sanford Thompson, his colleague from the pulp mill. "Can you not come in and see us on Sunday at the Vendome? We dine about 1:30. Come early as I have some business matters that I would like to talk over with you."

Sanford Eleazer Thompson, a thin, broad-shouldered young MIT graduate, had been Taylor's most trusted assistant in Maine. Hired by the Investment Company in September 1890, he first came to Taylor's admiring attention when a slow "cook," which required regular attention for forty hours, didn't work; immediately, he set out to repeat it. That impressed Taylor—who, Thompson wrote later, "was always on the lookout for traits in others which embraced [the] principle of carrying a thing through to its conclusion." Soon, Thompson, twenty-three when he joined the Investment Company and eleven years Taylor's junior, was overseeing the redesign of the mill and had forty machinists and carpenters answering to him.

Taylor took the younger man in tow and, long after both had left the company, issued fatherly injunctions much like those he had received from his own father while at Exeter. "I am very much interested in your success," he wrote Thompson, then working for another paper mill, in August 1893,

and have no doubt you will "get there" all right if you only do not
allow yourself to be diverted from the main object of the business
by things which are really more interesting but do not tell
financially. That is to say, be sure and find out what scheme the
owners are after most and work to accomplish that ahead of almost
anything else. I know that hard work will not be lacking on your
part, but what I am most afraid of, to be perfectly frank, is that
some of your work will be misdirected. That is, misdirected as far
as your own best interests are concerned. And while on this point,
as long as I am lecturing, I would warn you about the Sunday side
of the matter. You will certainly, for a good while to come, have to
subordinate your own inclinations and religious tendencies to the
interests of the mill—that is, if you place success as your goal. I
scarcely think it is possible to succeed in any manufacturing
enterprise without giving up almost all of one's Sundays to the mill
work, and take Monday for your religious devotions rather than
Sunday. At least I have found this to be the case in every

manufacture that I have had anything to do with. I hope you will pardon my intrusion upon your affairs and know that you will appreciate what I say is said in a spirit of friendly well wishing and not impertinent criticism.

The two men had maintained their correspondence and now, meeting at the Vendome, Taylor had a proposition for him, about time study. He had developed time study in the machine shop at Midvale and applied it at the pulp mill. Why not the building trades, as well, Sanford Thompson's bailiwick? That Sunday, Taylor broached the idea of collaborating on a series of books offering time study data in trades like plastering, shoveling, masonry, and carpentry.

Thompson, employed by a Boston engineering firm, hesitated. The Investment Company experience had soured him on lofty talk and big promises, and he was not sure about Taylor. At the pulp mill, he wrote later, "I was a little in doubt as to what was the real Taylor—whether he was essentially the taskmaster that he sometimes appeared, that he seemed to be when he would require the attainment of the apparently insurmountable, when he [would haul] us over the coals as man never did before." Did he really want to work for this difficult man again? The following Tuesday, Thompson wrote Midvale, presumably for information about Taylor's record there; five days later, responding to the company's invitation, he said he hoped to visit that week. Taylor, also going to Philadelphia, suggested they coordinate their trips; that way, he could show Thompson around himself.

In Philadelphia, probably staying at what he would remember as the "quiet mansion" on Rose Street that was the Taylor family home, Thompson had "the great privilege of meeting [Taylor's] father and mother, an accomplished gentleman and a gentlewoman of the type rarely met with in the younger generations." He saw Midvale and came away a believer—as much in Taylor, apparently, as in whatever he'd seen at the works. "My trip to Midvale," he wrote Taylor on December 27, "practically decided the matter."

Three days later, they signed a contract. Thompson would work for Taylor, earn a hundred dollars a month plus expenses, gather time-study data and, as it turned out, make a new stab at the old problem Taylor had tackled fifteen years before at Midvale: how much work could a man do in a day? Thompson was to share equally with Taylor in profits from sale of the information collected and, in lesser measure, from book royalties; they would share any byline, too.

On January 9, Thompson wrote his new employer:

I am on the hunt for stop watches. As I understand it, the kind we want are arranged so that by pressing one spring, the hands will fly back to 0, or by pressing another spring, they will go ahead from the point at which they were last stopped. How fine must it read? You told me but I did not make a note of it.

Taylor replied, from the Virginia Hotel in Chicago, on his way back to Wisconsin for another stint with Northern Electric: "The watch which I have used is a cheap silver one and reads, I think, to seconds, certainly not closer than half seconds . . . [and has] a minute hand as well as a second hand, so that it would record at least 60 minutes in addition to the regular number of seconds."

"I 'made a find' yesterday," wrote Thompson on March 6. "I accidentally ran across the very watch we have been hunting for at a wholesale jewelers. They have three or four that have been on hand for some time."

On March 25, Taylor advised Thompson to order the special dial faces he had mentioned in a previous letter, reading in tenths and hundredths of a minute, not in seconds; these made computations easier.

The stopwatch that would become the hated symbol of all the reputed evils of Taylorism was here the subject of the most banal technical correspondence. Through Thompson, with whom he would remain professionally close all his life, Taylor was placing new kinds of work under time study's magnifying lens.

By early 1896, Thompson was renting an office, making up letterheads and business cards, rooting around for a stenographer and typist, and sending Taylor the bills. All across the following year their correspondence thickened, Thompson working out of his home in Newton Highlands, Massachusetts, outside Boston, Taylor writing from Cleveland, or Chicago, or Johnstown, Pennsylvania.

Early in this period, Thompson camped out at the Boston Public Library, pursuing old French and American texts on the science of human work. But mostly, he did time studies, arranged through friends in the construction industry. These proved trickier than he'd expected.

Say you were clapboarding a house, to use an example Thompson cited later. A wall with many window openings plainly needed more time for cutting and fitting, per square foot, than a blank wall. But how much more? To find out, "clapboarding" had to be broken down much farther, into times for measuring, sawing, nailing, and all the other tasks it comprised.

The work dragged. "My out-of-door work is comparatively little relaxation," wrote Thompson on February 10,

> because watching three or four 'timers' and every motion of six or eight men requires no little labor. I have not said much about this because I thought I could worry through another year and because if there is one thing I cannot abide it is commencing a thing and not completing it, but the thought of two or three more years is formidable.

Indeed, the whole project proved formidable, occupying him in part for the next seventeen years. Ultimately, he would establish the time needed to fill one wheelbarrow, walk one foot, drive one nail. He'd conclude that one sort of hammer was better than another, one way to build concrete forms cheaper than others, that money could be saved when nails were standardized, that when a laborer did the heavy work, freeing up the carpenter, the savings amounted to so much. "I am not yet through with [time studies of] plastering in the Tremont Bldg," Thompson wrote Taylor in March. "If other branches of construction work have as much to them we shall have to write separate books on each."

Taylor peppered Thompson with suggestions, advice, criticism, and encouragement. He was much interested in what Thompson had dug up about the French studies of human work, but, he assured his young friend, "your work ... will be vastly more thorough than anything which has gone before, and I think we can have the satisfaction of feeling that in this respect we are almost pioneers."

One area they studied, later to become famous, was the shoveling of coal, sand, and other loose materials. Taylor had begun work on this "subject," if it can thus be dignified, at Midvale and forwarded details to Thompson: "I mean to chase this matter home." Thompson should get a spring balance with which to measure how much force it took to press a shovel into a heap of coal, and so figure how much energy it consumed. He'd heard from Midvale, Taylor wrote Thompson later, that a man shoveling coal averaged twelve shovelfuls per minute while actually working.

Thompson did most of the work. Taylor paid for it, directed it, and laid down the rules, one of which was secrecy. In their contract, witnessed by Taylor's father, Thompson promised not to reveal information without Taylor's approval; he was "to use his best endeavors to prevent other parties from knowing the nature and objects" of their joint work. Later, they worked out the design of a hollow book into which a stopwatch could be discretely secured and time study forms stored. And they conferred on how Thompson might extract information from friends without revealing what he was up to.

One time, Thompson expressed dissatisfaction with the data forms he'd had made. "They are rather small," he wrote, "but I did not dare to make them any larger for fear my notebook would attract too much attention."

Don't worry, Taylor wrote back. "Speak of yourself as writing for papers [which he had done earlier]. You would be perfectly safe in mentioning Paper Trade Journal. When they find that you are a reporter [as opposed, presumably, to a prying competitor], I do not think that they will worry over you."

A little later, Taylor urged further deception. Thompson could have cards printed up, with his name and college degree, "and down in one corner, 'corespondent for the Paper Mill Journal'; this I think may prove of very great benefit and you can use it with safety in a great many cases."

Thompson might also consider taking contractors, "or even the leading workmen if they are the right kind," to dinner. "Do not spare expense on what you get, as I think one of your best ways of gaining information will be to get all you can out of those most skilled in their trades."

When Thompson submitted to Taylor tables and charts of data, Taylor invariably approved but, also invariably, made suggestions:

> When you speak of two men working together on a job you should make it clear beyond a question as to whether the time given is that which would be required by one man if he were doing the whole

job by himself, or whether it is the time taken by each man. You must treat the public whom you are talking to as if they were children about 3 years old and were sure to misunderstand everything told them.

Later, he expressed concern about a percentage Thompson had established for brickwork. "I do not exactly like . . . the 66²/₃ percentage"—precisely two thirds. "This looks as if we had the law down a little too fine. I think 65 or 70 percent would be . . . better."

For Taylor, it was never just the truth or the facts that counted but the effect they were apt to have on readers and listeners. Out there, in the back rows of the audience to which he always played, were the ordinary folk, and one always had to keep in mind their limitations. Tables filled with their collected data, he counseled Thompson, must be "so simple in their form that ordinary mechanics can use them."

～

Johnstown, Pennsylvania. February 1896.

Taylor's next job brought him to Johnstown, Pennsylvania.

Seven years before, on May 31, 1889, a dam burst high in the hills over Johnstown, a town of about ten thousand east of Pittsburgh. A wall of water seventy feet high tumbled down the river valley, destroying all in its path. The town was wiped clean. The churning waters swept away homes, boxcars, trees, farm animals, and people. More than twenty-two hundred people died, some of them borne downstream into a mountainous pile of debris that caught fire and burned for days.

The day after the tragedy, survivors crowded into a schoolhouse, one of the few structures still standing. Everywhere lay the dead; the living cowered on the hills above the town, hungry and cold. A single clear voice of authority was needed. They turned to a young Welshman, new to town but already well respected, Arthur J. Moxham. To supervise removal of the dead, Moxham selected Tom Johnson, his partner in a company that manufactured streetcar rails. "No words can describe the horror and reluctance with which I approached the gruesome task," Johnson wrote later. "The sight of the first few bodies recovered moved me to tears."

A tousled big boy of a man, prematurely rich, later a two-term congressman and mayor of Cleveland, Johnson was a protege of Alfred Victor du Pont, of the Delaware du Ponts, makers of gunpowder. When du Pont, owner of a big piece of the rail manufacturing company, died in 1893, his stake passed to three young du Pont cousins. Two of them, Coleman and Pierre, became actively involved in the company, which in 1895 moved its rail operation to Lorain, Ohio, near Cleveland, and set up to build streetcar motors in Johnstown. Pierre, twenty-six, presided over the company's financial affairs from Delaware. Coleman, thirty-three, managed the Johnstown works.

But the senior man was really Moxham, who ran the Lorain operation and whom Pierre du Pont saw as "a master of cost sheets and orderly management." And Moxham was worried. The Lorain expansion and the long, lingering business depression had weakened the company. Electric motor manufacture, transferred from Cleveland, had yet to resume in Johnstown; the company would not even be hiring until early the following year. They needed to organize, cut costs, establish order. Late in 1895, Moxham contacted Taylor.

Just after the new year, Taylor spent two days in Johnstown, then visited Lorain. He came away impressed and either uncharacteristically diffident or determined to lower expectations. In a letter to Moxham written from Wisconsin, where he was finishing up at Northern Electric, he worried he'd be unable "to do your company nearly as good service as I can for nine out of ten companies who employ me." But Moxham wanted him and assured him he'd have free rein. On January twenty-fourth, he agreed—the better to pry Taylor free from his commitments—to pay him fifty dollars a day until June 1, the usual thirty-five dollars only after that.

By February 25, Fred and Lou were in Johnstown. On their arrival, Lou recalled, "the roads were ankle deep in mud and a drummer's hotel showed signs of the devastating Johnstown flood along the top of the dining room ceiling." Their trunks had all been dumped into one room until they could find better accommodations.

Soon, as Taylor wrote his friend Steele, Lou had secured "with a considerable amount of cheek and a great amount of tact" a spot at the top of the mountain, behind the Cambria Iron Company, intended as the site for a hotel; here the Taylors would build what Lou called their "shack," though we know what Taylor shacks are like. A few minutes' walk brought them to an inclined railroad that dropped nine hundred feet to the flood plain; they were pleasantly removed from what Lou wrote off as "the dismal town" below, yet convenient to it. On two sides of their home, they had wooden awnings built, which could be lifted by cord and pulley to grant a sudden rapturous view of the surrounding mountains. "We find this," Taylor wrote Steele of Johnstown, "one of the most agreeable places that we have ever stayed in."

They took to bicycle riding, tennis, and, especially, golf, which was now the height of fashion and which Taylor had taken up the previous fall with his usual gusto. His notebook recorded the yardage for each hole of the local course. He wrote back to Philadelphia for new golf gear. His correspondence began to include chatty, lighthearted exchanges with friends who also played. "Lou and I have been practicing a little golf on the hill with a captive ball," he wrote Goodrich in June. "This is very fair for practicing, but of course we lose most of the fun of the game. Do you continue to like the sport?" Taylor would for the rest of his life.

It was a fine time, his progress at the works no doubt contributing to his mood. By March 4, the shop employed 220 men and women and was still hiring. By April 14, a rush of orders had added a second shift. The energetic shop manager absorbed Taylor's thinking with astonishing ease. The faith that Moxham's fellow citizens had placed in him after the flood was soon shared by Taylor; he wrote Goodrich, with what sounds like mingled annoyance and respect, that Moxham was "a man who wants the most minute information regarding everything and wants it right away."

Moxham had outlined a rough plan: Taylor would first organize the switch and motor works in Johnstown, then the steel plant in Lorain, then work on the books for both companies. And that's about what Taylor did. When he started, he wrote Goodrich, he found "some hundred and fifty thousand dollars worth of valuable stores and supplies dumped down in a shed helter-skelter, without even protection from the weather, and each workman dived into this pile for whatever he wanted." So he set up an elaborate stores system, a way of keeping track of everything. The new scheme met with "great opposition" from the men, who preferred things as they were, but soon it was in place.

In the planer shop, he recommended old Midvale standbys like water-cooled cutting tools, higher cutting speeds, and an automatic tool grinder, like the one he had developed at Midvale. While visiting the planer shop, he wrote Coleman du Pont, "I noticed that your planers were idle" too much of the time, while work was being clamped in place. "You should have a special gang of men to set the work in the jigs" and later remove it, thus freeing the machinists from such routine chores and keeping the planers cutting more of each day.

Through wide precincts of the shop, he installed differential rates. In August, he wrote Axel Petre back at Midvale, wondering whether he might bring around some Johnson Company foundry foremen to see some "first class hustling piece work." As at Midvale, piece rates at Johnson were broken down by operation but were apparently not based on stopwatch studies. Taylor wrote A. O. Fox at Northern Electric on October 22, "We have saved enough in the wages of armature winding alone to pay for all the cost of introducing the system and running it."

Taylor introduced a cost accounting system based on all he had learned from Basley at the Investment Company, which, he boasted, could detect "if gang bosses or sub-foremen have employed one extra laborer." Late in his nine-month stint at Johnson, he suggested to Coleman du Pont new work rules for the accounting clerks: Well-defined tasks, no smoking, "no talking above a whisper," shorter hours. More work could be done "by having men work at their best while they are in the office and then giving them all extra time for recreation rather than have them intersperse their recreation with their work."

All this remained far from what Taylor had preached in his Detroit paper. Detroit represented a platonic ideal, the factory ruled by a clear, coherent system undergirded by science. But since leaving Midvale, limited time, money, and tolerance for his managerial overkill had forced him to pick and choose from his menu of management dishes—thicker belting, Basley's accounting system, the differential rate, time study, and so on. At Johnstown, time study simply never got served. Just before he left, he wrote Coleman du Pont recommending "a central rate fixing and time studying department." But that, apparently, was as far as it went. By now, Taylor must have felt like a *cordon bleu* chef employed by a succession of fast-food restaurants.

Still, Taylor was having such a good time, or was so caught up in the work, or both, that the time he charged the company mounted alarmingly. On July 9, Moxham reminded him that while "I was under the impression that you would be unable to give us more than six days a month," Taylor had been working nearly full time. He had so far received some seven thousand dollars, this just a few months after the company had had to frantically raise three quarters of a million dollars to pay its bills. "Can you not arrange your future work to do less of it yourself and do more of it through the clerks?"

Indeed, the company and the whole town were in real trouble. "Almost the whole of Johnstown is shut down now," Taylor wrote Steele on September 9, while Lou was back in Plymouth with her mother. "The Cambria Iron Company is all down except two blast furnaces, and the Johnson Company . . . [is] barely moving along." And yet, Moxham's plea had little effect, at least if the bills Taylor submitted in subsequent months are any indication: 22 days in July, $15^1/_2$ in September, $25^1/_2$ in October, or essentially full-time.

But if Taylor worried little about spending his client's money, in his own mind, at least, his costly services paid the company back. In early September, he wrote Steele, "I have been very successful in reorganizing their works. I have got just about through with their electrical department, which is quite a large one," with four hundred workers,

> and have started on their steel and iron foundries. I think that I have made enough saving already to pay for all the expense which they have gone to, which is a large one, including my salary. . . . [They now] have complete and elaborate returns each month of just what they have produced and the cost, not only of every piece made, but of every operation on every piece.

In October, just before he left and with the works virtually shut down, Taylor wrote Steele that his system had been "opposed bitterly by all but a few of the leading men, but the results are so satisfactory and so very apparent now that the opposition has almost entirely ceased." Indeed, if his sanguine assessment was anywhere close to the mark, perhaps only the deeply troubled economy stopped him, in the words of one Taylor scholar, Daniel Nelson, "from completing the development of scientific management at that time and making the Johnson Company the first truly 'Taylorized' firm."

In any case, the impact of his work at Johnstown extended far beyond the little town on the floodplain. Taylor was not alone in going on to bigger things; so did Moxham, Coleman du Pont, and, especially, Pierre du Pont. After Taylor left, Pierre went out to Lorain for a year and became intimate with Taylor's methods. In 1902, when the old family firm of Du Pont Powder joined more than a hundred others to become the E. I. Du Pont de Nemours conglomerate, Moxham—who would be called "the most imaginative of the new consolidation's founders"—and Pierre and Coleman du Pont presided over its creation. The du Pont cousins "had become intimately acquainted with Taylor's costing and control methods at Lorain Steel," writes Alfred Chandler, in his seminal study, *The Visible Hand: The Managerial Revolution in American Business*, and applied them at the new Du Pont, which business historians today view as a prototype of the modern firm. "Pierre, his cousin Coleman, and their associates," Chandler (with Stephen Salsbury) writes elsewhere, "brought the ways of both Carnegie and Taylor to the Du Pont Company."

Later, in the 1920s, Pierre du Pont became chairman of the board of General Motors.

~

Fitchburg, Massachusetts. December 1896.

In the months before Taylor, fresh from Johnstown, returned to Fitchburg, Simonds had been shut down. Old buildings were razed, new ones erected in their place, and new machinery installed. The company's general manager was forty-six-year-old George Weymouth, who, with his bland good looks beginning to yield to prosperous fat, seemed made for the part of local muckety-muck. Weymouth had moved to Fitchburg in 1882, started up a carriage business on Main Street, and became trustee of one local savings bank and director of another. Active in Republican politics, he'd been elected, in turn, to city council, state legislature and, in the November elections just past, Congress. During most of this time he had served on the Simonds board of directors. When, in about 1891, the previous superintendent left to start a rival company in Cleveland, Weymouth had been named in his place, though his job qualifications remain unclear. For the past several years, Taylor had urged him to introduce piece rate in the shop, but to no avail.

On December 11, 1896, Simonds' president Alfred Bowditch fired Weymouth, ordering him to turn over charge of the shop to Taylor. That same day, a letter went out to Taylor naming him to the company's executive committee.

Demand for balls just then was high, and the five million balls per month Simonds produced in 1896 might need to rise still more. Yet the failure of the ball combination meant a likely drop in prices. The two together, higher production and lower prices, virtually cried out for a dose of Fred Taylor, and Bowditch and the others on the board must have realized as much.

Within less than three weeks, Taylor had issued a memo setting out "conditions governing 'Permanent Piece Work' under the differential rate system for the Simonds Rolling Machine Company." To a point, it was Midvale all over again: high and low rates depended on output, and the high rate could never be cut "even if a workman earns two or three times as much as his usual pay." Only improved methods or new machines might justify a rate cut. (That, or the substitution of women for men; in that case, the memo declared without missing a beat, "the high rate can be lowered.")

But the new rates were not based on time study. If a year and a half before, in Detroit, Taylor was selling scientific rate setting, just now he seemed content—as he had been in Johnstown—to rely on the psychic bludgeon that was the differential rate: "If a man is either unwilling or unable to turn out a large day's work," read Taylor's memo, "or if he turns out any but the best quality of work, it is intended that he shall earn very low wages."

By February he had introduced piecework to the rough grinding department, where the balls went, their little metal tits still attached, after leaving the rolling machines. Finish grinding, the next step, had piecework by March. Workmen grinding 28,000 or fewer eighth-inch balls per day earned 5.1 cents per thousand; up to 36,000, 5.3 cents; beyond 36,000, 5.8 cents. A workman turning out just 28 percent more saw his pay increase from $1.43 to $2.09 per day, or almost half.

But at least one obstacle to higher production remained, in the inspection department, where the workers were mostly women in their early twenties. To the untrained eye, the dazzling steel spheres came from the long row of grinding and polishing machines looking alike and looking perfect. It took months for the women, who were paid about four dollars a week for five 10½-hour days and another half day on Saturday, to see past the balls's superficial shimmer. Much could go wrong—fire cracks from heat treating, soft spots, rough spots, flat spots—sometimes due to faulty steel, sometimes to the machines. Here, where so much rode on the balls' being perfect, inspection was inseparable from production. And, as Taylor wrote in a progress report later that year, inspection was "the stumbling block."

Typically, the woman placed a row of balls on the back of her hand, in the crease between two fingers. To and fro she rolled them, viewing them carefully under a strong light, using a magnet to pluck out defective balls, which she tossed into appropriately marked bins. This was close, nerve-racking work. The women examined tens of thousands of balls per day. With piecework mercilessly pitting quality against quantity, Taylor set up a system in which other inspectors examined balls passed by the first group. Small samples from this second group went to an "over-inspector." And to check her, the foreman would, every few days, surreptitiously introduce a few defective balls into a lot of otherwise perfect ones.

Early in the year, probably around March, Taylor brought in Sanford Thompson, who was already working for him on their building trades project. Thompson, stopwatch in hand, timed each step of the inspection. This, Taylor wrote later, "showed that the girls spent a considerable part of their time either in partial idleness, talking and half working, or in actually doing nothing." The remedy was inspired. No one could do such close work hour after hour; *of course* they were goofing off—who wouldn't? So Taylor cut the workday: the women would work fewer hours but when they worked they'd really work.

As Taylor recounted it later, he first made the mistake of asking the girls—that, of course, is how both he and Thompson referred to them—whether they wished to reduce their hours to ten per day. "The writer had not been especially noted for his tact," he wrote, "so he decided that it would be wise for him to display a little of this quality by having the girls vote on the new proposition." This, to hear him tell it, was an egregious mistake. The women were such hopeless stick-in-the-muds that "when the vote was taken the girls were unanimous that 10½ hours was good enough for them and they wanted no innovation of any kind."

Could it be that they simply preferred a long, leisurely, shmoozing sort of day to one that was shorter but flat-out? In any case, Taylor didn't. He'd had his fling with workplace democracy. "Now, girls," he reports telling them, "you are going to do just as much work in ten hours as you did in ten and a half, and if any girl doesn't like that she can step out and go somewhere else." Over succeeding months, the work day was cut, in half-hour increments, to eight and a half hours. Take-home pay remained the same. "And with each shortening of the working day," Taylor reported, "the output increased instead of diminishing."

One other change may have helped: the women were seated so far apart that they could no longer talk to one another. Taylor appreciated that some might fail to see the lofty motives behind this change and deem his girls "brutally treated." So two ten-minute work breaks were added each morning and afternoon, when the women "were obliged to stop work, and were encouraged to leave their seats and get a complete change of occupation by walking around and talking, etc." Here, scholar Mark Seltzer has suggested, was the first cigarette break.

Finally, Taylor introduced differential piece rates, based not only on output but on how well the balls they passed fared at the next level of inspection. Performance was measured hourly, any falloff prompting a visit from one of the foreman's assistants. Certainly the women had every reason to cooperate: their jobs were on the line. At one point, Thompson conducted tests of a "personal coefficient," which, from Taylor's sketchy description, sounds like a crude measure of reaction time. Those scoring insufficiently high weren't hired and, as Taylor acknowledged, "many of the most intelligent, hardest working, and most trustworthy girls" were fired. But here, in embryonic form, was the "scientific" selection of workers, which Taylor would come to see as a hallmark of his system.

By fall, thirty-five women were doing the work that a hundred and twenty had done before, making sometimes almost double their previous wages, or about what the most menial male laborer earned on day work. Maybe they weren't chatting much among themselves any more, maybe the hour-and-a-quarter periods between the "cigarette breaks" were like little prisons in time, given over utterly to the balls. But they were earning more than they ever had in their lives.

~

On June 28, 1897, came the Weymouth coup. On that day, George Weymouth, who had remained on the board after being replaced as general manager, abruptly resigned and formed a rival company. He took with him, Taylor wrote later to his friend Charles Humphries, "every foreman and assistant foreman in the place, as well as the superintendent, all of the salesmen, and the head man in the office." A company memo later suggested he exerted his influence "through political and secret society organizations." In any case, Taylor saw it as Weymouth's way to get Walter Simonds, the young son of George Simonds, to fire him.

The coup failed; all but one of the board sided with Taylor, and by early October, Weymouth was pleading to come back. But apparently he had planted a seed in the mind of "young Mr. Simonds who," as Taylor wrote, "is a very nice young fellow but has no experience whatever in business." The price of balls had dropped in half, dividends had been slashed to zero, and Taylor had, as usual, been spending lavishly. Had *he* remained in charge, Weymouth intimated, none of this would have happened. He "spread no end of lies broadcast about me," Taylor groused to Humphries, "saying that I never have made a success of anything, that I had always been fired wherever I have been, that I had not friends, and was a very general kind of damned fool." To determine the validity of Weymouth's charges, and intimating his own displeasure with Taylor, Simonds wrote to several of Taylor's former employers.

"No money nor success that I can possibly have from this Company," Taylor wrote a former colleague whom he sought to enlist in his defense, "will at all pay me for the damage which such a statement as this inflicts upon my reputation and I feel most bitter that this should have been done, and particularly so since I have been working myself sick almost for this Company for the past nine months."

One of those getting the Walter Simonds letter was Midvale's Charles Harrah, who wrote back that Taylor's innovations at Midvale were very much still in place and that he and everyone else at Midvale had the highest regard for him as an engineer and as "an honorable gentleman." But the same day, Harrah wrote Taylor in a style more natural to him:

> For God's sake don't bring your Uncle William Sellers, or should I say, Walter A. Simonds into any controversy with me. I have got lots of this stuff to attend to myself. For God's sake give him a job, give him a dividend, buy something for him; do anything under heaven, but don't let him write me letters.

Taylor wrote him back with thanks, and Harrah replied in still a third voice, this time with something like comradely warmth. Taylor's thanks were entirely unnecessary, he said:

> I think you and I know one another sufficiently well to know
> who we are and what we are at. Don't let those fellows bother you.
> The best evidence of your success is the hostility which you have
> inspired and the criticisms to which you have been subjected. I
> have known people to speak ill even of *me* and of *John
> Wanamaker*.

Wanamaker was Philadelphia's relentlessly do-good department store magnate.

In October 1897, Taylor testified in Simonds's patent suit against Hathorn Manufacturing and, in November, was sanguine about the company's future. Never, he wrote, had it been "in anything like as good condition as it now is." Output per worker, at almost every stage of production, was more than double. They had bought the most modern new machinery—even, when necessary, from their competitors. Then, too, he wrote a friend, "the new superintendent, who will take my place when I leave here on the first of next April, is a first rate manager and is familiar with all my methods, having been brought up under me at Midvale." (He meant H. L. Gantt, whom he'd brought to Simonds from the American Steel Casting Company around the time of the Weymouth coup, and from whose house at the west end of Main Street, at the far end of town from the works, he was writing.) Simonds was strong. "I have never," wrote Taylor, "been able to accomplish as much in so short a time."

But in June 1898, after Cleveland Machine Screw, a Simonds competitor, again cut prices—to seventy-five cents a thousand for eighth-inch balls—Bowditch wrote Taylor that the board had voted to shut down. Taylor remonstrated with him to reconsider. A few months later Simonds won its suit against Hathorn, which was later sustained by an appeals court. But it was too late. "The ball business, wrote Bowditch, "is pretty well played out."

But by now, Taylor was in a new business. Bowditch's letter was addressed to "Frederick W. Taylor, Esq., South Bethlehem, Pennsylvania," where, at the invitation of Joseph Wharton, he'd been working since early spring.

7

"FINISH EXCELLENT, CHIPS BLUE"

~

PHILADELPHIA QUAKER JOSEPH WHARTON was the first American to produce zinc commercially. He made a fortune in the nickel business, lobbied with William Sellers, among others, for protective tariffs, and founded a school of business at the University of Pennsylvania that became the Wharton School of Finance and Commerce. He'd begun acquiring stock in the Bethlehem Iron Company of South Bethlehem soon after its formation and became its largest stockholder. Now, spare and trim at seventy, he showed no diminution of energy or acumen. "I have read with care your treatise in 'A Piece Rate System,' and find it interesting," he wrote Taylor, on April 26, 1895, two months before the paper was presented in Detroit. "There ought to be opportunity at Bethlehem for the introduction of such a plan, and I am forwarding your treatise to our people there that they may consider it."

Maybe they considered it or maybe they didn't; Wharton said later he'd long pushed piece rates on the rest of the board, to no avail. Taylor, in any event, heard nothing from them.

Two years later, he did.

Following William Collins Whitney's stint as secretary of the navy, the government had resolved to modernize the nation's arms industry. Bethlehem was among those welcomed into the business. But in 1895, word got out that while the company sold armor plate to Russia for two hundred and fifty dollars a ton, it charged the U.S. government six hundred. Was some slight greed at work here? An angry Congress threatened to put up a government-run armor plant and suggested a cap on prices of, say, three or four hundred dollars a ton. The squeeze was on, the days of easy money over. Young Bethlehem president Robert P. Linderman was a banker by temperament and experience, not a manufacturer. What, he asked the board, should they do?

Reduce costs, the answer came back.

There certainly was room to do so. The company, launched in the

1850s to supply rail for the anthracite-hauling Lehigh Valley Railroad, and for years a testament to the mechanical prowess of legendary steel man John Fritz, was by now a case study in inefficiency. Its machine shop couldn't keep up with its forge; the floor was always littered with giant forgings yet untouched. Foremen among the company's three thousand employees clung to their own little fiefdoms, workmen to their long-outmoded practices. The place bore the mark of an ossified bureaucracy, management's upper ranks filled with friends and relatives of company directors.

Indeed, the company was more like a big incestuous family than a modern corporation, Lindermans and Leiberts and Packers and Sayres hopelessly entwined through blood and marriage. On the board with Linderman and Wharton, for example, sat Robert Sayre, formerly chief engineer of the Lehigh Valley Railroad. A daughter by his first marriage was Linderman's wife. His own second wife was an aunt by marriage of Linderman's father, who was the son-in-law of Asa Packer, who had formed the Lehigh Valley Railroad. The company elite made their homes in Fountain Hill, upwind from the coke ovens and blast furnaces; after Robert Sayre, Sr., built on Delaware Avenue in the 1860s, the top echelons of the company followed. Most of them belonged to the local Episcopal congregation, the Church of the Nativity, or sat on the board of Lehigh University, also the creation of Asa Packer.

Infusing a few drops of new blood in the clannish Bethlehem board was Russell Davenport, Taylor's old boss from Midvale. He'd joined the company in 1888, expecting to replace John Fritz as general superintendent, only to be passed over in favor of Owen Leibert, another Bethlehem old boy. A few years before, in recognition of his achievements in metallurgy, Davenport had received an honorary degree from Harvard. Now he was Bethlehem's second vice president and on its board of directors. Who, Davenport must have thought, could reduce costs better than Fred Taylor, whose "Piece Rate System," that summer of 1897, he was passing around?

On November 22, he wrote his old Midvale colleague:

> I have been directed by our President, Mr. R. P. Linderman,
> to communicate with you in reference to the possibility of
> arranging to secure your services at an early date in connection

with the proposed establishment of [a] piece work system in our Machine Shop.

I should like therefore to hear from you at your early convenience as to whether your present engagements will allow you to consider this question, and if so when you can make it convenient to come to Bethlehem and have a preliminary talk with Mr. Linderman.

Awaiting your early reply, I remain

> Yours very truly,
> R. W. Davenport
> Second Vice President

Discussions ensued. In December, Taylor met with Wharton in Philadelphia, talked about piecework, stressed that his system implied higher wages, and left Wharton, he felt sure, convinced of his system's merits. Writing to Davenport, he affected a breezy, indifferent demeanor. If Bethlehem wanted him, he could start in the spring; if not right away, then perhaps eight months or a year later. In any case, he had another company on the string and would need to know.

But Linderman was skeptical. Early in the new year, letters shuttled between them, Linderman seeking details, Taylor furnishing them. But always the Bethlehem president wanted to know more: "Write me more fully regarding your methods." In March, Taylor wrote Charles Harrah at Midvale, wondering whether he might bring Linderman around for a visit. To even this routine request, the inimitable Harrah brought his brand of swagger. "Of course we shall be happy to see you and your friend [Linderman]," he replied, "and as we always adapt our exhibition to the level of the visitor's mental ability, we shall show him the operations in the yard, such as unloading coal, sand, pig [iron], etc., etc., which has been so successfully inaugurated and established by you."

Perhaps lending urgency to the negotiations were the roiling tensions between the United States and Spain, of no slight interest to an arms maker like Bethlehem. In February, the battleship *Maine* was blown up in Havana harbor. Congress declared war on April 25. The Spanish fleet in Manila was destroyed by Admiral Dewey's battleships on May 1.

By the time the last shells screamed across Manilla Bay, Taylor had arrived in Bethlehem.

∽

Bethlehem was almost schizoid in its personality. The original town, situated on the north shore of the Lehigh River in eastern Pennsylvania, fifty miles north of Philadelphia, was settled in 1741 by pious immigrants from Moravia, in what is now the Czech Republic. The town grew more important in 1829, with the opening of the Lehigh Canal and the regular passage of anthracite-bearing canal boats to Philadelphia. In 1855, Asa Packer's Lehigh Valley Railroad reached town, and by 1863 a progenitor of Bethlehem Steel was making iron there.

But the iron making was all on the south side of the river, in South Bethlehem, across a covered bridge built atop heavy stone piers from the original settlement. The still largely Moravian north shore in 1888 witnessed America's first performance of Bach's *St. John Passion* and became a quaint tourist center; South Bethlehem, on the other hand, was all smoke, steel, and sweat. Rolling mills, coke mills, forging mills, and machine shops snaked along the riverfront for two miles, forming a skyline of tall, black-belching smokestacks.

Near the middle of the complex, between a wide ribbon of railroad track flanking the river to the north and the open-hearth furnaces to the south, sprawled Machine Shop No. 2, the axis of Taylor's life for the next three years. It was "the largest building of its kind under one roof in the country," *Iron Age* declared in 1891, "and possibly in the world." A quarter mile long, it was built up, like a giant erector set, from cast-iron structural shapes bolted together. Down the shop's great central bay ran railroad tracks. Heavy cranes passed overhead, the pulleys suspended from them bearing cannon-in-the-making bound for warships. Along either side squatted huge lathes, planers, and other metal-working tools, some of them two hundred feet long. Cannon, supported at intervals along their lengths by rollers, turned slowly in the lathes. Long boring bars inserted deep within their muzzles, cantilevered out from tool posts fifty feet away, cut the finest steel America could produce.

It was a sight to see, but also Bethlehem Steel's worst bottleneck. And to it, that summer of 1898, Taylor prescribed much the same stern medicine he had at Cramp's four years earlier, issuing a stream of reports laden with recommendations. He called for "abandoning your present system of having each machinist grind his own tools, and [instead] delivering tools already ground to the proper shape and in large numbers to your machinists . . . so that no machine shall ever lie idle." He called for new belting standards, for water-cooled tools, for new clerks and assistant superintendents to do the planning his system required. These, of course, were merely prerequisites to the piece-rate system, rooted in time study, to come.

Early on, however, Taylor was waylaid from the orderly imposition of his plans. From the start, he had urged upon Linderman "the use of the best self-hardening tool steel for all roughing cuts," the sometimes hours-long turning and planing operations that removed large masses of metal without heed to the jewel-like finish and precise dimensions required only at the end. But which steel was best? His experiments at Cramp's left room for doubt. Now, though, with the resources of Bethlehem behind him, he aimed to settle the matter.

He had a special experimental lathe built, modified from a stock model. Its bed, saddle, headstock, tailstock, and other key parts were all beefed up. Its forty-horsepower electric motor, much bigger than any regular lathe would need, could overcome the resistance offered even by a tool that had lost its edge. It could accommodate a forging more than four feet in diameter; tests could be run on a single homogeneous cylinder of steel for days at a stretch, with fewer results-confounding metallurgical variations. And you could set its cutting speed for anything from three to three hundred feet per minute, wide enough to embrace any conceivable situation. All these features ensured that the machine itself disappeared as a variable and that the hot, violent encounter of tool and work could freely proceed.

They set up the lathe against a wall of the shop and began tests in late summer. By October 19, Taylor was convinced that, among five different tool steels, Midvale's—containing, among other elements, 8 percent tungsten and $1^1/_2$ percent chromium—was best. He scheduled a demonstration for October 22, to introduce the new shop standard to company superintendents and foremen. And before all of them, the very steel he touted as best proved, by a wide margin, worst.

A "humiliating failure," Taylor later described it. The blacksmiths preparing the tools had probably overheated them—maybe by accident, maybe as a practical joke, maybe to discredit the troublemaking newcomer. In any case, the inexplicably poor showing cast doubt on Taylor's work at Cramp's and undermined his hopes for Bethlehem. Having the best tool steel—and knowing it was best—was crucial to getting more work out of Machine Shop No. 2.

Taylor prevailed on Davenport to authorize new tests that would systematically run samples of the Midvale steel through the gamut of heat-treating temperatures, in an effort to restore their cutting properties. Veteran Bethlehem metallurgist Maunsel White was placed in charge.

White and Taylor, born within days of one another in 1856, weren't quite the odd couple they seemed. Raised on his grandfather's antebellum Louisiana plantation, where he had a private tutor, White graduated from Georgetown University, studied metallurgy at Stevens, then went straight to work for Bethlehem. A bachelor, mostly bald, he lived across the covered bridge from South Bethlehem, at the Eagle Hotel on Main Street, near the original Moravian center of town. He loved food, drink, theater, poetry. His friends saw him, in Taylor's words, as "a littérateur, a poetical dreamer." He probably saw himself as a bon vivant, ever fond of "a hot bird and cold bottle," as he once put it in a letter to his brother.

"I am glad to see that you are enjoying yourself with golf tournaments," he once wrote Taylor, "and from the fact that you put no date on your letter I really think there are hopes for your joining the crowd of real pleasure seekers who forget all about business while pursuing pleasure." On another occasion, Taylor, uncertain of White's whereabouts, wrote him in care of his Bethlehem hotel, "I have no doubt that if you are South you are having the time of your life. Let me only give you one piece of advice: while you are there, devote about four fifths of your time to the game of golf and a very small percentage to liquids of any kind except H_2O."

But for all his dissipation, real or imaginary, White brought to his work the utmost seriousness. A few years before, his duties had taken him to England, Germany, and Russia to witness ballistic tests on armor plate; and his letters to Taylor, while light in tone, never strayed far from steel. He was terribly bright and could, it was said, recite *Hamlet*, in its entirety, from memory. At Georgetown, he'd been valedictorian of his class. Now this "brilliant and entertaining man," as Taylor would remember him, presided over the tests Davenport had authorized.

Blacksmiths worked to the "colors" that steel reached when plunged deep into the hottest part of the fire. First it turned a dull red—"black red"—then more and more intense red, through orange, yellow, and almost white. Each color corresponded to a temperature, but shop old-timers didn't think that way; the color it reached *was* the heat at which, for example, to pull it from the fire and hammer it on the anvil. Indeed, for most of human history color and temperature had never been correlated at all. By 1898, pyrometers—high-temperature thermometers were available, and the Bethlehem works had one. But it lacked a key part.

Taylor and White ordered it but, impatient to begin the tests, decided, in Taylor's words, "to take what may be called a preliminary canter through this field by heating tools to successive temperatures throughout this range, and judging these heats merely with our eyes." In the first series of tests, they would heat four tools, one each to a "barely visible red," a "full blood heat," a "low cherry," and a "bright cherry."

On the morning of October 31, four of the failed tools were systematically heated to these "colors," allowed to cool, then set to work on the lathe. The results were as they had been a week before, disappointingly low cutting speeds.

But that afternoon, the four tools were heated still hotter—two of them, denoted L3 and L4, to "salmon" and "bright yellow" respectively, well beyond the temperatures known to ruin tool steel. And yet these now cut faster, one of them slicing through fine steel at twenty-five feet per minute and coming out none the worse for wear. For the last five minutes of the cut, White's assistant recorded, the chips came off the tool visibly blue from the heat of cutting.

But there was more. Back at Cramp's, Taylor had established a twenty-minute run on the lathe as the fittest measure of a tool's cutting ability: that is, he defined its "standard" speed as the highest speed at which it could cut for a full twenty minutes without being driven to ruin. (The figure was a practical compromise: less than twenty minutes was too short to prove much, while more took too long and reduced too much fine steel to chips.) To test a tool, you ran it at, say, fifteen feet per minute; if it cut for twenty minutes without incident, you'd regrind it and then run it at maybe eighteen feet per minute. And so on, raising the cutting speed until finally it failed to last the full twenty minutes. In the afternoon tests on October 31, then, L3's and L4's "standard" speeds had not yet been established; that they could cut at twenty-five feet per minute didn't mean they had reached their limit, only that their "standard" speeds were at least that high.

In succeeding days, then, White's men pushed them further. On November 2, at 1:41 P.M., they mounted tool L3 in the tool post and drove it against the work at a rate of thirty-nine feet per minute; the tool endured. At 2:06 they mounted L4, set the speed a little higher, to forty-one: "Tool in good condition, finish excellent, chips blue [for the] last ten minutes." On November 4, L3 having been heated to a salmon-hued glow, they used it to cut at more than fifty feet per minute.

This in a shop where, on average, day after day, work was cut at nine feet per minute. A tool made from ordinary Midvale self-hardening steel—heat-treated at a temperature every machinist and blacksmith in the place knew with certainty would reduce it to rubble at the first swipe against the work—was cutting four or five times that fast.

"These results were so extraordinary in their novelty," Taylor said later, "that during the last few experimental runs . . . the machinists and foremen in the shop flocked around the experimental lathe until, finally, we were obliged to appoint one man to drive them away from the lathe and make them attend to their work . . .

"Before night of the first day of these phenomenal speeds," Taylor continued, "it was known to hundreds of mechanics all over Bethlehem that this remarkable occurrence had taken place. I had never before seen anything of this nature, nor do I believe anyone else had." Heating the tools to beyond the temperature known to ruin them mutated them into supertools. It was as surprising as if, after years of watching graphite pencil points break off, you broke one with particular violence only to see it metamorphosed into diamond.

Within days, they began to get letters and inquiries. Company higher-ups came around to see. "I went down to the Mill to see Taylor's experiment with new shaped cutting tools, new tool steel and increased speed," board member Robert Sayre, Sr., recorded in his diary on November 30. "Wharton came later. The experiment showed that great improvement could be made in the output of the machine shops."

But otherwise, Taylor and White let no outsiders in; their discovery was still too tentative. It was one thing to stumble on a few specimens of steel that cut as no tool ever had before, quite another to make them afresh, confident they would cut the same way. They began by taking inch-and-a-half-square lengths of Midvale steel, slicing them up into tools, and variously heat-treating them. Then, the tools would be clamped in the lathe and set to cutting.

All that fall, winter, and spring the experiments continued. The big lathe ran twenty-four hours a day.

8

UNCOMMON LABOR

∼

MIDWAY THROUGH THE TOOL STEEL EXPERIMENTS, early in the spring of 1899, in a remote yard of the Bethlehem property far from Machine Shop No. 2, Henry Noll stepped onto the stage of the world. He would become the most famous laborer in history. His name—or, rather, the name Fred Taylor gave him, Schmidt—would appear in sworn congressional testimony and be invoked as a symbol of brutal Taylorist oppression. His story—or, rather, Taylor's version of it—would be translated into a dozen languages.

Noll, twenty-eight years old, was a laborer—"common" was the adjective, then as now, that went with the word—clinging to the nethermost rung of the working-class ladder, a human drudge. All through the late nineteenth century millions of such men worked in road gangs, in the holds of ships, along railroad sidings—lifting, bearing, digging, heaving. Of steelworkers, one scholar has estimated, they accounted for four in ten. They came out of the countryside, off the ruined farms, or direct from steerage, after long ocean voyages, from Hungary, Sicily, Ireland.

A few years before, Princeton University sociologist Walter A. Wyckoff had sought a break from academe and a taste of "real work." So he signed on for a variety of jobs and wrote about his experience in an 1897 book entitled *The Workers: An Experiment in Reality*. For a time he worked as a laborer, in a gang hauling debris from a building site:

> You could hear the muttered oaths of the men, as they swore softly
> in many tongues at the boss, and cursed him for a brute. But

ceaselessly the work went on. We worked as though possessed by a curious numbness that kept us half-unconscious of the straining effort, which had become mechanical, until we were brought to by some spasm of strained muscles.

By day's end,

I was hungry, not with the hunger which comes from a [sportsman's day of] shooting, and which whets your appetite to the point of nice discriminations in an epicure's dinner, but with a ravenous hunger which fits you to fight like a beast for your food, and to eat it raw in brutal haste for gratification.

Such, or something like it, was the lot of the common laborer, most of whom could look forward only to food and sleep at the end of the day, a few dollars at the end of the week. In a time before forklifts and jackhammers, their powerful shoulders and strong, muscled backs helped build America. Most were forgotten.

Noll will never be.

〜

Among the laboring ranks at Bethlehem Iron (which became Bethlehem Steel only in 1899), Irish immigrants constituted the first wave. Later, beginning in the 1880s, came southern and eastern Europeans, especially Slovaks from northeast Hungary. Some, the story goes, sailed for twelve days from Bremen or Hamburg, landing at Castle Garden in New York with labels on their coats marked South Bethlehem. They'd arrive on the train a half day later, and soon be shuttling between the mill, local bars, and boardinghouses, where they sometimes lived ten or twelve to a room. The town's other major ethnic group, representing perhaps a third of the population, was the Germans, whose broad tent sheltered Protestants from northern Germany, Catholics from southern Germany and Austria, and native-born Pennsylvania Dutch who traced their ancestry back to colonial days and still spoke a German-flavored patois. Henry Noll—his name was sometimes spelled Knolle or Knoll—was among these last.

He had started at Bethlehem Iron in 1896, just as the big depression, which had driven some local unemployed to pocket their savings and return to Europe, was waning. A sloppy demographer might toss him and John Griffith, Taylor's friend from the pump works, into the same lumpish category, that of workingman. Neither had much education. Neither would ever have much occasion to wear a collar, at least on the job. Neither, all through their lives, could long stop worrying about where his next pay was coming from. But there the similarities end. Griffith was a skilled, highly intelligent craftsman who, after he left the pump works, got a good job at Midvale and ran Taylor's tennis post business on the side. Noll was neither skilled nor notably intelligent. He was, Taylor would write, "a man of the mentally sluggish type . . . , a man so stupid that he was unfitted to do [even] most kinds of laboring work." It was almost required of a man doing such work, Taylor wrote at another point, "that he shall be so stupid and so phlegmatic that he more nearly resembles in his mental make-up the ox than any other type."

In fact, Noll was more than a muscled brute and exhibited traits not wholly alien to today's middle-class sensibilities. For starters, he was a jogger, before the word existed; he would, as Taylor noted, "trot back home for a mile or so after his work in the evening, about as fresh as he was when he came trotting down to work in the morning." He was alive enough to a future beyond today to hold onto his money; it was said of him that "a penny looks about the size of a cart-wheel." He avoided trouble with the law. He could read and write and had attended grammar school at least until he was eleven. He would serve as a volunteer fireman and was utterly trustworthy; later, while working as a teamster, his dutifulness moved his employer to promise to provide for him when he was too old to work.

Indeed, for all the dim-wittedness Taylor imputed to him, by 1899 he had bought a tiny parcel of land and begun to build a house, apparently on his own, during hours squeezed from before and after work. It was a tiny one-and-a-half-story clapboard affair on Martin's Lane, an alley on the other side of the river, far from the mill. And it was built soundly enough that it defied the wrecker's ball until 1960 when, pitched over the alley on which it was built, its foundation at last disintegrating, it finally had to be torn down.

Noll was a small, regular-featured man, a little sad-eyed, perhaps 135 pounds, wiry and athletic. Paraded before a camera, standing tall, he could seem quite dapper in his striped pants and derby, watch chain dangling from his vest; to the women, we may guess, he cut a fine figure. He married a few years later, only to soon be divorced when his wife lost patience with his undue fondness for women and drink. He was, indeed, as one report described him, "a hard drinker." He was also, whatever else he was, more than the leaden ox of Taylor's description.

Most Bethlehem employees, Henry Noll among them, lived in a strip beyond Second Street that ran parallel to the works and just south of it, about a quarter mile deep and two miles across. South Mountain rose behind it to the south; the railroad tracks blocked off the east. Earlier in the 1890s, just starting out, Noll had boarded within this area, in a house on Church Alley; boarding, the single man's lot, meant paying as little as fifty cents a week for meals and a bed. So, working steadily, without a family to support and any profligacy perhaps limited to drink, he managed to amass a modest stake. By 1899, he was probably already living a few blocks away on Laufer, a narrow, gently sloping street of sturdy brick row houses, each perhaps a dozen feet wide and built up to within a few feet of the curb. Noll lived at 814 Laufer. At 810 lived John Souders, whom the town directory listed as a laborer. At 812 lived Charles Schwartz, a laborer. Across the alley, at 813, lived Frank Hugh, a laborer. At 815, lived Jacob Knopp, a laborer.

In the next block, Laufer Street butted up against a cemetery. Here, from the top of a little hill, South Mountain behind him, Kitatinny Ridge across the river in the distance, Noll could see all of Bethlehem: houses climbing up from the Lehigh, gabled windows and peaked roofs suggesting small domestic comforts. In the basin at the bottom of the hill, the great steelworks, with its scores of smokestacks, stretched out below him for miles.

In the late winter of 1899, a change in market conditions that some day would register as only a blip on a graph reached down to touch the life of Henry Noll. Over the past decade, the price of pig iron had dropped to below ten dollars a ton, less than the cost to produce it. But now, thanks partly to the short but furious Spanish-American War of the previous year, it began to climb.

The price had been so low for so long that the company had let eighty thousand tons of it accumulate in a big yard at the far eastern edge of its property known as the farm. But with pig iron supplies now dwindling and its price edging up to about $12.50 a ton, Bethlehem began selling it off. In March, some ten thousand tons, duly sold, lay in two large piles of "pigs"—gray iron bars about four by four in cross section, thirty-two inches long, and weighing ninety-two pounds each. They had now to be loaded onto railcars for shipment. Frederick Taylor decreed that the job, at least some of it, was to be done on piece rate.

Here was work far distant from that of the skilled machinist, and yet the problem in setting rates was, at bottom, the same: what was a full day's work? It was Taylor's old question, the one he'd started with back at Midvale. He delegated James Gillespie, whom he had brought over about the beginning of February from moribund Simonds, along with an assistant, Hartley C. Wolle, to observe and time the work.

On Saturday, March 11, they started, with a dozen men picked from among a group of "large, powerful Hungarians," as a later report had it, in the regular yard gang. The pigs sat in two piles, one about eighteen feet from the freight car, its topmost layer reaching to a few feet below the car's floor. Wooden planks were laid between the pile and the car. Up the walkway the men walked, bearing the heavy bars. Waiting for them at the top, other men took each one and piled it into the car.

The Hungarians, asked to simply work as they normally did, managed to load up the car in fifty-four minutes. This, Gillespie calculated, worked out to twenty-four tons per man in a ten-hour day. Of course, it was only a single hour and didn't include time lost in setting up the planks or in other delays. So the figure was much higher than the thirteen tons long averaged around the Bethlehem yards; higher than the sixteen tons that miners, in the words of the popular song, presumably hauled from the earth each day; higher than the fifteen to twenty tons that, scholars estimate, represented an average day's work, by the average laborer, since time immemorial.

On a comfortably cool Monday, ten of the best men in the regular yard gang were ordered to work as flat-out fast as they could, for the time it took to load one car. They did it, literally running up and down the planks, in fourteen minutes: $16^{1}/_{2}$ tons' worth. That worked out to seventy-one tons per man per day. Timings of individual men, some probably by Taylor, stopwatch in hand, followed. He recalled, "It took me about a day and a half to be sure what those people could do"— which he set at seventy-five, not seventy-one, tons per day. Of course, the men were drained; these industrial marathoners had had to sprint for their pay. "It was quite evident," wrote Gillespie and Wolle, "that this gait could not be kept up for any considerable length of time."

Yet somehow, this wildly artificial figure became the basis for fixing piece rates. Through reasoning entirely opaque a century later, Taylor lopped off 40 percent, to allow for rest and unavoidable delay, and set forty-five tons per day as each man's daily stint. This was at least double—and probably closer to triple—what laborers had been able to manage throughout history.

Lift the pig, its ninety-two pounds straining biceps, back, and legs. Then, eight or ten steps up the plank. Pass the pig to the man in the car. Then, down the plank, and back to the pile. Twice each minute. Eleven hundred times a day.

What was the basis for the 40 percent allowance that led to Taylor's standard? Why not 60, or 80, or 10 percent? The report that Gillespie and Wolle prepared later grants no insight. The stopwatch timing, the careful "observations," the pages of numbers and calculations, might feebly suggest "science." But the 40 percent was sheer witchcraft.

Nonetheless, on the basis of these numbers, Davenport and Taylor set as the new piece rate 3.75 cents per ton. At that rate, anyone actually loading forty-five tons per day would take home $1.69, almost 50 percent more than the $1.15 or so that most of them got, reflecting Taylor's experience in what it took to get men to work much harder than usual. But anyone managing only thirteen tons a day, the yard's historical average, would earn less than fifty cents a day.

Were Gillespie and Wolle surprised when, three days later, ten men who had agreed to try piecework reneged, reporting instead to the day-rate gang? Confronted with their promise, and told they could work only at piecework, the men quit in a body and were directed to the office to collect their final pay.

When assistant superintendent Robert Sayre, Jr., met up with them and the situation was explained to him, he told them they could work by the day for the time being. This was a potentially explosive situation; a strike had to be avoided.

Word of a battle brewing in the yard reached the president, Robert Linderman, who approached Sayre's father. Let them go back and work the old way, Sayre, Sr., counseled.

Then, Taylor heard about it. Ten men had defied his orders. If they were not fired, he would quit.

The next morning, they were fired.

"Fri. Mar. 17," Robert Sayre, Sr., recorded in his dairy. "Taylor in to see me about the trouble among the loaders. I told him the men had been discharged, and he went off satisfied."

And so matters stood for the next two weeks. During this period, another foreman, who enjoyed notably good relations with the laborers under him, personally recruited seven from among them to try piecework. They were to show up, ready to work, on March 30. Five of them did; one was Henry Noll.

Noll and the other four worked all day, loading a hundred and sixty tons of pig iron, or thirty-two tons each. "At the conclusion of the day's work," wrote Gillespie and Wolle, "the men appeared to be much fatigued, especially Miller and Strohl." The following day neither one showed up for work.

That left Noll and two others.

The next day, Noll and his fellow stalwarts were worked no longer as a gang but individually, each to his own car, simply throwing the pigs aboard. Each was separated by perhaps two hundred feet and a virtual cordon of Taylor's men from the others. It may have been at this time that, as Taylor told it later, he took Noll off to the side and gave him a pep talk, reminding him that if he did just as he was told he could prove himself a "high priced man" and earn much more than the $1.15 or so he had earned before. In any case, Noll loaded 45^3/$_4$ tons and earned $1.71. The two others managed between thirty-five and forty tons.

Of these two, one quit the next day. The other, Gillespie realized, would not last long either, "owing to his youth and [the] slightness of his build."

So then there was one, Noll.

Other men were recruited, some of whom could keep up with him. But most just gave up after a few eighty- or ninety-cent days, or else after earning more but deciding they couldn't endure such grueling work. A whole succession of strong men, accustomed to brute labor, put in stints on piecework. But almost all, it turned out, were just not strong enough, as the Gillespie report observed:

"We found that [Gruen] was not fitted for such heavy work."

"Roth on this day loaded 43 tons, earning $1.63, but after this day did not return to work."

"Koch and Howarth [claimed] that they could not earn a fair day's wages at this work."

For the next month and a half the experiments continued, "our gang sometimes being reduced to one man and sometimes consisting of five or six." Holding men was difficult, they said, because of the influence "brought to bear by some of the Hungarians who had been discharged on March 16th," and who had "threatened [would-be pieceworkers] with bodily harm."

All the more reason to celebrate, as Gillespie and Wolle did, Noll's contribution: "He worked to his maximum from the beginning and . . . demonstrated that a good day's wages could be made at the existing rates by a good man." Taylor claimed later they had to walk him home each evening, to ward off stones and insults aimed at the man who was living proof that you *could* load 45 tons and earn $1.70 a day.

After about mid-May, resistance to piecework slackened perhaps, Gillespie felt, because the company was giving the men lighter jobs when hurt or "run down by excessive work." For his part, Taylor credited a meeting with an emissary from the men. "You just go and tell so-and-so," he remembered saying, "that I haven't begun at all; we have only been going about thirty days, and we will be at this three years." They could forget about trying to wear him down.

As piece rate took hold, more elaborate experiments were done. The weight of pig iron hauled in a day was plotted against the distance of the piles from the cars, and their height. Both factors appeared in equations in which the amount of work each man did—the word now used in its scientific sense and expressed in the physical unit known as the foot-pound—could be calculated. Tables were prepared showing how many foot-pounds of work each laborer did, broken down into that required to lift the pig, carry it, and finally heave it into the car. Soon, piece rates took into account such variables as height of lift and the angle of the plank. Hot summer work got a 15 percent premium, the figure probably about as "scientific" as the 40 percent allowance for rest and delay on which the original rates were based.

By May 31, the piece-rate gang had loaded almost seventy-five hundred tons of pig iron for less than a nickel a ton, half the cost of day rate; pig iron sold just then for about fifteen dollars a ton. Of course, Gillespie and Wolle wrote, "we have had considerable difficulty in getting men who are able to stand this work." Most broke down after a couple of days. Of forty men especially "selected as being strong enough for the work," only ten ranked as "good"; this meant that for just a few cents a day more, they loaded about twice as much. Only three of the forty qualified as "first-class men," earning substantially more. One was Henry Noll.

Over the next two years, piece rates were extended to other sorts of labor in the Bethlehem yards and were defined ever more precisely. By late July 1899, rates for unloading pig iron were being set to three decimal places; iron carried less than fifteen feet from the side of the car went for $.0731 per ton. By the time Taylor was through, the number of yard laborers had plummeted from 600 to 140; the remaining men, Taylor would write, "constituted the finest body of picked laborers that the writer has ever seen together." Among them, we trust, was Henry Noll, still building his little house and earning $1.70 a day. But for the time being, his arduous days remained invisible to history.

⌒

Fred and Lou Taylor lived in a rented house known as Bishop's Palace, a mansard-roofed affair with a big porch occupying a steeply sloped, tree-shaded site in South Bethlehem. It was cold and wet that spring and they got out little. But their first winter in Bethlehem, he wrote Captain Goodrich in April, had been "quite a gay" one. They'd entertained much, Lou "having given quite extensive concerts at our house."

Fred, forty-three at the time of the pig iron experiments, began keeping shorter hours, typically leaving the office by four. He took to cycling between home and work. He joined the South Bethlehem Golf Club, tried getting in at least a little golf daily. The sport—"a most satisfactory amusement and exercise," he called it—became an important part of his life. He posed, in golf cap and knickers, winding up for a swing. He played in tournaments. Golf even sidled into his working hours; one time, he kept an aide waiting, and boiling, while he gabbed with friends about the sport.

Around this time, the Taylors began visiting his sister Mary and her husband, Clarence Clark, his old doubles partner, at the big summer house in Manchester, Vermont, they'd bought in 1898. For fifty years, marble-sidewalked Manchester had been an exclusive resort, drawing wealthy summer visitors from New York, Philadelphia, and Boston. The Clark place, Wyndhurst, occupied a site just out of town, at the top of a wide sloping lawn from the main road. A mountain rose behind it. Down the long driveway and across the dirt road, a few minutes' walk away, was the new Ekwanok Country Club, opened in 1900, its greens and fairways studded with glacial outcroppings. Clarence Clark had helped found the club, and by 1901 Taylor had won a silver cup there, for first prize.

A photograph taken a little after the pig iron experiments, on the Fourth of July, 1899, shows the Taylor and Clark families together in the shade of a stand of slim-trunked trees, perhaps at Wyndhurst. Sister Mary sits against a rock, knitting. Her husband, Clarence, with his dark, handlebar mustache, lies on a blanket, propped on one elbow. Their three boys, Fred Taylor's nephews, ranging from six through fourteen, sit in front. Emily Richards—"Aunt Millie," a deaf, forty-six-year-old distant cousin of the family and housekeeper for Franklin Taylor—leans against a tree, reading. Frank Taylor, now seventy-seven, looks hale, erect, and, as ever, somehow avuncular. Lou sprawls languorously on the grass beside her father-in-law, a winning little smile on her face. Fred sits in a rocker with a dog on his lap, in collar and tie, his pants freshly pressed, his shoes gleaming.

But Emily is missing. Two years before, she'd suffered a stroke that left her paralyzed, confined to a wicker-backed wheelchair and in the care of a full-time nurse. She had undergone a "total change of character," Taylor wrote a friend. "My mother, from being a very happy woman, and always most philosophical, has changed to directly the reverse, and has been really miserable ever since her stroke."

In January of the new century, Taylor heard from a carriage maker back in Philadelphia, in response to his inquiry about a pretty carriage he wanted made up for Lou. It would take nine weeks to complete, cost two hundred and fifty dollars; sketch and fabric swatch were enclosed. The figure rose to almost three hundred dollars with changes Taylor ordered. It had a wicker cab, rubber-tired wheels, and—after Lou's change of heart—seats upholstered in blue. In April, he arranged to see it on his way back through Philadelphia from Lakewood, New Jersey, one of their regular getaway spots.

Around May, the Taylors moved to a house in Fountain Hill, a neighborhood of great homes on the north side of town upwind from the mill; in the modern style, the name of the community was pure invention, fountains of any sort being notably absent. But since the 1860s, it had been the home of the mill elite, especially along Delaware Avenue. Robert P. Linderman, president, lived at 603 Delaware Avenue. Robert H. Sayre, Jr., son of the neighborhood's pioneer settler and now superintendent of the blast furnace, at 685; Russell Davenport, 705; now, Fred and Lou moved to 739.

The previous year, Taylor's friend from the paper mill, Frank Steele, wrote him from Chicago, boasting that he had just received seventy-five thousand dollars due him from his employer, Deering Harvester, "which is a pretty good return, over and above salary for the past five years." Taylor had his own success to report. "I know you will be pleased to hear that I have also done well during the last five years." Going on to supply the figures, he added, "We have done one pretty nearly as well as the other in our two different lines."

Plainly, Taylor was comfortably fixed, the paper mill losses long behind him. And now a new fortune was coming to him, through high-speed steel.

9

A SCIENCE OF WORK?

~

ALL THROUGH THE PIG IRON EXPERIMENTS and on into the summer and fall of 1899, work with the new tool steel continued. Following their fluke success with tools L3 and L4 that past November, Taylor and Maunsel White now sought to refine their first Eureka discovery.

In *Sixty Years*, a 1947 memoir of his life in industry, former *American Machinist* editor Fred Colvin observed that during this period "the budding science of metallurgy was looked upon as a secret art," in which

every job of heat-treating, or of hardening and tempering, took on the nature of sorcery and black magic. Most of the heat-treating work was done in an open forge with a hand-operated rotary blower, and every operator had his own personal technique of "coking up" the fire and applying the draft. There was much solemn hokum about the carbon composition of various steels, the proper ingredients to be used in the hardening bath, and even the kind of weather that should prevail during the ritual.

All this, of course, described the familiar world of carbon steels. More mysterious yet were the new alloy steels, with their whiff of exotic tungsten, chromium, and molybdenum. Taylor and White probably had only a glimmer of what they were doing. So mistrustful were they of their heretical, high-temperature heat treatment, for example, that at first they clung to their old, low-temperature ways.

They tried everything. They heated tools "in a blacksmith's coke fire, a blacksmith's soft coal fire, in muffles over a blacksmith's fire, and in gas heated muffles," Taylor wrote in his 1906 opus, *On the Art of Cutting Metals*. A pyrometer with a platinum wire thermocouple translated the hot steel's first blush of color, "blood red," into 1050 degrees Fahrenheit, "salmon" into 1650 degrees.

Likewise for cooling. "After being heated close to the melting point," he wrote, "tools were immediately buried in lime, in powdered charcoal, and in a mixture of lime and powdered charcoal. . . . We tried cooling them partly in water and then slowly for the rest of the time . . ." In the end, they relied for cooling on a bath of molten lead, cold by the steel's standards, whose temperature could be minutely calibrated. To slightly cool the bath, they lowered into it a pipe supplied with cold water; to raise its temperature, they injected air into the glowing coke fire beneath.

Overseeing the metal cutting, the acid test for their tools, was Dwight Merrick, twenty-eight, a family friend of the Taylors from back in Germantown who'd come up as a machinist's apprentice, gone to Drexel to study engineering, and wound up in the drafting room at Cramp's, before coming to Bethlehem. Before they were through, Taylor figured later, a dozen men had performed sixteen thousand individual experiments and reduced some two hundred tons of steel to chips.

But after close to a year, they knew what was happening. Midvale's chromium-tungsten tool steel did "break down" or become "ruined," to use the shop argot of the day, when heated beyond a "bright cherry red," or 1550 degrees; that, apparently, was the fate of the tools that had failed Taylor so publicly the year before. When heated to any temperature short of 1725 degrees, the tool remained useless, able to cut but slowly. Beyond that point, however, cutting speed turned back the other way, soon equaling that achieved below 1550, and rose, and rose, and rose still further with rising temperature until, past 2200 degrees or so, the steel approached its melting point.

The tools this regimen now reliably produced could cut at twice the old speeds; and the cuts themselves were 40 percent deeper. Altogether, they could take great chomping bites from the work at triple the old rate. Chips came off the tool so hot, Maunsel White recounted, that workmen lit their cigarettes with them. The result was high-speed steel, and today you can go into a hardware store and buy drill bits so labeled that are the lineal descendants of those born in Machine Shop No. 2. Late that year, Taylor and White applied for a patent on the process and on August 10, 1900, widening its scope, a second.

How can we imagine the impact of high-speed steel today, when computers, not machine tools, excite our wonder? When new materials, processes, and tools have robbed the machine shop of its luster? When entrepreneurs cut their losses, editors cut manuscripts, but few, it can seem, cut metal? The gain that high-speed steel promised wasn't one of a few percent but a doubling, tripling, or more. All the trouble to which England's Robert Mushet had gone to protect his self-hardening steel from competitors, all its honored place in metallurgical history, rested on cutting speeds half again higher than existing tools; Taylor-White steel, under the right conditions, quadrupled them.

～

But how to extract from the new steel all its potential? Taylor's old problem, of how to use the metal-cutting data to set speed and feed for any particular job, had with high-speed steel become more urgent. You didn't want to use some safe, leisurely speed that let the tool cut merrily along, hour after hour, without regrinding; that was too conservative, robbing the new steel of its value. You wanted, rather, to push the tool to its limit.

This meant, for a particular job, determining what that limit was— and fast. For with the cutting itself so rapid, you were cycling through each job more quickly now. Setup—swinging it onto the lathe, lining it up, clamping it down, setting speed and feed—consumed a larger proportion of each job and so offered more opportunity for waste; you didn't want to be figuring and reckoning when you could be cutting.

To hear Taylor tell it, for years he'd cast about for a mathematician who, "offered any reasonable fee," could take the tables, graphs, and curves that embodied the metal-cutting data and make speed and feed calculations quicker and more routine. Seven, by his count, had taken a shot at it. It can't be done, came their collective answer; there were just too many variables: the hardness of the metal to be cut, its diameter, the power the machine tool must furnish, the mechanical forces the tool had to bear, and many more. It might take a good mathematician two to six hours, Taylor estimated, to solve each problem, way too long to be of any use. At Bethlehem, Gantt and another man had worked on a slide rule aimed at speeding up the calculations, but by the summer of 1899, they had achieved little.

Enter Carl Barth.

Four years younger than Taylor, Barth was a short, dark Norwegian with a scraggly little beard and, in one scholar's words, "keen, sharp, snapping blue eyes." He brimmed over with intelligence. He was honest, headstrong, rabidly individualistic, and a socialist; he said of millionaires, "I would rather see them drowned." Yet he was profoundly elitist and could say in the same breath, "I believe there are very few men who have a right to their opinions." One earned a right to them only through study and effort. Of opinions, he declared, "I have got mighty few; but by the Almighty, they are strong."

He was unforgettable. When he appeared before the Commission on Industrial Relations in 1914, he was asked to identify himself. "Before I do I would like to get a little more air," the official record notes. "I am pretty nearly smothered." Someone opened a window.

"Is that better?" he was asked.

> Mr. Barth: I have not felt the effect as yet, but in anticipation of some improvement, I will proceed. My name is Carl—written with a C and not a K—Carl G. Barth. There is more to it, but it is too long to state.
>
> Mr. Thompson: Where do you live?
>
> Mr. Barth: Well, ask me where my wife lives, and I can tell you. I live where she lives—6151 Columbia Avenue, Philadelphia.
>
> · · ·
>
> Mr. Thompson: What is your business?
>
> Mr. Barth: Well, that is an awfully hard question to answer, but as people insist that a man assume a title in order to cover a

multitude of sins, I assumed the title of consulting engineer, because I can do anything under the sun under that title.

Mr. Thompson: Are you acquainted with what has been called by Mr. Taylor "scientific management shops," as relating to the workingman?

Mr. Barth: I should certainly say I was, if any man is. . . . It will be 15 years this summer since I got in touch with that work . . .

He was born in Christiania, now Oslo, and was probably living there when Taylor and his family passed through in 1870 on their way up to the fjord country. When he was twelve, an older boy took him to visit a brass foundry's machine shop, where the sight of chips flying off candlesticks being turned enthralled him. When he got through school, he resolved, he'd work in a machine shop. His father, a university-trained forester, wanted him to attend the university in Christiania. But Barth held out instead for Norway's famously theoretical technical school at Horten, at the mouth of a fjord near the capital; he was fifteen and, to hear him tell it later, the youngest boy ever admitted. From school, it was into the shop for what would normally have been a five-year apprenticeship. But he was already marked as prodigiously bright and when an instructor at the school quit, Barth was asked to take his place.

Friends would later recall how Barth could work out complicated gear trains in his head. Whatever he got near he wanted to reduce to graphs and formulas. In America, he studied mathematics on his own and in 1894 would present "The Principles of the Calculus in a New Light" before the Engineers Club of Philadelphia. He puttered with mathematical curves and equations all his life. And his talent for it was apparent to all, even in his teens.

Yet Barth made the equivalent of only three cents an hour at Horten and was forever getting into trouble with his boss. So, like many a troublemaker, he began studying English in earnest and emigrated to America, arriving in the New World on April 18, 1881. He wound up in Philadelphia, submitted examination drawings from Horten that impressed both Coleman Sellers, Jr., and Williams Sellers, and was offered two dollars a day to start in the drafting room. Soon he was making twenty a week.

At Sellers, he met Wilfred Lewis. When, many years later, in 1898, Taylor cast about for help at Bethlehem, Lewis recommended him.

Barth was working at an Ethical Culture school in New York at the time, teaching manual training and mathematics. "An opportunity has come up at the Works here," Taylor wrote him. "Can you not come over to Bethlehem in the near future and talk the matter over with me?" The two met. On June 15, when some of the yard laborers were threatening to strike, he reported for work. Word of trouble reached Taylor, Barth recalled, but "he did not betray the slightest perturbance," acting as if nothing had happened. Taylor put Barth to work on the experimental lathe under Merrick; Barth was a veteran machine tool designer, but to Taylor he was a novice and needed to get his hands dirty all over again.

Within a few months, Barth was doing what he'd been hired to do, pulling down twenty-five hundred dollars a year, and employed at what personnel records described as "calculations." "I shall never forget the intense delight evinced by Mr. Taylor one morning," Barth wrote later, on being presented a formula embodying results of the metal-cutting experiments. Soon, Barth had taken the primitive slide rule devised by Gantt and made it into one that coughed up answers almost instantly.

The ordinary slide rule, with its system of fixed and sliding scales, had been popular since around 1850 and remained so up to the 1970s, when its place in the engineer's affections was usurped by the pocket calculator. But while the typical slide rule was an all-purpose instrument, Barth's did just one thing, calculate speeds and feeds for a particular machine tool. Boasting five individual slides, it had to accommodate an enormous range of factors. The shape of the tool exerted an effect on cutting speed of 6 to 1, depending on whether you used a round-nosed tool or a pointed one, as in cutting a thread. Chip thickness, a factor of 3.5 to 1. The kind of metal you were cutting, whether soft or hard, 100 to 1. And, of course, whether you cut with high-speed steel or ordinary carbon steel, a factor of 7 to 1.

But with the Barth slide rule, you could slip through the calculations easily. Cutting speed had to satisfy two broad constraints: the machine tool's ability to exert power and the cutting tool's ability to bear it. Roughly, the rule's upper section dealt with the former, its lower part with the latter. Each, independently figured, gave a range of possible solutions. A check of the central scale revealed the one or very few solutions that satisfied both ends of the problem. All this in twenty of thirty seconds.

By the end of the year, the new Barth slide rules were being used with a dozen of the giant machine tools in Machine Shop No. 2. And their use, wrote Taylor, meant more than all the other metal-cutting improvements combined, because it achieved

> the original object for which in 1880 [at Midvale] the experiments were started; that of taking the control of the machine shop out of the hands of the many workmen, and placing it completely in the hands of management, thus superseding "rule of thumb" by scientific control.

So readily did the slide rules furnish optimum settings, and so briskly did high-speed steel tools dispose of the work, that at least twice Machine Shop No. 2 was left with nothing to do. This was in sharp contrast to a time not long past when, to relieve the shop's backlog, the purchase of a million dollars' worth of new machine tools had been seriously contemplated.

The slide rule's success placed Barth squarely among Taylor's favored few. After the inevitable fighting between them had convinced Taylor that Barth knew what he was about, he became one of a handful of men from whom he could take criticism; sometimes Taylor introduced him as "the man who right along proves that every darned thing I have ever done is wrong."

Soon Taylor was pushing more on him. "Now, Barth," he said, calling him into his office one day, "I want you to take these data we have here on laboring and try to work out the law." "These data" referred to the pig iron studies. "The law"—in this case of human physiology—referred to Taylor's efforts, going back to Midvale, to define a full day's work.

At least in Taylor's memory, Barth wanted no part of it. "I will not do it," he pictured Barth replying. "There is nothing in it. . . . Everyone will tell you so. Mr. Gantt warned me you would have me on that fool thing."

"Barth," Taylor told him, "you will either . . . do as I say or get out."

So Barth acquiesced, and Taylor piled the data on him. Maybe Barth figured, like everyone else, that there was "some relation between foot-pounds, or energy, and a day's work"? There wasn't, Taylor assured him. He had sought such a relation from the beginning, and concluded it didn't exist; the "law" simply wasn't that neat. But he had not given up the search for something hard, definite, and quantifiable in the data amassed over the years. Gantt, Gillespie, and others urged him to forget it. "But I was sure the thing was there," he would say, and now he wanted Barth to find it.

He was giving him everything he might need, Taylor told him, "even the temperature of the day, the moisture in the air, anything that may in any way remotely affect what constitutes a day's work." Not so, concluded Barth. To him, the data were "so inconsistent that no use could be made of it," and he launched new studies. From these, together with the original data, he did find something.

One day, recalled Taylor, Barth "came back in a great state of excitement," the coveted law in hand. Later, Taylor would challenge contractors, who drove men to their limits every day, to guess its form. None could. And yet this presumably astonishing scientific truth merely added a patina of arithmetical legitimacy to common sense: people need to rest, and the harder they work the more rest they need. More specifically, Barth's "law of heavy laboring" proposed that, in handling ninety-two-pound pigs, "a first-class workman can only be under load 43 per cent of the day. He must be entirely free from load during 57 per cent of the day. And as the load becomes lighter, the percentage of the day under which the man can remain under load increases."

Had Barth not come along, Taylor would have had to order him up from Central Casting; Barth's son once called him "even more of a Taylorite than Taylor." For he'd helped restore to the Taylor system what had almost gotten lost in the roving years since Midvale—*science*. And not just science, but science wrapped in the flag of mathematics. With his help and that of Gantt and the others, Taylor was fashioning a science of work. This science was less than he made it out to be, of course. Yet he was at least bringing a strategy, and a readiness to employ mathematical tools, to problems of human work left virtually untouched by legions of workmen, foremen, and managers over the centuries.

Among the areas he probed was, of all things, shoveling, which, with Noll's heroic pig iron handling, would one day furnish one of the two stories Taylor relied on most to impress his ideas on the public. "Now, gentlemen, shoveling is a great science compared with pig-iron handling," he would tell his inquisitors on the House Special Committee in 1912, no doubt pausing for appreciative titters.

Soon after arriving at Bethlehem, it seems, he'd looked out the office window and seen men shoveling rice coal—anthracite in nuggets about the size of fine gravel. Once they finished, "they walked to another part of the yard where there was a pile of ore from Mesabi, and with the same shovel they shoveled that ore." Now, a shovelful of rice coal might weigh four or five pounds, one of iron ore thirty-five pounds. Would the one shovel that Bethlehem yard laborers brought with them from home serve equally well for both? Might you not want larger shovels for lighter material, smaller ones for heavier?

Soon, Taylor's men were weighing the pile that a man shoveled in a day, dividing by the number of shovelfuls counted, and calculating an average weight per shovelful. Next day, they'd trim the edge of the shovel, to reduce the weight per shovelful, and note the effect on the day's output.

Was there one best shovel load?

Taylor's interest in this simple art, as we've seen, went all the way back to Midvale; since 1896, Sanford Thompson had been working on it in Boston. Back then, when still convinced that foot-pounds measurements would bear fruit in laws of work, Taylor's letters to Thompson revealed remarkable intimacy with what most others had written off over the centuries as simple brute labor, unworthy of study. "I note your figures on the foot-pounds of energy in unloading coal," he'd written Thompson on February 15, 1896:

> I think, however, you are perhaps a little wrong on one point. The coal, as it is unloaded over the side of the car, leaves the shovel while the latter is turned almost upside down. It is not thrown, for instance, as most laborers would throw dirt into a cart—that is, keeping the dirt always over the shovel and shooting the shovel out in the air at an angle of about 45 degrees in a comparatively straight line. In unloading coal, the men at Midvale bring the shovel up through a curved path, and I think in the average case, when the coal leaves the shovel the bottom of the shovel would be rather higher in the air than the coal. This, of course, means that the coal is raised very considerably above the top of the car as it goes over the side of the same; I should say on an average a foot to eighteen inches . . .

There was much more like this, and now, at Bethlehem, Taylor took it further yet. He and his assistants collected data on shoveling from the body of the pile, from the dirt bottom of it, from a wooden bottom, and from an iron bottom. They timed even the backward swing of the shovel needed to throw a load a given distance. For four months this went on, the results reduced to tables and graphs.

Taylor had guessed the optimum shovel load at fourteen pounds, but the data clustered around twenty-one. That is, furnish a laborer with a shovel that, for a particular material, held about twenty-one pounds and, at day's end, you'd have a bigger pile than for a shovel holding any other weight. At one point, Gantt and Taylor almost came to blows when Gantt insisted that shovels big enough to hold twenty-one pounds of rice coal couldn't be had. Nonsense, said Taylor, the gain in using them would justify any cost or trouble to get them—even having them custom-made. They got them.

In the end, through time study, piece rates, and other measures, the cost for each ton of material handled in the Bethlehem yards was halved, and the place was being run as no such place ever had before. Taylor and his minions built a telephone system. They hired clerks. They set up a bulletin board, along with big maps that let them plan the most efficient movements of men around the yard. As Taylor testified, "It was practically like playing a game of chess in which the four to six hundred men were moved about so as to be in the right place at the right time."

A man reporting for work in the morning went straight to the shovel room, where he was issued one of ten types of shovel, told where to report, and given a colored slip of paper. White meant he had earned his premium the day before, which left him with wages about 60 percent higher than otherwise, or about $1.85. Yellow meant he had failed, which presumably spurred him to greater effort. After a few such days, he might get remedial "instruction" in good shoveling technique, perhaps be reminded that only Henry Noll–style "high-priced men" could hold their jobs for long.

AFTERTHOUGHT

~

O N JANUARY 25, 1900, in a letter making due allowance for certain gaps in the company president's technical knowledge, Bethlehem general superintendent Archibald Johnston wrote Robert Linderman to recap progress on high-speed steel. It had long been accepted that self-hardening steel had to be worked and hardened at relatively low temperatures. But Taylor—he did not mention Maunsel White—had found otherwise. The results were astonishing. Steel once cut at twenty to thirty feet per minute could now be cut at sixty. A cannon tube that had taken seventy five hours to machine now took twenty-two. Labor time was down dramatically, of course. But more, the shop's great capital-devouring machine tools, some costing thirty thousand dollars (the equivalent today of close to a million dollars), did so much more work that the company could get by with fewer of them.

The machine shop as a whole—in the past, well behind the forge that supplied it work—was now sometimes kept waiting. They'd had to let some machinists go. The remaining men were watching and tending less, busy more. The shop even sounded different now: everything clacked and whirred faster. The main lines of shafting that, through belts, powered virtually every machine tool in the great cavernous shop, had been speeded up from ninety revolutions per minute to two hundred and fifty; they could have made it faster yet, Taylor said later, were it not for the infernal racket. There, in Machine Shop No. 2, the world was speeding up. It would never slow down again.

By now, in January 1900, everybody had heard about what was going on. "We have been giving an exhibition about every other day," Maunsel White wrote his brother in November 1899. Taylor testified later that

more than two hundred and fifty prominent engineers,
superintendents of works, and managers of machine shops, came

from all parts of the world to see these tools run in the Bethlehem shops. One man came from Australia, another from South Africa, others from almost every country in Europe, and one or two from South America, as well as many from Canada, and all parts of the United States.

In many demonstrations, Bethlehem kept a man by the lathe just to knock the helical ribbons of thick chips out of the way—presumably so visitors could better see, but also, no doubt, to dramatize their sheer profusion.

Some visitors brought their own tools to run against those of Bethlehem. They'd return home, report on what they'd seen—only to find their testimony disbelieved. A Carnegie Steel superintendent, back in Pittsburgh, showed his subordinate, a Mr. Frye, a box of steel chips he'd brought back from Bethlehem, and told him they'd been cut at a white heat. Said Frye later, "I frankly told him I didn't believe it."

Early on, Bethlehem began receiving offers to buy shop rights to the new process. By this time, Westinghouse had approached the company. So had the Gisholt Machine Company and Taylor Iron & Steel (no ties to Fred Taylor). Wm. Sellers & Company had talked to Taylor himself, as had Brown & Sharpe, Pratt & Whitney, Lorain Steel, and others. Sellers weighed buying shop rights for six thousand dollars but for a time held back. Finally, though, the venerable firm capitulated.

That, apparently, sold Linderman on the strength of the market for Taylor-White tools; if Sellers was parlaying up the money, the prospects for many more customers was great. Taylor had suggested to Archibald Johnston that maybe the company might want to buy him out. Johnston wrote Linderman that he thought that fifty-thousand dollars would do it. The offer went out. Taylor and White accepted— that is, for their American rights; foreign sales were to be divided fifty-fifty between them and the company. Indeed, in February, the English rights were sold to Vickers and Maxim, the big arms makers, for one hundred thousand dollars.

Early in April, while Fred and Lou were vacationing in Lakewood, Lou was stricken with appendicitis. She underwent surgery in the German Hospital back in Philadelphia. The operation, Taylor wrote Goodrich in June, "was entirely successful but . . . left her physically weak and with her nerves run down." Nonetheless, he went on, they planned to travel to Europe for two months in August.

That summer, a great international exposition was to be held in Paris, in which American machine tools would get their own building in the Bois de Vincennes, on the east side of the city. Around March, Bethlehem decided its new high-speed tools ought to be shown there. It was late, most other American exhibitors having long since packed up their machinery and shipped it; *American Machinist* called Bethlehem's decision "an afterthought." But somehow, the company arranged for space in a corner of the exhibit hall.

A twenty-ton lathe just like the experimental one back in Bethlehem, complete with its own forty-horsepower electric motor, was loaded along with the rest of the exhibit onto three freight cars and hauled to New York overnight for shipment overseas. Upon arrival in Le Havre, whose wharves were a chaos of packing crates bound for the fair, it was loaded on to railcars. Through the kind of tortuous odyssey that was the talk of the American exhibitors, it reached the Vincennes exhibit grounds about the end of May, a month after the opening of the fair.

PART FIVE

HOUSE ON THE HILL

(1900–1910)

1

AT THE BOIS DE VINCENNES

∿

WHEN DIRECTORS OF THE PARIS EXPOSITION first allotted space at their main exhibition site near the Eiffel Tower, American machine tool manufacturers got almost none. A big New England tool builder was offered a parcel just two feet by three and a half, smaller than its smallest lathe. Did the French fear American competition? So some Americans grumbled. A furor erupted, and America's machinery exhibit director, Francis Drake, gained permission to put up a separate building, in an annex to the fair in the Bois de Vincennes, a park on the east end of the city, six miles from the Eiffel Tower.

Vincennes, plainly stated, was the sticks; on the official, otherwise colorful exposition map, it was represented at half scale and reduced to a monochromatic blue. You got there by the brand-new Paris Métro, or by an electric tram that ran along the northern edge of the park, or by boat, steaming down the Seine—picturesque but, with all the stops, time-consuming. One American journalist called it "the desert of Vincennes." Some fretted that no one would come.

They needn't have worried.

True, the broad, sandy expanse of the Bois, prone to dust when it didn't rain, was a little ragtag; to a correspondent from *Iron Age*, it presented a "somewhat forlorn appearance." The Beautiful People were elsewhere, strutting in top hat and finery across the magnificent steel arch of the new Pont Alexandre across the Seine, or through the vaulted sculpture court of the Grand Palais. Certainly, Vincennes never got as infernally crowded as the main site, which some commercial exhibitors preferred, because it meant the curiosity seekers were elsewhere.

And yet, Vincennes was a success. The site housed exhibits of locomotives from a dozen nations. It displayed automobiles from America, England, Italy, and Germany, as well as France. It had windmills, a shooting gallery, an area for balloon ascents, a Restaurant des Sports along the lakefront of Lac Daumesnil. And along one side of a flat, sandy, triangular plot across from the municipal velodrome, it accommodated the American machinery building.

The building was supposed to represent a typical American machine shop, though this pristine vision was tainted when space-hungry outsiders to the industry horned in and claimed part of a hastily constructed wood-beamed annex. The main hall itself was a long, low structure, a model of prefabrication; fourteen men erected its steel shell in eight days. (At one point, in June 1899, construction was endangered by the same abrupt rise in the price of iron and steel that, back in Bethlehem, had left Henry Noll hauling pig iron.) It was simple yet quietly stylish, with rose windows and pennants atop flagpoles giving it a festive air.

Inside, exhibitors were arrayed along one of two long aisles. Browne & Sharp, Pratt & Whitney—all the big American machine-tool powerhouses were there, with shapers, turret lathes, surface grinders, milling machines. Air-driven power tools on exhibit made a deafening racket that reduced sober technical discussions to shouting matches.

If you came in through the main entrance, on the velodrome side, you found the Bethlehem exhibit at the end of an aisle near Pratt & Whitney. But you could come in from the Route des Glacières side, too, passing through a simple columned entrance under a rose window. There, immediately to your left, at the head of the main aisle, was the Bethlehem exhibit. The sign overhead said:

BETHLEHEM STEEL COMPANY,
South Bethlehem, Pennsylvania, U.S.A.
High Speed Cutting Tools
Made by the Taylor-White Process

along with smaller notices in French and German.

To run the exhibit, Taylor had picked Dwight Merrick and another man, who reached Vincennes before the carloads of equipment from Le Havre did; neither spoke French. But while other exhibitors waited patiently for French workmen to get to them, as exposition rules decreed, Taylor's men ordered bricks, mortar, and shovels, unloaded supplies at night, and began digging a foundation for the heavy lathe themselves. This, in Taylor's telling, occasioned "great horror" among the other exhibitors. When the lathe finally arrived, they were ready for it with tackle and rigging gear. They unloaded it with the help of a few laborers and had it up and running when many machines that had reached Vincennes earlier were still uncrated piles of parts.

The exhibit occupied an L-shaped corner of the hall. Its long leg, where the big lathe sat on its foundation, extended back about thirty feet toward windows on the north wall. An electric motor, mounted atop a wooden platform, drove the lathe whose cutting tools each day sliced at a ten-foot-long cylinder of solid steel. Under a trio of small French and American flags hung a photo of Machine Shop No. 2 in Bethlehem. A display case stood on the other side of a low railing from the aisle.

And between the posts of this railing had been hung—were they the fruit of an idle moment's playfulness or a master publicist's genius?— long, looping helices of steel chips, like cables of a suspension bridge. Across a break in the railing was draped a velvet rope; and beyond that, in from the aisle half the length of the lathe, a second one. Here, allowed in a few at a time, visitors could witness the spectacle up close.

For fear that their eyes deceived them, *everyone* wanted a closer look. Merrick would run a tool for twenty minutes, take a ten-minute break, then take another cut. And each time he did, Taylor would recall, people rushed from all over the building "to see the tools cutting with their noses red hot, and turning out blue chips. And the entire exhibit, together with all the space around it, was jammed with people trying to get a view." Other exhibitors complained that Bethlehem siphoned off attention from them.

Britain's Iron and Steel Institute held its annual meeting in Paris that summer, to coincide with the exposition, and word of the Bethlehem demonstrations filtered back to the technical sessions during the conference's first two days. On the third day, when they could go to Vincennes themselves, many members headed straight for the Bethlehem stand, to watch the tools churn out steel chips so thick they had to be broken up by hammer blows.

No one who saw the sight ever forgot it. For many, it was a defining moment of their careers, when they watched the world speed up before their eyes. When they told their colleagues about it or talked about it among themselves, technical restraint gave way to simple wonder, the very sight of those billowing coils of hot blue chips burned into their brains forever.

According to a French account, "The news spread rapidly in

the machine shops [of Paris] that one could, in this 'desert' [of Vin-cennes], see metal cut at a speed [previously] unsuspected"—by this inflated report, six times faster. "Engineers, technicians, lathe workers everywhere flocked to the stand of the Bethlehem Steel Company" to watch.

Albert Butler, a technical editor for the Crescent Steel Company of Pittsburgh, "wrote to the president of our company that a revolution in steel manufacture and in the use of steel tools for metal cutting had occurred, and that he must look to his laurels or we could no longer hold our preeminence as fine tool steel makers."

An English company, Armstrong Whitworth, sent ten of its fore-men to Paris to see the Taylor-White tools. Germany's largest machine shop, Ludwig Loewe, sent seven of its managers and superintendents. Visitors brought back chips to show their bosses and colleagues.

A British engineer, J. Hartley Wicksteed, was reminded of Edison's electric lamp. To see

> the cuttings coming off in long continuous pieces colored purple
> with heat . . . was about as surprising as when it was discovered
> that a carbon filament could be used for electric current without
> consuming itself. The whole idea of a tool preserving its edge when
> in a state of dull red heat was, I think, to all of us a revelation. . . . I
> consider that it is by far the greatest revolution that has taken place
> in my life.

Away from Vincennes, the reports were dismissed as ridiculous until they could be dismissed no longer. In Sheffield, world capital of tool steel, word reached Samuel Osborn & Company, which had long made traditional Robert Mushet tool steel under license. Its American representative in Boston tried to put a good face on the news; Taylor-White steel, he wrote Osborn on September 18, was "utterly imprac-tical. Even if successful RMS [Robert Mushet Steel] would still be wanted." Then, two weeks later:

> Large railroad under nose of Bethlehem told me genuine RMS
> good enough for them.

> Mr. Olp, master blacksmith of Bethlehem, told G. Williams,
> "You keep quiet—we will have RMS back here again ere long."

But other reports reaching Osborn that October held back none of the new truth. One said that Bethlehem was ridding itself of the Mushet it had on hand, selling off £12,000 of it. A hundred American shops, it was said, were already using the Taylor-White tools. Another, on October 3, to Osborn: "WCB fears RMS is done for!!"

Astonishment among those who had seen the exhibit, outright disbelief among those who had not—these were the reactions around the industrial capitals of the world. As the distinguished French metallurgist Henri-Louis Le Chatelier would write, "Nobody quite believed at first in the prodigious result . . . claimed by the Bethlehem Works, but we had to accept the evidence of our eyes."

~

They are gone now, the exhibit halls and palaces built for the exposition that once lined the Seine and attracted fifty million visitors. "A riot of color and an extravaganza of shape," someone called it. Science and technology figured large in the spectacle—as servants of man, to advance his ideals and lead him toward prosperity. That son and grandson of American presidents, Henry Adams, came to Paris and saw in the fair's almost silent, irresistibly turning dynamo a metaphor for the new age. French President Émile Loubet, borne across Paris by a golden carriage, could declare that "Soon, perhaps, we shall have completed an important stage in the slow evolution of work towards happiness, and of man towards humanity. It is under the auspices of such a hope that I declare the Exposition of 1900 open."

It would never be like that again. The fair could have been conceived, Richard Mandell would write, only "during a time that still had faith in optimistic philosophical systems, hopes for social reform, joy in expanding material wealth, and confidence in the moral benefits of art." Here was almost the last historical moment when the idea of progress, fueled by science, on the march to human happiness, could still be taken seriously.

Was there some monstrous excess here that might have foretold the excesses of the century? Viewed just a little differently, after all, the fair could be seen as mostly show and spectacle, a fever of grandiose dreams. The enormous figure of *La Parisienne*, flanked by Egyptian obelisks, loomed over its monumental entrance. On both sides of the Seine, along the Quai des Nations, clustered the national pavilions of Italy, Turkey, Bosnia, Britain, each more ornate then the next, bearing some of what Mandell would call the fair's "exaggerated and banal ornamentation, half École des Beaux-Arts, half Kursaal, with its flying figures, friezed pediments, and pinnacles," all ablaze in color, shape, and design. Except for a few permanent pavilions, most of these phantasms of architectural hubris were actually little more than stage sets, designed to come down the instant the last visitor left.

Later, lawyers contesting the Taylor-White patents would speak of "the Paris Exposition 'Show,' " and picture Bethlehem's demonstration as an exercise in stagecraft. Charles Hennig, a chemist who at Vincennes collected chips to show to a metallurgical engineer in Dresden, testified that the Bethlehem exhibit stood in a corner "about 60 feet from the light"—the better, implied Bethlehem's court foes, to show off the tool's red glow. "Appreciating the value of such a display," they argued, "and with due regard for the niceties of theatrical effect, the lathe was placed in a dark corner." Later, one of Taylor's French critics, Émile Pouget, would also see theater at work in the Paris demonstrations. "This truly American staging (*mise en scène*)," with its glowing tools and steaming blue chips, made for quite a "spectacle."

But whether a theatrical success or purely a technical one, Paris made the name of Frederick Winslow Taylor well known; poor Maunsel White was largely overlooked, one report giving his name as "Maunsel Hoyt." Scholars might look back at the exposition and see intimations of decline, its tinsel obscuring the grim century to come. But only in hindsight could one know of the Great War, the Depression, the death camps, and the Bomb. Engineers and industrialists fresh from Bethlehem's exhibit would have dismissed such dark thoughts with a wave. They had seen the future at Vincennes—and it was very, very fast.

2

THE RIDDLE OF THE SPHINX

~

AROUND MID-OCTOBER, Fred and Lou sailed back aboard the *Kaiser Wilhelm der Grosse* from a two-month trip that, besides Paris, had included a visit to England, Scotland, and Wales that Lou's relatives had mapped out for them. In Wales, they toured a coal mine and, one moonlit evening, visited an old castle, where a massed chorus of hundreds of voices performed. In picturesque Clovelly, along the north coast of Devon, in England, Lou rode donkey-back down steep, narrow lanes flanked by tiny gardens. In Dunster, Taylor played skittles, a local game like bowling.

In France, they visited Le Havre, saw Fred's French relatives, the descendants of grandfather Isaac Winslow's brother. During their three weeks in Paris, Fred went to the fair, saw his tools demonstrated, talked to potential buyers. He also found time for golf, in one Paris tournament earning a silver medal.

It was a delightful trip, perhaps tinged with adventure and romance. At one point, in Edinburgh, they went their separate ways for the day, the plan being to meet at the station when Fred's train pulled in. But the train was late, and would stop but momentarily, leaving no time to reach the agreed spot. "Knowing Fred's belief in the traits of Casablanca," Lou remembered, referring to a legendary French naval officer's son who stood by his post during a battle and went down with his father's ship, "I dreaded to break the agreement and to fail to meet him." Besides, she had spent all her money on antiques. Rushing to the platform as the Paris-bound through-train approached, she was thrilled to see "Fred leaning out of the coach to grab me."

Back in Bethlehem, it was one of the loveliest autumns he could remember, Taylor wrote a cousin. But frictions of shop floor and executive suite alike, which went back almost to the moment he'd arrived in town two years before, persisted.

347

As early as February 27, 1899, just before the pig iron experiments with Noll, Taylor had written company president Linderman with a

Report on the Slow Progress Which Is Being Made on
Improvements Which Have Been Authorized Upon
Recommendation of the Writer

He was angry. He had made recommendations and they had been ignored.

Machines due to be speeded up had not been. The new office adjoining Machine Shop No. 2, where centralized control of the works was to reside, remained incomplete. No one had been made available to help him introduce piece rate; he'd had to rely instead on men he'd brought with him to Bethlehem. Moreover, "the men at the head of your Engineering Department do not appreciate the importance of the work . . ."

Even the high-speed steel success left Taylor feeling unappreciated. By May 1899, the new tools used in Machine Shop No. 2 had dramatically reduced the times needed for rough turning. In the wake of Paris, and of well-publicized demonstrations staged at Bethlehem for the engineering press, sales of shop rights rolled in, each for three to five thousand dollars. By the spring of 1901, foreign rights had been sold in England, Germany, Austria, Hungary, and Scandinavia. High-speed steel promised so much lower costs that even small firms could afford to buy the rights. One company had only five machine tools in its shop; and yet, Taylor wrote, "after three months of use they have cut their piece work rates in two, and . . . expect to pay for the entire shop rights inside of three months more."

But that high-speed steel made both Taylor and the company money seemed to warm their relationship not at all. On February 27, Linderman sent Taylor a brisk letter complaining that his attention to the sale of American rights, which Linderman had previously asked him to oversee, "interferes considerably with the work which you were engaged to do for this company." He was, accordingly, relieving him of that job and asking that he "confine your entire time and attention to the work which was expected of you when you came to this Company."

In his reply, Taylor noted the profits coming Bethlehem's way and observed that the new tool steel's role in advertising the company had given it "a prestige it never before had." Moreover, Machine Shop No. 2 had become "the Mecca of those interested in machine shop practice," hundreds of engineers, shop owners, and managers from around the world coming to see the new tools and Taylor's system of shop management.

All this was preamble. "It is a curious psychological fact, and one for which the writer can find no explanation," he went on, "that of all the parties who have visited the works and are acquainted with what has been done here, the only ones who have failed to congratulate the writer upon the results accomplished are with one or two exceptions the leading officers of the company." Taylor was bitter and making no bones about it.

Around the same time, Taylor wrote his old friend Frank Steele in Chicago. The past year had gone well financially, he reported; but health problems had intervened, including Lou's appendectomy, and the stress he felt at Bethlehem had "overworked my nerves so that my stomach has given me a great deal of trouble." The company held it against him, he felt, that he had "succeeded in making money out of the sale of the tool steel patents. It seems to break their heart to think that anyone else gets anything out of it."

But Linderman and the other Bethlehem directors did have cause to cavil. Taylor had not been tending to business, at least not the business for which he had been hired: introducing piece rate. "I must confess," Taylor would testify in 1908, "that my personal interest in the art [of metal-cutting] was, at times, quite as great as in the other more important practical aspect of the work." So it could seem—as it must have seemed to Linderman—that the inventor, entrepreneur, and showman in Taylor had become too engrossed in high-speed steel for his own good and for that of the company; if he was introducing piecework, it was only with glacial slowness.

"The high degree of perfection demanded by Mr. Taylor" is how Henry Gantt later accounted for the delay. One must not too precipitously install piecework, Taylor held; much else had to be done first— and was being done. An office that brought "all of the planning and purely brain work of the establishment close together" had gone up near Machine Shop No. 2; the company's general offices, formerly a mile and a half away, were moved adjacent to it. Taylor's cost accounting system, grown all the more elaborate, was in use. "Standard

Orders" proliferated; No. 27 listed rules for filling out time cards, even down to the penmanship required: "Excepting only a man's signature, plain letters with straight lines must in all other cases be written upon the time notes. The letters *should* be like the following," wherein a whole block alphabet was recorded. "They must *not* be like the following," which showed script with the prohibited flourishes. Conferring with oculists, Taylor had established brown and green as standard colors for all lined forms.

In a memo to Linderman dated May 29, 1899, Taylor had outlined his ideas for breaking down the foreman's job—traditionally many-sided, hectic, nerve-racking, exciting, and impossible—into smaller, more specialized jobs, each assigned to separate men. In Taylor's scheme, one foreman would oversee the large lathes:

> Another man will see that the work is done in the proper order of precedence; another that proper tools are provided for the work; another that the machines are pulling the heaviest possible cut and running at the highest speed practicable.

A year later, the system was substantially in effect. On May 14, 1900, Standing Order No. 55 specified that the speed boss had charge of everything related to:

> The cutting speed of machine tools.
> The feeds to be used.
> The depth of cuts.
> The kind and shape of tool to be used.
> The method of setting, clamping and securing tools.

Similar memos went out for the other pieces of the foreman's old job, now parceled out among eight distinct classes of men.

What Taylor called "functional foremanship" made a kind of sense at a time when good foremen of the old school were hard to find. A Worcester, Massachusetts, engineer, M. P. Higgins, told his ASME colleagues that "200 young men suitable for foremen for foundries could be placed at once. . . . Nothing is more difficult than to find men capable of filling such positions." Taylor's solution? If you can't find good foremen, stop looking. Change the job. Simplify it, limit it, thereby leaving it within the grasp of many.

Looked at another way, Taylor was applying the division of labor to white- as well as blue-collar work. Bethlehem laborers were being trained up to become "handymen" and so replace veteran machinists; with machine settings furnished by the slide rule man in the planning office, these semiskilled, lower-paid operatives could take the roughing cuts, leaving skilled men for the fine work to follow. "The potential of functional foremanship," Taylor would write, "will not have been realized until almost all of the machines in the shop are run by men who are of smaller caliber and attainments, and who are therefore cheaper than those required under the old system." "Deskilling," labor economists would dub it later. But functional foremanship meant, as University of Akron historian Daniel Nelson astutely observes, that it was "the supervisors and foremen—the managers rather than the workers—who now worked under scientific management." Taylor was helping to create the modern white-collar workforce.

By late in Taylor's tenure at Bethlehem, instruction cards used in Machine Shop No. 2 spelled out the order in which each operation should be done and how long it should take. According to H. L. Gantt, they prescribed better methods "than the ordinary workman or foreman could devise on the spur of the moment." Speeds and feeds could be read right off the Barth slide rules, cutting times calculated: To face the end of a particular piston rod, the machinist should use tool of shape "PVM," and set the machine's speed to "2BF," which specified a particular combination of pulleys; the operation should take four minutes.

But these figures were not drawn from the kind of "elementary time studies" Taylor had pioneered at Midvale. The edifice of knowledge that he deemed essential for permanent, scientific piece rates remained incomplete. More to the point, the much sought dollars-and-cents productivity gains his client expected of him had not yet materialized. One fact, obvious to Linderman no less than anyone, remained: though slide rules and instruction cards had been used since 1899, Gantt wrote, "the monthly output of the shop during the year from March 1, 1900 to March 1, 1901 had been but little more than the monthly average for the five years preceding"—this, three years after Taylor's arrival in Bethlehem.

The men had no trouble cutting metal in the times set by the slide rule pushers in the planning office. The problem came when the tool wasn't cutting, which was entirely too often. "One would frequently find many of the machines idle," wrote Gantt, "and yet every workman could give a more or less plausible excuse why his machine was not running." Tools were ground for them, the work prepared for them, but still the machines lay idle.

Around Machine Shop No. 2, as elsewhere at Bethlehem, ill feeling was rife. At one point after the introduction of high-speed steel, six skilled machinists were fired. A *Bethlehem Globe* reporter looking into the incident cited union organizing and poor workmanship as possible reasons. "As to defective work," he noted,

> many of [the men] claim that good and accurate work is hardly possible under the system of rules governing them, which makes it incumbent on their part to work steel revolving at a tremendous speed, which is so great that the tools in use are unable to stand the strain. The system, they say, is one inaugurated by an individual, whom they call 'Speedy' Taylor, which has converted the day rule into one of piece work.

Or was trying to. For by early 1901, absorbed with high-speed steel, he had not yet placed the whole works on piece rate. Before Taylor left for Paris the previous summer, Barth had for a time threatened to quit if certain piece rates, even if too roughly reckoned to suit his boss, were not approved. For Taylor, the differential rate demanded that they really know what a man could do in a day, and for most jobs around Machine Shop No. 2, they didn't know.

But the adaptable Henry Gantt felt, as he wrote later, "that we should not wait for perfection" but should offer the workmen something now. On March 11, he suggested they pay a bonus of fifty cents per day—think of it as about ten dollars—to any worker who did all he was given to do. E. P. Earle, machine shop superintendent, suggested they also pay the gang boss and speed boss for each of their men who earned a bonus—doubling, as it were, the pressure to produce. Taylor, under pressure himself, acceded.

It was astonishing what the promise of extra pay—and extra pay alone—could do. Beginning on March 18 with Lathe No. 76, the big machines in Machine Shop No. 2 went under the plan a few at a time. Less than two months later, on May 13, assistant superintendent R. J. Snyder wrote that errors and machine breakdowns had been drastically reduced. "To earn his bonus a man must utilize his brains and faculties to the fullest." He must focus his attention. "Every move must be made to count. He thus has no time for dreaming." Production shot up. In January the shop had shipped 624,000 pounds of rough-machined work; in April, a month after the start of Gantt's plan, the figure was 1.6 million pounds, a third higher than the previous record—all without formal time study or the differential rate.

Was Taylor abashed? Gantt's simple bonus system had jump-started the shop, bypassing his own too-elaborate methods. Yet later, he would laud the work of his lieutenant, minimizing the differences between the differential rate and Gantt's "task-plus-bonus." After all, in both cases management set a specific quantitative task, not the workman himself. Management set the terms of the reward. Management specified how the work was to be done.

Publicly, Taylor and Gantt both pictured task-plus-bonus as strictly transitional, a way station toward the permanent rates that would reduce a job's time to its Platonic ideal. But this ideal, wrote Gantt in an ASME paper on his system, demanded the discipline and fine-grained analysis of formal time study, an often "long and tedious operation." Task-plus-bonus served in the meantime; as Taylor wrote, it "is especially useful during the difficult and delicate period of transition" between the old system and the new.

In fact, it was much better than that: it worked like a charm. And all the high-sounding, mutually respectful talk just papered over the truth—that Gantt's presumably ad hoc system was gentler, provoked less worker outcry, and could make the differential rate unnecessary even after time study had fixed a day's task with greater precision.

But Gantt's emergency measures came too late. What he, Taylor, and their confederates had done at Bethlehem cost plenty. Opinion had hardened against them. "Went through No. 2 and No. 3 shops with [fellow Bethlehem executives] Archie Johnston & Owen Liebert," Robert Sayre wrote in his diary on March 12. "Do not see where the $1,100,000 went to in the last two years. Think the bringing of Taylor here and placing all the manufacturing under Davenport was and is a failure." Taylor was in trouble.

All along, there had been Taylor men and anti-Taylor men, the two camps continually at war. Taylor forever defended his record, insisting on a free rein, while the entrenched leadership of Sayres, Leiberts, and

Lindermans looked critically over his shoulder, like time-study men with stopwatches. Over the years, the mutual bitterness only deepened. One time Taylor showed up for an appointment with Linderman half an hour late, swinging a golf club, prattling on about his game, heedless of the president's business. Another time, company directors tried to taunt him into resigning. Sorry, he as much as told them. They could fire him, but he wouldn't quit.

Taylor was a volcano that could erupt at any time, for any reason. Once, a visitor heard him mercilessly lambaste a subordinate. "Now look here," Taylor ranted, "I don't want to hear anything more from you. You haven't got any brains, you haven't got any ability—you don't know anything. You owe your position to your family pull, and you know it. Go on and work your pull if you want to, but keep out of my way."

Much later, when the Taylor system was being considered for use in the navy, Archibald Johnston would concede that "many of the schemes proposed by Fred Taylor had a great deal of merit, [but he] personally did not seem to have the ability to carry them out in a reasonable time. This was due principally to the antagonistic methods used by him in handling men." He fought with everyone. In May 1899, he ordered a bookkeeper to make up a special accounts-payable voucher. The bookkeeper thought it too much bother, refused, and secured Linderman's backing. Taylor stopped work on the accounting system for ten weeks.

He had a genius for making enemies. Even Copley, always in Taylor's corner, had to admit he was

> too ready to believe that people were opposed to him, and too
> much inclined to act in the spirit of "he who is not with me is
> against me," and at Bethlehem these defects of his immense
> sincerity and earnestness were exhibited at their worst.
>
> . . .
>
> As time went on, he exhibited a fighting spirit of an intensity
> almost pathological. Men in his own little group were shocked by
> some of his outbursts. "If I know that a man is going to stab me,"
> he said, "I'll stab him first, and if he hits me, I'll hit him twice."

On March 15, just before launching Gantt's bonus system and with Linderman and the board turning up the heat, Taylor wrote his patron,

Joseph Wharton, asking if they could meet. Twice that month they did meet, Taylor seeking Wharton's advice on how to deal with Linderman. His authority, he wrote, must "not be subject to continual appeals." Since responsibility for results lay with him, he could not allow himself to be merely one of several clamoring management voices. He'd not be henpecked by Linderman, the board, or anyone else.

"I do not want any authority in any matters except those immediately affecting my system of management and accounting," he wound up writing Linderman on April 14, "but I respectfully request that the various officers of the Company be instructed to carry out all orders" he gave them.

Two days later, Linderman replied with a letter that Taylor found waiting for him on his return from a week's vacation on the Jersey shore: "I beg to advise you that your services will not be required by this Company after May 1st, 1901."

~

A month later, Andrew Carnegie's protege Charles Schwab, first president of the United States Steel Corporation, bought Bethlehem Steel and largely threw out Taylor's brand of shop management. Out went sixty specialized foremen, out went Barth, Gantt, and the other Taylor men. When Gantt sent Johnston an advance copy of a paper about task-and-bonus that he planned to deliver at an upcoming ASME meeting, Johnston's reply was frosty. "Since you have severed your connection with the company," he wrote, "a great part of the system as described by you has been done away with." Foremen no longer got bonuses for each man who completed his day's task. Detailed instruction cards were gone. The great improvements Gantt claimed, Johnston said, were "misleading"; he and Taylor had actually achieved little.

In fact, Taylor's influence lingered at Bethlehem. When, during a bitter three-month machinists' strike in 1910, people wanted to know whether the Taylor system, by then better known, was to blame, Taylor distanced himself from the company, stressing that its policies were none of his doing. Yet at other times, he would claim that while Schwab opposed his system, an underground community of disciples, including a quietly sympathetic Archibald Johnston, maintained it surreptitiously.

"The slide rules were operated in a room back of the kitchen, which

Schwab never visited," Taylor wrote in reply to a query about why, if scientific management was so good, Bethlehem had abandoned it. "All of the slide rules, time study men, planners, etc., were carried on the payrolls as mechanics." Indeed, in talks with the navy, Johnston allowed that Taylor's innovations, "thoroughly boiled down and greatly modified, had resulted in considerable good."

∿

Despite Johnston's discouragement, Henry Gantt delivered his paper—with all due bowing and scraping to his mentor, Mr. Fred W. Taylor, whom he acknowledged no fewer than four times—at the ASME's December 1901 meeting in New York, sparking a lively debate in the engineering press over the next few months.

Among those hearing Gantt was Tecumseh Swift, a contributor to *American Machinist* in the tradition of Chordal. Wry and biting by turn, Swift pictured Gantt as a "hypnotist" who had worked "into the minds of his subjects" an insidious assumption: "No workman knows anything or, in this scheme, is to be expected or even permitted to know anything. Every operation is to be directed by a boss." One to pick the tool, another to set the speed, another to line up work for each machine. He was describing, of course, "functional foremanship," for which his contempt was palpable.

But this was just the beginning. Two weeks later, W. A. Warman sounded themes that would dog Taylorism even to the present day. In Taylor's system "a well-designed automaton could be operated with perforated cards [an early form of automatic control and a precursor of computers] to perform most of the functions." Taylor and Gantt failed to pay due heed to the brains of the machinist, who sometimes "has hidden away, under his dirty cap and greasy jumper, ideas and ideals of his own." Taylor's thinking was "antagonistic to our democracy."

"Mr. Taylor and His Methods," was the headline an editor gave a thoughtful letter in response to Tecumseh Swift's epistle, which had never mentioned Taylor or Gantt by name. Taylor's "radical suggestions," he lamented, had never "been discussed in the thorough way they deserve." Some engineers ridiculed his ideas, dismissing them as impracticable or absurd. Yet others "have been carried away by Mr. Taylor's principles and reports and look upon him as the herald of a new era." As for himself, he had witnessed improvements that Taylor's system had wrought. But what about overhead costs? And besides, giving another foretaste of future criticism, "Can the human, or at least American, element of demanding some opportunity for individual thought and freedom of action on the part of the workingman be ignored?" He was genuinely perplexed. "I have set the riddle," he wound up. "Can you give me the answer?" And he signed himself Sphinx.

On March 20 came a harsh and emphatic answer, from a Bethlehem machinist who signed himself Trigger:

> First, I want to tell Sphinx that his admiration of Mr. Taylor's abilities and virtues is not exceeded by mine. He is no doubt honest and sincere, energetic and resourceful, over-enthusiastic and wrong-headed in the right direction; for I believe that his ultimate purpose is for the good of mankind.

He could not speak of stopwatches, slide rules, and rotameters, Taylor's instrument for measuring a tool's cutting speed. But, he wondered,

> if the system promised any glimmering hope of success, why were its author, his assistants and a host of satellites dismissed from there about six months ago? Why was the management, from general superintendent down, superseded by hard-headed practical men—men who have worn overalls, who graduated from the "college of hard knocks," who obtained their education through their fingers, with the aid of some gray matter and a lot of midnight oil? Why were the speed bosses and rate-setters cheerfully chased back to productive work and scheming? Why were the rotameters and stop-watches relegated to dusty shelves? Why were the slide-rule compilers banished to other fields of usefulness? Why has the tonnage output for a given time exceeded that of any similar time during the Taylor swing of the pendulum? Why is the quality of the work better now? And why do good men who left under the former system show a willingness to return? Why does the present management show a disposition to hire folks who "can do things and then let them alone to do them"?
> It is true that the system still obtains in part, but it is gasping— evidently the dying swing of previously acquired momentum.

A few days later, an editor at *Iron Trade Review* called Taylor's attention to Trigger's letter. Trigger's insinuations, Taylor snapped back in a letter, were "without exception false. They are absolute and distinct misrepresentations. For this you merely have my word as against that of 'Trigger' "—a gentleman against that of a mere workman, he as much as said.

Particularly riling him, of course, was Trigger's intimation that "practical men" were now in charge at Bethlehem, replacing Taylor and his dreamy minions. "I served my apprenticeship, and a long one, both as a pattern maker and as a machinist. . . . I worked for many years with my hands, and the same is true of more than half of the sixteen assistants who have left Bethlehem." Here was the key to Taylor's identity: the workingman's past of which he was so proud and which he was always so quick to invoke.

Like the artist who transforms life into art, Taylor had a way of extracting from his own experience a central core of meaning and transforming it into message, if not exactly art. Scientific management, in anything like the form in which he had introduced it, did not last at Bethlehem Steel. His scientific time studies weren't very scientific. He had left a legacy not of harmony but turmoil. And he had been ignominiously fired. Yet these elements of the story would, in his telling and retelling, recede into a dark corner of the stage. Meanwhile, bathed in floodlight would be another version, close enough to the events to be "true," yet sufficiently rearranged and reconstituted to be seen with equal justice as the product of Taylor's art. He'd tell of the magical new steel, and the shoveling experiments that yielded the twenty-one-pound ideal, and the triumphant victory over himself of Noll, the redoubtable pig iron handler. All this would become the stuff of story, myth, and drama.

As for Fred Taylor himself, he was stepping off the shop floor, with its facts of steel and fire, leaving behind the world he had entered a quarter century before at the pump works. In November 1901, a little before Trigger's letter to *American Machinist*, he retired to Germantown, to begin a new phase of his life, one decisively influenced by events in Savannah, Georgia, earlier that year.

3

EXPLOSION IN SAVANNAH

~

FROM DOWN THE HALL, the sounds of his mother and father fighting had awoken the red-haired eleven-year-old once again. His New England–born parents, Dr. and Mrs. William Aiken, had moved here, to Savannah, in hopes that the softer South might better nurture the doctor's fragile mental condition. They lived on Oglethorpe Avenue, in a big, three-story brick house, with their four children and their black nannies. They were a handsome young couple, blessed with fine children, respected figures in the life of the old colonial capital.

But Dr. Aiken was madly jealous. His wife, Anna, had been unfaithful, was that not true? No, she protested, it wasn't.

And she was trying to put him away in an insane asylum, wasn't she? No, she pleaded.

The day before, the familiar litany of offenses had started up again, he insinuating, she denying. But a little before seven on the morning of February 27, 1901, came the terrible spluttered Yes.

A gunshot exploded through the house. A silence. Then another explosion.

The boy, as he described it later,

> got out of bed and went through the children's bedroom, where
> my sister and two brothers were in their cribs, and closed the
> folding doors between the nursery and my father's room, and
> stepped over my father's body. . . . He'd sprung all the way across
> the room from the bed, and was lying on his face with his pistol
> still in his hand, and I went to see if my mother was still alive—and
> of course she wasn't. Her mouth was wide open in the act of
> screaming.

He closed the doors, told his young siblings to stay in bed, assured them their nurses would be up for them shortly, and descended to the basement. He woke the nurses. Then, barefoot, he left the house for the police station across the street.

On the way, he stopped a patrolman and told him what had happened. After notifying others at the station, they entered through the basement office door and climbed the staircase. The officer pushed open a door to the room, shuttered against the feeble early light, and lit a match. There, in its flicker, he could see Mrs. Aiken, a bloody wound in her right temple; pillows, blankets, and walls splattered with blood; beside the bed, Dr. Aiken, an almost identical wound to his head, clutching the pistol.

Now the events in the house on Oglethorpe Avenue spiraled out beyond the dark bedroom. Other police arrived, along with a neighbor and the city coroner. The neighbor took the younger children to his house two doors away. Mrs. Aiken's brother in New England was notified; he would leave for Savannah at once, he wired back, as would Dr. Aiken's sister. An undertaker came to prepare the bodies for burial.

On the morning of March 1, the New Englanders arrived. The bodies remained in the house where they had died. "The tragedy of Wednesday morning," the *Savannah Evening Press* reported on the day of the funeral,

> was still the subject of almost universal comment yesterday, among people everywhere and in every walk of life. No happening of recent years has so shocked, grieved and unnerved the people of Savannah. There is sorrow for Dr. Aiken's untimely end and for the even sadder story of his wife's death, but the deepest sympathy is reserved for the four little children, who are left with this frightful heritage.

The oldest of the children, the almost preternaturally self-possessed boy who'd stepped over his father's body and gazed into his mother's silent scream, was Conrad Aiken, who would become among America's most distinguished writers and whose poetry and fiction would forever bear the imprint of that February morning. "I was eleven," he would say in old age, "and I think in a way . . . I've never gotten over it." Neither would his siblings, Elizabeth, eight, Kempton, seven, and Robert, six.

On March 5, a cousin of Mrs. Aiken, Julia Delano, reached Savannah from her home in New Bedford, Massachusetts, to preside over the care of the orphaned children. Miss Delano was the strong-willed daughter of a wealthy clipper ship master and first cousin of Sara Delano, Franklin Delano Roosevelt's mother. She brought word that a couple distantly related to the family was prepared to adopt the Aiken children.

Mrs. Aiken's brother was Alfred C. Potter, a Harvard University librarian.

And Alfred C. Potter's mother-in-law had a first cousin, Hannah, who had married Edward Spooner.

Their daughter, Louise, was the wife of Frederick Winslow Taylor.

～

Six months passed. His older brothers and sister elsewhere, six-year-old Robert Aiken had been staying with his great-aunt Jane, another cousin of Julia Delano. One day in October 1901, up the porch steps of Aunt Jane's big old house on County Street in New Bedford, the Quaker whaling town whose streets had borne the tread of Winslows a century before, came Frederick Taylor. He was there to get his new son, armed only with a box of lead soldiers.

Soon, it was the two of them together in the Pullman car heading back to Pennsylvania. "I was fascinated by these lead soldiers," Robert remembered later, "so I went along with him. I liked him right off the bat. It was love at first sight. I adopted him, rather than he adopting me."

In time, they reached South Bethlehem, where the Taylors still lived, six months after Fred's dismissal. Robert remembered going "up" to the house, perhaps recalling the long slope of Delaware Avenue up from the center of town near the covered bridge.

In his new home, he immediately made a friend, the Taylors' cat. A few weeks before, alerted by noise at the back of the house, Fred had found a cat dragging a young, long-necked weasel up the back steps. The Taylors took him in and, in homage to his backyard battle grit, named him Herr Paul Kruger, for the pugnacious Afrikaner leader whose ultimatum to the British had sparked the Boer War. The name didn't take; Put Mut, a corruption of Pussy Mussy, did. Over the years, hundreds of industrialists would see Taylor declaim on scientific management, Put Mut perched atop his left shoulder. For now, though, he was a boy's playmate.

Asked about it as an old man, Robert Potter Aiken Taylor couldn't say for sure how the Taylors came to adopt him and two of his siblings. "They had no children and I guess he could see things coming to the end," he hazarded. Taylor was forty-four at the time of the Savannah killings and well-off from years of fat consulting fees and smart investments, largely managed by his banker brother-in-law Clarence Clark. He had bought for as little as fifteen dollars each some fifteen hundred shares of Flat Top Coal Land, which owned coal fields in West Virginia; selling them for $165 per share, he'd realized a profit of perhaps $100,000. His holdings in Greene Consolidated, which had a big copper mine south of the Arizona border in Mexico, came to around $50,000. And now the high-speed steel money was rolling in, too. On July 18, 1901, Bethlehem issued him a voucher for another $22,625, proceeds from foreign sales for the first six months of the year. This at a time when the average worker, according to the 1900 census, earned thirteen dollars a week.

On November 16, soon after bringing Robert back to Bethlehem, Taylor wrote Ernest Wright that later in the week they were moving back to Germantown, to the old Kimball house on School Lane, which they planned to rent for a year. He mentioned the enlargement of his family in a strange, elliptical way, as if it had nothing to do with him: "Lou has two little children living with her this winter (cousins of hers) so that she is very much tied down by this." Maybe he didn't quite believe it was happening, but soon, Fred Taylor was indeed very much a father of three.

But not of four.

Conrad, now twelve, went his own way, staying with his uncle in Cambridge, Massachusetts. "I'm sure the Old Man went to see him and talk with him," said Robert later. "But I think he realized this arrangement probably wouldn't be a good thing." One Aiken biographer, Edward Butscher, blames Taylor for the breakup of the Aiken clan, citing his "cruel insistence that all four children adopt his name or he would refuse to accept responsibility." But it may have been for the best in any case: imperious Mr. Taylor and sensitive yet headstrong Conrad, on the eve of manhood, might have made for an explosive mix.

Before Christmas, 1901, Elizabeth—"a nervous, irritable child," is how Kempton thought of her—joined the family. The following spring, after school let out, it was Kempton's turn; Taylor went to get him at his Aunt Grace's house in Cambridge, just as he had Robert six months earlier in New Bedford. Over the years, Conrad saw his siblings probably fewer than a dozen times each, their relationship confined largely to the exchange of Christmas cards. Once, around 1904, when he did visit the Taylor home, Rob, about nine, and Kemp, about ten, were playing catch and invited him to join them. Conrad, then almost fifteen, threw one too hard. The ball tore through Rob's glove, struck him in the head, and knocked him unconscious. Taylor stormed from the house and, as Rob tells the story, "gave Conrad hell."

For all their horrific childhoods, all the children, including Conrad, had their mother's cherubic look, with round, sweet, bland faces that made them seem younger. They had grown up in a house that shook with a husband's rage. But that was not all they would remember. They were children of the South. They had grown up amid palmetto pines, across the street from a colonial graveyard. Robert remembered bathing with his mother when he was three, her thighs looming; remembered the two of them with scarlet fever, locked into upstairs bedrooms, the house quarantined, a big red sign on the front door; remembered troops in front of their house, bound for Cuba during the Spanish-American war, tents pitched and campfires burning.

Now it was a new century, new mother, new father, new lives. Kempton always remembered that lavish Christmas of 1902, his first with the Taylors, with the big tree and the toy stable. They lived at Red Gate, a brick house with gables and jutting angles set on six acres in Germantown, not far from Cedron, Taylor's boyhood home. They played with the children of coachmen and gardeners. They rode their bicycles to school. They played baseball on the big lawn. Sometimes their father, star pitcher for the Exeter nine, joined them for an impromptu catch, removing his coat, vest, collar, and cuffs. "At first he would simply toss the ball underhand," Robert recalled. "As we grew older, he put more steam on his pitched ball."

One afternoon, out for a walk with their father, the boys said they wanted a Lee-goo ball. Whatever were they talking about? asked Fred. There was no such thing.

Yes, there is.

No, there isn't.

So they showed him—a baseball, visible through the window of a neighbor's house, stamped League Ball.

Often they'd visit the Franklin Taylor house on Ross Street (which the city had renamed Magnolia Street), redolent with the old Quaker "thee" and "thou" their adoptive grandparents still used. Rob, for one, didn't relish the visits. His grandfather was "a very quiet, sweet man," but his grandmother "didn't like any of these three new kids. She'd sit there and look at us," perhaps a consequence of her stroke, which had turned her personality sour.

At age eight, Kempton was enrolled at Germantown Academy, where his father had gone. From early on, he showed intimations of the doctor he was to become. "He was putting splints on squabs that had fallen out of their nests when he was under 10," his brother remembered, "and was continually fixing up Put Mut, our maltese cat, after fights or accidents or illnesses."

Robert, meanwhile, in 1902 and 1903 went to Miss Knight's School. Since his bout with scarlet fever back in Savannah, he had fallen behind in school. But now, he bloomed. One day he went out to pick up the morning paper and "all of a sudden it meant something to me. I was elated." He could read.

Into his old age, he would have sharp memories of his father from this period, in particular of his sheer physical presence, all one hundred and sixty tight pounds of it. "He was 46 years old then but was husky— all over, legs, chest, arms, wrists, and hands. Not bulging muscles, but those like modern collegiate swimmers." Sometimes he'd take the boys sledding or ice-skating at a local lake. Robert, for one, never got the hang of it. Both boys were, in Kempton's phrase, "indifferent to out-door sport." But Fred kept pushing.

Whatever Taylor's failings, niggardliness in expressing love was not one of them. A photograph from this period shows Fred and the boys sitting on a step, he in the middle, in coat and collar, flanked by Rob and Kemp, his arms around each, pulling them to him with all the vehemence of his nature. Rob, who when he was still small sat on his father's lap at dinner, remembered in him tremendous warmth. One day, probably soon after moving to Red Gate, he noted the maid's morning ritual of bringing coffee or tea to his parents' room, and scurried in after her. "They were in bed and he was drinking it and so I just crawled in bed between them," encountering no protest from his father. "Of course," he added, a smile in the memory, "if you got away with it once, you did it again."

But while Fred embraced his new children, Lou held back. Robert detected "some resentfulness on her part that we took some of his attention and love," which he chalked up to "selfishness and jealousy." Certainly she was the frostier of the two. Frank Wallace, a grandson of Fred's brother Win, remembered her from a later period as "very self-contained and distant and, to a little boy, kind of scary. . . . She didn't cotton much to small children." She was tall, stately, and aloof. "Others in the family would hug you and give you a kiss when you'd meet. Aunt Lou would never do that. . . . She didn't know how to unwind." When Kemp first arrived at the Taylor house, sister Elizabeth warned him, almost before he got in the door, that their new mother was to be addressed as Ma-*ma*, not *Ma*-ma; each pronunciatory offense cost a nickel. As for Robert's early climbing-into-bed fun, she soon put a stop to it. "No!" he remembered her putting her foot down one day. "I'm not going to have a grubby boy next to me in the morning."

To Robert, "The Old Man was father and mother to us. I mean if we were in trouble we went to him." Once, when Robert was about nine, he got a bad case of poison ivy; Fred attended him, not Ma-*ma*. "If anybody was sick, she didn't want to see them. It was the Old Man who came in and sat on the edge of your bed and asked you how you were doing." When Rob had his adenoids taken out, he persisted in breathing through his mouth instead of through his nose. Each evening when he went in to say good night, "the Old Man—it must have been for five years every night—would . . . put a strip of adhesive tape across my lips and seal them shut."

"No one," Robert wrote a relative as an old man, "could have a better father than FWT. . . . He was a wonderful person. We were lucky to be adopted by them."

In the family as in the shop, Taylor was adamant and insistent. He was determined that his boys be vigorous and robust, even if he had to tease them into it. "For years, brother and I were 'runts,'" Kemp recalled. "No matter what occasion, or who present, we were laughingly hailed as 'runts,' and often torn from a chosen book and sent outside to play." The campaign worked. "From a book worm of pronounced stamp my disbelief in 'general' reading gradually became so strong that during my four years at college I can only recall three or four books read solely for pleasure."

Come winter, his father "never lost an opportunity to spill us in the snow," Kempton remembered. His taste for battle, however playfully expressed, surfaced even with Elizabeth. She had a way "of puckering up her lips in an impish way and squealing 'weedy-weed' at the top of her small lungs," which grated on him. So he'd tickle her, "a very painful process to judge from the vaulting fracas," Kempton recalled. One time, "she 'weedy-weedied' and streaked for the open door, thinking thusly to escape punishment. . . . [But] Papa's eyes widened with anticipative glee as he sped across the lawn" and caught her.

At the age of forty-five, Fred Taylor had stepped into something like his own parents' way of life. He was back in Germantown, enjoying his new family, near his father and invalid mother, with all the money anyone could want, and no apparent inclination to work. It could almost seem as if he had retired. He took to speaking at the men's club of the Unitarian church his mother had helped found three decades before and was advisor to the church's Nicetown Club for boys and girls. (Only rarely, however, did he attend services.) His love of golf burned ever more brightly. At Red Gate, he installed his own putting green. The ground was "thoroughly soaked until marshy," recalled Harold van du Zee, who later managed Taylor's property and was distantly related to both the Taylors and the Aikens. Then it was pounded flat with iron rammers and riddled with thousands of holes by a board studded with large nails. These holes were then filled with a germinating mixture.

But none of this could compare with what Taylor did at Boxly, to which the family moved in 1904.

~

While at Red Gate, the way Lou told it later in fragmentary notes intended to become an autobiography, "we were told of a deserted place at Chestnut Hill where there was an old boxwood garden." The property, which flanked a rail line that snaked through one of the poshest parts of the community, had once been part of the estate of a wealthy banker, Owen Sheridan. But its history went back much further, having once been used to cultivate silk by a Colonel Du Barry, a refugee from the French Revolution. Du Barry had planted elaborate gardens, including boxwood hedges along the walks, reminiscent of the royal gardens at Versailles. Roses erupted everywhere. "How beautiful! Just the spot we wanted," wrote Lou later. "Flora, our bay horse, was hitched to the red-wheeled dog-cart, and Fred and I and the children hunted the enchanted spot."

You reached Chestnut Hill, about ten miles outside of Philadelphia, by taking Germantown Avenue north and west from Germantown itself, past Mount Airy. Until 1854, when the original village was annexed to Philadelphia, it was still mostly rural, but in that year, the railroad reached out to it from the city, spurring development. A second rail line, driven up the community's west side in 1884, promoted further growth. In the years since, it had become among the city's most desirable suburbs, north Philadelphia's answer to the Main Line suburbs across the Schuykill. Here, except for modest colonial houses and shops on Germantown Avenue, the homes were grand Gothic affairs, or Victorian, or Italian villa, each bigger and finer than the next.

The old Sheridan place, Lou wrote, "exceeded our expectations." It was studded with old mulberry trees, commanded a lovely view of the Wissahickon valley and nearby hills, and included a ruined wall and two small stone houses in which silkworm cocoons had been boiled. Here they would build. At Red Gate, they fitted up a small room with two large drawing desks, "and there, perched on high stools, we drew our plans for our new home. Our working hours were long, and many were our arguments"—to the consternation of Lou's mother, who had lived with them off and on since the death of her husband—"trying to make science and artistic features work."

But in the end, they had crude plans, on scraps of wallpaper and backs of envelopes, that they could hand over to their architect, Mantle Fielding, a boyhood friend of Fred. Their design rested on the house's precise placement on the lot; they wanted it to lie between the vast tentacles of boxwood vegetation, which had so entranced them from the start, and the steep gorge down to Wissahickon Creek that began just beyond it. There—precisely there—it must go.

Problem: Fielding's clients wanted the house to face the old garden straight on. And from the back, they wanted to be able to look down over the Wissahickon. But if the house sat with its broad frontage facing the garden, the view out back was not of the Wissahickon at all, but of a protuberant chunk of earth, an inconvenient hillock that sat at exactly the wrong spot, right in your face, blocking the view.

Move it, said Taylor.

Move thirteen thousand cubic yards of dirt, a volume of earth triple that of the house they planned to build?

When no contractor bid less than fifty-five cents a yard for the job,

Taylor decided to superintend the work himself. He hired four foremen and a couple of dozen, mostly Italian laborers and placed them on Gantt's task-plus-bonus scheme: if the laborers moved the requisite amount of dirt, they'd each get an extra thirty cents a day. Good, strong horses were a must. Taylor weeded out the "old skates" first foisted upon him and wound up with, in his words, "the finest lot of working horseflesh ever assembled in these parts."

They moved the hill, and Fred and Lou got their view.

For fifteen cents a yard.

∼

While they worked on plans for the house, their family physician counseled a vacation, and soon, obligingly, Fred and Lou were on a train for California. In four days, they were visiting Fred's Aunt Emma in Pasadena. The trip, Lou wrote, "gave us renewed life." They played golf, thoroughly enjoying the climate. At one point, he spent several days touring underground tunnels of the copper mine whose stock he held in Cananea, about forty miles south of the Arizona border, where one of his Bethlehem assistants served as his personal spy.

On January 12, 1903, from South Orange Grove Avenue in Pasadena, Taylor wrote Ernest Wright, who had inquired about becoming a management consultant. He would be delighted to help, Taylor wrote back. But, he warned, the work was "most difficult and particularly trying for the nerves, and calls for a very extraordinary amount of endurance and strength." In closing, he added that he was writing a paper "on the subject of Shop Management," and would forward him a copy of it when it was out.

When he wrote Wright again three months later, he was "still buried in the work of writing the paper, but can see the end of it now."

Finally, though, it was finished, ready for him to present on the afternoon of Wednesday, June 23, 1903, at the forty-seventh meeting of the American Society of Mechanical Engineers, in the ballroom of the United States Hotel in Saratoga, New York.

THE NEW ORDER

~

SINCE BEFORE THE CIVIL WAR, when aristocratic Southerners came north for the summer in great coaches, with families, slaves, and thoroughbred racehorses in tow, Saratoga, just north of Albany, New York, had been a favorite summer destination of the rich. Now, at the turn of the century, it rivaled Newport. The wealthy came for the waters, the spa that had first given the town its name. Like millionaire sportsman William Collins Whitney, the former navy secretary and social lion who kept elaborate stables here and whose horse had won the Kentucky Derby at Epsom Downs two years before, they came for the racing. And they came to see and be seen, to promenade up Broadway, and sit at their ease on the broad porches of the hotels lining it, crowded with parasoled ladies and men with diamond-studded watches.

Perhaps the grandest of Saratoga's grand hotels was the United States, built in 1874 over the ashes of its predecessor of that name. Its deep porch, graced by high, arched columns, ran for more than two hundred feet along Broadway. From both ends of the Broadway frontage, it reached back an eighth of a mile, forming a U-shaped, three acre private park, complete with bandstand and fountain, shaded by elm trees. Marble washstands, black walnut furniture, and lace curtains filled the hotel's nine hundred high-ceilinged rooms. Some were in attached private "cottages," arrayed along the north side of the enclosed park, each a little mansion. Here, meals could be delivered, and carriages could discharge their passengers, all without passing through the main entrance—a convenience for rich men seeking private pleasures away from wives and children vacationing in Europe. Everyone knew about the cottages, and no one cared enough to upset a millionaire's composure or invite a millionaire's wrath.

It was here, in this setting of luxury and release, that three hundred and fifty mechanical engineers gathered in late June 1903. In the hotel's marble lobby, in its corridors, offices, and parlors, on its wide porches thick with rocking chairs, they traded talk of tests and turbines, gauges and gears. They attended receptions and dances in the ballroom, which could seat a thousand at a time, and smokers on the adjoining balcony. They laughed uproariously at a minstrel show performed by the Schenectady Jest and Song club, and they heard Fred Taylor deliver a paper whose influence would reach all across the century and all around the world.

"There is scarcely a feature of modern management," it would be said almost forty years later, "that is not touched upon in this epoch-making document." A half century after that, a scholar in a field far distant from engineering or management, Martha Banta, an English professor and cultural critic, would pronounce it "one of the key documents shaping . . . modern industrialization."

The coming of the engineers was a big enough event that the *Daily Saratogian* carried word of their arrival on its front page:

MECHANICAL ENGINEERS
IN ANNUAL CONFERENCE
First Session Held in Ball Room of
United States Hotel

Tuesday evening and Wednesday morning sessions were routine affairs, devoted to the likes of elevator testing and turbine flow. But then, on Wednesday afternoon, came three much anticipated papers on shop management. Two were by Taylor disciples—Charles Day, a Philadelphia engineer, and Henry Gantt, both of whom publicly acknowledged their debt to him. Taylor's own was called simply "Shop Management."

"It is not wide of the mark to assert," management scholar Harlow S. Person would write, "that Taylor never made more than one statement of his philosophy of management," all his papers being "essentially one and the same, differing only in emphasis." Of them all, however, the Saratoga paper was the most comprehensive and, at a hundred and twenty pages in the ASME *Transactions*, the longest.

Compared to later efforts, it was less evangelical. The differential rate that had siphoned off attention in Detroit became subservient to the goal that Taylor now advanced above any other, "that *scientific time study* will receive the attention which it merits." The paper included a sketch of a Sanford Thompson decimal-dial stopwatch. It took you through a sample time study and laid out equations into which time-study data could be plugged. Midvale, the sins of soldiering, payment schemes, instruction cards, and all the rest from 1895 were still here, but there was much new material from Simonds and especially Bethlehem—like ball bearing inspection, pig iron handling, slide rules, and functional foremanship. Compared to the Detroit paper, this was a paper you could sink your teeth into. It bore the most solid information. And, coming just three years after the Paris demonstrations of high-speed steel, it exerted the greatest impact on engineers and managers—first at Saratoga, where attendance was almost triple that of Detroit, then through its publication in the society's *Transactions*, and later in book form.

One night more than a decade later, early in World War I, a young British lieutenant named Lyndall Urwick, stationed in Rouen, got some advice from another officer: "If you survive this war, which I admit . . . seems improbable . . . , you ought to read a book called *Shop Management*. It's by an American engineer named F. W. Taylor; he can't write for nuts. But he's got something." Urwick did read it—and devoted his life to the new science of management.

Yet if Taylor couldn't "write for nuts," what accounted for his book's power? Extracted from a tangle of material originally three times larger, it was repetitive and wretchedly organized, its transitions from one idea to the next inelegant or nonexistent. Parts of it were pulled intact without apology from the Detroit paper or owed to letters Sanford Thompson had written him. Time study was treated in no fewer than four places. No reader of "Shop Management" could feel he was in the hands of a literary craftsman.

Still, he'd come away hypnotized. Taylor's paper droned on to a slow, steady background beat—inescapable, implacable, inevitable: the control of work must be taken from the men who did it and placed in the hands of a new breed of planners and thinkers. These men would think everything through beforehand. The workmen—elements of production to be studied, manipulated, and controlled—were to do as they were told. Everyone thereby prospered: workers got better pay, the company earned higher profits, the public paid lower prices. This great good flowed almost inevitably from a single, presumably

unobjectionable act: the irreversible and complete handover of all
planning, control, and decision making from the workmen to the new
class of scientific managers.

It was "Shop Management" 's rhetorical drumbeat that was so
mesmerizing, weaving its spell through relentless repetition, like the
advance and retreat of the waves. Individually, each point might be
debated and discussed, rebutted or defended. Yet together, as expressions of a single compelling logic, they left one fairly breathless with the
terror and the thrill of a new day dawning:

> After the men acquiesce in the new order of things and are willing
> to do their part toward cheapening production, it will take time for
> them to change from their old easy-going ways to a higher rate of
> speed, and to learn to stay steadily at their work, think ahead, and
> make every minute count. A certain percentage of them, with the
> best of intentions, will fail in this and find that they have no place
> in the new organization, while still others, and among them some
> of the best workers who are, however, either stupid or stubborn,
> can never be made to see that the new system is as good as the old;
> and these, too, must drop out.
>
> . . .
>
> In reaching the final high rate of speed which shall be steadily
> maintained, the broad fact should be realized that the men must
> pass through several distinct phases, rising from one place of
> efficiency to another until the final level is reached. First they must
> be taught to work under an improved system of day work. Each
> man must learn how to give up his own particular way of doing
> things, adapt his methods to the many new standards, and grow
> accustomed to receiving and obeying directions covering details,
> large and small, which in the past have been left to his individual
> judgment.
>
> . . .
>
> It may be accepted as an unquestioned fact that no gang boss is
> fit to direct his men until after he has learned to promptly obey
> instructions received from any proper source, whether he likes his
> instructions and the instructor or not, and even though he may be
> convinced that he knows a much better way of doing the work.
>
> . . .

All employees should bear in mind that each shop exists, first, last, and all the time, for the purpose of paying dividends to its owners. They should have patience, and never lose sight of this fact.

. . .

Certain men are both thick-skinned and coarse-grained, and these individuals are apt to mistake a mild manner and a kindly way of saying things for timidity or weakness. With such men the severity both of words and manner should be gradually increased until either the desired result has been attained or the possibilities of the English language have been exhausted.

If it is unfair to extract a succession of such quotes from their original context and pile them together, it was just this piling-up, this sense that an elemental force of nature had been unleashed, that left the deepest mark. As a correspondent for *American Machinist* correctly observed, "Mr. Taylor writes with an air of absolute conviction and as one who is dealing with absolute truth."

There was a Machiavellian tinge to what he said, too:

The first changes, therefore, should be such as to allay the suspicions of the men and convince them by actual contact that the reforms are after all rather harmless and are only such as will ultimately be of benefit to all concerned. Such improvements, then, as directly affect the workmen least should be started first.

In selecting workers, one must first ask which class of work, complex or routine, is to be their lot. For the first class, "men should be selected who are too good for the job"—those able, in other words, to adjust to the new, and cope with problems as they come up. But for routine work,

in which the same operations are likely to be done over and over again, with no great variety . . . a man should be selected whose abilities are barely equal to the task. Time and training will fit him for his work, and since he will be better paid than in the past, and will realize that he has been given the chance to make his abilities yield him the largest return—all of the elements for promoting contentment will be present; and those men who are blessed with cheerful dispositions will become satisfied and remain so.

Did some of "Shop Management" 's appeal rest in the heady sense of power and control it was apt to arouse? Its typical reader, we may guess, saw himself as the puller of strings, not as the marionette dangling from them. You could read it—as Lieutenant Urwick doubtless did, as any reader would—and come away feeling like a god, a shaper and molder of human material. Yet through its invocations of higher pay and work-place harmony, it came with its own, built-in social legitimacy.

The system embodied in "Shop Management" broke free from the old chains of labor versus capital. On the one hand, it could scarcely be distinguished from the "satanic mills" breed of capitalism: workers were expected to work—and work hard, those unable to bear up being replaced by those who could. On the other hand, it promised higher wages; and sometimes, as at Simonds, shorter hours; and maybe the chance to wind up in the planning office with a white collar. "Shop Management," it could seem, defied old categories of thought. With it, something new had come into the world.

Among those receiving advance copies of Taylor's paper was Harrington Emerson, who had met its author two years before and was something of an early efficiency expert himself. "For two days I have been studying the advance sheets of your paper 'Shop Management,' " he wrote Taylor. "I began by marking important passages. This was a mistake, as nearly every page is marked from top to bottom." As Emerson put it publicly at Saratoga, Taylor's was nothing less than "the most important contribution ever presented to the Society, and one of the most important papers ever published in the United States."

Frank Gilbreth, a former bricklayer and contractor who would go on to an international renown that paralleled Taylor's, devoured "Shop Management" when it appeared in the society's *Transactions*. He called it his Bible, ordered that his own followers read it three times, had his office staff take typing tests from a page of it, and pronounced it, in the words of one account, "a work of genius."

If there was a beginning to the cult surrounding Taylor, a time when disciples began to cluster about him, it was the Saratoga meeting and the publication of "Shop Management."

∽

Among those impressed by Taylor's paper was ASME president James Mapes Dodge, who was said to hold the Wednesday afternoon on which it was presented "the most interesting afternoon in the history of the Society" and became one of Taylor's most ardent champions.

Dodge, four years Taylor's senior, had for more than twenty-five years been associated with the Link-Belt Company. Like Simonds Rolling Machine Company, it had grown from a single wonderful idea: a chain-and-sprocket drive that, compared to belt drives, cut frictional losses in half. Link-Belt products helped haul coal cars up steep inclines, lift ashes from boiler rooms, handle barrels and sacks in sugar refineries. The company logo showed a bearded angel cranking a winch, which turned a sprocket, which drove a Link-Belt chain, which spun the world around. By now, the company had three factories, and employed fifteen hundred workers. Dodge presided over its engineering division in Philadelphia; by 1906, he would head the whole company.

Dodge—whose mother, Mary Mapes Dodge, was an esteemed writer of children's stories, creator of the Hans Brinker character, and longtime editor of *St. Nicholas* magazine—stood out boldly from the common run of engineers and industrialists. An owl-eyed man with thick, black eyebrows, prominent mustache and goatee, he boasted what one account describes, and all his correspondence confirms, as "a genial liveliness." He was expressive, wise, and witty. No less an authority than Mark Twain, who contributed to his mother's magazine, was supposed to have once called him "the greatest story teller in America."

Dodge's receptivity to Taylor and his ideas went back long before Saratoga, at least to the late 1880s, when a veteran Midvale hand, Louis Wright, joined Link-Belt and began to talk up Taylor's ideas. So when, in 1899, news of high-speed steel drifted down from Bethlehem, Dodge went there to see for himself and watched a Taylor-White tool "ripping heavy nickel steel faster than we were in the habit of turning off [much softer] brass." Its edge glowing "with a dull red heat," it cut at a hundred and forty feet per minute. "The wonderfully valuable mechanical training I had had and my twenty years of experience," he concluded, were "obsolete from that moment onward."

The next day, he returned to Philadelphia, where the modest Link-Belt factory occupied a triangle of land just across the tracks from Midvale Steel. Ruefully, Dodge surveyed his shop; after Bethlehem, it seemed a vestige of the Dark Ages, but the thought of sinking horrific sums into an innovation that might not pan out made him waver. Back to Bethlehem he went with some of his own toolmaker's best tools— only to witness "the instant failure of our samples alongside of the Taylor-White product." No option remained; he would have to join the twentieth century. A few days later Link-Belt bought shop rights to the new steel.

But just as today's computers beget new problems even as they solve old ones, so did high-speed steel at Link-Belt. For one thing, it didn't work as well on cast iron, whose chips didn't peel off the tool but crumbled. Second, the new wonder steel meant higher power consumption; whereas before, a fifty-horsepower engine sufficed, now the shop "was absorbing over 150 horsepower and calling for more." The old machine tools couldn't take it; they had to be replaced or rebuilt. Long-established piece rates meant nothing and had to be refigured. Moreover, Dodge related, some old-timers—men at Link-Belt twenty or thirty years and used to the lathe's leisurely turning—quit. With work spinning furiously faster now, "it was such a nervous strain on the men that they could not stand it."

Accounting, receiving, the toolroom, stores, routing—nothing worked as it had. It was as if admitting high-speed steel to the shop let in the edgy, overbearing ghost of Taylor himself—who, as always, brought with him trouble. Ultimately, "we called in the man who had been instrumental in getting us into our difficulties and asked him to get us out." But Taylor, with a new family and on the verge of moving into a new home, saw himself as retired.

Enter, once again, Carl Barth.

After leaving Bethlehem, Barth had found a job, through Taylor, with Wm. Sellers & Company. After fifteen months there, he joined Link-Belt, working on the purely mechanical problems that high-speed steel brought with it. After Saratoga, probably around October, his job broadened—to introducing, under his mentor's tutelage, the Taylor system of shop management. Dwight Merrick, another old Bethlehem hand, joined him, first in the drafting room, then on time studies. Barth ran tests, respeeded the machines, reorganized the toolrooms, rebuilt tools, introduced instructions cards and the differential rate, made his special slide rules, and much else—all according to the gospel of St. Frederick, which was about how he viewed it. He even set up a system of standard wage scales for those still paid by the day, based—Barth's mathematical mind at work again—on geometric series, each step a fixed 15 percent above the one below.

But, as at Bethlehem and everywhere else it was introduced, Taylor-style management met resistance. Link-Belt veterans, even Dodge himself, did not always do precisely as Barth and Taylor decreed. After two years of strife, Taylor had had it. The success of his system, he wrote Dodge angrily, "rests primarily upon two important elements:

> 1st: Absolutely rigid and inflexible standards throughout your establishment.
>
> 2nd: That each employee of your establishment should receive every day clear-cut, definite instructions as to just what he is to do and how he is to do it, and these instructions should be exactly carried out, whether they are right or wrong.

That wasn't happening. Among their other sins, Dodge's men had dared alter Taylor's routing system, dropped functional foremanship, and substituted another pay scheme (presumably Halsey's) for the bonus plan (presumably Gantt's) that he had ordained. "In making alterations of this type," Taylor concluded, "you have taken steps to entirely emasculate the system of management which I advocate."

Taylor wanted it done his way, and poor, loyal, earnest Barth was caught in the middle. Later he would call his first two years at Link-Belt "the last part of my apprenticeship." "Except in the mere engineering phases of the work," he wrote, "I often had a very hard time between [Taylor] and some of that company's officials. Had it not been for the encouragement and influence of my faithful wife I would never have gone through with it, and that would have been the end of the Taylor System."

That, of course, was not the end of the Taylor system; it operated at Link-Belt for years in about as pure a form as ever existed. And in June 1906, Barth turned to Link-Belt's Chicago plant.

During all this, it was not Taylor who issued the orders and dealt with the men, but Barth. It was Taylor whose ideas Barth translated into new machine settings and work rules, Taylor who advised and counseled. But as Barth recalled later, the man himself "did not visit us any too often," remaining at one remove—or maybe two or three—

from the shop floor. Since the spring of 1904, he had retired to Boxly, the name he'd given his new house on the old Sherwood estate in Chestnut Hill.

~

The previous winter, while still at Red Gate, troubles and calamities had beset the Taylor household. The coachman drove too fast around a corner, encountering an icy patch; Flora, the horse that had borne them on their maiden visit to Boxly, fell and broke her hip. She had to be shot.

Caspar Goodrich, who had just qualified for promotion to admiral, came to visit, mistook his way to the bathroom in the dark, and fell down the stairs. He landed on his head in the kitchen and, as Taylor wrote, "was lucky in not breaking his neck."

On March 4, Taylor's old friend from Midvale and Bethlehem, Russell Davenport, now general manager and vice president at Cramp's Shipyards, died of pneumonia; he'd been ill three days.

On Wednesday, March 9, 1904, seven years after the stroke that disabled her, Taylor's mother died, at the age of eight-one. Services were held that Saturday. After enduring her long death-in-life, Ernest Wright wrote Taylor, "It must be a blessed release."

On April 9, Clarence Clark's father, the banker Edward White Clark, also died.

It was probably with mingled relief and sadness, then, that, as Taylor wrote a friend on May 16, "We are now engaged in moving to the new house."

Boxly took its name from its almost century-old boxwood gardens, whose luxuriant growth had originally drawn them to the place. But after thirty years of neglect, the gardens were now more dilemma than delight. They had decayed into what one account described as "a wild tangle of box, overgrown with vines and interspersed with small trees, wild rose bushes, and weeds." The flower beds bordered by the boxwood hedges were by now obliterated; so were the paths through the garden. It was no longer a garden at all but, rather, "a wilderness of box."

How to restore its original beauty?

One way was to transplant the hedges, in conformity to some new aesthetic plan. Aesthetics was the easy part; for inspiration, the Taylors visited Mount Vernon, George Washington's estate in Virginia. But transplant them? Can't be done, Taylor heard from gardeners and landscape architects; the hedges would die, as they had whenever the previous owner had tried to do it. Undaunted, Taylor had deep trenches dug beside some hedges. The horizontal spread of their roots, he and the gardener discovered, was more than anyone had thought. Earlier transplant efforts had failed because they'd been hacking off the roots.

With this knowledge in hand, Taylor recruited a small army of laborers, had them dig trenches far enough from each bush to clear the roots, then use a thirty-ton jackscrew to drive huge knives—sharpened steel plates nine feet long and five feet wide—beneath the root-stuffed soil. On the sides, they supported each root pack with wooden planks. They lifted the whole mass of dirt, roots, hedge, wood, and steel on hydraulic jacks—a thirty-foot section weighed thirty tons—and moved it to a new bed prepared for it. Kempton remembered his father superintending the work, sometimes down in a trench himself showing a workman how to use the jack. Between March and November, the house going up around them, they moved twelve hundred feet of box. Only a handful of bushes died.

Their new house at Boxly was enormous, maybe ten or twelve thousand square feet. A first-floor wing, comprising kitchen, servant's dining room, and butler's pantry, occupied an area larger than most Philadelphia workers' houses. You'd drive up from St. Martin's Lane, or else stroll up from Highland Station of the Chestnut Hill Railroad, four or five minutes away, and face an edifice whose pedimented, colonnaded entrance was reminiscent of nothing so much as the White House. Stone steps led to a small foyer and then the main hall, dominated by a magnificent staircase. Across the great hall to the left were the living room and library.

Southern Colonial, as architect Mantle Fielding defined the new house's style, would normally dictate small window panes. But in the back, Taylor decreed, they'd have to violate stylistic constraints. He wanted nothing obstructing the panorama of the Wissahickon valley from the dining room or the view of the conservatory, lush with fern and flower, from the library. These, Mr. Fielding must understand, would have to be huge, unobstructed picture windows. And so they were, nine feet across and seven high, swinging on ball bearings.

The house boasted such inventive touches as a cooling chamber around the eaves and a hydraulic lift that brought up firewood or fresh flowers from the basement. "Boxly was a magic carpet," Lou would gush. "You pressed a button and a shutter came up from the cellar by hydraulic power" to protect the picture windows. A fireplace screen set within the chimney could be dropped into position by a touch.

~

And yet, for all the delights of Boxly, its grounds, its gardeners, and its servants, Fred Taylor always stressed what he called not "putting on lugs." The children were surrounded by millionaires even richer than they, Robert Taylor would note—the Disstons of the Disston Saw fortune, and the Houstons, developers of Chestnut Hill, and the Wanamakers, of the great department store. "Our father tried to keep us on the low side in all expenditures—we didn't have quite as fancy clothes as some of the other kids had." He went so far as to check with their rich neighbors and set the allowances of his boys a little lower. While the neighbors' boys went to school by carriage or auto, Kempton recalled, "only on the most inclement days were we allowed this luxury." And Rob sometimes wore Kemp's hand-me-downs. "I am sure," Taylor once wrote the boys when they were teenagers, "that Robert would not be such a snob as to care what any boy said about his suit."

He was determined that the boys not have it too good. "When I was 10, and my brother Kempton was 12," Robert remembered—which places the incident around 1905—"we were asked to meet with our father in his office at 6:30, a half hour before supper. He informed us that he had drawn up a new will that day," whose principles he wished them to understand. He himself had declined any of his mother's estate; the Winslow money had gone to Mary and Win when she died. And he was not about to ruin his own boys with excess: upon his death, they were each to get twenty thousand dollars—worth perhaps half a million dollars in today's money but paltry compared to his total worth.

Of course, Fred Taylor could afford to play down the importance of money; he had so much of it and always had. One day at Boxly, Robert remembered, they were standing in the great hall when his father opened a letter with a check for $87,500 in high-speed steel royalties.

"He told me I probably never would get a check that large in my lifetime."

5

PRESIDENT AND DR. TAYLOR

~

As JIM DODGE OF LINK-BELT could have testified, high-speed steel shattered the complacency of the industrial world. Everyone began scurrying about for new steels with which to compete against Taylor-White, even at the risk of trespass upon its patents. To Sheffield's Harry Brearley, at least, it made for a pathetic spectacle. In a 1933 memoir, *Steel-Makers*, the English inventor of stainless steel recalled how, after Paris, "faced by demonstrated fact at variance with his established rules . . .

> every maker of tool steel was busy with his mixtures and labels and catalogues. Those steel-makers who understood the subject, if any, were followed by those who made no pretensions to understand it. One of the most important moves in the game was to find a "brand": some name suggesting tireless, rapid efficiency which would look well on a tastefully printed label.

By 1907, high-speed steel was available in twenty or more brands, with names like Novo and Blue Chip, many of them imported. The stuff went for about twelve hundred dollars a ton, as compared to ordinary steel's thirty; it was practically gold. Total American consumption was less than four thousand tons, a tiny fraction of 1 percent of all steel production; Bethlehem itself made 330 tons, which could fit in a good-sized kitchen. And yet these trifling quantities wrought disproportionate results, which radiated from the hot cutting edge itself, to the rest of the machine, the whole shop, and throughout modern industry.

"Should the use of such tools tend to spread," the Paris exposition's international jury had written of Taylor-White tools, "it would necessitate, in order to obtain the maximum output, the use of lathes equipped in ways a little different from those we see today." In ways a little different? You had to redesign every big machine tool in the world! To exploit a tool that let you cut at triple the old speed, you needed power sources, belts, and machine parts muscular enough to drive the work into that implacable cutter. As Jim Dodge had learned at Link-Belt, a machine tool using high-speed steel could easily use ten or twenty horsepower; that, observes German historian Ulrich Wengenroth, "was a whole factory in 1890."

"We are on the eve," declared a 1903 booklet, *Points for Buyers and Users of Tool Steel*, "of a complete revolution in shop practice." At the Sheffield, England, engineering firm of Davy Brothers, after 1900, "practically the whole of the machine tools have been replaced in all cases by new tools of the most up-to-date type, suitable for high speed steel." An account from 1930 reads like Darwinian evolution at work on living metal:

> During the first decade of the 20th century we see high-speed steel
> revolutionizing the lathe—as it does all production machine tools.
> Beds and slides rapidly become heavier, feed works stronger, and
> the driving cones are designed for much wider belts than of old.
> The legs of big lathes grow shorter and shorter, and finally
> disappear as the beds grow down to the floor.

Not only the machines changed, however, but also the men working them, the shops where they worked, the means by which they were managed. After Paris, technical journals, American and foreign, large and small, were filled with papers dealing with repercussions of the new tools. "Metal Cutting with the New Tool Steels" in *Engineering Magazine* of April 1903 was one. "The New Tool Steel and Its Effect on Machine Shop Methods" in *Wisconsin Engineer* of June 1903 was another. Any priest of steel, like any computer expert today, found audiences hungry for his knowledge.

Beginning at Bethlehem, then more rapidly after Paris, the new tools influenced the mood of every shop they touched. Now, suddenly, the leisure was gone. The superintendent of an English mill, J. M. Gledhill, would observe that high-speed tools,

> throwing off shavings from steel and iron as one usually sees in
> turning wood, and imparting a life and energy to the whole

establishment in remarkable contrast to the sleepy rate at which
metals used to be turned and machined for so many years past . . .
[exerted] an influence on everybody therein to get "a hustle on"
that is positively exhilarating in its effects.

Exhilarating for the boss, perhaps, but what of the workers? They
spent less time now just watching their tools cut, more in setting up to
cut; now it was their time, not the machine's, that worried management most. At a meeting of Philadelphia's Franklin Institute in April
1901, Link Belt's Charles Day noted that a cast-iron ring once taking
fourteen hours to machine now took three and a half; what he called
"the age of intensified production" had arrived, and in this new age the
workman counted as much as the machine. Accordingly, "he should be
just as carefully watched, his welfare attended to, his physical and
mental conditions looked after." In too many shops, machinery got
attention while the worker, "keynote of the whole scheme, is ignored."
This had to change.

The new air of speed and urgency left less room for human guesswork, error, and delay; a worn belt, or a man standing around, stood
out all the more boldly. "The Taylor-White process of treating tool
steel," said Day—whose report to the Franklin Institute led to the two
men receiving its prestigious Elliott Cresson Medal the following
year—"has already wakened up machine shops all over the country to
the fact that methods frequently known as 'good shop practice' are anything but *good* and if they expect to keep up with the times they must
adopt . . . more radical methods."

Machinists felt the pressure. To show a visitor that his men were not
loafing, a Chicago plant superintendent stopped at a lathe, the floor
around which was sheathed in iron sheets. Remove them, he ordered.
When the machinist did so, chips flying from the hot cutting tool set
the floor on fire. His message was clear: no man running a tool that hot,
that fast, was malingering.

The industrial world was speeding up. Men would have to speed up
with it. If Taylor preferred to see high-speed steel as a footnote to the
larger cause he championed, out in the real world the influence often
went the other way: Link-Belt bought rights to the new tool steel, only
then introduced the Taylor system. However great its early promise,
high-speed steel proved more pivotal yet—as the opening into which
the earth-moving wedge of the Taylor system could be slipped. No

mere technical breakthrough, it made Taylor's brand of shop management seem not merely interesting but indispensable.

~

On March 20, 1906, Fred Taylor was fifty years old. To mark the occasion, his mother-in-law penned something of a biography in verse:

> By some he was called an Iconoclast,
>   As his ideas were new and not of the past
> While others, less original and bold,
>   Are content with their ways, let them be ever so old.
>   . . .
> He has now reached the half centenarian stage
>   With glories unusual to one of his age;
> But with all his triumphs and medals won
>   He has ever proved a faithful son;
> And now from his association sent
>   Comes his well earned honor, the President.

And president he was, of the American Society of Mechanical Engineers. To hear Taylor tell a Washington commission about it later in his best mock-humble form, he'd scarcely known what he was letting himself in for:

> For about three months, while the nomination was on, before the
> election, my chest got larger and larger, and I had to have
> somebody back of me to hold up my head to keep me from falling
> over backward. Four days after the election I was given a dinner.
> My head and chest suddenly contracted when I was told I had been
> elected because the society needed reorganizing and it was believed
> I was the man to do it.

When he'd joined the ASME two decades before, the society was still young and fresh. Now, though, it was weakened by the dead weight of past practice: 542 engineers showed up for its annual New York meeting in 1904, versus 129 in 1884. Yet during all that time, its administrative methods had scarcely changed. Many grumbled about the expensive New York office and general inefficiency.

Taylor, it was later said of his presidency, "threw himself whole-heartedly into the work, allowed nothing to stand in his way, and brought about, mainly by his own efforts, though not without assistance from others, a complete reformation in the Society's methods of administration."

The assistance was largely that of Morris Llewellyn Cooke, a young engineer Taylor had met at the home of Link-Belt's Jim Dodge. A graduate of Lehigh University in Bethlehem, Cooke had not exactly sailed through school. He'd been suspended for a year in a hazing incident. His family had money problems, forcing him to work for a while as a cub reporter in Philadelphia, New York, and elsewhere. When, after six years, he finally graduated, this youngest of six boys from an old Germantown family went to work at the Cramp's ship-yards, which impressed him with its shameless inefficiency. He worked as a machinist, served in the Spanish-American War as chief engineer aboard a navy ship, married, and went into the printing business in Philadelphia.

Along the way, he grew interested in Taylor's ideas and tried to apply them to his own work. At one company, his boss reminded him later, he virtually worked himself out of a job every few months by reducing to routine clerical tasks the work of a department he had "chewed up and systematized." Around the time of the Saratoga paper, thirty-one-year-old Cooke, with an introduction from a mutual friend in hand, wrote Taylor, expressing a wish to meet. At the Dodge house, "the two talked for hours," wrote Cooke's biographer, Kenneth E. Trombley. "Taylor, impressed with Cooke's zeal and his knowledge . . . , gripped his hand warmly upon parting."

Some time later, the new ASME president contacted Cooke, then working for a publisher. Would he help him reorganize the Society? "It was like offering honey to a bee," wrote Trombley, though neither man had "realized to what archaic depths the administration of the ASME had descended." A committee of three was formed. Cooke did most of the work; Taylor, out of his own pocket, paid his salary. Volumes of new office standards came out of that year. Carl Barth designed new accounting forms. The shaping idea, as Taylor explained it later, was to free up the society's top officers, "the men who were busy men . . . , the high-priced men, from all routine work, from all drudgery, from all trivial decisions; so as to leave them absolutely free from harassing details." Many "trivial decisions" were so standardized that clerks, their work inspected daily or weekly, could do them as well as their bosses had before.

It was a good year for Taylor, as he stepped ever more decisively from the dark shop floor onto a floodlit public stage. He testified against the Littauer Bill, which would have had American industry adopt the metric system. There, he regaled his listeners with his early experiences as a patternmaker, brandishing his workingman's past like a diploma: "I know these men well; many of them are my personal friends, and I have worked with them."

In May, when the society met in Chattanooga, Taylor made polite noises about how, after forty years of poverty and reconstruction since the Civil War, the South was perhaps now ready to take its rightful place in American industry.

In October, at the dedication of its new engineering building, the University of Pennsylvania conferred upon him an honorary doctorate, the basis for the Dr. Taylor with which his disciples often dignified him (and which he apparently didn't discourage). "Thorough and industrious in preparation for his life work," the citation read, "patient in investigation and experiment, logical in analysis and deduction, versatile in invention, his labors have brought system out of disorder in the organization of industrial establishments."

Taylor gave an address for the occasion. Its full title was:

A COMPARISON OF
UNIVERSITY AND INDUSTRIAL
DISCIPLINE AND METHODS
Being a protest against the excesses of the elective system and loose
university discipline; and a plea for bringing students early into
close contact with men working for their living

That, of course, said it all: every engineering student needed six months in a shop, right after freshman year. "He should have the same hours and be under the same discipline as other employees, and should receive no favors."

One other duty devolved upon the president of the American Society of Mechanical Engineers, to deliver a formal address at the end of his term. "Not being able to write in an ornamental way," he said later—and some of those presidential addresses were ornamental indeed—he chose to write about metal cutting. Around March, about the time of his birthday, he began reviewing his notes.

On June 14, with Sanford Thompson coming to visit Boxly, Taylor wrote him that "I shall have very little to say to you except on the subject of golf, as all my working time is taken up with my paper on the Art of Cutting Metals." The work dragged, four solid hours of dictation a day advancing it but slowly.

On August 23, he wrote Thompson from the Equinox Hotel in Manchester, Vermont, down Main Street from Clarence and Mary's summer home; perhaps he escaped there to work free of family distractions. There was barely time to finish before the December meeting, he fretted. "With plenty of time it would have been a distinct pleasure to write the paper, but with the constant anxiety lest it may not be finished on time, it is anything but a pleasure." Fred Taylor didn't like being rushed.

Not until two weeks before he was to present it in New York was the prodigious paper finished. Somebody, Morris Cooke recalled, suggested he call it "The Art of Cutting Metals," but Taylor countered with "On the Art . . . ," which was more modest—everything the paper as a whole was not; the society had never heard anything on so operatic a scale. The Taylor boys, Kempton and Robert, were there for opening night and remembered the huge slide rule, wide as a room, erected on the stage of the auditorium, with Barth on hand to demonstrate. Their father's paper comprised all he had learned about metal cutting since his first Midvale experiments twenty-five years before. It filled an entire volume of the *Transactions*, demanding 248 pages. It included two dozen foldout charts, a two-page index of definitions, and a seven-page table of contents. Indeed, in fitting resonance with Taylor's years in industry, the cost of printing this one paper, according to ASME historian Bruce Sinclair, "ate up all the savings Cooke had achieved in the publication department!"

The paper's Part II was stuffed with technical detail—on the design of the experimental lathe, on lip and clearance angles, on tool chatter, on heat treatment—and filled with formulas, charts, and figures. Part I, by contrast, was a short, semipopular exposition in which Taylor reviewed his work and recounted its history. This was no mere greasy lathe work, its every page intimated, but an enterprise of great and heroic proportion. "We have made between thirty and fifty thousand recorded experiments," he wrote,

> and many others of which no record was kept. In studying these laws we have cut up into chips with our experimental tools more than 800,000 pounds of steel and iron. More than sixteen thousand experiments were recorded in the Bethlehem Steel Company. We estimate that up to date between $150,000 and $200,000 have been spent upon this work.

Of those helping him over the years, he noted, Barth was the mathematician, Maunsel White the metallurgist, Gantt the all-around manager. "And the writer of this paper," he allowed, "has perhaps the faculty of holding on tighter with his teeth than any of the others."

Of course, Taylor got in a plug for his system. Barth slide rules could not "be left at the lathe to be banged about by the machinist. They must be used by a man with reasonably clean hands, and at a table or desk." Indeed—here it comes—"the correct use of slide rules involves the substitution of our whole task system of management for the old style management, as described in our paper on 'Shop Management.'"

And yet, may we not pardon Taylor for his rhetorical detour? "On the Art of Cutting Metals" was a tour de force; if Part I was good theater, Part II was good science. For decades it would be deemed the last word on the subject and on high-speed steel; in 1981, the ASME devoted a volume to it from the perspective of seventy-five years. Nor was its significance lost on anyone at the time. Henry Towne called it "a masterpiece." *Iron Trade Review* called it "the most important contribution ever made to engineering literature. . . . No manufacturer engaged in the working of iron and steel in machine tools can afford to neglect the lessons it presents." And in making his results freely available, it went on, "Mr. Taylor's work is a service not only to engineering but to mankind in general."

Soon, Taylor was hearing from old friends—tribute that, he wrote William Fannon, gave him "greater satisfaction than anything in connection with the work which we have done." One who wrote, lauding him for "the great honors that have been conferred on you," was John Griffith. Another was Admiral Goodrich. Reading the metal-cutting paper and imagining Taylor's triumph in New York, "We pictured you in our minds driving the imperial chariot about your arena and smiling to the assembled multitude from under your well-earned victor's wreath of laurel, as they shouted, 'Ave! Imperatore!' "

Goodrich, it seems, knew his friend well.

On June 30th, 1907, Taylor heard from Ernest Wright, now living in Pasadena, California, and who, after a few pleasantries, got straight to the point: He was writing on behalf of the leadership of the future Throop Polytechnic School," which became California Institute of Technology in 1920. "They are looking for a bigger man to organize the new school and be its president. Your name has been mentioned, and if you will entertain the suggestion a couple of the trustees will call upon you some time this summer."

Taylor replied that he was "unfit for work of this kind," adding that he had "recently had a similar suggestion made to me by one of the largest technical institutions in this country"—probably Massachusetts Institute of Technology. Still, these offers testified to how far he had come. Outside the industrial and engineering communities, he was still unknown. Inside, he was a very important man.

6

"I AM GOING TO POINT A WAY"

≈

EVEN WERE HE AN APPROPRIATE CHOICE to head Throop, Taylor told Wright, he felt he could do more good by advancing his system, which, he believed, represented "a permanent benefit to the community." This sounds suspiciously philanthropic, a sensibility that Taylor, who fancied himself distant in spirit from the effete rich of Chestnut Hill and Germantown, disdained. Later, testifying in a patent suit, he described his efforts, all at no slight personal expense, to advance his cause. So, he was asked, "You are something of a philanthropist?"

"I should say not," he replied. "I am very much interested in the subject of modern, scientific shop management and believe that I can do more for my friends and the world at large" by giving it his time and money. (Of course, this still sounds like philanthropy.)

Headquarters, as it were, for Taylor's benevolent foundation was his estate at Boxly, to which he invited anyone showing the slightest interest in his ideas. "Many were the mornings," Lou would recall,

> when I counted twenty or thirty well-known executives walking
> down the box paths to our doorway. My mother and I counted
> them from the second floor gallery as they came in, and wondered
> if they would stay for luncheon, what to have, and what would the
> cook say! I can recall the charmed circle of men listening to Fred's
> explanation of "Scientific Management" while he held his pet cat,
> "Put Mut," on his shoulder.

They came by the hundreds to hear him. The Boxly talks, as they became known, extended from about 1904 to 1912. But one of them, on a late spring evening in 1907, differed from the others. For on that day, stenographers were present to transcribe every word Taylor said, unburnished by an editor's pencil, in all its maddening repetition, across sixty-two typewritten pages.

"I am going to point a way," Taylor began, "and one lying right straight ahead:

> It may be monotonous, but I am going to try to keep on that single
> idea, so as to convince you in that if I possibly can. What I want to
> try to show is that, in the first place, the idea which is back of our
> scheme of management is radically different, and that it is not only
> radically different, but that it must be in almost every case
> overwhelmingly better. That is what I am going to try to prove.
>
> I ought to say at the start that what I am going to say will sound
> extremely conceited. It will sound as though we were very much
> stuck on ourselves, but we are not so much stuck on ourselves as
> we are on the idea . . .
>
> I want to try to convince you that the task idea—because that is
> what is back of everything we do—is overwhelmingly better than
> the other idea in its practical results. The best that there is in the

other scheme, the antithesis of our scheme, is asking for the initiative [of the workers] . . . their workmanship, their best brains and their best work . . .

I want to say, brutally speaking, and I am purposely brutal in my presentation, our scheme does not ask any initiative in a man. We do not care for his initiative. That is not true when we analyze it into its last limitation, but it is true as to the form in which we arrange, plan and lay out. I am going to try to prove to you that that scheme of not asking any initiative of our workmen will beat the other one all to pieces . . .

And so began the monologue, the two-hour, nonstop exhortation he would give, in various forms, for years.

"The company assembled in the early morning, in the beautiful large living room at Boxly, to be greeted by Taylor and often by his two young sons," one visitor recalled; then it was lunch and a factory tour downtown. In another pattern, guests were invited to dine at six thirty, then get down to business right after dinner.

He worked from notes and almost always gave the same talk, practically verbatim. He could not abbreviate it, he insisted. His listeners must give it no less than two hours and must ask no questions until the end; they were issued paper and pencil with which to jot them down for later. Nothing must interrupt the performance.

Anyone who saw him at Boxly—or lecturing anywhere, for that matter—remembered Taylor in the flesh as quite different from Taylor in print. Whereas his papers were relatively reserved, "in his speech," it was said of him later, "he was detailed, pell-mell and overwhelming." Only in person, attired in a well-cut, blue serge suit, before a rapt audience, did he entirely come into his own—not because he was especially eloquent, but because he was on fire. He believed, and people came away believing in him and in what he said. They came sometimes skeptical and left changed—warmed by the house and the grounds, by the view of the valley, by the fire crackling in the fireplace, mesmerized by Taylor's words, captivated by his passion.

"If I close my eyes," Lillian Gilbreth wrote of Taylor, "I can see him again, in his beautiful home, telling of the principles of management. . . . The fire of the enthusiast was there, but always, too, the close thinking of the scientist."

On this particular spring evening, as on so many other occasions, Taylor began—after eight transcript pages of preliminaries—with what had become his pet parable, that of Henry Noll, the pig iron loader. At Saratoga, Taylor had briefly referred to a "very quick and wiry fellow" whom he had taken to the side and instructed. Now, though, by the verdant gardens of Boxly, the Pennsylvania Dutchman appeared by name and not merely in a walk-on role; Noll got his own lines and probably (though the transcript doesn't say) an accent.

As Taylor told the story now, he and his aides had "studied" the Bethlehem yard workers and selected one among them, Noll, as capable of loading the forty-seven tons that previous "studies" had fixed as a proper day's work. But, he digressed, "it requires quite an art . . . to make these men do that 47 tons and be content, and not kick . . . , not have labor trouble on your hands." The old way,

> you would go to a workman and say, "Now, John, you are a mighty strong fellow. Don't you think you can do 47 tons of pig iron a day?"
>
> John would immediately say, "Why, hell, I have only done 12 ½. No man can do 47 tons."
>
> Then there would be an argument between you and John, and you would compromise on about 20 or 18, or whatever it was. John would have just as much to do in the argument as you . . . because if you ask for his initiative you presuppose he knows what he can do.

But John didn't know what he could do, and Taylor, presumably, did. Science had spoken: forty-seven tons. There was no need to negotiate, argue, or discuss. "We do not even talk about the number of tons." Getting him to do that much was all that counted. And achieving that, he emphasized, meant "it is up to us to do all the talking, and John to do all the listening."

At Bethlehem, he went on, "I picked out a Pennsylvania Dutchman . . . I went to him and said, 'Noll, are you a high-priced man?'

> He said, "I don't know what you mean."
>
> I said, "Of course you know what I mean. Are you a high-priced man?"
>
> "I don't know what you mean."

I said, "Don't trifle with me. Of course, you know what I mean.
I want to know whether you are really a high-priced man, or one of
those cheap workers satisfied with $1.15 a day," the wages paid up
there at that time . . . . "I am looking for fellows I can pay $1.85
to."

He said, "I will take $1.85 a day any time."

"You are making a joke out of this thing. You are not treating
this matter seriously. I want to know whether you are a high-
priced man. You know what I mean."

"I don't know what you mean. I will take $1.85 a day."

"You seem to be very stupid. There is something wrong with
you. I want to find out whether you are a high-priced man. If you
are, see that pile of pig iron. See that car. If you are a high-priced
man you can load that iron on that for $1.85 a day."

Taylor finally recapitulated the deal to the hapless Noll, adding one
final, crucial element:

"Hold on, there is another thing to this. Do you see that fellow
there?

"Yes."

"A high-priced man does just as he is told and don't go jawing
back. . . . When he tells you to pick up a pig you pick it up and
walk with it. When he tells you to sit down and rest, you sit down
and rest. That is the difference between a high-priced man and
these fellows that get $1.15 a day."

In the end, Noll was won over, did as he was told, and became a
high-priced man. And all the while, in Taylor's telling, he "had no
notion he was handling four times as much as before. We did not propose to let him know it."

The Boxly talks were a succession of such parables. In another,
Taylor told of a Pittsburgh company that sent an agent authorized to
offer Bethlehem shovelers 4.9 cents a ton, or 50 percent more than they
were getting. Taylor's assistant importuned him: shouldn't they pay
more? No, he replied, "We will let every one of them go." In fact, *they'd*
tell them of the offer first; "We might as well get the credit." But, the
departing men were reminded, they could always come back.

And, recounted Taylor, they did come back, most within six weeks, because they made less money in Pittsburgh at 4.9 cents a ton than in hard-charging Bethlehem, under scientific management, at 3.2 cents.

Boxly itself figured in Taylor's stories. He told about moving the hill behind the house; how they ran tests to see how much a horse and driver could haul, selecting them much as they had pig iron handlers; how the men were promised bonuses for each hour in which they achieved a given task, and a bonus on top of that for a whole day of met tasks. They had only to do as they were told, even to taking rests:

> They were thoroughly astounded when they were ordered off the job to go and rest.
> "I want my bonus."
> "We will attend to you and see you get the bonus. Go over there, you and your horse, and sit down!"
> We put up a little bench for them under the trees, and a place to tether the horse.

And the moral? "We did three times the work we were doing before, and twice the work any contractor would do." Toward the end, he said, local contractors would come around each day to witness this marvel of human and animal effort.

Then there was the one about how Henry Towne cautions Taylor's man, Barth, not to expect as much improvement at smooth-running Yale & Towne as he achieves elsewhere. "We can double the output of your hoist shop," Barth shoots back.

"But you have never been in my shop."

"No, I don't have to go in. I can tell you that without going in."

"That is the most arrogant thing I ever heard said."

"Well, you asked me something. I tell you we can double it sure." Finally, in Taylor's telling, Towne shows him around. "Now, Mr. Barth, having been in my shop, do you still say that?"

"No, I have changed my mind. Certainly we can do two and a half or three times the work."

In the end, Barth triumphs, production soars, and Taylor has his moral. "The man who has been there for years has not one chance in a thousand of hitting the one condition which will do the greatest work," he says, exhibiting a Barth slide rule. How could any one man's experience match this instrument's cool scientific authority?

And so, one after another, the day's little dramas played out. Finally, it was question time. But by now, sedated by the elixir of Boxly and the hypnotic drumbeat of Taylor's stories, his guests asked only the lamest questions, which Taylor fielded with practiced ease.

Next came the tour. Sometimes that afternoon, sometimes the following morning, his guests would head off to see one of two Philadelphia companies that had installed Taylor's system: Link-Belt and the Tabor Manufacturing Company.

Tabor, located in an old rented building near the great Baldwin Locomotive complex, was a small manufacturer of power-driven molding machines, which took some of the grunt work out of the molder's job. Taylor had become tangled in its fortunes in 1903 when his old friend Fred Lewis, who had joined Tabor in 1900, sought his help. The company had labor troubles, was suffering all sorts of business reverses, and risked going under. Taylor agreed to lend the company money if it would install his system. Placed in charge was Carl Barth, who was also working at Link-Belt.

"One day," blacksmith H. A. Connelly remembered, "a notice was posted in the shop stating that the company had adopted the Taylor System and the cooperation of the employees was desired." Some men quit on the strength of that alone, but most stayed just to see how the experiment would play out. As usual, there were Taylor forces and anti-Taylor forces. The stopwatch stirred almost universal enmity; so, too, among some union men of egalitarian stripe, did bonuses.

Gradually, however, they came around. Connelly, who at first resisted the whole idea of instruction cards, for example, used them to good effect to teach a newly hired blacksmith, "thereby doing the very thing I had always been opposed to." Other workers were similarly won over.

For a time, only large infusions of Taylor's cash kept the company afloat. But ultimately, wrote Lewis, "a better spirit prevailed, better wages were earned, and production increased so rapidly that I was lost in astonishment at the potency of the engine gratuitously placed in our hands." In the old days, before Taylor and Barth, Tabor had employed three bosses—superintendent, foreman, and assistant foreman—to oversee 126 men. In 1907, with ninety-six workmen watched over by no fewer than twenty-six planners, bosses, and clerks, the company turned out two and a half times as much work and made a handsome profit.

For visitors to Boxly, seeing Tabor and Link-Belt up close clinched the impressions made by Taylor's talk. Over the years, scholars would distinguish between the intellectual legacy and broad social influence of Taylorism on the one hand, and, on the other, its application to real workplaces. Only down on the shop floor did its abstract formulations, otherwise just so much talk, become detailed, infinitely elaborated work practices; ruled time-study forms; bulletin boards filled with instruction cards; toolrooms with every wrench, jig, and bolt sorted by mnemonic classification; wage schemes that established pay rates down to a fraction of a cent; machine tools modified to carry the loads of high-speed steel; slide rules custom-made for each planer, lathe, and milling machine; accounting forms that broke down charges by narrow category; stopwatches, belt gauges, special tools—and always rules, standing orders, instructions, and lists.

For the system to work in any company, these and many more details needed tending. At Tabor and Link-Belt, they were tended, more completely than anywhere else. Both companies benefited from Taylor's personal attention and gave him access to the chief executive. At both, more than at any company hiring him during the 1890s, he could do much as he pleased, at the more measured pace he preferred, as thoroughly as he liked.

And it was these model firms that Taylor's guests, after soaking up Boxly, saw up close. Link-Belt and Tabor, their examples shouted out, did work. Taylor's ideas weren't harebrained, theoretical stuff but the living flesh of industrial life—which here, down from the heights of Chestnut Hill, you could see breathe and pulse with vitality.

~

Of course, there was an element of smoke and mirrors to the Boxly show. If you looked at Taylor's life the wrong way, a little cynically, skewed just a bit, you might wonder how he could make so much out of a career riddled with failure, disappointment, and rejections. Whatever his achievements, he had infuriated thousands of workers, foremen, and bosses. He had been quietly relieved of his duties by one client, Cramp's, and fired by another, Bethlehem. At Simonds, a whole staff quit on him. He had made enemies wherever he'd gone.

Few left Boxly, it is safe to say, much aware of this. Like a tent revivalist who pries a congregation's worth of offerings out of one sick man grown well, Taylor made much of successes that could be interpreted as modest. Indeed, it was really the promise of scientific shop management, hitched to examples of real accomplishment, that Taylor, through the force of his conviction, had made into something. From his own work history, marked by hellish strife, he'd imagined a heaven of workplace fellowship.

The stories that cast a spell at Boxly were often exaggerated, distorted, or otherwise less than strictly true. For example, scholars have found serious discrepancies between Taylor's tale of the pig iron handlers and documentary accounts from the time. Taylor spoke of having "picked out" Henry Noll, when the evidence suggests Noll was merely one of the few laborers able to endure his forty-seven tons. He bragged that his search for "first class men" was the talk of a hundred miles around, and that he was lambasted by the newspapers. But no scholar has ever found a single newspaper clipping to that effect. As for the dialogue—"Noll, are you a high-priced man?"—it was almost certainly invented or, at best, re-created from vague, half-remembered snatches of conversation.

Likewise, Barth's encounter with Henry Towne. "One of the worst distortions of a story told by Mr. Taylor that I have ever come across," Barth would pencil onto the blue cover of the transcribed Boxly talk.

"This whole page is absolutely nothing but fiction," he scribbled in the margins of one page, referring to Taylor's version of events in which he, Barth, had taken part.

On the top of another page: "I am pretty well convinced that a lot of the forgoing is also fiction, but as I was not present . . . , I can't say how much."

And at another point: "From here on, there is a semblance to the facts, but they are badly mixed up."

Was all this surprising in a man who professed strict adherence to science, law, reason, and fact? Was there not some slight, gnawing inconsistency? Here was a thoroughgoing rationalist who metamorphosed a few bare facts into fables worthy of Aesop; a scientist who, once he mounted his pulpit, sounded like an evangelist; a plainspoken, shop-bred engineer who'd go to Machiavellian lengths to create the desired impression. Was there a discrepancy between all this showmanship, this choreography of effect, and the principled searcher after truth he purported to be?

Taylor held publicly to a single, sharp, exacting split between science, facts, and light on the one hand, and tradition, guesswork, and darkness on the other; he asked of his men ten hours of work that departed not one whit from the one best way fixed by fact and reason.

And yet, he made up stories or, at least, freely ornamented them.

Was Taylor simply swept along on the tide of his own enthusiasm? Certainly, the same man who held others to strict work rules and stopwatch-timed hundredths of a minute could be, toward himself, remarkably indulgent. He was routinely late for dinner and meetings, cursed at the slightest provocation, bellowed when crossed, belted out "A Warrior Bold" *con spirito*, wrote letters to his house cat, and doctored stories when it suited him. When his wife lovingly displayed a pewter platter that he didn't like, he hung a pair of dirty golf shoes in front of it—just in time for the dinner guests. Taylor enjoyed constraints on his freedom no more than anyone else and probably less. All his life, he indulged his whims, gave his enthusiasms free vent. "Almost everything I am doing is done for my own amusement," he once wrote a friend—including, presumably, his industrial tall tales.

Perhaps Taylor felt absolved from the dictates of literal truth by the larger cause that he championed. In *The Republic*, which Taylor had doubtless read at Exeter, Plato gave his philosopher-kings just such leeway: "It will be for the rulers of our city, then, if anyone, to use falsehood in dealing with citizen or enemy for the good of the State." Perhaps Taylor saw himself as acting within this genteel tradition.

Or might we better see Taylor as an artiste who can't be bothered by petty details but seeks only a higher truth? For most people, after all, precise chronology and who-said-what-to-whom slip from memory with the years. Events collapse one upon the other, new motivations are assigned past actions, inconvenient facts fade. Taylor was no different. And onstage at Boxly was hardly the place to become factually fastidious. Taylor, one scholar would say, "wrote to convince, and dramatic appeal was his method, regardless of errors of fact." In person, at Boxly, this was all the more true.

Taylor's flirtations with fiction didn't normally stretch over the line into outright falsehood. The events he described probably happened something like the way he told them, the discrepancies mostly in emphasis and detail—small enough for a sympathetic observer to dismiss them as dramatic license.

And that's just how one can best view the Boxly talks: as exercises in stagecraft. Taylor was, at heart, as much actor as engineer, and at Boxly he was in his element, all eyes upon him, commanding attention; you could no more interrupt him during those two mesmerizing hours than you could a Shakespearean soliloquy. Taylor at Boxly was how he'd be best remembered by hundreds of industrialists. There, in that great house, surrounded by spacious, flowered grounds, the whole setting served to impress his visitors with his wisdom and authority.

When Taylor gave his guests a tour of the place, the grand finale came on the balcony overlooking the valley of the Wissahickon below. Here, as Kenneth Trombley, Morris Cooke's biographer, writes, "as the assembled guests gazed in rapture at the surroundings, scores of pigeons swooped down from over the mansion and fanned out in many directions." How, Cooke wondered, did the birds all materialize, as if on cue? One day he discovered the answer:

> When everything was set, Taylor gave a signal to a maid who
> rushed post haste through the house to a window in the rear.
> There, by the wave of a handkerchief, the keeper of the pigeons was
> notified to open the doors of the bird houses.

Boxly, for Frederick Taylor, was the great stage from which he delivered his message to the world.

~

Dramatic actor was one way to view what Taylor had become since 1900, evangelist another, huckster of ideas perhaps a third. But in any case, he was no longer an engineer, and certainly he was no machinist or patternmaker. As an eighteen-year-old apprentice, he had taken that first, tentative step into the gloom of the shop where he'd met John Griffith. But that cherished time was now thirty years past, a blurred and distant memory.

Over the years, Taylor had kept in touch with Griffith, who ran their little tennis pole business for him and had done modestly well for himself. In 1899, after the death of his first wife, he had married a woman named Anna, an immigrant from England twenty years his junior and friend of his former wife. They had a house in a north Philadelphia neighborhood of clerks, carpenters, and machinists in which they lived with an Irish maid, two borders, their two young children and, in 1904, another on the way.

"Can you not come up and take supper with me some evening?"

Taylor, back from Bethlehem about a year, wrote him on October 8, 1902. "I am now living at Red Gate on School Lane. It is the old place in which Mr. Fred Kimball lived."

"I should like very much to come to see you some time," Griffith wrote back on November 20. "But when I cannot tell. I do not know where Red Gate is. What trolley will take me near it?"

He'd have his carriage pick him up, Taylor offered.

But Griffith declined. "It is very kind of you . . . but I would not like to put you to that trouble, for something might turn up that I could not go." One thing or another, mostly from Griffith's end—sick children, the press of work—kept them apart.

In his early fifties now, Griffith still grappled with money problems. The house was mortgaged and needed much care, the children always coming down sick. In 1902, he importuned Taylor, about to sink thousands into moving his boxwood, for advice on going into business to supplement his Midvale wages. It was something he'd long wanted to do but hadn't "on account of not having the cash. . . . Do you know where I could get $2000.00 on a second mortgage?"

Over the next several years, Griffith tried raising pigeons as a sideline, kept abreast of the box transplanting, and spoke often of visiting Boxly but rarely, if at all, made it to Taylor's estate. In August 1904, he invited Taylor and the boys to see his pigeons, but the visit apparently never came off. Indeed, none of their long correspondence refers to any visit that actually materialized. There is much talk, much business, but also a remoteness, as if, since their Race Street days, their paths had diverged too sharply to reconcile, as if Griffith knew his place and felt loath to trespass on Taylor's.

This last is speculation. More certain is that Taylor's first rush of mingled elation and bewilderment in Griffith's pattern shop was now only a memory, and that he'd left the factory floor long behind. Being foreman at Midvale had exiled him a little. As chief engineer he was further distanced. As a consultant he was forever the hired outsider. Even his most recent brush with a workingman's life—the winter of 1894 when he heat-treated tools and ran them on the lathes at Sellers and at Cramp's—was more than a decade past. Now, retired to Boxly, he was probably more removed from the lives of ordinary workmen than at any time since leaving Exeter.

"I can no longer afford to work for money," he'd say to anyone who'd listen. It was one of those memorable lines that, quoted again and again, contributed to his mystique, like the one about how he had worked his way up from laborer. It suggested lofty detachment and higher purpose—in a sense justly so: now, at that point in life when you begin to think of what will remain of you once you're gone, to work for money would only draw off energy properly directed to nobler ends. His system now seemed more important to him than anything as fleeting as, say, his consultant's business of the 1890s.

Over the decade before 1901, a succession of moves to towns like Fitchburg, Johnstown, and Bethlehem had introduced him to new industries and new problems, but he'd never stayed long enough to see his work reach fruition. Always there'd been trouble—Whitney breathing down his neck at the paper company, late accounting reports at Johnstown, Weymouth quitting on him at Simonds, Linderman firing him at Bethlehem. Always there'd been ignorant workmen, slimy detectives, greedy financiers. Now he needn't bother with any of them. "The years which Mrs. Taylor and I spent away from Philadelphia were at the time very trying ones," Taylor would write, in which they found themselves "obliged to mingle with people from all parts of the country . . . and in all ranks of society, and in the smallest and most out of the way places." Those trying middle years could now be transfigured into something finer—the great system that, first at Midvale, then rising up from reeking paper mills, smoky foundries, and whirring machine shops, and finally taking intellectual form in the papers he had begun to distill from his experience, now filled his life.

Taylor could well afford to devote his life to his calling. He had money enough to indulge his whims; the boxwood transplanting alone had cost something like seventeen thousand dollars, the equivalent today of a quarter million or more, and apparently he'd scarcely felt it. "After leaving Bethlehem, he was offered fabulous sums for the reorganization of other large concerns," Fred Lewis wrote later, but he considered his health and equanimity more important "to himself and to the cause for which he stood than any monetary compensation."

In a sense, Taylor was living out the Old Philadelphia tradition of genteel retirement. Just as his father retired from the law, and brother Win retired from medicine, Taylor had retired from business. Franklin Taylor didn't have to work at something for which he apparently cared little; Win didn't have to suffer irksome patients. Similarly, Fred didn't have to endure griping workers and ungrateful clients. It might have peeved him to hear it put this way, but at Boxly he had reverted to something like the life for which he had been groomed.

This overstates the case, perhaps, but not by much. For the rest of his life, Taylor struggled to advance his system, building up his idea as devotedly as any nineteenth-century millwright built a machine. "[I] now have so much work in connection with our shop management, etc.," he wrote Maunsel White during this period, "that I am nearly as busy as I used to be when introducing the system." But he no longer did it himself; he had Barth, Gantt, and later many others to do it for him. The bruising battles were now at one remove, below him, down in the fetid valley of industrial strife. Meanwhile, from his house on the hill overlooking the Wissahickon, amid the rosebushes and boxwood-lined paths, removed from the workaday trials of the shop, he was left free to pronounce the truth of the Taylor system.

7

A MERE NOTHING?

~

S INCE 1906, Taylor had corresponded with French metallurgist Henri-Louis Le Chatelier, who became the prime instrument for the diffusion of his views in France. He could scarcely have wished for a more ardent champion or one of more august reputation.

Tall, with close-cropped white hair and aristocratically chiseled cheekbones, Le Chatelier, six years older than Taylor, was a lion of French science. He had graduated from college at the head of his class in mathematics and science; enrolled at the École Polytechnique, France's elite engineering university, where he absorbed the science-rooted positivism of Auguste Comte; became full professor at the École des Mines in 1877 at the almost unseemly age of twenty-seven. He developed the platinum-rhodium thermocouple that was the basis for the pyrometer Taylor and White used at Bethlehem. He suggested the principle of the oxyacetylene torch. He proposed a law of chemical equilibrium today enshrined as the Le Chatelier principle. By 1900, he was on the faculty of the Sorbonne and an esteemed member of the French scientific pantheon.

As a young man, Le Chatelier had been deeply troubled by the roiling crowds and bloodshed of the revolutionary Paris Commune that followed France's defeat in the Franco-Prussian War. He had, by one account, "little faith in popular democracy. . . . Like Hippolyte Taine whom Le Chatelier greatly admired"—and whom Taylor had grown up hearing his father read in French at the table—"the Le Chatelier family believed it was the duty of the educated and privileged classes to provide the leadership and discipline to maintain social stability."

Le Chatelier was fifty when he visited the Paris exposition, where the high-speed steel exhibit left an indelible mark on him. Four years later, he founded the *Revue de Métallurgie* in hopes of injecting that field with "a better understanding of scientific methods of work," and soon was publishing articles on high-speed steel. One was by a Sheffield engineer who chalked up the discovery to luck. No, Le Chatelier said in a 1904 lecture, this was science at work. After all, he said later, "it had certainly required a high order of scientific observation . . . to draw such an important discovery from the carelessness of a workman."

Taylor, not surprisingly, was pleased to learn of this opinion by the esteemed Frenchman, whom he had never met. He wrote him, expressing gratitude and promising to send him the metal-cutting paper he was to present in New York. "As soon as I received the study," Le Chatelier wrote later, "I was impressed with its extraordinary importance," and he asked Taylor for permission to translate and publish it in full in his *Revue*.

Taylor was happy to grant permission and took the opportunity to include a copy of "Shop Management," which had the same seismic impact on Le Chatelier as it had on so many others. It was to apply science to industry that he'd started his *Revue*; but to him that meant industrial laboratories and the like. "I had not foreseen the possibility of extending the domain of science over all the realm of industry, including questions of organization, commercial questions, labor questions, etc."—which is just what the Taylor system promised to do. Le Chatelier was "ashamed to find the science of a practical man infinitely more developed than my own. From that day on I felt myself obliged . . . [to become] an apostle of the Taylor System."

In the *Revue*, he published virtually all Taylor wrote. When the metal-cutting, belting, and shop management papers were translated into French in late 1907, Le Chatelier's introduction to them, Taylor wrote Maunsel White, was "complimentary and flattering." Especially pleasing was Le Chatelier's insight that "all three papers are intimately related . . . and merely represent examples of the larger work in which we are engaged."

Among those inspired by reading "Shop Management" in the *Revue* was Georges de Ram, mechanical director of the Renault automobile factory in Billancourt, outside Paris, who soon was adapting some of its methods. The following fall, he wrote Taylor with a copy of his own *Revue* article, "Some Notes on a Trial Application of the Taylor System." This "trial" had yielded a 100 percent production increase in a shop employing about a hundred and thirty workers. Stopwatch study in other Renault shops had convinced him that the average worker "rarely furnishes, even while working under piece rate, more than three or four hours of effective work per day," which was about what Taylor had said of Midvale workers.

Stopwatch-set piece rates, said de Ram, meant that only truly able workers earned high wages, a "fact of natural selection" that quashed favoritism; mediocre workers, weeded out by the stopwatch's relentless objectivity, simply gave up. Early on, many workers had quit, "either because they didn't want to work at the rapid speed imposed on them" or couldn't.

Taylor wrote to Carl Barth and others about the de Ram article. "This is certainly a very good showing," he said. The translation of his papers was paying off. Taylorism had its first beachhead in Europe.

∽

After "On the Art of Cutting Metals" came out in 1906, Nils Lilienberg, a Swedish engineer who'd met Taylor in Bethlehem, wrote its author wondering whether he could translate it into Swedish, in time for a conference of iron makers the following May. That would be fine, replied Taylor.

∽

In 1901, the journal of the Verein Deutscher Ingenieure, the ASME's counterpart in Germany, issued a lengthy report on high-speed steel, which many of its members had seen demonstrated in Paris the previous year. It was the VDI, under the leadership of Georg Schlesinger, a design engineer with the Loewe Company, a large machine tool maker, that would take the lead in introducing Taylorism to Germany. In a VDI lecture in Cologne in 1914, Schlesinger would term the Paris demonstrations of high-speed steel nothing less than "a landmark in the history of mankind."

In 1904, the year after Taylor delivered it in Saratoga, "Shop Management" appeared in German translation.

On September 10, 1907, Taylor wrote Maunsel White, " 'On the Art of Cutting Metals' is now being translated into German, to be published by Julius Springer & Co. of Berlin."

~

But back in the States, paradoxically, high-speed steel, the breakthrough that had brought Taylor world attention, was under attack in the courts. In February 1903, Bethlehem brought a patent infringement suit against Bement-Miles, a large machine tool maker, for using the Taylor-White process to make its own tool steel. The case proved anything but open-and-shut.

Aligned with Bement was most of the powerful English tool steel industry based in Sheffield. After Paris, Sheffield steelmakers were "aghast, even disbelieving" about what they'd seen, writes English historian Geoffrey Tweedale. But soon they realized that the power of the Taylor-White tools was owed to special heat treatment of familiar steels, not to some mysterious new alloy. "Galvanized by the Taylor-White findings and faced with a major challenge to their livelihood," they embarked on research of their own and developed improved fast-cutting steels, including the tungsten-chromium-vanadium alloy known today as 18-4-1. Within a few years, they had regained much of the market.

Should the Bethlehem patents be judged valid, however, their success stood at risk. So the Sheffielders established—formally, if secretly—a High Speed Steel Association, which "marshaled its evidence, recruited the best metallurgical and legal brains . . . and sent them to America," all to sing the same chorus: that Taylor-White steel was nothing new and hence not protectable by patent.

"At last," White wrote Taylor on August 29, 1905, "the suit on the T.W. patents is to begin." Whether or not Taylor knew of the forces gathering against Bethlehem, he could not have been too sanguine.

Years before, in a letter to Ernest Wright, he had written, "I have very little confidence, in ninety-nine cases out of one hundred, in getting any decent return from an invention. . . . [Usually], the improvement is stolen even if it is patented."

On January 16 of the following year, Taylor, subpoenaed by the defendants—that is, Bethlehem Steel's courtroom foe—was sworn in. How, defendant's counsel, F. P. Warfield, wanted to know, did he first get the idea for the new heat treatment?

"I have had no practical connection with the treatment of tool steel for several years," Taylor replied, "and my memory has grown rather hazy." The inventor couldn't recall the origins of his invention? Here was the first of many answers that would enrage the presiding judge.

A week later he was asked, "You are the Frederick W. Taylor who on October 20, 1899, filed an application for Letters Patent of the United States for metal cutting tool and method of making the same, are you not?

"I am unable to state without seeing a copy of the application whether I am the Frederick W. Taylor whom you refer to or not," replied the witness, whoever he was. "I have entirely forgotten the date on which I filed an application for any patent relating to tool steel."

So it went. He couldn't answer the questions because he hadn't various reports and memoranda in front of him and so couldn't "swear to exact facts and dates." He did "not remember with sufficient exactness." He didn't know what Mr. Warfield meant by the "etc." of his question.

After many such exchanges, Taylor was handed a copy of the patent and asked whether it "embodies the subject matter" to which his testimony referred. No, said Taylor, toying with his interrogator; the patent referred to the heat treatment of tools, while his testimony had so far focused on his memory.

Uncooperative? He was being impossible.

After this abortive appearance in 1906, whether Taylor might appear for the plaintiff, Bethlehem, lay in doubt; he plainly did not want to. "I do not propose to bother myself and possibly injure my health in worrying over the affairs of the Bethlehem Steel Co.," he wrote Maunsel White—unless they paid him well for his trouble. Failing payment, he would insist on "a substantial interest in the patent," through a license to make saws and milling cutters from the patented steel.

The money didn't matter to him, he told White, but he'd be damned if he would give Bethlehem anything. His firing five years before still rankled. Besides, what had he to gain from a Bethlehem victory? He had sold the American rights long before (though he retained half the foreign). So while he hoped, out of simple pride, to see the patents sustained, he preferred not to lift a finger on Bethlehem's behalf. It was almost fair to say he was at war with both sides—which for Taylor, of course, was nothing new.

"I hope that they may win without either of our testimony," he wrote White on April 9, 1907. "If they win at all, they will certainly win without mine, except on the terms already offered, and I should feel sorry if these were accepted."

The high-stakes case went on forever; the testimony of dozens of witnesses would fill some five thousand typewritten pages. Not until February 12, 1908, did Taylor walk up the steps from Walnut Street to the three-story brick structure in downtown Philadelphia that housed the offices of Francis T. Chambers, Bethlehem's counsel, to again submit himself to questioning. But he was not doing so, he'd reiterated to White six days before, "out of sentimental regard for the Bethlehem Steel Company . . . , when they have done nothing but be as mean as they could to me whenever they had the chance."

Once on the stand, however, Taylor poured prodigious effort into his testimony, keeping two or three stenographers busy for four days. He came away exhausted; he didn't like being questioned or challenged. His friend Fred Lewis remembered that "The intense strain of this ordeal had immediately a detrimental effect upon his health and it took him some time to recuperate."

He and Lou headed south, for a golf vacation at the Hotel Bon Air, in Augusta, Georgia. "The weather was like midsummer," he wrote White on his return. "We both improved in health, and I got thoroughly rested from the overstrain in testifying." As to the case, he felt "very strongly that the Bethlehem Co. will win."

All through the summer and fall of 1908, his optimism persisted. Should White visit him in Philadelphia, he added in a letter that September, he must come see "the latest product of high speed steel"— new milling cutters that cut swathes eighteen inches wide and could chew up almost a ton of steel an hour.

The verdict came on January 29, 1909: Judge Joseph Cross of the Circuit Court of New Jersey overturned the patents. The judge questioned the basis of Taylor's "breaking-down point," the heat-treating temperature that the Taylor-White steel was supposed to magically transcend. He cited testimony from England that Taylor and White had "discovered" only what was well known among half the shops of Sheffield. And he found that if Taylor and White had done anything, it was to perfect an apparatus, presumably the temperature-controlled lead bath. The tight control it afforded represented the real breakthrough, he ruled—yet of this the patents said nothing. "If in the race, the patentees have surpassed others, it has not been through novelty or procedure, but by means of special facilities, apparatus and methods not embraced in the patents."

"This was one of the greatest surprises that I have ever had," Taylor wrote White on February 5, 1909. He suspected "influence of some kind" at work, pictured the judge as "completely partisan," and expressed confidence in a successful appeal.

What Taylor didn't mention was Judge Cross's extraordinary condemnation of him and another witness. "Steel Witnesses Rebuked by Court," the *New York Times* headline read. Subpoenaed by the defendant, Cross wrote, Taylor "showed a lack of memory, and an unwillingness to testify, as to matters concerning which . . . he must have had more knowledge than he chose to reveal." When called by Bethlehem, he first demanded a "prohibitive" fee, then testified only when he had secured his patent license—whereupon "a marked improvement in his attitude [became] noticeable."

To the Bethlehem lawyers in their appeal, Judge Cross's ruling was "the most amazing document ever handed down by a court as its opinion." Taylor's request for payment, they pointed out, had been intended to be prohibitive; he preferred not to testify at all and consented in the end only to relieve his friend White, who was ill. As for presumably secret licensing agreements, they had never been secret at all. And of course Mr. Taylor's facility with the facts was greater the second time, since he had spent the past year reviewing them for his metal-cutting paper.

"Having utterly and absurdly failed to shake [Taylor's] testimony by cross-examination," Bethlehem's lawyers concluded,

> defendant's counsel . . . [threw] mud at him and [tried] to blacken
> a character and reputation which stand as high as those of any man

in America and are recognized all over the world as ranking this
American engineer among those great men

—by now they were fairly falling all over themselves—

who have, during the last half century, been mainly instrumental
in the wonderful forward strides of the civilized world in material
prosperity.

This last assertion, one could argue, was actually true. But it was
also true that, throughout the whole business, Taylor had proven himself no paragon of principle. At one point, White had written him
about some molybdenum tools that lay outside the terms of the patent
and cut as fast as an improved grade of Taylor-White steel. Steer clear
of the whole area, Taylor wrote back. "Until you have personally investigated this matter, of course, you have no knowledge of it"—and so
could answer no embarrassing questions about it. Moreover, White
should urge Bethlehem not to make such tools. "If we win our suit . . . ,
molybdenum tools should for as long a period as possible be given a
black eye." Judge Cross may have had the details a little off, but he had
seen into Fred Taylor.

Around this time, Taylor received a second blow, if from another
quarter entirely. An odd-looking, Y-shaped putter he had patented in
1905 and freely used in golf tournaments, he wrote White on May 17,
1909, "has just been declared beyond the pale of the law by the Golf
Committee at St. Andrews [in Scotland], so that I am in mourning to
this extent. I think it would be the last straw if the courts were also to go
back on the tool steel business."

That is just what they did. On July 21, the Third Circuit Court of
Appeals affirmed Judge Cross's ruling. "I have been so thoroughly disgusted ever since . . . that I don't want to hear anything of the subject,"
Taylor wrote White in September. And Bethlehem had decided not to
appeal further, so "it is finally settled, and our patent is declared null
and void."

∾

Such was the ruling of the court. The ruling of history was otherwise.

In 1904, Harvard professor of metallurgy Albert Sauveur had argued "that the Taylor-White process constitutes the most important advance made in the metallurgy of steel since the invention of the Bessemer" and open-hearth processes. More than a quarter century later, the comparison to Bessemer found support from an unlikely source. Renowned Sheffield metallurgist Harry Brearley allowed that

> the unbiased student is impressed by the importance of Taylor and
> White's work. After the publication and demonstration of their
> results, it was easy for steel manufacturers to claim prior
> knowledge of their disclosures; but . . . those who claimed to know
> before the event either did not know what they knew, or were
> singularly lacking in commercial aptitude.
>
> . . .
>
> [The Taylor-White] process is delightfully simple, a mere
> nothing one might say, which had been done many times before,
> but the merit of the discovery and the feature of it which compels
> admiration lies in the courage to ignore time-worn precept and
> reach success by roads which, "according to Cocker," should lead
> to direct failure. In this respect the Taylor-White discovery may
> presumably stand alongside that of Henry Bessemer.

In 1925, engineering journalist Fred Miller declared the "court's decision entirely at variance with common knowledge and informed conviction. Taylor and Maunsel White will always be credited as the real inventors of high speed steel, as they really were, the courts notwithstanding."

More recently, English steel historian Tweedale has observed that while it might be simplistic to say Taylor and White had "invented" anything as evolutionary as high-speed steel, nonetheless "the claim that the crucible steel men knew all along about the heat treatment for high speed steel is not entirely supported by the facts. Otherwise," he asks tellingly, "why did Paris come as such a shock to them?"

Months after the final ruling, it still rankled both of the men whose names would be forever linked to the discovery. On April 29, 1910, White wrote Taylor, "The failure to sustain our patent so filled me with disgust that I retired into the hole of silence and tried to forget it."

On May 2, Taylor wrote back, "I have been in the same frame of mind as you regarding the loss of the Taylor-White patents. I simply don't allow myself to think about the subject, or I should be in a perpetual rage."

8

BEHOLD THE SOWER

~

CLIMB THE NARROW STAIRS at the back of the church, open a small wood door, enter the organ room, wend your way along a narrow passage flanked by organ pipes of every size and shape, and enter a second, smaller room even more cluttered with pipes. Step along a narrow catwalk, open yet another door, and there, abruptly, is the Taylor window, set aglow by the light of the sun.

"Presented in Loving Memory of Frederick Winslow Taylor," it reads along the base of this tall window of stained and painted glass. It is a handsome piece of work, alive with color. But it omits all reference to the industrial world in which Taylor toiled; there are no smokestacks, machine tools, or stopwatches in this artist's vision. Rather, we see a muscled, blond Adonis resembling Mikhail Baryshnikov clad in a flowing robe, strolling along a country road, with the sun, low on the horizon, at his back. The artist has frozen him in midstride, as he reaches across his body to a basket at his hip.

BEHOLD A SOWER WENT FORTH TO SOW

reads the ribbon of words emblazoned across the top of the window. And mirroring it at the bottom:

THE SOWER SOWETH THE WORD

The reference is to Mark 4 and its parable of the sower: The seeds of divine truth, says Jesus, sometimes alight on stony ground, sometimes among thorns destined to grow up and strangle them, sometimes are devoured by birds, only occasionally find fertile, receptive earth.

The window was installed in 1929 in the new Lincoln Drive home of the Unitarian church that Taylor's mother had helped found in 1865. And in both its religious flavor and its omission of industrial content, it deftly sums up Taylor's life after Bethlehem: he had left the shop behind but had abstracted from his experiences there truths he felt could save the world. At Boxly, and for the rest of his life, he became the zealous purveyor of a new gospel of industrial enlightenment.

Rarely has an ostensibly secular movement so embraced religious language and imagery. Words like creed, cult, gospel, dogma, faith, and prophet dog any account of its history. To one Swedish visitor, Taylor's relationship to scientific management was "akin to that of Luther in Protestantism." To Glenn Porter, writing in a multivolume *History of Technology*, "Scientific management took on some of the trappings of a kind of secular religion; Taylor was the messiah, and his followers, who spread the word, were (and still are) commonly referred to as 'disciples.'" They showed greater or lesser obedience to his doctrines, at times went out on their own independently of him; but always Taylor was their acknowledged master. Even papers that clashed with his views would often include an almost ritualized nod of obeisance, as toward a Jesus, Luther, or Marx beyond criticism.

"Let me tell you, my friends," one disciple, Robert T. Kent, would recall of the early days, "that no group of crusaders ever battled for their cause with greater energy, greater faith, than the men in this movement in those early days battled for scientific management." Kent quoted Jim Dodge to the same effect: "'Taylor in this movement is comparable to the Almighty. There are a few apostles, Gantt and Barth and some others. There are a number of disciples, such as myself, and you, and you, and you. The rest are all members of the church.' That was the spirit that sustained us."

Whatever their proper ecclesiastical category, it was these men who spread the gospel after Taylor retired. At first, Taylor had apparently not yet decided to quit consulting entirely. In a letter to a Western Electric Company official in late 1901, he said only that he planned "to take a long vacation, probably lasting one or two years"; it lasted the rest of his life. And with it began his practice of passing on jobs to colleagues. "The best man whom I know of now for the introduction of this system of piece work," his letter went on, "is Mr. H. L. Gantt, who has been my assistant for a number of years."

Indeed, Gantt was now a consultant himself and, over the next few years, took on such clients as the American Locomotive Company in Schenectady, New York; Sayles Bleachery in Rhode Island, where his four-year stint was marred by strikes; and Brighton Mills, in Passaic, New Jersey. Many of these jobs came through Taylor, and at each Gantt introduced one or another variant of the Taylor system.

By early 1906, only three men had the Taylor imprimatur. "After making a number of what may be called almost failures, at least very qualified successes," he wrote an old Bethlehem associate, Gantt

> has at least learned the art so well that he is now engaged in systematizing two companies and making a very great success of the work. Mr. Barth has given his whole time ever since leaving Bethlehem to learning how to introduce our system of management, and only last March undertook to systematize the first company on his own account [Yale & Towne]—that is, without my continual direct supervision.

The third man was Horace King Hathaway. As an eighteen-year-old native of San Francisco, Hathaway had ten years earlier hitched a freight car and wound up in Philadelphia. He got a job as an apprentice machinist at Midvale, then still suffused with Taylor's spirit. By 1902, he had worked his way up to foreman. In time, he landed at Tabor, learned mathematics, cost accounting, and the rudiments of the Taylor system from Barth, emerged as one of Taylor's fair-haired boys and, ultimately, became vice president of the firm under Fred Lewis. He later helped introduce the Taylor system to other companies.

Normally, a Taylor lieutenant would tour a prospective client's plant and submit a preliminary report. Toward the end of 1907, Barth and Gantt, along with Taylor, toured Pennsylvania's Lehigh Coal and Navigation Company. They would start slowly, Barth and Gantt wrote two weeks later, at first keeping the men on day rate. In time, they'd issue instruction cards for machining, introduce functional foreman-ship, a planning room, and the rest of Taylor's managerial parapher-nalia. Their fee was fifty dollars a day each, plus living expenses. They'd expect to put in about fifteen days per month.

This job apparently didn't materialize, but dozens of others did. Over twenty years, his son would later estimate, Carl Barth introduced scientific management to some fifty companies. From 1901, when he left Bethlehem, to his death a few years after Taylor's, Gantt did about the same.

Meanwhile, outside the immediate Taylor circle stood others who embraced his ideas but never earned his imprimatur. Among these was the unforgettable Frank Gilbreth, a big bulldog of a man who, with his wife, Lillian, would become as celebrated in some countries as Taylor.

Gilbreth had started out as an apprentice bricklayer in 1885. On his first day on the job, the story goes, the seventeen-year-old was placed under two men who were supposed to show him how to lay bricks. But, he noticed, they didn't do it the way they said to do it; they didn't even do it the same way. What, he wondered, was the right way? Before long, Gilbreth was foreman. By age twenty-seven he'd set up his own construction company. In the years since, he'd made bricklaying into a small science and introduced numerous refinements to the ancient craft, including an adjustable scaffold that reduced the bricklayer's stooping and reaching.

Gilbreth, whose gushing enthusiasm and prodigious fathering of twelve children would inspire that minor classic of a memoir, *Cheaper by the Dozen* (made into a 1950 motion picture), was the consummate showman. A favorite stunt, his son recounted later, was to arrive at a construction site with his wife and start mouthing off to the bricklayers about how easy their work was. *Awright, mister, maybe you wanna try it?* someone would say. With a show of reluctance, Gilbreth would remove his coat and tie and hand them to his wife. Then he'd take trowel in hand and give it a flip to test its weight. "And with that," his son recorded, "bricks and mortar would start to fly."

Along the way, Gilbreth fell into the orbit of Taylor's thinking. One day in the late 1890s, Sanford Thompson had been doing time studies at a construction site in Cambridge, Massachusetts, where Gilbreth was contractor. The two men met. "He was much interested in the [time] studies," Thompson wrote, "but the idea was new to him." Later, Gilbreth read "Shop Management" and, as we've seen, was smitten. One late fall day in 1907, Jim Dodge's second-in-command at Link-Belt, Conrad Lauer, introduced him to Taylor.

Gilbreth was not long back from San Francisco, to which, after the earthquake the previous year, he had gone in pursuit of the big construction jobs he thought would make him rich; "I should not be surprised," he wrote home from amid the rubble, "if I land 10—20—or even 30 million dollars worth of work here in the next year or two." He didn't, and returned back east. Now he was attending an ASME meeting in the new Engineering Center in New York that Andrew Carnegie had lavished upon the profession, a thirteen-story building located near the city's new public library off Fifth Avenue, that brought together the offices, libraries, and meeting rooms of several engineering societies. You came in off Thirty-ninth Street, into a broad foyer tiled in Tennessee marble, flanked by a dozen columns and furnished with couches and chairs in red leather. And there, in a corner of the lobby, beside a bas-relief of Carnegie and a large bronze tablet honoring his gift, Frank Gilbreth met Frederick Taylor. For years, at least until their friendship soured, he would declare, "Here on this spot I met the only man who has brought a message to the world in the last twenty-five years."

For Taylor, the meeting was not quite that memorable, though he was impressed by the younger man. "I had two or three hours talk with our friend Mr. Gilbreth, the contractor," Taylor wrote Sanford Thompson. Gilbreth, it seems, had brought the costs of reinforced concrete to below that of brick or wood. "He is very much interested in our work, particularly the study of unit costs." Thompson wrote back, perhaps a little jealous, "Gilbreth is one of the brightest men I know in the line of construction work, and understands details the most thoroughly. [But] he is a great bluffer, and has the reputation of not being always 'on the square.' "

When the two men met again that December, Gilbreth outlined his method of studying a task, teasing apart its individual motions, and reconstituting it more efficiently. "Motion study," he called it, and if not fundamentally different from what Taylor had done since at least 1884, it surely differed in emphasis. Gilbreth didn't bother timing a task; for him the idea was to eliminate its nonessential motions—which was only a by-product of Taylor's time study, not the focus. He claimed to have reduced the number of motions needed to lay bricks from eighteen to five, increasing a skilled man's output from 175 to 350 per hour.

Perhaps, Taylor suggested, Gilbreth could collaborate on the bricklaying book Sanford Thompson was writing (replacing him, Taylor, as Thompson's coauthor). No thank you, said Gilbreth. "He did not want motion study presented as a tail to Taylor's kite, and he was satisfied with his collaborator at home," his biographer, Edna Yost, wrote later.

The collaborator was his wife, who would earn a doctorate in psychology from Brown, outlive him by many years, and garner her own distinct place in industrial engineering. At the time, "when to be an affiliate of Taylor in any way was a great honor and gave one a certain stamp," his wife wrote in 1954, Gilbreth's decision to go it alone was a bold one.

A month later, Gilbreth paid his first visit to Boxly and toured Tabor. At first, Gilbreth said later, he "fought Dr. Taylor early and often," finding few parallels between construction work and that of "a machine shop, inspecting bicycle balls, and a half dozen other things that I wasn't much interested in." In time, however, he was won over. "I am absorbing the ideas that you have given me as fast as I am mentally capable," he wrote Taylor in February 1908, "but I am afraid that the whole thing will result in my having 'Tayloritis.' " By March, he was planning to install the Taylor system on a construction job in Massachusetts. For the next few years, he would be among Taylor's most zealous supporters.

In the 1910s and later, Barth, Gantt, Hathaway, Morris Cooke, Gilbreth, and ultimately many others descended on factories and mills, doing much as Taylor had done back in the 1890s. They studied the machines, standardized, classified, organized, timed operations, designed forms, set up accounting systems. Here was the advance guard for the waves of efficiency experts and management consultants that were to become a permanent feature of America's industrial landscape.

Even Taylor's most loyal lieutenants often dispensed with functional foremanship; this was one frequent deviation from purity, and there were others. Inevitably, each gave Taylor's principles his own twist or emphasis. Gilbreth emphasized the motion study he would always claim as his intellectual property. Barth concentrated on machine shops, his earliest and most congenial home. Gantt, possessed by black depressions that sometimes erupted in terrible rages, was surprisingly flexible, willing to deviate from the rule of abstract system in ways Taylor was not.

And yet all in all, Daniel Nelson concluded in a 1974 study of dozens of "installations" of the Taylor system, his disciples hewed to the Taylorist line with surprising fealty. Even Gilbreth, on the periphery, could write Taylor of his work for one client that, in Nelson's words, "he was following ' "Shop Management" from cover to cover,' and a detailed account of his activities indicates that he was thoroughly conventional in most areas."

When Barth had been at Yale & Towne for a while, an anonymous artist drew a lighthearted cartoon entitled "The Planning Dept. Baseball Line-up," which caricatured company men in the field or at bat. One was a time-study man, complete with clipboard and stopwatch, absorbed in a study of batting. Another was Carl Barth, with his small tense face, glasses, and goatee, ruminating, "I will have that speeded up." In the background, a stack billows smoke, identified as "Taylor System records." Taylor himself is nowhere to be seen, the butt of no barbs, no in-jokes. His spirit informs the scene, but he is gone in body.

Abstracted into ideas, principles, methods, cautions, sayings, aphorisms, and advice, one man's years of shop experience was now, through the work of his disciples, seeping into the life of the modern factory. First Midvale and Bethlehem. Then Link-Belt and Tabor. Tomorrow, America and the world.

9

Λ STILLNESS

〜

CONRAD AIKEN, oldest of the four siblings left orphans in Savannah, grew up with his uncle in Cambridge, Massachusetts, and went to school in Concord, where, he wrote later, the stain of his father's murderous act felt ineradicable. Then, it was off to Harvard and literary distinction. In his lightly fictionalized *Ushant*, Aiken described himself as "orphaned and further orphaned by the adoption of [brothers] R. and K. by Cousin Ted [Fred Taylor]." Rob Taylor, for one, suspected that despite twenty thousand dollars inherited from a rich aunt and a similar amount from his parents, Conrad resented the still more comfortable circumstances of his brothers and sister. On the other hand, it seemed to one relative that growing up as Taylors made Rob and Kemp into "a couple of nice stuffed shirts."

Staffed by a cook, a downstairs maid, an upstairs maid, and a half dozen gardeners forever mowing the grass and manicuring the grounds, Boxly was indeed well-ordered, its rhythms set by rule. For the children, first thing every morning, it was prunes—big fat ones in a jar, Rob recalled. Then a bath, and breakfast at seven. They all had to be down for meals on time; the hour was tolled by three tall clocks, in the dining room, the living room, and on the staircase, which could be heard all over the house. "So there was no excuse."

Always, after dinner, came a half hour or so of reading at the table—Dickens, perhaps, or a Hopalong Cassidy story—with Put Mut perched on their father's shoulder. Even this came under rules of law. No reading ahead—that was cheating—and every book, once begun, must be finished. Each child got an allowance and had to itemize his expenditures. "It had to balance or you were sent back to reconcile your accounts," Rob remembered. Rules covered everything, and infractions, as at the service academies, had to be "walked off"—fifty, a hundred, or more times around the big driveway in front of the house. Occasionally, as rebuke for youthful lying or cheating, Taylor hauled out his razor strop, doubled it up, and laid to.

None of this seems to have particularly devastated Rob or Kemp. Kempton went off to Exeter, where he did well, later attended Haverford College and Penn medical school, and had a career as a surgeon. Robert graduated as an engineer from Cornell but spent most of his life as an investment banker. Both served the shop stints their father favored; both led long, productive lives. Elizabeth, who went to boarding school at the age of about twelve, later suffered from mental illness. In her thirties, after her adoptive father was dead, she was committed to a mental hospital. Aiken biographer Edward Butscher has suggested that Taylor "might have contributed to Elizabeth's eventual breakdown, at least by maintaining his household in strict conformity with unbending genteel mores." But flimsy speculation is all this seems to be, and it takes scant account of her condition's possible hereditary origins or of the impact of the horrific events in Savannah.

Of course, Taylor's rigidities, excesses, and idiosyncrasies were enough to drive anyone a little crazy. "When I am away from home," he replied in 1909 to an invitation to stay at a Harvard professor's house in Cambridge, "I am very apt to get sleepless, and to avoid this I have to actually lie down for a considerable time during each day." This sleeplessness was apparently a code word for a range of afflictions suffered during these years and doubtless earlier. All his life, he had been plagued with insomnia and by nightmares, some of them recurring. In one, he found himself trapped within a maze of machinery. One piece of the machine angled off this way, another attached to something else, and so on. As Robert, whom he told about this nightmare machine, recalled, "he was spending the whole night trying to find out why the damned thing worked or didn't work."

Since retiring, Taylor had become preoccupied with his health. Talk of illness and death troubled him, Copley tells us, and a species of fatalism, or so it seemed to Robert, marked him during these years. Through worry and overwork, he felt, he'd depleted his vital energy; indeed, it was so as not to sap it further that he'd ostensibly shied away from the patent fight. Somehow, he saw himself as having a delicate constitution. Commiserating with an English correspondent toward the end of 1907, he wrote that he needed his afternoon naps

in order to sleep properly at night. It is certainly a most distressing trouble, and you have my sympathy. Be sure, however, not to break down more than once or twice in this way, or it will be likely to leave you more or less permanently disabled, as I am.

But if Frederick Taylor was disabled, it was in ways invisible to mere mortals. When a magazine tracked him down a few years later, he struck its reporter as "a hale, ruddy man. . . , a royal boniface, a hypnotic talker, and a wag in his way." When he pursued new interests it was always the Taylor way. Finding it difficult to maintain Boxly's putting green, he studied grass growing for twelve years with the same single-mindedness he'd once poured into metal cutting. He had prime turf imported from all over the country. With his gardener, he performed hundreds of experiments the results of which, toward the end of his life, he distilled into a five-part treatise for *Country Life* magazine that could have made a substantial book.

Letters dictated to his children while vacationing with Lou in Georgia in 1909 erupt with vitality, are rife with opinions, impressions, and advice. He'd played golf in a foursome with the president of Columbia University, but that worthy "did not display any very vast ability at the game." He wanted his boys "to do some good solid work this Spring in baseball, I mean really practicing and working hard over it, so that in a year or so you will be able to make one of the teams."

At least twice during this period, he wrote, through the boys, to his cat. "Dear Put," he began.

> I was very much pleased to note the progress you are making on the typewriter, as well as to see the improvement in your English style. At times I have thought that your diction was not altogether plain and that your style was somewhat involved, but this letter shows a marked improvement . . .
>
> By this time I think you must be pretty well convinced that your policy on using excessive tact and giving delicate suggestions to those boys is not working altogether satisfactorily. Of course you are right in doing everything possible to make them less runty and stop them from reading newspapers and get them out of doors . . .
>
> . . .
>
> Those boys require different treatment. My suggestion is to give them five minutes grace at every meal and then simply bite. You will find this will beat tact all hollow.

Fred Taylor, as 1910 neared, had lost little of his old verve.

Essential to Taylor's well-being during the Boxly years was golf, which he pursued relentlessly and urged on anyone who'd listen. He often told Barth, for example, that golf would improve his health; Barth, an avid cyclist who would outlive him by many years, couldn't be bothered. "If you would only take up that game," Taylor wrote hard-drinking Maunsel White, "I feel very sure that your future happiness and success in life would be entirely assured, and I should be most delighted to act as your guide, philosopher and friend in initiating you into proper methods."

Taylor's "proper methods," of course, struck other golfers as bizarre, prompting titters like those his spoon-shaped tennis racket had aroused years before at Newport. His driver was close to a foot longer than most; with shoulder raised and leg bent, he'd screw up into a strange and fearful position that reminded onlookers of a watch spring or else a human grasshopper. Of course, he'd regularly drive the ball two hundred and fifty yards. Besides, he'd say to the boys of such ridicule, "Look at the [tournament] mugs I've got."

Some of his clubs had a specially roughened face, which imparted backspin, so that when the ball landed on the green it was apt to stop dead. That was fine, except that it mercilessly tore up the covers of the balls.

His two-handled putter, barred by golf authorities in 1909, looked like none before or since. *American Golfer* ran a photo of him using it. "Mr. Taylor does not putt in the orthodox manner," its caption dryly noted. Patented in 1905, the putter was Y-shaped with forked projections on either side that rested against his arms; he'd face the hole—ball between his feet, putter gripped in front where the three legs of the Y met—and swing it like a croquet mallet. His nephew Edward Clark, with whom he played for the rest of his life and who was by now a strapping six-foot-four adult, referred to it as "that thing you putt with—which is indeed too sad for words."

In May 1909, on their twenty-fifth wedding anniversary, young Clark sent his aunt and uncle a congratulatory telegram along with a gift that Taylor, in thanking him, described as "very practical. . . . Knowing your strong inclination toward strong liquors, particularly sarsaparilla and root beer, we are not at all surprised." One can only imagine. Wrote Lou, "We celebrated our Silver Wedding standing in our wedding costumes before the open fireplace [at Boxly], surrounded by family and friends."

Even before moving to Boxly, Taylor had placed himself in the care of Dr. Judson Daland, who kept offices on South Eighteenth Street, near fashionable Rittenhouse Square. At least by 1905, he was bringing in the whole family for yearly checkups. "You went in to his office in Philadelphia, and he had urine and blood samples analyzed and gave everyone a complete examination," recalled Robert. "This Dr. Daland was really a lad who was way ahead of his time."

A few years younger than Taylor, he had earned his M.D. from the University of Pennsylvania in 1882 and five years later was elected to a fellowship in the College of Physicians of Philadelphia; his sponsors included, among other medical lights, Dr. William Osler, soon destined for fame at Johns Hopkins. At the time Taylor became his patient, he was professor of clinical medicine at the Medico-Chirurgical College of Philadelphia and had written articles across a broad range of subjects, from nephritis, dysentery, and cholera to hysterical seizures.

Daland attacked medicine as Taylor did work, bringing to it all the power of an emerging science and, to his patient care, a measured, coolly scientific style attractive to Taylor. Writing in 1904 to Sanford

Thompson, who sought advice on behalf of his sister, Taylor described Daland as "very slow in making a diagnosis and I doubt whether he would be willing to give any opinion without seeing and talking with your sister several times."

Daland diagnosed Taylor as slightly diabetic and ordered him to cut his sugar intake. Robert remembers his father's diet as remarkably regular: an orange for breakfast, which he cut into sixths with a special serrated knife; shredded wheat, milk, and some sugar substitute, probably saccharin or glycerin. For dinner, it was meat and potatoes with vegetables from the Boxly garden, which grew "wonderful asparagus and peas that were out of this world," recalled Robert. "You could eat these right out of the pod they were so sweet."

Easeful, healthy living: Fred Taylor had got religion. He was through with the long hours and the stress that were his lot in the 1890s. It was a person's *duty* to take care of himself, he'd corral his friends to tell them. Once, while ill, Sanford Thompson heard from Taylor that he should take it easy on that book about concrete he was supposed to be finishing. "It is really of comparatively little consequence whether the book comes out, while it is of great moment that you should not draw too much on your nervous energy." He, Taylor, had always overdone things, allowed his enthusiasms to run away with him. But no more; his health came first.

Later, when Frank Copley began his Taylor biography, he asked a physician "to lay down the law as to how I should live and work." The prescription: smoke only so many cigarettes a day, drink no alcohol, keep scrupulously to his diet, walk two or three miles daily, and exercise three afternoons at the YMCA. "When I told Mrs. Taylor something of this," he wrote Morris Cooke in 1917, "she allowed that the spirit of Mr. Taylor must be taking possession of me."

In 1910, John D. Rockefeller donated a hundred million dollars to the foundation that would bear his name. Mark Twain and Mary Baker Eddy, founder of Christian Science, died. Halley's Comet passed the sun. Nineteen persons were killed when, during a labor dispute, a bomb went off at the *Los Angeles Times*. Charlie Chaplin, a British music hall performer, toured the U.S. with a vaudeville act. The population of the United States stood at ninety million, New Mexico and

Arizona were invited into the Union, and Woodrow Wilson was elected governor of New Jersey.

Meanwhile, visitors kept coming to Boxly, the mother church of Taylorism, the Vatican from which the new faith spread. From the house on the hill over the Wissahickon, lines of influence radiated to the world. By May 1910, "Shop Management" had been translated into French, German, Russian, Dutch, and Swedish. The Taylor system, as many now called it, was spreading.

~

In September 1910, Taylor's father died.

Just the previous Thanksgiving someone—perhaps the Taylor children, perhaps the Clark cousins—wrote a bit of doggerel in honor of their grandfather, to the tune of "Billy Boy":

> It is you we toast today, Grandpa T, Grandpa T!
> It is you we toast today, Grandpa Taylor!
> We are thankful for a lot,
> Of the things that we have got,
> But most of all for you, dear Grandpa Taylor!

And so it went, telling how this beloved old man had mended their toys, watched their investments, enjoyed a good life, and been blessed with a fine wife and children.

> We will set our watch by yours, Grandpa T, Grandpa T,
> We will set our watch by yours, Grandpa Taylor,
> Then when we are eighty-six
> We perhaps will have your tricks,
> For cheating Father Time, dear Grandpa Taylor.

But he couldn't cheat Father Time forever. He was up in Manchester, visiting Mary, Clarence, and the children, when the stroke seized him, as he sat in a chair near the first tee of the Ekwanok golf course, set within a bowl of breathtaking mountain greenness. His right side paralyzed, "he carefully arranged his right hand and leg so that no one would know that anything had happened," Taylor recounted, and waited while the boys finished their round.

A little later, bound for the last green, Edward Clark heard his grandfather call to him. How was his round doing, Grandpa T wanted to know. Oh, and once he finished, could he then please return to his side? "His manner was so absolutely simple," wrote Taylor, "that it took Edward some time to realize what had happened."

Later, driven by automobile up the hill to Wyndhurst, Mary sat beside him. "Well, Mary," he smiled at her, "I am all in. This is the last of me." On September 10, he died. "However well one may be pre-pared," wrote Taylor, "the end always brings with it a great sorrow. . . . I can hardly think of any man of his age who will be more missed than father. He has been so much in personal sympathy with every one of us, I am sure that throughout the winter I shall feel his loss constantly."

On learning of the stroke, Fred had rushed home from England, arriving two days before his father's death. He had been attending a joint meeting of the ASME and its British counterpart, the Institution of Mechanical Engineers, in Birmingham.

~

Two months earlier, on a cloudless afternoon in mid-July, the SS *Celtic* left its dock on New York's North River and steamed toward England, loaded with 144 ASME members and their guests. Jim Dodge was among them; so were Gantt, Gilbreth, and Fred Lewis. Dodge delivered a lecture in which, by one account, "he assumed to controvert the theo-ries of all other scientists"; it was entitled, "An Exhaustive Review of the Formation of the Earth and its Oceans, with Some Conclusive Educa-tional Remarks on the Solar System and Prognostications on the Ulti-mate End of the Universe." Someone else read an "Engineer's Reverie," written by a Detroit member. "What's the use?" it asked.

> If your ultimate ambition is to roll a ton of rails,
> To build an automobile or to make a keg of nails,
> You will find that life's a burden, you will find existence stale,
> If you live by rule and precedent you pretty sure will fail,
> And if you only work and sleep and take three meals a day
> Why there isn't any answer and it really doesn't pay.

Taylor was not on hand for these festivities; one wonders what he might have thought. With Lou and daughter Elizabeth, nineteen, he had gone ahead on another ship, reaching England some days earlier. Together with the president of the British Institution, he was there to greet his ASME friends in Liverpool, where they all boarded trains for Birmingham. And it was in Birmingham, the Midlands industrial center, that a historic event of a peculiar sort may be said to have taken place.

The joint meeting got under way in the lecture hall of the Birmingham and Midland Institute, with Taylor among those representing the American delegation. The British conferred upon their visitors a framed letter written in 1777 by James Watt, inventor of the steam engine. Americans and British together visited the British Museum, toasted king and president, professed undying solidarity. Taylor himself had prepared a speech—it is not clear for what occasion or even whether he gave it—called "Sentiment," which celebrated the ties of "mental kinship" that joined engineers everywhere. Whereas lawyers and clergy, for example, dealt in words, engineers created mental pictures, the materials for which "are the great truths and principles of science and the mechanic arts . . . [which] materialize into the machines, the structures and the great engineering works which mark the progress of the world."

Among papers presented in Birmingham was one on "High Speed Tools and Machines to Fit Them," by H. I. Brackenbury, from Newcastle-on-Tyne. Engineers seeing high-speed steel in Paris, he began, "felt that they were witnessing the beginning of a revolution in tool steel and in machines fitted for its use. This revolution," he added, "has now taken place," whereupon he surveyed its progress in the ten years since.

It was not surprising, of course, that after a paper on high-speed steel, Frederick Winslow Taylor should rise to comment. What was surprising was what he had to say—and not say. "The proceedings of the American Society have been burdened to such an extent with what I have said on the subject of high-speed steel," he began, "that I feel it would be improper for me to make any further remarks on that point."

But he wasn't about to sit down, either: "I do, however, welcome the opportunity of speaking upon the far broader subject of which the art of cutting metals and the proper use of machine tools is but one of the small elements"—that is, his system of shop management. He proceeded to do so at length, along the way citing Frank Gilbreth's innovations in bricklaying. He got some facts wrong; but what did mere details matter to Taylor when he was onstage? At the end, he invited Gilbreth to get up and say something, but Gilbreth declined. "Had he sensed a coolness and lack of interest in the reception given to Taylor's contribution?" wondered British management historian Lyndall Urwick later.

Indeed, as soon as Taylor sat down, everyone got right back to tool steel and Brackenbury's paper, as if he had said not a word. As for Brackenbury, he "entirely agreed" with Taylor's comments. But "unfortunately the paper did not deal with that subject and he would very much have valued any remarks Dr. Taylor might have made on tools and machines, of which he had had such great experience."

And so, this day in late July 1910 was a historic one of sorts. For it may have been the last time that what Fred Taylor had to say about scientific management was ignored.

PART SIX

JUDGMENT DAY

(1910–1915)

1

A MILLION DOLLARS A DAY

~

IN NOVEMBER 1910, Fred Taylor became famous.

A group of powerful railroads petitioned a federal agency for a rate hike. You don't need it, they were told; they could save far more than the millions they sought by embracing the efficiency methods of a Philadelphia genius named Frederick Winslow Taylor, who for thirty years had been quietly perfecting them. Over the course of months, a dramatic, high-stakes battle played out in the pages of the nation's newspapers and magazines. By the end, Taylor and scientific management were on every lip, and efficiency was a national ideal.

The instrument of this shift in Taylor's fortunes was a Boston lawyer named Louis Brandeis, whom President Woodrow Wilson would name to the Supreme Court six years later. The son of European Jews who had come to America in the early 1800s and settled in Louisville, Kentucky, Louis Dembitz Brandeis was born in 1856, the same year as Taylor. Like Taylor's, his family was abolitionist. Like Taylor's, his parents took him to Europe after the Civil War. Back in America, the brilliant Mr. Brandeis entered Harvard Law School, earning his degree by age twenty. By thirty, he had a large practice.

But raised on liberal social values and, as a Jew, perhaps feeling the onus of the outsider in conservative Boston, Brandeis began taking on public interest cases outside his regular practice. In 1897, he appeared at a tariff hearing on behalf of "the consumer," an entity never before represented. He fought against handing over a trolley monopoly to private interests. Before the Supreme Court, he defended a state law limiting the hours of women workers. In that case, his argument relied on social and economic arguments, not just narrowly legal ones; this, to generations of lawyers, became known as a Brandeis brief.

In June 1910, alarmed by sharply rising prices, Congress passed the Mann-Elkins Act, which shifted onto the railroads and other carriers the burden of proving that they needed higher freight rates. Later that year, the big railroads east of the Mississippi and north of the Potomac and Ohio rivers petitioned the Interstate Commerce Commission for twenty-seven million dollars in increases. Among them were the Pennsylvania, the New York Central, and the Baltimore and Ohio. Railroad workers, their unions, and insurance companies (which represented small investors holding railroad bonds) were on their side. Opposed were the shippers who'd have to foot the bill, including the New York Merchants Association and the Boston Chamber of Commerce. Brandeis, accepting no fee, set out to fight the rate hike and soon established himself as foremost among the dozens of lawyers on both sides.

At first, Brandeis said later, he'd planned to contest the increase on technical grounds. But early in the hearings before ICC examiners that got under way at New York's Waldorf-Astoria Hotel on August 15— before what the *New York World* called "the most extraordinary aggregation of legal talent ever assembled"—he changed course. As railroad officials fumbled in response to straightforward questions about their costs, he concluded they didn't know what their costs were and so could scarcely claim they'd reached the heights of efficient management. Were the people to subsidize the inefficiency of the railroads?

Brandeis, fifty-four years old, had prominent cheekbones, a high forehead, deep-set eyes. He was tanned from sailing. Hands thrust into his pants pockets, he asked James McCrea, president of the Pennsylvania Railroad, about the road's locomotive repair costs and determined that McCrea knew nothing about them.

"What evidence have you," he asked McCrea, "that these costs, however they may be made up, represent not merely what was actually paid, but what should have been paid?"

"I do not know, quite, how I can answer that," replied McCrea. Through such measures as reduced grades, larger locomotives, and more capacious freight cars, his years of knowledge and experience convinced him, the limits of railroad efficiency had been reached.

In effect, he and other railroad executives said, "Trust me."

But Brandeis, the people's lawyer, would not.

Charles Daly, New York Central vice president, said: "From the best of our knowledge and belief, based on great experience, we do not feel that the rate which it is proposed to inaugurate . . . is unduly high."

Brandeis wanted to know what this knowledge and belief were based on.

"The basis of my judgment," Daly replied, "is exactly the same as the basis of a man who knows how to play a good game of golf. It comes from practice, contact and experience."

"I want to know, Mr. Daly, just as clearly as you can state it, whether you can give a single reason based on anything more than your arbitrary judgment."

And Daly answered, "None whatever."

Early in the hearings, as one executive after another conceded he couldn't pin down this cost or that, Brandeis must have remembered what he had learned about a management system that countered guesswork with facts. One of his own clients, a shoe manufacturer, had gotten the Taylor treatment. And over the years, Brandeis had spoken with Gantt and with Harrington Emerson, an efficiency expert outside the Taylor orbit.

Emerson—"a born salesman with the mind of an intellectual," someone once called him—had gone through piles of his father's money trying to establish himself variously in teaching, banking, and real estate. Around 1899, he finally found his niche, as a management consultant, and soon fell under the spell of Taylor's Saratoga paper. "I would rather have your approval . . . than [that] of any other man living or dead," he wrote Taylor. Between 1904 and 1907, he reorganized the Santa Fe Railroad, saving it tons of money. Taylor saw him as a blowhard, didn't like him much, and apparently even told him so one day on a train bound for Boston. And yet it was Emerson who, through a single memorable utterance, would catapult Taylor to fame.

Brandeis went to see Emerson, whose Santa Fe experience made him a real railroad man. And Emerson reminded him of Taylor, whose "Shop Management" Brandeis had already read. Right there, from Emerson's office, he telephoned Taylor and arranged to meet him in Philadelphia. "I quickly recognized," he said later, "that in Mr. Taylor I had met a really great man." Through Taylor and Gantt, he met Cooke, Barth, Hathaway, and the others.

Brandeis galvanized the Taylor devotees. In the weeks before the hearings were to resume, Frank Gilbreth's wife, Lillian, wrote later, "Small feuds were forgotten; ancient friendships revived; new members were being admitted into the cult, everything in the field that could be used to further the cause was being gathered together and prepared."

In October, Brandeis met at Gantt's apartment in New York with Frank Gilbreth, Jim Dodge, and others. "It seemed to me important

that all differences between the various advocates of efficiency should
be eliminated," he recalled. For starters they needed something to call
it. The Taylor system? Functional management? Shop management?
Just plain efficiency? In the end, they adopted scientific management.
Taylor, among others, had used the term before; that his system was
scientific was its central claim.

The budding movement took institutional form during these
months, too. Behind it was Frank Gilbreth, the former bricklayer, that
big, insatiably energetic man with the bowling ball of a skull. Brandeis
had sent him and another engineer, Robert Kent, to Montreal, to
report back on Gantt's work for the Canadian Pacific Railroad. One
night, they took the boat for Trois Rivières, Quebec, arrived at two
thirty in the morning and, too tired to sleep, stayed up all night,
smoking and talking. This Brandeis fellow was going to make scientific
management big, Gilbreth prophesied; they needed an organization to
hold the ground that would be won. Soon, a fledgling Taylor Society, at
first known as the Society to Promote the Science of Management, was
meeting at Keen's Chop House in New York. "Not one of us," recalled
Kent,

> dreamed that in less than a quarter of a century the principles of
> scientific management would be so woven into the fabric of our
> industrial life that they would be accepted as a commonplace, that
> plants would be operating under the principles of scientific
> management without knowing it, plants perhaps that had never
> heard of Taylor.

In the weeks before resumption of the hearings on November 21,
Brandeis remained in close touch with Taylor and his circle. Taylor furnished him with copies of his writings, sought cooperation from
would-be witnesses, and fed Brandeis debate ammunition, such as how
a strike in Philadelphia had spurred sympathy strikes at most nearby
manufacturers, but not at Tabor or Link-Belt.

In Philadelphia, Brandeis spent a day at Link-Belt, interviewing
Jim Dodge and other company officials, working up questions and
answers of likely use later, "We are satisfied," Dodge wrote Taylor on
November 3, "that Mr. Brandeis is on the right track."

Brandeis began marshaling publicity. When the *Indianapolis Sun*
ran an article about him, he wrote its editor suggesting the paper have

its Washington correspondent on hand for the hearings set to begin later that month. Plainly, Brandeis's devotion to the cause was no mere whim. "Of all the social and economic movements with which I have been connected," he wrote, "none seems to me to be equal to this in its importance and hopefulness."

In his brief, Brandeis reminded the commission of the railroads' insistence that further improvements in efficiency were impossible, and of the seemingly endless rounds of price increases from which shippers, carriers, and consumers alike suffered. "To these declarations of despair involving a vicious circle of ever-increasing cost of living," declared Brandeis, "we [offer instead] the gospel of hope. . . . We offer cooperation to reduce costs and hence to lower prices. This can be done through the introduction of scientific management."

Then came a litany of specific claims. "We shall show you how scientific management, when applied to the simple operation of loading a railroad car with pig iron, increased the performance of the individual worker from 12 1/2 to 47 tons"; he referred, of course, to Henry Noll. He would further show "how, when applied to shoveling coal, it doubled or trebled the performance of the shoveler. How, when applied to the operations of a machine shop it developed, in certain operations, increases ranging from 400 to 1,800 per cent. How, when applied to brick laying, the day's accomplishment rose from 1,000 to 2,700 brick. We shall show that the principles of scientific management are general in their application."

On November 10, Brandeis dropped his bombshell. A *New York Times* headline proclaimed:

ROADS COULD SAVE
$1,000,000 A DAY

———

Brandeis says Scientific Management
Would Do It—Calls
Rate Increases Unnecessary

Brandeis's witnesses over the next few days included Henry Towne, H. L. Gantt, Jim Dodge, Harrington Emerson, and Frank Gilbreth. Taylor himself chose not to speak, but in one firm, insistent voice his disciples spoke on his behalf.

Gilbreth especially made an impression. The commissioners,

someone recalled, "hung over their desks and watched, in a sort of fascination, as he seized law books and illustrated his points about the motion study of bricklaying." The books were bricks, the commissioners putty in his hands. "This," one of them said to Gilbreth, "has become a sort of substitute for religion with you." And the witness agreed.

Two days later it was Emerson's time to sustain Brandeis's million-dollar-a-day claim. When asked how $300 million a year in savings, out of total railroad expenses of $1.6 billion, could be effected, he was ready with an answer—or, rather, four; he had arrived at the figure in that many different ways. In one, he merely extended his experience with the Santa Fe to the industry as a whole. In another, he gathered instances of stellar railroad performance—ABC Railroad's record in locomotive maintenance, say—then used each best case as a standard against which to hold its competitors. Arithmetic hokum? It could seem that way. But all four converged, within a few tens of millions, on three hundred million dollars a year—suggesting just the sort of scientific precision of which the new movement boasted.

∽

On November 25, Taylor wrote Brandeis that he was sorry he'd been unable to get to Washington for the show. "Please let me congratulate you most warmly upon the masterly way in which you marshaled your forces and presented your testimony, and also upon the publicity which your testimony has received and the interest shown by the papers all over the country."

Suddenly Taylor, scientific management, and efficiency were household words. "Few of those present" at the hearings, wrote muckraking journalist Ray Stannard Baker, "had ever even heard of scientific management or of Mr. Taylor, its originator, and the testimony, at first, awakened a clearly perceptible incredulity." But that turned to real interest, Baker went on, in part thanks to "the extraordinary fervor and enthusiasm expressed by every man who testified. Theirs was the firm faith of apostles."

A group of railroads not party to the case wired Brandeis that if he could show *them* how to save so much money, he could name his own price. This was mockery, of course, but Brandeis affected not to notice. He'd be happy to show them, he wrote back. But, he added in a master public relations stroke, he could accept no pay for this public service.

"Sincerity Answers Sarcasm," declared a *New York Times* editorial. Brandeis, that paragon of social virtue, who had brought scientific management to the attention of the nation, was now a media star. Long feature articles appeared in Sunday sections:

BRANDEIS, TEACHER OF BUSINESS ECONOMY

Personality and Theories of the Man Who Volunteers to Tell Railroads How to Save
$300,000,000 a Year.

"By a single stroke," as one engineer had it later, "Brandeis caused a greater advance in scientific management than would otherwise have come in the next quarter of a century." The railroads offered rebuttals, technical and otherwise: you could, for example, scarcely compare the operations of a farflung railroad system with the tight little world of the machine shop, where scientific management began. But none of this stuck with the public. What did was that original headline-grabbing claim, a million dollars a day, and Brandeis's high-mindedness and zeal.

At first, it was Brandeis who got the attention. A *Boston Post* cartoon showed supplicants tearing at his coat and thrusting bags of money at him. "I'll make you manager, president, or anything you say," said one, holding out a check for half a million dollars. Even a sweating J. P. Morgan clamored for him. "Please help a poor downtrodden million-aire," he pleaded, proffering a contract to run the Morgan railroads for a million a year. The headline? "THEY ALL WANT BRANDEIS NOW."

But soon, attention shifted to the new movement itself. Just what was scientific management, this elemental force that could find hidden springs of dollars, millions of them, in every factory, mill, and shop? The eyes of the nation turned to Philadelphia.

On December 3, a long letter to the editor, under the head "Scientific Management," appeared in the *New York Times*, written by Robert Kent, editor of *Industrial Engineering* and charter member of the Society to Promote the Science of Management. "The world owes a debt of gratitude to Fred W. Taylor, the man who reduced the principles of management to a science, and who almost singlehandedly for a quarter of a century worked on in the face of opposition and discouragements that would have appalled an ordinary man."

This was not the first time he had been named, of course. All through the hearings he had been heralded as the founding genius behind this next industrial revolution. A writer from the *Boston Transcript* called Taylor "a man big enough to be called by his last name without any handle." A few days after the end of testimony, a *New York Tribune* writer tracked him down in Philadelphia. Though Taylor asked him to keep his name out of it, he wrote, "it seems about as possible to do so and tell the story properly as it would be to tell the story of the discovery of the North Pole and leave out the name of Peary."

Weeding Waste Out of Business
Is This Man's Special Joy

Perhaps Our Railways
Might Save One Mil-
lion Dollars a Day By
Listening to Him

read the headline that graced the story.

Taylor, his correspondence suggests, was reduced to fairly pinching himself that all this was really happening. Perhaps now deeming his earlier thanks to Brandeis insufficient, Taylor wrote him again a week later, "I want to again congratulate you most warmly upon your achievement in Washington. You have started a movement which I am very sure will be of immense service to the country. Already four magazine editors have been here."

In its anticlimactic ruling on February 23, 1911, the Interstate Commerce Commission denied the rate increase but not, at least publicly, on the basis of Brandeis's arguments on behalf of scientific management, which the commissioners deemed only a "theory." Neither the decision nor the reasoning behind it, of course, mattered anymore: the hearings had already reached deep into American life. As an *American Machinist* editorial put it, they had "produced a profound and, from some points of view, a wholly unexpected impression. . . . The testimony of the 'efficiency' witnesses opened the whole matter of American effectiveness in the use of capital, of labor, of materials, and of time." At least ten editors flocked to Boxly. Letters, including many requests to speak, arrived by the hundreds.

On a Saturday afternoon in January, Taylor and Jim Dodge appeared before two hundred merchants, manufacturers, editors, and other local luminaries at Philadelphia's City Club. Dodge described the introduction of scientific management at Link-Belt; Taylor gave a version of his Boxly talk. When, after citing industries to which his system had been applied, and recounting Gilbreth's bricklaying successes, he reached the story of the Simonds bicycle-ball inspectors, he paused. His time was growing short, he said; further illustrations might take too much of their time. No, cried his audience, "Go on!" And he did.

At the end, he submitted to questions. Might his training of shovelers, say, "tend to make them more automatic in their general actions, and stunt their intelligence?"

Oh, no, replied Taylor. Did a surgeon, at the top of the skills heap, stunt his intelligence by adhering to well-proven techniques?

In February, the *American Magazine* promised for the following month's issue "the first complete and authoritative account of 'scientific management,' written . . . by Frederick W. Taylor, of Philadelphia, the originator of the system." In the wake of the rate hearings, "much has appeared, in a fragmentary form, in the daily and weekly newspapers, regarding the work of Mr. Taylor and his associates." This, however, would be "the first authentic presentation of the whole subject."

∽

Spread over three issues of the *American Magazine*, readers found a long essay Taylor had been working on with the editorial help of Morris Cooke. Cooke was an ex-reporter who, during the depression of 1893, had tracked down a failed sugar speculator to his Brooklyn home, where he found the man despondent, slumped over a table, weeping; the scoop got him a promotion. Cooke knew how to tell a story and knew how to help Taylor tell his.

Already writing a Carnegie Foundation–commissioned book on scientific management in higher education, he had begun fashioning Taylor's ideas into a book he planned to call *Industrial Management*. Its starting point was Taylor's Boxly talks, one of which, as we've seen, he'd had transcribed in full back in 1907. This, with much new material and Cooke's substantial help, now became *The Principles of Scientific Management*, Taylor's most popular treatment of his ideas. Here, the stories Taylor told so many times at Boxly were tidied up and polished.

Here, Henry Noll, the pig iron handler, vanished, only to be replaced by "a man we will call Schmidt," complete with the Pennsylvania Dutch dialect Taylor had presumably given him at Boxly:

> "Schmidt, are you a high-priced man?"
> "Vell, I don't know vat you mean."
> "Oh yes, you do. What I want to know is whether you are a high-priced man or not."
> "Vell, I don't know vat you mean."
> "Oh, come now, you answer my questions . . ."

On it went, generally following the Boxly version, with all the imperiousness in Taylor's original dialogue retained and sometimes heightened. This was the version that caught the imagination of the public, that was translated into a dozen languages ("Schmidt, êtes-vous un. . . ?"), reprinted in countless management texts, pored over by generations of business students, and plumbed for affinities with such literary works as Stephen Crane's *Red Badge of Courage* and Mark Twain's *A Connecticut Yankee at King Arthur's Court*.

It was here, in the *Principles*, that Taylor declared, "In the past the man was first; in the future the system must be first." In so saying, observed Michael W. Munley in a University of Massachusetts doctoral dissertation,

> Taylor topples priorities that had prevailed over centuries of
> humanist thought, from its first outburst in the Italian Renaissance
> and its animation of the Protestant Reformation, through its
> elaboration of political reform based on the sovereignty of the
> individual.

This is not the arrant hyperbole it might seem.

In what Munley depicts as this "bible of American management," Taylor raised the stakes on his life's work. While asserting that he wrote for engineers and managers, he hoped it would be clear that

> the same principles can be applied with equal force to all social
> activities: to the management of our homes; the management of
> our farms; the management of the business of our tradesmen, large

and small; of our churches, our philanthropic institutions, our universities, and our governmental departments.

The Principles of Scientific Management was no ordinary technical paper, which may explain why the ASME, to which Taylor first submitted it, had such trouble deciding what to do with it. What do you do when an esteemed colleague, a former society president, submits a paper offering little, technically speaking, that's new? That crosses over into social commentary far removed from your discipline? What the ASME did was sit on it, neither rejecting nor accepting it.

When, a little before the rate case, the society's intentions became clear, Taylor decided to publish it himself and distribute it privately to ASME members, ultimately withdrawing it from formal consideration. Then, after the rate case, with Taylor in demand and magazines clamoring for anything he had to say, Cooke sought magazines that might serialize the book. "I think during the course of the coming week we will be forced to reach a decision," he wrote Taylor on December 10. He had been in touch with several journals; the choice came down to the *Atlantic* and the *American Magazine*, circulation 340,000.

Representing the *American* in long conversations over dinner with Cooke was a handsome forty-one year old man with straight, dark hair and demonically intense eyes, Ray Stannard Baker. Baker was a muckraker, a word Theodore Roosevelt had coined to describe journalists who reported on the evils of the big trusts, inhumane social conditions, the plight of the poor, and the like. As a group, they were of liberal sentiments, their big, progressive hearts firmly in the right place. They included such noted figures as Lincoln Steffens and Ida Tarbell, who had almost single-handedly broken up the Standard Oil monopoly through her exposés.

But as one student of the breed, C. G. Regier, has shown in *The Era of the Muckrakers*, they were not radicals, revolutionaries, or even reformers: they were reporters. Some were simply sensation-mongers. They were squarely middle-class. Few were "in any way connected with trade unions; few of them wrote in the interest of trade-union development. . . . They attacked injustice wherever they discovered it; but beyond that they did not go."

To this pattern Ray Stannard Baker precisely conformed. As a Chicago reporter, he had marched over the Alleghenies with Coxey's impoverished army to Washington, and reported on labor disturbances such as the bloody Pullman strike of 1894. But he had exposed labor corruption, too, and, writes Regier, "he had no program of reform, nor was he fundamentally critical of American life. He described both the good and the bad as he saw them, fully confident that in the end the good would prevail." He was quiet, a superb listener, blessed of what a colleague remembered as "a joyous laugh." When Taylor's name came up early in the rate case hearings, Baker's editor, John Phillips, wondered just who Frederick Taylor was. No one knew.

"Baker," he said, "you better find out."

Cooke worried about the *American*. It had published articles by philosopher William James and reformer Jane Addams. of Chicago's Hull House. But, he wrote Taylor, "in the same issue have appeared articles on baseball," and "a good deal of it has been dangerously near the line of sensationalism." The manuscript was better off at the *Atlantic*. They'd have to abridge its thirty-two thousand words, but reaching that magazine's literary readership would be a coup.

Taylor disagreed. The *Atlantic* might get the "professors and literary men," he wrote back, but the *American* would reach more of those actually doing the work of the world. It was a muckracking magazine? No matter. "I think that any magazine which opposed the 'stand-patters' and was not under the control of the moneyed powers," opined Mr. Taylor of Boxly, "would now be classed among the muck-rakers."

So the *American* it was. There, in big, illustrated spreads stretched across three issues between March and May of 1911, the *Principles* appeared. The first issue was introduced by a wildly laudatory piece by Baker about Taylor. "For three days last November," he began, "I sat in the court room of the Interstate Commerce Commission at Washington, listening to one of the most remarkable cases ever presented before that distinguished body. . . . What is this scientific management?" he asked, "and who is Mr. Taylor?"

His answers could scarcely have pleased Taylor more. "One day, some thirty-six years ago, a young man named Taylor began work in a Philadelphia machine shop. He swept up the shavings in the morning . . ." Taylor, in other words, came off just as he wished to be seen. Indeed, Baker often used language borrowed from autobiographical notes that Taylor had furnished Cooke a little earlier. All in all, Baker's piece was puffery on the grand scale. Taylor, he wrote, was a rare, high type of American, a public servant in the best sense. . . . There have been times in recent years when it seemed as though our civilization were being throttled by things, by property, by the very weight of industrial mechanism, and it is no small matter when a man arises who can show us new ways of commanding our environment.

This by Baker, that clear-eyed enemy of injustice, malfeasance, and sham.

On February 22, Taylor wrote Cooke from the Hotel Bon Air in Augusta, Georgia. Daughter Elizabeth, now twenty, had taken up tennis and would soon start horseback riding. In golf, he was burning up the links; in one tournament, he'd scored an 83. And, he added, "The *American* article has just arrived. Baker has done it in fine shape."

Three days later, Cooke wrote Taylor that he'd subscribed to a clipping service, "to keep in closer touch with what is being said about you and scientific management in the daily press." And over the next few years the clips poured in. An incomplete reckoning by the New York Public Library counted thirty-one articles bearing on scientific management in 1910, fifty-eight in 1911, and two hundred and twenty in 1912.

All of the world's botchery and mismanagement seemed to reveal itself at once. One correspondent wrote *American Machinist* about how he'd once sent out for bids on a machine shop job and got estimates that ranged all the way from sixteen minutes to eleven hours. Now wasn't *that* a case of Taylor's despised rule-of-thumb guesswork at its worst? Didn't the average machine shop need "a little more science"?

And didn't the legal profession need some science, too? asked a writer to the *New York Times*. Mr. Brandeis ought to "get Mr. Taylor to take a few stop watch observations in a typical court, and in a typical lawyer's office, and make an estimate of the existing and obtainable efficiencies."

In March 1911, Edward Mott Woolley wrote of scientific management at the Link-Belt Company for the magazine *System*. His article was called "Finding the One Best Way," perhaps the first time that phrase, which came to be associated with Taylor and the efficiency movement as a whole, reached the general public.

During 1911, other efficiency movement notables came out with books. There was Harrington Emerson's *Twelve Principles of Efficiency*; H. L. Gantt's *Work, Wages, and Profits*; and the Gilbreths' *Motion Study*.

Would it be possible to overstate the euphoria that greeted the nation's discovery of efficiency? Catapulted to prominence first by the rate case, then the *American*'s lavish play (along with that in dozens of other magazines), and the publication by Harper & Row of *Principles*—all within a few months—Taylor and his way of seeing the world were, suddenly, everywhere.

Taylor was seeing forty or fifty people a week, all of them peppering him with questions, seeking comment and advice. He gave lectures everywhere, running up to Amherst on April 20, to Cornell on April 27. At a conference of the American Society of Machine Tool Builders in May, he was introduced as nothing less than "a deliverer of mankind."

Around this time, on June 5, Maunsel White wrote him from Newark, where he was working, wondering whether they might get together for an evening in New York. Sorry, Taylor wrote back, "Almost every minute of my time is taken up with engagements to speak and men coming to see me relating to this infernal activity about scientific management."

So many were the questions in response to the *American Magazine* series alone—well into the hundreds—that the editors asked Taylor what to do about them. Taylor gave them Gilbreth's name. And he, with his wife, Lillian, wrote a *Primer on Scientific Management* in question-and-answer form, which came out the following year:

> How can you expect every laborer to understand Scientific Management when it takes an engineer so many years to learn it?

The Gilbreth answer:

> The laborer does not understand it, nor is he expected to understand it. He simply understands the assistance he receives from the functional foreman, in learning how to do his work more efficiently.

Louis Brandeis himself was recruited to write a foreword. "Under Scientific Management," he declared, "men are led, not driven. Instead of working unwillingly for their employer, they work in cooperation with the management," thus securing "a very large share of the industrial profits arising from improved industry."

The party line—simplified, popularized, digested—was going out across America. "I am glad to live in such a wonderful age," somebody wrote the *American*.

In the spring of 1911, hope surged through an America still reeling from the cruel dislocations of the industrial revolution. As the moving spirit behind scientific management and the *ism* that already bore his name, Taylor represented progress, stood in the advance guard of a movement that would secure prosperity for all and rid the industrial world of its inequities.

It was too good to last, of course. The efficiency movement resembled some of today's spiritual cults—all bliss on the surface—and, like some of them, also had a dark side. Indeed, were it more irreproachably benign, Taylorism might never have left so indelible a mark on our age. Its sunny vision of prosperity and workplace harmony was only part of its appeal.

On May 24, 1911, sounding worried that the burgeoning movement might get completely out of hand, Taylor wrote the British ambassador, James Bryce, "The interest is growing so fast in this country that I am afraid that the final result may be, as in many things with us, that there will come an extensive reaction."

He was right; in fact, the reaction had already set in.

2

STORM CLOUDS

∾

ALL THROUGH HIS CAREER, Taylor had been a target of attack. But usually it had come from business owners who saw him as belligerent, tactless, and inept at gaining workers' cooperation; or a hopeless spendthrift; or a purveyor of costly red tape; or a dreamer. Now, though, it was different. Alongside the tributes heaped on him came savage condemnation from the ranks of labor; a foreigner might have felt that one hand of American public opinion didn't know what the other was doing, or else, that there were two Taylors. It was a time of high rhetoric, pro and con, and little in the way of cool, reasoned judgment about the new movement loosed on America.

After the rate case hearings, for example, mine workers' union expresident John Mitchell, citing the authority of the superintendent of the Manhattan State Hospital for the Insane, asserted that job specialization, encouraged by scientific management, was "a frequent cause of insanity." It seems that brain cells not employed in monotonous labor "finally go dead from lack of use, and then the worker is ready for the insane asylum." The workman who could no longer take time to sharpen his tools lost a break from deadly routine. "There is nothing," said Mitchell, "so restful as variety."

On March 27, 1911, Louis Brandeis met James Duncan, first vice president of the American Federation of Labor, at the Economic Club of New York for a debate on "Efficiency." The "promoters of the new cult," allowed Duncan, did not intend harm to come of it. But harm did come of it, in the form of "blood-money," to men brutally driven to achieve output that then becomes the new, higher standard. An expert presumably devised these improved work methods? It didn't matter, said Duncan, who was also an officer of the granite cutters' union. "As a skilled workman I want no task nor task setter to harass me at my work. That . . . would reduce me to an automaton." Workingmen didn't understand the new scheme? Oh, yes they did. The new workplace efficiency aimed at " 'remaking' workmen in a new mold, trimmed, polished, with bulging muscles, swift of hand and foot, improved eyesight, shop value seventy-five per cent more. . . , governed by thought from the speeding boss, and for what? We repeat, for what?"

Taylor treated workers as less than human; so labor charged. Sometimes the accent was on how mercilessly the human machine was driven. Sometimes, on being treated as a machine at all, robbed of independence, judgment, and thought. Sometimes on being likened to intelligent gorillas like Schmidt. Sometimes on being deemed little more than slaves, or puppets, or industrial serfs. But always it was a diminished humanity that Taylor's critics saw in his system.

Among crimes attributable to scientific management, wrote an *American Machinist* correspondent, was the assumption of "a monopoly of brains" among experts who schedule "every movement so that a man is simply one of the gears in the operation of the machine." A man made the "puppet of a planning department will soon cease to think of much else beside 'quitting time and pay day.' "

Time study, said another critic, "practically eliminates the operator's or mechanic's personality, transforming him from a skilled mechanic into that of *factotum* or machine, and the foreman in charge only one grade higher but in the same class." This, be it noted, more than a year before Henry Ford's first assembly line.

Sometimes, the hostility took a lighter form. Someone wrote a charming essay entitled "Applying the Taylor Process to Painting Blinds"; another, identified only as "The New York Bo'," affected a working-class dialect in the *International Molders Journal*:

> W'en dis Taylor guy, de great discov'rer o' de lost motion in
> workin' guys, foirst introduces his syst'm, Slim gets a job at it, so as
> to keep 'breast wid de times . . .

whereupon we learn of Slim's fate at the hands of the time-study man, already a despised figure.

Taylor's own words—"certain infelicities of speech and illustration," as one management scholar, Harlow Person, referred to them— often got him in trouble. He referred to the yard laborers whose ranks he'd trimmed at Bethlehem as "the finest body of picked laborers that the writer has ever seen together," as if they were so much horseflesh. He asserted that a "task should be made so difficult that it can only be accomplished by a first-class man," a term that imputed inferiority to those lower on the scale. (No one seemed to remember that ads in Philadelphia papers—during Taylor's apprenticeship, say—routinely sought "a first class sheet iron worker," or "two first class furniture upholsterers.")

But it was the Schmidt story that enraged people the most.

WHAT HAS HAPPENED TO SCHMIDT?

read the headline *American Magazine* gave one letter writer inquiring of his fate. It was one thing to charm a group of sympathetic industrialists at Boxly and talk about how poor, dumb Henry Noll just wasn't smart enough to know when to rest and needed an expert to tell him. It was quite another when the story was reduced to print, and those more apt to identify with Noll than with his boss could see just how Taylor viewed him.

On February 24, 1911, Upton Sinclair, whose *The Jungle* had almost single-handedly spurred reform of the meatpacking industry, wrote *American Magazine* in response to its first installment of Taylor's book. "I shall not soon forget the picture which he gave us," wrote Sinclair, "of the poor old laborer who was trying to build his pitiful little home after hours, and who was induced to give 362 per cent more service for 61 per cent more pay." Why, he asked, should Schmidt "receive $1.85 for the work, instead of, let us say, $2.85."

Pay workers too much, Taylor wrote in reply, and they "work irregularly and tend to become more or less shiftless, extravagant and dissipated. Our experiments showed . . . that for their own best interest it does not do for most men to get rich too fast."

When Samuel Gompers, the cigar maker who now headed the American Federation of Labor, read about Schmidt, he was struck not by Schmidt's victory in the yard at Bethlehem but by the defeat of seven out of eight of his laboring brethren:

> This experiment of Doctor Taylor, in ascertaining with scientific
> accuracy the breaking point of seven out of eight laborers, presents
> novelty only in its cold-bloodedness and its endeavor to transfer
> mathematical observations of the strength of metals to those of the
> strength of men's muscles and spirit.
>   [The Taylor system makes] every man merely a cog or a nut or
> a pin in a big machine, fixed in the position of a hundredth or a
> thousandth part of the machine, with no need to employ more
> than a few mechanical motions nor any brain power except the
> little required in making those motions.

An *American Machinist* correspondent calling himself Entropy made it a point to restore to Schmidt the brains Taylor denied him: "It is not muscle, nor height, nor weight that enables a man to perform great feats; it is that intangible control of muscle by the mind that makes a man run a hundred yards in ten seconds—or," he added with a lift of his cap to Schmidt, "that enables him to carry 47 tons of pig iron to a pile."

Sometimes, those commenting on Schmidt got this or that detail wrong; Upton Sinclair, for example, pictured him lifting forty-seven pounds, rather than forty-seven tons per day. But the fury roused by the Schmidt story was scarcely conducive to careful fact-checking. Taylor's science, wrote Samuel Gompers in another bitter editorial, fixed

> not only your length, breadth, and thickness as a machine, but your grade of hardness, malleability, tractability, and general serviceability. . . . Science would thus get the most out of you before you are sent to the junk pile.

Ambition, pride, and fear of job loss had once sufficed to goad the worker. But now, it seemed, he must be taught

> the economical lifts, pushes, jumps, steps, stoops and bends, the quickest looks and thinks, the most dexterous fingering, the most supple wrist-play, the finest elbow work . . .

The new Taylorized worker thus learned to "do his twentieth century best." A grim prospect this was—but perversely, Gompers had to admit, one "gripping in its fascination."

∼

That was February 1911 and just so much talk. But a few months later, labor's fury found a concrete object.

Among enterprises to which scientific management had been introduced were arsenals, shipyards, and other governmental installations. Just after the rate case hearings, a committee convened by Army Chief of Ordnance William B. Crozier had proposed, based on more than a year's experience with the Taylor system at Watertown Arsenal in Massachusetts, that it be applied to other arsenals. When workers at Rock Island Arsenal in Illinois got wind, they protested. A delegation was sent to Washington to meet with government officials. Adoption of scientific management, they warned, would grant government sanction to "Mr. Taylor's methods of treating workmen," which overworked and enslaved them, replaced skilled mechanics with drones, and caused unemployment.

With all this, Taylor at first affected a lack of concern. Congress had been "flooded with resolutions from mass meetings in the Rock Island Arsenal protesting against scientific management," he wrote Morris Cooke on March 17, but "no harm has been done so far." But on April 14, Representative Pepper of Iowa, whose district lay on the other side of the Mississippi from the arsenal in Illinois, submitted House Resolution 90, which began:

> Whereas it has been disclosed that the United States Government has partially installed in certain Government work a system of shop management known as the "Taylor system"; and
>
>   . . .
>
> Whereas the said "Taylor system" appears to be of such a character and nature as to be detrimental to the best interests of American workingmen, being in its essential parts a "high-speed" process, where none but the strong survive and they being crowded constantly to the maximum point of physical exertion . . .

the Committee on Labor should investigate.

A little later, James O'Connell, the slim, dapper machinists' union president, issued a broadside to six hundred locals, alerting them to the danger posed by the Taylor system: Its originator "is a former master mechanic of the Midvale Steel Co., Philadelphia, Pa., and is well qualified by disposition and education to undermine our trades." His "insidious" system reduced men "to virtual slavery and low wages," and spawned such suspicion among them that each looked to his fellow as a would-be traitor and spy. Now Taylor had turned his malign gaze to arsenals and navy yards. He had to be stopped.

For four days beginning on April 28, the House Labor Committee, Congressman William B. Wilson of Pennsylvania presiding, held hearings. Only Herbert Stimpson, a self-styled efficiency expert, represented management, and he had never even met Taylor. Otherwise, the testimony read like all the other unremittingly sinister pronouncements hurled at scientific management thus far. "The whole scheme of the system is to remove the head of the workmen," said James O'Connell:

> Taylor and his assistants declare: "Give us big physical men and we will do the thinking for them." The scheme tends to wipe out all

the manhood and genius of the American workman and make him a mere machine, to be driven at a high speed until he breaks down, and then to be thrown into the scrap heap.

Samuel Gompers, in rare rhetorical form, was among those to testify; the Taylor system spelled higher production of "goods and things, but in so far as man is concerned it means destruction." What Taylor deemed wasted motion "is frequently that moment when the divine spark of a new thought" comes to the worker. Had James Watt not had the leisure "to watch a kettle boil, we might not have known of the power of steam."

But with all the rhetorical sound and fury, nothing came of the hearings. No investigation was launched. The pro- and anti-Taylor camps had not yet joined in battle.

Of course, it was only May. For the next three months, it would be possible to say in retrospect, the industrial world waited for the other shoe to drop.

And in August it did.

3

THUNDERCLAP

~

ON AUGUST 12, 1910, Carl Barth wrote Taylor that a group of molders had struck the government arsenal at Watertown, Massachusetts, six miles outside Boston. Time-study man Dwight Merrick, who had worked for Taylor at Bethlehem and then with Barth at Link-Belt, had entered the foundry, pulled out his stopwatch, and begun timing a man. That, wrote Barth, "turned the devil loose."

Barth, overseeing the work at Watertown and Taylor's most devoted disciple, was mortified. "I can't tell you how bad I feel about this matter for your own sake, for in the eyes of the world I fear you can never again say that you have never caused a strike."

That had been one of Taylor's claims—he had said as much in the Detroit paper in 1895 and again in "Shop Management" in 1903. In

Principles of Scientific Management, published just a few months earlier, he had declared, "During the thirty years that we have been engaged in introducing scientific management there has not been a single strike." When reminded that Bethlehem Steel had suffered a long one, he snapped back, "They never struck while I was there."

"I believe that under the circumstances you had better come down and talk the situation over," Barth wrote Taylor; he could be reached by wire, letter, or phone. Or, "if you prefer to have me come to you, I will come at once."

By August 15, Barth was growing uneasy. "WHY NO ANSWER TO LETTER REGARDING MOULDERS STRIKE AT WATERTOWN OR YOUR COMING DOWN?" he wired Taylor, for whom the summer, taken at a stroll and filled with golf, had proved "the most restful that Mrs. Taylor and I have had for more than a year."

That afternoon Barth at last heard from Taylor, who had written the day before. "I am exceedingly sorry to hear of the strike at Watertown," Taylor began. Time studies had been introduced to the foundry with insufficient groundwork; *that* was the problem. "There is only one course to pursue, namely, to fight the thing right straight through. . . . This strike hits at the very foundation of scientific management."

∽

In 1911, the world wars that would so expand the scale of Watertown Arsenal and make its high-walled, cavernous shops so familiar to drivers along Arsenal Street lay in the future. Arriving at the little steeple-topped guardhouse, just inside the iron gate from Arsenal Street, a visitor was within five minutes of everything. The arsenal employed only about four hundred people. Cattle still freely grazed on its open fields. Its brick buildings mostly went back to before the Civil War, when men and women sat around wood tables in small rooms assembling munitions. An early commandant, Thomas J. Rodman, had built himself a twelve-thousand-square-foot mansion on the arsenal grounds, complete with parquet floors, marble fireplaces, and fine views of the Charles River. Sitting on the veranda of Rodman's mansion now, the current commandant, Lieutenant Colonel Charles B. Wheeler, could look out upon the river, unmindful of the clatter from the shops. Asked whether a man watched by a time-study expert might feel "he had to get a move on him," he would reply, "I never thought of it in that way."

Then as now, government arsenals enjoyed no reputation for efficiency; but Watertown, of them all, was perhaps the most backward. Pig iron, steel billets, and copper ingots came into the arsenal. Large seacoast gun carriages went out, their cost almost entirely the sheer labor of making their hundreds of parts. But it was too much labor. Workmen lost time looking for tools or waiting at grinders, because machines broke or equipment was not at hand, or because casting left too much metal to be cut away. Almost half the machine tools had been around for more than fifteen years, which meant they predated high-speed steel and hence were obsolete. No reliable system for ordering material was in place. When a foreman needed something for a job, he'd order it, and order it again when it didn't come in right away, winding up with twice what he needed, which of course hung around the shop forever. Like Bethlehem Steel in 1898, the arsenal cried out for a shot of Taylorism.

Through General William Crozier, Army Chief of Ordnance (weapons and munitions), the arsenal got it. Like Louis Brandeis, Crozier was an age-mate of Taylor's, born within a year or so of him. The son of a senator from Kansas, he had attended West Point, where he topped his class academically, fought in the Indian wars against the Sioux, served at Watertown as a young officer in the late 1880s, and designed cannons that became fixtures of American defense for years. By 1909, he had known Taylor for almost two decades, read his books, and visited him in Philadelphia. "I concluded that Mr. Taylor's system would hold water and was well worth trying," he said later.

Two years later, after investing in machine tools rebuilt to handle high-speed steel, in standardized bolts for holding work in place (a seeming trifle but universally applauded), in a toolroom with its ordered rows of bins and boxes, in a new routing system to stop overbuying, in forms to keep track of everything, and in Carl Barth's fifty-dollars-a-day consulting fees, Watertown was ready for time study. Dwight Merrick was brought in at fifteen dollars a day. Soon, of a hundred fifty men in the machine shop, about a dozen had been stopwatch-timed.

Merrick's next stop was the foundry. This crowded hulk of a building, constructed as a lumber storehouse in 1852, had witnessed none of the preparatory measures that, in the machine shop, had taken up nearly two years. Earlier efforts to increase production had come to nothing. One was a premium plan based not on time study but solely on past output; it had only stirred resentment. The foundry persisted in what would later be described as its "old pattern of comfortable disorganization."

On August 10, Merrick began to time molder John Hendry as he worked on bench molds for a steel part called a pommel. A molder, recall, set pieces of the pattern in a two-piece frame, rammed sand around them, removed the pattern, inserted any baked-sand cores necessary, cleaned up the mold, and closed it up, ready to receive molten metal. Hendry, a molder of twenty years standing, didn't like someone standing over him with a stopwatch. "I could not do my work right," he testified later.

Merrick determined that, to earn a premium of one third over his daily wage, Hendry should be able to finish two and a half molds per hour; that is, one every twenty-four minutes. Any longer than that and he'd begin to lose his extra pay, until at forty minutes per mold he'd be back at ordinary day wages.

But forty minutes was too little, Hendry complained.

After an appeal from the foreman, Major C. C. Williams, Colonel Wheeler's senior aide, raised the figure to fifty, about as long as Hendry had taken before; no one ever tried to claim that Williams's action was anything but arbitrary or that anything like "science" entered into it.

But it was too late in any case. Merrick's original time study had sown seeds of discord. Another molder, working nearby, had informally timed Hendry, finding he needed forty-nine minutes per mold. To Joseph R. Cooney, seventeen years past his apprenticeship and seven years at Watertown, Merrick's figures constituted nothing less than "an untruthful statement." Besides, Merrick was not a molder himself. They were going to be timed, their work methods called into question, their livelihoods threatened, by someone who knew next to nothing about a craft they'd followed all their lives?

That evening, after supper, they drew up a petition to Colonel Wheeler:

Dear Sir:
The very unsatisfactory conditions which have prevailed in the foundry among the molders for the past week or more reached an acute stage this afternoon when a man was seen to use a stop watch on one of the molders. This we believe to be the limit of our endurance. It is humiliating to us, who have always tried to give to

the Government the best that was in us. This method is un-American in principle, and we most respectfully request that you have it discontinued at once.

General Crozier had promised them, the petition went on,

that he would not install any part of the Taylor system that might be objectionable to the men; and we assure you that this part of the system will not be tolerated by the molders.

Each of the twenty-four molders signed it, and all agreed, in Cooney's words, "that any man on whom the stop watch was pulled should refuse to continue work."

The next morning, Friday, Cooney had been working for about fifteen minutes when Merrick and the foreman approached him. The foreman described Cooney's job to Merrick and left. The time-study man remained. Cooney ceased work. Did Merrick intend to time him?

Seconds passed. Well, yes, he did, replied Merrick at last. Was there some trouble with that?

"Nothing in particular," replied Cooney, "only that we don't care to stand for this."

Merrick tried jollying him into submission. "Now, my good fellow," Cooney recalled him saying, "go right along just as though I wasn't here at all."

But Cooney would not budge. "Either you or I will have to be on the floor alone."

"I don't care to enter into any argument with you," Merrick said.

And they did not argue. Cooney pulled out the petition, which was taken to foreman John Larkin with the request that it go to Colonel Wheeler.

Merrick rushed in to Larkin's office soon after, telling him, "There is trouble. It is all off. Cooney refuses to work under observation."

About twenty minutes later, Major Williams appeared, called Cooney into his office, explained the reasons for the time study, and asked whether he would agree to it.

When Cooney said that he could not, he was fired.

On the way to the washroom to change clothes, Cooney told the other molders, who joined him in protest.

The next day, the Boston papers bore the news:

MOLDERS QUIT
AT WATERTOWN
Arsenal Men Balk at
"Spy" System

———

One Who Objected Discharged
by Maj. Wheeler
Others Protest and Leave
Government Shops

On Wednesday afternoon, a committee of strikers arrived at the arsenal to meet with Colonel Wheeler. They were met at the gate and escorted under guard to the commandant's office. Soldiers stood just outside while they conferred—to no avail. The men were not permitted to get their personal tools and work clothes. Instead, Major Williams and two others carried out their belongings—stuffed in boxes, piled atop sand sieves or wrapped in the men's shirts and pants—and dumped them onto the ground for them to retrieve.

That burned. "We felt," Cooney said later, that "we were self-respecting, law-abiding citizens, and that we did not need an escort or guard. . . . We felt that having worked there as long as we had that we certainly had the privilege of going to our lockers. There were no ex-convicts among the men that I know of."

Feelings were hurt and tensions ran high, yet no one wanted a strike; the molders had at first denied that they were on strike at all and hadn't bothered to inform the local in Boston. Meanwhile, Wheeler was learning that skilled molders were hard to come by. Besides, the molders asked for so little, only that someone listen to them. General Crozier in Washington acceded, ordering his aide, Lieutenant Colonel John Thompson, to investigate. In scarcely more than a week, the men were back at work and giving vent to their grievances.

From August 21 to 26, the men's recreation room at the arsenal became a hearing room, and even in those few days of testimony, you could hear themes raised that would dog Taylorism over the years, could hear views of life and work in seemingly irreconcilable conflict, could hear men speaking to one another but hearing nothing.

Sanford Thompson, Taylor's right-hand man at the paper mill, who later collaborated with him on time-studies in the construction trades.

Boomtown on the Kennebec: The paper mill, over which Taylor presided from 1890 to 1893, goes up in Madison, Maine.

Taylor at rest: In the sitting room of his rented house in Bethlehem, Pa., 1899.

Machine Shop No. 2, at Bethlehem Steel Works in Bethlehem, Pa., may have been the largest such shop in the world. Here visitors came to see the high speed steel cutters developed by Taylor and Maunsel White ripping through metal at triple the speed of other tool steels.

One version of the Barth slide rule, first developed at Bethlehem Steel around 1899, which permitted cutting speeds dependent on many variables to be calculated quickly.

Fourth of July, 1899. *Adults from left:* Taylor on rocking chair, Clarence Clark, Millie Richards (Franklin Taylor's housekeeper), Louise, Franklin, Mary Taylor Clark. The Clark kids sit in front.

Henry Noll, or Knoll, or Knolle, but to the world best known, through Taylor's tale of him in *The Principles of Scientific Management*, as "Schmidt." He is probably the most famous laborer in the world, generations of business students having heard how Taylor got him to carry 47 tons of pig iron a day.

At the Paris Exposition, 1900, the Bethlehem exhibit that brought high speed steel, and Frederick Taylor, to the attention of the world. Note the curlicued ribbons of steel shavings in foreground, left and right of the entrance.

Taylor with his two adoptive sons, probably around 1905.

Left: The Taylor family, around 1903. Lou and Fred, with Kempton in front, Robert at right, Elizabeth in the back. The children's brother, not adopted by the Taylors, was Conrad Aiken, the poet and novelist.

Boxly, Taylor's estate in Chestnut Hill, on the outskirts of Philadelphia, named after the boxwood hedges in foreground. Only the right hand section of the house still stands. The columned entrance is gone.

Taylorized order, standardization, and control.

Above: Link-Belt, one of Taylor's two prime showcase companies. Industrialists would come to Boxly to hear Taylor in the morning, then head down to Link-Belt after lunch to see scientific management in something like pure form. *Left:* Instruction card for the machining of a simple roller, each process assigned a time down to the hundredth of a minute.

Machinist at work at Tabor Manufacturing, the other Taylor showcase company.

Carl Barth. This brilliant Norwegian immigrant, more of a Taylorite than Taylor, introduced scientific management to Link-Belt and other companies. Of opinions, he declared, "I have got mighty few; but by the Almighty, they are strong."

Taylor, left of flower girl, a smiling Andrew Carnegie behind her, James Mapes Dodge between them, at the cornerstone laying of the Engineers Building in Manhattan. Here, two years later, Taylor met Frank Gilbreth, hero of the popular memoir *Cheaper by the Dozen*.

Taylorism spread across the world. Here, a poster, "Work and Savings in All Professions Through Taylorism," from Weimar Germany.

62D CONGRESS,
1ST SESSION.

H. RES. 90.

IN THE HOUSE OF REPRESENTATIVES.

APRIL 14, 1911.

Mr. PEPPER submitted the following resolution; which was referred to the Committee on Labor and ordered to be printed.

RESOLUTION.

Whereas it has been disclosed that the United States Government has partially installed in certain Government work a system of shop management known as the "Taylor system"; and

Whereas it is now proposed and determined that the said "Taylor system", or parts thereof, shall be extended to and installed in other branches of Government work; and

Whereas the said "Taylor system" appears to be of such a character and nature as to be detrimental to the best interests of American workingmen, being in its essential parts a "high-speed" process, where none but the strong survive and they being crowded constantly to the maximum point of physical exertion, to the end that an increased output may be obtained and at a low labor cost; and

Whereas it has ever been recognized that one of the highest functions of any Government is to guard with zealous care the happiness and welfare of its great army of producers; and

Whereas the partial or complete installation of the said "Taylor system" in Government work is a matter of tremendous importance to the people of the United States, and may be

First page of House Resolution 90.

One response to Taylorism.

Louis Brandeis, after the Eastern Rate Case, which brought scientific management, the larger cause of efficiency, and Frederick Winslow Taylor to public attention.

Workers at Watertown Arsenal, some years before arsenal molders went out on strike against stop-watch timing of their work. The strike culminated in a full-blown Congressional investigation of the Taylor System.

Left: The building on Rac Street in Philadelphia tha once housed the pump works where Taylor serve his apprenticeship, now made into offices.

Right: Taylor's grave in West Laurel Hill Cemetery, high over Philadelphia's Schuykill River.

The tracks, overgrown with weeds, that swept just south of Midvale Steel.

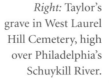

In scientific management, Wheeler, Williams, Merrick, and Barth saw higher output benignly attained; the workmen, on the other hand, felt harassed. "I have to watch every move I make and every time I move," said Ed Sherman, thirty-three years a molder:

Every time I turn I find a man with a watch watching me; if I go after anything he is watching me; when I come back he is watching me; and if it is any kind of a half-decent job at all that man would get me so nervous that I really would not know what I would be doing.

They didn't like being watched, they didn't like being timed, and they didn't like the fact that the man timing them wasn't one of their own. "We understood from him," Cooney said of Merrick, "that he intended to instruct us as to unnecessary labor. . . . Our claim is that, not being a capable man, he is not able to do that."

Merrick's own account of how he did time study raised the Emperor's New Clothes question that would always mock its claim to scientific legitimacy. For each element of a molder's job—put board in place, place pattern on board, and so on—he would take perhaps five measurements. Then he'd note the best time for each, add all the best times together, and come up with "a theoretical time which it is impossible for a man to make."

Not possible but impossible, because it was calculated by adding up the absolute bare minimum for each work element. To square it with real life, Merrick would add a "percentage of allowance," like 60 percent, that made the job practical and that acknowledged inevitable hitches and delays. But "how does this percentage vary?" he was asked. Where did it come from? How did he establish it?

"That is a very difficult question to answer," he allowed. "I have no fast or set rules."

The molders had other gripes as well. Their pay depended not only on their own merits, they objected, but also on the vagaries of a shop where they sometimes had a helper to mix sand and sometimes did not; where some helpers were vastly better than others; where the crane used for heavy lifting was often in use by someone else, three or four men lined up to use it next. This was no smooth-clacking production shop, they emphasized. The Watertown foundry, said twenty-five-year

veteran molder G. E. Lawson, was really a "jobbing shop," manufacturing almost custom-made articles, in small quantities, that weighed
anywhere from a pound to twenty-five tons.

Most of all, the men objected that their experience as molders,
which told them what was fit, right, and safe, was being challenged.
Said Cooney, "We make it a principle to work safe; that is, take no
chances. While [sometimes] we do things that could be left undone, for
the purpose of being positively sure we put in this extra labor."

The men took the small-eyed stares of the efficiency expert as
demeaning. "I think I have worked long enough for anyone to tell that I
have been faithful in my work," said Joe Hicklin, thirty-eight years a
molder, who pulled down $3.52 a day. "I could not do any more if I
was getting $5 per day than I am at present."

But what was so un-American about having a stopwatch "used on
you," Edward Joyce was asked, or about working under a premium
system? It drove you toward the big money, he answered, "and in
course of time [you] cannot stand it." Joyce would go home, have
supper, and find he "was all tired out and would not feel like going anywhere, whereas while working by the day I feel as though there was
something to live for, and feel like going out for a walk evenings."
There was more to life than money, he was saying. There was more to
work than work.

All these were truths of a sort, and yet other truths, painful to the
molders, were revealed in the course of the investigation. Some outsiders hired during the strike, it seems, had been kept on. And while
Hendry, whose resistance to the stopwatch had prompted the strike,
made nine pommels a day, one of these new men made twenty-four.
That stark number came up again and again.

"Did you, or did you not, make the statement that . . . you preferred
to use your judgment rather than measure by means of a watch?"
Major Williams asked John Larkin, the foreman, who thought the old
ways, pre-Taylor, were just fine.

"Yes, sir."

"Therefore you have a great deal of confidence in your judgment?

"Yes, sir."

Now, Williams reminded him, when Merrick fixed two and a half
pommels an hour as within a molder's capabilities, "Did you not
protest to me that . . . a man could not do it?"

"Yes, sir."

"With full confidence in your judgment?"

"Yes, sir."

Yet hadn't the new man been able to do twenty-four per day?

Yes.

"Does not that shake your confidence in your judgment??

Well, Larkin allowed, Edgecomb, this tornado of a molder, was "an exceptional man." Indeed, the following month, while most of the men earned premiums of a few percent beyond their regular pay, none of them more than about a third, Edgecomb tripled his; in one two-week span he earned more than most veteran molders made in a month. Some said he monopolized the crane, that he left out steps, that his slapdash work would cost as much to finish later as he had saved. Still, there it was—twenty-four! Maybe the time-study man wasn't so far off after all.

~

As strikes go, this first one against the Taylor system was nothing much: a handful of men, few lapses from civility, the men back to work after a week. And yet its impact spiraled out from Watertown. The *Boston Globe* had reported, right up in its headline, that here was the "First Action Against Use of Taylor System in U.S. Work." The molders' union local in Boston had petitioned their congressmen. The local secretary had written the national American Federation of Labor. John P. Frey, editor of the molders' union journal, came to Watertown, where he found the arsenal gates patrolled by soldiers with fixed bayonets. On his return to Washington, the federation's executive board formally sanctioned the strike. By August 18, when the arsenal hired four scabs to replace striking molders, the strike was as good as over and General Crozier's emissary, Lieutenant Colonel Thompson, was bound for Watertown. But the ensuing investigation settled nothing.

In his testimony before Thompson—given in the arsenal's administration building, since "it was not considered desirable to detain this expert any longer than necessary"—Carl Barth applied spin control, vintage 1911, to protect the Taylor system as an abstract ideal. "We will both be found guilty," he had closed his letter to Taylor advising him of the strike, "though neither of us had had a thing to do with it." But, of course, he was Taylor's man, and the strike had come on his watch.

Now, Barth claimed that "agitation caused by the investigation undertaken by the [House] Committee on Labor" back in April had biased the men against time study. Besides, he had been away when it happened. And as for Dwight Merrick, he was just a time-study man, "whom neither Mr. Taylor nor I look upon as in any way competent to prepare the way for time study or to install the Taylor system." Merrick's mistakes, in other words, couldn't be charged against the system.

Still, it was the system that took the hit. A mass meeting was called of arsenal workers, among whom feeling against the Taylor system was said to remain "strong and bitter." Stay at work, the molders' union president told his men, document conditions, and plan to present them to a special congressional subcommittee due to arrive in Boston the following month.

For indeed, by August 21, the House had overcome a filibuster led by Illinois Congressman James Mann (better known for the Mann Act that outlawed "white slave" trafficking) and passed Resolution 90, authorizing a Special Committee to Investigate the Taylor and Other Systems of Shop Management. The committee, chaired by William B. Wilson of Pennsylvania, included the majestically muttonchopped William C. Redfield, a New York manufacturer and former public works commissioner in Brooklyn, who represented the city's Fifth Congressional District; and John Q. Tilson, a New Haven, Connecticut, congressman chosen, Taylor would observe, "as a sort of umpire, because he knew nothing about the subject."

General Frederick Winslow Taylor began to marshal his forces. They needed "a plan of campaign," he wrote Jim Dodge on September 6. "We should spare no effort to try to make the best possible impression upon the committee." They should bring the committee to Philadelphia before the formal hearings, closet them one on one—"off the record, where you don't have to worry about every word"—and show them around Tabor and Link-Belt. And they should see to it that the committee called as witnesses Link-Belt employees friendly to scientific management.

A little later, Taylor wrote Louis Brandeis. Did he know anyone on the committee? "I am anxious to learn everything that I can about the men whom we are likely to have to deal with."

Taylor saw the hearings for precisely what they were, a judgment of his life's work—and all along he worked behind the scenes to orchestrate a favorable one. He peppered committee members with literature on scientific management and corresponded with them. He lined up favorable witnesses and coached them. He met personally with his judges. "I want very much to consult [with] you about a few matters" related to the hearings, he wrote Congressman Redfield at one point. "It has occurred to me that you might not object to my joining you on your train from New York to Philadelphia." Later, given the opportunity to check the stenographic record of his own testimony, Taylor went so far as to rewrite portions of it.

On September 19, Taylor received a letter on House of Representatives letterhead. "Dear Sir," it began, "I am directed by the Special House Committee authorized to investigate the Taylor and other systems of shop management to inform you that the Committee will begin its investigation at the Watertown Arsenal on October 4th, 1911." It was signed, "W. B. Wilson, Chairman."

4

THE SPECIAL COMMITTEE

~

"**I**S IT NOT A MATTER OF FACT that no property or no title to property can be created or maintained except by virtue of law?" Chairman Wilson asked witness Henry Towne.

"Surely."

"And that law is created by society for its own welfare and that a manufacturing establishment could not be maintained unless a title to property existed somewhere?"

"That is absolutely right," replied Towne.

"So that in its final analysis a manufacturing establishment is maintained primarily for the welfare of society and secondarily for the welfare of those who are immediately the owners."

"That is right."

This was not the only time Special Committee testimony would read as if pulled straight from one of Plato's dialogues, or that the hearings otherwise took a philosophical turn. A little later, Wilson asked

Herbert Stimpson, the sole efficiency engineer to testify back in April, whether he would "class a man in the same category that you would an ordinary machine?" Stimpson replied that he looked upon a man

> as a little portable power plant . . . a mighty delicate and complicated machine. . . . The physical body of the man is constructed on the same mechanical principles as the machine is, except that it is a very much higher development. Take the human arm; look at the flexibility of motion there . . .

And like any machine, you could push a man right up to his limits, so long as you figured in a factor of safety.

"How would you arrive at the factor of safety in a man?" Wilson asked.

"By a process analogous to that by which we arrive at the same factor in a machine," he replied.

"Who is to determine this for a man?" asked A. J. Coyle, a union representative.

"Specialists," replied Stimpson. "We employ the specialist who knows what the machine can stand, and we should use the specialist who knows what the human frame can stand."

If these are familiar ideas today, when knees, hips, and optic lenses are surgically replaced and ergonomics counts as a real science, they were more novel in 1911. And so was much else surrounding the new ideas of Taylorism during those five months of hearings before Chairman Wilson.

Was work simply an exchange of labor and skill in return for pay? Was it best written off as a necessary evil, the other fourteen or sixteen hours of the day left for the real business of living? Or did it encompass a spiritual and moral dimension? Did the worker's own experience—as he shoveled into the sandpile or measured the depth of a groove he was turning on a lathe—count in the reckoning, too? Or ought workers simply to obey orders? How hard and how fast should we work? Who is to say, and to what end? How was one to use time? In whose control was work to reside? Did the owner of a company have license to do as he wished, or did he bear a responsibility to his workers and to the community? What was real democracy? What was the nature of science? What did it mean to be rational? What constituted the good life?

The introduction of the Taylor system to Watertown Arsenal, historian of technology Hugh Aitken has written, represented no mere technical innovation. "There in miniature were all the stresses of an industrial society exposed to constant revolution in technology and organization." Indeed, the hearing that grew out of the molders' strike threw open all of modern work, and much else of modern life besides, to study, dissection, and debate. The Special Committee investigated a doctrine, management scholar Harlow S. Person stressed in 1926; it was one thing for Congress to take on some specific instance of misconduct, quite another to publicly investigate a social, ethical, and economic doctrine—Taylorism. On the surface, this was just another public hearing, meant to influence legislation, steeped in politics, riddled with rhetorical flourishes and all the "Mr. Chairman this" and "Mr. Chairman that" you could want. But it was much more.

~

It started out modestly enough in Boston and Watertown, where friends of scientific management could see what they were up against in Chairman Wilson of Pennsylvania. While Congressman Redfield stood on scientific management's side and Congressman Tilson remained largely mute, Wilson sympathized openly with labor. The former coal miner, risen through the ranks to a high union position and then to Congress (and later to secretary of labor under Woodrow Wilson), proved every bit Taylor's match.

In testimony taken at the arsenal itself, he noted a mold sitting on a bench and asked, "The workman has to bend over the mold?"

"Yes, sir," replied Major Williams.

So wouldn't having to walk a distance to fetch nails or other supplies—"inefficient" in a scientifically managed shop—afford a chance to straighten up? Wilson understood this better than most, he explained, because he'd spend his early life as a coal miner.

At fifty, boyishly benign in appearance, Wilson was alive to any potential abuse of the worker; even Taylor respected him. Plunked down onto the foundry floor, molding lingo flying around him, he let nothing go. "What is a gagger?" he asked, of a tool placed in a mold to secure the sand against the molten metal's pressure. At another point, questioning pertained to how the two halves of a mold were nailed together. "Is the term 'nail' the same term as is used generally," he asked, "or is it a technical term?"

Wilson profitably pursued points that to others were self-evident.

When Major Williams stated that "a time once properly set will not be reduced," Wilson, after some intervening questions, seized upon "properly." So time study might *not* be properly made; scientific management, however imposing its edifice of science, could err.

Most of the issues raised by Taylorism over the years rear up at least in embryonic form in the hearings' 1,935 pages of printed transcript. "Is it a part of the system," Wilson asked Colonel Wheeler, "that all of the work, with the exception of the mere mechanical work of caring for the machine, is carried on in that planning department?"

"Yes, sir," replied the colonel.

"Leaving no discretion other than simply the mechanical work of caring for the machine to the workmen?"

"That is practically so."

What if that spread generally throughout industry? Would it not reduce the skilled workforce "and thereby tend to lower the general standard of work?" Wilson was already worried about the insidious "deskilling" of which Taylorism would later stand accused.

Just as some scholars would question Taylorism's seemingly axiomatic guilt, so did Colonel Wheeler. "I have thought that possibly the effect would be just the reverse of that, Mr. Chairman," he replied. The machinists got instructions prepared by men more expert than themselves. These were the skilled men now, even if they never got their hands dirty and wore white collars instead of blue.

When Wheeler argued that scientific management encouraged suggestions, the chairman wondered if whether, on the contrary, it discouraged them. For weren't workers now "nothing more nor less than human machines to carry out . . . instructions?" The planning room was now the repository of all knowledge and skill. The shop itself would be denuded of both.

In questioning a witness later, Congressman Redfield tried to refute this argument. "When something comes out of the planning department to you," he asked Willard Barker, a machinist and sometime foreman, "are you free to criticize it . . . and to make suggestions?"

Yes, replied Barker, he was.

Didn't the man on the machine thereby profit from "the combined wisdom of the planning room and of yourself?"

"Yes, sir."

So the workman is in a position to constantly learn?

Yes.

And "that adds to his ability as a workman, does it not?"

"I think so."

"And by adding to his ability as a workman you add to his capacity to earn, whether in your shop or any other shop, do you not?"

(Now it was Redfield exploiting the Socratic method.)

"That is the way it seems to me."

"Now, I ask you, and I think it is a very important question, whether a man who graduates from that system is not better fitted to face the world on his own feet than he was before?"

And to this, too, Barker had to agree.

Listen to Redfield, then, and the Taylor system produced not automatons bereft of skill but ever more capable, knowledgeable workers.

Chairman Wilson didn't let it go at that. "Do you believe," he asked Barker, that the workman's skill profits from having "all the details of his work mapped out for him by somebody else, giving him no latitude to exercise his skill?"

"I think it would hurt a workman."

Bound by detailed, written instructions, "would not a man naturally hesitate about . . . suggesting any other process?"

"It seems to me he would," replied Barker

About an hour and a half later, a labor representative asked Barker whether the arsenal's machine shop really needed outside experts to modernize it: "Mr. Barker, could you have done as well or better . . . if given the same latitude as the so-called experts?"

But before he could answer, Major Williams interposed a twist to the question that left Barker less maneuvering room: "Could you have redesigned those lathes . . . that we put motors on?"

Well, he'd never tackled a job like that, but he could.

And that was the beginning of the end for poor Barker, whom the forces of knowledge and light now proceeded to humiliate.

"Now, Mr. Barker, have you ever installed any electrical machinery?" asked Redfield.

"No, sir."

"You are familiar with the conditions of speed required by direct current motors?"

"No, sir."

"Would you go out and seek employment yourself as a mechanic versed in the erection and installation of electrically driven machinery?"

"No, sir."

"Mr. Barker," Col. Wheeler put in, "could you have prepared the specification" for the motors they'd bought?

"Probably it would have taken me some time, but I think I could have told how fast I wanted the motor to go."

"Would you have called for a compound motor or a series motor?"

"I could not say that I know about that."

"How are the motors wound, Mr. Barker?" This time it was Redfield again.

"I could not say."

"You don't know the winding of motors?"

"No, sir."

Was he familiar with construction differences between General Electric speed controllers and those made by Cutler-Hammer?

No.

"Would you be prepared to draw a specification giving one or the other, and the reasons why?

No.

"Then, as a matter of fact," Redfield cinched the case, "would you say to the committee that . . . you would be prepared in the electrical equipment [area] to do anything that the experts did?"

"Not in the electrical line," Barker replied.

Major Williams took over, addressing presumably more familiar mechanical areas: "Could you calculate the strength of the gearing needed?"

"Probably not scientifically."

"Then you would probably have to just guess at the dimensions of the gear?"

Wheeler pressed home the attack. Suppose they did metal-cutting tests, which severely tried the lathe's gearing. "Can you tell me what the downward pressure on that tool is when the cut is being taken?"

"No, sir."

"Would not that kind of information be necessary in order to deter-mine the strength of your teeth and gears?

"Yes sir; I suppose it would."

"Can you tell me how much stress is being brought on the lead screw in feeding the tools into that metal?" asked Wheeler.

"No, sir."

"Then you would not be prepared to undertake the design or redesign of a lathe tool, would you?"

"Probably not, scientifically."

Barker was beaten, but the jackals only sank their fangs deeper. "Would you be prepared, Mr. Barker"—it was Redfield again—"to explain the advantage or disadvantage . . . of what is known as an epicycloid gear?" Barker hesitated. Redfield reassured him, "I should not expect you to, but I want you to answer me whether you do or not."

And of course he didn't know. The man who could do without the experts couldn't.

With high-speed steel, Taylor had shown that he—not the man down on the floor—made the best cutting tools. Barth's slide rules showed that the machinist who set speed and feed knew less than the man in the planning office. Now, Wheeler and the others had shown that this veteran foreman knew almost nothing at all.

Guesswork, habit, and hunch were on the run.

At other times, though, science was on the run, or at least scientific management's claim on it. Much as scholars today often find ambiguity in areas of knowledge that had once seemed fixed and certain, Chairman Wilson repeatedly pointed up the arbitrariness he saw in the Taylor system, questioned its objectivity, consistency, and fairness.

When Colonel Wheeler described the Taylor system as "based on common sense," for example, Wilson fairly pounced on him: If it were just common sense, wouldn't it vary with "different standards of common sense" around the country and thus, in a sense, be arbitrary? Wasn't common sense really just "Mr. Taylor's ideas and standards of common sense?"

To this, Colonel Wheeler had to agree.

Later came a replay of the awkward questions Merrick had faced in the Thompson investigation two months earlier, first with Major Williams in the hot seat. The time-study man added to his raw stopwatch times a percentage, anywhere from 10 to 100 percent. But how, Chairman Wilson wanted to know, "do you arrive at it?"

"This is somewhat a matter of judgment and experience," Williams replied.

"It is not based, then, upon any known scientific system?" Wilson asked.

"It is based upon careful observation."

Then, Merrick himself fielded the questions. Wasn't the allowance "arbitrarily determined, depending solely upon the judgment of the man setting the time?" Merrick could only fumble awkwardly.

"Then it is a matter of his judgment based upon observation?" asked Wilson.

"Yes, sir," said Merrick, mere judgment.

The stopwatch itself, the very symbol of Taylorism, exposed the biggest breach between the workers and their masters. To the managers it was just a tool; to the workers it was a hideous invasion of privacy, an oppressive all-seeing eye that peered into their work lives, ripping at their dignity.

It was the difference in viewpoint between the watcher and the watched.

"When a man stands over me all day, I get very nervous," Watertown machinist Richard Stackhouse said in reply to a question. Very few could do their work properly with someone standing over them. "I think a man's nerves cannot stand it. I know mine cannot."

But what if management had no wish to fix the workman's pay at all, but simply wanted to make improvements and needed the times to help them? Would he object then?

No, said Stackhouse, unless they used a stopwatch on him.

So then he would object!

What if the observer had no stopwatch but merely watched? Chairman Wilson wondered.

"It would have the same effect on me."

The watching *itself* was the problem; to Stackhouse and the others, surveillance with a stopwatch seemed not mere seeing but judgment, prying, intrusion. George White, a machinist of ten years' standing at Watertown, testified that he, too, felt uncomfortable with Merrick's attentions on him. But why, Merrick himself asked. Had he spoken harshly to him?

No, not exactly. But "I have seen times when you would come up and go over how many I had done in half a day, and you would not feel just right over it. You would kind of scowl."

~

On October 11, 1911, a labor representative asked the committee to give Boston navy yard workers more time to testify. Impossible, said

Wilson. Their report was due by December 10, and they'd already spent three days longer in Boston than planned. The committee would adjourn and meet in New York on October 25.

There, over three days, they heard from Harrington Emerson, the man whose million-dollar-a-day claim had boosted scientific management into orbit. And from H. L. Gantt, Henry Towne, Edith Wyatt (whom a magazine had commissioned to look into conditions of women under scientific management), sheet metal workers from the Brooklyn navy yard, and others.

The evening of the first day in New York, Taylor wrote Hathaway that, while both Emerson and Gantt had done well, "the star witness of the day was Miss Wyatt, who testified in the greatest detail, and evidently carried the committee with her." Taylor had already had her to Boxly, of course. Behind the scenes, he was still trying to choreograph events.

The following Monday, he wrote Hathaway that they should gather instruction cards that showed a high percentage allowance for delay— the witch's brew factor of time study. "The Committee want to know, among other things, how it is that we arrive at the proper marginal allowance for unavoidable delays. . . . So that if you have any logical way in which you do this, I hope you will be able to tell them."

Taylor was hugely confident. He wrote Brandeis, "The labor leaders who have appeared before the Committee have been tamed in quite a wonderful way, and I think the Committee is practically convinced already that scientific management is a good thing for the workmen and for the Government as well."

I can find in the testimony no basis for Taylor's assertion, though, in the long run, labor was indeed tamed. If anything, the situation was heating up. Secretary of War Henry Stimson had called the Watertown experiment "highly gratifying and full of promise." But in a statement issued in Washington on November 3, machinists' union president James O'Connell declared:

> If the Taylor system is put into operation in government shops by
> Secretary Stimson, as he has stated, one of two things will result—
> either Congress will enact legislation relieving machinists of the
> unjust rigors of the so-called "scientific management," or there will
> be a cessation of work.

On December 8, Chairman Wilson was granted a ninety-day extension for the committee report and asked for more money for travel and per diem expenses. "The battle to be fought out before the committee," *Iron Age* predicted two weeks before the hearings were to resume, "will doubtless be an interesting one."

This phase of the hearings, from January 4 almost nonstop to February 12, 1912, brought to Washington more than forty witnesses. In the first two weeks, it was metal polishers, machinists, and carpenters from the Rock Island Arsenal; blacksmiths, riveters, and electricians from the navy yard at Norfolk. General Crozier testified, as did Carl Barth and Jim Dodge. So did Taylor.

On January 20, Wilson wrote Taylor, who had attended the hearings religiously, that he was directed to appear on January 25.

Two days later, Taylor wrote back saying, "It will give me pleasure to appear before your committee."

It gave him none.

~

The day he heard from Wilson, Taylor called in an old debt.

Ten months earlier, around the time the *American Magazine* articles were coming out, Taylor got a letter of introduction from a thirty-six-year-old West Medford, Massachusetts, man named Hollis Godfrey.

Godfrey had graduated from Tufts College in Massachusetts, done graduate work at MIT, and was just then, as he wrote Taylor in March 1911, "head of the Department of Science in the School of Practical Arts, Boston." He had written monographs on public health and popular books on scientific subjects, as well as children's books, short stories, and even a novel that predicted a coming world war. An earnest, neat young man with a pince-nez, he "struck nearly everyone who met him more than briefly," according to a later account, "as slightly mad." Now, said his letter to Taylor, he wished to become "more efficient" and better prepared to organize "the rather disorganized field of education." Could scientific management work for him? Could he get Mr. Taylor's help?

Taylor sometimes took on new recruits, paying them to work at Tabor or Link-Belt and learn the ropes before going out on their own in the service of scientific management. Godfrey became one of them. He made the pilgrimage to Boxly and began a correspondence with

Taylor notable for its servile flattery: "It is a very great thing to evolve an idea which seems likely to prove of such great value to the industries of the world," he wrote his new mentor. He gave up his sideline advertising business, declared his obeisance to scientific management, and expressed willingness to "get into the game from the standpoint of the beginner."

But he did have this one little problem. "The only difficulty in my way is that my family must be considered. I can give up three months to a low wage or no wage at all, but I must then begin to earn money." Taylor had him meet Morris Cooke. He was full of himself, but smart, Cooke wrote Taylor. "If you handle him right, you can get him to do almost anything you tell him to do for the next two or three years." After that, "he might do some things that we would all be glad to have done." Soon Godfrey was at Tabor, Taylor paying him four thousand dollars a year.

Now, in January, Taylor had been called down from the mountaintop. There, in the miasma of Washington politics, he would need help. He wired Godfrey:

I MUST TESTIFY BEFORE HOUSE COMMITTEE THURSDAY, TEN
O'CLOCK. THINK YOU HAD BETTER COME DOWN TO WASHINGTON
TO HEAR TESTIMONY AND SO FORTH. HAVE WRITTEN YOUR HOUSE.

He needed Godfrey, his letter explained, to help "take charge of our case and see that the proper testimony is brought out from our witnesses." Having followed the hearings closely, he knew best how "to give certain shades to my testimony" and what might influence the committee. "Therefore it seems to me important for you to be in Washington to hear my testimony.

He did not ask Godfrey to come: this was a summons.

I shall be at the New Willard Hotel, and would suggest that you be
at the Capitol, in the room of the Labor Committee, at ten o'clock
on Thursday morning. Of course I shall be pleased to pay all of
your expenses, etc.

∼

The New Willard, which rose two stories over the corner of Pennsylvania Avenue and Fourteenth Street, practically across from the White House, had on its completion in 1901 instantly joined the ranks of the capital's best hotels. Taylor was accustomed to the kind of opulence it offered, but now he would have found it matched by the grand scale of a new *public* Washington. About the time he was there, *Scribner's* magazine described the recent "evolution of a Virginian village into a city worthy to be the capital and show-place of the nation." Everywhere stood columns and pediments, new expanses of granite and marble. The Library of Congress, with its great circular reading room, had gone up in 1897. Recent construction, at enormous public expense, had created new office buildings for the House and Senate, a new Department of Agriculture, and the monumental Union Station, with its arched facade stretching across the front and its echoing vaults within. "If our republic is by no means like Cicero's in 'hating private luxury,' " *Scribner's* writer Montgomery Schuyler observed, "it resembles it at least in 'loving public magnificence.' " And if all this could seem like too liberal an expenditure of the public treasury, it could likewise be seen as honoring "the people," before whom Taylor had, in effect, been summoned to testify. As he stepped out from the Willard lobby onto a Pennsylvania Avenue sprinkled with horse-drawn carriages and motor-cars alike, he could see to his left the dome of the Capitol. There, in a first-floor committee room, he was to testify.

In 1912, labor-management strife hung heavy in the air. A strike of twenty thousand textile workers in Lawrence, Massachusetts, had brought out the militia and filled every front page. Cardinal John Murphy Farley of New York, speaking before a convention at New York's Astor Hotel, lamented that employer and employee stood "like two galleries of statues, facing one another, having no sympathy with one another whatever, no tie, no bond, each one independent. . . , like two armies in battle array, waiting for the order to attack one another."

Earlier, the Boston papers and trade journals like *Iron Age* had covered the hearings. But by the time Taylor took the stand, after almost fifty previous witnesses, with testimony having already ground on for a month in Washington alone, and with the troubles in Lawrence drawing the nation's gaze, "the papers have lost interest in it," wrote Taylor. For most of his testimony, probably only a dozen or fifteen people were on hand: the three congressmen, Taylor himself, Hollis

Godfrey, Carl Barth for a while, labor representatives, stenographers, and a few others. It was an intimate battle, fought hand to hand and bloody.

"Mr. Taylor," the chairman began at a quarter to eleven on the morning of Thursday, January 25, "are you the author or compiler of the system of shop management generally known as the 'Taylor System'?"

No simple "I am" would do for Taylor. "I have had a very great deal to do with the development of the system of management which has come to be called by certain people the 'Taylor system,' " he replied, "but I am only one of many men who have been instrumental in the development of this system. I wish to state, however, that at no time have I personally called the system the 'Taylor system.' "

Almost immediately, Wilson gave Taylor his head. The resulting monologue lasted all that morning and afternoon and on into the following day. Rarely did anyone break in for a question or even suggest that he hurry up. His opening statement, reprinted in book form, extended over 106 pages. Here was the Boxly talk all over again—only not quite the Boxly talk. Whereas at Chestnut Hill he played mainly to business leaders, here it was labor he tried to sway with his awkwardly endearing mix of shop floor plain talk and Germantown idealism.

"While I shall have to say quite a little in the way of blame as to the views and acts of certain labor leaders during my talk," he allowed, "in the main I look upon them as strictly honest, upright, straightforward men."

He would speak of class but only to mean "groups of men and women with somewhat similar aims in life, and not at all with the 'upper and lower class' distinctions which are sometimes given to these words."

Back in 1840, he told his audience, five thousand Manchester weavers resisted the power loom for fear of losing their jobs to it. Now Manchester employed a quarter million. "Has the introduction of labor-saving machinery"—which is how he broadly classed scientific management—"thrown men out of work?"

Checks on production hurt not the rich, he said, but the poor, who consumed "nineteen-twentieths" of everything. Soldiering was nothing less than a "robbing of the poor."

He knew that many viewed workmen "as greedy, selfish, grasping, and even worse," he said a little later. "But I don't sympathize with this view in the least."

He reminded the room of a time "when I was a workman" and that he, too, had soldiered.

Taylor's performance included some of his most oft-quoted utterances on scientific management. "I want to clear the deck," he said at one point, and "sweep away a good deal of rubbish first by pointing out what scientific management is not." Then commenced the astonishing litany:

> Scientific management is not any efficiency device, not a device of any kind for securing efficiency; nor is it any group of efficiency devices. It is not a new system of figuring costs; it is not a new scheme of paying men; it is not a piecework system; it is not a bonus system; it is not a premium system; it is no scheme for paying men; it is not holding a stop watch on a man and writing things down about him; it is not time study; it is not motion study nor an analysis of the movements of men; it is not the printing and ruling and unloading of a ton or two of blanks on a set of men and saying, "Here's your system; go use it." It is not divided foremanship or functional foremanship; it is not any of the devices which the average man calls to mind when scientific management is spoken of.

These were merely tools, "adjuncts." Scientific management was more, demanding "a complete mental revolution" on the part of workers and management. "And without this complete mental revolution on both sides scientific management does not exist."

A mental revolution. All through his testimony, he'd repeat the phrase. This revolution would—indeed, must—"produce results which are magnificent for both sides." In the past, workingmen and management worried about "the proper division of the surplus resulting from their joint efforts," each side looking to maximize its take and viewing the other as its enemy. But under scientific management that would change:

> The great revolution that takes place in the mental attitude of the two parties under scientific management is that both sides take

their eyes off of the division of the surplus as the all-important matter, and together turn their attention toward increasing the size of the surplus until this surplus becomes so large that it is unnecessary to quarrel over how it shall be divided.

Pulling together, they hugely increase production and the resulting "surplus." Wages and profits rise. Everyone goes home happy. "This, gentlemen, is the beginning of the great mental revolution," which results in

the substitution of peace for war; the substitution of hearty brotherly cooperation for contention and strife; of both pulling hard in the same direction instead of pulling apart; of replacing suspicious watchfulness with mutual confidence; of becoming friends instead of enemies.

This mental revolution required a radical change in viewpoint, one "absolutely essential to the existence of scientific management"—the sovereignty of science. "Both sides must recognize as essential the substitution of exact scientific investigation and knowledge for the old individual judgment or opinion," in all matters bearing on work. "This applies both as to the methods to be employed in doing the work and the time in which each job should be done." Required was

the deliberate gathering in on the part of those on the management's side of all of the great mass of traditional knowledge, which in the past has been in the heads of the workmen, and in the physical skill and knack of the workmen, which he has acquired through years of experience.

It was this knowledge—recorded, tabulated, reduced "to laws, rules, and even to mathematical formulae"—that bestowed its bounty on worker, boss, and public.

What followed, on into Friday afternoon, were some of Taylor's favorite stories. But that of Schmidt was not among them; it was getting him into trouble, he must have realized, and suffered from overexposure, besides. "For some reason, I don't know exactly why, this illustration has been talked about a great deal. So much, in fact, that some people seem to think that the whole of scientific management consists in handling pig iron." This time, he offered the tale of the twenty-one-pound shovel load instead, but not before getting in one parting gibe at the Schmidts of the world. Shoveling was quite a science, and "the ordinary pig-iron handler" is not well suited to it. "He is too stupid; there is too much mental strain, too much knack required."

From there it was on to Gilbreth's bricklaying and finally, the pièce de résistance, the metal-cutting experiments, complete with Barth slide rules and three of the empirical formulas they embodied, duly certifying scientific management's scientific legitimacy:

$$P = 45,000 \ D^{\frac{14}{15}} F^{\frac{3}{4}}$$

$$V = \frac{90}{T^{\frac{1}{8}}}$$

$$V = \frac{11.9}{F^{0.665} \left(\dfrac{48}{3} D\right)^{0.2373} + \frac{2.4}{18 + 24D}}$$

How could such baroque specimens fail to impress?

Finally, after seven hours, Taylor's soliloquy was over. The following morning, a Saturday, Wilson set to work on the cross-examination.

"How long did you serve as an apprentice?"

"I started in 1874 and finished in 1878."

"Making four years?"

"Four years of work; yes sir."

"How old were you when you began your apprenticeship?"

"About 18 years old."

Now the conversation was no longer just a monologue. Back at Boxly, Taylor faced no dissent; but here, in the committee room, he contended with workmen, union leaders, and others sympathetic to them, like Wilson, on something like equal terms. Here he faced mistrust and skepticism from those of background and life experience foreign to his own—men who'd insisted they be formally subpoenaed by Congress lest they lose their jobs back at Rock Island or Watertown, and for whom the five-cents-a-mile and two-dollars-a-day traveling allowance made the difference in whether they could come to Washington at all. Was this what Taylor found so exhausting—this maddening, intransigent countervoice taking issue with him and his ideas, peppering him with questions whose content, pacing, and direction he could not control? Was this what left him, after four days in that vaulted committee room almost beneath the Capitol dome, shaking with rage and frustration?

Taylor spoke of the long-term benefits of scientific management. But, Wilson wondered, what about in the meantime when, during "a disturbed condition in the trades affected by the improvements," workers bore "the entire burden?"

Taylor admitted that labor-saving machinery, for example, had often left workers not benefiting as they should. Under his system, though, they gained immediately, through wages 30 to 100 percent higher.

But what of those who lose their jobs entirely, who have no wages?

Scientific management never came in suddenly, Taylor answered. There would be a period of adjustment, during which prices fell, thus increasing consumption and, in turn, employment.

"But is it not true," asked Wilson, that any increased consumption, with its new jobs, likewise did not come suddenly?

Taylor cited history and statistics, but Wilson held firm. He was thinking of men and women trapped in that intellectually uninteresting "short term" where they actually lived and suffered. What would happen to them? How did scientific management propose to relieve their suffering?

Wilson's dark scenario didn't materialize often, Taylor insisted. Blue-collar jobs were lost, but management jobs were gained, many workers becoming "teachers, guiders, and helpers."

When the hearings resumed on Tuesday, Wilson took up Taylor's notion of soldiering. "Who," he wondered, "is to determine what constitutes soldiering?"

The question would resound throughout the hearings and across the years. To Taylor, the answer was simple: a proper day's work was a matter of "accurate, careful scientific investigation." Science would determine.

But wasn't the employer an interested party to this scientific investigation? Wouldn't that influence the results? How "could the workman protect himself?"

"By simply refusing to work at the pace set," Taylor replied, in which case his wage would revert to the regular day rate. Besides, rate setters had typically been workmen themselves six months or a year before. "You must remember, Mr. Chairman . . . that under scientific management the workmen and the management are the best of friends." Workers had but to bring any seeming injustice to the attention of management and an "impartial and careful investigation will be made."

Wilson's antennae were buzzing. Tasks were set "by men who have come fresh from the ranks?"

"Yes, sir."

But wasn't a man selected by management likely picked precisely because he would protect the interests of management? And wasn't it true "that the very essence of scientific management is that there must be one directing head," who brooked no interference?

Yes, the witness allowed, no interference could be tolerated, though worker and management could cooperate.

But under Taylor's system, didn't such cooperation have to conform "with the judgment and direction and policy" of the boss?

By now, Taylor was sorely put out. "No, sir; most emphatically no." The system imposed standards that were fair and just.

And true collective bargaining? In which "the workmen collectively [help determine] the wages, the task, and the conditions under which they shall work?" Did scientific management have room for it?

Not in the "old sense," said Taylor. Under his system, workers and management join as one, and "collective bargaining, instead of becoming a necessity, becomes of trifling importance." Should some injustice arise, workers had only to protest and receive "a careful scientific investigation" into the case."

Taylor was offering a vision of worker and boss united in harmony under the banner of science. But, Chairman Wilson asked, as long as management was "the sole and arbitrary judge" of workplace issues, wasn't that "very much like the lion and the lamb lying down together with the lamb inside?"

No, "the lion is proverbial of strife, arrogance—of everything that is vicious. Scientific management cannot exist in establishments with lions at the head of them. It ceases to exist when injustice knowingly exists. Injustice is typical of some other management, not of scientific management."

May we expect, asked Wilson, that employers, motivated by profit, would then "immediately, voluntarily, and generally enforce the golden rule?"

"If they had sense they would," replied Frederick Taylor.

But what penalty, the chairman asked, would be incurred by the head of a company who didn't live by its precepts? Wasn't he immune from harmful consequence?

But his system could not be used that way, said Taylor. "It is possible to use the *mechanism* of scientific management, but not scientific management itself. It ceases to be scientific management the moment it is used for bad." This was about like saying that a steam engine, at its first departure from the ideal, at the first sign of heat loss or mechanical friction, was no longer a steam engine.

Taylor resorted to this rhetorical device again and again. Time study or other such "mechanisms" might be abused, but then, whatever tolerated them was no longer scientific management—which, accordingly, could not be held to account.

It was a disingenuous trick, as Taylor's own correspondence shows. Writing a potential witness a week later, he called it "the most effective weapon that we have all of us found as a foil against inconvenient questions." By now, Wilson "perfectly detests the statement that scientific management is mainly a state of mind, and that it ceases to exist when anyone on the management side gets into the wrong state of mind." Writing Hollis Godfrey around this time, he called the notion of a "mental revolution"—the altered state of mind that presumably bars its harmful use—as one "method of protecting scientific management from attack."

"Weapons," "methods," "devices," and "shields" for use against the "lies," "wiles," and "traps" of his foes; this was the language Taylor was using now. His rhetoric pictured a benign system, a workplace at peace. But now, down from the mountaintop, on reality's fetid plains, Fred Taylor was, as usual, at war.

Taylor had explained that in time studies for railroad car axles, say, he tacked on an allowance, of 20 to 27 percent, for unavoidable delays and interruptions. But "by what scientific formula or mathematical calculation" did he arrive at that figure? asked Wilson. He was cutting to the heart of the Taylor system's vaunted science.

"Through a very careful study," Taylor replied—by studying a man for sometimes days on end.

But what about the actual numbers? "Is not that 20 to 27 per cent arbitrarily arrived at by the judgment of a person watching the operation?"

"No, sir," insisted Taylor, "not the arbitrary judgment of anyone. An arbitrary judgment would be something that a man guessed at. But this is a scientific investigation, a careful, thorough scientific investigation of the facts."

But scientific *how*? Weren't the old, informal ways "just as scientific and just as arbitrary as the method employed [by you] in securing this 20 to 27 per cent?" He never got an answer that satisfied him.

Taylor testified that, in timing a man, "you are very apt to put three or four teachers around him at once to see that he does not skip out from under anywhere."

But wouldn't that distort the would-be science of the measurement? Wouldn't time study's accuracy be undermined by "the abnormal conditions created by that power being brought to bear on the individual workman?"

No, because in making the time study, workers and management cooperate "in the most friendly manner."

But where was the cooperation, Wilson wanted to know, if choosing not to cooperate placed the worker's livelihood in danger? If refusal, while of no account to his employer, meant starvation to him?

"I must say, Mr. Chairman, that I do not exactly catch your meaning; I do not think I understand you." He really didn't get it. He didn't see the asymmetry in the position of labor and management that, to Wilson, undermined his system's very foundation. By now, the chairman may have thought he was dealing with a child, or a naïf, or a cynic of Machiavellian proportion. "I will give you an illustration," he said wearily, going on to construct a scenario in which a worker, "starvation staring him in the face," is forced to capitulate to any terms the employer may demand.

There were still hours to go before Wilson was finally through with him. They talked about what could happen to men who were not, in Taylor's phase, "first class men," and what constituted such a species.

And they talked about whether society was so exquisitely balanced that it always provided the working population with just the right mix of jobs.

At one point, Taylor advanced a vision of a more productive world offering plenty to all. "In my judgment, the best possible measure of the height in the scale of civilization to which any people has arisen is its productivity."

But if, as was true by 1912, the American worker was already more productive than his counterparts abroad, or his counterparts two hundred years before, yet still often lived in misery, why, asked Wilson, squeeze still more work out of him? And if higher production was supposed "to add to the comfort and well-being of mankind," hadn't Taylor, in pressing the worker to his limit and exacerbating his discomfort, "thereby destroyed the very purposes of your production?"

What discomfort, Taylor as much as said. "I do not look upon it as anything of a misfortune" that a man should "spend his working time in useful effort instead of in useless exertion."

But who was to decide? Did Mr. Taylor think the employer "should have the power to determine absolutely . . . what constitutes comfort" for their employees? Despite every disavowal by Taylor, here was how scientific management seemed to Wilson: the boss firmly in charge as usual. "Under our laws," said Wilson, "no judge would be permitted to sit in a case in which he had a personal interest." Yet "with the power centered in the head of the establishment," that was precisely the situation under the Taylor system.

∽

When, after seven hours of brawling, Taylor finally stepped down late Tuesday night, probably around midnight, he was angry and exhausted. "As the hearings have progressed," he'd written Henry Towne back in October, it seemed to him "that the labor leaders were growing less and less bitter in their opposition; in other words, that they were becoming tamed." They had, he was sure, only to "be held in the room for a day or two, listening to testimony," to come away more sympathetic.

By now, they'd been held in a room with him for four days and still were untamed. "A more agile intellect, or one skilled in disputation would have perceived early in the cross-examination . . . that minds were not meeting, and would have framed his replies differently," said Harlow Person, then director of the Taylor Society, to explain Taylor's unraveling. But it could be argued as easily that he was simply unnerved by the rough-and-tumble of free and open debate.

Washington was not Boxly. Here, he was out in the open, exposed, rebutted and provoked by men not in any way his intellectual inferior.

Toward the end of his testimony, Taylor fell into pitched battle with two of the labor leaders. Insults and provocations threatened to escalate to blows. Wilson shouted a stop to it and struck everything said in anger from the record.

When Taylor was finally excused, Godfrey went with him to get a cab to Union Station, a few blocks away. When no cab materialized, Taylor fumed. Godfrey, alarmed by his want of mental equanimity, accompanied him to the train himself.

When they had trouble getting into the station, Taylor lashed out. At station personnel? At Godfrey? At the goddamned union leaders? At the whole stupid, unseeing world? The record is not clear. What is clear is that Taylor was a forlorn hulk of nerves, frustrated and defeated.

By the next day, Taylor was installed at the Hotel Brighton in Atlantic City, New Jersey. He and Lou—she was "very much run down" and plagued with trouble sleeping—were already booked aboard the Cunard liner *Caronia*, set to sail on February 20 for Naples. In a letter written that evening, Godfrey didn't mention Taylor's outbursts, but concluded, "I hope you had a good trip and [that you will have] a few days of less strenuous life."

But Taylor had too much to do. Eighteen men were still to testify, which would take up most of the next two weeks, and he wanted to keep abreast of it. In the meantime, he was supposed to correct his own testimony as it came back from the stenographer. Godfrey remained at the New Willard as his emissary, attending sessions, serving as liaison to the committee, writing him daily reports.

On February 1, Barth went on the stand, delivering a performance that, in Taylor's words to James Dodge the next day, was "contrary to all our expectations." From the New Willard, Godfrey had written him how Barth

> bared his great heart, told of his own struggles and of his deep and abiding interest in the workman, showed by concrete case after case where he had stood for justice and right and seemed almost inspired in his appeal for justice and recognition of his values. He moved Wilson more than I could have believed him moved and left with an admirable feeling all around.

The same day as Barth's testimony, the committee clerk wrote Taylor with the stenographic copy of his January 26 testimony, asking that he return it, corrected, as soon as possible. Next day, Taylor wrote subpoenaed witness David Van Alstyne, former shop manager of the American Locomotive Company, that once in Washington he should look up Godfrey, who would furnish him "the best general tactics to follow in giving your testimony before the Committee. The labor people are very keen in setting traps for every one of our witnesses."

All that day, Taylor dictated letters. He wrote William Barba, super intendent back at Midvale, with a list of four Midvale men subpoenaed "by the union side. . . . Can you not give me some history of these men, something which would be of help in cross-examining them when they get on the stand?" Better yet would be finding men friendly to scientific management. "I shall be glad personally to pay the expenses of any such men. . . . I will have subpoenas issued for them, and will see that they are well-treated when they get to Washington."

Taylor sought to influence not just the course of the hearings but also how they were represented in the official record. For the next two weeks, he worked at correcting his testimony, often staying up late each night. Here was his last chance to put it in the best light and perhaps make up for that terrible last night on the stand. "It takes me about four days to correct one day's testimony, he wrote Barth, "and even then it is pretty poor reading." He would "rather dictate the whole thing all the way over again from the start."

And, amazingly, that's what he tried to do. On February 12, he wrote the committee secretary lamenting that he'd had much trouble "correcting the record, so that you will find some of the pages pretty badly scarred up, and in some cases I was obliged to entirely rewrite the page."

Obliged to rewrite the page? He was taking his sworn testimony and rewriting it?

But Wilson missed nothing. "I note that the testimony of the afternoon [of January 26] is entirely revised, rather rewritten," he wrote Taylor on February 13, "and as you have failed to return the original testimony, the committee is not in a position to determine whether or not they can accept the revision. Kindly return, as soon as possible, the original testimony."

Two days later, Taylor wrote Godfrey of Wilson's complaint,

lamented he had no time to go over his testimony properly, and made a request:

> If I were you, I should not say anything to any of them about this, but if you happen to have a chance to temporarily get away with Wilson's copy of the Principles of Scientific Management, and keep it until after my testimony has gone to the printer, all the better. I dare say that this may not be practicable, but if it were, it would not be a bad idea.

In revising his testimony, it seems, Taylor planned to use language from his book, where he had presumably said it best. But Wilson might notice, and take the trouble to compare the "revision" to the book. Couldn't have that. So, spirit away the book. Here was the Fred Taylor who ran a spy ring back at Simonds. Godfrey replied that he would "try to carry out your instructions in the second paragraph."

"I am still struggling along trying to get my testimony corrected," Taylor wrote Cooke in a scrawled postscript to a letter on February 15. "Shall just about finish it as I get on the steamer."

That proved about right. He was already aboard the *Caronia*, perhaps just before it steamed out of port, when he wrote Cooke that the testimony was

> now in much better form than it would have been if the stenographic notes had been better taken. That they were so bad gave me the chance to ring in a good many very useful sentences. And I feel that they will all have too much to do at Washington to kick much about anything.

The man was shameless.

$\sim$

On balance, the committee's report sustained Taylor's critics. "Neither the Taylor system nor any other should be imposed from above on an unwilling work force," it affirmed. "Any system of shop management ought to be the result of . . . mutual consent."

A fair day's work can't be fixed by a stopwatch, which could "determine the time in which a piece of work can be done, but [not] . . . the length of time in which it ought to be done." This was a formula dear to Wilson, one he'd used all through the hearings.

A workman was not a machine. "He would be less than a man if he did not resent the introduction of any system which deals with him in the same way as a beast of burden or an inanimate machine."

As to the improved "mental attitude" Taylor touted as the sine qua non of his system, the committee deemed it nothing of the sort. A spirit of cooperation didn't emerge automatically from "any particular system of management" but rested on the personalities of all concerned. "The mere mental attitude of the employer is too variable and unsubstantial a basis upon which to rest the material welfare of the wage worker."

The *Machinists' Monthly Journal* concluded, "On the whole, organized labor, and that part of it marshaled under the banner of the International Association of Machinists, will get a great deal of satisfaction from the report." On what basis, then, could Taylor and his friends take comfort from it?

For they did. On January 30, while Taylor testified, Fred Lewis had written Frank Gilbreth that a witness just back from Washington had concluded that scientific management faced "a pre-determined decision mapped by the labor leaders." Given that, things hadn't turned out so bad. While much in the report was "unsatisfactory," Taylor wrote James Dodge later, still "it was the best of politics on the part of Redfield and Tilson to so modify their report that old man Wilson would sign it. The report as it is will probably prevent all legislation."

And you could see what he was getting at. The report was toothless, a model of unavailing compromise. Standardization and systematization, both pivotal to scientific management, were fine, the committee ruled. So was motion study that rid work of needless effort. Routing work through the shop more efficiently, ending instances where a machine backed up today had nothing for it tomorrow—behind this, all could rally. And as Gantt had contended all along, such prosaic measures as these represented most of scientific management.

And time study? It "should not be made of workmen without their consent," the report declared. But recommend anything substantive? This the committee forswore to do, finding it neither "advisable nor expedient to make any recommendations for legislation." It pointed a finger at the Taylor system and clucked a little but, in the end, did nothing to retard its spread through American industry. As Taylor wrote Tilson in September, it was "a wonderful achievement that you succeeded in getting Mr. Wilson to sign as mild a report as you did, and I read the report as a distinct victory on your part."

On the day the committee issued its report, Fred and Louise Taylor had already reached Europe on the *Caronia*. He was just shy of fifty-six and had three years to live—painful years, sullied by controversy, struggle, disappointment, and the illness of his wife.

It was March 9, 1912.

~

Report from
the End of the Century

~

THE GREAT DIFFUSION

In 1919, the French poet Paul Valéry, looking out over a postwar Europe haunted by the ghosts of the dead and memories of mindless production in death's service, concluded a "Letter from France" by writing, "The world, which calls by the name of 'progress' its tendency towards a fatal precision, marches on from Taylorization to Taylorization."

In 1929, those attending meetings of the American Academy of Political and Social Science heard how scientific management was being applied to "the clerical functions." There was now one best way for inserting paper into a typewriter, for pinning pages together, and for secretaries to sit at their desks.

In 1933, FBI director J. Edgar Hoover helped choose the new superintendent for Alcatraz prison, James A. Johnston. Johnston, writes Jay Stuller in the *Smithsonian*, "pushed penology into the realm of mad science." Up at 6:30 A.M. Twenty minutes to brush teeth, make beds, and dress. Twenty minutes to eat. Utensils counted. Marched back to their cells. Inmates counted. Under Johnston, writes Stuller, Alcatraz "bore the imprint of Frederick Winslow Taylor."

In 1986, the Japanese industrialist Konosuke Matshushita predicted that America would lose in the race for international markets because it was infected with a disease, the disease of Taylorism.

~

Most of a century has passed since the house Special Committee to Investigate the Taylor and Other Systems of Shop Management issued its report. In the years since, Taylor's system has spread around the world.

The first eruption of interest in scientific management led to an efficiency craze that reached into home, farm, and office, as well as factory, its impact heightened by World War I. "Efficiency," wrote Samuel Haber in his study of *Efficiency and Uplift: Scientific Management in the Progressive Era*, "became a patriotic duty." Both conservatives and liberals waved the standard of efficiency like a flag. "Taylor's advocacy of unrestrained production became common sense."

Upon America's entry into the war in 1917, Morris Cooke wrote later, Army Chief of Ordnance William Crozier brought into his department "every member of the Taylor Society on whom he could lay his hands." Most played key roles in wartime preparedness. Cooke himself held a high position with the War Industries Board. Gantt helped speed ship production through the Emergency Fleet Corporation. Hollis Godfrey served on President Woodrow Wilson's Council of National Defense.

The need to produce at previously unheard-of levels made Taylor's preoccupations those of the nation. As Edward Eyre Hunt wrote in the introduction to his 1924 book *Scientific Management Since Taylor*, people "who had never heard his name were enrolled among his followers." Labor and capital were thrown into unexpectedly intimate embrace; forced to cooperate, they did.

The realization that cooperation was possible blunted labor's resistance to scientific management. Morris Cooke became friends with, of all people, American Federation of Labor president Samuel Gompers, whom he largely credited for labor's warming.

Scientific management warmed, too. "The group around the Taylor Society," according to one account, formed "a sort of left wing management group" more open to the notion that the feelings of workers just might matter, too; maybe shop floor communication could go both ways. Industrial democracy was in the air; and Taylorites, including Louis Brandeis, were among those to champion it. After the war, Cooke, Gompers, and ASME president Fred Miller—an unlikely trio just a few years before—together edited a series of papers on industrial problems.

"From the bitterest sort of opposition to Taylor and all his works," Stuart Chase could write in the *New Republic* in 1925, organized labor now virtually embraced it. "The garment trades, the machinists, many miners and railroad workers have learned that there can be no increase in real wages until industrial waste is checked." The International Ladies Garment Workers' Union, for one, subscribed to principles that included "fair minimum standards of amounts of work on a basis of careful study of jobs," which sounds suspiciously like time study. In the 1950s, historian Milton Nadworny was so struck by what some saw as labor's "capitulation" that he devoted a book to it, *Scientific Management and the Unions, 1900–1932.*

The great rapprochement left few obstacles to scientific management's spread. Even by 1920, when Sten Rockstrom visited the United States on behalf of industrial patrons in Sweden, he noted that its proponents no longer took the trouble to defend it. During Taylor's lifetime, Morris Cooke wrote in 1924, he faced "opposition from a thousand quarters. . . . Then the Great War came and we saw all that Mr. Taylor had stood for in production proved out on a gigantic scale. Opposition to scientific management rightly conceived is no longer heard in responsible quarters."

He wasn't far from wrong. Time and motion study and other Taylorist paraphernalia spread all through industry, along with planning departments, standardization, and other features once virtually the intellectual property of Taylor's disciples. By 1929, Westinghouse's East Pittsburgh works had a time-study staff of a hundred and twenty; they set more than a hundred thousand rates per month. U.S. Rubber, Western Electric, International Harvester, General Motors—the time and motion experts were everywhere. Something like a consensus had emerged that Taylor's methods represented the one best way to run a shop.

But not *just* the shop.

During the late teens and twenties, scientific management split off into pieces and parts, factions, specialties, new disciplines, nascent social movements. Gantt rounded up fifty engineers in a group he called the New Machine, which sought to establish an "aristocracy of the capable"; engineers, efficiency experts, and their friends would take the helm of society from know-nothing financiers and politicians. The New Machine proved short-lived, but the young Columbia University engineering professor who was its secretary, Walter Rautensrauch, later helped fashion the much broader technocracy movement, to which our word "technocrat" is owed.

Whole new academic and business fields, novel at the time but with names that trip easily off the tongue today, grew from that one idée fixe of Frederick Taylor. "Personnel management," for example, went Taylor's call for the "scientific selection" of workers one better. Personnel departments replaced the foreman's role in hiring with formal selection procedures, written employment histories, and batteries of aptitude tests. Taylor, one management text testifies, "was in great part responsible for the very existence of the field."

William Leffingwell, a midwestern woodworker's son trained as a stenographer, applied scientific management to the office, experimenting with typists and clerks the way Taylor had with machinists and shovelers. "Taylor could not have had a more devoted disciple," writes Sharon Hartman Strom in *Beyond the Typewriter*, her study of the origins of modern American office work. Leffingwell saw malingerers behind every file cabinet, just as Taylor did behind every lathe. And a Leffingwell story about rousing typists to greater heights of productivity uncannily resembled Taylor's saga about Schmidt. One of the new field's journals was *System: The Magazine of Business*, which went weekly in 1929 and became *Business Week*.

Efficiency reached into the doctor's office and operating suite, too. "Where could the rationality of business better be joined to the rationality of science," wrote one historian of medicine, "than in increasing the efficiency of the hospital?"—or, for that matter, that of medical care generally? Medical journals carried articles like "The Efficiency of Out-Patient Work" and " 'Efficiency Engineering' in Pelvic Surgery: One and Two-Suture Operations"; the latter told how to save time and motion through better suturing technique and operating room organization. "Beyond any other craft," wrote Robert Latou Dickinson, "the surgeon's work demands the new 'scientific management.' " Frank Gilbreth, meanwhile, went into the operating room himself, observing dozens of operations. "If you were laying brick for me," he told one surgeon, "you wouldn't hold your job ten minutes."

And if the body, why not the mind? German psychologist Hugo Munsterberg, another admirer of Taylor, helped launch the field of industrial psychology. His pioneer textbook, *Psychology and Industrial Efficiency*, was studded with references to pig iron handling, bicycle ball inspection, and others of Taylor's classic tales.

Inspired in part by the example of Morris Cooke—who, recommended by Taylor, had been named head of Philadelphia's department of public works, where he'd saved the city millions—scientific management was soon being applied to the public sphere as well as the private, giving birth to a new discipline, public administration, with its own terminology, university courses, and journals.

In May 1908, the first dean of Harvard's graduate school of business, Edwin F. Gay, visited Taylor, got the Boxly treatment, toured Tabor, and was soon introducing "industrial organization" to the curriculum. Taylor and Barth, among others, regularly lectured there. Penn State's was among the first engineering programs to absorb Taylorist ideas, through Hugo Diemer, a Taylor devotee formerly at the University of Kansas; by 1909, he had begun the country's first true industrial engineering department. Cornell and Purdue followed. By 1930, writes historian Daniel Nelson, "scientific management had become a central feature of the practical curriculum. . . . From the 1910s to at least the 1940s a large percentage of business students and a smaller but not inconsiderable number of engineering students were exposed to the tenets of scientific management, whether they realized it or not."

Even academia became a candidate for scientific management when Morris Cooke was asked by the Carnegie Foundation for the Advancement of Teaching to undertake a study of efficiency in colleges and universities. In academia, his 1910 report led off, "one is struck with the absence of any gauge of efficiency which even remotely resembles, for instance, profits in an industrial undertaking." It urged measurement of faculty "production" in terms of "student-hours" and other quantitative measures, that teachers be inspected in class, that faculty work fewer but more intense hours, that comparing the efficiency of colleges and universities demanded standardization among them. Predictably, Cooke's report appalled academicians. Predictably, its effects are felt today, as any college professor who's ever filled out a state-mandated faculty productivity form can attest.

By the late 1920s, it could seem that all of modern society had come under the sway of a single commanding idea: that waste was wrong and efficiency the highest good, and that eliminating one and achieving the other was best left to the experts. The 1928 election of mining engineer Herbert Hoover, secretary of commerce in the Harding and Coolidge administrations and author of the influential 1921 report "Waste in Industry," brought scientific management into the White House itself.

∾

Taylorism never much respected the old Left-Right ideological divide or barriers between industries or political systems; it reached everywhere. So, too, did it diffuse across international borders. Almost from the beginning, it was a worldwide movement.

Yukinori Hoshino, a Japanese bank director, was traveling in America in 1911 when the furor over scientific management broke. Taken with *Principles of Scientific Management,* he sought and received permission to translate it. It was published in Japan in 1913 to Taylor's considerable pleasure. Soon, Japanese students, industrialists, and educators were making the pilgrimage to Boxly and touring Link-Belt and Tabor—one of them played on the Tabor baseball team—before returning to Japan with the received gospel.

Shipyards, cotton mills, and government factories became the sites of time studies and other experiments in scientific management. In 1920, efficiency expert Yoichi Ueno worked on a dentifrice-packing operation at a Tokyo company; measured amounts of tooth powder were ladled into small paper bags themselves packed in wooden boxes, the operation taking place, as Ueno remembered later, amid "a pretty cloud of the powder." After time and motion studies on the fifteen female workers "exactly as it was explained in textbooks of scientific management," production shot up.

Three years later, the Mitsubishi Electric Company reached a technical cooperation agreement with Westinghouse, sent people to the United States to learn time-study methods, analyzed hundreds of the tasks involved in electric fan manufacturing, and were soon spreading the new technique through Japan.

In June 1929, Ueno led the Japanese contingent to the Fourth International Congress of Scientific Management in Paris. There, at a reception in honor of Taylor's widow, he presented her with a map of sorts, a strange graphic representation of the history of management in which "rivers" and "tributaries" represented each of the early management pioneers. The largest river, surging out from a "Cradle of Civilization" in Philadelphia, represented Taylor, with Midvale, Bethlehem, the Paris exposition, and his key papers points along its course. Cooke, Hathaway, Barth, and the others got tributaries, each joining Taylor's Mississippi at a site corresponding to when they'd come under his influence.

Ueno's bizarre map reflected Taylor's substantial influence in Japan. Before Pearl Harbor, a Japanese publication noted that virtually all scientific management literature published in the United States had appeared in Japan as well. Japanese popular magazines reported on the work of Taylor, Gilbreth, and the others. A fictionalized pamphlet, "The Secrets of Saving Lost Motion" sold more than a million copies. During the 1920s, Barth, Harrington Emerson, Hathaway, Wilfred Lewis, and Lillian Gilbreth all went to Japan to lecture, inspect factories, and otherwise help guide the embryonic movement.

So when, following World War II, W. Edwards Deming brought to Japan the quality-management techniques that would help make Japanese consumer electronics the envy of the world, the way had been cleared by an earlier generation of American management leaders. Taiichi Ohno, father of the vaunted Toyota production system, himself acknowledged his intellectual debt to scientific management. As Daniel Wren writes in a popular management history textbook, *The Evolution of Management Thought*, "The phenomenon that modern authors call 'Japanese-Style Management' is not a recent creation, but a product of the introduction of scientific management into Japan" early in the century.

∾

As Taylorism touched each of the world's industrial nations, the story was never quite the same yet never altogether different: The first thrill among a few people taken with Taylor's ideas; letters back and forth to America; translation and publication of Taylor's writings; industrial experiments; controversy and debate; some form of institutionalization; the spread of his ideas.

Within a few years of its American publication, *Principles of Scientific Management* had been translated into Chinese, Italian, Russian, and Dutch, as well as French and German. Soon a stream of correspondence was reaching Boxly from abroad. "I am born an Italian, belonging to Austria," wrote Carlo Saiz, a shipyard owner in Trieste. "I consider your book of such importance that it should be a duty for any honest man . . . to collaborate with you in bringing your ideas" to public attention.

Even before the war, his ideas were being put into practice, if not always orthodoxly so. In the summer of 1912, Édouard Michelin, coowner of the tire company, sent his nephew Marcel to visit Taylorized factories in America; but in the end, he hired a French engineer to introduce something only barely recognizable as scientific management. In Germany, Siemens and General Electric experimented with Taylorist ideas. Switzerland's Bally shoe factory sent a four-man delegation to the United States in the autumn of 1913, leaving behind an engineer to continue his study of scientific management in Philadelphia.

Their tallish tales surviving translation well, Taylor's books fueled controversy abroad no less than in America. So did efforts to apply his precepts to working factories. When Henri Le Chatelier wrote in 1924 of the French success of *The Principles of Scientific Management*—twenty thousand copies reaching French engineers within a few years—he noted that progress would have been greater yet but for "many mistakes." Among them he doubtless had in mind the debacle at the Renault car factory at Billancourt, outside Paris.

Renault had gotten its first whiff of scientific management a few years before, through Georges de Ram's modest efforts. In 1911, Louis Renault visited America, met Taylor, and returned to France eager to Taylorize the big assembly plant. Three to five years ought to do it, Taylor had said. But Monsieur Renault seemed not to hear and rushed ahead with time studies, ignoring preparatory steps that Taylor deemed essential. A brief strike in December 1912 was followed by a bitter, six-week one in 1913. Taylor was understandably vexed but came around to Le Chatelier's view that the furor could only help spread the word. (Maybe it did. Early in 1914, Taylor learned that a Parisian cleric, Père Sertilanges, had begun a sermon with "The love of God is the Taylor system of our spiritual life.")

For the belligerents in World War I, their very fate as nations depended on replenishing the artillery shells and machine gun ammunition they hurled at the enemy; they turned to Taylorism, if again in bastardized form. In Britain, one scholar has written, management's prior coolness to scientific management was "transformed into a veritable heat wave of enthusiasm for it after the outbreak of the First World War." In France, Le Chatelier wrote, "Taylor's books are being sold as though they were appearing for the first time." Late in the war, Premier Georges Clemenceau ordered that the Taylor system be introduced into all government departments. By war's end, French industry was primed for modernization.

As Europe began to recover during the 1920s, it looked enviously to America's production miracle and saw the looming figures of Frederick Taylor and Henry Ford. In France, popular booklets issued by Michelin included one with excerpts from Taylor's testimony before the house special committee; another, contrasting a French plant with one in Milltown, New Jersey, showed how time and motion study promised French workers the prosperity enjoyed by their American cousins. In the Netherlands, World War I had spawned much talk of scientific management, but little action; now, the trade unions warmed toward it, and 1925 saw the creation of a national Efficiency Institute. In England, His Majesty's Stationery Office issued a pamphlet steeped in Taylorist thought, *Scientific Business Management*, that one writer saw as completing "the process of

Anglicizing scientific management." Germany, fairly hypnotized by *Taylorismus* and *Fordismus*, produced a yet more encompassing idea, "rationalization," that reached everywhere into its national life. In the twenty years after World War I, Taylor's principles were applied to the manufacture of rubber goods, automobile bodies, beauty products, clothing, ceramics, and much else.

Of course, they were often twisted out of all recognizable shape in the process. One observer, C. Bertrand Thompson, wrote in 1940 that in France, as in America, "the wider [scientific management] spread, the thinner it got." Many industrial organizers specialized only in time study or premium systems. At the bottom of the barrel could be found "a larger group of shameless fakers, mostly unemployed bookkeepers, who solicited clients from house to house." Scientific management in England, meanwhile, "encountered the almost invincible conservatism of the British temperament and was so emasculated that when I first saw some so-called examples of the Taylor System in England in 1922 I could not recognize them." One factor was the entrenched class system, which resisted what scholar Judith Merkle has called "the *arriviste* bustle of a rising class of Taylorite efficiency engineers." Still, the American import influenced British work practice enough to leave a record thick with accounts of disaffected workers bemoaning how "a good job done in my own time" was no longer the workplace standard.

All through the interwar years, world scientific management congresses, attracting an average of thirteen hundred people each, were held in Prague, Brussels, Rome, Paris, and Amsterdam. Every nation had offices and agencies to advance the movement. In Czechoslovakia, there was the National Committee for Scientific Management; in Germany, the Reichskuratorium für Wirtschaftlichkeit; in Italy, the Ente Nazionale Italiano per l'Organizzazione Scientifica del Lavoro. And while organizations dissolved, companies went out of business and ideas out of fashion, in the end, Taylorism made its mark.

In England and the Netherlands, the mark was relatively light; in France and Japan, heavier. Likewise, as we will see, in Italy, Soviet Russia, and Germany scientific management left an enduring imprint.

∾

"At no time has the influence of Fred Taylor been so great or his memory so secure as at this moment," the dean of Cornell University's engineering school, Dexter Kimball, observed in 1927, "when the factories of the United States are pouring forth a stream of industrial wealth such as mankind has never witnessed."

But did this pouring forth owe to Frederick Taylor or to that other icon of the industrial age, his contemporary Henry Ford? To judge by how often their names have appeared together, one might suspect that their legacies, Taylorism and Fordism, were one and the same, or else that Taylor had somehow invented the assembly line. They weren't, and he didn't. But despite Ford's greater visibility, it's probably Taylor who exerted broader influence. In 1977, when three groups of historians and managers were asked to rank contributors to American business and management thought, all ranked Taylor first; no group scored Ford higher than seventh.

By 1913, the Ford Motor Company, which had been making automobiles since 1903, had outgrown a three-story plant on Piquette Avenue in Detroit and moved into a new factory in Highland Park, a Detroit suburb. That spring, Ford began assembling magnetos, an electrical system component, by a new system: a moving conveyor brought the work to stationary workers, each of whom added a part or performed one of twenty-nine operations. Soon the chassis for the Model T was being built on an assembly line, too. Through interchangeable parts and special-purpose machine tools, Ford production had even by 1911 reached fifty-three thousand a year. Now, thanks to the assembly line, it shot up to 230,000 by 1914. Prices fell from $690 to $490; later, the cheapest Model T could be had for less than $400.

Scholars have subjected the revolution at Highland Park to searching study. Oliver Evans's nineteenth-century flour mill in Delaware has sometimes been cited as a progenitor of the assembly line. So have the conveyor-driven mold carriers of the Westinghouse Airbrake Company, and the conveyors and grain elevators of breweries; and, especially, the "disassembly" lines of Chicago meatpackers, which Henry Ford had seen. "If they can kill pigs and cows that way, we can build cars that way," he supposedly said. As for scientific management, Ford denied its influence on him, as did his chief engineer, Charles Sorensen. Nor has anyone else close to Ford ever stepped forward to say that Taylor's *Shop Management* made the scales fall from his eyes.

Five years before the first Ford line, scientific management was already being applied to automobile production, at the Franklin Manufacturing Company of Syracuse, New York. In 1914, Taylor wrote Charles de Freminville, a French disciple, crowing over Franklin's success: cost reductions of $350 per car, with greater gains imminent, lower selling price, rising sales. "I think there is only one other maker of first class cars in the country selling more cars than the Franklin people. . . . I do not, of course, refer," he added, "to the Ford car or any of the other very cheaply and roughly made cars." At the time, Franklin was making three hundred cars a month, Ford twenty thousand.

Nothing spoke so plainly to the differences between the two men. The assembly line was indeed a landmark achievement and could probably never have spluttered up from the brain of Frederick Taylor. His defenders' assertions to the contrary, he was no revolutionary. Ford, you could argue, was. "I will build a motor car for the great multitude," he had declared in 1908 on introducing the Model T. Whatever a Taylor might think of the result ("very cheaply and roughly made"), Ford's engineers wrung every last bit of skilled labor out of the car, through ever more elaborate machinery. No Wm. Sellers & Company drill press straight from the packing case for Ford. A self-taught tinkerer who'd grown up on the family farm in Dearborn, Michigan, he'd turn instead to a custom-built machine that drilled sixteen holes at once and could never be used for anything else (which was one reason the Model T stayed unchanged on into the late 1920s). Taylor, on the other hand, took production largely as he found it, ridding it of needless elements and directing the worker how to do it better and faster, but leaving its machinery largely intact.

This, at least, is the canonical scholarly distinction between Taylor and Ford; in fact, the split is more one of nuance. The tool grinder that Taylor designed at Midvale was created expressly to make an unskilled job out of a skilled one. A Taylor invention used for maneuvering and steadying work on the anvil of a steam hammer was intended, in the words of his 1889 patent, "to substitute [mechanical devices] for the skilled and disciplined labor required of the smith or foremen by the old method." Likewise at Simonds, Taylor introduced a machine that automatically gauged balls down to a ten-thousandth of an inch. "We are building a tempering machine which will turn out with one man our entire product of balls in ten hours," he wrote in an 1897 progress report. Planned, too, were new automatic counting machines and conveyors for delivering balls to the drying ovens. This sounds like Ford fifteen years later.

But it was not a mechanical contribution but a conceptual one—the breakdown of work, the teasing apart of time—that secures Taylor's position in history. French historian Yves Cohen, who has studied the early Renault, Peugeot, and Citroën assembly lines, notes that "to make the movement along the line really continuous, proper timing was crucial; each position had to be balanced in relation to numerous other operations of short duration. . . . The distribution of the work could no longer be left to the whim of the foreman, and a new generation of work organizers had to be created." This step, crucial to any assembly line, owed much to Taylor.

Ford engineers had broken up magneto assembly into twenty-nine distinct operations? Well, Taylor had minutely broken up the machining of railroad tires at Midvale thirty years before; and Dwight Merrick and other time-study men, along with Barth and Gilbreth in their own ways, made a veritable profession of it. By the time of the revolution at Highland Park, this habit of thought was densely part of the American industrial air.

Taylor, a national figure among mechanical engineers at least since the Saratoga paper of 1903, was hardly unknown in Detroit. Most top Ford engineers, writes Ford biographer Allan Nevins, had by the early days at Highland Park "doubtless caught some of [Taylor's] ideas," including time study. The company had a time-study department by 1912 or 1913. *American Machinist* editor Fred Colvin's observations of rear axle assembly at Highland Park in early 1913, just before the first line started up, convinced him "that motion study has been carefully looked into, whether it is called by that name or not." Meanwhile, the man Nevins pictured as most responsible for development of the chassis assembly line, Clarence Avery, a young University of Michigan–trained former manual training teacher, "read widely, knew the latest European and American advances in engineering, and kept in touch with the ideas of men like Frederick W. Taylor."

But Taylor's influence on automotive mass production went beyond any influence he had on Ford. After *The Principles of Scientific Management* came out, it was said, you could hardly buy a stopwatch in Detroit, so swiftly were they snapped up. In 1909, he'd given a four-hour monologue at a Packard auto plant there; by 1913, Packard was largely Taylorized, reducing workers needed for each car by almost half. Visiting Detroit again in 1914, he addressed a gathering of six hundred superintendents and foremen. One engineer entranced by his ideas even before Brandeis and the rate case, E. K. Wennerlund, joined the new General Motors in 1911 and later became its director of production engineering. "All that the rest of us have done," he said, "is simply to take [Taylor's] basic ideas, refine them, and adapt them to big-scale modern production."

Both Taylor and Ford raised production, cut costs—and reduced the judgment and skill needed by the average worker. At Ford, it might be through a machine that cut holes of particular diameter and surface finish, at set locations, to set depths, at set speeds; in a Taylorized plant, it was special slide rules, stopwatches, instruction cards, and standard operating procedures. In either case, the worker was left with eight or ten hours whose minute-by-minute course was more closely prescribed and scrutinized than ever. After Ford and Taylor got through with them, most jobs needed less of everything—less brains, less muscle, less independence.

Just as Taylor raised pay to get people to submit to his methods, so did Ford. In 1913, that annus mirabilis of the assembly line, labor turnover ran 380 percent at Highland Park. People couldn't or wouldn't stand the work and quit; Ford had to hire four thousand people a year for each thousand jobs. "So great was labor's distaste for the new machine system," writes Keith Sward in *The Legend of Henry Ford*, that toward year's end, turnover exceeded 900 percent. On January 5, 1914, the company announced wages of five dollars a day, about double the prevailing figure, higher even than the most skilled toolmakers at, say, Watertown Arsenal. "MEN WILL NOT DO AN EXTRAORDINARY DAY'S WORK FOR AN ORDINARY DAY'S PAY," Taylor had warned in "A Piece-Rate System." Coming in at the high end of the 30 to 100 percent increase Taylor ordained, the five-dollar day kept workers hitched to the line—and made Ford the folk hero Taylor never was.

Yet Taylor's was probably the more powerful idea. While the assembly line remains a common if tired metaphor, it defines surprisingly little of modern manufacturing. The Taylorized workplace, on the contrary, appears everywhere, heedless of the lines between one industry and the next; by 1917, bleaching, bookbinding, bricklaying, canning, textile dyeing, lithography, lumber, publishing, wire-weaving machinery, and many other industries had all gotten a taste of scientific management. A French scholar, Robert Linhart, has described Fordism as simply "an application of the Taylor system to mass production": Fordism was the special case, Taylorism the universal.

As Judith Merkle has pointed out in *Management and Ideology*, Taylorism, as compared to Fordism, has an "immense advantage in its ability to absorb new technologies and to adapt itself over time." The assembly line, then, might be likened to a biological species adapted, through evolution, to its own peculiar ecological niche, like a Galápagos tortoise. Scientific management, on the other hand, adapts the way a virus does, fitting in almost everywhere. To listen to Taylor and his friends, it could be applied to anything.

∾

"Imagine," wrote a reporter in the opening paragraph of a newspaper article about Taylor in 1911,

> a machine of universal efficiency—a combination gasoline engine, electric dynamo, wireless apparatus; reaper, binder and thresher; coal miner, ore digger, smelter, forging plant and scissors grinder; linotype machine, reporter, editor and advertising hustler . . .

It went on and on like this.

> Imagine all these, and all other forms of human productiveness, co-ordinated into a single machine, known to increase the output of every branch affected from two to three or four times what it is now . . .
>
> It is the machine of efficiency, proclaimed as universally applicable, from making a lawn to making a jewsharp.

Here was the sheer power and range of Taylor's vision. And indeed, over the course of the century it has insinuated itself into every area of modern work. Consider:

In the 1940s, a University of Iowa team designed a work area for dentists performing orthodontics. Into a tight little area around the patient's chair they stuffed equipment formerly spread around the room. They succeeded in saving 29 percent of the dentist's time and reducing the distance traveled in making an orthodontic band from 186 feet to 75.

A veteran steelworker recalled how, after the efficiency experts came through, "You were told when to do something, how to do something, how far you could go. Every job was broken down to its smallest integral part."

In 1990, the National Center on Education and the Economy found that the typical American bank was organized along factory lines. Low-paid tellers accepted deposits, cashed checks, and recorded bill payments—but little else. For a more complex banking problem the customer was routed to a college-educated service rep. "The entire 'front office' system . . . is organized by operations managers to move customers in and out of the bank as quickly as possible. It is highly 'Tayloristic' work design."

After World War II, a time and motion study done at a 350-bed hotel reduced the time needed to make beds from 3.21 minutes to 1.81 minutes.

In 1979, a sheet metal worker saw a computer-controlled punch press installed in the factory where he worked. He looked forward to learning how to use it but was told it was for "managers only" and that responsibility for making the tapes to run the machine lay in the new programming department. When, on his own, he learned how to program, the foreman installed a lock that denied access to the machine's computer memory. The worker protested but to no avail. The work he wished to do, he was sternly advised, was best left to a "small, specialized group" of programmers.

In the 1970s, the playwright and political activist Barbara Garson spent months interviewing workers in tuna-processing plants and automobile factories, and working as a keypuncher herself. "Today," she wrote darkly in *All the Livelong Day*, referring to Taylor's pig iron handler,

> we type, assemble and even talk under routines like those worked out for Schmidt. . . . Since Frederick Taylor's day, the division of labor has continued in its soul-destroying direction. Some large categories of work seem difficult at first to reduce to small job modules, but gradually stenographers are replaced by tapes, secretaries are relegated to the typing pool, and look what McDonald's has done to the highly individualized jobs of waiters and short order cooks.

As Garson's language suggests, and as we shall see, dark clouds have all along threatened Taylorism's sunlit vision. But they little interfered with its spread. It was as if, early in the century, a concentrated gas of immense potency, until then trapped within a corked vial, had suddenly been released and had ever since been wafting across the world.

In a 1974 paper delivered before the Fourteenth International Congress of the History of Science, meeting in Tokyo, historian Edwin Layton used just such a metaphor—that of a substance freely diffusing across boundaries—to explain the influence of Taylor and Ford. An American anthropologist, Alfred L. Kroeber, had decades earlier shown how the concrete details of a cultural system may face resistance to its spread, while the system itself—as an idea, a spirit, a sensibility—drifts freely from one culture to the next, taking new forms. Stimulus diffusion, he'd called it; and something like it, Layton argued, helped explain the spread of Taylor's and Ford's ideas. Taylor had his time-study sheets, doctrinaire texts, and mnemonic systems; these were hard to transfer. But the essence of Taylorism was vastly more portable.

Layton applied the diffusion idea to Taylorism's influence abroad, but the idea applied perhaps even better to its spread outside industry and into other areas of modern life. High-speed steel? Functional foremanship? These had little to say even a few steps off the shop floor. But many of Taylorism's core ideas—standardization, the split of planning from doing, the use of experiment to study the seemingly unstudiable, the setting of precisely defined tasks, the emphasis on efficiency and productivity to the exclusion of all else—were peculiarly seductive.

As historians probed the early years of our century and critics and thinkers asked why we live as we do, their gaze fell again and again on Frederick Taylor, finding that his ideas had seeped into some of the narrowest, most seemingly remote niches of modern life. At Taylor's door they laid the emergence of modern time consciousness, leisure's transformation from genuinely free time to organized recreation, the Reagan administration's approach to managing the federal bureaucracy, and even what one critic, Christopher Lasch, has called "a new interpretation of the American Dream." They saw Taylor's hand in the work of poet William Carlos Williams and in French modernist writer Louis-Ferdinand Céline's support for a public-hygiene police intended to prevent the health-insured from "playing sick."

In his 1994 book *Post-Capitalist Society*, management guru Peter Drucker reasserted his view that Taylor, not Karl Marx, warranted a place in the trinity of makers of the modern world, along with Darwin and Freud. Even America's victory in World War II, he said, could properly be credited to Taylor's influence. After Pearl Harbor, Hitler declared war on the United States because he reasoned that, lacking a merchant marine, modern destroyers, and a good optics industry, America could scarcely wage war at all—much less wage it in Europe. Hitler was right, said Drucker. America did lack those things:

> But by applying Taylor's Scientific Management, U.S. industry trained totally unskilled workers, many of them former sharecroppers raised in a pre-industrial environment, and converted them in sixty to ninety days into first-rate welders and ship-builders. Equally, the United States trained the same kind of people within a few months to turn out precision optics of better quality than the Germans ever did.

(One of those hurriedly built ships, identical to hundreds of others churned out during the war, was the 7,176-ton SS *Frederick W. Taylor*, launched in South Portland, Maine, in 1942.)

Drucker's intimation that it was Taylor who won the war for America recalls management consultant C. Bertrand Thompson's recognition of how loose and ill-defined a concept Taylorism had become, even by 1940:

> As the number of those talking and writing about scientific management has increased, the principles have become vaguer and the spirit more tenuous, until now they are taken to cover every supposed improvement in managerial practice. I have myself seen the installation of an adding machine, or even of a telephone, referred to as "Taylorization."

But Taylorism was always much more than a bundle of tools and techniques: it was a vision and a hope. To Anson Rabinbach, writing in *The Human Motor*, Taylor shared with certain European thinkers "the utopian hope" that industrial conflict could be resolved scientifically for the good of all. The irony was that Taylor dismissed professors and theorizers and saw himself as the most practical of men. And yet, utopian visionary he was. Like Karl Marx, for example, he was the author of a powerful, ostensibly scientific system that ensnared the imagination. Like Marx, too, his influence resided not in how his ideas actually worked in this factory or that country, but in the way they seemed to sweep away all objections, cover every situation, glow with an aura of spiritual certainty.

Between fifty and a hundred thousand people worked under scientific management, Morris Cooke would claim in 1913. When Taylor testified before the Industrial Relations Commission in April 1914, he put the figure at between a hundred fifty and two hundred thousand but acknowledged it as no more than a guess. Another tally, in 1917, estimated 172 factories, construction companies, banks, and publishing houses, with fifty-nine thousand employees. These are relatively unimpressive numbers, causing many scholars to remark on the seeming split between Taylorism's pervasive impact and the modest scale at which it was applied in anything like pure form.

The answer was that the numbers represented only that part of the great iceberg of Taylorism which broke the surface. Beneath the waves loomed the hulking mass of the idea that powered it, sloughing off its influence wherever it drifted. Horace Drury, an early historian of scientific management, reported that "missionaries fresh from India and Japan" had told him it could be applied even to mission industrial work. "We suppose there are few important factories where the influence of scientific management has not been felt."

Indeed, Sten Rockstrom, reporting back to his Swedish patrons after a tour of the United States, spoke of a "very large body of so-called organization experts of various estimated reputation and standing" already at work by 1919—thousands of them, well paid, and so busy you could scarcely get one to come to Sweden. Here were the shock troops of scientific management and the broader efficiency movement, fanning out across America, spreading Taylor's ideas as well as those of his imitators.

The imitators and usurpers didn't understand real scientific management, purists like Carl Barth caviled; and many *were* sloppy or superficial. But they passed on some taste of the original—a stopwatch study here, a motion study there; tools and fixtures standardized at one company, a Gantt premium system at another. Distorted, popularized, simplified, and bastardized, the master's teachings spread.

Forging the twentieth century on an anvil of his own making, Taylor helped make modern life what it is—not only in the factory or even in the broader workplace but everywhere.

II

MR. PROGRESSIVE

It can be hard to remember today that Taylor was once seen as a benign and progressive influence. The liberal elements of the day, who looked out for the worker, sought to check privilege and bestow the blessings of industry on all, saw Taylor as one of their own. Taylor had worked his way up from the shop floor, been written up glowingly by the muckrakers, declared he could no longer afford to work for money, distanced himself from the moneyed classes. A progressive through and through, no? *The Principles of Scientific Management*, writes Daniel Nelson, a biographer of Taylor, can be seen as "above all a reform tract, a progressive manifesto," one pointing up the evils of the existing factory and offering a way out, through science. Indeed, when American history courses teach Taylorism today, it is often within the context of the Progressive movement.

When Louis Brandeis was nominated to the Supreme Court in 1916, an opponent carped, "He always acts the part of a judge toward his clients instead of being his client's lawyer." Brandeis, he was saying, had to be convinced of the rightness of his client's cause. And in the rate case he *was* convinced—that the railroads were wrong, that in scientific management lay the solution to their problems. "The coming *science of management* in this century," he would declare, "marks an advance comparable only to that made by the coming of the *machine* in the last." Mechanization had profited the worker little. But of the blessings "to come from the new scientific management, the people are to have their share."

Brandeis—this man of crystalline intellect, sterling principle, and bottomless sympathy for the underdog—had embraced scientific management heart and soul. And so did many others of progressive stamp, who saw Taylor leading humanity toward a new industrial utopia.

"No man in the history of American industry has made a larger contribution to genuine cooperation and juster human relations than did Frederick Winslow Taylor," Ida Tarbell wrote in 1924. "He is one of the few—very few—creative geniuses of our time." Another tribute after his death recalled how, on first encountering his ideas, "it did not take me long to realize that at last we had found the man the industrial world had been waiting for."

Many of Taylor's disciples identified more with the traditional left than the right. Carl Barth, for example, professed himself a socialist, declared his wish to see millionaires drowned. Morris Cooke, the "happy liberal" to his biographer, brought scientific management to the reform administration of Mayor Blankenburg in Philadelphia, and later held high posts in the New Deal administration of Franklin D. Roosevelt. Even that distinguished daughter of Germantown, Florence Kelley—translator of Friedrich Engels, champion of child labor laws, defender of the downtrodden—joined the Taylor Society before she died.

Taylor's insistence that scientific management implied a more enlightened attitude toward workers impressed at least one correspondent to *American Machinist.* "That repeated admission from a man of the class to which Mr. Taylor belongs means the awakening among employers of a sense of responsibility that they have not felt in the past." As for Taylor's sometime tactlessness, "let us . . . forget his mistakes, overlook his unfortunate inferences, but take home and defend at every turn the sound, humane principles of scientific management."

Sound and humane is how many viewed them. And to the extent that Taylorism was dangerous, as its critics charged, it could still be rendered harmless, like a magnificent viper from which the venom is extracted. In *The Socialist,* one writer called scientific management "in harmony with Socialism, in so far as it will eliminate unnecessary labor and produce more wealth with less energy expended." Taylor himself had capitalist sympathies? So what? Under the socialist commonwealth, his system would benefit the world.

In Italy, the influential political thinker Antonio Gramsci embraced Taylor's ideas; his "factory councils" placed such emphasis on efficiency, production, discipline, and sobriety as would have made Taylor smile. But Gramsci, whose left-wing credentials were unassailable, was a founder of the Italian Communist Party. Indeed, no less a Communist than Lenin himself saw in Taylorism a way to modernize archaic Russian industry after the revolution; Taylorism's good, he believed, could be embraced, its evil expunged.

This discussion, I am bound to note, slavishly follows those well-trod forking paths of Left and Right of two centuries' standing to which even today much political debate conforms. But it was just this old divide that Taylorism ignored, drifting across it as if it weren't there.

With Taylorism, it could seem, everyone stood to gain—consumer, worker, and boss. "Taylor believed, like Henry Ford," wrote Ida Tarbell, "that the world could take all we could make, that the power of consumption was limitless." To give the world all it needs, he fairly shouted at her one day at Boxly, was industry's true mission. After thousands of years of never enough to go around, where if everyone worked hard the king wound up with enough to suit his needs but no one else did, Taylorism's promise of more for everyone was too good to pass up.

In Taylor's day even those enjoying middle-class lives, with homes of their own and a little money socked away, lived simply. $1.85 a day, rather than $1.15, was what Taylor promised Henry Noll; and yet even well-off three-dollar-a-day workers still didn't have much. Over one four-week period in 1908 a family of seven in Homestead, Pennsylvania, bought oil, coal, a lamp wick, a shovel, a basin, a brush, soap, paint, a broom, some clothes, thread, ribbon, candy, and "flowers for the dead." That, besides food, furniture payments, and a roof over their heads, was about it. Yet this family lived on $16.38 a week—much toward the high end in Homestead; more than one in four workers in town, their families mostly crowded into two-room shacks, made less than $12.00.

All this smacks of the old codger regaling his bored listeners with tales of a childhood spent in bleak privation. But in fact, ignoring this or that year's economic blips and squiggles, and excepting a persistent underclass that suffers today as much as anyone ever did, industrialized countries today enjoy material abundance so great we no longer see it. Many living today have never known life without radios, TVs, home freezers, power mowers, and computers; without hot water at the tap, electricity at the outlet, and a car in the driveway. Collective memory fades, and it becomes hard to imagine a time, before Taylor and Ford, when things weren't so plentiful and so cheap.

In 1840, cotton shirts and dresses were a luxury, Taylor told the Special Committee; by 1912 they had become a necessity. One day, he hoped, "the luxuries of one generation [will become] the necessities of the next [and] the working people of our country will live as well and have the same luxuries, the same opportunities for leisure, for culture, and for education, as are now possessed by the average business man."

That day has largely come. It has come even in Lubbenau, Germany, in the marshy, wooded region south of Berlin known as the Spreewald that thirteen-year-old Fred Taylor visited with his family in 1869. Back then, as he wrote in his journal, the local peasants were "very primitive in their ways. The women look as if they worked very hard, and I should think that they got very little for the labor which they expend on their farms." But in 1992, in this recently East German town near the Polish border, shopwindows were stuffed with food, clothes, electronic gear. Children rode bicycles, motorcyclists exploded through narrow streets. Foul-smelling Trabants shared the road with BMWs and Mercedeses. Near where Taylor and his family stepped off the train from Berlin stood the big blue sign of a HITECH VIDEO AUDIO SHOP. Everywhere were *things*, and everybody had them. Along the canals of the Spree, guest houses had sprung up. Across from an old baronial estate now squatted Camping am Schlosspark, as ugly a camper heaven as ever you'd see in Tampa or Topeka, but affordable. Meanwhile, the traditional workboats that once plied the canals with tired peasants hauling their meager crops were now fitted with seats for tourists—not for a few rich Americans, like the Taylors in 1869, but pretty much everyone. The vast, leveling productivity that Taylor had prophesied, his dream of ordinary people living like the rich of long ago, had even here, a few miles from the Polish border, come to be.

$\sim$

Scientific management would achieve its productive miracle, of course, through science, which in the late nineteenth and early twentieth centuries came draped in a white robe of virtue. That the world was ruled by natural law and that human beings could discover it, Edwin Layton writes in *The Revolt of the Engineers*, served as an article of the engineer's faith. Taylor absorbed this intellectually mainstream position, as usual, without demur.

Sometimes, in the last years of his life, he and his son Robert would go over to the Philadelphia Cricket Club, abutting Boxly, for a round of golf. Robert, who hung on his father's every word, one day resolved to "find out what he thought this world was all about." Over the next few days, he netted at least one morsel he'd carry with him always. "As far as what I have seen in my life," his father said, "any time you start poking under the cover of something or looking into something you begin to find laws. These are the laws of creation, or of nature, or *something*. They're there." Such laws were neither passed by legislatures nor matters of opinion; they derived from physical fact.

It was just such inviolable laws of human work that Taylor had sought at Midvale and pursued all his life. How much work could a man do in a day? Sanford Thompson had tracked down French and German students of the problem in the Boston Public Library in the 1890s. At Bethlehem, the yard shovelers and the pig iron handlers represented further mileposts on the way to industrial truth.

Taylor's work complemented what scholar Anson Rabinbach calls a "European science of work" peopled by distinguished theorists like Hermann von Helmholtz, one of the first to formulate the law of conservation of energy. Among them, too, was Étienne Marey, who, back in the 1880s, began using a contrivance of his own design to photograph moving figures against a black screen, yielding a succession of images, separated by small fractions of a second, that broke down running or fencing into discrete stop-moments of time (and which inspired Marcel Duchamp's *Nude Descending a Staircase*).

Both Taylor and the Europeans, wrote Rabinbach in *The Human Motor*, "took as their starting point the decomposition of each task into a series of abstract, mathematically precise relations, calculable in terms of fatigue, time, motion, units of work, and so forth. . . . Both rested their claims on the authority of science."

Of course, some would say that to this science Taylor himself made few lasting contributions. In a spasm of overstatement, the French statesman Édouard Herriot once compared him to such luminaries as the physicist Charles Augustin de Coulomb, the biologist Claude Bernard, and even Descartes. But in *From Taylorism to Fordism: A Rational Madness*, French psychiatrist Bernard Doray argued more reasonably that "it is . . . difficult to find any major discovery in the work of Taylor." No one cites his work science, for example, the way they did for many years his metal-cutting experiments.

At the height of the efficiency craze, a Boston consulting engineer, A. Hamilton Church, asked in an *American Machinist* article, "Has 'Scientific Management' Science?" His answer was no. Apart from certain useful "mechanisms," presumably time study, it had "nothing tangible behind it." Taylor's "Shop Management" struck him as scientifically vague. Even so firm a believer as Carl Barth found Taylor's experiments at Bethlehem so flawed he'd had to redo them.

Of course, if Taylor did little that was scientifically unprecedented, he admitted as much. After "Shop Management" came out, James Dodge noted later, many stepped forward to claim "prior knowledge of some element in the paper," often with some justice. For Taylor had woven his new system from many stray strands of existing practice. "Hardly a single piece of original work was done by me in Scientific Management," Taylor said at a 1911 conference at Dartmouth College. "Everything that we have has come from a suggestion by someone else. . . . And, gentlemen," he added in a twist suggesting both modesty and the reverence for fact, truth, and law he demanded of others, "I am proud of it; I am not ashamed of it, because the man who thinks he can place himself against the world's evolution, against the combined knowledge of the world, is pretty poor stuff."

To Taylor and to his defenders, his seeming want of originality took nothing from his contribution. Harlow Person, a dean at Dartmouth's Amos Tuck School who became a sober student of scientific management, compared Taylor to the Wright Brothers:

> If the Wright brothers had brought each part of the first aeroplane separately before the public and declared it to be something new, they would have been ridiculed. Not a single part of the physical structure of the aeroplane represented a new principle. But the design, the integration of the parts, the functional capacity of the whole, was one of man's greatest inventions.

The same, he said, applied to Taylor and scientific management. It was the system as a whole that was new.

And this system, its proponents believed, promised a new era of workplace democracy.

～

Scientific management, concluded one report on the troubles at Watertown Arsenal, "lacks the spirit of democracy." And given what could seem Taylor's autocratic leanings, maybe the report was on to something. Here's Taylor, in a lecture, telling how to get a man in line: "Rarely reason with him, never match wits with him, throw him onto the defensive, take short steps one after another in quick succession without talking about them, at least until after they are taken." Pointing to his "brutal conversation" with Schmidt, a correspondent to *American Machinist* once described Taylor as someone "whose idea of class distinction belongs to the Middle Ages." And yet classless, scrupulously fair, and utterly democratic was just what proponents of the Taylor system claimed it to be.

Just before his death, Taylor told his son Kempton how he had urged on Harvard University the elimination, in Kempton's words, of "the prevailing club system, with its disorder and drunkenness. He advocated a strict supervision of the undergraduate body. . . . One of Papa's characteristics was the readiness with which he subjected human activity to law and regulation." No one was exempt from these laws, the student gentry no more than anyone else. This, to Kempton and other friends of scientific management, was real democracy.

Democracy meant freedom from capricious rule by princes of industry. It meant no one getting special breaks. It didn't mean argument, negotiation, debate, voting, or strikes. For science was at the helm now, consigning such cumbersome baggage to the past.

His system, Taylor wrote a Harvard engineering professor not long before his death, "prevents arbitrary and tyrannical action on the part of the foremen and superintendents quite as much as it prevents 'soldiering' or loafing or inefficiency on the part of the workmen." Science held management in the same benign embrace as it did workers. Indeed, workmen could hold their bosses to account and were even supplied printed forms on which to complain about them, which were "invariably" acted upon by management. "Thus you see we have under scientific management a greater democracy than has ever before existed in industry."

No tenet of scientific management was held more firmly among Taylor's disciples. "Natural law is not any respecter of persons, while arbitrary law is the conserver of privilege," said H. L. Gantt. "If we follow Taylor's injunction and base everything on fact, we are all judged by the same standard, and that is the basis of democracy."

All this pleased the Progressives. "The scientific spirit is the discipline of democracy, the escape from drift, the outlook of a free man," wrote Walter Lippmann in *Drift and Mastery* in 1914. But was there, perhaps, a problem? The new workplace democracy held that science had the answers and that scientific management embodied them; that there was a best way to work and that for all the confusion of shop and office you could learn what it was; and that everyone, keen-minded and large-hearted, would agree on it. But was that asking too much?

One union foe pointed to Taylor's dictatorship of the experts as "an indication to our minds that there is really no place in scientific management for two people's opinions." But you didn't need two people's opinions, Taylor held, for the simple reason that scientific management rested upon the bedrock of science.

But did it?

III

THE FIFTEEN UNNECESSARY MOTIONS
OF A KISS

Testifying before the U.S. Industrial Relations Commission in 1914, Taylor, fencing with his inquisitors, said it was not really the time-study man who decided anything but a "code of laws."

But, he was pressed, "A code of laws is an inanimate thing and can not decide anything."

"There is nothing in the world more powerful than a code of laws," replied Taylor with what reads like real feeling. "The whole United States is run by a code of laws. . . . The code of laws is above all people."

But how are these laws to be ferreted out? And how are we to know that we have all of them? Might there lurk within these laws and truths, as in any science, surprises that confound our understanding? Finally, how are we to know when we have erred? Perhaps the expert, expert as he is, is not infallible—or perhaps he misses some larger truth.

The experts, of course, did err.

After he left Bethlehem, A. B. Wadleigh wrote Taylor about an error they'd made in the early shoveling experiments. A man could shovel eleven times a minute, they'd decided back then, and on that basis fixed his pay at 4³/₄ cents a ton. But the numbers were wrong: eight shovelsful per minute was more like it. "The reason for this mistake," Wadleigh wrote Taylor, was that "the man we had was a wonder and could not keep up this rate . . . , [and] the conditions were better than average." But for a year, by Wadleigh's reckoning, the men had been stuck making barely thirteen cents an hour—about what they'd earned before, but for greater effort.

On its face, time study was hard to refute. Stopwatch, clipboard, and ruled sheets, all wielded with mathematical exactitude by the expert, screamed out their scientific legitimacy. One study, for "Putting Wheels in Gear Cutters and Removing," made by Dwight Merrick at Link-Belt in 1907, recorded times down to the hundred-thousandth of an hour: "Remove bushing from wheel—.00083 hours." (Of course, that works out to a nice round three seconds and maybe started out that way.)

But for all its props, time study was as easy to get wrong, and as dependent on the skill and good faith of ordinary mortals, as anything else. It was not easy to discern in the worker's blurred movements those which were essential and those which were not, establish "elements," and time them. Then, too, the worker might resent the expert's presence, fear his judgment, and do what he could to thwart him. So much could go wrong that Taylor always insisted that until you'd laid the groundwork by revamping the whole shop, you should hardly bother. In his consulting days, time study was often the last thing he'd do; at Bethlehem, he never got to it at all.

And then there was the great fudge factor, Taylor's allowance for fatigue and unavoidable delay. In 1921, a Johns Hopkins School of Public Health expert, Reynold A. Spaeth, reminded the Taylor Society how any time study built up from both stopwatch timings and crude estimates was profoundly flawed. Say a chemist must determine the weight of a substance. If he weighs one portion of it on a chemical balance to five decimal places, then hefts the rest of it in his palm "and guesses it to weigh about a pound and a half," the final accuracy profits not at all from his precision measurement and rests almost entirely on his guess. The same applied to time study. If the fatigue allowance was way off, the final result was way off.

Again and again members of the Special Committee returned to this question. They got answers but never ones that placated them. Even Tilson, the easygoing one of the three, was bothered. "I have not been satisfied as yet with the omniscience of anybody to know what the standard time should be," he said in questioning Gantt. Chairman Wilson, of course, was preoccupied with the issue. Scientific management, he understood, allowed for a margin between the theoretical best time of the best worker, as revealed by stopwatch study, and the standard set for the average worker. But how wide a margin? How, he asked Gantt, might you arrive at it?

"You have got to have a certain amount of experience in this thing before you can arrive" at it, Gantt said. But "experience" was just the sort of vague, unscientific, trust-me reply that had gotten the railroads in trouble with Brandeis. The Taylor system was supposed to dispense workplace justice rationally, working in obedience to scientific law. Yet here Gantt invoked mere experience. Maybe time study, the crown jewel of scientific management, was as vulnerable as any other human endeavor to trickery, self-delusion, error, and guess.

Of course, hammer any theory on the merciless anvil of practice, and it was sure to come away battered. In a review of *Principles of Scientific Management*, a Boston religious journal reminded readers not to "suppose that here is a self-regulating remedy for poverty and other social ills." Inevitably, scientific management depended "upon the character, the fairness, the humaneness of the men who do the managing."

But Taylor denied even this modest caveat. "In the past the man was first," he wrote in the *Principles*. "In the future the system will be first." Once men and women placed themselves in the system's benign hands, the industrial evils of the past would fade away. And this benefit inhered in the system itself, resting but slightly on the talents or failings of those who ran it. Taylor's Italian correspondent from Trieste wrote him that under scientific management "one man must be the soul of it, to see that it is always kept alive and does not sink to bureaucratics and insignificant writings. This man must be rather an extraordinary man." No, Taylor replied. "Under the ordinary management, a man must be . . . a born manager. That is to say, he must have a special intuitive knowledge of men." Not so under his system; there, science reigned.

To Taylor, this was no trifling point. At Midvale, he had battled with the machinists, almost come to blows; the metal-cutting experiments and time studies had, to his mind, rescued him. System had worked there and would work everywhere—but only if it remained insulated from passion, pettiness, and human judgment. The moment it didn't, he was right back in the pit from which he had extricated himself at Midvale.

It was illusion, of course, to think you could ever slip the chains of human judgment. An editorial in one engineering journal noted that

Taylor, Gantt, and their friends tried "to explain their successes by the discovery of new principles of management, instead of attributing it to personality." History suggested they were wrong. "The explanation of Napoleon is found in Napoleon, rather than in his procedures." Likewise Taylor.

Behind the system at work in any shop, under scientific management or not, "is the personality of a man," observed another journal, *American Machinist.* "It is [too] easy to credit the results obtained to the system."

Maybe somewhere was a science of work as independent of human judgment as Taylor imputed to scientific management, expressible in pounds per square inch and hundred-thousandths of an hour, that couldn't be tainted by grasping human prejudices. But his was not it and never would be.

~

"The first truth the so-called 'efficiency engineers' proclaim," wrote Congressman Redfield, "is that neither owners nor operators, taken at large, know very much about the details of the business in which both are engaged." They needed the scientific managers to tell them.

That threatened every worker's, every foreman's, sense of self and worth. Experts could go where generations of craftsmen had gone before and do the work better and faster? All the worker's years on the job counted for less than what the outsiders could learn in a few days or weeks? In their humiliating cross-examination of foreman Willard Barker, the Watertown officers had driven home just this point—how little he knew and how much he needed the experts.

Yet maybe, critics held, human work held secrets that Taylor and his experts could never see, was influenced by factors to which their science was blind.

In 1913, *Life* carried a cartoon showing a man and woman in an office, their workplace embrace broken up by the "Efficiency Crank": "Young man, are you aware that you employed fifteen unnecessary motions in delivering that kiss?" That same year, an article in the *Nation* imagined the time accounting demanded of, say, a young minister:

9:30 to 10:27, visited the widow and the fatherless
10:27 to 11:03, bound up three brokenhearted

Efficiency methods, such spoofs deftly noted, left something out, whose omission, whatever it was, rendered the results ridiculous.

Taylor himself became a target of ridicule. His fondness for golf, for example, provoked a letter to the *New York Sun* representing his putting style:

> After computing angles, distances, grades, the right foot was brought provisionally into position, a whirl upon the toe then brought it definitively so and simultaneously the left. . . . By this method it is understood Mr. Brandeis will offer to save the golfers of Boston 100,000,000 strokes in a single half holiday.

Barbed stories grew up around the poisonous logic of the efficiency expert. Nelson Algren's character Highpockets, a hardworking "hillbilly from way back at the fork of the crick," was a time-study man's dream come true:

> The time-study man, that mother-robbing creeper that watches you from behind dolly trucks and stock boxes, he's always trying to figger a way to get more work out of you at the same pay. He'll even ask you if they ain't some way you could do a little more than you are. He never expects you should say yes.

But Highpockets does say yes. Let him run another machine with his left hand, he pleads. Soon he's turning out twice as much as before, which spurs the time-study man to new depths of fiendish ingenuity. Soon a block and tackle is attached to Highpockets's right leg, and then a band to his left leg with which to pick things off a conveyor. Finally, with a rod stuck between his teeth, he's jerking his head back and forth to run something else. The time-study man is thrilled, and Highpockets has caught the spirit. *"If you want to stick a broom someplace,"* he cries, leaving scant doubt where "someplace" is, *"I think I could be sweeping the floor!"*

No figure in industry was more reviled than the time-study man in particular or the efficiency expert in general. In one large plant, a trade magazine reported,

> a number of young "efficiency engineers" were employed and placed in almost complete charge of the works and they busied themselves

for about six or eight months by drawing a large salary, smoking cigarettes, holding a stop watch, looking wise, asking fool questions and
making themselves generally ridiculous

They left the works "in a state of complete disorganization."

A veteran canoe maker told how one day the boss installed "Brown,
the efficiency man. . . . He was a young fellow, just out of college, telling
old canoe-makers how to go about their work." Force-dry the canoes, he
said; that would cut a ten-day job to four hours. They did. Orders came
in, canoes went out. And then two months after the last of them was
shipped, they began coming back with warped ribs and splintered
gunwales.

The priests of efficiency, in their temples of formula and rule, seemed
to possess science's secrets. Yet didn't it seem they always got things
wrong? Maybe you couldn't say just what they didn't know, but the bitter
derision, the seeming delight in pointing up their errors, hinted at some
higher job wisdom that the experts missed and that mattered a great deal.

The "human element," this missing factor would invariably be called:
nuances of method and technique not obvious to the outsider, tangled
on-the-job allegiances just beneath the workplace's seemingly placid
surface, fuzzy unquantifiables like dignity, pride, and independence—
anything, in short, that fell outside the experts' gaze. "It's easy for them
time-study fellows to come down there with a stop watch and figure out
just how much a man can do in a minute and fifty-two seconds," said one
thirty-seven-year-old auto worker. "There are some things they can see
and record with their stop watch. But they can't clock how a man feels
from one day to the next."

American Machinist editor Fred Colvin likewise noted how he'd
become "fed up" with a scientific management purveyed as "a set of
rules, many of which utterly ignored some of the real fundamentals of
management, such as the personal or human factor." Taylor's "science"
fell short of its own ideals, he was saying, precisely because it overlooked
a "variable," as it were, that figured heavily in every real work setting.

Taylor was justly proud to have identified no fewer than a dozen variables that bore on metal cutting. Yet in the worker's customs, prejudices,
and psyche lay a crucial variable that scientific management largely
ignored. That's how it struck Felix Frankfurter, the future Supreme Court
justice, when he suggested in 1917 that scientific management had yet to
"become completely scientific."

But if scientific management wasn't completely scientific, what about its claim to being democratic? That claim rested on the assertion that you need never negotiate, debate, or otherwise sink to angry workplace bickering, because its powerful science resolved every issue objectively. What if, as Frankfurter and others said, it didn't? What if it left room for disagreement after all?

Suppose you did a time study, commissioner James O'Connell asked James Dodge at an Industrial Relations Commission hearing in 1914, and the workman disputes it, saying, "No, it cannot be done in that time." What then?

"We bring a man in there to show him that it can be done," replied Dodge.

"And if he still disagrees with you?"

"You do not mean to say that he will disagree after he has been shown that the thing can be done?" replied Dodge. Surely the commissioner did not mean that.

"I am afraid I do," said the commissioner.

"If I say two and two is four and a man disagrees with me, and I bring a mathematician or a professor to tell him so, and show him in every way that it is so, and he still disagrees, he is hopeless."

Hopeless? Or maybe he so distrusts the experts brought in to prove him wrong, so yearns for his small voice to be heard, that out of sheer, ornery spite, he holds fast. Then again, maybe the experts do get it wrong. "You know what some men can say and what they can do with figures," replied Commissioner O'Connell, heavy with implication.

But on this point, Taylor and Company never wavered. Workers didn't need a say in the shop; they could suggest, and they could quit. But otherwise, their views did not warrant a voice; they simply lacked the knowledge. "The truth is," wrote Morris Cooke, "that after scientific management has made any material progress in a plant it becomes increasingly difficult for those not making a special study of any given matter to make suggestions." If you didn't know what the experts knew, how could your opinion count?

Unless, as Taylorism's critics argued, the basis for making a decision was not so cut-and-dried as it might seem. What, for example, was soldiering? What did it mean to "restrict" output? As Hugh Aitken soundly observed in *Taylorism at Watertown Arsenal*, "Restriction of output is not restriction unless measured against some relevant standard, and the standards of the engineer and employer have no more claim" to validity than do those of the worker. The tools of scientific management alone could supply no certain answer, even in principle. The truth they discovered was only a limited truth that must be balanced against others.

Balanced how?

Balanced by negotiations between groups that might have wildly differing notions, based on wildly differing assumptions, of what a full day's work, for example, really was. Collective bargaining, labor called it.

After Taylor's death, as we've seen, a more liberal wing arose that did acknowledge a place for collective bargaining. "Out of a cult which insisted somewhat stridently that 'facts' and 'science' were the solvents of industrial ills," Ordway Tead, a leader of this group, wrote in the *New Republic* in 1920, "grows a spirit daily sweeter and more reasonable which points out that if our economic institutions are to be truly scientific, they must also be democratic and human." Not surprisingly, Louis Brandeis was among the first to preach this view. "We cannot reach our goal without . . . [material] things," Brandeis said in 1915. "But we may have all those things, and have a nation of slaves."

This needed corrective, however, came late, mostly after Taylor was dead, and represented merely a spur line to his thinking; Taylor's vision remained the trunk. As late as 1915, when Robert Valentine, one of the first to argue for more democratic scientific management, came before the Taylor Society to say as much, he was met, Tead noted, "with an almost abusive absence of sympathy." It was this hard, unyielding streak in Taylorism that gave it its early energy and direction, that dominated Taylor's own writings, and that left its stamp indelibly on the world.

IV

THE STOPWATCH AND THE JACKBOOT

Plaszów concentration camp in German-occupied Poland, during World War II. Attached to the camp is a factory ostensibly producing goods for the German war machine, but which its benign director, Oskar Schindler, a Nazi party member, actually uses to protect Jews with "essential skills" from going to Auschwitz. On this day, however, Schindler is away and

Plaszów's sadistic commandant, Amon Goeth, has come to inspect. As Thomas Keneally tells it in *Schindler's List*, Amon pauses besides a machine manned by Rabbi Levartov:

> "What are you making?" asked the Commandant.
> "Herr Commandant," said Levartov, "I am making hinges." The rabbi pointed, in fact, to the small heap of hinges on the floor.
> "Make me one now," Amon ordered. He took a watch from his pocket and began timing.

Levartov strains, thinking thereby to demonstrate his value to the German war effort and stay at Plaszów instead of going to his death.

Fifty-eight seconds.

Amon asks for another. Again about a minute.

But now, in unassailable numbers on the watch face, Levartov's abilities have been laid bare. Amon Goeth looks down at the few hinges at the rabbi's feet:

> "You've been working here since six this morning," said Amon, not raising his eyes from the floor. "And you can work at a rate you've just shown me—and yet, such a tiny little pile of hinges?"
> Levartov knew, of course, that he had crafted his own death.

In the end, Levartov is spared when he offers a convincing excuse for his low output. But the scene shows how raw, seemingly neutral knowledge can serve cruel power.

A Dundee, Scotland, factory worker in 1887 reminisced:

> Masters and managers did with us as they liked. The clocks at the factories were often put forward in the morning and back at night, and instead of being instruments for the measurement of time, they were used as cloaks for cheatery and oppression. . . . A workman then was afraid to carry a watch, as it was no uncommon event to dismiss any one who presumed to know too much about the science of horology.

Knowledge in the wrong hands, it seems, could bully and coerce. And it was knowledge—the craftsman's secrets, the mysteries of the guilds— that Taylorist management set out to gather, concentrate in its own hands, and use for its own ends. In knowledge lay power; more knowledge, more power; too much knowledge, too much power. Most of Taylor's critics never quite found words to define the danger, but Nels Alifas did.

At the time Alifas briefly appeared on the historical stage, he was the American Federation of Labor's representative for machinists employed in government arsenals and navy yards. A Danish immigrant, he had started as a machinist with a Rockdale, Illinois, company, then gone to Rock Island Arsenal in 1904, where he became a toolmaker. His work had earned praise, his pay climbing to four dollars a day by 1911, when he was thirty-one, despite a pronounced tendency to speak his mind; one boss labeled him "a disturber." Wherever labor fought scientific management during these years, Alifas the disturber was usually there to question what to Taylor seemed self-evident truths.

In 1914, he shared a speaker's platform with Taylor at a Wisconsin labor meeting. Why did labor oppose time study? One means "by which an employee has been able to keep his head above water and prevent being oppressed by the employer," he explained,

> has been that the employer didn't know just exactly what the employee could do. The only way that the workman has been able to retain time enough in which to do the work with the speed with which he thinks he ought to do it, has been to keep the employer somewhat in ignorance of exactly the time needed.

Yes, workers did try to keep knowledge to themselves and for good reason: to exercise control over their work lives. They wished to set how fast they worked, not leave it to others. What was wrong with that?

> The people of the United States have a right to say we want to work only so fast. We don't want to work as fast as we are able to. We want to work as fast as we think it's comfortable for us to work.

He wanted to be comfortable?!

> We haven't come into existence for the purpose of seeing how great a task we can perform through a lifetime. We are trying to regulate our work so as to make it an auxiliary to our lives.

As unlikely as it might seem to the Taylors of the world, other things besides work mattered. Maybe time and energy left for drinking and carousing, in which Taylor didn't indulge, or hunting and fishing, in which he did; or reading, singing, tennis, or golf, all of which Taylor also enjoyed. Maybe workers could go faster; but maybe they didn't want to and shouldn't have to:

> Most people walk to work in the morning, if it isn't too far. If some-body should discover that they could run to work In one third the time, they might have no objection to have that fact ascertained, but if the man who ascertained it had the power to make them run, they might object to having him find it out.

Here was the antithesis of what every scion of the Enlightenment, every Taylor and every Gantt, knew with absolute certainty In knowl-edge lay truth, freedom, progress? No, to Alifas, knowledge menaced.

~

On the eve of the Billancourt strike at Renault in 1913, the story went around that a Frenchman, touring an American factory and seeing only young men, asked where the older workers were. "Let me show you," said the boss, directing his guest to the cemetery. "Down there," he pointed.

The tale, issued as an alarm against Taylorism, was actually drawn from an Englishman's 1906 account of factory work near Pittsburgh and had nothing to do with scientific management. But it caught on among striking Renault workers who saw, in time and motion studies, a threat to their health, independence, and livelihood. Similarly frightful visions—of slavery, totalitarianism, and worse—have dogged Taylorism from the start, its more histrionic critics seeing in it not just a want of democratic spirit but something akin to the demonic.

At the time of the Watertown strike, a committee of molders charged the Taylor system with functioning like "a slave driver's whip on the Negro, as it keeps him in a constant state of agitation." An English paper depicted scientific management in a headline as "Another Step Towards Industrial Slavery." And in an outburst its author must have enjoyed, the AF of L said of the Taylor system:

No tyrant or slave-driver in the ecstasy of his most delirious dream ever sought to place upon abject slaves a condition more repugnant to commonly accepted notions of freedom of action and liberty of person.

Most of this was just so much rhetoric, good for a debating point or pumping up the crowd. Still, such denunciations must have rankled Taylor and his friends, to whom scientific management meant slavery averted, not inflicted.

H. L. Gantt, whose family had held slaves in Maryland, pictured scientific management as a giant step up from "the time of slave labor," when the best foreman was one who drove his men the hardest.

In 1914, Taylor reminded an audience that personal freedom was quite a new idea:

Only a few hundred years ago a great part of the world's work was done by actual slaves, by men every one of whose acts were completely governed and regulated by other men, their masters. And this slavery was of the very worst type—far worse than that of our own country in which the black man (on the whole an inferior race) were made the slaves of the white men.

In Rome and Greece, "white men of equal intelligence and abilities with their masters" lived at their every whim. And it was cruel whim that scientific management proposed to banish.

Banish, not uphold. Where, then, was the slavery its foes imputed to it?

In 1973, a Queens College, New York, professor, R. Keith Aufhauser, contributed a paper to the *Journal of Economic History* in which he proposed "to show the extent to which the theory and practice of the slaveholders [of the American South] conformed to F. W. Taylor's school of scientific management."

He did indeed find likenesses. Taylor, he wrote, "views the average worker as sluggish, incapable of individual initiative, insensitive to individual incentive, too stupid to produce efficiently without the constant supervision of a mentally superior supervisor." This, of course, was how even enlightened planters saw their slaves. Indeed, their correspondence often cited "experiments in ascertaining the maximum work that could be expected from their field laborers under various soil and weather conditions; the tasks were always designed to drive slaves close to this maximum."

Aufhauser quoted rules, intended to guide overseers, worthy of Taylor:

Order and System must be the aim of everyone on the plantation, and the maxim strictly pursued of a time for everything and everything done in time, a place for everything and everything kept in its place, a rule for everything and everything done according to rule.

Aufhauser ignored the mechanics of scientific management and conflated worlds distant in time, place, and historical circumstances. Still, one wonders, *was* there some peculiar affinity between Taylorism and oppression, the stopwatch and the jackboot?

∽

In September 1927, the Third International Management Congress came to Rome. Benito Mussolini, Il Duce, spared no effort in welcoming Taylorism to Fascist Italy. The Campidoglio, crowning the Capitoline Hill, was decked out in tapestries and flags; soldiers lined the stairway to the Senate chamber.

Scientific management's roots in Italian soil never went terribly deep. "The Italian, notwithstanding eighteen years of Fascism, is still somewhat the same easy-going, skeptical, and individualist personality that he has always been, and ill disposed to take orders," an American partisan of scientific management wrote on the eve of World War II; its prospects there, he believed, were poor.

But not for want of trying.

"The role of the Fascists in creating an environment favorable to the introduction of Taylorism should not be underestimated," writes Perry R. Willson in *The Clockwork Factory: Women and Work in Fascist Italy*. An enfeebled trade union movement left employers free to do as they wished. In 1926, the government established a propaganda arm, known as ENIOS, for promoting scientific management. It did this especially among small and medium-size firms, though its reach extended into the home, with a campaign to make housework more efficient.

Among large firms, the two most Americanized—that is, influenced by Ford and Taylor—were the carmaker Fiat and Willson's subject, Magneti Marelli, a manufacturer of radios, magnetos, and other electrical equipment. *The Principles of Scientific Management* had been translated into Italian in 1915, and Magneti managers read Taylor and visited American factories, bringing back with them ideas for introducing scientific management. "The complete reorganization of our production methods," the company newspaper reported in 1929, "dates, in fact, from this period."

What Willson called Magneti's clockwork factory, which was regularly visited by dignitaries from abroad, Fascist muckety-mucks, and Mussolini himself, boasted new automatic machine tools, more efficient factory layout, and technical managers bent on relieving workers of their skills. "As in all the best foreign firms," a company newsletter boasted, Magneti workers need not "worry about either the way work is organized or how to obtain the necessary tools, etc. All this is taken care of by special departments created for the purpose," Taylorized planning departments where the brains of the firm now resided.

For the 1927 congress's closing ceremonies, the Campidoglio was yet more gloriously done up, the soldiers were there in even greater numbers, and government officials and high military officers, two thousand of them, crowded the Senate chamber. Suddenly, in the words of one account,

> the murmur of conversation was hushed by a fanfare of trumpets on the Piazza outside. . . . There were several moments of almost breathless silence, and Il Duce, Benito Mussolini, gravely and quickly entered, releasing sharp cries of welcome and a burst of applause from the audience. A forward thrust of his right arm finally secured silence . . .
>
> As Mussolini rose to speak he was again greeted by vociferous applause. His vigorous and deeply serious address, given successively in English, French and German, left no one in doubt as to the value he placed on scientific management.

The scene impressed itself on Taylor's widow, who was also present. It was wonderful, Lou wrote later,

> to be escorted by members of the Taylor Society to the brilliantly decorated capital, and to have Fred's photo flashed on the screen . . . !

Later, I was invited to [Mussolini's chambers] to be received by him and to receive his photo in exchange for one of my husband's. As he said, he wanted one of the great man who had revolutionized industry and management.

∼

It was probably sometime in 1916 that Lenin came under Taylor's spell.

World War I raged and he was living in Zurich, where he encountered Adolf Wallichs's German translation of *Shop Management,* as well as a paean to the Taylor system by a German, Rudolf Seubert, who had spent eight months at Tabor before the war.

Forty-six-year-old Lenin made numerous marginal notes in Taylor's books, recorded excerpts in his notebooks. Before the war, he had charged scientific management with "enslavement of humankind to the machine," but that, apparently, was before he'd actually read Taylor. Now it seemed to him that Taylorism offered hope for modernizing backward Russian industry.

During the revolution itself, writes Judith Merkle in *Management and Ideology: The Legacy of the International Scientific Management Movement,* "the influence of the Taylor system of scientific management . . . appears to have been pervasive." With the country laid waste, industrial production fell to a third of prewar levels. Russia must be rebuilt and capitalist science would help do it, declared Lenin, by raising productivity and improving labor discipline. Taylorism, he said in a speech published in *Pravda* in 1918, blended "the refined cruelty of bourgeois exploitation with a number of most valuable scientific attainments. . . . We must introduce in Russia the study and the teaching of the Taylor system and its systematic trial and adaptation." When a "Left Communist" faction opposed Taylorism's application to Russian industry, Lenin wrote a polemic against them.

Leon Trotsky, Lenin's partner in revolution, embraced Taylorism, too, and probably did more to work Taylorism into Soviet life. Trotsky, in turn, influenced Stalin—who, writes Merkle, "stole [from him] . . . Taylorism, ready-made, and forced [it] into Russian industry by all the coercive power at the command of a totalitarian regime."

Not that Taylorism made Russia into a five-million-square-mile Midvale; Russia had too far to go. An American described Russian trains as "strings of match boxes coupled with hairpins and drawn by samovars."

Russian workers, peasants straight off the farms, had often never seen a watch, much less a stopwatch. Mechanical breakdowns were written off to bourgeois sabotage, not technical problems easily remedied. One American engineer who'd come to help the new Soviet state was arrested as he tried to leave the country in 1920 and languished in jail for a year before being returned to the United States.

Still, Taylorism stuck. Robert Linhart, author of a long essay entitled "Lenine, Les Paysans, Taylor," found "traces of [Taylorism] not only in the structure of the work process, but in Soviet society as a whole." By 1921, the young Soviet Union was home to twenty institutions that bore the stamp of scientific management. The "Russian Taylor," Alexei Gastev, an early Bolshevik exiled in France—where, as a metalworker at Renault, he had apparently seen scientific management up close—became vice president of the Council for Scientific Management. The infamous Soviet Five-Year Plans, their progress tracked by the special scheduling charts pioneered by Gantt, fairly reeked of Taylorism, which seeped so deeply into Russian organization, writes Merkle, that it took on "the appearance of a native phenomenon."

~

In Germany just before World War I, a client bragged of his Taylorized plant's success to Wilfred Lewis. "Other concerns were doing the same thing," Taylor's old friend recalled, "and it cannot be doubted that the Taylor system of scientific management will ultimately become an integral part of the German 'Kultur,' which stands for efficiency and the survival of the fittest." Indeed, despite its author's dislike for Germans (though his Germantown roots led some to think he bore their blood), Taylorism's influence in Germany was especially strong, both before the First World War and in the years leading up to the Second.

GERMANY ADOPTS
AMERICAN SYSTEM

———

Scientific Shop Management
Devised by F. W. Taylor
Makes a Big Hit

———

BIG CONCERNS CONVERT

So read a headline in the *New York Tribune* before the war. Taylorism's ideas "are destined within a comparatively short space of time to revolutionize German industrial methods."

They didn't, at least not right away. German industry, which boasted of its quality, precision, and small-scale handwork, resisted. Workers opposed the loss of their prerogatives, manufacturers the coming of a new bureaucracy. And yet, Taylorist sensibilities came to hang heavily in the German air, perhaps more so even than in America's.

German engineers, for one, loved Taylor. The historian of technology Ulrich Wengenroth pictures his "messianic and undemocratic" attitude as "dear to many engineers," who saw it leaving them in firm control of the workplace. More prosaic factors applied, too. Taylor's books had been translated early on. High-speed steel still bathed him in its reflected glow. The university-trained were drawn to the "science" in scientific management. And in the person of Georg Schlesinger, longtime head of Germany's premier engineering society, the Verein Deutscher Ingenieure, *Taylorismus* had a devoted champion. "We Germans as a people," he told a joint meeting of the VDI and the ASME in 1913, "have been accustomed for centuries to obedience to superiors, to methodical instruction, and to observing written orders of the fullest description." It was a perfect fit.

During the war, two backers of scientific management, Walther Rathenau and Wichard von Moellendorff, played key roles in the German economics ministry; their technocratic ideas heavily influenced postwar reconstruction. By 1920, a booklet by Taylor disciple Gustav Winter, *How to Introduce the Taylor System in Germany*, had sold a hundred thousand copies. Big companies, like Berlin's Siemens and Stuttgart's Bosch, experimented with Taylorist measures. Vestag, the iron-and-steel trust, established a Committee for Time and Motion Studies. German engineers flocked to the United States to see American economic muscle up close and tour the Ford assembly line, which impressed many of them, writes Judith Merkle, as "the physical manifestation of Taylorism." One Weimar era poster showing men and women, military officers and merchants, together around a table, exhorted, "Work and Savings in all Professions Through the Taylor System." By 1927, a scholarly bibliography on scientific management in Germany was forty pages long.

Germany now bestowed a new word on the world, *Rationalisierung*, or "rationalization." This heroically scaled idea went scientific management one better by setting out to fuel the whole national economy with order, system, and efficiency. Harmonizing the workaday concerns of the shop floor with the Enlightenment tradition, it invested mere production with Reason. Central to the new idea, writes Detlev J. Peukert in *The Weimar Republic*, "were the managerial principles of Taylorism . . . which were now beginning to be implemented on a broad scale."

In *Visions of Modernity*, her study of American business influence on German modernization between the wars, Mary Nolan notes that Germans, while not alone in applying Taylorism to the home, did so more ardently than anyone else. At international management congresses, the "unquestioning endorsement [by German delegates] of economic efficiency as the highest goal and scientific management as the best means," she writes, "strikes later readers as abstract, austere, and almost dehumanized."

Rationalization was seeping down into the soil of everyday German life.

Did it seep a little too thoroughly?

"Germans grabbed the theory of scientific management with great enthusiasm," a Czech immigrant to America would write after World War II, but "with the cruelty natural to them, exploited the system against the workers, which culminated in the Nazi state and their slave labor camps." This brusque pronouncement was imperfect history at best, fair to neither Germany nor the German people. But did it contain some small seed of truth? Did a misshapen Taylorism somehow culminate in, or otherwise contribute to, the dark National Socialist night?

The extermination of the Jews horrifies not alone by its unparalleled scale, nor by the hatred it represented, but by the brutal efficiency with which it was done—from Adolf Eichmann's collection points and smooth-running trains at one end, to gaping ovens for consuming the corpses at the other, with gas chambers for efficiently dispatching the victims in-between. Blind hatred that exploded in paroxysms of violence was one thing; quite another was the systematic murder of millions of Jews, Gypsies, and others through a vast machinery of death. So when Wengenroth pictures Auschwitz as "the Taylorization of the killing of the Jewish people," is he, in any sense, right?

In *Reactionary Modernism*, his study of attitudes toward technology in the Weimar Republic and Nazi Germany, Jeffrey Herf gives us reason to pause before blaming Taylorist reason for evils done in passion's name.

Engineers most drawn to the Nazi movement, he argues, hailed from a strain in early twentieth-century German thought he calls "reactionary modernism," which, far from embracing Enlightenment rationality, rejected it.

For example, to Heinrich Hardensett, one of reactionary modernism's premier thinkers, Herf writes, "the rationalization movement of the 1920s, Taylorism, and time and motion studies were indicative of a 'soulless demonism of labor' that eliminated from the workplace all 'comradely playful transcendence, all joyful, plastic sensuality.' " This sounds like a liberal critique of Taylorism yet comes from a Nazi apologist. Engineers like Hardensett preferred technology embodying, in Herf's words, "irrational and instinctual forces that fought the good fight" against modern capitalism; that rejected the shabby materialist values of both America and a Russia that "idealized some of the worst aspects of American capitalism (Taylorism, for example)."

The Nazis needed the wiliest rhetorical tricks of propaganda minister Joseph Goebbels to forge ideological permission, as it were, to exploit modern technology. In a speech reprinted in a 1939 German journal, the cover of which shows the Nazi propaganda minister flanked on one side by Hitler and on the other by a new Volkswagen, Goebbels warned that technology risked making men "soulless." National Socialism didn't reject technology but set as its task "to fill it inwardly with soul.

> We live in an age that is both romantic and steel-like, that has not lost its depth of feeling. On the contrary, it has discovered a new romanticism in the results of modern inventions and technology. . . . National Socialism [has] understood how to take the soulless framework of technology and fill it with the rhythm and hot impulses of our time.

Here, Goebbels reconciled the Reich's need for the newest and best in technology with its dark, brutish urges. But it was irrationality that most indelibly stamped Nazism, Herf argues, not rationality run amok.

In any case, the Third Reich was no Taylorist examplar. And German war production was not notably efficient, though it became more so after Albert Speer became armaments minister in 1942. Then, engineers trained in scientific management moved into war factories. Production processes were simplified and standardized, special-purpose machine tools introduced, semiskilled labor relied upon more heavily. But workers resisted piece-rate systems, and a dearth of time-and-motion study experts hindered their introduction. Even in that most successful of Nazi endeavors, the death camps, writes Michael Allen in a doctoral dissertation, mismanagement was more the rule than a "rhetoric of well-oiled 'machineries of extermination' or the 'technocrats of death' would imply."

Plainly, Nazism on the one hand and scientific management on the other did not go hand in hand. Walther Rathenau, the World War I economics minister who championed rationalization, was murdered by right-wing extremists in 1922. His colleague, Wichard Moellendorff, committed suicide in 1937, despondent over the perversion of his ideals by the Nazis. And ardent Taylorite Georg Schlesinger, whom Wengenroth calls "the pope of the rationalization movement," migrated to England soon after the Nazis came to power. Meanwhile, among high Nazis most hostile to the "American" production methods introduced by Speer and most drawn to the romantic streak in Nazi ideology was SS General Otto Ohlendorf, who commanded an Einsatzgruppe that murdered Jews and Gypsies on the Eastern front in 1941. His acts were not those of a Taylorist engineer but of a blood-crazed killer.

If anything, Nazi ideology can be seen as a brutal reaction to the implacable currents of rationalism that swirled through early twentieth-century life and that Taylor and scientific management embodied. "Germany did not suffer from too much reason, too much liberalism, too much Enlightenment, but rather from not enough of any of them," Jeffrey Herf concludes. "Auschwitz remains a monument to the deficit and not the excess of reason in Hitler's Reich."

Even in a form twisted beyond any resemblance to itself, then, Taylorism was in no sense "responsible" for the Final Solution. On the other hand, might the Taylorist sensibilities that Germany sopped up between the wars—a hallowed efficiency, the exploitation of technology in its behalf, the split between planning and doing—have helped mold a society in which the Final Solution was more possible and more final?

"When put in charge of the new concentration camp at Auschwitz," writes Joan Campbell in *Joy in Work, German Work*, Rudolf Hoess "did his best to remain true to the *Arbeit macht frei* principle which he brought with him from Dachau," whose entrance gate bore the identical slogan, Work will make you free. While killing thousands daily, he nonetheless tried "to run Auschwitz as a labor camp, dedicated to production and run according to enlightened principles of scientific management."

It was Hoess who settled on Zyklon B, hydrogen cyanide, for more expeditious killing, replacing such inefficient means as shooting and carbon monoxide gassing. Even after the war, writes Robert Jay Lifton in *The Nazi Doctors*, he "remained proud of the efficiency of 'his' gas: 'Experience had shown,' " he quotes the commandant, that it

> caused death with far greater speed and certainty, especially if the rooms were kept dry and gas-tight and closely packed with people, and provided they were fitted with as large a number of intake vents as possible.

Its use, added Hoess,

> set my mind at rest, for the mass extermination of the Jews was to start soon and at that time neither Eichmann nor I was certain how these mass killings were to be carried out. . . . Now we had the gas, and we had established a procedure.

The factory of death was ready to run.

In Germany between the wars, writes Mary Nolan, the rationalized factory became "the model for everyday life." The depression of the 1930s and the Nazi seizure of power left Americanism less in favor. But Hitler still admired Henry Ford enough to award him a medal. And, Nolan writes, "elements of Americanism were inserted discretely but firmly into Nazi society, where they coexisted with distinctly Nazi innovations—consumption and concentration camps, technological rationalization and racial annihilation."

To Monika Renneberg and Mark Walker, in their essay "Scientists, Engineers and National Socialism," Nazi technocratic leanings "played an important role in the history of the Third Reich. How else can we explain the transition from mass shootings to gas chambers?" And they add:

> If a Party technocrat, an SS technocrat, technocrats from a special agency like the Four Year Plan, the General Government, or Speer's Ministry, and a technocrat from the Armed Forces were to meet together—as, for example, such technocrats did at the Wannsee Conference—they would . . . all agree that scientific, technological and bureaucratic rationality and efficiency was the way to solve their and

Germany's problems, in this case the "Final Solution of the Jewish Question."

At Auschwitz, Lifton reports, camp doctors coolly debated technical facets of their gory work, endeavoring always to make things run smoothly. "Which is better," Lifton quotes a camp doctor reconstructing a debate, "to let mothers go with their children to the gas or to select the mothers later by separating them from their children?' " Or else, what to do when the crematoriums broke down, as they sometimes did. "Thousands were lying there and had to be burned," another camp doctor told him. "How does one do that?" Ditches around the piles, wooden planks beneath, and gasoline on top? Or perhaps gasoline beneath and wood in between? Which way was best?

At the Buchenwald concentration camp, a survivor recalled how

> long, heavy iron beams . . . were not carried, say, on wagons or carts but rather on the shoulders of the prisoners. The supervisors and Kapos [prisoner watchmen] had experimented to establish how many men could carry one beam. Not one additional man was assigned to ease the burden for support or assistance, although plenty of men were available.

Michael Allen, who relates this story in his study of Nazi concentration camp administration, describes it as "an evil parody of Frederick Taylor's classic tale of Schmidt."

At the least, then, Germany's infatuation with Taylorism and efficiency between the wars, followed by National Socialism's mechanized killing, sounds a cautionary note. Eichmann, says Ulrich Wengenroth, can be seen as "a perfect Taylor engineer."

LOST PARADISE

In America, the Special Committee's 1912 report constituted not the final judgment of the Taylor system but only the first of many. Over the years, a whole litany of grievances was voiced in books, scholarly articles, union broadsides, platform addresses, and works of literature and film.

Scientific management, it was said, sang the same old capitalist tune; it was just another in a long line of brutal "speedup" systems designed to extract more from labor. The worker crawled home exhausted at day's end, while any pay increase was temporary at best. Besides, with Taylor boasting that 120 yard laborers now did the work of 400, what were the other 280 supposed to do?

All this, of course, was standard labor-movement fare. But objections to scientific management regularly took unfamiliar turns as well. In March 1911, two United Textile Workers Union representatives toured a scientifically managed mill in Passaic, New Jersey—probably Brighton Mills, with H. L. Gantt at the helm—where it found not capitalist ogres but caring superintendents, a pleasant lunchroom, clean washrooms, and a regular fifty-hour week. And yet, of the mill's 635 employees, most seemed unhappy.

One group of them made $2.41 a day if their output exceeded a certain figure, $1.47 if not. It was a big difference, and it took a big toll. "Yes, we get a little more money," union investigators heard. "But we are pushed to the limit. The mental strain under which we work, and our anxiety and fear that we shall fall below the standard, makes the job scarcely worth while." Workers lost weight, came home drenched in sweat. The same went for their overseers, whose pay was tied to that of their "help," and who seemed eternally irritable. "It is drive, drive, drive every minute of the day," one weaver said. "I am ready to go to bed the moment I get home at night, often without supper." These workers had jobs, claimed no physical duress, and were relatively well paid. But if you believed the union, they were miserable, suffering from "mental strain," nervous and fretful.

Charges aimed at Taylorism frequently raised just such apparent paradoxes. Maybe it delivered wages close to those it promised, and physically, it might not drive you so much harder. Yet it exacted other tolls, less tangible ones—mental, emotional, social, and even spiritual.

Scientific management, the charge went, pitted workers as individuals against one another, made them claw at each other for the privilege of becoming one of Taylor's "first class men." It broke up the comradely fellow-feeling, the respect of one man for his brother, that lay behind the labor movement at its best and that alone raised the worker above the moneygrubbing capitalist who was his master.

Scientific management was degrading. In reducing work to instructions and rules, it took away your knowledge and skill. In standing over you with a stopwatch, peering at you, measuring you, rating you, it treated you like a side of beef. You weren't supposed to think. Whatever workmanly pride you might once have possessed must be sacrificed on the altar of efficiency, your role only to execute the will of other men paid to think for you. You were a drone, fit only for taking orders.

Scientific management, then, worked people with scant regard not only for the limitations of their bodies but for the capacities of their minds. In the great Taylorist equation that spat out the Good News of high wages, high profits, and low prices, the quality of those eight or ten hours on the job itself had been banished from the calculation.

During the Special Committee hearings, William D. Hemmerly, once of Tabor, mentioned a mechanic just promoted to the planning department. "Does he have to work harder?" wondered Congressman Redfield.

"That depends on what you mean by working harder," said Hemmerly. Maybe he worked longer, but not really harder, "because he is able to arrange his work to some extent to suit his own dictates. . . . In that respect you might say that he is a little more his own boss."

Autonomy it is called today—this, anyway, is the five-dollar word for it—the chance to exert a say-so in your job, to do it your way. Work was more than how hard you worked, more than how much you earned, more than the skill you possessed. What counted also was your freedom to exercise skill as you wished, in your own time, subject to your own judgment. And while Hemmerly's ex-mechanic had more independence as a planner—he was one of the brains now, he issued the orders—many under scientific management, probably most, had less.

A fifty-nine-year-old steelworker who used an air hammer to scrape off the bad spots on a billet complained, after thirty-one years on the job, how "now they have inspectors who make chalk marks on the places they want scraped off. [In the past], I looked at the slab of steel and decided for myself the spots that needed chipping."

"My job is all engineered out," said an auto worker. "The jigs and fixtures are all designed and set out according to specifications. There are a lot of little things you could tell them, but they never ask."

"Too much direction is not a good thing," a sheet metal worker, thirteen years at the Brooklyn navy yard, told the Special Committee. "If I am to simply punch holes when I should not only punch the holes but also make the marks where the holes ought to go, I am certainly doing something that is not profitable."

It was a revealing choice of words. Might "profit" reside in something beyond the weekly pay envelope? Might prescribing another's work too minutely deplete it of something vital—like skill, or the pleasure in its use, or judgment—and so make it less "profitable"?

Scientific management gathered knowledge and fed it back to the worker in the form of instruction cards, books of standard operating procedures, standing orders, standardized jigs and fixtures, fixed machine settings, printed forms, posted work rules, and so on. The worker need only check off the right blank, or press the right block on the computer touch screen, or otherwise follow simple rules. Here, roughly, was the "deskilling" argument advanced by Harry Braverman in his influential 1974 book, *Labor and Monopoly Capital: The Degradation of Work in the Twentieth Century.* In it, Frederick Taylor emerged as chief villain.

At an ASME meeting, someone once asked Taylor about trouble with unions; didn't have any, he replied. "If the operator objects to increasing the feed from one sixty-fourth of an inch to one-eighth, he is told that he is to obey orders! If he objects to the shape of a tool, he gets the same answer."

The boss had always been the one to give the orders, observed Braverman, who had apprenticed as a copper worker and worked at that and other trades for fourteen years. "But Taylor raised the concept of control to an entirely new plane when he asserted as an *absolute necessity for adequate management the dictation to the worker of the precise manner in which work is to be performed.*" Taylor insisted that management's job was incomplete "so long as it left to the worker any decision about the work."

Maybe the new machine tenders Taylorism brought up from the laboring ranks earned more now, and presided over big machines, whereas before they had only their shovels. But were they any more masters of their work than before? Many of these lucky ex-laborers actually lost independence, suggests Andrea Graziosi, an Italian who studied the history of common laborers in America. Once, she wrote in a 1981 essay, laborers were supervised "from above and from outside"; they might be driven hard by more or less despotic foremen, but were otherwise left alone. Under scientific management, on the other hand, any remaining "elements of self-direction" were eliminated. Like Schmidt, they learned to do just as they were told and so gave up what little autonomy they'd once enjoyed.

At the high end of the skills ladder, the story was much the same. Harley Shaiken, a machinist turned academician, wrote in 1985 how a two-year study of the U.S. metalworking industry—drawn from the experience of hundreds of experts but no workers or union representatives—had recommended that industry should "reduce the skill levels required to operate or maintain certain machine tools."

Shaiken quoted *Iron Age*'s observation that numerical control, an early form of machine tool automation, "embodies much of what the father of scientific management, Frederick Winslow Taylor, sought back in 1880." But now, even planning itself was having skill sucked out of it. One software program, Shaiken quoted its developers,

> provides a means of reducing the individual skill and experience generally necessary for a process planner to function productively. It is a vehicle for standardizing and optimizing production methods by removing individual decision-making.

∾

And why not, Taylor or any of his disciples might have asked. "It is impossible to permit the workmen to use their judgment as to the best methods of work," Henri Le Chatelier said at the opening of the French Congress of Management in 1924. His argument bore a pristine logic of its own: "No workman is going to learn by five minutes of reflection before a turning lathe . . . [what] it took Taylor twenty-five years of research to discover." Surely, that much was incontrovertible.

Having planners and experts on the one hand, and operatives on the other, imputed neither superiority to the one nor inferiority to the other, Taylor always insisted. You couldn't expect one person to do both—not at the same time, anyway. It was the old division of labor taken just one more step.

Besides, what did scientific management really strip from work? Nothing, said the Taylorites. On the contrary, it brought workers up, into better jobs. The floor sweeper learned to run a grinding wheel. The grinder learned to run a drill press; the drill press man, a lathe. The lathe-man became a toolmaker, the toolmaker wound up in the planning office. Taylor furnished the Special Committee with charts showing just such progress among Watertown Arsenal workers. He told later of a man who came to America on the first day of the new century, worked as a laborer at fifteen cents an hour, and moved up through a succession of jobs to become foreman and head of the whole department. "We had taught that fellow five or six trades. That is what we propose to do for every man."

The new men coming up from below replaced skilled men? Maybe so, allowed Taylor, but now the "high-class mechanics become our teachers. Our factories are all managed by the workmen," who graduate into management. Once, at a meeting of the Taylor Society, King Hatha-way mentioned several men present who had come up through the ranks at Tabor and had moved on to better jobs at bigger companies. "That does not look as if we stifled initiative," he said.

Indeed, scientific management turned out whole armies of white-collar workers. In the early days, they were route clerks, time-study and instruction-card men, but over the years their ranks broadened. Scientific management, wrote Taylor's son Kempton, twenty-two at the time, in a paper for college not long after his father's death, was "one of the most powerful elevating influences that civilization has developed. Machinery took the workman from the field and the bench; scientific management takes him from the machine and puts him in the planning department." This metamorphosis "marks a step in the 'uplift' of mankind."

Many of those new white-collar workers, of course, were now fairly stranded in the office, cut off from the work of the shop. During the Special Committee hearings, foreman Barker agreed it was good that planners, in their own area, were less readily interrupted—but maybe not so good: "If they could see their castings as well as a drawing, it would help out sometimes." No abstract representation on paper (much less a computer screen) conferred the knowledge that sight and touch did. If the stock Taylorized drone had become "mindless," his white-collar counterpart, lost to numbers, forms, charts, and rules—no longer repacking a bearing, no longer hoisting a casting onto a planer bed—had become "bodyless."

Still, it was enhanced, not withered, opportunity that scientific management promised. In a paper written in 1913, Morris Cooke stressed that "if we are to reach the highest point in productivity . . . , [we must] have every individual use his or her highest powers to advantage." Half the brains in the world, said Cooke, lay in the working classes, blocked by want of opportunity. Under scientific management, "this great storehouse of wealth will be tapped, not we hope for the benefit of the few, but for the benefit of all."

This sunny view of scientific management was, of course, almost unrecognizable to its critics, but Taylor and his disciples were not alone to see it that way. For one thing, while Braverman's "deskilling" ideas were provocative, some scholars came to feel that the loss of skill among some workers was matched by a growth in jobs requiring additional skill. It was easy to mythologize the old days, before that old devil Taylor came along, but did anyone really want to go back to the creaking changelessness of Cramp's, the crooked favoritism of Renault, the nepotism at Bethlehem, the sheer industrial slovenliness from which consumer, boss, and worker suffered alike? Snicker all you want at compulsive Taylorist order, but did anyone really prefer dirty shops with machines set up every which way, discarded castings and other odd junk littering the floor, workers waiting for harried foremen to give them something to do?

So maybe the Bravermans of the world were wrong. They imagined an Arcadian industrial past that never existed. One skeptic, Jean Monds, archly entitled the tale they told "The Lost Paradise of Craft Autonomy: with F. W. Taylor as Serpent."

By the end of World War I, writes Daniel Nelson, unionists were "more impressed with the promise of order, planning, and security from capricious rule-of-thumb management than with the dangers of time study." And as the unions came around, as wages climbed, as the bicycles, cars, pumps, and widgets poured out of America's factories, it became easy to forget that there'd ever been a price to pay for the productive miracle Taylorism wrought.

In a 1911 article in *System*, "Putting the 'One Best Way' Into Practice," Edward Mott Woolley described a shop before and after scientific management:

> Formerly, as in most shops, the mechanics did a large part of the planning how work was to be done. They studied their blue-prints and decided what operations were necessary, which should come first and how they should be accomplished. They hunted up the . . . tools they needed, borrowing them with or without permission. They drove their planers or lathes at whatever feed and speed they thought right.

This was written, it bears reminder, to point up the egregious waste of such practices. And yet some might read it today as the nostalgic evocation of a worker's heaven that granted ached-for independence; many, in white-collar jobs and blue, would *die* for it.

In the scientifically managed shop, the author went on, such archaic practices vanished:

> Today the workmen do no planning. Every detail of work on every job is thought out for them and put down in unmistakable black and white. Not merely general directions but the specific instructions indicating operations necessary on each part and the factors bearing on these operations—the character and number of cuts, the depth of each, the tool to be used, the speed, the feed, the time allowed if a bonus or premium is to be earned, the hourly rate if the bonus time is not attained.

On it continued, devoid of irony, without a hint that the transformation might not be entirely benign.

A BARGAIN RECONSIDERED

In 1915, Katie Richards O'Hare, a colorful working-class journalist won over to socialism by no less a figure than the fabled Mother Jones herself, came away from a tour of Ford's Highland Park plant determined to give Taylor's redoubtable Schmidt new life. While hefting pig iron for Taylor, the way she told her story in a publication known as *The National Rip-Saw*, Schmidt got pneumonia, which "not only swept away all his savings but took the scrap of waste land" on which he had been building his little house:

> When Schmidt could stand upon his shaky legs he got a job on rail-road construction work, drifted out to Detroit and today is working eight hours per day screwing a certain nut on a certain bolt in each automobile engine that passes him on the endless chain in the Ford Motor plant. He receives five dollars per day; his three thousand dollar six-room cottage is one-third paid for, his three children are in school, and two are taking music lessons; his garden is the pride of the block.

All this was fiction, and yet, in a sense, every word of it was true. Concluded O'Hare, "I met thousands of Schmidts in the Ford plant in Detroit."

And millions more, over the rest of the century, would accept versions of the deal that Ford offered the fictional Schmidt at Highland Park or that Taylor offered Henry Noll at Bethlehem: make big money, enjoy the good life, but in return submit to the implacable rhythms of the assembly line or to a squinty-eyed efficiency man. Nobody liked working the line or submitting to the Taylor system—single-mindedly, following directions, ever aware of the clock. But it was worth it, right? Low wages were a steep price to pay for the dubious pleasure of working at one's own pace, in one's own way.

Fred Taylor had come up during the worst depression of his generation, the one following the panic of 1873 and extending to about 1878. All around him, while he served his apprenticeship at the pump works, men were out of work. Those who still had jobs earned a third less than they had a few years earlier. Autonomy? Independence? Big words for what didn't count, Taylor might have fired back. What workers wanted were secure jobs and high wages. And high wages were what he offered those willing to do his bidding.

Sten Rockstrom, the Swede who came away a believer after seeing scientific management in the United States, admitted that "everyone who is controlled by a stop-watch has unquestionably the same disagreeable feeling," that of being a "machine . . . in possession of no initiative." But, he went on, "Is it not better to work eight or nine hours and resign [one self] to this disagreeable feeling, which will no doubt not last very long, and earn one third more?"

Then, too, labor and management were not the only parties to the deal. There was also, as Taylor called it, the whole public. The same breakneck pace and adherence to rule that presumably eviscerated jobs also, through greater efficiency, brought prices down for everyone. The beauty of the social deal that Ford and Taylor offered was that the new, rising tide of prosperity was borne up on *two* strong shoulders, high wages and low prices, both bought by those cramped hours of withered choice.

Still, murmurs of protest could be heard. One nameless but passionate correspondent wrote that it was

a far cry from the apprentice of former years who mastered every detail of his trade . . . to the workman in the factory under "scientific management," who spends his days in the monotonous, unthinking, mechanical performance of some, perhaps, unimportant part of a work . . . [in which he sees nothing] that thrills him with the pride of producer.

And, he went on:

There are some economies that are dear at any price. . . . What, indeed, will compensate the nation for the weakening of the mental and moral fiber of a large body of its citizens?

And with two lines from Oliver Goldsmith's "The Deserted Village," he concluded:

> Ill fares the land, to hastening ills a prey
> Where wealth accumulates and men decay.

Few people, it seems apparent by century's end, agonized much that way; most just took the money, Taylor's and Ford's, and ran. But a few individuals did spurn the great bargain. In 1927, Geoffrey Brown, a New Jersey consulting engineer, recalled how, sixteen years earlier, he'd worked at a preassembly line car factory. He had been machining brass bushings, a job he found "mildly interesting" and to which he had made a few improvements. Then, one morning, a few months into the job, appeared "a stranger armed with a board having a stop watch mounted in its upper corner."

Brown suffered no ordeal in being timed; it took about an hour. But soon after, they changed pulleys on him, so the lathe would turn faster. He was instructed to use a tool with a different shape. He was handed a typewritten instruction card with times indicated for each phase of the job. Any future improvements in the job would come from the planning office, he was told.

"From my standpoint," Brown wrote, "it was a little as if the substance of the job had suddenly vanished in thin air. I had become like one of the mannequins that we sometimes see crossing the vaudeville stage on invisible wires operated by someone in the wings." He worked like that for a few weeks, then quit and got "work in another shop where I received less money but regained much of [my] old freedom."

Most, however, simply toiled on, inexpressive and mute. The good things of this life, on the back of Taylor's $1.85 a day in 1899 (or Ford's $5.00 a day in 1915), were simply too good to pass up. Few wound up either in premature graves or like the hapless Charlie Chaplin in *Modern Times*—his body, tightening bolts all day, left spasmodically twitching. Still, weren't there other ways to suffer physical, mental, and nervous pain? And wasn't the very idea of time study to first establish, and then push you hard up against, your limits?

If at day's end a worker is "exhausted, does not eat his meal with relish, cannot read his newspaper in ease, [and] pushes the baby away from him with annoyance, he is not an efficient citizen," however efficient he may be on the job. So wrote Miner Chipman, delegated by three hundred Watertown Arsenal workers to look into conditions there in 1915; Taylor's notion of efficiency, he was saying, was hopelessly narrow, since he looked only at the workday itself. What about the rest of life? "It is not the purpose of efficiency engineering," another labor sympathizer, Frank T. Carlton, pointed out, to leave the worker "with more than a minimum of surplus energy for recreation, for family life, for civic duties, or for trade-union activities."

But as the century passed, and the workday dropped to eight hours, many did have something left at day's end. By the 1950s, bowling alleys, amusement parks, and shopping centers pulled in workers who had money and time enough to enjoy them; the great bargain looked, if anything, better than ever. While the artist or professional might be "entirely absorbed by his work," French sociologist Georges Friedmann wrote in 1961 in *The Anatomy of Work*, the average worker reserved "his best efforts, his energy, for what he will do out of working hours." Through what was, even by this time, a "fantastic mushrooming" of hobbies, arts, crafts, and sports, the worker sought "to regain in his leisure hours the initiative, responsibility and sense of achievement denied to him in his work." Pleasure was taken, control exercised, choices made—outside work.

Some, of course, still found what they needed at work. In a Taylorized plant like Tabor, for instance, the drawing room, with its engineers, draftsmen, and designers, was a place of privilege, "less affected by the new order of things than any other," wrote Wilfred Lewis:

> Here the work is . . . more or less original and, of course, no time can be set for the completion of that which is not definitely known, and which grows into shape by a process of trial and error. . . . Being an artist in his line [the designer] cannot be held to a time schedule. In original work, the incentive . . . must come from within rather than from without.

Some few, then, were exempt from scientific management's grip. Lewis's designers, and maybe artists, scholars, scientists, and top executives, needed their independence, whereas most others, presumably, did not. But do we err—did Fred Lewis err? did Taylor err?—in presuming that the freedom indispensable to the few is not a deeper, more universal need?

At an ASME meeting in 1906, Taylor was asked how his system

worked "for a new and difficult piece of work, say the pattern work job which requires ingenuity and thought." Here was work Taylor had done as a teenager, alongside John Griffith at the pump works. "The gentleman has hit upon the most difficult class of work to be done in any establishment," he replied. "I used to be a patternmaker myself, and I have never yet attempted to do pattern work under this system."

So patternmaking was exempt. Was anything else?

Might even Schmidt have ached for some little chance to go his own way on the job? Was the iniquitous soldiering that Taylor sought to stop neither aberrant nor corrupt but the expression of an innate human need to preserve a bastion of personal autonomy?

In April 1911, John Golden of the United Textile Workers was talking at the New York Civic Forum about scientific management. Weavers today produced more cloth and ran more looms, he told them, but,

> my friends, it is also true that the old time weaver of twenty-five years ago could sit down and read his newspaper. And many a hundred old weavers I saw asleep at their looms twenty-five years ago. Do they sleep any today?

Do they sleep? On the job?

It would have set poor Taylor's teeth grinding to hear it. And yet Golden told it with something like longing, achingly, for a time now sadly past.

Have you ever stopped off at an infrequently visited next-door neighbor's house, looked out from his porch at familiar streets and gardens, only to see the whole scene from a skewed perspective that made it look strange and new?

In *Rivethead*, a riotous memoir drawn from his columns in a Flint, Michigan, newspaper, autoworker Ben Hamper recorded his exploits in a General Motors paint shop. He learned to "blaze my way through [most of his assigned work] in the morning, be finished by lunch and spend the rest of the afternoon reading paperbacks and listening to the oldies station on my latex-splattered transistor radio."

In " 'doubling-up,' [another] time-honored tradition throughout the shop," one man sprinted through two jobs at once, while his partner loafed, read the paper, did crosswords; then they'd switch.

Sometimes, Hamper would spirit himself out of the plant altogether and wind up in his "sweetheart's bed, shakin' off the post-ejaculatory sweat, gigglin' like a schoolboy, a paroled hedonist smiling from a third-story window far removed from the numbness and drudgery of Greaseball Mecca . . .

"I liked the idea of outsmarting all those management pricks with their clean fingernails and filthy bonuses."

Getting workers to obey orders was hard, H. L. Gantt said in an ASME paper, because "a large percentage of men seem so constituted as to be apparently unable to do as they are told." Was Rivethead's soldiering on the grand scale perhaps more "normal" than any Taylorized work regimen could ever be?

In his seminal study of "Time, Work-Discipline and Industrial Capitalism," E. P. Thompson found that work before the industrial revolution was marked by

> alternate bouts of intense labor and of idleness, wherever men were in control of their own working lives. This pattern persists among some self-employed— artists, writers, small farmers, and perhaps also with students—today, and provokes the question whether it is not a "natural" human work-rhythm.

We don't want to work too hard? Yes, but maybe we don't want to work too steadily or too compliantly either. A bricklayer told author Kenneth Lasson why he loved being in business for himself: "You set your own hours, work your own pace. If you want to bust balls one day and slack off another, you can."

As the century wore on and more work fell under the dominion of white- or blue-collar forms of Taylorism, it was liberation from stopwatch and work rule that some came to cherish more than high pay. In his long, curmudgeonly essay "Class," Paul Fussell pictures the "mid- and low proles" of the class structure

> as people who feel bitter about their work, often because they are closely supervised and regulated and generally treated like wayward children. . . . The degree of supervision, indeed, is often a more eloquent class indicator than mere income, which suggests that the whole class system is more a recognition of the value of freedom than a proclamation of the value of sheer cash. The degree to which your

work is overseen by a superior suggests your real class more accurately than the amount you take home from it. Thus the reason why a high school teacher is "lower" than a tenured university professor: The teacher is obliged to file weekly "lesson plans." . . . The professor, on the other hand, reports to no one.

For most of his life, Taylor, too, reported to no one. He worked hard but, mostly, when it suited him. He was as far from today's image of the engineer as corporate drudge as you can get. Back in the 1890s, he'd been an industrial knight for hire, a fifty-dollar-a-day man who took clients or didn't, when and under the circumstances he wished. His was work of pleasure in its own doing. He was justly acclaimed for the metal-cutting experiments he pursued, indefatigably, for twenty-six years; but he did it because he wished to, not because he was ordered to.

Taylor had the best job in town. He got his hands dirty or kept them clean, cut steel or dictated letters or harangued subordinates, whenever he liked. He made lots of money. When he'd had enough of troublesome clients, he stopped taking them on. He kept working, but always on projects of his own choosing. For Taylor, said Louis Brandeis, work was "the greatest of life's joys." Given his circumstances, we need hardly wonder why.

> We shall work for an age at a sitting,
>   And never be tired at all:
> And no one shall work for money,
>   And no one shall work for fame;
>   But each for the joy of working.
> And only the Master shall praise,
>   And only the Master shall blame.

To H. L. Gantt, Taylor perfectly exemplified these lines from Kipling.

Though said to look in blind incomprehension at works of art, and little drawn to "the finer things," Taylor had by no means a withered, narrow life. He was not a man of gargantuan appetites, but he was no ascetic, either. That he didn't drink and that no accounts of sexual escapades come down to us doesn't mean he denied himself. Boxly was not the house of a man who denied himself. He enjoyed what money could buy, traveled widely, vacationed often, stayed at the best places.

And he literally took time to smell the roses; in later life, his rose garden at Boxly was his special pleasure.

He esteemed himself practical and down-to-earth. Yet critics called his most influential book, *Principles of Scientific Management,* "a vision of industrial reform" and "a utopian dream." Visions and dreams erupt not from dead routine but from a soul that soars. And Taylor's had always been free to do so, spurning in his life just that machinelike regularity demanded of those who worked under scientific management. As a boy visiting a palace in Berlin, he'd scooted around on the king's wheeled throne and played "Yankee Doodle" on the piano. And pleasure in life's small, spontaneous delights never left him. His life was full, unchecked, free.

Indeed, here was the cruel irony of his life's work: we can scarcely imagine Taylor himself, or anyone cast in his mold, or anyone of independent spirit, or anyone who simply exulted in his own orneriness as Taylor did, willingly working under his system.

The latitude of thought and action he so enjoyed and prized, he did not grant others. A contributor to the *Bulletin of the Taylor Society,* Irving Fisher, put it this way in 1925:

> He never seemed clearly to realize that other workmen needed the same sort of interests in workmanship to be happy at work. . . . The Taylor System, after all, harps chiefly on one string, the instinct of self preservation. [But] a complete life must satisfy many other instincts, such as the instincts of workmanship, self-respect, home making, reverence, loyalty and play. These are among the things men live by and not by bread alone.

But to such claims, Taylor remained deaf. A workplace of fixed tasks, strict orders, tight control, and generous wages suited workers best. He knew, he would have said, because he'd come up the same way they had.

But, of course, he had not.

He had paid his dues as apprentice, swept the floor of the shop each morning, toiled at Midvale; so he was privileged to demand the same of others. He really believed that. You can come away from Taylor's papers over a lifetime convinced he never once doubted the keenness of his insight into the worker's mind. After all, had he not been a workman?

Some of his critics, at least, were not deceived. "Like Taylor, Cooke had served a brief apprenticeship in the ranks of labor," writes Morris Cooke biographer Jean Christie, "but unlike Taylor he did not delude himself that he had thus become a workingman."

In his sly, vituperative 1912 essay, "The Organization of Overwork," Taylor's French nemesis, Émile Pouget, saw more deeply yet into him:

> It has been said of Taylor that he is a worker who is a "self-made man." But while in the United States, it may not be rare for a "prolo" to start with nothing and gain fortune and fame—Carnegie, Rockefeller, Edison are examples—the assertion is imprecise for our man. . . . He was made apprentice, later a workman . . . not by the need to earn a living . . . but simply to *complete his education* . . . , so that he could say later, "a factory chief formed at his trade."

So did Frank Gilbreth see Taylor's labor credentials for what they were. In 1924, after Copley's biography came out, Gilbreth got a copy and would read it on the train, often writing comments in the margins. At one point, Copley wrote a little too cloyingly of Taylor's affection and sympathy for the workers. Gilbreth, who had his own reasons to resent Taylor, lost all patience, scribbling in the right-hand margin, "But none came to his funeral, nor to his memorial service one year later."

In a Harvard lecture in about 1909, on "Workmen and Their Management," Taylor said:

> Those of us whose acquaintance with workmen consists chiefly in seeing them slouching along the street on their way back from work, with dirty clothes, chewing tobacco, in many cases hardly looking up as they pass one by, stolid and indifferent-looking, almost inevitably come to the conclusion (not usually in words, none the less definite) that these men are a different kind of animal from you and from me. On the other hand, the workman who sees in men of our class merely the outward signs of prosperity—good clothes, and the possession of carriages and automobiles, the careless holiday look, accompanied by short working hours—the workman who sees these outward signs is apt to conclude that men of our class are a different kind of animal from himself.

Under their skin, he assured his audience, they were much the same kind of animal. The differences stemmed from "the effect of the surroundings of each. . . . We must not forget that workmen have spent their lives obeying other people's orders."

But these insights, seemingly so liberal in their appreciation of the environment as a shaper of lives, Taylor meant only as a description of things as they were, not something begging to be changed. Never, here or elsewhere, did he suggest that a worker might yearn for what he, Taylor, had enjoyed all his life: freedom to live his dreams, indulge his excesses, be gloriously inefficient, do as he wished. Never did he imagine a world with class boundaries so much more permeable that all people could lead lives closer to their potential.

In 1917, Horace Drury, a Columbia University professor, posed what seemed to him a crucial question facing scientific management, how it might draw out the ability of the worker. Children are "full of life, and enterprise, and the spirit of investigation." But parents, school, custom, and lack of opportunity, crush it out of them, except, that is, for the "comparatively few" who enjoy "the benefits of real freedom, of leisure, travel, education, of responsibility, of authority."

Drury's vision? That "industry could find no greater opportunity, and life could have no greater end, than to extend and make universal" this richer kind of life.

Taylor, one of Drury's comparatively few, never expressed any affinity for such sentiments. Busy until his death promoting the system that bore his name, he never understood how well it buttressed the status quo. For scientific management took workers who, as Drury put it, were too often "timid, obedient, unenterprising, [and] unthinking"—and kept them that way.

Taylor fancied himself a radical; he was not. He reminded some of Theodore Roosevelt, their common traits including fortitude, self-confidence, and zeal. But in one way, at least, the comparison breaks down. In *Mornings on Horseback*, David McCullough tells how Samuel Gompers once took the young Roosevelt through the homes of poor cigar workers; Roosevelt came away deeply moved. But Taylor never showed evidence of having been penetrated by the lives of others. Management scholar Harlow Person saw in his House testimony "evidence that Taylor was not thinking of management for a new social order. . . . He was concerned only with better management under the present system."

Taylor's inclination to grasp only what lay before him, the ease with which he accepted the values of his day, ran all through his life, crimping his vision. If there was tragedy to his life, it was that his empathy did not run deeper, that he couldn't see just a little larger, that he hadn't the imagination to conceive a world in which many might share the freedom and autonomy he took for granted.

"It seems probable," machinist-turned-academician Harley Shaiken has written, "that the large ships that once plied the Mediterranean, propelled by legions of slaves in the galley, were designed by people who had no expectation of doing any rowing."

DEATH AND LIFE

~

AFTER HIS ORDEAL BEFORE THE SPECIAL COMMITTEE in Washington and his flight to Atlantic City, Fred and Lou boarded the Cunard ship *Caronia,* bound for Europe. It was February 20, 1912.

On the way over, they stopped briefly at Portuguese Madeira, Algiers, and Monte Carlo. Finally, they reached Naples, where, as Taylor wrote, Lou "began sight-seeing in earnest." The scheduled two-month trip stretched into four. "Mamma was gaining [in health] so much here," Taylor wrote daughter Elizabeth on May 10, around the time of her twenty-first birthday, that they'd decided not to rush back home.

Taylor wrote from the northern Italian town of Cadenabbia, on Lake Como, populated by "only the highest class English and a few Americans," many of them retired army officers and their families. It would be a good object lesson in taste," this faithful democrat wrote his daughter,

> to see how simply they all dress and what beautiful lives they lead. It is a good contrast to most of the other hotels we have been at, and also to much of our fashionable society at home. . . . We have only seen one single woman who powders and paints, and she has now left the hotel.

One day they rowed across the lake to Bellagio and climbed the hill to Villa Serbellini, its terrace overgrown with magnificent salmon-hued roses that made them think of Boxly:

> We are both very sorry and greatly disappointed, darling, not to be with you on your birthday, especially this one. We shall think of you and from the bottom of our hearts wish you many happy

returns. Mamma joins me in best wishes for the present and for years to come, with love and kisses, your

Papa.

The visit to the villa was the high point of their trip. From Como, it was up through the Haute-Savoie of France, to Aix-les-Bains, south of Geneva. Then, on to Paris and a visit with Le Chatelier, and finally Cherbourg, there to board a steamer back to America.

Taylor returned in early June to letters stacked "mountains high." He went up to Hobart College, where he was inducted into Phi Beta Kappa and received an honorary degree. The European trip, it turned out, had neither done Lou good nor proven restful to him. Tending her, he'd "hardly had a minute to myself" and was beset with "continuous worry and anxiety." But as he wrote Jim Dodge later that month, Lou at least "now realizes she is sick and is willing to take care of herself."

What, exactly, ailed her? It had struck, whatever it was, the previous fall. In a letter to a French relative in August, after their return from Europe, Fred described it as "something very much resembling nervous prostration," which left her "so run down and miserable" she couldn't so much as write. To Taylor's secretary, Frances Mitchell, it was plain enough; Lou had suffered a "nervous breakdown."

Pinning down what afflicted Lou would occupy Taylor and their doctors for the rest of his life. "Neither Dr. Daland nor Kemp [who later became a physician] really could say what went wrong with our mother," Robert said later. Europe and its amusements would cure her, Lou had thought at first. "She knew better than any doctor what she needed," Taylor wrote Dodge on their return, a little testily. But instead, she'd only deteriorated.

Taylor's letter to a friend after their return sounds almost like a lab report. "We have . . . acquired while abroad most useful knowledge as to her limitations," he wrote. More than ten minutes' exercise during the day? She'd sleep poorly that night. "It was hard for us to realize that physical exertion tended quite as much to making her sleepless as mental exertion." What she needed, Taylor concluded, was total rest. That meant "absolute freedom from excitement," seeing no one other than Fred himself, "and doing very little if anything except leading what might be almost called a vegetable life." Two doctors concurred.

It was a time when neurasthenia, a mysterious disease, or condition, or *something,* of the nerves, had become fashionable, striking especially the high-born and the well off. No one knew what it was; some chalked it up to simple nervousness. In *American Nervousness, 1903*, Tom Lutz writes that it was "a mark of distinction, of class, of status, of refinement," of a sensitive nature unsettled by the pace of modern life. Sure enough, Lou would write of "pressure . . . too great for my constitution," though with no hint as to the pressure's source. Certainly, Lou struck some as brittle and self-indulgent. "Vain and shallow," someone called her once. "Not the most stable person in the world," said another. Even small household upheavals could undo her. "Lou has had a complete change of servants since returning," Taylor had written an old friend years before, while still at Red Gate. This, he said, had been "very upsetting to her."

The established treatment was the rest cure. In a short story about a neurasthenic by feminist and economist Charlotte Perkins Gilman, the narrator was ordered to bed by her doctor, forbidden any activity, allowed no visitors. Such, precisely, was Lou's fate.

It was no easy regimen to maintain for this "ambitious woman," as Taylor called her, by which he apparently referred to her pleasure in activity, not any larger life goals. By early July 1912, they'd stationed themselves for the summer in Plymouth, where, "she and I together, with two servants who have been with us for many years," stayed in a small gray cottage two doors down from her mother's house. She was to see and talk to no one but him and the doctor, Taylor wrote:

> She lies in bed now until about half past eleven in the morning,
> goes to bed again at half past two and gets up at five, and receives
> very gentle massage again at quarter of nine. . . . For the small time
> she is up I talk to her very mildly, or read to her from some
> quieting story.

By early August, Lou was sometimes sleeping straight through the night, without sleeping pills. After a month of the regimen—during which she at first saw no one but Fred, then had brief visits from her mother, daughter Elizabeth, and the doctor—she "finds herself distinctly better than at the beginning." The mystery, though, remained. "It is such an intangible illness," lamented Taylor, "that one does not know which way to turn."

Back in Philadelphia on Dr. Daland's orders by October 21, the

Taylors stayed at the new Bellevue-Stratford, where Daland could see Lou regularly and better diagnose her case. "A serious intestinal derangement" was Daland's latest diagnosis, Taylor wrote his boyhood friend, Birge Harrison, on November 20. "For this she has been receiving a very severe, but effective, treatment. She is worked over by two doctors and a nurse every day, and sometimes three doctors"; just what they worked over, and how, is not clear. Sometimes the two of them went for a drive in the car. Sometimes Fred got out to Boxly for an hour or two. But for the most part, he was still "pretty closely confined on account of Lou," who, on doctor's orders, could see no one but him.

With the next year, Lou's health improved. They spent two months in South Carolina, some of it with the Harrisons in Charleston. The two of them played golf, indulged in little putting matches, took walks through a countryside alive with color and the music of birds.

By May, they were back at Boxly in its fullest garden glory, Lou seemingly as well as ever, her "intestinal poisoning" gone, sleeping well, seeing her friends, attending meetings of the garden club.

On July 12, 1913, they headed off for Europe again, this time with Elizabeth and, at least for part of the trip, Dr. Daland. Their automobile accompanied them; a French chauffeur drove them around. In September, they returned to America, aboard the *Imperator*, Lou seasick and unable to eat but otherwise fine.

But by now, Fred himself was afflicted with some malaise.

~

A little before their trip, in May, you could see some want of strength or spirit in Taylor's letter to Birge Harrison. "Every minute of my day here is filled up," he wrote, "and yet somehow I don't seem to accomplish much of anything. Studying the growth of grass plots," for putting greens, "is a great time-consumer and although I believe the work to be valuable, still it may—like many other things I have undertaken— prove after all to amount to but little." This was not the Fred Taylor we have known.

If compared to the time of the rate case or the House hearings things were quiet, interest in scientific management remained strong. Articles and books appeared by the hundreds; controversy swirled. Link-Belt had so many people trekking through that it finally had to limit visits to one day a week. Barth, Merrick, Hathaway, and a corps of new disciples kept busy introducing scientific management, giving lectures, talking up the new movement.

But Taylor himself, was not at top form. He was busy, he wrote Goodrich toward the end of 1913, but "I have been unable to keep up with my work, and am away back with my correspondence." His reserves of energy and will were not infinite. He was tired, his hip bothered him enough to interfere with golf, he came down with the first bad bronchial cold he could ever remember. When he belatedly learned that William B. Wilson lost his seat in Congress, he wrote him with a condolence note in which he added, "I have been practically out of touch with what has been going on in the country."

Many looking back at those years of a drawn and depleted Fred Taylor were apt to obliquely blame Lou. His personal secretary, Frances Mitchell, spoke of Taylor's care of her and his diminished vitality in two juxtaposed sentences, back to back, as if to imply cause and effect. Mary Clark likewise described Lou's health problems as a burden on her brother: "The sorrow weighed him down."

Son Robert was less circumspect. His mother, whose illness he could explain no better than anyone else, was endlessly demanding, jealous of any attention Fred gave him, Kemp, or Elizabeth. "There's no question that it killed the Old Man. He was under terrific pressure all the time. Here he was trying to carry on his work, [which had just] come to fruition. Yet she would demand things done." And he complied; the same energy he brought to everything he now poured into Lou's care. "She ran him ragged," Robert said. Her weakness, moral or spiritual as much as physical, he as much as said, brought him low.

"He was on duty twenty-four hours a day," Robert recalled of the summer of 1913. His parents lived in a little cottage perched in the middle of a golf course in Rockland, Maine, where they had meals sent over from the hotel, three quarters of a mile away. He didn't see his mother at all. His father, who seemed to him to have aged ten years, reserved a room for him at the hotel; they'd meet for breakfast before she got up. During the last three years of his father's life, Robert saw him rarely. The last time was in Philadelphia at Christmas, 1914: "It wrung your heart to see how he had failed in that last year."

But was there, perhaps, an element of complicity in Taylor's role, a degree to which he took on this new caretaker role willingly?

Was he hiding behind Lou's skirts?

When Taylor had just begun to settle into Lou's care, soon after his return to the States, he wrote Goodrich from Plymouth that he was "leading a very monotonous life, but to me this is infinitely preferable" to the trouble he'd had with Lou in Europe. "I expect to do a lot of reading, and perhaps some writing, this summer, which I have wanted to do for a good many years, and I am also hoping once a day to get in a round of golf." He was hardly fighting it.

Certainly his friends were not used to seeing him like this. Fred Lewis wrote that during the last few years of his life, "Taylor exhibited a spirit of devotion which few who had known him, chiefly in a professional way, suspected him of possessing. . . . All of his engagements," Lewis noted, "were made conditional upon his wife's health permitting him to keep them."

Was he, in a sense, clinging to Lou? Was he so wearied by a lifetime of struggle that, after the House hearings and with the prospect of more trouble to come, he now embraced a role, of devoted husband, apt to keep him out of battle? After all, with Lou so in need of his care, he couldn't don armor, mount charger, and ride off to war. Her illness gave him sanction to turn to the safer, quieter world of her convalescent bed, away from irksome conflicts outside.

For all the uncertainty about Lou's complaint, none exists about when it surfaced: the fall of 1911. This was right after the Watertown strike and about the time the House hearings were getting under way; just then she became ill, demanding his attention. Over the next two years, she wrote later, "Fred almost entirely gave up his life's work and gave me all care and devotion," at just that time when he was most under attack and the world outside their narrow domestic orbit was most troubled.

The chickens, it could be said, had come home to roost. Taylor had always made enemies; now they were legion. The tall tales of Schmidt with which he had regaled his audiences at Boxly now earned him rebukes for his heartlessness. He became testy, critical, even of his disciples. He saw Gantt as insufficiently pure, Gilbreth as financially disreputable; in August 1914, he wrote a friend that for Gilbreth and Harrington Emerson "their chief interest in the movement consists in the dollars and cents which they can get out of it." Meanwhile, the two rejected children, Gantt and Gilbreth, became chummy and lived nearby in New Jersey; the huge Gilbreth clan referred to Gantt as Father, a term of endearment. Taylor, reports Gantt's grandson, Laurence G. Taber, was "a name not mentioned too much around the house."

Taylor was important, successful, famous—and hated. "A devil incarnate" was how some steel executives and labor leaders viewed him, his friend Scudder Klyce, a navy lieutenant, reported. "Extremely egotistical and frequently vindictive. He craved personal credit and admiration to an extreme degree." That appraisal came from Fred Colvin, longtime editor of *American Machinist*. Indeed, the man Frank Copley met in July 1912, soon after Taylor's return from Europe after the House hearings and long before Copley became his authorized biographer,

> did not reveal himself to be the possessor of a nature that
> ordinarily would be called lovable. . . . Mr. Taylor undoubtedly
> had a large circle of warm and admiring friends, and as I continued
> on my travels I here and there encountered one. Nevertheless,
> most of the men with whom I talked about Fred Taylor and his
> work either spoke of him personally with significant reserve or
> denounced him with a bitterness which sometimes was really
> remarkable in its intensity.

Taylor's defenders pictured this ill will as the price he paid for firm adherence to principle. "We have the anomaly of Scientific Management fighting to keep two antagonists from fighting," Kempton observed later, "and experiencing the unpopularity that has always fallen to the lot of the mediator." Whatever the spin put on it, though, it was painful—how could it not be? Taylor knew of the hatred felt for him, Klyce recalled, "and I have certain knowledge that it hurt him."

He seemed increasingly volatile and defensive. One time, while showing some bank executives interested in scientific management through Link-Belt, they were virtually accosted by a Link-Belt employee, "Don't you know that no one is allowed in . . . without special permission?" he said.

"My name is Taylor and I am showing some of my friends through the works and I am very sure that Mr. Dodge would not object." This, however, carried no weight with the man.

Taylor wrote Dodge complaining about his treatment, adding, "I am quite used to holding my own with men of this sort and it makes exceedingly little difference to me what he says or thinks about me." But it did make a difference to him—to be treated so shabbily, to not be recognized as *the* Mr. Taylor, to be embarrassed in front of the men from the bank.

Taylor's equanimity, one suspected, could be shattered by the right blow or succession of them; this haughty leader of a great industrial movement was more fragile than he seemed.

~

During these years, 1912 to 1915, Frederick Taylor pulled back from the larger, peril-ridden world to the relative sanctuary of his wife's care, to projects around Boxly, and to the small circle of close friends who gave him undiminished respect, love, and loyalty.

He got caught up in his grass experiments, which culminated in a mammoth three-part exegesis, "The Making of a Putting Green," published in *Country Life in America* just before his death. He studied how roses grew, selected the best strains, developed formulas for the sprays and food they needed, wrote treatises on their care. "We have already succeeded in growing the finest autumn roses that have ever been grown around Philadelphia," he wrote Goodrich in November of 1913, "and are hoping next year to do still better."

Seeing his boyhood chum Birge Harrison led to a reflowering of their friendship, and Harrison talked of giving him one of his paintings. "There is no one in the world to whom I would rather give one of my pictures than to your good self," he wrote Taylor in October 1912. "Our long talks this summer have been a great joy to me, for there is no pleasure in this rather patchy and uneven life greater than that of finding an old comrade who has ripened well—who is as sound at heart at fifty and over as he was at twenty."

Taylor was touched:

> It does not often fall to one's lot to receive a letter such as you
> wrote me, and I can assure you that it has given me far more
> pleasure and real satisfaction than anything which has happened
> this fall. Our friends are of course the greatest possession which we
> have in this life, and when, at our time of life, we can combine a

mutuality of interest with all of the associations accompanying an early friendship, it is something rare and greatly to be prized.

A little later, they visited for a few days, Harrison's wife commenting, as he wrote Taylor, that "it was as if we were wrapped in cotton-wool by your constant hospitable kindness."

In two letters to Barth early next year, Taylor took a distinctly fatherly tone with his most loyal disciple, his advice sounding as if it had profited from sad experience: "Never tell them that what they are doing is rotten, or that they are wrong in any way, but simply say, 'This is our way and we do it this way because we think it is best.' "

And the ever voluble Barth should not blow his own horn about the work he was doing for a company. "If you keep quiet about the important things you are doing and let other people talk about them, it carries much more weight." Fred Taylor was dispensing savvy and tact!

"I dare say you are tired of the lectures from me," declared Papa Fred, "but I am sure you realize that at heart I only am considering your welfare and best interests."

Taylor was looking back now—he was fifty-seven in 1913—as much as looking ahead, defending and consolidating more than starting anything new. On his return from Europe after the House hearings, Taylor had written Chairman Wilson, for whom he felt a grudging fondness, with a copy of the recently published *Concrete Costs*, which he had written with Sanford Thompson. "Do not be alarmed on receiving it," he said with a smile, from his mother-in-law's place in Plymouth, "because you will be in no way called upon to read it." He had to point out, however, that all its data came from "detailed study with a stop watch" of men in the building trades, and that none of them had objected to it. He was still justifying his life's work.

By now, Taylor was intent on securing his place in history. When an ASME committee in late 1912 issued a report on the "present state of the art of industrial management" that looked back to the antecedents of scientific management and found them a hundred and fifty years before in Adam Smith and Charles Babbage, among others, Taylor was incensed. L. P. Alford, its author, got congratulations from Taylor on "the very fine report" he'd written. But to General William Crozier, Taylor could be more candid: "It is so colorless and insipid that it seems hardly worth discussing." In a formal response, he wrote, "Time studies began in the machine shop of the Midvale Steel Company and in 1881." Period.

~

Remember the carnival game with the animal figures that pop back up however fast you whack them down? It was October 1913, and Schmidt had popped back up.

Schmidt was already part of the national consciousness. But what of the real Schmidt, Henry Noll? Before the Special Committee hearings two years before, Taylor had briefly sought to track him down but got no cooperation from Bethlehem officials just digging out from an ugly strike. Now, though, General Crozier advised him, Taylor's foes in Congress had decided that he was probably dead from overwork. Efforts to block the use of stopwatches in government facilities had continued, and new hearings on scientific management were in prospect. Well, Taylor resolved, they'd find Noll this time, have a doctor examine him, and pronounce him fit before the world, no worse for hauling pig iron under the Taylor system.

(Of course he wouldn't actually testify. "Such men . . . as Henry Knolle," Taylor had earlier written, "are all of them too stupid to testify properly before any committee anywhere"—what did he mean by "properly"?—"so that it would be nonsense to get them on the witness stand.")

Conceivably, Noll was dead, Taylor wrote Crozier, "but I do not believe it, as he was a very tough little customer." Could Crozier have his man at Bethlehem look him up?

A little later, Crozier wrote back that they'd found him. After some years at Bethlehem Steel, he was now working for another company. His wife couldn't stand his drinking and had left him about ten years before. Otherwise, he was apparently fine.

Just before Christmas, Taylor wrote A. B. Wadleigh, who'd worked for him at Bethlehem, spied for him in Arizona, advised him of their time-study error with the shoveler, and now, if his stationery was to be believed, was a gentleman farmer, presiding over Mount Joy Manor Farm in Norristown, Pennsylvania. Taylor wrote him

> about our friend H. Knoll, who you will remember was the first pig iron handler whom we trained in at Bethlehem. The amount of work which he did in a day has been considered by lots of the

philanthropists and trades unionists, etc., to be nothing short of scandalous, and they think he must have been killed by it.

Could Wadleigh go to Bethlehem and "get next" to him—get into his good graces?

Noll was employed by Pettinos Brothers, a small graphite manufacturer, as a teamster. He was out with his horses when Wadleigh and John Stahr, Crozier's man at Bethlehem, called. Noll's employers didn't trust these outsider spies but, on Noll's return, sent him to the office, instructing him to answer questions but sign nothing. After supper, Wadleigh took Noll over to Noll's own physician to be examined. "The doctor told me he had known Knoll for several years," he wrote Taylor on January 3, "and that so far as he knew his only trouble was drink and women."

The next stop was in nearby Allentown for a picture of their man; the photograph shows him a little hollower in the cheek than fifteen years before, wearing a mustache now, flanked by Wadleigh and Stahr, all three of them in derbies. In his letter, Wadleigh briefly recounted Noll's history since the pig iron days of 1899 and enclosed the doctor's three-sentence pronouncement that the forty-four-year-old Noll was in "good physical condition."

Taylor was delighted, except for one small matter. In his report, Wadleigh said something about how "most men of [Noll's] class are old men at his age." This would never do. The socialists, congressmen, and trade unionists, he wrote back, would be on them in a minute, making it out to mean "that scientific management made men old at 44." So he had gone ahead and had Wadleigh's report typed up with that sentence expunged. If that was all right, Wadleigh should sign two of the three copies enclosed, return them, and accept the enclosed check, for fifty dollars—a thousand or more today—"with my warmest thanks." The embattled Taylor was taking no chances.

A few days later, the signed copies were in Taylor's hands, a trap ready to spring at the first intimation that poor Schmidt was disabled or dead.

∾

On a snowy day a few months later, in March 1914, Taylor was host to Abraham Jacob Portenar, a fifty-year-old Brooklyn typographer. Portenar had written a book on labor problems, published two years before, that had impressed Morris Cooke with its open-mindedness. Cooke brought it to the attention of Taylor, who likewise thought well of it. Could they win over this articulate, well-read labor advocate?

That day, their talk turned to how workers really felt about scientific management, and Portenar said what must have struck him as obvious: Taylor just couldn't know.

"How do you know I cannot?" he snapped. "I have been a workingman."

A few months later, Portenar took up their debate once more; he was at work, during a lapse in the flow of copy for him to enter, so he composed his letter on the Linotype machine. In the intervening months, he'd read *Shop Management* but now was more skeptical than ever. "You give the workmen no voice whatever in the fixing of wages. You tell the manager over and over again that he shall do such and such things to enable him to fix a fair wage. . . . *But you make one party to the agreement the sole judge of what is fair,*" he continued, switching over to italic type, and thus "*show that you have not comprehended human nature.*"

Taylor just didn't get it, he was saying. The presumably contented workers' faces visible on a Link-Belt tour meant nothing; "A walk through a plant under the aegis of the boss is not the best way to get at the truth."

Taylor was incensed. Did Portenar mean to impugn his motives? All he did, including the expenditure of "every cent of [my] surplus income," he wrote back, had been "done entirely with the idea of getting better wages for the workmen . . . to help them to live better lives and, above all, to be more happy and contented. This," he concluded, "is a worthy object for a man to devote his life to."

To this typesetter in Brooklyn, Frederick Winslow Taylor of Chestnut Hill was attempting to justify his life.

Portenar must have realized he had struck a nerve. For in his reply, this time on a typewriter, he was gentler. "I give full credence to your statement that you have not sought personal profit in your work. . . . Whatever I may think of your system, I do not hesitate to say that your motives are sincere and unselfish."

Still, to him the Taylor system was nothing but feudalism in modern dress:

The generous, but arrogant overlord and his loyal and well-treated but subservient vassals are the precise types of your managers and workmen . . .

But that was not cooperation—not as the twentieth century defines cooperation. The baron allotted to each man his task—so do you. The baron took a large part of the task upon himself as leader—so do you. The baron allotted to each his share of the usufruct in spoils or produce—so do you. The baron was the sole judge of whether a man was right or wrong—so are you . . .

An enterprise in which the workman has no voice in fixing anything can never be cooperative.

The same went for pay. "If you decided the pay was too little, I would be glad; if too much, I might growl. Either way—*I have no say.*"

About a month later, from the Samoset Hotel in Maine, Taylor answered in a two-sentence letter. With his stenographer away, he said, he'd had no chance to reply but would. There is no record that he ever did.

~

On March 14, Taylor wrote Goodrich that he had "been more closely confined than ever this winter, owing to Lou's illness. She had an exceedingly wretched time all through January, sicker I think than she has ever been." Now, though, she was improved, managing to work in the potting shed, transplanting flowers and the like for an hour or so every afternoon. On doctor's orders, the house was empty: Lou's mother was back in Boston, Elizabeth in Bermuda, the boys at school. "The house is really turned into a rest cure." That winter it had snowed interminably. He had scarcely seen the neighbors or even his sister.

But that spring, with Taylor all but withdrawn into complete retirement, events pulled him into the outside world once more. On March 20, Taylor wrote Barth that he had been asked by Chairman Walsh of the Commission on Industrial Relations to testify on April 13.

The nine-member commission had been created by Congress in 1912 to "discover the underlying causes of dissatisfaction in the industrial situation." Workers' safety, the condition of women and children, and the illegal immigration of "Asiatics" were among the areas it examined. Another was "efficiency systems and labor"; at hearings convened in the assembly room of Washington's Shoreham Hotel, Taylor was the first to testify.

There was little new to Taylor's testimony; to anyone who'd listened to him much since 1910 it must have seemed stale. Moreover, he'd hardly learned to sweeten his language in the intervening years. "We sent for two good shovelers, big, powerful fellows; well suited for their work. Mark my words," he said at one point, "we never take a human instrument that is badly suited for its work any more than we would take a bad machine. We take a proper human animal, just as we would take a proper horse to study." This was vintage Taylor, if scarcely apt to endear him to his enemies.

If Taylor thought labor's opposition had stilled in the two years since the House hearings, he was mistaken. Testimony from boot and shoe union officials, the AF of L, Nels Alifas from the machinists, and others revealed what the final report called labor's "almost unqualified opposition" to scientific management; so much so that it became the object of a separate investigation by Robert F. Hoxie, a distinguished forty-six-year-old University of Chicago economist.

Later, in the fall, Taylor met at the Touraine Hotel in Boston with Hoxie and navy engineer H. G. Coburn, a short-lived candidate to become scientific management's official representative on Hoxie's three-man panel. Someone raised the issue of whether labor and scientific management might ultimately cooperate. Taylor was horrified by the notion and said so in what Coburn recalled as "his most characteristically peppery manner." Later, Taylor delivered what Coburn remembered as "the most rigid, clean-cut description of his inflexible, unbending, uncompromising position as to scientific management."

In June, the Wisconsin State Federation of Labor, before which both Taylor and his nemesis, Alifas, had spoken, weighed in with another indictment of scientific management. Taylor was left "very indignant at the conclusions" and issued a bitter retort. Barth reassured him, "Let your consolation be that eventually your work must and will be universally recognized."

But Taylor had few other consolations during these months. In August, he wrote that Lou's "continued and serious illness has prevented me from doing anything whatever this summer. I have been almost worried to death."

By September, Lou's illness seemed "nothing but a series of relapses.

The moment she gets the least bit better she . . . undertakes some wild foolish thing, such as going to a big reception, when she ought to be in bed." By now he sounded a little disgusted.

In October, his brother's wife died, leaving Win "very much depressed. . . . He never will recover from Lily's loss and will feel it more and more as time goes on."

Family friend Edward Wright suffered a paralytic stroke around this time, too. "It is sad to see him stricken down in this way."

Taylor took the outbreak of war in Europe almost personally, as stupidity triumphant; like many Americans, he blamed Germany. "I do not see how it is possible for you men to have thoughts for anything except this horrible war," he wrote one Englishman about a month after it had begun. "To me the whole thing is absolutely unthinkable. I lie awake at night worrying over it and am sure no greater calamity could overtake the world than the success of the German arms." He wrote one friend that the Germans were "destined to be very much crippled and broken down through this horrible war and, in fact, they deserve to be."

Worry about Lou and the war's outcome, he wrote Goodrich, "has so overwhelmed me that I have hardly been able to do anything for several weeks and have myself been very much run down." Taylor hardly able to do anything? This was serious. Even money problems nagged at him. Some of his investments no longer spat out their usual dividends, and Taylor found himself, relatively speaking, "cramped for income."

Taylor was taking blow after blow. Gloom permeates his letters.

~

From the fall of 1914 through the end of the winter, Fred and Lou stayed at the Hotel Brighton, in Atlantic City. This shore community sixty miles southeast of Philadelphia was no blue blood's retreat; the "Newport of the Nouveaux Bourgeois," someone called it. Its stretch of coastline had been picked as a potential resort because it was a straight shot from Philadelphia; it was just an hour and a half on the train— through pine forests, cranberry bogs, and finally the salt marshes of Absecon Island—from the big city and its swarming millions. In tourist season, the boardwalk teemed with promenaders; the beach with men and women in flannel bathing costumes, dressed up to the neck and down to the ankles, but having a grand time.

To ease the off-season doldrums, the town had long billed itself as the place to go for one's health; in the fevered imagination of its boosters, at least, it was "the only place on the coast which is visited all the year round by health-seekers." The climate was supposed to be ideal; no one mentioned the mosquitos. The air was supposed to be restorative, in particular the "ozone"—though one cynic, unloved by the city fathers, attributed it to "the combined smell of rotting seaweed, derelict oyster-shells, and other marine flora." To Taylor's friend Birge Harrison the town was "most curative and restful to overstrained nerves—though socially a strange and impossible hurly burly."

It was here that Taylor had retreated once the Special Committee was finished with him two years before, and it was here that Taylor lived most of the last months of his life. Spread over spacious grounds where the Sands Casino stands today, the Hotel Brighton departed from the town's middle-class ways. A *Social Register* hotel, open to new guests only by introduction, it boasted saltwater baths and an adjoining casino, with sundeck, dance floor, and swimming pool.

Undaunted by the cold, Taylor played golf, only snow itself keeping him off the links. He wrote his articles on putting greens. He strolled along the boardwalk with visiting businessmen. Mostly, though, he was alone with Lou, like Napoleon in exile or Hitler in his bunker, the booming battles over scientific management distant and remote. In the Senate, New Jersey's William Hughes was saying that "a gentleman named Taylor arrived at the conclusion that the laboring people of the United States are not working hard enough" and sought "dividends for manufacturers at the expense of the bones and tissue and the lives" of the workers. To Taylor, it must have been maddening that so many could say so much that was so stupid.

And now, was even Jim Dodge saying stupid things? Dodge was one of his earliest champions; his company, Link-Belt, was the Taylor system's premier showcase. And yet, toward the close of 1914—as Robert Hoxie, whom the two of them met in December, investigated scientific management—he was straying, too.

Hoxie had been trying to establish a list of scientific management's formal claims that in the end took up ten pages. On January 18, Dodge wrote Taylor suggesting they omit several references to "soldiering" that were apt to incite their enemies. "You know I have never been in sympathy with making a feature of this."

That was bad enough, but Dodge went further. "It would be perfectly possible," it seemed to him, "to harmonize scientific management with trade unionism if an earnest effort were made by both parties."

Heresy—and there was more of it:

I believe that we are making a mistake in saying that scientific
management is based on exact science when, as a matter of fact,
the base rates and the percentages we add to our time studies are
matters of human judgment and cannot, in my judgment, be
arrived at sufficiently well to be called "scientific" determinations.

But that's what the union leaders and Chairman Wilson had said all along. And now Jim Dodge was saying it, too?

Setting wage rates, Taylor had told the Industrial Relations Commission, was strictly a scientific problem, one tackled with all the precision of, say, astronomy: "It is a scientific investigation, just as a man who figures there will be an eclipse of the moon and says it is so-and-so and writes it down."

Now, in a letter to Dodge on January 27, 1915, Taylor allowed that while "one or two elements" of scientific management were not based on "full and exact knowledge," the same was true of any science. Those few holdouts would ultimately succumb to science's power.

A little later, Dodge wrote Taylor that the Link-Belt board had decided to permit shop committees, "elected by the workmen for the purpose of permitting and encouraging our men to take an interest in the determination of base rates and piece rates." The idea behind this nod to industrial democracy? It might "disarm organized labor in their claim that we are all arbitrary and heartless."

No! Under scientific management, orders went one way and one way only: from the top down, never back up the other way. "I think you are making a great mistake in doing this," Taylor wrote back. "I do not believe there is the slightest dissatisfaction among your men." These shop committees would only encourage trade unionism.

Taylor's letter was dated February 25. The following Tuesday through Friday, he noted, he would be in Ohio. After a long winter in which he had refrained from public speaking outside Philadelphia, he had arranged a trip west to give some talks.

That Tuesday, probably just before heading off for the station a few blocks from the hotel, he wrote Birge Harrison. It was too bad, Birge had written, that Fred's brother Win, who had just lost his wife, lacked "some compelling and absorbing occupation, for work is the one great comforter—the greatest of all doctors—a blessing above all others to the sick at heart and a sedative such as there is none other in the world."

On this Taylor gratefully seized. "I heartily agree with your views regarding the curative effect of hard work. I look upon it as the greatest blessing which we have and almost every day of my life thank my stars that, in spite of Lou's illness, I have enough work to occupy all of my spare time."

On March 3, Taylor was in Cleveland, touring the Clothcraft Shops, a men's clothing manufacturer employing about two thousand men and women. Clothcraft was friendly territory, a model of scientific management at its enlightened best. Taylor deemed Richard Feiss, at its helm, "a very high class man and feel that he is already a great credit to our system and likely to become even more so. All we can do for him," he wrote Dwight Merrick before he left, "will come back to us many fold."

Clothcraft pulled out the stops for its esteemed guest. The visitor's book, covered in leather and graced by a geometric design that incorporated the company's little heraldic shield, bore the signatures of a succession of industrial leaders. Most, like Lillian Gilbreth, signed in one after another, half a dozen or so to a page, with their hometown and a brief comment. Taylor, though, got a page to himself. His bare, thin-nibbed signature sat in the middle, alone, the white of the page framing it. One imagines the book held open for him: Won't you please sign right here, Mr. Taylor?

That evening, he delivered a talk to the Cleveland Advertising Club on scientific management. It went on for about two hours, was interrupted frequently by laughter and applause. He was altogether charming.

At some point, he had contracted a cold. He brushed it off at first, successfully getting through his talk in Cleveland and then another in nearby Youngstown. But the following morning, he felt terrible—the grippe, he called it. "I was so hoarse with a bronchial cough that I was almost unable to speak," he wrote Feiss a few days later.

Heading home from Youngstown, Taylor likely boarded a train

leaving Cleveland's dreary depot about 5:30 P.M., bound for Pittsburgh. Arriving there about four hours later, his car would have sat in the station, then been hitched to a train from Chicago bound for arrival in Philadelphia the next morning. For one reason or another, Taylor hadn't gotten a sleeper and was stuck in the regular "open section car." All night he sat up, blanket wrapped around him, coughing.

By March 9, he was back at the Hotel Brighton in Atlantic City, neither fever nor cough any better.

Probably the next day, he went back to Philadelphia to spend a few days with Mary and Clarence at Cedron.

But the day after, on the eleventh, he was admitted to the city's Medico-Chirurgical Hospital with pneumonia.

On March 15, he got a letter from Professor Hoxie inviting him to meet with him next time he was out west. He probably never saw it. "Mr. Taylor is very sick in the hospital," Taylor's secretary wrote Hoxie, "so that he will not be going west or, in fact, will not be able to attend to any business whatever for some time."

Around this time, Lou's mother wrote relatives in New England that Fred had a bad cold.

When she wrote again a few days later, around the seventeenth or eighteenth, his condition had worsened. The news was taken as of "a somewhat alarming nature."

On Saturday, his fifty-ninth birthday, he grew weaker. Early the following morning, he was heard to wind his watch.

Some time later, he fell into a coma.

That same day, March 21, telegrams went out with the news. Robert Taylor heard it at Cornell:

YOUR FATHER PASSED AWAY THIS MORNING.

∼

The funeral took place at Cedron on March 24; James Dodge and Morris Cooke spoke. "He was the bearer of the only flag of truce that was ever carried upon the battlefield of industrial strife," said Dodge. Robert, Kempton, and Taylor's four nephews were the pallbearers.

He was buried a few feet from the graves of his parents at West Laurel Hill Cemetery, across the Schuykill River from where he'd started out as an apprentice forty years before.

The papers carried his obituary. Magazines carried remembrances.

In October, a memorial meeting was held at the University of Pennsylvania. The mayor of Philadelphia came. A military attaché from the French embassy brought a letter from Le Chatelier. Sanford Thompson spoke. So did Barth and Brandeis. They made a book out of what people said there, bound it up and published it, said what a great man he was.

Except for those mutual claims of love and humanity that he exerted on his wife, children, family, and friends, none of this mattered. Nature, it is said, loses interest once an individual has passed along its seed; then it can die and, in the evolutionary scheme of things, it doesn't matter. So it was with Taylor. By the time of his death he had already sired, and nurtured, Taylorism.

Taylor spoke tactlessly. He was a troublemaker. But mostly, this was just theatrical veneer. Deep down, he was a conventional man, at home in his time, safe behind walls of class and circumstance that were firm, solid, impenetrable.

The coming of Taylorism made our age what it was going to become anyway—only more so, more quickly, more irrevocably. Taylor died relatively young. But he lived long enough to take currents of thought drifting through his own time—standards, order, production, regularity, efficiency—and codify them into a system that defines our age.

In its thrall, and under its blessing, we live today.

ACKNOWLEDGMENTS

My greatest debt is owed my wife and son. I cannot possibly express my gratitude for their forbearance and understanding, nor my regret for injuries done them in the book's name, nor my love.

I wish to thank the following scholars for allowing me to see their papers and works-in-progress, sharing with me leads and ideas, making introductions, submitting to interviews, and otherwise aiding me: Mike Allen, Walter Licht, Thomas Hughes, Pete Petersen, John Higham, Rob Roy, Hugo Kijne, J. C. Spender, Geoffrey Clark, Susan Lindee, Bill Leslie, Christopher McKenna, Thomas Misa, Arwen Mohun, Daniel Nelson, Archie Green, Edwin Layton, Lindy Biggs, John Breeze, Rick Stager, Robert Rodden, John K. Brown, Katherine Kish Sklar, Stephen P. Waring, Herb Harwood, Jim Dilts, Joan K. Burton, Richard Adelstein, Larry Ingle, Edward T. Morman, Gottfried Riemann, Friedrich Meyer-Hirsch, Walter Koenig, Irene Helmreich-Schoeller, Helmuth Trischler, Robert Friedel, Ulrich Wengenroth, and Alexandre Herlea.

It is impossible to survey the mass of research material available on Frederick Taylor without noting the contribution of Charles D. Wrege. For four decades, Mr. Wrege has, along with his students and associates (in particular his late colleague Ronald G. Greenwood), tracked down valuable materials on Taylor and other early management pioneers, reporting on their findings in numerous papers and one book. One need not agree with Mr. Wrege's conclusions in every respect to admire his remarkable tenacity.

Peter Liebhold and Steve Lubar made the resources of the Smithsonian available to me and greatly helped me early in my research.

Lance Metz, Hugh Moore Historical Park and Museum and John Fielding, Bethlehem Steel, arranged a richly informative tour of Machine Shop No. 2; Martha Capwell introduced me to the town of Bethlehem.

I learned a great deal about machine shop, forge, and foundry practice at an industrial living history workshop at the Knight Foundry, Sutter Creek, California, organized by Ed Arata.

Dennis Zembala of the Baltimore Museum of Industry granted me access to the museum's machine shop, where Mark, Frank, Chet, Leon, and Everett were endlessly patient with my questions and taught me much.

I also want to thank the staffs of the following for helping me learn something of the crafts of machinist, patternmaker, and molder: Hagley Museum machine shop; Appomattox Iron Works, Petersburg, Virginia; General Pattern and Tooling, Baltimore; Deutsches Museum, Munich; American Precision Museum, Windsor, Vermont.

Jane Morley went to much trouble on my behalf to gather material from the Gilbreth Archive.

Jane Mork Gibson introduced me to Philadelphia and Chestnut Hill and has been a rich trove of knowledge about nineteenth century industrial Philadelphia.

John Rumm let me see his fine unpublished study of machine shop apprenticeships.

Geoffrey Clark shared with me an unpublished draft of his study of Taylor's roots in the nineteenth century machine shop.

Geoffrey Tweedale sent me material from his steel industry research, read portions of the manuscript, and has been a good pen-pal and friend.

Yisrael Mayer furnished memories of Lillian Gilbreth and has supplied much useful information about the early scientific management movement.

Myron Johnson has researched Taylor's family and New England roots, let me examine the fruits of his work at his house in Connecticut and, with his wife, showed me every kindness during my stay there.

Members of the Taylor family have generously shared with me their memories, family stories, and photographs. These include Charlotte and the late Bayard Clark, Tony Wallace, Frank Wallace, Jr.; J. Thierry du Pasquier; Claiborne T. Smith; Marie Clark Hodges, to whom I owe much thanks for her kindness and hospitality in Manchester; and Lisa Carr, who let me see her early Taylor family letters, has worked toward making her collection an important rersource for research on the early abolitionists, and has been unfailingly helpful and kind.

Thanks are also due the following, who have helped in ways large and small: Frederick Blodi, Roger Harrison, Andrew Janca, Ann & Tom Schoonmaker, Amy Bernstein, Jay Tolson, Bryant Simon, Russ Miller, Richard A. Mulford, Daniel F. Danzl, Emilie Priebsch of Finstermunz, Austria, the late William Sellers of Chestertown, Md., William T. Delamar, Pat McNees, William Craig, Fred Carrigan, Laird Harrison, and Warren and Helen Buhler.

Hearty thanks to everyone at the Taylor Collection, S. C. Williams Library, Stevens Institute of Technology, including Nydia Cruz, Ourida Oubraham, Ellen Zamir and, above all, the late Jane Hartye, who extended me every courtesy in my many visits to Stevens and whose knowledge of the collection's holdings far exceeded that of any electronic data base, known or imaginable. I am sorry she didn't live long enough to see this book.

Thanks to Elise Hancock, Dennis O'Shea, Ross Jones, and Ed Rosenfeld, who made available to me the extraordinary resources of the Milton S. Eisenhower Library, Johns Hopkins University; and also, to the staffs of the library's government publications, interlibrary loan, and special collections departments.

Thanks also to the directors and staffs of the following libraries, archives, and other research institutions: Germantown Historical Museum Library; Roy Goodman and Elizabeth Carroll-Horrocks, American Philosophical Library, Philadelphia; Joanne Barry, archivist, Philadelphia Academy of Music; Gail Pietrzyk, University of Pennsylvania archives; Albert F. Bartovics, Special Collections, Baker Library, Harvard School of Business; Gladys Breuer, archivist, Franklin Institute Science Museum; Stephanie Morris, Franklin Institute; Edouard Desrochers, Phillips Exeter Academy; Franklin D. Roosevelt Library (Morris L. Cooke Papers); Richard Strassberg, Catherwood Library, Cornell University; Lori Finkelstein, Bopst Library, New York University and Dorothy Wick, of the Bopst's Tamiment Institute of Labor History; Marilyn Massaro, Museum of Natural History, Providence, R. I.; Friends Historical Library, Swarthmore College; Lloyd Kiff, Western Foundation of Vertebrate Zoology; Irene W. Church, Madison (Maine) Public Library; Edwin N. Probert II, Germantown Academy; Tom Smith, Sellers Memorial Library, Upper Darby, Pa.; Marvin Rosen, Elwyn Institute, Elwyn Pa.; University of Maryland, Baltimore County; Hagley Museum and Library; Free Library of Philadelphia; Enoch Pratt Free Library, Baltimore; Atwater Kent Museum, Philadelphia; Historical Society of Pennsylvania; Atlantic City Free Public Library; Urban Archives at Temple University; Pennsylvania State Archives, Harrisburg, Pa.; National Museum of American History and Dibner Library; Historical Society of Washington, D. C.; Martin Luther King Library, Washington, D. C.; Welch Medical Library, Baltimore; Engineeering Societies Library, New York; Steamship Historical Society Collection, University of Baltimore. Also, libraries and historical societies in: Fitchburg, Mass., Watertown, Mass., Manchester, Vermont, Saratoga Springs, N.Y., Greenville, Maine; Bethlehem, Pa. And, of course, the Library of Congress.

In Europe: Spreewald Museum, Lubbenau, Germany; Alte Pinakothek and Deutsches Museum, Munich; Management Institute and Stadtarchiv, Zurich; Swiss Transportation

Museum, Lucerne; Bibliotheque Historique de la Ville de Paris, Musee National des Techniques, Conservatoire des Arts et Metiers, La Cite des Sciences et de l'Industrie, Paris; Sheffield City Council Library, Lisa A. Atkinson, archivist.

Finally, a word of thanks to Neil Kleinman, Carol Pierce and Stephen Matanle for furnishing so congenial an academic home at the Yale Gordon College of Liberal Arts, University of Baltimore; to Ginny, Jane, Jennifer, Kendra, Stephanie, and my other colleagues there; and to Marge Holmes, Diane Wood Cameron, the time-study man's daughter, and others among my students in the Publications Design program.

Thanks to my mother, father, and sister, and to the Pearl boys, for their encouragement and interest; to Vicky Bijur, most excellent agent, for bearing up with me through another book. And to everyone at Viking, including Gail Belenson for allowing a writer into the sacred precincts of design; and Barbara Grossman, for her indefatigable energy and commitment. Barbara astutely assigned me to editor Beena Kamlani, who in a thousand ways made this book a better one and who, in her devotion to it, exemplifies the old craft values at their best.

I also wish to acknowledge Hugh G. J. Aitken, whom I met in Amherst not long before his death, and whose *Taylorism at Watertown Arsenal* is a model of the historian's craft; and my old teacher, the late Isadore Traschen, long-time professor of English at Rensselaer Polytechnic Institute, who taught me as an undergraduate long ago and then, decades later, alerted me to Yevgeny Zamiatin's Taylor-inspired novel.

A grant by the Alfred P. Sloan Foundation permitted me to research this book with a thoroughness impossible without its help. My thanks to Arthur Singer and the others at Sloan who have helped to make this experience such a rewarding one, and whose generosity freed me from the cramped "efficiency" this book might otherwise have required.

NOTES

Letters and reminiscences not otherwise identified may be found in the Frederick Winslow Taylor Collection, Samuel C. Williams Library, Stevens Institute of Technology, Hoboken, N.J.

The following running titles appear in the Notes:

Bulletin: Bulletin of the Taylor Society.

Carr: Elise W. Carr private collection, about 250 letters passed down through the Taylor family. Letters with doubtful dates are supplemented by numbers, referring to the collection's own numbering system.

Catherwood: Kheel Center for Labor-Management Documentation & Archives, Martin P. Catherwood Library, New York State School of Industrial and Labor Relations, Cornell University.

Collection: Taylor Collection.

Chordal: James W. See, *Extracts from Chordal's Letters.*

Copley: Frank Barkley Copley, *Frederick W. Taylor: Father of Scientific Management.* Two vols.

Dartmouth: *Addresses and Discussions at the Conference on Scientific Management Held October 12, 13, 14, 1911,* Dartmouth College, Amos Tuck School of Business Administration, Easton, Pa.: Hive Publishing Co., 1985.

Hearings: Testimony before Special House Committee to Investigate the Taylor and Other Systems of Shop Management. When Taylor is on the stand—in the form "FWT-Hearings, xx"—the page numbering refers to: *Scientific Management,* comprising *Shop Management, The Principles of Scientific Management,* and *Testimony Before the Special House Committee,* New York: Harper & Brothers, 1947.

For the testimony of all others—in the form "Hearings, xx"—the page numbers refer to: *U. S. House of Representatives—Special Committee to Investigate the Taylor and Other Systems of Shop Management,* 3 vols. Taylor's testimony appears on pp. 1377–1507.

Industrial Relations: Commission on Industrial Relations, *Industrial Relations,* vol. 1, *Final Report and Testimony.*

Journal: The journal young Taylor kept in Europe, 1869–1870. Two vol. Taylor Collection.

Kempton Taylor: Kempton P. A. Taylor letter, recalling his father. Taylor Collection.

Littauer: Taylor's testimony at congressional hearings on the Littauer Bill, concerning adoption of the metric system, 1906. Taylor Collection.

Louise Fragment: Louise Taylor's fragmentary autobiography. Taylor Collection. Because its pagination is unclear and appears in handwritten and several typewritten forms of unknown priority, the citation goes no further.

Machinist: American Machinist.

Merkle: Judith A. Merkle, *Management and Ideology.*

Midvale Collection: Midvale Steel Company Collection, 363-A-1 to 371-A-1, in *The Franklin Institute and the Making of Industrial America: Guide to the Microfiche Collection,* ed. Stephanie A. Morris, Bethesda, Maryland: Academic Editions.

Nelson: Daniel Nelson, *Frederick W. Taylor and the Rise of Scientific Management.*

Robert Taylor, 1976: John A. Bromer, J. Myron Johnson, and Richard P. Widdicombe, "A Conversation with Robert P. A. Taylor." Paged within chapters.

Robert Taylor, 1979: J. Myron Johnson and Richard P. Widdicombe, "*An Avocation that Became a Vocation.*"

Robert Taylor, 1983: "Dr. [Myron] Johnson's Visit to Robert P. A. Taylor," June 24, 1983.

Steel Patent: Bethlehem Steel vs. Niles, Bement, Pond Company, United States District Court, District of New Jersey, Case 4641, 1906–1909. National Archives-Northeastern Region, New York City.

Taylor Memorabilia: Material found within books titled "A Brief Description of the Eight Large Gray Canvas Covered Books of Taylor Memorabilia Compiled in Their Present Form by Carl G. Barth, 1933." Taylor Collection. The page numbering refers to the pages of these canvas books, not the page numbers of the documents pasted into them.

Taylor Memorial: *Frederick Winslow Taylor: A Memorial Volume.*

Thesis: Thesis of Fred W. Taylor, 1883. Unless otherwise indicated, all references are to Part II. Taylor Collection.

Transactions Asme: Transactions of the American Society of Mechanical Engineers.

Vestpocket: Four vestpocket notebooks, described in the text, now in the Taylor Collection. These are a mass of unpaged scribbles, not always in chronological order, and are difficult to cite in a useful way. However, when Taylor's whereabouts are not otherwise cited during the period from 1890 to 1898, they derive from here.

Wrege & Greenwood biography: Charles D. Wrege and Ronald G. Greenwood, *Frederick W. Taylor, the Father of Scientific Management: Myth and Reality.*

PROLOGUE

1 COMMITTEE ROOM. Glenn Brown, *History of the United States Capitol,* vol. 1, Washington: Government Printing Office, 1900; *Congressional Directory,* 62nd Congress, 2nd sess.; material on Room II-163 (room 70 in 1912) furnished by Art and Reference division, architect of the Capitol.

CONGRESSMAN WILSON. Clarke L. Wilhelm, "William B. Wilson: The First Secretary of Labor, Ph. D. dissertation, Johns Hopkins University, 1967, Ann Arbor, Mich.: University Microfilms, no. 68–6582; Roger W. Babson, *W. B. Wilson and the Department of Labor,* New York: Brentano's, 1919; W. Anthony Gengarelly, "Secretary of Labor William B. Wilson and the Red Scare, 1919–1920," *Pennsylvania History,* 47 (4), 1980, 311–330. Wilson papers (which I have not seen) are at the Historical Society of Pennsylvania.

SHOULD BE DONE. FWT-Hearings, 123.

3 EFFECT ON THE MAN. Ibid., 223.

SMOOTH OLD FELLOW. FWT to J. T. Wallis, February 5, 1912.

CANNOT ANSWER THAT QUESTION, FWT-Hearings, 169.

4 BIG DRAY HORSE. Ibid., 173.

I GIVE IT UP. Ibid., 175.

NOR SINGING BIRDS. Ibid., 176.

5 THIS SORT OF SYSTEM. Investigation of Taylor System of Shop Management, House Committee on Labor, April 28, 1911, 18.

OUT FOR BLOOD. Copley, "Taylor and Trade Unions," Bulletin. August 1925,

6 FLUSHED FACE. Copley, II, 348.

TOMBSTONE. West Laurel Hill Cemetery, Philadelphia.

COMMONPLACES. Don D. Lescohier, *Working Conditions,* 315 (vol. III of *History of Labor in the United States, 1896–1932,* New York: Macmillan, 1935). See also

Braverman, 87: "If Taylorism does not exist as a separate school today, that is because, apart from the bad odor of the name, it is no longer the property of a faction, since its fundamental teachings have become the bedrock of all work design."

7 MORAL INHERITANCE. Hunt, xiv.

BOOKS WITH TITLES. Ralph Keyes, *Timelock: How Life Got Hectic and What You Can Do About It*, New York: HarperCollins, 1991; Diana Hunt and Pam Hait, *The Tao of Time*, New York: Henry Holt & Co., 1990.

8 EVEN ON VACATION. Munley, 60.

ANY OTHER SINGLE INDIVIDUAL. Rifkin, 106.

NO OTHER DEVELOPMENT. Rabinbach, 238.

LOGICAL EXTENSION. Peter Drucker, "Technology and Society in the Twentieth Century," in Kranzberg and Pursell, Jr., 26.

LIKE CRAZY. Interview with Yisrael Mayer.

TOUCHED OR HANDLED. Robert Taylor to Richard P. Widdicombe, October 9, 1981, Myron Johnson papers; see also Robert Taylor, 1976, VI-4.

OUT OF FASHION. "Return of the Stopwatch," *The Economist*, January 23, 1993: " 'Taylorism' is now vilified as the epitome of a hierarchical, authoritarian style of management which caused decades of labour strife. No right-thinking manager today would describe himself as a disciple of Taylor."

CONFERENCE IN LITTLE ROCK. "Remarks by John Sculley, President-Elect Bill Clinton's Economic Conference, December 15, 1992," typescript furnished by Apple Computer.

JARRING. Paul Adler, "Time-and-Motion Regained," *Harvard Business Review*, January–February 1993, 103.

9 TAYLORIZATION OF MANAGEMENT. Charles Heckscher, *White-Collar Blues*, New York: Basic Books, 1995, 16.

IMPORTANCE OF THIS SPLIT. Robert B. Reich, *The Next American Frontier*, New York: Times Books, 68.

GENIUSES AND MORONS. Gomberg and Dubinsky, 97.

10 ANTI-TAYLORISM. Maurice de Montmollin, "Taylorism and Anti-Taylorism," trans. Verdalee Tombelaine, *International Studies of Management & Organization*, Fall 1975, 13.

TAYLORIST COIN. Waring, 187.

WON HANDILY. Daniel A. Wren and Robert D. Hay, "Management Historians and Business Historians: Differing Perceptions of Pioneer Contributors," *Academy of Management Journal*, September 1977, 470.

SAW THAT IT WORKED. Haber, xi.

11 THE AMERICAN PLAN. John Dos Passos, *The Big Money*, volume 3 of *U.S.A.*, Boston: Houghton, Mifflin, 1946, 21–26.

FEDERALIST PAPERS. Peter Drucker, *The Practice of Management*, New York: Harper, 1954, 280.

BATTLE-SCARRED CHÂTEAU. Arthur G. Bedeian, "Kismet!: A Tale of Management," *Proceedings*, 32nd Annual Meeting, Academy of Management, 1972.

RHYTHM OF HIS THOUGHT. "Economists Honor 'Genius' of Taylor," *New York Times*, December 8, 1933.

THE AMERICAN LESSON. Taylor Memorial, 53.

CHARACTERISTIC FEATURE. Cited in Maier, 27.

TAYLORISM + FORDISMUS. Hughes, 285.

FORD'S ASSEMBLY LINE. See Part VI.

12 CERTAIN INDUSTRIAL SETTINGS. Montgomery, *The Fall of the House of Labor*, 233.

APPLIED WITH EQUAL FORCE. Taylor, *Principles*, 8.

VISIONARY CLARITY. Hubert Zapf, "Taylorism in D. H. Lawrence's *Women in Love*," *D. H. Lawrence Review* 15 (1–2; Spring–Summer 1982), 130.

62 SECONDS. "Time Study of the Mixing and Baking of Biscuits," Mary Pattison, in Charles D. Wrege, "Achieving Social Change Through Scientific Management: Mary Pattison and 'Domestic Engineering': 1909–1916," for Management History Division, Academy of Management, 1981, Collection.

CHRISTINE FREDERICK. See her *Household Engineering: Scientific Management in the Home*, Chicago: American School of Home Economics. 1920.

13 SITUATION OF READINESS. Callahan, 18.

APPLIED TO TEACHING MUSIC. Ibid., 61.

ALL OF AMERICAN EDUCATION. Ibid., 41. See also Kenneth Gray, "Why We Will Lose: Taylorism in America's High Schools," *Phi Delta Kappan*, January 1993.

DARWIN, MARX, FREUD. See Giedion, 100.

MOMENTARY DOUBT. Quoted in Callahan, 68.

REDUCE TO AN EQUATION. Martha Bensley Bruere, "What Is the Home For?" *The Outlook*, December 16, 1911, 910.

LIBRARIES. Marion Casey, "Efficiency, Taylorism, and Libraries in Progressive America," *Journal of Library History* 16 (2; Spring 1981), 265–279.

PROTESTANT CHURCHES. Peter B. Petersen, "Scientific Management in American Protestant Churches," *Proceedings of Eastern Academy of Management*, May 14, 1988, 214–216.

14 LITERARY FIGURES. See Tichi; Banta. See also Lisa M. Steinman, *Made in America: Science, Technology, and American Modernist Poets*, New Haven, Conn.: Yale University Press, 1978; James F. Knapp, *Literary Modernism and the Transformation of Work*, Evanston, Ill.: Northwestern University Press, 1988.

LITTLE DOUBT. Hubert Zapf, "Taylorism in D. H. Lawrence's *Women in Love*," 136.

MECHANICAL INSTRUMENTS. D. H. Lawrence, *Women in Love*, New York: Penguin, 1976, 223.

LITERARY ANCESTOR. Carolyn H. Rhodes, "Frederick Winslow Taylor's System of Scientific Management in Zamiatin's *We*," *Journal of General Education* 28 (1; Spring 1976), 31–42.

15 TEN CENTURIES AHEAD. Eugene Zamiatin, *We*, trans. Gregory Zilboorg, New York: Dutton, 1924, 32.

BOOK OF THE YEAR. Robert Rogers, "This Is Life," *Boston American*, December 12, 1933.

HELD HIM IN RESERVE. Rudolf Brunngraber, *Karl und die Twentieth Century*, trans. Eden and Cedar Paul, New York: William Morrow, 1933, 3.

16 NEW METHODS WERE BETTER. Ibid., 4.

DESTROYED THEM. D. H. Lawrence, *Women in Love*, 223.

INWARD GOODS. Brunngraber, 291.

TECHNOLOGY AS FAITH. Postman, 50.

FIRST CLEAR STATEMENT. Ibid., 52.

17 ALL ITS UGLINESS. Richard M. Pfeffer, *Working for Capitalism*, New York: Columbia University Press, 1979, 285.

HUMAN MACHINERY. Braverman, 87.

FORD DIDN'T CARE. Interview with Ulrich Wengenroth.

PROGRESSIVE MOVEMENT. See Part VI.

SUPPLANT THE PRICE SYSTEM. Robert Reich, 99.

18 INTRODUCE IN RUSSIA. See Part VI.

AGRICULTURE OF THE TWENTY-FIRST CENTURY. Anson Rabinbach commented

on this view at a conference on "Industrialization and the Human Body," Hagley Museum and Library, March 19, 1993.
INCALCULABLE PROPORTION. Lyndall Urwick, "The Integrity of Frederick Winslow Taylor," *Advanced Management*, March 1958, 15.
19 SYSTEM MUST BE FIRST. Taylor, *Principles*, 7.

PART I

A PERSON OF GENTLE BREEDING

23 FINSTERMUNZ. Journal, July 25–26, 1869; John Forbes, *Sight-Seeing in Germany and the Tyrol in the Autumn of 1855,* London: Smith, Elder, and Co., 1856.
24 FATHER INDUCED HER. Journal, August 16, 1869.
25 EDITH HAD HER WATCH. Ibid., August 23, 1869.
WINDOWS THOROUGHLY WASHED. Ibid., March 18, 1869.
HE GOT A BOAT. Franklin Taylor to FWT, May 15, 1873.
FINE BOOTS. Franklin Taylor to FWT, October 24, 1872.
26 FATHER HAD SOME MEANS. FWT-Hearings, 112.
PROMPTLY DISSIPATED. Charles de Freminville, "How Taylor Introduced the Scientific Method into Management of the Shop," *Bulletin,* February 1925, 32.
OBLIGED TO MINGLE. FWT to Morris Cooke, December 2, 1910.
27 BROOKDALE FARM. Interview with Frank Wallace, Jr.
TAYLOR FAMILY. See Francis Bazley Lee, *Genealogical and Memorial History of the State of New Jersey,* vol. IV, New York: Lewis Historical Publishing Company, 1910; materials furnished by Myron Johnson; interviews with Frank Wallace, Jr., Tony Wallace, Bayard Clark, Marie Clark Hodges, and Lisa Carr.
28 HESSIAN MERCENARIES. Interview with Myron Johnson.
SUNBURY. Book excerpt, "Shadows over Sunbury," n.p., n.d., depicts Sunbury as haunted by an "Uncle Caleb." Could this be Fred's uncle Caleb?
MY ALMOST MOTHER. Franklin Taylor to Emily, May 7, 1850. Carr.
29 BORN RETIRED. Burt, 67.
DIPLOMA TO HIS BELOVED. Ibid., 100.
BIGGER AND BIGGER. Robert Taylor, 1976, III-2.
MORE MISSED. FWT to King Hathaway, September 14, 1910.
RETREATED TO FRENCH. Copley, I, 46.
NOT THE LEAST A GO-GETTER. Robert Taylor, 1976, I-2.
30 CARRIAGE AVAILABLE. Copley, I, 46.
PENNSYLVANIA TRAINING SCHOOL. *Eighth Annual Report of the Pennsylvania Training School for Feeble-Minded Children,* Philadelphia, 1861; Mabel E. Talbot, *Edouard Seguin: A Study of an Educational Approach to the Treatment of Mentally Defective Children,* New York: Bureau of Publications, Teachers College, Columbia University, 1964; *Proceedings of Association of Medical Officers of American Institutions for Philadelphia: 1876–1886.*
Why Franklin's interest in the "feeble-minded"? Conceivably—this is pure speculation—his older brother William was retarded. His mother's will of October 29, 1862 (Collection), made special provision for the "support and maintenance of my son William Taylor." In a letter to Emily, September 17, 1850, (Carr), Franklin wrote that four older brothers lived at home, "some of them confirmed in their odd ways. Nor are all their peculiarities the most agreeable for family life and social intercourse." That could mean anything but is at least compatible with one of them being physically or mentally disabled.

HOPELESS IDIOCY. Scharf, 1458.

TRUE TO YOURSELF. Franklin Taylor to FWT, October 16, 1872.

31 WHERE . . . STUDY? Franklin Taylor to FWT, January 30, 1873.

EVIL PASSIONS. "On Self-Control," furnished by J. Thierry du Pasquier.

ACT UNFAIRLY. Franklin Taylor to FWT, October 16, 1872.

EVER AGAIN COPY. Franklin Taylor to FWT, November 14, 1872.

GENTLE BREEDING. Franklin Taylor to FWT, November 28, 1872.

32 WINSLOW HISTORY. See, for example, Bibber; Holton; Copley, I, chapter 1.

33 TIGHT-FISTED, CRUEL, AND RUTHLESS. Quoted in Russell Bourne, *The View From Front Street: Travels Through New England's Historic Fishing Communities.* New York: W.W. Norton, 1989.

FOR SALE AT THEIR STORES. Bibber, 192.

IN COMMAND OF THE BOURBON. Du Pasquier, 130.

DELAROCHE. Ibid., 95.

CHANSON DU PÈRE WINSLOW. Ibid., 82. See also Charles de Freminville to Morris Cooke, April 6, 1926, Franklin D. Roosevelt Library.

NATIONALISTIC BACKLASH. Interview, J. Thierry du Pasquier.

34 LITTLE FRENCH TRUNK. Louise Fragment.

DEAR LITTLE EMILY. Isaac Winslow to Sarah and Emily Winslow, July 1829, Carr.

LONELY AND SOLITARY. Isaac Winslow to Sarah Winslow, February 1, 1830, Carr.

AROUND 1833. Copley, I, 37, says Isaac Winslow returned to the United States in 1829; in fact, his wife and child returned, but he didn't. Du Pasquier, 130, reports that Isaac, living in Le Havre, applied for French citizenship in that year, and that he returned to the United States only "some years later," which Du Pasquier later fixes as "1833 or the beginning of 1834." See also Bibber, 197.

HUNDRED THOUSAND DOLLARS' WORTH. Du Pasquier, 131.

TONIC MIXTURE. Ibid., 130.

FOOD IN SEALED CANS. Bibber, 200–203.

WROTE A FRIEND. Du Pasquier, 131.

I WILL BE HEARD. *The New Encyclopaedia Britannica,* 15th ed., vol. 5, 132.

BANKROLLED GARRISON. Ruchames, 209.

EARLY AND ATTACHED FRIEND. Walter M. Merrill, 530.

ATTENDED 1833 FOUNDING SESSION. Ruchames, 209.

SAVAGE TRIUMPH. Committee report signed by Isaac Winslow and four others, Boston, March 8, 1837, Pennsylvania Abolition Society Papers, Historical Society of Pennsylvania.

35 IN 1840. Copley, I, 41, incorrectly gives the date as 1842, and Emily Winslow as twenty.

ROSCOE. See Tolles, 14, for Lucretia Mott's account of the voyage.

NEAT LITTLE GALE. Emily Winslow's diary, Carr.

ANIMATED . . . DISCUSSIONS. Quoted in Ira Brown, 24.

STAYED WITH THE MOTTS AND GARRISON. Ruchames, 655.

36 AMONG THE SIGNERS WAS ISAAC WINSLOW. Tolles, 44.

BEGINNING OF WOMEN'S RIGHTS MOVEMENT. Ira Brown, 27.

ALIAS LORD SOMEBODY. Elizabeth Neall to Emily Winslow, April 11, 1843, Carr.

SLAVEHOLDING PASSENGERS. Elizabeth Neall to Emily Winslow, October 20, 1840, Carr.

HOW MUCH ASTONISHMENT. Elizabeth Neall to Emily Winslow, April 11, 1843, Carr.

SIX-MONTH TRIP TO THREE YEARS. Sarah Southwick to Emily Winslow, July 30, 1843, Carr.

COMMON PROPERTY. Harriet Winslow to Emily Winslow, December 6, 1840, Carr.

MUCH ENJOYMENT. Sarah Southwick to Emily Winslow, July 30, 1843, Carr.

FUTURE MISERY. Isaac Winslow to Emily Winslow, June 25, 1843, Carr.

BY 1843 IN BUSINESS. Ibid.

FOURTEEN HUNDRED JARS. Isaac Winslow to Emily Winslow, September 6, 1845, Carr.

EARLY IN 1844. Nelson, 22, puts the time as "in the 1840s." My estimate is based on letters (Carr) to Emily Winslow in France dated as late as December 12, 1843 (Isaac Winslow to Emily Winslow); and on the fact that Emily was one of the signers of the Constitution of the Philadelphia Female Anti-Slavery Society, some time before January 9, 1845 (Minutes of Philadelphia Female Anti-Slavery Society, Pennsylvania Abolition Society Papers).

UNRELENTING QUAKER ABOLITIONIST. Quoted in Bibber, 197.

37 DEPARTING FROM PLAINNESS. Ibid., 200.

CHIEF SUBJECT OF CONVERSATION. Louisa Winslow Sewall to Emily Winslow, April 16, 1840, though the postmark and internal evidence implies 1841, Carr.

EMILY MET EMERSON. Copley, I, 40.

DOWRY OF TEN THOUSAND DOLLARS. Isaac Winslow to Emily Winslow, June 25, 1843, Carr.

BEAUTY . . . SMILE . . . CONQUESTS. Harriet Winslow to Emily Winslow, undated, 1848 (#81); Anna Southwick to Emily Winslow, January 16, 1848; Anna Southwick to Emily Winslow, November 19, 1847. All, Carr.

PLEASANT IMPRESSION. Anna Southwick to Emily Winslow, October 29, 1843, Carr.

YOUNG PATRICIAN. Ibid.

ENGAGED TO CHARLES WRIGHT. Sarah Southwick to Emily Winslow, August 19, 1846, Carr.

AWKWARD, UGLY JOB. Sarah Southwick to Emily Winslow, November 5, 1846, Carr.

38 BEAUTIFUL EYES AND FINE HAIR. Harriet Winslow to Emily Winslow, January 3, 184[?], Carr, #205.

EARLY 1846 IS THE BEST GUESS. "When we lived in the same house," Franklin Taylor writes Emily Winslow, April 29, 1850. In her draft reply (see below), Emily speaks of "daily contact during six months." In a letter to Emily on May 30, 1846, Isaac Winslow writes: "I have not seen Mr. Taylor" (though here we must beware the ubiquity of the Taylor name). Other evidence hints that they'd met some time earlier, in a boardinghouse run by a Mrs. Crim: In letters to Emily on August 31, September 1, and September 6, 1845, Isaac writes of Mrs. Crim making rooms and a parlor ready for Emily, while in a letter to Emily on September 13, 1850, Franklin also mentions Crim: "I have been looking for board, but have re-engaged my old room at Crim Castle." "Castle" sounds like a private joke. These and other letters between Emily and Franklin, spanning April 29 to September 26, 1850, can be found in Carr.

MAKE THE EXPERIMENT. Kate Wilkeson to Emily Winslow, August 4, no year, Carr, #177. The reference to Stanton and Mott, Emily's attendance at the West Newton Normal School through mid-1849, Wilkeson's urgency, the suggestion that Emily and Abby Southwick come around mid-September, and the school's official opening in October 1849, which we know from the flyer (see below), all suggest 1849 for the year of the letter.

(Money, writes Wilkeson here, is "a disagreeable subject, but it is better for us women to get used to it before Lib [her sister, Elizabeth Cady Stanton] and Lucretia Mott assure our rights to us," as they had begun to do at the Seneca Falls conference of 1848. "The right to earn money without feeling degraded is one I long to see acted upon by our sex.")

GLOWING REFERENCES. Barnum Field, September 28, 1849; C. Pierce, July 4, 1849, and unsigned reference, July 24, 1849, Carr.

YOUNG LADIES' SCHOOL. Flyer in Carr.

I LOVE YOU. Franklin Taylor to Emily Winslow, April 29, 1850, Carr.

39 MINGLED FEELINGS. Franklin Taylor to Emily Winslow, May 7, 1850, Carr.

IMMENSITY OF THE STEP. Franklin Taylor to Emily Winslow, May 20, 1850, Carr.

FORETASTE OF BLISS. Franklin Taylor to Emily Winslow, September 8, 1850, Carr.

40 WEDDING. A fragment of family record, Collection, that supplies biographical material about Franklin Taylor has a handwritten addendum supplying these details.

BROKE OFF FROM THE MAINSTREAM. It was a messy split, one long brewing. Isaac Winslow's brother Jeremiah, back in New Bedford during the winter of 1823, wrote how he was "disgusted by the slander, the denigration, and the religious squabbling I witnessed." Du Pasquier, 126.

TWO THIRDS. Benjamin, 19.

"DISORDERLY" MARRIAGE. Copley, I, 45.

41 ATTENDED QUAKER MEETING. Journal, August 21, 1870.

ALL THEE AND THOU. Robert Taylor to Myron Johnson, November 1, 1979, Myron Johnson Papers.

A QUAKER FACADE. Burt, 72.

SATIN BANNER. Interview with Marie Clark Hodges.

ALL HIS DRIVE. Robert Taylor, 1976, I-2. See also Copley, I, 16: "It has been said that his mother had the stronger personality, and that it apparently was through her that he acquired most of his characteristics."

FERVENT ABOLITIONIST. Dos Passos, 21.

42 ANTI-SLAVERY AGITATOR. Copley, "Frederick W. Taylor: Revolutionist," 3.

UNUSUAL FORCE OF CHARACTER. Du Pasquier, 131.

PLEASED TO ATTEND. Elizabeth Neall to Emily Winslow, April 11, 1843, Carr.

SOUL-STIRRING MEETINGS. Sarah Southwick to Emily Winslow, January 31, 1842, Carr.

FROM WHAT SHE ONCE WAS. Ruth Morrell to Emily Winslow, January 27, 1843, Carr.

NO LONGER TAKE AN INTEREST. Isaac Winslow to Emily Winslow, July 25, 1841, Carr.

TIME AND CIRCUMSTANCES. Franklin Taylor to Emily Winslow, May 20, 1850, Carr.

43 YIELD NOT A CERTAINTY. Franklin Taylor to Emily Winslow, May 7, 1850, Carr.

PRIVATE CIRCLE. Franklin Taylor to Emily Winslow, May 20, 1850, Carr.

COLLECT SUBSCRIPTION MONEY. March 13, 1845, Minutes of Philadelphia Female Anti-Slavery Society.

HELPED SARAH PUGH. Ibid., February 13, 1851.

ARRANGEMENTS COMMITTEE. Ibid., February 9, 1854.

NEARER SARAH PUGH. Copley, I, 50, says that Sarah Pugh was Mrs. Isaac Pugh. In fact, she was the sister of Isaac Pugh, who by the time of the Civil War was partner in a wallpaper manufacturing company (Kelley, 10). For most of her life Sarah lived with her brother and his wife, Elizabeth. See Sklar, *Florence Kelley and the Nation's Work,* chapter 1; *Memorial of Sarah Pugh,* 105; Otelia Cromwell; Ira Brown.

SILENT LITTLE QUAKERESSES. Kelley, 10.

44 GROWN BY SLAVES. Ibid.

GERMANTOWN LIBRARY. *Philadelphia Press,* July 19, 1895. See also Minutes of Germantown Library Association, Germantown Historical Society.

COMMITTEE ON ENTERTAINMENTS. December 11, 1873, Minutes of Germantown Library Association.

DARNED SORRY. *Industrial Relations*, 810.

DEPENDING ON THE TEMPERAMENT. *Memorial of Sarah Pugh*, 102. See also Minutes of Philadelphia Female Anti-Slavery Society, January 8, 1863.

CONTEMPTUOUS RECOLLECTION. See also Soderlund, 68: The Philadelphia Female Anti-Slavery Society "eventually became a narrow, introspective circle of anti-slavery veterans who spent much of their time preparing for the annual fair."

45 GOOD IMPRESSION. Emily Taylor to FWT, January 8, 1873.

SILK IS HANDSOME. Emily Taylor to FWT, November 2, 1873.

SUFFRAGE MAN. Emily Taylor to FWT, December 6, 1872.

UNSELFISH, USEFUL LIFE. Emily Taylor to FWT and Winslow Taylor, December 18, 1873.

46 EQUANIMITOUS. Dictionaries fail to list this word, but I wish to offer it as more fitting than "equanimous," the established adjective, much as "calamitous" is the adjectival form for "calamity."

WILLOW AVENUE HOUSE. Copley, I, 49; street maps, Philadelphia Free Public Library.

AESTHETIC CHARM. Frank B. Copley to Morris L. Cooke, May 22, 1930, Franklin D. Roosevelt Library.

47 GERMANTOWN. Charles F. Jenkins, *Guide Book to Historic Germantown*, 5th ed., Germantown, Pa.: Site and Relic Society, 1973; exhibit at Germantown Historical Society. For impact of horsecars, see Hershberg, chapter 4. Horsecar ridership figure from Germantown Historical Society.

CEDRON. "Cedron: Historic and Beautiful," *Germantown Independent*, 1919. Redwood Wright was actually William Redwood Wright, born 1846. His father was not Thomas K. Wright, as the article states, but Robert K. Wright, born 1820. See notes below on Wright family.

RELIGIOUS MINISTRATION. Clarence C. Brown, *History of the Unitarian Society of Germantown*, Part I, 1865–1945, Philadelphia: Unitarian Society of Germantown.

48 WRIGHTS. The important ties between the Wrights and Taylors have gone largely unnoted. See Edward Needles Wright, "The Story of Peter Wright & Sons," *Quaker History*, Autumn 1967; Ernest Neall Wright, *Peter Wright and Mary Anderson: A Family Record*, Ann Arbor, Michigan: Edwards Bros, 1939 (reprint, Pasadena, Calif., 1947).

WE CHILDREN. Ernest N. Wright to Franklin de R. Furman, November 1, 1933.

DISTANT KINSHIP TIES. In his parents' letters to Fred at Exeter, James A. Wright, Jr., was "Cousin Jamie," but the precise relation is unclear.

49 CLARKS. For the Clarks as bankers see Fritz Redlich, *The Molding of American Banking: Men and Ideas*, New York: Johnson Reprint Corporation, 1968; Vincent P. Carosso, *Investment Banking in America*, Cambridge, Mass.: Harvard University Press, 1970; interviews with Bayard Clark, Marie Clark Hodges, Frank Wallace, Jr., and Tony Wallace.

CIVIL WAR. Chronology of events in Germantown during the Civil War from Germantown Historical Society.

MYSTERIOUS APPEARANCE. Birge Harrison reminiscence, August 24, 1915.

50 FORMER SLAVES. September 11, 1862, Minutes of Philadelphia Female Anti-Slavery Society.

BANGED AT THEIR DRUMS. Weigley, 408.

FRED'S "ENTHUSIASM." Birge Harrison Reminiscence, August 24, 1915.

GERMANTOWN ACADEMY. See William Travis, *History of the Germantown Academy*, Philadelphia: Ferguson Bros., 1882.

51 ISAAC WINSLOW'S DEATH. *Augusta, Hallowell and Gardiner Directory*, Augusta, Me.: Pierce Brothers, 1867, supplies details of the Insane Hospital. Hospital records establish his dates of admission and death. Holton and Du Pasquier incorrectly give the year of death as 1868.

SEEMED IN GOOD HEALTH. Garrison to Samuel May, Jr., August 20, 1867, in Walter M. Merrill.

LESS THAN A YEAR LATER. Copley, I, 49, says the Taylors went to Europe "four years after the war ended," or 1869. But Fred's journal entries from 1869 make several references to what are plainly a previous summer's travels. While in Schandau, near Dresden, on June 8, 1869, he calls the rock formations there "larger and more [illegible] than in Switzerland," which they had not yet visited that summer. While in Munich, on June 18, 1869, Taylor writes that his mother and sister "met the three Miss Pierces, with whom we traveled last summer." Most likely the Taylors had come to Europe the *previous* year, 1868. In Industrial Relations, 765, Taylor gives three and a half years as his time in Europe. If he returned with his family in about August 1871, the time of Elizabeth Pugh's welcome home letter of August 10, 1871, they must have left around the spring of 1868.

WOKE UP THIS MORNING. Journal, March 20, 1969.

TRAVEL BY CARRIAGE. See Andres Furger, *Der Gotthard-Postwagen*, Zurich: Schweizerische Landesmuseum, 1990; Transportation Museum, Lucerne.

55 MIST THICKENED. Journal, August 28, 1869.

SIGHTSEEING GUIDE. Forbes, *Sight-Seeing*.

56 NOTED THEIR ARRIVAL. *Tageblatt der Stadt Zürich*, August 3–5, 1869.

RALLYING POINT AND RENDEZVOUS. Junius Henri Browne, *Sights and Sensations in Europe*, Hartford, Conn.: American Publishing Co., 1871, 127.

COLLECTING BIRD'S EGGS. See Lloyd Kiff, "The Egg Came First," *Terra* (Natural History Museum of Los Angeles County), Winter 1991; and, by the same author, "Oology: From Hobby to Science," *The Living Bird Quarterly*, Winter 1989.

A RITE OF PASSAGE. Kiff, "The Egg Came First," 5.

57 JAHN. A monument to Jahn stands in the Hasenheide, a park on the outskirts of Berlin.

VELOCIPEDES. See *Jeux de Velos*, Paris: Musée national des techniques, Conservatoire national des Arts et Métiers, Paris, 1992; Albert A. Pope, "The Bicycle Industry," in Depew, 550: "The popularity of the velocipede in America reached its height about 1869 or 1870 . . . and yet—so suddenly come the changes of public sentiment—two years later these machines had entirely disappeared." Original velocipedes on display at Arts et Métiers in Paris and Transportation Museum, Lucerne.

RIDE A LITTLE ALONE. Journal, August 16, 1869.

59 AMERICAN CONSUL. Ibid., July 22, 1870.

ROCK FORMATIONS. Ibid., June 8, 1869.

CRYSTAL PALACE. Ibid., August 14, 1870.

BOARDING HOUSE KEEPER. Ibid., June 3, 1869.

EXTREMELY DIRTY. Ibid., July 25, 1870.

FULL OF PEASANTS. Ibid., September 10, 1870.

RICH LADIES. Ibid., June 24, 1869.

LAZY LIFE HERE. Ibid., August 19, 1870.

60 CHERRIES VERY CHEAP. Ibid., June 14, 1869.

THICK AND SOFT. Ibid., August 30, 1870.

TWO GROSCHENS A TICKET. Ibid., April 19, 1869.

CHEAPEST I HAVE YET SEEN IT. Ibid., May 3, 1869.

"WOUNDED HUNTSMAN." Ibid., July 1, 1869.

61 1400 GUILDENS WORTH. Ibid., July 3, 1869.
   A SINGLE PAGE. Ibid., April 6–9, 1869.
   BEST BAT. Journal, vol. II.
62 POTSDAM. Journal, May 25, 1869.
63 NARROW SEATS OF THE SCHAUSPIELHAUS. Henry Vizetelly, *Berlin Under the New Empire,* 2 vols., London: Tinsley Brothers, 1879, II, 249.
   TYROLEAN PEASANTS. Journal, June 24, 1869.
   GOOD TALKER. Journal, vol. II, following main chronological section.
   RUTHLING. Ibid.
64 SMALL PALACE. Journal, May 25, 1869.
   CARLO DOLCI. Ibid., June 25, 1869. "I think the prettiest picture in the gallery is the head of Christ when a boy by Carla dolche." *Verzeichnis der Gemälde in der königlichen Pinakothek du München* (Munich, 1853) lists among the museum's holdings *Jesus als Knabe mit einem Blumenbouquet.* So does a museum catalog published in 1908.
   RELIGIOUS FANATIC. Beverly Louise Brown and Arthur K. Wheelock, Jr., *Masterworks from Munich: Sixteenth-to Eighteenth-Century Paintings from the Alte Pinakothek,* Washington, D.C.: National Gallery of Art, 1988, 54 and Charles P. McCorquodale, "A Fresh Look at Carlo Dolci," *Apollo* 97 (1973), 477–488.
   MOST BEAUTIFUL PICTURES. Journal, April 2, 1869.
65 CIVILIZATION OF THE HUMAN RACE. Vizetelly, II, 150; Karl Baedeker, *Berlin and Its Environs,* Leipzig: Karl Baedeker, 1910, 79, uses similar language, the Treppenhaus murals representing "important epochs in the history of mankind."
   STAMP ALBUM. Collection.
   SIEGESÄULE. Having visited Berlin in 1872, Vizetelly (II, 20) remarks on "the abundance of its outdoor statues of a bellicose type. Effigies of military or mythological heroes embellish the Linden and the Lustgarten, surmount most of the palaces and public buildings, crown the Brandenburg Gate, grace the entrance to the old Schloss and adorn its courts, scale the steps of the Museum, flank the classic guard-house and the opera," etc.
66 THOROUGH GERMAN. Journal, following chronological section.
   DISLIKED THE GERMANS EXCEEDINGLY. Copley, I, 66.
   VISITED THE BATTLE MONUMENT. Journal, March 25, 1869.
   FRED DIDN'T NOTICE. Ibid., June 21, 1869.
   INLAID WITH GOLD. Ibid., June 23. 1869.
   DEAD BODIES OF THEIR FRIENDS. Ibid., June 30, 1869.
67 UNHOLY JOY. Copley, I, 60.
   THOSE TAYLOR BOYS. Louise Fragment.
   STRASSEN JUNGEN. Journal, May 2, 1869.
   LOCKING ARMS. Interview with Frank Wallace, Jr.
   RUE DE BOULOGNE. The street no longer exists.
68 HIS REAL CHARACTER. Journal, following chronological section.
   BAGGAGE STRAPPED UP BEHIND. Journal, July 25, 1870.
   HARD AS A BRICK. Ibid., July 26, 1870.
69 HE WAS DEAD. Journal; see also Wright, *Peter Wright and Mary Anderson.*
70 PERFECTLY UNNOTICED. Journal, September 12, 1870.
   UNIFORM INSIGNIA. Interview with Frank Wallace, Jr.
71 I DISAPPROVE. FWT to Morris Cooke, December 2, 1910.
   FLUENTLY. FWT to George B. Wendell, December 15, 1910.
   PASS KNOWINGLY ON ITS TRANSLATION. FWT to H. K. Hathaway, May 12, 1910.
72 WELCOME YOUR RETURN. Elizabeth Pugh to "my very dear friends," the Taylors, August 10, 1871. Copley, I, 69, incorrectly asserts an 1872 return.

GERMANTOWN DETAILS. Germantown Historical Society.

73 HEALTHY OUT-OF-DOOR LIFE. FWT to Morris Cooke, December 2, 1910.

BOYHOOD FRIENDS. Birge Harrison reminiscence, August 24, 1915.

GERMANTOWN SCIENTIFIC SOCIETY. Germantown Historical Society.

STUDYING MATH. Inscription of FWT's name and the date "Jan 4th 1872" in FWT's copy of Greenleaf's *New Higher Algebra,* Collection; FWT to Professor Byerly, undated draft copy, Collection.

PEYTON IMPROVING. Franklin Taylor to FWT and Winslow Taylor, October 2, 1873.

ED AND PHOEBE HOUGHTON. Copley (I, 69) says the Taylors "returned from Europe in 1872, to settle in Ross Street." But family letters (1871–1874) reveal that they bounced around Germantown first, for a while staying with the Houghtons. In the meantime, they planned and oversaw construction of their new house, which went up at the same time as, and next door to, that of Alfred Jones. Jones, nine years her junior, was Emily's first cousin on her father's side.

NEW ENGLAND. I owe this insight to Myron Johnson.

74 TWENTY TO THIRTY BOYS. Cunningham, 312. For more on Exeter, see McLachlan, chapter 8; Charles Bell; Echols; Williams.

413 FROM HARVARD. Crosbie, 104.

75 EXCESSIVE AMOUNT OF MONEY. *Catalogue,* Phillips Exeter Academy, 1872–1873, Cambridge, Mass.: John Wilson & Son, 1873.

OLD PHOTOGRAPHS. See, for example, Echols, 57.

KIND MOTHERLY PERSON. Franklin Taylor to FWT, October 24, 1872.

LAUNDERING. See "Washing Accounts," Collection.

76 EXETER CULTURAL LIFE. Accounts in *Exeter News-Letter* during this period. See also McLachlan, 225.

FIEND OF FIENDS. *Exeter News-Letter,* November 8, 1872. Evans was executed on February 17, 1874; *Exeter News-Letter,* February 20, 1874.

77 EXCITING CIRCUMSTANCES. Emily Taylor to FWT, "Monday 11th P.M." the only date. Someone's hazarded "[May 1874]" is doubtful. Based on the reference to Evans, February 1873 seems likely, perhaps Monday, February 10, with Emily off by a day.

DEFALCATION. *Exeter News-Letter,* January 24 and 31, 1873. The same edition reported news of the Evans murder trial.

ORATIONS AGAINST CATILINE. *Catalogue,* Phillips Exeter Academy, 1872–1873.

LATIN ANY EASIER? Emily Taylor to FWT, October 9, 1872.

GRADES. Phillips Exeter Academy grades register for term of September 14 to December 16, 1872.

TEN THOUSAND TIMES. Franklin Taylor to FWT, November 14, 1872.

NO RULES. Crosbie, 95, 98.

ENLIGHTENED CONSCIENCE. Franklin Taylor to FWT, November 28, 1872.

78 DIME NOVELS. Franklin Taylor to FWT, May 21, 1873.

WEAK INJURIOUS NOVELS. Ibid., note from Emily Taylor appended.

MORE THAN A YEAR. Tufts reminiscence attached to letter to Kempton Taylor, October 13, 1915, a fuller version appearing in *Bulletin of the Phillips Exeter Academy,* 1915. For more on Tufts, see Cunningham, 201.

MUDFLATS. Henry A. Shute, "Student Life in the Seventies," *PEAN,* 1906, 192.

FRED WANTED A BOAT. See Franklin Taylor to FWT, September 24, 1872; May 15, 1873; May 21, 1873.

CHURCH CELLAR. Cunningham, 268.

79 THRONGED. *Exeter News-Letter,* October 24, 1873.

BASEBALL. Henry A. Shute, "Student Life in the Seventies," 191.

STUDENTS DROPPED. FWT to Morris Cooke, December 2, 1910.
HARD WORK. Olmstead reminiscence, April 5, 1910, Exeter archives.
FORTY OR FIFTY DESKS. Dartmouth, 373.
80 THE CURRICULUM. McLachlan, 228.
COLLINS INCIDENT. Olmstead reminiscence, April 5, 1910.
THE GREAT TRIUMVIRATE. Crosbie, 110.
CILLEY AND WENTWORTH. Ibid., chapter IX.
81 FINISHED APPEARANCE. Ibid., 113.
CONFIDANT OF EVERY TROUBLEMAKER. McLachlan, 224.
CONGRESSIONAL COMMITTEE. FWT-Hearings, 258.
MADE A FORTUNE. McLachlan, 233.
TENDERLY AS A MOTHER. Crosbie, 115.
SAVAGERY AND TENDERNESS. Ibid., 114.
82 NO EXCUSE WAS TAKEN. FWT to Morris Cooke, December 2, 1910.
VERY BEST EXPERIENCE. Ibid.
LAST MOMENTS. Emily Taylor to FWT, May 26, 1872.
BANK OF ENGLAND FAILED. McCullough, *Mornings,* 134.
TERRIBLE PANIC. Franklin Taylor to FWT, October 2, 1873.
83 SUFFERING. Emily Taylor to FWT, November 2, 1873.
I AM OBLIGED TO SELL. Ibid.
FIVE HOURS A NIGHT. Robert Taylor, 1976, IV-1.
TOO SEVERE. Ibid.
FRED'S GRADES. Phillips Exeter Academy grades register for term of September 14 to December 16, 1872.
EXERCISE. Franklin Taylor to FWT, September 24, 1872.
SICK BY STUDY. Emily Taylor to FWT, [September] 26, [1872].
84 PAGES OF ADVICE. Franklin Taylor to FWT, October 24, 1872.
SHOULD IT BE STORMY. Franklin Taylor to FWT, December 5, 1872.
ENVIABLE CHILDHOOD. In "Too Great Stress: Exeter and Frederick Taylor," former Exeter student Andrew Janca looked at Taylor's upbringing and came to broadly similar conclusions. Unpublished manuscript, Collection.
85 PERHAPS THE WRIGHTS. This is a guess. Win "worked on the waterfront for a family friend whose name I don't know," Frank Wallace, Jr., Winslow Taylor's grandson, told Myron Johnson. In an interview with the author, Wallace said it was an export-import business, probably on the Delaware waterfront. The company of Peter Wright & Sons, then presided over by close family friend James A. Wright, was an import-export business with offices at 307 Walnut Street, close by the Delaware. (Edward Needles Wright, "The Story of Peter Wright & Sons," *Quaker History,* Autumn 1967, 73.)
SMOKING CIGARS. Interview with Frank Wallace, Jr.
TOOK DOWN HIS SHINGLE. Robert Taylor, 1976, I-3. Frank Wallace, Jr., in interview with Myron Johnson, suggests this came some time after Win was thirty-five.
A DAMN THING. Robert Taylor, 1976, I-3.
TELLTALE BLACK DOTS. Interview with Frank Wallace, Jr.
86 SHOT FOUR QUAIL. John Peet to Edward Winslow Taylor, September 9, 1872.
GUNS, AMMUNITION, KILLS. Sarah Allen, Franklin Taylor's sister, to FWT, September 23, 1872.
TO HER ROOM IN TEARS. Interview with Marie Clark Hodges.
EGO IN HIS COSMOS. Copley, "Frederick W. Taylor: Revolutionist," 4.
87 RUIN YOUR HEALTH. Franklin Taylor to FWT, September 25, 1873.
TROY, HOBOKEN. Emily Taylor to FWT, September 29, 1873.

88 REGULATE BOILERS. See, for example, Annual Catalogue of the Stevens Institute of Technology, Hoboken, N.J., 1881.
HEADACHES EASED. Franklin Taylor to FWT and Winslow Taylor, October 2 and 9, 1873.

89 SCREAM AT HIM. Copley, I, 60.
TRAIN TO HAMBURG. Journal, July 8, 1870
SPELLS OF SEASICKNESS. Ibid., August 13, 1870.
EMILY WENT TO SEE ONE. Ibid., July 16, 1869.
NOTED EYE SPECIALIST. Louise Fragment.

90 15 MINUTES CONSULTATION. Emily Taylor to FWT and Winslow Taylor, "Thursday morning," probably January or February 1874.
ASTIGMATISM. See Henry W. Williams, *The Diagnosis and Treatment of The Diseases of the Eye*, 2nd ed., rev., Boston: Cupples, Upham & Co., 1886; Charles Snyder, *Our Ophthalmic Heritage*, Boston: Little, Brown, 1967; Frans Cornelis Donders, "Astigmatism," in James E. Lebensohn, ed., *An Anthology of Ophthalmic Classics*, Baltimore: William & Wilkins, 1969. Also, Gerald B. Kara, M.D., to the author.
DONDERS'S BREAKTHROUGH. Henry W. Williams, *Diagnosis and Treatment*, 392.
INSTINCTIVE CRAVING. S. Weir Mitchell, "Headaches from Eye Strain," in Lebensohn, *Anthology*. See also Henry W. Williams, 349: "Asthenopia [eye fatigue often accompanied by headaches] also occurs in asigmatism, because of the confusion produced by unsymmetrical refraction. It frequently follows long use upon small objects or in an insufficient light."
STUDYING TOO HARD. Emily Taylor to FWT and Winslow Taylor, December 10, 1873.
PULLING DOWN 9's and 10's. Phillips Exeter Academy grades register for term September 3 to December 23, 1873.
DULL BOYS. Franklin Taylor to FWT, January 30, 1873.

91 BROKE MY EYES DOWN. FWT to Morris Cooke, December 2, 1910. Taylor added: "The three other men who led the class before I did also broke down and had to leave Exeter, on account of poor health," though how reliable this is we cannot say.
WEAKNESS OF MY EYES. Franklin Taylor to FWT and Winslow Taylor, February 22, 1874.
PROBABLY IN MARCH. The term Fred failed to complete ended March 24, 1874. The last letter to Fred from home is his father's of February 22.

PART II

IRON, FIRE, SAND, AND SMOKE

96 DULL AND HEAVY MATERIAL. Chordal, 279.

97 ENTERPRISE HYDRAULIC WORKS. Manufacturer's Census, May 31, 1879, Roll 12, T956, p. 145. See also 1875 Philadelphia city atlas by G. M. Hopkins, C.E., vol. 6, 10th ward, and other maps from the period, Philadelphia Free Public Library. The adjoining buildings on Race Street still stand. Enterprise Hydraulic Works had no connection to another Philadelphia concern, Enterprise Manufacturing Co., which made household hardware.
DIVERSITY SCARCELY MATCHED. "Philadelphia's Industrial History: A Context and Overview," by Philip B. Scranton, *Workshop of the World*, ii-2. See also Blodget, *Census of Manufacturers*.
BALDWIN. See John K. Brown.

98 ELEVEN THOUSAND. Blodget, *Census of Manufacturers*, 6; Licht, 7, gives a figure of 9,163 for 1880.
   THIRTY-FIVE PEOPLE. Manufacturer's Census, May 31, 1879, roll 12, T956, p. 145.
   PROBABLY SMALLER. R. G. Dun Credit Ledgers, Philadelphia, vols. 147 and 277, Hagley Museum and Library, Accession 1413. Ferrell was worth about $15,000 during this period, Jones probably contributing little capital.
   WILLIAM H. JONES. *Gopsill's* Philadelphia City Directory for these years. Dun Credit Ledgers, vols. 147 and 277.
   TWENTY-THREE THOUSAND PEOPLE. Blodget, *Census of Manufacturers*, 34.
   PHALANX. 1875 Philadelphia city atlas by G. M. Hopkins, C.E., vol. 6, 10th ward, and other maps from the period, Philadelphia Free Public Library.
99 TRANSMITTING PIECE OF METAL. Chordal, 227.
   HALF DOZEN OR SO. *Boyd's Philadelphia City Business Directory,* 1878.
   ELEVATOR MACHINERY. Blodget, *Census of Manufacturers,* 147.
   KNOW THE RULE? Littauer, 16.
100 BIOGRAPHICAL ACCOUNT. H.P.J. Porter, "Frederick Winslow Taylor: President, American Society of Mechanical Engineers," proof, set January 11, 1906, for *Engineering News*, Collection.
101 SALT MINE. Journal, July 18, 1869.
103 REJECTION OF HIS FATHER. Kakar incorrectly claims (26) that Taylor complained of eye problems only after—rather than long before—passing the Harvard entrance examination. He suggests that Taylor "chose" his father's illness—Franklin wrote of a "great weakness of the eyes"—when, in fact, Taylor's headaches long predated this letter.
   OVERLOOKS THE POSSIBILITY. Edwin T. Layton, Jr., *Technology and Culture*, vol. 12, 1971, 666–668. See also Geraldine Joncich Clifford, " 'Psyching' Psycho-History," *History of Education Quarterly*, Winter 1971, 413–425; James T. Patterson, "The Uses of Techno-Psychohistory," *Journal of Interdisciplinary History*, 2 (4; 1972), 473–477: Kakar "dangles his thesis from a rather thin thread. By Kakar's own evidence Taylor's parents were far from autocratic, and they showed a warm understanding of their unconventional son."
104 SCIENTIFIC SOCIETY. Chronology of events in Germantown during March 1871, Germantown Historical Society.
   FRED'S LEADERSHIP. Birge Harrison reminiscence, August 24, 1915.
   MRS. PRENTICE'S HELP. Journal, August 7, 1869.
   100 ORIGINAL WAYS. Ibid., August 11, 1869.
   DREW THE FIGURE. Ibid., August 21, 1869.
   PIECE OF ENGINEERING. Ibid., July 25, 1869.
105 PIGGESTAD, ETC. Ibid, July 27, 1870.
   MARKED WITH A STAR. Ibid., August 10, 1870.
   BOTTLE CAP. U. S. Patent No. 6,963, December 18, 1849.
   CORN-STRIPPING KNIFE. U. S. Patent No. 51,279, December 5, 1865.
   LONG-TOOTHED RAKE. Copley, I, 57.
   CEASED TO BE A VICTIM. Birge Harrison reminiscence, August 24, 1915.
106 DOGGEREL. Collection.
   TROUBLOUS PERIOD. Haber, 5. Thomsen, 11, is among others to raise the issue.
   ACCOUNT OF MY EYES. FWT to James A. Tufts, dated February 23, 1882, but more likely 1883. See note on p. 597 of this book, SPECIAL STUDENT AT PENN.
   FRENCH INTERVIEWER. "Quelques Minutes avec Mme Taylor," Collection.
   FRED'S DISAPPOINTMENT. Louise Fragment.
107 DEAD LANGUAGES. FWT's exam booklet, "Time Is Not Well Spent in the Study of the Classics," n.d., Collection.

HARVARD EXAM. Reminiscence of FWT, accompanying letter by James. A. Tufts to Kempton Taylor, October 13, 1915. Date of exam drawn from Harvard catalogue, 1873–1874.

GREEK TRANSLATION. Harvard catalogue, 1874–1875.

108 WITHOUT LOSS OF SOCIAL POSITION. *Every Evening,* in Rumm, 2.

MECHANICAL ENGINEERING DEGREE PROGRAMS. R. H. Thurston, "Technical Education in the United States," *Transactions ASME,* XIV, 855.

FAMILY'S WISHES. Carl Barth, "Inception," 2.

START AT THE BOTTOM. FWT to Paul L. Reed, January 21, 1907.

FOURTEEN HUNDRED . . . LOST THEIR JOBS. John K. Brown, 33.

109 PERHAPS THROUGH FERRELL. Wrege & Greenwood biography, 8. Ferrell was the more educated, wealthy, and socially connected of the partners. He was a member of the Franklin Institute (*Journal of the Franklin Institute,* 1876, v.) and in 1880 became an early member of the Engineers Club of Philadelphia. (*Proceedings of the Engineers Club of Philadelphia,* 1881, II, 200). See also R. G. Dun Credit Ledgers, Philadelphia, vols. 147 and 277.

SHORTLY JOIN HIM. Ernest N. Wright to Franklin de R. Furman, November 1, 1933.

IF W GOES. Franklin Taylor to FWT, December 5, 1872.

HEFTING STONES. Copley, I, 76.

POURING DAY. My understanding of patternmaking, molding, and sand casting was aided by visits to Knight Foundry, Sutter Creek, California; Appomattox Iron Works, Petersburg, Virginia; General Pattern and Tooling, Baltimore; Deutsches Museum, Munich. See also *Patternmaking, 1905,* Manteno, Illinois: Lindsay Publications, 1982 (reprinted from American School of Correspondence, "Modern Engineering Practice," 1902, 1903, and 1905); Joshua Rose, *The Pattern Maker's Assistant,* New York: D. Van Nostrand, 1878; William H. Parry, "The Foundry Patternmaker," *Machinest,* May 4, 1911.

111 TOO SMALL. Blodget, *Census of Manufacturers,* 145, indicates manufacturers that have "large foundries attached, or a foundry department." It does not so indicate for Ferrell & Muckle, successor to Ferrell & Jones.

CRESWELL FOUNDRY. Oliver Evans Chapter of The Society for Industrial Archeology, *Workshop of the World.* Philadelphia: 1990. See also Blodget, *Census of Manufactures,* 139.

115 IMAGINE THE CASTING. *Patternmaking, 1905,* 63.

MEN OF INTELLIGENCE. Paul Gohre, *Three Months in a Workshop: A Practical Study,* New York: Charles Scribner's Sons, 1895, 46.

116 BOB'S BUSINESS. Chordal, 225.

LORDLY ENGINEERS. Ibid., 226.

THREE OR FOUR OF THEM. Taylor, "Why Manufacturers," 85.

JOHN R. GRIFFITH. Ernest N. Wright to Franklin de R. Furman, November 1, 1933. Griffith's movements come from *Gopsill's Philadelphia City Directory* during this period. See also 1900 Census, enumerated June 12, 38th div., 12th ward, enumeration district 514, supervisor's district 1 PA; for later FWT-Griffith correspondence, see Hayward, comp., "Tennis Poles and Sockets, Correspondence, 1890–1906," 17.

117 JONES . . . A PATTERNMAKER. R. G. Dun Credit Ledgers, Philadelphia, vols. 147 and 277.

WAGES DROP. See, for example, Ken Fones-Wolf, *Trade Union Gospel: Christianity and Labor in Industrial Philadelphia, 1865–1915,* Philadelphia: Temple University Press, 1989, 78.

VERY BEST TRAINING. FWT to Morris Cooke, December 2, 1910.

MANY A YOUNG ENGINEER. During the three years I worked as an engineer in the late 1960s, I met several such men, one of them a wise, immensely skilled quality-control technician named Louis ("Jack") Griffith.

STAN SHAW. See Geoffrey Tweedale, *Stan Shaw, Master Cutler,* Sheffield: Hallamshire Press, 1993.

118 WILLIE. See Douglas Harper, *Working Knowledge: Skill and Community in a Small Shop,* Berkeley: University of California Press, 1987.

INTEREST IN THINGS MECHANICAL. Ernest N. Wright to Franklin de R. Furman, November 1, 1933.

119 IF YOU WANT SUCCESS. Copley, I, 77.

SWEEPING THE FLOOR. Taylor, "Comparison," 7.

BLACK IMMENSITY. Chordal, 127.

THREE QUARTERS OF . . . PHILADELPHIA BOYS. Licht, 21.

LARGELY NATIVE-BORN. Licht, 14.

120 INDUSTRIAL CONDITIONS. FWT to Morris Cooke, December 2, 1910.

VALE OF TEARS. Robert V. Bruce, *1877: Year of Violence,* Indianapolis: Bobbs-Merrill, 1959, 17.

ASHTON PLACE . . . CHAMBERMAID. Philadelphia *Public Ledger,* September 10, 1874.

75 CENTS A DAY. Blodget, "Industrial Employment," 27.

DROUGHT-RIDDEN FALL. Philadelphia *Public Ledger,* September 10, 1874.

NOT ORDINARY WORKERS. Theodore Hershberg at al., "The 'Journey-to-Work': An Empirical Investigation of Work, Residence and Transportation, Philadelphia, 1850 and 1880," in Hershberg, ed., 128–173.

PASCHALL IRON WORKS ACCIDENT. Philadelphia *Public Ledger,* September 19, 1874.

121 HYNEMANN ACCIDENT. Ibid., September 12, 1874.

HOUR OF WEARINESS. Theodore Dreiser, *An Amateur Laborer,* ed. Richard W. Dowell, Philadelphia: University of Pennsylvania Press, 1983, 121.

MCKIM. Franklin Taylor to FWT, February 1, 1873.

ROSS STREET. Row houses have replaced the old Taylor home.

122 MORE LIKE ROOMS THAN CLOSETS. Emily Taylor to FWT, undated.

RHUBARB. Louise Fragment. Lou records what Taylor's father read to him as "the history of the French revolution by Taine." Most likely it's the first volume of Taine's *Les Origines de la France contemporaine,* which goes up to the eve of the revolution and appeared in 1876. See also "Quelques Minutes avec Mme Taylor," Collection.

ERECT A SIGN. Minutes, Germantown Library Association, December 11, 1874.

VALUABLE PART OF MY EDUCATION. Taylor, "Comparison," 7.

SLOUCH ALONG THE STREET. Taylor, "Workmen," 15.

123 PERFECTLY ASTONISHING AWAKENING. Taylor, "Why Manufacturers," 85. FWT repeats this line in "Success," 11.

COMPLEX PERSON. David Lodge, *Nice Work,* London: Secker & Warburg, 1988, 88 and 151.

LUNCH PAIL. "Quelques Minutes."

COMMUNITY OF FEELING. Taylor, "A Piece-Rate System," 115.

APPRENTICESHIP. See Rorabaugh; Calvert; Rumm; James S. Whitney, "Apprenticeship, and a Boy's Prospect of a Livelihood," Philadelphia Branch, American Social Science Association, 1872; E. H. Parks, "The Question of Apprentices," *Cassier's Magazine,* XXIII, 199–204; Dexter S. Kimball, "Industrial Schools and Apprenticeship," *Machinist,* November 24, 1910; Entropy, "Industrial Schools and Apprenticeship," ibid., December 29, 1910; John R. Godfrey, "Training vs. Production of Apprentices," ibid., August 17, 1911; C. C. Howe, "A Few Recollections of an Apprentice

Machinist," ibid., August 4, 1910; *Final Report of the Industrial Commission,* 587–590, 809–813; Addison B. Burk, "Apprenticeship as It Was and Is," Philadelphia Social Science Association, June 1, 1882.

124 CONFUSED MANY AMERICANS. Rorabaugh, 74.
THREE DOLLARS A WEEK. FWT-Hearings, 112.
NOT UNUSUAL. John K. Brown, 141, reports that from 1854 to 1868 apprentice pay at Baldwin was $2.25 a week the first year, $3.25 by the fifth.
SPECIAL OPPORTUNITIES. FWT-Hearings, 112.

125 PERHAPS EARLY IN 1876. In "Success," 8, Taylor relates how, at the centennial, he told Lucian Sharpe he hoped to become a $2.50-a-day machinist.
CENTENNIAL. See Lynne Vincent Cheney, "1876, Its Artifacts and Attitudes, Returns to Life at Smithsonian," *Smithsonian,* May 1976, 37. J. S. Ingram, *The Centennial Exposition, Described and Illustrated,* Philadelphia: Hubbard Bros., 1876, Robert C. Post, ed., *1876: A Centennial Exhibition,* Washington, D.C.: National Museum of History and Technology, 1976; John Maass, "When the New World Dazzled the Old," *American Heritage,* June 1976; John Maass, *The Glorious Enterprise,* Watkins Glen, N.Y.: American Life Foundation, 1973; *Report of the Chief of the Bureau of Machinery,* International Exhibition, 1876.
SUNDAY CLOSINGS. Margaret Hope Bacon, "Lucretia Mott: Pioneer for Peace," *Quaker History,* Fall 1993, 77.

126 NICHOLSON. On view today at the Smithsonian.

127 FERRELL & JONES EXHIBIT. *Official Catalogue,* International Exhibition, 1876, Philadelphia: John R. Nagle, 1876 (Dept. V, Machinery, 41); exhibit location established through map in *Report of the Chief of the Bureau of Machinery,* International Exhibition, 1876.

128 HOWELL. Copley, I, 78; see also Clarence C. Brown, *History of the Unitarian Society of Germantown,* Part I, 1865–1945, Philadelphia: Unitarian Society of Germantown, 11 and 30.

129 BROWN & SHARPE. Luther D. Burlingame, "The Universal Milling Machine," *Machinist,* January 5, 1911, 9–13; Roe, chapter XVI; Rosenberg, 431–433; Rolt, 180; *Iron Age,* November 2, 1899. Conceivably, the death of Sharpe's partner Brown, on July 23, 1876, the exposition then in progress, left him in a reflective mood and inclined to reminisce with young Fred Taylor.
GET TO BE A MACHINIST. Taylor, "Success," 8.

130 GENIUS OF INVENTION. Maass, "New World," 76.
HITLER . . . ENTOURAGE. Ibid., 77.

131 REPRODUCE THEMSELVES. Colvin, 6. See also Roe; Rolt; Rosenberg; William Sellers, "Machinery Manufacturing Interests," in Depew, II, 346–352; Merritt Roe Smith, "The Origins of the American Machine Tool Industry, 1817–1860," Research Seminar Paper #9, May 6, 1993, Center for the History of Business, Technology, and Society, Hagley Museum, 39; Strassmann.

133 THOMAS EDISON. *History of Technology* 16 (1991), 156.

134 FEEL LIKE PETTING IT. Charles Stelzle, *A Son of the Bowery: The Life Story of an East Side American,* New York: George H. Doran Company, 1926, 42.
HAVEN'T GOT STARTED YET. Chordal, 318.
DRILLING SET SCREW HOLES. Ibid., 11.

135 BELLOWS AND . . . SLEDGEHAMMER. Rorabaugh, 140.
SHOP-TRAINED BOY. Entropy, "Industrial Schools." Two years into his apprenticeship, writes Entropy, the brighter boy "may begin to suspect there is a connection between the time spent in building a machine and its cost."
ALL OF MY READING. *Industrial Relations,* 774.

136 JOSHUA ROSE. Joshua Rose, *The Complete Practical Machinist*, Philadelphia: Henry Carey Baird, 1876.
    TWO HOURS AND A HALF. *Industrial Relations*, 774.
    NOT VERY LIBERAL. C. C. Howe, "A Few Recollections of an Apprentice Machinist," *Machinist*, August 4, 1910.
    APPRENTICE LEARNED PLENTY. Ibid.

137 SO BOB BOLTON SAYS. Quoted in Rumm, 15.
    HIT IT A CRACK. Dartmouth, 48.
    MIDDLE AGES. *Industrial Relations*, 774.
    GENTLER MANNER. W. D. Graves, "How Shall Our Boys Learn a Trade," *Machinist*, September 22, 1910.

138 HAVING A FRIEND. *Industrial Relations*, 810.
    NEARLY THE CONTRARY. *Transactions ASME*, VII, 771.
    HANDLED RATHER BRUTALLY. FWT to Paul L. Reed, January 21, 1907.

139 DISAGREEABLE THINGS. Taylor, "Why Manufacturers," 84.
    ALIEN TO MECHANICAL WAYS. Ernest N. Wright to Franklin de R. Furman, November 1, 1933.
    AVERSION TO MANUAL WORK. Carl Barth, "Inception," 2.

140 EASIEST AND HAPPIEST YEAR. FWT-Hearings, 125.
    STATED THEIR SIDE. Littauer, 6.
    NONE OF YOU GENTLEMEN. Ibid., 15.
    INTIMATE PERSONAL CONTACT. Ibid., 27.

141 NOT LIKE A LOOM. Ibid., 17.
    PRACTICALLY UNIVERSAL. FWT-Hearings, 114. For more on restriction of output, see Mathewson; *Final Report*, 817–821.

142 MEET THEIR FAMILIES. Birge Harrison (August 24, 1915, reminiscence) recalls "a little dinner at the Hotel Bellevue-Stratford in Philadelphia, where the guests present, besides [him and Taylor], were Mr. Taylor's sons and a young iron worker from one of the big steel mills in which he was interested. This youth's mother was a washer woman, but he was a fine manly fellow, and the three boys went off to the theatre together at the end of the repast." Harrison told the story to demonstrate his friend's democratic instincts. But it occurred more than three decades after Taylor's apprenticeship and scarcely changes the picture.
    BEFORE THE WORKMEN FOUND OUT. FWT to Paul L. Reed, January 21, 1907. Copley (I, 160) writes how when Taylor soldiered with the other men at Midvale, he probably "made no bones of letting them know how abhorrent this practice was to him." "Not so," Frank Gilbreth wrote in the margins of his copy of the Copley biography (Gilbreth Archives). "Taylor told me the contrary."

143 EVERY INCH THE 'DUDE'. McCullough, *Mornings*, 276.
    STIFF GERMAN PROFESSOR. Copley, I, 88. See also Robert Taylor, 1976, III-21; Louise Fragment: "An Englishman once said to him while playing golf, 'You don't speak like most Americans,' not detecting his love of mimicking the English accent."
    CULTIVATED SWEARING. Copley, I, 89.
    COLD PRINT. Harlow Person, "Final Memorandum on Manuscript of Copley's 'Taylor,' " Collection.
    CHESTERFIELDIAN MANNERS. Copley, I, 91.
    WHATEVER ADVANTAGE. Ibid., 90.

144 PRESENCE OF A HOUSEMAID. Marcel Proust, *Swann's Way*, vol. 1 of *Remembrance of Things Past*, translated by C. K. Scott Moncrieff and Terence Kilmartin, New York: Vintage, 1982, 209.
    PUZZLED AND THEN AMUSED. Copley, I, 90.

THE WORD 'GANG BOSS'. FWT to Morris Cooke, March 23, 1911. Franklin D. Roosevelt Library.

CANNOT SAY TEN SENTENCES. Taylor, "Why Manufacturers," 86.

145 TALKED TO ON THEIR OWN LEVEL. Taylor, "Workmen and Their Management," 17.

WAGON WHEELS. Graves, "How Shall Our Boys."

DEMONSTRATE MASTERY. Whitney, 10.

TAYLOR'S STEAM PUMP. Collection.

WORKED SATISFACTORILY. Robert Taylor to Carl Barth, December 1, 1933.

146 WILFRED LEWIS. See *Bulletin*, February 1930, 45; Morris Llewellyn Cooke, "Remarks at Memorial Service for Wilfred Lewis," Franklin D. Roosevelt Library; *Mechanical Engineers in America Born Prior to 1861: A Biographical Dictionary*, New York: American Society of Mechanical Engineers, 1980, 209. Lewis was a founding member of the Engineers' Club of Philadelphia, some of its earliest meetings taking place at his home (Ray M. Fuller, *"Through the Years": A Historical Outline of the Engineers' Club of Philadelphia*, 1970, 6 and 16.)

BOND OF SYMPATHY. Wilfred Lewis to Kempton Taylor, July 26, 1915.

LOVED HIM AS A BROTHER. Wilfred Lewis to Louise Taylor, June 23, 1915.

BOSTON TRIP. M. R. Muckle, Jr., to Wilfred Lewis, November 24, 1915.

SELLERS FAMILY. For William Sellers and the Sellers family generally, see Sinclair; Calvert; Freedley, *Philadelphia*, 364; Bishop, 28; *Journal of the Franklin Institute*, May 1905, 365–381; for Coleman Sellers, see *Transactions ASME* 29, 1163; *Transactions ASME* 30, 130–137.

147 PROBABLY IN LATE 1878. The April 1879 *Proceedings of the Engineers' Club of Philadelphia* lists Taylor, employed at Midvale Steel, as having joined the club on April 20, 1878. But this needn't mean, and probably doesn't, that he worked at Midvale at the time he joined. For more on the Engineers' Club, see Fuller, *"Through the Years"*.

THANKFUL FOR A JOB. Chordal, 21.

MADE GOOD AS A CLERK. FWT-Hearings, 78.

TWO MONTHS. FWT-Hearings, 113. Barth ("Inception," 3) says "for a few weeks or months."

PART III

THE CREATION

151 WOODEN FENCE. See Hexamer General Survey Map #1332–1333, survey of January 1878, Philadelphia Free Public Library, which gives many details of the early Midvale. For more, see *Midvale Safety Bulletin*, July 1921, 7; A. L. Holley and Lenox Smith, "American Iron and Steel Works," *Engineering*, March 30, 1877; Wrege and Greenwood, "Origins of Midvale Steel" and "Early History of Midvale Steel"; Tweedale, *Sheffield Steel*, chapter 9; and three company histories—*The Midvale Steel Company: Fiftieth Anniversary, 1867–1917*; Nalle; and *Seventy-Five Years: The Midvale Company*.

152 NEVER CLEANED. J. B. King, "Retrospection," *Midvale Safety Bulletin*, April 1915. See also FWT to William Redfield, August 31, 1912: "The original old shop at the Midvale Steel Works . . . was of this kind, almost falling down."

TWO MEN TRUDGED. Guillemeau Aertsen, "Retrospection," *Midvale Safety Bulletin*, December 1914.

NICETOWN. *Philadelphia Magazine*, August 1951.

PHILLIP SYNG JUSTICE. Freedley, *Philadelphia*, 360; Wrege & Greenwood biography, 9.

153 EXPAND A SIXTY-FOURTH. See "Shrinkage Allowance for Locomotive Tires," *Catalogue of Midvale Steel Tires*, Philadelphia: The Midvale Company, 1928, 18.

FIVE TIMES. Tweedale, *Sheffield Steel*, 113; Robert H. Thurston, review of *The Materials of Engineering*, in *Proceedings of the Engineers' Club of Philadelphia*, 1883, III, 342.

CLIMBED PRECIPITOUSLY. Tweedale, *Sheffield Steel*, 113. For similar figures, see also Strickland Kneass, "Annual Address," *Proceedings of the Engineers' Club of Philadelphia*, 1882, III, 12.

STEEP IMPORT TARIFFS. Aertsen, "Retrospection," *Midvale Safety Bulletin*, January 1915, 7.

PROPOSED TO START. Tweedale, *Sheffield Steel*, 113.

MIDVALE VETERANS. Aertsen, "Retrospection," *Midvale Safety Bulletin*, December 1914.

BLACK DIAMOND. Robert E. Rogers, *Commemorative Exercises at the Fiftieth Anniversary of the Franklin Institute*, February 6, 1874. Philadelphia: Hall of the Institute, 1874, 61. For more on anthracite, see Freedley, *Philadelphia*, 74–80; *Final Report of the Industrial Commission*, 444–447.

154 CARS RATTLED BY. Brinley, 37.

BUTCHER AD. Freedley, *Philadelphia*, 361.

155 IRON AND STEEL. See, for example, Freedley, *Leading Pursuits*, chapter IX; Temin; Strassmann; Misa.

156 BESSEMER STEEL. An American, William Kelly, had earlier hit upon something similar.

OPEN-HEARTH STEEL. See J. R. Adams, "The Manufacture of Iron and Steel: 11th installment—Open Hearth Steel," *Midvale Safety Bulletin*, n.d.; Strassmann, 36; Temin, 457.

BESSEMER PRICE CUTS. H. B. Bope, "Some Memories of Earlier Days in the Steel Industry," *Midvale Safety Bulletin*, August 1922, 13.

STEEL RAILS PRICES. Temin, 459.

MIDVALE TIRE MANUFACTURING. See Aertsen, "The Manufacture of Weldless Steel Tires for Locomotives and Car Wheels," *Midvale Safety Bulletin*, August 1917; G. K. Flavell, "Manufacture of Iron and Steel," 36th installment, *Midvale Safety Bulletin*, September 1922; "A Farewell to Midvale," *Iron Age*, August 2, 1888.

157 NO EQUAL IN THIS COUNTRY. See also Aertsen, "Retrospection," *Midvale Safety Bulletin*, January 1915, 7.

CUPFUL OF METAL. Aertsen, "Retrospection," *Midvale Safety Bulletin*, February 1915, 8.

THE RAILS BROKE. Wrege and Greenwood, "Origins of Midvale Steel," 209.

GOOD AND WILLING MEN. "A Farewell to Midvale," *Iron Age*, August 2, 1888.

PAYMENT IN STOCK. *Midvale Steel Company: Fiftieth Anniversary*, 12.

158 MIDVALE NAME. *Midvale Safety Bulletin*, April 1938.

SELLERS WENT TO ENGLAND. "Samuel Huston vs. E. W. Clark, et al.," Israel H. Johnson's Minority Report, p. 6, Reading Railroad file, Historical Society of Pennsylvania.

LITTLE OR NOTHING WAS KNOWN. "A Farewell to Midvale," *Iron Age*, August 2, 1888.

BRINLEY. *Obituary Record of Yale Graduates, 1918–1919*, New Haven: Yale University, 1920. See also Midvale Collection, 363-A-1, "Daily Notes of Charles A. Brinley."

SILK HANDKERCHIEF. Taylor, "Workmen," 17.

STAND OR FALL BY IT. Brinley, 39.

BY CAREFUL SELECTION. Aertsen, "Retrospection," *Midvale Safety Bulletin,* February 1915, 9.

159 FROM THIS TIME FORWARD. *Midvale Steel Company: Fiftieth Anniversary,* 18.
RUSSELL DAVENPORT. See Brinley.
BESIDE A MECHANICAL TESTING MACHINE. Brinley, 37.
NOT A NIGHT PASSED. Ibid.
INTERESTING AND CAPRICIOUS MATERIAL. Ibid., 44.
LARGE LABORATORY. Nalle, 12.
SELLERS. See note on p. 593 of this book, SELLERS FAMILY.
NINETY PATENTS. Roe, 248.

160 SEVEN HUNDRED PEOPLE. Blodget, *Census of Manufacturers,* 134.
WITHOUT A PARALLEL. *Report of the Chief of the Bureau of Machinery,* International Exhibition, 1876: Report by François Perrier for "Group XXI, Machine Tools for Metal, Wood, and Stone," 14.
EXPONENTS OF PERFECTION. Chordal, 146.
STANDARD THREAD. Sinclair, "At the Turn of a Screw"; Roe, 249; Rolt, 126.

161 CHASTE LINES. Merritt Roe Smith, "Origins," 39. See also Wosk, *Breaking Frame,* 201; Strassmann, 132; Rolt, 126.
PLEASINGLY FANCIFUL. To my eye, anyway.
WHAT IS RIGHT, LOOKS RIGHT. *Bulletin,* October 1929, 232.
MACHINE GRAY. Roe, 256.
NAVY ORDER FOR HOWITZERS. Brinley, 40.

162 DAMN PIECE-WORK HOG. FWT-Hearings, 79.
PIECE RATE. See, for example, Mathewson, 735; Stelzle, 42.
PAYING THE MEN TOO MUCH. (Philadelphia) *City Club Bulletin,* January 18, 1911, 25.
LOCKED UP. Dartmouth, 355.

163 THIRD OF A DAY'S WORK. *Industrial Relations,* 782; FWT-Hearings, 122.
GALLAGHER'S NAP. Trombley, 87.
NO 'SOGERING'. Richard Henry Dana, *Two Years Before the Mast:* See *Oxford English Dictionary.*

164 WORK THEIR SKINS OFF. Chordal, 138. See also Mathewson.
NATURAL INSTINCT. Taylor, "Shop Management," 30.
THAT MEANS WAR. *Industrial Relations,* 782.
HAD IN MIND. FWT-Hearings, 114.
REFUSED TO DO ANY MORE WORK. Ibid., 81.

165 BROOKLYN BRIDGE CONTRACT. Aertsen, "Retrospection," *Midvale Safety Bulletin,* March 1915, 6.
SCRAPED UP OFF THE STREET. Brinley, 45.
WORK FAST AND RIGHT. FWT-Hearings, 82

166 NIGGER DRIVER. Ibid., 83.
HE'D BEST BE CAREFUL. Taylor, *Principles* 51; Copley, I, 167.
BESIDE THE RAILROAD TRACKS. Route reconstructed from G. M. Hopkins ward maps, Philadelphia Free Public Library.
CRICKET GROUNDS. Wilfred Lewis to Kempton Taylor, July 26, 1915.
SHOOT AND BE DAMNED. Taylor, *Principles,* 52.
INGENIOUS ACCIDENTS. FWT-Hearings, 84.
THESE MEN WILL SHOW YOU. FWT-Hearings, 80.

167 WORKING PARENTS. Taylor, *Principles,* 50.
YOU WILL PAY ALL THE SAME. FWT-Hearings, 84. See also Taylor, *Principles,* 51.
HEAVY FINES. Copley, I, 168.

SIDE OF MANAGEMENT. Taylor, *Principles*, 49.

TRIM, TIGHT FRAME. See Phelps; Robert Taylor to Frank Phelps, April 2, 1984, Myron Johnson Papers.

168 LEGENDARY STEELMEN. Taylor, "Workmen," 12.

HARDLY SENSE HIS POWER. Taylor Memorial, 14.

EYES, KEEN AND PENETRATING. Lillian M. Gilbreth, *Quest*, 32.

NOT AS TACTFUL. Copley, I, 155.

FEW . . . COURAGE TO DO SO. Taylor, "A Piece-Rate System," 100.

169 TOTTERING TO HIS GRAVE. Ibid., 103.

DO IT QUICK. Taylor, "Boxly Talk," 3.

PATENT CASE REJOINDER. Steel Patent, 184.

GET THROUGH FIRST? Littauer, 14.

WILLING TO COMBAT. Taylor Memorial, 107.

FIGHTING BLOOD. FWT-Hearings, 83.

A FRIENDLY WAR. Taylor, *Principles*, 49.

170 TWICE AS MUCH AS BEFORE. Ibid., 52. See also *Industrial Relations*, 782.

YOUNG MAN IN YEARS. FWT-Hearings, 85. See also *Industrial Relations*, 782.

TEN TIMES MORE. *Industrial Relations*, 782.

171 STUDYING. FWT-Hearings, 119.

172 CORRECT SOME IMPERFECTION. Thesis, 1.

174 TENDER, NIBBLING CUTS. Chordal, 290.

FALLING FAR SHORT. Rose, *Practical Machinist*, 35.

175 COULDN'T HAVE NAMED. In Thesis, 7–8, Taylor did list factors that seemed to him important, but for this early work kept them "sensibly constant."

SOME MEN WERE SURE. Thesis, 2.

ENTERPRISING FOREMAN. Egbert P. Watson, *The Modern Practice of Machinists and Engineers*, London, 1867. Quoted in Geoffrey W. Clark, 22.

PROMISCUOUS PRACTICE. Joshua Rose, *The Complete Practical Machinist*, Philadelphia: Henry Carey Baird, 1876, p. 8.

SCIENCE IN THE AIR. See, for example, Ordway Tead, "Comment" (on the twenty-fifth anniversary of FWT's death), *Advanced Management* V (4; 1940), 145.

COMMANDING PRESENCE. Wilfred Lewis, appended to obituary of Sellers in *Journal of the Franklin Institute*, May 1905, 375.

BETTER WORK THAN HERETOFORE. Coleman Sellers, *Journal of the Franklin Institute* LXIV, 1872, 106–108. Quoted in Geoffrey W. Clark, 32.

176 SCARCELY . . . AS RADICAL. Geoffrey W. Clark, 16, observes that Taylor's experiment was "of inherent interest to William Sellers as a technical and labor problem."

COMPROMISE CUTTING ANGLES. Carl Barth to Frank B. Copley, April 18, 1921.

SPECIAL MACHINE.. For one Sellers drill-grinding machine, see *A Treatise on Machine-Tools as Made by Wm. Sellers & Co.*, 4th ed., rev., Philadelphia: J. B. Lippincott, 1877, 40.

CONVICTION . . . SO STRONG. Taylor, *Art of Cutting Metals*, I, 245.

SIX MONTHS. Taylor, *Principles*, 105.

DIDN'T MUCH MATTER. *Industrial Relations*, 783.

177 TOP OF THE GOLD MINE. Ibid.

SPRING OF 1881. Steel Patent, 2384.

ONE EARLY SERIES. What follows is largely drawn from Thesis.

AS NEARLY ALIKE. Thesis, 8.

UNAVOIDABLE BIAS. Ibid., 20.

178 DECLINE INTO USELESSNESS. Ibid., 17.

PRODUCT OF SPEED AND FEED. Ibid., 33.

CONTRADICTED. Taylor, "Art of Cutting Metals," I, 249.
REAL NUISANCE. Ibid., 246.
179 BANCROFT SUGGESTION. Dartmouth, 48.
30 PERCENT MORE WORK. Thesis, 49.
FROM A LOWER CLASS. Ibid.
UNACCOUNTABLE PREJUDICE. Ibid., 52.
180 ENGINEERS CLUB ADMISSION. *Proceedings of the Engineers' Club of Philadelphia,* April 1879.
COLLEGE DEGREE. J. Myron Johnson, 4; FWT to Morris Cooke, December 2, 1910: "Throughout my early days at Midvale I found myself very much short of a scientific education."
ONE AMERICAN ENGINEER IN NINE. Samuel C. Florman, *The Civilized Engineer,* New York: St. Martin's Press, 1987, 58.
181 PROFESSORS AT HARVARD. FWT to Morris Cooke, December 2, 1910.
KNOWLEDGE OF CALCULUS. FWT to Professor Byerly. An undated draft of this letter is in the Collection.
EARLY IN 1881. In FWT to Stephen B. Phelps, April 10, 1911, Taylor claims he started at Stevens "after I was foreman in the Midvale Steel Works." In Steel Patent, 2398, he writes that he became foreman "in the latter part of [1880]." See also letter to Morris Cooke, December 2, 1910, where Taylor notes that he graduated in June 1883, "about two and a half years" after starting at Stevens.
HENRY MORTON. Coleman Sellers and A. R. Leeds, "Biographical Notice of President Henry Morton," February 15, 1892; obituary, *Machinist,* May 15, 1902; entry in *Dictionary of American Biography.*
SNOW-CAPPED MOUNTAINS. Address of Henry Morton, *Commemorative Exercises at the Fiftieth Anniversary of the Franklin Institute,* February 6, 1874, 80.
MORTON DIARIES. J. Myron Johnson, 6.
CLASS OF '81 . . . VISITS. Annual Catalogue of the Stevens Institute of Technology, 1881, 26–27.
182 ALTOGETHER INADEQUATE. Stevens faculty minutes, January 24, 1879, 112.
TWO DAYS A WEEK. Ibid., June 11, 1881, 146.
UNUSUAL TERMS. Franklin de R. Furman, "Taylor's Contacts with Stevens and Stevens Men," 2, Collection.
CLAIMED TO HAVE TAKEN ENTRANCE EXAMS. FWT to J. E. Moultrop, January 10, 1914; to T. J. Foster, October 3, 1905; to Stephen B. Phelps, April 10, 1911. See also Robert Taylor, 1976, VIII, 5–6.
SPECIAL ARRANGEMENT. Alexander Humphreys to Kempton Taylor, July 23, 1915; see also Ernest N. Wright to Franklin de R. Furman, November 1, 1933.
YOUNG MAN. Stevens *Indicator,* December 1933.
KNEW CLASSMATES. FWT to J. E. Moultrop, January 10, 1914; see also Morgan Brooks to F. de R. Furman, October 26, 1933.
183 NO RECORD OF TUITION. Alexander Humphreys to Kempton Taylor, July 23, 1915.
PASSED PHYSICS EXAM. Ibid.; see also Stevens faculty minutes, January 14, 1882.
PLAISTED RECALLED. H. M. Plaisted to F. de R. Furman, November 25, 1933.
STEVENS ACADEMIC REQUIREMENTS. Annual Catalogue of the Stevens Institute of Technology, 1881.
REARRANGE HIS NOTES. Thesis, introductory note to Part I.
PERIODICALLY WARNED. For example, Stevens faculty minutes, May 7, 1880: "Wrote to Wright's father. No improvement."
MARK THOSE AREAS. Ernest N. Wright to Franklin de R. Furman, November 1, 1933.

THETA XI. Ernest N. Wright to Franklin de R. Furman, November 1, 1933.

184 MOTHER READ TO HIM. J. Myron Johnson, 6.

SPECIAL STUDENT AT PENN. University of Pennsylvania Catalogue and Announce-ments, 1882–1883, 39; for Penn's "chemical section," see p. 33. Another Penn publica-tion, from the early 1890s and supplying amended information on Penn matriculates, declares that Taylor "entered as a special student 1883 and left 1884." But the contem-poraneous source seems more credible. In any case, Taylor never mentioned his Penn studies.

In a letter to James A. Tufts, dated February 23, 1882, Taylor predicted he'd graduate from Stevens that June. Given that he didn't graduate until June 1883, this seems to suggest some school difficulty, a possibility that his enrollment at Penn might seem to support. However, the date of this letter is suspect. In it, FWT speaks of having entered Stevens "about two years ago"—which suggests early 1880. However, other evidence (see note on p. 597 of this book, EARLY IN 1881.) suggests he enrolled early in 1881, making the date of the letter more likely February 1883. Other evidence supports this guess. Taylor mentions being engaged to Miss Spooner; since he married in 1884, the 1882 date makes for a two-year engagement—a little long. He speaks of his brother marrying "this fall." But Winslow actually married in 1883. He calls himself chief engi-neer; but company records accord him a title of "engineer" only in 1883. During the first weeks and months of a new year, of course, many people keep writing the old year. Very likely, that is the case here.

TAYLOR AS CHEMIST. Annual Catalogue of the Stevens Institute of Technology, 1883–1884.

ARDUOUS SCHEDULE. The various accounts derive respectively from Copley, I, 128; Wilfred Lewis, "Versatile Genius"; Myron Johnson, biographical account of FWT, 18, Collection.

COMPLETELY FILLED MY TIME. FWT to James A. Tufts, dated February 23, 1882 (see above note, SPECIAL STUDENT AT PENN).

185 BRITANNICA ENTRY. *The New Encyclopaedia Britannica,* 15th ed., vol. 11, 172.

HISTORY OF TENNIS. Burt, 309; Ted Tinling, "Philadelphia's Proud Tennis Story," 1980, 68–69 and 152–153, Taylor Collection.

186 SPIRITED DINNER PARTIES. Copley, I, 143.

TAYLOR TENNIS. Phelps. See also correspondence between Robert Taylor and Frank Van Rensselaer Phelps between January 16 and April 11, 1984, Myron Johnson Papers.

CLARENCE CLARK. Interview, Marie Clark Hodges. See also *National Cyclopedia of American Biography;* alumni records, University of Pennsylvania Archives; obituaries in Philadelphia *Inquirer* and *New York Times,* June 30, 1937.

DESPERATE CONTEST. Tinling, 152.

TENNIS ASSOCIATION. See *American Cricketer,* May 5 and June 2, 1881.

LUSTRE DIMMED. Ibid., June 19, 1881.

IMPECCABLE TEAMWORK. Ibid., May 26, 1881; June 2, 1881.

187 NEWPORT FINALS. *New York Times,* September 1–3, 1881.

ROSS STREET HOME. Wilfred Lewis to Kempton Taylor, July 26, 1915.

SPOON-SHAPED RACKET. U. S. Patent No. 335,656, issued November 26, 1886.

ABUNDANT MERRIMENT. Wilfred Lewis to Kempton Taylor, July 26, 1915.

TENNIS POSTS. U.S. Patent No. 401,082, April 9, 1889, and No. 415,825, Novem-ber 26, 1889.

MADE MONEY ON THEM. Robert Taylor, 1979, 36.

188 YOUNG AMERICA CRICKET CLUB. John A. Lester, ed., *A Century of Philadelphia Cricket,* Philadelphia: University of Pennsylvania Press, 1951, 23; George M. Newshall,

The Cricket Grounds of Germantown and a Plea for the Game, Germantown: The Site and Relic Society, 1910.
CONTENTIOUS LOT. Lester, *Century,* 24.
CLARET CUP AND SUN-LIT CHINA. Ibid., 138.
189 NOW, LOOK HERE. Copley, I, 89.
ACADEMY OF MUSIC. See John Francis Marion, *Within These Walls: A History of the Academy of Music in Philadelphia,* Philadelphia: The Academy of Music, 1984.
AMUSING MONOLOGUE. Wilfred Lewis, "Versatile Genius."
INVITATION TO THE DANCE. Copley, I, 87.
SCORE INSTRUCTS. William C. Bridgman, *Basic Songs for Male Voices,* New York: American Book Co., 1936. Thanks to Amy Bernstein for her interpretation.
"A WARRIOR BOLD." Copley I, 88.
SANG WITH DAVID BISPHAM. Copley, I, 88.
GOLDEN-HAIRED GERTRUDE. David Bispham, *A Quaker Singer's Recollections,* New York: Macmillan, 1920, 43.
190 LOUISE MARIE SPOONER. See Louise Fragment.
FAMILY HISTORY. *Plymouth Cordage Company: One Hundred Years of Service,* Plymouth, Mass.: Plymouth Cordage Company, 1924, 77. Plymouth Cordage brushed with history again later, when Bartolomeo Vanzetti, of Sacco and Vanzetti fame, tried to organize a strike there and was blacklisted.
191 PRETTIEST. Journal, final undated entry, after September 18, 1870.
NOT HALF PRETTY ENOUGH. Ibid., June 29, 1869.
YOUNG LADIES. E. N. Wright to FWT, November 8, 1872.
INTEREST IN THAT LINE. Ibid., November 29, 1872.
192 BEAUTIFUL FIGURE. Robert Taylor, 1976, IV-7.
DAYS OF YOUR ENGAGEMENT. Louise Fragment.
UNHAPPIER PERSON. Frank B. Copley to Mrs. Morris Cooke, February 6, 1917.
FULL OF TURMOIL. F. W. Clark to J. Myron Johnson, August 10, 1987. Myron Johnson Papers.
COMPLETE TURNAROUND. Robert Taylor, 1976, III-8. See also ibid., VIII-1; Louise Fragment; F. W. Clark to J. Myron Johnson, August 10, 1987, Myron Johnson Papers; Morris Cooke to Edward W. Clark, May 12, 1930, Franklin D. Roosevelt Library: "I have seen Mrs. Taylor twice since she returned. It is remarkable the way she keeps up her health and interests."
LONG-LOST HAPPY GIRLHOOD. Frank B. Copley to Morris Cooke, January 14, 1917.
193 GOUGEVILLE. Ernest N. Wright to Franklin de R. Furman, November 1, 1933.
MOOSEHEAD LAKE TRIPS. Copley, I, 144.
GREENVILLE. Emma J. True, ed., *History of Greenville,* n.p., 1936. For more on Maine woods trips, see Lew Dietz, *The Allagash,* New York: Holt, Rinehart and Winston, 1968; Mary R. Calvert, *The Kennebec Wilderness Awakens,* Lewiston, Me.: Twin City Printery.
AX ALONG THE TRAIL. Wilfred Lewis to Henry R. Towne, November 27, 1915.
INCUBATION PERIOD. Robert Taylor, 1976, III-3.
194 CANOE TIPPED OVER. Ibid., III-5.
HYPOTHERMIA. See Derek Maclean and Donald Emslie-Smith, *Accidental Hypothermia,* Oxford: Blackwell, 1977.
STOMACH PROBLEMS. Robert Taylor, 1976, III-21.
ASKED TO GO. Wilfred Lewis to Henry R. Towne, November 27, 1915.
BALSAM BOUGHS. Louise Fragment.
WHOLLY RENOUNCE. Wilfred Lewis, "Versatile Genius."
RIDICULOUS NONSENSE. Copley, I, 158.

LED THE LIFE OF FIVE MEN. Louise Fragment.
195 NARROW-MINDED TO EXCEL. McCullough, *Mornings*, 201.
196 IN EARLY 1883. See note on p. 597 of this book, SPECIAL STUDENT AT PENN.
"COLONEL" JAMES THOMPSON. *Midvale Safety Bulletin*, April 1920, 10.
FROM THIS DATE. Midvale Collection, February 2, 1884.
A DOZEN YOUNG MEN. Taylor, "Success," 6.
MIDVALE DRINKING PROBLEM. FWT to E. S. Stackhouse, March 6, 1914; FWT to
Willard Price, September 17, 1914. See also Midvale Collection, General Orders,
December 28, 1881.
197 LEANING TOWER. *Midvale Steel Company: Fiftieth Anniversary*, 28; Taylor, "Success," 9.
PUT ON OVERALLS. Ibid.
198 EXCESSIVELY IMPATIENT. FWT to Morris Cooke, December 2, 1910.
MOST WEARING. FWT to Sanford E. Thompson, February 9, 1887.
SOME GREAT THING. Taylor, "Success," 5.
BUSHEL OF DIRT. Ibid., 10.
199 VERY WELL SATISFIED. Ibid., 5.
WELL, FREDDY. FWT, Address to Cleveland Advertising Club, March 3, 1915, 14,
Collection.
COMMON SENSE GUIDE. Taylor, "Success," 10.
TRADE CATALOGS. These and correspondence bearing on them are in the
Collection.
MIDVALE ON A ROLL. Midvale financial statements from January 1, 1881, to October 31, 1885, Collection.
PREPARED TO FORGE. Wrege & Greenwood biography, 46.
200 NEW MACHINE SHOP. See circa 1887 photos of Midvale, through Mrs. William
Hearne, Collection; *Midvale Safety Bulletin*, April 1915.
SPECIFICATIONS. Collection.
STREAM OF WATER. FWT, "Art of Cutting Metals," I, 249.
201 BELTS. FWT, "Art of Cutting Metals," I., 261; FWT, "Notes on Belting." For more on
belting, see: "General Report of the Judges of Group XX," *Report of the Chief of the
Bureau of Machinery*, International Exhibition, 1876, 56–63; Dennis E. Howe. "The
Page Belting Company: A Study of 19th Century Power Transmission Belting Manufacturing," *IA: The Journal of the Society for Industrial Archeology*, 19 (1; 1993).
BETTER CHERISHED. Alexander Bros. to FWT, January 31, 1895.
WIDTH OF THE BELT. Chordal, 246.
202 PULLEYS OF LARGER DIAMETER. Taylor, "Notes on Belting," 142.
NOTES OF IMPORTANCE. Collection.
NOT RELIABLE. "Notes of Importance," 29.
203 SAFE TO ALLOW. Ibid., 39.
GUESSES AT THE TIME. Taylor, "A Piece-Rate System," 56.
DAY'S WORK. Taylor, "Boxly Talk," 27, and *Principles*, 54.
MAREY. Marta Braun, *Picturing Time: The Work of Etienne-Jules Marey*, Chicago: University of Chicago Press, 1992.
NYSTROM. Geoffrey W. Clark, 32; see also Rabinbach.
204 A MAN'S OUTPUT. Geoffrey W. Clark, 34–35.
COME TO NOTHING. Taylor, *Principles*, 53.
TWO GOOD WORKERS. Ibid., 54.
EIGHTH OF A HORSEPOWER. Ibid., 55.
EACH OF THE ELEMENTS. Taylor, "A Piece-Rate System," 57.
205 CASTING ILLUSTRATION. Ibid., 60.

206 HIDDEN PAYOFF. Taylor, "A Piece-Rate System," 72.
     SINGLE SETTING. Taylor, "Shop Management," 84.
207 OVERHAULING BOILERS. "Standing Orders for Inspection, with Routine of Work
     and Reports, for A Set of Boilers at Midvale Steel Works," Collection; see also unpub-
     lished discussion of H. L. Gantt's paper before ASME, December 5, 1901, Collection: "I
     ... devoted every minute of my spare time [to the job].... We climbed inside and
     chipped the scales off with little picks.... I had to go in and clean the ashes, take out
     the manhole covers, apply new gaskets, and so forth."
     MUCH LAUGHED AT. Taylor, "Shop Management," 182.
     THICK PADS. Ibid., 181.
208 ART OF MANAGEMENT. Taylor, "Shop Management," 180.
     CHAIN IS DRAWN TIGHT. "Observations of Hand-Work on Machine Tools,"
     similar to form folded into "Shop Management" at page 166, but dated "1-24-84" and
     annotated, Collection.
     GREAT OPPOSITION. Taylor, "A Piece-Rate System," 59.
     PRETTY WITH THE PLAIN. Copley, I, 88.
209 ENTIRELY DIFFERENT MATTER. Taylor, "A Piece-Rate System," 62.
     BUSTING HIMSELF ALL DAY LONG. G. F. Steele to James Deering, April 28, 1894, 9.
     WORK LIKE THE DEVIL. Taylor, "Boxly Talk," 15.
     IRRITABLE AT THE LEAST THING. Hearings, 1811.
210 IN ALL PROBABILITY. William A. Fannon reminiscence, 1.
     SHARTLE. *Middletown Journal,* September 22, 1932, and, about the same time, *Cincin
     nati Enquirer.*
211 OWED MUCH TO BRINLEY. J. B. King, "Retrospection," *Midvale Safety Bulletin,*
     January 1915, 8.
     $2.67 A DAY. Midvale Collection, Daily Notes of Charles A. Brinley, 91.
     TO ONE-AND-A-QUARTER. Ibid., 88.
     CHIMERICAL AIR-CASTLE. G. F. Steele to James Deering, April 28, 1894, 9. See also
     Taylor, "A Piece-Rate System," 75.
212 HIGH FAVOR. Taylor, "A Piece Rate System," 71.
     TWO TO THREE TIMES AS MUCH. Taylor Memorial, 100.
     TAYLOR DISAPPOINTED. Taylor, "A Piece-Rate System," 124.
     AN EXTRAORDINARY DAY'S WORK. Ibid., 64.
213 SUBJECT TO BE THEORIZED OVER. Taylor, "Shop Management," 25; see also FWT-
     Hearings, 264; "Boxly Talk," 16; *Industrial Relations,* 788.
     ESPECIAL SKILL. Taylor, "Shop Management," 26.
214 PAID FOR ITSELF. Taylor, "A Piece-Rate System," 58.
     COMPLETELY HARMONIZING, Ibid., 59.
215 PURELY MENTAL. FWT-Hearings, 258.
     FIFTY OR SO CLASSMATES. Dartmouth, 373.
216 LEARNING WHAT IS TO BE DONE. "Observations of Hand-Work on Machine
     Tools."
     NICELY FITTED. Wilfred Lewis, "Versatile Genius."
217 MOTIONS OF HABIT. Coleman Sellers, *Journal of the Franklin Institute* LXIV,
     106–108. Quoted in Geoffrey W. Clark, 32.
     GATHERING IN. FWT-Hearings, 40.
219 FIRST PALS. Copley, I, 189.
220 IMPERSONAL ARBITER. See Theodore Porter, *Trust in Numbers,* Princeton, N.J.:
     Princeton University Press, 1995. "Quantification," as one summary of Porter's argu-
     ment goes, "grows from attempts to develop a strategy of impersonality in response to

pressures from outside. . . . [It becomes] most important where elites are weak, where private negotiation is suspect, and where trust is in short supply."
TAYLOR WEDDING. *Transactions ASME* 37, 1478.
HOW PROUD I WAS. Louise Fragment.
FEELINGS OF JEALOUSY. Ibid.
BLUES AND YELLOWS. Ibid.

221 SEVEN THOUSAND DOLLARS A YEAR. Robert Taylor, 1979, 5.
A LITTLE OUT OF JOINT. Louise Fragment.
MORAL SCRUPLE. Robert Taylor, 1976, III-17.
GAY DINNERS. Louise Fragment.
THREE MEAGER CHOPS. Ibid.
STRENUOUS FOR THE YOUNG BRIDE. Ibid.
SORREL. "Quelques Minutes."
A NATURE LIKE FRED'S. Louise Fragment.
STRAIN HE WAS UNDER. Ibid.

222 MECHANICAL HEAVEN. Copley, I, 171.
SUPERINTEND THE DESIGN. Taylor, "A Piece-Rate System," 73.
BEYOND THAT PREVAILING. King Hathaway, "Methods Study," *Bulletin*, October 1930, 212.
JIGS, TEMPLATES, GAUGES. G. F. Steele to James Deering, April 28, 1894, 7.
USEFUL FEATURES. U. S. Patent 565,644, August 11, 1896.
YOUNG BOYS. G. F. Steele to James Deering, April 28, 1894, 9.

223 MORE SUCH OLD MACHINES. FWT to William C. Redfield, August 31, 1912.
SINCLAIR. Franklin de R. Furman, "Taylor's Contacts with Stevens and Stevens Men." See also Bradley T. Shaw, "Notes on George Marshall Sinclair," 1987, Collection.
SUBMITTED HIS REPORT. George M. Sinclair, "To Index the Drawings in the Drawing Room of the Midvale Steel Co.," November 20, 1886, Collection.
PIECE OF CHALK. Copley, I, 101.

224 CAREFUL AND SYSTEMATIC STUDY. Taylor, "A Piece-Rate System," 73.
ORDER SCREWS OR TAPS. Chordal, 53.
COINAGE ANALOGY. Chordal, 166.
INDUSTRIAL STANDARDS. James W. See, "Standards," *Transactions ASME*, X, 542.
EARLIEST ORIGINATORS. William F. Muhs, Charles D. Wrege, and Arthur Murtuza, "Extracts from Chordal's Letters: Pre-Taylor Shop Management," *Academy of Management Proceedings*, 1981, 96.

225 LOADS NO MAN WITH LABOR. Chordal, 242.
FOREMAN TO SUPPLY THE JUDGMENT. Chordal, 71.
FOREMAN'S ROLE. See Nelson, *Managers;* Montgomery, *House of Labor;* Taylor, "Shop Management," 94.
FIVE SPECIALIZED FUNCTIONS. Taylor, "Shop Management," 107.

226 RUSH ORDER. Copley, I, 132.
OILING REGIMEN. Taylor Memorabilia, Book I, 32, "Description of System of Oiling Machine, etc. in the Works of the Midvale Steel Co. June 16, 1885."
TIN TAGS AND PLUGS. J. B. King, "Retrospection," *Midvale Safety Bulletin*, February 1915, 6.
ANTIPATHY OF THE MEN. Taylor Memorabilia, Book 1, 34.

227 PRETTY HOT ARGUMENTS. Charles Shartle to William A. Fannon, May 2, 1916.
AS MAD AS I EVER SAW HIM. Ibid.
RESOURCES OF THE ENGLISH LANGUAGE. Copley, I, 165.
DUTCH UNCLE. William A. Fannon to FWT, June 30, 1903.

YELLOW DOG. Copley, I, 188.
228 CONTRADICTORY CHARACTER. Taylor Memorial, 108.
USELESS UNDERTAKING. Copley, I, 232.
MORE BENEFIT TO ME. Charles Shartle to William A. Fannon, May 2, 1916.
TRUE DEMOCRAT. See Part VI for full discussion.
WANTED TO PLEASE. Charles Shartle to William A. Fannon, May 2, 1916.
229 SWEEP OUT THE SHOPS. G. F. Steele to James Deering, April 28, 1894, 11.

PART IV

A WIDENING WORLD

233 NATIONAL INITIALS. *Transactions ASME*, VII, 428.
YALE AND TOWNE. See Urwick, ed., 25; Fritz Hirschfeld, "Henry R. Towne: A Talent for Management," *Mechanical Engineering*, April 1980; Joshua L. Chamberlain, ed., *University of Pennsylvania: Its History, Influence.* . . . Boston, 1901, 131–133; Giedion, 59.
234 SELLERS INTRODUCED HIM TO LINUS YALE. Roe, 258.
NOT A DEAD LEAF. Henry Roland, "Six Examples of Successful Shop Management," *Engineering Magazine*, 1896, 402.
MUSIC WITHOUT NOTES. *Transactions ASME*, VII, 440; see also Chandler, 272.
SYSTEM VERY SIMILAR. *Transactions ASME*, VII, 475.
235 ONLY WITH MISGIVINGS. Hirschfeld, "Henry R. Towne", 34.
RELATIVE VALUE OF WATER GAS. *Transactions ASME*, VII, 669.
PRACTICE HAD PRECEDED THE THEORY. FWT, Address to Cleveland Advertising Club, March 3, 1915, Collection.
REASON FOR THE BELIEF. Henry Towne to Frank B. Copley, May 2, 1921.
236 LONG-STANDING SUIT. Wrege & Greenwood biography, 61.
HARRAHS, FATHER AND SON. *Midvale Safety Bulletin*, March 1915; see also the standard Midvale company histories; Copley, I, 118; Wrege & Greenwood biography, 59.
ENDORSEMENT OF STATUS QUO. Midvale Collection, General Orders, March 29, 1887.
NO SMOKING. Ibid., April 1, 1887.
WITH COATS ON. Ibid., July 23, 1888.
GREAT INDUSTRIAL LEADERS. Taylor, "Workmen," 11.
237 MANY ASSISTANTS AND HELPERS. Steel Patent, 2399.
BLUE ORDER 221. Midvale Collection, General Orders, May 17, 1887; see also *Midvale Safety Bulletin*, January 1927, 7.
GANTT. See Alford; Urwick, ed., 89; Urwick and Brech, 71; Drury, 122; *Journal of Industrial Engineeering*, January-February, March-April, and May-June, 1961. Peter Petersen is preparing a new biography of Gantt.
SHARP-TONGUED CHAP. Alford, 39; see also Fred J. Miller to Henry J. McFarland, March 30, 1927, Henry Laurence Gantt Papers, New York University.
238 LABORIOUS. Taylor, "Art of Cutting Metals," II, 246.
QUITE RAPID APPROXIMATIONS. Ibid., 247.
BIG CANNON. Wrege & Greenwood, "Early History of Midvale Steel," 163.
NO APPARATUS CAPABLE. Hirsch, 324.
STEAM HAMMERS. Robert Routledge, *Discoveries and Inventions of the Nineteenth Century*, London: George Routledge and Sons, 1891, 24–27; see also Edward V. Fieran, "The Manufacture of Iron and Steel," *Midvale Safety Bulletin*, February 1921.
239 SCARLET AND YELLOW YEAST. Quoted in Routledge, 27.

ERECTOR SET. Copley, I, 196; U.S. Patent 424,939, April 1, 1890; William Fannon to Frances Mitchell, April 21, 1915.

SHOOK TIOGA. *Midvale Safety Bulletin,* January 1927, 7.

240   COMMENTED ON COLLEAGUE'S PAPER. *Transactions ASME,* IX, 151.

SPEAKING UP. *Transactions ASME,* VIII, 24 and 228.

TAYLOR PATENTS. See Hayward, 14–16.

CONTRACTED WITH A. G. SPALDING. Ibid., 16.

GRIFFITH AND TENNIS POST BUSINESS. See Hayward, 17: "Tennis Poles and Sockets, Correspondence, 1890–1906."

MOVING FAREWELL SPEECH. *Iron Age,* August 2, 1888.

SELLERS DRAFTING ROOM OFF LIMITS. Stevens *Indicator,* December 1933, 152.

241   WILLIAM COLLINS WHITNEY. See Hirsch.

BOMB MADISON SQUARE. Quoted in Hirsch, 263.

LONG RECORD OF CROOKEDNESS. Quoted in Hirsch, 262.

242   WHITNEY AND WASHINGTON YARD. Caspar Goodrich reminiscence.

FIRST PAPER MILL. Macfarlane, 67. For early photo of the Madison mill, see Horace Weeks, *A History of Paper-Manufacturing in the United States,* New York: Lockwood Trade Journal, 1916.

ENTREATED FOR THEIR OLD CLOTHES. Warner Miller, "American Paper Mills," in Depew, 303.

HUNDRED AND FIFTY MILLION POUNDS. Bolles, 460.

STRAW FOR PAPER. Miller, "American Paper Mills", 305.

243   RAGS ARE NO LONGER KING. Freedley, *Leading Pursuits,* 68.

WOOD PULP. "Pulp" is fiber prepared for papermaking, though it may be used to make other products.

MITSCHERLICH PROCESS. See Charles Thomas Davis, *The Manufacture of Paper,* Philadelphia: Henry Carey Baird, 1886, 244 and 263; Edwin Sutermeister, *The Story of Papermaking,* Boston: S. D. Warren Company, 1954, chapter VI.

WHITNEY INVESTORS. Copley, I, 372.

FLATTERING OFFERS. William Fannon to S. E. Thompson, December 25, 1895, Catherwood.

SO MUCH RESPONSIBILITY. Wilfred Lewis to Kempton Taylor, July 26, 1915.

FOUR THOUSAND. E. A. W. Jefferies to FWT, June 14 and December 1, 1890.

244   FIFTEEN THOUSAND DOLLARS. FWT to Wiliiam C. Whitney, January 20, 1890; Contract between FWT and Manufacturing Investment Co., May 26, 1890; amendment to the contract dated November 7, 1890. In the end, Taylor drew $10,000 in salary and bought common and preferred stock in the firm whose dividends were supposed to bring his income up to $15,000. He was loaned $30,000 for the stock purchase. See notes beginning "Original contract provided . . . ," on Investment Co. financial arrangements, undated and unsigned, Collection.

GORGED EVERY APPETITE. Henry Adams, *The Education of Henry Adams,* Boston: Houghton Mifflin Company, 1961, 347.

THERMOMETER GOES TO 20 BELOW. Louise Fragment.

FRAGRANCE OF BALSAM. Ibid.

MADISON. See Emma Folsom Clark, comp., *History of Madison.* N.p., n.d.

245   DRUMMERS' HOTEL. Louise Fragment.

ALL BUT FANNON REFUSED. William Fannon to Frances Mitchell, April 8, 1915. See also FWT to Wm. H. Colby, October 17, 1890, to which handwritten note is appended: "I hope you will decide to come with me and think you will have no cause to regret doing so." But Colby didn't.

PERFECTLY CONTENTED. William Fannon to S. E. Thompson, December 25, 1895, Catherwood.

LEFT EVERY COMFORT. Ibid.

STONE STREWN ABOUT. Emma Folsom Clark, 68. Photos of dynamiting, Collection.

CIRCULAR TIERS. *Madison Bulletin,* November 27, 1890.

246 MADISON BOOMING. Ibid., January 29, 1891.

LONG BEFORE FALL. Vestpocket.

THROWN FROM CARRIAGE. *Madison Bulletin,* October 30, 1890.

APPLETON. See Glaab & Larsen.

247 NOT CALLED UPON TO HELP. Louise Fragment.

NO PRETENSION TO FINISH. *Madison Bulletin,* July 2, 1891.

CABIN COST MORE THAN FIVE THOUSAND. The above article estimated "not less than $3000 or $4000," but the cabin was sold back to the company a few years later for five thousand.

LOU AND HER MOTHER. *Madison Bulletin,* July 16, 1891.

NEAR OLD POINT CROSSING. Ibid., July 23, 1891.

COLONEL TAYLOR. Ibid., July 2 and 23, 1891.

STERN AND STEELY GAZE. "The Sailor on Horseback," clipping perhaps from *Madison Bulletin,* October 16, 1941, Madison Public Library.

GOODRICH. See Caspar F. Goodrich, *Rope Yarns From the Old Navy,* New York: Naval History Society, 1931.

UNUSUAL CHARM. Nelson, "Progressive Engineer," 451, 453.

SAILOR ON HORSEBACK. "The Sailor on Horseback."

248 STREAMS OF WINE. Ibid.

QUARRELED WITH ARCHITECT. "Madison Mill, Manufacturing Investment Co.," notebook kept by S. E. Thompson, Catherwood.

CALL IT INTIMATE. Taylor Memorial, 81.

249 LONG, BLACK CURVE OF THE RIVER. Louise Fragment.

LUMBER COLLECTED. See Emma Folsom Clark, 67; "Manufacture of Sulphite Fibre," notebook kept by Sanford E. Thompson, Catherwood; "Sailor on Horseback"; numerous accounts in *Madison Bulletin* of early 1890s.

DERISION AND PROTEST. Copley, I, 383.

HAUL CAMERAS TO THE TOP. Emma Folsom Clark, 56.

HEAR THE RUMBLE. "Sailor on Horseback."

HELLFIRE AND BRIMSTONE. Ibid.

250 THREE OR FOUR DOLLARS. Price list in Vestpocket.

APPLETON MILL. Glaab and Larsen, 285.

PULP IS DIRTY. FWT to William L. Putnam, quoted in John E. McLeod, history of Great Northern Paper Company, 1974, chapter 6, Collection.

MY SOUL REJOICED. Caspar Goodrich to FWT, December 3, 1891.

LOCAL BOYS. "Sailor on Horseback."

REPORTED TO THE ... BOARD. Report #1105, New York, October 26, 1892, Catherwood.

FORTY-ONE CARLOADS. Emma Folsom Clark, 196.

251 ENORMOUS FRAUD. FWT to George Hammond, May 18, 1893.

PATENT RIGHTS. Fannon, 8.

HORSEPOWER ESTIMATES. "Report on the Relative Cost of the Madison Mill to that of Other Similar Mills," Report #1111, December 19, 1892, Catherwood.

MISREPRESENTATIONS. FWT to George Hammond, August 9, 1893.

50,000 OR SO GALLONS PER TON. Glaab & Larsen, 80.

CAME TO MADISON. Emma Folsom Clark, 188; David C. Smith, 251.

SHORTNESS IN WATER. FWT to Stanford E. Thompson, May 16, 1891; see also Fannon, 8.

DIRECTED TO ERECT. Robley D. Evans, *A Sailor's Log: Recollections of Forty Years of Naval Life*, New York: D. Appleton & Co., 1901, 241.

252 COMPETITION BETWEEN TWO MEN. Fannon, 9.

MACHINERY IS PACKED. "Report on Relative Cost," 6.

SHAFTING AND BELTING WORE OUT. Ibid., 7; FWT to Edward Sawyer, August 4, 1893.

BIN . . . COLLAPSED. *Madison Bulletin*, November 19, 1891.

PULLEY BURST. Ibid., February 11, 1892.

HEAT SO INTENSE. Ibid., November 14, 1892.

$3000. Report #1105.

MORE THAN A HUNDRED THOUSAND DOLLARS. S. E. Thompson to FWT, March 1, 1893.

TRADE JOURNALS. David C. Smith, *A History of Lumbering in Maine, 1861–1960* (Orono, Me., 1972), 251.

A LITTLE TOO THOROUGH. Copley, I, 382.

LENGTHY REPORT. "Report on the Relative Cost."

253 SLIGHTEST EFFECT. FWT to Caspar Goodrich, December 13, 1892.

SHAFT REVOLVING. Quoted in Nelson, 50.

IF A BELT BREAKS ONCE. Taylor Memorial, 67.

WHY WASN'T IT DONE? Ibid., 66.

UNDERSTAND ENGLISH. C. B. Thompson, *Taylor System*, 135.

DIGESTER FLUID. Ibid.

254 DIFFICULT CLASS OF LABOR. Copley, I, 383.

ABSOLUTELY CERTAIN. FWT to George Hammond, May 18, 1893.

EVERY OPERATION . . . ON PIECEWORK. Ibid.

THESE RATES. "Standing Order Number Twenty," January 3, 1893, Collection.

ARBITRARY. C.A.L. Smith report, July 8, 1893, Collection.

STOVE PIPE HAT AND FROCK COAT. Louise Fragment.

255 WHITE GLOVES AND JACKET. Ibid.

OBLIGED TO INVITE. See notes beginning "Original contract provided . . . ," (op cit.)

MUSICAL EVENINGS. Louise Fragment.

RIDE HORSES. FWT to Caspar Goodrich, December 13, 1892.

ROMANTIC WILDERNESS. "Tributes to Frederick W. Taylor," *Transactions ASME* 37, 1478.

FAUST AT THE METROPOLITAN. Louise Fragment.

FANNON HAD WARNED HIM. William Fannon to S. E. Thompson, December 25, 1895, Catherwood.

PHOTO RECIPIENTS. W. H. Golby to FWT, December 6, 1890.

256 SEE THE HAMMER START. W. H. Colby to FWT, November 2, 1890.

QUITE A CROWD. W. E. Firth to FWT, February 2, 1891.

STARTED IN EARNEST. John Cox to FWT, January 10, 1892.

257 FIFTY CENTS MORE. Joseph Entwistle to FWT, May 15, 1891.

SECRETARY OF WAR. Charles Harrah to FWT, February 18, 1893.

258 WHY DO YOU STAY UP IN MAINE? Axel Petre to FWT, August 14, 1893.

GOODRICH AND HIS CREW DEPARTED. "Sailor on Horseback."

LEFT LONG BEFORE. *Madison Bulletin*, October 8, 1891. Robley Evans, *Sailor's Log*, 243, puts it even before that.

PULP . . . WON PRIZE. Virginia C. Meredith to FWT, May 17, 1895.

259 PLEASED TO HEAR. FWT to George Hammond, May 18, 1893.

ASKED HIM TO STAY ON. Copley, I, 386.

FREE FROM CARE. FWT to John H. King, June 14, 1893.

SAVINGS FOR THE PAST 20 YEARS. Notes beginning "Original contract provided . . . ." See also FWT to George Hammond, May 18, 1893.

BUY BACK THEIR HOUSE. Sales contract between Louise M. S. Taylor and Manufacturing Investment Co., June 27, 1894, Collection.

AFFECTED HIS HEALTH. Fannon, 10. But, Fannon to S. E. Thompson, December 23, 1895, Catherwood: "I think Mr. Taylor will bob up again alright and in the end may be better off."

NERVOUS BREAKDOWNS. Kakar, 130; FWT to Scudder Klyce, December 22, 1911.

260 COMPLETELY BREAK DOWN. Benjamin Frick to FWT, June 23, 1893.

CAUGHT THE MALADY. FWT to Caspar Goodrich, August 20, 1892.

ALL THE COAL, WOOD. FWT to George Hammond, May 18, 1893.

GETTING ON TO PIECE WORK. Ibid.

261 REMAIN IN MADISON. Ibid.

CURIOUS COINCIDENCE. FWT to George Hammond, June 14, 1893.

262 PACK AND UNPACK. Louise Fragment.

TRYING. FWT to Morris Cooke, December 3, 1910.

YANKEE CONTRACTORS. Chordal, 29.

263 POCKET WAS PICKED. Vestpocket.

ILLUSIONS LEFT. Copley, I, 120.

264 PIECE OF WORK. FWT to Chauncey Smith, August 25, 1893.

SIMONDS. See D. Hamilton Hurd, comp., *History of Worcester County, Massachusetts*, Philadelphia. J.W. Lewis, 1889; Doris Kirkpatrick, *The City and the River*, Fitchburg, Mass.: Fitchburg Historical Society, 1971, 300 and 390; William A. Emerson, *Fitchburg, Massachusetts, Past and Present*, Fitchburg: Blanchard & Brown, 1887.

265 HALF A CENTURY. Fitchburg *Sentinel*, February 23, 1888.

COIN WEALTH LIKE A MINT. Ibid.

BALL BEARINGS. George F. Simonds, "Anti-Friction Ball Bearings," *Iron Age*, October 26, 1893; "Making Balls for Bearings," *Machinist*, October 1, 1896.

LICK OBSERVATORY. Testimonial brochure, Collection.

1890s BICYCLE BOOM. Schlereth, 221; Albert A. Pope, "The Bicycle Industry," in Depew, 549. For bicycle's impact on precision manufacturing, see Peter Liebhold, "Bicycle Wheels and Grinding Tools," *Cutting Tool Engineering*, August 1989.

VOLUMINOUS PETTICOATS. Kirkpatrick, *City and the River*, 358.

266 FORGING PATENTS. George F. Simonds to FWT, December 16, 1889, in Wrege & Greenwood, "Early Work at Bethlehem," 104.

SIMONDS STOCK. Chauncey Smith to FWT, October 21, 1889.

COMPANY'S MANAGEMENT HEADACHES. George F. Simonds to FWT, August 20, 1890, quoted in Wrege & Greenwood biography, 73.

BEG LEAVE TO ENCLOSE. FWT to Chauncey Smith, December 1892.

267 MANAGERIAL ACCOUNTING. See H. Thomas Johnson and Robert S. Kaplan, *Relevance Lost: The Rise and Fall of Management Accounting*, Boston: Harvard Business School Press, 1987; For Taylor's role, see Charles D. Wrege, "Nineteenth Century Origins of 'Bookkeeping Under the Taylor System,'" *Proceedings, Academy of Management*, 43rd annual meeting, 1983; Rosita S. Chen and Sheng-Der Pan, "Frederick Winslow Taylor's Contributions to Accounting," *Accounting Historians Journal*, Spring and Fall 1980; King Hathaway, "Accounting as a Tool of Management," *Bulletin*, October 1932 to April 1934.

SOONER KILL HIMSELF. Copley, I, 363.

268 SET ABOUT TO MASTER. FWT to Edward Sawyer, August 4, 1893: "I have spent the

last two weeks in New York studying the system of bookkeeping there"; Morris Cooke, *Stevens Indicator*, November, 1933: Taylor "took six months off to study accounting."
VALUABLE SYSTEM. FWT to Chauncey Smith, August 4, 1893.
BASLEY. Wrege, "Nineteenth Century Origins," 107.
CARNEGIE. Chandler, 268.
RAILROAD ACCOUNTING. Ibid., 465.
ALL BOOK ENTRIES. William Basley to FWT, July 12, 1893.

269 STAMP. *Bulletin*, February 1923, 1.
MODERN INDUSTRIAL ACCOUNTING. *Transactions ASME* 37, 1469.
MISLEADING. FWT to Chauncey Smith, August 4, 1893.
HOW LONG? Edward Sawyer to FWT, August 7, 1893.
ISLE OF SHOALS. FWT to George Hammond, August 9, 1893.
IDLE MOMENTS ROCKING ON THE PIAZZA. Louise Fragment.
BUSY . . . NEAR BOSTON. FWT to George Hammond, August 25, 1893.

270 BELT RECORD. FWT to Joseph King, March 22, 1893.
EMPHATIC GROUND. FWT to John H. Cooper, June 9, 1893.
WISH HE HAD NEVER PRESENTED. S. M. Snow to S. E. Thompson, December 10, 1894, Catherwood.
BASIS FOR ALL SUBSEQUENT STUDIES. "Publisher's Note" to Taylor, "Notes on Belting." See also S. E. Thompson to FWT, December 27, 1895: "Your paper on 'Belting' is widely quoted in the papers, in Kent's Pocket Book and at the [Massachusetts] Institute of Technology."
TREATISE. Taylor, "Notes on Belting," 190.
NO. 23. Ibid., 135.

271 LOSS AND INCONVENIENCE. Ibid., 198.
TIED BY 3¹/₂-INCH SHAFT. Example drawn from sketch in S. E. Thompson's notebook, Catherwood.
8:30 IN THE MORNING. Vestpocket.
GREATEST NAVAL ARSENAL. Charles Cramp, December 21, 1900, quoting 1894 company history, in *Final Report of Industrial Commission*.

272 CRAMP'S. See Charles Morris, *Makers of Philadelphia*, Philadelphia: L. R. Hamersly & Co., 1894, 126–127; Bishop, 65.
ALTER MY JUDGMENT. FWT to Edwin S. Cramp, September 19, 1894, 4.
OCEAN BREEZES. FWT to S. E. Thompson, July 15, 1894.

273 EVERYDAY WORK. FWT to E. S. Cramp, September 27, 1894.
SHROUDED IN SECRECY. Tweedale, *Sheffield Steel*, 67.
FIRST SEEN SELF-HARDENING STEEL. Steel Patent, 2403.
CAREFUL EXPERIMENT. FWT to E. S. Cramp, September 27, 1894.
NEVER A DAY THAT I WAS OVERWORKED. FWT-Hearings, 125.

274 DIRECTION OF THE ARROW. Sketch, Cramp's folder, Collection.
LABELS REMOVED. Steel Patent, 2404.
NORTHERN EXPOSURE. Ibid., 2366.
LAUGHED AT BY THE TOOL DRESSERS. Ibid., 2367.

275 BIG NEWS WAS BURIED. "Report on Speeding Up All of the Lines of Shafting in Your Machine Shop," FWT to Edwin S. Cramp, March 12, 1895.
EXACT WEIGHT. FWT to Edwin S. Cramp, March 11, 1895.
TESTED THE PATIENCE. Copley, I, 439.
SPIRIT UNWOUNDED. Ibid., 444.
TOOLROOM HAD BEEN EXPANDED. Leighton Lee to FWT, August 10, 1898.

276 WORSE THAN USELESS. FWT to Leighton Lee, August 12, 1898.
GEORGE F. SIMONDS HAD DIED. *Transactions, ASME*, XVI, 1189.

CONSOLIDATE THE PROFITS. Draft constitution in Collection.
277 CONSUMPTION OF BALLS. FWT to George Weymouth, April 20, 1895.
INTENSE SUSPICION. Ibid.
OVER-PARTICULAR. E. M. Clarke to Alfred Bowditch, June 24, 1895.
RUSSELL HOUSE. Alfred Bowditch to E. M. Clark, June 24, 1895.
FOUR-DAY GAP. Vestpocket.
278 BREAKFAST AT BALTIMORE. *Transactions ASME*, II, 424; see also "Mechanics—
Introductory," Coleman Sellers, *Journal of the Franklin Institute*, March 1884, 162.
THUNDERBOLTS OF JOVE. *Transactions ASME*, IX, 3.
280 DISCREDITABLE CONTRAST. *Transactions ASME*, IV, 95.
CHEAP LABOR IS NOT NOT ALWAYS PROFITABLE. *Transactions ASME*, VII, 468.
HIGH WAGES . . . A SOLUTION. *Transactions ASME*, VIII, 269–294.
281 HOMESTEAD STRIKE. See William Serrin, *Homestead: The Glory and Tragedy of an
American Steel Town*, New York: Times Books, 1992.
A PERMANENT ANTAGONISM. Taylor, "A Piece-Rate System," 33.
PROMOTES A MOST FRIENDLY FEELING. Ibid., 37.
TOWNE'S GAIN SHARING. *Transactions ASME*, X, 600.
282 HALSEY PREMIUM PLAN. *Transactions ASME*, XII, 755.
KNOW MORE . . . THAN THE MEN THEMSELVES. Drury, 86.
283 EDITH WRIGHT'S MODEL COMMUNITY. "Record of Wrightsville: An Experiment
in the Care of Property," Philadelphia, January 19, 1889. Urban Archives. Temple
University. John Fulton Sutherland, "A City of Homes: Philadelphia Slums and Re-
formers, 1880–1918," Ph.D. dissertation, Temple University, 1973.
FLORENCE KELLEY. See Sklar, Kelley.
284 STRICTEST MORALISTS. Taylor, "A Piece-Rate System," 64.
REMARKABLE THING OF ITS KIND. Ibid., 95.
FULLEST POSSIBLE DETAILS. Ibid., 90.
HARMONIZING OF LABOR AND CAPITAL. Ibid., 100.
SOCIAL SIDE OF THESE QUESTIONS. Ibid., 117.
SURPRISED AND DISAPPOINTED. Ibid., 124.
286 CREST OF THE WAVE. Ibid., 84.
QUITE ASHAMED OF IT. Kempton Taylor, 6.
AMERICAN ECONOMIC ASSOCIATION. F. W. Taussig to FWT, April 27, 1896.
ALTOGETHER SATISFACTORY. *Electrical Review*, August 9, 1895.
287 DO NOT PRETEND. FWT to H. S. Shadbolt, July 3, 1895.
DIRECT EVIDENCE. FWT to Alfred Bowditch, May 25, 1895.
FARM LABORER. FWT to H. S. Shadbolt, July 3, 1895.
INDUSTRIAL ESPIONAGE. See Wrege & Greenwood, "Frederick W. Taylor and
Industrial Espionage: 1895–1897," *Business and Economic History*, second series,
vol. 15, 1986, 183; Vestpocket makes numerous references to Shadbolt and the other
spies.
A LITTLE MONEY. H. A. Willard to FWT, July 3, 1895 (second letter of this date).
288 DARE TO BE VERY BOLD. H. A. Willard to FWT, July 3, 1895 (first letter of this date).
Original spelling and punctuation left intact.
CARLTON. Wrege & Greenwood, "Industrial Espionage," 186.
ADVERTISING. H. S. Shadbolt to FWT, November 13, 1895.
SHORT, THIN MAN. FWT to Pinkerton Detective Agency, October 27, 1896.
HARDENED ME. Newcomb Carlton to FWT, November 22, 1895.
BRITISH PATENT. FWT to Philip M. Justice, May 4, 1897.
EXPERT TESTIMONY. FWT to Coleman Sellers, May 4, 1897.

ENGINEER'S LICENSE. Commonwealth of Massachusetts, Engineer's License, issued August 30, 1897.

289 THRILLING AND AMUSING. Wilfred Lewis to Frances Mitchell, November 25, 1915.
SEND PIECEWORK PAPER TO FOLLOWING. Vestpocket.
PIECE ROAD SYSTEM. N. Miller to FWT, March 17, 1896.
RUNNING AROUND. John A. Markoe to FWT, June 10, 1896.
TWO HUNDRED DOLLARS. FWT to John A. Markoe, June 15, 1896.

290 STARTED RIGHT. A. O. Fox to FWT, August 6, 1895.
STEPPED OFF THE TRAIN. Vestpocket.
A DECIDED ADVANTAGE. FWT to Frank Steele, June 26, 1896. FWT heavily influenced Steele, one of his assistants back at the paper mill. "You taught me more than schools or colleges," Steele wrote him on December 2, 1911. "You taught me things which I little appreciated at the time and came to understand in later years."

291 BUSINESS MATTERS. FWT to S. E. Thompson, November 27, 1895.
SANFORD THOMPSON. See Drury, 136; Urwick, ed. 126; "Copy of application sent to Chas. Warren Hunt," in effect Thompson's resume, 1896, Catherwood.
ALWAYS ON THE LOOKOUT. Taylor Memorial, 66.
MUCH INTERESTED IN YOUR SUCCESS. FWT to S. E. Thompson, August 3, 1893, Catherwood.

292 A LITTLE IN DOUBT. Taylor Memorial, 70.
WROTE MIDVALE. Secretary, Midvale Steel Co., to S. E. Thompson, December 5, 1985, Catherwood.
COORDINATE THEIR TRIPS. FWT to S. E. Thompson, December 7, 1895.
QUIET MANSION. Taylor Memorial, 70.
PRACTICALLY DECIDED THE MATTER. S. E. Thompson to FWT, December 27, 1895. Thompson had apparently sought advice from William A. Fannon. Fannon wrote him (December 23, 1895, Catherwood), speaking well of Taylor and adding, "I hope you will decide wisely in your choice, although I am not familiar with what you have in view or in what line Mr. Taylor is working."
TAYLOR-THOMPSON CONTRACT. Catherwood.

293 HUNT FOR STOP WATCHES. S. E. Thompson to FWT, January 9, 1896, Catherwood.
CHEAP SILVER ONE. FWT to S. E. Thompson, January 13, 1896, Catherwood.
MADE A FIND. S. E. Thompson to FWT, March 6, 1896, Catherwood.
SPECIAL DIAL FACES. FWT to S. E. Thompson, March 25, 1896, Catherwood.
BOSTON PUBLIC LIBRARY. S. E. Thompson to FWT, February 10, 1896, Catherwood.

294 CLAPBOARDING. S. E. Thompson, *Stevens Indicator*, November 1933, 151.
OUT-OF-DOOR WORK. S. E. Thompson to FWT, February 10, 1896, Catherwood.
SEPARATE BOOKS ON EACH. S. E. Thompson to FWT, March 19, 1896, Catherwood.
ALMOST PIONEERS. FWT to S. E. Thompson, February 17, 1896, Catherwood.
CHASE THIS MATTER HOME. FWT to S. E. Thompson, January 27, 1896, Catherwood.
GET A SPRING BALANCE. FWT to S. E. Thompson, February 22, 1896, Catherwood.

295 TWELVE SHOVELFULS PER MINUTE. FWT to S. E. Thompson, February 26, 1896, Catherwood. See also T. Coonahan to FWT, February 20, 1896.
BEST ENDEAVORS. Contract between Thompson and Taylor, Catherwood.
HOLLOW BOOK. S. E. Thompson to FWT, February 21, 1896, Catherwood.
TOO MUCH ATTENTION. S. E. Thompson to FWT, February 29, 1896, Catherwood.
WRITING FOR PAPERS. FWT to S. E. Thompson, March 11, 1896, Catherwood.
VERY GREAT BENEFIT. FWT to S. E. Thompson, March 25, 1896, Catherwood.
DO NOT SPARE EXPENSE. Ibid.
CLEAR BEYOND A QUESTION. FWT to S. E. Thompson, May 6, 1896, Catherwood.

296 I DO NOT EXACTLY LIKE. FWT to S. E. Thompson, January 18, 1897, Catherwood.
JOHNSTOWN FLOOD. See McCullough, *Johnstown Flood.*
TURNED TO MOXHAM. McCullough, *Johnstown Flood*, 190.
NO WORDS CAN DESCRIBE. Tom Johnson, *My Story*, New York: B. W. Huebsch, 1911, 38. For two months after the flood, Johnson ran the town railway free. At least, he jibed his stockholders, they'd eliminated the problem of crooked fare collectors.

297 MASTER OF COST SHEETS. Chandler and Salsbury, 29.
WEAKENED THE COMPANY. Ibid. For more on the company, see Nelson, "Scientific Management in Transition"; Michael Massouh, "Technological and Managerial Innovation: The Johnson Company, 1883–1898," *Business History Review*, Spring 1976, 46; Johnstown *Tribune*, January 21, 1896.
NINE OUT OF TEN. FWT to A. J. Moxham, January 22, 1896.
PRY TAYLOR FREE. A. J. Moxham to FWT, January 24, 1896.
ANKLE DEEP IN MUD. Louise Fragment.
CHEEK AND . . . TACT. FWT to G. F. Steele, June 26, 1896.
THEIR "SHACK." Louise Fragment. See also FWT to Caspar Goodrich, June 3, 1896, and FWT to G. F. Steele, June 26, 1896.

298 AGREEABLE PLACES. Ibid.
TAKEN UP THE PREVIOUS FALL. FWT to Spaulding Bros., July 20, 1896. Copley, I, 453, asserts, wrongly, that Taylor took up the sport on July 4, 1896.
YARDAGE FOR EACH HOLE. A notation in one of the vestpocket notebooks begins, "Links at Johnstown: 1, 699. 2, 569. . . . 18 holes 15,358 = 2.91 miles."
NEW GOLF GEAR. FWT to Spaulding Bros., July 20, 1896.
CAPTIVE BALL. FWT to Caspar Goodrich, June 23, 1896.
STILL HIRING. Johnstown *Tribune*, March 4, 1896.
SECOND SHIFT. Ibid., April 14, 1896.
ASTONISHING EASE. FWT to Frank Steele, October 14, 1896.
WANTS IT RIGHT AWAY. FWT to Caspar Goodrich, June 3, 1896.
MOXHAM'S ROUGH PLAN. A. J. Moxham to FWT, January 29, 1896.
HELTER-SKELTER. FWT to Caspar Goodrich, June 3, 1896.

299 PLANERS WERE IDLE. FWT to Coleman du Pont, April 6, 1896.
HUSTLING PIECE WORK. FWT to Axel Petre, August 8, 1896.
ARMATURE WINDING. FWT to A. O. Fox, October 22, 1896.
NO TALKING. FWT to T. C. du Pont. October 21, 1896.
RATE FIXING. FWT to T. C. du Pont, November 2, 1896.
UNDER THE IMPRESSION. A. J. Moxham to FWT, July 9, 1896.

300 THREE QUARTERS OF A MILLION. Chandler and Salsbury, 31.
CAN YOU NOT ARRANGE? A. J. Moxham to FWT, July 9, 1896.
BARELY MOVING. FWT to G. F. Steele, September 9, 1896.
BILLS. Taylor billed at thirty-five dollars per day plus expenses, Collection.
ENOUGH SAVING. FWT to G. F. Steele, September 9, 1896.
OPPOSED BITTERLY. FWT to G. F. Steele, October 14, 1896.
TRULY "TAYLORIZED" FIRM. Nelson, "Scientific Management in Transition," 472.

301 MOST IMAGINATIVE OF THE . . . FOUNDERS. Chandler, 444.
INTIMATELY ACQUAINTED. Ibid., 445.
BOTH CARNEGIE AND TAYLOR. Chandler and Salsbury, xxi.
SIMONDS HAD BEEN SHUT DOWN. FWT testimonry, Simonds Rolling Machine Company vs. Hathorn Manufacturing Company, Circuit Court of the United States, Boston: Alfred Mudge & Son, 1898, Pleadings and Evidence, vol. 1, 429.
GEORGE WEYMOUTH. *Fitchburg Daily Sentinel*, Souvenir Edition, June 18, 1892.
PREVIOUS SUPERINTENDENT. Nelson, 56.

TURNOVER CHARGE. Alfred Bowditch to FWT, December 11, 1896.

302 PERMANENT PIECE WORK. Taylor, "Permanent Rates," Simonds memo, December 29, 1896, Collection.

28,000. Rates for grinding balls, November 25. Simonds memo, Collection. Whether these rates were merely proposed or actually instituted is not clear.

STUMBLING BLOCK. "Report in Progress Made in Manufacture of the Simonds Rolling Machine Company, date uncertain, but probably 1897, Collection; Sanford E. Thompson, "The Quality of Product in Piece-Work," *Cassier's Magazine* 23, 233; Taylor, "Shop Management," 85–92; Taylor, *Principles*, 86–97. For similar ball inspection problems at another ball maker, see "Making Balls for Bearings," *Machinist*, October 1, 1896, 920: "One glance at this shimmering field of balls in the tray is simply maddening to any but the strongest eyes, and such a serious lot of girl-workers are seldom seen elsewhere."

303 DOING NOTHING. Taylor, "Shop Management," 88.

CUT THE WORKDAY. Taylor, *Principles*, 87. See also *Industrial Relations*, 793: "Without waiting for any system or anything else, I just knew that it was inhuman to work girls 10 hours a day."

NOTED FOR HIS TACT. Taylor, *Principles*, 88.

GO SOMEWHERE ELSE. Taylor, "Principles and Methods of Scientific Management," *Journal of Accountancy*, adapted from address before the Civic Forum, New York, April 28, 1911.

WITH EACH SHORTENING. Taylor, *Principles*, 88.

304 BRUTALLY TREATED. Ibid., 92.

FIRST CIGARETTE BREAK. Mark Seltzer, *Bodies and Machines*, New York: Routledge, 1992, 221.

PERSONAL COEFFICIENT. Taylor, *Principles*, 89. See also Taylor, "Principles and Methods."

MOST TRUSTWORTHY. Taylor, *Principles*, 90. See "The Four-Hour Day is a Long Way Off Yet . . . ," Philadelphia *North American*, July 16, 1911, where FWT is quoted: "A group of philanthropic ladies called on me and told me that my kind, philanthropic soul couldn't be aware of the dire plight of the ninety girls who had been laid off at the bicycle factory. I hastened to give them a list of those poor, persecuted girls." All had jobs, said Taylor, having been "snapped up by the local cotton mills" at higher wages than they'd earned under him.

WEYMOUTH COUP. FWT to J. J. Porter, July 21, 1897.

EVERY FOREMAN. FWT to Charles Humphries, October 27, 1897.

305 SECRET SOCIETY ORGANIZATIONS. Simonds company memo accompanying financial report of September 10, 1898, Collection.

DAMNED FOOL. FWT to Charles Humphries, October 27, 1897.

PAST NINE MONTHS. FWT to A. H. Couden, November 22, 1897.

HONORABLE GENTLEMAN. Charles Harrah to Walter A. Simonds, October 22, 1897.

FOR GOD'S SAKE. Charles Harrah to FWT, October 22, 1897.

306 SUFFICIENTLY WELL. Charles Harrah to FWT, October 28, 1897.

AS GOOD CONDITION. FWT to A. H. Couden, November 22, 1897.

BALL OUTPUT MORE THAN DOUBLE. "Progress Made," 13.

FAMILIAR WITH ALL MY METHODS. FWT to A. H. Couden, November 22, 1897. Gantt became superintendent in July 1897: FWT testimony, Simonds vs. Hathorn, 407.

AGAIN CUT PRICES. FWT to Alfred Jones, June 27, 1898.

PLAYED OUT. Alfred Bowditch to FWT, June 14, 1898.

307 WHARTON. See Yates; B. S. Stephenson, "Eminent Men of the Iron World: Jos. Wharton," *Iron Trade Review*, March 3, 1906.

READ WITH CARE. Joseph Wharton to FWT, April 26, 1895.

ANGRY CONGRESS. Yates, 284.

308 CASE STUDY IN INEFFICIENCY. Nelson, chapter 4; Nelson, "Taylorism at Bethlehem Steel," 488–491; Wrege & Greenwood, "Frederick W. Taylor's Early Work at Bethlehem."

BIG INCESTUOUS FAMILY. Thomas Patrick Vadasz, *The History of an Industrial Community: Bethlehem, Pennsylvania, 1741–1920*, doctoral dissertation, Ann Arbor, Mich.: University Microfilms, 1975, chapter 5; Copley, II, 6; Burton W. Folsom, *Urban Capitalists: Entrepreneurs and City Growth in Pennsylvania's Lackawanna and Lehigh Regions, 1800–1920*, Baltimore: Johns Hopkins University Press, 136–139.

PASSED OVER. Brinley, chapter V.

PASSING AROUND. H.F.J. Porter to FWT, June 30, 1897.

DIRECTED BY OUR PRESIDENT. Russell Davenport to FWT, November 22, 1897.

309 MET WITH WHARTON. FWT to R. W. Davenport, January 4, 1898.

COULD START IN THE SPRING. Ibid.

MORE FULLY. Robert P. Linderman to FWT, January 6, 1898.

MENTAL ABILITY. Charles Harrah to FWT, March 4, 1898.

310 LARGEST BUILDING OF ITS KIND. *Iron Age*, 1891.

311 EVER LIE IDLE. FWT to Robert P. Linderman, August 17, 1898.

FOR ALL ROUGHING CUTS. Ibid.

EXPERIMENTAL LATHE. Steel Patent, 2342; Taylor, "Art of Cutting Metals," II, 58–61.

BY OCTOBER 19. Maunsel White, "Statement," January 5, 1900, Collection; Steel Patent, 2343.

HUMILIATING FAILURE. Steel Patent, 2343; Taylor, "Art of Cutting Metals," I, 260.

312 MAUNSEL WHITE. Chris P. Neck and Arthur G. Bedeian, "Maunsel White III: Louisiana Inventor and Victim of the Matthew Effect," *New Orleans Genesis*, October 1988, 399–404; Sidney White to Charles C. Phelps, October 30, 1912, Catherwood.

EAGLE HOTEL. Sholes's *Directory of the Bethlehems*, 1900–1901, lists White at Eagle Hotel, whose location is shown in 1886 map in *Bethlehem of Pennsylvania: The Golden Years*, publication in Bethlehem public library, n.p., n.d.

POETICAL DREAMER. Taylor, unsigned "Obituary Notice of Mr. Maunsel White," Collection.

HOT BIRD. Maunsel White to Sidney White, November 29, 1909, Catherwood.

PURSUING PLEASURE. Maunsel White to FWT, August 3, 1901.

GAME OF GOLF. FWT to Maunsel White, February 8, 1902.

EUROPEAN TRIP. R. W. Davenport to Hermann Weding, August 27, 1896; and to F.E.D. Ackland, August 28, 1896.

HAMLET . . . FROM MEMORY. Neck and Bedeian, "Maunsel White III," 401.

BRILLIANT AND ENTERTAINING. Taylor, "Obituary Notice."

313 THE HEAT. Misa, 190. See also Maunsel White and F. W. Taylor, "Colors of Heated Steel Corresponding to Different Degrees of Temperatures," *Transactions ASME*, XXI, 1.

PRELIMINARY CANTER. Steel Patent, 2345.

DENOTED L3 AND L4. I've rendered the awkward original (L/ . . . and L/. . . .) into more reader-friendly form.

TWENTY-MINUTE TESTS. Taylor, "Art of Cutting Metals," I, 255.

314 FINISH EXCELLENT, CHIPS BLUE. Wrege & Greenwood, "FWT at Bethlehem, II," 150.

NINE FEET PER MINUTE. Archibald Johnston to Robert Linderman, January 25, 1900, Hagley Museum and Library, 5.

SO EXTRAORDINARY. Steel Patent, 2345.

GREAT IMPROVEMENT COULD BE MADE. Yates, 294.

315 HENRY NOLL. Much of what we know about Noll owes to Wrege and Perroni; see also Robert T. Brown and Charles D. Wrege, "The Search for 'Schmidt,' " *The American Cemetery*, September 1964.

COMMON LABORERS. See Graziosi.

FOUR IN TEN. Montgomery, *House of Labor*, 64.

MUTTERED OATHS. Walter Wyckoff, *The Workers: An Experiment in Reality*, New York: Scribner's, 1897, 47.

316 I WAS HUNGRY. Ibid., 49.

TWELVE DAYS. Mark M. Stolarik, *Growing Up on the South Side: Three Generations of Slovaks in Bethlehem, Pennsylvania, 1880–1976*, Lewisburg: Bucknell University Press, 25–32.

317 MENTALLY SLUGGISH TYPE. Taylor, *Principles*, 46. See also "Report on Henry Knolle of Bethlehem, Pa," submitted by A. B. Wadleigh, January 3, 1914, Collection; A. B. Wadleigh to FWT, January 3, 1914, referring to the assessment of Mr. Yokum, superintendent of Pettinos Bros., Noll's employer.

RESEMBLES . . . THE OX. Ibid., 59.

TROT BACK HOME. Ibid., 43.

SIZE OF A CART-WHEEL. Ibid., 44.

VOLUNTEER FIREMAN. Harold R. Ziegenfuss to Charles D. Wrege, October 1, 1963.

PROVIDE FOR HIM. A. B. Wadleigh to FWT, January 3, 1914.

BEGUN TO BUILD A HOUSE. Taylor, *Principles*, 44.

318 HARD DRINKER. William Crozier to FWT, November 26, 1913; A. B. Wadleigh to FWT, January 3, 1914.

STRIP BEYOND SECOND STREET. Stolarik, *Growing Up*, 23.

CHURCH ALLEY. *Directory of the Three Bethlehems*, J. E. Williams, Bethlehem: 1893.

LAUFER STREET. Sholes's *Directory of the Bethlehems*, 1900–1901.

PIG IRON PRICES. Victor S. Clark, 286, 566; see also *Final Report of Industrial Commission*, 215 (and, in different forms, 1109, 1113).

EIGHTY THOUSAND TONS. Taylor, *Principles*, 42.

319 GILLESPIE. The following account is largely drawn from James Gillespie and H. C. Wolle, "Report on the Establishment of Piecework in Connection with the Loading of Pig Iron, at the Works of the Bethlehem Iron Co., South Bethlehem, Pa," Collection; and Taylor's own various accounts.

DAY'S TONNAGE. Graziosi, 517; Montgomery, *House*, 58.

DAY AND A HALF. FWT, "Boxly Talk," 9: "It was such an important job I took a stop watch and observed myself."

320 EIGHT OR TEN STEPS. Gillespie and Nolle, 5, report that the pile was situated eighteen feet from the car.

STRIKE HAD TO BE AVOIDED. Montgomery, *House*, 93: When, a few years before, the Detroit water board announced plans to pay by the cubic yard instead of the day, five hundred laborers protested and killed the sheriff. Eighteen were killed by police gunfire.

WENT OFF SATISFIED. Yates, 295.

321 CORDON. American Society of Mechanical Engineers, unpublished discussion, June 24, 1903, Collection.

TOOK NOLL OFF TO THE SIDE. Taylor, *Principles*, 44.

322 WALK HIM HOME. American Society of Mechanical Engineers, unpublished discussion, June 24, 1903, Collection.

HAVEN'T BEGUN AT ALL. Ibid.

ELABORATE EXPERIMENTS. See " 'Pig Iron' " Report No. 2 and accompanying piece rates, July 10, 1899, and Report No. 3, July 26, 1899, Collection; "Work Done by Two

Extraordinary Laborers in Carrying Pig Iron," March 1915 (its diagrams are copies of those Barth prepared in late 1899), Catherwood.
323 THREE DECIMAL PLACES. Report No. 3.
PICKED LABORERS. Taylor, *Principles*, 72.
BISHOP'S PALACE. FWT to Goodrich, June 16, 1900, speaks of a coming move to a new house, while FWT to Caspar Goodrich, January 15, 1901, confirms that they moved into it "last spring." Sholes's *Directory of the Bethlehems*, published in September 1900, gives Taylor's address as Delaware Avenue, making this their *second* house in Bethlehem. Meanwhile, Louise Fragment gives the name of the Taylor house in Bethlehem as Bishop's Palace, referring to a time soon after reaching town—*before* the move to Delaware Avenue; a photo of the Taylor house in the possession of Marie Clark Hodges is dated 1899, making it the Bishop's Hostel of Lou's account, and the source of my description.
QUITE A GAY ONE. FWT to Caspar Goodrich, April 3, 1899.
SHORTER HOURS. Copley, II, 15 and 71–72. See also FWT to G. F. Steele, March 11, 1901.
GABBED WITH FRIENDS. Copley, II, 71.
MANCHESTER. See Edwin L. Bigelow and Nancy H. Otis, *Manchester, Vermont: A Pleasant Land Among the Mountains*, Town of Manchester, 1961.
324 EKWANOK. See *A History of Ekwanok: Commemorating its 75th Year*, Manchester-in-the-Mountains: Ekwanok Country Club, 1974.
FOURTH OF JULY PHOTO. Marie Clark Hodges.
EMILY RICHARDS. Robert Taylor, 1983, 5.
CHANGE OF CHARACTER. FWT to Clem Rutter, March 27, 1901.
CARRIAGE. FWT to Caspar Goodrich, July 6, 1900; letters between FWT and Collings Carriage Co., January through May 1900.
PURE INVENTION. Tinsley Jeter, "Fountain Hill's History," *Daily Times* Sesquicentennial Industrial Edition, June 1892, 8.
DELAWARE AVENUE HOMES. Sholes's *Directory of the Bethlehems*, 1900–1901.
325 GOOD RETURN. G. F. Steele to FWT, June 15, 1899.
ALSO DONE WELL. FWT to G. F. Steele, June 19, 1899.
SCIENCE OF METALLURGY. Colvin, 43.
326 GAS HEATED MUFFLES. Taylor, "Art of Cutting Metals," II, 200.
PARTLY IN WATER. Ibid., 201.
GLOWING COKE FIRE. *Journal of the Franklin Institute*, February 1903, 127.
DWIGHT MERRICK. Hearings, 536–537. See also Dwight Merrick to Kempton Taylor, August 16, 1915.
327 CIGARETTES. Tweedale, *Sheffield Steel*, 217, n. 20.
HIGH-SPEED STEEL PATENTS. U.S. Patents 668,269 and 668,270.
HALF AGAIN HIGHER. Tweedale, *Sheffield Steel*, 66.
328 ANY REASONABLE FEE. Taylor, *Principles*, 110.
CARL BARTH. See Manning; Bjork; Hearings, 1539. See also Gilson, 125: "I can see Carl Barth now, impatient, emitting richly profane phrases directed at charlatans.... He was resentful of any who would bring the name of Frederick Taylor or the Taylor Society into disrepute."
SNAPPING BLUE EYES. Manning, 44.
RATHER SEE THEM DROWNED. *Industrial Relations*, 893.
BY THE ALMIGHTY. Ibid., 888.
PRETTY NEARLY SMOTHERED. Ibid., 886.
LEWIS RECOMMENDED HIM. Carl Barth to FWT, August 7, 1898.
330 AN OPPORTUNITY HAS COME UP. Copley, II, 25.

SLIGHTEST PERTURBANCE. *Transactions ASME* 37, 1474.

TWENTY-FIVE HUNDRED DOLLARS A YEAR. Barth earned $208.34 a month, according to material deposited in Collection by Charles D. Wrege in 1966: "Data in Davenport File from H. L. Gantt on persons working with Taylor at B[ethlehem] S[teel], September 8, 1899."

INTENSE DELIGHT. *Transactions ASME* 37, 1473.

BARTH SLIDE RULE. See U. S. Patent No. 753,840, March 8, 1904; Carl G. Barth, "Betterment of Machine-Tool Operations by Scientific Metal Cutting," *Engineering Magazine* 42, 586; Taylor, *Principles*, 111; Taylor, "Art of Cutting Metals," II, 246; FWT-Hearings, 100.

331 SUPERSEDING "RULE OF THUMB." Taylor, "Art of Cutting Metals," I, 252.

EVERY DARNED THING. Manning, 48.

WORK OUT THE LAW. Taylor, "Boxly Talk," 29. See also Taylor, *Principles*, 55–58.

332 SO INCONSISTENT. Taylor, "Boxly Talk," 29, copy annotated by Carl Barth, Baker Library, Harvard University.

LAW OF HEAVY LABORING. See also Taylor, *Principles*, 57; Taylor, "Boxly Talk," 31.

SHOVELING IS A GREAT SCIENCE. FWT-Hearings, 50.

333 PILE OF ORE FROM MESABI. *Industrial Relations*, 777; Taylor, "Boxly Talk," 35; FWT-Hearings, 50–65.

YOUR FIGURES. FWT to S. E. Thompson, February 15, 1896.

334 ALMOST CAME TO BLOWS. Taylor, "Boxly Talk," 38.

COST . . . HALVED. FWT-Hearings, 65.

LIKE PLAYING A GAME OF CHESS. Ibid., 57.

335 RECAP PROGRESS. Archibald Johnston to Robert Lieberman, January 25, 1900, Hagley Museum and Library.

NINETY REVOLUTIONS PER MINUTE TO TWO HUNDRED FIFTY. FWT to William A. Murray, February 21, 1900.

MADE IT FASTER. Steel Patent, 2349.

GIVING AN EXHIBITION. Maunsel White to Sidney White, November 29, 1899, Catherwood.

336 ALL PARTS OF THE UNITED STATES. Steel Patent, 2349.

MAN BY THE LATHE. Ibid., 2445.

DIDN'T BELIEVE IT. Bethlehem Steel Company vs. Niles-Bement-Pond Company, United States Circuit Court, District of New Jersey, Brief of Complainant, 26.

VENERABLE FIRM. Correspondence between FWT and William Sellers, January 18–22, 1900; Archibald Johnston to Robert Linderman, January 25, 1900, Hagley Museum and Library, 10.

THOUGHT THAT FIFTY THOUSAND DOLLARS WOULD DO IT. Ibid.

ENTIRELY SUCCESSFUL. FWT to Goodrich, June 16, 1900.

337 AFTERTHOUGHT. *Machinist*, July 5, 1900.

LOADED . . . ONTO THREE FREIGHT CARS. Ibid. See also *Machinist*, May 10, 1900.

PART V

HOUSE ON THE HILL

341 AMERICAN MACHINE TOOL. *Report of the Commissioner General*, III, 122.

NEW ENGLAND TOOL BUILDER. *Machinist*, May 10, 1900.

SO SOME AMERICANS GRUMBLED. *Iron Age*, July 12, 1900.

EXPOSITION MAP. The Guide-Boussole series of maps can be seen at the Bibliothèque Historique de la Ville de Paris.

VINCENNES ANNEX. Edmund Mitchell, "The Paris Exposition as a Mechanical Achievment," *Engineering Magazine*, 1900, 399–410.

DESERT OF VINCENNES. See Mandell, 63: "The atmosphere in Vincennes was probably similar to that of the more bucolic parts of a great Middle Western state fair."

FORLORN APPEARANCE. *Iron Age*, July 12, 1900.

CURIOSITY SEEKERS ELSEWHERE. *Iron Age*, April 19, 1900, 2.

342 TYPICAL AMERICAN MACHINE SHOP. *Iron Age*, December 14, 1899, 12, and April 19, 1900, 2.

SPACE-HUNGRY OUTSIDERS. *Report of the Commissioner General*, III, 130.

ERECTED ITS STEEL SHELL. *Iron Age*, July 12, 1900, 8. But see *Report of the Commissioner General*, III, 134–135, which implies twelve days.

RISE IN PRICE OF IRON. *Report of the Commissioner General*, III, 127.

DEAFENING RACKET. *Machinist*, July 5, 1900

LAYOUT OF MACHINERY BUILDING. *Report of the Commissioner General*, III, 130.

PICKED MERRICK. Dwight Merrick to Kempton Taylor, August 16, 1915.

GREAT HORROR. Taylor, "Success," 7.

343 TEN-FOOT-LONG CYLINDER. *The Engineer*, September 7, 1900.

BETHLEHEM EXHIBIT. Description culled from photo, Collection; map in *Report of the Commissioner General*.

JAMMED WITH PEOPLE. Steel Patent, 2350.

IRON AND STEEL INSTITUTE. *Engineering*, September 28, 1900.

HAMMER BLOWS. *The Engineer*, September 7, 1900.

NEWS SPREAD RAPIDLY. A. Garanger, "Au sujet de l'invention de l'acier rapide," *Documents pour l'Histoire des Techniques*, Cahier No. 6, Paris: Centre de documentation d'histoire des techniques (special issue of *Revue d'Histoire des Sciences*, XX [2; 1967]).

344 LOOK TO HIS LAURELS. Steel Patent, 752.

VICKERS AND LOEWE. Steel Patent, 2351.

REVOLUTION IN MY LIFE. *Transactions ASME*, XXV, 680.

YOU KEEP QUIET. Sheffield City Archives, Ref. Os. 103, where the other British responses may also be found.

345 EVIDENCE OF OUR EYES. Copley, II, 116.

RIOT OF COLOR. *Iron Age*, April 5, 1900.

AMBITIOUS INTERNATIONAL GATHERING. Mandell, xi.

DYNAMO. Adams, *The Education of Henry Adams*, chapter 25.

EVOLUTION OF WORK TOWARDS HAPPINESS. Mandell, 60.

STILL HAD FAITH. Ibid., xi.

346 BANAL ORNAMENTATION. Ibid., 72.

PARIS EXPOSITION "SHOW." Bethlehem Steel Company vs. Niles-Bement-Pond Company, United State Circuit Court, District of New Jersey, Brief for Defendant, 729.

60 FEET FROM THE LIGHT. Steel Patent, 2069.

NICETIES OF THEATRICAL EFECT. Bethlehem Steel Company vs. Niles-Bement-Pond Company, Brief for Defendant, 731.

A SPECTACLE. Pouget, 9–13. A similar flavor runs through the account in Fred M. Osborn, *The Story of the Mushets*, London: Thomas Nelson & Sons, 102: "To demonstrate their claims an exhibit was staged in the Engineering Section of the Paris Exhibition of 1900. . . . The show was wonderful, but every condition was made favourable, the lathe perfect, the tool post like a rock, the steel machined very 'soft.' "

MAUNSEL HOYT. *Report of the Commissioner General*, III, 154.

347 MAPPED OUT. Louise Fragment.

THREE WEEKS IN PARIS. Steel Patent, 2350.

SILVER MEDAL. Hayward, 10.

CASABLANCA. Louise Fragment. See "Casablanca," *Poetical Works of Mrs. Felicia Hemans*, Philadelphia: Grigg & Elliot, 1845. The poem was inspired by the Battle of the Nile in 1798.

348 SLOW PROGRESS. Report No. 9, February 27, 1899.

DRAMATICALLY REDUCED. FWT to Robert P. Linderman, May 29, 1899.

THREE MONTHS MORE. FWT to Joseph Welden, January 2, 1901.

INTERFERES CONSIDERABLY. Robert P. Linderman to FWT, February 27, 1900. See also Steel Patent, 2353.

349 CURIOUS PSYCHOLOGICAL FACT. FWT to Linderman, March (no date on typescript) 1901.

OVERWORKED MY NERVES. FWT to Frank Steele, March 11, 1901.

I MUST CONFESS. Steel Patent, 2369.

DEGREE OF PERFECTION. Gantt, *Work, Wages, and Profit*, 106.

PURELY BRAIN WORK. Taylor, "Shop Management," 110.

350 PENMANSHIP REQUIRED. Standing Order No. 27, in Taylor Memorabilia, Book 8. Taylor had done much the same at Simonds; see "Directions for Issuing, Returning and Entering Time Notes," Simonds Rolling Machine Co., Collection.

OCULISTS. Taylor Memorabilia, Book 8, introductory page.

HIGHEST SPEED PRACTICABLE. Report No. 10, "Progress Made in No. 2 Machine Shop and Further Improvements Needed," FWT to Robert P. Linderman, May 29, 1899.

STANDING ORDER NO. 55. Collection. In FWT to Robert P. Linderman, May 29, 1899, Taylor says such a system "is now being inaugurated."

200 YOUNG MEN. *Transactions ASME*, XXI, 647. See also Richard M. Rupley, ed., "Taylor's Notes for a Talk on Management He Gave to the Leading Officials of the Bethlehem Steel Co. in the Fall of 1899," Collection: "It is impossible to obtain, for any sum of money, enough qualified foremen and superintendents who are capable of performing all the functions demanded of them."

351 MEN . . . OF SMALLER CALIBER. Taylor, "Shop Management," 105.

SUPERVISORS AND FOREMEN. Nelson, "Taylorism and the Workers at Bethlehem Steel, 1898–1901," 491.

SPUR OF THE MOMENT. Gantt, "Bonus System," 342.

SHAPE "PVM." Ibid., 349, for this example.

ELEMENTARY TIME STUDIES. See Carl Barth, "Inception," where he states unequivocally of Bethlehem: "No Time Studies."

FIVE YEARS PRECEDING. Gantt, *Work, Wages, and Profits*, 106. See also Gantt, "Bonus System," 359.

352 MORE OR LESS PLAUSIBLE EXCUSE. Gantt, "Bonus System," 351.

"SPEEDY" TAYLOR. *Bethlehem Globe*, August 19. Year unknown, but almost certainly 1899 or 1900.

THREATENED TO QUIT. Copley, II, 79.

WAIT FOR PERFECTION. Gantt, *Work, Wages, and Profits*, 107.

353 DREAMING. R. J. Snyder to E. P. Earle, May 13, 1901.

624,000 POUNDS. Report by H. L. Gantt, "Task Work with a Premium," May 13, 1901, Collection.

MINIMIZING THE DIFFERENCES. Taylor, "Shop Management," 77.

TEDIOUS OPERATION. Gantt, "Bonus System," 346.

DELICATE PERIOD OF TRANSITION. Taylor, "Shop Management," 77.

WENT THROUGH . . . SHOPS. Yates, 297.

354 SWINGING A GOLF CLUB. Copley, II, 47.

TAUNT HIM INTO RESIGNING. Ibid.

OUT OF MY WAY. Spencer Klaw, "Frederick Winslow Taylor: The Messiah of Time and Motion," *American Heritage*, 1979, 30.

ANTAGONISTIC METHODS. Archibald Johnston memorandum, November 18, 1909, Hagley Museum and Library.

STOPPED WORK. Copley, II, 144–145; FWT to Robert P. Linderman, December 21, 1898, with note of August 2, 1899, appended, Collection.

INTENSITY ALMOST PATHOLOGICAL. Copley, II, 148.

355 TWICE THAT MONTH. Yates, 297.

CONTINUAL APPEALS. FWT to Joseph Wharton, April 4, 1901.

CARRY OUT ALL ORDERS. FWT to Robert Linderman, dated April 4, 1901—but which Yates, 297, argues went to Linderman ten days later and so did not influence Linderman's decision.

BEG TO ADVISE. Robert Linderman to FWT, April 17, 1901.

OUT WENT. Archibald Johnston memo.

ACHIEVED LITTLE. Archibald Johnston to H. L. Gantt, November 27, 1901.

356 ON THE PAYROLLS. FWT to William Crozier, April 16, 1910. See also Hearings, 1587, William D. Hemmerly testimony.

CONSIDERABLE GOOD. Archibald Johnston memo.

GANTT DELIVERED HIS PAPER. Gantt, "Bonus System."

HYPNOTIST. *Machinist,* January 2, 1902.

AUTOMATON. Ibid., January 16, 1902.

357 SIGNED HIMSELF SPHINX. Ibid., February 13, 1902.

SYSTEM . . . GASPING. Ibid., March 20, 1902.

358 MY WORD. FWT to Robert J. Clegg, March 27, 1902.

359 SAVANNAH TRAGEDY. *Savannah Morning News,* February 28, 1901; *Savannah Evening Press,* February 28 and March 1, 1901; Butscher, chapters 1 and 2.

ACT OF SCREAMING. Quoted in Butscher, 45.

360 FRIGHTFUL HERITAGE. *Savannah Evening Press,* March 1, 1901.

NEVER GOTTEN OVER IT. Butscher, 52.

361 DAUGHTER, LOUISE. For genealogy, see Robert Taylor to J. Myron Johnson, November 1, 1979, and November 3, 1982, Myron Johnson papers.

BOX OF LEAD SOLDIERS. Robert Taylor, 1976, II-3.

HOMAGE TO . . . BATTLE GRIT. Louise Fragment: "His real name was Herr Paul Kruger on account of his successful hunting and fighting accomplishments."

362 COMING TO THE END. Robert Taylor, 1976, II-3.

FLAT TOP COAL. FWT to Caspar Goodrich, January 15, 1901. See also Robert Taylor, 1976, VIII-6, and Robert Taylor, 1979, 4.

GREENE HOLDINGS. FWT to Ernest Wright, November 16, 1901.

TWO LITTLE CHILDREN. Ibid.

HE REALIZED. Robert Taylor, 1976, II, 4. In Lorenz, 50, Robert is quoted as saying that Conrad "chose not to join us."

CRUEL INSISTENCE. Butscher, 50, 333.

NERVOUS, IRRITABLE CHILD. Kempton Taylor, 1.

363 FEWER THAN A DOZEN. Butscher, 333. See also Robert Taylor to Myron Johnson, November 1, 1979, Myron Johnson Papers.

GAVE CONRAD HELL. Butscher, 66; Lorenz, 51.

BIG RED SIGN. Robert Taylor, 1976, II-4.

LAVISH CHRISTMAS. Kempton Taylor, 1.

RED GATE. Photo in Collection. See also Robert Taylor, 1976, III-1.

CHILDREN OF COACHMEN. Kempton Taylor, 1.

MORE STEAM. Robert Taylor to Frank van Rensselaer Phelps, April 2, 1984, Myron Johnson papers.

364 SIT THERE AND LOOK AT US. Robert Taylor, 1983, 15.

ELATED. Robert Taylor, 1976, III-12.

COLLEGIATE SWIMMERS. Robert Taylor to Frank van Rensselaer Phelps, April 2, 1984, Myron Johnson papers.

VEHEMENCE OF HIS NATURE. Photo in Collection.

CRAWLED IN BED BETWEEN THEM. Robert Taylor, 1976, III-4.

365 RESENTFULNESS ON HER PART. Ibid., III-7.

KIND OF SCARY. Interview with Frank Wallace, Jr.

PRONUNCIATORY OFFENSE. Kempton Taylor, 1.

GRUBBY BOY. Robert Taylor, 1976, III-4.

FATHER AND MOTHER TO US. Robert Taylor, 1976, III-14.

SEAL THEM SHUT. Ibid., III-16.

LUCKY TO BE ADOPTED. Robert Taylor to Bayard Clark, June 26, 1983, Myron Johnson papers.

RUNTS. Kempton Taylor, 2.

366 WEEDY-WEED. Kempton Taylor, ibid.

MEN'S CLUB. Oscar B. Hawes to Frank Copley, n. d.

SOAKED UNTIL MARSHY. Taylor Memorial, 89.

DESERTED PLACE. Louise Fragment. Lou's recollections were a little off; they had purchased the eleven-acre spread before moving to Red Gate. See FWT to G. F. Steele, November 19, 1901.

CHESTNUT HILL. See David R. Contosta, *Suburb in the City: Chestnut Hill, Philadelphia, 1850–1990*, Columbus, Ohio: Ohio State University Press, 1992; Willard S. Detweiler, *Chestnut Hill: An Architectural History*, Philadelphia: Chestnut Hill Historical Society, 1969.

367 HIGH STOOLS. Louise Fragment.

INCONVENIENT HILLOCK. Claude H. Miller, "Moving a Century-Old Boxwood Hedge," *Country Life in America*, August 1909; "The Four-Hour Day is a Long Way Off Yet . . ." Philadelphia *North American*, July 16, 1911.

368 WORKING HORSEFLESH. Ibid.

RENEWED LIFE. Louise Fragment.

TOURING UNDERGROUND TUNNELS. FWT to Ernest N. Wright, January 10, 1903.

ENDURANCE AND STRENGTH. Ibid., January 12, 1903.

BURIED IN THE WORK. Ibid., April 23, 1903.

369 SARATOGA. See George Waller, *Saratoga: Saga of an Impious Era*, Englewood Cliffs, New Jersey: Prentice-Hall, 1966.

UNITED STATES HOTEL. Waller, *Saratoga*, 160–161, 171; Leslie Dorsey and Janice Devine, *Fare Thee Well: A Backward Look at Two Centuries of Historic American Hostelries, Fashionable Spas & Seaside Resorts*, New York: Crown Publishers.

370 EPOCH-MAKING DOCUMENT. Dexter S. Kimball, "The Significance of the CIOS Gold Medal," accompanying presentation of medal of the Comite International de l'Organisation Scientifique to Harry Arthur Hopf, April 11, 1940, Collection.

KEY DOCUMENTS. Banta, 93.

FRONT PAGE. *Daily Saratogian*, June 24, 1903.

ONLY IN EMPHASIS. Harlow Person, "The Early Steps of Taylor's Technical Advance," *Bulletin*, October 1920, 197.

SARATOGA PAPER. *Transactions ASME*, XXIV, 1337–1456. But page numbers following refer to "Shop Management," in *Scientific Management*. See Bibliography.

371 RECEIVE THE ATTENTION. Taylor, "Shop Management," 58.

CAN'T WRITE FOR NUTS. L. Urwick quoted in Bedeian, "Kismet!: A Tale of Management," see note on p. 576 of this book, BATTLE-SCARRED CHATEAU.
WRETCHEDLY ORGANIZED. Nelson, 116–119; Wrege & Greenwood biography, 172–175; Wrege & Greenwood, "Discovering Some of the Roots of Taylor's Shop Management."
372 MEN ACQUIESCE. Taylor, "Shop Management," 132.
PLACE OF EFFICIENCY. Ibid., 133.
PROMPTLY OBEY INSTRUCTIONS. Ibid., 139.
373 DIVIDENDS TO ITS OWNERS. Ibid., 143.
POSSIBILITIES OF THE ENGLISH LANGUAGE. Ibid., 196.
ABSOLUTE TRUTH. *Machinist*, July 2, 1903, 953.
ALLAY THE SUSPICIONS. Taylor, "Shop Management," 137.
374 CHEERFUL DISPOSITIONS. Ibid., 142.
IMPORTANT PASSAGES. Quoted in Quigel, Jr., 105.
MOST IMPORTANT CONTRIBUTION. *Transactions ASME*, XXIV, 1463. See also H. K. Hathaway, *Journal of the Efficiency Society*, April 1915, 7.
BIBLE. Morris Cooke to Margaret Ellen Hawley, February 17, 1927, Gilbreth Archive.
WORK OF GENIUS. Frank B. Gilbreth, Jr., 114; Yost, 155.
375 JAMES MAPES DODGE. See George P. Torrence, *James Mapes Dodge (1852–1915): Mechanical Engineer, Inventor, Pioneer in Industry*, New York: Newcomen Society in North America, 1950.
GREATEST STORY TELLER. Ibid., 14.
LINK-BELT. See *Modern Methods*, Book No. 37, Philadelphia: Link-Belt Engineering Co., 1904; L. P. Alford, "Scientific Management in Use," *Machinist*, April 4, 1912, 548; "Methods of Management That Made Money," *Engineering Digest*, January 1911, 21; Margaret Dunning Day, "Charles Day: A Memory," 1934, Catherwood.
FROM THAT MOMENT ONWARD. *Transactions ASME* 27, 721.
376 INSTANT FAILURE. Ibid.
CALLING FOR MORE. Ibid., 722.
NERVOUS STRAIN. (Philadelphia) *City Club Bulletin*, January 18, 1911, 24.
377 BASED . . . ON GEOMETRIC SERIES. Manning, 91.
RIGID AND INFLEXIBLE. FWT to James Dodge, October 23, 1905.
LAST PART OF MY APPRENTICESHIP. Manning, 36.
DID NOT VISIT US. Hearings, 1545.
378 BREAKING HIS NECK. FWT to S. E. Thompson, March 4, 1904, Catherwood.
BLESSED RELEASE. Ernest Wright to FWT, March 14, 1904.
NEW HOUSE. FWT to S. E. Thompson, May 16, 1904.
TANGLE OF BOX. Claude H. Miller, "Moving a Century-Old Boxwood Hedge"; Copley, II, 190–196.
379 VISITED MT. VERNON. Louise Fragment.
DOWN IN A TRENCH. Kempton Taylor, 3.
BOXLY HOUSE. See Copley, II, 186–201; John Nartowicz, *Nite Beat*, Rutgers University, November 1978; Louise Fragement; blueprints, Collection.
380 MAGIC CARPET. Louise Fragment.
LOW SIDE. Robert Taylor, 1979, 1.
INCLEMENT DAYS. Kempton Taylor, 3.
SUCH A SNOB. FWT to Kempton and Robert, March 3, 1909.
DRAWN UP A NEW WILL. Robert Taylor to his grandson Gilbreth (Gilbey) Taylor Brown, about January 1983, Myron Johnson papers.
381 CHECK THAT LARGE. Robert Taylor, comments on paper by Myron Johnson, Myron Johnson papers.

TASTEFULLY PRINTED LABEL. Brearley, *Steel-Makers*, 121–123.

TWELVE HUNDRED DOLLARS A TON. "Memoranda re Taylor-White Tool Steel," August 6, 1907, Hagley Museum and Library, 7, refers to "present selling price of sixty cents per pound."

TOTAL AMERICAN CONSUMPTION. Ibid., 1.

382 WAYS A LITTLE DIFFERENT. *Rapports du Jury International. Paris: Imprimerie Nationale*, 1903, 210.

A WHOLE FACTORY. Interview, Ulrich Wengenroth.

SUITABLE FOR HIGH SPEED STEEL. Quoted by Geoffrey Tweedale in letter to the author.

DOWN TO THE FLOOR. Guy Hubbard, "Metal Working Plants," *Mechanical Engineering*, April 1930, 411, quoted in Rosenberg, 44.

383 EXHILARATING IN ITS EFFECTS. Quoted in Thomas Misa, "Science, Technology and Industrial Structure: Steelmaking in America, 1870–1925," Ph. D. thesis, University of Pennsylvania, 1987, 182.

INTENSIFIED PRODUCTION. Charles Day, "The Taylor-White Process of Treating Tool Steel, And Its Influence on the Mechanic Arts," *Journal of the Franklin Institute*, September 1901.

SHEATHED IN IRON SHEETS. Carroll D. Wright, 111.

HABIT OF THOUGHT. Wilfred Lewis, "An Object Lesson in Efficiency," in C. B. Thompson, ed., 232.

384 BIOGRAPHY IN VERSE. Collection.

CHEST GOT LARGER. *Industrial Relations*, 787.

385 REFORMATION. *Bulletin*, February 1925.

MORRIS LLEWELLYN COOKE. See Trombley; Christie; Layton, "Revolt," chapter 7.

CHEWED UP. "Extract from a letter from John D. Morris," included in resume of Morris Cooke, about 1905, Catherwood.

GRIPPED HIS HAND WARMLY. Trombley, 7.

HONEY TO A BEE. Ibid., 8.

FREE FROM HARASSING DETAILS. Dartmouth, 374.

386 PERSONAL FRIENDS. Littauer, 11.

RIGHTFUL PLACE. *Transactions ASME* 27, 310.

RECEIVE NO FAVORS. Taylor, "A Comparison," 7.

ORNAMENTAL WAY. Steel Patent, 2341.

387 ALL MY WORKING TIME. FWT to Sanford Thompson, June 14, 1906, Catherwood.

FOUR SOLID HOURS. FWT to Ernest Wright, July 20, 1906, postscript.

PLENTY OF TIME. FWT to Sanford Thompson, August 23, 1906.

METAL-CUTTING PAPER TITLE. *Bulletin*, April 1919, 4.

HUGE SLIDE RULE. Robert Taylor, 1976, III-3; Kempton Taylor, 5.

ATE UP ALL THE SAVINGS. Sinclair, *Centennial History*, 92.

388 SPENT UPON THIS WORK. Taylor, "Art of Cutting Metals," I, 247.

TIGHTER WITH HIS TEETH. Ibid., 246.

OUR WHOLE TASK SYSTEM. Ibid., 263.

MASTERPIECE. Ibid., 267.

SERVICE . . . TO MANKIND. *Iron Trade Review*, April 25, 1907.

SATISFACTION. FWT to William Fannon, December 20, 1906.

GREAT HONORS. John Griffith to FWT, December 31, 1906.

389 AVE! IMPERATORE! Caspar Goodrich to FWT, December 16, 1906.

A BIGGER MAN. Ernest Wright to FWT, June 30, 1907.

UNFIT FOR WORK. FWT to Ernest Wright, July 8, 1907.

MASSACHUSETTS INSTITUTE OF TECHNOLOGY. Wilfred Lewis to Henry Towne,

November 27, 1915: "I know also . . . that Taylor was asked at one time to accept the presidency of the M.I.T."
PERMANENT BENEFIT. FWT to Ernest Wright, July 8, 1907.
A PHILANTHROPIST? Steel Patent, 2401.
390 MANY WERE THE MORNINGS. Louise Fragment.
POINT A WAY. Taylor, "Boxly Talk," 1.
391 COMPANY ASSEMBLED. Lillian M. Gilbreth, 34.
CLOSE MY EYES. Lillian Gilbreth to Dean F. de R. Furman, November 23, 1933.
392 WIRY FELLOW. American Society of Mechanical Engineers, unpublished discussion, June 24, 1903, Collection.
STUDIES. Taylor, "Boxly Talk," 10; Taylor, *Principles*, 43.
AS TAYLOR TOLD THE STORY. Wrege & Greenwood, "Frederick W. Taylor's Early Work at Bethlehem Steel," 124, picture the story as "completely fictional," Morris Cooke and an editor writing it in 1909. But plainly, Taylor told the story first, at Boxly, in 1907; and it was the Boxly talk from which Cooke worked.
WOULD GO TO A WORKMAN. Taylor, "Boxly Talk," 10.
393 LET EVERY ONE OF THEM GO. Ibid., 22.
GET THE CREDIT. Ibid., 23.
394 THOROUGHLY ASTOUNDED. Ibid., 42.
DOUBLE THE OUTPUT. Ibid., 47.
395 TABOR. Wilfred Lewis, "Object Lesson."
NOTICE WAS POSTED. Connelly reminiscence, April 18, 1915, in Kempton P. A. Taylor, "Some Aspects of Scientific Management," Haverford College paper, May 15, 1915, Collection.
LOST IN ASTONISHMENT. Wilfred Lewis, "Object Lesson," 234.
397 DISCREPANCIES. See Wrege & Perroni.
PICKED OUT. Taylor, *Principles*, 43, and "Shop Management," 50.
LAMBASTED BY THE NEWSPAPERS. Taylor, "Boxly Talk," 14. But see Wrege & Greenwood, "Frederick W. Taylor's Early Work at Bethlehem Steel," 127.
WORST DISTORTIONS. Taylor, "Boxly Talk," copy annotated by Carl Barth, Baker Library, Harvard University.
398 DIRTY GOLF SHOES. Robert Taylor, 1976, III-21; Louise Fragment.
OWN AMUSEMENT. FWT to Scudder Klyce, quoted in Copley, II, 433.
RULERS OF OUR CITY. See also Revell, 56: Taylor saw himself "as a law-giver, or to use Daniel Bell's apt characterization, as a philosopher king."
WROTE TO CONVINCE. Mariann Jelinek, *Business History Review*, 1981, 429.
399 PIGEONS SWOOPED DOWN. Trombley, 10.
GRIFFITH REMARRIED. FWT to John R. Griffith, April 15, 1899. (See also note on p. 589 of this book, JOHN R. GRIFFITH.)
400 KIND OF YOU. John R. Griffith to FWT, December 8, 1902.
GET $2000.00. John R. Griffith to FWT, November 21, 1902.
SEE HIS PIGEONS. John R. Griffith to FWT, August 11, 1904.
401 OBLIGED TO MINGLE. FWT to Cooke, December 2, 1910.
SEVENTEEN THOUSAND DOLLARS. Copley, II, 195.
FABULOUS SUMS. *Transactions ASME* 37, 1477.
402 NEARLY AS BUSY. FWT to Maunsel White, April 9, 1907.
LE CHATELIER. See Urwick & Brech, chapter 9; Urwick, ed., 32; Humphreys, 49.
403 MAINTAIN SOCIAL STABILITY. Humphreys, 52.
BETTER UNDERSTANDING. "Frederick W. Taylor to Henri Le Chatelier," *Bulletin*, October 1928, 206.
CARELESSNESS OF A WORKMAN. Taylor Memorial, 18.

EXTRAORDINARY IMPORTANCE. "Frederick W. Taylor to Henri Le Chatelier," *Bulletin*, October 1928, 206.
FELT MYSELF OBLIGED. Taylor Memorial, 19.
404 FLATTERING. FWT to Maunsel White, September 10, 1907.
TRIAL APPLICATION. Georges de Ram, "Quelques Notes sur un Essai d'Application du Système Taylor dans un Grand Atelier de Mecanique Français," *Revue de Metallurgie*, September 1909, 929.
RARELY FURNISHES. Ibid., 932.
GOOD SHOWING. FWT to Barth, September 20, 1909.
TRANSLATE IT INTO SWEDISH. Nils Runeby, "Americanism, Taylorism and Social Integration," *Scandinavian Journal of History* 3, 21–46, 1978.
405 LANDMARK. G. Schlesinger, Lecture to the Verein Deutscher Ingenieure, Cologne, April 8, 1914. Quoted in F. Koenigsberger, "Production," chapter 43 of Trevor I. Williams, ed., *A History of Technology*, vol. VI, Oxford: Clarendon Press, 1978.
AGHAST, EVEN DISBELIEVING. Geoffrey Tweedale, quoting from article in press, letter to the author.
REGAINED MUCH OF THE MARKET. See Geoffrey Tweedale, *Sheffield Steel*, chapter 5, and *Steel City*, 113–119.
MARSHALED ITS EVIDENCE. Geoffrey Tweedale, letter to the author.
SUIT . . . IS TO BEGIN. Maunsel White to FWT, August 29, 1905.
406 LITTLE CONFIDENCE. FWT to Ernest Wright, March 29, 1900.
MEMORY . . . GROWN. Steel Patent, 168.
ARE YOU NOT? Ibid., 171, and continuing to 174.
BOTHER MYSELF. FWT to Maunsel White, March 20, 1907.
407 WIN WITHOUT MINE. FWT to Maunsel White, April 9, 1907.
AS MEAN AS THEY COULD. Ibid., February 6, 1908.
TIME TO RECUPERATE. Wilfred Lewis to Henry Towne, November 27, 1915.
BETHLEHEM CO. WILL WIN. FWT to Maunsel White, March 21, 1908.
LATEST PRODUCT. FWT to Maunsel White, September 28, 1908.
408 IN THE RACE. 166 Federal Register, Bethlehem Steel Co. vs. Niles-Bement-Pond Co., Circuit Court, District of New Jersey, January 29, 1909, 896. Writing to Bethlehem president Linderman (January 25, 1900, Hagley Museum and Library), Archibald Johnston had earlier cited the need "to control, with great accuracy and uniformity, the temperatures employed, and in order to do this, an apparatus containing novel features has been developed, under Mr. Taylor's directions." But this apparatus did not figure in the patent claim.
PARTISAN. FWT to Maunsel White, February 5, 1909.
MARKED IMPROVEMENT. Judge Cross's ruling.
MOST AMAZING DOCUMENT. United States Court of Appeals for the Third Circuit, Bethlehem Steel Company vs. Niles-Bement-Pond Company, Brief for Apellant, 2.
409 MATERIAL PROSPERITY. Ibid., 130.
PERSONALLY INVESTIGATED. FWT to Maunsel White, May 9, 1906.
DISGUSTED. FWT to Maunsel White, September 20, 1909.
410 BESSEMER. *Iron and Steel Magazine*, November 1904, 1259.
A MERE NOTHING. Brearley, *The Steel-Makers*, 121.
AT VARIANCE. *Bulletin*, February 1925. See also Townsend, 779.
AS SUCH A SHOCK. Geoffrey Tweedale to the author, April 5, 1993.
HOLE OF SILENCE. Maunsel White to FWT, April 29, 1910.
411 PERPETUAL RAGE. FWT to Maunsel White, May 2, 1910.
INSTALLED IN 1929. *Bulletin*, December 1930, 288.
412 AKIN TO THAT OF LUTHER. Rockstrom, 23.

TAYLOR WAS THE MESSIAH. Glenn Porter, "Management," in Williams, ed., *A History of Technology*, vol. VI, Oxford: Clarendon Press, 1978.

CRUSADERS. *Bulletin*, February 1932. See also Gilson, 140: "Those Frederick Taylor lectures left me in the state of a person who has suddenly 'got religion.' "

LONG VACATION. FWT to Theodore Jessup, December 11, 1901. (As late as August 19, 1901, in a letter to W. M. Dollar, of a Buffalo, New York, iron works, Taylor was still in business, quoting a rate of fifty dollars a day and expressing a willingness to visit his would-be client.) For Gantt's work see Peter B. Petersen, "Henry Gantt's Work at Bancroft: The Option of Scientific Management," *Academy of Management Proceedings*, August 12, 1985; Paul J. Kelly and Peter B. Petersen, "Scientific Management and the Williams & Wilkins Company (1908–1909)," *Academy of Management Best Papers Proceedings*, August 9–12, 1992.

413 LEARNED THE ART. FWT to H. F. J. Porter, February 21, 1906.

HATHAWAY. Drury, 129; Urwick, ed., 201.

TAYLOR'S SPIRIT. H. K. Hathaway, "Mr. Taylor as I Knew Him," *Journal of the Efficiency Society*, April 1915, 6.

PROPOSITION. H. L. Gantt and Carl Barth to Lehigh Coal & Navigation Company, December 30, 1907, Baker Library, Harvard.

FIFTY COMPANIES. J. C. Barth, "List of Numbered Lantern Slides," Collection; Urwick and Brech, I, 74; Alford, 108.

414 FRANK GILBRETH. See Yost; Price; Frank B. Gilbreth, Jr.; Lillian M. Gilbreth.

MORTAR WOULD START TO FLY. Frank B. Gilbreth, Jr., 103.

IDEA WAS NEW TO HIM. Sanford Thompson to Margaret Ellen Hawley, November 23, 1927, Gilbreth Archive.

SHOULD NOT BE SURPRISED. Price, 39.

415 HERE ON THIS SPOT. Frank B. Gilbreth, Jr., 115; see also Yost, chapter 12; Lillian M. Gilbreth, 32; Wm. T. Magruder to Margaret Ellen Hawley, February 15, 1927, Gilbreth Archive. See also "Engineering Societies Building in New York," *Iron Trade Review*, April 4, 1907.

TALK WITH OUR FRIEND. FWT to Sanford Thompson, December 9, 1907, Catherwood.

GREAT BLUFFER. Sanford Thompson to FWT, December 13, 1907, Catherwood.

MOTION STUDY. See Hugo Kijne, "Time and Motion Study: Beyond the Taylor-Gilbreth Controversy," seen in manuscript. Brian Price, "Frank and Lillian Gilbreeth and the Manufacture and Marketing of Motion Study, 1908–1924," *Business and Economic History*, second series, vol. 18, 1989, 88–98; William R. Spriegel and Clark E. Myers, *The Writings of the Gilbreths*, Homewood, Illinois: Richard D. Irwin, 1955, chapters 5–7.

TAIL TO TAYLOR'S KITE. Yost, 156.

416 A CERTAIN STAMP. Lilliam M. Gilbreth, 35.

HALF DOZEN OTHER THINGS. Frank Gilbreth, "The Theory at Work," address before the Civic Forum, New York City, April 28, 1911, printed in the *Journal of Accountancy* soon after.

ABSORBING THE IDEAS. Frank Gilbreth to FWT, February 1, 1908, quoted in Price, 49.

CONGENIAL HOME. To Taylor, Barth was the group's mathematical genius, but Barth himself said (Manning, chapter VIII) that "a real professional mathematician would make me look like less than thirty cents in one minute."

SURPRISINGLY FLEXIBLE. Alford, 130; Copley, II, 23.

COVER TO COVER. Nelson, "Scientific Management, Systematic Management, and

Labor," 494. See also Morris Cooke to Margaret Ellen Hawley, February 17, 1927, Gilbreth Archive.

417 BASEBALL LINE-UP. Cartoon in Collection.

ORPHANED. Conrad Aiken, *Ushant*, Boston: Little, Brown & Co. 1952, 72.

CONRAD RESENTED. Lorenz, 50.

NICE STUFFED SHIRTS. Quoted in Butscher, 67.

BOXLY STAFFING. Robert Taylor, 1976, III-4

418 PRUNES. Ibid., III-3.

NO EXCUSE. Ibid., III-2.

NO READING AHEAD. Ibid., III-7.

HAD TO BALANCE. Ibid., III-8.

WALKED OFF. Ibid., III-17.

UNBENDING GENTEEL MORES. Butscher, 67. Elizabeth's problems with her parents may have lain more with her mother. "I think my mother was jealous of her," Robert Taylor (1983, 7) told Myron Johnson. "She had an artistic streak which my mother didn't encourage at all; he [FWT] did. He stood up for her."

AWAY FROM HOME. FWT to Ira N. Hollis, March 29, 1909.

419 MAZE OF MACHINERY. Robert Taylor, 1976, III-14.

DISABLED. FWT to H. C. H. Carpenter, October 7, 1907.

RUDDY MAN. Gordon Blodgett Jones, "The Gospel of Efficiency," *The Forecast*, probably 1912, Collection.

TREATISE. Taylor, "The Making of a Putting Green," *Country Life in America*, five-part series ending June 1915; "Brings Grass Plot from Connecticut," *Post-Gazette*, July 14, 1911, Germantown Library; Taylor Memorial, 87–97; Kempton Taylor, 4.

ANY VERY VAST ABILITY. FWT to Robert Taylor, March 12, 1909.

420 BEAT TACT ALL HOLLOW. FWT to "Putmut P. A. Taylor" c/o Kempton Taylor, March 8, 1909.

IMPROVE HIS HEALTH. Manning, 52.

PROPER METHODS. FWT to Maunsel White, March 21, 1908.

HUMAN GRASSHOPPER. Kempton Taylor, 4.

LOOK AT THE MUGS. Robert Taylor, 1976, III-9.

ROUGHENED FACE. Phelps; see also Robert Taylor to Richard P. Widdicombe, October 9, 1981, Myron Johnson papers.

421 Y-SHAPED PUTTER. U. S. Patent No. 792, 631. See also Kempton Taylor, 4.

SAD FOR WORDS. Edward C. Clark to FWT, December 5, 1908.

SARSAPARILLA. FWT to Edward C. Clark, May 10, 1909.

SILVER WEDDING. Louise Fragment.

JUDSON DALAND. See Arthur C. Morgan, "Memoir of Judson Daland, M. D." *Transactions of the College of Physicians of Philadelphia*, series 4, vol. 6, 48–50; Philadelphia *Evening Bulletin*, August 16, 1937.

WAY AHEAD OF HIS TIME. Robert Taylor, 1976, III-5.

422 SLOW IN MAKING A DIAGNOSIS. FWT to Sanford Thompson, August 11, 1904.

SLIGHTLY DIABETIC. Robert Taylor, 1976, III-6.

FATHER'S DIET. Ibid.

WONDERFUL ASPARAGUS. Ibid.

TAKING POSSESSION. Frank Copley to Morris Cooke, March 15, 1917, Franklin D. Roosevelt Library.

423 1910. Sullivan, 559–573.

TRANSLATIONS. FWT to H. K. Hathaway. May 12, 1910.

GRANDPA T. Collection.

ARRANGED. FWT to H. K. Hathaway, September 14, 1910.

424 STEAMED TOWARD ENGLAND. *Transactions ASME* 32, 588–791.
    ENGINEER'S REVERIE. Ibid., 605. The author was Granger Whitney.
425 MENTAL KINSHIP. Taylor, "Sentiment," Collection.
    NOW TAKEN PLACE. *Transactions ASME* 32, 727. See also Urwick & Brech, II, 93–96;
426 FACTS WRONG. Yost, 184;
    COOLNESS. Urwick & Brech, II, 93–96.
    ENTIRELY AGREED. Ibid.

PART VI

JUDGMENT DAY

429 BRANDEIS AND RATE CASE. See *North American,* November 22, 1910, February 2,
    1916; *New York Times,* December 4, 1910; Brandeis, *Scientific Management and and
    Railroads;* Bullock; Ernest Poole, foreword to Louis D. Brandeis, *Business—A Profession;*
    Oscar Kraines, "Brandeis' Philosophy of Scientific Management," *Western Political
    Quarterly* XIII (1960), 191–201; Mason, *Free Man's Life;* "What Is Scientific Manage-
    ment, and What Does it Do?" *Industrial Engineering and The Engineering Digest,*
    January 1911.
430 AGGREGATION. Quoted in Mason, *Free Man's Life,* 316.
    SHOULD HAVE BEEN PAID. Bullock, 140.
    KNOWLEDGE AND BELIEF. Ibid., 112.
431 SHOE MANUFACTURER. Adelstein, 648.
    HARRINGTON EMERSON. See Quigel; Carl Graves, "Applying Scientific Manage-
    ment Principles to Railroad Repair Shops—the Santa Fe Experience," *Business and Eco-
    nomic History,* second series, vol. 10, 124–136.
    BORN SALESMAN. Merrill, 178.
    ANY OTHER MAN LIVING OR DEAD. Harrington Emerson to FWT, November 17,
    1905.
    BOUND FOR BOSTON. Alford lecture notes, Catherwood. FWT to Carl Barth, Janu-
    ary 13, 1910: "We cannot afford to let Harrington Emerson's name be associated with
    our work." On the other hand, FWT to Morris Cooke, May 26, 1910: "He is a very
    earnest man, and a hard worker, and I believe an honest worker."
    SMALL FEUDS. Lillian M. Gilbreth, 33.
432 ALL DIFFERENCES. Louis Brandeis to Horace Bookwalter Drury, January 31, 1914, in
    Urofsky and Levy, eds., *Letters of Louise D. Brandeis,* III, 241.
    USED THE TERM BEFORE. See Holden A. Evans, "Scientific Factory Management,"
    Machinist, June 16, 1910, 1108: "The term 'scientific management' is now generally
    accepted as referring to the type of management advocated by Fred W. Taylor." Indeed,
    the year before, a freelance writer had approached a magazine editor this way: "There is
    a man named Fred W. Taylor, living in Philadelphia, who has developed and really for-
    mulated the science of shop management. . . . Scientific management," he went on to
    call it. The writer failed to land the assignment (*Bulletin,* April 1932, 86).
    NOT ONE OF US. *Bulletin,* February 1932, 39. See also Yost, 187; Robert T. Kent to
    Margaret E. Hawley, December 31, 1926, Gilbreth Archive.
    SYMPATHY STRIKES. FWT to Louis Brandeis, November 11, 1910.
    RIGHT TRACK. James Dodge to FWT, November 3, 1910.
433 IMPORTANCE AND HOPEFULNESS. Louise Brandeis to Rudolph Gaar Leeds,
    November 9, 1910, in Urofsky and Levy, eds., *Letters of Louis D. Brandeis,* II, 383–385.
    GOSPEL OF HOPE. *New York Times,* November 22, 1910.

ROADS COULD SAVE. Ibid.

434 HUNG OVER THEIR DESKS. Charles Going to Margaret Ellen Hawley, March 13, 1927, Gilbreth Archive.

SUBSTITUTE FOR RELIGION. Ray Stannard Baker, "Frederick W. Taylor—Scientist in Business Management," *American Magazine*, March 1911, 565.

OR, RATHER, FOUR. Brandeis, *Scientific Management and the Railroads*, 83.

MASTERLY WAY. FWT to Brandeis, November 25, 1910.

FAITH OF APOSTLES. Baker, "Scientist in Business Management," 565.

WIRED BRANDEIS. "Invite Brandeis to Manage Their Roads," *New York Times*, November 24, 1910.

COULD ACCEPT NO PAY. "Brandeis to Teach Roads Without Pay," *New York Times*, November 30, 1910.

435 ANSWERS SARCASM. *New York Times*, December 1, 1910.

BRANDEIS, TEACHER. *New York Times*, December 4, 1910.

BY A SINGLE STROKE. Quoted in Poole, foreword to *Business—A Profession*, xlviii.

ALL WANT BRANDEIS NOW. *Boston Post*, February 25, 1911.

436 WITHOUT ANY HANDLE. Bullock, 106.

THIS MAN'S SPECIAL JOY. *New York Tribune*, November 27, 1910.

AGAIN CONGRATULATE. FWT to Louis Brandeis, December 4, 1910.

ONLY A "THEORY." Kraines, "Brandeis' Philosophy", 195.

WHOLLY UNEXPECTED IMPRESSION. *Machinist*, December 15, 1910.

437 GO ON! (Philadelphia) *City Club Bulletin*, January 18, 1911, 32.

FAILED SUGAR SPECULATOR. Christie, 4. For more on Cooke's role, see Wrege & Stotka.

438 A MAN WE WILL CALL SCHMIDT. Taylor, *Principles*, 44.

ÊTES-VOUS. See, for example, André Vielleville, *Le Système Taylor*, University of Paris thesis, Imprimerie Viellville, Paris, 1914, 58.

CRANE, TWAIN. Mulcaire; Munley; see also Banta.

SYSTEM MUST BE FIRST. Taylor, *Principles*, 7.

TAYLOR TOPPLES PRIORITIES. Munley, 308.

BIBLE OF AMERICAN MANAGEMENT. Ibid., 286.

SAME PRINCIPLES. Taylor, *Principles*, 8.

439 SIT ON IT. See FWT to Carl G. Barth, October 17, 1910: "I insisted [to the ASME meetings committee] that the members of our Society would be interested in my paper, and they thought not."

REACH A DECISION. Morris Cooke to FWT, December 10, 1910.

RAY STANNARD BAKER. See Regier, 146.

ATTACKED INJUSTICE. Regier, 147.

440 NO PROGRAM OF REFORM. Ibid., 156. See also Tarbell, *Day's Work*, 281.

JOYOUS LAUGH. Tarbell, *Day's Work*, 197.

BETTER FIND OUT. Ibid., 292.

ARTICLES ON BASEBALL. Morris Cooke to FWT, December 10, 1910.

AMONG THE MUCK-RAKERS. FWT to Morris Cooke, December 10, 1910.

WHO IS MR. TAYLOR. Baker, "Scientist in Business Management," 564–570.

AUTOBIOGRAPHICAL NOTES. FWT to Morris Cooke, December 2, 1910: "The very best training I had was in the early years of apprenticeship in the pattern shop, when I was under a workman of extraordinary ability, coupled with fine character." Baker: "He regards the early years of his apprenticeship as the best training he ever had and the workman under whom he served, who was a man of extraordinary ability, coupled with fine character, as one of the best teachers."

441 FINE SHAPE. FWT to Morris Cooke, February 22, 1911, Franklin D. Roosevelt Library.

KEEP IN CLOSER TOUCH. Morris Cooke to FWT, February 25, 1911, Franklin D. Roosevelt Library.

MORE SCIENCE. *Machinist,* April 6, 1911, 656.

OBTAINABLE EFFICIENCIES. *New York Times,* April 21, 1911.

THE ONE BEST WAY. Edward Mott Woolley, *System,* March 1911. Brandeis had used the term the year before in his rate case brief: "Scientific management seeks to ascertain and apply in every process the best attainable methods, practices, tools, and machines. It necessarily follows that all must be standardized. There is but one best way."

442 FORTY OR FIFTY A WEEK. FWT to W. O. Webber, May 26, 1911.

DELIVERER OF MANKIND. *Official Report,* National Machine Tool Builders Association convention, May 18–19, 1911, 110, Collection.

GET TOGETHER. Maunsel White to FWT, June 5, 1911.

EDITORS ASKED TAYLOR. Yost, 192.

MEN ARE LED, NOT DRIVEN. Brandeis foreword to *Primer of Scientific Management,* New York: D. Van Nostrand, 1914, viii.

443 WONDERFUL AGE. *The American Magazine,* May 1911, 139.

EXTENSIVE REACTION. FWT to James Bryce, May 24, 1911.

444 CAUSE OF INSANITY. *New York Times,* December 11, 1910.

REDUCE ME TO AN AUTOMATON. James Duncan, *Journal of Accountancy,* May 1911, 26–34.

MONOPOLY OF BRAINS. *Machinist,* April 13, 1911, 674.

445 FACTOTUM OR MACHINE. Wilson E. Symons, *Journal of the Franklin Institute,* January 1912, 14.

BLINDS. "Con Wise," *Machinist,* April 6, 1911, 634.

DIS TAYLOR GUY. Francis Alberts, "The 'New York Bo' Talks About the Taylor System," *International Molders Journal,* August, 1911, 602.

INFELICITIES. Harlow Person, "Scientific Management: A Brief Statement of Its Nature and History," in Hunt, 12.

PICKED LABORERS. Taylor, *Principles,* 72.

ROUTINELY CARRIED ADS. The examples are from the *Public Ledger,* September 15 and 17, 1874, respectively.

WHAT HAS HAPPENED TO SCHMIDT? *The American Magazine,* May 1911, 140.

EXPERT TO TELL HIM. Taylor, *Principles,* 59.

446 NOT SOON FORGET. Upton Sinclair (letter dated February 24, 1911), *American Magazine,* June 1911, 243; Taylor's reply, 244. Ernest Wright to FWT, July 2, 1911: "I've just read your and Upton Sinclair's remarks in the June American; really, you are becoming quite mild and tactful in your old age!"

BREAKING POINT. *Federationist,* April 1911, 94.

INTANGIBLE CONTROL. *Machinist,* May 18, 1911.

447 TWENTIETH CENTURY BEST. *Federationist,* February 1911. .

OTHER ARSENALS. See Hearings, 1161.

MR. TAYLOR'S METHODS. Letter to Secretary of War Dickinson, in Investigation of Taylor system of shop management, House Committee on Labor, April 28, 1911, 18.

448 MASS MEETINGS. FWT to Morris Cooke, March 17, 1911.

VIRTUAL SLAVERY. Investigation, 26. See also Hearings, 1222, 1235. For more on O'Connell, see Robert G. Rodden, *The Fighting Machinists: A Century of Struggle,* 18.

BIG PHYSICAL MEN. Investigation, 36.

449 DIVINE SPARK. Ibid., 32.

THE DEVIL LOOSE. Carl Barth to FWT, August 12, 1911. My account owes much to Hugh Aitken's masterful *Taylorism at Watertown Arsenal.* See also *Iron Age,* August 31 and November 9, 1911; *Machinist,* September 12 & 19, 1912.

450 NOT BEEN A SINGLE STRIKE. Taylor, *Principles*, 135.
     WHILE I WAS THERE. Hearings, 932.
     UNDER THE CIRCUMSTANCES. Carl Barth to FWT, August 12, 1911.
     WHY NO ANSWER. Carl Barth to FWT, telegram, August 15, 1911.
     MOST RESTFUL. FWT to Morris Cooke, August 2, 1911.
     RIGHT STRAIGHT THROUGH. FWT to Carl Barth, August 14, 1911.
     WATERTOWN ARSENAL. See Judy Dobbs, *A History of the Watertown Arsenal, 1816–1967*, Watertown, Massachusetts, 1977.
     NEVER THOUGHT OF IT. Hearings, 62.
451 PERHAPS THE MOST BACKWARD. Hearings, 1122.
     WILLIAM CROZIER. See Peter B. Petersen, "The Pioneering Efforts of Major General William Crozier (1855–1942) in the Field of Management," *Journal of Management* 15 (3; 1989), 503.
     WELL WORTH TRYING. Hearings, 1124.
     MERRICK WAS BROUGHT IN. Hearings, 1172.
     ABOUT A DOZEN. Hearings, 88, 91.
452 COMFORTABLE DISORGANIZATION. Aitken, 142.
     DO MY WORK RIGHT. This account is drawn from Aitken and Hearings, 1868–1935, the testimony taken during the original investigation.
     UNSATISFACTORY CONDITIONS. Hearings, 1879.
454 MOLDERS QUIT. *Boston Globe*, August 12, 1911.
     DUMPED THEM ONTO THE GROUND. Hearings, 230; Watertown *Tribune-Enterprise*, August 18, 1911.
     NO EX-CONVICTS. Hearings, 244.
455 EVERY TIME I TURN. Ibid., 1892.
     WE UNDERSTOOD. Ibid., 1891.
     IMPOSSIBLE FOR A MAN. Ibid., 1914.
     NO FAST OR SET RULES. Ibid.
456 JOBBING SHOP. Ibid., 1889.
     EXTRA LABOR. Ibid., 1891.
     FAITHFUL IN MY WORK. Ibid., 1905.
     FOR A WALK EVENINGS. Ibid., 1886.
457 SHAKE YOUR CONFIDENCE? Ibid., 1921.
     PATROLLED BY SOLDIERS. Aitken, 154.
     DETAIN THIS EXPERT. Hearings, 1884.
     BOTH BE FOUND GUILTY. Carl Barth to FWT, August 12, 1911.
458 AGITATION. Hearings, 1885.
     ANY WAY COMPETENT. Ibid. See also FWT to Morris Cooke, May 5, 1910: Merrick "was a third-class man in almost every kind of work that he was put to, and everyone was delighted when he developed into an excellent time study man."
     STRONG AND BITTER. Watertown *Tribune-Enterprise*, September 8, 1911.
     SORT OF UMPIRE. FWT to William Barba, February 9, 1912.
     CAMPAIGN. FWT to James Mapes Dodge, September 6, 1911.
     ANXIOUS TO LEARN EVERYTHING. FWT to Louis Brandeis, September 14, 1911.
459 ON YOUR TRAIN. FWT to William C. Redfield, January 1, 1912.
     INFORM YOU. William B. Wilson to FWT, September 19, 1911.
     SPECIAL COMMITTEE. For accounts of the hearings, see Max H. C. Brombacher, "The Watertown Arsenal Labor Trouble," *Iron Age*, January 11 and 25, 1912, and "The Rock Island Arsenal Labor Trouble," *Iron Age*, February 2, 1912.
     EXCEPT BY VIRTUE OF LAW. Hearings, 649.
460 PORTABLE POWER PLANT. Ibid., 650.

461 THERE IN MINIATURE. Aitken, 12.
DOCTRINE. Harlow Person, *Bulletin* XI (3/4; 1926).
BEND OVER A MOLD? Hearings, 126.
TECHNICAL TERM? Ibid., 142.
462 PROPERLY. Ibid., 147.
LEAVING NO DISCRETION? Ibid., 100.
463 FITTED TO FACE THE WORLD. Ibid., 369.
NO LATITUDE. Ibid., 373.
464 NOT IN THE ELECTRICAL LINE. Ibid., 400.
465 COMMON SENSE. Ibid., 340.
MATTER OF JUDGMENT. Ibid., 505.
466 ARBITRARILY DETERMINED. Ibid., 506.
NERVES CANNOT STAND IT. Ibid., 307.
KIND OF SCOWL. Ibid., 442.
467 STAR WITNESS. FWT to King Hathaway, October 24, 1911.
ANY LOGICAL WAY. Ibid., October 30, 1911.
TAMED. FWT to Louis Brandeis, November 3, 1911.
FULL OF PROMISE. *Iron Age*, November 9, 1911.
CESSATION OF WORK. Ibid.
468 AN INTERESTING ONE. *Iron Age*, December 14, 1911.
GIVE ME PLEASURE. FWT to William Wilson, January 22, 1912.
HOLLIS GODFREY. *National Cyclopedia of American Biography.*
SLIGHTLY MAD. Robert D. Cuff, "The Cooperative Impulse and War: The Origins of
the Council of National Defense and Advisory Commission," in Jerry Israel, ed.
Building the Organizational Society, New York: Free Press, 240.
MORE EFFICIENT. Hollis Godfrey to FWT, March 15, 1911.
469 VERY GREAT THING. Ibid., April 27, 1911.
GET INTO THE GAME. Ibid., May 6, 1911.
GLAD TO HAVE DONE. Morris Cooke to FWT, May 6, 1911.
FOUR THOUSAND DOLLARS A YEAR. Hollis Godfrey to FWT, May 15, 1911; FWT
to Godfrey, May 18, 1911; Godfrey to FWT, August 31, 1911.
TAKE CHARGE OF OUR CASE. FWT to Hollis Godfrey, January 22, 1912. Letter con-
tains text of telegram.
NEW WILLARD. See Richard Wallace and Marie Pinak Carr, *The Willard Hotel: An
Illustrated History*, Washington, D.C.: Dicmar Publishing, 1986; Dorothy Ames Marks,
"A Statcly Willard Proudly Receives Guests Once More," *Smithsonian*, February, 1987.
470 EVOLUTION OF A VIRGINIAN VILLAGE. Montgomery Schuyler, "The New Wash-
ington," *Scribner's Magazine*, February 1912.
LAWRENCE STRIKE. "Fail to End Strike at Lawrence Mills," *New York Times*, Janu-
ary 28, 1912.
ARMIES IN BATTLE ARRAY. "New Cardinal Talks on Labor Problem," *New York
Times*, January 28, 1912.
LOST INTEREST. FWT to James T. Wallis, February 5, 1912.
471 ARE YOU THE AUTHOR? FWT-Hearings, 5.
STRAIGHTFORWARD MEN. Ibid., 11–40.
473 GATHERING IN. Ibid., 40.
DON'T KNOW EXACTLY WHY. Ibid., 48. For Taylor not to tell the Schmidt story was
like a Tony Bennett concert without "I Left My Heart in San Francisco."
474 HE IS TOO STUPID. Ibid., 50.
BAROQUE SPECIMENS. Ibid., 102.
HOW LONG DID YOU SERVE. Ibid., 112.

TRAVELING ALLOWANCE. *Iron Age*, December 28, 1911.
475 DISTURBED CONDITION. FWT-Hearings, 132–141.
WHO IS TO DETERMINE? Ibid., 143–153.
477 USED FOR BAD. Ibid., 191.
EFFECTIVE WEAPON. FWT to James T. Wallis, February 5, 1912.
FROM ATTACK. FWT to Hollis Godfrey, February 2, 1912.
WHAT SCIENTIFIC FORMULA. FWT-Hearings, 162.
478 CATCH YOUR MEANING. Ibid., 166.
479 BEST POSSIBLE MEASURE. Ibid., 209.
MORE PRODUCTIVE. Ibid. See *Final Report of the Industrial Commission*, 537: "The productiveness of [industrial] labor was multiplied, on the average, not less than three or four times, and in some departments many fold, in the brief period from 1865–1889."
ANYTHING OF A MISFORTUNE. Ibid., 211.
UNDER OUR LAWS. Ibid., 213.
BECOMING TAMED. FWT to Henry Towne, October, 30, 1911.
MORE AGILE INTELLECT. Harlow Person, *Bulletin* XI, (3/4; 1926).
480 WILSON SHOUTED A STOP. Copley, II, 348.
MUCH RUN DOWN. FWT to James T. Wallis, February 5, 1912.
LESS STRENUOUS LIFE. Hollis Godfrey to FWT, January 31, 1912. Godfrey's next few letters further attest to Taylor's ordeal. February 1: "I am very glad you are going to have the rest of a trip abroad." February 4: "I hope that Mrs. Taylor is better and that you are getting rested."
CONTRARY TO ALL OUR EXPECTATIONS. FWT to James Mapes Dodge, February 2, 1912.
HIS GREAT HEART. Hollis Godfrey to FWT, February 1, 1912.
481 SETTING TRAPS. FWT to David Van Allstyne, February 2, 1912.
CROSS-EXAMINING. FWT to William Barba, February 2, 1912.
PRETTY POOR READING. FWT to Carl Barth, February 6, 1912.
ENTIRELY REWRITE. FWT to House Labor Committee secretary, February 12, 1912.
RATHER REWRITTEN. William Wilson to FWT, February 13, 1912.
482 NOT BE A BAD IDEA. FWT to Hollis Godfrey, February 15, 1912.
YOUR INSTRUCTIONS. Hollis Godfrey to FWT, February 16, 1912.
STRUGGLING ALONG. FWT to Morris Cooke, February 15, 1912, postscript.
KICK MUCH. FWT to Morris Cooke, February 20, 1912.
MUTUAL CONSENT. Report printed in *Iron Age*, March 21, 1912.
483 GREAT DEAL OF SATISFACTION. *Machinists' Monthly Journal*, 1912, 300.
PRE-DETERMINED DECISION. Wilfred Lewis to Frank Gilbreth, January 30, 1912.
BEST OF POLITICS. FWT to James Dodge, June 20, 1912.
484 DISTINCT VICTORY. FWT to John Q. Tilson, September 20, 1912.
486 TOWARDS A FATAL PRECISION. Paul Valery, "Letters From France: 1. The Spiritual Crisis," *The Athenaeum*, April 11, 1919.
CLERICAL FUNCTIONS. Davies, 109.
ALCATRAZ. Jay Stuller, "There Never Was a Harder Place Than 'The Rock,'" *Smithsonian*, September 1995, 84.
DISEASE OF TAYLORISM. Konosuke Matsushita, "A Secret Is Shared," *Manufacturing Engineering*, February 1986, quoted in Kenneth Gray, "Why We Will Lose: Taylorism in America's High Schools," *Phi Delta Kappan*, January 1993.
487 PATRIOTIC DUTY. Haber, 119.
LAY HIS HANDS. *Advanced Management*, January–March 1943.
ENROLLED AMONG HIS FOLLOWERS. Hunt, ed., xi.

LARGELY CREDITED. *Advanced Management*, January–March 1943, 34. See also Gomberg and Dubinsky, 18.

LEFT WING MANAGEMENT GROUP. Ibid.

BITTEREST SORT OF OPPOSITION. *New Republic*, March 25, 1925.

FAIR MINIMUM STANDARDS. Frank B. Copley, "Taylor and Trade Unions," *Bulletin*, August 1925, citing review by Ordway Tead of history of International Ladies Garment Workers' Union.

488 CAPITULATION. Steven Fraser, *Labor Will Rule: Sidney Hillman and the Rise of American Labor*, New York: Free Press, 1991, 171.

TOOK THE TROUBLE. Rockstrom, 30–31.

NO LONGER HEARD. *Bulletin*, February 1924, 38.

WESTINGHOUSE. Quoted in Nelson, "Scientific Management and the Workplace," 82.

ARISTOCRACY OF THE CAPABLE. See Peter B. Petersen, "Henry Gantt and the New Machine (1916–1918)," *Academy of Management Proceedings*, 1986; and "Correspondence from Henry L. Gantt to an Old Friend Reveals New Information About Gantt," *Journal of Management* 12 (3; 1986), 339–350.

TECHNOCRACY. See Akin.

VERY EXISTENCE. Whitsett & Yorks, 83.

489 PERSONNEL MANAGEMENT. See Bruce E. Kaufman, *The Origins and Evolution of the Field of Industrial Relations in the United States*, Ithaca, New York: ILR Press, 1993, 21–25.

DEVOTED DISCIPLE. Strom, 233; see also Davies, chapter 6.

ROUSING TYPISTS. Davies, 116.

BUSINESS WEEK. Davies, 110.

BETTER BE JOINED. Edward T. Morman, ed., *Efficiency, Scientific Management, and Hospital Standardization: An Anthology of Sources*, New York: Garland, 1989, introduction.

BETTER SUTURING TECHNIQUE. Reprinted in Ibid.

BEYOND ANY OTHER CRAFT. Ibid., 149.

WOULDN'T HOLD YOUR JOB. Charles D. Wrege, "Medical Men and Scientific Management: A Forgotten Chapter in Management History," *Review of Business and Economic Research*, Spring 1983, 38. See also Morris Cooke to Margaret Hawley, February 17, 1927, Gilbreth Archive; Charles D. Wrege, "The Efficient Management of Hospitals: Pioneer Work of Ernest Codman, Robert Dickinson, and Frank Gilbreth, 1910–1918," *Academy of Management Proceedings*, 1980, 114–118.

STUDDED WITH REFERENCES. Whitsett & Yorks, 82.

PUBLIC ADMINISTRATION. See Schacter.

490 REALIZED IT OR NOT. Nelson, *Mental Revolution*, 96.

GAUGE OF EFFICIENCY. Dartmouth, 301; see also Morris Cooke, *Academic and Industrial Efficiency: A Report to the Carnegie Foundation for the Advancement of Teaching* (Bulletin No. 5), New York: Carnegie Foundation, 1910. Taylor once told authorities at Harvard (Kempton Taylor, 8): "You have fifty odd instructors giving courses whose average attendance is three or four students. Do away with these little-sought courses."

IDEOLOGICAL DIVIDE. FWT, writes Peter Drucker ("The Coming Rediscovery of Scientific Management," *The Conference Board Record*, June 1976, 25), "committed the unpardonable offense of proving the 'isms' to be irrelevant. . . . The 'system,' Taylor implies, hardly matters. Job, task and work do. The economy is not made by 'capitalism' or 'socialism.' It is made by productivity." Giedion, 126, makes a like point: "The assembly line and scientific management can be put to work within quite opposite economic systems."

JAPANESE SCIENTIFIC MANAGEMENT. See Seishi Nakagawa, "The Introduction and Development of Scientific Management and the Rise of Japanese Management," *Fukuoka University Review of Commercial Sciences* 36 (1; 1991), 89–120; Satoshi Sasaki, "The Introduction of Scientific Management by the Mitsubishi Electric Engineering Co. and the Formation of an Organized Scientific Management Movement in Japan in the 1920s and 1930s," *Business History* 34 (2; 1992), 12–27; Horace King Hathaway, "Scientific Management in Japan," *Bulletin*, August 1929, 182; Ronald G. Greenwood and Robert H. Ross, "Early American Influence on Japanese Management Philosophy: The Scientific Management Movement in Japan," in Sang M. Lee and Gary Schwendiman, eds., *Management by Japanese Systems*, New York: Praeger, 43–50.

491 CLOUD OF POWDER. Greenwood and Ross, "Early American Influence", 47.
MAP OF SORTS. Ibid., 48.

492 OHNO ... ACKNOWLEDGED HIS ... DEBT. Nakagawa, "Scientific Management and the Rise of Japanese Management," 2.
NOT A RECENT CREATION. Wren, 205.
ANY HONEST MAN. Carlo Saiz to FWT, March 29, 1913.
BARELY RECOGNIZABLE. Humphreys, 93.
SWITZERLAND'S BALLY. Rudolf Braun, "The 'Docile' Body as a Growth Factor," in Patrice Higonnet, David S. Landes, and Henry Rosovsky, eds., *Favorites of Fortune: Technology, Growth, and Economic Development Since the Industrial Revolution*, Cambridge, Mass.: Harvard University Press, 1991, 132.
20,000 COPIES. Henri Le Chatelier, "The Philosophy of Taylorism," *Bulletin*, December 1928, 249. For more on Taylorism in France see, for example, Humphreys; Aimée Moutet, "Les Origines du système de Taylor en France: Le point de vue patronal (1907–1914)," *Le Mouvement Social*, October–December 1975, 15, and her "La Première Guerre mondiale et le taylorisme," in Montmollin and Pastre.

493 MANY MISTAKES. Le Chatelier, "Philosophy of Taylorism".
RENAULT STRIKE. See Patrick Fridenson, *Histoire des Usines Renault: Naissance de la Grande Entreprise, 1898–1939*, Paris: Editions du Seuil, 1972; Moutet, "Système de Taylor en France."
SPREAD THE WORD. Charles de Freminville to FWT, May 5, 1913, referring to conversation with Le Chatelier.
LOVE OF GOD. Charles de Freminville to FWT, January 16, 1914: "Last Sunday but one, Father Sertilanges, having made a specialty of addressing people of high culture and science, began his sermon saying: "L'amour de Dieu est le système Taylor de notre vie intérieure."
HEAT WAVE. Geoff Brown, 159.
CLEMENCEAU ORDERED. See "Taylor Methods in French War Ministries," *Bulletin*, June 1919, 29.
MICHELIN BOOKLETS. See, for example, "Prospérité, ou Sam et François," 1927. Another included Taylor's House testimony.
UNIONS WARMED. E.S.A. Bloemen, *Scientific Management in Nederland, 1900–1930*, Amsterdam: Neha, 1988, English-language "Summary," p. 190.

494 ANGLICIZING SCIENTIFIC MANAGEMENT. Urwick and Brech, 102.
THINNER IT GOT. C. B. Thompson, "The Taylor System in Europe," *Advanced Management*, October–December 1940, 173.
EMASCULATED. Ibid., 171.
ARRIVISTE BUSTLE. Merkle, 240.
DONE IN MY OWN TIME. Geoff Brown, 149.
WORLD ... CONGRESSES. See Devinat; Erik Bloemen, "The Movement for Scientific Managment in Europe," seen in manuscript.

495 NEVER WITNESSED. *Bulletin*, June 1927.

RANKED TAYLOR FIRST. Daniel A. Wren and Robert D. Hay, "Management Historians and Business Historians: Differing Perceptions of Pioneer Contributors," *Academy of Management Journal*, September 1977.

FORD. See Hounshell, Nevins; Nelson Lichtenstein and Stephen Meyer, *On the Line: Essays in the History of Auto Work*, Urbana, Illinois: University of Illinois Press, 1989; Keith Sward, *The Legend of Henry Ford*, New York: Rinehart, 1948; Stephen Meyer III, *The Five Dollar Day: Labor Management and Social Control in the Ford Motor Company, 1908–1921*, Albany: State University of New York Press; Robert Lacey, *Ford: The Men and the Machine*, Boston: Little, Brown, 1986.

FORD DENIED. But see Fred J. Miller, "Mass Production Versus Scientific Management," *Manufacturing Industries*, December 1926, 427–428, Franklin D. Roosevelt Library. Miller takes Ford's principles of mass production and shows how each were "from the first, parts of scientific management."

FRANKLIN MANUFACTURING. See George D. Babcock, *The Taylor System in Franklin Management*, 1918, reprint, Easton, Pa.: Hive Publishing Co. 1972.

496 ONE OTHER MAKER. FWT to Charles de Freminville, January 27, 1914.

TOOL GRINDER. U.S. Patent 565,644, issued August 11, 1896.

SUBSTITUTE MECHANICAL DEVICES. U. S. Patent 400,143, issued March 26, 1889.

GAUGED BALLS. "Report in Progress Made in Manufacture of the Simonds Rolling Machine Company," 1897, 6, Collection.

TEMPERING MACHINE. Ibid., 7.

497 TIMING WAS CRUCIAL. Yves Cohen, "The Modernization of Production in the French Automobile Industry Between the Wars," *Business History Review* 65 (Winter 1991), 768.

DOUBTLESS CAUGHT. Nevins, 468.

BY 1912 OR 1913. Hounshell, 250.

CAREFULLY LOOKED INTO. Quoted in Hounshell, 236.

READ WIDELY. Nevins, 474–475. See also Merkle, 97.

HARDLY BUY A STOPWATCH. Edward K. Miller to the author.

FOUR-HOUR MONOLOGUE. FWT to Edward Clark, March 12, 1909. For more on Packard, see Nevins, 468.

SIX HUNDRED SUPERINTENDENTS. FWT to Carl Barth, December 4, 1914.

498 BIG-SCALE MODERN PRODUCTION. Bjork, 309.

LABOR'S DISTASTE. Sward, 49.

WATERTOWN TOOLMAKER. Hearings, 1170.

APPLICATION OF THE TAYLOR SYSTEM. Linhart, 85. See also John P. Hoerr, *And the Wolf Finally Came: The Decline of the American Steel Industry*, Pittsburgh: University of Pittsburgh Press, 1988, 313: "Although a Tayloristic division of labor most readily evokes the visual image of an assembly line ... its principles were applied in many industries, such as steel, which had no assembly lines."

499 IMMENSE ADVANTAGE. Merkle, 95.

MACHINE OF UNIVERSAL EFFICIENCY. "The Four-Hour Day Is a Long Way Off Yet ...," Philadelphia *North American*, July 16, 1911.

DENTISTS. Ralph M. Barnes, *Motion and Time Study Applications*, New York: John Wiley & Sons, 1948, 22.

SMALLEST INTEGRAL PART. Hoerr, *And the Wolf*, 313.

500 HIGHLY TAYLORISTIC. National Center on Education and the Economy, *America's Choice: High Skills or Low Wages*, 1990, 39.

MAKE BEDS. Barnes, *Motion and Time Study Applications*, 26.

WORKED OUT FOR SCHMIDT. Garson, 266.

501 1974 PAPER. Edwin Layton, "The Diffusion of Scientific Management and Mass Production from the U.S. in the Twentieth Century," *Proceedings #4*, XIVth International Congress of the History of Science, 1974. Typescript courtesy Edwin Layton.

MODERN TIME CONSCIOUSNESS. Steven A. Battaglia, "Measuring Time: Railroads, Taylorism, and the Emergence of a Modern Time Consciousness," *Techne* (Spring 1992), 34–37.

LEISURE'S TRANSFORMATION. Robert Goldman and John Wilson, "The Rationalization of Leisure," *Politics and Society* 7 (2; 1977) 157–187.

REAGAN. Bert A. Rockman, "Tightening the Reins: The Federal Executive and the Management Philosophy of the Reagan Presidency," *Presidential Studies Quarterly*, 1991, 103–114.

NEW INTERPRETION. Christopher Lasch, *The True and Only Heaven*, New York: W. W. Norton, 1991, 224.

WILLIAM CARLOS WILLIAMS. Cecilia Tichi, "William Carlos Williams and the Efficient Moment," *Prospects* 7 (1982), 267–279.

CÉLINE. Philippe Roussin, "Getting Back from the Other World: From Doctor to Author," *South Atlantic Quarterly* 93 (2; Spring 1994), 243–264.

PLACE IN THE TRINITY. Drucker, *Post-Capitalist Society*, 39.

502 SIXTY TO NINETY DAYS. Drucker, "The Rise of the Knowledge Society," 62.

S S *FREDERICK W. TAYLOR*. American Bureau of Shipping *Record*, 1945.

PRINCIPLES . . . BECOME VAGUER. C. B. Thompson, "The Taylor System in Europe."

UTOPIAN HOPE. Rabinbach, 243.

503 NO MORE THAN A GUESS. *Industrial Relations*, 792; C. B. Thompson, *The Taylor System of Scientific Management*, 7.

SEEMING SPLIT. Consider, for example, Sanford M. Jacoby, "The Workplace as an Expressive Totality," *Labor History* 30, 108: Taylorist engineers "had more of an impact on management ideology than on actual industrial practice."

MISSIONARIES FRESH FROM INDIA. Drury, 187.

SO-CALLED ORGANIZATION EXPERTS. Rockstrom, 30.

504 PROGRESSIVE MANIFESTO. Nelson, 170.

PART OF A JUDGE. Quoted in Revell, 53.

ADVANCE COMPARABLE. Brandeis, *Business—A Profession*, xlviii. See also Adelstein, 649.

505 FEW CREATIVE GENIUSES. Quoted in Strom, 127.

DID NOT TAKE ME LONG. Joseph French Johnson, *Journal of the Efficiency Society*, April 1915, 9.

JOINED THE TAYLOR SOCIETY. *Bulletin* XVII (1), 38.

SOUND, HUMANE PRINCIPLES. *Machinist*, July 27, 1911.

IN HARMONY WITH SOCIALISM. *The Socialist*, May 20, 1911.

GRAMSCI. See Martin Clark, *Antonio Gramsci and the Revolution That Failed*, New Haven, Conn.: Yale University Press, 1977.

506 POWER OF CONSUMPTION LIMITLESS. Tarbell, *Day's Work*, 293.

HOMESTEAD. Margaret F. Byington, *Homestead: The Households of a Mill Town*, Pittsburgh: University of Pittsburgh Press, 1974, 83. See also Licht, 240.

COTTON SHIRTS. FWT-Hearings, 18.

SAME LUXURIES. Ibid., 209.

507 PRIMITIVE IN THEIR WAYS. Journal, June 3, 1869.

ARTICLE OF THE ENGINEER'S FAITH. Layton, *Revolt of the Engineers*, 140.

START POKING. Robert Taylor, 1976, III-11.

DUCHAMP. Ibid., 115.

508 DECOMPOSITION OF EACH TASK. Rabinbach, 242.

COMPARED TO COULOMB. Doray, 184.

TANGIBLE BEHIND IT. A. Hamilton Church, "Has 'Scientific Management' Science?" *Machinist*, July 20, 1911.

509 PRIOR KNOWLEDGE. James M. Dodge, YMCA talk, December 8, 1913, Collection.

SINGLE PIECE OF ORIGINAL WORK. Dartmouth, 48.

WRIGHT BROTHERS. Harlow Person, "The Genius of Frederick W. Taylor, *Advanced Management*, January–March 1945, p. 3. See also Carl Barth, *Bulletin*, December 1921, 229: Taylor "warned his disciples to remember that his system was an evolution of years and *not a brilliant invention* [emphasis in original] either on his own part or on that of anybody else."

LACKS THE SPIRIT. *New York Times*, February 26, 1916.

RARELY REASON WITH HIM. FWT, notes beginning with "Most of what I shall say . . ." Collection, file 81C.

510 MIDDLE AGES. Frank C. Hudson, "The Machinist's Side of Taylorism," *Machinist*, April 27, 1911, 773.

PREVAILING CLUB SYSTEM. Kempton Taylor, 7.

TYRANNICAL ACTION. FWT to Lionel Marks, August 29, 1914.

CONSERVER OF PRIVILEGE. H. L. Gantt, *Bulletin*, February 1917. See also Theodore M. Porter, "Objectivity as Standardization: The Rhetoric of Impersonality in Measurement, Statistics, and Cost-Benefit Analysis," *Annals of Scholarship* 9 (1–2; 1992), 28: "It is not by accident that the authority of numbers is linked to a particular form of government, representative democracy. Calculation is one of the most convincing ways by which a democracy can reach an effective decision in cases of potential controversy, while sumultaneously avoiding coercion and minimizing the disorderly effects of vigorous public involvement."

OUTLOOK OF A FREE MAN. Walter Lippmann, *Drift and Mastery: An Attempt to Diagnose the Current Unrest*, 1914; rev. ed., Madison: University of Wisconsin Press, 1985, 151.

511 TWO PEOPLE'S OPINIONS. N. P. Alifas, quoted in John R. Commons, ed., *Trade Unionism and Labor Problems*, Boston: Ginn and Company, 1921, 147.

CODE OF LAWS. *Industrial Relations*, 804.

A WONDER. A. B. Wadleigh to FWT. See also T. Coonahan to FWT, February 20, 1896: "A man will throw 12 shovels a minute while working" but typically loafs a third of the time.

512 REMOVE BUSHING. L. P. Alford, "Scientific Management in Use," *Machinist*, April 4, 1912, 549.

GUESSES IT TO WEIGH. *Bulletin* VI (3; 1921), 114.

513 CERTAIN AMOUNT OF EXPERIENCE. Hearings, 582.

SELF-REGULATING. *The Congregationalist*, May 20, 1911.

THE SOUL OF IT. Carlo Saiz to FWT, May 2, 1913.

BORN MANAGER. FWT to Carol Saiz, May 16, 1913.

514 NAPOLEON. *Engineering News Record*, March 23, 1911.

EASY TO CREDIT. *Machinist*, April 6, 1911. See Wilfred Lewis, *Bulletin*, December 1921: "We [at Tabor] were fortunate in the beginning to have the personal help and guidance of Mr. Taylor himself. . . . We had faith in our leader and his magnetic personality carried us safely through a multitude of storms."

FIRST TRUTH. William Redfield, *New Industrial Day*, New York: The Century Co., 1913, 35.

FIFTEEN UNNECESSARY MOTIONS. *Life*, 1913. For two similar examples, see Sullivan, 76 and 83.

VISITED THE WIDOW. *Nation*, October 1912, 402–403, quoted in Callahan, 46.

515 LEFT SOMETHING OUT. See Max H. C. Brombacher, "The Watertown Arsenal Labor Trouble," *Iron Age*, January 25, 1912: When intelligent foremen "see a system that has been incorrectly or impossibly labelled 'scientific' fall down in application, they laugh. They reason that if the system were really scientific it would hardly be likely to break down, since science is fact; hence, its breaking down demonstrates that it is almost anything but scientific."

100,000,000 STROKES. *New York Sun*, June 1, 1911.

HIGHPOCKETS. "Highpockets," Ann Banks, *First-person America*, New York; Knopf, 1980. Thanks also to folklorist Archie Green, who furnished several other stories in this spirit.

516 FOOL QUESTIONS. *Machinists' Monthly Journal*, 24, 1912, 406.

OLD CANOE-MAKERS. "Henry Mitchell," in Banks, *First-person America*.

THE HUMAN ELEMENT. On many a bricklayer's scaffold, writes Sullivan, 82, "occurred combats between orthodoxy and reformation not inferior in dignity and certainly not less white-hot in emotion than Martin Luther before the diet of Worms."

CAN'T CLOCK HOW A MAN FEELS. Robert H. Guest, "Men and Machines," *Personnel*, May 1955.

FED UP. Fred H. Colvin to Margaret Ellen Hawley, February 8, 1927, Gilbreth Archive.

COMPLETELY SCIENTIFIC. *Bulletin*, November 1917, 6.

517 HOPELESS. *Industrial Relations*, 869.

MAKE SUGGESTIONS. Morris Cooke, "The Spirit and Social Significance of Scientific Management," *Journal of Political Economy*, June 1913, 493.

RELEVANT STANDARD. Aitken, 47.

518 SPIRIT DAILY SWEETER. Ordway Tead, *New Republic*, January 28, 1920. See also Robert Valentine, "The Progressive Relation Between Efficiency and Consent," *Bulletin*, January 1916, 7.

NATION OF SLAVES. *Industrial Relations*, 991–1011.

ABUSIVE ABSENCE OF SYMPATHY. Tead, *New Republic*.

519 WHAT ARE YOU MAKING? Thomas Keneally, *Schindler's List*, New York: Touchstone, 1993, 209.

SCIENCE OF HOROLOGY. In E. P. Thompson, 86.

520 NELS ALIFAS. See Hearings, 1262–1264.

521 MAKE THEM RUN. Quoted in John R. Commons, ed., *Trade Unionism and Labor Problems*, Boston: Ginn and Company, 1921, 149.

ENGLISHMAN'S 1906 ACCOUNT. Versions of this story appear in Henri Le Chatelier, "The Philosophy of Taylorism," *Bulletin*, December 1928, 249; Vielleville, *Le Système Taylor*, 114. See also editor, *Mon Bureau*, to FWT, March 5, 1913; Humphreys, 111; Merkle, 225.

SLAVE DRIVER'S WHIP. Hearings, 1934. See also D.H.M., "More Light on the Gospel of 'Efficiency,'" *Machinists' Monthly Journal* 24, 1912, 408.

ANOTHER STEP. *The Clarion*, December 20, 1912.

522 TYRANT OR SLAVE-DRIVER. Quoted in Urwick & Brech, II, 103.

FAMILY HAD HELD SLAVES. Fred J. Miller, "Henry L. Gantt—An Appreciation," *Management Review*, April, 1930.

TIME OF SLAVE LABOR. Hearings, 571. James Dodge ("Scientific Management: Progressive and Irresistible," December 8, 1913, typescript in Collection): Scientific management "was born to the world in the first cry of anguish that escaped the lips of the lashed slave, and followed up by untold myriads of others expressing the sufferings of those oppressed by the cruelty of the task master."

FEW HUNDRED YEARS AGO. FWT, YMCA talk, October 12, 1914, Collection.

INFERIOR RACE. There is reason to doubt Nathaniel Burt and Wallace E. Davies, in Weigley, 492 (repeated in Licht, *Getting Work,* 46, and *Labor History,* Winter 1994), that FWT "hired 200 blacks to work with his white "gangs' at Midvale Steel in 1896." See Robert Kanigel, *Labor History,* Spring 1996, 300.

AUFHAUSER. R. Keith Aufhauser, "Slavery and Scientific Management," *Journal of Economic History* 33 (4; 1973), 811–824.

523 MUSSOLINI WELCOME. Eleanor Cooke, "The Third International Management Congress," *Bulletin,* October 1927, 486–490.

EASY-GOING, SKEPTICAL. C. B. Thompson, "The Taylor System in Europe," 175.

ROLE OF THE FASCISTS. Willson, 39.

524 DATES . . . FROM THIS PERIOD. Quoted in Willson, 43.

TAKEN CARE OF. Quoted in Willson, 52.

MURMUR OF CONVERSATION. Eleanor Cooke, "Third International," 488.

FLASHED ON THE SCREEN. Louise Fragment.

LIVING IN ZURICH. Merkle, 178, specifies Zurich. The city cites a six-story gabled house at 14 Spiegelgasse as Lenin's during this period.

525 ENSLAVEMENT OF HUMANKIND. Linhart, 84, 87; R. Traub, "Lenin and Taylor: the Fate of 'Scientific Management' in the (Early) Soviet Union," *Telos* 37 (1978), 82.

THIRD OF PREWAR LEVELS. Traub, "Lenin and Taylor," 83.

REFINED CRUELTY. *Pravda,* April 28, 1918. See John R. Commons, *Trade Unionism and Labor Problems,* Boston: Ginn and Company, 1921, 179.

POLEMIC AGAINST THEM. Merkle, 114.

FORCED IT INTO RUSSIAN INDUSTRY. Ibid., 116.

DRAWN BY SAMOVARS. Quoted by Kendall E. Bailes, "The American Connection: Ideology and the Transfer of American Technology to the Soviet Union, 1917–1941," *Comparative Studies in Society and History* 23(3), 425.

526 NEVER SEEN A WATCH. Traub, "Lenin and Taylor", 85.

ONE AMERICAN ENGINEER. The engineer in question was Royal Keely, whom Taylor had taken on as an acolyte. See Daniel A. Wren, "Scientific Management in the U.S.S.R., with Particular Reference to the Contribution of Walter N. Polakov, *Academy of Management Review* 5 (1; 1980), 3.

TRACES. Linhart, 78.

TWENTY INSTITUTIONS. Traub, "Lenin and Taylor", 91.

GASTEV. See Hughes, 257–259; Nelson, *Mental Revolution,* 18.

GANTT CHARTS. Whitsett and Yorks, 78; See Peter B. Petersen, "The Evolution of the Gantt Chart and Its Relevance Today," *Journal of Management Issues,* Summer 1991, 131–155.

NATIVE PHENOMENON. Merkle, 121.

'KULTUR.' Wilfred Lewis, *Transactions ASME* 37, 1477.

GERMANY ADOPTS. *New York Herald,* probably June 3, 1912. (The handwritten reference to 1907 on the Collection's clipping doesn't fit its contents.)

527 MESSIANIC. Interview with Ulrich Wengenroth. See also Thomas Hughes, "Technology," in *The Holocaust: Ideology, Bureaucracy, and Genocide* [The San Jose Conference on the Holocaust, 1977–1978], edited by Henry Friedlander and Sybil Milton, Millwood, N.Y.: Kraus, 1980.

OBEDIENCE TO SUPERIORS. *Iron Age,* June 24, 1913.

HUNDRED THOUSAND COPIES. Hughes, *American Genesis,* 285.

BIG COMPANIES. Nolan, 43, 146.

PHYSICAL MANIFESTATION. Merkle, 193.

WEIMAR ERA POSTER. Hughes, *American Genesis,* 287.

FORTY PAGES. Devinat, Appendix II. In 1913, a cartoon in a popular magazine

(*Jugend* 42), showed a professor lecturing a group of young washerwomen. "Dr. Striese," read the caption, "has decided to offer popular lectures, the Psychology of the Senegalese Early Romantic Period, at the workplace, so as not to reduce the precious time of the working women and girls" (tran. Friedrich Meyer-Hirsch, Berlin). This was true efficiency: the girls would simultaneously work and learn, while the professor enjoyed their company. The caption was headed, "System Taylor."

RATIONALIZATION. See Edward Eyre Hunt, "Scientific Management and World Economics, *Bulletin*, June 1927, 383: " 'Rationalization' is a new word to American ears, and has not been satisfactorily defined. It is a slogan which expresses with a certain vagueness, perhaps, what we mean by science in management"; see also Charles Adamiecki, "Scientific Management or Rationalization," Franklin D. Roosevelt Library.

528 BROAD SCALE. Peukert, 113.

ALMOST DEHUMANIZED. Nolan, 231. See also Nicholas Bullock, " 'First the Kitchen—then the Façade'," *Journal of Design History* 1 (3–4; 1988), 177–192.

CRUELTY NATURAL TO THEM. Stan Spacek, "Who Is F. W. Taylor?" Collection.

529 PLASTIC SENSUALITY. Herf, 183.

INWARDLY WITH SOUL. Quoted in Herf, 196.

AFTER ALBERT SPEER. Overy, 360–365. See also Tilla Siegel, "Rationalizing Industrial Relations: A Debate on the Control of Labor in German Shipyards in 1941," in Thomas Childers and Jane Caplan, eds., *Reevaluating the Third Reich*, New York: Holmes & Meier, 1993, 139–160; Anson G. Rabinbach, "The Aesthetics of Production in the Third Reich," in George L. Mosse, ed., *International Fascism*: New Thoughts and New Approaches, London: Sage Publications, 1979.

530 MISMANAGEMENT WAS MORE THE RULE. Michael Allen, "Engineers and Modern Managers in the SS: The Businesss Administration Main Office," dissertation, University of Pennsylvania, 1995, 255.

PERVERSION OF HIS IDEALS. Merkle, 201.

POPE OF RATIONALIZATION MOVEMENT. Interview with Ulrich Wengenroth. See also Campbell, 135–137.

OHLENDORF. Ibid., 373.

NOT EXCESS OF REASON. Herf, 234.

ENLIGHTENED PRINCIPLES. Campbell, 347.

531 EFFICIENCY OF HIS GAS. Robert Jay Lifton, *The Nazi Doctors*, New York: Basic Books, 1986, 160.

SET MY MIND AT REST. Ibid., 162.

MODEL FOR EVERYDAY LIFE. Nolan, 213.

ELEMENTS OF AMERICANISM. Ibid., 233.

IF A PARTY TECHNOCRAT. Monika Renneberg and Mark Walker, *Science, Technology, and National Socialism*, Cambridge, Engl.: Cambridge University Press, 8.

532 WHICH IS BETTER. Lifton, *Nazi Doctors*, 176.

HEAVY IRON BEAMS. Michael Allen, "Engineers and Modern Managers in the SS," 81.

PERFECT TAYLOR ENGINEER. Interview with Ulrich Wengenroth.

533 TO THE LIMIT. John Golden, " 'Scientific Management' in the Textile Industry," *American Federationist*, August 1911, 603.

534 HAVE TO WORK HARDER? Hearings, 1588.

535 CHALK MARKS. Eli Ginzberg, *The American Worker in the Twentieth Century*, New York: Free Press of Glencoe, 165.

ENGINEERED OUT. Ibid., 285.

TOO MUCH DIRECTION. Hearings, 691.

OBEY ORDERS. *Transactions ASME* 27, 729.

ENTIRELY NEW PLANE. Braverman, 90.

536 ABOVE AND . . . OUTSIDE. Graziosi, 542.
REDUCE THE SKILL LEVELS. Shaiken, 46.
SOUGHT BACK IN 1880. Ibid., 49.
MEANS OF REDUCING . . . SKILL. Ibid., 55.
FIVE MINUTES OF REFLECTION. Henri Le Chatelier, "The Philosophy of Taylorism," *Bulletin*, December 1928, 252.
537 JUST SUCH PROGRESS. FWT-Hearings, 276–277.
FIVE OR SIX TRADES. *Industrial Relations*, 797.
MANAGED BY THE WORKMEN. Ibid.
STIFLED INITIATIVE. H. King Hathaway, *Bulletin*, February 1917, 17.
UPLIFT OF MANKIND. Kempton P. A. Taylor, "Some Aspects of Scientific Management," Haverford College B. S. degree paper, May 15, 1915, Collection.
SEE THEIR CASTINGS. Hearings, 392.
538 HIGHEST POWERS. *Journal of Political Economy*, 1913, 485.
GREAT STOREHOUSE. Ibid., 486.
MATCHED BY A GROWTH. See, for example, Paul Attewell, "Skill and Occupational Changes in U. S. Manufacturing," in Adler, 46–88; Andrew Dawson, "The Paradox of Dynamic Technological Change and the Labor Aristocracy in the United States, 1880–1914," *Labor History*, 20, 325–351.
LOST PARADISE. Jean Monds, "Workers' Control and the Historians: A New Economism," *New Left Review*, May–June 1976, 85.
PROMISE OF ORDER. Nelson, *A Mental Revolution*, 20.
539 THEY THOUGHT RIGHT. Edward Mott Woolley, "Putting the 'One Best Way' Into Practice," *System*, April 1911, 356–365.
540 PRIDE OF THE BLOCK. Katie Richards O'Hare, *National Rip-Saw*, January 1916.
541 SAME DISAGREEABLE FEELING. Rockstrom, 172.
PRIDE OF PRODUCER. Undated article, "Scientific Management," in clipping file, Collection.
542 STRANGER ARMED. Geoffrey C. Brown, "Workers' Participation in Job Study," *Bulletin*, June 1927. See also Gomberg and Dubinsky, 22.
NOT AN EFFICIENT CITIZEN. *New York Times*, February 26, 1916. See also Miner Chipman, "Efficiency, Scientific Management, and Organized Labor," read at the annual meeting of the Efficiency Society, January 21, 1916, Collection.
543 MINIMUM OF SURPLUS ENERGY. Frank T. Carlton, *Journal of Political Economy*, October 1912, 838.
HIS BEST EFFORTS. Friedmann, *The Anatomy of Work*, 105.
NEW ORDER OF THINGS. Wilfred Lewis, "An Object Lesson in Efficiency," in C. B. Thompson, ed., 240.
544 MOST DIFFICULT CLASS. *Transactions ASME* 27, 726.
SLEEP TODAY? John Golden, "The Attitude of Organized Labor."
BLAZE MY WAY. Ben Hamper, *Rivethead: Tales from the Assembly Line*, New York: Warner, 1992, 24.
DOUBLING UP. Ibid., 35.
545 GREASEBALL MECCA. Ibid., 191.
AS THEY ARE TOLD. H. L. Gantt, *Transactions ASME* 30, 1041.
ALTERNATE BOUTS. E. P. Thompson, 71. Max Weber noted in *The Protestant Ethic and the Spirit of Capitalism* (London: Harper Collins Academic, 1991, 60) how for some workers earning more is simply not so appealing as working less: "A man does not 'by nature' wish to earn more and more money."
SLACK OFF ANOTHER. Kenneth Lasson, *The Workers*, New York: Bantam, 1972, 145.

LOW PROLES. Paul Fussell, *Class*, New York: Ballantine, 1984, 43. See also Richard Sennett and Jonathan Cobb, *The Hidden Injuries of Class*, New York: Vintage, 1973, 236.
546 GREATEST OF LIFE'S JOYS. Taylor Memorial, 72.
MASTER SHALL BLAME. Ibid., 65.
547 VISION OF INDUSTRIAL REFORM. Mulcaire, 66.
UTOPIAN DREAM. Munley, 34.
YANKEE DOODLE. Journal, May 15, 1869. Caspar Goodrich to Kempton Taylor, July 23, 1915: "No man ever lived who was more the 'captain of his soul' " than Taylor.
NOT BY BREAD ALONE. *Bulletin*, February 1925, 59.
548 DID NOT DELUDE HIMSELF. Christie, 22
SELF-MADE MAN. Pouget, 3.
MEMORIAL SERVICE. See copy of Copley's biography (II, 437) annotated in the margins by Gilbreth, Gilbreth Archive, courtesy of Jane Morley.
549 MUST NOT FORGET. Taylor, "Workmen and Their Management," 15.
EXTEND AND MAKE UNIVERSAL. Drury, *Bulletin*, February 1917.
TIMID, OBEDIENT. Ibid.
DEEPLY MOVED. McCullough, *Mornings on Horseback*, 259–260.
THE PRESENT SYSTEM. Harlow Person, *Bulletin*, June–August 1926, 94. In "Shop Management," 146, Taylor acknowledges that some might disapprove of a planning department intended to think for the men, "on the ground that this does not tend to promote independence, self-reliance, and originality." But if so, they "must take exception to the whole trend of modern industrial development"—which apparently he did not. Wilfred Lewis, 3, wrote of Taylor that he was "a reformer of the first magnitude who took life as he found it, and . . . sought to improve the social fabric of which he formed a part. He was not a blatant demagogue bent upon destruction for the sake of an imaginary reconstruction of society."
550 SLAVES IN THE GALLEY. Shaiken, 64.
551 CARONIA. See Arnold Kludas, *Great Passenger Ships of the World*, vol. 1, Cambridge: Patrick Stephens, 1975, 112; "Cunard Floating Hotels," Cunard brochure, Steamship Historical Society Collection, University of Baltimore.
HIGHEST CLASS ENGLISH. FWT to Elizabeth Taylor, May 10, 1912. See also FWT to Caspar Goodrich, July 13, 1912.
552 MOUNTAINS HIGH. FWT to I. Minis Hays, June 25, 1912.
WORRY AND ANXIETY. FWT to Caspar Goodrich, July 13, 1912.
TAKE CARE OF HERSELF. FWT to James Dodge, June 20, 1912.
PROSTRATION. FWT to Marcel de Coninck, August 21, 1912.
NERVOUS BREAKDOWN. Frances Mitchell to William A. Fannon, May 17, 1915.
WRONG WITH OUR MOTHER. Robert Taylor to Bayard Clark, June 26, 1983, Myron Johnson papers. See also Robert Taylor, 1976, IV-7.
EUROPE AND ITS AMUSEMENTS. FWT to Langdon C. Stewardson, July 12, 1912.
KNEW BETTER. FWT to James Dodge, July 12, 1912.
VEGETABLE LIFE. FWT to Langdon C. Stewardson, June 21, 1912.
553 MARK OF DISTINCTION. Tom Lutz, *American Nervousness, 1903: An Anecdotal History*, Ithaca: Cornell University Press, 1991, 6.
PRESSURE . . . TOO GREAT. Louise Fragment.
VAIN AND SHALLOW. Kakar, 209, n. 16.
SERVANTS. FWT to Ernest N. Wright, October 29, 1902.
GILMAN STORY. Lutz, *American Nervousness*, 224.
AMBITIOUS WOMAN. FWT to Langdon C. Stewardson, June 21, 1912. Lou's condition emerges from FWT's letters to James Dodge (July 12, 1912), Ned Wright (Sep-

tember 26), Edward and Frank Clark (August 3), Stewardson (July 12 and August 10), and Gaston de Coninck (August 21).

QUIETING STORY. FWT to Langdon C. Stewardson, July 12, 1912.

INTANGIBLE ILLNESS. FWT to Langdon C. Stewardson, August 10, 1912.

554 INTESTINAL DERANGEMENT. FWT to Birge Harrison, November 30, 1912.

INTESTINAL POISONING. FWT to Langdon C. Stewardson, May 14, 1913. Lou's condition during this later period comes from FWT's letters to G. F. Steele (February 12, 1913), Caspar Goodrich (April 7 and June 2), and Birge Harrison (May 26).

FRENCH CHAUFFEUR. FWT to Caspar Goodrich, June 23, 1913.

EVERY MINUTE. FWT to Birge Harrison, May 26, 1913.

555 UNABLE TO KEEP UP. FWT to Caspar Goodrich, November 20, 1913.

HIP BOTHERED HIM. FWT to Birge Harrison, May 26, 1913; FWT to Caspar Goodrich, June 2, 1913.

BRONCHIAL COLD. FWT to Caspar Goodrich, April 7, 1913.

OUT OF TOUCH. FWT to William B. Wilson, December 17, 1912.

CAUSE AND EFFECT. Frances Mitchell and William A. Fannon, May 17, 1915.

WEIGHED HIM DOWN. Mary Clark to Frank Gilbreth, May 3, 1916. Gilbreth Archive.

KILLED THE OLD MAN. Robert Taylor, 1976, IV-7.

RAN HIM RAGGED. Ibid., IV-5.

TWENTY-FOUR HOURS A DAY. Ibid.

ROCKLAND. Robert Taylor to Jane Hartye, January 30, 1984. See also Robert Taylor, 1976, IV-8.

WRUNG YOUR HEART. Robert Taylor to Bayard Clark, June 26, 1983, Myron Johnson papers.

556 MONOTONOUS LIFE. FWT to Caspar Goodrich, July 13, 1912.

SPIRIT OF DEVOTION. Wilfred Lewis, *Transactions ASME* 36, 1478.

CARE AND DEVOTION. Louise Fragment

CHIEF INTEREST. FWT to Lionel Marks, August 29, 1914. See also FWT to Barth, October 12, 1912. On the other hand, see Robert Taylor, VI-13: "I think the Old Man rather liked [Gilbreth] and thought that he was doing pretty good work." In the same vein, see Robert T. Kent to Margaret Ellen Hawley, December 31, 1926, Gilbreth Archive.

557 "FATHER". Lillian M. Gilbreth, "As I Remember Him," *Journal of Industrial Engineering*, March–April 1961, 137; interview, Laurence G. Taber.

NAME NOT MENTIONED. Interview, Laurence G. Taber.

DEVIL INCARNATE. Quoted in Copley, II, 435.

EGOTISTICAL AND ... VINDICTIVE. Fred H. Colvin to Margaret Ellen Hawley, April 6, 1927, Gilbreth Archive.

REMARKABLE IN ITS INTENSITY. Copley, "Revolutionist," 4.

LOT OF THE MEDIATOR. Kempton P. A. Taylor, "Some Aspects of Scientific Management," Haverford College B. S. degree paper, May 15, 1915, p. 32, Collection.

CERTAIN KNOWLEDGE. Quoted in Copley, II, 435.

MY NAME IS TAYLOR. FWT to James Dodge, November 23, 1914.

558 PUTTING GREEN. Taylor, "The Making of a Putting Green," five-part series ending June 1915.

AUTUMN ROSES. FWT to Caspar Goodrich, November 20, 1913.

RIPENED WELL. Birge Harrison to FWT, October 14, 1912.

559 TO BE PRIZED. FWT to Birge Harrison, November 20, 1912.

COTTON-WOOL. Birge Harrison to FWT, January 1913.

THIS IS OUR WAY. FWT to Carl Barth, March 27 and 29, 1913.

CALLED UPON. FWT to William B. Wilson, July 16, 1912.

STATE OF THE ART. "The Present State of the Art of Industrial Management," in C. B. Thompson, ed., 153–174.

VERY FINE REPORT. FWT to L. P. Alford, December 11, 1912.

INSIPID. FWT to William Crozier, November 14, 1912.

TIME STUDIES BEGAN. FWT response to "The Present State of the Art of Industrial Management," in C. B. Thompson, ed., 194.

560 NO COOPERATION. FWT to William Crozier, October 8, 1913.

DEAD FROM OVERWORK. FWT to Morris Cooke, December 6, 1913.

LITTLE CUSTOMER. FWT to William Crozier, October 8, 1913.

APPARENTLY FINE. William Crozier to FWT, November 26, 1913.

561 KILLED BY IT. FWT to A. B. Wadleigh, December 22, 1913.

WITH HIS HORSES. A. B. Wadleigh to FWT, January 3, 1914.

DRINK AND WOMEN. Ibid.

GOOD PHYSICAL CONDITION. Ibid., with Dr. C. L. Johnstonbaugh's note, January 2, 1914, appended to letter.

WARMEST THANKS. FWT to A. B. Wadleigh, January 6, 1914.

562 IMPRESSED MORRIS COOKE. Copley, II, 236.

HOW DO YOU KNOW? A. J. Portenar to FWT, June 1, 1914.

WORTHY OBJECT. FWT to A. J. Portenar, June 10, 1914.

GIVE FULL CREDENCE. A. J. Portenar to FWT, June 27, 1914.

563 ARROGANT OVERLORD. Ibid.

NO CHANCE TO REPLY. FWT to A. J. Portenar, July 28, 1914.

REST CURE. FWT to Caspar Goodrich, March 14, 1914.

ASKED BY CHAIRMAN WALSH. FWT to Carl Barth, March 20, 1914

UNDERLYING CAUSES. *Industrial Relations*, 6.

564 PROPER HUMAN ANIMAL. Ibid., 777.

UNQUALIFIED OPPOSITION. Ibid., 128.

HOXIE. Urwick, ed., 144; John P. Frey, "Robert F. Hoxie: Investigator and Interpreter," *Journal of Political Economy*, November 1916, 884–896.

PEPPERY MANNER. H. G. Coburn to Kempton Taylor, September 16, 1915.

VERY INDIGNANT. FWT to Carl Barth, June 13, 1914.

UNIVERSALLY RECOGNIZED. Carl Barth to FWT, June 15, 1914.

RELAPSES. FWT to Caspar Goodrich, September 14, 1914.

565 MORE AND MORE. FWT to Birge Harrison, February 20, 1915.

SAD TO SEE HIM STRICKEN. Ibid.

HORRIBLE WAR. FWT to E. C. Allingham, September 4, 1914.

DESERVE TO BE. FWT to G. F. Steele, November 10, 1914.

OVERWHELMED ME. FWT to Caspar Goodrich, September 14, 1914.

CRAMPED FOR INCOME. FWT to Birge Harrison, March 2, 1915. See also Copley, II, 444.

HOTEL BRIGHTON. Photos and other material furnished by Atlantic City Free Public Library and Bryant Simon. See also Charles Funnell, *By the Beautiful Sea: The Rise and High Times of That Great American Resort, Atlantic City*, New Brunswick: Rutgers University Press, 1983.

566 ONLY PLACE ON THE COAST. Quoted in Funnell, *By the Beautiful Sea*, 135.

ROTTING SEAWEED. Ibid, 136. See also *Handy Guide to Philadelphia and Environs* Chicago: Rand McNally & Co., 1913, chapter XII.

HURLY BURLY. Birge Harrison to FWT, November 27, 1914.

ONLY SNOW ITSELF. FWT quoted in Copley, II, 446.

BONES AND TISSUE. *Congressional Record*, Senate, 4343 (February 23, 1915).

FORMAL CLAIMS. See Hoxie, *Scientific Management and Labor*.

IN SYMPATHY. James Dodge to FWT, January 18, 1915.

567 ECLIPSE OF THE MOON. *Industrial Relations*, 800.

ONE OF TWO ELEMENTS. FWT to James Dodge, January 27, 1915.

HEARTLESS. James Dodge to FWT, February 18, 1915.

GREAT MISTAKE. FWT to James Dodge, February 25, 1915.

568 GREAT COMFORTER. Birge Harrison to FWT, February 27, 1915.

GREATEST BLESSING. FWT to Birge Harrison, March 2, 1915.

CLOTHCRAFT. See Nelson, *Mental Revolution*, chapter 2; Gilson; Tarbell, *New Ideals*, 214.

HIGH CLASS MAN. FWT to Dwight Merrick, March 4, 1915.

VISITOR'S BOOK. Located at Catherwood Library.

CLEVELAND ADVERTISING CLUB. Typescript of Address, March 3, 1915, in Collection.

ALMOST UNABLE TO SPEAK. FWT to Feiss, March 11, 1915 (dictated March 9, 1915).

HEADING HOME. This is speculative but is drawn from interview with railroad historian Herb Harwood; Peter T. Maiken, *Night Trains: The Pullman System in the Golden Years of American Rail Travel*, Baltimore: Johns Hopkins University Press, 1989; Robert Taylor, 1976, IV-5; and related correspondence. Events in succeeding days are pieced together from Copley, II, 447–453; *Philadelphia Press* and Philadelphia *Public Ledger*, March 22, 1915.

569 NOT BE GOING WEST. Frances Mitchell to Robert Hoxie, March 15, 1915.

ALARMING NATURE. Herbert Hamilton Chandler to Emily Richards, March 19, 1915.

WIND HIS WATCH. Copley, II, 452.

FATHER PASSED AWAY. Collection.

INDUSTRIAL STRIFE. Taylor Memorial, 4. Said Morris Cooke, 6: "In every part of the world—in the mines of Mozambique, in far-off Japan, and among each of the contending armies on the Continent, and all over this country—were those who called him 'Master.' "

570 MADE A BOOK. Taylor Memorial.

SELECT BIBLIOGRAPHY

Adams, Jr., Graham. *Age of Industrial Violence, 1910–1915*. New York: Columbia University Press, 1966.

Addresses and Discussions at the Conference on Scientific Management Held October 12, 13, 14, 1911. Darmouth College. Amos Tuck School of Business Administration. Easton, Pa.: Hive Publishing Co., 1985.

Adelstein, Richard P. " 'Islands of Conscious Power': Louis D. Brandeis and the Modern Corporation," *Business History Review* 63 (Autumn 1989): 614–656.

Adler, Paul S. *Technology and the Future of Work*. New York: Oxford University Press, 1992.

Aitken, Hugh G. J. *Taylorism at Watertown Arsenal: Scientific Management in Action, 1908–1915*. Cambridge, Mass.: Harvard University Press, 1960.

Akin, William E. *Technocracy and the American Dream: The Technocracy Movement, 1900–1941*. Berkeley: University of California Press, 1977.

Alford, L. P. *Henry Lawrence Gantt*. New York: Harper Brothers, 1935.

Baltzwell, E. Digby. *Philadelphia Gentlemen: The Making of a National Upper Class*. Philadelphia: University of Pennsylvania Press, 1979.

Banta, Martha. *Taylored Lives: Narrative Productions in the Age of Taylor, Veblen, and Ford*. Chicago: University of Illinois Press, 1993.

Barth, Carl. "The Inception and Early History of Scientific Management." Lecture typescript. Baker Library, Harvard University, 1924.

Bell, Charles H. *Phillips Exeter Academy in New Hampshire: A Historical Sketch*. Exeter, N.H.: William B. Morrill, 1883.

Bell, Daniel. *Work and Its Discontents*. Boston: Beacon Press, 1956.

Benjamin, Philip S. *The Philadelphia Quakers in the Industrial Age, 1865–1920*. Philadelphia: Temple University Press, 1976.

Bibber, Joyce. "Nearly All in the Family: Nathan Winslow and His Family Network. *Maine Historical Society Quarterly* 28 (4; Spring 1989): 186–208.

Bishop, J. Leander. A *History of American Manufactures*. Philadelphia: Edward Young & Co., 1868.

Bjork, Kenneth. *Saga in Steel and Concrete: Norwegian Engineers in America*. Northfield, Minnesota: Norwegian-American Historical Association, 1947.

Blodget, Lorin. "The Census of Industrial Employment, Wages, and Social Condition in Philadelphia, in 1870." Philadelphia Social Science Association, April 25, 1872.

———. "The Social Condition of the Industrial Classes of Philadelphia." Philadelphia Social Science Association, November 8, 1873.

———. *Census of Manufacturers of Philadelphia*. Philadelphia: Dickson & Gilling, 1883.

Bolles, Albert S. *Industrial History of the United States*. 3d. ed., 1881. Reprint, New York: Augustus M. Kelley, 1966.

Brady, Robert A. *The Rationalization Movement in German Industry: A Study in the Evolution of Economic Planning*. Berkeley: University of California Press, 1933.

Brandeis, Louis. *Scientific Management and the Railroads*. 1911. Reprint, Easton, Pa.: Hive Publishing Co., 1981.

———. *Business—A Profession*. Boston: Small, Maynard & Company, 1914.

Braverman, Harry. *Labor and Monopoly Capital*. New York: Monthly Review Press, 1974.

Brearley, Harry. *Knotted String: Autobiography of a Steel-Maker.* London: Longmans, Green and Co., 1941.

———. *Steel-Makers.* London, 1933. Reprinted in *Steel-makers and Knotted String,* London: Institute of Materials, 1995.

Brinley, C. A. *Russell Wheeler Davenport.* New York: G. P. Putnam's Sons, 1905.

Brody, David. *Steelworkers in America: The Nonunion Era.* Cambridge, Mass.: Harvard University Press, 1960.

Bromer, John A., J. Myron Johnson, and Richard P. Widdicombe. "A Conversation with Robert P. A. Taylor." Interview conducted in Providence, R.I., October 14 and 15, 1976. Taylor Collection. Hoboken, N.J.: Stevens Institute of Technology. Taylor Collection.

Brown, Geoff. *Sabotage: A Study in Industrial Conflict.* Nottingham, England: Spokesman Books 1977.

Brown, Ira. *Mary Grew: Abolitionist and Feminist, 1813–1896.* Selinsgrove, Pa.: Susquehanna University Press, 1991.

Brown, John K. *The Baldwin Locomotive Works, 1831–1915.* Baltimore: Johns Hopkins University Press, 1995.

Bullock, Harry A. *Higher Railroad Rates vs. Scientific Management.* 1911. Reprint, Easton, Pa.: Hive Publishing Co., 1981.

Bumbrey, Jeffrey Nordlinger. *A Guide to the Microfilm Publication of the Papers of the Pennsylvania Abolition Society at the Historical Society of Pennsylvania.* Philadelphia: The Pennsylvania Abolition Society and the Historical Society of Pennsylvania, 1976.

Burt, Nathaniel. *The Perennial Philadelphians.* Boston: Little, Brown & Company, 1963.

Butscher, Edward. *Conrad Aiken: Poet of White Horse Vale.* Athens, Ga.: University of Georgia Press, 1988.

Callahan, Raymond E. *Education and the Cult of Efficiency: A Study of the Social Forces That Have Shaped the Administration of the Public Schools.* Chicago: University of Chicago Press, 1962.

Calvert, Monte A. *The Mechanical Engineer in America, 1830–1910.* Baltimore: Johns Hopkins University Press, 1967.

Campbell, Joan. *Joy in Work, German Work: The National Debate, 1800–1945.* Princeton, N. J.: Princetown University Press, 1989.

Chandler, Alfred D., Jr. *The Visible Hand.* Cambridge, Mass.: Belknap Press of Harvard University Press, 1977.

Chandler, Alfred D., Jr., and Stephen Salsbury. *Pierre S. Du Pont and the Making of the Modern Corporation.* New York: Harper & Row, 1971.

"Chordal" (See, James W.). *Extracts from Chordal's Letters.* New York: American Machinist Publishing Co., 1880.

Christie, Jean. *Morris Llewellyn Cooke: Progressive Engineer.* New York: Garland, 1983.

Clark, Geoffrey W. "Machine-shop Engineering Roots of Taylorism: Efficiency of Machine-tools and Machinists, 1865–1884." Unpublished paper.

Clark, Victor S. *History of Manufactures in the United States, 1860–1914.* Washington, D.C.: Carnegie Institution, 1928.

Clawson, Dan. *Bureaucracy and the Labor Process: The Transformation of U. S. Industry, 1860–1920.* New York: Monthly Review Press, 1980.

Colvin, Fred H. (with D. J. Duffin). *Sixty Years with Men and Machines: An Autobiography.* 1947. Reprint, Bradley, Ill.: Lindsay Publications, 1988.

Commission on Industrial Relations. *Industrial Relations.* Vol. 1. *Final Report and Testimony.* 64th Cong., 1st sess. S. Doc. 415. Washington, D.C.: Government Printing Office, 1916.

Copley, Frank Barkley. *Frederick W. Taylor: Father of Scientific Management.* Two vols. New York: Harper and Brothers, 1923.

————. "Frederick W. Taylor: Revolutionist," in *Two Papers on Scientific Management*. London: George Routledge & Sons, 1919.

Cromwell, Otelia. *Lucretia Mott*. Cambridge, Mass.: Harvard University Press, 1958.

Crosbie, Laurence M. *The Phillips Exeter Academy: A History*. Exeter, N. H.: Phillips Exeter Academy, 1923.

Cunningham, Frank H. *Familiar Sketches of the Phillips Exeter Academy*. Boston: James R. Osgood & Co., 1883.

Danbom, David B. *"The World of Hope": Progressives and the Struggle for an Ethical Public Life*. Philadelphia: Temple University Press, 1987.

Davies, Margery. *Women's Place Is at the Typewriter: Office Work and Office Workers, 1870–1930*. Philadelphia: Temple University Press, 1982.

Depew, Chauncey M. *One Hundred Years of American Commerce*. Two vols. New York: D. O. Haynes & Co., 1895.

Devinat, Paul. *Scientific Management in Europe*. Geneva: International Labour Office, 1927.

Doray, Bernard. *From Taylorism to Fordism: A Rational Madness*. Trans. David Macey. London: Free Association Books, 1988.

Drucker, Peter F. *Post-Capitalist Society*. New York: Harper Business, 1993.

————. "The Knowledge Society," *Wilson Quarterly*, Spring 1993.

Drury, Horace Bookwalter. *Scientific Management: A History and Criticism*. New York: AMS Press, 1915.

DuBreuil, H. *Robots or Men? A French Workman's Experience in American Industry*. New York: Harper & Brothers, 1930.

Du Pasquier, J. Thierry. *Les Baleinièrs Français au XIXe Siècle (1814–1868)*. Grenoble: Terre et Mer, 1982.

Echols, Edward C., ed. *The Phillips Exeter Academy: A Pictorial History*. Exeter, N.H.: Phillips Exeter Academy Press.

Edwards, Richard. *Contested Terrain: The Transformation of the Workplace in the Twentieth Century*. New York: Basic Books, 1979.

Evans, Holden A. *One Man's Fight for a Better Navy*. New York: Dodd, Mead, 1940.

Fannon, William A. Untitled reminiscence of FWT, April 20, 1916. Taylor Collection. Edited version appears in Taylor Memorial, 98.

Final Report of the Industrial Commission, Washington, D.C.: Government Printing Office, 1902.

Fladeland, Betty. *Men and Brothers: Anglo-American Antislavery Cooperation*. Urbana: University of Illinois Press, 1972.

Freedley, Edwin T. *Leading Pursuits and Leading Men*. Philadelphia: Edward Young, 1856.

————. *Philadelphia and its Manufacturers*. Philadelphia: Edward Young, 1867.

Friedmann, Georges. *Problèmes Humains du Machinisme Industriel*. Paris: Gallimard, 1946.

————. *The Anatomy of Work*. New York: Free Press of Glencoe, 1961.

Fritz, John. *The Autobiography of John Fritz*. New York: John Wiley & Sons, 1912.

Fry, Louis. "The Maligned F. W. Taylor: A Reply to His Many Critics," *Academy of Management Review*, July 1976, 124–129.

Gallman, J. Matthew. *Mastering Wartime: A Social History of Philadelphia During the Civil War*. Cambridge: Cambridge University Press, 1990.

Gantt, Henry L. *Work, Wages, and Profit*. Easton, Pa.: Hive Publishing Co., 1974.

————. *How Scientific Management is Applied*. 1911. Reprint, Easton, Pa.: Hive Publishing Co., 1974.

————. "A Bonus System of Rewarding Labor," *Transactions of the American Society of Mechanical Engineers*, XXIII, 341–372.

Garson, Barbara. *All the Livelong Day*, rev. ed. New York: Penguin Books, 1994.

Giedion, Siegfried. *Mechanization Takes Command.* New York: Oxford University Press, 1948.

Gilbreth, Frank B. *Primer of Scientific Management.* 1914. Reprint, Pa.: Hive Publishing Co., 1985.

Gilbreth, Frank B., and Lillian M. Gilbreth. "An Indictment of Stop Watch Time Study," *Bulletin of the Taylor Society,* June 1921, 91.

Gilbreth, Frank B., Jr. *Time Out for Happiness.* New York: Thomas Y. Crowell, 1970.

Gilbreth, Frank B., Jr., and Ernestine Gilbreth Carey. *Cheaper by the Dozen.* 1948. Reprint, New York: Bantam, 1988.

Gilbreth, Lillian M. *The Quest of the One Best Way: A Sketch of the Life of Frank Bunker Gilbreth.* 1954(?). Reprint, Easton, Pa.: Hive Publishing Company, 1985.

Gilson, Mary Barnett. *What's Past Is Prologue.* New York: Harper & Brothers. 1940.

Glaab, Charles N., and Lawrence H. Larsen. *Factories in the Valley: Neehah-Menasha, 1870–1915.* Madison, Wis.: State Historical Society of Wisconsin, 1969.

Goldmark, Josephine. *Fatigue and Efficiency.* New York: Russell Sage Foundation, 1912.

———. *Impatient Crusader: Florence Kelley's Life Story.* Urbana: University of Illinois Press, 1953.

Gomberg, William, and David Dubinsky, *Trade Union Analysis of Time Study.* New York: Prentice-Hall, 1955.

Goodrich, Caspar F. *Rope Yarns from the Old Navy.* New York: Naval History Society, 1931.

Graziosi, Andrea. "Common Laborers, Unskilled Workers: 1880–1915," *Labor History,* Fall 1981.

Greenbaum, Joan M. *In the Name of Efficiency: Management Theory and Shopfloor Practice in Data Processing Work.* Philadelphia: Temple University Press, 1979.

Haber, Samuel. *Efficiency and Uplift: Scientific Management in the Progressive Era, 1890–1920.* Chicago: University of Chicago Press, 1964.

Halpern, Rich. "Industrial Apprenticeship in Nineteenth-Century Philadelphia." Unpublished paper, University of Pennsylvania, 1984.

Hayward, Elizabeth Gardner, *A Classified Guide to the Frederick Winslow Taylor Collection.* Hoboken, N.J.: Stevens Institute of Technology, 1951.

Herf, Jeffrey. *Technology, Culture, and Politics in Weimar and the Third Reich.* Cambridge: Cambridge University Press, 1984.

Hershberg, Theodore, ed. *Philadelphia: Work, Space, Family, and Group Experience in the Nineteenth Century.* New York: Oxford University Press, 1981.

Hindle, Brooke, and Steven Lubar. *Engines of Change: The American Industrial Revolution, 1790–1860.* Washington, D.C.: Smithsonian Institution Press, 1986.

Hirsch, Mark D. *William C. Whitney: Modern Warwick.* New York: Dodd, Mead, and Co., 1948.

Holton, David Parson, and Frances Holton. *Winslow Memorial.* New York: Mrs. F.K. Holton, 1888.

Hounshell, David A. *From the American System to Mass Production, 1800–1932.* Baltimore: Johns Hopkins University Press, 1984.

Howard, Robert. *Brave New Workplace.* New York: Viking, 1985.

Hoxie, Robert Franklin. *Scientific Management and Labor.* 1915. Reprint, New York: Augustus M. Kelley, 1986.

Hughes, Thomas P. *American Genesis: A Century of Invention and Technological Enthusiasm, 1870–1970.* New York: Penguin, 1990.

Hunt, Edward Eyre, ed. *Scientific Management Since Taylor: A Collection of Authoritative Papers.* New York: McGraw-Hill, 1924.

Ingle, H. Larry. *Quakers in Conflict: The Hicksite Reformation.* Knoxville: University of Tennessee Press, 1986.

Johnson, J. Myron. "Fred Taylor, '83: Giant of Non-repute." *Stevens Indicator,* Spring 1980, 4–8.

Johnson, J. Myron, and Richard P. Widdicombe. "An Avocation that Became a Vocation." Interview with Robert P. A. Taylor, at Providence, R.I., October 1979. Taylor Collection.

Jordan, John M. *Machine-Age Ideology: Social Engineering and American Liberalism, 1911–1939.* Chapel Hill: University of North Carolina Press, 1994.

Jurgens, Ulrich, et al. *Breaking from Taylorism: Changing Forms of Work in the Automobile Industry.* Cambridge: Cambridge University Press, 1993.

Kakar, Sudhir. *Frederick Taylor: A Study in Personality and Innovation.* Cambridge, Mass.: MIT Press, 1970.

Kelley, Florence. "My Philadelphia," *Survey Graphic,* October 1926.

Killorin, Joseph. *Selected Letters of Conrad Aiken.* New Haven, Conn.: Yale University Press, 1978.

Klyce, E.D.H. "Scientific Management and the Moral Law," *The Outlook,* November 18, 1911, 659.

Kranzberg, Melvin, and Carroll Pursell, Jr., eds. *Technology in Western Civilization.* Vol. 2: *20th Century.* New York: Oxford University Press, 1967.

Layton, Edwin T., Jr. *The Revolt of the Engineers; Social Responsibility and the American Engineering Profession.* Baltimore: Johns Hopkins University Press, 1986.

Leuchtenburg, William E. *The Perils of Prosperity, 1914–1932.* Chicago: University of Chicago Press, 1958.

Lewis, Wilfred. "The Versatile Genius of Taylor." Typescript, November 25, 1915. Taylor Collection.

Licht, Walter. *Getting Work: Philadelphia, 1840–1950.* Cambridge, Mass.: Harvard University Press, 1992.

Linhart, Robert. *Lenine, Les Paysans, Taylor.* Paris: Editions du Seuil, 1976.

Locke, Edwin. "The Ideas of Frederick Taylor: An Evaluation," *Academy of Management Review,* vol. 7, 1982, 14–24.

Looney, Robert F. *Old Philadelphia in Early Photographs, 1839–1914.* New York: Dover, 1976.

Lorenz, Clarissa M. *Lorelei Two: My Life with Conrad Aiken.* Athens, Ga.: University of Georgia Press, 1983.

Maier, Charles S. "Between Taylorism and Technocracy: European Ideologies and the Vision of Industrial Productivity in the 1920s," *Journal of Contemporary History* 1990 5(2): 27–61

Mandell, Richard D. *Paris 1900: The Great World's Fair.* Toronto: University of Toronto Press, 1967.

Manning, Florence Myrtle. "Carl Barth: A Sketch." Master's thesis, University of California, 1927.

Mason, Alpheus Thomas. *Brandeis: A Free Man's Life.* New York: Viking, 1946.

———. *Brandeis: Lawyer and Judge in the Modern State.* Princeton,: N.J., Princeton University Press 1933.

Mathewson, Stanley B. *Restriction of Output Among Unorganized Workers.* New York: Viking, 1931.

May, Henry F. *The End of American Innocence: A Study of the First Years of Our Own Time, 1912–1927.* New York: Knopf, 1959.

McCullough, David. *Mornings on Horseback.* New York: Touchstone/Simon & Schuster, 1981.

———. *The Johnstown Flood.* New York: Touchstone, 1968.

MacFarlane, John J. *Manufacturing in Philadelphia: 1683–1912.* Philadelphia: Philadelphia Commercial Museum, 1912.

McKelvey, Jean Trepp. *AFL Attitudes toward Production, 1900–1932.* Ithaca, New York: Cornell University Press, 1952.

McLachlan, James. *American Boarding Schools: A Historical Study.* New York: Charles Scribner's Sons, 1970.

Memorial of Sarah Pugh: A Tribute of Respect from Her Cousins. Philadelphia: J. B. Lippincott, 1888.

Merkle, Judith A. *Management and Ideology: The Legacy of the International Scientific Management Movement.* Berkeley: University of California Press, 1980.

Merrill, Harwood F., ed. *Classics in Management.* New York: American Management Association. 1960.

Merrill, Walter M., ed. *Let the Oppressed Go Free,* volume V, 1861–1867, of *The Letters of William Lloyd Garrison.* Cambridge, Mass.: Belknap Press of Harvard University Press, 1979.

The Midvale Steel Company: Fiftieth Anniversary, 1867–1917. Philadelphia, 1917.

Misa, Thomas J. *A Nation of Steel: The Making of Modern America, 1865–1925.* Baltimore: Johns Hopkins University Press, 1995.

Montgomery, David. *Workers' Control in America: Studies in the History of Work, Technology, and Labor Struggles.* Cambridge: Cambridge University Press, 1979.

————. *The Fall of the House of Labor: The Workplace, the State, and American Labor Activism, 1865-1925.* Cambridge: Cambridge University Press, 1987.

Montmollin, Maurice de, and Olivier Pastré. *Le Taylorisme: Actes du colloque international sur le taylorisme organisé par l'Université de Paris-XIII,* May 2–4, 1983. Paris: Éditions La Découverte, 1984.

Mulcaire, Terry. "Progressive Visions of War in *The Red Badge of Courage* and *The Principles of Scientific Management,*" *American Quarterly* 43. (1; March 1991), 46–72.

Munley, Michael W. *American Literature and the Rise of Management: From the Mill Girls, Emerson, Thoreau and Melville to Rebecca Harding Davis, Bellamy, Twain and Frederick Taylor.* Dissertation, University of Massachusetts, 1991.

Nadworny, Milton J. *Scientific Management and the Unions, 1900–1932.* Cambridge, Mass.: Harvard University Press. 1955.

————. "Frederick Taylor and Frank Gilbreth: Competition in Scientific Management," *Business History Review* XXXI (1957), 23–34.

Nalle, Richard T. *Midvale—and its Pioneers.* New York: Newcomen Society of England, American Branch, 1948.

Nelson, Daniel. *Managers and Workers: Origins of the New Factory System in the United States, 1880–1920.* Madison: University of Wisconsin Press, 1975.

————. *Frederick W. Taylor and the Rise of Scientific Management.* Madison: University of Wisconsin Press, 1980.

————. "Taylorism and the Workers at Bethlehem Steel, 1898–1901. *Pennsylvania Magazine of History and Biography* 101 (October 1977), 487–505.

————. "The Making of a Progressive Engineer: Frederick W. Taylor," *Pennsylvania Magazine of History and Biography* 103 (October 1979), 446–466.

————. "Scientific Management in Transition: Frederick W. Taylor at Johnstown, 1896," *Pennsylvania Magazine of History and Biography* 99 (October 1975), 460–475.

————. "Scientific Management, Systematic Management, and Labor, 1880–1915," *Business History Review* (Winter 1974), 479–500.

————. "Scientific Management and the Workplace, 1920–1935," in Sanford M. Jacoby, ed., *Masters to Managers: Historical and Comparative Perspectives on American Employers.* New York: Columbia University Press, 1991.

————, ed. *A Mental Revolution: Scientific Management since Taylor.* Columbus: Ohio State University Press, 1992.

Nelson, Daniel, and Stuart Campbell. "Taylorism vs. Welfare Work in American Industry: H. L. Gantt and the Bancrofts," *Business History Review* 46 (Spring 1972), 10.

Nevins, Allan. *Ford: The Times, the Man, the Company.* New York: Charles Scribner's Sons, 1954.

Noble, David. *Forces of Production: A Social History of Industrial Automation.* New York: Knopf, 1984.

Nolan, Mary. *Visions of Modernity: American Business and the Modernization of Germany.* New York: Oxford University Press, 1994.

Oliver Evans Chapter of the Society for Industrial Archeology. *Workshop of the World: A Selective Guide to the Industrial Archeology of Philadelphia.* Wallingford, Pa.: Oliver Evans Press, 1990.

Overy, R. J. *War and Economy in the Third Reich.* Oxford: Clarendon Press, 1994.

Perrot, M., et al. *Les Techniques de la Civilisation Industrielle.* Paris: Press Universitaires de France. 1979.

Person, Harlow, ed. *Scientific Management in American Industry.* 1929. Reprint, Easton, Pa.: Hive, 1972.

Peukert, Detlev J. K. *The Weimar Republic: The Crisis of Classical Modernity.* Trans. Richard Deveson. New York: Hill and Wang, 1987.

Phelps, Frank V. Frederick W. Taylor entry in encyclopedia of sport. Taylor Collection.

Pichierri, Angelo. "Diffusion and Crisis of Scientific Management in European Industry," in Salvador Giner and Margaret Scotford Archer, eds. *Contemporary Europe: Social Structures and Cultural Patterns.* London: Routledge & Kegan Paul, 1978.

Postman, Neil. *Technopoly: The Surrender of Culture to Technology.* New York: Knopf, 1992.

Pouget, Emile. *L'Organisation du Surmenage (Le Système Taylor).* Paris: Librairie des Sciences, Marcel Rivière et Cie, 1914.

Price, Brian. *One Best Way: Frank and Lillian Gilbreth's Transformation of Scientific Management, 1885–1940.* Doctoral dissertation. Ann Arbor, Mich.: University Microfilms, 1987.

Pursell, Carroll. *Technology in America: A History of Individuals and Ideas,* 2nd ed.. Cambridge, Mass.: MIT Press, 1991.

"Quelques Minutes avec Mme Taylor." Question-and-answer interview with Louise Taylor. N.p., n.d. Taylor Collection.

Quigel, James P., Jr. "The Business of Selling Efficiency: Harrington Emerson and the Emerson Efficiency Engineers, 1900–1930." Dissertation, Pennsylvania State University, 1992. Diss. Abstr. Int., 1993, 53:2491-A.

Rabinbach, Anson. *The Human Motor: Energy, Fatigue, and the Origins of Modernity.* New York: Basic Books, 1990.

Regier, C. G. *The Era of the Muckrakers.* Chapel Hill: University of North Carolina Press, 1932.

Report of the Commissioner General for the United States to the International Universal Exposition, Paris, 1900, in 6 vols.

Revell, Keith Douglas. *Professionalism and Public Service: The Taylor/Brandeis Alliance of 1910.* Master's thesis, University of Virginia, 1989.

Rifkin, Jeremy. *Time Wars.* New York: Henry Holt, 1987.

Rockstrom, Sten. "Some Points of Interest Collected During an Investigation of Industrial Conditions in U.S.A., 1 Dec. 1919–1 May 1920." Taylor Collection.

Rodgers, Daniel T. *The Work Ethic in Industrial America: 1850–1920.* Chicago: University of Chicago Press, 1978.

Roe, Joseph Wickham. *English and American Tool Builders.* New Haven: Yale University Press, 1916.

Rolt, L.T.C. *Tools for the Job: A History of Machine Tools to 1950.* London: Her Majesty's Stationery Office, 1986.

Rorabaugh, W. J. *The Craft Apprentice: From Franklin to the Machine Age in America.* New York: Oxford University Press, 1986.

Rosenberg, Nathan. "Technological Change in the Machine Tool Industry, 1840–1910," *Journal of Economic History* 33 (1963), 422.

Roy, Charles. *La Formule Allemande de Production Rationnelle dans l'Industrie.* Paris: Librairie Felix Alcan, 1929.

Ruchames, Louis, ed. *A House Dividing Against Itself,* volume II, 1836–1840, of *The Letters of William Lloyd Garrison.* Cambridge, Mass.: Belknap Press of Harvard University Press, 1971.

Rumm, John C. "The Nineteenth-Century Machine Shop Apprenticeship: Acquiring Knowledge, Acquiring Culture." Unpublished manuscript, October 1981.

Schachter, Hindy Lauer. *Frederick Taylor and the Public Administration Community: A Reevaluation.* Albany, N.Y.: State University of New York Press, 1989.

Scharf, J. Thomas, and Thomas Westcott. *History of Philadelphia, 1609–1884.* Philadelphia: L. H. Everts & Co., 1884.

Schlereth, Thomas J. *Victorian America: Transformations in Everyday Life, 1876–1915.* New York: Harper Collins, 1991.

Schor, Juliet B. *The Overworked American: The Unexpected Decline of Leisure.* New York: Basic Books, 1991.

Schrank, Robert. *Ten Thousand Working Days.* Cambridge, Mass.: MIT Press, 1978.

Scranton, Philip, and Walter Licht. *Work Sights: Industrial Philadelphia, 1890–1950.* Philadelphia: Temple University Press, 1986.

Seventy Five Years: The Midvale Company Philadelphia, 1942.

Shadwell, Arthur. *Industrial Efficiency: A Comparative Study of Industrial Life in England, Germany and America.* Two vols. London: Longmans, Green, & Co., 1906.

Shaiken, Harley. *Work Transformed: Automation and Labor in the Golden Age.* Lexington, Mass.: Heath, 1986.

Sinclair, Bruce. *Philadelphia's Philosopher Mechanics: A History of the Franklin Institute, 1824–1865.* Baltimore: John Hopkins University Press, 1974.

———. *A Centennial History of the American Society of Mechanical Engineers, 1880–1980.* Toronto: University of Toronto Press.

———. "At the Turn of a Screw: William Sellers, the Franklin Institute, and a Standard American Thread," *Technology and Culture,* January 1969, 20–34.

Sklar, Kathryn Kish. *Florence Kelley and the Nation's Work: The Rise of Women's Political Culture, 1830–1900.* New Haven: Yale University Press, 1995.

Spriegel, William R., and Clark E. Myers, eds. *The Writings of the Gilbreths.* Homewood, Ill.: Richard D. Irwin, 1953.

Strassmann, W. Paul. *Risk and Technological Innovation: American Manufacturing Methods during the Nineteenth Century.* Ithaca: Cornell University Press, 1959.

Strom, Sharon Hartman. *Beyond the Typewriter: Gender, Class, and the Origins of Modern American Office Work, 1900–1930.* Urbana: University of Illinois Press, 1992.

Sullivan, Mark. *Our Times: The United States, 1900–1925,* Part IV, 1909–1914. New York: Charles Scribner's Sons, 1935.

Tarbell, Ida M. *New Ideals in Business.* New York: Macmillan, 1916.

———. *All in the Day's Work: An Autobiography.* New York: Macmillan, 1939.

Taylor, Frederick Winslow. "Boxly Talk," June 4, 1907. Taylor Collection.

———. "A Comparison of University and Industrial Methods and Discipline." Address delivered at the University of Pennsylvania, October 19, 1906.

———. "A Piece-Rate System," in *Two Papers on Scientific Management.* London: George Routledge & Sons, 1919. Reprint of paper in *Transactions of the American Society of Mechanical Engineers* XVI.

————. "Notes on Belting," in *Two Papers on Scientific Management*. Reprint of paper in *Transactions of the American Society of Mechanical Engineers* XV.

————. "On the Art of Cutting Metals," *Transactions*, American Society of Mechanical Engineers, vol. 28 (3; mid-November 1906). Part I reprinted in C. B. Thompson, ed. *Scientific Management: A Collection of the More Significant Articles Describing the Taylor System of Scientific Management*, and referred to in the Notes as FWT, "Art of Cutting Metals," I, with the Thompson page numbering. Part II referred to in the Notes as FWT, "Art of Cutting Metals," II, with the *Transactions* page numbering.

————. *Scientific Management* [comprising *Shop Management, The Principles of Scientific Management*, and *Testimony Before the Special House Committee*]. Foreword by Harlow S. Person. New York: Harper & Brothers, 1947.

————. "Shop Management," in *Scientific Management*, above.

————. "Success: A Lecture to Young Men Entering Business." Lecture to engineering students at the University of Illinois, February 1909. *Bulletin of the Taylor Society* XI (2; 1926).

————. Thesis of Fred W. Taylor, 1883. I. Comparison of Fan and Steam Blast for Heating Furnace. II. Experiments Made to Determine Efficiency of Tire-Boring Mill. Taylor Collection.

————. "Workmen and Their Management." Lecture given at Harvard University, ca: 1909. Taylor Collection.

————. "Why Manufacturers Dislike College Students," *Proceedings of the Society for the Promotion of Engineering Education*, XVII, 1909.

————. *The Principles of Scientific Management*, in *Scientific Management*, above.

Taylor, Frederick W., and Sanford E. Thompson. *Concrete Costs*. New York: John Wiley & Sons, 1912.

Taylor Society. *Frederick Winslow Taylor: A Memorial Volume*. 1920. Reprint, Easton, Pa.: Hive Publishing Co., 1985.

Temin, Peter. "The Composition of Iron and Steel Products, 1869–1909, Journal of Economic History 23 (1963), 447–471.

Thompson, C. B. *The Taylor System of Scientific Management*. 1917. Reprint, Easton, Pa.: Hive Publishing Co., 1974.

————, ed. *Scientific Management: A Collection of the More Significant Articles Describing the Taylor System of Scientific Management*. 1914. Reprint, Easton, Pa.: Hive Publishing Co, 1972.

Thompson, E. P. "Time, Work-Discipline, and Industrial Capitalism," *Past and Present* 38, 56–97.

Thomsen, E. G. "F. W. Taylor—A Historical Perspective," in L. Kops and S. Ramalingam, eds., *On the Art of Cutting Metals—75 Years Later: A Tribute to F. W. Taylor*. New York: American Society of Mechanical Engineers, 1982.

Tichi, Cecilia. *Shifting Gears: Technology, Literature, Culture in Modernist America*. Chapel Hill, N.C.: University of North Carolina Press, 1987.

Tolles, Frederick B., ed. *Slavery and "The Woman Question": Lucretia Mott's Diary of Her Visit to Great Britain to Attend the World's Anti-Slavery Convention of 1840*. Supplement 23 to *Journal of the Friends' Historical Society*, 1952.

Towne, Henry R. "The Engineer as Economist," *Transactions ASME*, 7 (1886), 428–432.

Townsend, Arthur S. "Alloy Tool Steels and the Development of High Speed Steel," *Transactions of the American Society for Steel Treating*, September 1933, 769–795.

Trombley, Kenneth. *The Life and Times of a Happy Liberal: A Biography of Morris Llewellyn Cooke*. New York: Harper & Brothers, 1954.

Tweedale, Geoffrey. *Steel City: Entrepreneurship, Strategy, and Technology in Sheffield, 1743–1993*. Oxford: Clarendon Press, 1995.

———. *Sheffield Steel and America: A Century of Commercial and Technological Interdependence, 1830–1930*. Cambridge: Cambridge University Press, 1987.

———. "Metallurgy and Technological Change: A Case Study of Sheffield Specialty Steel and American, 1830–1930," *Technology and Culture,* April 1986, 27:2.

Urofsky, Melvin I. and David W. Levy, eds. *Letters of Louis D. Brandeis.* Three vols. Albany, N.Y.: State University of New York Press. 1972, 1973.

Urwick, L., ed. *The Golden Book of Management.* London: Newman Neame Ltd.

Urwick, L., and E.F.L. Brech. *The Making of Scientific Management.* Two vols. London: Management Publications Trust, 1949.

U. S. House of Representatives—Special Committee to Investigate the Taylor and Other Systems of Shop Management. Three vols. Washington, D.C.: U. S. Government Printing Office, 1912.

Wallace, Anthony F. C. *Rockdale: The Growth of an American Village in the Early Industrial Revolution.* New York: Knopf, 1978.

Waring, Stephen P. *Taylorism Transformed: Scientific Management Theory Since 1945.* Chapel Hill, N.C.: University of North Carolina Press, 1991.

Weigley, Russell F., ed., *Philadelphia: A 300-Year History.* New York: W. W. Norton, 1982.

Weisbord, Marvin R. *Productive Workplaces: Organizing and Managing for Dignity, Meaning, and Community.* San Francisco: Jossey-Bass, 1987.

Whitsett, David A., and Lyle Yorks. *From Management Theory to Business Sense: The Myths and Realities of People at Work.* New York: AMACOM, 1983.

Williams, Myron R. *The Story of Phillips Exeter.* Exeter, N.H.: The Phillips Exeter Academy, 1957.

Willson, Perry, R. *The Clockwork Factory: Women and Work in Fascist Italy.* Oxford: Clarendon Press, 1993.

Wilson, Joseph M. *Masterpieces of the Centennial International Exhibition.* Vol. III: *History, Mechanics, Science.* New York: Garland Publishing, 1977.

Wood, Stephen, ed. *The Degradation of Work? Skill, Deskilling and the Labour Process.* London: Hutchinson, 1983.

Wosk, Julie. *Breaking Frame: Technology and the Visual Arts in the Nineteenth Century.* New Brunswick, N.J.: Rutgers University Press, 1992.

Wrege, Charles D., and Ronald G. Greenwood. *Frederick W. Taylor, the Father of Scientific Management: Myth and Reality.* Homewood, Ill.: Business One Irwin, 1991.

———. "Discovering Some of the Roots of Taylor's *Shop Management:* Taylor's Secret Six-Year Study of the Building Trades." In Thomas N. Martin and Richard N. Osborn, eds. *Organizational Analysis for the 1980s: The View from the Midwest,* Midwest Academy of Management, 24th annual conference, 1981.

———. "Origins of Midvale Steel (1866–1880): Birthplace of Scientific Management," *Essays in Economic and Business History,* VII (1989).

———. "The Early History of Midvale Steel and the Work of Frederick W. Taylor: 1865–1890," *Canal History and Technology Proceedings* XI, 145–176.

———. "Frederick W. Taylor's Work at Bethlehem Steel, Phase II: The Discovery of High-Speed Tool Steel, 1898—Was It an Accident?" *Canal History and Technology Proceedings* XIII, 115–164.

———. "Frederick W. Taylor at Bethlehem Steel, Phase III: Sale of the 'Taylor-White' Patent and the Initiation of the High Speed Steel Patent Suit: 1902–1905," *Canal History and Technology Proceedings* XIV, 105–128.

Wrege, Charles D., Ronald G. Greenwood, and Ti Hsu. "Frederick W. Taylor's Early Work at Bethlehem Steel Company, First Phase—1898 to 1899: Some New Insights," *Canal History and Technology Proceedings* XII, 102–138.

Wrege, Charles D., and A. Stotka. "Cooke Creates a Classic: The Story Behind F. W. Taylor's

Principles of Scientific Management," *Academy of Management Review* 3 (October 1978), 736–749.

Wrege, Charles D., and A. Perroni. "Taylor's Pig-Tale: A Historical Analysis of Frederick W. Taylor's Pig-Iron Experiments, *Academy of Management Journal* 17 (1974), 6–27.

Wren, Daniel A. *The Evolution of Management Thought,* 3d ed. New York: John Wiley and Sons, 1987.

Wright, Carroll D. *Regulation and Restriction of Output.* Eleventh Special Report of the Commissioner of Labor. Washington, D.C.: Government Printing Office, 1904.

Yates, W. Ross. *Joseph Wharton: Quaker Industrial Pioneer.* Bethlehem, Pa.: Lehigh University Press, 1987.

Yellin, Jean Fagan, and John C. Van Horne, eds. *The Abolitionist Sisterhood: Women's Political Culture in Antebellum America.* Ithaca, N.Y.: Cornell University Press, 1994.

Yost, Edna. *Frank and Lillian Gilbreth: Partners for Life.* New Brusnwick, N.J.: Rutgers University Press, 1949.

Zuboff, Shoshana. *In the Age of the Smart Machine.* New York: Basic Books, 1988.

Zunz, Olivier. *Making America Corporate, 1870–1920.* Chicago: University of Chicago Press, 1990.

INDEX

ILLUSTRATION CREDITS

First section:

Pages 1 (top and center), 6 (below), 7 (top right, center, and below), 8 (center and below): Frederick Winslow Taylor Collection, Stevens Institute of Technology, Hoboken, NJ

Pages 1 (below) and 6 (top right): Marie Clark Hodges

Pages 2 (top right), 3 (below), 4 (below), 5 (top right and below): Robert Kanigel

Page 2 (below right): Elise W. Carr

Page 3 (top): Bayard Stockton Clark

Page 4 (top): Archives of Germantown Academy

Page 4 (center): Photograph by G. H. Hastings, courtesy of Phillips Exeter Academy

Page 7 (top left): Map Collection, Free Library of Philadelphia

Page 8 (top): Amanda Patten

Second section:

Page 1 (top left): Sanford E. Thompson Papers, Kheel Center for Labor-Management Documentation and Archives, Cornell University

Pages 1 (top right), 2 (center), 3 (both), 4 (all), 5 (top right, below left and right): Frederick Winslow Taylor Collection, Stevens Institute of Technology, Hoboken, NJ

Pages 1 (below) and 2 (below): Marie Clark Hodges

Page 2 (top): Bethlehem Steel Corporation Collection, National Canal Museum

Page 5 (top left): Courtesy of Hagley Museum and Library

Page 6 (top): IEEE Center for the History of Electrical Engineering

Page 6 (below left): Thomas P. Hughes

Page 7 (top): Smithsonian Institution

Page 8 (top): Courtesy Watertown Free Public Library, Watertown, MA

Page 8 (below all): Robert Kanigel